COMPUTER GRAPHICS

PROCEEDINGS

Volume 26 Number 2 July 1992

SIGGRAPH '92
Conference Proceedings
July 26–31 1992
Papers Chair Edwin E. Catmull
Panels Chair Bruce H. McCormick

A publication of ACM SIGGRAPH
Production Editor Steve Cunningham

*Sponsored by the Association for
Computing Machinery's Special
Interest Group on Computer Graphics*

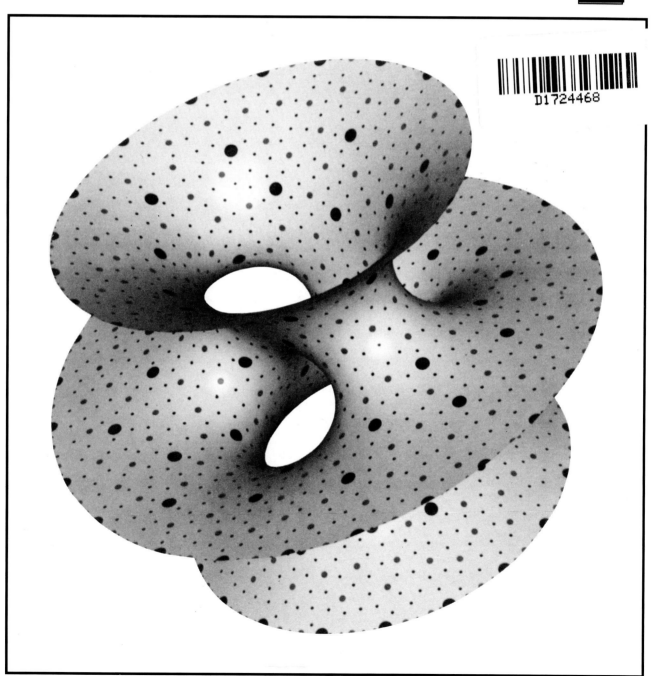

The Association for Computing Machinery, Inc.
1515 Broadway, 17th Floor
New York, NY 10036

Sample Citation Information:
...Proceedings of SIGGRAPH '92 (Chicago, Illinois, July 26–31, 1992). In *Computer Graphics*, 26, 2 (July 1992), ACM SIGGRAPH, New York, 1992, pp. xx–yy.

ORDERING INFORMATION

Orders from nonmembers of ACM placed within the United States should be directed to:

Addison-Wesley Publishing Company
Order Department
Jacob Way
Reading, MA 01867
Tel: 1-800-447-2226

Addison-Wesley will pay postage and handling on orders accompanied by check. Credit card orders may be placed by mail or by calling the Addison-Wesley Order Department at the number above. Follow-up inquiries should be directed to the Customer Service Department at the same number. Please include the Addison-Wesley ISBN number with your order:
A-W ISBN 0-201-51585-7

Orders from nonmembers of ACM placed from outside the United States should be addressed as noted below.

Latin America and Asia:
Addison-Wesley Publishing Company Inc.
Reading, MA 01867, USA
Tel: 617-944-3700
Cable: ADIWES READING
Telex: 94-9416

Canada: Addison-Wesley Publishing (Canada) Ltd.
36 Prince Andrew Place
Don Mills, Ontario M3C 2T8 Canada
Tel: 416-447-5101

Australia and New Zealand:
Addison-Wesley Publishing Company
6 Byfield Street
Norty Ryde, N.S.W. 2113
Australia
Tel: 888-2733
Cable: ADIWES SYDNEY
Telex: AA71919

United Kingdom, Republic of Ireland, Africa (excluding North Africa) and South Africa:
Addison-Wesley Publishers Ltd.
Finchampstead Road
Workingham
Berkshire RG11 2NZ, England
Cable: ADIWES Workingham
Telex: 846136

Continental Europe, the Near East, Middle East, and North Africa:
Addison-Wesley Publishing Company
Dr Lairesstraat, 90
1071 P J Amsterdam
The Netherlands
Tel: 020 76 40-44
Cable: ADIWES AMSTERDAM
Telex: 844-14046

Orders from ACM Members:

A limited number of copies are available at the ACM member discount. Send order with payment to:

ACM Order Department
P.O. Box 64145
Baltimore, MD 21264

ACM will pay postage and handling on orders accompanied by check.

Credit card orders only:
1-800-342-6626
Credit card orders may also be placed by mail.

Customer service, or credit card orders from Alaska, Maryland, and outside the United States: 301-528-4261

Electronic mail inquiries may be directed to acmpubs@acmvm.bitnet.

Single-copy orders placed by fax:
410-528-8596

Please include your ACM member number and the ACM order number with your order.

ACM Order Number: 428920
Soft Cover ACM ISBN:
    0-89791-479-1
Series Hard Cover ACM ISBN:
    0-89791-480-5
ISSN: 0097-8930

Contents

Papers Sessions, Wednesday, 29 July 1992

8:45–10:00   **Conference Opening Section**

ACM SIGGRAPH '92 Welcome
Maxine D. Brown

10:30–12:00   **Morphing**
Chair: Richard Chuang

1:30–3:00   **Efficient Polygonal Surfaces**
Chair: Marc Levoy

3:15–4:45   **Humans and Clothing**
Chair: Lance Williams

Papers Sessions, Thursday, 30 July 1992

Papers Sessions, Friday, 31 July 1992

Panel Sessions, Wednesday, 29 July 1992

Panel Sessions, Thursday, 30 July 1992

Panel Sessions, Friday, 31 July 1992

Preface

These proceedings contain the papers presented at the Technical Program of the 19th annual ACM Conference on Computer Graphics and Interactive Techniques, SIGGRAPH '92, in Chicago.

This year we added new categories of papers as part of our ongoing responsibility to adapt to this changing field. In particular we added calls for pedagogical papers, cross-disciplinary papers, video papers, and multi-media papers. The latter two types of papers were very experimental, but it is the kind of experiment that we should be making. We did receive three video papers and one multi-media paper.

We received 213 papers by the deadline on January 8, 1992. Forest Baskett, Jim Kajiya, and I spent a day dividing the papers up to distribute to the 25 senior reviewers. Each senior reviewer was responsible for finding two or three other reviewers to read the papers. Every paper was read by at least two senior reviewers. Thus every senior reviewer had to read about 16 papers and find additional reviewers for 8 papers. This is a fairly heavy load, as the process of reviewing a paper is difficult and time consuming.

The entire committee met in March to select those papers that were to be accepted. The committee tried conscientiously to find the jewels among the papers. The papers were discussed by the entire committee. If there was disagreement, then additional committee members read the paper at the meeting. One of the criteria for a paper was whether or not the reviewers believed that it would stimulate future work in the computer graphics field. The excellent reputation of the SIGGRAPH proceedings is a result of the volunteer work put forth by these leaders in computer graphics.

We are also deeply indebted to Kay Seirup who helped organize, communicate, and coordinate throughout this complex process. Thanks are also due to Ray Davis who put together the database system for keeping track of and sorting the papers. Dee Bell did a lot of the original support work until she left to have her baby. We also received help from Beth Sullivan and Susan Anderson in sorting and distributing the papers. A special note of thanks is due to Jim George who works behind the scenes to ensure high standards. My gratitude also goes to Steve Cunningham who helped maintain SIGGRAPH's color standards in an era of tighter budgets. He has been a pleasure to work with in producing these proceedings.

Read and Enjoy.

Ed Catmull
SIGGRAPH '92 Papers Chair

Conference Committee

CONFERENCE CHAIR

Maxine D. Brown
(University of Illinois at Chicago)

CONFERENCE COMMITTEE CHAIRS

Patti Harrison, *Conference Coordinator*
Edwin E. Catmull, *Papers*
(Pixar)
Bruce H. McCormick, *Panels*
(Texas A&M University)
Alan Norton, *Courses*
(IBM T.J. Watson Research Center)
Gray Lorig, *Electronic Theater/HDTV Events*
(Barking Trout Productions)
John Grimes, *Art Show*
(Institute of Design, Illinois Institute of Technology)
James E. George, *Exhibits/Showcase*
(Mesa Graphics, Inc.)
Branko J. Gerovac, *G-Tech*
(Digital Equipment Corp./MIT Media Laboratory)
Coco Conn, *SIGKids*
(Homer & Associates)
John Fujii, *Slide Sets*
(Hewlett-Packard Co.)
Steve Cunningham, *Proceedings*
(California State University Stanislaus)
Steven M. Van Frank, *Treasurer*
(Lynxys, Inc.)
Ellyn Gore, *Events Planning*
(Convex Computer Corp.)
Thomas I. Prudhomme, *Marketing*
(MCNC)

Kathryn R. Riemer, *Public Relations*
(IBM)
Michael H. Bigbee, *Registration Operations*
(Alternative Software, Inc.)
David Spoelstra, *Audio/Visual*
(Truevision)
Clark Dodsworth, *Speaker Materials*
(VideOcart, Inc.)
Mark Hall, *Student Volunteers*
(Rice University)
Walt Bransford, *Facilities Coordinator*
(Premisys Corp.)
Richard M. Mueller, *International Liaison*
(Dynamic Graphics, Inc.)
Ralph Orlick, *Computer Systems*
(University of Illinois at Chicago)
Thomas A. DeFanti, *as himself*
(University of Illinois at Chicago)
Kathryn McKee, *Promotional Materials*
(AT&T)
Adele Newton, *SIGGRAPH Director for Conferences*
(Alias Research, Inc.)

CONFERENCE PLANNING COMMITTEE

Adele Newton (Alias Research, Inc.)
Michael Bailey (San Diego Supercomputer Center)
Maxine D. Brown (University of Illinois at Chicago)
Carol Byram (Sony Computer Peripheral Products Co.)
Branko J. Gerovac (Digital Equipment Corp./MIT Media Lab)
Christopher F. Herot (Lotus Development Corp.)
Robert L. Judd (Los Alamos National Laboratory)
Mark Resch (Computer Curriculum Corp.)
Jacqueline M. Wollner (Convex Computer Corp.)

PAPERS COMMITTEE

Alan H. Barr (California Institute of Technology)
Forest Baskett (Silicon Graphics Computer Systems)
Richard J. Beach (Xerox PARC)
Loren Carpenter (Pixar)
Richard Chuang (Pacific Data Images, Inc.)
Elaine Cohen (University of Utah)
Robert L. Cook (Light Source Computer Images, Inc.)
Frank Crow (Apple Computer, Inc.)
Henry Fuchs (University of North Carolina at Chapel Hill)
Donald P. Greenberg (Cornell University)
Pat Hanrahan (Princeton University)
Paul Heckbert (Delft University of Technology)
James T. Kajiya (California Institute of Technology)
Marc Levoy (Stanford University)
Jock Mackinlay (Xerox PARC)
Nelson Max (Lawrence Livermore National Laboratory)
Don P. Mitchell (AT&T Bell Laboratories)
Darwyn Peachey (Pixar)
Craig Reynolds
Robert Sproull (Sun Microsystems, Inc.)
Craig Upson (Silicon Graphics Computer Systems)
Andries van Dam (Brown University)
Turner Whitted (Numerical Design, Ltd.)
Lance Williams (Apple Computer, Inc.)
Andrew P. Witkin (Carnegie Mellon University)

PANELS COMMITTEE

Richard J. Beach (Xerox PARC)
Donna Cox (National Center for Supercomputing Applications)
Robert L. Judd (Los Alamos National Laboratory)
Mike Keeler (Kubota Pacific Computer, Inc.)
Jaron Lanier (VPL Research, Inc.)
Richard L. Phillips (Los Alamos National Laboratory)
Vibeke Sorensen (California Institute of the Arts)
Steven L. Tanimoto (University of Washington)
James M. Winget (Silicon Graphics Computer Systems)

COURSES COMMITTEE

Frank Bliss (EDS)
Ed Council (Timberfield Systems)
Rich Ehlers (Evans & Sutherland)
Lauretta Jones (IBM T.J. Watson Research Center)
Nan Schaller (Rochester Institute of Technology)
Dino Schweitzer (U.S. Air Force Academy)

ART SHOW COMMITTEE

Peter Beltamacci (Institute of Design, Illinois Institute of Technology)
Paul Brown
Ron Clark (Institute of Design, Illinois Institute of Technology)
Geroge Kraft (Illinois Intitute of Technology)
Larry Kolasch (AT&T Bell Labs)
Irv Moy (Argonne National Laboratory)
Marla Schweppe (Tornado Productions)
Joan Truckenbrod (School of the Art Institute of Chicago)
Dietmar Winkler (Kansas City Art Institute)
Kirk Woolford (Techtron Imaging)

ART SHOW JURY

John Pearson (Oberlin College)
Patric Prince (California State University Los Angeles)
John Sturgeon (Rensselaer Polytechnic Institute)
Lynne Warren (Museum of Contemporary Art, Chicago)

ELECTRONIC THEATER COMMITTEE

Nancy St. John (Small Pond Productions)
Joel Welling (Pittsburgh Supercomputing Center)
Jonathan Luskin (Industrial Light and Magic)
John Hart (University of Illinois at Chicago)
Hugette Chesnais
Tom Cassey
Doug Lerner (Inpac Corporation)

Barabara Mones-Hattal (George Mason University)
Ken O'Connell (University of Oregon)

ELECTRONIC THEATER EVENING JURY

Brad DeGraf
Copper Giloth (University of Massachusetts)
Bill Reeves (Pixar)
Craig Upson (Silicon Graphics Computer Systems)

ELECTRONIC THEATER OPENING/PERFORMANCE JURY

Jamie Dixon (Pacific Data Images)
Michael Wahrman

SLIDE SETS JURY

Edwin E. Catmull (Pixar)
Bruce H. McCormick (Texas A&M University)
F. Kenton Musgrave (Yale University)
Alan Norton (IBM T.J. Watson Research Center)
John Wallace (3D/Eye, Inc.)

SIGKIDS COMMITTEE

Scott Kim
Judy Sachter (IBM)
Marla Schweppe (Tornado Productions)
Diane Schwartz (Northwestern University)

G-TECH COMMITTEE

Edwin E. Catmull (Pixar)
Coco Conn (Homer & Associates)
Thomas A. DeFanti (University of Illinois at Chicago)
James E. George (Mesa Graphics, Inc.)
John Grimes (Institute of Design, Illinois Institute of Technology)
John Fujii (hewlett-Packard)
Bruce H. McCormick (Texas A&M University)
Alan Norton (IBM)

SHOWCASE COMMITTEE

Tom DeFanti (University of Illinois at Chicago)
Branko Gerovac (Digital Equipment Corp./MIT Media Lab)
Andy Goodrich (RasterOps)
Larry Smarr (National Center for Supercomputing Applications)

SHOWCASE TEAM

Carolina Cruz-Neira (University of Illinois at Chicago)
David Curtis (National Center for Supercomputing Applications)
John Hart (University of Illinois at Chicago)
Tim Kuhfuss (Argonne National Laboratory)
Gary Lindahl (University of Illinois at Chicago)
Jonathon Miller (Advanced Network & Services)
Kathy O'Keefe (University of Illinois at Chicago)
Ralph Orlick (University of Illinois at Chicago)
Dana Plepys (University of Illinois at Chicago)
Maggie Rawlings (University of Illinois at Chicago)
Dan Sandin (University of Illinois at Chicago)
Lewis Siegel (University of Illinois at Chicago)

TECHNICAL LIAISONS

G. Scott Owen, *Education*
 (Georgia State University)
Irwin M. Jarett, *Financial Services*
 (Graphics MIS)
Lloyd Treinish, *Global Information Services*
 (IBM T.J. Watson Research Center)
David N. Levin, *Medical Imaging*
 (The University of Chicago)
T. J. O'Donnell, *Molecular Modeling*
 (O'Donnell Associates)
Hiram T. French, *Printing/Publishing*
 (Superset Inc.)
Renée LeWinter, *Printing/Publishing*
 (LeWinter Baron)

PROCEEDINGS PRODUCTION EDITORS

Steve Cunningham, *Conference proceedings*
(California State University Stanislaus)
Maureen Stone, *Conference proceedings color consultant*
(Xerox PARC)
Vicki Putz, *Visual proceedings*
(Vicki Putz Design)
Dietmar Winkler, *Visual proceedings design consultant*
(Kansas City Art Institute)

FUNDAMENTALS SEMINAR

Wayne E. Carlson, Chair (The Ohio State University)
Mike Bailey (San Diego Supercomputer Center)
Judith R. Brown (The University of Iowa)

PAPERS REVIEWERS

Salim Abi-Ezzi
Greg Abram
John Airey
Kurt Akeley
Al Alcorn
John Amanatides
Tony Apodaca
Matt Arrott
Jim Arvo
Dan Asimov
Larry Aupperle
Robert Bacon
Norm Badler
Chandrajit Bajaj
David Baraff
Joe Bates
Dan Baum
Barry Becker
Jeff Beddow
Thad Beier
Gary Bishop
Avi Bleiweiss
Jim Blinn
Jules Bloomenthal
John Bradstreet
David Breen
Tom Brigham
Wim Bronsvoort
Bob Brown
Marc Brown
Derrick Burns
Bill Buxton
Brian Cabral
Tom Calvert
A. T. Campbell
Stuart K. Card
Rikk Carey
Wayne Carlson
Judy Challinger
Sheue-Ling Chang
Eric Chen
Michael Chen
Michael Cohen
Sabine Coquillart
Bob Coyne
Paul Cross
Frank Crow
Mark Daly
John Danskin
Tom Davis
Philippe de Reffye
Michael Deering
Gary Demos
Tony DeRose
John Dill
Mike Dilts
David Dobkin

Julie Dorsey
Bob Drebin
Steve Drucker
Tom Duff
David Ellsworth
Kels Elmquist
David Em
Nick England
John Eyles
Eliot Feibush
Steve Feiner
Gordon Ferguson
Eugene Fiume
Kurt Fleischer
A. Robin Forrest
David Foulser
Alain Fournier
W. R. Franklin
Joseph Friedman
George Furnas
Donald Fussell
Steve Gabriel
Tinsley Galyean
Kicha Ganapathy
Larry Gelberg
Nader Gharachorloo
Charlie Gibson
Ziv Gigus
Copper Giloth
Greg Glass
Andrew Glassner
Michael Gleicher
Al Globus
Enrique Godreau
Jack Goldfeather
Ron Goldman
Andy Goris
David Gossard
John Goutsias
Mark Green
Ned Greene
Leslie Greengard
Trey Greer
John Gross
Leonidas Guibas
Charlie Gunn
Satish Gupta
Paul Haeberli
Eric Haines
Roy Hall
Mark Hannah
Patrick Hanrahan
Chuck Hansen
John Hart
Roy Hashimoto
Xiao D. He
Paul Heckbert

PAPERS REVIEWERS (Continued)

Jim Helman
Scott Hempill
Mark Henne
Shaun Ho
Christopher Hoffman
Randy Hoogerhyde
Leo Hourwitz
Donald House
Philip Hubbard
Bernardo Huberman
John Hughes
Kevin Hunter
Erik Jansen
Tom Jensen
George Joblove
Deven Kalra
Dave Kamins
Michael Kass
Arie Kaufman
Dave Kirk
Victor Klassen
Jeff Kleiser
Craig Kolb
Andy Kopra
S.V. Krishnan
Tosiyasu L. Kunii
David Kurlander
David Laidlaw
Jonathon Leech
Wm Leler
Bryan Lewis
John Lewis
Andy Lippman
James Lipscomb
Pete Litwinowicz
Charlie Loop
Bill Lorensen
Robert Lotufo
Tom Lyche
Jock Mackinlay
Larry Malone
Tom Malzbender
Abraham Mammen
Cameron Manoocheri
Martti Mantyla
Dan McCabe
Robert McDermott
Barb Meier
Teresa Meng
Gary Meyer
Gavin Miller
Don Mitchell
Steve Molnar
Ken Musgrave
Sandy A. Napel
Patrick Naughton
Bruce Naylor
Shawn Neely
Ulrich Neuman
Kevin Novins
Derek Nye
Gary Oberbrunner
Art Olson
Eben Ostby
Rick Parent
Frederic Parke
Nicholas Patrilakis
Randy Pausch
Alex Pentland
Ken Perlin
Cary Phillips
Flip Phillips

Clifford Pickover
Les Piegl
Steven Pieper
Tom Porter
Frits Post
John Poulton
Przemyslaw Prusinkiewicz
Marc Raibert
Lyle Ramshaw
John Rasure
Richard Redner
Bill Reeves
Mack Reichert
Gary Ridsdale
George Robertson
Warren Robinett
Alyn Rockwood
Michael Rodriguez
Holly E. Rushmeier
David Salesin
Hanan Samet
Ray Sarraga
Dietmar Saupe
Rick Sayre
Chris Schmandt
William Schroeder
Sally Sedelow
Tom Sederberg
Bob Sedgewick
Mark Segal
Hans-Peter Seidel
Carlo Séquin
Mike Shantz
Mike Shantzis
Peter Shirley
Ken Shoemake
Richard Shoup
François Sillion
Karl Sims
Robert Skinner
Kenneth Sloan
Eliot Smyrl
Bengt-Olaf Snyder
John Snyder
Dave Springer
Garland Stern
Maureen C. Stone
Steve Strassmann
Paul Strauss
Srikanth Subramaniam
K. R. Subramanian
Richard Szeliski
John Tang
Seth J. Teller
Demetri Terzopoulos
Daniel Thalmann
Spencer Thomas
Nick Thompson
David Tonnessen
Ken Torrance
David Tristram
Ben Trumbore
Pauline Ts'o
Allen Tuchman
Greg Turk
Ken Turkowski
Sam Uselton
Michiel van de Panne
Reinier van Kleij
Mark VandeWettering
Doug Voorhies
Jeff Vroom

PAPERS REVIEWERS (Continued)

Michael Wahrman
Janet Walker
John Wallace
Gregory J. Ward
Colin Ware
Joe Warren
Keith Waters
Gary Watkins
Robert Webber
Jerry Weil
Kevin Weiler
William Welch
Lee Westover
Turner Whitted

Lou Wicker
Jane Wilhelms
James Winget
Matthias Wloka
George Wolberg
Adam Woodbury
Brian Wyvill
Frances Yao
Gideon Yuval
Harold Zatz
Polle Zellweger
David Zeltzer
Michael Zyda

COURSE REVIEWERS

Scott E. Anderson
Tony Apodaca
Richard A. Becker
R. Daniel Bergeron
Garry Bierne
Tim Binkley
Teresa Bleser
Jules Bloomenthal
Walt Bransford
Wayne Brown
Al Bunshaft
Tom Calvert
Wayne Carlson
George S. Carson
Janet Chin
Michael Cohen
Steve Cunningham
Greg Daigle
Michael Ferraro
Andrew Glassner
Ned Greene
Eric Haines
Pat Hanrahan
Lou Harrison
John C. Hart
Edy Henderson
Mark Henderson
Marty Hess
Donald H. House
Francis X. Janucik
Dave Jordaini
Alyce Kaprow

Isaac Kerlow
Bill Kolomyjec
David Kramlich
Olin Lathrop
Lorene Lavora
Renée LeWinter
Tony Longson
Jeffrey J. McConnell
Andy Mickel
Maureen Nappi
Scott Nelson
Rick Parent
Frederic I. Parke
Thomas Porett
Theodore N. Reed
Earl Rennison
Judson Rosebush
Sylvie Rueff
Hans-Peter Seidel
William M. Shyu
Deborah Sokolove
Jon Steinhart
Roger T. Stevens
Demetri Terzopoulos
Steve E. Tice
Bruce Wands
Annette Weintraub
Lee Westover
Turner Whitted
Michael J. Wollman
Brian Wyvill
Kenneth Yapkowitz

PROFESSIONAL SUPPORT

ACM SIGGRAPH Conference Coordinators
Patti Harrison, SIGGRAPH '92
Molly Morgan-Kuhns, SIGGRAPH '93

ACM SIGGRAPH Senior Program Director
Lois Blankstein
Donna Goldsmith, *ACM SIGGRAPH Coordinator*

Administrative Assistants
Kay Seirup, *Papers*
Sherry Escalante, *Panels*
Glenn Cho, *Courses*
Alex Traube, *Art Show*
Sue Gardner, *Electronic Theater*
Maggie Rawlings, *Showcase*
Jo Dee McDonnell, *SIGGRAPH '92*
Barbara Hause, *SIGGRAPH '92 On-Site*

Audio/Visual Management
Audio Visual Headquarters Corporation
Jim Bartolomucci
Doug Hunt
Ritch Farnham
Paul Babb

Conference Accounting
Smith, Bucklin and Associates
Ruth Kerns
Roger Albert
Shelley Johnson

Conference Management
Smith, Bucklin and Associates
Cindy Stark
Diedre Ross
Jackie Groszek
Anne Lueck
Peggy Rohs
Maureen Baumann

Conference Travel Agency
Travel Planners, Inc.
Felix Mendez
Karen Trzcianka

Decorator/Drayage
Andrews-Bartlett and Associates, Inc.
John Patronski
Bob Borsz
John M. Loveless

Exhibition Management
Hall-Erickson, Inc.
Barbara Voss
Tom Corcoran
Mike Weil
Peter Erickson

Graphic Design
Vicki Putz Design
Vicki Putz

Promotional Materials Writer
In Any Event, Ltd.
Karla Kreblein

Public Relations
Smith, Bucklin and Associates
Sheila Hoffmeyer
Patricia Maloney
Sara Patterson
Leona Caffey

SIGGRAPH Show Daily
Computer Graphics World
Laureen Belleville

Exhibitors

Abekas
Academic Press, Inc.
Acrobat Graphics Ltd.
ADDA Technologies, Inc.
Addison-Wesley Publishing Company
Advanced Digital Imaging
Advanced Imaging
Advanced Technology Center
Advanced Visual Systems Inc.
AGFA
Alacron, Inc.
Alias Research, Inc.
Alias Research Inc., Style Division
Ameritech
Ampex
AmPro Corporation
Apple Computer, Inc.
Art Machines Inc.
Ascension Technology Corporation
Association for Computing Machinery
AT&T Graphics Software Labs
Audio Digital Imaging
Aura Technologies
Aurora Systems
Autodesk
Autodessys Inc.
Avid Technology Inc.
Aware, Inc.
Bit 3 Computer Corporation
Brooktree Corporation
Byte by Byte Corporation
Canon USA, Inc.
Chase Technologies, Inc.
Chromatek, Inc.
Computer Design, Inc.
Computer Graphics World
Computers in Physics
Comtec Automation Solutions
Convex Computer Corporation
Cyberware
Cymbolic Sciences International
Diaquest, Inc.
Digital Arts
Digital Equipment Corporation
Digital F/X, Inc.
Digital Micronics, Inc.
Discreet Logic Inc.
Double M Industries
Du Pont Pixel Systems
Dynamic Graphics, Inc.
Eastman Kodak Company
Electric Image, Inc.
Enhance Memory Products, Inc.
Esprit Projection Systems
Eurographics
Evans and Sutherland
Extron Electronics
Eyring Corporation
F and S, Inc. (FSI)

Focus Graphics Inc.
Folsom Research
FOR.A Corporation of America
Fraunhofer Computer Graphics Research Group (USA)
FRISC, Inc.
Geobyte
General Electric, PDPO
GIG Nederland
Helios Systems
Herstal Automation Ltd.
Hewlett-Packard Company
High Color
Hotronic, Inc.
Howtek, Inc.
IBM Corporation
IEEE Computer Society
IEEE Visualization '92
IGES Data Analysis
IICS
Image Manipulation Systems, Inc.
Imagine That
Imagraph
Impediment Incorporated
IMSL, Inc.
INA-Imagina
Infotronic SpA
Integrated Computer Solutions, Inc.
Intelligent Light
Intelligent Resources
Interactive Media Technologies (IMT)
Intergraph Corporation
IRIS Graphics, Inc.
Ithaca Software
C. Itoh Technology, Inc.
Jobo Fototechnic
Jones and Bartlett Publishers
JVC Professional Products Company
Kingston Technology Corporation
Kubota Pacific Computer, Inc.
Lasertechnics, Inc.
LAZERUS
Lead Technologies Inc.
Liant Software Corporation
Lightscape Graphic Software
Lightwave Communications, Inc.
Loviel Computer Corporation
Lyon Lamb Video Animation Systems, Inc.
Management Graphics, Inc.
Maximum Strategy Inc.
Meckler Group
Meta Corporation U.S.A.
Microfield Graphics, Inc.
Microtime, Inc.
Midwest Litho Arts, Inc.
Minolta Corporation
MIT Press
Mitsubishi Electronics
Mitsubishi Electronics America-Professional Electronics Division
Mitsubishi International Corporation

ModaCAD
Mondo 2000
Montage Publishing, Inc.
Morgan Kaufmann Publishers
Motorola, Inc.
Multimedia Plus
Multipoint Technology Corporation
National Computer Graphics Association
Network Computing Devices
Nippon Computer Graphics Association
NPES-Association for Suppliers of Printing & Publishing Technologies
Nth Graphics
Optibase Inc.
O'Reilly & Associates, Inc.
Oxberry
Panasonic Communications & Systems Company
Panasonic Industrial Company
Parallax Graphics, Inc.
Parsytec Inc.
Peritek Corporation
Photron Limited
Pinnacle Systems, Inc.
Pixar
Pixelvision
Pixsys
Polhemus Incorporated
Post Magazine
Pre-
Prentice Hall
Presentation Products
Primary Image Inc.
Quarterdeck Office Systems
Rainbow Technologies, Inc.
Ray Dream, Inc.
Raytheon Company Submarine Signal Division
ReproCAD
RFX Inc.
RGB Spectrum
Roche Image Analysis Systems, Inc.
Sampo Corporation of America
San Diego Supercomputer Center
Santos Technology Inc.
Science Accessories Corporation
Scientific Computing & Automation
Ron Scott, Inc.
Screen Magazine
Seiko Instruments USA, Inc.
Sharp Electronics Corporation
Shima Seiki USA., Inc.
SHOgraphics, Inc.
SIGGRAPH '93
SIGGRAPH Education Committee
SIGGRAPH Local Groups
SIGGRAPH Organization

SIGGRAPH Video Review
Sigma Electronics, Inc.
Signetics Company
Silicon Graphics Computer Systems
Sixty Eight Thousand Inc.
SOFTIMAGE Inc.
Software Security, Inc.
Sony Corporation
Specular International
Springer-Verlag, Inc.
StereoGraphics Corporation
Strata Inc.
Sun Microsystems, Inc.
Supercomputing '92
Supercomputing Review
Symbolics, Inc.
TaraVisual Corporation
Tech Images
Techexport, Inc.
Tech-Source, Inc.
Tektronix, Inc.
Texas Memory Systems, Inc.
Texnai Inc.
Thomson Digital Image (TDI)
Time Arts Inc.
Trident Microsystems, Inc.
Trix Company, Ltd.
Truevision
University of Lowell
Univision Technologies, Inc.
UNIX Review Magazine
UNIXWorld Magazine
Vertigo Technology Inc.
Video Graphic Technologies, Inc.
Video Systems Magazine
Videomedia, Inc.
VIDI
Viewpoint Animation Engineering
Virtual Realities Group
Visionetics International Corporation
Visual Software
The Vivid Group
Volumetric Imaging, Inc.
VPL Research, Inc.
Wacom Technology Corporation
Wasatch Computer Technology
Wavefront Technologies, Inc.
WaveTracer, Inc.
John Wiley & Sons, Inc.
Winsted Corporation
Wolfram Research, Inc.
Xaos Tools Inc.
Yamashita Engineering Manufacture, Inc.
Yarc Systems Corporation

1992 ACM SIGGRAPH Awards

Computer Graphics Achievement Award

Henry Fuchs

The 1992 SIGGRAPH Computer Graphics Achievement Award is presented to Dr. Henry Fuchs for his contributions to high performance, parallel display architecture. He was a pioneer who recognized the importance of parallelism for graphics processors and provided leadership to achieve a practical implementation of massively parallel high speed display processors — Pixel-Planes.

Increasing the performance of the hardware, upon which we depend so much, has been a vital ingredient, even a driving force, in Computer Graphics. Through an ongoing series of projects spanning the past fifteen years, Fuchs has contributed significantly to the goal of achieving truly interactive 3D graphics through work on the hardware for real-time rendering. In particular, he advanced the state of the architecture of image displays through the innovative use of parallelism. Among his numerous publications we find the initial paper showing the use of multiple processors working on a visible surface algorithm [1, 1977]. In a subsequent paper [2, 1979] with Brian Johnson, he outlined a parallel display architecture in which individual processors are interleaved on a pixel-by-pixel basis, and in which multiple memory units can be variably mapped to processors. This organization overcame the pitfalls of the one obvious scheme whereby a z-buffer is partitioned into contiguous regions. It reduced image memory contention and avoided usage imbalances when objects in a scene are unevenly distributed over the screen. Furthermore, this architecture easily permitted processors to be added to obtain improved performance.

His early work introducing the use of a binary space partitioning tree [3, 1980] also contributed to the development of the Pixel-Planes architecture [4, 1981]. By introducing the idea of Pixel-Planes, an elegant scheme for simultaneously evaluating a linear expression at every pixel in an image, he launched a series of practical experiments to explore the potential of massively parallel display system elements. Five generations of chips and three successively more powerful VLSI implementations of high speed research display systems were been built using Pixel-Planes rasterizers.

The most recent machine called Pixel-Planes 5 [5, 1989], developed under the direction of Fuchs and John Poulton, is a test-bed for evaluating design alternatives. The radically different architecture of this display system extends it well beyond the implied meaning of the label "Pixel-Planes." Although the Pixel-Planes rasterizer is an element of the system, the significance of its design is that it promotes exploration of the issues of paralleling all elements of the display process, not just the polygon tiling.

Henry Fuchs obtained his Ph. D. in Computer Science from the University of Utah in 1975. After graduation he joined the faculty of the University of Texas at Dallas as Assistant Professor of Mathematical Sciences. He has been a faculty member at the University of North Carolina at Chapel Hill since 1978 where he is Federico Gil Professor of Computer Science. As an indication of his cross-disciplinary interests, he was Adjunct Associate Professor in the Department of Medical Computer Science, University of Texas Southwestern Medical School (1979-82) and since 1988 is Adjunct Professor of Radiation Oncology at UNC School of Medicine. In addition, he has been an active consultant and advisor to industry and been a leader in many workshops and technical advisory panels.

The ideas developed in Fuchs's research over the past fifteen years have had a significant impact on the design of high-performance display systems. The research team that he has assembled continues to work towards innovative approaches for solving increasingly massive problems using parallel display systems. SIGGRAPH recognizes Henry Fuchs for his singular contributions to high performance, parallel display architectures as well as for his other ongoing contributions to Computer Graphics by presenting him the Computer Graphics Achievement Award.

Selected references

[1, 1977] Fuchs, Henry, "Distributing a Visible Surface Algorithm Over Multiple Processors," Proceedings of ACM '77, Seattle, October 1977, pp. 449–451.

[2, 1979] Fuchs, Henry, and Brian W. Johnson, "An Expandable Multiprocessor Architecture for Video Graphics," Proceedings of the Sixth Annual ACM-IEEE Symposium on Computer Architecture, 1979, pp. 58–67.

[3, 1980] Fuchs, Henry, Zvi M. Kedem and Bruce F. Naylor, "On Visible Surface Generation by A Priori Tree Structures," Proceedings of SIGGRAPH '80, in *Computer Graphics* 14:3 (July, 1980), pp. 124–133.

[4, 1981] Fuchs, Henry, and John Poulton, "Pixel-planes: A VLSI-Oriented Design for a Raster Graphics Engine," *VLSI Design*, vol. 2, no. 3, 3rd Quarter 1981, pp. 20–28.

[5, 1989] Fuchs, Henry, John Poulton, John Eyles, Trey Greer, Jack Goldfeather, David Ellsworth, Steve Molnar, Greg Turk, Brice Tebbs, and Laura Israel, "Pixel-Planes 5: A Heterogeneous Multiprocessor Graphics System Using Processor-Enhanced Memories," Proceedings of SIGGRAPH '89, in *Computer Graphics* 23:3 (July, 1989), pp. 79–88.

Previous award winners

1991	James T. Kajiya
1990	Richard Shoup and Alvy Ray Smith
1989	John Warnock
1988	Alan H. Barr
1987	Robert Cook
1986	Turner Whitted
1985	Loren Carpenter
1984	James H. Clark
1983	James F. Blinn

Keynote:
Communicating with Images
An Idea Whose Time Has Come

Robert W. Lucky
AT&T Bell Laboratories

For the better part of this century people have written about, dreamed of, and predicted videotelephony. Movies like *Star Trek N* and *2001* have made video telephones a staple of future life. Yet the technology for all this has existed for many years. World Fairs have featured them, and virtually every exposition has shown smiling people talking to their distant families on large screen color displays. In fact, the Bell System even marketed the Picturephone as a standard product more than twenty years ago. What happened then, and what gives us the belief that now is the time that people will begin to communicate with images? In answering this question we might begin with technology, though it is not by any means the whole story. However, this is a particularly fertile time in that three important technological factors have come together to make video transmission relatively inexpensive. They are cheap consumer video components, powerful compression algorithms. and plentiful bandwidth. The first factor, consumer video, is obvious, while the development of powerful, standard compression algorithms is the subject of several talks at this conference. This talk will focus on the question of available bandwidth for video, and then turn to questions relating to applications of image communications. The driving force behind the availability of bandwidth is optical fiber transmission, where the increase in achievable capacity on a single fiber is roughly doubling every year. A fiber has a bandwidth of approximately 25,000 GHz, leading to the belief that it might ultimately support transmission rates in the tens of terabits per second. No one knows this ultimate capacity of fibers, and current research experiments are showing that non-linear effects will make for interesting scientific challenges in achieving terabit capacities. However,

today's commercial systems that transmit at 2.5 gigabits per second are far from what will certainly be accomplished in the next half dozen years. Given this remarkable windfall in communications capacity, the telecommunications industry is looking to implement an infrastructure that will support inexpensive broadband services. The other pieces of this infrastructure are switching and local distribution. Progress on both of these fronts is rapid, as the world fashion in switching has turned to ATM (Asynchronous Transfer Mode) — a packet-switched system that can serve as a platform for bandwidth-on-demand services. Simultaneously, attention has been focussed on the classic last-mile problem, where the telephone companies are wrestling with the CATV providers to bring fiber into homes. With this firm vision of a new broadband communications infrastructure, the pervasive question is what will people do with all these plentiful bits? The only answer that echoes through the industry is video and image communications. There seems to be no other class of applications that require so much bandwidth. Thus, given that there will be an emphasis on image communications, what are the potentialities and the roadblocks? Some applications are obvious; for example, medical imagery and visualization are frequently mentioned. However, for more widespread applications, such as videotelephony, videoconferencing, and multimedia, there are difficult human factors that remain to be worked. Undoubtedly, the market itself will be the psychological testbed in which these services are developed. It will be an interesting time. The technology will evolve to meet our needs, but in turn, we will change the way we work and interact in order to take advantage of what we have been given.

A TeleComputer

Jim Clark
Silicon Graphics, Inc.

As digital computing costs decline over the next ten years, computer technology's most widespread use will be in consumer applications. The future digital television screen will be a natural visual control center for many new applications, such as normal television entertainment, virtual reality games, home control systems, interactive books, magazines and newsprint, and telephonic, televideo and data communications. A *client-server network* environment can exist in which the *network* is the merged cable-tv/telephone system, the *client* is a home *telecomputer* that controls the images seen, and the *server* is a multi-media computer system that is integral to the cable "head-end" or telecommunications "central-office." In this paper, I attempt to define the functionality of a telecomputer so that the broadest set of applications is possible.

Introduction.

"Multi-media" means the integration of audio, video, graphics and computing into a single digital environment. It promises many new applications that can utilize this combination of technologies.

Most people expect the integration to come in next generation personal computers, and many computer companies are working to this end. But for the ordinary consumer, a more likely possibility is that a "telecomputer" will bridge the gap between television and multi-media computing. Think of this "multi-media player" as the digital equivalent of the cable-tv decoder -- it will be the consumer's computer. It's central role will continue to be entertainment, such as movies, tv programs and interactive games, but it can also be capable of many functions, including:

- textbooks that teach through graphic simulation
     and animation coupled with audio and video
- media retrieval from databases and libraries
- newspaper and magazine retrieval
- multiparticipant virtual reality games
- digital television entertainment services
- digital audio retrieval
- media mail
- video telephones

A low-cost telecomputer in the home is important before authors will invest in writing interactive books. And interactive media services on demand, such as magazines, newspapers, books, encyclopedias, games, and digital audio/video entertainment, need a digital media player in the home before the services can develop.

Computer Industry Milestone. The computer industry can benefit enormously by defining telecomputer building blocks so that they can be used in standard multi-media computers. This will ensure compatibility between the consumer and computing worlds -- the client and the server. Also, the distribution volumes of consumer electronics can dramatically decrease the cost of computers, enabling portable (tele)computers far more powerful than possible today.

A telecomputer's main elements will come from the technologies of networking, computer systems, computer graphics, image processing and semiconductors, all with a focus on the economies of scale of consumer electronics. But to achieve a low-cost telecomputer for the cost of today's cable-tv decoder electronics, intermediate parts suppliers, distributors, gate array manufacturers, and expensive packaging common in the computer industry will be circumvented. Success might even require that a single company be able to integrate almost everything, from semiconductor fabrication to the telecomputer itself.

The computer industry, especially the workstation segment, has an advantage because it has already started to develop "multi-media" technology. Today's dominant consumer electronics companies do not yet fully grasp the range of digital imaging and graphics technologies necessary to create digital televisions, which helps explain why they continue to focus on analog approaches to HDTV.

Teleprocessing Power. An enormous amount of processing power is required to decode an incoming, high-resolution digital television signal. It will need to be scaled to a different output screen resolution and decompressed in real-time, and pay-per-view services will require encryption. The scaling function done generally requires significant image-processing power to properly sample and filter the incoming image. Compression and encryption are just as demanding.

The main message of this paper is that the power required for this is essentially the same as that required for "virtual-reality" quality 3D graphics. Moreover, building a telecomputer with the additional graphics capability can enable a broad range of markets that an ordinary digital television can not. The goal here is to functionally define and rationalize a $200 "building block" module that has the required capability. It is a combination of RISC processing power with multiple parallel data paths, caches, program memories, double-buffered full-color screen memories with z-buffer, generalized ultra high-speed interconnect for I/O, and suitable specialized hardware support for image processing, encryption, compression, and real-time 2D and 3D high-end, textured graphics.

The goal is achievable in 2-3 years. Semiconductor yields for *today's* most advanced CPU's allow about 100,000 transistors/dollar in high-volume fabrication cost -- the cost to the semiconductor company to fabricate the silicon chip and test it. By the end of the decade this number will approach one million. Likewise, the <u>fabrication cost</u> of memory is about 50,000 Bytes/dollar today, and it will approach 500 kByte/$ by the end of the decade.

Four million transistors devoted to RISC, encryption, compression, graphics and image processing would make a digital teleprocessor comfortably capable of everything discussed in this paper. Today, this can be combined with up to 20 megabytes of image memory, for HDTV resolutions, and packaged economically on a single low-power module for under $600 silicon manufacturing cost. Within two to three years, this number will fall below $200 and be compelling.

The Basic Technologies.

Four basic technologies are required for multi-media: digital audio, digital video/image processing, computer graphics and general-purpose processing.

Digital Audio.

Digital audio is the most thoroughly understood technology because of compact disks, which store two channels of 16-bit samples at the rate of 44 kHz, or 88 kBytes/sec/channel bandwidth. Sony Corporation has shown that 4:1 compression is achievable with no perceptible loss, so 22 kBytes/sec/channel is probably minimum to keep high-fidelity. Processing at this data rate is not difficult compared to the data rates of digital video.

Digital Video.

Digital television transmission standards have been slow to develop. I think much of the reason for this is because the problem is viewed from traditional analog television perspectives. Those involved don't fully comprehend the benefits and capabilities of digital imaging. Much of the motivation for this paper is to give a computer graphics perspective to this, because I am convinced that the computer graphics community can solve many of the issues confronting the development of digital television.

Transmission/Reception Decoupling. Analog systems are always in lock-step. For example, the vertical retrace pulse is transmitted and after a fixed phase delay related to the speed of signal travel to the receiver, it causes a retrace of the receiver. Similarly, if scan-lines are interlaced at transmission, the receiver must put them immediately to the screen in interlaced form as they arrive. In effect, buffering analog is very difficult.

In contrast, a digital television receiver's input parameters can be completely decoupled from its output to the viewing device. This means interleaving, for example, is not even related to transmission. A complete incoming digital tv frame would be stored in a frame buffer memory before it is output, i.e. it would be double-buffered. The complete frame data might even be transmitted over a fiber-optic link carrying several hundred other channels multiplexed onto the same carrier, which of course would require storing fragments of the image in a buffer until the complete frame is received. It might also be encrypted for selective pay-per-view reception and compressed to save bandwidth, both of which require real-time processing on the

incoming data. It might even be transmitted in a special color space. All of these can be altered by the telecomputer processor (teleprocessor) before display on the screen.

Resolution Decoupling. In a digital system, the transmitted resolution can be totally decoupled from the displayed resolution. Digital subsampling or supersampling and filtering can be done by a teleprocessor if necessary to suite any output resolution or scan-line interlace discipline. NTSC, PAL and digital standards D1 and D2 can easily be generated, no matter what the resolution of the incoming signal, for compatibility with existing standards. A digital receiver with the right processor can easily be made to filter a digital video transmission format to generate any output format. Compatibility with existing technology can be complete. The transmission resolution can be made irrelevant.

What's Important. Ignoring specifics related to the transmission network and protocols, a fairly small set of specifications are necessary for digital video transmission:

- resolution
- pixel aspect ratio
- number of bits per pixel
- encoding of these bits (HSV, RGB, ...)
- sequential or interlaced lines
- compression algorithm used
- encryption technique used
- and frame transmission rate.

Even some of these are unnecessary. For example, the pixel aspect ratio should be square. Nothing is gained from ratios other than 1:1 except for compatibility with the *analog* Highvision format out of Japan, and uniform horizontal and vertical computer generated lines are more important than conformity with an unestablished *analog* broadcast approach. Vertical and horizontal computer generated lines should be the same.

There also is no compelling reason to transmit scan lines in an interleaved manner, since input and output are naturally decoupled. The fact that this has been part of the HDTV debate points to the limitations of an analog perspective. If the output display requires interlaced scan lines, as with NTSC, the telecomputer processor will do this at output time. Sequential input simplifies everything and loses nothing.

Soft Digital Transmission Parameters. The remaining "soft" parameters should be transmitted to the digital receiver:

1. Resolution
2. Encoding and Bits/pixel
3. Frame Rate
4. Encryption Algorithm
5. Compression Algorithm

1. Resolution.. Transmission resolution should be completely independent of the display resolution on the output device. Any resolution should be allowed. High Definition Television (HDTV) resolutions now being considered by the FCC range from roughly 1000x700 to about 2000x1000. Aspect ratios of 16x9 are important for movie transmission, so perhaps the ideal "high-definition" resolution is 1820x1024. The important thing is that the transmission resolution should depend on the source material, and nothing else -- it should be "soft." The telecomputer should map <u>any</u> input resolution (up to some maximum, of course) to <u>any</u> output resolution. Normally, input and output aspect ratios would be the same, but a "window" on the television might be of any size, and subsampling or supersampling is necessary for different resolutions or aspect ratios. Any teleprocessor must be able to do these image processing functions.

2. *Encoding*. The particular color-space encoding and number of bits per color-space component should be specified by the transmitter, because some formats might yield better compression. Yet the output display might require a different format. The receiver's teleprocessor should accept a range of possible formats and number of bits per component. Conversion to output format should be automatically handled by the teleprocessing engine using a simple 3x3 color space transformation.

3. *Frame Rate*. The update rate for animated images varies according to the source, and it should always be transmitted to the receiver. For example, 30 frames per second is common for today's analog video, 24 is common for movies recorded on film, and 12 is common for animated cartoons. Any rate should be allowed -- 10 frames/sec might be adequate for videophones, for example. To save transmission bandwidth, the update rate should be part of the soft transmission parameters. Then the source material can be transmitted at its rate, not always at 30 frames/sec as with analog video -- this is another form of compression that costs nothing. Also, just as in today's workstations, the telecomputer can synchronize the *output refresh rate* with the *update rate* using conventional frame interleaving techniques.

4. *Encryption*. Encryption will be *essential* for digital television and future telecommunications. Encryption provides selective access to television programming, such as pay-per-view, and it will provide needed security for many types of on-line transactions that will be possible with telecomputing.

Public key encryption technologies, such as RSA are a natural fit. The teleprocessor should be able to encrypt and decode all transmissions and receptions at real-time rates, in addition to its other tasks. Specialized acceleration hardware will be necessary to do this in real-time.

5. *Compression Algorithms*. Compression is an area of considerable confusion and high expectation. Two things are driving it. First, cable television companies look to forthcoming digital optical fiber with compression as a solution to their bandwidth and signal degradation problems. Second, virtually all computer companies wish to compress video so that it can be stored and retrieved in real-time on CD-ROM's. Cable companies want to replace analog with a better product. Computer companies want video clips for multi-media.

This has limitations. Trying to force a CD to store and retrieve video at audio rates of 1.408 Mbits/sec is asking a lot. Perhaps as much effort should be exerted to cause a new "VideoCD" standard to be created. This could then replace old, sequential video tape, and consumer market volumes could be used to leverage into existence a powerful new storage mechanism.

MPEG I is supposed to compress a 352x240, 30 frames/sec signal into a 1 Mbit/sec transmission rate, plus another 200k bits/sec for sound. For general entertainment quality, this seems unrealistic. MPEG II allows 5 to 10 Mbits/sec on 720x480 resolution. Even this is only about one half to one bit per pixel.

MPEG II seems overly complicated. It compresses 8x8 tiles of the image using a Discrete Cosine Transform (DCT), combined with Huffman encoding and a time consuming, search-based, predictive tracking algorithm that is applied to these tiles during compression to try to predict their frame to frame trajectory, as in a scene with a panning camera. Not only does this seem overly *ad hoc*, but also the tiling pattern is evident in fast moving scenes. For entertainment, the consumer will not tolerate anything that actually looks worse than old analog technology -- CD's would have failed if digital audio had been worse than 33 rpm records. Although MPEG II will be useful for multi-media, it might not be adequate for digital video entertainment.

The important thing, however, is not the specifications for MPEG II, or any other compression scheme. Rather, it is that compression is an embryonic technology, and better compression methods will be invented. Moreover, there will be a variety of compression algorithms, some "high-compression" where it can be tolerated and others low-compression -- perhaps even "lossless" -- to maintain the highest quality, as for example in Sony's 4:1 audio compression. The proper approach is to build mechanisms in the teleprocessor to accelerate core elements of compression, such as perhaps cosine transforms and pattern recognition, but allow the general-purpose processor to control the algorithm. The decompression algorithm itself might even be downloaded before transmission. The challenge for the present is to invent a range of algorithms covering high to low compression applications.

If the objective were simply to specify a High-resolution Digital Television -- HDTV-- we could stop here and ignore advanced computer graphics. Current television has no graphics ability. But new markets are available, such as education and virtual-reality games, that will make the transition to digital tv more compelling for the consumer. Moreover, the real-time compute power and memory bandwidth required to sample, filter, store, retrieve, compress and encrypt digital video signals is essentially adequate for real-time 3D color graphics.

Computer Graphics.

Two approaches to computer graphics have developed over the last decade. The first is "bit-mapped" graphics, which is <u>static</u>, single-buffered, black and white, one bit/pixel, 2D, page-image oriented graphics, commonly found on an Apple Macintosh or Sun Workstation. It has revolutionized desktop publishing but is inappropriate for dynamic media. The other graphics approach is <u>dynamic</u>, double-buffered, real-time, color, 3D, simulation oriented graphics commonly found on workstations from Silicon Graphics.

As previously outlined, simple digital video requires dynamic, double-buffered, full-color frame storage and real-time image processing capability. This power is shared with real-time 3D graphics. For example, filtering, sampling and mapping incoming digital images from one resolution to another is identical to the computations required for anti-aliased mapping of textures onto three dimensional surfaces.

It is natural to minimize the graphics primitives in a telecomputer to the essentials. Today's graphics systems have lots of bells and whistles, but the four most important geometric graphics primitives are:

- characters
- points
- lines
- and surfaces.

These primitives should be

- arbitrarily scaled, rotated and translated
- illuminated from multiple light sources
- and have textures and transparencies mapped
  onto them

in real-time to provide a very general geometric graphics environment.

Add image processing capability to

- point-sample geometry
- filter and accumulate images
- store, retrieve and map anti-aliased textures.

The result is a graphics environment virtually as complete as the most expensive systems available today.

Note that characters, like points, lines and surfaces, are geometric, yet all real-time graphics systems made in the last ten years have treated characters as images -- previously "rendered" objects. As a result, only specific font sizes are available, and generalized rotations, scaling and other operations have not been possible in real-time. Geometric outline fonts are now commonplace, however, and they should be rendered in real-time like any other geometry. Additional hardware will be necessary to enable a screenful of characters to be rendered in a frame time, but fully interactive real-time print media will need it.

The Teleprocessor.

Today's workstations in complete form are too complex for a telecomputer, but some things should be in common between them. The most crucial for compatibility is the CPU instruction set and the multi-media environment. This doesn't mean, however, that we put a workstation or PC in every television. UNIX, MS-DOS, "NT", X-windows interfaces and keyboards are complicated and mean nothing for the most common consumer uses.

RISC Core. The programs that run on a telecomputer require a CPU, and the most efficient CPU is a Reduced Instruction Set CPU. It doesn't waste silicon space with microcode for unused instructions. Also, for a given semiconductor technology, CISC CPU's will typically run slower and use more power. A RISC CPU allows more space to be used for graphics, compression, encryption and network protocol hardware.

What would be an ideal RISC CPU configuration for graphics and image processing? A RISC CPU with 4 data paths, each

with 32-bit integer and floating-point capability, each data path capable of multiply-add in one cycle, clocked in excess of 100 MHz. This would enable 800 million arithmetic operations per second, which would help achieve virtual-reality graphics speeds. The CPU would also need caches and program memory sufficient for holding the essential algorithms, and it would have to control network I/O and the graphics, compression and encryption accelerators. It should also be compatible with a widely available RISC processor used in workstations, in order to leverage the available digital media development tools.

Operating System. A completely new Real-time Execution-only Operating System will be required, because no current operating system environment is efficient enough to do real-time image processing, graphics, compression, encryption and digital audio in a small amount of memory. UNIX and Microsoft's various OS flavors are too complex, and their "features" are unnecessary in a low-cost, consumer multi-media "player".

On the other hand, applications require a complete development environment. This means that conventional workstation/PC platforms will need a compatibility mode to support the Real-time Execution OS for program development and debugging.

The Memory System.

Current DRAM organizations are wrong for digital image generation, and computer graphics systems designers have struggled with this for over ten years. The market opportunity presented by telecomputers, however, is sufficiently large to finally motivate memory manufacturers to make high-density memories with a specialized organization for telecomputers, rather than just continuing to make chips that are compatible with the previous generation DRAM's. The main problem is bandwidth. The solution requires changes in DRAM design that are motivated by this new high-volume application. This paper cannot address the potential architecture of this new memory, but it is a very important requirement. For this paper and associated talk, I'll assume the right memory is available.

Basic Memory Requirements. A digital television image requires a minimum of about 2 bytes per pixel to store a static image. Using dithering techniques, it is possible to get by with somewhat less, but I believe the effort required to reduce the memory by a few percent is not worth it, because of the rate of decline in memory prices. Two buffers are required for a dynamic image, so 4 bytes/pixel are the minimum.

How much more storage does 3D graphics require? For the simplest case -- no texture mapping -- a total of about 4 bytes/pixel is required for z-buffer, transparency coefficient alpha and tags for window management. This doubles the memory requirements of a basic digital tv.

Conventional NTSC resolutions will fit within a 640x512 pixel image memory of 327,680 pixels. A basic digital tv with NTSC output would therefore need 1.32 MBytes, and the simplest 3D telecomputer requires twice this, not counting program storage.

Advanced 3D Capability. Adding texture mapping dramatically increases the realism of 3D images, thus enabling virtual-reality quality. The additional memory needed depends upon the sizes and number of different texture maps. If 2 bytes/pixel are needed to store an image, 4 bytes/pixel are required for a full-screen texture map using traditional MIP-map techniques for dealiasing treatment. But even very small, cyclic texture maps can considerably enrich a 3D scene, so 4 bytes/pixel is considerable texture storage.

A typical telecomputer with NTSC output resolution would therefore have 1.32 MByte of memory for image buffers, 1.32 MByte for z-buffer and transparency, 1.32 MBytes for textures and perhaps 2 MBytes of program memory. The total memory *costs* today for a virtual-reality, 3D telecomputer with NTSC output would be under $120, and can be under $30 in the mid 90's.

High-resolution Digital Television (HDTV). Digital television and telecomputers will finally allow variable transmission resolutions that can be different from receiver resolutions. Transmission resolutions can then be determined according to source material, not fixed for all time as with an analog system.

Receiver resolution is variable too. The incoming picture might be subsampled to fit within a small window on the receiver's screen. The maximum resolution of the output CRT (or flat-panel display) determines the size of memory needed in the image buffer. Higher resolution input signals are filtered, sampled and stored in the image buffer as they arrive. This requires a minimum of buffering if the incoming signal is not interlaced.

If all receivers use the same teleprocessor, the main difference between them is evidently the amount of memory they have. But as resolution is increased, more pixels require more processing in order to maintain the same image processing and graphics update speed. Ideally, we'd like a processor/memory module that can be replicated to make higher resolutions. Multiple copies would increase not only the memory available but also the processing power to change it.

A module with 640x512 resolution memory and sufficient computing power to handle this image size would work. First, it is adequate for NTSC output resolutions, which means it will work with standard televisions. Second, four modules would make 1280x1024, which is the commonly used resolution in color workstations. Finally, six modules makes 1920x1024, which is adequate for an 1820x1024 HDTV resolution, with about 100 Kpixels left over.

Each of these modules can have variable amounts of memory, according to the features desired, from plain digital television to virtual-reality capability.

Summary and Closing Comments

Over the next four to five years, unprecedented change will occur in the computer, telecommunications and television industries as multi-media technology enters the home via the *telecomputer*.

This will require the development of a digital fiber-optic data communications network that replaces both the cable tv system and the telephone system. While this will certainly take many years to complete, just as cable systems have grown incrementally, so will this new system. But it will require the telecomputer's capability to create a demand for the new services.

The present "local loop" of the telephone system and the "cable franchise" for television will become one Multi-media Server Loop. Each loop will represent several tens of thousands of "clients," each using a telecomputer. In the loop will be high-speed computer systems for serving audio and movies on demand, virtual reality games, digital forms of daily newspapers, weekly and monthly magazines, libraries, encyclopedias and interactive books. In time, all media will be available in dynamic form. Switching systems for video conferences and telecommunications will be integrated, as well.

A combination of semiconductor, computer graphics and computer industries have the capability to design a build a telecomputer with the power described in this paper. Current consumer electronics companies do not -- they are encumbered by analog thinking and by preserving an installed base. Yet a telecomputer can be made so that it can still use existing television, as well as grow to higher resolution and higher quality in a modular way. The challenge is ours.

A Physically Based Approach to 2–D Shape Blending

Thomas W. Sederberg
Eugene Greenwood
Brigham Young University[1]

Abstract

This paper presents a new algorithm for smoothly blending between two 2–D polygonal shapes. The algorithm is based on a physical model wherein one of the shapes is considered to be constructed of wire, and a solution is found whereby the first shape can be bent and/or stretched into the second shape with a minimum amount of work. The resulting solution tends to associate regions on the two shapes which look alike. If the two polygons have m and n vertices respectively, the algorithm is $O(mn)$. The algorithm avoids local shape inversions in which intermediate polygons self-intersect, if such a solution exists.

Categories and Subject Descriptors: I.3.3 [**Computer Graphics**]: Picture/Image Generation; I.3.5 [**Computer Graphics**]: Computational Geometry and Object Modeling.

General Terms: Algorithms

Additional Key Words and Phrases: Computer graphics, shape blending, animation, physically based algorithms.

1 Introduction

The topic of this paper is illustrated in Figures 1–3. Given

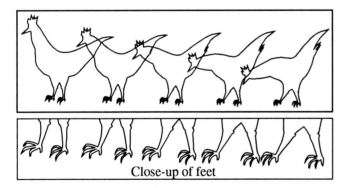

Close-up of feet

Figure 1: Shape blend example

Figure 2: Shape blend example

two polygonal shapes, the problem is to compute a continuous shape transformation from one to the other. For example, in Figure 1, the far left and far right sketches of a chicken are given, and the three intermediate shapes are automatically computed with no user interaction. This operation is known variously as shape averaging, shape interpolation, metamorphosis, shape evolving, and shape blending. It has widespread application in illustration, animation, and industrial design. 2–D shape blending is an increasingly popular feature in many commercial illustration software packages (such as [1], [6], [7], [17], [18]).

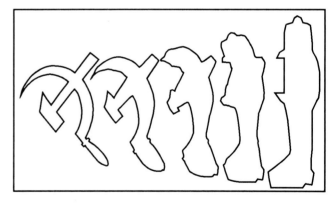

Figure 3: Shape blend example

Solutions to the 3–D shape interpolation problem have also been proposed ([4], [10], [14]). Indeed, the research effort reported in this paper initially focused on the 3–D problem. However, the authors soon realized that even the 2–D problem had many open questions, such as how can a shape blend algorithm avoid chaotic intermediate shapes and how can an

[1] Engineering Computer Graphics Laboratory
368 Clyde Building
Brigham Young University
Provo, UT 84602
(801)378-6330
(801)378-2478 FAX
tom@tws.ce.byu.edu

algorithm recognize similar, though not identical, features on the two terminal shapes (such as the feet and head of the chicken in Figure 1) and maintain those features throughout the blend.

We tested several commercial shape blending software packages on some of our shape examples. The best of any results for the chicken outline is shown in Figure 4 and the best E to F blend is shown in Figure 5. Notice how the chicken feet in Figure 4 degenerate to a self-intersecting scribble.

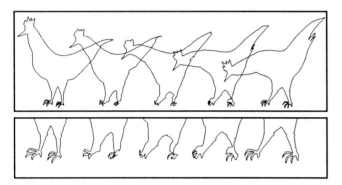

Figure 4: Shape blend of chicken using commercial software

Figure 5: Shape blend of E to F using commercial software

The algorithm presented in this paper is based on a physical model. Imagining that each shape is made of a piece of wire, the blend is determined by computing the minimum work required to bend and stretch one wire shape into the other. The user can specify some physical properties of the wire, which control the relative difficulty with which it can be bent or stretched. A severe penalty is charged for blends which experience a local self intersection due to the wire bending through an angle of zero degrees. This penalty nearly always prevents the self intersection problem in Figure 4. All of the blends in this paper were generated automatically with no user intervention (Figures 4 and 5 by commercial packages, the rest by our algorithm) except for initially specifying the physical attributes of the wire.

1.1 Related work

Shape blending is a problem which has been motivated by several different applications and attacked in several different ways. For example, if we envision the family of blend polygons as forming a ruled surface in (x, y, t) space, as shown in Figure 6, the shape blending problem bears strong similarity to the contour triangulation problem [5], [8], [9], [15]. This is the background from which we approached the problem, and our solution borrows graph theory concepts from [15] and [8]. The algorithms used in the commercial illustration software cited above probably resemble the triangulation algorithms in [5] and [9] since these are $O(n)$ in time and memory, thus more suitable for PC applications than ones based on graph theory.

The first paper on 3–D shape interpolation [4] was motivated by industrial design. It tackles the problem by slicing the two 3–D shapes into contours, blending corresponding contours, then reconstructing the 3–D blended surface. More recent solutions, [10] and [14], are based on Minkowski sums. These approaches give impressive results, but leave some room for further investigation. For example, two non-convex objects

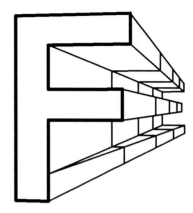

Figure 6: Family of blend polygons as a function of t

with similar features (such as a dog and a horse) will lose protruding details such as legs during intermediate shapes. In fact, the blend of a non-convex object with itself is not a constant shape.

Problems related to 2–D shape blending arise in shape recognition [2], [19] and curve matching for graphical search and replace [16]. In these applications, the primary concern is determining how similar two complete objects are. Shape blending also resembles the computer vision problem of contour identification, for which one solution is based on energy minimization [13], as is the shape blending algorithm described herein.

When the two shapes to be blended are taken to be keyframes in a character animation (such as in Figure 1) shape blending is similar to inbetweening — an important component of the general problem of computer-assisted animation [3]. The problem addressed in this paper, inbetweening of polygonal shape outlines, is simpler than the more general problem of inbetweening complete drawings.

1.2 Overview

Section 2 discusses geometric aspects of the shape blending problem. The physical work model is discussed in section 3. The minimum work solution is found by means of a directed graph, as discussed in section 4. Section 5 presents several examples and discusses the relative influence of stretching and bending work.

2 Geometric preliminaries

Given two polygons $\mathbf{P}_0$ and $\mathbf{P}_1$ with the same number of vertices, shape blending is accomplished by performing a linear interpolation between the corresponding vertices of the two polygons. If

$$\mathbf{P}^0 = [\mathbf{P}_0^0, \mathbf{P}_1^0, \ldots, \mathbf{P}_n^0]; \quad \mathbf{P}^1 = [\mathbf{P}_0^1, \mathbf{P}_1^1, \ldots, \mathbf{P}_n^1] \quad (1)$$

where $\mathbf{P}_i^k$ denote vertices, intermediate polygons in the blend can be defined

$$
\begin{aligned}
\mathbf{P}(t) &= u\mathbf{P}^0 + t\mathbf{P}^1 \\
&= [u\mathbf{P}_0^0 + t\mathbf{P}_0^1, u\mathbf{P}_1^0 + t\mathbf{P}_1^1, \ldots, u\mathbf{P}_n^0 + t\mathbf{P}_n^1] \\
&= [\mathbf{P}_0(t), \mathbf{P}_1(t), \ldots, \mathbf{P}_n(t)]
\end{aligned}
\quad (2)
$$

where $u = 1 - t$. The motion of three adjacent vertices undergoing a shape blend is shown in Figure 7.

Consider the simple example in Figure 8, where the vertex numbers are labeled. Each intermediate shape is determined by linearly interpolating each node as shown. The paths for vertices 1 and 3 are shown in dotted lines.

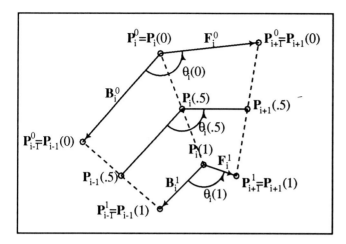

Figure 7: Blending of three adjacent vertices

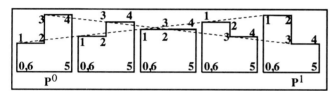

Figure 8: Simple example, solution 1

If the vertices are renumbered, a shape blend such as in Figure 9 can be obtained.

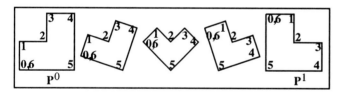

Figure 9: Simple example, solution 2

Different blends can be achieved if we insert new vertices in each polygon. In Figure 10, a vertex labeled "5" is inserted in $\mathbf{P}^0$ and a vertex labeled "1" is inserted in $\mathbf{P}^1$ as shown. Another variation is obtained by adding two new vertices at the same point. In Figure 11, vertices labeled "5" and "6" are inserted in $\mathbf{P}_0$ and vertices labeled "1" and "2" are inserted in $\mathbf{P}_1$ as shown.

Typically, two polygons to be blended do not initially have the same number of vertices, and even if they do, the correspondence will not generally produce a pleasing blend. The examples in Figures 8–11 suggest that the principle task in shape blending is that of adding vertices to each polygon such that each polygon ends up with the same number of vertices, and the resulting vertex correspondences produce the desired blend.

So, how can an algorithm automatically decide, with little or no human intervention, where to add the vertices? Section 2.1 shows two geometric conditions that an algorithm can identify and try to avoid, and section 3 discusses a physical model which can further guide an algorithm.

2.1 Angles

Consider the solution to the step problem shown in Figure 12. This blend serves little useful purpose (except to illustrate shape blending gone awry), because the angle at the circled vertex goes to zero, so that the two edges meeting at that

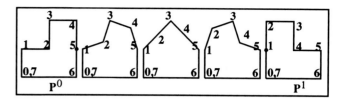

Figure 10: Simple example, solution 3

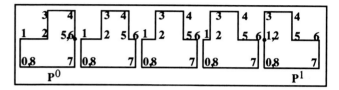

Figure 11: Simple example, solution 4

vertex pass over one another. When this happens, at least part of the shape is turning itself "inside out".

Another example of ill-behaved intermediate angles is shown in Figure 13. Here, the terminal angles at vertices 4 and 6 are both $90°$, yet those angles in the intermediate blends exceed $130°$. Also, vertex 5 begins and ends on a straight line, yet that line becomes noticeably bent during the blend operation.

Figures 12 and 13 suggest two angle constraints that should be imposed on blend solutions. First, if at all possible we should avoid

$$\theta_i(t) = 0 \qquad 0 \le t \le 1 \qquad (3)$$

at each vertex, since that implies that an intermediate shape is self-intersecting. Second, it seems preferable, when possible, for each intermediate angle to be bounded by its terminal angles. That is, $\theta_i(t)$ should change monotonically from $\theta_i(0)$ to $\theta_i(1)$.

It happens that there is an unexpectedly simple representation for the angle $\theta_i(t)$ which greatly aids the understanding and analysis of these two conditions. In the following,

$$\mathbf{P}_i \times \mathbf{P}_j \equiv (x_i, y_i) \times (x_j, y_j) \equiv x_i y_j - x_j y_i,$$

$$\mathbf{P}_i \cdot \mathbf{P}_j \equiv (x_i, y_i) \cdot (x_j, y_j) \equiv x_i x_j + y_i y_j,$$

and

$$||\mathbf{P}_i|| = \sqrt{x_i^2 + y_i^2}.$$

Letting $u = 1 - t$, the angle $\theta(t)$ can be computed

$$
\begin{aligned}
\theta_i(t) &= \angle[(\mathbf{P}_{i-1}^0 u + \mathbf{P}_{i-1}^1 t), (\mathbf{P}_i^0 u + \mathbf{P}_i^1 t), (\mathbf{P}_{i+1}^0 u + \mathbf{P}_{i+1}^1 t)] \\
&= \angle[(\mathbf{B}_i^0 u + \mathbf{B}_i^1 t), \mathbf{0}, (\mathbf{F}_i^0 u + \mathbf{F}_i^1 t)] \qquad (4)
\end{aligned}
$$

where $\mathbf{B}_i^k = \mathbf{P}_{i-1}^k - \mathbf{P}_i^k$ and $\mathbf{F}_i^k = \mathbf{P}_{i+1}^k - \mathbf{P}_i^k$ as shown in Figure 7. Recalling that

$$\sin(\angle \mathbf{P}_1, \mathbf{0}, \mathbf{P}_2) = \frac{\mathbf{P}_1 \times \mathbf{P}_2}{||\mathbf{P}_1|| \, ||\mathbf{P}_2||};$$

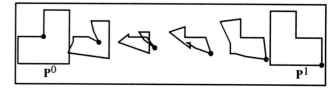

Figure 12: Simple example, "solution" 5

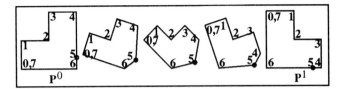

Figure 13: Simple example, "solution" 6

$$\cos(\angle \mathbf{P}_1, 0, \mathbf{P}_2) = \frac{\mathbf{P}_1 \cdot \mathbf{P}_2}{||\mathbf{P}_1|| \, ||\mathbf{P}_2||};$$

$$\tan(\angle \mathbf{P}_1, 0, \mathbf{P}_2) = \frac{\mathbf{P}_1 \times \mathbf{P}_2}{\mathbf{P}_1 \cdot \mathbf{P}_2}, \tag{5}$$

$$\tan(\theta_i(t)) = \frac{(\mathbf{F}_i^0(1-t) + \mathbf{F}_i^1 t) \times (\mathbf{B}_i^0(1-t) + \mathbf{B}_i^1 t)}{(\mathbf{F}_i^0(1-t) + \mathbf{F}_i^1 t) \cdot (\mathbf{B}_i^0(1-t) + \mathbf{B}_i^1 t)}$$

$$= \frac{y_0(1-t)^2 + y_1 2t(1-t) + y_2 t^2}{x_0(1-t)^2 + x_1 2t(1-t) + x_2 t^2} \tag{6}$$

where

$$x_0 = \mathbf{F}_i^0 \cdot \mathbf{B}_i^0; \quad x_1 = \frac{\mathbf{F}_i^1 \cdot \mathbf{B}_i^0 + \mathbf{F}_i^0 \cdot \mathbf{B}_i^1}{2}; \quad x_2 = \mathbf{F}_i^1 \cdot \mathbf{B}_i^1; \tag{7}$$

$$y_0 = \mathbf{F}_i^0 \times \mathbf{B}_i^0; \quad y_1 = \frac{\mathbf{F}_i^1 \times \mathbf{B}_i^0 + \mathbf{F}_i^0 \times \mathbf{B}_i^1}{2}; \quad y_2 = \mathbf{F}_i^1 \times \mathbf{B}_i^1. \tag{8}$$

Equation 6 can be interpreted as a degree two Bézier curve

$$\mathbf{Q}(t) = (x_0, y_0)(1-t)^2 + (x_1, y_1)2t(1-t) + (x_2, y_2)t^2$$

$$= \mathbf{Q}_0(1-t)^2 + \mathbf{Q}_1 2t(1-t) + \mathbf{Q}_2 t^2. \tag{9}$$

As illustrated in Figure 14, $\mathbf{Q}(t)$ has the important property that $\theta_i(t) = \angle((1,0), (0,0), \mathbf{Q}(t))$. Thus, $\theta_i(t) = 0$ only if $\mathbf{Q}(t)$

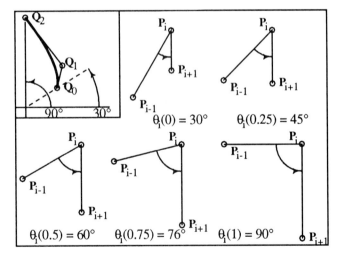

Figure 14: Relationship between $\theta_i(t)$ and $\mathbf{Q}(t)$

intersects the positive x axis (as shown in Figure 15).

Angle monotonicity is assured if no line through the origin intersects $\mathbf{Q}(t)$ more than once (as shown in Figure 16). The angle function $\theta_i(t) = \angle[(1,0), (0,0), \mathbf{Q}(t)]$ has four possible extrema: $\theta_i(0)$, $\theta_i(1)$, $\theta_i(t_1)$, or $\theta_i(t_2)$ where t_1 and t_2 satisfy the equation

$$(\mathbf{Q}(t) - 0) \times \mathbf{Q}'(t) = 0.$$

This produces a cubic polynomial which always degree reduces to a quadratic polynomial in Bernstein form:

$$d(t) = d_0(1-t)^2 + d_1 2t(1-t) + d_2 t^2 = 0; \tag{10}$$

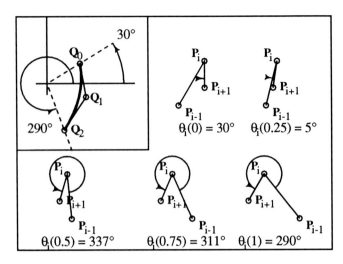

Figure 15: $\theta_i(t)$ goes to zero

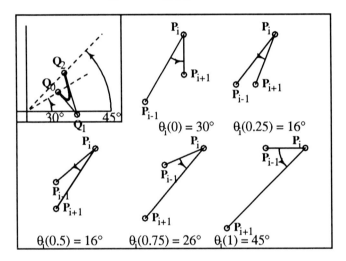

Figure 16: $\theta_i(t)$ is not monotonic

where

$$d_0 = \mathbf{Q}_0 \times \mathbf{Q}_1;$$

$$d_1 = \frac{\mathbf{Q}_0 \times \mathbf{Q}_2}{2};$$

$$d_2 = \mathbf{Q}_1 \times \mathbf{Q}_2.$$

$\theta_i(t)$ changes monotonically if and only if equation 10 has no real roots in the unit interval.

The work model in section 3.2 requires us to compute the angle change $\Delta\theta_i$. If triangle $\triangle \mathbf{Q}_0\mathbf{Q}_1\mathbf{Q}_2$ does not contain the origin, then $\Delta\theta_i = |\theta_i(1) - \theta_i(0)|$ mod $180°$. If triangle $\triangle \mathbf{Q}_0\mathbf{Q}_1\mathbf{Q}_2$ *does* contain the origin, it's possible for $\Delta\theta_i$ to exceed $180°$ as illustrated in Figure 17. Necessary and sufficient conditions for $\Delta\theta_i$ to exceed $180°$ is for $\triangle \mathbf{Q}_0\mathbf{Q}_1\mathbf{Q}_2$ to contain the origin, and $d_1^2 - d_0 d_2 < 0$ (the discriminant of the quadratic formula in equation 10). Thus,

$$\Delta\theta_i = \begin{cases} 360° - |\angle(\mathbf{Q}_0, (0,0), \mathbf{Q}_2)| & \text{if } d_1^2 - d_0 d_2 < 0 \text{ and} \\ & \triangle \mathbf{Q}_0\mathbf{Q}_1\mathbf{Q}_2 \supset (0,0) \\ |\angle(\mathbf{Q}_0, (0,0), \mathbf{Q}_2)| & \text{otherwise} \end{cases} \tag{11}$$

where $\angle(\mathbf{Q}_0, (0,0), \mathbf{Q}_2) \leq 180°$.

If $\theta_i(t)$ is not monotonic, the development in section 3.2, needs to know *how far* $\theta_i(t)$ deviates from monotonicity. This deviation is a non-negative angle denoted by $\Delta\theta_i^*$ as shown

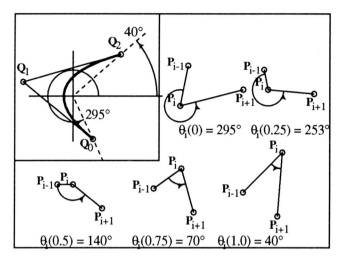

$$\theta_i(0) = 295° \quad \theta_i(0.25) = 253°$$

$$\theta_i(0.5) = 140° \quad \theta_i(0.75) = 70° \quad \theta_i(1.0) = 40°$$

Figure 17: $\Delta\theta_i$ exceeds $180°$

in Figure 18(a) for a single deviation, and Figure 18(b) for a double deviation.

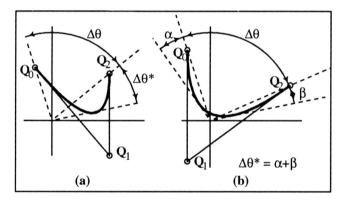

(a)   **(b)**

Figure 18: Measurement of $\Delta\theta_i^*$ for non-monotonic $\theta_i(t)$

2.2 Coincident vertices

Coincident vertices are a common occurrence which invite special attention. When n adjacent vertices on one polygon lie at the same point, $n-1$ edges on the other polygon collapse to that point. Since $\angle(\mathbf{P}_{i-1}, \mathbf{P}_i, \mathbf{P}_{i+1})$ is undefined if $\mathbf{P}_i$ is coincident with either of its neighbors, the angle *change* when such a case is involved in a shape blend is also undefined, as is the bending work discussed in section 3.2. Our tests verify that the following heuristic for assessing angle change when vertices are coincident gives good results.

We imagine that coincident vertices actually lie evenly spaced along the base of an infinitesimal isosceles triangle, as shown in Figure 19. In this case, $\theta_2 = \theta_4 = 90° + \frac{\alpha}{2}$ and $\theta_3 = 180°$ in radians. In general, if vertices $\mathbf{P}_i, \ldots, \mathbf{P}_j$ are coincident, $\theta_i = \theta_j = 90° + \frac{\alpha}{2}$ and $\theta_{i+1} = \theta_{i+2} = \cdots = \theta_{j-1} = 180°$.

In Figure 20, all three vertices of one polygon are coincident. However, as portrayed in Figure 19, those vertices are treated as though they are infinitesimally spaced along a line segment. Thus, in such cases, control point $\mathbf{Q}_2$ (or $\mathbf{Q}_0$) of the $\mathbf{Q}$ curve will always be located an infinitesimal distance from the origin along the $-x$ axis. Figure 21 shows the $\mathbf{Q}$ curve for vertex $i = 2$ in Figure 20. In this case, $\mathbf{Q}_2$ lies an infinitesimal distance from the origin along a ray $110°$ from the $+x$ axis as shown, and $\Delta\theta = 38°$. Figure 22 shows an example of coincident vertices in which an intermediate angle goes to zero.

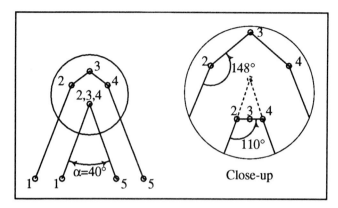

Figure 19: Treatment of coincident vertices

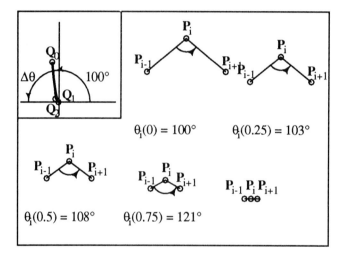

$$\theta_i(0) = 100° \quad \theta_i(0.25) = 103°$$

$$\theta_i(0.5) = 108° \quad \theta_i(0.75) = 121°$$

Figure 20: $\mathbf{Q}$ curve for three coincident vertices

3 Physically based model

Section 2 defined the shape blending problem to be one of deciding where to add vertices to two polygons so that intermediate polygons in the blend could be defined by interpolating corresponding vertices on the given polygons. The decision on where to add vertices must be guided by some heuristic. The heuristic we propose is to model polygon $\mathbf{P}^0$ as a piece of wire made of some idealized metal. The "best" shape blend is the one which requires the least work to deform $\mathbf{P}^0$ into $\mathbf{P}^1$ through bending and stretching.

This section discusses a simplified model for assessing the work involved in moving each vertex and line segment through the shape blend. Section 4 shows how to compute a globally optimal least work solution for all possible vertex correspondences.

We distinguish between work which causes bending, and work which causes stretching. Stretching work is computed for each line segment (that is, each adjacent pair of vertices) whereas bending work is computed for each adjacent pair of line segments (that is, for each set of three adjacent vertices).

3.1 Stretching work

A force P will stretch an actual wire of length L_0 [12] an amount

$$\delta = \frac{PL_0}{AE} \tag{12}$$

where A is the cross sectional area and E is the *modulus of elasticity*, a constant of the material (for example, E for steel

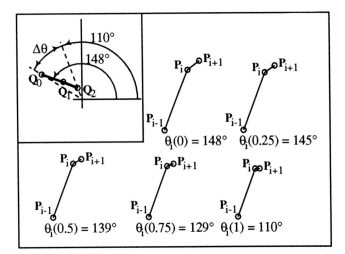

Figure 21: $\mathbf{Q}$ curve for two coincident vertices

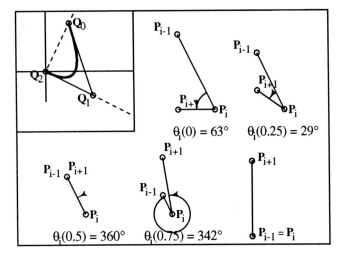

Figure 22: Coincident vertices with $\theta(.5) = 0$

is 29,000,000 psi). The work expended in stretching a real piece of wire an amount δ is [12]

$$W = \frac{\delta^2 AE}{2L_0}. \tag{13}$$

Since AE is a constant for the wire, for our purposes we replace it with a single user-definable "stretching stiffness constant" k_s. If L_0 is the initial length of a section of wire, and if L_1 is its final length, equation 13 will compute different values if the initial and final shapes are swapped ($\frac{\delta^2 AE}{2L_0}$ in one case and $\frac{\delta^2 AE}{2L_1}$ in the other). Furthermore, if an edge collapses to a single vertex (i.e., $L_0 = 0$), equation 13 requires infinite work. These two considerations motivate the following modification to equation 13:

$$W_s = k_s \frac{(L_1 - L_0)^2}{(1 - c_s)\min(L_0, L_1) + c_s\max(L_0, L_1)} \tag{14}$$

where $\delta = L_1 - L_0$ and c_s is a user definable constant which controls the penalty for edges collapsing to points.

The exponent 2 in equations 13 and 14 assumes the wire is *linearly elastic*, which is the case if the wire has not stretched very much. If excessive stretching occurs, less work is required to elongate the wire because it undergoes *plastic deformation*

[12]. In this case, an exponent of 1 more closely expresses the work expended. Thus, we make one final modification to our stretching work equation:

$$W_s = k_s \frac{|L_1 - L_0|^{e_s}}{(1 - c_s)\min(L_0, L_1) + c_s\max(L_0, L_1)}, \tag{15}$$

where k_s, c_s, and e_s are user definable constants.

In physical reality, these work equations only make sense if the wire is getting longer ($L_1 > L_0$), not if it is getting shorter ($L_1 < L_0$). For our purposes, we compute both stretching and compressing work using equation 15.

Section 4 calls for notation which expresses which segment of wire is being stretched. Letting $L_0 = \|\mathbf{P}_{i_1} - \mathbf{P}_{i_0}\|$ and $L_1 = \|\mathbf{P}_{j_1} - \mathbf{P}_{j_0}\|$, we denote by

$$W_s([i_0, j_0], [i_1, j_1]) = \frac{k_s|L_1 - L_0|^{e_s}}{(1 - c_s)\min(L_0, L_1) + c_s\max(L_0, L_1)} \tag{16}$$

the stretching work required to map $\mathbf{P}_{i_0}$—$\mathbf{P}_{i_1}$ to $\mathbf{P}_{j_0}$—$\mathbf{P}_{j_1}$, where $i_1 = i_0$ or $i_1 = i_0 + 1$ and $j_1 = j_0$ or $j_1 = j_0 + 1$.

3.2 Bending work

Analogous to the equation for stretching work developed in section 3.1, work which causes bending is defined in equation 18 for angle $\angle(\mathbf{P}_{i_0}^0, \mathbf{P}_{i_1}^0, \mathbf{P}_{i_2}^0)$ bending into angle $\angle(\mathbf{P}_{j_0}^1, \mathbf{P}_{j_1}^1, \mathbf{P}_{j_2}^1)$:

$$W_b([i_0, j_0], [i_1, j_1], [i_2, j_2]) = \tag{17}$$
$$\begin{cases} k_b(\Delta\theta + m_b\Delta\theta^*)^{e_b} & \text{if } \theta(t) \text{ never goes to zero} \\ k_b(\Delta\theta + m_b\Delta\theta^*)^{e_b} + p_b & \text{if } \theta(t) \text{ does go to zero} \end{cases}$$

where $\Delta\theta$ and $\Delta\theta^*$ are measured in radians and are defined in sections 2.1 and 2.2. k_b, m_b, e_b, and p_b are user definable constants. The constant k_b indicates bending stiffness, m_b penalizes angles which are not monotonic, e_b is an exponent which plays a role similar to e_s, and p_b penalizes angles from going to zero.

3.3 Normalization

Notice that the work due to bending is independent of the size of the shapes. Thus, if the two shapes are scaled uniformly, the bending work computation does not change. However, the stretching work varies with the scale of the shapes. To make the constants k_s and e_s independent of scale, it is a good idea to map each shape to a unit *rectangle*, scaling the same amount in x and y, so that the largest dimension of the bounding box is one. It is important to scale uniformly, or else the angles will change, along with the bending work computation.

It is noteworthy that uniform scaling of the shapes *does* affect the $\mathbf{Q}(t)$ curves, but not the bending work computation. If $\mathbf{P}^1$ is scaled by a constant c, then $\mathbf{Q}_0$ is unchanged, $\mathbf{Q}_1$ is scaled by c, and $\mathbf{Q}_2$ is scaled by c^2. This creates a different $\mathbf{Q}(t)$ curve, but the angle function $\angle((0, 1), (0, 0), \mathbf{Q}(t)) = \theta(t)$ does not change.

3.4 Numerical examples

This section provides two numerical examples of the work required to transform a unit isosceles right triangle into a unit square. In Figure 23, there is no stretching work in line segments 0–1 and 3–4 and no bending work in angle 0. The

stretching work in legs 1–2 and 2–3 is each $k_s \dfrac{|1 - \frac{\sqrt{2}}{2}|^{e_s}}{\frac{\sqrt{2}}{2} \cdot (1 - c_s) + 1 \cdot c_s}$.

The bending work in angles 1 and 3 is each $k_b(\frac{\pi}{4})^{e_b}$ and in vertex 2 is $k_b(\frac{\pi}{2})^{e_b}$. Thus, the total work is

$$W_1 = 2k_s \frac{.293^{e_s}}{.707 + .293 c_s} + 2k_b .785^{e_b} + k_b 1.571^{e_b}. \quad (18)$$

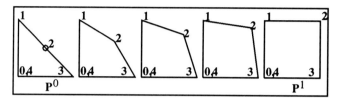

Figure 23: Work computation example, blend 1

In Figure 24, there is also no stretching work in line segments 0–1 and 3–4 and no bending work in angle 0. The stretching work in line segment 1–2 is $k_s \frac{|1-0|^{e_s}}{0 \cdot (1-c_s)+1 \cdot c_s} = \frac{k_s}{c_s}$ and in line 2–3 is $k_s \frac{|1-\sqrt{2}|^{e_s}}{1(1-c_s)+\sqrt{2}c_s}$. The bending work in angles 1 and 2, based on section 2.2, is $k_b \left[\left(\frac{1}{2}\frac{\pi}{4} + \frac{\pi}{2}\right) - \frac{\pi}{2} \right]^{e_b} = k_b \left(\frac{\pi}{8}\right)^{e_b}$. Angle 3 has a $\Delta\theta$ of $\pi/4$ and hence a bending work of $k_b \frac{\pi}{4}^{e_b}$. Thus, the total work to perform the transformation in Figure 24 is

$$W_2 = k_s \left(\frac{1}{c_s} + \frac{.414^{e_s}}{1 + .414 c_s} \right) + k_b [2(.393)^{e_b} + .785^{e_b}]. \quad (19)$$

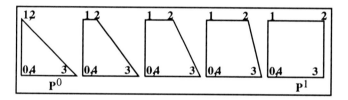

Figure 24: Work computation example, blend 2

By selecting different coefficients k_s, k_b, e_s, e_b, and c_s, we can coerce either blend to have a smaller work requirement. For example if $k_s = k_b = .5$, $e_s = e_b = 1$ and $c_s = 0.5$, $W_1 = 1.91$ and $W_2 = 1.96$. However, if we change $k_s = 0.4$ and $k_b = 0.6$, then $W_1 = 2.16$ and $W_2 = 1.88$. So, if the wire stretches more easily than it bends, blend 2 uses less work.

4 Least work solution

This section presents a method for determining where to insert vertices so that the shape transformation is accomplished with the least work.

This method determines a globally optimal least work solution for all possible correspondences of *existing* vertices, so vertices can only be inserted at existing vertices. As a preprocessing step, additional vertices can be added to break up long line segments. The reason the optimization search is restricted to existing vertices is that otherwise it becomes a non-linear constrained optimization problem whose solution is very expensive and whose global optimality is difficult to verify. By contrast, the discrete solution presented here can be solved in $O(mn)$ time in the number of respective vertices, and global optimality is assured.

One of the first papers written on contour triangulation, [15], employs a directed graph to compute an optimal triangulation between a pair of contour lines. [8] further refined the use of the directed graph for that problem. Our least work solution is primarily based on those two excellent papers. This section briefly reviews the use of directed graphs, giving only enough detail to explain how the ideas in [8] are adapted.

Given two polygons $\mathbf{P}^0 = [\mathbf{P}_0^0, \mathbf{P}_1^0, \ldots, \mathbf{P}_m^0]$ and $\mathbf{P}^1 = [\mathbf{P}_0^1, \mathbf{P}_1^1, \ldots, \mathbf{P}_n^1]$, all vertex correspondences can be represented in an $m \times n$ rectangular matrix, or "graph". The columns of the graph represent vertices on $\mathbf{P}^0$ and the rows of the graph represent vertices on $\mathbf{P}^1$. The point at which column i meets row j signifies a correspondence between $\mathbf{P}_i^0$ and $\mathbf{P}_j^1$.

Denote by $[i,j]$ a correspondence between $\mathbf{P}_i^0$ and $\mathbf{P}_j^1$, which can be represented on the graph as a dot at the junction of column i and row j. A complete shape transformation requires every vertex in $\mathbf{P}^0$ to correspond to at least one vertex in $\mathbf{P}^1$ and vice versa. Furthermore, we only allow $[i,j]$ to be a correspondence if $[i-1,j]$, $[i,j-1]$, or $[i-1,j-1]$ is also a correspondence — else intermediate polygons in the shape transformation would split apart. Given that $[0,0] = [m,n]$ is a correspondence, a complete solution can be represented on the graph as a string of dots starting at $[0,0]$ and ending at $[m,n]$, with each subsequent dot positioned one step East, South, or Southeast from the preceding dot. This is illustrated in Figure 25, where the dots are connected by arrows. We will refer to such a sequence of dots as a *path*, denoted by

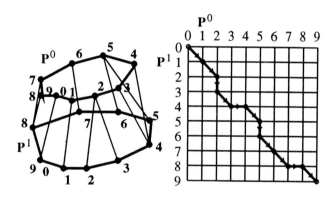

Figure 25: Graph representation of a shape transformation

$\{c_0, c_1, \ldots, c_k\}$. In Figure 25, $c_0 = [0,0]$, $c_3 = [2,3]$, etc. Note that k is the number of vertices in each intermediate polygon in the blend, with $\max(m,n) \leq k \leq m+n$.

We do not allow a South step to be immediately followed by an East step, or an East step to be followed by a South step, because such a combination is more expensive than a single Southeast step, except possibly under unusual work coefficients. The main reason for this rule is to save some computation. Thus, we may say that a path must travel in a Southeasterly direction, and make no 90° turns.

Consider how to evaluate the bending and stretching work for the example in Figure 25. Stretching work is computed for each pair of neighboring dots on the path (c_{l-1}, c_l), since each such pair of dots on the path represents two points on $\mathbf{P}^0$ transforming to two points on $\mathbf{P}^1$. Bending work must be computed using *three* neighboring dots on the path (c_{l-1}, c_l, c_{l+1}), since an angle change involves three points on $\mathbf{P}^0$ moving to three points on $\mathbf{P}^1$.

For large $m = n$, there are $O\left(\frac{m^m}{m!}\right) = O\left(\frac{\epsilon^m}{\sqrt{m}}\right)$ legal paths. However, using a graph, the least work solution can be determined by visiting each junction only once ($O(m^2)$

computation expense). The basic strategy proceeds by considering polygon fragments consisting of vertices $0, \ldots, i$ of $\mathbf{P}^0$ and vertices $0, \ldots, j$ of $\mathbf{P}_1$. Denote these polygon fragments $\mathbf{P}^0(i)$ and $\mathbf{P}^1(j)$. We wish to compute the minimum work required to transform $\mathbf{P}^0(i)$ into $\mathbf{P}^1(j)$, according to the work equations in section 3. In graph theory language, we want to find the path which connects $[0,0]$ to $[i,j]$ using the minimum amount of work, denoted $W(i,j)$. This is easily accomplished using the simple observation that if we know the minimum work values $W(i-1,j)$, $W(i,j-1)$, and $W(i-1,j-1)$, then $W(i,j)$ must equal one of those three predecessors plus the incremental work involved in connecting that predecessor with $[i,j]$.

To accomplish this, we must actually concern ourselves with *three* values of $W(i,j)$, denoted by $W_\uparrow(i,j)$, $W_\nwarrow(i,j)$, and $W_\leftarrow(i,j)$, which indicate the minimum work required to transform $\mathbf{P}^0(i)$ into $\mathbf{P}^1(j)$ if $[i,j-1]$, $[i-1,j-1]$, or $[i-1,j]$ respectively is the preceding dot on the path. These three values are required because each bending work computation relies on three dots on the path. We thus proceed by assigning $W_\uparrow(0,0) = W_\leftarrow(0,0) = W_\nwarrow(0,0) = 0$ and computing for $j = 0, \ldots, n$ and for $i = 0, \ldots, m$ (i and j not both $= 0$):

$$W_\leftarrow(i,j) = W_s([i-1,j],[i,j]) + \qquad (20)$$
$$\min\{W_\leftarrow(i-1,j) + W_b([i-2,j],[i-1,j],[i,j]),$$
$$W_\nwarrow(i-1,j) + W_b([i-2,j-1],[i-1,j],[i,j])\}$$

$$W_\uparrow(i,j) = W_s([i,j-1],[i,j]) + \qquad (21)$$
$$\min\{W_\uparrow(i,j-1) + W_b([i,j-2],[i,j-1],[i,j]),$$
$$W_\nwarrow(i,j-1) + W_b([i-1,j-2],[i,j-1],[i,j])\}$$

$$W_\nwarrow(i,j) = W_s([i-1,j-1],[i,j]) + \qquad (22)$$
$$\min\{W_\uparrow(i-1,j-1) + W_b([i-1,j-2],[i-1,j-1],[i,j]),$$
$$W_\nwarrow(i-1,j-1) + W_b([i-2,j-2],[i-1,j-1],[i,j]),$$
$$W_\leftarrow(i-1,j-1) + W_b([i-2,j-1],[i-1,j-1],[i,j])\}$$

where $W_b([i_1,j_1],[i_2,j_2],[i_3,j_3]) = \infty$ for $i_1 < 0$ or $j_1 < 0$.

The value $\min(W_\leftarrow(m,n), W_\nwarrow(m,n), W_\uparrow(m,n))$ is the global least work. This is of secondary interest; what we *really* want to know is what path results in this minimum work. The path is determined by backtracking through the graph, a process discussed in [8]. Actually, our backtracking is slightly more complicated because each graph node must keep track of *three* backpointers, one for each direction from which the node can be approached in the backtrack.

4.1 Implementation

There is no need to store more than two rows of $W_\leftarrow(i,j)$, $W_\nwarrow(i,j)$, $W_\uparrow(i,j)$ information. Once a complete row of work values has been computed, the previous row can be discarded.

The algorithm as stated goes to a lot of effort to assure that it has found a path of globally minimal work. In particular, the bending work costs much more to compute than does the stretching work, since each node in the graph can represent the middle vertex of seven different angle changes. A much more economical (three times faster!) implementation is possible, which no longer assures a global minimum work solution, but which provides virtually identical results to the rigorous algorithm dicussed above. The simplified algorithm uses only one value of $W(i,j)$ (instead of calculating $W_\uparrow(i,j)$, $W_\nwarrow(i,j)$, and $W_\leftarrow(i,j)$) as follows.

For purposes of discussion, if point $[i,j]$ lies on a path, the preceding point on the path is indicated using the functions $west(i,j)$ and $north(i,j)$. If the preceding point is directly West of $[i,j]$, then $west(i,j) = 1$ and $north(i,j) = 0$. If the preceding point is straight up from $[i,j]$, then $west(i,j) = 0$

and $north(i,j) = 1$. If the preceding point is North-West of $[i,j]$, then $west(i,j) = 1$ and $north(i,j) = 1$. Define

$$w_0 = W(i-1,j) + W_s([i-1,j],[i,j]) + \qquad (23)$$
$$W_b([i-1-west(i-1,j), j-north(i-1,j)],$$
$$[i-1,j],[i,j])$$

$$w_1 = W(i,j-1) + W_s([i,j-1],[i,j]) + \qquad (24)$$
$$W_b([i-west(i,j-1), j-1-north(i,j-1)],$$
$$[i,j-1],[i,j])$$

$$w_2 = W(i-1,j-1) + W_s([i-1,j-1],[i,j]) + \qquad (25)$$
$$W_b([i-1-west(i-1,j-1), j-1-north(i-1,j-1)],$$
$$[i-1,j-1],[i,j])$$

where w_0 is undefined for $i = 0$, w_1 is undefined for $j = 0$, and w_2 is undefined for $i = 0$ or $j = 0$. Then

$$\text{if } w_0 \leq w_1, w_2 \quad : \quad W(i,j) = w_0; \quad west(i,j) = 1;$$
$$north(i,j) = 0 \qquad (26)$$

$$\text{if } w_1 \leq w_0, w_2 \quad : \quad W(i,j) = w_1; \quad west(i,j) = 0;$$
$$north(i,j) = 1 \qquad (27)$$

$$\text{if } w_2 \leq w_0, w_1 \quad : \quad W(i,j) = w_2; \quad west(i,j) = 1;$$
$$north(i,j) = 1 \qquad (28)$$

The algorithm for computing the least work solution amounts to setting $W(0,0) = 0$ and from equations 23 — 28 computing $W(i,j)$; $i = 0, \ldots, m$; $j = 0, \ldots, n$. $W(m,n)$ is then the optimal total least work, and the *north* and *west* information can be used to backtrace the path which leads to this least work solution.

We recommend using this simplified algorithm, because it is easier to implement, it runs three times faster than the theoretically precise algorithm, and the results are visually similar.

4.2 Starting points

The above discussion assumes that point $\mathbf{P}_0^0$ corresponds to point $\mathbf{P}_0^1$. A globally minimum work solution for *any* initial correspondence can be computed in $O(mn \ln n)$ time (see [8]). The example in Figure 9 shows a zero work solution which was found by considering all possible starting correspondences. All the other Figures in the paper had the initial correspondence specified.

5 Examples and discussion

The work equations in section 3 contain seven user definable constants: k_s, k_b, e_s, e_b, p_b, m_b, and c_s. k_s and k_b can be restricted to the unit interval. Table 1 shows the coefficients used by our algorithm to blend the figures in this paper. The meaning of diagonal deviation dd is discussed in section 5.2.

Figures 8–11 underscore the inherent ambiguity of the shape blending problem. Without human guidance, no algorithm could discern which of these four solutions is appropriate, since one can think of specific instances in which each of them might be preferred. Note that for these shape pairs, parameter adjustment can achieve the different desired results. As mentioned, the only user intervention for the examples in this paper is the specification of starting points and of the seven constants. However, it is easy to contrive examples where no set of seven constants will produce a prescribed blend (such as in Figure 26, which consists of a combination of Figures 8 and 11). In some cases, it may be needful for the user to specify a few other correspondences as well.

Figure	dd	k_s	k_b	e_s	e_b	p_b	m_b	c_s
1	.06	1	.2	2	2	1000	10	.5
2	.09	0	1	2	2	1000	10	.5
3	.09	1	1	2	.5	1000	10	.5
8	0	0	1	2	.8	1000	10	.5
10	0	1	0	2	1	1000	10	.5
11	.125	0	1	2	1	1000	10	.5
27	.245	.3	1	2	.3	1000	10	.5
28	.04	1	.1	2	.1	1000	10	.5

Table 1: Coefficients for various example figures

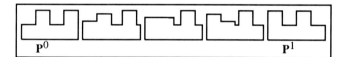

Figure 26: Unattainable example

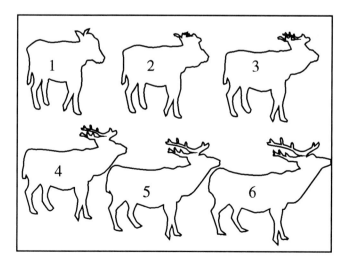

Figure 27: Cow to deer

Figure 27 shows a blend from a cow to a deer. Notice that some of the antlers cross each other in the intermediate shapes. A high value of p_b prevents *local* self-intersections (angles going to zero) but not global self intersections.

Figure 28 involves excessive movement of the dancer's arm. Due to the linear motion between corresponding vertices, the arm shortens as it moves.

Figure 28: Dancer

5.1 Preprocessing

The heuristic described in this paper relies on a reasonable initial distribution of polygon vertices. For example, Figure 2 requires additional vertices to be inserted along some of the straight segments of the F shape in order to provide a pleasing correspondence with the base of the E.

Since the work equations are more realistic for distinct vertices than for coincident vertices, the algorithm tends to work best if the two polygons have roughly the same number of vertices. This tends to reduce the number of coincident vertices in the final solution, since there must be a minimum of $|m-n|$ coincident vertices.

5.2 Speedups

We timed an example in which each polygon has 100 vertices, and the execution time on an IBM RS6000 Model 530 workstation is 8 seconds using unoptimized code. Using the simplified alorithm in section 4.1, the execution time is 3 seconds.

In most cases, the graph of the least work solution has a path (see Figure 25) which does not deviate very far from the diagonal of the graph. Recall that a polygon $\mathbf{P}^0$ with m vertices and a polygon $\mathbf{P}^1$ with n vertices create a graph with m columns and n rows. The amount which graph point $c[i,j]$ deviates from the graph diagonal is

$$\left| \frac{i}{m} - \frac{j}{n} \right|. \tag{29}$$

The diagonal deviation of an entire path is

$$dd = \max_{[i,j] \in \text{path}} \left| \frac{i}{m} - \frac{j}{n} \right|. \tag{30}$$

The cow-to-deer blend path (see Figure 27) is shown in Figure 29. Its diagonal deviation of .245 is the largest of any of the examples in this paper (see Table 1). Thus, instead of searching the entire rectangular graph, the least work solution can generally be determined by visiting only those elements of the graph within a distance dd from the diagonal.

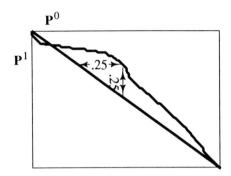

Figure 29: Cow to deer least work path; diagonal deviation

6   Future Work

This research seems to have generated more questions than it has answered. The authors are currently looking at several follow-up problems. For example, to make this process useful for keyframe animation and morphing, an interior preserving map is needed for interpolating raster images which are enclosed by the terminal polygons. We are currently studying how well Schwartz-Christoffel transformations solve this problem.

How do we deal with cases where a scene composed of m number of polygons blends into a scene composed of n polygons, perhaps including holes? Ideas from [5] may help decide.

What about using periodic B-splines instead of polygons? An easy answer is to simply polygonize the curves and apply the current algorithm, but a more satisfying answer is to develop energy minimization methods which work directly on the curves. The calculus of variations may provide help here.

All the blends in this paper involve moving corresponding vertices along linear paths. This can create some undesirable effects, such as the withering arm in blend 4 of Figure 28. **Q** curves are easily extended to express angle change and segment length when vertices travel along Bézier curves of any degree. Study is underway in identifying curved paths which relieve the withering arm problem.

The work model assumes that each wire has uniform stiffness. There may be merit to specifying that some portions of the wire are more stiff than others, suggesting a relative discouragement towards altering those portions. For example, in the cow-to-deer blend, it may be helpful to assign a smaller stiffness to the antlers than to the rest of the deer.

Of course, extending this algorithm to polygonal surfaces in 3-D is a worthwhile goal.

Applications to other fields such as pattern and signature recognition are also being studied.

More detail on the material in this paper can be found in [11].

Acknowledgements
Peisheng Gao sketched several of the illustrations in the paper. Thanks to Andrew Glassner for motivating discussions and for the initial shapes in Figure 3. Bruce Brereton provided valuable assistance in evaluating commercial illustration software that supports blending. This work was supported under NSF grant DMC-8657057, and under a grant from IBM.

References

[1] Adobe Systems, Inc. *Adobe Illustrator 88*.

[2] Bruce G. Baumgart. *Geometric Modeling for Computer Vision*. Phd thesis, Stanford University, Computer Science Department, 1974.

[3] Edwin Catmull. The problems of computer-assisted animation. *Computer Graphics*, 12(3):348–353, 1978.

[4] Shenchang Eric Chen and Richard Parent. Shape averaging and its applications to industrial design. *IEEE CG&A*, 9(1):47–54, 1989.

[5] Henry N. Christiansen and Thomas W. Sederberg. Conversion of complex contour line definitions into polygonal element mosaics. *Computer Graphics (Proc. SIGGRAPH)*, 12(3):187–192, 1978.

[6] Computer Support Corporation. *Arts & Letters 3.01*, 1991.

[7] Corel Systems Corporation, Ottawa, Canada. *Corel-Draw! 2.0*, 1990.

[8] Henry Fuchs, Z. M. Kedem, and S. P. Uselton. Optimal surface reconstruction from planar contours. *Comm. ACM*, 20(10):693–702, 1977.

[9] S. Ganapathy and T. G. Dennehy. A new general triangulation method for planar contours. *Computer Graphics (Proc. SIGGRAPH)*, 16(3):69–75, 1982.

[10] Andrew Glassner. Metamorphosis. *preprint*, 1991.

[11] Eugene Greenwood. A physically based approach to 2–d shape interpolation. Master's thesis, Brigham Young University, Department of Mechanical Engineering, 1992.

[12] Archie Higdon, Edward H. Ohlsen, William B. Stiles, John A. Weese, and William F. Riley. *Mechanics of Materials*. John Wiley & Sons, Inc., New York, 1976.

[13] Michael Kass, Andrew Witkin, and Demetri Terzopoulos. Snakes: Active contour models. *International Journal of Computer Vision*, 1(3):321–331, 1988.

[14] Anil Kaul and Jarek Rossignac. Solid-interpolating deformations: Construction and animation of PIPs. In F.H. Post and W. Barth, editors, *Proc. Eurographics '91*, pages 493—505. Elsevier Science Publishers B.V, 1991.

[15] E. Keppel. Approximating complex surfaces by triangulation of contour lines. *IBM Journal of Research and Development*, 19:2–11, 1975.

[16] David Kurlander and Eric A. Bier. Graphical search and replace. *Computer Graphics*, 22(4):113–120, 1988.

[17] Micrografx, Inc., Richardson, TX. *Designer 3.1*.

[18] Software Publishing Corp., Sunnyvale, CA. *Harvard Graphics 3.0*, 1991.

[19] Naonori Ueda and Satoshi Suzuki. Automatic shape model acquisition using multiscale segment matching. In *Proc. 10th ICPR*, pages 897—902. IEEE, 1990.

Feature-Based Image Metamorphosis

Thaddeus Beier

Silicon Graphics Computer Systems
2011 Shoreline Blvd, Mountain View CA 94043

Shawn Neely

Pacific Data Images
1111 Karlstad Drive, Sunnyvale CA 94089

1   Abstract

A new technique is presented for the metamorphosis of one digital image into another. The approach gives the animator high-level control of the visual effect by providing natural feature-based specification and interaction. When used effectively, this technique can give the illusion that the photographed or computer generated subjects are transforming in a fluid, surrealistic, and often dramatic way. Comparisons with existing methods are drawn, and the advantages and disadvantages of each are examined. The new method is then extended to accommodate keyframed transformations between image sequences for motion image work. Several examples are illustrated with resulting images.

Keywords: Computer Animation, Interpolation, Image Processing, Shape Transformation.

2   Introduction

2.1   Conventional Metamorphosis Techniques

Metamorphosis between two or more images over time is a useful visual technique, often used for educational or entertainment purposes. Traditional filmmaking techniques for this effect include clever cuts (such as a character exhibiting changes while running through a forest and passing behind several trees) and optical cross-dissolve, in which one image is faded out while another is simultaneously faded in (with makeup change, appliances, or object substitution). Several classic horror films illustrate the process; who could forget the hair-raising transformation of the Wolfman, or the dramatic metamorphosis from Dr. Jekyll to Mr. Hyde? This paper presents a contemporary solution to the visual transformation problem.

Taking the cutting approach to the limit gives us the technique of stop-motion animation, in which the subject is progressively transformed and photographed one frame at a time. This process can give the powerful illusion of continuous metamorphosis, but it requires much skill and is very tedious work. Moreover, stop-motion usually suffers from the problem of visual strobing by not providing the motion blur normally associated with moving film subjects. A mo-

tion-controlled variant called go-motion (in which the frame-by-frame subjects are photographed while moving) can provide the proper motion blur to create a more natural effect, but the complexity of the models, motion hardware, and required skills becomes even greater.

2.2   3D Computer Graphics Techniques

We can use technology in other ways to help build a metamorphosis tool. For example, we can use computer graphics to model and render images which transform over time.

One approach involves the representation of a pair of three-dimensional objects as a collection of polygons. The vertices of the first object are then displaced over time to coincide in position with corresponding vertices of the second object, with color and other attributes similarly interpolated. The chief problem with this technique is the difficulty in establishing a desirable vertex correspondence; this often imposes inconvenient constraints on the geometric representation of the objects, such as requiring the same number of polygons in each model. Even if these conditions are met, problems still arise when the topologies of the two objects differ (such as when one object has a hole through it), or when the features must move in a complex way (such as sliding along the object surface from back to front). This direct point-interpolation technique can be effective, however, for transformations in which the data correspondence and interpolation paths are simple. For example, the technique was successfully used for the interpolation of a regular grid of 3D scanned data in "Star Trek IV: The Voyage Home" [13]. Methods for automatically generating corresponding vertices or polygons for interpolation have been developed. [5][6]

Other computer graphics techniques which can be used for object metamorphosis include solid deformations [1] [12] and particle systems [10]. In each case the 3D model of the first object is transformed to have the shape and surface properties of the second model, and the resulting animation is rendered and recorded.

2.3   2D Computer Graphics Techniques

While three-dimensional object metamorphosis is a natural solution when both objects are easily modeled for the computer, often the complexity of the subjects makes this approach impractical. For example, many applications of the effect require transformations between complex objects such as animals. In this case it is often easier to manipulate scanned photographs of the scene using two-dimensional image processing techniques than to attempt to model and render the details of the animal's appearance for the computer.

The simplest method for changing one digital image into another is simply to cross-dissolve between them. The color of each pixel is

©1992   ACM-0-89791-479-1/92/007/0035 $01.50

interpolated over time from the first image value to the corresponding second image value. While this method is more flexible than the traditional optical approach (simplifying, for example, different dissolve rates in different image areas), it is still often ineffective for suggesting the actual metamorphosis from one subject to another. This may be partially due to the fact that we are accustomed to seeing this visual device used for another purpose: the linking of two shots, usually signifying a lapse of time and a change in place [7].

Another method for transforming one image into another is to use a two-dimensional "particle system" to map pixels from one image onto pixels from the second image. As the pixel tiles move over time the first image appears to disintegrate and then restructure itself into the second image. This technique is used in several video effects systems (such as the Quantel Mirage) [11].

Another transformation method involves image warping so that the original image appears to be mapped onto a regular shape such as a plane or cylinder. This technique has limited application towards the general transformations under consideration in this paper, but has the advantage of several real-time implementations for video (such as the Ampex ADO) [11]. Extensions include mapping the image onto a free-form surface; one system has even been used for real-time animation of facial images [8].

Other interesting image warps have been described by Holzmann [3] [4], Smith [14], and Wolberg[16].

2.4 Morphing
We use the term "morphing" to describe the combination of generalized image warping with a cross-dissolve between image elements. The term is derived from "image metamorphosis" and should not be confused with morphological image processing operators which detect image features. Morphing is an image processing technique typically used as an animation tool for the metamorphosis from one image to another. The idea is to specify a warp that distorts the first image into the second. Its inverse will distort the second image into the first. As the metamorphosis proceeds, the first image is gradually distorted and is faded out, while the second image starts out totally distorted toward the first and is faded in. Thus, the early images in the sequence are much like the first source image. The middle image of the sequence is the average of the first source image distorted halfway toward the second one and the second source image distorted halfway back toward the first one. The last images in the sequence are similar to the second source image. The middle image is key; if it looks good then probably the entire animated sequence will look good. For morphs between faces, the middle image often looks strikingly life-like, like a real person, but clearly it is neither the person in the first nor second source images.

The morph process consists of warping two images so that they have the same "shape", and then cross dissolving the resulting images. Cross-dissolving is simple; the major problem is how to warp an image.

Morphing has been used as a computer graphics technique for at least a decade. Tom Brigham used a form of morphing in experimental art at NYIT in the early 1980's. Industrial Light and Magic used morphing for cinematic special effects in *Willow* and *Indiana Jones and the Last Crusade*. All of these examples are given in Wolberg's excellent treatise on the subject[15].

Wolberg's book effectively covers the fundamentals of digital image warping, culminating in a mesh warping technique which uses spline mapping in two dimensions. This technique is both fast and intuitive; efficient algorithms exist for computing the mapping of each pixel from the control grid, and a rubber-sheet mental model works effectively for predicting the distortion behavior. It will be compared to our technique in detail below.

2.5 Field Morphing
We now introduce a new technique for morphing based upon fields of influence surrounding two-dimensional control primitives. We call this approach "field morphing" but will often simply abbreviate to "morphing" for the remainder of this paper.

3 Mathematics of Field Morphing

3.1 Distortion of a Single Image
There are two ways to warp an image [15]. The first, called forward mapping, scans through the source image pixel by pixel, and copies them to the appropriate place in the destination image. The second, reverse mapping, goes through the destination image pixel by pixel, and samples the correct pixel from the source image. The most important feature of inverse mapping is that every pixel in the destination image gets set to something appropriate. In the forward mapping case, some pixels in the destination might not get painted, and would have to be interpolated. We calculate the image deformation as a reverse mapping. The problem can be stated "Which pixel coordinate in the source image do we sample for each pixel in the destination image?"

3.2 Transformation with One Pair of Lines
A pair of lines (one defined relative to the source image, the other defined relative to the destination image) defines a mapping from one image to the other. (In this and all other algorithms and equations, pixel coordinates are **BOLD UPPERCASE ITALICS**, lines are specified by pairs of pixel coordinates(***PQ***), scalars are ***bold lowercase italics***, and primed variables (***X'***, ***u'***) are values defined relative to the source image. We use the term *line* to mean a directed line segment.)

A pair of corresponding lines in the source and destination images defines a coordinate mapping from the destination image pixel coordinate ***X*** to the source image pixel coordinate ***X'*** such that for a line ***PQ*** in the destination image and ***P'Q'*** in the source image.

$$u = \frac{(X - P) \cdot (Q - P)}{\| Q - P \|^2} \tag{1}$$

$$v = \frac{(X - P) \cdot Perpendicular\,(Q - P)}{\| Q - P \|} \tag{2}$$

$$X' = P' + u \cdot (Q' - P') + \frac{v \cdot Perpendicular\,(Q' - P')}{\| Q' - P' \|} \tag{3}$$

where *Perpendicular( )* returns the vector perpendicular to, and the same length as, the input vector. (There are two perpendicular vectors; either the left or right one can be used, as long as it is consistently used throughout.)

The value ***u*** is the position along the line, and *v* is the distance from the line. The value ***u*** goes from 0 to 1 as the pixel moves from ***P*** to ***Q***, and is less than 0 or greater than 1 outside that range. The value for *v* is the perpendicular distance in pixels from the line. If there is just one line pair, the transformation of the image proceeds as follows:

For each pixel X in the destination image
    find the corresponding u,v
    find the X' in the source image for that u,v
    destinationImage(X) = sourceImage(X')

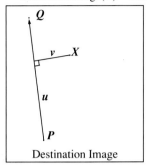 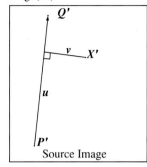

Figure 1: Single line pair

In Figure 1, X' is the location to sample the source image for the pixel at X in the destination image. The location is at a distance v (the distance from the line to the pixel in the source image) from the line $P'Q'$, and at a proportion u along that line.

The algorithm transforms each pixel coordinate by a rotation, translation, and/or a scale, thereby transforming the whole image. All of the pixels along the line in the source image are copied on top of the line in the destination image. Because the u coordinate is normalized by the length of the line, and the v coordinate is not (it is always distance in pixels), the images is scaled along the direction of the lines by the ratio of the lengths of the lines. The scale is only along the direction of the line. We have tried scaling the v coordinate by the length of the line, so that the scaling is always uniform, but found that the given formulation is more useful.

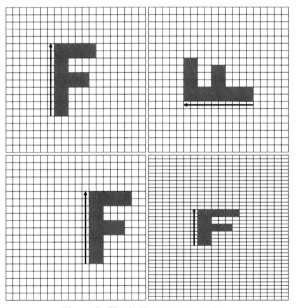

Figure 2: Single line pair examples

The figure on the upper left is the original image. The line is rotated in the upper right image, translated in the lower left image, and scaled in the lower right image, performing the corresponding transformations to the image.

It is possible to get a pure rotation of an image if the two lines are the same length. A pair of lines that are the same length and orientation but different positions specifies a translation of an image. All transformations based on a single line pair are affine, but not all affine transformations are possible. In particular, uniform scales and shears are not possible to specify.

3.3 Transformation with Multiple Pairs of Lines

Multiple pairs of lines specify more complex transformations. A weighting of the coordinate transformations for each line is performed. A position X_i' is calculated for each pair of lines. The displacement $D_i = X_i' - X$ is the difference between the pixel location in the source and destination images, and a weighted average of those displacements is calculated. The weight is determined by the distance from X to the line. This average displacement is added to the current pixel location X to determine the position X' to sample in the source image. The single line case falls out as a special case of the multiple line case, assuming the weight never goes to zero anywhere in the image. The weight assigned to each line should be strongest when the pixel is exactly on the line, and weaker the further the pixel is from it. The equation we use is

$$weight = \left(\frac{length^p}{(a + dist)} \right)^b \qquad (4)$$

where *length* is the length of a line, *dist* is the distance[†] from the pixel to the line, and *a*, *b*, and *p* are constants that can be used to change the relative effect of the lines.

If *a* is barely greater than zero, then if the distance from the line to the pixel is zero, the strength is nearly infinite. With this value for *a*, the user knows that pixels on the line will go exactly where he wants them. Values larger than that will yield a more smooth warping, but with less precise control. The variable *b* determines how the relative strength of different lines falls off with distance. If it is large, then every pixel will be affected only by the line nearest it. If *b* is zero, then each pixel will be affected by all lines equally. Values of *b* in the range [0.5, 2] are the most useful. The value of *p* is typically in the range [0, 1]; if it is zero, then all lines have the same weight, if it is one, then longer lines have a greater relative weight than shorter lines.

The multiple line algorithm is as follows:

For each pixel X in the destination
    $DSUM = (0,0)$
    weightsum = 0
    For each line $P_i Q_i$
        calculate u,v based on $P_i Q_i$
        calculate X'_i based on u,v and $P_i'Q_i'$
        calculate displacement $D_i = X_i' - X_i$ for this line
        dist = shortest distance from X to $P_i Q_i$
        weight = ($length^p$ / (a + $dist$))^b
        $DSUM$ += D_i * *weight*
        weightsum += *weight*
    $X' = X + DSUM$ / *weightsum*
    destinationImage(X) = sourceImage(X')

---

† Note that because these "lines" are directed line segments, the distance from a line to a point is abs(v) if $0 < u < 1$, the distance from P to the point if $u < 0$, and the distance from Q to the point if $u > 1$.

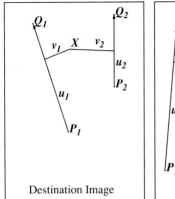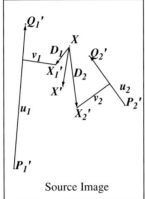

Destination Image | Source Image

Figure 3: Multiple line pairs

In the above figure, X' is the location to sample the source image for the pixel at X in the destination image. That location is a weighted average of the two pixel locations X_1' and X_2', computed with respect to the first and second line pair, respectively.

If the value a is set to zero there is an undefined result if two lines cross. Each line will have an infinite weight at the intersection point. We quote the line from *Ghostbusters*: "Don't cross the streams. Why? It would be bad." This gets the point across, and in practice does not seem to be too much of a limitation. The animator's mental model when working with the program is that each line has a field of influence around it, and will force pixels near it to stay in the corresponding position relative to the line as the line animates. The closer the pixels are to a line, the more closely they follow the motion of that line, regardless of the motion of other lines. This mental model gives the animator a good intuitive feel for what will happen as he designs a metamorphosis.

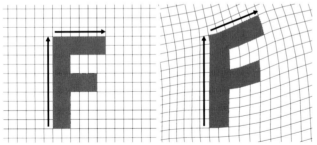

Figure 4: Multiple line pair example

With two or more lines, the transformation is not simple. The figure on the left is the original image, it is distorted by rotating the line above the F around its first point. The whole image is distorted by this transformation. It is still not possible to do a uniform scale or a shear with multiple lines. Almost any pair of lines results in a non-affine transformation. Still, it is fairly obvious to the user what happens when lines are added and moved. Pixels near the lines are moved along with the lines, pixels equally far away from two lines are influenced by both of them.

3.4 Morphing Between Two Images

A morph operation blends between two images, *I0* and *I1*. To do this, we define corresponding lines in *I0* and *I1*. Each intermediate frame *I* of the metamorphosis is defined by creating a new set of line segments by interpolating the lines from their positions in *I0* to the positions in *I1*. Both images *I0* and *I1* are distorted toward the position of the lines in *I*. These two resulting images are cross-dissolved throughout the metamorphosis, so that at the beginning, the image is completely *I0* (undistorted because we have not yet begun to interpolate away from the line positions associated with *I0*). Halfway through the metamorphosis it is halfway between *I0* and *I1*, and finally at the end it is completely *I1*. Note that there is a chance that in some of the intermediate frames, two lines may cross even if they did not cross in the source images.

We have used two different ways of interpolating the lines. The first way is just to interpolate the endpoints of each line. The second way is to interpolate the center position and orientation of each line, and interpolate the length of each line. In the first case, a rotating line would shrink in the middle of the metamorphosis. On the other hand, the second case is not very obvious to the user, who might be surprised by how the lines interpolate. In any case, letting the user see the interpolated position helps him design a good set of beginning and end positions.

3.5 Performance

For video-resolution images (720x486 pixels) with 100 line pairs, this algorithm takes about 2 minutes per frame on a SGI 4D25. The runtime is proportional to the number of lines times the number of pixels in the image. For interactive placement of the lines, low resolution images are typically used. As is usually the case with any computer animation, the interactive design time is the dominant time; it often takes 10 times as long to design a metamorphosis than to compute the final frames.

4   Advantages and Disadvantages of this Technique

This technique has one big advantage over the mesh warping technique described in Wolberg's book[15]: it is much more expressive. The only positions that are used in the algorithm are ones the animator explicitly created. For example, when morphing two faces, the animator might draw line segments down the middle of the nose, across the eyes, along the eyebrows, down the edges of the cheeks, and along the hairline. Everything that is specified is moved exactly as the animator wants them moved, and everything else is blended smoothly based on those positions. Adding new line segments increases control in that area without affecting things too much everywhere else.

This feature-based approach contrasts with the mesh warping technique. In the simplest version of that algorithm, the animator must specify in advance how many control points to use to control the image. The animator must then take those given points and move them to the correct locations. Points left unmodified by mistake or points for which the animator could not find an associating feature are still used by the warping algorithm. Often the animator will find that he does not have enough control in some places and too much in others. Every point exerts the same amount of influence as each of the other points. Often the features that the animator is trying to match are diagonal, whereas the mesh vertices start out vertical and horizontal, and it is difficult for the animator to decide which mesh vertices should be put along the diagonal line.

We have found that trying to position dozens of mesh points around is like trying to push a rope; something is always forced where you don't want it to go. With our technique the control of the line segments is very natural. Moving a line around has a very predictable effect. Extensions of the mesh warping technique to allow refinement of the mesh would make that technique much more expressive and useful[2].

Another problem with the spline mesh technique is that the two-pass algorithm breaks down for large rotational distortions (bottleneck problem)[14][15]. The intermediate image in the two pass algorithm might be distorted to such an extent that information is lost. It is possible do mesh warping with a one-pass algorithm that would avoid this problem.

The two biggest disadvantages of our feature-based technique are speed and control. Because it is global, all line segments need to be referenced for every pixel. This contrasts with the spline mesh, which can have local control (usually the 16 spline points nearest the pixel need be considered).

Between the lines, sometimes unexpected interpolations are generated. The algorithm tries to guess what should happen far away from the line segments; sometimes it makes a mistake. This problem usually manifests itself as a "ghost" of a part of the image showing up in some unrelated part of the interpolated image, caused by some unforeseen combination of the specified line segments. A debugging tool can be useful in this case, in which the user can point to a pixel in the interpolated image and the source pixel is displayed, showing where that pixel originated. Using this information, the animator can usually move a line or add a new one to fix the problem.

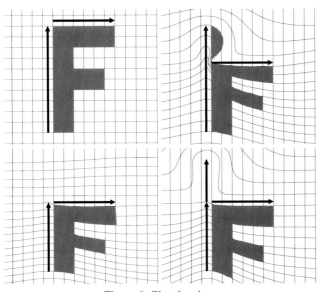

Figure 6: Ghostbusting

In Figure 6, the top left image is the original. Moving the horizontal line down creates a ghost above the line, that is made from pixels copied from the top edge of the F. The bottom left image shows one fix, shrinking the vertical line to match the horizontal one. If the vertical line must maintain its length for some other reason, then the ghost can be eliminated by breaking the vertical line into two parts, as shown on the lower right.

5   Animated Sequences

It is often useful to morph between two sequences of live action, rather than just two still images. The morph technique can easily be extended to apply to this problem. Instead of just marking corresponding features in the two images, there needs to be a set of line segments at key frames for each sequence of images. These sets of segments are interpolated to get the two sets for a particular frame,

and then the above two-image metamorphosis is performed on the two frames, one from each strip of live action. This creates much more work for the animator, because instead of marking features in just two images he will need to mark features in many key frames in two sequences of live action. For example, in a transition between two moving faces, the animator might have to draw a line down the nose in each of 10 keyframes in both sequences, requiring 20 individual line segments. However, the increase in realism of metamorphosis of live action compared to still images is dramatic, and worth the effort. The sequences in the Michael Jackson video, *Black or White*, were done this way.

6   Results

We have been using this algorithm at Pacific Data Images for the last two years. The first projects involved interpolation of still images. Now, almost all of the projects involve morphing of live-action sequences.

While the program is straightforward and fun to use, it still requires a lot of work from the animator. The first project using the tool, (the *Plymouth Voyager* metamorphosis), involved morphs between nine pairs of still images. It took three animator-weeks to complete the project. While it was very quick to get a good initial approximation of a transition, the final tweaking took the majority of the time. Of course, it was the first experience any of us had with the tool, so there was some learning time in those three animator-weeks. Also, a large amount of time was spent doing traditional special effects work on top of the morph feature matching. For example, the images had to be extracted from the background (using a digital paint program), some color balancing needed to be done, and the foreground elements had to be separated form each other (more painting). These elements were morphed separately, then matted together. On current morph production jobs at PDI, we estimate that about 20-40 percent of the time is spent doing the actual metamorphosis design, while the rest of the time is used doing traditional special effects.

7   Acknowledgments

Tom Brigham of the New York Institute of Technology deserves credit for introducing us to the concept of morph. The magicians at Industrial Light and Magic took the idea to a new level of quality in several feature films, and provided inspiration for this work. Jamie Dixon at PDI was a driving force behind the creation of the tools, and the rest of the animators at PDI have been the best users that we can imagine. The great animation created with this program is mostly their work, not ours. Finally, Carl Rosendahl, Glenn Entis, and Richard Chuang deserve credit for making Pacific Data Images the creative, fun environment where great new things can happen, and for allowing us to publish details of a very profitable algorithm.

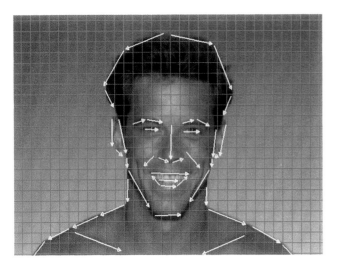

Figure 7

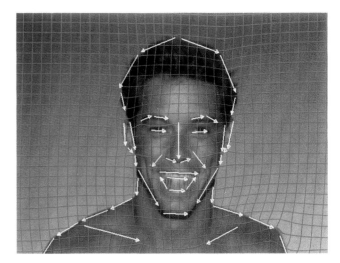

Figure 10

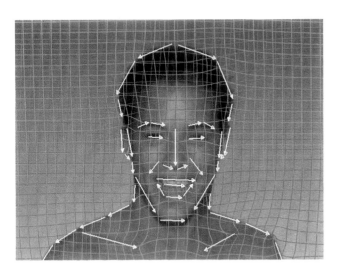

Figure 8

Figure 7 shows the lines drawn over the a face, figure 9 shows the lines drawn over a second face. Figure 8 shows the morphed image, with the interpolated lines drawn over it.

Figure 10 shows the first face with the lines and a grid, showing how it is distorted to the position of the lines in the intermediate frame. Figure 11 shows the second face distorted to the same intermediate position. The lines in the top and bottom picture are in the same position. We have distorted the two images to the same "shape".

Note that outside the outline of the faces, the grids are warped very differently in the two images, but because this is the background, it is not important. If there were background features that needed to be matched, lines could have been drawn over them as well.

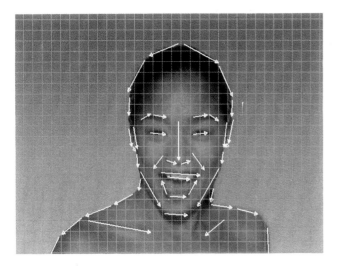

Figure 9

Figure 11

Figure 12

Figure 14

Figure 12 is the first face distorted to the intermediate position, without the grid or lines. Figure 13 is the second face distorted toward that same position. Note that the blend between the two distorted images is much more life-like than the either of the distorted images themselves. We have noticed this happens very frequently.

The final sequence is figures 14, 15, and 16.

Figure 15

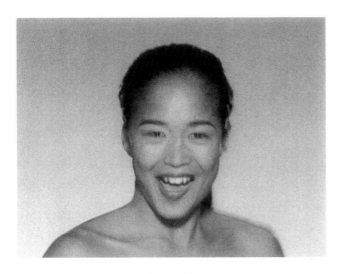

Figure 13

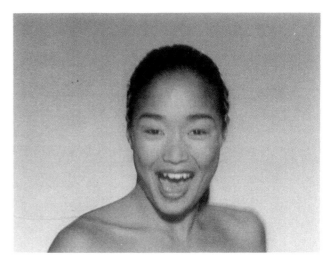

Figure 16

8 References

[1] Barr, A.H., Global and Local Deformations of Solid Primitives. In "Proc. SIGGRAPH '84" (Minneapolis, July 23-27, 1984). Published as "Computer Graphics", 18(3) (July 1984), pp. 21-30.

[2] Forsey, D. R., Bartels, R. H., Hierarchical B-Spline Refinement. In "Proc. SIGGRAPH '88" (Atlanta, August 1-5, 1988). Published as "Computer Graphics", 22(4) (August 1988), pp. 205-211

[3] Holzmann, G.J., PICO --- A Picture Editor. "AT&T Technical Journal", 66(2) (March/April 1987), pp. 2-13.

[4] Holzmann, G.J., "Beyond Photography: The Digital Darkroom". Prentice Hall, 1988.

[5] Kaul, A., Rossignac, J., "Solid-Interpolating Deformations: Constructions and Animation of PIPs," *Proceedings of EUROGRAPHICS '91*, September 1991, pp. 493-505

[6] Kent, J.,Parent, R., Carlson, W. "Establishing Correspondences by Topological Merging: A New Approach to 3-D Shape Transformation", *Proceedings of Graphics Interface '91*, June 1991, pp. 271-278

[7] Oakley, V., "Dictionary of Film and Television Terms". Barnes & Noble Books, 1983.

[8] Oka, M., Tsutsui, K., Akio, O., Yoshitaka, K., Takashi, T., Real-Time Manipulation of Texture-Mapped Surfaces. In "Proc. SIGGRAPH '87" (Anaheim, July 27-31, 1987). Published as "Computer Graphics", 21(4) (July 1987), pp. 181-188.

[9]Overveld, C.W.A.M. Van A Technique for Motion Specification."Visual Computer". March 1990

[10] Reeves, W.T., Particle Systems: A Technique for Modeling a Class of Fuzzy Objects. "ACM Transactions on Graphics", 2(2) (April 1983). (Reprinted in "Proc. SIGGRAPH '83" (Detroit, July 25-29, 1983). Published as "Computer Graphics", 17(3) (July 1983), pp. 359-376.)

[11] Rosenfeld, M., Special Effects Production with Computer Graphics and Video Techniques. In "SIGGRAPH '87 Course Notes #8 - Special Effects with Computer Graphics" (Anaheim, July 27-31, 1987).

[12] Sederberg, T.W. and Parry, S.R., Free-Form Deformation of Solid Geometric Models. In "Proc. SIGGRAPH '86" (Dallas, August 18-22, 1986). Published as "Computer Graphics", 20(4) (August 1986), pp. 151-160.

[13] Shay, J.D., Humpback to the Future. "Cinefex 29" (February 1987), pp. 4-19.

[14] Smith, A.R., Planar 2-Pass Texture Mapping and Warping. In "Proc. SIGGRAPH '87" (Anaheim, July 27-31, 1987). Published as "Computer Graphics", 21(4) (July 1987), pp. 263-272.

[15] Wolberg, G., "Digital Image Warping". IEEE Computer Society Press, 1990.

[16] Wolberg, G., Skeleton Based Image Warping, "Visual Computer", Volume 5, Number 1/2, March 1989. pp 95-108

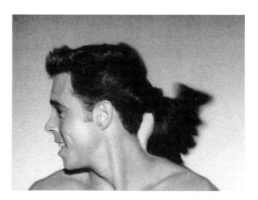

Figure 17
A sequence from Michael Jackson's *Black or White*
(Courtesy MJJ Productions)

Scheduled Fourier Volume Morphing*

John F. Hughes

Department of Computer Science, Box 1910, Brown University
Providence, RI 02906.

(401) 863-7638; jfh@cs.brown.edu

Abstract

We describe an easily implemented and computationally feasible method for smoothly transitioning from one sampled volumetric model to another. This induces a transition between isosurfaces of the two models. The technique is based on interpolating smoothly between the Fourier transforms of the two volumetric models and then transforming the results back. A linear interpolation between the transformed datasets yields unsatisfactory results in some cases. We use a *schedule* for the interpolation in which the high frequencies of the first model are gradually removed, the low frequencies are interpolated to those of the second, and the high frequencies of the second model are gradually added in. Such scheduling yields more satisfactory results. We give several examples and comment briefly on preprocessing models to make the morphing smoother.

CR Categories: I.3.5 [Computer Graphics]: Computational Geometry and Object Modeling; Curve, surface, solid, and object representations; Hierarchy and geometric transformations; I.3.6 [Computer Graphics]: Graphics data structures and data types.

Additional Keywords: Fourier transformation, morphing, smooth interpolation, sampled volumetric models.

1 Introduction

A volumetric model is an entity that can provide a value at each point in 3-space, either by computing the value of some analytically expressed function or by computing a value indirectly from some other description. They are being used more frequently as workstation memories grow and processor speeds increase. Such volumetric models may come from external sources, such as MRI, or they may be created directly with the intent of modeling shapes [1] [2] [5]. In the latter case, the shape being constructed is typically an *isosurface* of a function on 3-space. For Blinn's blobby objects [1] and Wyvill et. al.'s soft objects [4], the function on 3-space is derived from the model indirectly; for sampled data, such as that stored in sculpted models [5], the function values at the sample points are known exactly, and the values elsewhere must be interpolated.

If we have two volumetric models, we can interpolate from one to the other directly: if the first model gives a function $g(x, y, z)$ on 3-space and the second gives a function $h(x, y, z)$, then we can define a function $K_t(x, y, z) = (1 - t)g(x, y, z) + t\,h(x, y, z)$. By looking at the functions K_t for values of t between 0 and 1, we get models that could reasonably be said to be "between" the two original models[1]. Computing the isosurfaces of K_t for a sequence of t values gives a sequence of surfaces that change from the surface represented by the first model to that represented by the second, or a *morphing*[2] between the models. This is difficult to do with conventional polygonal or spline-based models, because of the possibly different topologies of the starting and ending models.

This simple form of morphing yields an interesting interpolation between the models, but difficulties can arise, in part from the high-frequency components of the sampled data and in part from the nature of the data values away from the particular isosurface level (see Section 4). We therefore use a slightly more complex interpolation between the models, involving Fourier transforms, which we describe in the next section.

The examples in this paper are all based on $32 \times 32 \times 32$ volume data, primarily for speed and because of the storage requirements for larger datasets. The operations involved in blending datasets or rendering an image from a dataset of size $n \times n \times n$ are of order n^3, so the time spent in the Fourier transforms ($O(n^3 \log n)$) is not substantially greater than that spent in other operations.

2 Implementing Volumetric Morphing

Very roughly speaking, high-frequency components of the function represented by sampled data tend to generate small wiggles in the isosurfaces of the function. In a two-dimensional analogy, a contour line for the ocean surface has more wiggles on a windy day (when there are lots of ripples) than on a calm one (when only large swells remain). Figure 1 shows this situation in one dimension: in part (a) showing a function with some high-frequencies, the set of points at a constant height consists of many points, while in part (b), a function made up of just one low-frequency term, the set of points at a constant height consists of just a few widely spaced points.

Because interpolating between the wiggles on one object and on another seems unimportant compared to the larger-scale process of interpolating between the general shape of one object and of another, we have devised a slightly more subtle scheme for interpolation. We take the first sampled volumetric model, gradually remove the high frequencies, interpolate over to the low frequencies of the second model, and then blend in the high frequencies of the second model. (See Figures 5–7 for examples.) The order in which the high frequencies are removed and the blending is done we call the *schedule*; its exact design is discussed in Section 3.

*This work was supported in part by grants from NSF, DARPA, IBM, NCR, Sun Microsystems, DEC, and HP.

[1]The range of values in the models should be the same, e.g., from 0 to 1; the isosurfaces will be at the halfway level, i.e., at 0.5.

[2]The word "morph" is derived from "metamorphosis," or "morphogenesis." "Morphing" was originally used to describe manipulation of *images* rather than the underlying models [3].

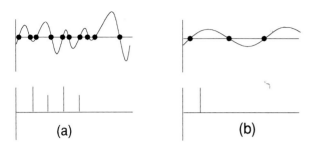

Figure 1: The level sets of two different functions and their Fourier transforms.

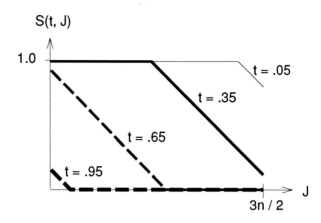

Figure 2: A blending function with $W = 32$.

To understand this scheduled blending mathematically, suppose that we have a function $S_1(t, f_x, f_y, f_z)$ that describes how much of the information at frequency (f_x, f_y, f_z) should remain from the first model at time t, and another such function S_2 for the second model. Then, letting $\mathcal{F}$ denote the fast Fourier transform and once again using g and h to denote our two sampled volumetric datasets, we define the blended version of g and h, according to the schedules S_1 and S_2, to be

$$K_t = \mathcal{F}^{-1}(S_1(t, f_x, f_y, f_z)\mathcal{F}(g) + S_2(t, f_x, f_y, f_z)\mathcal{F}(h)))$$

In explicit terms, the pseudocode is the following:

```
Compute G = FFT of dataset g
Compute H = FFT of dataset h
for several values of t between 0 and 1{
    for (fx = -omega; fx <= omega ; fx++){
        for (fy = -omega; fy <= omega ; fy++){
            for (fz = -omega; fz <= omega ; fz++){
                K[fx][fy][fz] =
                    G[fx][fy][fz] * S_1(t, fx, fy, fz) +
                    H[fx][fy][fz] * S_2(t, fx, fy, fz);
            }
        }
    }
    compute k = inverse FFT of K
}
```

If we let

$$J = |f_x| + |f_y| + |f_z| \tag{1}$$

denote the total frequency of a component of the signal, then our schedule functions can be rewritten as $S_1(t, J)$, representing the fraction of the signal at total frequency J that should be present at time t, and the pseudocode (for datasets of size $n \times n \times n$) becomes this:

```
Compute G = FFT of dataset g
Compute H = FFT of dataset h
for several values of t between 0 and 1{
    for (i = 0; i < n; i++) {
        for (j = 0; j < n; j++) {
            for (k = 0; k < n; k++) {
                K(i, j, k) =
                    G(i, j, k) * S_1(t, J) +
                    H(i, j, k) * S_2(t, J);
            }
        }
    }
    compute k = inverse FFT of K
}
```

where the dependence of J on the frequencies f_x, f_y, and f_z, is given by Equation 1, and the relationship between f_x, f_y, and f_z and i, j, and k, which depends on the implementation of the FFT.

3 The Design of the Schedule

The simplest schedule (the one described in the introduction) was

$$S_1(t, J) = 1 - t \tag{2}$$
$$S_2(t, J) = 1 - S_1(t, J) \tag{3}$$

Equation 3 can be used in general; that is to say, we can simply design S_1 and let S_2 be determined from it by Equation 3. In fact, if the sum of S_1 and S_2 is not 1, then in particular the DC[3] term of

[3]The DC term is the $f_x = f_y = f_z = 0$ term in the Fourier transform, and corresponds to the average value of the data.

the signal will not be blended uniformly. Assuming for the moment that this DC term is the same at both ends, the failure of Equation 3 would cause a change in the average value of the volume data. If the isosurface value is constant, then changing this average value has the same *net* effect as keeping the average value the same and varying the isosurface level. The results can be problematic: if we make the isosurface level too high, we may get no isosurface at all. (In Figure 1, this would correspond to moving the horizontal lines up, so that they miss the graphs of the functions altogether).

By contrast, Equation 2 is not particularly general. Strict linear interpolation is just one of many possibilities. For example, the schedule used in producing the pictures here is

$$a(t, J) = (W + \frac{3n}{2})(\frac{1 - t}{W}) - \frac{J}{W} \tag{4}$$
$$S(t, J) = \max(0, \min(a(t, J), 1.0)) \tag{5}$$
$$S_1(t, J) = S(t, J) \tag{6}$$
$$S_2(t, J) = 1 - S(t, J) \tag{7}$$

where the parameter W determines the shape of the function[4]. We call W the "notch width." The idea in the design of the function S was to have it look like a constant function on the interval $[0, \frac{3n}{2}]$ when $t = 0$, and then get a notch in its right end (representing *high* frequencies) as t increases.

Figure 2 shows this schedule function when $W = 32$ as t takes on the values .05, .35, .65, and .95. Figure 3 shows the schedule, but with $W = 16$. From these, we see that this schedule implements the plan described in Section 2—it first trims down the high frequencies of the first model, then blends the low frequencies over to become those of the second model, and then adds in the high frequencies of the second model. Varying the width of the notch W affects the rate at which this blending takes place. For a wide notch, the low frequencies may begin to be blended before all the high frequencies are gone from the first model, so that the overall shapes begin to interpolate while the details of the models are still present. For a narrow notch, the high frequencies (and even some of the middle frequencies) of the first model are gone well before the low-frequency blending starts. This means that the first model becomes "softer" or "blobbier" before it begins to change its overall shape to that of the second model, which then begins to show its fine details and features.

The precise schedule required to make the model change at the right rate can depend on the model. For example, Figure 4 shows

[4]The number $\frac{3n}{2}$ is the largest possible value for J: frequency $(0, 0, 0)$ is $\frac{3n}{2}$ steps away from $(\frac{n}{2}, \frac{n}{2}, \frac{n}{2})$, which is the highest frequency in the dataset.

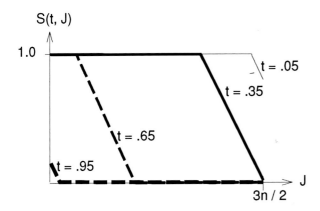

Figure 3: A blending function with $W = 16$.

two functions p and q whose level sets look identical at some level e, even though their values away from e are quite different. Analogous behavior in three dimensions leads to different underlying models with the same isosurfaces. Interpolating from p to another function r gives different results, even with the same schedule, from interpolating from q to r. Thus one must either do some experimentation with different schedules for two particular models, or else alter the models a priori so that one knows how the values away from the isosurface look. We discuss one way of doing this next.

4 Problems with Data

Normally when one extracts an isosurface from a dataset, the values far from the isosurface level are unimportant. In volume morphing, however, they may play a part. For example, in the sphere-to-torus morphing shown in the accompanying videotape, it is important the the torus have moderately high density (though less than 0.5, of course) in the hole, so that the hole will fill in smoothly during the morphing, instead of having the ring shrink rapidly to a thin band and disappear all at once. The function describing the sphere decays rapidly outside the sphere, which accounts for the sudden bulge that appears about a quarter of the way through the morphing.

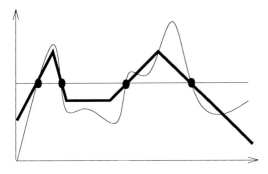

Figure 4: Two functions whose level sets are identical but whose values elsewhere are very different.

The problem of making a model better behaved away from an isosurface can be partly solved by techniques from image processing, but there is much work left to be done. We mention just one method here. We create a new dataset from the original as follows: for each point, determine the shortest path along the integer lattice

to a point of the isosurface. Call this distance d. Then let

$$\text{newValue} = 0.5 + k\, d \operatorname{sgn}(\text{oldValue} - 0.5)$$

for some value of k that causes the value to fade away from 0.5 at the desired rate.

5 Remarks

If one does a long sequence of the morphing transformations described in this paper, passing among a sequence of volumetric datasets, high frequencies will be present at certain moments (the "keyframes") and will be absent the rest of the time, at least if a filter with a narrow notch is used. The effect thus produced–a sort of sequential crystallization into different forms–could be useful to an animator, but it may also be distracting. Some method of splining the blending schedules may be able to reduce this emphasis of keyframes, except at the start and finish.

The approach taken here has been to try to remove the features of the model and then interpolate the general shape. One can, instead, *add* features randomly, by adding high-frequency noise to the data, then interpolate the underlying volumes and finally reduce the high-frequency noise. This tends to cause the surface to ripple and even to have bits break off and then later reassemble. In this case, the morphing between the details of the models is hidden behind noise; rather than having the details of the model fade into a blob, they become hidden in a forest of noise. The accompanying video shows this kind of noisy morphing between a two-holed torus and a teapot.

Volume morphing is not a general solution to interpolation. For example, a metamorphosis between two identical objects, one displaced from the other, is *not* a smooth translation.

Finally, we should remark that until volumetric and surface-based modeling methods are unified, we see no way to apply this technique to anything but volumetric models. We therefore look forward to the unification of volumetric models with surface-based techniques.

6 Conclusion

Despite the complexity (or at least the size) of sampled volumetric models, the task of changing smoothly between widely varying topologies is particularly easy in this case. With appropriate texture mapping, the results can be quite impressive. The method described in this paper can be implemented in a few hours.

7 Acknowledgments

Thanks to Brian Cole for continually interesting me in Fourier transforms. Tinsley Galyean at MIT, and members of the Brown Computer Graphics Group, particularly Tom True, Brook Conner, and Scott Snibbe, made many helpful suggestions. Finally, the work would not have been possible without the generous support of our sponsors.

References

[1] Blinn, J.F. A Generalization of Algebraic Surface Drawing. *ACM TOG*, 1(3):235–256, 1982.

[2] Bloomenthal, J. and Shoemake, K. Convolution Surfaces. *Computer Graphics*, 25(4):251–256, July 1991. Proceedings of SIGGRAPH '91 (Las Vegas, Nevada, July 29 - August 2, 1991).

[3] Carolco Productions. Terminator 2, 1991.

[4] G. Wyvill, C. McPheeters and Wyvill, B. Data Structures for Soft Objects. *The Visual Computer*, 2(4):227–234, August 1986.

[5] Galyean, T. and Hughes, J. Sculpting: An Interactive Volumetric Modeling Technique. *Computer Graphics*, 25(4):267–274, July 1991. Proceedings of SIGGRAPH '91 (Las Vegas, Nevada, July 29 - August 2, 1991).

  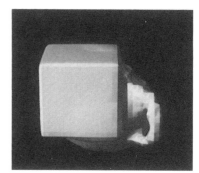

Figure 5: A sculpted teapot becomes a cube.

 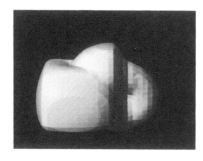 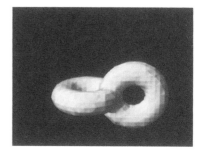

Figure 6: A cube becomes a 2-holed torus.

Figure 7: A spherical isosurface becomes toroidal.

Shape Transformation for Polyhedral Objects

James R. Kent
Wayne E. Carlson
Richard E. Parent
Department of Computer and Information Science
Advanced Computing Center for the Arts and Design
The Ohio State University
Columbus, Ohio 43210

Abstract

Techniques that transform one two-dimensional image into another have gained widespread use in recent years. Extending these techniques to transform pairs of 3D objects, as opposed to 2D images of the objects, provides several advantages, including the ability to animate the objects independently of the transformation. This paper presents an algorithm for computing such transformations. The algorithm merges the topological structures of a pair of 3D polyhedral models into a common vertex/edge/face network. This allows transformations from one object to the other to be easily computed by interpolating between corresponding vertex positions.

Keywords: Computer Animation, Computer-Aided Geometric Design, Interpolation, Shape Transformation.

CR Categories: I.3.5 [Computer Graphics]: Computational Geometry and Object Modeling; I.3.7 - [Computer Graphics]: Three-Dimensional Graphics and Realism

1.0 Introduction

In recent years, image processing techniques, popularly known as "morphing", have achieved widespread use in the entertainment industry. Morphing involves the transformation of one 2D image into another 2D image. These techniques involve first specifying some function that maps points from one image onto points of the other image, then simultaneously interpolating the color and the position of corresponding points to generate intermediate images. When viewed in sequence, these intermediate images produce an animation of the first image changing into the second. Variations of these techniques have been used to create astonishing special effects for commercials, music videos, and movies.

While morphing is useful for many applications, the fact that the intermediate stages of the transformation are images with no 3D geometry limits its use. In order to fully realize the benefits of transformations in animation and design, 3D models of the objects must be transformed, instead of just 2D images of these objects. Transforming 3D models as opposed to images allows for the objects to be animated independently of the transformation, using computer animation techniques such as keyframing. In addition, 3D transformations can be used in design to create objects that combine features of the original objects ([4], [8], [14]).

This paper presents an algorithm that, given two 3-D polyhedral models, generates two new models that have the same shape as the original ones, but that allow transformations from one to another to be easily computed. A previous paper [9] described an early version of the algorithm that was limited to star-shaped[1] polyhedral solids. Since then, the algorithm has been extended to allow for transformations between more complex polyhedral models. In addition, the computational complexity and robustness of the algorithm have been improved.

After some fundamental concepts are defined in Section 2, a description of the shape transformation problem for 3D objects is given in Section 3. This is followed by a brief review of previously published research in Section 4. Section 5 provides a detailed description of the algorithm. Section 6 addresses interpolation issues, including transforming non-geometric attributes, such as surface color. Sample transformations are presented in Section 7. The paper concludes with a discussion of open issues and future research in Section 8.

2.0 Fundamental Concepts

In order to discuss the shape transformation problem, it is useful to carefully define a few key terms. Throughout this discussion, the term *object* will be used to refer to an entity that has a 3D surface geometry. The *shape* of an object refers to the set of points in object space that comprise the object's surface. The term *model* will be used to refer to any complete description of the shape of an object. Thus, a single object may have many different models that describe its shape.

Following the terminology used by Weiler in [16], *topology* refers to the vertex/edge/face network of a model. *Geometry* refers to an instance of a topology for which the vertex coordinates have been specified. Vertices, edges, and faces are collectively referred to as *topological elements*.

Some concepts from mathematical topology also need to be defined. Two objects are said to be *homeomorphic*, or *topologically equivalent*, if a continuous, invertible, one-to-one mapping between

---

1. *Star-shaped* refers to models for which at least one interior point, p, exists such that any semi-infinite ray originating at p intersects the surface of the object at exactly one point.

©1992   ACM-0-89791-479-1/92/007/0047 $01.50

points on the surface of the two objects exists. Such a mapping is referred to as a *homeomorphism*. Finally, an object is said to be *Euler-valid* if its topology obeys the generalized Euler formula:

$$V - E + F = 2 - 2G$$

where V, E, and F are, respectively, the number of vertices, edges, and faces of the topological network, and G is the number of passages through the object (i.e. its *genus*).

3.0 The Shape Transformation Problem

A common approach to transforming one shape into another is to divide the problem into two steps. The first step is to establish a mapping from each point on one surface to some point on the second surface. Once these correspondences have been established, the second step is to create a sequence of intermediate models by interpolating corresponding points from their position on the surface of one object to their position on the surface of the other. The first step will be referred to as the *correspondence problem*, and the second step will be referred to as the *interpolation problem*. The two problems are interrelated since the method used to solve the interpolation problem is dependent upon the manner in which the correspondences are established.

This paper presents a solution to the correspondence problem for Euler-valid, genus 0, polyhedral objects. By restricting ourselves to polyhedral objects, the correspondence step does not need to explicitly specify the mapping for every point on the surface. A sufficient solution is to specify correspondences for each vertex of the models. The interpolation problem is then solved by interpolating the positions of corresponding vertices. Since the main contribution of this paper is an algorithm for establishing correspondences, the majority of the paper is concerned with the solution to the correspondence problem. Issues that arise during the interpolation are briefly discussed in Section 6.0.

4.0 Previous Work

As mentioned in Section 1.0, "morphing" techniques for transforming images have demonstrated remarkable results and have achieved widespread use. Wolberg provides an excellent introduction to image morphing in [17]. These techniques rely on the user to specify pairs of points in the two images that correspond.

Several approaches to three-dimensional shape transformation have been published. Wyvill [18] describes a transformation algorithm for implicit surfaces (i.e. blobby objects). Brute force approaches for polyhedral models, such as that described by Terzides' [14], essentially require the user to specify, for every vertex, a corresponding vertex from the other model. Hong et al. [7] propose a solution for polyhedra based on matching the faces of the objects whose centroids are closest. Bethel & Uselton [1] describe an algorithm that adds degenerate vertices and faces to two polyhedra until a common topology is achieved. Chen & Parent [4] present a transformation algorithm for piecewise linear 2D contours, then briefly address an extension for 3D lofted objects. Parent [10] describes a solution for polyhedra that establishes correspondences by splitting the surface of the models into pairs of sheets of faces, then recursively subdividing them until the topology of each pair is identical. Kaul & Rossignac [8] transform pairs of polyhedra by computing the Minkowski sum of scaled versions of the models. By gradually scaling one model from 100% to 0% while simultaneously scaling the other from 0% to 100%, a transformation is obtained. Payne & Toga [11] first convert each polyhedra into a distance-field volumetric representation, interpolate the values at each point of the 3D vol-

ume, then find a new isosurface that represents some combination of the original objects.

Techniques that make use of the topology and geometry of the models tend to yield better results. For example, since Hong et al. and Payne & Toga do not make full use of the topological information, the surfaces of the models generated at intermediate steps are not guaranteed to remain connected. Similarly, Bethel & Uselton and Parent rely primarily on the topology to establish correspondences, ignoring most of the geometric information. This often results in severely distorted intermediate models.

Kaul & Rossignac's technique, as well as the one described in this paper, make full use of both the topology and the geometry of the models, resulting in intermediate models that have connected surfaces and that exhibit small amounts of distortion. One principal advantage of the method described herein is that our correspondence algorithm describes a homeomorphism. This provides a straightforward method for interpolating the surface attributes of the objects along with the geometry. In addition, it seems likely that our approach can be more easily extended to allow for greater user control over the transformation.

5.0 An Algorithm for Establishing Correspondences

Suppose that two genus 0 solid objects are specified. Now, imagine that it were possible to inflate these objects with air like balloons until they became spherical. Each point on the surface of each object maps onto a unique point on the surface of the sphere. Associating each point from one object with the point from the other object that maps to the same point on the sphere establishes a one-to-one correspondence between points on the surface of the two objects.

The above observations form the basis for the correspondence algorithm. First, the surface of each object is projected onto a unit sphere. This mapping is used to identify correspondences between points on the two original objects by associating pairs of points that map to the same location on the sphere. This approach can potentially be applied for non-polyhedral genus 0 objects (e.g. spline surface models) as long as a mapping from the surface of the object to the surface of the unit sphere can be found.

Bier and Sloan [2] describe a similar approach for solving the problem of wrapping a 2D texture onto a 3D object. The first step maps the texture onto an intermediate surface, such as a sphere or a cylinder. The second step maps the intermediate surface to the surface of the 3D object. Unfortunately, the techniques used to map the intermediate surface to the 3D object are not always one-to-one, and thus are not appropriate for our application.

This section describes an implementation of the correspondence algorithm for genus 0 polyhedral solids. The first step is to project the topology of both models onto the unit sphere. Next, the two topologies are merged by clipping the projected faces of one model to the projected faces of the other. The merged topology is then mapped onto the surface of both original models. This generates two new models that have the same shape as the original two models, but that share a common topology. This allows a transformation between the two shapes to be easily computed by interpolating the coordinates of each pair of corresponding vertices. Figure 1 shows a pair of models and the same pair with the merged topologies mapped onto their surfaces

Throughout the discussion, the original objects are referred to as A and B. The original polyhedral models of these objects are referred to as M_a and M_b. M_a has vertices, V_a, edges, E_a and faces, F_a. Similarly, M_b has vertices, V_b, edges, E_b, and faces, F_b. The projection of M_a and M_b onto the unit sphere are referred to as $(M_a)_p$ and

$(M_b)_p$, respectively, with vertices $(V_a)_p$ and $(V_b)_p$. When referring to a specific topological element of one of the models, lower case letters will be used. For example, e_a refers to a specific edge of object M_a, and $(v_b)_p$ refers to a specific projected vertex of M_b. The results of the correspondence algorithm (i.e. the two new models of A and B that share a common topology) are referred to as M_a^* and M_b^*.

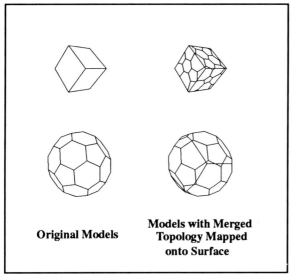

Original Models

Models with Merged Topology Mapped onto Surface

Figure 1 - An Example of The Correspondence Algorithm

5.1 Projection Methods

The first step of the correspondence algorithm is to project the surface of the two polyhedra onto the surface of the unit sphere. The projection must satisfy two conditions. First, it must be one-to-one, so that each point on the surface of the object projects to a unique point on the surface of the sphere. Second, the projection must be continuous in the sense that points within a small radius of a given point project to within a small radius of the projection of that point. Any method for projecting an object that satisfies these two conditions is acceptable.

The projected polyhedral models are completely specified by the topology of the original model together with the coordinates of the projected vertices. This enables the projected models to be saved, eliminating the need to recompute them each time the model is used.

Since the correspondences between the models are established by their mappings onto the sphere, different mappings result in different transformations. Thus, providing different projection methods gives the user some degree of control over the transformation. Sections 5.1.1 through 5.1.4 describe a collection of projection methods that allow a wide variety of polyhedral models to be transformed. While no completely general method has been found, the techniques presented work for a large number of commonly encountered types of models.

5.1.1 Convex and Star-Shaped Objects

The definition of a star-shaped polyhedral object is that at least one interior point of the polyhedron exists from which all the vertices of the object are visible. This definition suggests a method for projecting such an object. First, specify such an interior point, O, to be the center of the object, and translate the object so that O coincides with the origin. Then, move each vertex in or out along the ray from O through the vertex until it lies at unit distance from O.

A suitable center point can be algorithmically selected by first computing the intersection of the interior half spaces of all the planes of the faces of the model. The resulting volume is called the *kernel* of the polyhedral model. If the original polyhedron is star-shaped, its kernel is a non-empty convex polyhedron. Averaging the vertices of the kernel yields a suitable center point for the projection. The complexity of computing the kernel of a three-dimensional polyhedron is O(NlogN) [12].

Since the choice of center point affects the location of the projected vertices, providing the ability to select a center point gives the user some control over the transformation. Verifying that the selected point satisfies the vertex visibility condition can be performed in O(N) time by testing that the outward normal of each face is directed away from the point.

Note that convex polyhedra are a special case of star-shaped polyhedra for which all interior points satisfy the visibility condition. Thus, for convex polyhedra, any interior point may be specified as the center.

Some of the projection methods described in the following sections project the model onto a convex polyhedron (usually the convex hull of the object). To complete the projection to the sphere, the star-shaped projection is applied to this convex polyhedron.

5.1.2 Methods Using Model Knowledge

Polyhedral models are often constructed using techniques such as revolving a contour about an axis, or extruding a planar polygon along a line [3]. By using information about how the model is constructed, efficient methods for projecting the object to the unit sphere can be found. This approach naturally lends itself to an object-oriented methodology, where "ProjectToSphere" could be one of the methods attached to an object.

The class of polyhedral models known as objects of revolution consist of a set of planar contours (ribs) arranged at angular increments around an axis. Such a model can be projected to a sphere in O(N) time by positioning the points of each rib along a longitudinal arc of the sphere whose "north/south" axis matches the axis of the model. Each arc should lie in the plane of the rib, have its endpoints on the axis, and be on the same side of the axis as the rib.

Two methods for spacing the rib points along a semicircle have been developed. The first positions them so that the arc lengths between points on the semicircle are proportional to the distance between the corresponding points on the rib. The second method first projects the rib onto its convex hull using a recursive method similar to that described by Ekoule et al. in [5]. Once the rib is mapped onto its convex hull, each point is moved in or out to the unit sphere along a ray from the midpoint of the axis through the point.

Any technique that maps a rib to a semicircle can be used for spacing the points with different transformations resulting. However, methods that preserve geometric information from the original model, such as the two described above, generally lead to more aesthetic transformations.

Another common class of polyhedral models, known as extruded objects, are generated by moving a planar polygon along a straight line, sweeping out a solid volume. Two copies of the polygon are used to cap the ends of the object. This class of models can be projected by mapping each of the two caps to its convex hull, using Ekoule's method as above. The resulting convex model can be projected to the unit sphere using the star-shaped projection from Section 5.1.1.

It is important to note that the above techniques work for any model that can be described in an appropriate format, whether or not the object was originally modeled using the described techniques. For example, data from 3D digitizers can often be easily converted into the object of revolution format.

5.1.3 Physically-Based Methods

As mentioned in Section 5.0, the inspiration for the shape transformation algorithm involves an analogy with inflating the objects like a balloon. This idea led to experimentation with projection methods based upon physically-based simulation. The goal is to have the simulation convert the object into a convex object with the same topology while preserving as much of the geometric information contained in the model as possible. The simulations, based on the work of Haumann [6], treat the surface of the model as a flexible object. Each vertex of the topology is modeled as a mass and each edge of the topology as a spring.

Several types of simulations were tried. One approach was to model the forces involved in inflating a balloon. Weak spring forces were applied along the edges together with internal air pressure forces. The air pressure forces had a magnitude that was proportional to the area of each face and were applied to the centroid of each face in the direction of its outward normal. For some models, this approach worked well, but in general, the simulation did not always produce a convex model. This was usually due to the presence of cycles of short edges in the models. When stretched, these edges generated large forces that resisted further stretching. In addition, vertices would tend to drift around, which diminished the relationship between the geometry of the original objects and their projections.

Another approach that has been more successful is to first determine which vertices of the model lie on its convex hull. Fixing these points, and treating the non-hull vertices as free masses connected by springs along the edges to each other and to the hull vertices, a simulation is run to "snap" the model outward to its convex hull. Setting the strengths of the springs to be inversely proportional to their original lengths preserves the ratios of edge lengths as much as possible. In addition, fixing the hull vertices minimizes the drifting problem. Although this approach generally works better than the first, it does not work for arbitrary models.

In performing the above experiments, one scenario that consistently yields the desired results was discovered. This situation occurs whenever a concave region of the model is completely surrounded by a planar convex ring of edges that lie on the convex hull. Running a simulation by fixing the vertices that lie on this ring, and treating the network of edges and vertices that lie inside as a mass/spring system quickly "snaps" out the interior into the plane of the surrounding ring. In the following, this scenario will be referred to as a "surrounded region".

To better understand this situation, consider the following analogy. Suppose you were to build a planar, convex wooden frame with a nail pounded into each corner. Next, attach a mesh of rubber bands to the nails. No matter how one pulls upon the rubber band mesh, as soon as it is let go, it snaps back into the plane of the wooden frame. In this analogy, the wooden frame corresponds to the surrounding ring of edges. The nails correspond to the vertices of the surrounding ring. The edges of the interior network are the rubber bands, and the vertices correspond to places where rubber bands are joined.

An approach that shows promise for solving the projection problem for arbitrary genus 0 polyhedra is to attempt to divide the projection into a set of subproblems, each of which involves a surrounded region. A heuristic approach to subdividing the problem in this manner is to use the faces of the convex hull of the model to define the set of surrounded regions as follows. Start by computing the convex hull of a model. Next, find a set of non-intersecting paths of edges that connect each pair of vertices connected by an edge of the hull. Finally, space the points of each path along the corresponding hull edge. If a set of non-intersecting paths is found, each face of the convex hull will now define a surrounded region. Although this algorithm works for many models, it is not too difficult to create models for which no appropriate set of paths can be found. Further research is being conducted into algorithmically finding a suitable subdivision for any genus 0 polyhedra.

Figure 2 shows a polygonal model of a goblet in the upper left. The set of paths of edges found by the algorithm are shown in the upper right. Spacing the vertices of each path along the corresponding edge of the convex hull yields the object in the lower left. The results of the simulation are shown in the lower right. In this case, the simulation causes the network of vertices and edges that form the inside of the goblet's bowl to snap out onto the plane defined by the rim of the goblet.

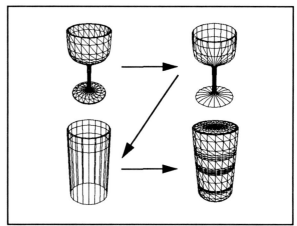

Figure 2 - "Snapping" an Object to its Convex Hull

5.1.4 Hybrid Methods

In addition to the projection methods described in the proceeding three sections, two other techniques have been developed that combine model knowledge with physical simulation.

Lofted and tubular objects consist of a series of planar contours that are joined along a (possibly curved) path. Combining the methods of Section 5.1.2 and 5.1.3 generates an algorithm for projecting this class of models. Select two adjacent contours. If the contours are not convex, project them to their convex hull using Ekoule's method. The two contours define a pair of surrounded regions as described in Section 5.1.3. Running a "rubber-band mesh" simulation with the contour points fixed causes the interior of each region to snap onto the plane of the contour. Figure 3 shows a tubular object with the selected contours highlighted and the same object after the simulation is completed.

Two features of this technique may not be evident. First, the two contours do not have to contain an equal number of points. The only requirement is both contours are a simple planar polygon. Second, the entire procedure can be performed with no user interaction, provided that knowledge of the manner in which the models are stored is available. However, it is desirable that the user be allowed to specify the pair of contours which are to remain fixed.

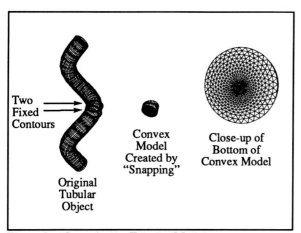

Figure 3 - "Snapping" a Tubular Model

The second hybrid method involves the user directly specifying the surrounded regions of the model. For example, to project a model of a man, the user might specify rings of edges around each arm at the shoulder, around each leg at the hip, and around the head at the base of the neck. A "rubber-band mesh" simulation is then run to snap in the extremities. It is up to the user to select surrounded regions that result in a convex model after the simulation is performed. Techniques for assisting the user in specifying the regions are currently being investigated.

Using this technique, the surrounded regions appear to "grow" out of the other model during the transformation. This interesting effect is due to the fact that points on the ends of the extremities have much larger distances to cover than do those at the base, and hence move at a greater velocity.

5.2 The Merging Algorithm

Once both models have been projected, the second step of the correspondence algorithm is to merge the topologies of the two models by clipping the projected faces of one object to the projected faces of the other. In an earlier paper [9], an $O(N^2)$ algorithm based on Weiler's polygon clipping algorithm ([15]) is described. The algorithm requires each projected edge of one model to be intersected with each projected edge of the other. Since the edges of the projected models map onto great circles of the unit sphere, these computations involve finding the intersection of pairs of circular arcs.

This algorithm works well for merging the projected topologies of objects that are not overly complex. However, for large models (> 1000 vertices) small numerical inaccuracies in the arc intersection calculations often result in an improper ordering of the intersection points along an edge. Since the algorithm is dependent upon maintaining a valid topological structure, improper ordering can cause the merging process to fail.

The original merging algorithm was also quite slow. If the number of edges of the models are N_a and N_b, respectively, in the worst case, there are $O(N_a N_b)$ intersections. However, for most models, since the faces are spread out across the entire surface of the sphere, an edge from one model only intersects a small number of edges of the other model. Thus, in the vast majority of cases, the number of intersections is much less than $N_a N_b$. This suggests that an algorithm whose execution time is dependent upon the number of intersections could significantly reduce the overall execution time.

This observation led to the development of a new merging algorithm that is faster and more robust than the original one described in [9]. The improvements are the result of exploiting the topological information contained in the models. The algorithm is similar in nature to the planar overlay algorithm described by Seidel in [13].

The following paragraphs describe the steps of this new algorithm and analyze its complexity. The description assumes that the faces of the model have been triangulated prior to execution. It also assumes that no projected vertices of the two models are coincident, and that no projected vertex of one model lies on a projected edge of the other. These degenerate cases can be handled by simple extensions of the basic algorithm.

Figure 4 contains a pseudocode description of the algorithm. The pseudocode assumes that arrays are used to store structures for each vertex, edge, and face of the models. For each vertex, this structure contains the original and projected locations of the vertex, as well

```
(Step 1)
Read in the Topology and Geometry of Ma and Mb, as
well as the Coordinates of the Projected Vertices,
(Va)p and (Vb)p.Translate the models so their cen-
ters are at the origin.

(Step 2)
v1a <-- first vertex of Ma
MapToB[v1a] <-- face of (Mb)p that contains (v1a)p
Add the edges originating at v1a to Work List (WL)
Mark those edges Used
While (WL) is Not Empty
    ea <-- next edge of WL
    v1a, v2a <-- endpoints of e1a
    fb <-- MapToB[v1a]
    Add edges of fb to Candidate List (CL)
    While CL is Not Empty
        eb <-- next edge of CL
        Intersect ea and eb
        If Successful
            Add Intersection Point, i, to Model
            Create links from ea and eb to i
            fb <-- Face of Mb on other side of eb
            Add two other edges of eb to CL
        End If
    End While
    MapToB[v2a] <-- fb
    Add the unused edges originating at v2a to WL
    Mark those edges Used
End While

(Step 3)
For each edge, eb, of Mb
    v1b, v2b <-- endpoints of eb
    Sort the intersections of eb using topological
        Information from Ma
    Set MapToA[v1b] and MapToA[v2b] to faces con-
        taining v1a and v2b, respectively
End For

(Step 4)
For each vertex, va, of Ma
    Calculate the barycentric coordinates of (va)p
        with respect to the projected vertex coordi-
        nates of the face, MapToB[va], of Mb
    Use these barycentric coordinates and original
        vertex coordinates of the face, MapToB[va]
        to determine where va maps to on the surface
        of Mb
End For

(Step 5)
Repeat Step 4 for each vertex of Mb, using the faces
stored in array MapToA to identify the face of Ma
that contains each vertex of Mb

(Step 6)
Output the combined geometry and topology of both
models, Ma* and Mb*
```

Figure 4 - Pseudocode for the Merging Algorithm

as the edges beginning at that vertex, stored in clockwise order. Each edge structure includes the indices of the two endpoints and the indices of the two faces it separates. The edge structure also contains a pointer to the list of intersections of that edge. The face structure includes the indices of the three vertices and the three edges that comprise the face. In addition to these structures, as each intersection point if found, it is stored in an array of structures that contain the indices of the two edges that intersect, the parametric values of the intersection point relative to those edges, and pointers used to order the intersections along the edge.

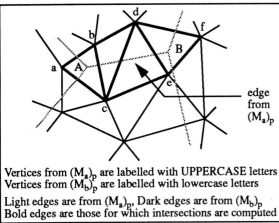

Vertices from $(M_a)_p$ are labelled with UPPERCASE letters
Vertices from $(M_b)_p$ are labelled with lowercase letters

Light edges are from $(M_a)_p$, Dark edges are from $(M_b)_p$
Bold edges are those for which intersections are computed

Figure 5 - Calculating the Intersections of an Edge

The first step is straightforward and can be performed in O(N) time. Step 2 involves intersecting each edge of $(M_a)_p$ with a subset of the edges of $(M_b)_p$, as illustrated in Figure 5. First, vertex v_A of $(M_a)_p$ is determined to lie inside face f_{abc} of $(M_b)_p$. This can be done in O(N) time by casting a ray from the origin through v_A and finding the face of $(M_b)_p$ it intersects. Once this is done, the edges originating at v_A are added to a list of edges to be processed, the work list. Assume e_{AB} is the first edge on this list. Since it is known that v_A lies on face f_{abc} of $(M_b)_p$, the first intersection of that edge must be with one of the edges of that face. Thus, e_{ab}, e_{ac}, and e_{bc} from $(M_b)_p$ are added to a list of candidate edges that e_{AB} might intersect. In this case, e_{AB} intersects e_{bc}. The topology of M_b can be used to determine that e_{AB} crosses over to face f_{bcd} at the intersection point. Thus, edges e_{bd} and e_{cd} are added to the candidate list. Similarly, at the intersection of e_{cd} and e_{AB}, edge e_{AB} crosses onto face f_{cde}, and edges e_{ce} and e_{de} are added to the candidate list. At the intersection of e_{de} and e_{AB}, edge e_{AB} crosses onto face f_{def}, and edges e_{df} and

e_{fb} are added to the candidate list. Since e_{AB} does not intersect either of these edges, vertex v_B must lie on face f_{def}. This fact is recorded and the edges originating at v_B are added to the work list. This continues until the work list is empty.

Step 3 of the algorithm sorts the intersections of each edge of $(M_b)_p$ using topological information from $(M_a)_p$ to ensure that the ordering is valid. As shown in Figure 6, basing the sort on this information avoids inconsistencies in the topology due to small numerical errors in the intersection calculations. This step is also used to determine which face of $(M_a)_p$ contains each vertex of $(M_b)_p$.

Steps 4 and 5 use the information that indicates which face of $(M_b)_p$ contains each vertex of $(M_a)_p$, and vice versa, to determine where the vertices of one model map onto the surface of the other. This is done using barycentric coordinates as shown in Figure 7. Step 6 involves tracing out of the faces of the combined models using the original topologies and the sorted intersections of each edge and can be performed in O(N) time.

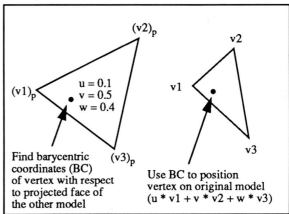

Figure 7 - Determining the Vertex Locations

5.2.1 Analysis of the Merging Algorithm

Steps 1, 4, 5, and 6 can all be performed in O(N) time. The time required to complete Steps 2 and 3 is dependent upon the number of edges that intersect and is analyzed below. As in previous sections, N_a and N_b represent the number of edges of M_a and M_b.

In step 2, each edge of M_a is intersected with exactly $3 + 2 * I_e$ edges, where I_e is the number of intersections of the edge. Since this must be done for each edge, the total number of intersections is $3 * N_a + 2 * I_{tot}$, where I_{tot} is the total number of edge-edge intersections. Thus the running time of step 2 is $O(N_a + I_{tot})$. For complex models, the distribution of the faces on the sphere ensures that $I_{tot} \ll N_a N_b$.

In step 3, the intersections of each edge of M_b must be sorted. If I_e is the number of intersections of an edge, the sorting of that edge requires time $O(I_e \log I_e)$. Since in the worst case, each edge can be intersected $O(N_a)$ times, the worst case complexity is $O(N_b N_a \log N_a)$. However, in terms of the total number of intersections, since the sum of $(I_e \log I_e)$ for each edge is less than or equal to $(I_{tot} \log I_{tot})$, the complexity is $O(I_{tot} \log I_{tot})$.

Thus, the overall complexity of the algorithm in terms of output size equals that of step 3, $O(I_{tot} \log I_{tot})$. Although in the worst case, I_{tot} is $O(N^2)$, the distribution of the edges on the sphere causes I_{tot} to be much smaller than this in most cases.

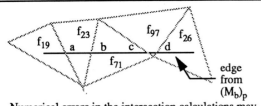

Numerical errors in the intersection calculations may indicate that the ordering of the intersection points is a-b-d-c.

Using topological information about the intersected edges yields the correct ordering a-b-c-d, based upon the faces along the edge, f_{19}-f_{23}-f_{71}-f_{97}-f_{26}

It also indicates which faces contain the endpoints of the edge being intersected (i.e. f_{19} and f_{26}).

Figure 6 - Sorting the Intersections

6.0 Interpolation Issues

Up to now, this paper has concentrated on the correspondence step of the shape transformation problem. Once the combined models, M_a^* and M_b^* have been created, the transformation is computed by interpolating between each pair of corresponding vertex locations. In addition to linear interpolation, the use of a Hermite spline for the path of each vertex, with the tangent vectors of the spline set equal to the vertex normals, has proven effective.

Two potential problems may arise during the interpolation. First, for faces with more than three edges[2], interpolating vertices from one position to another will not guarantee that all faces remain planar. This problem can be solved by triangulating the faces of M_a^* and M_b^*, prior to the interpolation. Second, an object may penetrate itself during the interpolation. This may or may not be a problem, depending on the application. Possible solutions of this problem are being investigated.

Interpolating non-geometric surface attributes, such as color, texture, or transparency, along with the geometry of the models produces interesting effects. This can be easily done since the correspondence algorithm specifies a homeomorphic mapping between the two objects. Given a point on the surface of some intermediate model, barycentric coordinates can be used to locate that point relative to the vertices of the face that contain it. From these coordinates, the corresponding points on the original objects can be found. The value of the attribute for the point on the intermediate model is found by interpolating the values of the attribute for these two points.

7.0 Results

Figures 8 to 11 present some examples of the transformation algorithm. The examples were rendered using faceted shading and neutral colors to better illustrate the topological structure of the intermediate models.

Figure 8 shows a glass transforming into a spiral tube. The projections used for the two objects are those illustrated in Figure 2 and Figure 3, respectively. The spiral is used again in Figure 9, this time transforming into a 3D digitized sculpture. The sculpture data was obtained from a 3D digitizing device and is organized as a set of

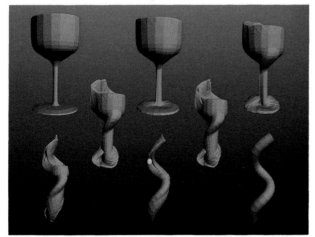

Figure 8 - Transforming an Object Using the Convex-Hull Snapping Technique into a Tubular Object

___

2. Although M_a and M_b must be triangulated, the faces of M_a^* and M_b^* will, in general, have up to six sides.

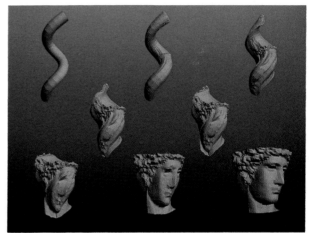

Figure 9 - Transforming a Tubular Object into an Object of Revolution

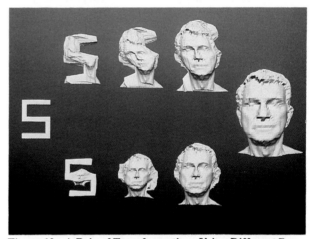

Figure 10 - A Pair of Transformations Using Different Projection Methods for the "S"-shaped Object

Figure 11 - Each Column Illustrates the 0%, 25%, 50%, 75%, and 100% Points of a Transformation

planar ribs revolved around an axis. Thus, the object of revolution technique from Section 5.1.2 was used for the projection.

Figure 10 illustrates the results of using different projection methods upon the transformation. In the upper sequence, the extruded letter 'S' was projected using the convex hull snapping technique described in Section 5.1.3. In the lower sequence, the hybrid method for tubular objects described in Section 5.1.4 was used to project the 'S'. The object of revolution method was used to project the digitized head in both sequences. The two sequences illustrate that radically different results are possible by altering the projection method used.

Figure 11 shows three columns, each of which represents a transformation between a a pair of objects of revolution. The objects in the middle of each column are the models obtained at the 25%, 50%, and 75% points of the transformation. The base objects of the left and middle columns are objects of revolution. The base object of the rightmost column is an extruded 6-pointed star.

As a final note, the following statistics for the transformations in Figures 8 to 11 are provided to support the claim made in Section 5.2.1 that the total number of intersections, I_{tot}, is much less than $N_a N_b$ for complex models.

	N_a	N_b	$N_a N_b$	I_{tot}
Figure 8	1.8K	2.7K	4.9M	6.5K
Figure 9	2.7K	18.7K	50.5M	19.9K
Figure 10				
-- top	66	18.4K	1.2M	4.0K
-- bottom	66	18.4K	1.2M	1.9K
Figure 11				
-- left	864	18.7K	16.2M	14.7K
-- middle	102	18.7K	1.9M	5.0K
-- right	72	18.7K	1.3M	3.9K

8.0 Future Research

Future research will focus on three areas. First, extensions of the algorithm to handle wider classes of polyhedra will be investigated. For genus 0 objects, this involves developing new ways to project the surface of a model onto a sphere. For non-genus 0 objects, cutting the objects to eliminate the passages through them, or replacing the sphere with a representative manifold (e.g. a torus for objects with one hole) are possibilities.

The second area of interest is to examine the problem of self-intersections during the interpolation. A good solution to this problem has applicability for many other problems that involve interpolation, not just shape transformation.

The third area of investigation involves providing user control of the transformation. The remarkable results obtained by morphing are possible because the user maintains complete control over the transformation. Unlike the other published techniques for 3D shape transformation, the algorithms presented in this paper allow some control over the transformation through mechanisms such as selecting the center of the object and choosing the projection technique. However, to achieve results equivalent to those obtained by morphing images, techniques that provide a finer level of control over the transformation are needed. One possibility is to add a warping step after the models are mapped to the sphere, but before the topologies are merged.

Acknowledgments

We wish to thank the Department of Computer and Information Science, the Advanced Computing Center for the Arts and Design and the Ohio Supercomputer Center for the use of their facilities, and Hewlett-Packard and AT & T for equipment grants that make this research possible. We also wish to thank Dr. Rephael Wenger, Kevin Rodgers, Steve May, and Stephen Spencer for useful ideas and criticism, and Professor Charles Csuri for the use of his head.

Bibliography

1. Bethel, E. and Uselton, S. Shape Distortion in Computer-Assisted Keyframe Animation. In *State of the Art in Computer Animation*. Magnenat-Thalmann, N. and Thalmann, D., eds., Springer-Verlag, New York, 1989, 215-224.

2. Bier, E. and Sloan, K. Two-Part Texture Mappings. *IEEE Computer Graphics and Applications 6*, 9 (Sept. 1986), 40-53.

3. Carlson, W. An Advanced Data Generation System for Use in Complex Object Synthesis For Computer Display. *Proceedings of Graphics Interface '82* (1982) 197-204.

4. Chen, E., and Parent, R. Shape Averaging and Its Applications to Industrial Design. *IEEE Computer Graphics and Applications 9*, 1 (Jan. 1989) 47-54.

5. Ekoule, A., Peyrin, F. and Odet, C. A Triangulation Algorithm from Arbitrary Shaped Multiple Planar Contours. *ACM Transactions on Graphics 10*, 2 (April, 1991) 182- 199.

6. Haumann, D. and Parent, R. The Behavioral Test-Bed: Obtaining Complex Behavior from Simple Rules. *Visual Computer 4*, 6 (Dec. 1988) 332-347.

7. Hong, T., Magnenat-Thalmann, N. and Thalmann, D. A General Algorithm for 3-D Shape Interpolation in a Facet-Based Representation. *Proceedings of Graphics Interface '88* (June 1988) 229-235.

8. Kaul, A. and Rossignac, J. Solid-Interpolating Deformations: Construction and Animation of PIPs. Proceedings of Eurographics '91. In *Computers and Graphics* (1991).

9. Kent, J, Parent, R. and Carlson, W. Establishing Correspondences by Topological Merging: A New Approach to 3-D Shape Transformation. *Proceedings of Graphics Interface '91* (Calgary, Alberta, June, 1991) 271-278.

10. Parent, R. Shape Transformation by Boundary Representation Interpolation: A Recursive Approach to Establishing Face Correspondences. Technical Report OSU-CISRC-2/91-TR7. Computer and Information Science Research Center. The Ohio State University (1991).

11 Payne, B. and Toga, A. Distance Field Manipulation of Surface Models. *IEEE Computer Graphics and Applications 12*, 1 (Jan. 1992) 65-71.

12. Preparata, F. and Shamos, M. *Computational Geometry - An Introduction.* Springer-Verlag, New York, 1985.

13. Seidel, R. *Output-Size Sensitive Algorithms for Constructive Problems in Computational Geometry.* Ph.D. Thesis, Cornell University, 1986.

14. Terzides, C. Transformational Design. *Knowledge Aided Architectural Problem Solving and Design,* NSF Project #DMC-8609893, Final Report, (June 1989).

15. Weiler, K. Polygon Comparison Using a Graph Representation. Proceedings of SIGGRAPH '80 (Seattle, Washington, July 1980). In *Computer Graphics 14*, 3, (Aug. 1980), 10-18.

16. Weiler, K. Topology as a Framework for Solid Modeling. *Proceedings of Graphics Interface '84,* (May, 1984).

17. Wolberg, G. *Digital Image Warping.* IEEE Computer Society Press, Los Alamitos, CA, 1990.

18. Wyvill, B. Metamorphosis of Implicit Surfaces. *Notes from SIGGRAPH '90 Course 23 - Modeling and Animating with Implicit Surfaces,* (Dallas, Texas, Aug. 1990).

Re-Tiling Polygonal Surfaces

Greg Turk

Department of Computer Science

University of North Carolina at Chapel Hill

Abstract

This paper presents an automatic method of creating surface models at several levels of detail from an original polygonal description of a given object. Representing models at various levels of detail is important for achieving high frame rates in interactive graphics applications and also for speeding-up the off-line rendering of complex scenes. Unfortunately, generating these levels of detail is a time-consuming task usually left to a human modeler. This paper shows how a new set of vertices can be distributed over the surface of a model and connected to one another to create a re-tiling of a surface that is faithful to both the geometry and the topology of the original surface. The main contributions of this paper are: 1) a robust method of connecting together new vertices over a surface, 2) a way of using an estimate of surface curvature to distribute more new vertices at regions of higher curvature and 3) a method of smoothly interpolating between models that represent the same object at different levels of detail. The key notion in the re-tiling procedure is the creation of an intermediate model called the *mutual tessellation* of a surface that contains both the vertices from the original model and the new points that are to become vertices in the re-tiled surface. The new model is then created by removing each original vertex and locally re-triangulating the surface in a way that matches the local connectedness of the initial surface. This technique for surface re-tessellation has been successfully applied to iso-surface models derived from volume data, Connolly surface molecular models and a tessellation of a minimal surface of interest to mathematicians.

CR Categories and Subject Descriptors: I.3.3 [**Computer Graphics**]: Picture/Image Generation – Display algorithms; I.3.5 [**Computer Graphics**]: Computational Geometry and Object Modelling – Curve, surface, solid, and object representations.

Additional Key Words and Phrases: model simplification, automatic mesh generation, constrained triangulation, levels-of-detail, shape interpolation.

© 1992   ACM-0-89791-479-1/92/007/0055 $01.50

1 Introduction

This paper shows how a simplified polygonal model can be automatically created from an initial polygonal description of an object. We use the term *re-tiling* to describe the process of simplifying a polygonal model. The notion of representing a model at multiple levels of detail is a common thread that runs through much work in computer graphics and image processing. These levels of detail can be found in a number of forms, such as multiple collections of polygons, different collections of bicubic surface patches or variously filtered levels of a raster image. There are several benefits to having more than one representation of an object. One benefit is that it is often unnecessary to use a fully-detailed model of an object during rendering if the object will cover a small portion of the screen. Using a smaller model can significantly shorten the time it takes to render an image. It is this ability to increase the rendering rate, especially for interactive applications, that motivates the work presented in this paper. Another benefit of having more than one representation of an object is that this is often a graceful way to avoid sampling problems when rendering an image. Probably the best-known example of this in computer graphics is the texture anti-aliasing work of Lance Williams [Williams 83]. A third reason for using multiple levels of detail is that features of an object can be classified by following the features through successively more coarse representations of the object. This method of feature recognition appears in much of the recent work being done in image processing and pattern recognition. Computer graphics has yet to make much use of feature tracking and elimination, and we will return to this issue in the future work section of this paper.

Polygonal descriptions of objects are currently the most widely-used forms of model representation in computer graphics. One reason for this is the availability of graphics workstations that can rapidly render polygons. Another reason is that there are a large numbers of techniques for translating a given model into a polygonal dataset. For these and other reasons, it is likely that polygonal representations of objects will continue to be important to computer graphics. This serves as motivation for finding automatic methods of creating new polygonal models of the same object that have a fewer number of polygons than the original description.

Because there is such a wide range of objects that can be represented by polygonal tessellations, it may be impossible to find one technique that can do a good job of re-tiling any given polygon dataset. For instance, techniques that are successful at reducing the number of polygons in a model of a building may not necessarily be applicable to re-tiling of medical datasets such as those derived from CT scans. This paper's re-tiling method is best suited to models that represent curved surfaces. Examples of such models include iso-surfaces from medical data and from molecular graphics, smooth mathematically-defined manifolds and digitized or hand-modelled organic forms such as animals or people. This technique is poorly suited to models that have well-defined corners and sharp edges such as buildings, furniture and machine parts.

This paper begins with an overview of related work in creating levels of detail, and, in particular, work that deals with polygonal models. The rest of the paper describes the basic steps taken to re-tile a given model and several extensions to this basic method. The first section on re-tiling describes how to distribute a given number of points evenly over a polygonal surface. These points will eventually become the vertices of the new model. Next, the notion of *mutual tessellation* followed by *vertex removal* is presented as a robust method of completely replacing the original set of vertices with the new points. This is how a completely new triangulation of the model is created. The next section shows how local estimates of maximum curvature can be used to concentrate more new vertices at regions that need more points to faithfully represent the surface. The paper then describes how the polygons from a more fine representation of an object can be flattened onto the surface of a more coarse polygonal model. Using this method, we can interpolate between this flattened version of the model and the original high-detail representation to give a smooth transition between the coarse and the fine versions of an object. The next section describes how re-tiled models can aid the interactive task of radiation treatment planning. The final section discusses future topics of research in representing multiple levels of detail in polygonal models.

2 Previous Work

James Clark's paper on hierarchical geometric models describes the benefits of using more than one representation of a model for image rendering [Clark 76]. Clark points out that objects that cover a small area of the screen can be rendered from a simplified version of the object and that this allows more efficient rendering of a scene. This same benefit of having both simple and complex representations of an object is given by Frank Crow in his paper on an image generation environment [Crow 82]. Crow gives the example of a chair that is represented in high detail, medium detail and very low detail. The three models in his example were created by hand, but Crow suggests that creating the lower levels of detail is a process that should be automated. A guaranteed frame-rate is essential in flight simulators, and for this reason models of objects such as airplanes are often made at several levels of detail by hand [Cosman & Schumacker 81].

The creation of lower levels of detail has been automated for some well-behaved polygonal datasets. Lance Williams showed how a regular mesh of quadrilaterals can be used to represent surfaces such as a human face, and how such meshes can be filtered down to smaller resolutions in the same manner as he used for texture filtering [Williams 83]. This is similar to how flight simulators use coarse versions of terrain data when a ground feature is far away and use a more detailed terrain model when the feature is closer to the viewer. The flight simulator literature describes how new features of the terrain can be gradually introduced as the viewer moves closer by first adding new vertices in the plane of a terrain polygon and then moving each vertex's elevation smoothly until it reaches the correct elevation [Zimmerman 87]. With a gridded terrain model it is easy to know which vertices need to be joined to form new polygons when a new vertex is added or when an old vertex is removed. This problem is more difficult for polygonal models with arbitrary topology.

Another polygonal data format that has been automatically re-tiled is the laser-scanned data from Cyberware Laboratories of Monterey, California. Their digitizing method results in a large collection of regularly joined quadrilaterals. Schmitt and co-workers have adaptively fit bicubic patches to such models by starting with a rough approximation of the surface and then adaptively refining the surface

at locations where the model is not yet well fit [Schmitt 86]. This method generates models at varying levels of detail by specifying a set of increasingly fine tolerance levels for the surface fit. Extensions to this method have been explored to adapt the technique to creating polygonal models and to more closely bound the error [DeHaemer & Zyda 91]. DeHaemer and Zyda's methods reduced a 112,128 polygon image of a human head to 12,821 polygons. As with terrain data, the Cyberware format makes it easy to decide which vertices become neighbors when a vertex is added or removed.

To reduce the large numbers of polygons often found in medical data, Kevin Novins implemented a method of identifying and removing vertices that are in relatively flat portions of a polygonal object [Novins 92]. His program examines the variance in surface normals of triangles that share a given vertex and uses this to decide which vertices to remove. When a vertex is removed, the region immediately surrounding the vertex is re-triangulated. The user gives a target number of vertices and the program removes vertices until this number is reached. Schroeder and his co-workers have also used an approach of vertex removal and local re-triangulation for simplifying polygonal models [Schroeder et al 92]. They remove vertices that are within a distance tolerance of a plane that approximates the surface near the vertex. Their method also identifies sharp edges and sharp corners and makes sure that such features are retained in order to better represent the original data. They show how these techniques can be used to drastically reduce the number of polygons in large medical and terrain models and still retain feature detail.

There is a large body of literature on automatic mesh generation for use in finite element techniques. An overview of this work is given in [Ho-Le 88]. Here the problem is how to sub-divide the surface or volume of an object to provide a mesh over which some physical properties of the material can be simulated, such as heat dissipation or stress and strain. It is assumed that all the edges and faces of a model are to be accurately reflected in the re-meshed version of the object. This is the main difference between meshes used in finite element methods versus smooth surface models for rendering in computer graphics. The exact placement of vertices and edges in a polygonal representation of a cat are not as important as the placement of the edges separating the copper and iron portions of a machine part being analyzed for heat conductivity. There are some issues, however, that do touch upon the problems that are found in mesh generation in both domains. For example, many finite element meshing routines use local re-meshing operators to improve the shapes of triangles in an initial mesh. Similar local operations can be used to improve re-tilings for computer graphics.

There is a good deal of material in computational geometry that is relevant to the re-tiling problem. Specifically, the properties of Voronoi regions and the associated Delaunay triangulation are relevant to the question of "goodness" of triangle shape in a triangulation of a collection of points [De Floriani et al 85].

3 Choosing New Vertices for Re-Tiling

3.1 Input Surface and the Results of Re-Tiling

The re-tiling method described in this paper begins with a polygonal surface and creates a triangulation of this surface with a user-specified number of vertices. There are few restrictions on the initial polygonal surface. The polygons may be either concave or convex, and may in fact have holes. The major restriction is on the number of polygons that share any given edge. The method described below is suitable for polygonal models in which each edge is shared by either one or two polygons. If a model satisfies this restriction, the algorithm is guaranteed to produce a new model with the same topology as the original model. The method will not introduce tears

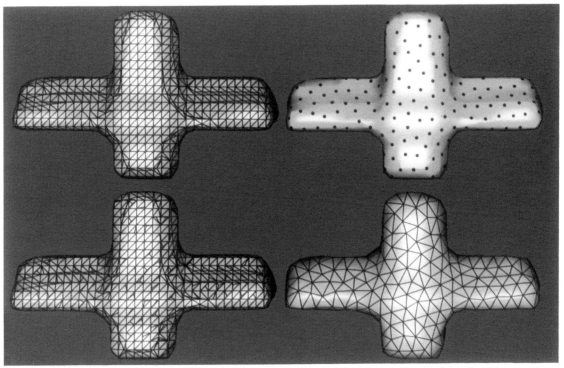

Figure 1: Re-tiling of a radiation iso-dose surface. Upper left: Original surface. Upper right: Candidate vertices after point-repulsion. Lower left: Mutual tessellation. Lower right: Final tessellation.

in the surface and will not connect regions of the surface that were unconnected in the original model. The next two sections outline the basic re-tiling method.

3.2 Positioning Vertices by Point Repulsion

The first step in re-tiling is to choose a set of points that will, at a later step, become the vertices of a new triangular tessellation of the surface. These new points are chosen to lie in the planes of the original polygons, and some of them may in fact be coincident with the vertices of the original model. The underlying assumption of this re-tiling approach is that the original polygonal surface gives a good indication of the location of the surface to be represented, but that the original placement of vertices on this surface may be poor choices for vertex positions of a re-tiled version of the surface. Allowing the new vertices to be placed anywhere on the surface lets them be placed in a manner that will give well-shaped triangles in the new representation of the surface. Placing the points fairly uniformly over the surface, as described in this section, is the portion of the re-tiling responsible for faithfully representing the *geometry*, the location and curvature, of the re-tiled surface. Joining these points together to form a triangular mesh, described in the following section, is that part of the re-tiling method responsible for faithfully representing the original surface's *topology*, that is, which parts of the surface connect to which other parts of the surface.

The basic method of placing these new points on the surface is taken directly from work on mesh generation for texture synthesis [Turk 91], and is described briefly below. This method places points uniformly over a given polygonal surface by distributing points at random over the surface and then having each point repel all of its neighbors. Sometimes, however, it is not desirable to have the distribution of points be uniform over the surface. This subject is addressed in a later section of this paper.

The re-tiling begins by having a given number of points (specified by the user) placed randomly over the surface of the polygonal model. Each point is placed by first making a random, area-weighted choice

from among all the polygons in the model and placing the point at a random position on this polygon. Once all the points have been randomly placed on the surface, a relaxation procedure is applied to move each point away from all other nearby points. The basic operation of this relaxation procedure is to fold or project nearby points onto a plane tangent to the surface at one point, to calculate the repelling force that each nearby point has on the given point and then to move this point over the polygonal surface based on the force exerted against it. A point that is pushed off one polygon is moved onto an adjacent polygon. For the sake of speed, the repelling force that one point has on another is a force that falls off linearly with distance, and thus becomes zero at a fixed radius. Because points farther apart than this distance do not affect one another, the search for nearby points can be made constant-time by placing all of the points in a three-dimensional grid data structure. The upper right portion of Figure 1 shows 400 points that have been positioned on a polygonal surface by this relaxation procedure. The original model, with its polygons outlined in black, is shown in the upper left of the same figure. This model is a tessellation of a radiation dose level surface that has been used to help visualize radiation treatment beams. The original model contains 1513 vertices.

4 Re-Tiling by Mutual Tessellation

4.1 Some Pitfalls of Re-Tiling

Once the points that will become new vertices (the *candidate vertices*) have been placed on the model's surface, the next task is to find how these vertices can be connected together to form a triangular mesh that reflects the topology of the original surface. This is a difficult task because of the many pitfalls that a complicated surface can present. The need for a robust algorithm cannot be overly stressed. One problem case in connecting the candidate vertices is when two portions of a surface that are far from one another as measured over the surface are actually near to each other in 3-space because the surface folds back on itself (see Figure 2a). Any algorithm for connecting together the candidate vertices must not

Figure 2: Problems encountered when connecting new vertices. (a) Connecting regions that fold back near one another. (b) "Bubbles" resulting from incorrect joining of vertices.

join together a pair of vertices that reside on two such separated regions (the thin lines in Figure 2a). Another pitfall is the creation of small surface "bubbles", where two sets of polygons are created that both tile the same portion of a surface (see Figure 2b). Groups of polygons that meet at a sharp corner also present difficulties when re-tiling.

Two distinct approaches were tried for connecting the candidate vertices before the method described below (mutual tessellation) was found. Both of these earlier methods failed because they relied on heuristics to choose which candidate vertices were neighbors and which of these neighbors should be connected together to form triangles. The first of these failed methods used a planar approximation to a point's Voronoi region to determine neighbors. The second failed technique used a global greedy algorithm. This method added a new edge to the list of edges in the re-tiling if it was the shortest edge not already on the list and if it did not intersect any other edge in planar approximation to the surface in the area near the edge. Below we will see how a *local* greedy algorithm is used to give a robust re-tiling method.

4.2 Mutual Tessellation

The key notion in creating a re-tiling of the surface is to form an intermediate polygonal surface, called a *mutual tessellation*, that incorporates both the old vertices of the original surface and the new points that are to become vertices in the re-tiled surface. After the mutual tessellation is made, the old vertices are removed one at a time and the surface is re-tiled locally in a manner such that the new triangles accurately reflect the connectedness of the original surface. Creating the mutual tessellation is a straightforward task. Each polygon of the original model is replaced by a collection of triangles that exactly tiles the polygon but that also incorporates the candidate vertices that lie in the polygon. This re-triangulation of a given polygon is performed by first gathering together the vertices of the polygon along with the candidate vertices that lie on this polygon. This collection of points (original vertices and candidate vertices) is then triangulated, subject to the constraint that the edges of the original polygon are to be included in the final triangulation. The triangulation is performed in the plane of the given polygon. For

example, a square polygon containing exactly one candidate vertex would be removed from the model and replaced by a set of four triangles that all meet at the one candidate vertex. If the square face contained n candidate vertices then it would be replaced by a set of $2n+2$ triangles.

The method of constrained triangulation used for this paper is greedy triangulation, but this is just one of several ways to form such a triangulation [Preparata & Shamos 85]. There is no chance for misrepresenting the original surface at this stage because each polygon is replaced by a set of triangles that exactly tile the original polygon. An added benefit to using mutual tessellation is that the original surface can include concave polygons or even polygons with holes since constrained triangulation algorithms easily handle these cases.

The lower left object of Figure 1 shows the mutual tessellation of the original model shown in the upper left portion of the figure. The candidate points that have been used to create this tessellation are those shown in the upper right of the same figure.

4.3 Removing Old Vertices

The next task is to remove the old vertices in a way that guarantees that the newly-created triangles follow the topology of the original surface. This can be done by invoking the same triangulation routine that was used to create the mutual tessellation. Given an old vertex R to be removed, we collect together all vertices that share a triangle with R. Call this collection of neighboring vertices V, and give the name T to the set of triangles that the vertices in V share with the vertex R. Then this collection of neighboring vertices, *without* the vertex R, are projected onto a plane that is tangent to the surface at R. Now a few tests are made to see if this region can be re-tiled without compromising the topology of the surface. These tests are described later. If the tests check out, then the vertices V are triangulated along with the additional constraints that all edges of the triangles in T that do not contain R must be included in the final triangulation. Call these additional constraint edges the set E. This set of edges E form a closed polygon surrounding the vertex R. The triangulation is performed along with the final constraint that no new edges are to be introduced outside of the polygon formed by the edges in E.

Figure 3a shows a vertex R to be removed and its set V of neighbors: A, B, C, D, E, F and G. In this example there are seven triangles in the set T, and the set E consists of the edges AB, BC, CD, DE, EF, FG and GA. Figure 3b shows the result of removing R and triangulating the neighbors in V to give five new triangles. These new triangles completely replace the triangles in the set T, and all the triangles in T are removed from the model. Notice that performing this triangulation in a plane assures us that the new triangles match the topology of that local portion of the original surface. The newly-created triangles are constrained to have a common border that is just the edges in E, so they will be adjacent to the same triangles that used to border the triangles in T.

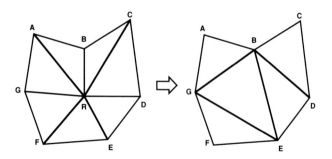

Figure 3: Removing a vertex from a mutual tessellation.

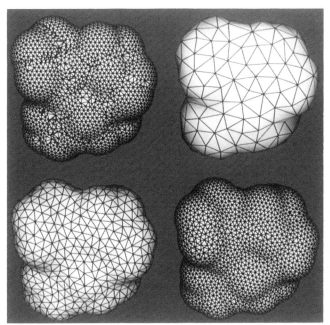

Figure 4: Re-tiling a molecular model. Original model is shown in the upper left. Other models are re-tilings of the same object.

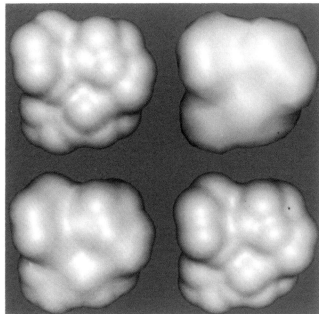

Figure 5: Phong-shaded rendering of the models in Figure 4.

The lower right portion of Figure 1 shows the result of removing all the old vertices from the mutual tessellation that is shown in the lower left. Figure 4 illustrates how several models of various levels of detail can be generated using the above re-tiling method. The model in the upper left of Figure 4 is the original model, a polygonal representation called a Connolly surface of a manufactured carbohydrate. The models shown in the upper right, lower left and lower right are increasingly more detailed re-tilings of the original surface, and they contain 201, 801 and 3676 vertices respectively. The original model contains 3675 vertices. Notice that the most detailed re-tiled version of the model has more evenly-sized polygons than the original model. This demonstrates how successful the point-repulsion method is at placing points uniformly over a surface. Figure 5 shows a Phong-shaded rendering of the same four models.

4.4 Topological Consistency Checks

As mentioned above, two checks must be made before removing an old vertex. If either of these two tests fail, then the vertex R must not be removed. A failing of either check is not a failing of the algorithm, but is instead an indication that the vertex R needs to be retained in the re-tiled model to faithfully represent the topology of the original surface. In practice, nearly all old vertices can be safely removed from a mutual tessellation. The first check is to see that the edges in the set E do not intersect one another except at their endpoints (the vertices in V) when projected into the plane for triangulation. If any pair of these edges do intersect, then R is not removed. This check assures us that the planar triangulation of the points in V will not fold the surface near R. If this check fails we can try projecting the neighborhood of R onto planes at other orientations to see if the edges in E intersect in these cases. If there is a projection onto a plane in which these edges do not intersect, we can remove R and perform the triangulation in this plane. The re-tiling code used to make the images in this paper tries 13 alternate projections before giving up and deciding that a vertex R should be retained.

The second check makes sure that we do not accidentally join the portion of the surface surrounding R to another portion of the surface in front of or behind this region. This can occur when three or four polygons form a narrow neck-like region. For example, Figure 6 shows an old vertex R that we want to remove and the solid lines show

the triangles that surround R. The dotted triangles BDF and BDG are two triangles that form a portion of the surface on the other side of the model. Imagine that the six edges radiating from R are removed and that the region is triangulated. It is likely that one of the new triangles will have BD as an edge, which would cause this edge to be shared by three triangles. It is also possible that the triangulation would create the triangle BDF, so that this triangle would be present twice in the model. Neither of these situations should be permitted because they would change the topology of the surface. The potential for these problems can be checked by examining triangles near R before the triangulation. If a situation like that of Figure 6 is detected, then the region surrounding R is left alone. This is the approach used to create the re-tiled models in this paper. Another solution is to triangulate the region surrounding R and then see if any of the new triangles would lead to a change in surface topology. If they would, then the vertex R is retained.

4.5 Triangle Shape

There is one additional, optional step that may be performed to assure that the triangles in the re-tiling are well-shaped. This clean-up step examines each vertex of the re-tiled model and attempts to re-triangulate in its neighborhood. This is similar to the vertex removal stage, except that the vertex is not removed but rather is included in the re-triangulation. Figure 7a shows the triangles surrounding a vertex Q whose neighboring vertices are examined during the clean-

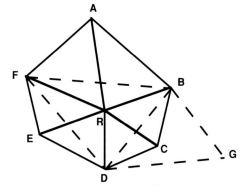

Figure 6: Problem that must be checked during vertex removal.

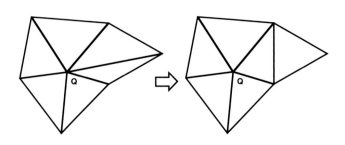

Figure 7: Improving triangle shape by local re-triangulation.

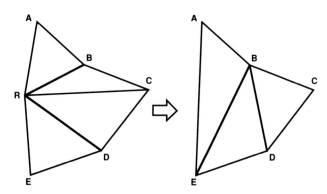

Figure 8: Removing a vertex on the boundary of a surface.

up stage. Figure 7b shows the same vertices, along with Q, after local re-triangulation. Any reasonable approximation to a tangent plane to the surface at the vertex Q can be used for the plane in which to perform the triangulation. Here again, the same two checks should be performed to avoid re-tiling at a fold and to avoid creating edges shared by three or more triangles. One or two clean-up passes were used in creating all the re-tiled models shown in this paper. The same greedy triangulation routine described earlier was used in this improvement step.

4.6 The Special Case of Boundaries

The re-tiling process can be augmented to handle polygonal models where some of the edges belong to only one polygon. Each of the three steps of mutual tessellation, vertex removal and clean-up must treat these boundary edges specially. When incorporating candidate vertices into a mutual tessellation, any candidate vertex that lies on a boundary edge must be incorporated into the boundary of the polygon that is being triangulated instead of into the interior of the polygon. This means that such a candidate vertex must be an endpoint in two of the constraint edges. During the vertex-removal stage, we choose not to remove an old vertex if it is at the corner of a polygon where two boundary edges meet that are part of the *same* polygon. Likewise, a vertex will be retained if more than two boundary edges meet at that vertex. If exactly two boundary edges from *different* polygons meet at a old vertex, that vertex may be removed. Figure 8a shows such a vertex R where the edges AR and RE belong only to the triangles ABR and RDE, respectively. Figure 8b shows the triangles formed after removing R.

4.7 Re-Tiling Robustness and Extensions

It is worth examining at this point how this re-tiling approach avoids the possible pitfalls involved in connecting candidate vertices. The central strength of the above method is that it breaks the surface re-tiling problem into many small *planar* triangulation problems. Planar triangulation of vertices with constraints is a well-understood problem from computational geometry. Casting the problem into two dimensions avoids the ambiguities found in three dimensions when trying to determine if a point is inside a polygon or whether two edges intersect. Constraining each triangulation sub-problem to include the edges E surrounding a vertex R that is being removed guarantees us that the collection of newly-created triangles will have the same common boundary as the old triangles T. This common boundary is just E, the set of constraint edges. These same observations apply to the triangulations performed during the clean-up step. One way to think of the re-tiling process is that the mutual tessellation allows the vertices and polygons of the original model to act as guides for how different portions of the surface will be connected to one another in the re-tiled model.

There is the opportunity within the framework of mutual tessellation and vertex removal to choose a measure of triangle quality for the triangulation sub-problems. The re-tilings shown in this paper were made with a greedy triangulation routine, where the shortest edges that do not intersect already chosen edges are picked to be included in the final triangulation. More specifically, although the triangulation is always performed in a plane, the edge distances used in the greedy algorithm are determined from each vertex's unprojected 3-space position. This greedy algorithm has created well-shaped triangles in the re-tilings that we have performed. If another measure of triangle goodness is desired then another triangulation routine can be incorporated into the basic framework described above. For example, one might use a triangulation routine that attempts to maximize the most acute angle in the potential collection of triangles [De Floriani et al 85].

5 Surface Curvature

5.1 Curvature Approximation

The basic method of point-repulsion gives surface re-tilings in which the new triangles are all roughly the same size across the model. This is quite adequate for surfaces that do not vary greatly in the amount of curvature at different locations. If, however, the variation in surface curvature is relatively large, then the features of the surface would be more accurately reflected in a re-tiling by increasing the density of vertices in regions of high curvature.

Ideally, we would like to have an exact measure of curvature from the object that the polygonal model is meant to represent. Often, however, this information is not available, either because the object being represented is not available (e.g. the volume data was not

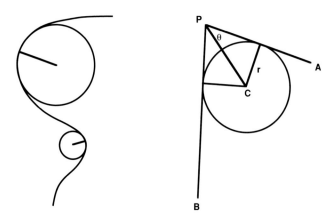

Figure 9: Curvature. (a) Radius of curvature in the plane.
(b) Approximation to curvature in the plane at a vertex.

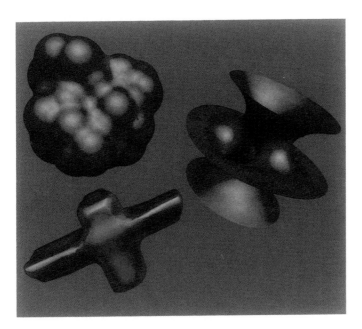

Figure 10: Surface curvature. Red specifies regions of higher curvature and blue shows regions that are relatively flat.

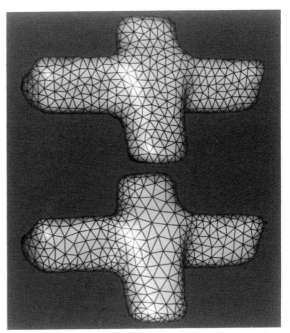

Figure 11: Top surface was created using the same radius of repulsion across the model. Bottom model used curvature to determine the repulsion radius.

retained) or because there never was an exact description of the object (e.g. a cat model was created freehand by a human modeler). For these reasons it is useful to have a way to approximate surface curvature from the polygonal data alone. More precisely, we want to know the maximum principle curvature at any given point on the model. See any text on differential geometry for a mathematical description of principle curvature, such as [O'Neill 66]. Intuitively, this is asking for the radius of the largest sphere that can be placed on the more curved side of the surface at a given point without being held away from the surface by the manner in which the surface curves. Figure 9a shows the radius of curvature at two points along a curve in the plane.

Figure 9b illustrates the curvature approximation used in this paper. This figure shows the two-dimensional version of the curvature estimate near a point P. Here a circle has been drawn that is tangent to the edge PA at its mid-point and that is also tangent to the longer edge PB. The radius of this circle is $r = \tan(\theta) \, |P - A| / 2$. In this figure, the line segment PC bisects the angle APB. This figure will act as a starting point for approximating the curvature of a polygonal surface in 3-space at a vertex P.

In the three-dimensional case, the line segment PC is replaced by an approximation to the surface normal N at the vertex P. Then, each edge in the polygon mesh that joins the vertex P to another vertex Q_i is examined, and an estimate of the radius of curvature from each of the n edges PQ_1, PQ_2,... PQ_n can be computed. Let V be the normalized version of the vector $Q_i - P$, that is, a unit vector parallel to the edge PQ_i. Then an estimate for θ_i is $\arccos(N \cdot V)$, and the radius estimate for the edge PQ_i is $r_i = \tan(\theta_i) \, |P - Q_i| / 2$. The final estimate r of minimum radius of curvature at the vertex P is the minimum of all the r_i. This estimate of curvature is a little noisy for some models, so we can smooth the estimate by averaging a vertex's radius r with that of all of its neighbors, and we can take this to be the minimum radius of curvature at the vertex. Figure 10 shows the results of this estimate, where each surface is colored red in areas of high curvature (small radius) and is colored blue in the regions that are more nearly flat.

5.2 Concentrating Vertices at Locations of Higher Curvature

Using the above curvature estimate, we can modify the first step of the point-placement method so that more points are distributed to those places of higher curvature when the points are initially placed on the surface. Recall that the random point placement is area-weighted, so that more points are initially placed on larger polygons. We can increase the density of points on a particular polygon if the polygon's stored value of its area is increased while other polygons' stored area values are held at their correct value. Therefore, to double the density of points on polygons of high curvature, we can multiply the stored area value of these polygons by a factor of two before the area-weighted point-placement step.

Armed with an estimate of curvature over the surface, we can use this value to choose the radius of repulsion in the point-placement routine. We want points that are at very curved areas (small radius of curvature) to push less on their nearby points than points that are on nearly flat regions. This will result in placing more points at the more curved areas. The curvature-adjusted radius of repulsion for a point can be derived from an average of the curvature measures at each of the vertices of the polygon that the point is on. This average is weighted by the distance of the point from each of the polygon's vertices. When computing the force between two points close to one another, the average of their curvature-adjusted radii of repulsion is used instead of using one fixed radius of repulsion for all points. The top portion of Figure 11 shows the re-tiling from 800 points distributed by using the same repulsive radius over all points, and the bottom portion shows the re-tiling given by 800 points that were distributed using curvature-weighted repulsive radii.

6 Interpolation Between Models

6.1 Nested Models

There is a natural nesting of levels of detail in polygonal datasets that are arranged in a rectangular grid of cells, and this nesting of levels can be used to smoothly interpolate between the different levels of detail. If the most detailed version of a terrain model is arranged in

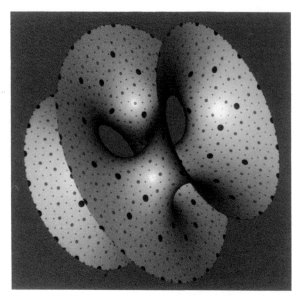

Figrure 12: Spots on minimal surface show the positions of three nested candidate vertex sets.

a 256×256 array of cells, then a 128×128 version of the data can be made by sampling the data at every other vertex of the original cell mesh in each of the x and y directions. Each of the vertices in this reduced grid is also present in the more detailed grid. This section describes how a similar nesting of levels of detail can be made when re-tiling *arbitrary* polygonal models and how we can smoothly interpolate from one level of detail to another. The technique we will use to interpolate between the levels of detail is to flatten some of the vertices and triangles of a higher-detailed model onto the triangles of a model with less detail.

Assume we have a detailed polygonal model and we wish to create three versions of this model that contain 200, 800 and 3200 vertices, and that we want all the vertices in the lower-detailed models to be present in the models with more detail. The first step is to position 200 points on the original polygonal surface using point-repulsion. The 800 vertex model can be created by fixing the positions of the first 200 points, then placing 600 additional points on the object's surface and finally by allowing these new points to be repelled by one another as well as by the 200 fixed points. The most detailed model is then made by fixing these 800 vertices and adding 2400 more in the same manner in which we added the previous 600. Now we have 200 vertices that have the same position in all three models and 800 vertices that are present in the same location in two of the models.

Figure 12 shows the positions of the points from three such levels of detail that were created in the manner just described. The large black spots are the 200 initial points, the red spots are the 600 additional points, and the cyan spots are the final 2400 points. The original object is a portion of a minimal surface of mathematical interest that was modelled using 2040 vertices. The spots in this figure were rendered by changing the color at a given surface position if it is inside a sphere centered at one of the 3200 points. Now the issue is to determine how to interpolate between pairs of these models.

6.2 Polygon Fragment Tracking for Interpolation

There are two sub-tasks involved in deciding how to interpolate between a high- and a low-detail model. First, for each vertex V that is present only in the high-detail model, we need to choose a triangle in the low-detail model onto which V may be flattened. Once such a triangle is determined for each such vertex V, we must split each triangle T from the high-detail model by each edge in the low detail model that intersects T. Figure 13 shows a high-detail and a low-detail model drawn together. Vertices A, B, C and D belong to the low-detail model and the edges AB, BC, AC, CD and DA are the edges that will be formed in the low-detail model. These same vertices A, B, C and D are also part of the initial high-detail model. The thinner edges in this figure are the edges of triangles in the high-detail model, and the vertices V, W and X are three of the vertices that are only present in the high-detail model. We require a way of determining that the vertex V can be flattened onto the low detail triangle ACD and that W can be flattened onto ABC. We also want to learn that the high-detail triangle AWV crosses the low-detail edge AC, so that we can split AWV into two triangles for later use in the interpolation procedure. The way to determine this information is to track each vertex such as V and each triangle such as AWV through the entire process of vertex removal as we change the high-detail model into the low-detail model.

The nested point sets shown on the surface in Figure 11 were created by moving from low to high detail. That is, first the low-detail points were placed, then the next higher level, etc. This process is now reversed by working from the high-detail model down to the low-detail model to provide the information we will need to flatten the high-detail triangles on the low-detail model. We begin with the vertices and triangles of the high-detail model and track how some triangles are split and re-formed when the high-detail vertices are removed from the model. Call the set of triangles in the high-detail model H, and let L denote the set of low-detail triangles that make up the model we are working towards. Ultimately, each triangle in L will

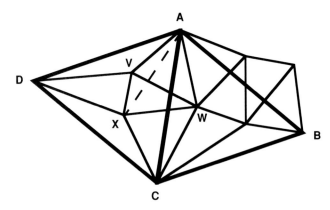

Figure 13: Fragment tracking when removing the high-detail vertices from a model.

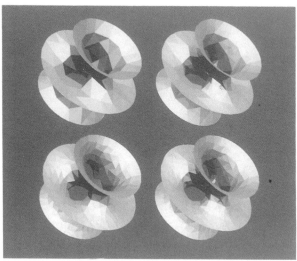

Figure 14: Clockwise from upper left is smooth interpolation between low-detail and high-detail models.

have a pointer to a list of polygon fragments of several triangles from *H*. These polygon fragments retain the positions of their original 3-space vertices from when they were a part of the high-detail model, and they also save their final, flattened position on one of the triangles in *L*. Each of these polygon fragments will also remember what original high-detail triangle they descended from, and this tag will be used to determine which fragments may be re-united after the process of vertex removal.

The polygon tracking process begins as follows. First, each triangle in the high-detail model is initialized with a list of polygon fragments that contains just a single element, and this element is a copy of the original triangle. Each triangle also retains a list of flattened points which is initially empty. Several steps are followed when a high-detail vertex is removed from the model, and these steps all take place in the plane. This lets us unambiguously determine where one edge intersects another and when a point is inside a given triangle. First, when a high-detail vertex *V* is removed then the triangles surrounding *V* must be split by the new edges that are introduced by the re-triangulation of the area surrounding *V*. For instance, assume that the four triangles surrounding *V* in Figure 13 will be replaced by two triangles that share a new edges *AX* (dotted line). This new edge splits each of the old triangles *AWV* and *VWX* into two pieces. The new triangle *AWX* is given a list containing the two polygon fragments that lie within *AWX*. Similarly, the new triangle *AXD* keeps the other two fragments and the undivided polygons *AVD* and *VXD* in its list. Now we must determine which of the new triangles *AWX* or *AXD* the old vertex *V* should be flattened onto. In this example, the new, flattened position of *V* is on triangle *AXD*. This same process of vertex removal, triangle splitting and vertex flattening is carried out for all the high-detail vertices in the model. The result is a set of low-detail triangles *L*, each of which has a list of fragments from the original triangles of the high-detail model. Some of the fragments in a list may be fragments of the same triangle of the high-detail model, and such fragments may be coalesced to give fewer final polygons. Such sibling fragments are found in the same list when a polygon is split at an early stage in the fragment tracking process by an edge that is later removed from the model.

6.3 Performing the Interpolation

When the above work is finished, we have a large collection of polygon fragments that know where they came from in the original, high-detail model and that also know what their current, flattened position is on the surface of the low-detail model. It is now a simple task to interpolate the vertices of each of the polygon fragments between these two positions. At one end of the interpolation they will all lie flat on the low-detail model, and together they will have exactly the same shape as the low-detail model. At the other end of the interpolation, they have a shape identical with the high-detail model. The process of interpolating between these two positions has the effect of "inflating" the low-detail model into the model with more triangles. We have found that linear interpolation between these two positions is sufficient to make smooth transitions between models. There are no jumps or discontinuities during this interpolation. This provides a seamless way of switching from one level of detail to another, and could be useful in both in interactive applications and for rendering frames for animating a complex scene. Figure 14 shows this form of shape interpolation between two models that are re-tiled versions of the minimal surface shown in Figure 12.

7 An Application of Re-Tiling

We have immediate plans to use re-tilings of polygonal surfaces in research on radiation-treatment planning being done at the University of North Carolina at Chapel Hill. Planning the placement of radiation beams for the treatment of tumors is an intensely geometric task [Chung 92]. The problem is how to aim several radiation beams at a tumor while at the same time keeping too much radiation from impinging on the organs surrounding the tumor. James Chung has prototyped a beam-placement application program where the user wears a head-mounted display and places radiation beams around a polygonal representation of the anatomy containing the tumor. The models used to represent the tumor and the surrounding organs (lungs, kidneys, etc.) often contain many thousands of polygons. There is a trade-off that can be made between the accuracy of representation of the anatomy and the frame update rate of the display. One possible solution is to give the user direct control over this update rate [Holloway 91]. The graphics engine would use a more coarse set of polygonal models when the user wishes to make broad motions (e.g. walking around the simulated patient) and would then switch to the more detailed models when fine adjustments are being made to the final beam placements. We plan to make use of the re-tiling techniques described here to provide the variously detailed models.

8 Future Work

One possible extension of the re-tiling method would be to use information about the *direction* of minimum and maximum curvature at each point to help guide the local re-triangulation of the surface. The point-repulsion step could take direction of higher curvature into account by having the points repel in a direction-dependent manner. This would amount to changing the shape of a point's field of repulsion from a circle to an ellipse. The directional curvature measure should also guide which edges between points are created during triangulation. Polygon edges should be created preferentially along the direction of lesser curvature.

There are several more broad issues that should be addressed in future work on re-tiling of polygonal models. One issue is whether there are better ways to estimate the surface curvature on a polygonal model. Another topic is finding measures of how closely matched a given re-tiling is to the original model. Can such a quality measure be used to guide the re-tiling process? Perhaps the biggest issue to explore is the opportunity for elimination of features at very low levels of detail. How can small features of a model be automatically identified and under what conditions is it acceptable to remove a feature completely from a model? For example, no triangles need to be used to represent the shape of a person's ear if the size of the person in the final image will be three pixels high.

Acknowledgments

Many people provided ideas, aid and encouragement for this work, and these people include: David Banks, Henry Fuchs, Marc Olano, Penny Rheingans, John Rhoades, Brice Tebbs and Terry Yoo. Several of the anonymous reviewers made excellent suggestions for improving this paper. Thanks also goes to Kevin Novins and Michael Zyda for discussions about other work that has been done in this area. The radiation dose volume data was provided by the UNC Department of Radiation Oncology and the iso-dose surface was created by Victoria Interrante and James Chung. The molecular model of the carbohydrate called "Wilma" was provided by Mark Zottola. The model of the Costa genus one minimal surface was created by James T. Hoffman using his adaptive mesh algorithm and the mathematical description of this surface is due to Celso Costa, David Hoffman and William Meeks III.

This work was supported by a graduate fellowship from IBM and by the Pixel-Planes Project. Pixel-Planes is funded by DARPA Grant No. DAEA 18-90-C-0044, NSF Cooperative Agreement No. ASC 8920219 and ONR Grant No. N00014-86-K-0680.

References

[Chung 92] Chung, James C., "A Comparison of Head-Tracked and Non-Head-Tracked Steering Modes in the Targeting of Radiotherapy Treatment Beams," *1992 Symposium on Interactive 3D Graphics*, Cambridge, Massachusetts, 29 March - 1 April 1992, pp. 193-196.

[Clark 76] Clark, James H., "Hierarchical Geometric Models for Visible Surface Algorithms," *Communications of the ACM*, Vol. 19, No. 10, pp. 547-554.

[Cosman & Schumacker 81] Cosman, M. and R. Schumacker, "System Strategies to Optimize CIG Image Content," *Proceedings of the Image II Conference*, Scottsdale, Arizona, 10-12 June, 1981.

[Crow 82] Crow, Franklin C., "A More Flexible Image Generation Environment," *Computer Graphics*, Vol. 16, No. 3 (SIGGRAPH '82), pp. 9-18.

[De Floriani et al 85] De Floriani, L., B. Falcidieno and C. Pienovi, "Delaunay-based Representations of Surfaces Defined over Arbitrarily Shaped Domains," *Computer Vision, Graphics and Image Processing*, Vol. 32, pp. 127-140.

[DeHaemer & Zyda 91] DeHaemer, Michael J., Jr. and Michael J. Zyda, "Simplification of Objects Rendered by Polygonal Approximations," *Computers & Graphics*, Vol. 15, No. 2, pp. 175-184.

[Ho-Le 88] Ho-Le, K.," Finite Element Mesh Generation Methods: A Review and Classification," *Computer Aided Design*, Vol. 20, No. 1, pp. 27-38.

[Holloway 91] Holloway, Richard, untitled technical presentation, University of North Carolina at Chapel Hill, December 1991.

[Novins 92] Novins, Kevin, personal communication.

[O'Neill 66] O'Neill, Barrett, *Elementary Differential Geometry*, Academic Press, 1966, New York.

[Preparata & Shamos 85] Preparata, Franco P. and Michael Ian Shamos, *Computational Geometry: An Introduction*, Springer-Verlag, 1985, New York.

[Schmitt et al 86] Schmitt, Francis J. M., Brian A. Barsky and Wen-Hui Du, "An Adaptive Subdivision Method for Surface-Fitting from Sampled Data," *Computer Graphics*, Vol. 20, No. 4 (SIGGRAPH 86), pp. 179-188.

[Schroeder et al 92] Schroeder, William J., Jonathan A. Zarge and William E. Lorensen, "Decimation of Triangle Meshes," *Computer Graphics*, Vol. 26 (SIGGRAPH 92, these proceedings).

[Turk 91] Turk, Greg, "Generating Textures on Arbitrary Surfaces Using Reaction-Diffusion," *Computer Graphics*, Vol. 25, No. 4 (SIGGRAPH 91) pp. 289-298.

[Williams 83] Williams, Lance, "Pyramidal Parametrics," *Computer Graphics*, Vol. 17, No. 3 (SIGGRAPH 83), pp. 1-10.

[Zimmerman 87] Zimmerman, Stephen A., "Applying Frequency Domain Constructs to a Broad Spectrum of Visual Simulation Problems," Evans & Sutherland Technical Document, Presented at the IMAGE IV Conference, Phoenix, Arizona, 23-26 June, 1987.

Decimation of Triangle Meshes

William J. Schroeder, Jonathan A. Zarge, *William E. Lorensen*

General Electric Company Corporate Research and Development
*ConSolve, Inc

ABSTRACT

Computer graphics applications routinely generate geometric models consisting of large numbers of triangles. We present an algorithm that significantly reduces the number of triangles required to model a physical or abstract object. The algorithm makes multiple passes over an existing triangle mesh, using local geometry and topology to remove vertices that pass a distance or angle criterion. The holes left by the vertex removal are patched using a local triangulation process. The decimation algorithm has been implemented in a general scientific visualization system as a general network filter. Examples from volume modeling and terrain modeling illustrate the results of the decimation algorithm.

Keywords: computer graphics, geometric modeling, medical imaging, terrain modeling, volume modeling

1 INTRODUCTION

The polygon remains a popular graphics primitive for computer graphics application. Besides having a simple representation, computer rendering of polygons is widely supported by commercial graphics hardware and software. However, because the polygon is linear, often thousands or millions of primitives are required to capture the details of complex geometry. Models of this size are generally not practical since rendering speeds and memory requirements are proportional to the number of polygons. Consequently applications that generate large polygonal meshes often use domain–specific knowledge to reduce model size. There remain algorithms, however, where domain–specific reduction techniques are not generally available or appropriate.

One algorithm that generates many polygons is *Marching Cubes* [10]. *Marching Cubes* is a brute force surface construction algorithm that extracts isodensity surfaces from volume data, producing from one to five triangles within voxels that contain the surface. Although originally developed for medical applications, *Marching Cubes* has found more frequent use in scientific visualization where the size of the volume data sets are much smaller than those found in medical applications. A large computational fluid dynamics volume could have a finite difference grid size of order 100 by 100 by 100, while a typical medical computed tomography or magnetic resonance scanner produces over 100 slices at a resolution of 256 by 256 or 512 by 512 pixels each. Industrial computed tomography, used for inspection and analysis, has even greater resolution, varying from 512 by 512 to 1024 by 1024 pixels. For these sampled data sets, isosurface extraction using *Marching Cubes* can produce from 500k to 2,000k triangles. Even today's graphics workstations have trouble storing and rendering models of this size.

Other sampling devices can produce large polygonal models: range cameras, digital elevation data, and satellite data. The sampling resolution of these devices is also improving, resulting in model sizes that rival those obtained from medical scanners.

This paper describes an application independent algorithm that uses local operations on geometry and topology to reduce the number of triangles in a triangle mesh. Although our implementation is for the triangle mesh, it can be directly applied to the more general polygon mesh. After describing other work related to model creation from sampled data, we describe the triangle decimation process and its implementation. Results from two different geometric modeling applications illustrate the strengths of the algorithm.

2 RELATED WORK

The decimation algorithm applies to discrete modeling: the synthesis, analysis and manipulation of objects contained within sampled data. Approaches to synthesizing these objects can be either adaptive or filter–based.

Adaptive techniques produce more primitives in selected areas. For example, Fowler [7] creates triangulated irregular networks (TIN) of terrain by finding ridges and channels, performing a Delaunay triangulation of these features and then adaptively adding points from the dense elevation grids. In implicit modeling, Bloomenthal [2] produces isosurfaces from implicit models by adaptively evaluating the implicit equations as long as the surface intersects his sampling cubes. In finite element mesh generation, the CATFEM system [6] uses octree techniques to create 3D finite elements directly from volume samples, generating more elements in areas of fine detail. Deformable models [11, 15] use an initial surface model that is repeatedly deformed to fit the implicit surface that exists within a sampled volume. The original model resolution controls the number of primitives in the final, deformed model. Fitting techniques approximate a surface with one or more primitives using error criteria to measure the goodness of fit. Schmitt [13] starts with rough bi–cubic patch approximations to sample data, then subdivides those patches that are not sufficiently close to the underlying samples. Recent work by DeHaemer [4] extends this

Author address:
GE CRD, KW/C211, 1 River Road, Schenectady, NY 12345
schroeder@crd.ge.com

© 1992   ACM-0-89791-479-1/92/007/0065 $01.50

work to reduce the number of polygons in a polygonal mesh. Turk [16] uses a re–triangulation technique that introduces new points onto a polygonal mesh, and then discards the old points to create a new mesh.

Filter–based techniques start with a large number of samples or primitives and remove or replace samples to reduce model size. Two naive approaches are sub–sampling and averaging. Sub–sampling uses every n^{th} point in the data to reduce the size of the data, while averaging resamples the data using neighboring points.

The bulk of published work on reducing the number of primitives for modeling addresses the two–dimensional approximation of curves with line segments. Dunham [5] compares nine techniques for the piecewise linear approximation of 2D planar curves. These algorithms seek approximations that satisfy a uniform error criterion. The points produced by each algorithm all lie on the digitized curves. Recent work [8] uses dynamic programming to approximate 3D space curves. Kalvin et. al. [9] describe a technique called *Adaptive Face Merging* that removes co–planar polygons. They report substantial polygon reduction for binary voxel data sets.

3 THE DECIMATION ALGORITHM

The fundamental goal of the decimation algorithm is to reduce the total number of triangles in a triangle mesh, while preserving as accurately as possible important features. Here we define a triangle mesh to be a collection of triangles in three–space, joined along common edges and vertices. Typically the topology of the mesh is 2–manifold [17], but non–manifold forms are possible and must be treated by the algorithm.

Any reduced mesh must meet two requirements [14]. First, the reduced mesh must preserve the original topology of the mesh, including non–manifold forms. Second, the decimated mesh must form a good geometric approximation to the original mesh. Optionally, the vertices of the decimated mesh can be a subset of the original vertices. Hence new vertices are never created, instead relatively unimportant vertices (and associated triangles) are removed from the mesh, forming new approximations to the original. This optional requirement, although not essential to forming an effective approximation to the original mesh, is useful in practice because it provides a way to use the auxiliary vertex data such as normals or texture coordinates.

3.1 OVERVIEW

The decimation algorithm is simple. Multiple passes are made over all vertices in the mesh. During a pass, each vertex is a candidate for removal and, if it meets the specified decimation criteria, the vertex and all triangles that use the vertex are deleted. The resulting hole in the mesh is patched by forming a local triangulation. The vertex removal process repeats, with possible adjustment of the decimation criteria, until some termination condition is met. Usually the termination criterion is specified as a percent reduction of the original mesh (or equivalent), or as some maximum decimation value. The three steps of the algorithm are:
1. characterize the local vertex geometry and topology,
2. evaluate the decimation criteria, and
3. triangulate the resulting hole.

3.2 CHARACTERIZING LOCAL GEOMETRY / TOPOLOGY

The first step of the decimation algorithm characterizes the local geometry and topology for a given vertex. The outcome of this process determines whether the vertex is a potential candidate for deletion, and if it is, which criteria to use.

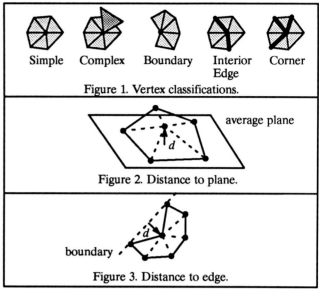

Figure 1. Vertex classifications.

Figure 2. Distance to plane.

Figure 3. Distance to edge.

Each vertex may be assigned one of five possible classifications: simple, complex, boundary, interior edge, or corner vertex. Examples of each type are shown in Figure 1.

A simple vertex is surrounded by a complete cycle of triangles, and each edge that uses the vertex is used by exactly two triangles. If the edge is not used by two triangles, or if the vertex is used by a triangle not in the cycle of triangles, then the vertex is complex. These are non–manifold cases.

A vertex that is on the boundary of a mesh, i.e., within a semi–cycle of triangles, is a boundary vertex.

A simple vertex can be further classified as an interior edge or corner vertex. These classifications are based on the local mesh geometry. If the dihedral angle between two adjacent triangles is greater than a specified *feature angle*, then a *feature edge* exists. When a vertex is used by two feature edges, the vertex is an interior edge vertex. If one or three or more feature edges use the vertex, the vertex is classified a corner vertex.

Complex vertices are not deleted from the mesh. All other vertices become candidates for deletion.

3.3 EVALUATING THE DECIMATION CRITERIA

The characterization step produces an ordered loop of vertices and triangles that use the candidate vertex. The evaluation step determines whether the triangles forming the loop can be deleted and replaced by another triangulation exclusive of the original vertex. Although the fundamental decimation criterion we use is based on vertex distance to plane or vertex distance to edge, others can be applied.

Simple vertices use the distance to plane criterion (Figure 2). An average plane is constructed using the triangle normals, $\vec{n}_i$, centers, $\vec{x}_i$, and areas A_i,

$$\vec{N} = \frac{\sum \vec{n}_i A_i}{\sum A_i}, \quad \vec{n} = \frac{\vec{N}}{|\vec{N}|} \quad \vec{x} = \frac{\sum \vec{x}_i A_i}{\sum A_i}, \qquad (1)$$

where the summation is over all triangles in the loop. The distance of the vertex $\vec{v}$ to the plane is then $d = |\vec{n} \cdot (\vec{v} - \vec{x})|$. If the vertex is within the specified distance to the average plane it may be deleted. Otherwise it is retained.

Boundary and interior edge vertices use the distance to edge criterion (Figure 3). In this case, the algorithm determines the distance to the line defined by the two vertices creating the boundary or feature edge. If the distance to the line is less than d, the vertex can be deleted.

It is not always desirable to retain feature edges. For example, meshes may contain areas of relatively small triangles with large feature angles, contributing relatively little to the geometric approximation. Or, the small triangles may be the result of "noise" in the original mesh. In these situations, corner vertices, which are usually not deleted, and interior edge vertices, which are evaluated using the distance to edge criterion, may be evaluated using the distance to plane criterion. We call this edge preservation, a user specifiable parameter.

If a vertex can be eliminated, the loop created by removing the triangles using the vertex must be triangulated. For interior edge vertices, the original loop must be split into two halves, with the split line connecting the vertices forming the feature edge. If the loop can be split in this way, i.e., so that resulting two loops do not overlap, then the loop is split and each piece is triangulated separately.

3.4 TRIANGULATION

Deleting a vertex and its associated triangles creates one (simple or boundary vertex) or two loops (interior edge vertex). Within each loop a triangulation must be created whose triangles are non–intersecting and non–degenerate. In addition, it is desirable to create triangles with good aspect ratio and that approximate the original loop as closely as possible.

In general it is not possible to use a two–dimensional algorithm to construct the triangulation, since the loop is usually non–planar. In addition, there are two important characteristics of the loop that can be used to advantage. First, if a loop cannot be triangulated, the vertex generating the loop need not be removed. Second, since every loop is star–shaped [12], triangulation schemes based on recursive loop splitting are effective. The next section describes one such scheme.

Once the triangulation is complete, the original vertex and its cycle of triangles are deleted. From the Euler relation [12] it follows that removal of a simple, corner, or interior edge vertex reduces the mesh by precisely two triangles. If a boundary vertex is deleted then the mesh is reduced by precisely one triangle.

4 IMPLEMENTATION

The decimation algorithm has been implemented as a filter in our object–oriented LYMB/VISAGE visualization environment. Usually we apply the algorithm repeatedly to eliminate vertices and triangles from a mesh until a specified reduction threshold is achieved. The decimation is controlled by slowly adjusting the distance and feature angle criterion. It is also possible to limit the total number of iterations, as well as modify other parameters such as the triangulation aspect ratio. We often specify an initial distance of zero to first remove triangles within strictly planar regions.

Two major challenges were addressed to create a successful implementation of the decimation algorithm. First, the data structures had to be carefully crafted since the size of the data (i.e., millions of triangles) demands both efficient access to and storage of data. Second, the triangulation algorithm was designed to be simple and efficient, and to take advantage of the particular characteristics of the triangulation process.

It should be noted that this algorithm, while expressly described with triangle meshes in mind, is directly applicable to polygon meshes. Only minor modifications need be made in the implementation of the data structures and loop evaluation.

4.1 DATA STRUCTURES

The data structure must contain at least two pieces of information: the geometry, or coordinates, of each vertex, and

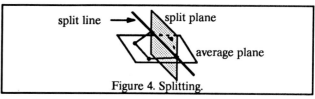
Figure 4. Splitting.

the definition of each triangle in terms of its three vertices. In addition, because ordered lists of triangles surrounding a vertex are frequently required, it is desirable to maintain a list of the triangles that use each vertex.

Although data structures such as Weiler's radial edge [17] or Baumgart's winged–edge data structure [1] can represent this information, our implementation uses a space–efficient vertex–triangle hierarchical ring structure. This data structure contains hierarchical pointers from the triangles down to the vertices, and pointers from the vertices back up to the triangles using the vertex. Taken together these pointers form a ring relationship. Our implementation uses three lists: a list of vertex coordinates, a list of triangle definitions, and another list of lists of triangles using each vertex. Edge definitions are not explicit, instead edges are implicitly defined as ordered vertex pairs in the triangle definition.

4.2 TRIANGULATION

Although other triangulation schemes can be used, we chose a recursive loop splitting procedure. Each loop to be triangulated is divided into two halves. The division is along a line (i.e., the split line) defined from two non–neighboring vertices in the loop. Each new loop is divided again, until only three vertices remain in each loop. A loop of three vertices forms a triangle, that may be added to the mesh, and terminates the recursion process.

Because the loop is non–planar and star–shaped, the loop split is evaluated using a split plane. The split plane, as shown in Figure 4, is the plane orthogonal to the average plane (Eqn. 1) that contains the split line. In order to determine whether the split forms two non–overlapping loops, the split plane is used for a half–space comparison. That is, if every point in a candidate loop is on one side of the split plane, then the two loops do not overlap and the split plane is acceptable. Of course, it is easy to create examples where this algorithm will fail to produce a successful split. In such cases we simply indicate a failure of the triangulation process, and do not remove the vertex or surrounding triangle from the mesh.

Typically, however, each loop may be split in more than one way. In this case, the best splitting plane must be selected. Although many possible measures are available, we have been successful using a criterion based on aspect ratio. The aspect ratio is defined as the minimum distance of the loop vertices to the split plane, divided by the length of the split line. The best splitting plane is the one that yields the maximum aspect ratio. Constraining this ratio to be greater than a specified value, .e.g., 0.1, produces acceptable meshes.

Certain special cases may occur during the triangulation process. Repeated decimation may produce a simple closed surface such as a tetrahedron. Eliminating a vertex in this case would modify the topology of the mesh. Another special case occurs when "tunnels" or topological holes are present in the mesh. The tunnel may eventually be reduced to a triangle in cross section. Eliminating a vertex from the tunnel boundary then eliminates the tunnel and creates a non–manifold situation.

These cases are treated during the triangulation process. As new triangles are created, checks are made to insure that duplicate triangles and triangle edges are not created. This preserves the topology of the original mesh, since new connections to other parts of the mesh cannot occur.

5 RESULTS

Two different applications illustrate the triangle decimation algorithm. Although each application uses a different scheme to create an initial mesh, all results were produced with the same decimation algorithm.

5.1 VOLUME MODELING

The first application applies the decimation algorithm to isosurfaces created from medical and industrial computed tomography scanners. *Marching Cubes* was run on a 256 by 256 pixel by 93 slice study. Over 560,000 triangles were required to model the bone surface. Earlier work [3] reported a triangle reduction strategy that used averaging to reduce the number of triangles on this same data set. Unfortunately, averaging applies uniformly to the entire data set, blurring high frequency features. Figure 5 shows the resulting bone isosurfaces for 0%, 75%, and 90% decimation, using a decimation threshold of 1/5 the voxel dimension. Figure 6 shows decimation results for an industrial CT data set comprising 300 slices, 512 by 512, the largest we have processed to date. The isosurface created from the original blade data contains 1.7 million triangles. In fact, we could not render the original model because we exceeded the swap space on our graphics hardware. Even after decimating 90% of the triangles, the serial number on the blade dovetail is still evident.

5.2 TERRAIN MODELING

We applied the decimation algorithm to two digital elevation data sets: Honolulu, Hawaii and the Mariner Valley on Mars. In both examples we generated an initial mesh by creating two triangles for each uniform quadrilateral element in the sampled data. The Honolulu example illustrates the polygon savings for models that have large flat areas. First we applied a decimation threshold of zero, eliminating over 30% of the co-planar triangles. Increasing the threshold removed 90% of the triangles. Figure 7 shows the resulting 30% and 90% triangulations. Notice the transitions from large flat areas to fine detail around the shore line.

The Mars example is an appropriate test because we had access to sub-sampled resolution data that could be compared with the decimated models. The data represents the western end of the Mariner Valley and is about 1000km by 500km on a side. Figure 8 compares the shaded and wireframe models obtained via sub-sampling and decimation. The original model was 480 by 288 samples. The sub-sampled data was 240 by 144. After a 77% reduction, the decimated model contains fewer triangles, yet shows more fine detail around the ridges.

6 CONCLUSIONS

The decimation algorithm significantly reduces the number of triangles required to model an object to a given level of detail. Using local topological and geometric operations, the algorithm makes multiple passes over a triangle mesh, removing vertices and triangulating the resulting holes until user-specified decimation criteria are satisfied. The three step algorithm affords the opportunity to experiment with other data structures, surface approximation metrics, and triangulation schemes. For example, the first step of the decimation could be modified to allow the user to tag some vertices as not-removable. Also, other non-geometric vertex data such as scalar quantities could be used to control the decimation.

We have successfully applied the algorithm to two visualization areas: volume and terrain modeling. We expect that some surface-based analysis techniques, such as boundary element methods or radiosity, will also benefit from the model reductions we have achieved. Here, the computational reduction will be even more significant, since the complexity of analysis is often more than linear with the number of primitives.

7 ACKNOWLEDGEMENTS

Joe Ross, GE Aircraft Engines, supplied the turbine blade data. Lee Moore, Webster Research Center, Xerox Corporation, provided the digital elevation data to the UseNet community through anonymous ftp access. The Mars data, also obtained from Xerox, is courtesy of the NASA Goddard's National Space Science Data Center (NSSDC), the US Geological Survey Astrogeology Division, Flagstaff, Arizona, and the NASA Ames Aerospace Human Factors Division Visualization for Planetary Exploration project.

REFERENCES

[1] Baumgart, B. G., "Geometric Modeling for Computer Vision," PhD Dissertation, Stanford University, August 1974.

[2] Bloomenthal, J., "Polygonalization of Implicit Surfaces," *Computer Aided Geometric Design*, Vol. 5, pp. 341–355, 1988.

[3] Cline, H. E., Lorensen, W. E., Ludke, S., Crawford, C. R., and Teeter, B. C., "Two Algorithms for the Three Dimensional Construction of Tomograms," *Medical Physics*, Vol. 15, No. 3, pp. 320–327, June 1988.

[4] DeHaemer, M. J., Jr. and Zyda, M. J., "Simplification of Objects Rendered by Polygonal Approximations," *Computers & Graphics*, Vol. 15, No. 2, pp 175–184, 1992.

[5] Dunham, J. G., "Optimum Uniform Piecewise Linear Approximation of Planar Curves," *IEEE Trans. on Pattern Analysis and Machine Intelligence*, Vol. PAMI-8, No. 1, pp. 67–75, January 1986.

[6] Finnigan, P., Hathaway, A., and Lorensen, W., "Merging CAT and FEM," *Mechanical Engineering*, Vol. 112, No. 7, pp. 32–38, July 1990.

[7] Fowler, R. J. and Little, J. J., "Automatic Extraction of Irregular Network Digital Terrain Models," *Computer Graphics*, Vol. 13, No. 2, pp. 199–207, August 1979.

[8] Ihm, I. and Naylor, B., "Piecewise Linear Approximations of Digitized Space Curves with Applications," in *Scientific Visualization of Physical Phenomena*, pp. 545–569, Springer-Verlag, June 1991.

[9] Kalvin, A. D., Cutting, C. B., Haddad, B., and Noz, M. E., "Constructing Topologically Connected Surfaces for the Comprehensive Analysis of 3D Medical Structures," *SPIE Image Processing*, Vol. 1445, pp. 247–258, 1991.

[10] Lorensen, W. E. and Cline, H. E., "Marching Cubes: A High Resolution 3D Surface Construction Algorithm," *Computer Graphics*, Vol. 21, No. 3, pp. 163–169, July 1987.

[11] Miller, J. V., Breen, D. E., Lorensen, W. E., O'Bara, R. M., and Wozny, M. J., "Geometrically Deformed Models: A Method for Extracting Closed Geometric Models from Volume Data," *Computer Graphics*, Vol. 25, No. 3, July 1991.

[12] Preparata, F. P. and Shamos, M. I., *Computational Geometry*, Springer-Verlag, 1985.

[13] Schmitt, F. J., Barsky, B. A., and Du, W., "An Adaptive Subdivision Method for Surface-Fitting from Sampled Data," *Computer Graphics*, Vol. 20, No. 4, pp. 179–188, August 1986.

[14] Schroeder, W. J., "Geometric Triangulations: With Application to Fully Automatic 3D Mesh Generation," PhD Dissertation, Rensselaer Polytechnic Institute, May 1991.

[15] Terzopoulos, D. and Fleischer, K., "Deformable Models," *The Visual Computer*, Vol. 4, pp. 306–311, 1988.

[16] Turk, G., "Re-Tiling of Polygonal Surfaces," *Computer Graphics*, Vol. 26, No. 3, July 1992.

[17] Weiler, K., "Edge-Based Data Structures for Solid Modeling in Curved-Surface Environments," *IEEE Computer Graphics and Applications*, Vol. 5, No. 1, pp. 21–40, January 1985.

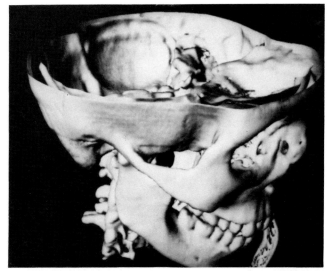

Figure 5a. Full resolution (569k Gouraud shaded triangles).

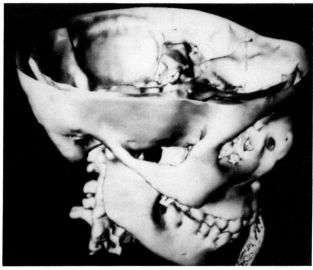

Figure 5b. 75% decimated (142k Gouraud shaded triangles).

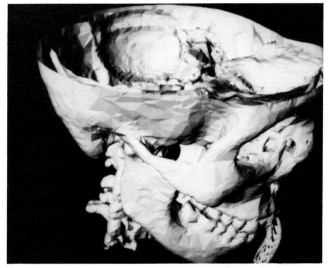

Figure 5c. 75% decimated (142k flat shaded triangles).

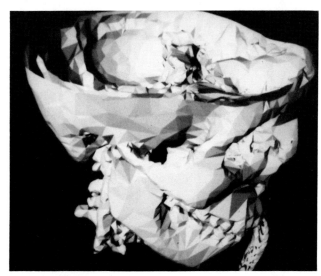

Figure 5d. 90% decimated (57k flat shaded triangles).

Figure 6a. 75% decimated (425k flat shaded triangles).

Figure 6b. 90% decimated (170k flat shaded triangles).

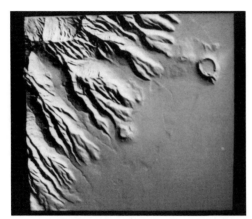

Figure 7a. 32% decimated (276k Gouraud triangles).

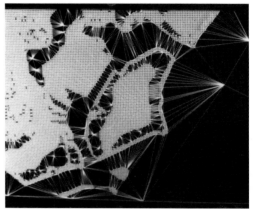

Figure 7b. 32% decimated, shore line detail.

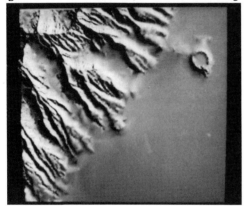

Figure 7c. 90% decimated (40k Gouraud triangles).

Figure 7d. 90% decimated (40k wireframe).

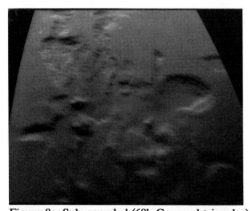

Figure 8a. Sub-sampled (68k Gouraud triangles).

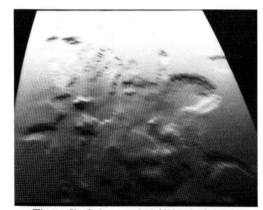

Figure 8b. Sub-sampled (68k wireframe).

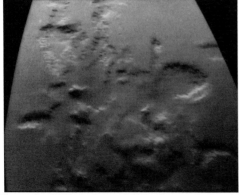

Figure 8c. 77% decimated (62k Gouraud triangles).

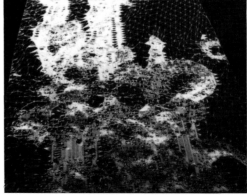

Figure 8d. 77% decimated (62k wireframe).

Surface Reconstruction from Unorganized Points

Hugues Hoppe*   Tony DeRose*   Tom Duchamp†
John McDonald‡   Werner Stuetzle‡

University of Washington
Seattle, WA 98195

Abstract

We describe and demonstrate an algorithm that takes as input an unorganized set of points $\{x_1, \ldots, x_n\} \subset \mathbb{R}^3$ on or near an unknown manifold M, and produces as output a simplicial surface that approximates M. Neither the topology, the presence of boundaries, nor the geometry of M are assumed to be known in advance — all are inferred automatically from the data. This problem naturally arises in a variety of practical situations such as range scanning an object from multiple view points, recovery of biological shapes from two-dimensional slices, and interactive surface sketching.

CR Categories and Subject Descriptors: I.3.5 [Computer Graphics]: Computational Geometry and Object Modeling.

Additional Keywords: Geometric Modeling, Surface Fitting, Three-Dimensional Shape Recovery, Range Data Analysis.

1 Introduction

Broadly speaking, the class of problems we are interested in can be stated as follows: Given partial information of an unknown surface, construct, to the extent possible, a compact representation of the surface. Reconstruction problems of this sort occur in diverse scientific and engineering application domains, including:

- *Surfaces from range data:* The data produced by laser range scanning systems is typically a rectangular grid of distances from the sensor to the object being scanned. If the sensor and object are fixed, only objects that are "point viewable" can be fully digitized. More sophisticated systems, such as those produced by Cyberware Laboratory, Inc., are capable of digitizing cylindrical objects by rotating either the sensor or the object. However, the scanning of topologically more complex objects, including those as simple as a coffee cup with a handle (a surface of genus 1), or the object depicted in Figure 1a (a surface of genus 3), cannot be accomplished by either of these methods. To adequately scan these objects, multiple view points must be used. Merging the data generated from multiple view points to reconstruct a polyhedral surface representation is a non-trivial task [11].

- *Surfaces from contours:* In many medical studies it is common to slice biological specimens into thin layers with a microtome. The outlines of the structures of interest are then digitized to create a stack of contours. The problem is to reconstruct the three-dimensional structures from the stacks of two-dimensional contours. Although this problem has received a good deal of attention, there remain severe limitations with current methods. Perhaps foremost among these is the difficulty of automatically dealing with branching structures [3, 12].

- *Interactive surface sketching:* A number of researchers, including Schneider [21] and Eisenman [6], have investigated the creation of curves in $\mathbb{R}^2$ by tracing the path of a stylus or mouse as the user sketches the desired shape. Sachs et al. [19] describe a system, called 3-Draw, that permits the creation of free-form curves in $\mathbb{R}^3$ by recording the motion of a stylus fitted with a Polhemus sensor. This can be extended to the design of free-form surfaces by ignoring the order in which positions are recorded, allowing the user to move the stylus arbitrarily back and forth over the surface. The problem is then to construct a surface representation faithful to the unordered collection of points.

Reconstruction algorithms addressing these problems have typically been crafted on a case by case basis to exploit partial structure in the data. For instance, algorithms solving the surface from contours problem make heavy use of the fact that data are organized into contours (i.e., closed polygons), and that the contours lie in parallel planes. Similarly, specialized algorithms to reconstruct surfaces from multiple view point range data might exploit the adjacency relationship of the data points within each view.

In contrast, our approach is to pose a unifying general problem that does not assume any structure on the data points. This approach has both theoretical and practical merit. On the theoretical side, abstracting to a general problem often sheds light on the truly critical aspects of the problem. On the practical side, a single algorithm that solves the general problem can be used to solve any specific problem instance.

*Department of Computer Science and Engineering, FR-35
†Department of Mathematics, GN-50
‡Department of Statistics, GN-22

This work was supported in part by Bellcore, the Xerox Corporation, IBM, Hewlett-Packard, the Digital Equipment Corporation, the Department of Energy under grant DE-FG06-85-ER25006, the National Library of Medicine under grant NIH LM-04174, and the National Science Foundation under grants CCR-8957323 and DMS-9103002.

1.1 Terminology

By a *surface* we mean a "compact, connected, orientable two-dimensional manifold, possibly with boundary, embedded in $\mathbb{R}^3$" (cf. O'Neill [17]). A surface without boundary will be called a *closed surface*. If we want to emphasize that a surface possesses a non-empty boundary, we will call it a *bordered surface*. A piecewise linear surface with triangular faces will be referred to as a *simplicial surface*. We use $\|\mathbf{x}\|$ to denote the Euclidean length of a vector $\mathbf{x}$, and we use $d(X, Y)$ to denote the Hausdorff distance between the sets of points X and Y (the Hausdorff distance is simply the distance between the two closest points of X and Y).

Let $X = \{\mathbf{x}_1, \ldots, \mathbf{x}_n\}$ be sampled data points on or near an unknown surface M (see Figure 1b). To capture the error in most sampling processes, we assume that each of the points $\mathbf{x}_i \in X$ is of the form $\mathbf{x}_i = \mathbf{y}_i + \mathbf{e}_i$, where $\mathbf{y}_i \in M$ is a point on the unknown surface and $\mathbf{e}_i \in \mathbb{R}^3$ is an error vector. We call such a sample X δ-*noisy* if $\|\mathbf{e}_i\| \leq \delta$ for all i. A value for δ can be estimated in most applications (e.g., the accuracy of the laser scanner). Features of M that are small compared to δ will obviously not be recoverable.

It is also impossible to recover features of M in regions where insufficient sampling has occurred. In particular, if M is a bordered surface, such as a sphere with a disc removed, it is impossible to distinguish holes in the sample from holes in the surface. To capture the intuitive notion of sampling density we need to make another definition: Let $Y = \{\mathbf{y}_1, \ldots, \mathbf{y}_n\} \subset M$ be a (noiseless) sample of a surface M. The sample Y is said to be ρ-*dense* if any sphere with radius ρ and center in M contains at least one sample point in Y. A δ-noisy sample $\{\mathbf{x}_1, \ldots, \mathbf{x}_n\} \subset \mathbb{R}^3$ of a surface M is said to be ρ-dense if there exists a noiseless ρ-dense sample $\{\mathbf{y}_1, \ldots, \mathbf{y}_n\} \subset M$ such that $\mathbf{x}_i = \mathbf{y}_i + \mathbf{e}_i$, $\|\mathbf{e}_i\| \leq \delta$, $i = 1, \ldots, n$.

1.2 Problem Statement

The goal of *surface reconstruction* is to determine a surface M' (see Figure 2f) that approximates an unknown surface M (Figure 1a), using a sample X (Figure 1b) and information about the sampling process, for example, bounds on the noise magnitude δ and the sampling density ρ.

We are currently working to develop conditions on the original surface M and the sample X that are sufficient to allow M to be reliably reconstructed. As that work is still preliminary, we are unable to give guarantees for the algorithm presented here. However, the algorithm has worked well in practice where the results can be compared to the original surface (see Section 4).

2 Related Work

2.1 Surface Reconstruction

Surface reconstruction methods can be classified according to the way in which they represent the reconstructed surface.

Implicit reconstruction methods attempt to find a smooth function $f : \mathbb{R}^3 \to \mathbb{R}$ such that $\{\mathbf{x}_1, \ldots, \mathbf{x}_n\}$ is close to the zero set $Z(f)$. They differ with respect to the form of f and the measure of closeness. Pratt [18] and Taubin [25] minimize the sum of squared Hausdorff distances from the data points to the zero set of a polynomial in three variables. Muraki [15] takes f to be a linear combination of three-dimensional Gaussian kernels with different means and spreads. His goodness-of-fit function measures how close the values of f at the data points are to zero, and how well the unit normals to the zero set of f match the normals estimated from the data. Moore and Warren [13] fit a piecewise polynomial recursively and then enforce continuity using a technique they call *free form blending*.

In contrast to implicit reconstruction techniques, parametric reconstruction techniques represent the reconstructed surface as a topological embedding $f(\Lambda)$ of a 2-dimensional parameter domain Λ into $\mathbb{R}^3$. Previous work has concentrated on domain spaces with simple topology, i.e. the plane and the sphere. Hastie and Stuetzle [9] and Vemuri [26, 27] discuss reconstruction of surfaces by a topological embedding $f(\Lambda)$ of a planar region Λ into $\mathbb{R}^3$. Schudy and Ballard [22, 23] and Brinkley [4] consider the reconstruction of surfaces that are slightly deformed spheres, and thus choose Λ to be a sphere. Sclaroff and Pentland [24] describe a hybrid implicit/parametric method for fitting a deformed sphere to a set of points using deformations of a superquadric.

Compared to the techniques mentioned above, our method has several advantages:

- It requires only an unorganized collection of points on or near the surface. No additional information is needed (such as normal information used by Muraki's method).

- Unlike the parametric methods mentioned above, it can reconstruct surfaces of arbitrary topology.

- Unlike previously suggested implicit methods, it deals with boundaries in a natural way, and it does not generate spurious surface components not supported by the data.

2.2 Surface Reconstruction vs Function Reconstruction

Terms like "surface fitting" appear in reference to two distinct classes of problems: surface reconstruction and function reconstruction. The goal of surface reconstruction was stated earlier. The goal of function reconstruction may be stated as follows: Given a surface M, a set $\{\mathbf{x}_i \in M\}$, and a set $\{y_i \in \mathbb{R}\}$, determine a function $f : M \to \mathbb{R}$, such that $f(\mathbf{x}_i) \approx y_i$.

The domain surface M is most commonly a plane embedded in $\mathbb{R}^3$, in which case the problem is a standard one considered in approximation theory. The case where M is a sphere has also been extensively treated (cf. [7]). Some recent work under the title *surfaces on surfaces* addresses the case when M is a general curved surface such as the skin of an airplane [16].

Function reconstruction methods can be used for surface reconstruction in simple, special cases, where the surface to be reconstructed is, roughly speaking, the graph of a function over a *known* surface M. It is important to recognize just how limited these special cases are — for example, not every surface homeomorphic to a sphere is the graph of a function over the sphere. The point we want to make is that function reconstruction must not be misconstrued to solve the general surface reconstruction problem.

3 A Description of the Algorithm

3.1 Overview

Our surface reconstruction algorithm consists of two stages. In the first stage we define a function $f : D \to \mathbb{R}$, where $D \subset \mathbb{R}^3$ is a region near the data, such that f estimates the signed geometric distance to the unknown surface M. The zero set $Z(f)$ is our estimate for M. In the second stage we use a contouring algorithm to approximate $Z(f)$ by a simplicial surface.

Although the *unsigned* distance function $|f|$ would be easier to estimate, zero is not a regular value of $|f|$. Zero is, however, a regular value of f, and the implicit function theorem thus guarantees that our approximation $Z(f)$ is a manifold.

The key ingredient to defining the signed distance function is to associate an oriented plane with each of the data points. These *tan-*

gent planes serve as local linear approximations to the surface. Although the construction of the tangent planes is relatively simple, the selection of their orientations so as to define a globally consistent orientation for the surface is one of the major obstacles facing the algorithm. As indicated in Figure 2b, the tangent planes do not directly define the surface, since their union may have a complicated non-manifold structure. Rather, we use the tangent planes to define the signed distance function to the surface. An example of the simplicial surface obtained by contouring the zero set of the signed distance function is shown in Figure 2e. The next several sections develop in more detail the successive steps of the algorithm.

3.2 Tangent Plane Estimation

The first step toward defining a signed distance function is to compute an oriented tangent plane for each data point. The tangent plane $Tp(\mathbf{x}_i)$ associated with the data point $\mathbf{x}_i$ is represented as a point $\mathbf{o}_i$, called the center, together with a unit normal vector $\hat{\mathbf{n}}_i$. The signed distance of an arbitrary point $\mathbf{p} \in \mathbb{R}^3$ to $Tp(\mathbf{x}_i)$ is defined to be $\text{dist}_i(\mathbf{p}) = (\mathbf{p} - \mathbf{o}_i) \cdot \hat{\mathbf{n}}_i$. The center and normal for $Tp(\mathbf{x}_i)$ are determined by gathering together the k points of X nearest to $\mathbf{x}_i$; this set is denoted by $Nbhd(\mathbf{x}_i)$ and is called the k-neighborhood of $\mathbf{x}_i$. (We currently assume k to be a user-specified parameter, although in Section 5 we propose a method for determining k automatically.) The center and unit normal are computed so that the plane $\{\text{dist}_i(\mathbf{p}) = 0\}$ is the least squares best fitting plane to $Nbhd(\mathbf{x}_i)$. That is, the center $\mathbf{o}_i$ is taken to be the centroid of $Nbhd(\mathbf{x}_i)$, and the normal $\hat{\mathbf{n}}_i$ is determined using principal component analysis. To compute $\hat{\mathbf{n}}_i$, the covariance matrix of $Nbhd(\mathbf{x}_i)$ is formed. This is the symmetric 3×3 positive semi-definite matrix

$$CV = \sum_{\mathbf{y} \in Nbhd(\mathbf{x}_i)} (\mathbf{y} - \mathbf{o}_i) \otimes (\mathbf{y} - \mathbf{o}_i)$$

where $\otimes$ denotes the outer product vector operator[1]. If $\lambda_i^1 \geq \lambda_i^2 \geq \lambda_i^3$ denote the eigenvalues of CV associated with unit eigenvectors $\hat{\mathbf{v}}_i^1, \hat{\mathbf{v}}_i^2, \hat{\mathbf{v}}_i^3$, respectively, we choose $\hat{\mathbf{n}}_i$ to be either $\hat{\mathbf{v}}_i^3$ or $-\hat{\mathbf{v}}_i^3$. The selection determines the orientation of the tangent plane, and it must be done so that nearby planes are "consistently oriented".

3.3 Consistent Tangent Plane Orientation

Suppose two data points $\mathbf{x}_i, \mathbf{x}_j \in X$ are geometrically close. Ideally, when the data is dense and the surface is smooth, the corresponding tangent planes $Tp(\mathbf{x}_i) = (\mathbf{o}_i, \hat{\mathbf{n}}_i)$ and $Tp(\mathbf{x}_j) = (\mathbf{o}_j, \hat{\mathbf{n}}_j)$ are nearly parallel, i.e. $\hat{\mathbf{n}}_i \cdot \hat{\mathbf{n}}_j \approx \pm 1$. If the planes are consistently oriented, then $\hat{\mathbf{n}}_i \cdot \hat{\mathbf{n}}_j \approx +1$; otherwise, either $\hat{\mathbf{n}}_i$ or $\hat{\mathbf{n}}_j$ should be flipped. The difficulty in finding a consistent global orientation is that this condition should hold between all pairs of "sufficiently close" data points.

We can model the problem as graph optimization. The graph contains one node N_i per tangent plane $Tp(\mathbf{x}_i)$, with an edge (i, j) between N_i and N_j if the tangent plane centers $\mathbf{o}_i$ and $\mathbf{o}_j$ are sufficiently close (we will be more precise about what we mean by sufficiently close shortly). The cost on edge (i, j) encodes the degree to which N_i and N_j are consistently oriented and is taken to be $\hat{\mathbf{n}}_i \cdot \hat{\mathbf{n}}_j$. The problem is then to select orientations for the tangent planes so as to maximize the total cost of the graph. Unfortunately, this problem can be shown to be NP-complete via a reduction to MAXCUT [8]. To efficiently solve the orientation problem we must therefore resort to an approximation algorithm.

Before describing the approximation algorithm we use, we must decide when a pair of nodes are to be connected in the graph. Since

the surface is assumed to consist of a single connected component, the graph should be connected. A simple connected graph for a set of points that tends to connect neighbors is the Euclidean Minimum Spanning Tree (EMST). However, the EMST over the tangent plane centers $\{\mathbf{o}_1, \ldots, \mathbf{o}_n\}$ (Figure 1c) is not sufficiently dense in edges to serve our purposes. We therefore enrich it by adding a number of edges to it. Specifically, we add the edge (i, j) if either $\mathbf{o}_i$ is in the k-neighborhood of $\mathbf{o}_j$, or $\mathbf{o}_j$ is in the k-neighborhood of $\mathbf{o}_i$ (where k-neighborhood is defined over $\{\mathbf{o}_1, \ldots, \mathbf{o}_n\}$ as it was for X). The resulting graph (Figure 1d), called the *Riemannian Graph*, is thus constructed to be a connected graph that encodes geometric proximity of the tangent plane centers.

A relatively simple-minded algorithm to orient the planes would be to arbitrarily choose an orientation for some plane, then "propagate" the orientation to neighboring planes in the Riemannian Graph. In practice, we found that the order in which the orientation is propagated is important. Figure 3b shows what may result when propagating orientation solely on the basis of geometric proximity; a correct reconstruction is shown in Figure 3c. Intuitively, we would like to choose an order of propagation that favors propagation from $Tp(\mathbf{x}_i)$ to $Tp(\mathbf{x}_j)$ if the unoriented planes are nearly parallel. This can be accomplished by assigning to each edge (i, j) in the Riemannian Graph the cost $1 - |\hat{\mathbf{n}}_i \cdot \hat{\mathbf{n}}_j|$. In addition to being non-negative, this assignment has the property that a cost is small if the unoriented tangent planes are nearly parallel. A favorable propagation order can therefore be achieved by traversing the *minimal spanning tree* (MST) of the resulting graph. This order is advantageous because it tends to propagate orientation along directions of low curvature in the data, thereby largely avoiding ambiguous situations encountered when trying to propagate orientation across sharp edges (as at the tip of the cat's ears in Figure 3b). In the MST shown in Figure 2a, the edges are colored according to their cost, with the brightly colored edges corresponding to regions of high variation (where $\hat{\mathbf{n}}_i \cdot \hat{\mathbf{n}}_j$ is somewhat less than 1).

To assign orientation to an initial plane, the unit normal of the plane whose center has the largest z coordinate is forced to point toward the $+z$ axis. Then, rooting the tree at this initial node, we traverse the tree in depth-first order, assigning each plane an orientation that is consistent with that of its parent. That is, if during traversal, the current plane $Tp(\mathbf{x}_i)$ has been assigned the orientation $\hat{\mathbf{n}}_i$ and $Tp(\mathbf{x}_j)$ is the next plane to be visited, then $\hat{\mathbf{n}}_j$ is replaced with $-\hat{\mathbf{n}}_j$ if $\hat{\mathbf{n}}_i \cdot \hat{\mathbf{n}}_j < 0$.

This orientation algorithm has been used in all our examples and has produced correct orientations in all the cases we have run. The resulting oriented tangent planes are represented as shaded rectangles in Figure 2b.

3.4 Signed Distance Function

The signed distance $f(\mathbf{p})$ from an arbitrary point $\mathbf{p} \in \mathbb{R}^3$ to a known surface M is the distance between $\mathbf{p}$ and the closest point $\mathbf{z} \in M$, multiplied by ± 1, depending on which side of the surface $\mathbf{p}$ lies. In reality M is not known, but we can mimic this procedure using the oriented tangent planes as follows. First, we find the tangent plane $Tp(\mathbf{x}_i)$ whose center $\mathbf{o}_i$ is closest to $\mathbf{p}$. This tangent plane is a local linear approximation to M, so we take the signed distance $f(\mathbf{p})$ to M to be the signed distance between $\mathbf{p}$ and its projection $\mathbf{z}$ onto $Tp(\mathbf{x}_i)$; that is,

$$f(\mathbf{p}) = \text{dist}_i(\mathbf{p}) = (\mathbf{p} - \mathbf{o}_i) \cdot \hat{\mathbf{n}}_i.$$

If M is known not to have boundaries, this simple rule works well. However, the rule must be extended to accommodate surfaces that might have boundaries. Recall that the set $X = \{\mathbf{x}_1, \ldots, \mathbf{x}_n\}$ is assumed to be a ρ-dense, δ-noisy sample of M. If there was no noise, we could deduce that a point $\mathbf{z}$ with $d(\mathbf{z}, X) > \rho$ cannot

---

[1]If $\mathbf{a}$ and $\mathbf{b}$ have components a_i and b_j respectively, then the matrix $\mathbf{a} \otimes \mathbf{b}$ has $a_i b_j$ as its ij-th entry.

be a point of M since that would violate X being ρ-dense. Intuitively, the sample points do not leave holes of radius larger than ρ. If the sample is δ-noisy, the radius of the holes may increase, but by no more than δ. We therefore conclude that a point z cannot be a point of M if $d(z, X) > \rho + \delta$. If the projection z of p onto the closest tangent plane has $d(z, X) > \rho + \delta$, we take $f(p)$ to be undefined. Undefined values are used by the contouring algorithm of Section 3.5 to identify boundaries.

Stated procedurally, our signed distance function is defined as:

$i \leftarrow$ index of tangent plane whose center is closest to p

$\{$ *Compute* z *as the projection of* p *onto* $Tp(\mathbf{x}_i)$ $\}$
$$z \leftarrow \mathbf{o}_i - ((\mathbf{p} - \mathbf{o}_i) \cdot \hat{\mathbf{n}}_i)\,\hat{\mathbf{n}}_i$$

if $d(z, X) < \rho + \delta$ **then**
$\qquad f(\mathbf{p}) \leftarrow (\mathbf{p} - \mathbf{o}_i) \cdot \hat{\mathbf{n}}_i \qquad \{= \pm \|\mathbf{p} - z\|\}$
else
$\qquad f(\mathbf{p}) \leftarrow$ **undefined**
endif

The simple approach outlined above creates a zero set $Z(f)$ that is piecewise linear but contains discontinuities. The discontinuities result from the implicit partitioning of space into regions within which a single tangent plane is used to define the signed distance function. (These regions are in fact the Voronoi regions associated with the centers $\mathbf{o}_i$.) Fortunately, the discontinuities do not adversely affect our algorithm. The contouring algorithm discussed in the next section will discretely sample the function f over a portion of a 3-dimensional grid near the data and reconstruct a *continuous* piecewise linear approximation to $Z(f)$.

3.5 Contour Tracing

Contour tracing, the extraction of an isosurface from a scalar function, is a well-studied problem [1, 5, 28]. We chose to implement a variation of the marching cubes algorithm (cf. [28]) that samples the function at the vertices of a cubical lattice and finds the contour intersections within tetrahedral decompositions of the cubical cells.

To accurately estimate boundaries, the cube size should be set so that edges are of length less than $\rho + \delta$. In practice we have often found it convenient to set the cube size somewhat larger than this value, simply to increase the speed of execution and to reduce the number of triangular facets generated.

The algorithm only visits cubes that intersect the zero set by pushing onto a queue only the appropriate neighboring cubes (Figure 2c). In this way, the signed distance function f is evaluated only at points close to the data. Figure 2d illustrates the signed distance function by showing line segments between the query points p (at the cube vertices) and their associated projected points z. As suggested in Section 3.4, no intersection is reported within a cube if the signed distance function is undefined at any vertex of the cube, thereby giving rise to boundaries in the simplicial surface.

The resulting simplicial surface can contain triangles with arbitrarily poor aspect ratio (Figure 2e). We alleviate this problem using a post-processing procedure that collapses edges in the surface using an aspect ratio criterion.[2] The final result is shown in Figure 2f. Alternatively, other contouring methods exist that can guarantee bounds on the triangle aspect ratio [14].

---

[2] The edges are kept in a priority queue; the criterion to minimize is the product of the edge length times the minimum inscribed radius of its two adjacent faces. Tests are also performed to ensure that edge collapses preserve the topological type of the surface.

4 Results

We have experimented with the reconstruction method on data sets obtained from several different sources. In all cases, any structure (including ordering) that might have been present in the point sets was discarded.

Meshes : Points were randomly sampled from a number of existing simplicial surfaces[3]. For instance, the mesh of Figure 3a was randomly sampled to yield 1000 unorganized points, and these in turn were used to reconstruct the surface in Figure 3c. This particular case illustrates the behavior of the method on a bordered surface (the cat has no base and is thus homeomorphic to a disc). The reconstructed knot (original mesh from Rob Scharein) of Figure 3d is an example of a surface with simple topology yet complex geometrical embedding.

Ray Traced Points : To simulate laser range imaging from multiple view points, CSG models were ray traced from multiple eye points. The ray tracer recorded the point of first intersection along each ray. Eight eye points (the vertices of a large cube centered at the object) were used to generate the point set of Figure 1b from the CSG object shown in Figure 1a. This is the point set used in Section 3 to illustrate the steps of the algorithm (Figures 1a-2f).

Range Images : The bust of Spock (Figure 3e) was reconstructed from points taken from an actual cylindrical range image (generated by Cyberware Laboratory, Inc.). Only 25% of the original points were used.

Contours : Points from 39 planar (horizontal) slices of the CT scan of a femur were combined together to obtain the surface of Figure 3f.

The algorithm's parameters are shown in the next table for each of the examples. The execution times were obtained on a 20 MIPS workstation. The parameter $\rho + \delta$ and the marching cube cell size are both expressed as a fraction of the object's size. The parameter $\rho + \delta$ is set to infinity for those surfaces that are known to be closed.

Object	n	k	$\rho + \delta$	cell size	time (seconds)
cat	1000	15	.06	1/30	19
knot	10000	20	∞	1/50	137
mechpart	4102	12	∞	1/40	54
spock	21760	8	.08	1/80	514
femur	18224	40	.06	1/50	2135

5 Discussion

5.1 Tangent Plane Approximation

The neighborhood $Nbhd(\mathbf{x}_i)$ of a data point $\mathbf{x}_i$ is defined to consist of its k nearest neighbors, where k is currently assumed to be an input parameter. In the case where the data contains little or no noise, k is not a critical parameter since the output has been empirically observed to be stable over a wide range of settings. However, it would be best if k could be selected automatically. Furthermore, allowing k to adapt locally would make less stringent the requirement that the data be uniformly distributed over the surface. To select and adapt k, the algorithm could incrementally gather points while monitoring the changing eigenvalues of the covariance matrix (see Section 3.2). For small values of k, data noise tends to dominate, the eigenvalues are similar, and the eigenvectors do not reveal the surface's true tangent plane. At the other extreme, as k becomes

---

[3] Discrete inverse transform sampling [10, page 469] on triangle area was used to select face indices from the mesh, and uniform sampling was used within the faces.

large, the k-neighborhoods become less localized and the surface curvature tends to increase the "thickness" λ_i^3 of the neighborhood. Another possible criterion is to compare λ_i^3 to some local or global estimate of data noise. Although we have done some initial experimentation in this direction, we have not yet fully examined these options.

If the data is obtained from range images, there exists some knowledge of surface orientation at each data point. Indeed, each data point is known to be visible from a particular viewing direction, so that, unless the surface incident angle is large, the point's tangent plane orientation can be inferred from that viewing direction. Our method could exploit this additional information in the tangent plane orientation step (Section 3.3) by augmenting the Riemannian Graph with an additional pseudo-node and n additional edges.

5.2 Algorithm Complexity

A spatial partitioning Abstract Data Type greatly improves performance of many of the subproblems discussed previously. The critical subproblems are (with their standard time complexity):

- EMST graph ($O(n^2)$)
- k-nearest neighbors to a given point ($O(n + k \log n)$)
- nearest tangent plane origin to a given point ($O(n)$)

Hierarchical spatial partitioning schemes such as octrees [20] and k-D trees [2] can be used to solve these problems more efficiently. However, the uniform sampling density assumed in our data allows simple spatial cubic partitioning to work efficiently. The axis-aligned bounding box of the points is partitioned by a cubical grid. Points are entered into sets corresponding to the cube to which they belong, and these sets are accessed through a hash table indexed by the cube indices. It is difficult to analyze the resulting improvements analytically, but, empirically, the time complexity of the above problems is effectively reduced by a factor of n, except for the k-nearest neighbors problem which becomes $O(k)$.

As a result of the spatial partitioning, the Riemannian Graph can be constructed in $O(nk)$ time. Because the Riemannian Graph has $O(n)$ edges (at most $n + nk$), the MST computation used in finding the best path on which to propagate orientation requires only $O(n \log n)$ time. Traversal of the MST is of course $O(n)$.

The time complexity of the contouring algorithm depends only on the number of cubes visited, since the evaluation of the signed distance function f at a point p can be done in constant time (the closest tangent plane origin o_i to p and the closest data point x_j to the projected point z can both be found in constant time with spatial partitioning).

6 Conclusions and Future Work

We have developed an algorithm to reconstruct a surface in three-dimensional space with or without boundary from a set of unorganized points scattered on or near the surface. The algorithm, based on the idea of determining the zero set of an estimated signed distance function, was demonstrated on data gathered from a variety of sources. It is capable of automatically inferring the topological type of the surface, including the presence of boundary curves.

The algorithm can, in principle, be extended to reconstruct manifolds of co-dimension one in spaces of arbitrary dimension; that is, to reconstruct $d - 1$ dimensional manifolds in d dimensional space. Thus, essentially the same algorithm can be used to reconstruct curves in the plane or volumes in four-dimensional space.

The output of our reconstruction method produced the correct topology in all the examples. We are trying to develop formal guarantees on the correctness of the reconstruction, given constraints on

the sample and the original surface. To further improve the geometric accuracy of the fit, and to reduce the space required to store the reconstruction, we envision using the output of our algorithm as the starting point for a subsequent spline surface fitting procedure. We are currently investigating such a method based on a nonlinear least squares approach using triangular Bézier surfaces.

References

[1] E. L. Allgower and P. H. Schmidt. An algorithm for piecewise linear approximation of an implicitly defined manifold. *SIAM Journal of Numerical Analysis*, 22:322–346, April 1985.

[2] J. L. Bentley. Multidimensional divide and conquer. *Comm. ACM*, 23(4):214–229, 1980.

[3] Y. Breseler, J. A. Fessler, and A. Macovski. A Bayesian approach to reconstruction from incomplete projections of a multiple object 3D domain. *IEEE Trans. Pat. Anal. Mach. Intell.*, 11(8):840–858, August 1989.

[4] James F. Brinkley. Knowledge-driven ultrasonic three-dimensional organ modeling. *IEEE Trans. Pat. Anal. Mach. Intell.*, 7(4):431–441, July 1985.

[5] David P. Dobkin, Silvio V. F. Levy, William P. Thurston, and Allan R. Wilks. Contour tracing by piecewise linear approximations. *ACM TOG*, 9(4):389–423, October 1990.

[6] John A. Eisenman. Graphical editing of composite bezier curves. Master's thesis, Department of Electrical Engineering and Computer Science, M.I.T., 1988.

[7] T.A. Foley. Interpolation to scattered data on a spherical domain. In M. Cox and J. Mason, editors, *Algorithms for Approximation II*, pages 303–310. Chapman and Hall, London, 1990.

[8] Michael R. Garey and David S. Johnson. *Computers and Intractability*. W. H. Freeman and Company, 1979.

[9] T. Hastie and W. Stuetzle. Principal curves. *JASA*, 84:502–516, 1989.

[10] Averill M. Law and W. David Kelton. *Simulation Modeling and Analysis*. McGraw-Hill, Inc., second edition, 1991.

[11] Marshal L. Merriam. Experience with the cyberware 3D digitizer. In *NCGA Proceedings*, pages 125–133, March 1992.

[12] David Meyers, Shelly Skinner, and Kenneth Sloan. Surfaces from contours: The correspondence and branching problems. In *Proceedings of Graphics Interface '91*, pages 246–254, June 1991.

[13] Doug Moore and Joe Warren. Approximation of dense scattered data using algebraic surfaces. TR 90-135, Rice University, October 1990.

[14] Doug Moore and Joe Warren. Adaptive mesh generation ii: Packing solids. TR 90-139, Rice University, March 1991.

[15] Shigeru Muraki. Volumetric shape description of range data using "blobby model". *Computer Graphics (SIGGRAPH '91 Proceedings)*, 25(4):227–235, July 1991.

[16] Gregory M. Nielson, Thomas A. Foley, Bernd Hamann, and David Lane. Visualizing and modeling scattered multivariate data. *IEEE CG&A*, 11(3):47–55, May 1991.

[17] Barrett O'Neill. *Elementary Differential Geometry*. Academic Press, Orlando, Florida, 1966.

[18] Vaughan Pratt. Direct least-squares fitting of algebraic surfaces. *Computer Graphics (SIGGRAPH '87 Proceedings)*, 21(4):145–152, July 1987.

[19] Emanuel Sachs, Andrew Roberts, and David Stoops. 3-Draw: A tool for designing 3D shapes. *IEEE Computer Graphics and Applications*, 11(6):18–26, November 1991.

[20] Hanan Samet. *Applications of Spatial Data Structures*. Addison-Wesley, 1990.

[21] Philip J. Schneider. Phoenix: An interactive curve design system based on the automatic fitting of hand-sketched curves. Master's thesis, Department of Computer Science, U. of Washington, 1988.

[22] R. B. Schudy and D. H. Ballard. Model detection of cardiac chambers in ultrasound images. Technical Report 12, Computer Science Department, University of Rochester, 1978.

[23] R. B. Schudy and D. H. Ballard. Towards an anatomical model of heart motion as seen in 4-d cardiac ultrasound data. In *Proceedings of the 6th Conference on Computer Applications in Radiology and Computer-Aided Analysis of Radiological Images*, 1979.

[24] Stan Sclaroff and Alex Pentland. Generalized implicit functions for computer graphics. *Computer Graphics (SIGGRAPH '91 Proceedings)*, 25(4):247–250, July 1991.

[25] G. Taubin. Estimation of planar curves, surfaces and nonplanar space curves defined by implicit equations, with applications to edge and range image segmentation. Technical Report LEMS-66, Division of Engineering, Brown University, 1990.

[26] B. C. Vemuri. *Representation and Recognition of Objects From Dense Range Maps*. PhD thesis, Department of Electrical and Computer Engineering, University of Texas at Austin, 1987.

[27] B. C. Vemuri, A. Mitiche, and J. K. Aggarwal. Curvature-based representation of objects from range data. *Image and Vision Computing*, 4(2):107–114, 1986.

[28] G. Wyvill, C. McPheeters, and B. Wyvill. Data structures for soft objects. *The Visual Computer*, 2(4):227–234, August 1986.

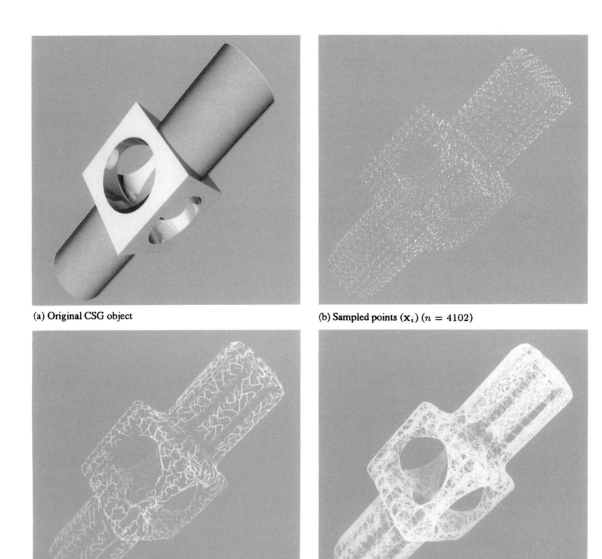

(a) Original CSG object

(b) Sampled points $(\mathbf{x}_i)$ $(n = 4102)$

(c) EMST of tangent plane centers $\mathbf{o}_i$

(d) Riemannian Graph over $\mathbf{o}_i$

Figure 1: Reconstruction of ray-traced CSG object (simulated multi-view range data).

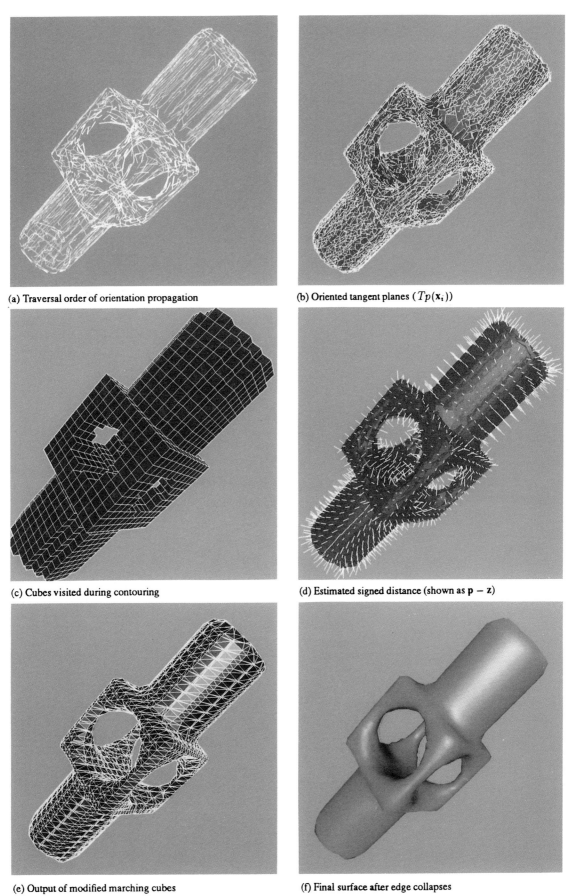

(a) Traversal order of orientation propagation

(b) Oriented tangent planes ($Tp(\mathbf{x}_i)$)

(c) Cubes visited during contouring

(d) Estimated signed distance (shown as $\mathbf{p} - \mathbf{z}$)

(e) Output of modified marching cubes

(f) Final surface after edge collapses

Figure 2: Reconstruction of ray-traced CSG object (continued).

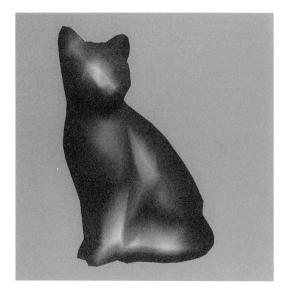

(a) Original mesh

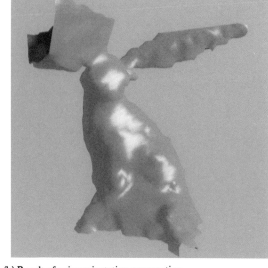

(b) Result of naive orientation propagation

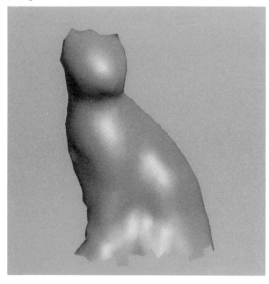

(c) Reconstructed bordered surface

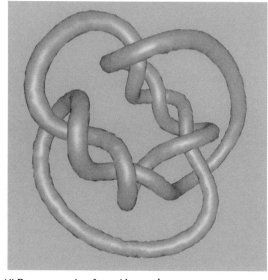

(d) Reconstructed surface with complex geometry

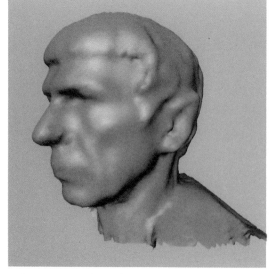

(e) Reconstruction from cylindrical range data

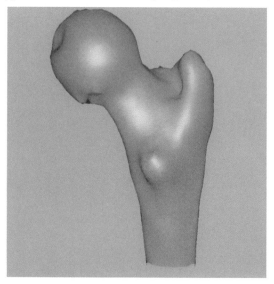

(f) Reconstruction from contour data

Figure 3: Reconstruction examples.

Smoothing Polyhedra using Implicit Algebraic Splines*

Chandrajit L. Bajaj   *Insung Ihm*

Department of Computer Sciences,
Purdue University,
West Lafayette, Indiana 47907

Tel: 317-494-6531
Fax: 317-494-0739
bajaj@cs.purdue.edu
ihm@cs.purdue.edu

Abstract

Polyhedron "smoothing" is an efficient construction scheme for generating complex boundary models of solid physical objects. This paper presents efficient algorithms for generating families of curved solid objects with boundary topology related to an input polyhedron. Individual faces of a polyhedron are replaced by low degree implicit algebraic surface patches with local support. These quintic patches replace the C^0 contacts of planar facets with C^1 continuity along all interpatch boundaries. Selection of suitable instances of implicit surfaces as well as local control of the individual surface patches are achieved via simultaneous interpolation and weighted least-squares approximation .

1 Introduction

The generation of a C^1 mesh of smooth surface patches or *splines* that interpolate or approximate *triangulated space data* is one of the central topics of geometric design. Two surfaces $f(x, y, z) = 0$ and $g(x, y, z) = 0$ meet with C^k-continuity along a curve C if and only if there exists functions $\alpha(x, y, z)$ and $\beta(x, y, z)$ such that all derivatives upto order k of $\alpha f - \beta g$ equals zero at all points along C, see for e.g., [13]. Chui [8], Dahmen and Michelli [10] and Hollig [18] summarize much of the history of multivariate splines. Prior work on splines have traditionally worked with a given planar triangulation using a polynomial function basis [1, 32, 35]. More recently surface fitting has been considered over closed triangulations in three dimensions using parametric surface patches [6, 7, 12, 15, 16, 17, 21, 24, 26, 27, 29, 33, 37].

---

*Supported in part by NSF grants CCR 90-00028, DMS 91-01424 and AFOSR contract 91-0276

Little work has been done on spline bases using implicitly defined algebraic surface patches. Sederberg [34] showed how various smooth implicit algebriac surfaces in trivariate Bernstein basis can be manipulated as functions in Bezier control tetrahedra with finite weights. Patrikalakis and Kriezis [25] extended this by considering implicit algebriac surfaces in a tensor product B-spline basis. However the problem of selecting weights or specifying knot sequences for C^1 meshes of implicit algebraic surface patches which fit given spatial data, was left open. Dahmen [9] presented a scheme for constructing C^1 continuous, piecewise quadric surface patches over a data triangulation in space. In his construction each triangular face is split and replaced by six micro quadric triangular patches, similar to the splitting scheme of Powell-Sabin [30]. Dahmen's technique however works only if the original triangulation of the data set allows a transversal system of planes, and hence is quite restricted. Moore and Warren [23] extend the marching cubes scheme of [22] and compute a C^1 piecewise quadratic approximation (least-squares) to scattered data. They too use a Powell-Sabin like split, however over subcubes.

In this paper we consider an arbitrary spatial triangulation $\mathcal{T}$ consisting of vertices $\mathbf{p} = (x_i, y_i, z_i)$ in $\mathbb{R}^3$ (or more generally a simplicial polyhedron $\mathcal{P}$ when the triangulation is closed), with possibly "normal" vectors at the vertex points. We present an algorithm to construct a C^1 continuous mesh of low degree real algebraic surface patches S_i , which respects the topology of the triangulation $\mathcal{T}$ or simplicial polyhedron $\mathcal{P}$, and C^1 interpolates all the vertices. Our technique is completetly general and uses a single implicit surface patch for each triangular face of $\mathcal{T}$ of $\mathcal{P}$, i.e. no local splitting of triangular faces. Furthermore, our C^1 interpolation scheme is local in that each triangular surface patch has independent degrees of freedom which may be used to provide local shape control. In this paper, we show how these extra parameters may be adjusted and the shape of the patch controlled by using weighted least squares approximation from additional points and normals, generated locally for each triangular patch.

Algebraic surfaces: For our polyhedron smoothing problem we only considered fitting with algebraic surfaces, i.e. two dimensional zero sets of polynomial equations. This was primarily motivated from the fact that manipulating polynomials, as opposed to arbitrary analytic functions, is computationally more efficient [3]. Furthermore, algebraic surfaces provide enough generality to accurately model almost all complicated rigid objects. A real algebraic surface S in $\mathbb{R}^3$ is implicitly defined by a single polynomial equation $\mathcal{F}$: $f(x, y, z) = 0$, where coefficients of f are over the real numbers $\mathbb{R}$. While **all** real algebraic surfaces have an implicit definition $\mathcal{F}$ only a small subset of these real surfaces can also be defined parametrically by the triple $\mathcal{G}(s, t) : (x = G_1(s, t), y = G_2(s, t), z = G_3(s, t))$ where each G_i, $i = 1, 2, 3$, is a rational function (ratio of polynomials) in s and t over $\mathbb{R}$. The primary advantage of the implicit definition $\mathcal{F}$ is its closure properties under modeling operations such as intersection, convolution, offset, blending, etc. The smaller class of parametrically defined algebraic surfaces $\mathcal{G}(s, t)$ is not closed under any of these operations. Closure under modeling operations allow cascading repetitions[1] without any need of approximation. Furthermore, designing with the complete class of algebraic surfaces leads to better possibilities (as we show here) of being able to satisfy the same geometric design constraints with much lower degree algebraic surfaces. The implicit representation of smooth algebraic surfaces also naturally yields half-spaces $\mathcal{F}^+ : f(x, y, z) \geq 0$ and $\mathcal{F}^- : f(x, y, z) \leq 0$, a fact quite useful for intersection and offset modeling operations. Finally, since prior approaches to scattered data fitting over triangulations had focused on the parametric representation of surfaces our aim here was to exhibit that implicitly defined algebraic surfaces were also equally (if not more) amenable to the task.

Why is low degree important ? Let the *geometric degree* of an algebraic surface is the maximum number of intersections between the surface and a line, counting complex, infinite and multiple intersections. It is a measure of the "wavi-ness" of the surface. This geometric degree is the same as the degree of the defining polynomial f of the algebraic surface in the implicit definition, but may be as high as n^2 for a parametrically defined surface with rational functions G_i of degree n. The *geometric degree* of an algebraic space curve is the maximum number of intersections between the curve and a plane, counting complex, infinite and multiple intersections. A well known theorem of algebraic geometry (**Bezout's** theorem) states that the the geometric degree of an algebraic intersection curve of two algebraic surfaces may be as large as the product of the geometric degrees of the two surfaces [36]. The use of low degree surface patches to construct models of physical objects thus results in faster computations for subsequent geometric model manipulation operations such as computer graphics display, animation, and physical object simulations, since the time complexity of these manipulations is a direct function of the degree of the involved curves and surfaces. Furthermore, the number of singularities[2] (sources of numerical ill-conditioning) of a curve of geometric degree m may be as high as m^2 [38]. Keeping the degree low of the curves and surfaces thus leads to potentially more robust numerical computations.

The main results of this paper are:

1. an efficient algorithm in sections 2, 3, 4 which computes

---

[1] The output of one operation acts as the input to another operation
[2] Points on the curve where all derivatives are zero

C^1 smooth models of a convex polyhedron using degree 5 algebraic surface patches, and of an arbitrary polyhedron using *at most* degree 7 algebraic surface patches,

2. a numerically stable method in section 5 for the simultaneous C^1 interpolation and weighted least squares approximation used for both the selection of a smooth, single-sheeted solution surface as well as local shape control,

Both our solution surface degree bounds 5 and 7 are also significantly better than the geometric degree 18, parametric bicubic surface patch solutions for the same problem achieved by Peters [26]. Note that this comparison is only between the prior known fitting algorithm which did not additionally split the meshed data and had the best degree bound. Details on the implementation of our algorithms and illustrative examples are given in the section 6.1.

2 The Polyhedron Smoothing Algorithm

In this section, we present an outline of the algorithm to smooth a simple polyhedron $\mathcal{P}$ with C^1-continuous implicit algebraic surface patches.

Algorithm

1. Triangulate each of the nontriangular polygonal faces of the given polyhedron $\mathcal{P}$. Each face of $\mathcal{P}$ is a simple polygon which can be triangulated by adding non-intersecting inner diagonals[31]. See Figure 2.

2. Specify a single "normal" vector at each vertex of $\mathcal{P}$. This provides a single tangent plane for all patches which shall interpolate that vertex with C^1 continuity.

3. Next, construct a curvilinear wire frame by replacing each edge of $\mathcal{P}$ with a curve which C^1-interpolates the end points of the edge and the specified "normals". Any remaining degrees of freedom of the C^1 interpolatory curve are used to select a desired shape of the curve and indirectly thereby a desired shape of the smoothing surface patch. See Figure 2.

4. Specify normal vectors along each of the edge curves. This provides the tangent planes for the two incident patches which shall C^1 interpolate the edge curves. See Figure 3.

5. Finally, C^1-interpolate the three edge curves and curve normals of each face. The remaining degrees of freedom for each individual patch are consumed via weighted least squares approximation to achieve a suitably shaped single-sheeted algebraic surface patch. The resulting surface patches yield a globally C^1 smooth curved model for the given polyhedron. See Figures 3 and 6.

Details of each of the steps 2 to 5 of the algorithm for specific classes of polyhedra (convex, non-convex) together with explicit degrees of the required curves and surfaces are presented in subsequent sections. Steps 2 to 4 are detailed in section 3 and step 5 in sections 4.

3 Wireframe Construction

3.1 Choice of Vertex Normals

The single "normal" vector assigned to each vertex of the triangulated polyhedron $\mathcal{P}$ can be chosen independently and quite arbitrarily. However the relative directions of each adjacent vertex normal pair can affect the degree of the C^1 interpolating edge curve which replaces th e straight edges of $\mathcal{P}$. Let the two normal vectors at the two end points of an edge be called an *edge-normal-pair*. Certain relative directions of an edge-normal-pair induce an inflection point for any C^1 interpolating curve. Since conics do not have inflection points one is then forced to either switch to cubic curves at the least or to artificially split the edge. Splitting an edge in turn induces splitting of the triangular face of $\mathcal{P}$. In this section, we restrict ourselves to surface fitting without the splitting of any triangular faces of $\mathcal{P}$.

We first derive a necessary and sufficient condition for the relative directions of an edge-normal-pair to allow a singly connected C^1 conic interpolating curve. Here, the interpolation is *strict* in that the curve's normal at the vertex points and the prescribed vertex normal are in the same direction and not opposite. This restriction guarantees the construction wire frames which are free of cusp-like connections. In the following definitions and lemmas we make all of this more precise.

Definition 3.1 *Let $P_0 = (p_0, n_0)$ and $P_1 = (p_1, n_1)$ be an edge-normal-pair. A conic segment $S(P_0, P_1)$ is said to C^1-interpolate P_0 and P_1 if there exists a non-degenerate quadratic surface a(quadric) $F : ax^2 + by^2 + cz^2 + dxy + eyz + fzx + gx + hy + iz + j = 0$ such that*

- *$S(P_0, P_1)$ is a singly connected conic segment on F,*

- *p_0 and p_1 are the end points of $S(P_0, P_1)$,*

- *the gradient of $f(x, y, z) = 0$ at p_0 and p_1 have the same directions as n_0 and n_1, respectively. In other words $\nabla f(p_0) = \alpha n_0$ and $\nabla f(p_1) = \beta n_1$ for constants $\alpha, \beta > 0$.*

For a given point-normal pair $P = ((p_x, p_y, p_z), (n_x, n_y, n_z))$, we have $T_P(x, y, z) = n_x(x - p_x) + n_y(y - p_y)n_z(z - p_z) = 0$ as the equation of the tangent plane that passes through (p_x, p_y, p_z) and has a normal direction (n_x, n_y, n_z). The tangent plane $T_P(x, y, z) = 0$ divides space into a positive halfspace $\{(x, y, z) \in \mathbf{R}^3 | T_P(x, y, z) > 0\}$, and a negative halfspace $\{(x, y, z) \in \mathbf{R}^3 | T_P(x, y, z) < 0\}$. Note also, that for a surface $f(x, y, z)$ if $\nabla f(p_x, p_y, p_z) = \alpha(n_x, n_y, n_z)$ then $T_P = T_{((p_x, p_y, p_z), \nabla f(p_x, p_y, p_z))}$.

Theorem 3.1 *There exists a single connected conic segment $S(P_0, P_1)$ on a non-degenerate quadric F that C^1-interpolates $P_0 = (p_0, n_0)$ and $P_1 = (p_1, n_1)$ if and only if $T_{P_0}(p_1) \cdot T_{P_1}(p_0) > 0$.*

Proof: ($\Rightarrow$) Let $f(x, y, z) = ax^2 + by^2 + cz^2 + dxy + eyz + fzx + gx + hy + iz + j = 0$ be the non-degenerate quadric F. From definition 3.1 of a C^1 interpolating conic segment on F, it follows that

$T_{P_0}(p_1) \cdot T_{P_1}(p_0) = T_{(p_0, \nabla f(p_0))}(p_1) \cdot T_{(p_1, \nabla f(p_1))}(p_0)$. Without loss of generality, assume that $p_0 = (0, 0, 0)$, and $p_1 = (1, 0, 0)$. Since $\nabla f(x, y, z) = (2ax + dy + fz + g, 2by + dx + ez + h, 2cz + ey + fx + i)$, $\nabla f(0, 0, 0) = (g, h, i)$ and $\nabla f(1, 0, 0) = (2a + g, d + h, f + i)$. Hence, $T_{(p_0, \nabla f(p_0))}(x, y, z) = gx + hy + iz$, and $T_{(p_1, \nabla f(p_1))}(x, y, z) = (2a + g)(x - 1) + (d + h)y + (f + i)z$. From the containment conditions of the two points, $f(0, 0, 0) = j = 0$, and $f(1, 0, 0) = a + g + j = a + g = 0$. Then, $T_{(p_0, \nabla f(p_0))}(p_1) \cdot T_{(p_1, \nabla f(p_1))}(p_0) = g(-(2a + g)) = -g(2(-g) + g) = g^2 > 0$, as g cannot be zero. For if $g = 0$, it would follow that $a = g = j = 0$, and either $T_{P_0}(p_1)$ or $T_{P_1}(p_0)$ or both would be zero (i.e. the tangent plane at p_0 contains p_1 or the tangent plane at p_1 contains p_0, both). In each such case the quadric $f(x, y, z) = by^2 + cz^2 + dxy + eyz + fzx + hy + iz = 0$ is a degenerate quadric as its intersection with any plane section through p_0 and p_1 yields a pair of lines (a degenerate conic).

($\Leftarrow$) If $T_{P_0}(p_1) \cdot T_{P_1}(p_0) > 0$, then the conic segment on $f(x, y, z) = L(x, y, z)^2 - \kappa \cdot T_{P_0}(x, y, z) \cdot T_{P_1}(x, y, z) = 0$ or $-f(x, y, z) = 0$ will C^1 interpolate the pair P_0 and P_1, where $L(x, y, z) = 0$ is a plane containing p_0 and p_1, and κ is a constant. ♠

The geometric interpretation of the inequality $T_{(p_0, \nabla f(p_0))}(p_1) \cdot T_{(p_1, \nabla f(p_1))}(p_0) > 0$ is that p_0 is on the positive (negative) halfspace of T_{P_1} if and only if p_1 is on the positive (negative) halfspace of T_{P_0}.

3.2 Generation of a Conic Wireframe

First, we give a definition of the term *quadric wire*.

Definition 3.2 *Let $C(t) = (\frac{x(t)}{w(t)}, \frac{y(t)}{w(t)}, \frac{z(t)}{w(t)})$ and $N(t) = (\frac{nx(t)}{w(t)}, \frac{ny(t)}{w(t)}, \frac{nz(t)}{w(t)})$ be two triples of quadratic rational parametric polynomials. Then, the pair $W(t) = (C(t), N(t))$ is called a quadric wire if there exists a quadric $q(x, y, z) = 0$ such that $q(C(t)) = 0$ and $\nabla q(C(t)) = \alpha N(t)$, for $\alpha > 0$ and all t.*

The rationale in our construction of a quadric wire is that a conic curve is naturally associated with curve normal vectors taken from a quadric. Our first step to smoothing a convex polyhedron is to compute a C^1 interpolating conic curve $C(t)$, from an edge-normal-pair (p_0, n_0), (p_1, n_1) and a normal npl of a plane Q which contains p_0 and p_1. In particular, we set $W(0) \equiv (p_0, n_1)$ and $W(1) \equiv (p_1, n_1)$, [3] and hence use the segment of $W(t), 0 \leq t \leq 1$. To compute $C(t)$, the normal vectors n_0 and n_1 are projected into the plane P on which $C(t)$ will lie. (See Figure 1). This projection results in a control triangle $p_0 - p_2 - p_1$. Lee [20] presents a compact method for computing a conic curve $C(t)$ from such a control triangle. In his formulation, the conic is expressed in Bernstein-Bézier form :

$$C(t) = \frac{w_0 p_0 (1 - t)^2 + 2w_2 p_2 t(1 - t) + w_1 p_1 t^2}{w_0 (1 - t)^2 + 2w_2 t(1 - t) + w_1 t^2},$$

where $w_i > 0$, $i = 0, 1, 2$ are shape control parameters. An often used parameterization, called the *rho-conic parameterization*, is

---

[3] By $\equiv$, we mean the points are the same, and the normal vectors are proportional, maintaining positivity.

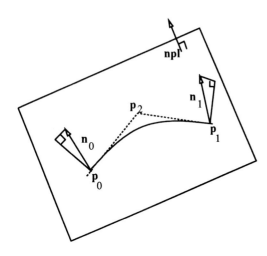

Figure 1: Computation of a Conic Curve

given by the special choice $w_0 = w_1 = (1 - \rho)$, $w_2 = \rho$, $\rho > 0$. Let $p_{01} = (p_0 + p_1)/2$ be the midpoint of the chord $p_0 p_1$. Then, ρ has a property that $C(0.5) - p_{01} = \rho(p_2 - p_{01})$. From this, we can see that as ρ is increased, the conic gets more curved. In particular, it can be shown that $\rho = 0.5$ for a parabola, $0 < \rho < 0.5$ for ellipses and $0.5 < \rho < 1.0$ for hyperbolas.

3.3   Assigning Normals along Edge curves

Once $C(t)$ is fixed, we find a quadratic surface $q(x, y, z) = 0$ such that $N(t)$ is proportional to $\nabla q(x, y, z)$ along $C(t)$ and interpolates n_0 and n_1. Consider a quadric surface $q(x, y, z) = c_0 x^2 + c_1 y^2 + c_2 z^2 + c_3 xy + c_4 yz + c_5 zx + c_6 x + c_7 y + c_8 z + c_9 = 0$. $q(x, y, z) = 0$ has 10 coefficients, and since dividing the surface by any nonzero coefficient does not change the surface, there are 9 degrees of freedom. The first requirement is that $q(x, y, z) = 0$ must contain the computed conic $C(t)$. The C^1 interpolation algorithm for algebraic surfaces [5] gives 5 linear equations in terms of the unknowns c_i for the containment requirement. That 5 constraints on c_i are required also follows from Bezout's theorem which says if a non-degenerate conic intersects with a quadric at more than 4 points, then the conic must lie on the quadric.

Hence, $4 (= 9 - 5)$ degrees of freedom in choosing c_i are left, and these are used to interpolate the normal vectors at the two end points. Interpolating n_0 and n_1 at p_0 and p_1, respectively, gives 2 more linear constraints which leaves 2 degrees of freedom in choosing the quadric. We now explain why specifying one more normal vector at a point on the C^1 interpolating conic fixes the normal vectors along the entire conic. Consider the gradient vector $\nabla q(x, y, z)$ of the quadric. Its components are linear and the vector function $\nabla q(C(t))$ is a degree 2 polynomial parametric curve in projective space. Hence, three independent constraints fixes the curve $\nabla q(C(t))$ and thereby the normal vector along $C(t)$.

Using similar reasons as above one obtains the following lemma.

Lemma 3.1 *Let $W(t) = (C(t), N(t))$ be a quadric wire. Then the quadrics which C^1 interpolate $W(t)$ comprises of a family of*

surfaces with one degree of freedom.

What we do in our implementation in order to fix the additional normal vector on the conic is the following. First, the average $n_{01} = (n_0 + n_1)/2$ is computed, and then n_{01} is projected onto the plane which contains $C(t)$. (All conics are planar). Next we require that the projected vector be perpendicular to the tangent at $C(0.5)$ i.e. the vector $C'(0.5)$. This then fixes all the normal vectors $N(t)$ along $C(t)$.

For a convex polyhedron, we can always specify a normal vector at each vertex such that the condition in Theorem 3.1 for each edge-normal-pair is satisfied. (For example, the average of normal vectors of incident faces of a vertex is one possible choice.) This implies that we can always construct a wireframe for a convex polyhedron whose curves and associated normal vectors are described in terms of quadric rational polynomials. Whether we can construct a similar conic wireframe for non-convex polyhedra is currently unresolved.

3.4   Generation of a Cubic Wireframe

The construction of a cubic wireframe follows along very similar lines as the conic wireframe construction. Each edge is now replaced by a polynomial parametric cubic curve, C^1 interpolating the vertex-normal pairs of the edge. Here no restrictions are imposed on the vertex-normal pairs as was the case for the conic wireframe of the earlier section. The construction of this cubic wireframe or cubic mesh of curves, see for example [11], is what has been used in the past and previously reported for example in [26]. We therefore omit further discussion of this construction and refer the reader to the earlier references.

4   Local Patch Generation

4.1 C^1 Interpolation of a Quadric Triangle

Definition 4.1 *An augmented triangle is an 9-tuple $T = (p_0, p_1, p_2, n_0, n_1, n_2, npl_{01}, npl_{12}, npl_{20})$ where the points p_i are three vertices of a triangle with the corresponding unit normal vectors n_i, and npl_{ij} is the normal of the plane which will contain the quadric wire made from (p_i, n_i) and (p_j, n_j).*

Definition 4.2 *A quadric triangle is a triple $QT = (W_0(t), W_1(t), W_2(t))$ of quadric wires such that $W_0(1) \equiv W_1(0)$, $W_1(1) \equiv W_2(0)$, and $W_2(1) \equiv W_0(0)$.*

Given an augmented triangle, each quadric wire is computed as described in the foregoing section. Next the quadric triangle is fleshed using a single algebraic surface $f(x, y, z) = 0$. For this we use the C^1 interpolation of Bajaj and Ihm [5]. This algorithm takes as input positional and first derivative information of points and space curves, given parametrically or implicitly, and characterizes, in terms of the nullspace of a matrix, the space of all the algebraic surfaces of a specified degree that C^1 interpolates the specified geometric data. For the quadric triangle the C^1 interpolation is applied to all three quadric wires and produces a homogeneous linear system $\mathbf{M_1 x} = \mathbf{0}$, where unknowns $\mathbf{x}$ are coefficients of $f(x, y, z) = 0$, such that any algebraic surface with coefficients that are solutions of the system C^1 interpolates the quadric triangle. The nontrivial solutions in the nullspace of $\mathbf{M_I}$ form a family of all possible algebraic surfaces of degree n, satisfying the given input constraints, whose coefficients are expressed by homogeneous combinations of q free parameters where $q = n_v - r$ is the dimension of the nullspace. Since dividing $f(x, y, z) = 0$ by a nonzero number does not change the surface, there are, in fact, $n_v - r - 1$ degrees of freedom in choosing an instance surface from the family. Hence, the rank r of $\mathbf{M_I}$ must be less than the number of the coefficients n_v, should there exist an interpolating surface.

We now derive general degree bounds for C^1 interpolatory triangular patches with degree m interpolatory curves and from this obtain lower bounds on the degree of surfaces which C^1 interpolate a quadric triangle. Assume that we use a degree n algebraic surface $f(x, y, z) = 0$ to C^1 interpolate a wire of degree m $W(t) = (C(t), N(t))$. According to Bezout's theorem, $mn + 1$ constraints on the coefficients of f are required for the algebraic surface f to contain $C(t)$ which is of degree m. Additionally for C^1 continuity, consider the restricted normal vector $\nabla f(C(t))$. Since the degree of each component of $\nabla f(x, y, z)$ is, at most $n - 1$, each component of $\nabla f(C(t))$ has degree $m(n - 1)$. Furthermore, the vector function $\nabla f(C(t)) - \alpha N(t)$ is a degree $m(n-1)$ parametric polynomial curve in projective space, with $N(t)$ of degree m and α any polynomial of degree at most $m(n - 2)$. Finally, since the surface $f(x, y, z) = 0$ contains $C(t)$ the component of the above vector function along the tangent direction of $C(t)$ is already satisfied. Hence $m(n - 1) + 1$ additional constraints are enough to guarantee C^1 continuity along $C(t)$.

Lemma 4.1 *Let $W(t) = (C(t), N(t))$ be a degree m wire. For an algebraic surface $f(x, y, z) = 0$ of degree n to smoothly interpolate $W(t)$, at most $2mn - m + 2 (= mn + 1 + m(n - 1) + 1)$ independent linear constraints on the f's coefficients must be satisfied.*

This lemma says that the rank of the matrix for Hermite interpolation of a degree m wire with a degree n surface is at most $2mn - m + 2$. For C^1 interpolation of a triangular patch, there exists a geometric dependency between the three wires which also leads to dependency amongst these linear C^1 contraints. First, since the curves intersect pairwise, there must be three rank deficiencies between the equations from the containment conditions (i.e. three equations are generated twice). For the same reasons there must be three rank deficiencies between the equations for the matching of normals. Secondly, at each vertex of the curvilinear triangle, two incident curves automatically determine the normal at the vertex. It is obvious, from the way the curve wire construction, this vector is proportional to the given unit normal vector at the vertex. So, satisfying the containment conditions for the 3 curves guarantees that any interpolating surface has gradient vectors at the three points as required. This fact implies that there are three rank deficiencies between the linear equations for the containment conditions, and the equations for the C^1 condition. This yields a total of 9 overall deficiencies.

Lemma 4.2 *Let $QT = (W_0(t), W_1(t), W_2(t))$ be a quadric triangle. The rank of the linear system $\mathbf{M_I x} = \mathbf{0}$ which is constructed by*

the Hermite interpolation for the algebraic surface $f(x, y, z) = 0$ of degree n that smoothly fleshes QT, is at most $12n - 9$.

Proof: For C^1 interpolation of all three quadric wires, $3(4n - 2 + 2) = 12n$ linear equations are generated according to Lemma 4.1. Subtracting 9 deficiencies from this yields $12n - 9$. ♠

Since $f(x, y, z) = 0$ of degree n has $\binom{n+3}{3}$ coefficients, and the rank of the linear system should be less than the number of coefficients for a nontrivial surface to exist, we see that 5 is the minimum degree required. In the quintic case, there are 56 coefficients (55 degrees of freedom) and the rank is at most 51, which results in a family of interpolating surfaces with at least 4 degrees of freedom in selecting an instance surface from the family.

Even though some special combination of three quadric wires can be interpolated by a surface of degree less than 5, for example, three quadric wires from a sphere, the probability that such spatial dependency occurs, given an arbitrary triple of conics with normals, is infinitesimal. Hence, we can say that 5 is the minimum degree required *with the probability one*.

Lemma 4.3 *Let $QT = (W_0(t), W_1(t), W_2(t))$ be a cubic triangle whose wires are cubic rational polynomials. The rank of the linear system $\mathbf{M_I x} = \mathbf{0}$ which is constructed by the Hermite interpolation for the algebraic surface $f(x, y, z) = 0$ of degree n that smoothly fleshes QT, is at most $18n - 12$.*

Proof: For C^1 interpolation of all three degree 3 wires, $3(6n - 3 + 2) = 18n - 3$ linear equations are generated according to Lemma 4.1. Subtracting 9 deficiencies, yields $18n - 12$. ♠

The minimum degree of the C^1 interpolating surface is 7. In the quintic case, there are 120 coefficients (119 degrees of freedom) and the rank is at most 114, which results in a family of interpolating surfaces with at least 5 degrees of freedom in selecting an instance surface from the family.

Lemma 4.4 *Let $QT = (W_0(t), W_1(t), W_2(t))$ be a quadric triangle with one edge a cubic wire. The rank of the linear system $\mathbf{M_I x} = \mathbf{0}$ which is constructed by the Hermite interpolation for the algebraic surface $f(x, y, z) = 0$ of degree n that smoothly fleshes QT, is at most $14n - 10$.*

Proof: For C^1 interpolation of two quadric wires and a cubic wire, $2(4n - 2 + 2) + (6n - 3 + 2) = 14n - 1$ linear equations are generated according to Lemma 4.1. Subtracting 9 deficiencies from this yields $14n - 10$. ♠

The minimum degree of the C^1 interpolating surface is 6. In the degree 6 case, there are 84 coefficients (83 degrees of freedom) and the rank is at most 74, which results in a family of interpolating surfaces with at least 9 degrees of freedom in selecting an instance surface from the family.

Lemma 4.5 *Let $QT = (W_0(t), W_1(t), W_2(t))$ be a cubic triangle with one edge a quadric wire. The rank of the linear system $\mathbf{M_I x} = \mathbf{0}$ which is constructed by the Hermite interpolation for the algebraic surface $f(x, y, z) = 0$ of degree n that smoothly fleshes QT, is at most $16n - 11$.*

Proof: For C^1 interpolation of two cubic wires and a quadric wire, $4n - 2 + 2) + 2(6n - 3 + 2) = 16n - 2$ linear equations are generated according to Lemma 4.1. Subtracting 9 deficiencies from this yields $16n - 11$. ♠

The minimum degree of the C^1 interpolating surface is 7. In the degree 7 case, there are 120 coefficients (119 degrees of freedom) and the rank is at most 101, which results in a family of interpolating surfaces with at least 18 degrees of freedom in selecting an instance surface from the family.

4.2   Surface Selection and Local Shape Control

The result of a C^1 interpolation of a quadric triangle QT is a family of degree 5 algebraic surfaces $f(x, y, z) = 0$ with at least 4 degrees of freedom. Similarly C^1 interpolation of a cubic triangle is achieved with a 5 parameter family of degree 7 surfaces. These families are expressed as a linear combination of the nontrivial coefficients vectors in the nullspace of M_I. To select a degree 5 or 7 surface from their respective families, values must be specified for these extra degrees of freedom.

We now show how weighted least squares approximation to additional points around the triangular patch, can be used for both selecting a suitable non-singular surface from the family as well as as local shape control. Let $S_0 = \{v_i \in \mathbf{R}^3 | i = 1, \cdots, l\}$ be a set of points which approximately describes a desirable surface patch. (These points can be selected for example from a sphere, paraboloid etc., centered around the curvilinear triangle). A linear system $M_A x = 0$, where each row of M_A is constructed from the linear conditions $f(v_i) = 0$ with x containing the undetermined coefficients of the family. Conventional least squares approximation is to minimize $\| M_A x \|^2$ over the nullspace of M_I. Though minimizing $\| M_A x \|^2$ does yield a good distance approximation it does not prevent the resulting surface from self-intersecting, pinching or splitting inside the triangle.

To rid our solution surfaces of such singularities and provide more geometric control , we instead approximate a monotonic trivariate function $w = f(x, y, z)$ rather than just the implicit surface $f(x, y, z) = 0$, the zero contour of the function. We first generate $S_0 = \{(v_i, n_i) | i = 1, \cdots, l\}$ where v_i are approximating points, and n_i are approximating gradient vectors at v_i. Then, from this set, we construct two more sets $S_1 = \{u_i | u_i = v_i + \alpha n_i, i = 1, \cdots, l\}$, and $S_{-1} = \{w_i | w_i = v_i - \alpha n_i, i = 1, \cdots, l\}$ for some small $\alpha > 0$. Next we set up the least squares system $M_A = b$ from the following three kinds of equations : $f(v_i) = 0$, $f(u_i) = 1$, and $f(w_i) = -1$. These equations give an approximating contour level structure of the function $w = f(x, y, z)$ near the inside of a quadric triangle. We found out that forcing well behaved contour levels rids the selected surfaces of self-intersection in the spatial region enclosed by the points. See Figures 6, 8, 9 and 10.

4.3   Compatibility and Non-Singularity Constraints

In this subsection, we briefly discuss why quintic surfaces which C^1-interpolate quadric triangles may be singular at the end vertices.

Ihm [19] gives a theorem which presents a necessary regularity condition on C^1 interpolating surfaces.

Theorem 4.1 *Let $C_1(u)$ and $C_2(v)$ be two parametric curves with parametric normal directions $N_1(u)$ and $N_2(v)$ such that $C_1(0) = C_2(0) = p$, and that $N_1(0)$ and $N_2(0)$ are proportional. Then, any surface S, which interpolates the curves with tangent plane continuity, is singular at p unless $\frac{(N_1'(0), C_1'(0))}{\| N_1(0) \|} = \frac{(C_2'(0), N_2'(0))}{\| N_2(0) \|}$.*

The above theorem implies that enforcing two curves to have the same normal vectors at intersection points, does not guarantee the regularity of an interpolating surface at those points. The equation in the theorem is a necessary condition for regularity, indicating that, if the given curves and their normals do not satisfy the equation, any smoothly interpolating surface must be singular at p. In most cases, the above condition is not met when quadric triangles are constructed, and hence we observe singularities at the vertices. A good side-effect of these vertex singularities is that the vertex enclosure problem is automatically resolved.

This issue has been also addressed in the literature of parametric surface fitting. Peters [27] showed that not every mesh of parametric curves with well-defined tangent planes at the mesh points can be interpolated by smooth regularly parametrized surfaces with one surface patch per mesh face (also known as the vertex enclosure problem). In [28], he used singularly parametrized surfaces to enclose a mesh points when mesh curves emanating from the point do not satisfy a constraint, called the vertex enclosure constraint.

5   Computational Details and Examples

5.1   Solution of Interpolation and Least-Squares Matrices

For an algebraic surface $S : f(x, y, z) = 0$ of degree n, the C^1 interpolation conditions of section 4.1 produces a homogeneous linear system $M_I x = 0$, $M_I \in \mathbf{R}^{n_i \times n_v}$ of n_i equations and n_v unknowns where x is a vector of the $n_v (= \binom{n+3}{3})$ coefficients of S. A matrix $M_A \in \mathbf{R}^{n_a \times n_v}$ for least-squares approximation is next constructed, similar to the construction of M_I, for the additional points generated around the triangular patch as described in section 4.2.

For the case of quintic algebraic surface patches we solve the following, simultaneous interpolation and weighted least-squares approximation problem below. The case of other low degree (6 or 7) C^1 algebraic surfaces is nearly identical, with only modified sizes of the matrices.

$$\begin{aligned} minimize \quad & \| M_A x - b \|^2 \\ subject\ to \quad & M_I x = 0, \end{aligned}$$

where $M_I \in \mathbf{R}^{n_i \times 56}$ is a Hermite interpolation matrix, and $M_A \in \mathbf{R}^{n_a \times 56}$ and $b \in \mathbf{R}^{n_a}$ are matrix and vector, respectively, for contour level approximation, and $x \in \mathbf{R}^{56}$ is a vector containing coefficients of a quintic algebraic surface $f(x, y, z) = 0$.

To find the nullspace of M_I in a computationally stable manner, the singular value decomposition (SVD) of M_I is computed [14] where M_I is decomposed as $M_I = U \Sigma V^T$ where

$U \in \mathbf{R}^{n_i \times n_i}$ and $V \in \mathbf{R}^{56 \times 56}$ are orthonormal matrices, and $\Sigma = diag(\sigma_1, \sigma_2, \cdots, \sigma_s) \in \mathbf{R}^{n_i \times 56}$ is a diagonal matrix with diagonal elements $\sigma_1 \geq \sigma_2 \geq \cdots \geq \sigma_s \geq 0$ $(s = min\{n_i, 56\})$. It is known that the rank r of $\mathbf{M_I}$ is the number of the positive diagonal elements of Σ, and that the last $56 - r$ columns of V span the nullspace of $\mathbf{M_I}$. Hence, the nullspace of $\mathbf{M_I}$ is expressed as :
$\{\mathbf{x} \in \mathbf{R}^{56} | \mathbf{x} = \sum_{i=1}^{56-r} w_i \mathbf{v}_{r+i}, \ where \ w_i \in \mathbf{R}, \ and \ \mathbf{v}_j \ is \ the \ jth \ column \ of \ V\}$, or $\mathbf{x} = V_{56-r}\mathbf{w}$ where $V_{56-r} \in \mathbf{R}^{56 \times (56-r)}$ is made of the last $56 - r$ columns of V, and $\mathbf{w}$ a $(56 - r)$-vector. [4] $\mathbf{x} = V_{56-r}\mathbf{w}$ compactly expresses all the quintic surfaces which Hermite-interpolate the three quadric wires.

After substitution for $\mathbf{x}$, we lead to $\| \mathbf{M_A}\mathbf{x} - \mathbf{b} \| = \| \mathbf{M_A} V_{56-r}\mathbf{w} - \mathbf{b} \|$. Then, an orthogonal matrix $Q \in \mathbf{R}^{n_a \times n_a}$ is computed such that

$$Q^T \mathbf{M_A} V_{56-r} = R = \begin{pmatrix} R_1 \\ 0 \end{pmatrix}$$

where $R_1 \in \mathbf{R}^{(56-r) \times (56-r)}$ is upper triangular. (This factorization is called a *Q-R factorization* [14]). Now, let

$$Q^T b = \begin{pmatrix} c \\ d \end{pmatrix}$$

where c is the first $56 - r$ elements. Then, $\| \mathbf{M_A} V_{56-r}\mathbf{w} - \mathbf{b} \|^2 = \| Q^T \mathbf{M_A} V_{56-r}\mathbf{w} - Q^T \mathbf{b} \|^2 = \| R_1 \mathbf{w} - c \|^2 + \| d \|^2$. The solution $\mathbf{w}$ can be computed by solving $R_1 \mathbf{w} = c$, from which the final fitting surface is obtained as $\mathbf{x} = V_{56-r}\mathbf{w}$.

5.2 Examples

In prior sections, we described how to compute low degree triangular algebraic surface patches from a given augmented curvilinear triangle. A polyhedron is smoothed by replacing its faces with the triangular patches meeting each other with tangent plane continuity. For the augmented triangles $T = (p_0, p_1, p_2, n_0, n_1, n_2, npl_{01}, npl_{12}, npl_{20})$ of the faces of a polyhedron, the normal data, i.e., three vertex normals and three edge normals, must be provided as well as the given three vertices. In some applications, the normal data may come with a solid, but, in general, only vertices and their facial information are provided.

The vertex normal $\mathbf{n}_i$ at each vertex $\mathbf{p}_i$ can be computed by averaging the normals of the faces incident to the vertex. Other assignment schemes which rely on the normals arsiing form a sphere or a paraboloid are also possible. For a convex triangulation $\mathcal{T}$ or polyhedron $\mathcal{P}$, the above choice of normals at vertices always yields compatible vertex-normal pairs (as per section 3) for C^1 conic interpolation and hence degree five surface patches suffice by results in section 4. However the above simplistic choice of vertex normals may yield incompatible vertex-normal pairs for a non-convex triangulation or polyhedron. To come up with a compatible vertex normal assignment for the non-convex case is an open problem. For

now, we use a C^1 interpolating cubic curve whenever an incompatible vertex-normal pair arises, as in the non-convex case. Hence in this case we may need to use algebraic surface patches of degree 7, (as per section 4). Also, we average the normals of the faces incident to each edge (p_i, p_j), and take its cross product with the vector $p_j - p_i$ to get the edge normal vector npl_{ij}. After the normal data is computed, quadric wires are generated for the ρ value which is interactively controlled by the user.

Example 5.1 *Construction of Quadric Wire Frames*

Figures 5 and 7 show two quadric wire frames for the same convex polyhedron[5] with the ρ values 0.4 (yielding ellipses) and 0.75 (yielding hyperbolas), respectively. □

Example 5.2 *Polyhedra Smoothed with Quintic Algebraic Surfaces*

Each of 32 faces of the polyhedron in Example 5.1 is replaced by a quintic implicit algebraic surface which smoothly fleshes its quadric triangle. Figures 6 and 8 respectively illustrate the C^1 surface meshes of $\rho = 0.4$ and 0.75. □

6 Remarks and Open Problems

6.1 Implementation Issues

We have presented a method that smooths out a polyhedron with C^1 continuous triangular algebraic surface patches. The polyhedron smoothing algorithms have been implemented in our distributed and collaborative geometric design environment SHASTRA [2], currently consisting of independent toolkit processes SHILP, GANITH and VAIDAK. For polyhedron smoothing, SHILP takes as input a polyhedron $\mathcal{P}$ and a user specified ρ value (for shape control), and computes quadric wires (if the normal condition is satisfied for the edge) or cubic wires. Next, for each triangular facet of curves, a GANITH computation is invoked via inter process communication and the facet C^1 fitted with a low degree (5 to 7) algebraic surface patch. Potentially, a separate GANITH process can be invoked for each individual facet on a network of workstations, to achieve maximal distributed parallelism. See Figure 10.

6.2 Open Problems

A number of open problems do remain. First, we need to devise a more robust way of generating the points and contour levels for the least squares approximation of section 4.2. While the heuristics for weighted least square approximation usually work well, sometimes we need to manually change, for example, the value of α in S_1 and S_{-1}. Secondly, we continue to work on smoothing an arbitrary polyhedron. We feel that quintic algebraic surfaces are also flexible enough for generating C^1 smooth nonconvex triangular surface patches. In this paper, we have shown that degree seven algebraic surfaces are sufficient, however not necessary. (See Figure 9 for a

---

[4]As mentioned before, in most cases, the rank r of $\mathbf{M_I}$ is 51. However, we keep the variable r because it is possible that there are more dependency between boundary curves and normal vectors though the chances are rare.

---

[5]This polyhedron is gyroelongated triangular bicupola with its rectangular faces triangulated.

C^1 mesh of quintic surface patches over a nonconvex combination of quadric wires.) An open problem is to construct a wire frame for a non-convex polyhedron with conic curves. In this paper, we have shown that cubic wires are sufficient for the non-convex case, however they are not shown to be necessary. On approach to accomodate incompatible adjacent normals in the non-convex case is to subdivide edges into sub-edges and thereby faces into subfaces. We are currently exploring this approach.

Our ultimate goal is to construct arbitrary curved solids with the lowest algebraic degree surface patches, and to manipulate them through geometric operations such as boolean set operations. This ability will provide a geometric modeling system with a complex way of creating and manipulating models of physical objects with various geometries. One current application of our polyhedron smoothing algorithms has been in the smooth reconstruction of skeletal structures from three dimensional CT/NMR imaging data, using the SHILP, GANITH and VAIDAK toolkits of our SHASTRA system [2]. See also [4] for algorithmic details of the skeletal model reconstruction via approximation of the imaging data, using relatively sparse number of curved patches.

Acknowledgements : We are grateful to Vinod Anupam, Andrew Royappa and Dan Schikore for their assistance in the implementation of the smoothing algorithms.

References

[1] Alfeld, P.,. Scattered Data Interpolation in Three or More Variables. In T. Lyche and L. Schumaker, editors, *Mathematical Methods in Computer Aided Geometric Design*, pages 1–34. Academic Press, 1989.

[2] Anupam, A., and Bajaj, C., and Royappa, A. *The SHASTRA Distributed and Collaborative Geometric Design Environment*. Computer Science Technical Report, CAPO-91-38, Purdue University, 1991.

[3] Bajaj, C. Geometric modeling with algebraic surfaces. In D. Handscomb, editor, *The Mathematics of Surfaces III*, pages 3–48. Oxford Univ. Press, 1988.

[4] Bajaj, C. Electronic Skeletons: Modeling Skeletal Structures with Piecewise Algebraic Surfaces. In *Curves and Surfaces in Computer Vision and Graphics II*, pages 230–237, Boston, MA, 1991.

[5] Bajaj, C., and Ihm, I. Algebraic surface design with Hermite interpolation. *ACM Transactions on Graphics*, 19(1):61–91, January 1992.

[6] Beeker, E. Smoothing of Shapes Designed with Free Form Surfaces. *Computer Aided Design*, 18(4):224–232, 1986.

[7] Chiyokura, H., and Kimura, F. Design of Solids with Free-form Surfaces. Computer Graphics, 17(3):289–298, 1983.

[8] Chui, C. *Multivariate Splines*. Regional Conference Series in Applied Mathematics, 1988.

[9] Dahmen, W. Smooth piecewise quadratic surfaces. In T. Lyche and L. Schumaker, editors, *Mathematical Methods in Computer Aided Geometric Design*, pages 181–193. Academic Press, Boston, 1989.

[10] Dahmen, W. and Michelli, C. Recent Progress in Multivariate Splines. In L. Schumaker C. Chui and J. Word, editors, *Approximation Theory IV*, pages 27–121. Academic Press, 1983.

[11] deBoor, C., and Hollig, K., and Sabin, M. High Accuracy Geometric Hermite Interpolation. *Computer Aided Geometric Design*, 4(00):269–278, 1987.

[12] Farin, G. Triangular Bernstein-Bézier patches. *Computer Aided Geometric Design*, 3:83–127, 1986.

[13] Garrity, T., and Warren, J. Geometric continuity. *Computer Aided Geometric Design*, 8:51–65, 1991.

[14] Golub, G., and Van Loan, C. *Matrix Computation*. The Johns Hopkins Univ. Press, Baltimore, MD, 1983.

[15] Gregory, J., and Charrot, P. A C^1 Triangular Interpolation Patch for Computer Aided Geometric Design. *Computer Graphics and Image Processing*, 13:80–87, 1980.

[16] Hagen, H., and Pottmann, H. Curvature Continuous Triangular Interpolants. *Mathematical Methods in Computer Aided Geometric Design*, pages 373–384, 1989.

[17] Herron, G. Smooth Closed Surfaces with Discrete Triangular Interpolants. *Computer Aided Geometric Design*, 2(4):297–306, 1985.

[18] Hollig, K. Multivariate Splines. SIAM J. on Numerical Analysis, 19:1013–1031, 1982.

[19] Ihm, I.,. *Surface Design with Implicit Algebraic Surfaces*. PhD thesis, Purdue University, August 1991.

[20] Lee, E. The rational Bézier representation for conics. In G. Farin, editor, *Geometric Modeling : Algorithms and New Trends*, pages 3–19. SIAM, Philadelphia, 1987.

[21] Liu, D., and Hoschek, J. GC^1 Continuity Conditions Between Adjacent Rectangular and Triangular Bezier Surface Patches. Computer Aided Design, 21:194–200, 1989.

[22] Lorensen, W., and Cline, H. Marching Cubes: A High Resolution 3D Surface Construction Algorithm. *Computer Graphics*, 21:163–169, 1987.

[23] Moore, D., and Warren, J. Approximation of dense scattered data using algebraic surfaces. In *Proc. of the 24th Hawaii Intl. Conference on System Sciences*, pages 681–690, Kauai, Hawaii, 1991.

[24] Nielson, G. A Transfinite Visually Continuous Triangular Interpolant. In G. Farin, editor, *Geometric Modeling Applications and New Trends*. SIAM, 1986.

[25] Patrikalakis, N., and Kriezis, G. Representation of piecewise continuous algebraic surfaces in terms of B-splines. *The Visual Computer*, 5(6):360–374, Dec. 1989.

[26] Peters, J. Local Cubic and BiCubic C^1 Surface Interpolation with Linearly Varying Boundary Normal. *Computer Aided Geometric Design*, 7:499–516, 1990.

[27] Peters, J. Smooth interpolation of a mesh of curves. *Constructive Approximation*, 7:221–246, 1991.

[28] Peters, J. Parametrizing singularly to enclose data points by a smooth parametric surface. In *Proc. of Graphics Interface*, Calgary, Alberta, June 1991. Graphics Interface '91.

[29] Piper, B. Visually Smooth Interpolation with Triangular Bezier Patches. In G. Farin, editor, *Geometric Modeling: Algorithms and New Trends*. SIAM, 1987.

[30] Powell, M., and Sabin, M. Piecewise Quadratic Approximations on Triangles. *ACM Trans. on Math. Software*, 3:316–325, 1977.

[31] Preparata, F., and Shamos, M. *Computational Geometry, An Introduction*. Springer Verlag, 1985.

[32] Ramshaw, L. Beziers and B-splines as Multiaffine Maps. In *Theoretical Foundations of Computer Graphics and CAD*. Springer Verlag, 1988.

[33] Sarraga, R. G^1 interpolation of generally unrestricted cubic Bézier curves. *Computer Aided Geometric Design*, 4:23–39, 1987.

[34] Sederberg, T. Piecewise Algebraic Surface Patches. *Computer Aided Geometric Design*, 2:53–59, 1985.

[35] Seidel, H-P. A New Multiaffine Approach to B-splines. *Computer Aided Geometric Design*, 6:23–32, 1989.

[36] Semple, J., and Roth, L. *Introduction to Algebraic Geometry*. Oxford University Press, Oxford, U.K., 1949.

[37] Shirman, L., and Sequin, C. Local Surface Interpolation with Bezier Patches. Computer Aided Geometric Design, 4:279–295, 1987.

[38] Walker, R. *Algebraic Curves*. Springer Verlag, New York, 1978.

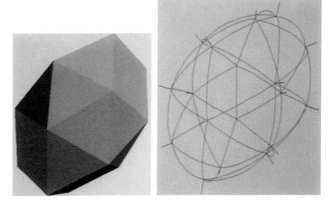

Figure 2: A Convex Polyhedron and its C^1 Conic Wireframe

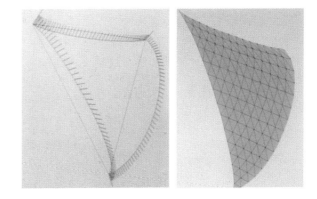

Figure 3: A Quadric Triangle and its C^1 Patch

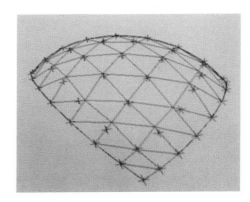

Figure 4: A Triangulation for Display and Additional (+) Points for Shape Control

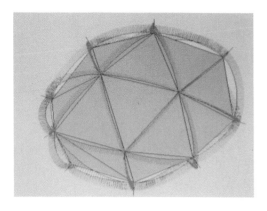

Figure 5: A Convex Polyhedron with Quadric Wires : $\rho = 0.4$

Figure 8: A C^1 Smooth Polyhedron with Quintic Algebraic Patches : $\rho = 0.75$

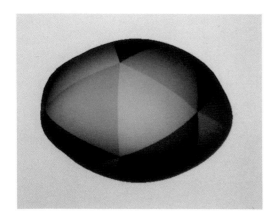

Figure 6: A C^1 Smooth Polyhedron with Quintic Algebraic Patches : $\rho = 0.4$

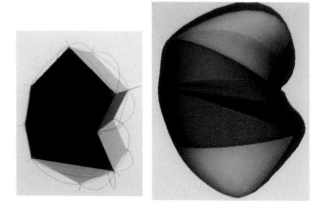

Figure 9: Smoothing the Non-Convex Polyhedron with Quintic Algebraic Patches

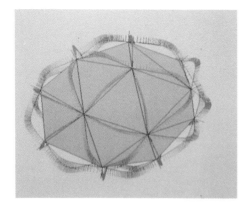

Figure 7: A Convex Polyhedron with Quadric Wires : $\rho = 0.75$

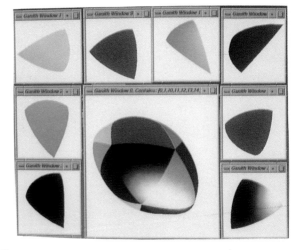

Figure 10: A Polyhedron Smoothed in the SHASTRA Distributed and Collaborative Geometric Design Environment

Pump It Up:
Computer Animation of a Biomechanically Based Model of Muscle Using the Finite Element Method

David T. Chen and David Zeltzer
Computer Graphics and Animation Group
The Media Laboratory
Massachusetts Institute of Technology
Cambridge, MA 02139

ABSTRACT

Muscle is the fundamental "motor" that drives all animal motion. We propose that changes in shape of moving human and animal figures will be accurately reproduced by simulating the muscle action and resulting forces that propel these figures. To test this hypothesis, we developed a novel computational model of skeletal muscle. The geometry and underlying material properties of muscle are captured using the finite element method (FEM). A biomechanical model of muscle action is used to apply non-linear forces to the finite element mesh nodes. We have tried to validate the FEM model by simulating well known muscle experiments and plotting out key quantities. Our results indicate that the twin goals of realistic computer animation and valid biomechanical simulation of muscle can be met using these methods, providing a principled foundation both for animators wishing to create anatomically based characters and biomechanical engineers interested in studying muscle function.

CR Categories: I.3.7 [Computer Graphics]: Three-Dimensional Graphics and Realism—Animation.

Additional Keywords: finite element method, non-linear dynamics, character animation.

1   INTRODUCTION

Modeling and animation of the human form has long been a research goal in computer graphics. The human figure is an important and ubiquitous expressive tool that we would like to use in computer animations: our bodies transmit information about ourselves, and we take cues, both narrative and physical, from what is seen of others. The human body, however, is a collection of complex rigid and non-rigid components that are difficult to model. Moreover, skeletal motions of the body are well coordinated and subtly complex. Muscles change shape due to the dynamic interactions of contraction and contact. The muscles, in turn, are covered by overlapping layers of living tissue, and modeling the ways in which this tissue interfaces to the outside world is also daunting.

Typically in character animation, only the surface geometry is modeled. Here we take a detailed look at modeling the important underlying structures, i.e., muscles and bone. Our immediate research goal is to accurately model individual three-dimensional muscles. This is a "bottom up" approach, but because a *physically-based* model is created, the results can be applied both to produce realistic-looking animations of human characters as well as to help create new bioengineering applications in which computer graphics display is vital. As computer workstations become more powerful, and rendering and computation times drop, it will be possible to extend the research results in a considered and straightforward way. The eventual goal then is not only character animation but to take a step towards the creation of an *artificial person* that can repond convincingly as its simulated muscles are activated.

1.1   Previous Work

The approaches taken to modeling the shape of the human figure include:

1. *geometric*—rigid links, like bones, in which only the static geometry is specified
2. *kinematic*—the geometry of a whole limb changes due to the kinematics of the underlying skeleton
3. *elastic*—modeling parts of the body as non-linear visco-elastic-plastic composite materials that change shape due to the action of forces

For the geometric case, the three methods most commonly used are polygonal meshes, volume primitives and surface patches. Fetter [7] used contours derived from biostereometric data to generate the polygons in his "Fourth Man and Woman". Human forms from standard volume primitives include Badler's Bubbleman [1], made from spheres, or Ginsberg and Maxwell's "cloud" figure [16], based on ellipsoids. In these examples, the shape of the limbs does not change as the character moves.

Examples of kinematic models include that of Komatsu, who parameterized spline patch control points to simulate a contracting biceps as the elbow is bent [14]. Komatsu used four major spline patch surfaces to cover the head, chest, abdomen and legs of a skeleton. Chadwick et.al. in [4], generalized this approach by using a "layered" technique based on *free-form deformations* (FFDs) to apply muscle effects onto a skeleton. Their model derives the shape of a whole limb from the kinematic skeletal state. Abstract muscles are parameterized as two sets of FFDs. These FFDs are controlled by the skeleton position to simulate the gross effects of muscle contraction at the body's surface. A simple elastic model based on discretized mass points joined by Hookean springs can be added on top of this to allow for automatic squash and stretch of the face or whole limbs.

©1992   ACM-0-89791-479-1/92/007/0089 $01.50

Elastic[1] models [23] comprise one form or another of displacement analysis of an elastic continuum. This analysis can be characterized as static or dynamic, linear or non-linear, isotropic or anisotropic, and so on. The particular shape of a deformation is a function of both the internal stresses and strains within the elastic object and the external forces applied to it. Examples include Gourret [9], who described a system for modeling the human hand with a finite element volume meshed around bone. He formulates and solves a set of statics equations for skin deformation based on bone kinematics and hand/object contact points in a grasping task. While bending and flexing of the hand flesh is nicely simulated, no muscle effects or changes in the underlying shape are calculated.

Pieper et.al. [19] [20], has developed a *surgical simulation* system that can be used both to create animation of the face and to simulate surgical reconstructions of the face. He performs a finite element analysis of the skin arranged as three different layers of material. Force generating muscles that control facial expression have also been implemented. Terzopoulos and Waters [22] have constructed a dynamic model of the face for computer animation based on a lattice of springs and masses. They too have implemented force generating muscles to provide realistic expressions. This paper concerns *skeletal* muscle, the anatomy for which is different than muscles of the face. Skeletal muscle makes up from 40 to 45 percent of the total human body weight, so we expect that our emphasis on modeling this muscle type will eventually allow us to simulate shape throughout much of the body.

2 MUSCLE ANATOMY

Muscle connects to bone through tendons, which are bundles of connective tissue. These connective tissues are composed largely of collagen, a fibrous protein found throughout the body. The center part of the muscle can be called the "belly", which is surrounded by a connective tissue sheath called the *epimysium*. The tendons are actually continuations of these connective tissue sheaths that hold the muscle together. The angle made by the muscle fibers relative to the tendon is the *pennation* angle. The whole muscle is held in place within the body by extensive connective tissue layers called *fascia* [13].

The connective tissue also penetrates the muscle and divides it longitudinally into groups of muscle fibers known as *fasciculi*. It is at this level of differentiation that the muscle is supported by capillaries, veins and nerve fibers. Muscle fibers come in many lengths—sometimes stretching the whole length of a muscle—and are usually 10 to 100 microns in diameter. The muscle fibers are composed of still smaller elements called *myofibrils* that run the whole length of the fiber. Each myofibril is about 1 to 2 microns thick. A single muscle fiber contains on the order of hundreds to thousands of myofibrils.

It is at the level of myofibril that a discussion of the contractile mechanism for a muscle usually begins. The myofibril is made up of *sarcomeres* arranged in a repeating pattern along its length. This repeating pattern is responsible for the striations or banding pattern often observed on skeletal muscles. The sarcomere is the actual functional unit of contraction for the muscle. Sarcomeres are short sections—only about 1 to 2 microns long—that contract upon suitable excitation, developing tension along their longitudinal axis. The shortening of a single muscle fiber then is due to the effect of many sarcomeres shortening in series. A bundle of

[1]i.e., visco-elastic-plastic models

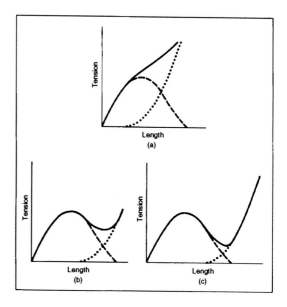

Figure 1: Tension-length curves. The dotted line shows the length-tension curve of the resting muscle. The total force recorded on fully activating the muscle is shown by the solid line. The extra force developed on stimulation is shown by the dashed line. The progression from (a) to (c) results from muscles with progressively less connective tissue [3].

muscle fibers can be thought to be many of these force generators arranged in parallel. Finally, the combined tension produced by bundles of muscle fibers is transmitted to the bones through the network of connective tissue and muscle tendons.

2.1 Sliding Filament Theory of Contraction

The discussion above has concerned the more or less macroscopic properties of muscle force generation. Here we will briefly touch upon the contractile mechanism within a single sarcomere. Muscles have been differentiated into at least eight separate protein structures, of which four play a role in contraction. The two most important of these are *actin* and *myosin*. These two contractile proteins form filaments within the sarcomere, and, when viewed in cross section, can be seen to be packed hexagonally, with six thin filaments surrounding each thick filament. The thick myofilaments are made of myosin, the thin myofilaments are made of actin.

The idea behind the sliding filament theory of muscle contraction is that as a muscle fiber shortens, the thin and thick myofilaments do not themselves get shorter, rather they slide across each other [11] [12].

2.2 Hill's Force Model

One of the simplest kinds of experiments that can be done to a prepared, isolated whole muscle is to measure the force output as the muscle is stretched through a number of constant lengths, see Fig. 1. If this is done with no stimulation, then the resulting plot of force or tension to length is said to represent the *passive* elastic properties of the muscle. This passive tension-length curve has an exponential shape in which the curve gets steeper and steeper the more the muscle is elongated. This behavior is very similar to a rubber band in which the material can be pulled very easily until it is all "stretched out", and then the rubber band can feel very stiff.

If the same kind of tension-length plot is then made with the muscle fully stimulated, then a different curve is produced that has components from both *active* and passive force components. This curve, of course, should always be greater than the passive force-length plot by itself and is called the total tension-length curve. Finally, the tension-length curve that represents only the active muscle force is found by subtracting the passive curve from the total curve. The length dependence of the developed force is altogether consistent with the sliding filament theory of muscle contraction [11].

Futhermore, from measurements on human subjects, A. V. Hill proposed that there is also a velocity dependent force component that counteracts the contraction force. That is, *the force exerted by the muscle decreases as the speed of shortening increases* [8]. It was supposed at first that this phenomenon depended on an automatic regulatory mechanism within the central nervous system, but Gasser and Hill showed through quick-release experiments on isolated frog muscle that this damping effect was part of the "fundamental character" of the muscle itself. A muscle held isometrically was suddenly allowed to shorten to a new length against no applied load. The force that was recorded fell below the amount that corresponded to the isometric equilibrium point of the new length and only slowly developed tension back up to that point. The observation that the measured muscle force did not instantaneously reach the level predicted by the new length indicated a damping effect within the contractile machinery. See Fig. 2.

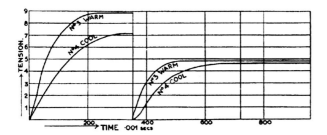

Figure 2: Quick-release curves, plotting tension versus time [8]

A simple mechanical model of muscle that takes into account the effects described above is shown in Fig. 3. This model is commonly attributed to A. V. Hill. The active state force T_0 is found, as discussed above, by subtracting the total force measured at different lengths for a stimulated muscle from that found to be due to passive effects alone. The notation $T_0(x_1, t)$ indicates that this force is a function of the muscle length and time-varying activation. The passive parallel stiffness K_{PE} has contributions due to the penetration of connective tissue through the muscle body resulting in the fasciculus divisions and also interfiber elasticity. The parallel damping component B is most likely due to the rate of the biochemical reactions that are responsible for contraction at the myofilament level. The series stiffness K_{SE} is primarily from the effect of tendon at the muscle attachment points, but is also probably partially due to the details of myofilament attachment within a sarcomere. The series element is very important in its ability to buffer the rapid change from inactive to active state and also provides a mechanical energy storage mechanism for the body in motion.

The Hill model, while very simple, has proven enormously

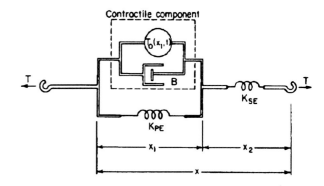

Figure 3: Hill's muscle model [18]

useful in practice in making calculations of the force generation of muscles working against different kinds of loads.

2.3 Zajac's Force Model

Zajac [25] [24] has developed a "dimensionless" lumped model of a *complete* musculotendon actuator that can be easily scaled to model particular whole muscles. Zajac's model is a refinement of the Hill model, and the normalized force curves that are presented directly reflect the non-linearities that result from the action of sliding filaments. The curves for the active and passive muscle force components are taken from measurements of single muscle fibers to ensure that tendon effects are not superimposed. Furthermore, pennation effects are directly included, while the series elastic element *not* associated with tendon is removed.

The isometric force generated in a particular actuator depends on one set of parameters that is considered constant over all actuators and another set that is musculotendon specific. The four specific parameters are,

α pennation angle
F_0 maximum isometric force of active muscle
l_0^M optimal muscle length at which F_0 is developed
l_s^T tendon rest length

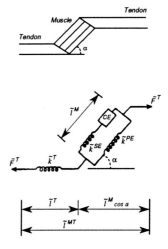

Figure 4: Musculotendon architecture [25]

The active muscle is represented in Fig. 4 by the contractile element CE. Force developed by passive muscle is from

$\tilde{k}^{PE}$ and is summed with the force from CE. The effect of the series elastic element $\tilde{k}^{SE}$ is lumped with the tendon model $\tilde{k}^T$. The dimensional units of interest are force and length. F_0 and l_0^M are the normalizing factors for these units. A *tilde* above a symbol denotes that it is a normalized quantity, for example,

$$\tilde{l}^M = \frac{l^M}{l_0^M} \quad \text{normalized muscle fiber length}$$

Other quantities and relationships used are,

$$
\begin{aligned}
&l^{MT} && \text{musculotendon length} \\
&l^T && \text{tendon length} \\
&l^{MT} = l^T + l^M \cos\alpha
\end{aligned}
$$

Zajac gives the non-specific, dimensionless functions to model a musculotendon actuator in [25]. We implemented the active muscle function $\tilde{F}_{fa}^{CE}(\tilde{l}^M)$ as an interpolating cubic spline through twelve control points from [6]. For the passive parallel force $\tilde{F}^{PE}(\tilde{l}^M)$, we use the quadratic function,

$$\tilde{F}^{PE}(\tilde{l}^M) = 4(\tilde{l}^M - 1)^2 \quad \text{if } \tilde{l}^M \geq 1, \text{ else } 0$$

Plots of these two functions are presented in Fig. 5.

The isometric muscle force functions can then be written,

$$
\begin{aligned}
\tilde{F}_{iso}(\tilde{l}^M, t) &= \tilde{F}_{fa}^{CE}(\tilde{l}^M)a(t) \\
\tilde{F}_M(\tilde{l}^M, t, \alpha) &= (\tilde{F}_{iso}(\tilde{l}^M, t) + \tilde{F}^{PE}(\tilde{l}^M))\cos\alpha
\end{aligned}
$$

where $a(t)$ is the time-varying normalized muscle activation function. This activation function results from a neural controller $u(t)$ and *excitation-contraction* dynamics—the process of calcium release and associated sarcomere shortening due to neural excitation. This effect can be safely ignored for our application as will be shown.

For tendon, the normalized force is $\tilde{F}_T(\varepsilon^T)$ where ε^T is the tendon strain defined by,

$$\varepsilon^T = \frac{l^T - l_s^T}{l_s^T} = \frac{(l^{MT} - l^M \cos\alpha) - l_s^T}{l_s^T} = \frac{(l^{MT} - \tilde{l}^M l_0^M \cos\alpha) - l_s^T}{l_s^T}$$

This we also implemented as a polynomial function, see Fig. 6.

To characterize the dynamic properties of a musculotendon actuator, it is necessary to consider the velocity dependent nature of the muscle forces. This damping force is represented by the dashpot element B in Hill's model and is typically formulated as a *force-velocity* relationship in which the force is scaled depending on the contraction velocity. Zajac presents such a curve in terms of the dimensionless form of velocity $\tilde{v}_r^{CE}$, which we implement with an arctan function, Fig. 7. The function is designed such that the normalized force will be 1 when the velocity is 0 and the force will be 0 when the velocity is -1.

Finally, the total active force from the contractile element is a function of the activation $a(t)$, the force function $\tilde{F}_{fa}^{CE}(\tilde{l}^M)$, and the normalized muscle velocity $\tilde{v}_r^{CE}$,

$$\tilde{F}^{CE} = f(\tilde{v}_r^{CE})\tilde{F}_{iso}(\tilde{l}^M, t) = f(\tilde{v}_r^{CE})a(t)\tilde{F}_{fa}^{CE}(\tilde{l}^M)$$

and the force in the whole muscle is

$$\tilde{F}_M = (\tilde{F}^{CE} + \tilde{F}^{PE}(\tilde{l}^M))\cos\alpha$$

3 MUSCLE SHAPE

In our research we have tried to test the hypothesis that to make a good simulation of the changes in shape that a contracting muscle experiences, it is sufficient to characterize

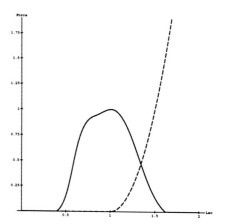

Figure 5: Plots of force vs. normalized muscle fiber length $\tilde{l}^M$. Solid line is active force function $\tilde{F}_{fa}^{CE}(\tilde{l}^M)$. Dashed line is passive force $\tilde{F}^{PE}(\tilde{l}^M)$.

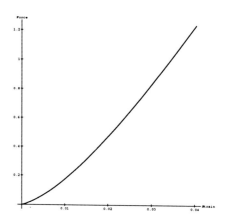

Figure 6: Normalized tendon force $\tilde{F}_T(\varepsilon^T)$ vs. tendon strain ε^T.

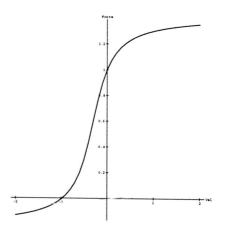

Figure 7: Amount of normalized force relative to isometric force vs. dimensionless velocity $\tilde{v}_r^{CE}$. Negative velocity is for muscle contraction, while lengthening muscle will have positive velocity.

both the resting material and the changes in force known to be important to the contractile process. The primary benefit of this approach is that if the forces are calculated properly, then not only will it be possible to visualize a muscle in action, but a valid biomechanical model will also be developed that can be used in further experimentation. For the purposes of visualization, however, it is important to obtain accurate geometric representations of the rest shapes of muscle masses upon which dynamic simulations will be run. We have constructed muscle rest shapes using the Swivel 3D™ Professional [17] modeling program on the Macintosh and from contour stacks derived from magnetic resonance imaging (MRI) systems.

3.1 Manual Shape Input

Since much of the experimental work reported in the muscle biomechanics literature is done using frog muscles, the *gastrocnemius* muscle from a prepared frog was digitized for use in the computer simulated biomechanical experiments discussed in Section 5. Some time was spent observing Dr. Simon Gitzer at MIT in the "frog lab" making force-length measurements from the gastrocnemius of an actual animal. After these were done, the muscle was fully dissected and the top and side dimensions measured. Swivel was then used to "lathe" a polyhedral model. See Fig. 10.

3.2 Contour Data

Imaging from CAT and MRI scanning systems is a relatively new but very important source of clinical data. These systems acquire three-dimensional objects as a series of 2D slices arranged along an axis in space. The "skinning" facility in Swivel can be used to operate on data sets of this kind, where anatomical forms are defined by varying the shape of the cross section along the length of the body. More sophisticated techniques such as the *marching cubes* algorithm [15] can automatically create polygonal models of constant density surfaces from 3D data arrays of this type, but it remains problematic to identify meaningful structures.

A polygonal data set from an entire human left calf was made available to us through Dr. Alan Garfinkel at UCLA. The source for the calf model was a long sequence of MRI scans that were carefully hand segmented into the individual, anatomical muscle masses and then "skinned" into triangles. Ten muscles, including the medial-gastrocnemius, the lateral-gastrocnemius, and the soleus, and one muscle group make up the data. The tibia and fibula bones are also included.

Because the leg data was received as files of triangle meshes, no further processing had to be done to ready them for simulation or display. Fig. 8 shows three different views of the reconstructed leg. The entire data set is shown in the middle view. In the left view, the overlying gastrocnemius muscles and the soleus are removed to show the underlying structures, and the tibia and fibula are shown on the right.

4 METHODS

We have presented Hill's muscle model and discussed Zajac's refinement. Our data sources have included Cyberware scans, MRI slices and direct geometric output from Swivel. All these are turned into a standard polyhedral representation for display.

To simulate the action of muscle for our computer graphics application, the biomechanical model and input data must be synthesized, and for this the *finite element method* [2] is used, Fig. 9. Thus the FEM serves as a vehicle for our muscle model. The polyhedral data is used to define

meshes of twenty-node isoparametric brick elements. Dynamic equilibrium equations are derived from the mesh. Zajac's model is used to apply non-linear forces to the mesh node points. The FEM model is then dynamically simulated forwards and the mesh automatically deforms in response. A free-form deformation defined by the mesh helps us visualize the resulting changes in shape due to the contraction. Unfortunately, a full discussion of our finite element system is beyond the scope of this paper; details can be found in [5].

The muscle model was constructed by dissecting the gastrocnemius from an anesthetized frog, measuring the top and side dimensions, then Swivel was used to make a polyhedral model as discussed. A user-assisted finite element mesh generator was then used to interactively construct the mesh shown in Fig. 10. Four twenty-node isoparametric bricks are used to approximate the gastrocnemius. The exact number of elements used represents a tradeoff of the quality of the simulation versus simulation time. The model then has 56 nodes or 168 total degrees of freedom.

From the mesh of twenty-node brick elements, equilibrium equations are derived that have the form

$$M\ddot{u} + C\dot{u} + Ku = R(t)$$

For a body having n nodal points, u is an $3n$ vector of nodal displacements, M, C and K are $3n$ x $3n$ matrices describing the mass, damping and stiffness between points within the body, and R is a $3n$ vector of forces applied to each node. The finite element matrices are specified in terms of Young's modulus E, Poisson's ratio, ν, and mass density, ρ.

The FEM equilibrium equations can be characterized as a coupled set of second-order differential equations. To solve for the displacements $u(t)$, first reduce to the equivalent first-order system,

$$\begin{aligned} \dot{u} &= v(t) \\ \dot{v} &= M^{-1}(R(t) - Ku - Cv) \end{aligned}$$

A standard ordinary differential equation solver like LSODE from NetLib, can then be used to compute the dynamic time-course of the nodal displacements. This is done in terms of a **derivs** function that first calculates $R(t)$ so that $\dot{u}$ and $\dot{v}$ can be found.

To simulate a muscle contraction, non-linear force generators are added to the node points of the finite element mesh that act along the longitudinal direction of the muscle. Wired in this way, there are eight generators per twenty-node brick, for a total of 32 for the whole muscle. Tendons are constructed in a similar fashion, see Fig. 11.

To allow the **derivs** function to calculate the world-space nodal force $R(t)$ due to the action of these fibers, the finite element data structures are augmented with information for the muscle state. For the muscle fibers, we add

1. **fibers**, a vector of integers, of length (nofibers*2): encodes nodal attachment of each fiber

2. **fiber_len0**, a vector of doubles, of length (nofibers): fiber rest length

3. **fiber_len**, a vector of doubles, of length (nofibers): current fiber length

4. **fiber_time**, a scalar: simulation time for which **fiber_len** was calculated

In addition, three scalar parameters define the muscle, as per Zajac's dimensionless model. The maximum isometric active force is **fiber_F0a**, the passive force scalar is **fiber_F0p** and the maximum normalized fiber velocity

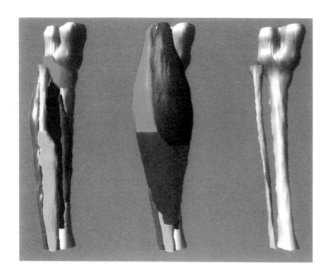

Figure 8: Reconstructed legs

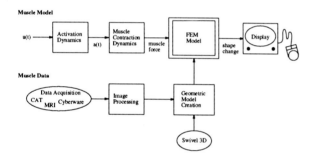

Figure 9: Muscle model and muscle data *after* [24] *and* [15].

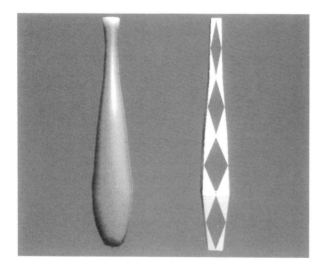

Figure 10: Frog gastrocnemius made from 576 polygons, *left*. *Right*, Finite element mesh made from polyhedral representation.

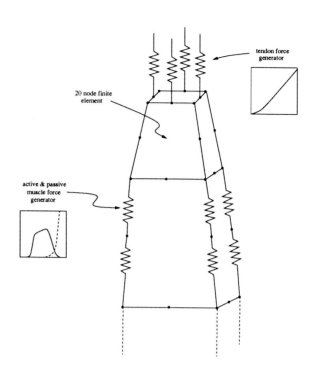

Figure 11: Force generators for muscle and tendon

is `fiber_Vmax`. The effects of the muscle activation function $a(t)$, directly scales the maximum active fiber force `fiber_F0a`. This is the mechanism used to turn the muscle on and off.

The current world space mesh nodal positions are found for each fiber. These are subtracted to yield a world space length. From this the normalized fiber length $\tilde{l}^M$ is

```
lm = len / fiber_len0[i];
```

The normalized length is used to find the isometric active and passive force functions and their derivatives, as discussed in Section 2.3.

```
zajac_passiveforce( lm, &Fmp, &dFm );
zajac_activeforce( lm, &Fma, &dFm );
```

The fiber velocity is determined through the following first-order approximation. Before the next time step is taken by LSODE, the lengths for each of the muscle fibers are found and saved in `fiber_len`. The simulation time before the next step is stored in `fiber_time`. When the next step is taken, the instantaneous simulation time t is accessed by **derivs** and the normalized velocity $\tilde{v}_r^{CE}$ computed,

```
if (t == fiber_time) vel = 0.;
else
{   vel =
        (len - fiber_len[i]) / (t - fiber_time);

    vel /= fiber_len0[i];
    vel /= Vmax;
}
```

from which the scale factor from the force-velocity curve is looked-up

```
zajac_forcevelocity( vel, &Fvc );
```

and the force generated by the fiber from the normalized quantities is

```
force  = Fmp * F0p;
force += Fma * F0a * Fvc;
force *= .5;
```

The final scale by .5 is done because half the force is applied to the element of $R(t)$ corresponding to the first node point of the fiber, and the other half of the force is summed with the second fiber node point.

The tendon fibers are modeled in much the same way as the muscle fibers, the main difference being that tendons connect mesh node points to external world space locations. For tendon, the finite element data structures are further augmented with

1. **tendons**, vector of integers, of length (notendons): encodes which nodes are tendon attached

2. **tendon_len0**, a vector of doubles, of length (notendons): the tendon rest length

3. **tendon_wsppt**, a vector of doubles, of length (notendons*3): the world space attachment points

4. **tendon_force**, a vector of doubles, of length (notendons*3): the amount of force generated by the tendon fibers

There is also a scalar that scales the normalized tendon force, **tendon_F0**.

For the four element approximation, the tendon fibers are placed at the edge midpoints of the bottom and top faces of the mesh assemblage. To calculate the tendon force, begin with the world space location of the node to which the tendon fiber is fixed. Subtract the position of the external attachment point defined by **tendon_wsppt**, and find the length **len** and direction of the resulting vector **d1**. Using the rest length of the current tendon fiber, the strain ε^T is,

```
strain = (len - len0) / len0;
```

Then the strain is used to look up the normalized tendon force. The vector **d1** is scaled by the force,

```
zajac_tendonforce( strain, &Ft, &dFt );
force = Ft * F0t;
```

This is repeated for each tendon fiber and again the computed force is summed into the world space external force vector $R(t)$ for the finite element mesh. In addition, the force generated by each of the tendon fibers is saved in the vector **tendon_force**. This is because the total force generated by the muscle is the sum of the reaction forces created by the tendon attachments. This total force is, of course, an important measure and is one of the quantities plotted in the subsequent experiments.

5   RESULTS

To test the biomechanical validity of the muscle model developed here, two well-known experiments are simulated and compared to results in the literature. First, tension-length curves were plotted of both active and relaxed muscle. Second, Gasser and Hill's quick-release experiment were simulated to reveal the dynamic time course of the forces generated by the finite element muscle model.

5.1   Tension-Length Experiment

The first experiment plots the characteristic tension-length relationship produced by the FEM muscle model. This is easy to do by attaching the top set of tendons to various positions to control the overall muscle length, measuring the amount of force generated by the whole muscle, then fully activating the muscle and measuring the force again. The

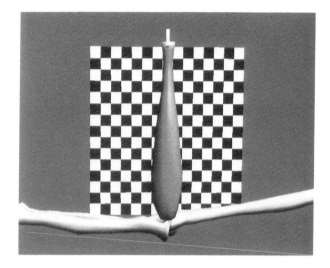

Figure 12: Setup for tension-length experiment

setup for this experiment is illustrated in Fig. 12. The muscle is attached with tendon to both the bone and the horseshoe shaped "clamp" in the figure.

Up to now, most of the development has concerned computing the non-linear muscle force functions defined by biomechanical models to apply at the finite element mesh nodal points. To fully specify the FEM model, however, the passive mechanical characteristics of muscle must also be set. Grieve and Armstrong in [10] publish stress-strain curves derived from compressing plugs taken from pig muscle. These curves are also non-linear, the plugs becoming stiffer the more they are compressed. The range of values for Young's modulus they present are from close to 0 up to 2.745×10^3 Pa at a strain of 40%. Or, in **cgs** units, 2.745×10^4 dyne/cm^2.

A major assumption currently made, in terms of these passive elastic properties, is that muscle can be approximated as a linear, homogeneous, isotropic material. This assumption is necessary because of simplifications we make in the derivation of the stiffness matrix K, but could be easily relaxed by implementing better constitutive models [2]. In any case, we feel this simplification is justified when examining muscle contraction because the contraction forces are orders of magnitude larger than the passive mechanical forces, and these non-linear, anisotropic forces are indeed modeled. An intermediate, convenient value is then chosen for Young's modulus, E. Poisson's ratio, ν, is set to approximate a volume preserving material. The density, ρ, of muscle was found by Grieve and Armstrong through careful weighing. Gravity, g, is turned off so as not to confound the force measurements. The physical constants for the simulation are as follows,

$$E = 1000 \text{ dyne/cm}^2 \quad \nu = .49 \quad \rho = 1.04 \text{ g/cm}^3 \quad g = 0 \text{ cm/s}^2$$

The frog muscle rest length is 6 cm long. The maximum isometric force generated by the gastrocnemius measured in the frog lab was 2.77 N or 2.77×10^5 dynes. This force is distributed evenly among the 32 fibers and so the fiber force is 8656.2 dynes.

The tension-length experiment is performed by first measuring the force for the passive muscle. This is done by examining the force generated in the tendons attached to the clamp through the **tendon_force** vector. The muscle is activated and the force measured again. The whole process

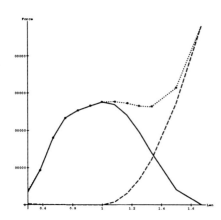

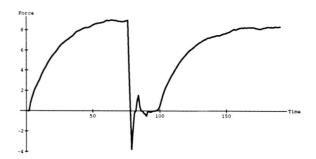

Figure 14: Simulation results for Gasser-Hill quick release experiment. Force vs. time. Force is scaled to match plot of Fig. 2.

Figure 13: Simulation results for tension-length experiment. Isometric muscle force vs. normalized length. Dotted line is total isometric force, dashed line is the force from passive muscle and the solid line is the developed force.

is repeated for the muscle set to different initial lengths. The resulting tension-length curves are presented in Fig. 13.

An examination of this plot shows a good correspondence to the published biological observations (see Fig. 1), with a local maximum for the muscle at its rest length. The other result taken from this simulation, interesting from the point of view of computer graphics, is that very little changes in shape are produced by a muscle undergoing purely isometric contraction. Another of the simplifying assumptions made in the muscle model is that all the fibers are homogeneous both in terms of the amount of force they can develop, and in their response to stimulus from the neural controller $u(t)$. The small observed shape change is then expected since the actions of all the series and parallel fibers should produce a net zero resultant force at the internal mesh faces, while producing a large force at the origin and insertion ends which is then canceled by the tendon forces. Hence, to produce larger shape changes for the purposes of computer animation requires either the muscle to lengthen or shorten, or for the contraction to work against shape changes due to external forces such as gravity.

5.2   Quick Release Experiment

The second experiment simulated is the quick release procedure carried out by Gasser and Hill to examine the velocity dependent effects within the muscle. The muscle is stimulated and made to work isometrically. Then the muscle is suddenly released and hits a 'knot' or new position constraint after a certain amount of time. A plot of force versus time for this experiment is presented in Fig. 14. The muscle begins at the rest length, 6 cm or $\tilde{l}^M = 1$. The amount of shortening that takes place is 1.3 cm so that the final normalized muscle length is $\tilde{l}^M = 0.7833$.

Fig. 14 shows a good correspondence with Gasser and Hill's plots of Section 2.2. In that section, the conclusion drawn from the shape of the curves is that the slow rise in the force both when the muscle is activated, and after the quick release, indicate that it is caused by a biochemical damping effect, rather than a central nervous system control mechanism. Furthermore, we feel the shape of this force function justifies another of the simplifying assumptions made in the model, namely that the effects of *excitation-contraction* dynamics are negligible for this application because they occur

on a much shorter time scale than what is being simulated.

As discussed above, a change of shape in the simulated muscle is only predicted for a situation in which the contraction works against shape changes produced by external forces. Such a case is presented in Fig. 15, in which the relaxed frog muscle bows downwards due to gravity. Upon contraction, the muscle pulls taut between its attachment points. If however, velocity dependent effects are not included, or the maximum velocity, $\tilde{v}_r^{CE}$, is set too high, the muscle will oscillate back and forth, much as a plucked string, in an amusing, albeit unrealistic manner. The arrows in the figure show the direction, but not the scale, of the world space forces acting at the finite element mesh node points.

5.3   Human Gastrocnemius Simulation

The FEM based muscle model is used in a similar way to simulate contraction of the medial gastrocnemius from a human subject. This muscle was chosen both because of its large size, and because it is on the outside, closest to the skin. Thus it should play a large part in determining the shape of the whole leg. The gastrocnemius is approximated with a four element mesh made of twenty-node bricks as in the frog simulations. The medial gastrocnemius model is 24 cm long. The maximum isometric force used is 1113 N from [6]. Each of the 32 fibers generates 34.78 N or 3.48×10^6 dynes. The passive mechanical parameters for the FEM mesh are set as before, with gravity equal to -980 cm/s^2.

To model fascia attachments to the rest of the leg, tendons are defined for nodes on the backside of the muscle. These are set so that the muscle can move freely, but not by a large amount. Furthermore, a *reaction constraint* [21] is defined so that the muscle will not penetrate the soleus. For the animation, the leg is rotated 45 degrees to horizontal and the relaxed muscle deforms due to gravity. Fig. 16 shows that muscle contraction causes the gastrocnemius to pull taut as expected. Again, the arrows only show the direction in which the world space forces are acting.

5.4   Human Biceps Simulation

The example above demonstrates muscle acting isometrically against external forces. In an effort to apply the research results to making computer animation of muscled characters, it is necessary that we be able to simulate non-isometric muscle action as well. Geometry for a human biceps was digitized from an anatomically accurate plastic model. A FEM mesh was constructed and contraction forces applied to the nodes as before. For this simulation, the biceps is attached at the shoulder, but the forearm end is left free. Activation causes the biceps to shorten; the forearm flexes *inverse kinematically* to track the end of the muscle, see Fig. 17.

6 CONCLUSIONS

For computer animation, the next step beyond kinematic simulations of skeleton movement must include realistic modeling and rendering of the muscle and skin. We have developed a novel finite element model of muscle that can be used both to simulate muscle forces and to visualize the dynamics of muscle contraction. Biomechanically, we have taken an existing model of muscle function, added complexity by making it 3D, and shown that under certain circumstances it still behaves like a muscle. We have tried to validate the model by doing biomechanical experiments and plotting out key quantities.

It is much harder to validate the shape changes produced by the force-based FEM muscle model. Videos of live frog and human subjects have been made to serve as checkpoints for the simulations, but these can do so only qualitatively. The clearest way to verify the shape changes produced by the muscle model would be to make a whole series of MRI reconstructions, with the limb held in different states of isometric tension while measuring the muscle force wherever possible. A series of reconstructions made in this way would be appropriate data against which to compare simulation results. This would be a big project, and just barely doable with the current MRI technology.

However, by emphasizing the *physical model*, we have taken a step beyond the original computer graphics goal of making a virtual actor, up to the goal of making an *artificial person*. By studying the anatomy, the form will be revealed through the function.

7 ACKNOWLEDGMENTS

This work was supported in part by NHK (Japan Broadcasting Corp.) and an equipment grant from Hewlett-Packard. Thanks to Dr. Joe Rosen, Betsy, Darcy and the SnakePit guys for help and support. Special thanks go to Dr. Simon Gitzer of the MIT Brain and Cognitive Science Department for sharing his experience and understanding of muscle function, and to Dr. Alan Garfinkel of UCLA for providing the human leg data.

References

[1] N.I. Badler, J. O'Rourke, and H. Toltzis. A spherical representation of a human body for visualizing movement. *Proceedings IEEE*, 67(10):1397–1402, 1979.

[2] Klaus-Jürgen Bathe. *Finite Element Procedures in Engineering Analysis*. Prentice-Hall, 1982.

[3] F. D. Carlson and D. R. Wilkie. *Muscle Physiology*. Prentice-Hall, Inc., 1974.

[4] John E. Chadwick, David R. Haumann, and Richard E. Parent. Layered construction for deformable animated characters. *ACM Computer Graphics*, 23(3):243–252, 1989.

[5] David T. Chen. *Pump It Up: Computer Animation of a Biomechanically Based Model of Muscle using the Finite Element Method*. PhD thesis, MIT, 1992.

[6] Scott L. Delp. *Surgery Simulation: A Computer Graphics System to Analyze and Design Musculoskeletal Reconstructions of the Lower Limb*. PhD thesis, Stanford University, 1990.

[7] William A. Fetter. A progression of human figures simulated by computer graphics. *IEEE Computer Graphics and Applications*, pages 9–13, November 1982.

[8] H.S. Gasser and A.V. Hill. The dynamics of mucular contraction. *Royal Society of London Proceedings*, 96:398–437, 1924.

[9] Jean-Paul Gourret, Nadia Magnenat-Thalman, and Daniel Thalman. Simulation of object and human skin deformations in a grasping task. *ACM Computer Graphics*, 24(3):21–30, 1989.

[10] Andrew P. Grieve and Cecil G. Armstrong. Compressive properties of soft tissues. *Biomechanics XI-A*, International Series on Biomechanics, Amsterdam, 1988. Free Unversity Press.

[11] A.F Huxley and R. Niedergerke. Structural changes in muscle during contraction. *Nature*, 173:971–973, 1954.

[12] H. Huxley and J. Hanson. Changes in the cross-striations of muscle during contraction and stretch and their structural interpretation. *Nature*, 173:973–976, 1954.

[13] David L. Kelley. *Kinesiology: Fundamentals of Motion Description*. Prentice Hall, Inc., 1971.

[14] Koji Komatsu. Human skin model capable of natural shape variation. Laboratories Note 329, NHK, Tokyo, March 1986.

[15] W.E. Lorensen and H.E. Cline. Marching cubes: A high resolution 3d surface construction algorithm. *ACM Computer Graphics*, 21(4):163–169, 1987.

[16] Delle Rae Maxwell. Graphical marionette: a modern-day Pinocchio. Master's thesis, MIT, 1983.

[17] S. McKenna, Y. Harvill, A. Louie, and D. Huffman. *Swivel 3D Professional User's Guide*. Paracomp, Inc., 1987-1990.

[18] Thomas A. McMahon. *Muscles, Reflexes, and Locomotion*. Princeton University Press, 1984.

[19] Steve Pieper, Joseph Rosen, and David Zeltzer. Interactive computer graphics for plastic surgery: A task-level analysis and implementation. *Proceedings of the ACM 1992 Symposium on Interactive 3D Graphics*, pages 127–134, 1992.

[20] Steven Donald Pieper. *CAPS: Computer-Aided Plastic Surgery*. PhD thesis, MIT, 1992.

[21] John C. Platt and Alan H. Barr. Constraint methods for physical models. *ACM Computer Graphics*, 22(4):279–288, 1988.

[22] D. Terzopoulos and K. Waters. Physically-based facial modelling, analysis, and animation. *The Journal of Visualization and Computer Animation*, 1(2):73–80, 1990.

[23] Demetri Terzopoulos and Kurt Fleischer. Modeling inelastic deformation: Viscoelasticity, plasticity, fracture. *ACM Computer Graphics*, 22(4):269–278, 1988.

[24] F. E. Zajac. Muscle and tendon: Properties, models, scaling, and application to biomechanics and motor control. *Critical Reviews in Biomedical Engineering*, 17:359–411, 1989.

[25] F. E. Zajac, E.L. Topp, and P.J. Stevenson. A dimensionless musculotendon model. *Proceedings IEEE Engineering in Medicine and Biology*, 1986.

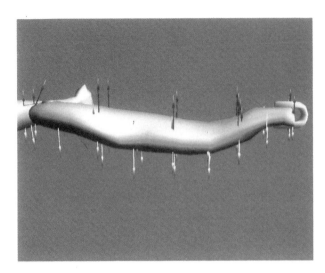 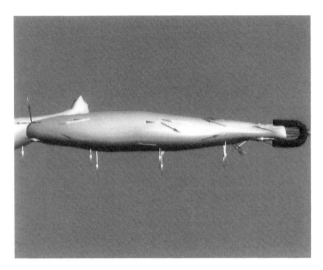

Figure 15: Relaxed muscle deforms due to gravity. Active muscle pulled taut.

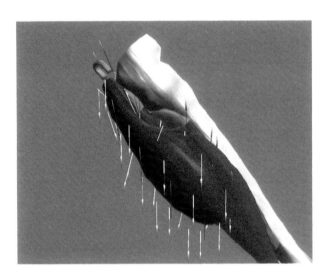 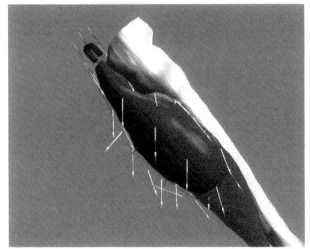

Figure 16: Human gastrocnemius deformed due to gravity, then pulled taut.

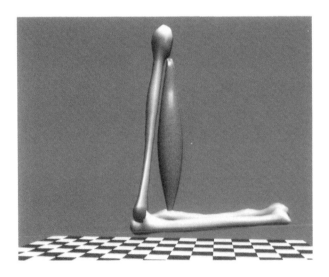 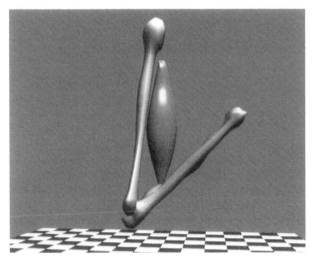

Figure 17: Biceps shortens upon activation, forearm motion is specified inverse kinematically.

Dressing Animated Synthetic Actors with Complex Deformable Clothes

Michel Carignan[1], Ying Yang[2], Nadia Magnenat Thalmann[2,1], Daniel Thalmann[3]

1. MIRALab, HEC, University of Montreal, Canada

2. MIRALab, University of Geneva

3. Computer Graphics Lab, Swiss Federal Institute of Technology

Abstract

This paper discusses the use of physics-based models for animating clothes on synthetic actors in motion. In our approach, cloth pieces are first designed with polygonal panels in two dimensions, and are then seamed and attached to the actor's body in three dimensions. After the clothes are created, physical properties are simulated and then clothes are animated according to the actor's motion in a physical environment. We describe the physical models we use and then address several problems we encountered. We examine how to constrain the elements of deformable objects which are either seamed together or attached to rigid moving objects. We also describe a new approach to the problem of handling collisions among the cloth elements themselves, or between a cloth element and a rigid object like the human body. Finally, we discuss how to reduce the number of parameters for improving the interface between the animator and the physics-based model.

Keywords and phrases:

cloth animation, garment design, discretization, dynamic constraints, collision responses, deformable surface model

1. Introduction

In recent years, several models [17,15,7,6,1,5,11] have been proposed to animate deformable and soft objects such as rubber, paper, cloth, and so on. However, no complete methodology has been proposed to perform cloth modelling and animation for the complex case of synthetic actors [9].

_____

1. 5255 Decelles, Montréal, H3T 1V6 Canada,
   tel: 1-514-340-6616, Email: miralab@crt.umontreal
2. 12 rue du Lac, CH 1207 Geneva, Switzerland,
   tel: +41-22-7876581, fax: 41-22-7353905,
   Email: thalmann@uni2a.unige.ch.
3. CH-1015 Lausanne, Switzerland, tel:+41-21-6935214,
   fax: 41-21-6935328, Email: thalmann@eldi.epfl.ch.

From our experience, we find that it is relatively easy [10] to use the elastic surface model to animate some simple-shaped objects. Flags, tablecloths, scarves, carpets and skirts (as shown in Fig.1), all of which consist of one or two surface panels, have few constraints. But it is somewhat difficult to realistically animate complex objects consisting of many surface panels like trousers or jackets without proper dynamic constraints. Problems include seaming the surface panels together, attaching them to other rigid objects, and calculating collision responses when cloth self-collides or collides with a rigid object. Some algorithms of collision response were described [7,13] but they are not effective in cloth animation except for special cases such as a single skirt.

Figure 1. A simple cloth: only the skirt is deformable and designed as a single panel.

In our approach, we work as a tailor does, designing garments from individual two-dimensional panels seamed together. The resulting garments are worn by and attached to the synthetic actors. When the actors are moving or walking in a physical environment, cloth animation is performed with the internal elastic force and the external forces of gravity, wind, and collision response.

In this paper, Section 2 explains the physics-based model used for the simulation of cloth motion. Section 3 describes the collision response algorithm. Section 4 discusses the algorithm of joining and attaching elements of the deformable panels. Finally in Section 5, we discuss how to reduce the number of parameters and how to choose values which provide realism and mathematical stability, thus improving the interface between the animator and the physics-based model.

2. The dynamic model

Our work is based on the fundamental equation of motion as described by Terzopoulos et al. [15] with the damping term replaced by a more accurate one proposed by Platt et al. [14]:

$$\rho(a)\frac{d^2r}{dt^2} + \frac{\delta}{\delta r}\iint_\Omega \|E\|^2 da_1\, da_2 + \frac{\delta}{\delta v}\iint_\Omega \|\dot{E}\|^2 da_1\, da_2$$

$$+\frac{\delta}{\delta r}\iint_\Omega \|B-B_0\|^2 da_1\, da_2 = \Sigma\, F_{ex} \qquad (1)$$

Because this equation is quite similar to Eq.1 of [15], we discuss only the modified third term and refer the reader to [15] for notation and explanations.

In the second term of Eq.1, $E = G - G^o$ is called the Lagrangian strain tensor. In the third one, $\dot{E}$ is the time rate of E and is defined as [14]:

$$\dot{E}_{ij}(r(a)) = \frac{d}{dt}E_{ij} = \frac{1}{2}\dot{G}_{ij} = \frac{\partial r}{\partial a_i}\cdot\frac{\partial v}{\partial a_j} + \frac{\partial r}{\partial a_j}\cdot\frac{\partial v}{\partial a_i} \quad (2)$$

This term works like a dissipative function. We choose to replace it because the one used in [15] is scalar. So, no matter where energy comes from, it will be dissipated. For example, gravitational energy is dissipated, resulting in a surface which achieves a limiting speed and is not continually accelerated. In our case, we use Raleigh's dissipative function [4] generalized for a continuum surface [14]. As E is the strain (a measure of the amount of deformation), dE/dt is the "speed" at which the deformation occurs. This means that the surface integral may be considered a rate of energy dissipation due to internal friction. This implies that the variational derivative with respect to velocity of the surface integral will minimize the "speed" of the deformation. With this approach, no dissipation occurs when the surface undergoes rigid body displacement like when falling in an air-free gravity field. This improves the realism of motion.

Taking the variational derivative in Eq.1 and keeping only terms of the first order, expression Eq.15 of [15] becomes, with the new dissipative function,

$$f_{in} = \sum_{i,j=1}^{2} -\frac{\partial}{\partial a_i}\{((\alpha_{ij}+\gamma_{ij})\frac{\partial r}{\partial a_j}\} + \frac{\partial^2}{\partial a_i\partial a_j}(\beta_{ij}\frac{\partial^2 r}{\partial a_i\partial a_j}) \quad (3)$$

This expression gives the internal forces — due to stretching, dissipation and bending — that act on an infinitesimal part of the surface located at r. In this expression, we define:

$$\alpha_{ij} = \eta_{ij}(G_{ij} - G^o_{ij}) \qquad (4a)$$

$$\gamma_{ij} = \varphi_{ij}(\dot{E}_{ij}) \qquad (4b)$$

$$\beta_{ij} = \xi_{ij}(B_{ij} - B^o_{ij}) \qquad (4c)$$

which are constitutive functions of the elastic properties of the material.

In Eq.4, G_{ij} and B_{ij} can be computed with the help of their definitions given in Eq.3 and Eq.4 of [15] respectively. $\dot{E}ij$ can be computed as in Eq.2 above. And η_{ij}, φ_{ij} and ξ_{ij} are physical constants which can be computed as shown later.

On the right side of Eq.1, we put all external forces. Contact forces coming from collisions with the cloth itself or any rigid object like an actor's body are described in the next section.

In reality, complex clothes or garments usually consist of many fabric panels. To apply the elastic deformable surface model, the polygonal panel should be discretized using the finite difference approximation method. The discretization of the cloth boundary follows the technique in [15].

3. Collision response

This problem is handled in two steps. The first one is collision detection. This means that we have to find any object's triangle (including those belonging to the cloth itself) within a threshold distance from cloth's vertices. Several algorithms have already been proposed [7, 16, 13]. When a collision is detected, we pass through the second step where we act on the vertices to actually avoid the collision. This may be done using a potential field method as suggested by Terzopoulos et al. [15]. A detailed algorithm is described by Lafleur et al. [7] for Marilyn's skirt in the film *Flashback* [8]. Although the method works, the use of this type of force is somewhat artificial and cannot provide realistic simulation with complex clothes. In fact, the effect degrades when the potential becomes very strong, looking like a "kick" given to the cloth. To improve realism, we propose the use of the law of conservation of momentum for perfectly inelastic bodies. This means that kinetic energy is dissipated, avoiding the bouncing effect.

Case 1: Self collision

We use a dynamic inverse procedure to simulate a perfectly inelastic collision. Such collisions between two particles are characterized by the fact that their speed after they collide equals the speed of their centers of mass before they collide.

Let p_o be a point from one part of the cloth that collides with a triangle on another part. Let p_1 be the point where the collision occurs on that triangle. All physical quantities at p_1 are obtained by linear interpolation from values at the triangle's vertices. Let us call u_i and v_i the speed before and after the collision where i stands for 0 and 1. F_i will be the resultant of external and internal forces at i and f_{u_i} is an unknown force which, when added to F_i makes v_i equal v_c, the speed of the centers of mass of particles 0 and 1 before they collide.

Assuming that forces are constant in the time interval, speed after the encounter will be

$$v_0 = u_0 + \frac{(F_0 + f_{u_0})\Delta t}{m_0} \qquad (5)$$

With

$$V_c = \frac{m_0\, u_0 + m_1\, u_1}{m_0 + m_1} \qquad (6)$$

and the soft collision criteria

$$v_0 - V_c = 0 \qquad (7)$$

we find for $\mathbf{f}_{u_0}$:

$$\mathbf{f}_{u_0} = \frac{m_0 \, m_1 \, (\mathbf{u}_1 - \mathbf{u}_0)}{(m_0 + m_1) \, \Delta t} - \mathbf{F}_0 \qquad (8)$$

Adding $\mathbf{f}_{u_0}$ at $\mathbf{F}_0$ and proceding similarly while replacing 0 by 1 and 1 by 0 in Eq.5, Eq.7 and Eq.8 will make the interaction perfectly inelastic.

Case 2: Collision between cloth and human body

In this case, to simulate perfectly inelastic collision, we cancel out the velocity and force components of p_0 that lie along the outward normal vector located at p_1. Now p_1 belongs to a triangle which composes a rigid object. Again physical quantities are interpolated from their values at the triangle's vertices.

Let us define the speed of p_0 relative to p_1. Then we have:

$$\mathbf{v} = \mathbf{v}_0 - \mathbf{v}_1 \qquad (9)$$

$$\mathbf{v}_{//} = (\, \mathbf{v} \cdot \mathbf{n}_1)\, \mathbf{n}_1 \qquad (10)$$

$$\mathbf{v}_\perp = \mathbf{v} - \mathbf{v}_{//} \qquad (11)$$

which are the components of v both along and perpendicular to $\mathbf{n}_1$, respectively. Then to cancel out speed, we add $-\mathbf{v}_{//}$ to $\mathbf{v}_0$ if the dot product between $\mathbf{v}_{//}$ and $\mathbf{d} = \mathbf{r}_1 - \mathbf{r}_0$ is positive.

For forces, we apply a similar procedure. Let

$$\mathbf{f}_{//} = (\mathbf{F}_0 \cdot \mathbf{n}) \, \mathbf{n} \qquad (12)$$

$$\mathbf{f}_\perp = \mathbf{F}_0 - \mathbf{f}_{//} \qquad (13)$$

which are the components of $\mathbf{F}_0$ both along and perpendicular to $\mathbf{n}_1$, respectively. But before cancelling out $\mathbf{f}_{//}$ from $\mathbf{F}_0$, we can add a frictional force:

$$\mathbf{f}_f = -\mu \, |\mathbf{f}_{//}| \, \frac{\mathbf{v}_\perp}{|\mathbf{v}_\perp|} \quad \text{if} \quad \frac{\mu |\mathbf{f}_{//}|}{m|\mathbf{v}_\perp|} \, \Delta t \leq 1$$

$$\mathbf{f}_f = -m \frac{\mathbf{v}_\perp}{\Delta t} \quad \text{else} \qquad (14)$$

where μ is a frictional constant characteristic of the interaction. The first condition ensures that $\mathbf{f}_f$ will prevent an increase of speed in the inverse direction. If the frictional force is too high, the second value is taken and makes $\mathbf{f}_\perp$ go to zero. Adding $\mathbf{f}_f$ and $\mathbf{f}_{//}$ to $\mathbf{F}_0$ when the dot product between $\mathbf{f}_{//}$ and $\mathbf{d}$ is positive and $-\mathbf{v}_{//}$ to $\mathbf{v}_0$ when the dot product between $\mathbf{v}_{//}$ and $\mathbf{d}$ is positive makes certain that p_0 and p_1 are never forced together when p_1 belongs to a heavy object.

4. Joining and attaching

In the animation of deformable objects which consist of many surface panels, the constraints that join different panels together and attach them to other objects are very important. In our case, two kinds of dynamic constraints [14, 2] are used during two different stages. When the deformable panels are separated, forces are applied to the elements in the panels to join them according to the seaming information. The same method is used to attach the elements of deformable objects to other rigid objects. When panels are seamed or attached, a second kind of constraint is applied which keeps a panel's sides together or fixed on objects. For example, in cloth creation and animation, all the polygonal deformable panels are designed in two dimensions. Seaming information is also indicated. The

polygonal panels are then transformed into a three-dimensional space. Then according to the seams, forces are applied to the elements on the edges of the panels to put them together. The direction and magnitude of a seaming force depends on the positions of the elements, their masses, and metric factors, etc. This procedure has to be performed dynamically to let panels deform as they encounter objects like an actor's body. When the elements are close enough, their positions are forced to be the same. The panels are similarly attached to the body of a synthetic actor. After the creation of the deformable objects, another kind of dynamic constraint is used to guarantee the seaming and attaching. Fig.2a shows an example of a complex dress with many panels while a texture is applied in Fig.2b.

(a)

(b)

Figure 2. (a) Complex deformable clothes: dresses are first designed with 2D panels; the panels are placed around the model's body, then external sewing forces are applied to the seam lines indicated on the panels while the physical deformation model is processed. (b) Texture mapping can also be applied to the garment; in this picture, spangle texture is used.

To put together sides of panels (or a side of a panel to a rigid object), we put constraints on points belonging to sides according to the seam information recorded at the creation stage of the garment.

In the process, as long as $|r_{01} - r_{02}| > d$ the constraint of the first type applied

$$f_i = k\eta_i m_i(r_j - r_i),\qquad (15)$$

making the distance decrease over time.

As soon as $|r_{01} - r_{02}| < d$, according to the momentum law:

$$m_1 v_{01} + m_2 . v_{02} = (m_1 + m_2)\, v_m \qquad (16)$$

we put the second type of constraint.

$$v_m = (m_1 v_{01} + m_2 . v_{02})\,/\,(m_1 + m_2)\qquad (17)$$

$$r_m = r_{01} + (r_{02} - r_{01}).m_2\,/\,(m_1 + m_2)\qquad (18)$$

Thereafter points on a seam stay together.

In formulas above, r_{0i}, v_{0i}, m_i $(i=1,2)$, are the position vector, velocity, and mass of element i (i =1,2) before the constraint is applied to them; r_m, v_m are the position vector and velocity of both points 1 and 2 after the constraint applied to them. d is the threshold combining distance, k is a constant, and $\eta_i = \eta_{i_{11}}$ (or $\eta_{i_{22}}$ depending if point i belongs to a vertical or horizontal side) is the metric factor of the material of the panel.

In the case where point 2 belongs to a rigid object, we make the assumption that mass is infinite and no constraints are applied. In this case Eq.17 and Eq.18 comes

$$v_m = v_{02}\qquad (19)$$

$$r_m = r_{02}\qquad (20)$$

5. Automatically computed parameters

Physics-based animation models are very powerful because they allow the production of realistic results. Unfortunately, models are generally too complex to be used by an animator with no background in physics. For example, in the physics-based cloth model from Eq.1, quite a few parameters should be specified by the animator. Each parameter has a physical meaning and controls a physical property. To model clothes made from different kind of fabrics, we should find parameter values which make clothes move realistically. In addition, these parameters control the mathematical stability of the model, so it is not a trivial task to put them all together.

To overcome these difficulties, we propose a way of computing all the parameters from just two which have more intuitive meaning to people with no background in physics. Our goal is to introduce a few user parameters intuitive in meaning and insensitive to discretization. This technique allows testing with very few points defining a cloth, and we can look for the physical properties to be modelled with little CPU time. Then, when satisfied, we may discretize as much as we want without searching for a new set of parameters.

The first parameter to calculate is the mass for each node. But, we consider density a more fundamental quantity than mass, because it is independent of how clothing panels are discretized. The animator should select, for example a value ranging from 0.005 gr/cm^2 for silk to 1.000 gr/cm^2 for heavy leather. Mass at a node is then calculated as follows:

$$m(a) = \rho(a)da_1 da_2 \qquad (21)$$

The second parameter controls the resistance to stretching. To compute it, we use an artificial criterion: the percentage a clothing panel will stretch when suspended under gravity. If the norm of gravity is g and if λ is the percentage of stretch tolerance, we have:

$$\eta_{11} = mgh_v/2/\lambda/100 \qquad (22a)$$

$$\eta_{22} = mgh_h/2/\lambda/100 \qquad (22b)$$

$$\eta_{12} = \eta_{21} = (\eta_{11} + \eta_{22})^{1/2} \qquad (22c)$$

In this expression, η_{ij} is a force multiplied by a squared length. For η_{12} and η_{21}, we take the mean value from η_{11} and η_{22} as it is shown in Eq.22c.

The third parameter to be calculated is Δt, used to control the step size in the numerical integration of Eq.1. Furthermore, Δt should be correlated with real-time or a video time unit. This means that in a simulation from t_1 to t_2 with a step size of Δt, we can record a video frame each $N\Delta t = 1/25$ sec. resulting in a cloth animation sequence that is neither too fast nor too slow. We should not forget that the time parameter also controls the mathematical stability of the numerical integration of Eq.1. The lower the Δt, the greater the accuracy and stability, but the larger the processing time. The best values are then a matter of compromise.

As a clothing panel in our model may be considered a suitable medium in which waves can travel, we can find [12] that phase speed of lower node waves can be calculated as:

$$v_v = (\eta_{11}/m)^{1/2} \qquad (23a)$$

$$v_h = (\eta_{22}/m)^{1/2} \qquad (23b)$$

where v_v and v_h are wave speeds in the vertical and horizontal directions, respectively. A good Δt could reasonably be chosen to make a wave travel only a fraction l of the inter-vertex space in one time step:

$$\Delta t = \min\,(h_v/v_v,\ h_h/v_h)\,/\,l \qquad (24)$$

where a good value for l is 2 or 3.

The fourth parameter is ξ_{ij}, which appears in Eq.1. This parameter controls the resistance to bending. A zero value corresponds to no resistance at all, which means a cloth moves very freely like satin. For greater values cloth appears like rigid cotton or even leather or plastic. Again, we are looking for values independent of discretization but in this case, we introduce a user parameter c that has no physical meaning for the user parameter, like η_{ij}. This value is given by

$$\xi_{11} = cmgh_v^4 \qquad (25a)$$

$$\xi_{22} = cmgh_h^4 \qquad (25b)$$

$$\xi_{12} = \xi_{21} = (\xi_{11} + \xi_{22})^{1/2} \qquad (25c)$$

The fifth parameter controls the rate at which the energy coming from stretching will dissipate. The computation is analogous to the problem of a mass attached to a damped spring [12]. This means that, for the ideal case of a single mass, the movement which results from a starting position out of its rest position is of three kinds, depending on the relative amplitude of η and γ (see [2]). In our problem, the best relations between η_{ij} and γ_{ij} are:

$$\gamma_{11} = 2h_v(m\ \eta_{11})^{1/2} \tag{26a}$$

$$\gamma_{22} = 2h_h(m\ \eta_{22})^{1/2} \tag{26b}$$

$$\gamma_{12} = \gamma_{21} = (\gamma_{11} + \gamma_{22})^{1/2} \tag{26c}$$

and a stretch panel will return to its rest position without oscillation.

To summarize, parameters m, η_{ij}, Δt, ξ_{ij} and γ_{ij} are all obtained with only three input values: the density ρ the elongation percentage λ and the number c. With such an approach, all physical parameters lose their tensor meaning and become scalar. This results in an isotropic cloth model; physical properties are the same in all directions. This is not the case in real life, but we consider this a small price to pay for such simple use of physical properties. To overcome this, the animator – with free control of these parameters – can act on other directions by means of multiplicative factors.

Fig.3 shows a fashion show sequence; the walking trajectory has been given using an interactive tool dedicated to the design of walking trajectories for human figures [3]. Fig.4 shows an example of cloth animation during a motion simulated using dynamics.

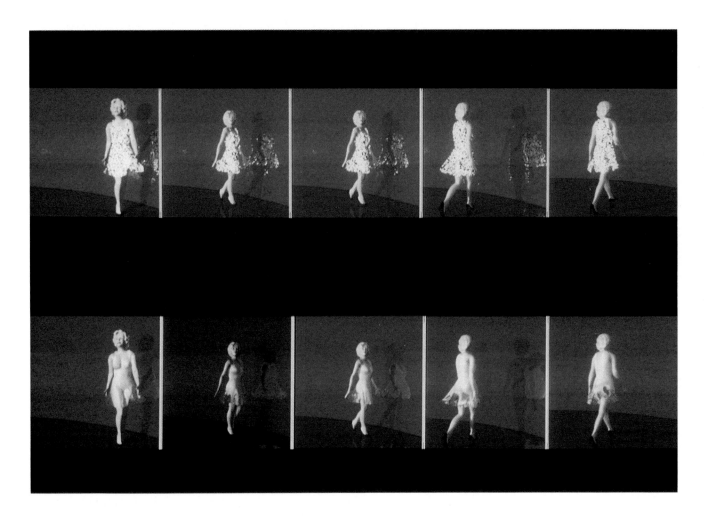

Figure 3. Fashion show sequence (film in preparation). The walking motion is performed using a global human free-walking model built from experimental data on a wide range of normalized velocities.

Figure 4. Marilyn as a trapezist is wearing a short 3D dress. The trapeze motion is calculated using dynamic simulation.

6. Conclusion

We have developed clothing software according to the above algorithms. First, polygonal cloth panels are interactively designed and edited in two dimensions. Then the panels are discretized in three dimensions and applied using the elastic model. Clothes are seamed and attached around the synthetic actor, and when the actor moves in space, external forces like gravity, wind, and collision responses are applied to the clothes. Clothes and garments are very complex deformable surfaces consisting of many differently shaped fabric panels joined together. Cloth modelling and animation have significant meaning in deformable object animation, and they have potential application in the garment industry. In our present research, we try to make clothes look more realistic, incorporating, for example, various textures, buttons, belts and other decorations.

7. Acknowledgments

The authors would like to thank Arghyro Paouri and Kyoko Kurihara for the design of the pictures and Hans Martin Werner for the development of a 2D interface. This research was supported by "Le Fonds National Suisse pour la Recherche Scientifique," the Natural Sciences and Engineering Council of Canada and the FCAR foundation in Quebec.

References

1. Aono Masaki. A Wrinkle Propagation Model for Cloth. In *Proc. Computer Graphics International '90*, Springer, Tokyo, 1990, pp.96-115.

2. Barzel R, Barr Alan H. A Modeling System Based on Dynamic Constraints. In *Proc. SIGGRAPH '88, Computer Graphics*, Vol. 22, No4, 1988, pp.179-188.

3. Bezault Laurent, Boulic Ronan, Magnenat Thalmann N, Thalmann D. An Interactive Tool for the Design of Human Free-Walking Trajectories. In *Proc. Computer Animation '92*, Springer, Tokyo, 1992.

4. Eringen AC, Suhubi, ES. *Elastodynamics*, Vol.1, Academic Press, NY.,1974.

5. Hinds BK, McCartney J. Interactive garment design, In *The Visual Computer*, 1990, Vol. 6, pp.53-61.

6. Kunii Tosiyasu L, Gotoda Hironobu. Modeling and Animation of Garment Wrinkle Formation Processes. In *Proc. Computer Animation'90*, Springer, Tokyo, 1990, pp.131-147.

7. Lafleur Benoit, Magnenat Thalmann Nadia, Thalmann Daniel. Cloth Animation with Self-Collision Detection. In *Proc. IFIP Conference on Modeling in Computer Graphics*, Springer, Tokyo, 1991, pp.179-187.

8. Magnenat Thalmann Nadia, Thalmann Daniel. Flashback. [videotape] *SIGGRAPH Video Review*, ACM SIGGRAPH, New York, 1990.

9. Magnenat Thalmann Nadia, Thalmann Daniel. Complex Models for Visualizing Synthetic Actors. In *IEEE Computer Graphics and Applications*, Vol.11, No5, 1991, pp.32-44.

10. Magnenat Thalmann Nadia, Yang Ying. Techniques for Cloth Animation. In *New Trends in Animation and Visualization*, edited by N. Magnenat Thalmann and D. Thalmann, John Wiley & Sons Ltd.,1991, pp.243-256.

11. Mangen Alain, Lasudry Nadine. Search for the Intersection Polygon of any Two Polygons: Application to the Garment Industry. In *Computer Graphics Forum*, 1991, Vol.10, pp.19-208.

12. Marion, J.B. *Classical Dynamics of Particles and Systems*. Academic Press, 1970.

13. Moore Matthew, Wilhelms Jane. Collision Detection and Response for Computer Animation. In *Proc. SIGGRAPH'88, Computer Graphics*, Vol.22, No.4, 1988, pp.289-298.

14. Platt Jone C, Barr Alan H. Constraints Methods for Flexible Models. In *Proc. SIGGRAPH'88 , Computer Graphics*, Vol.23, No.3, 1988, pp.21-30.

15. Terzopoulos Demetri, Platt John, Barr Alan, Fleischer Kurt. Elastically Deformation Models. In *Proc. SIGGRAPH'87, Computer Graphics*, 1987, Vol. 21, No.4, pp.205-214.

16. Von Herzen Brian, Barr Alan H, Zatz Harold R. Geometric Collisions for Time-Dependent Parametric Surface. In *Proc. SIGGRAPH'90, Computer Graphics*, Vol.24,No.4, 1990, pp.39-46.

17. Weil Jerry. The Synthesis of Cloth Objects. In *Proc. SIGGRAPH'86, Computer Graphics*, Vol.20, No.4, 1986, pp.49-54.

Three Dimensional Apparel CAD System

Hidehiko Okabe[1], Haruki Imaoka[2], Takako Tomiha[3] and Haruo Niwaya[1]

1: Research Institute for Polymers and Textiles, 1-1-4, Higashi, Tsukuba, 305 Japan

2: Nara Women's University, Kita-uoya-nisimachi, Nara, 630 Japan

3: Toray Industries, Inc., Engineering Research Labs., 3-3-1, Sonoyama, Otsu, 520 Japan

Abstract

We are developing a three dimensional (denoted 3D, hereafter) CAD system for garments to help the process of pattern making. This is a process to create a 3D form of a garment by designing a two dimensional (2D, hereafter) paper pattern that realizes the 3D form. The core of the system is a simulator that estimates the 3D form of a garment put on a body from its paper pattern (2D→3D process) and a developing program to obtain the 2D pattern that minimizes the energy required to deform it to the given 3D shape (3D→2D process). In both processes, the specific anisotropy of the mechanical properties of cloths is considered. In the 2D→3D process, the contact problem with body and geometrical nonlinearity are also taken into account. The preprocessor for the 2D→3D simulator is quite unique in that it converts an arbitrary 2D paper pattern into a 3D surface, considering the topological operation, 'sewing'. Both the 2D→3D process and the 3D→2D process are formulated as nonlinear energy-minimum problems, and they are solved by our original method in about 10 minutes with our workstations. Once the 3D form is obtained, the color pattern of a given cloth is mapped and displayed. As a consequence of the mechanical calculation, the distributions of the distortion and stress of the cloth are also visualized. Such information may contribute to the design of garments with consideration of physical attributes as well as visual beauty.

1. Introduction

The apparel industry is one of the fields where utilization of CAD systems dates back to the early age of computer graphics. However, still now, apparel CAD systems remain only for the treatment of 2D objects - paper patterns and color patterns of textiles, while CAD systems for other products can check the final results of designs by way of 3D views. This is mainly because of

1: Tel. 81(Japan) 298-54-6323, 6277   Fax. 298-54-6232
    Email S5603@jpnaist (BITNET)
2: Tel. 81(Japan) 742-20-3465   Fax. 742-26-5897
3: Tel. 81(Japan) 775-33-8465   Fax. 775-33-8466

the gap between the 2D paper patterns and the 3D form of the garments. In fact, the mechanical analysis of a dress draping along a human body bears most of the difficult problems found in structure analysis, such as contact and friction with the body, large deformation non-linearity, and extreme anisotropy of materials. Although there has been some research conducted to analyze or simulate the formation of a 3D form of garments on the basis of material mechanics[1,2,14], these studies did not take the form of applicative general purpose systems. On the other hand, there are some apparel oriented graphic editors that allow local distortions of the picture imitating the 3D view. Once such distortions are defined by hand, then any pattern of cloth can be substituted into these places. In some cases, the 3D coordinates of an actual garment corresponding to the lattice points of a 2D cloth are measured, and pattern mapping onto a true 3D surface is realized[13]. Though such systems are effective for designing color patterns of clothes, they lend no aid for the design of the 3D form itself. Also we cannot forget to mention about the attractive studies which have presented the motions of cloth in wind[9,15]. Though, the ultimate goal must be the same (i.e. true dynamical simulation of the dress, body and the air), the present direction of these studies seems to be different from ours.

Therefore, the system introduced here may be considered to be the first 3D apparel CAD system because it supports the mechanical analysis of draping from a 2D paper pattern to a 3D form, the development of a 3D surface to a 2D pattern, and the preprocessing which accepts arbitrary paper patterns for input. Although there is still a gap between our present system and commercial systems of the future, we are developing this system with the intention that it will be used by a wide variety of people. This is reflected in the fully automated preprocessor, where one need only to indicate the lines to be sewn together and the lines consisting of the waist or neck line, and our selection of robust methods all over the system, where no delicate regulation is required. But this does not mean that the true mechanics is sacrificed in this system. We rather believe that the fidelity to the natural process is a key for the clarity and easiness of such a system.

Due to the limitation of space, it is impossible to discuss the techniques used for the implementation of this system in detail. Several parts of the system including the formal mathematical expressions, have been published already[5,7,8,11]. However, we think that the concepts and structure of this system are more important than the implementation technique, and we believe that

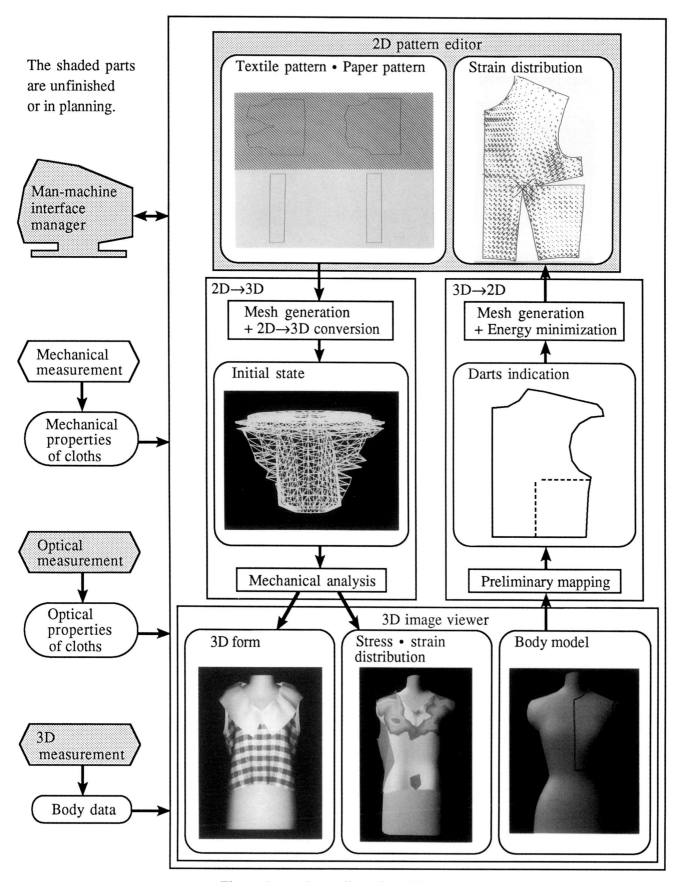

Figure 1   An outline of the 3D apparel CAD system

our system shows a basic framework for 3D apparel CAD. This means two things: First, this will provide a common ground or starting point for further discussions in this field. Second, the results of such discussions will be easily implemented and tested by refining or replacing some components of this system.

2. Overview of the system

An overview of the system including our future plan is shown in Fig.1. Though the textile editor and 2D pattern editor are expressed as different processes in the figure, it is only an expedient for explanation. As is observed in some programs for drawing, these two editors can be superimposed as two layers of a 2D graphic editor. Actually, our most important and urgent subject is to prepare an elegant and integrated interface between a user (designer) and our system. As a primitive form of such an interface, we have already developed a command procedure which provides the control of the execution of programs, file assignment and file management. But, with the ability of current graphic workstations, we can expect a much more comfortable and efficient work environment for designers. Especially, three graphic programs, textile color pattern editor, 2D paper pattern editor, and the 3D image viewer should be incorporated so as to reflect instantaneously the changes given in one view to others. That is, the cursors in the 2D view and 3D view should always point at the corresponding position of the cloth, and if one alters the color of a pixel of the cloth in the 2D view, it should be mapped to the 3D surface at the same moment, and vice versa.

The visualization of various mechanical properties of garments such as the distribution of normal stress (which is equal to the body contact pressure) must be especially useful for the design of underclothes and sportswear. In the future, provided with a more precise mechanical model for human bodies and a 3D measurement system, this ability of our system may contribute to furnish all clothing with a perfect fit of custom-tailoring.

In Fig.2, we show the position of our system in the whole process of the design and production of garments. It should be noted that both textile design and apparel design can be parallelly or synchronously processed by our system, though, traditionally, they are thought to be in serial relation. There is a special implication in the connection between our system and the manufacturing process of clothes. Our data structure for paper patterns contains the description of how the parts of a dress are sewn together and how the dress is to be put on the body. The fact that our CAD system can simulate the formation of the final shape of a dress, assures that the information given by this data structure is sufficient to indicate how the parts should be assembled and sewn in apparel CAM or an automated sewing system.

The old version of our system was written by FORTRAN and we utilized CORE for 3D views and PLOT10 for 2D views. The present version utilizes PHIGS or IDEAS for both 3D and 2D views. Now we are rewriting the whole program in C or C++ for the explicit treatment of the data structures, easy interface with advanced graphic libraries, and convenience for use at workstations.

The requirement for our system for the memory is very humble. The most demanding step is the mechanical analysis, but it requires no more than 3M bytes for the structure, including up to 4000 triangles (6000 variables). The most time consuming step (that is, of course, the mechanical analysis) is finished within 10 minutes for typical structures containing 1500 triangles by floating point calculation oriented workstations. We suppose that this is not an unbearable time for designers because the corresponding conventional process to sew up a prototype dress needs one day or more.

3. Preprocessor - conversion from 2D to 3D

Making a system that accepts various inputs is completely different from writing down a program that calculates a special problem. This preprocessor for mechanical analysis is the main source of the difference from other studies simulating cloths. In addition to the usual mesh generation, our preprocessor has a

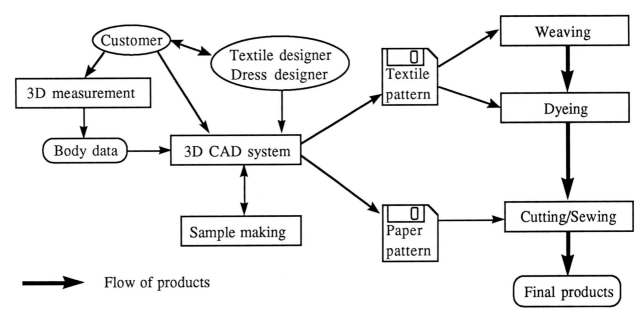

Figure 2   The position of the 3D CAD system in apparel industry in the future.

remarkable function to convert a 2D paper pattern into a 3D structure, which may be characteristic to 3D apparel CAD systems.

First, we input the 2D shape of each piece of a paper pattern as a collection of curved lines, assign the lines to be sewn together, and mark the lines which are to be put at some characteristic position of the human body (e.g., waist line). Precisely, this is a task of the 2D paper pattern editor.

Then the computer generates a triangular mesh on each piece, considering that the lines to be sewn together should be divided with the same proportion along each arc length, even though they have mutually different shapes and lengths. We call this mesh in the 2D plane the P-mesh. Next, the topological structure of the 3D garment (S-mesh) is obtained by unifying the edges and vertices of the P-mesh indicated to be sewn together. The correspondence between the triangles of the S-mesh and those of the P-mesh is one to one, while an edge or a vertex of the S-mesh may correspond to two or more elements of the P-mesh. At this point, the 3D coordinates of the vertices of the S-mesh are left open. The data structures for the P-mesh and S-mesh are designed to satisfy the definition of the two dimensional sim-plicial complex, and this facilitates the utilization of the concepts and results of elemental topology.

The last step is to fill in the 3D coordinates of the vertices of the S-mesh with appropriate values, providing a good initial state for the mechanical analysis. Let us take an example as in the case of a skirt. First, the vertices on the lines that are designated to be put at the waist line (we denote these vertices as the 0th layer vertices) are given the 3D coordinates along the waist line of the human body model. Then, each vertex adjacent to the $(i-1)$th layer vertices in the S-mesh is classified to be the ith layer, and they receive 3D coordinates $(k_i\,x, k_i\,y, z-a_i)$, where x, y and z are the average of the coordinates of adjacent vertices in the $(i-1)$th layer, and k_i and a_i are determined by the standard mesh size and the numbers of vertices in the $(i-1)$th and ith layers. We regard this step as an analog of the process to put a dress on a human body. As the standard characteristic portions of the human body for this step, we selected the neck line, arm holes, waist line (for skirts) and crotch-waist lines (for pants).

4. Mechanical analysis

The mechanical elements considered in the present version of our system are expressed by the following energy terms:

$$E = E_{au} + E_{av} + E_{sh} + E_{bu} + E_{bv} + E_{tw} + E_g + E_p\,,$$

where E_{au} and E_{av} are elongation energies, E_{sh} is the shearing energy, E_{bu} and E_{bv} are bending energies, E_{tw} is the twisting energy, E_g is the gravitational energy and E_p is the energy of a potential function of which the value is 0 at the outside of the body and Kd^2 inside the body, where d is the distance from the surface of the body and K is an appropriate large value. Note that the deformation energy terms $E_{au}, E_{av}, E_{sh}, E_{bu}, E_{bv}$ and E_{tw} should be calculated by referring to the original position of each triangle in the P-mesh, because the directions of the warp (u-axis) and weft (v-axis) in the 2D pattern determine the anisotropic properties of each triangular element in the S-mesh. The term E_p is known as the penalty function for the violation of the boundary condition. From the viewpoint of treating the human body as a deformable object, the penalty function method is not an expedience, but is the first order approximation, while a completely hard surface corresponds only to the 0th order approximation.

We do not take into account the mutual interference of each part of cloth, because it requires a large amount of calculation[4]. So, it sometimes happens that two different parts of cloth penetrate each other, causing a destructive effect for the 3D view. Presently, the appearance is covered by shifting one part upward, but we recognize that this is not the true resolution, and we are determined to take up this problem in the near future.

Our method for finding the minimum point of the energy function highly contributed to the development of this system, with its robustness, efficiency and compactness by means of both the program size and data memory area. It can be classified as a mutant of the steepest descent method, but, since we control the size of the step in each variable independently, the total vector of one step is no more directed to the gradient of the energy function. The spirit of the step control is very simple. One step is tried to the decreasing direction of the energy. If the value of the partial derivative of energy by that variable does not widely change, one can proceed more boldly, i.e. with a larger step. If the value of the partial derivative widely changes (for example, the sign changes), then one should reduce the scale of the step the next time. Though it is not mathematically proven for general cases, many experiments showed that this method never loses control and it ends in a certain minimum solution. Moreover, we tested this method with many classical sample functions known to be difficult to attain the minimum, and its robustness and efficiency were well confirmed.

5. Development from 3D to 2D

It is natural to think that it would be quicker and more straightforward to make a 2D pattern directly from a 3D form by developing or flattening it. However, with more consideration, it is noticed that the process to flatten a curved surface to a plane is different from the process to force a pattern on a plane to take the form of the given curved surface, and the real process to make a dress from an undeformed cloth is equivalent to the latter. So, we solved a sort of inverse problem to obtain a 2D pattern that will take the given 3D form after its spontaneous deformation, as follows.

Although there are some trials[3], it is not easy to define and edit a curved 3D surface of a human body or a garment with standard I/O devices of present graphic workstations. Therefore, we project the domain of the 3D surface with a preliminary mapping Φ, in order to obtain an initial shape of the 2D pattern. Here, we use a very simple Φ that maps a point on the body expressed as (r,θ,z) by the cylindrical coordinate system to a point $(r_0\theta, z)$ by the two dimensional Cartesian coordinate system, where $r_0 = 10$cm. Then we define some darts in the initial 2D pattern and generate a P-mesh on it. Next, we operate the inverse map of Φ to the vertices of the P-mesh to obtain the S-mesh. This time, we consider the energy E required to deform the P-mesh to the S-mesh as a function of the 2D coordinates of the vertices of the P-mesh, and the minimization problem of E is solved by the same method for the 2D $\rightarrow$ 3D simulation. Since E_p is independent from the uv coordinates of vertices, it is omitted in the minimization. We also neglect $E_{bu}, E_{bv}, E_{bv}, E_{tw}$ and E_g since the changes of these terms are higher order functions of the infinitesimal deformation of the S-mesh. As a result, the final shape of the 2D pattern and the distribution of the

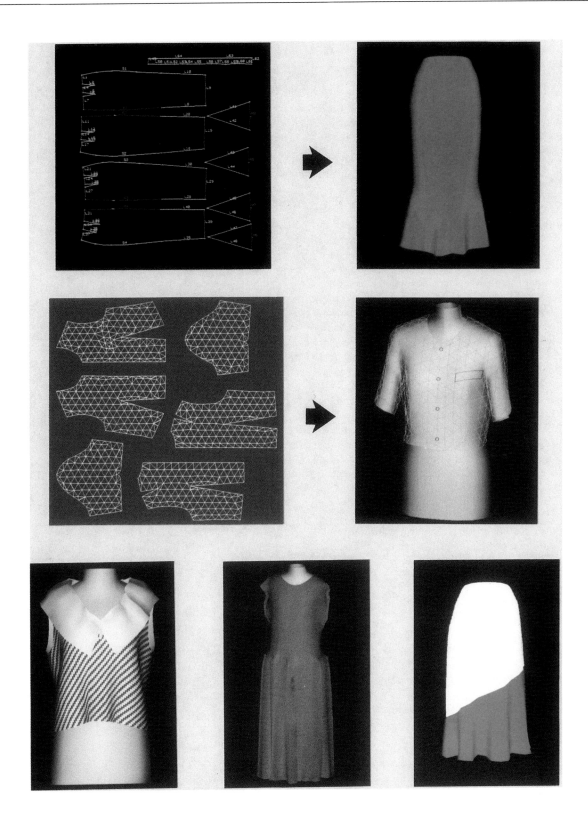

Figure 3   Examples of simulated garments and their paper patterns

residual strain that could not removed by the darts are displayed.

There is no guarantee that the developed 2D pattern will take the very indicated 3D form because the cloth is no more constrained on the indicated surface in the natural draping process. In other words, there are 3D forms that can never be realized by draping. Therefore, the developed pattern should be checked by the 2D→3D simulator, and it should be modified until a satisfactory 3D drape form is obtained.

6. Further results and future problems

Some experiments were made to check the agreement between the real material and the results of the calculations[6]. The differences of the draped shapes were no more than 3% of the length of the cloth in the standard experiments using rectangular specimens and less in the experiments using actual skirts. Considering that displacement of specimens by deformation is very large and that some percentages of variance in the mechanical properties of a given cloth are usual, the agreement is satisfying. The results of the measurement of the contact pressure were more striking. We observed that even the smallest sensor embedded in the contacting object caused a concentration of pressure, and the total stress always exceeded the weight of the specimen. On the other hand, the total stress and the weight agreed precisely in our simulation[10].

The mechanical parameters of fabrics used in our system were measured by KES, a fabric measuring system developed by S. Kawabata. But when compared with hard materials like metals, our knowledge about the mechanical properties of cloths is still very incomplete and there are many problems in deducing mechanical parameters for our simulation from the results of measurements.

Although they are not considered much in our present system, the optical surface character and 'matière' of cloths are very diverse, and they are important factors in the appearance of garments. There are some trials to model and visualize the touch of cloths[16,17], but recognizing the variety from velvet to gossamer and from silk to leather, we realize that this is still a vast area to be explored.

Precise and quick measurement of a 3D form of an object is very important in obtaining human body shapes and comparing the forms of actual garments with computed ones. At present, our model for the human body is based on a dress dummy measured by a contact type 3D digitizer. But in the future, the measurement of a customer's body in various postures or even in motion may be required. In response to such a request, we are now engaged in the research of a 3D measurement system based on color pattern recognition and multi-TV camera stereoscopy[20].

Our system may have more applications. Paper is another highly deformable 2D material widely used to produce 3D forms and we have a special concern in simulating paper crafts or origami, a highly geometrical traditional art of Japan. Our system may be interesting from the viewpoint of computational topology. As sewing and draping accompany large deformations, the mesh structures and their operations defined in our system should be firmly based on topology. In turn, our system can help the visualization of topological operations since it can simulate the widely used rubber film model in topology.

References

†: in Japanese

1. J. Amirbayat and J. W. S. Hearle, "The Complex Buckling of Flexible Sheet Materials - Part I. Theoretical Approach", *International Journal of Mechanical Sciences* 28 (1986), 339.
2. M. Aono, "A Wrinkle Propagation Model for Cloth", *Proceedings of CG INTERNATIONAL'90* (1990), 95.
3. J. -L. Delaporte and R. Soenen, (personal communication).
4. B. V. Herzen, A. H. Barr and H. R. Zatz, "Geometric Collision for Time-Dependent Parametric Surfaces", *Proceedings of SIGGRAPH '90* (August 1990). In *Computer Graphics* 24, 4 (August 1990), 39.
5. H. Imaoka, H. Okabe, H. Akami, et al., "Analysis of Deformations in Textile Fabrics", *Sen-i Gakkaishi* 44 (1988)†, 217.
6. H. Imaoka, H. Okabe, R. Matsuda, et al., "Estimation Method of Textile Deformation - In the Case of Two-Dimensional Problem", *Sen-i Gakkaishi* 44 (1988)†, 229.
7. H. Imaoka, H. Okabe, T. Tomiha, et al., "Prediction of Three-Dimensional Shapes of Garments from Two-Dimensional Paper Patterns", *Sen-i Gakkaishi* 45 (1989)†, 420.
8. H. Imaoka, A. Shibuya, N. Aisaka, "Automatic Paper Pattern Making Using Mechanical Development Method of a Curved Surface on a Plane Surface", *Sen-i Gakkaishi* 45 (1989)†, 427.
9. B. Lafleur, N. Magnenat-Thalmann and D. Thalmann, "Cloth Animation with Self-Collision Detection", *Proceedings of IFIP WG5.10 - Modeling in Computer Graphics* (1991), 179.
10. H. Niwaya, H. Imaoka, A. Shibuya and N. Aisaka, "Predicting Method of Contact Pressure of Fabrics", *Sen-i Gakkaishi* 45 (1989)†, 427.
11. H. Okabe, H. Imaoka, T. Tomiha, et al., "Transformation from Paper Pattern to Spatial Structure of Dress by Computer - Simulation of Sewing and Dressing", *Sen-i Gakkaishi* 44 (1988)†, 129.
12. H. Okabe and T. Ikawa, "Point Matching for Stereoscopy by Bayesian Inference", *Computer Vision Graphics and Image Processing* (submitted).
13. T. Sengan, (personal communication)†.
14. W. J. Shanahan, D. W. Lloyd and J. W. S. Hearle, "Characterizing the Elastic Behavior of Textile Fabrics in Complex Deformations", *Textile Research Journal* 48 (1978), 495.
15. D. Terzopoulos, J. Platt, A. Barr and K. Fleischer, "Elastically Deformable Models", *Proceedings of SIGGRAPH '87* (July 1987). In *Computer Graphics* 21, 4 (July 1987), 49.
16. J. Weil, "The Synthesis of Cloth Objects", *Proceedings of SIGGRAPH '86* (August 1986). In *Computer Graphics* 20, 4 (July 1986), 49.
17. T. Yasuda and S. Yokoi, "Shading Model to express the texture of cloth", *Nikkei Computer Graphics* 1990, 2 (February 1990)†, 150.

A Simple Method for Extracting the Natural Beauty of Hair

Ken-ichi Anjyo*‡   Yoshiaki Usami*   Tsuneya Kurihara†

Hitachi, Ltd.

ABSTRACT

A simple differential equation method is proposed for modeling the aesthetic features of human hair. In the method, a simplified cantilever beam simulation is employed for hairstyle modeling, which allows hairdressing variations with volumetric and realistic appearance. In order to describe the dynamical behavior of hair in an animation, one-dimensional projective differential equations of angular momenta for linked rigid sticks are also derived. For the problem of collision detection between hair and a human head, the "rough" approximate solution is provided, which gives visually satisfactory results by solving the projective equations under a pseudo-force field. The hair's pliability can be controlled by using a set of stiffness parameters in the method. In addition, a fast rendering technique for anisotropic reflection is introduced, which is derived from Blinn's specular model. The efficiency of the proposed method is illustrated by the still images and short animations obtained.

CR Categories and Subject Descriptors: I.3.3 [**Computer Graphics**]: Picture/Image Generation; I.3.7 [**Computer Graphics**]: Three-dimensional Graphics and Realism.
General Terms: Algorithms, Graphics
Additional Keywords and Phrases: human modeling, hair, differential equation, simulation, collision detection, anisotropic reflection

* Hitachi Research Laboratory, 4026 Kuji, Hitachi, Ibaraki 319-12

† Hitachi Central Research Laboratory, 1-280 Higashi-Koigakubo, Kokubunji, Tokyo 185

‡ Current address: Systems Engineering Division, Hitachi, Ltd., 4-6 Kanda-Surugadai, Chiyoda Tokyo 101

1. Introduction

Modeling human characters is one of today's most challenging issues in computer graphics [6]. In particular realistic representation of human hair presents many problems to overcome, which appear in all aspects of computer graphics technologies, i.e. rendering, shape modeling and animation.

In the late 1980's several new techniques appeared relating to synthetic hair representation, but most of them were only for rendering furry objects, such as a teddy bear [4] or spider [7], rather than human hair. More recent works [5, 8] have shown that naturalistic human hair rendering can also be performed as variations of previous research, including the above techniques. These successful results for rendering have led us to achieve more realistic syntheses of human characters, along with the development of modeling and animation techniques. However research for hairstyle modeling or for describing dynamical behavior of hair is not completed yet.

In an actual hairstyling process, many artificial techniques are provided by a hairdresser, such as shearing, perming, and combing. These may be very important factors in selecting a desirable hairstyle. Other essential factors lie in the natural and physical properties of hair, which include hair color, width, pliability and volumetric appearance. Therefore a hairstyle modeling method for our purpose should be computationally tractable, while considering these two aspects of actual hairstyling: artificial and intrinsic factors. A previous work [11] proposed models for describing some artificial factors. The intrinsic factors may be achieved partly by the rendering techniques mentioned above. However, for *shape* modeling of hair, a novel technique dealing with the intrinsic factors as well as the artificialities is desired.

In order to model the dynamical behavior of hair in an animation, a physically based modeling approach [9] may not be applicable. In a physically meaningful simulation, the number of unknown functions appearing in the derived differential equations must be too large to obtain satisfactory results at reasonable computational cost. In particular it is impossible to numerically treat self-interaction or collision detection of a large amount of hair, typically tens of thousands of hairs. On the other hand, supposing several simplifications, such as disregard for inter-hair collision, a variation on the philosophies of physically based modeling has been recently proposed [8]. In any case physically faithful dynamics of hair can be considered to reflect an aspect of the hair's beauty, so that a differential equation approach would not be avoided. Consequently the differential equation approach for our purpose should employ easy-to-solve equations which still hold some aesthetics of hair as the physically faithful realities.

This paper is therefore intended to provide a step forward in modeling the aesthetic features of human hair, focusing on hairstyling and dynamics. However, we do not emphasize the rigorous physics necessary for modeling. The heart of the proposed method lies in deriving simple differential equations as the *visual analogies*, while abandoning a physically rigorous formulation or its simplification [9, 8]. This allows the method to employ several simple and intuitive ideas for fast processing while preserving a visually satisfactory reality.

The organization of the paper is as follows: In section 2 we describe the hairstyle modeling technique, which employs a simple ordinary differential equation governing cantilever beam deformation. The obtained hairstyle variations illustrate the efficiency of the proposed technique. In section 3, we introduce simple differential equations of one-dimensional angular momenta for describing dynamical behavior of hair. Collision detection or avoidance of hair strands is then discussed. The animation examples are also shown. In section 4 the rasterization process in our method is briefly presented. The computational costs are also discussed along with the examples obtained. In addition a fast rendering method for representing anisotropic reflection of hair is derived. Concluding remarks are made and further work is discussed in section 5.

2. Hairstyle modeling

In our case a geometrical model of a human head with texture is obtained from the three-dimensional digitized data of an actual mannequin, whereas the textures of such items as eyes, mouth, and teeth are made by a designer using interactive operations. The hairstyle modeling then consists of the following steps:

[α] Define an ellipsoidal hull of the head model, which can be considered as a rough approximation to the head. Then also specify the region of hair pores on the ellipsoid.
[β] Calculate hair bending, based on a simplified simulation of *a cantilever beam*. This process also includes collision detection between each hair and the ellipsoid.
[γ] Cut hair and modify with slight adjustment, in order to get the desired shape in the final stage.

In step [α], the ellipsoid is employed simply for convenience in the design and calculation of hairstyle. For example, the pore positions are easily specified on the ellipsoidal hull, rather than on the original (polygonal) head model. This is because a polar coordinate system for the ellipsoid is available, which provides global guidance for explicit positioning. In addition, collision detection between the ellipsoid and hair is readily done at a low computational cost, compared to checking between the polygonal head model and hair. Though of course the "ellipsoidal" approximation is not accurate for general purposes, we believe that it is still valid and efficient for extracting the beauty of hair which is

described in this paper.

The central idea of the modeling method is the use of a cantilever beam simulation for the hair bending calculation, which allows variations in hairdressing with volumetric and realistic appearance. The following sections are mainly devoted to describing the hair bending method.

2.1 The cantilever beam simulation for hair bending

In the field of material strengths [10], the cantilever beam is originally defined as a straight beam with a one-sided and fixed support, as shown in Fig.1 (a). Let us employ the cantilever beam as our hair model, which is also shown later to give an efficient analogy for volumetric representation of hair.

The hairstyle modeling method then involves the process of hair bending, which is actually interpreted as the numerical simulation of the cantilever beam deformation. In order to describe the simulation technique, a two-dimensional case is first treated for simplicity. Suppose that the cantilever beam of two-dimensions in an initial state is set as shown in Fig. 1 (a), where one end of the beam is fixed. (This actually corresponds to the pore of a hair). Let us consider a typical case in which the beam is loaded by the external force g uniformly distributed on the whole beam, such as gravity. Then two types of model deformation may occur: one is caused by bending moment and the other is by shearing force. The former deformation is principally activated, whereas the latter does not affect our purpose. Thus we just consider the bending momentum deformation. Let the x-axis be along the initial beam direction, and the y-axis be vertical to the direction. The y-axis indicates the deflectional direction, with the variable y representing deflection of the beam. Assuming that the model is elastically deformed, the following equation governs the

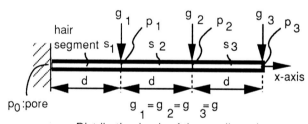

(a) Distribution loads of the cantilever beam for hair model

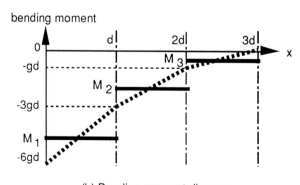

(b) Bending moment diagram

Fig. 1 Bending moment of the cantilever beam

deformation process:

$$d^2y/dx^2 = -M/(E*I), \qquad (1)$$

where E is Young's modulus, and I denotes the second momentum of area. The term E*I is usually referred to as the flexural rigidity, which depends on the beam material. Theoretically equation (1) does not hold in dealing with large deformation, but can be considered to be valid for our purpose of hairstyle modeling.

The calculation method of the above bending moment is illustrated in Fig. 1. Fast calculation is derived from the idea that the distributed load g is approximated by the finite sum of the *segmentally averaged* concentrated loads. For this idea, we suppose that the cantilever beam consists of finite linear segments with the same length. Let $p_0, p_1, ..., p_k$ be the node vectors of the segments, where p_0 is the pore and p_k is the free end of the beam. In Fig. 1 (a), the beam consists of three segments s_0, s_1, and s_2, so that s_i corresponds to the vector $\overrightarrow{p_{i-1}p_i}$. and the magnitude $\|\overrightarrow{p_{i-1}p_i}\|$ is equal to d, for $1 \le i \le 3$. Let g_0, g_1, and g_2 be the copies of the force g, where each g_i is supposed to be a concentrated load at the node p_i. Then the bending moment at point x on the model would be represented by the graph of broken line in Fig. 1 (b). However, for simplicity, we assume the bending moment as being constant on each segment, as shown in Fig. 1 (b). The constant values M_i on the segment s_i are defined as:

$$M_i = -\|g\| d(\sum_{p=1}^{k-i+1} p + \sum_{p=1}^{k-i} p)/2 = -\|g\|d(k-i+1)^2/2. \qquad (2)$$

The displacement y_i of the node p_i can be easily evaluated, using the following formula:

$$y_i = (-1/2)*(M_i/E*I)*d^2, \qquad (3)$$

which is derived from equation (1). Suppose that p_{i-2} and p_{i-1} are known using formula (3). Then let us obtain the new position of the node p_i. To do so, get the vector e_i such that e_i

$= \overrightarrow{p_{i-2}p_{i-1}} + y_i$, where the x-axis for the calculation is defined as being along the segment vector $\overrightarrow{p_{i-2}p_{i-1}}$ and the vector y_i is in the deflectional direction with its magnitude being equal to y_i in (3). The new node p_i is consequently defined as $p_i = (d/\|e_i\|)e_i + p_{i-1}$, satisfying $\|\overrightarrow{p_{i-1}p_i}\| = d$. The vectors are successively obtained from p_1 to p_k.

Let us now extend the calculation method to a three-dimensional case. First we introduce the coordinate system suitable for the method. The a_0-axis in Fig. 2 corresponds to the x-axis described above, that is, the a_0 axis is defined as being along the segment vector $\overrightarrow{p_{i-2}p_{i-1}}$. Let $p*_i$ be a point which is a distance d along the a_0-axis from p_{i-1}. Also $p*_{i-1}$ denotes a point which is far from p_{i-1} by a certain distance, so that the three points $p_{i-1}, p*_{i-1}$, and $p*_i$ span a plane. Then the a_1-axis is defined as being vertical to the a_0-axis and on the plane. The a_2-axis is specified such that it is orthogonal to both axes. Now we apply the two-dimensional method to obtaining the deflections y_1 along the a_1-axis and y_2 along the a_2-axis, considering a respective component of the force. Supposing there is no compression of the beam, the desired deflectional vector y_i is obtained as $y_1a_1 + y_2a_2$, where the vectors a_1 and a_2 are from the orthonormal basis of the a_0-a_1-a_2 coordinate system. Similar to the two-dimensional case, a new sequence of the beam nodes is obtained, using the deflectional vectors.

In applying the above cantilever beam simulation to hairstyle modeling, we should consider collision detection to prevent the hair model from intersecting the head or body. As is well

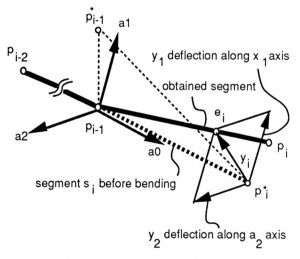

Fig. 2 Deflection of 3D hair model

Fig. 3 Bobbed hair

known, the problem of collision detection is very difficult to solve in a general situation. The collision detection process in physically based modeling is generally rather time-consuming, compared to other calculation processes. Even if we concentrate only on collisions between the hair and the head, neglecting hair-hair collisions, it would still require a high computational cost. This is because it must be checked whether each segment of the hair intersects any polygon of the head, though in total the hair model typically consists of over 400,000 segments and the polygon head has about 10,000 polygons. So let us use the ellipsoidal approximation again. Then we avoid the hair model intersecting the ellipsoid in a very inexpensive way. The collision detection and avoidance are performed while obtaining the new sequence of the nodes $\mathbf{p}_i$. Suppose that the two nodes $\mathbf{p}_{i-2}$, $\mathbf{p}_{i-1}$ of the hair model are newly defined using the cantilever beam simulation and then modified to be out of the ellipsoid. Subsequently, it is easy to know whether the next node $\mathbf{p}_i$, which is again the result of the beam simulation, is intersecting the ellipsoid. This is done by checking the signature of the quadric form $E(\mathbf{p}_i)$, which defines the ellipsoid: $E(\mathbf{p}) = 0$. If the node $\mathbf{p}_i$ is intersecting, then it is moved out in such a way that the resultant node is near the original point of $\mathbf{p}_i$ and it is on the plane spanned by the three points $\mathbf{p}_{i-2}$, $\mathbf{p}_{i-1}$ and $\mathbf{p}_i$ (or an appropriate plane containing $\mathbf{p}_{i-2}$ and $\mathbf{p}_{i-1}$, if these three vectors degenerate).

2.2 The modeling process and examples

Though the hair bending process plays a central role in our hairstyle modeling, it just shows one physically faithful aspect of hair. Actually a hairdresser creates many artificial aspects, such as shearing, combing, tying up into a ponytail, etc. In this paper, relatively simple techniques are developed to model such artificial techniques to beautify hair. These are very naive and elementary, and they may become insufficient for achieving more accurate and realistic hairstyle modeling, but the sophisticated approaches for this have not been established yet to our knowledge.

Our modeling method is introduced through several examples. As a typical case, the modeling process of bobbed hair shown in Fig.3 is described. First, the initial state is defined, as shown in Fig. 4 (a), where the pore positions and the initial length of hair are specified. Since there is no external force or gravity applied to the initial hair beams, they stand radially. By adding gravity, the hair beams go down, as illustrated in Fig. 4 (b). The hair near the top of the head is not deformed much, since the strands are essentially parallel to the gravity vector and the bending momentum is relatively small. The undulation of hair in front of the face is also observed in Fig. 4 (b), which is caused by the collision avoidance mentioned above. Then cutting, combing or brushing makes the hair more attractive in actual hairdressing. For the bobbed hair in Fig. 3, these kinds of techniques would give the short bangs, parting the hair at the middle of the head, and so on. Instead of using shears or a comb, cutting operations and bending calculations

(a)   (b)

(c)   (d)

Fig. 4 Hairdressing process

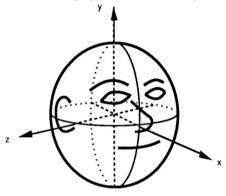

(a) Head positioning in the local coordinate system

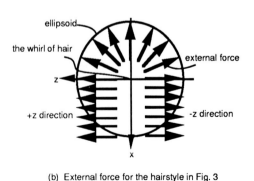

(b) External force for the hairstyle in Fig. 3

Fig. 5 Head coordinate system and examples of external force

Fig. 6 illustrates some other hairdressing examples generated by our method. Fig. 6 (a) shows a hairstyle relatively similar to that of Fig. 3, while the drooping bangs and proper fluctuation of hair lengths are successfully produced. As for making the hairdo in Fig. 6 (b), the external force applied indicates the negative x direction, that is, from the face backwards. The tuft of hair at the side of the temple is also added. A tied hairstyle, or "ponytail" is represented in Fig. 6 (c), where the ponytail and other parts of the hair are individually designed. In making the short haircut in Fig. 6 (d), the cutting operation is somewhat elaborate as the number of hair segments not to be displayed is arranged depending on the height of the hair pore (i.e., the y value of the pore). These examples visually demonstrate the variety· of realistic appearances achievable with the method.

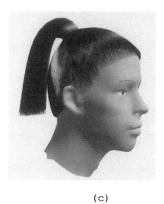

(c)   (d)

Fig. 6 Example hairstyles

with additional external forces are used for the hairstyle modeling. In the cutting operations specification of the hair to be cut is performed using the polar coordinate system of the approximating ellipsoid and the threshold along the vertical direction, i.e. the y-axis direction shown in Fig. 5 (a). For instance the pore positions of the hair to be cut are specified by the range of the azimuth ϕ and zenith angles θ such as $\phi_0 \le$ $\phi \le$ and $\theta \le \theta_0$. Then the segments of the hair whose pores are in the range are not displayed if the y coordinate values of their nodes are less than the designated threshold. (In a rendering step, each hair is displayed as a polyline. For more details, see section 4). To comb the hair, some external forces in addition to gravity are selected. To illustrate this, suppose that the face indicates the positive x direction, and the y-axis is in the vertical direction, using the coordinate system shown in Fig. 5 (a). The external force field shown in Fig. 5 (b) is then applied to the hair segments that are located higher than the eyes. Fig. 4 (c) shows the result, in applying the cantilever beam simulation using force to the hair segments in the positive z region, where cutting is done during postprocessing. After this, the hair model in Fig. 4 (d) is obtained, by adding similar results for the hair in the negative z region. Again by shearing the back hair in Fig 4 (d), the hairstyle in Fig. 3 is consequently made, which illustrates well the efficiency of the method in representing a volumetric appearance of hair.

3. Dynamical behavior of hair

An aesthetic feature in hair dynamics seems to appear typically in scenes where long hair is *gently* blowing in the wind or is swaying according to human movement, such as, running or looking back quickly. (Then the highlighted areas of the hair are also moving, which again fascinates us, but the rendering technique for this is described later). Considering these actual impressions of hair dynamics, the equation(s) to be employed here should at least control the *inertial* property of hair. In other words, some aesthetic features in hair animation are extracted by the method, which are obtained as the result of *inertia vs applied force*. To do so, simple ordinary differential equations are introduced in the following way.

In the previous section each hair strand is represented as a deformed beam, and is actually a collection of linked linear segments. For the purposes of animation, the hair model also has such a geometrical structure, whose segments may be considered to be rigid sticks this time. The proposed technique for pursuing dynamical behavior of hair is essentially reduced to solving the simple one-dimensional differential equation(s) of angular momentum for each hair. Then collision and interaction, such as a friction effect, of the hair strands with themselves and with the head are not rigorously considered. However, the technique gives a "roughly" approximate solution of these difficult problems. The solution simply means utilizing a pseudo-force field in solving the differential equations, beside rigorous treatments of applied forces and some other physical conditions. The pliability of hair is also described using a parameter for controlling the angles of adjacent segments of hair, which copes with the differential equations.

3.1 One-dimensional projective equations for hair dynamics

Let us now consider the dynamics of a single hair, since hair self-interaction is not treated rigorously in the method. Then, taking the polar coordinate system as shown in Fig. 7, the behavior of the zenith angle θ_i and the azimuth ϕ_i of the i-th segment s_i of the hair are observed. Particular consideration is given to the shadows of the segment on the θ and ϕ planes

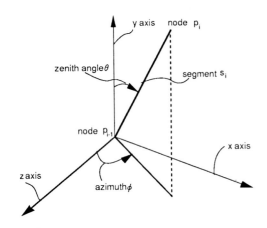

Fig. 7   The polar coordinate system for a hair segment

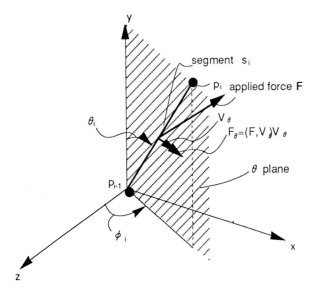

Fig. 8 Definitions of θ plane and F_θ

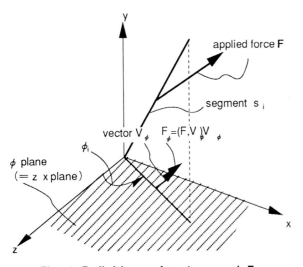

Fig. 9 Definitions of φ plane and F_ϕ

which are defined as shown in Figs. 8 and 9. The θ plane is the plane spanned by the y-axis and the segment s_i. If s_i is almost parallel to the y-axis, then the θ plane is defined using the y-axis and an applied force **F** instead of s_i. The φ plane is defined as the zx plane. Then, on these planes, the variables $θ_i(t)$ and $φ_i(t)$ with the time parameter t may be governed by the ordinary differential equations:

$$d^2θ_i/dt^2 = c_i u_i F_θ , \qquad (4)$$

$$d^2φ_i/dt^2 = c_i v_i F_φ, \qquad (5)$$

where c_i corresponds to the reciprocal number of the inertia moment of s_i;

u_i is $(1/2)\|s_i\|$;

v_i is the half length of the segment that is the projection of s_i onto the φ plane; and

$F_θ$, $F_φ$ are the "θ, φ -components" of the applied force **F** respectively, as shown in Figs. 8 and 9.

The above θ component $F_θ$ of the applied force field **F** is the scalar value defined by $F_θ = \|F_θ\| =(F, V_θ)$, where $V_θ$ is the unit vector (i.e. the magnitude is equal to one) on the θ plane that is perpendicular to the segment s_i. Similarly the φ component $F_φ$ is defined by $F_φ = \|F_φ\| =(F, V_φ)$, where $V_φ$ is the unit vector on the φ plane which is perpendicular to the projection segment of s_i onto the φ plane. Our idea is that we employ *one-dimensional projective equations* (4) and (5) for describing hair dynamics, though originally these govern *projective* behaviors of our hair model.

In the numerical simulation, these equations mean simple recurrence formulae of second order. Using the known values $θ_i^{n-1}$ and $θ_i^n$, the new value $θ_i^{n+1}$ at the time $(n+1)Δt$ is obtained by

$$θ_i^{n+1} -2θ_i^n + θ_i^{n-1} = (Δt)^2 c_i u_i F_θ . \qquad (4)'$$

Similarly, from $φ_i^{n-1}$ and $φ_i^n$, the new value $φ_i^{n+1}$ is given by

$$φ_i^{n+1} -2φ_i^n + φ_i^{n-1} = (Δt)^2 c_i v_i F_φ . \qquad (5)'$$

The calculation starts with the segment s_1, and the new position of s_i is successively determined, using (4)' and (5)'. It should be noted that, in the calculation of (4)' and (5)', the discrete time loop concerning the parameter n can be set as the inner loop while the outer loop is the segment number i. This would be useful for saving time in calculating many frames of a huge amount of hair. An example of the initial condition is that $θ_i^0 = θ_i^{-1} =θ_i^{init}$; $φ_i^0 = φ_i^{-1} = φ_i^{init}$, which means that the hair is still at the beginning. Other conditions for the parameters or input information about (4)' and (5)' are described next, which also involves rough treatment of collision avoidance or self-interaction of hair.

3.2 Introducing a rough approximation of physics

3.2.1 Inertia moment and its modification

Consider the straight stick S with length kd and line density ρ. Then its inertia moment I_S is given by $I_S = (1/3)\rho(kd)^2$. For our hair model, the terms c_iv_i and c_iu_i in (4) and (5) closely relate to this I_S. For example, suppose that the inertia moment I_i of s_i is proportional to $1/i$ ($1 \le i \le k$) and that I_k is equal to I_S (see [1] for a more mathematical treatment). Then I_i is given as $I_i = (\rho/3i)k^3d^2$. The term $(\Delta t)^2c_iu_i$ in (4)' is consequently represented as $\{3(\Delta t)^2i\}/(2k^3\rho d)$. (For the term $(\Delta t)^2c_iv_i$ in (5)', a similar expression is obtained). This expression may be used for numerically estimating the magnitude of the righthand side of equation (4)'. In addition, it is noted that the kind of self-interaction effect can be described by arranging the c_i's values. For example, if the c_i's are selected as rather small for the segments near the top of the head, the hair near the top moves relatively slowly, when affected by an applied force field. This can be thought of as a "rough" approximation of the hair's frictional effect. Therefore in the method, the coefficients are appropriately arranged according to the situation.

Fig. 10 shows the four frames taken from a very short film representing a wind gust scene. The animation is made under the condition that $\Delta t = 0.1$, $d = \rho = 1.0$ and $k = 18$, where the number k is the maximum number of the segments used for the hair model shown in Fig. 10 (a). About 10,000 individual hairs are described for the scene. Then the applied force field **F** is quite simple: From the first to the 15th frame, **F** is defined as (-200, 0, 0) with the coordinate system in Fig. 5 (a). From the 16th frame, **F** is (-20, -250, 0). The discontinuous change of the force field corresponds to the drastic change of an actual

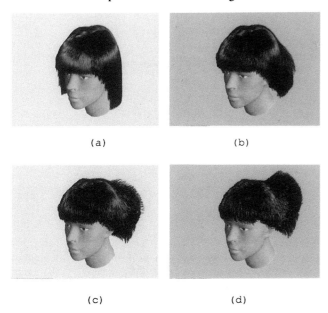

(a)   (b)

(c)   (d)

Fig. 10 A wind gust scene

(a)

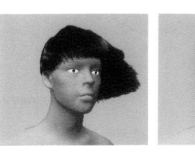 

(b)   (c)

Fig. 11 Example of dynamic collision avoidance

wind gust. The 10th frame is shown in Fig. 10 (b) and the 15th frame is in Fig. 10 (c). The hair undulation is observed in the 20th frame, as shown in Fig. 10 (d). This is caused by the drastic change of the wind vector field, which illustrates the effect of inertia vs applied force by the method. Note also that the bangs do not go through the forehead. This is achieved by using the pseudo-force field, which is described in the next section.

3.2.2 Pseudo-force field

The method also provides a simple technique for avoiding in the mass hair collisions with the head. The technique implies introducing a pseudo-force field, instead of the specified force field. Let **F** be the force field specified by a user. In solving equations (4) and (5) for **F**, let us define the segment direction D_i of the hair segment s_i, using the ellipsoid equation E(**p**): $D_i = (E_x(p_i), E_y(p_i), E_z(p_i))$, where E_x, E_y, and E_z are partial derivatives of the algebraic polynomial. For a prescribed value α ($|\alpha| \le 1$), it should be examined whether the inner product (D_i, F) is smaller than $\alpha \|D_i\| \cdot \|F\|$. If so, it means that the segment s_i is roughly in the opposite direction of **F**. In addition, if the segment is near the head model, then replace **F** by the *pseudo-force* ε_iF, where $0 \le \varepsilon_i \le 1$. The *pseudo-force constants* ε_i for the segments near a pore are usually assigned smaller values, whereas those for the segments near the endpoint p_k are equal to 1. The pseudo-force ε_iF near the pore can be understood as the simplification of the composite force of **F** and the repulsive force.

An applied example of the pseudo-force field is found in Fig.11. The initial state with **F** = 0 is shown in Fig. 11 (a).

The result without the pseudo-force effect, which means all ε_i are set at 1.0, is shown in Fig. 11 (b), where many hairs on the left side go through the head by the force $\mathbf{F} = (0, 0, -500)$. Fig. 11 (c) shows the pseudo-force effect, where $\alpha = -0.75$ and the coefficients ε_i of the segments near the head are assigned 0.1.

3.2.3 Joint angle adjustment controlling stiffness

For our hair model, the joint angle ϑ_i at the node $\mathbf{p}_i$ is the angle between $\overrightarrow{\mathbf{p}_i\mathbf{p}_{i-1}}$ and $\overrightarrow{\mathbf{p}_i\mathbf{p}_{i+1}}$. Then the stiffness of the hair model is prescribed by the parameters σ_i ($0° \le \sigma_i \le 180°$). The i-th *stiffness* parameter σ_i works after the new $\mathbf{p}_{i+1}$ is determined using the recurrence formulae (4)' and (5)'. If ϑ_i is greater than σ_i, the node $\mathbf{p}_{i+1}$ is then adjusted such that the joint angle is equal to σ_i. Usually the stiffness parameters whose nodes are near a pore are set at 180°(that is, no adjustments of the nodes are done). And, in describing a smoother curve of hair, the parameters σ_i would be rather small, such as 10° or 15°, for the nodes far from a pore.

A typical application of this technique is the description of gently blowing hair with locally subtle fluctuations, as shown in Fig. 12. In this case each hair strand fluctuates according to the given uniform random numbers, after obtaining the new node positions by (4)' and (5)'. The use of the random numbers is made not for each frame, but for one per ten frames, to avoid excess fluctuations. Then, using the stiffness parameters, the obtained hair strand is rearranged in order to maintain the curve's smoothness. The local fluctuations are caused by the short haircut and the drastic change of the force field (similar to the case of Fig. 10). In Fig. 12 (a), the fluctuations are not observed clearly, since the stiffness parameters are set at 180°. On the other hand, if the parameters σ_i are set rather small as described above, then the fluctuations are exaggerated while preserving the hair's smoothness, as described in Fig. 12 (b). The efficency of the stiffness parameters is obvious, but a careful choice of the parameters' values is currently required to obtain a desired result.

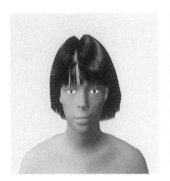 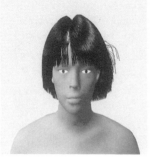

(a)   (b)

Fig. 12 Effect of joint angle control

4. Rendering technique and numerical results

4.1 Anisotropic reflection model for a three-dimensional curve

The rendering method are rather restrictive for fast processing, whereas the main contribution of this paper is toward modeling and animating hair. In particular shadowing effect is disregarded. As stated in the introduction, alternative rendering techniques [5, 8] would be helpful for more accurate description of hair.

The color of the hair treated in this paper is relatively dark brown or black, which allows the simplified rendering model described here still to be powerful. At the rendering stage the geometry of our hair model is represented as a collection of three-dimensional curves, which consequently consists of the polylines. Let us now consider a standard illumination equation involving ambient, diffuse and specular components. In order to describe glossy hair, the specular component seems to be dominant among the three components, whereas the diffuse term is neglected for simplicity. The resulting intensity of hair is supposed to be the sum of the ambient constant and specular component.

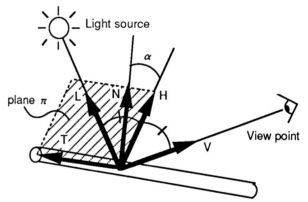

Fig. 13 Specular lighting geometry

Mathematically the hair model consists of polylines which have ill-defined normal vectors, since they have no volumes. To derive an illumination model, suppose that each hair segment is a cylinder with very small radius. Then a simple technique for calculating the specular term is introduced, which is motivated by Fig.13. The technique is based on Blinn's specular model [2], that is, the specular term Φ_S at the point $\mathbf{P}$ on a surface is defined by:

$$\Phi_S = k_S \, (\mathbf{N}, \mathbf{H})^n, \qquad (6)$$

where k_S is the specular reflection coefficient, $\mathbf{N}$ is the surface normal at $\mathbf{P}$, $\mathbf{H}$ is the halfway vector of the light vector $\mathbf{L}$ and the vector $\mathbf{V}$ pointing to the eye, and n is the exponent indicating the sharpness of the highlight. In our case, since the point $\mathbf{P}$ is on a very thin cylinder, it would be more accurate to get an integral around its circumference based on the model (6). However, the specular component proposed here is represented as the above Φ_S in (6), taking the normal $\mathbf{N}$ on the plane π spanned by the vector $\mathbf{H}$ and the cylinder's tangent $\mathbf{T}$.

Then, as shown in Fig.13, the term (N, H) in (6) is easily evaluated using the known vectors:

$$(N, H) = \cos \alpha = \sqrt{1 - (T, H)^2} \qquad (7)$$

Another algebraic proof of (7) is again easy to see. Since the vectors N and T constitute the orthonormal basis of the plane π, the following vector expression is obtained : $H = (N, H)N + (T, H)T$. Then, by taking an inner product on both sides, the scalar relation holds: $1 = (N, H)^2 + (T, H)^2$, which leads us to equation (7). Thus the resultant specular term at P is defined as

$$\Phi_s (P) = k_s \{1 - (T, H)^2\}^{n/2} . \qquad (8)$$

The expression simply means that the actual highlight intensity is approximated by the strongest one in varying the surface normal at P. This also gives an alternative formulation of the specular distribution based on Phong's model [4], but produces different effects in general [3].

The total intensity at a point P on a cylinder is consequently given as

$$I(P) = I_a k_a + I_s \Phi_s (P), \qquad (9)$$

where I_a is the intensity of the ambient light, k_a is the ambient reflection coefficient, I_s is the intensity of the light source and $\Phi_s (P)$ is of the form in (8). In rendering the hair model, the ambient reflection coefficient k_a also plays an important role.

The coefficient k_a is a material property, so that it should be distinguished in rendering each hair, since the actual ambient color of hair is usually heterogeneous. In our situation, introducing a normal distribution, k_a fluctuates so randomly that it takes the same value on each hair strand, but differs between strands. The qualities of the resultant images derived from these simplifications are illustrated in Figs. 3-6, where anisotropy of hair reflection is observed, for example, like a halo. The quantitative effect for fast processing is demonstrated in the next section.

4.2 Rasterization process and computational costs

The z-buffer algorithm is now available as a hardware facility of current graphics workstations. The above rendering algorithm can be combined with the hardware benefit in the rasterization process. Let us suppose that the width of the hair segment on the screen is a multiple of the pixel size. As described before, let p_0, p_1, ..., and p_k be the nodes of the hair segments s_1, s_2, ..., and s_k. The color of the nodes is first defined by $I(p_i)$ in equation (9), where the tangent vector T is defined as $\overrightarrow{p_{i-1} p_i}/\|\overrightarrow{p_{i-1} p_i}\|$. Then the color at each point on the segment is linearly interpolated by the hardware support. Thus the z-buffer algorithm can deal with the hair

Fig. 14 Blowing in the wind

segments, along with polygon data. It should also be noted that the technique can be extended to the case where the hair width in the obtained image is less than the pixel size. This is easily achieved by a oversampling technique. In Fig. 14, about 50,000 hair strands are described whose width is 1/4 pixel size and the image resolution is 1024×783.

The presented method for modeling, rendering and animating of hair is implemented on a Silicon Graphics Iris Power Series workstation with a VGX graphics board. The provided hardware supports involves the z-buffer algorithm, anti-aliasing and linear color interpolation. Typically the generated model has about 20,000 hairs, each of which is at most 20 linear segments. The wall clock time for the hairstyle modeling (mainly for the hair bending calculation) was about 50 seconds, whereas it averaged around 40 seconds per frame in the animation calculation. As for a rendering time, it was usually several seconds. In particular, the image with a different camera angle was obtained in almost real time. Even in adding the anti-aliasing process, it took less than 15 seconds on average at 1024 × 1024 pixels resolution.

Finally we note that the fast processing facilities of the method allow quick feedback in previewing. In particular, an animation preview is easily done under the condition that the number of hairs is less than a few hundred. Then hair segment data generation by the method for making an animation takes less than 2 seconds per frame. Consequently, after stacking the hair data for hundreds of frames, the near real time animation preview is performed by the fast rendering method. The projective equations allow numerically stable simulations, so that longer animations can be produced than those illustrated in this paper. However interactive facilities would be desired for explicit specification of the external forces in pursuing more complex hair dynamics.

5. Concluding remarks

This paper has presented a simple method for describing human hair, which is essentially a combination of simple ordinary differential equations and some intuitive heuristics. The obtained images have demonstrated well the efficiency of the method. It should then be noted that these differential equations are directly combined with the aesthetic observations, sacrificing rigorous formulation of physics. Moreover this allows to easily introduce fast processing and several efficient heuristics to the method, which is evident in particular for hair dynamics. The one-dimensional projective equations are solved under a pseudo-force field. Consequently the method provides a big advantage over existing approaches, in fast processing and descriptive power of hair's natural beauty. We are currently working on extending the method, giving "rough" approximate solutions of the problems in collision detection between hair and a human body or other objects, in order to deal with the long hair in a more general situation.

The available range of the proposed method may still be small, compared to the diversity and variety of actual human hair. It is also understood that several assumptions used for the method do not hold in general. Nevertheless we feel the method is valuable as a first trial for extracting some aesthetic features of hairstyle modeling and animation of hair dynamics.

Acknowledgements

The authors would like to thank Ryozo Takeuchi, George Nishiyama, Akio Yajima and Masao Yanaka for their continuous encouragement and support. Thanks to Munetoshi Unuma, Kiyoshi Arai and Hiroaki Takatsuki for helpful discussions. The first author thanks Takeshi Sato for his programming support. The authors also wish to thank Dr. Carol Kikuchi for proofreading and suggestions.

Reference

[1] Arnold V. I. *Mathematical Methods of Classical Mechanics (2nd ed.)* Springer Verlag New York, 1989

[2] Blinn J. Models of Light Reflection for Computer Synthesized Pictures *Computer Graphics* 11, 3 (July 1977) 192 -198.

[3] Foley J., van Dam A., Feiner S. and Hughes J. *Computer Graphics: Principles and Practice*, Addison-Wesley, 1990.

[4] Kajiya J. T. and Kay T. L. Rendering Fur with Three Dimensional Textures *Computer Graphics* 23, 3 (July 1989) 271 -280.

[5] LeBlanc A. M., Turner R., and Thalmann D. Rendering Hair using Pixel Blending and Shadow Buffers *The Journal of Visualization and Computer Animation* 2, 3 (1991) 92-97.

[6] Magnenat-Thalmann N. and Thalmann D. Complex Models for Animating Synthetic Actors *IEEE Computer Graphics and Applications* 11, 5 (September 1991) 32-44.

[7] Miller, Gavin. S. P. From Wire-Frame to Furry Animals *Proceedings of Graphics Interface '88* (October 1988) 138-146.

[8] Rosenblum, R. E., Carlson, W. E. and Tripp, III, E. Simulating the Structure and Dynamics of Human Hair: Modelling, Rendering and Animation. *The Journal of Visualization and Computer Animation* 2, 4 (October-December 1991), 141-148.

[9] Terzopoulos D. and Fleischer K. Deformable Models *The Visual Computer* 4, 6 (December 1988) : 306 -331.

[10] Timonshenko S. *Strength of Materials : Part I Elementary Theory and Problems* D. Van Nostrand Company, Princeton, New Jersey, 1955

[11] Watanabe, Y. and Suenaga, Y. A Trigonal Prism-Based Method for Hair Image Generation *IEEE Computer Graphics and Applications* 12, 1 (January 1992), 47-53.

Interval Analysis For Computer Graphics

John M. Snyder

California Institute of Technology

Pasadena, CA 91125

Abstract

This paper discusses how interval analysis can be used to solve a wide variety of problems in computer graphics. These problems include ray tracing, interference detection, polygonal decomposition of parametric surfaces, and CSG on solids bounded by parametric surfaces. Only two basic algorithms are required: SOLVE, which computes solutions to a system of constraints, and MINIMIZE, which computes the global minimum of a function, subject to a system of constraints.

We present algorithms for SOLVE and MINIMIZE using interval analysis as the conceptual framework. Crucial to the technique is the creation of "inclusion functions" for each constraint and function to be minimized. Inclusion functions compute a bound on the range of a function, given a similar bound on its domain, allowing a branch and bound approach to constraint solution and constrained minimization. Inclusion functions also allow the MINIMIZE algorithm to compute global rather than local minima, unlike many other numerical algorithms.

Some very recent theoretical results are presented regarding existence and uniqueness of roots of nonlinear equations, and global parameterizability of implicitly described manifolds. To illustrate the power of the approach, the basic algorithms are further developed into a new algorithm for the approximation of implicit curves.

CR Categories: I.3.5 [Computer Graphics]: Computational Geometry and Object Modeling; G.4 [Mathematical Software]: Reliability and Robustness

Additional Key Words: constraint solution, constrained minimization, interval analysis, inclusion function, approximation, implicit curve

1 Introduction

Interval analysis is a new and promising branch of applied mathematics. A general treatment can be found in [MOOR66] and [MOOR79], by R.E. Moore, the originator of this field. The main benefit of interval analysis is that it can solve problems so that the results are guaranteed to be correct, even when computed with finitely precise floating point operations. This is accomplished by using inclusion functions that compute bounds on functions relevant to the problem, thus controlling approximation errors.

Although the application of interval methods to computer graphics is not new, it has been applied only to a limited class of computer graphics problems. Mudur and Koparkar [MUDU84] have presented an algorithm for rasterizing parametric surfaces using interval arithmetic. They also suggest the utility of such methods for other operations in geometric modeling. Toth [TOTH85] has demonstrated the usefulness of interval based methods for the direct ray tracing of general parametric surfaces. Most recently, interval methods have been used for error bounding in computing topological properties of toleranced polyhedra [SEGA90], for contouring 2D functions

and rendering implicit surfaces [SUFF90], and for ray tracing implicit surfaces [MITC90]. Several researchers have also used Lipschitz bounds, a special case of an interval method, in their algorithms: to approximate parametric surfaces [VONH87], to compute collisions between time-dependent parametric surfaces [VONH89,VONH90], and to ray trace implicit surfaces [KALR89].

This paper extends the work of these researchers by showing how a general set of problems in computer graphics can be solved using only two algorithms that employ interval analysis: constraint solution (SOLVE) and constrained minimization (MINIMIZE). Many of the ideas presented here are borrowed from recent work in the area of interval analysis ([RATS88, ALEF83]), but are new to computer graphics. These ideas include the actual algorithms for SOLVE (Section 3.1) and MINIMIZE (Section 3.3), and a robust test for the solution of nonlinear systems of equations (Section 3.2). Section 2 presents background information necessary for the understanding of these ideas. Using the techniques described, Section 4 presents a new, robust algorithm for the approximation of implicit curves, an important algorithm in shape modeling operations such as CSG.

1.1 Problem Definition for SOLVE and MINIMIZE

SOLVE computes solutions to a *constraint problem*, which seeks points from a domain,[1] $D \subset \mathbf{R}^n$, that satisfy a logical combination of equalities and inequalities. That is, it seeks the set given by

$$\operatorname*{SOLVE}_{x \in D} F \equiv \{x \mid x \in D, F(x) = 1\}$$

where $F: \mathbf{R}^n \to \{0, 1\}$ represents the constraint to be solved. For example, $F(x)$ may be given by the simultaneous satisfaction of the $r + s$ constraints

$$
\begin{aligned}
g_i(x) &= 0 & i &= 1, \ldots, r \\
h_j(x) &\leq 0 & j &= 1, \ldots, s
\end{aligned}
$$

The scalar functions $g_i(x)$ and $h_j(x)$ are called the *constraint functionals*, and are assumed to be continuous.

Related to the constraint problem is what we call the *constrained partitioning problem*, which seeks to partition a domain D into a collection of hyper-rectangles, $\{R_i\}$, such that each partition R_i satisfies a given set constraint. A *set constraint* is a mapping from a hyper-rectangle to $\{0, 1\}$. For example, let $S: \mathbf{R}^2 \to \mathbf{R}^3$ be a parametric surface, and let $R \subset \mathbf{R}^2$. Define the distance function of the surface, $d(R)$, as the maximum distance between two surface points, mapped from R:[2]

$$d(R) \equiv \sup\{\|S(p_1) - S(p_2)\| \mid p_1, p_2 \in R\}$$

A useful set constraint for the surface approximation problem, $G(R)$, is

$$G(R) \equiv (d(R) < \epsilon) \tag{1}$$

which requires that no two points on S from R be farther apart than ϵ. A constrained partitioning problem can also be combined with a constraint problem, in order to partition the constraint problem's solution set. We will later show how SOLVE can be applied to the constrained partitioning problem.

---

[1] We will assume the domain of all problems is a hyper-rectangle, also called a vector-valued interval in Section 2.1.

[2] sup denotes supremum, the least upper bound of a set.

MINIMIZE computes solutions to a *constrained minimization problem*, which seeks the global minima of a scalar function, $f(x)$, called the *objective function*, over the points in a given domain that satisfy a system of constraints. Two possible solutions may be required, the minimum value of the objective function:[3]

$$\underset{x \in D, F(x)=1}{\text{MINIMUM}} f \equiv \inf \{f(x) \mid x \in D, F(x) = 1\}$$

or its set of global minimizers:

$$\underset{x \in D, F(x)=1}{\text{MINIMIZERS}} f \equiv \{x \mid f(x) = \underset{x \in D, F(x)=1}{\text{MINIMUM}} f\}$$

Note that the MINIMUM operator is well-defined only if the feasible set of the constraint system is nonempty. We assume the continuity of the objective function as well as the constraint functionals involved in the definition of $F(x)$. This, together with the compactness of D, guarantees that the MINIMIZERS operator is well-defined when the feasible set is nonempty.

We will use the term *global problem* for a constraint problem, constrained partitioning problem, or constrained minimization problem.

1.2 SOLVE and MINIMIZE in Computer Graphics

SOLVE and MINIMIZE can be applied to a wide variety of problems in rendering and geometric modeling. We shall describe an important, but by no means exhaustive, set of examples in the following paragraphs. Further applications of the algorithms to computer graphics include scan conversion of parametric surfaces, parametric/implicit representation conversion, selection of feasible/optimal parameters for parameterized shapes, and computation of toleranced geometric queries such as point enclosure.

Ray Tracing Ray tracing a parametric surface, $S(u, v) : \mathbf{R}^2 \rightarrow \mathbf{R}^3$, involves a minimization problem over (u, v) space. Let o and d be the origin and direction, respectively, of a given ray. As in [TOTH85], to find the first intersection of this ray with S, we may solve

$$\underset{\substack{(u,v) \in D_S \\ F(u,v)=1}}{\text{MINIMUM}} t(u, v)$$

where the objective function, $t(u, v)$, is given by[4]

$$t(u, v) \equiv \min\left\{ \frac{S_x(u, v) - o_x}{d_x}, \frac{S_y(u, v) - o_y}{d_y}, \frac{S_z(u, v) - o_z}{d_z} \right\}$$

and the constraint function $F(u, v)$ is given by

$$(S(u, v) - o) \times d = 0 \text{ and } t(u, v) \geq 0$$

Ray tracing of implicit surfaces can be accomplished with a similar, 1D minimization problem [MITC90].

Polygonal Decomposition Approximating a shape, such as a curve or surface, as a collection of simple pieces is a fundamental operation in computer graphics. For example, we may wish to produce a collection of triangles that approximate a parametric surface, $S(u, v)$, to some error tolerance. Such an approximation can be accomplished using constrained partitioning with the set constraint, $G(R)$, from Formula (1). For each resultant (u, v) partition, a set of triangles can be formed joining the partition's four corner vertices, as well as any vertices from more highly subdivided neighbor partitions (Figure 1). The whole collection of triangles approximates the surface without deviating from it more than a distance of ϵ. Set constraints can be also be defined that bound each partition's surface area, maximum variation of surface normal, or any other function over the surface. Figure 10 compares polygonal decomposition using set constraints with simple uniform sampling.

Interference Detection Let $S(u, v)$ and $T(r, s)$ be two parametric surfaces, with D_S and D_T their respective domains. To compute whether these surfaces intersect, the following 4D constraint problem is appropriate:

$$\underset{\substack{(u,v) \in D_S \\ (r,s) \in D_T}}{\text{SOLVE}} \quad (S(u, v) = T(r, s))$$

---

[3] inf denotes infimum, the greatest lower bound of a set.

[4] If any ray direction components are equal to 0, the corresponding quotient is taken to be ∞, and so is ignored in the min.

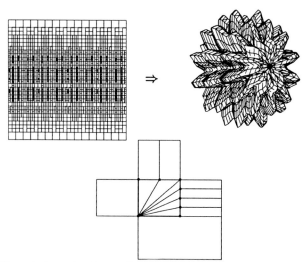

Figure 1: Approximating a surface as a triangular mesh – The surface's parameter space is first broken into rectangles each of which satisfies a set constraint, controlling the approximation quality. A collection of triangles is then generated connecting points at the corners of the rectangle or its neighbors.

In this case, evaluation of the points of intersection is unnecessary; we need only compute whether or not the feasible set is empty. Similar constraint problems can be solved to determine whether two moving surfaces intersect, by solving a 5D constraint problem given the time-dependent surfaces $S(u, v, t)$ and $T(r, s, t)$ [VONH90].

A related problem is to determine the minimum distance between two parametric surfaces, which may be expressed as the unconstrained minimization problem

$$\underset{\substack{(u,v) \in D_S \\ (r,s) \in D_T}}{\text{MINIMUM}} \|S(u, v) - T(r, s)\| \qquad (2)$$

Figure 11 shows the results of the unconstrained minimization problem to compute the minimum distance between two parametric surfaces.

CSG Computing CSG operations on solids represented by their parametric surface boundaries involves computing the curve of intersection between pairs of parametric surfaces. The resulting curve can be projected into the respective parameter spaces of the two surfaces, and used to perform trimming operations. The curve of intersection is an implicit curve solving a system of three equations in four variables, of the form

$$\underset{\substack{(u,v) \in D_S \\ (r,s) \in D_T}}{\text{SOLVE}} \quad (S(u, v) = T(r, s))$$

where S and T are the two intersecting parametric surfaces. This problem is similar to the one presented for interference detection, except that an approximation of the solution is desired rather than a mere indication of solution existence. Such an approximation can be computed using the algorithm in Section 4, which is built on the SOLVE algorithm. Figure 8 shows the results of CSG operations computed in this way.

2 Inclusion Functions

The interval analysis approach to solving global problems works by recursively subdividing an initial hyper-rectangle of the parameter space of the global problem. Inclusion functions are used to test whether a particular region satisfies the constraints (constraint and minimization problems), contains points with a small enough value of the objective function (minimization problem), or satisfies the set constraint (partitioning problem), by computing a bound on the function over the region. For example, to test whether a region X includes a solution to the equation $f(x) = 0$, an inclusion function for f is evaluated over the region X. If the resulting bound on f does not contain 0, then X may be rejected. The following section defines inclusion functions more precisely, discusses some of their properties, and explains how they may be implemented.

2.1 Terminology and Definitions

An *interval*, $A = [a, b]$, is a subset of $\mathbf{R}$ defined as

$$[a, b] \equiv \{x \mid a \leq x \leq b, \; x, a, b \in \mathbf{R}\}$$

The numbers a and b are called the *bounds* of the interval; a is called the *lower bound*, written $\mathrm{lb}[a, b]$, and b, the *upper bound*, written $\mathrm{ub}[a, b]$. The symbol $\mathbf{I}$ denotes the set of all intervals.

A *vector-valued interval of dimension n, $A = (A_1, A_2, \ldots, A_n)$*, is a subset of $\mathbf{R}^n$ defined as

$$A \equiv \{x \mid x_i \in A_i \text{ and } A_i \in \mathbf{I} \text{ for } i = 1, 2, \ldots, n\}$$

For example, a vector-valued interval of dimension 2 represents a rectangle in the plane, while a vector-valued interval of dimension 3 represents a "brick" in 3D space. An interval A_i that is a component of a vector-valued interval is called a *coordinate interval of A*. The symbol $\mathbf{I}^m$ denotes the set of all vector-valued intervals of dimension m. Hereafter, we will use the term interval to refer to both intervals and vector-valued intervals; the distinction will be clear from the context.

The *width* of an interval, written $w([a, b])$, is defined by

$$w([a, b]) \equiv b - a$$

Similarly, the width of a vector-valued interval, $A \in \mathbf{I}^n$, is defined as

$$w(A) \equiv \max_{i=1}^{n} w(A_i)$$

Given a subset D of $\mathbf{R}^m$, let $\mathbf{I}(D)$ be defined as the set of all intervals that are subsets of D:

$$\mathbf{I}(D) \equiv \{Y \mid Y \in \mathbf{I}^m \text{ and } Y \subseteq D\}$$

Let $f: D \rightarrow \mathbf{R}^n$ be a function. An *inclusion function* for f, written $\Box f$, is a function $\Box f: \mathbf{I}(D) \rightarrow \mathbf{I}^n$ such that

$$x \in Y \Rightarrow f(x) \in \Box f(Y) \quad \forall Y \in \mathbf{I}(D)$$

In other words, $\Box f$ is a vector-valued interval bound on the range of f over a vector-valued interval bound on its domain. Many possible inclusion functions may be defined for a given function f, each having different properties. For example, an inclusion function $\Box f$ is called *convergent* if

$$w(X) \rightarrow 0 \; \Rightarrow \; w(\Box f(X)) \rightarrow 0$$

Note that f must be continuous for its inclusion function to be convergent.

2.2 Inclusion Functions for Arithmetic Operators

To see how inclusion functions can be evaluated on a computer, let us first consider functions defined using arithmetic operations. Let g and h be functions from $\mathbf{R}^m$ to $\mathbf{R}$, and let $X \in \mathbf{I}^m$. Let inclusion functions for g and h be given and evaluated on the interval X

$$\begin{aligned} \Box g(X) &= [a, b] \\ \Box h(X) &= [c, d] \end{aligned}$$

Given these interval bounds on g and h, we can bound an arithmetic combination, $g \star h$, where $\star$ represents addition, subtraction, multiplication or division. This bound may be computed by bounding the set $Q_\star$, defined as

$$Q_\star \equiv \{x \star y \mid x \in [a, b], y \in [c, d]\}$$

$Q_\star$ can be bounded within an interval using the well-known technique of *interval arithmetic*, which defines the operators $+_\Box$, $-_\Box$, $*_\Box$, and $/_\Box$ according to the rules

$$\begin{aligned} [a, b] +_\Box [c, d] &\equiv Q_+ &\equiv& [a + c, b + d] \\ [a, b] -_\Box [c, d] &\equiv Q_- &\equiv& [a - d, b - c] \\ [a, b] *_\Box [c, d] &\equiv Q_* &\equiv& [\min(ac, ad, bc, bd), \max(ac, ad, bc, bd)] \\ [a, b] /_\Box [c, d] &\equiv Q_/ &\equiv& \left[\min(\tfrac{a}{c}, \tfrac{a}{d}, \tfrac{b}{c}, \tfrac{b}{d}), \max(\tfrac{a}{c}, \tfrac{a}{d}, \tfrac{b}{c}, \tfrac{b}{d})\right] \\ && & \text{provided } 0 \notin [c, d] \end{aligned}$$

The inclusion functions defined above rely on an infinitely precise representation for real numbers and arithmetic operations. To perform interval analysis on a computer, an interval $A = [a, b]$ must be approximated by a *machine interval $A_M = [a_M, b_M]$* containing A, so that a_M and b_M are members of the machine's set of floating point numbers. We can not assume that an inclusion function for $g + h$ can be constructed by producing the interval $[a +_M c, b +_M d]$, where $+_M$ denotes the hardware addition operator. Because of addition rounding errors, $a +_M c$ may not be a lower bound for $a + c$. This problem can be solved on machines that conform to the IEEE floating point standard using using round-to-$-\infty$ mode for computation of interval lower bounds, and round-to-$+\infty$ mode for interval upper bounds.

2.3 Natural Interval Extensions

It is clear that the interval bounds of the previous section can be recursively applied to yield an inclusion function for an arbitrary, nested combination of arithmetic operators on a set of functions with known inclusion functions. For example, an inclusion function for $f + (g + h)$ is given by

$$\Box(f + (g + h)) \equiv \Box f +_\Box (\Box g +_\Box \Box h) \tag{3}$$

Furthermore, this notion can be extended to non-arithmetic operators. For each operator, $P(f_1, f_2, \ldots, f_n)$, that produces a function given n simpler functions, we must define a method, $P_\Box$, that evaluates an inclusion function for P, depending only on the interval results of the inclusion functions $\Box f_i$. Let each of the functions f_i be defined on a domain D and let $X \in \mathbf{I}(D)$. Given $P_\Box$, an inclusion function for $P(f_1, \ldots, f_n)$ is then given by

$$\Box P(f_1, f_2, \ldots, f_n)(X) \equiv P_\Box(\Box f_1(X), \Box f_2(X), \ldots, \Box f_n(X))$$

In a generalization of Equation 3, given a set of operators, $P_1, P_2, \ldots, P_N$, an inclusion function can be evaluated for any function formed by their composition (e.g., $P_1(P_2(f_1, f_2), P_3(f_3))$). Inclusion functions constructed in this way are called *natural interval extensions*.

Construction of an operator's inclusion function method may not be difficult if the operator's monotonicity intervals are known. For example, an inclusion function evaluation method can be defined for the cosine operator, based on the observation that the cosine function is monotonically decreasing in the interval $[\pi 2n, \pi(2n + 1)]$, and monotonically increasing in the interval $[\pi(2n + 1), \pi(2n + 2)]$, for integer n. Let f be a function from $\mathbf{R}^m$ to $\mathbf{R}$, and let $X \in \mathbf{I}^m$. Let an inclusion functions for f be given and evaluated on the interval X, yielding the interval $[a, b]$. An inclusion function for $\cos(f)$ can be evaluated on X according to the following rules:

$$\cos_\Box([a, b]) \equiv$$
$$\begin{cases} [-1, 1], & \text{if } 1 + \left\lceil \frac{a}{\pi} \right\rceil \leq \frac{b}{\pi} \\ [-1, \max(\cos(a), \cos(b))], & \text{if } \left\lceil \frac{a}{\pi} \right\rceil \leq \frac{b}{\pi} \text{ and } \left\lceil \frac{a}{\pi} \right\rceil \bmod 2 = 1 \\ [\min(\cos(a), \cos(b)), 1], & \text{if } \left\lceil \frac{a}{\pi} \right\rceil \leq \frac{b}{\pi} \text{ and } \left\lceil \frac{a}{\pi} \right\rceil \bmod 2 = 0 \\ [\min(\cos(a), \cos(b)), \\ \max(\cos(a), \cos(b))], & \text{otherwise} \end{cases}$$

The numerical cosine evaluations implied by $\min(\cos(a), \cos(b))$, for example, must be computed so that they are a lower bound for the theoretical result. Similar inclusion functions can be constructed for operators such as sine, square root, exponential, and logarithm.

Inclusion functions for vector and matrix operations are also easy to construct. For example, an inclusion function method for the dot product operator can be defined via

$$\Box(f \cdot g) \equiv (\Box f_1 *_\Box \Box g_1) +_\Box (\Box f_2 *_\Box \Box g_2) +_\Box \ldots +_\Box (\Box f_n *_\Box \Box g_n)$$

Similarly, interval arithmetic can be used to define inclusion function methods for the matrix multiply, inverse, and determinant operators, and for vector operators like addition, subtraction, length, scaling, and cross product.

2.4 Inclusion Functions for Relational and Logical Operators

Inclusion functions can also be defined for relational and logical operators, allowing natural interval extensions for functions used as constraints.

A relational operator produces a result in the set $\{0, 1\}$, 0 for "false" and

1 for "true". The operators **equal to, not equal to, less than,** and **greater than or equal to** are all binary relational operators. An inclusion functions for a relational operator, such as **less than**, can easily be defined. Let f and g be functions from $\mathbf{R}^n$ to $\mathbf{R}$, with given inclusion functions, $\Box f$ and $\Box g$. Let $X \in \mathbf{I}^n$, and

$$\Box f(X) = [a, b]$$
$$\Box g(X) = [c, d]$$

Then we have

$$\Box(f < g)(X) \equiv \begin{cases} [0, 0], & \text{if } d \le a \\ [1, 1], & \text{if } b < c \\ [0, 1], & \text{otherwise} \end{cases}$$

Logical operators, such as **and, or,** and **not,** combine results of the relational operators in Boolean expressions. Their inclusion functions are also easily defined. For example, if r_1 and r_2 are two relational functions from $\mathbf{R}^n$ to $\{0, 1\}$, and $\Box r_1$ and $\Box r_2$ are their corresponding inclusion functions, then an inclusion function for the logical **and** of the relations, $r_1 \wedge r_2$, is given by

$$\Box(r_1 \wedge r_2) \equiv \begin{cases} [0, 0], & \text{if } \Box r_1 = [0, 0] \text{ or } \Box r_2 = [0, 0] \\ [1, 1], & \text{if } \Box r_1 = [1, 1] \text{ and } \Box r_2 = [1, 1] \\ [0, 1], & \text{otherwise} \end{cases}$$

2.5 Mean Value Forms

Given a differentiable function $f: \mathbf{R}^m \to \mathbf{R}^n$, with parameters $x_1, x_2, \ldots, x_m$, an inclusion function, called the *mean value form*, can be constructed for f as follows:

$$\Box f(Y) \equiv f(c) +_\Box \Box f'(Y) \cdot_\Box (Y -_\Box c) \qquad (4)$$

where $c \in Y$, $Y \in \mathbf{I}^m$ and $\Box f'$ is an inclusion function for the Jacobian matrix of f, i.e.,

$$\Box f'(Y) \equiv \left[\Box \frac{\partial f_i}{\partial x_j}(Y) \right]$$

That the above formula represents a valid inclusion function for f is an immediate consequence of Taylor's theorem. The mean value form has the useful property that, under certain conditions, the resulting bound on f quadratically converges to the ideally tight bound as the width of Y shrinks to 0 (Krawczyk-Nickel 1982, for a formal statement and proof, see [SNYD92b]). Note that the addition, subtraction and matrix-vector multiplication operations implied by this definition are computed using interval arithmetic. [5] The ensuing treatment of interval analysis will drop the $\Box$ subscripts for interval arithmetic operations; it should be clear by the context whether the standard operations or their interval analogs are meant.

The idea of a mean value form can be generalized to produce inclusion functions that incorporate more terms of a function's Taylor expansion, called *Taylor forms*. A related inclusion function, called the *monotonicity-test inclusion function*, is also defined using inclusion functions on the partial derivatives of f [MOOR79]). By testing whether these derivatives exclude 0, (i.e., the function is monotonic with respect to a given parameter), very tight bounds can be produced. Mean value forms can also be defined for functions which are only piecewise differentiable (see [RATS88]).

3 Solving Global Problems

3.1 Constraint Solution Algorithm

A system of constraints can be represented as a function, $F: \mathbf{R}^n \to \mathbf{R}$, that returns a 1 if the constraints are satisfied and a 0 if they are not. Such a function can incorporate both equality and inequality constraints, and can be represented with the relational and logical operators whose inclusion functions were examined in Section 2.4. As discussed in Section 2.4, an inclusion function for F, $\Box F$, over a region $X \subset \mathbf{I}^n$ can take on three possible values:

$$\Box F(X) = [0, 0] \quad \Rightarrow \quad X \text{ is an infeasible region}$$

$$\Box F(X) = [0, 1] \quad \Rightarrow \quad X \text{ is an indeterminate region}$$
$$\Box F(X) = [1, 1] \quad \Rightarrow \quad X \text{ is a feasible region}$$

An *infeasible region* is a region in which no point solves the constraint system. A *feasible region* is a region in which every point solves the constraint system. An *indeterminate region* is a region in which the constraint system may or may not have solutions. We now present an algorithm to find solutions to this constraint system.

Algorithm 3.1 (SOLVE) We are given a constraint inclusion function $\Box F$, an initial region,[6] X, in which to find solutions to the constraint problem $F(x) = 1$, and the solution acceptance set constraint, $\Box A$, specifying when an indeterminate region should be accepted as a solution.

```
place X on list L
while L is nonempty
        remove next region Y from L
        evaluate □F on Y
        if □F(Y) = [1, 1] add Y to solution
        else if □F(Y) = [0, 0] discard Y
        else if □A(Y) = [1, 1] add Y to solution
        else subdivide Y into regions Y₁ and Y₂,
                and insert into L
endwhile
```

Subdivision in Algorithm 3.1 can be achieved by dividing each candidate interval in half along the midpoint of a single dimension. By storing the index of the last subdivided dimension with each region, the algorithm can cyclically subdivide all dimensions of the initial region, ensuring that the width of candidate regions tends to 0 as the number of iterations increases. On the other hand, by knowing properties of the constraint system whose solutions are sought, we can often deduce smaller regions that bound the solutions, especially through the use of interval Newton methods [TOTH85,RATS88,SNYD92b]. The Hansen-Greenberg algorithm is an efficient method for finding zeroes of a function [RATS88] and uses exhaustive subdivision, interval Newton methods, and local Newton methods.

3.1.1 The Problem of Indeterminacy

Algorithm 3.1 finds a set of intervals bounding the solutions to the constraint system. In particular, by the property of inclusion functions, if this algorithm finds no solutions, then the constraint system has no solutions, because a region Y is rejected only when $\Box F(Y)$ shows that it is infeasible. It can also be proved that the constraint solution algorithm converges to the actual solution set, when the inclusion functions used in the equality and inequality constraints are convergent (see, for example, [SNYD92b]).

Unfortunately, a computer implementation of the constraint solution algorithm can not iterate forever; it must terminate at some iteration n and accept the remaining regions as solutions. Especially when equality constraints are used, the algorithm may accept some indeterminate regions, which may contain zero, one, or more solutions, when these regions satisfy the solution acceptance set constraint. This problem is mitigated by several factors.

First, it may be enough to distinguish between the case that the constraint problem possibly has solutions (to some tolerance), and the case that it has no solutions. For example, to compute interference detection between two parametric surfaces, $S_1, S_2: \mathbf{R}^2 \to \mathbf{R}^3$, a constraint system of three equations in four variables can be solved of the form

$$S_1(u_1, v_1) = S_2(u_2, v_2)$$

If we instead solve the relaxed constraint problem,

$$\|S_1(u_1, v_1) - S_2(u_2, v_2)\| < \epsilon$$

the algorithm can hope to produce feasible solution regions, for which the constraints are satisfied for every point in the region.[7] Such relaxed con-

---

[5] It should also be noted that to implement this mean value form on a computer, the interval $\Box f([c, c])$ should replace $f(c)$. This is because the computer can not *exactly* compute $f(c)$ and must instead bound the result.

[6] The initial region X can be infinite if the technique of *infinite interval arithmetic* is used (see [RATS88]).

[7] Note that the solution to the unrelaxed system is typically a curve of intersection between the two parametric surfaces. Any neighborhood of a point on this curve will also contain points for which the two surfaces do not intersect and hence do not solve the system of equations. The relaxed problem, on the other hand, has solutions for which a neighborhood of small enough size is completely contained within the solution space.

straint problems are called ϵ-collisions in [VONH89]. If any feasible regions are found, the surfaces interfere, within the tolerance. If all regions are eventually found to be infeasible, the surfaces do not interfere within the tolerance, and in fact come no closer than ϵ. It is also possible that only indeterminate regions are accepted as solutions. In this case, we may consider the two surfaces to interfere to the extent that our limited floating point precision is able to ascertain.

Second, we may know a priori that the system has a single solution. Let the solution acceptance set constraint have the simple form

$$\Box A(Y) \equiv (w(Y) < \epsilon)$$

If the inclusion functions bounding the constraint equality and inequality functions are convergent, then the solution approximation produced by Algorithm 3.1 achieves any degree of accuracy as ϵ goes to 0.

Third, we may be able to compute information about solutions to the constraint system as the algorithm progresses. Section 3.2 presents a theorem specifying conditions computable with interval techniques under which a region contains exactly one zero of a system of equations.

Finally, we can relax the constraints of a constraint system and/or accept indeterminate results of the algorithm. In practice, although we can not guarantee the validity of such results, they are nevertheless useful.

3.1.2 Termination and Acceptance Criteria for Constraint Solution

SOLVE can be applied to five specific problems:

1. find a bound on the set of solutions
2. determine whether a solution exists
3. find one solution
4. find all solutions
5. solve a constrained partitioning problem

The following discussion analyzes the application of Algorithm 3.1 to these specific problems, making the distinction between *heuristic* approaches, in which the results are not guaranteed to be correct, and *robust* approaches, in which the results are guaranteed to be correct.

Algorithm 3.1 never rejects a region unless it contains no solutions to the constraint problem. Therefore, an unmodified Algorithm 3.1 can be used to robustly find a set of regions bounding the solutions to the constraint system. Such a solution superset is often useful in higher-level algorithms, such as the implicit curve approximation algorithm of Section 4. The solution superset can also be visualized to obtain a rough idea of the nature of the solutions, even if the solutions form a multidimensional manifold rather than a finite set of points.

To determine whether a solution exists, if the algorithm terminates with an empty list of solutions, then the algorithm should return the answer "no". If at any point the algorithm finds a feasible region, then the algorithm can immediately terminate with the answer "yes". If the algorithm finds only indeterminate regions, then nothing can be concluded with certainty. A heuristic solution is to return "yes" anyway. This heuristic approach can be made more robust through the choice of an appropriate solution acceptance set constraint. For example, in solving the system $f(x) = 0$ for a continuous function f, it is reasonable that a region, Y, before being accepted as a solution, should satisfy

$$w(\Box f(Y)) < \delta$$

for some small δ. The algorithm should report an error when none of the indeterminate regions satisfy the acceptance criteria, before the machine precision limit is reached during subdivision. A robust solution to the problem can be achieved by testing indeterminate regions for the existence of solutions, using the test of Section 3.2.

To find any single solution to a constraint system, Algorithm 3.1 may conclude that the entire starting region is infeasible, or find a feasible region. In the latter case, any point in the feasible region is chosen as a representative solution and the algorithm is halted. Indeterminate regions are heuristically accepted when they satisfy the solution acceptance set constraint. They may also be tested for the existence of solutions, again using the test of Section 3.2.

Algorithm 3.1 can also be applied to the problem of finding all solutions to a constraint system, when a finite set of solutions is expected. Again, if

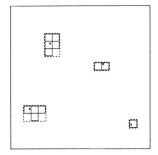

Figure 2: Solution aggregation – The solution regions returned by Algorithm 3.1 are the collection of nondashed squares. The actual solutions are marked by dots. An adequate level of subdivision has been achieved so that sets of contiguous regions encompass each of the four solutions, and each contiguous region may be bounded in an interval (dashed boxes) that is disjoint from other such regions.

the algorithm terminates with an empty solution list, there are no solutions. If a feasible region is found, an infinite number of solutions exist. If only indeterminate regions are found, then a useful heuristic approach is to union all contiguous solution regions into a set of mutually disjoint aggregate regions, as shown in Figure 2. A point inside each aggregate region is picked as a solution. If the number of solutions is known beforehand, then the algorithm can be terminated with an error condition if the machine precision is reached in subdivision with a number of aggregated regions unequal to the number of solutions. Of course, we note that although this approach almost always works correctly, it is still heuristic, since, for example, one region may contain no solutions while another contains two. A robust approach is to test for solution existence in each aggregated region. In this case, reaching the machine precision limit during subdivision without being able to verify solution existence should result in an error termination.

Finally, to solve a constrained partitioning problem, Algorithm 3.1 must be slightly modified so that it adds a region to the solution only when $\Box A$ is true, regardless of the value of $\Box F$. Alternatively, the constraint inclusion can be set so that it returns true (i.e., the constant $[1, 1]$) for all regions. The solution acceptance set constraint then becomes the set constraint of the constrained partitioning problem.

3.2 Interval Tests for Solution Existence and Uniqueness

An interesting and useful result can be proved that guarantees the existence of a unique zero of the function $f: \mathbf{R}^n \to \mathbf{R}^n$ in an interval domain X.

Theorem 3.1 (Bao-Rokne 1987) Let $f: \mathbf{R}^n \to \mathbf{R}^n$ be continuously differentiable in an interval domain X, and let $c \in X$. Let $\Box J$ be the interval Jacobian matrix of f over X, i.e.,

$$\Box J \equiv \left\{ J \mid J_{ij} \in \Box \frac{\partial f_i}{\partial x_j}(X) \right\}$$

Let Q be the solution set of the linear interval equation in x

$$f(c) + \Box J(x - c) = 0$$

That is,

$$Q \equiv \{x \mid \exists J \in \Box J \text{ such that } f(c) + J(x - c) = 0\}$$

If $Q \neq \emptyset$ and $Q \subseteq X$, then f has a unique zero in X.

A proof of this theorem can be found in [SNYD92b]. The hypothesis of the theorem can be verified using practical computations in several ways. First, if the interval determinant of $\Box J$ is not 0, then

$$Q \subset c - \Box J^{-1} f(c)$$

where $\Box J^{-1}$ is the interval matrix inverse of $\Box J$. We can therefore compute the interval inverse of the Jacobian matrix $\Box J$, compute

$$Q^* \equiv c - \Box J^{-1} f(c)$$

and verify that $X \subset Q^*$, in order to show the existence of a unique solution in X. Other methods involve Gauss-Sidel iteration on the linear equation [RATS88], or use of linear optimization [SNYD92b].

We note that the theorem is not useful in every case, since if there is a zero of f in X at p, and the determinant of the Jacobian of f at p is 0, then we can never verify solution uniqueness using this theorem. We also note that an interval test for solution existence (but not necessarily uniqueness) can be found in [MOOR80]. The appendix discusses a test that indicates when a region has **at most** one zero.

3.3 Minimization Algorithm

The constrained minimization problem involves finding the global minimum (or global minimizers) of a function $f: \mathbf{R}^n \to \mathbf{R}$ for all points that satisfy a constraint function $F: \mathbf{R}^n \to \{0, 1\}$. This constraint function is defined exactly as in Section 3.1.

Algorithm 3.2 (MINIMIZE) We are given a constraint inclusion function $\Box F$, a solution acceptance set constraint, $\Box A$, an inclusion function for the objective function, $\Box f$, and an initial region, X. The variable u is a progressively refined least upper bound for the value of the objective function f evaluated at a feasible point. Regions are inserted into the priority queue L so that regions with a smaller lower bound on the objective function f have priority.

```
place X on priority queue L
initialize upper bound u to +∞
while L is nonempty
        get next region Y from L
        if □A(Y) = [1, 1] add Y to solution
        else
                subdivide Y into regions Y₁ and Y₂
                evaluate □F on Y₁ and Y₂
                if □F(Yᵢ) = [0, 0] discard Yᵢ
                evaluate □f on Y₁ and Y₂
                if lb □f(Yᵢ) > u discard Yᵢ
                insert Yᵢ into L according to lb □f(Yᵢ)
                if Yᵢ contains an identified feasible point q
                        u = min(u, f(q))
                else if Yᵢ contains an unidentified feasible point
                        u = min(u, ub □f(Yᵢ))
                endif
        endif
endwhile
```

Let the region U_n^i be the i-th region on the priority queue L after n while loop iterations of the algorithm. Let u_n be the value of u at iteration n, and let l_n be given by

$$l_n \equiv \text{lb } \Box f(U_n^1)$$

The interval U_n^1 is called the *leading candidate interval*, and has the smallest lower bound for the value of f. Let f^* be the minimum value of the objective function subject to the constraints. We note that if a region X contains feasible points for the constraint function F, then f^* exists. Given existence of a feasible point, an important property of Algorithm 3.2 is

$$l_n \leq f^* \leq u_n \quad \forall n$$

Algorithm 3.2 suffers the same problems that Algorithm 3.1 does, in that an indeterminate region (i.e., a region Y for which $\Box F(Y) = [0, 1]$), may or may not include feasible points of the system of constraints. This implies that the algorithm may accept indeterminate regions as solutions that are, in fact, infeasible. Moreover, if the constraints can never be satisfied exactly, (e.g., they are represented using equality constraints), then all candidate regions are indeterminate, so that u is never updated. In this case, the algorithm is unable to reject any of the candidate regions on the basis of the objective function bound and accepts all indeterminate regions as solutions.

A robust solution to this problem is to use an existence test, such as the one presented in Section 3.2, to verify that a region contains at least one feasible point. A heuristic approach is to consider indeterminate regions of small enough width as if they contained a feasible point. These indeterminate regions may be subjected to an appropriate acceptance test that provides more confidence that the region contains a feasible point.

Algorithm 3.2 can be enhanced with techniques that find feasible points, feasible points with a smaller value of the objective function, or feasible regions in which the objective function is monotonic with respect to any input variable [RATS88].

3.3.1 Termination and Acceptance Criteria for Minimization

A constrained minimization problem can be "solved" in three ways:

1. find the minimum value of the objective function

2. find one feasible point that minimizes the objective function

3. find all feasible points that minimize the objective function

Slight modifications to Algorithm 3.2 regarding when the algorithm is halted and when indeterminate regions are accepted as solutions can make it applicable to each of these specific subproblems.

To find the minimum value of the objective function, f^*, Algorithm 3.2 should be terminated when a leading candidate interval, U_n^1, is encountered with $w(\Box f(U_n^1))$ sufficiently small, given that U_n^1 contains at least one feasible point.[8] In this case, the value $f(q)$ should be returned for some $q \in U_n^1$. This approach is justified because if U_n^1 contains a feasible point then

$$\text{lb } \Box f(U_n^1) \leq f^* \leq \text{ub } \Box f(U_n^1)$$

This approach presumes that we can verify the presence of a feasible point in an indeterminate region before the machine precision is reached in subdivision. Lack of this verification should result in some form of error termination. A heuristic approach is to accept indeterminate regions of small enough width (and, possibly, satisfying other criteria) as though they contained a feasible point.

Finding one or all minimizers of the objective function is a difficult problem that is currently not amenable to completely robust solution. Under certain conditions[9], Algorithm 3.2 converges, in a theoretical sense, to the set of global minimizers of the minimization problem. In practice however, we obtain a bound on the set of global minimizers after a finite number of iterations. Although techniques exist to verify whether a given interval in this bound contains a local minimizer of the minimization problem, we will not know, in general, if these local minimizers are also global minimizers.

If we know, a priori, that a single global minimizer exists, then the technique of solution aggregation (Section 3.1.2) can be used to collect candidate solutions into a single interval. We can then verify that the width of this interval tends to zero as the algorithm iterates. If we expect a finite set of global minimizers, then a reasonable heuristic approach is to aggregate solutions, and pick a point in each aggregated region as a global minimizer. Such an aggregated region should be small enough in width and satisfy other acceptance criteria that increase confidence that it contains a global minimizer.

4 Example: Approximating Implicit Curves

An implicit curve is the solution to a constraint system $F(x) = 1$, $x \in X \subset \mathbf{R}^n$, such that the solution forms a 1D manifold. Implicit curves are extremely useful in geometric modeling, especially for CSG and trimming operations on parametrically described shapes. They represent, for example, the intersection of two parametric surfaces in $\mathbf{R}^3$, or the silhouette edges of a parametric surface in $\mathbf{R}^3$ with respect to a given view.

The robustness of the algorithm presented here is superior to local methods such as [TIMM77,BAJA88]. Timmer's method, for example, separates implicit curve approximation into a hunting phase, where intersections of the implicit curve with a preselected grid are computed, and a tracing phase, where the curve inside each grid cell is traced to determine how to connect the intersections.

The new algorithm computes points on the implicit curve using Algorithm 3.1, guaranteeing a bound on the result. This method is superior to

---

[8]If all candidate intervals are rejected, then no feasible points exist in the original region, so f^* does not exist.

[9]A sufficient condition is the existence of a sequence of points in the interior of the feasible domain that converges to a global minimizer [RATS88].

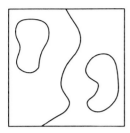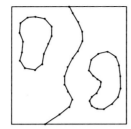

Figure 3: Implicit curve approximation – The figure on the left shows an implicit curve satisfying the algorithm's assumptions. It consists of three segments: two closed segments, and one segment intersecting the boundary of the interval of consideration. The figure on the right shows an approximation of the implicit curve. In this case, the algorithm produces three linked lists of points as output, one for each segment of the implicit curve.

local methods, such as Newton iteration, which are not guaranteed to converge. Timmer's method also fails to find a disjoint segment of the curve if it lies completely within one grid cell, while the proposed algorithm uses a global parameterizability criterion that subdivides parameter space until no curve segment can be lost. The algorithm is similar to the one described in [SUFF90], but differs in three respects: it uses this global parameterizability criterion, it handles multivariate implicit curves, and it incorporates an approximation quality metric.

4.1   An Implicit Curve Approximation Algorithm

The following are inputs to the approximation algorithm:

1. an interval $X \in \mathbf{I}^n$, called the *interval of consideration*, in which to approximate the implicit curve.

2. an inclusion function $\Box F(Y)$, $Y \in \mathbf{I}(X)$ for the constraint system defining the implicit curve.

3. an inclusion function $\Box A(Y)$, $Y \in \mathbf{I}(X)$, called the approximation acceptance inclusion function. This inclusion function tells when an interval Y is small enough that each segment of the implicit curve it contains can be approximated by a single interpolation segment between a pair of solution points.

The algorithm works by subdividing the region X into subregions, called *proximate intervals*, that contain the implicit curve, satisfy the approximation acceptance inclusion function, and allow simple computation of the local topology of the curve. The algorithm makes the following assumptions:

1. The solution to the constraint system $F(x) = 1$ is a continuous, 1D manifold. This implies that the solution contains no self-intersections, isolated singularities, or solution regions of dimensionality greater than 1. It further implies that each disjoint curve segment of the solution is either closed or has endpoints at the boundary of the region X.

2. The intersection of the solution curve with a proximate interval's boundaries is either empty or a finite collection of points, not a 1D manifold. This assumption is unimportant for implicit curves with no segments entirely along the parametric axes. When the implicit curve does have such segments, the constraint system must be reposed (often simply by a linear transformation of the parametric coordinates) as discussed in [SNYD92b].

Under these assumptions, each point on the implicit curve is linked to two neighbors, or possibly a single neighbor if the point is on the boundary of X. The output of the approximation algorithm is a list of "curves", where each curve is a linked list of points on a single, disjoint segment of the implicit curve, as shown in Figure 3.

Algorithm 4.1 (Implicit Curve Approximation)

1. **Subdivide X into a collection of proximate intervals bounding the implicit curve and satisfying the approximation acceptance inclusion function.** This can be accomplished using Algorithm 3.1. Figure 4 shows an example of a collection of proximate intervals.

2. **Check each proximate interval for global parameterizability.** The implicit curve contained in a proximate interval Y is called *globally parameterizable in a parameter i* if there is at most one point in Y on the curve for any value of the i-th parameter (see Figure 5). If the implicit curve is not globally parameterizable in Y for any parameter, then Y is recursively subdivided and tested again.

3. **Find the intersections of the implicit curve with the boundaries of each proximate interval, using Algorithm 3.1.** Assumption 2 implies that this intersection will be empty or a finite collection of points.

4. **Ensure that the boundary intersections are disjoint in the global parameterizability parameter.** Let i be the global parameterizability parameter for a proximate interval Y, computed from Step 2. This step checks that intersections of the implicit curve with Y's boundary are non-overlapping in coordinate i, as shown in Figure 6, so that they can be unambiguously sorted in increasing order of coordinate i.

   If Y's boundary intersections are not disjoint in parameter i, Y is recursively subdivided and retested.

5. **Compute the connection of boundary intersections in each proximate interval.** If an interval Y contains no boundary intersections, it can be discarded, because the global parameterizability condition implies that the solution cannot be a closed curve entirely contained in Y. Nor can the solution be a curve segment that does not intersect Y's boundary, by Assumption 1. If Y contains a single boundary intersection, then the solution is either tangent to a boundary of Y or passes through a corner of Y, but does not intersect the interior of Y.

   If Y contains more than one boundary intersection, the boundary intersections are sorted in order of the global parameterizability parameter i. For each pair of boundary intersections adjacent in parameter i, Algorithm 3.1 is used to see if the solution curve intersects the i-th parameter hyperplane midway between the two boundary intersections, as shown in Figure 7. If so, the boundary intersections are connected in the local curve topology linked list.

6. **Find the set of disjoint curve segments comprising the implicit curve.** After the implicit curve has been traced inside of each proximate interval, the list of connected boundary intersections is traversed, using the following algorithm

   ```
   let S be the set of boundary intersections
   while S is nonempty
         remove an intersection point P from S
         find and remove all points Q in S that are
               (indirectly) connected to P
         associate P and the set Q with a new curve
   endwhile
   ```

We note that in accumulating the set of points on a particular curve using this algorithm, if a point $P' \in Q$ is eventually found such that $P = P'$ then the curve is closed. Otherwise, the curve has two endpoints on the boundary of X by Assumption 1.

Step 1 of the algorithm combines the constraint inclusion with the approximation acceptance inclusion to create an initial collection of proximate intervals bounding the implicit curve (subproblem 1 in Section 3.1.2). Step 2 ensures that each proximate interval satisfy a global parameterizability criterion. The appendix presents a theorem identifying conditions for global parameterizability, computable with interval techniques already discussed. This theorem pertains to the special case of a system of $n - 1$ continuously differentiable equality constraints in n parameters. We have also developed a more general but heuristic test for global parameterizability, discussed in [SNYD92b].

Step 3 of the algorithm computes the intersections of the implicit curve with the boundary of each proximate interval. Algorithm 3.1 is used with the original constraint inclusion, $\Box F$, and an initial region formed by one of the $2n$ $(n - 1)$-dimensional hyperplanes bounding the proximate interval. For each boundary hyperplane, Algorithm 3.1 searches for all the constraint system's solutions, producing a set of intervals bounding the solutions, called *boundary intersection intervals*. Boundary intersection intervals that are shared along edges or corners of contiguous proximate intervals should be merged, as discussed in [SNYD92b].

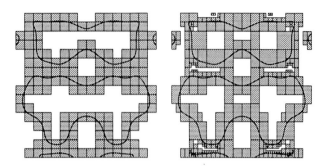

Figure 4: Collection of proximate intervals bounding an implicit curve – In these examples, the constraint system is given by the equation

$$x^2 + y^2 + \cos(2\pi x) + \sin(2\pi y) + \sin(2\pi x^2)\cos(2\pi y^2) = 1$$

The interval of consideration is $[-1.1, 1.1] \times [-1.1, 1.1]$. The approximation acceptance inclusion function for the left example simply requires that the width of the parameter space interval should be less than 0.2, while that on the right guarantees the global parameterizability of the solution in each interval.

I. Examples Globally Parameterizable in x

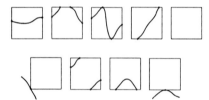

II. Examples Not Globally Parameterizable in x

III. Examples Not Allowed by Assumptions

Figure 5: Global parameterizability – The figure illustrates some of the possible behaviors of an implicit curve in an interval.

Steps 4 and 5 link boundary intersection intervals that are connected by the same segment of the implicit curve. Boundary intersection intervals are sorted in the global parameterizability parameter, and each pair of adjacent intersections is tested. The test uses Algorithm 3.1 to discover whether the implicit curve intersects a hyperplane midway between the pair of intersections. This application of the constraint algorithm need only ascertain whether a solution exists; the location of the intersection point is not required. On the other hand, the intersection point can be used to better approximate the implicit curve's behavior between the boundary intersections, at little extra computational cost.

Finally, after all proximate intervals have been examined, Step 6 associates each of the boundary intersection intervals with a disjoint segment of the implicit curve. A point inside each of the boundary intersection intervals should be chosen to represent the actual point of intersection of the proximate interval's boundary with the implicit curve. This point can be chosen arbitrarily (e.g., midpoint of the interval) or computed using a local iterative technique such as Newton's method.

We note that an algorithm similar to Algorithm 4.1 can be used to generate approximations of implicit surfaces [SNYD92a]. This algorithm also uses the global parameterizability criterion described in the appendix, for the case

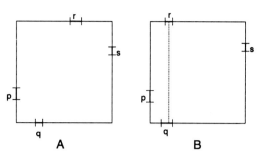

Figure 6: Boundary intersection sortability – Figure A illustrates a 2D interval containing four boundary intersections that are disjoint in the x parameter (horizontal axis). They can therefore be sorted in x, yielding the ordering p, q, r, s. In figure B, boundary intersections q and r are not disjoint in x (the dashed line shows a common x coordinate).

I. Boundary Intersections of an Implicit Curve

II. Eight Cases of Implicit Curve Behavior

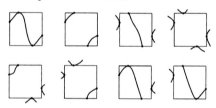

III. Not Allowed by Global Parameterizability

Figure 7: Global parameterizability and the linking of boundary intersections – In this figure, we assume an implicit curve defined in $\mathbf{R}^2$ is globally parameterizable in x in an interval. The implicit curve has four intersections with the interval's boundary, as shown in I. Because of global parameterizability and the curve approximation algorithm's assumptions, there are only eight possible ways the implicit curve can connect the boundary intersections, as shown in II. The possibilities shown in III are not globally parameterizable in x, and are therefore excluded. To disambiguate between these eight cases, we need only see if the implicit curve intersects the x hyperplane (dashed vertical line in I) between each pair of adjacent boundary intersections.

of a 2D manifold rather than a 1D manifold.

5 Results

Figures 8 through 11 illustrate the results of the interval analysis algorithms. Running times for the examples ranged from about 5 seconds for the computation of the minimum distance between two parametric surfaces (Figure 11) to several minutes for the CSG example (Figure 8) on a HP9000 Series 835 Workstation.

6 Conclusions

We have shown how a variety of important problems in computer graphics can be solved using the technique of interval analysis. These problems include ray tracing, computation of toleranced polygonal decompositions, detection of collisions, computation of CSG operations, approximation of silhouette curves, and many others. We have described two general algorithms, constraint solution and constrained minimization, which can solve these problems either directly, or when used in a higher level algorithm such as the implicit curve approximation algorithm of Section 4.

The advantage of the approach advocated here is twofold. Robust solution of computer graphics problems is achieved because interval analysis controls numerical error. A simple implementation is achieved because only two basic algorithms are necessary, which require inclusion functions for functions relevant to the problem. Definition of inclusion functions is not difficult; natural interval extensions, a particular type of inclusion function, can be defined by implementing an inclusion function method for each operator used in the relevant functions (e.g., the arithmetic operators and the cosine operator of Section 2.3). Mean value forms, another type of inclusion function, can be defined using natural interval extensions and a derivative operator. An entire, very powerful geometric modeling system can be built upon a set of operators each having an inclusion method, such as the system described in [SNYD92a,SNYD92b].

Acknowledgments

I would like to thank Al Barr for his support and encouragement of the publication of this research. Al Barr and Ronen Barzel have provided many helpful comments and suggestions. This work was funded, in part, by IBM, Hewlett-Packard, and the National Science Foundation.

References

[ALEF83]   Alefeld, G., and J. Herzberger, *Introduction to Interval Computations,* Academic Press, New York, 1983.

[BAJA88]   Bajaj, C., C. Hoffman, J. Hopcroft, and R. Lynch, "Tracing Surface Intersections," *Computer Aided Geometric Design,* 5, 1988, pp. 285-307.

[KALR89]   Kalra, Devendra, and Alan H. Barr, "Guaranteed Ray Intersections with Implicit Surfaces," *Computer Graphics,* 23(3), July 1989, pp. 297-304.

[MITC90]   Mitchell, Don, "Robust Ray Intersections with Interval Arithmetic," Proceedings Graphics Interface '90, May 1990, pp. 68-74.

[MITC91]   Mitchell, Don, "Three Applications of Interval Analysis in Computer Graphics," Course Notes for Frontiers in Rendering, Siggraph '91.

[MOOR66]   Moore, R.E., *Interval Analysis,* Prentice Hall, Englewood Cliffs, New Jersey, 1966.

[MOOR79]   Moore, R.E., *Methods and Applications of Interval Analysis,* SIAM, Philadelphia.

[MOOR80]   Moore, R.E., "New Results on Nonlinear Systems," in *Interval Mathematics 1980,* Karl Nickel, ed., Academic Press, New York, 1980, pp. 165-180.

[MUDU84]   Mudur, S.P., and P.A. Koparkar, "Interval Methods for Processing Geometric Objects," *IEEE Computer Graphics and Applications,* 4(2), Feb, 1984, pp. 7-17.

[RATS88]   Ratschek, H. and J. Rokne, *New Computer Methods for Global Optimization,* Ellis Horwood Limited, Chichester, England, 1988.

[SEGA90]   Segal, Mark, "Using Tolerances to Guarantee Valid Polyhedral Modeling Results," *Computer Graphics,* 24(4), August 1990, pp. 105-114.

[SNYD91]   Snyder, John, *Generative Modeling: An Approach to High Level Shape Design for Computer Graphics and CAD,* Ph.D. Thesis, California Institute of Technology, 1991.

[SNYD92a]   Snyder, John, "Generative Modeling: A Symbolic System for Geometric Modeling," to be published in Siggraph '92.

[SNYD92b]   Snyder, John, *Generative Modeling for Computer Graphics and CAD: Symbolic Shape Design Using Interval Analysis,* to be published by Academic Press, summer 1992.

[SUFF90]   Suffern, Kevin G., and Edward Fackerell, "Interval Methods in Computer Graphics," Proceedings of Ausgraph '90, Melbourne, Australia, 1990, pp. 35-44.

[TIMM77]   Timmer, H.G., *Analytic Background for Computation of Surface Intersections,* Douglas Aircraft Company Technical Memorandum CI-250-CAT-77-036, April 1977.

[TOTH85]   Toth, Daniel L., "On Ray Tracing Parametric Surfaces," *Computer Graphics,* 19(3), July 1985, pp. 171-179.

[VONH87]   Von Herzen, Brian P. and Alan H. Barr, "Accurate Sampling of Deformed, Intersecting Surfaces with Quadtrees," *Computer Graphics,* 21(4), July 1987, pp. 103-110.

[VONH89]   Von Herzen, Brian P., *Applications of Surface Networks to Sampling Problems in Computer Graphics,* Ph.D. Thesis, California Institute of Technology, 1989.

[VONH90]   Von Herzen, B., A.H. Barr, and H.R. Zatz, "Geometric Collisions for Time-Dependent Parametric Surfaces," *Computer Graphics,* 24(4), August 1990, pp. 39-48.

Appendix – A Robust Test for Global Parameterizability

Consider an r-dimensional manifold defined as the solution to a system of $n - r$ equations in n parameters ($r \in \{0, 1, \ldots, n - 1\}$):

$$f_1(x_1, x_2, \ldots, x_n) = 0$$
$$\vdots$$
$$f_{n-r}(x_1, x_2, \ldots, x_n) = 0$$

Given a set of r parameter indices, $A = \{k_1, k_2, \ldots, k_r\}$, and an interval $X \in \mathbf{I}^n$, we define a *subinterval* of X over A as a set depending on r parameters ($y_1, y_2, \ldots, y_r$), $y_i \in X_{k_i}$, defined by

$$\left\{ x \in X \mid \begin{array}{ll} x_i = y_j & \text{if } i = k_j \in A \\ x_i \in X_i & \text{otherwise} \end{array} \right\}$$

Thus, a subinterval is an interval subset of X, r of whose coordinates are a specified constant, and the rest of whose coordinates are the same as in X.

The solution to a system of $n - r$ equations in n parameters is called *globally parameterizable* in the r parameters indexed by A over an interval X if there is at most one solution to the system in any subinterval of X over A. Put more simply, the system of equations is globally parameterizable if r parameters can be found such that there is at most one solution to the system for any particular value of the r parameters in the interval.

We define $\square J_{\{k_1, k_2, \ldots, k_r\}}(X)$, called the *interval Jacobian submatrix*, as an $(n - r) \times (n - r)$ interval matrix given by

$$\square J_{\{k_1, k_2, \ldots, k_r\}}(X) \equiv \left[\square \frac{\partial f_i}{\partial x_j}(X) \right]_{j \notin \{k_1, k_2, \ldots, k_r\}}$$

For an $n \times n$ interval matrix $\square M$, we write $\det \square M \neq 0$ if there exists no matrix $M \in \square M$ such that $\det M = 0$. The following theorem guarantees the global parameterizability of the solution in an interval X (for a proof, see [SNYD92b]).

Theorem A.1 (Interval Implicit Function Theorem) Let the constraint functions $f_i(x)$, $i = 1, 2, \ldots, n - r$ be continuously differentiable. Let a region $X \in \mathbf{I}^n$ exist such that

$$\det \square J_{\{k_1, k_2, \ldots, k_r\}}(X) \neq 0$$

Then the solution to the system of equations $f_i(x) = 0$ is globally parameterizable in the r parameters indexed by $\{k_1, k_2, \ldots, k_r\}$ over X.

In the case of approximation of a 1D solution manifold, $r = 1$; i.e., a system of $n - 1$ equations in n variables is to be solved. The theorem guarantees that if, in an interval X, we can find $n - 1$ parameters such that

$$\det \square J_{\{k\}}(X) = \det \left[\square \frac{\partial f_i}{\partial x_j} \right]_{j \neq k} \neq 0$$

then the solution manifold is globally parameterizable in X over the parameter x_k, and thus satisfies the constraint of Step 2. We can verify that

$$\det \square J_{\{k\}}(X) \neq 0$$

by forming an inclusion function for the determinant of any of the n interval Jacobian submatrices using the interval arithmetic presented in Section 2.2.

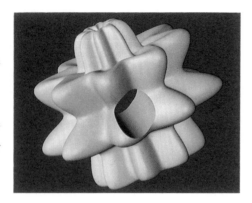 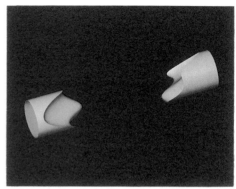

Figure 8: CSG Example. Algorithm 4.1 was used to find the curve of intersection between a bumpy sphere surface and a cylinder surface. The output of the algorithm was used in a parametric trimming operation, resulting in the subtraction of the cylinder from the bumpy sphere on the left, and the subtraction of the bumpy sphere from the cylinder on the right.

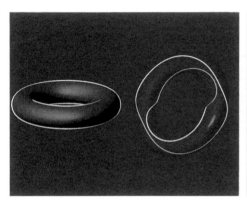 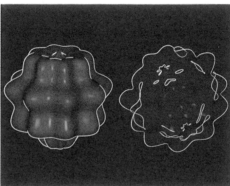

Figure 9: Silhouette Edge Detection Example. The figures show the results of the implicit curve approximation algorithm to approximate the silhouette curve of a parametric surface, $S(u, v)$, with respect to a given (in this case, orthographic) view. The implicit curve is the solution in two variables, u and v, of the equation $E \cdot \left(\frac{\partial S}{\partial u} \times \frac{\partial S}{\partial v} \right) = 0$ where $S(u, v)$ is the parametric surface and E is the viewing direction.

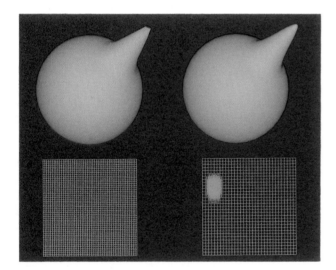 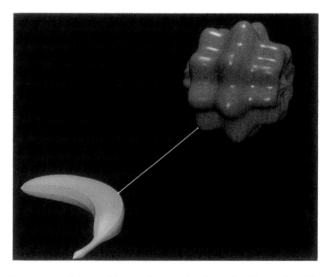

Figure 10: Polygonal Decomposition Example. The figure on the left shows polygonal decomposition based on uniform sampling in parameter space. On the right, the same surface has been decomposed using a slightly smaller number of triangles, using the constrained partitioning algorithm, which subdivides the parameter space (shown below the two surfaces) until the maximum variation in the surface normal is below a threshold. Polygonal artifacts on the highly curved projection are much reduced.

Figure 11: Minimum Distance Computation Example. The results of the minimization algorithm to find the minimum distance between two parametric surfaces is displayed. The green line connects the points on the two surfaces closest to each other. In this case, a single global minimizer was found for the unconstrained minimization problem of Formula 2 in Section 1.2.

Interval Arithmetic and Recursive Subdivision for Implicit Functions and Constructive Solid Geometry

Tom Duff†

AT&T Bell Laboratories
600 Mountain Avenue
Murray Hill, New Jersey 07974

Abstract

Recursive subdivision using interval arithmetic allows us to render CSG combinations of implicit function surfaces with or without anti-aliasing. Related algorithms will solve the collision detection problem for dynamic simulation, and allow us to compute mass, center of gravity, angular moments and other integral properties required for Newtonian dynamics.

Our hidden surface algorithms run in 'constant time.' Their running times are nearly independent of the number of primitives in a scene, for scenes in which the visible details are not much smaller than the pixels. The collision detection and integration algorithms are utterly robust — collisions are never missed due to numerical error and we can provide guaranteed bounds on the values of integrals.

CR Categories and Subject Descriptors: G.1.0 [Numerical Analysis] Numerical Algorithms I.3.3 [Picture and Image Generation] Display algorithms, Viewing algorithms, I.3.5 [Computational Geometry and Object Modeling] Curve, surface, solid and object representations, I.3.5 [Computational Geometry and Object Modeling] Hierarchy and geometric transformations. I.3.7 [Three-Dimensional Graphics and Realism] Visible line/surface algorithms, Animation

General Terms: Algorithms

Additional Keywords and Phrases: anti-aliasing, compositing, computer-aided animation, recursive subdivision, image synthesis, dynamic simulation, collision detection

1. Introduction

The most commonly-used geometric representations in computer graphics are local. Polygonal models, for example, specify which points are on an object's surface, and tell us nothing substantial about the rest of the space in which the object is embedded, except by omission. It requires substantial mental effort to formulate answers tp questions like "Do these objects intersect?", or "What parts of this object are visible?" or even something as simple as "What is the volume of this object?". More elaborate surface representations, like Bezier patches or NURBS don't make these questions any easier—since they only describe the objects locally, they make it difficult to answer global questions about them.

Likewise, the computational methods we normally use are mostly local. The ray-tracing algorithm, for example, tries to

†Phone (908) 582-6485, email td@research.att.com

compute an image one pixel at a time by testing every primitive in the scene for intersection with a ray from the eye-point through the pixel's center. Of course any decent ray-tracer goes to a lot of trouble to avoid most of this work. But an algorithm that had decent access to global information about the scene wouldn't need go to the trouble—it would know immediately what parts of the scene were relevant to what parts of the screen.

A good example of a global representation is the BSP tree [11]. Each node of a BSP tree gives useful information about the object's relationship to the whole of the space it's embedded in. The nodes effectively say about their subtrees, "in this half of space, you need only think about this half of the model." BSP trees naturally engender simple algorithms for all sorts of geometric tasks, from hidden surface removal to object intersection [23] to shadow generation [6], that make natural, effective use of the global information stored in the model.

This paper will examine in detail another global object representation and its algorithms, based on implicit functions, Constructive Solid Geometry and interval arithmetic.

Briefly, implicit functions are test functions for classifying points in space as inside, on or outside an object. Interval arithmetic allows us to extend those tests to whole chunks of space at once. Constructive Solid Geometry allows us to combine simpler objects, keep unwieldy primitives (like infinite cylinders) under control and model many important industrial and natural processes that go into creating geometric forms.

2. Implicit Functions

Implicit functions are an indirect representation of solid objects. Given a function of three variables $F(x,y,z)$, we can use the equation $F(x,y,z)=0$ to specify the points on a surface. The representable surfaces range from the mundane to the exotic: from planes $(ax+by+cz+d=0)$ and quadrics—the spheres, cones cylinders and paraboloids of elementary geometry—to more exotic polynomial surfaces like those of Kummer and Dupin [10] to Barr's downright weird twisted, bent and tapered super-ellipsoids [4].

If F is continuous, we can classify points as inside, on or outside the object depending on whether $F<0$, $F=0$ or $F>0$. This is the global property we are after: F classifies every point in space in its relationship to the surface. In regions of space not crossed by the surface, the fact that F's sign does not change is a source of coherence useful in hidden-surface and other geometric algorithms that can be exploited by using interval arithmetic to quickly obtain bounds on $F(x,y,z)$ for whole ranges of x, y and z.

3. Interval Arithmetic

Interval arithmetic [16] generalizes ordinary arithmetic to closed, bounded ranges of real numbers. If $\underline{X}$ and $\bar{X}$ are real numbers with $\underline{X} \le \bar{X}$, then X is an interval

$$X = [\underline{X}, \bar{X}] = \{ x \mid \underline{X} \le x \le \bar{X} \}$$

The natural interval extensions of the elementary operations of arithmetic are

$$X + Y = [\underline{X} + \underline{Y}, \overline{X} + \overline{Y}]$$

$$X - Y = [\underline{X} - \overline{Y}, \overline{X} - \underline{Y}]$$

$$X \times Y = [\min(\underline{XY}, \underline{X}\overline{Y}, \overline{X}\underline{Y}, \overline{XY}), \max(\underline{XY}, \underline{X}\overline{Y}, \overline{X}\underline{Y}, \overline{XY})] \quad (1)$$

$$X / Y = [1/\overline{Y}, 1/\underline{Y}], \text{ but undefined if } \underline{Y} \leq 0 \leq \overline{Y}$$

These definitions give tight bounds on the range of the corresponding real functions with arguments chosen in the given intervals. In particular, for degenerate intervals like $[a,a]$, interval arithmetic reproduces ordinary arithmetic. We can use these rules to compute bounds on the value of a rational expression $F(x,y,z)$ inside any box (X,Y,Z).

Unfortunately, the achievable bounds on general arithmetic expressions are not as tight as on the arithmetic operators. For example, $x^2 \in [0,1]$ when $x \in [-1,1]$, but, by (1), $x \times x = [-1,1]$. Generally, for intervals X, Y, Z,

$$\{F(x,y,z) \mid x \in X, y \in Y, z \in Z\} \subseteq F(X,Y,Z)$$

but we cannot replace $\subseteq$ by $=$ except in special circumstances.

A second source of looseness is that when using finite precision floating-point arithmetic, we must be sure to round the upper and lower bounds in the appropriate directions. Doing this is not the practical problem that it used to be — machines claiming to do IEEE arithmetic [12] are required to provide control of the rounding direction of floating-point calculations. If instead you use improperly-rounded interval arithmetic, the errors introduced will not often be noticeable. Of course, such an implementation voids the warranty of robustness.

Any $F(X,Y,Z)$ composed using the rules (1) above is an *interval extension* of the corresponding real function. That is, $F([x,x],[y,y],[z,z]) = [F(x,y,z), F(x,y,z)]$. Furthermore, F is *inclusion monotonic*. That is, if $X' \subseteq X$, $Y' \subseteq Y$ and $Z' \subseteq Z$, then $F(X',Y',Z') \subseteq F(X,Y,Z)$. Moore [16] is a good general introduction to interval methods, and discusses these properties and their implications in detail. For purposes of this paper, it is sufficient that if $x \in X$, $y \in Y$ and $z \in Z$ that $F(x,y,z) \in F(X,Y,Z)$. This is true for every inclusion monotonic interval extension of $F(x,y,z)$.

We can easily construct interval extensions of most standard transcendental functions. For monotonic functions like e^x, $\ln x$, $\sqrt{x}$, we have $F(X) = [F(\underline{X}), F(\overline{X})]$, or if $F(x)$ is monotone decreasing, $F(X) = [F(\overline{X}), F(\underline{X})]$. Continuous functions that have maxima and minima in known places, like sin and cos, can be handled by taking the union of their values over monotonic pieces. For example

$$X^n = \begin{cases} [\underline{X}^n, \overline{X}^n] & n \text{ odd or } \underline{X} \geq 0 \\ [\overline{X}^n, \underline{X}^n] & n \text{ even and } \overline{X} \leq 0 \\ [0, \max(-\underline{X}, \overline{X})^n] & n \text{ even and } \underline{X} < 0 < \overline{X} \end{cases}$$

These interval extensions all give tight bounds on the underlying transcendental functions, and expressions involving them yield inclusion monotonic interval extensions of the underlying real expressions.

If $\overline{F}(X,Y,Z) < 0$, we know that all points (x,y,z) with $x \in X$, $y \in Y$ and $z \in Z$ are located inside the implicit function surface F, and if $\underline{F}(X,Y,Z) > 0$ they are all outside. If $\underline{F}(X,Y,Z) \leq 0 \leq \overline{F}(X,Y,Z)$, we can guess that the surface might intersect the cell (we cannot be sure unless we know that the bounds we've computed are tight) and that it deserves closer examination.

4. Constructive Solid Geometry

A powerful and natural tool for taming implicit functions and building useful geometric models from them is Constructive Solid Geometry (CSG). Since implicit functions describe volumes as point-sets, we can use them as primitives and build more complicated models using set-theoretic union, intersection, complement and difference operators. The union and set-difference operators can model the most important ways that people build real objects. Milling machines, saws, drills, routers and chisels are all (restricted) set-difference engines. Glue, nails, soldering irons and Velcro are set-union agents—in the world of real solids, all unions are of disjoint sets. Set intersection allows us to focus attention on interesting or useful local features of implicit functions that may extend to infinity or otherwise behave wildly at a distance.

In general, we will represent an object or scene as a tree with implicit functions at its leaves and CSG operators at its interior nodes. We will assume that the only operators in the tree are union ($S \cup T$) and intersection ($S \cap T$). Set difference ($S - T$) and complement ($\neg S$) operators can be eliminated by repeatedly applying the rules

$$S - T \rightarrow S \cap \neg T$$

$$\neg(S \cup T) \rightarrow \neg S \cap \neg T$$

$$\neg(S \cap T) \rightarrow \neg S \cup \neg T$$

$$\neg F \rightarrow -F, \text{ where } F \text{ is a leaf function}$$

The first rule converts set differences into intersections. The second two (deMorgan's laws) push complement operators toward the leaves. The third absorbs complement operators into the leaf functions.

5. Rendering

Suppose we wish to make shaded images of a scene described as a CSG combination of implicit-function primitives. For simplicity, we will make an image by parallel projection in the z direction into the xy plane. (Perspective is a simple extension — we can either incorporate the viewing transformation directly into the CSG tree's leaf functions or decorate the CSG tree with transformation matrices and transform coordinates as we walk the tree.)

We are given a CSG tree and a rectangular viewing volume described by three intervals (X,Y,Z). For each leaf of the tree, we can do an interval computation to bound the value of the leaf's function in the viewing cell. If the upper bound is negative or the lower bound is positive, we can replace the leaf by the empty set $\varnothing$ or its complement U and simplify the tree by repeatedly applying the rules

$$\varnothing \cap S \rightarrow \varnothing, \quad U \cap S \rightarrow S$$

$$\varnothing \cup S \rightarrow S, \quad U \cup S \rightarrow U$$

Now we can divide the viewing cell into 8 pieces by dividing X, Y and Z at their midpoints and repeat this procedure recursively. At each level of subdivision, replacement of primitives by constants will further reduce the CSG tree—if we are lucky, the whole tree will reduce to a constant, in which case we need consider the cell no further, since it contains no surface. (We should always keep in mind that the reduced CSG trees are valid only within the corresponding cells.) Subdivision terminates when the bases of the cells are pixel-sized, at which point the reduced CSG tree should be very small—typically only the one or two primitives contributing to the image at the pixel.

At each level of subdivision we should first examine the sub-cells closest to the viewpoint and use a quad-tree or some equivalent data structure to keep track of which pixels are completely covered, allowing us easily to avoid examining more distant cells that will contribute nothing to the image. (This algorithm follows directly from the *vole* algorithm, described by Woodwark and Quinlan [25]. They use a similar subdivision scheme, but for CSG models whose only primitives are planar half-spaces, for which they need not resort to interval arithmetic to classify cells.)

The total expenditure required to sample the surface is nearly independent of the number of primitives in the model. This obviously cannot be true in the limit. Let us call a model "realistic" if by-and-large no more than a few primitive surfaces cross each pixel. (On a 1000×1000 screen, a model can have several million (small) primitives and still satisfy this requirement.) For realistic models, small cells will by-and-large contain reduced CSG trees with only a few nodes. Large cells, containing more complex trees, are *much* fewer in number — depending on how many cells are culled by the coverage quadtree, there are between three and seven times as many pixel-sized cells as there are cells of all other sizes combined. The great majority of the computation occurs in small cells, in which the size of the reduced CSG trees does not strongly depend on the complexity of the original model.

When we have subdivided to the pixel level, we can sample the image using ordinary ray-casting methods. We substitute the ray's parametric equation $(x,y,z) = A + \alpha(B - A)$, where A and B are appropriate points on the near and far planes of the subdivided cell, into each primitive of the reduced CSG tree and find all values of α where the primitives go to zero. We discard values of α for which the corresponding point is outside the object, as determined by substituting point coordinates into the leaves and evaluating the CSG operators. The smallest remaining α, if any, denotes the visible point on the surface. Papers by Amanatides and Mitchell ([14], [15], [1]) answer in much more detail questions that may arise in implementing this sort of ray-casting procedure.

6. Anti-aliasing

If point-sampling dissatisfies you (as it ought to!) then interval arithmetic can help do better. If we ignore for now the problems of highlight and texture aliasing (see [7], among numerous others, for apposite approaches to these aspects of the problem), then the anti-aliasing question hinges on identifying silhouette edges of primitives and intersection edges of CSG combinations.

Ideally, we would compute in their entirety the visible portions of all significant edges and use an exact convolution method like that of [9] to compute an anti-aliased image. As this appears to be too much to hope for, we must satisfy ourselves with a careful treatment of the simple cases that affect most pixels, approximating the rest as well as we can afford. (For simplicity, we will assume that we are using a box filter to sample the image although that is by no means a limitation of the method—see [9] for more relevant discussion. That is, we compute pixel values by integrating the scene's intensity across pixel-sized squares.)

As above, we will subdivide the viewing volume, reducing CSG trees as we go. When we reach pixel resolution, we will concentrate our best attention on cells that are completely covered by one primitive (figure 1a) or are crossed by a single visible edge. This edge will be either the silhouette edge of a tree with a single leaf (figure 1b) or an intersection edge in a two-leaf tree (figure 1c). We will treat more complicated situations (figure 1d) by subdividing the pixel, hoping to find a simpler situation in the

subpixels and giving up when their contribution to the image is tiny.

Suppose that each implicit function F at the leaves of our CSG tree has continuous partial derivatives. The silhouette of the surface $F = 0$ is precisely those points at which $\partial F / \partial z = 0$. So, let us use interval arithmetic to evaluate $\partial F / \partial z$ in our pixel-sized cell, calling the result S. If $0 \notin S$, the surface has no edge inside the cell. It may, however, protrude through the cell's front or back surface (figure 1e), giving a spurious edge crossing the pixel where the surface is clipped. An interval computation can alert us to this possibility. If $0 \in F(X, Y, [\bar{Z}, \bar{Z}])$ then F may pass through the far surface of the cell (X, Y, Z). Whenever we come to process a cell that contains such a surface, we save the CSG tree and the cell coordinates and defer processing the cell. When later we return to the cell behind it, we can merge the two cells and their trees before processing them. (Of course, if the CSG tree in the cell behind has been reduced to $\varnothing$ or U, we will not return to it. When later we return to the pixel for farther cells, we should first dispose of the saved tree by treating it as one of the more complicated cases mentioned above. You might, as I did initially, naively believe that this circumstance cannot occur — after all, if there is nothing in the cell behind, how could a surface cross the cell boundary? However, if one surface of an intersection passes through the back of a cell and the other does not, the cell behind may easily reduce to $\varnothing$.)

Now we are ready to handle the simple cases:

If the reduced CSG tree has only one leaf and $0 \notin S$, the primitive has no edges inside the cell (figure 1a) and may trivially be rendered by casting a ray through the pixel's center.

If the CSG tree has two leaves and $0 \notin S$ for each, then we have two possibly intersecting primitives F and G, neither with an edge in the cell (figure 1c). We will approximate their intersection curve by a straight line that runs from edge to edge of the pixel. We can cast four rays to find the Z coordinates at which the surfaces pass through the pixel corners. Then, following [8], we compare the z values at each corner. Along each pixel edge where the z's compare differently we linearly interpolate the z's to find a point at which they are equal. In any cell there will be zero, two or four such points. We join them up as in figure 2 (taken from [8]) and compute the quantity β, the total fraction of the pixel in which F is in front of G, according to our approximation. Now we need only determine which surface, if any, is visible in each part of the cell and compute their contributions, weighted by β, to the color of the cell. We can determine visibility by considering the CSG operator connecting the two surfaces, and whether the two surfaces face the viewer. For example, if F faces the viewer and G faces away, and the CSG operator is $\cap$, then we can see F inside the part of the pixel where it is in front, and nothing in the other part. The following table summarizes the contributions in all cases:

	F toward G toward	F toward G away	F away G toward	F away G away
$\cup$	$\beta F + (1-\beta)G$	$(1-\beta)G$	βF	$\beta G + (1-\beta)F$
$\cap$	$\beta G + (1-\beta)F$	βF	$(1-\beta)G$	$\beta F + (1-\beta)G$

If the reduced CSG tree has only one leaf and $0 \in S$, then there may be a silhouette edge in the cell, as in figure 1b. As before, we wish to approximate the edge by a segment running from edge to edge of the pixel. Again, we can cast rays through the pixel corners, but now we are interested only in identifying cell faces through which the edge must pass because the surface intersects one edge of the face but not the other. Having identified these faces (again there must be zero, two or four of them), we can find the silhouette's endpoints by solving systems

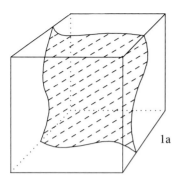 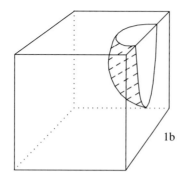 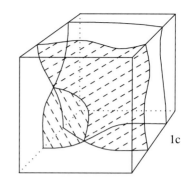

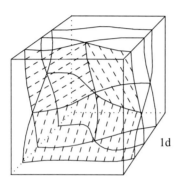 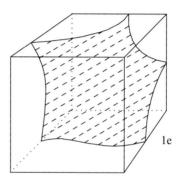

Figure 1 − Simple and non-simple cells

Figure 1a illustrates a cell completely covered by a single surface. 1b has a cell containing a single surface with a silhouette edge. 1c has a cell covered by a pair of intersecting surfaces. 1d is too complicated to be handled without subdivision. 1e illustrates a cell with a surface passing through its back face. Its processing will be deferred for merging with the cell behind it.

of three simultaneous equations: $F(x,y,z)=0$, $\partial F/\partial z=0$ and the plane equation of the cell face, one of $x=\underline{X}$, $x=\overline{X}$, $y=\underline{Y}$ or $y=\overline{Y}$. A useful optimization is to eliminate the cell face equation by substituting into the other two. Moore ([16] pp 62-68) outlines robust interval methods for producing these solutions.

As in the previous case, we can join these points by line segments (see figure 3) to find the fraction of the pixel covered by the surface. Note that this computation is not particularly robust — it is entirely possible for an edge to protrude a pixel without the surface passing through any vertex. Indeed, the whole surface may be contained within a single cell. But, we stated up front that we intended to approximate the silhouette by a sequence of line segments passing from pixel edge to pixel edge, and neither of these situations admits a reasonable approximation in those terms. A more robust computation that could identify these situations

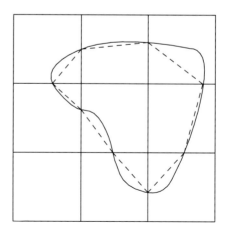

Figure 2 − Joining endpoints of edges

Each square represents a pixel. The corners are marked with the sign of $F-G$. The label in each pixel fragment indicates which surface is in front in it. β is the total area of the fragments labeled F.

Figure 3 − silhouette edge approximation

The squares are pixels. The closed curve is the a silhouette edge of a surface that intersects each pixel as in figure 1a. The dashed lines are our piecewise linear approximation to the silhouette.

and allow us to subdivide would be straightforward, if tedious, to implement.

Any situation not handled above we manage by further subpixel subdivision. We subdivide only in x and y, not z, further reducing the CSG tree as we go, stopping when we find a subpixel satisfying one of the above cases or in any case at some fixed depth. The contributions of the subpixel cells, weighted by subpixel area, are added to determine the color of their pixel-sized ancestor.

Since cells that partly cover pixels must allow the color of cells behind them to show through the uncovered parts, we store colors in the rgbα representation of Porter and Duff [19], using α-blending to composite each cell's color with the accumulated color of the cells in front of it. This can make mistakes in pixels that contain multiple visible edges. If this worries you, you can use a more elaborate compositing scheme, saving a list of previously-encountered edges against which to clip the newly-computed regions or keeping at each pixel a sub-pixel bit-mask (as in Carpenter's A-buffer [5], but simpler because we know depth order *a priori*) against which to clip the newly-computed regions.

7. Collision detection

Let us now turn our attention to motion computations for animation purposes. Suppose we have a scene composed of a number of CSG objects, and that we wish to compute their motion. At any point in time, we need to decide whether objects in the scene have collided, in order to prevent interpenetration and to compute the forces resulting from any collision.

Let the objects in the scene (considered as point-sets) be O_i, $0 \le i < n$. Then to compute an image we would run one of the above algorithms on the CSG tree for

$$\bigcup_{i=0}^{n-1} O_i \qquad (2)$$

To decide whether there has been a collision, we must decide whether there are points occupied by more than one object. To do this, we first build a CSG tree in which each of the top-level union operators (see equation 2) is specially marked. Now, we recursively subdivide a cell surrounding the entire scene, reducing the CSG tree at each subcell as before, except that for specially-marked top-level union operators we rewrite the tree using only the rule

$$\varnothing \cup S \rightarrow S$$

We do not reduce top-level instances of U using the rule $U \cup S \rightarrow U$ because we wish to count them. If at any level of subdivision the reduced CSG tree contains two or more top-level U's, we have detected a collision. Likewise, if the tree has no marked top-level union operator, there can be no collision in this cell and we need subdivide no further.

If we subdivide down to cells smaller than some tolerance without reaching a decision, we can declare the question unanswerable to within the given tolerance. This may strike you as unsatisfactory, and in fact we can make a much stronger statement. For all functions computed by sequences of arithmetic operations and transcendental functions, their natural interval extensions satisfy an *interval Lipschitz condition* (under certain mild assumptions.) That is, there is an easy-to-compute constant c, depending only on F and the domain of interest (say a viewing volume (X_0, Y_0, Z_0)), such that if $(X,Y,Z) \subseteq (X_0, Y_0, Z_0)$ then $\overline{F}(X,Y,Z) - \underline{F}(X,Y,Z) \le c \max(\overline{X} - \underline{X}, \overline{Y} - \underline{Y}, \overline{Z} - \underline{Z})$. (Again, we refer you to [16] pp 33-35 for further details, including a proof.) Informally, the size of the intervals $F(X,Y,Z)$ decreases at worst

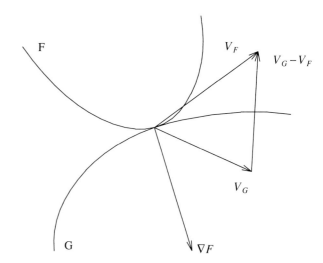

Figure 4 — collision

F and G are two colliding surfaces. ∇F is the normal to F at the point of collision. V_F and V_G are their velocities at the point of collision. Since the angle between ∇F and $V_G - V_F$ is larger than 90 degrees, surfaces are separating and the collision will be rejected.

linearly with the size of (X,Y,Z). Thus, when we abandon subdivision at a tolerance ε, we know that the surfaces touch to within some easily-computable tolerance $c\varepsilon$.

8. Dynamic Collision Detection

If we can describe the motion of O_i as a function of time, we can extend the above algorithm to find the earliest time in an animation at which a collision occurs. We need only subdivide in x, y, z and t, looking at subcells earlier in time before later cells and stopping when we first find a cell smaller than a collision tolerance ε that still contains parts of two intersecting objects.

At this point we will presumably do a momentum-transfer calculation and restart the collision detector with $t = t_{collision}$. But this will just re-detect the previous collision. We must reject collisions at which the objects are not approaching one another. Let the two objects be F and G, and let their velocities at the point of collision by V_F and V_G — see figure 4. G is moving towards F if the angle between its velocity (relative to F) and F's normal at the point of collision is larger than 90 degrees, that is if $\nabla F \cdot (V_G - V_F) < 0$. In an edge-to-edge or other complicated collision, F's gradient may be undefined. In that case, we must use the normal to the collision tangent plane as described by Baraff [3].

The sorts of motion that this scheme can accommodate are fairly general. Any time-varying coordinate mapping will do, as long as its inverse can be expressed in a closed form that admits an inclusion monotonic interval extension. For example, points on a rigid body tumbling and moving under gravity are transformed by

$$P = \text{rot}(\omega t, A) R(P' - C) + C + P_0 + V_0 t + \begin{bmatrix} 0 \\ -1/2 g t^2 \\ 0 \end{bmatrix} \qquad (3)$$

where

    $P = (x,y,z)^T$ is the transformed point,
    $\text{rot}(\theta, axis)$ is a rotation matrix,
    ω is the object's rate of rotation,
    A is the axis about which it rotates,

R is a rotation matrix describing its orientation at $t = 0$,
P' is a coordinate in model-definition space,
C is the object's center of mass,
P_0 is its position at time $t = 0$,
V_0 is its velocity at time $t = 0$, and
g is the acceleration due to gravity.
The inverse of (3) is just

$$P' = R^T \text{rot}(-\omega t, a)(P - C - P_0 - V_0 t - \begin{bmatrix} 0 \\ -1/2 g t^2 \\ 0 \end{bmatrix}) + C$$

So, the implicit function $F(P')$ is just F as transformed by its motion.

More complex motions, like the modal deformations of Pentland and Williams [18] can be handled similarly. Constrained motions like those described by Barzel and Barr [2] and Baraff [3] for which the associated ODEs are generally insoluble in closed form are beyond the scope of the work reported here. Interval methods for ODEs are an interesting research problem and would be extremely helpful here. In their absence, we must use conventional ODE methods and accept the loss of robustness that they entail.

Pentland and Williams [18] claim to do collision detection of implicit functions (but not their CSG combinations) by converting one of a pair of objects to be tested into polygons. The objects intersect if any of the vertices gives a negative value when substituted into the other function. Sclaroff and Pentland [20] repeat this claim. But, their scheme does not work—it is easy for an object to pass through a polygonal face without meeting any of its edges. Even testing the polygonal representation of each object against the other will not work, as they can easily meet edge-to-edge with no vertex of either polygonization penetrating the other object. The methods presented here are utterly robust—interval arithmetic always provides guaranteed bounds on the functions we compute.

When we discover that two objects meet, we need to calculate the collision forces and their effects on the bodies' motions. To do this, we need to know in what direction the force is applied and some physical properties of the colliding bodies—particularly their masses and moments of inertia.

The information needed to calculate the direction of applied force is readily available when the collision is detected. Inside the cell in which the collision occurs the reduced CSG trees will include one or more surfaces from each of the colliding objects. If a single surface from one object or the other is involved, we need only compute its normal direction. If each object has two surfaces active, we have an edge-to-edge collision. We can find the edge directions by looking at intersections of tangent planes, and transmit the force as in [3]. More complicated situations represent indeterminate cases that can also be linearized by working with the tangent planes and handled as in [3].

9. Integral Properties

Mass and moments of inertia are *integral properties* of solid objects. Computing them involves evaluating simple definite integrals inside the objects' volumes. For example, to compute the mass of a body B, we need to evaluate

$$\iiint_B \rho(x, y, z) \, dx \, dy \, dz$$

where ρ is the density of the material. If ρ is easy to integrate over rectangular prisms (often it will be constant), we can recursively subdivide a cell surrounding B, reducing B's CSG tree

as we go, and accumulate the integral's value over those cells in which the reduced CSG tree is U. Cells whose reduced CSG trees are $\varnothing$ contribute nothing, and partially occupied cells will contain a vanishingly small fraction of B's volume as the subdivision limit decreases. (The fraction may not decrease as quickly as you'd like if the Hausdorff dimension of B's surface is larger than 2, but then you have worse problems since, for example, B's partial derivatives will be undefined.)

Other integral properties can be computed similarly. For example, B's moment of inertia about a particular axis is just

$$\iiint_B r^2 \rho(x, y, z) \, dx \, dy \, dz$$

where r is the distance from (x, y, z) to the axis in question.

10. Examples

Figures 5-9 show a variety of objects as rendered by our algorithms. Figure 5 is Kummer's surface with 16 real double-points (4 are at infinity) with malachite texture. This beautiful surface extends to infinity in 8 directions and would be useless for real applications without some sort of trimming. Figure 6 is the intersection of Kummer's surface and a sphere. Figure 7 is the intersection of a Parabolic Spindle Cyclide and a sphere with hideous orange marble texture. (Fischer [10] gives good detailed descriptions of these surfaces.) Figure 8 is an image of a face made using a 48×48 raster of intersecting marbles of varying sizes, just to show that we can handle scenes with a larger number of primitives. Figures 5-8 were all computed at 1024×1024 resolution using the point-sampling renderer described in section 5. Figure 9 is an anti-aliased rendering of a compound of 3 spheres, done at 256×256 resolution using the algorithm of section 6.

The videotape accompanying this paper shows two simple animations made using our dynamic collision detection and rendering algorithms. The first scene shows 9 balls falling onto a sphere with a dish carved out of its top. You can see the balls collide with the dish and, in one case, with each other. The second scene is similar, but with 25 balls. There are 80 collisions in this shot, mostly between pairs of balls.

11. Conclusion

We have presented a wide range of algorithms that use interval arithmetic and recursive subdivision of object space to process geometric objects described as CSG combinations of implicit function primitives.

The algorithms are all suited to manipulating extremely complex objects because they discard parts of the objects that are irrelevant to the subdivided cells. Their running times are only mildly influenced by the size of their inputs because small cells typically contain at most one or two surfaces. Presumably when the number of primitives in the original model is a large fraction of the number of pixels on the screen we will start to see greater dependence, as this assumption will begin to break down.

The algorithms of sections 7, 8 and 9 are quite robust—it is impossible to lose track of parts of objects due to rounding error when using interval arithmetic. The bounds it provides are absolutely guaranteed to enclose the exact function values. We can only run into trouble when we terminate subdivision at some *a priori* level, and even then the existence of interval Lipschitz conditions can help us set that level to bound the unavoidable error in our computations however we wish.

In retrospect, the work most closely related to ours is work by Al Barr and his colleagues on rendering and collision detection of functions with Lipschitz conditions [13], [24]. A Lipschitz condition (not to be confused with an interval Lipschitz condition) is a bound on a function's variation. Given an appropriate Lipschitz constant, one can easily bound a function's value on an interval, a sort of "interval arithmetic without the intervals." In fact, Lipschitz constants can be computed by interval evaluation of a function's derivatives, and those bounds converted into bounds on the original function using the mean value theorem. In this light it is perplexing that Kalra and Barr [13] put the question of 'identifying ... useful implicit functions and computing Lipshitz constants' for them first on their list of important problems to attack.

Recursive subdivision using interval arithmetic is a natural and versatile scheme to use for implicit function CSG models. We have only begun to scratch the surface of its potential applications. Our anti-aliased rendering method should be easily convertible into a polygonization algorithm. (Indeed, Snyder [22] gives an interval polygonization algorithm, along with many other applications of interval arithmetic.) Interval function minimization methods can provide global optima for many problems and should be applicable to some of the control problems in animation, and, as Don Mitchell has pointed out in conversation, to a range of global illumination problems as well.

Another problem that must be better addressed before we can consider wider use of implicit function surfaces is the problem of using them to model sculpted surfaces, a realm in which Bezier surfaces and NURBS reign. There is some hope that this situation will improve. [17] and [21] are two recent papers describing ideas that show a great deal of promise.

12. Acknowledgements

Don Mitchell is always a good friend and source of ideas and criticism. His paper on interval root-finding [14] put this bee in my bonnet, and his interval arithmetic routines made it possible to get the first version of this stuff going in a couple of days.

Andy Witkin suggested looking at collision detection.

A detailed and insightful referee's report contributed greatly to the paper's clarity and correctness.

13. References

[1] John Amanatides and Don P. Mitchell, "Some Regularization Problems in Ray Tracing," *Proc. Graphics Interface '90*, 1990

[2] Ronen Barzel and Alan H. Barr, "A Modeling System Based on Dynamic Constraints," *Computer Graphics* 22(3), July 1988, 179-188

[3] David Baraff, "Analytical Methods for Dynamic Simulation of Non-penetrating Rigid Bodies," *Computer Graphics* 23(3), July 1989, 223-231

[4] Alan H. Barr, "Global and Local Deformations of Solid Primitives," *Computer Graphics* 18(3), July 1984, 21-30

[5] Loren Carpenter, "The A-Buffer, An Anti-Aliased Hidden Surface Method," *Computer Graphics* 18(3), July 1984, 103-108

[6] Norman Chin and Steven Feiner, "Near Real-Time Shadow Generation Using BSP Trees," *Computer Graphics* 23(3), July 1989, 99-106

[7] Franklin C. Crow, "Summed Area Tables for Texture Mapping," *Computer Graphics* 18(3), July 1984, 207-212

[8] Tom Duff, "Compositing 3-D Rendered Images," *Computer Graphics* 19(3), July 1985, 270-275

[9] Tom Duff, "Polygon Scan Conversion by Exact Convolution," *Raster Imaging and Digital Typography '89*, Cambridge University Press, London, 1989

[10] Gerd Fischer, *Mathematische Modelle/Mathematical Models*, Friedr. Vieweg & Sohn, Braunschweig/Wiesbaden, 1986

[11] H. Fuchs, Z. M. Kedem and B. F. Naylor, "On Visible Surface Generation by *A Priori* Tree Structures," *Computer Graphics* 14(3), July 1980, 124-133

[12] *IEEE Standard for Binary Floating-Point Arithmetic*, ANSI/IEEE Std 754-1985, Institute of Electrical and Electronics Engineers, New York, 1985

[13] Devandra Kalra and Alan H. Barr, "Guaranteed Ray Intersections with Implicit Surfaces," *Computer Graphics* 23(3), July 1989, 297-306

[14] Don P. Mitchell, "Robust Ray Intersection with Interval Arithmetic," *Proc. Graphics Interface '90*, 1990

[15] Don P. Mitchell, "Spectrally Optimal Sampling for Distribution Ray Tracing," *Computer Graphics* 25(3), July 1991, 157-164

[16] Ramon E. Moore, *Methods and Applications of Interval Analysis*, Society for Industrial and Applied Mathematics (SIAM), Philadelphia, 1979

[17] Shugeru Muraki, "Volumetric Shape Description of Range Data using "Blobby Model"," *Computer Graphics* 25(4), July 1991, 227-235

[18] Alex Pentland and John Williams, "Good Vibrations: Model Dynamics for Graphics and Animation," *Computer Graphics* 23(3), July 1989, 215-222

[19] Thomas Porter and Tom Duff, "Compositing Digital Images," *Computer Graphics* 18(3), July 1984, 253-259

[20] Sclaroff and Alex Pentland, "Generalized Implicit Functions for Computer Graphics," *Computer Graphics* 25(4), July 1991, 247-250

[21] Thomas W. Sederberg and Alan K. Zundel, "Scan Line Display of Algebraic Surfaces," *Computer Graphics* 23(3), July 1989, 147-156

[22] John Snyder, *Generative Modeling: An Approach to High Level Shape Design for Computer Graphics and CAD*, Ph.D. Thesis, California Institute of Technology, 1991

[23] W. Thibault and B. F. Naylor, "Set Operations on Polyhedra Using Binary Space Partitioning Trees," *Computer Graphics* 21(4), July 1987, 153-162

[24] Brian von Herzen, Alan H. Barr and Harold R. Zatz, "Geometric Collisions for Time-Dependent Parametric Surfaces," *Computer Graphics* 24(4), August 1990, 39-48

[25] J. R. Woodwark and K. M. Quinlan, "Reducing the effect of complexity on volume model evaluation," *Computer-Aided Design* 14(2), March 1982, 89-95

Figure 5 — Kummer surface

Figure 6 — Sphere-Kummer intersection

Figure 7 — Sphere-Cyclide intersection

Figure 8 — 2304 Spheres

Figure 9 — Combination of 3 spheres, anti-aliased

Computing the Antipenumbra
of an Area Light Source

Seth J. Teller
University of California at Berkeley[‡]

Abstract

We define the *antiumbra* and the *antipenumbra* of a convex area light source shining through a sequence of convex areal holes in three dimensions. The antiumbra is the volume from which all points on the light source can be seen. The antipenumbra is the volume from which some, but not all, of the light source can be seen. We show that the antipenumbra is, in general, a disconnected set bounded by portions of quadric surfaces, and describe an implemented $O(n^2)$ time algorithm that computes this boundary, where n is the total number of edges comprising the light source and holes.

The antipenumbra computation is motivated by a visibility scheme in which we wish to determine the volume visible to an observer looking through a sequence of transparent convex holes, or *portals*, connecting adjacent cells in a spatial subdivision. Knowledge of the antipenumbra should also prove useful for rendering shadowed objects. Finally, we have extended the algorithm to compute the planar and quadratic surfaces along which the rate of areal variation in the visible portion of the light source changes discontinuously due to occlusion. These surfaces are relevant in polygon meshing schemes for global illumination and shadow computations.

CR Categories and Subject Descriptors: [Computer Graphics]: I.3.5 Computational Geometry and Object Modeling – *geometric algorithms, languages, and systems*; I.3.7 Three-Dimensional Graphics and Realism – *color, shading, shadowing, and texture*.

Additional Key Words and Phrases: Radiosity, aspect graph, discontinuity meshing, stabbing lines, Plücker coordinates.

1   Introduction

1.1   Penumbrae and Antipenumbrae

Suppose an area light source shines past a collection of convex occluders. The occluders cast shadows, and in general attenuate

[‡]Computer Science Department, Berkeley, CA 94720 (seth @cs.berkeley.edu)

or eliminate the light reaching various regions of space. There is a natural characterization of any point in space in this situation, depending on how much of the light source can be "seen" by the point. Figure 1 depicts a two-dimensional example. If the point sees none of the light source (that is, if all lines joining the point and any part of the light source intersect an occluder), the point is said to be in *umbra*. If the point sees some, but not all, of the light source, it is said to be in *penumbra*. Otherwise, the point may see all of the light source.

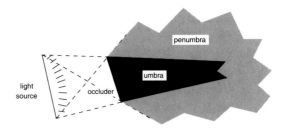

Figure 1: Umbra and penumbra of an occluder in 2D.

Imagine that the occluders are replaced by convex "holes," or transparent areas, in otherwise opaque planes. In a sense complementary to that above, every point in space can again be naturally characterized. We define the *antiumbra* cast by the light source as that volume from which the entire light source can be seen, and the *antipenumbra* as that volume from which some, but not all, of the light source can be seen (Figure 2). For a given light source and set of holes or occluders, the umbra is the spatial complement of the union of antiumbra and antipenumbra; similarly, the antiumbra is the spatial complement of the union of umbra and penumbra. Both the antiumbra and antipenumbra may be vacuous beyond the plane of the final hole, i.e., they may contain no points.

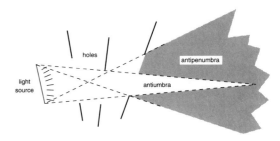

Figure 2: Antiumbra and antipenumbra of a series of holes in 2D.

For a *point* light source and a set of polygonal occluders in three

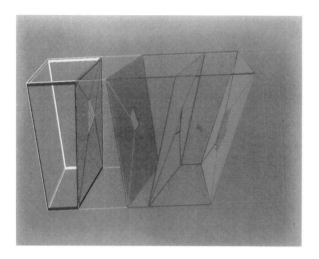

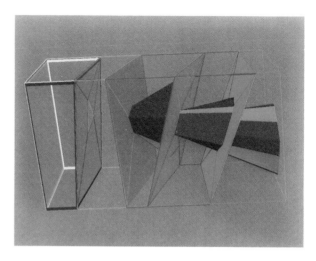

Figure 3: A spatial subdivision, the convex polyhedral cells of which are linked by convex polygonal transparent portals.

Figure 4: Successively narrowing antipenumbrae cast by the light source (here, the leftmost portal) through the cells of the subdivision.

dimensions, the penumbra is vacuous, and computing the umbra is straightforward [1, 7]. The problem becomes substantially more complex when the light source is lineal or areal. In general, as few as two occluders can give rise to shadows bounded by *reguli*, ruled quadric surfaces of negative Gaussian curvature [23], whose three generator lines arise from non-adjacent hole or light-source edges. Reguli were first used in the context of occlusion for the *aspect graph* computation, which catalogues all qualitatively distinct views of a polyhedral object under orthographic or perspective projection [14, 20]. At present, the best time bound for computing the aspect graph of a general polyhedral object with n vertices is $O(n^4 \lg n + m \lg m + c_t)$, where m is the number of qualitatively distinct views, at worst $O(n^6)$, and c_t the total number of changes between these views [10].

For a convex lineal or areal light source and a *single* convex occluder in 3D, the umbra and its union with the penumbra are convex. Such first-order shadows have been employed to yield convincing renderings of shadowed scenes [15, 16]. These penumbra algorithms, however, extend to multiple occluders only by effectively approximating the light source as a point or as a set of points. Several algorithms approximating multiple-occluder shadow boundaries have been described.

For example, in [16], the penumbra cast by multiple occluders is approximated by casting each occluder's penumbra individually, then performing polyhedral union and intersection operations on the result. An analogous approach is described in [4], where the light source is treated as a discrete set of point light sources, and the shadows of collections of occluders are cast and combined. An algorithm proposed in [19] replaces the area light source with a point at its center, and describes an error metric that bounds the spatial discrepancy between the computed and true penumbra. This error metric can then be used to control adaptive subdivision of the light source or occluders. Another recent algorithm approximates umbra volumes by constructing "penumbra trees" and "umbra trees"; these are BSP trees [8] whose polyhedral leaf cells bound polygon fragments in partial or complete shadow [5].

For polygonal light sources, holes, and occluders, the boundary between total illumination (antiumbra) and partial illumination (penumbra, antipenumbra) is piecewise-planar. The boundary between partial illumination (penumbra, antipenumbra) and no illu-

mination (umbra), however, generally consists of portions of reguli. Generically, any connected portion of a regulus is non-convex, and any volume bounded by a portion of a regulus must be non-convex. Consequently, no algorithm that uses only polyhedral primitives or aggregations of convex objects can exactly represent the antipenumbra or umbra of an area light source for arbitrary polygonal occluders in three dimensions.

1.2 Motivation

Antipenumbra determination is motivated by visibility computations in a polygonal environment. Space is subdivided into polyhedral cells, which are mutually visible only through sequences of *portals*, or convex polygonal holes [9, 26, 27]. Figure 3 depicts five cells of one such polyhedral subdivision, and the portals linking adjacent cells. An observer constrained to a given *source* cell can see out of the cell only through a portal (say, that of the leftmost cell in Figures 3 and 4). If this portal is treated as an area light source, the antipenumbra cast by the portal beyond the plane of any further portal in a sequence bounds the volume visible to the constrained observer. For an observer determined to be inside the source cell, only objects inside this antipenumbral volume can be potentially visible.

A description of the antipenumbra may also prove useful for radiosity computations. For example, only polygons mutually visible through a portal sequence (i.e., in each other's antipenumbrae) can interact directly by exchanging luminous energy. Knowing a light source's antipenumbra would also be useful in the polygonal subdivision that shadowing and global illumination algorithms employ to model shadow boundaries [3, 4, 12, 13, 21].

Finally, the algorithm is of theoretical interest for two reasons. First, for the class of input described here, the algorithm computes "strong" (antiumbral) and "weak" (antipenumbral) polygon visibility [17] with respect to a polygon (area light source) in 3D. Second, again for this input class, the algorithm demonstrates an upper time and storage bound of $O(n^2)$ on the aspect graph computation.

1.3 Overview

It can easily be shown that, in three-space, the antiumbra is convex, polyhedral, has complexity $O(n)$, and can be computed in $O(n \lg n)$ time, where n is the total polygon edge complexity of a convex light source and some number of convex areal holes. Here, we show that the three-space antipenumbra is, in general, non-convex and disconnected, but has at most quadratic complexity in n. We present an implemented $O(n^2)$ time algorithm that computes the piecewise-quadratic boundary of the antipenumbra.

We also describe an extension of the algorithm that computes linear and quadratic *event surfaces* [10]. These are the loci at which the rate of areal variation in the visible portion of the light source, and therefore the derivative of illumination intensity, changes discontinuously due to occlusion. Such surfaces are useful, for example, in polygon meshing schemes for global illumination and shadow computations.

The algorithm uses Plücker coordinates, a five-dimensional line representation, to transform the edges of the light source and holes into hyperplanes bounding a five-dimensional polytope. The face structure of this polytope is then intersected with a four-dimensional quadric surface, the Plücker quadric. The resulting intersections or *traces* are remapped to 3D objects such as stabbing lines and portions of planar and quadric surfaces, some of which are shown to bound the antipenumbra. The remaining traces correspond to surfaces of illumination rate discontinuity lying within the antipenumbra.

2 Plücker Coordinates

We use the Plücker coordinatization [23] of directed lines in three space. Any ordered pair of distinct points $p = (p_x, p_y, p_z)$ and $q = (q_x, q_y, q_z)$ defines a directed line ℓ in 3D. This line corresponds to a projective six-tuple $\Pi_\ell = (\pi_{\ell 0}, \pi_{\ell 1}, \pi_{\ell 2}, \pi_{\ell 3}, \pi_{\ell 4}, \pi_{\ell 5})$, each component of which is the determinant of a 2×2 minor of the matrix

$$\begin{pmatrix} p_x & p_y & p_z & 1 \\ q_x & q_y & q_z & 1 \end{pmatrix} \quad (1)$$

We use the following convention dictating the correspondence between the minors of Equation 1 and the $\pi_{\ell i}$:

$$\begin{aligned}
\pi_{\ell 0} &= p_x q_y - q_x p_y \\
\pi_{\ell 1} &= p_x q_z - q_x p_z \\
\pi_{\ell 2} &= p_x \quad - q_x \\
\pi_{\ell 3} &= p_y q_z - q_y p_z \\
\pi_{\ell 4} &= p_z \quad - q_z \\
\pi_{\ell 5} &= q_y \quad - p_y
\end{aligned}$$

(this order was adopted in [18] to produce positive signs in some useful identities involving Plücker coordinates).

If a and b are two directed lines, and Π_a, Π_b their corresponding Plücker *duals*, a relation $side(a, b)$ can be defined as the permuted inner product

$$\Pi_a \odot \Pi_b = \pi_{a0}\pi_{b4} + \pi_{a1}\pi_{b5} + \pi_{a2}\pi_{b3} + \pi_{a4}\pi_{b0} + \pi_{a5}\pi_{b1} + \pi_{a3}\pi_{b2}. \quad (2)$$

This sidedness relation can be interpreted geometrically with the right-hand rule (Figure 5): if the thumb of one's right hand is directed along a, then $side(a, b)$ is positive (negative) if b goes by a with (against) one's fingers. If lines a and b are coplanar (i.e., intersect or are parallel), $side(a, b)$ is zero.

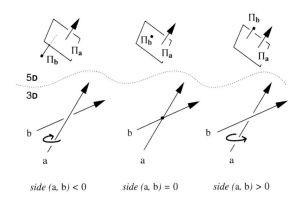

side $(a, b) < 0$ side $(a, b) = 0$ side $(a, b) > 0$

Figure 5: The right-hand rule applied to $side(a, b)$.

The six-tuple Π_ℓ can be treated either as a homogeneous point in 5D, or (after suitable permutation via Equation 2) as the coefficients of a five-dimensional hyperplane. The advantage of transforming lines to Plücker coordinates is that detecting incidence of lines in 3D becomes equivalent to computing the inner product of a homogeneous point (the dual of one line) with a hyperplane (the dual of the other).

Plücker coordinates simplify computations on lines by mapping them to points and hyperplanes, which are familiar objects. However, although every directed line in 3D maps to a point in Plücker coordinates, not every point in Plücker coordinates corresponds to a *real line*. Only those points Π satisfying the quadratic relation

$$\Pi \odot \Pi = 0 \quad (3)$$

correspond to real lines in 3D. All other points correspond to *imaginary lines*.

The six Plücker coordinates of a real line are not independent. First, since they describe a projective space, they are distinct only to within a scale factor. Second, they must satisfy Equation 3. Thus, Plücker coordinates describe a four-parameter space. This confirms basic intuition: one could describe all lines in three-space in terms of, for example, their intercepts on two standard planes.

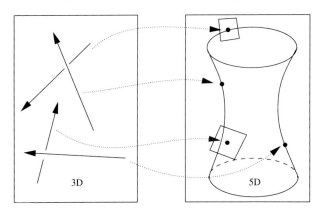

Figure 6: Directed lines map to points on, or hyperplanes tangent to, the Plücker surface.

The set of points in 5D satisfying Equation 3 is a quadric surface called the *Plücker surface* [23]. One might visualize this set as a four-dimensional ruled surface embedded in five dimensions, analogous to a quadric hyperboloid of one sheet embedded in three-space (Figure 6).

Henceforth, we use the notation $\Pi : \ell \to \Pi(\ell)$ to denote the map Π that takes a directed line ℓ to the Plücker point $\Pi(\ell)$, and the notation $\mathcal{L} : \Pi \to \mathcal{L}(\Pi)$ to denote the map that takes any point Π on the Plücker surface and constructs the corresponding real directed line $\mathcal{L}(\Pi)$. For any plane or hyperplane h, we denote the closed nonnegative halfspace of h as h^+, and say that a point in this halfspace is *on* or *above* h.

3 Extremal Stabbing Lines

We wish to describe the set of light rays originating at the light source and passing through each of a sequence of holes. Our algorithm exploits the fact that the holes are *oriented* by the sense in which they are traversed during a directed graph search through the portals of a spatial subdivision. For a particular hole sequence, each hole can be considered to admit light in only one direction.

In the following analysis, we call the light source and holes the *generator polygons*. In total, these polygons have n directed *generator edges* E_k, $k \in 1, \ldots, n$ (we assume at first that no two edges from different polygons are coplanar). Each edge E_k is a segment of a directed line e_k. Since the polygons are oriented, the e_k can be arranged so that if some directed line s *stabs* (intersects) each polygon, it must have the same sidedness relation with respect to each e_k. That is, any stabbing line s must satisfy (Figure 7):

$$side(s, e_k) \geq 0, \qquad k \in 1, \ldots, n.$$

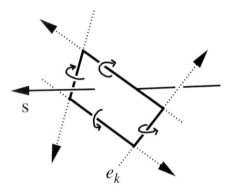

Figure 7: The stabbing line s must pass to the same side of each e_k.

Define h_k as the oriented Plücker hyperplane corresponding to the directed line e_k:

$$h_k = \{\mathbf{x} \in \mathbf{P}^5 : \mathbf{x} \odot \Pi_k = 0\}.$$

For any stabbing line s, $side\,(s, e_k) \geq 0$. That is, $S \odot \Pi_k \geq 0$, where $S = \Pi(s)$, and $\Pi_k = \Pi(e_k)$. Thus, S must be on or above each hyperplane h_k (Figure 8), and inside or on the boundary of the convex polytope $\bigcap_k h_k^+$.

The face structure of the polytope $\bigcap_k h_k^+$ has worst-case complexity quadratic in the number of halfspaces defining it [2], and can be computed by a randomized algorithm in optimal $O(n^2)$ expected time [6]. Define the *extremal* stabbing lines as those lines incident on four generator edges [18]. Since four lines (i.e., constraints) are necessary to determine a line, if *any* stabbing lines exist, then at least one must be extremal. The structure of the polytope $\bigcap_k h_k^+$ yields all extremal stabbing lines [18, 25]. Each such line ℓ is incident, in 3D, upon four of the e_k. Consequently, the Plücker point Π_ℓ must

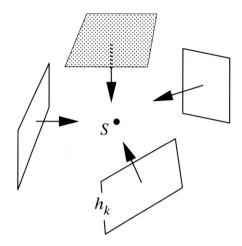

Figure 8: The 5D point $S = \Pi(s)$ must be on or above each h_k.

lie on four of the hyperplanes h_k in 5D, and must therefore lie on a *1D − face*, or edge, of the polytope $\bigcap_k h_k^+$. Thus, we can find all extremal stabbing lines of a given polygon sequence by examining the edges of the polytope for intersections with the Plücker surface. The extremal stabbing line corresponding to each intersection can be determined in constant time from the four relevant generator edges E_k [24].

Figure 9 depicts the output of an implementation of this algorithm. The input consists of nine polygons, with $n = 39$ edges total. The 5D convex polytope $\bigcap_k h_k^+$ has 755 edges, which together yield 82 intersections with the Plücker surface, and thus 82 extremal stabbing lines. All stabbing lines, considered as rays originating at the plane of the final hole, must lie within the antipenumbra of the "light source" (here, the leftmost polygon in the sequence). Some extremal stabbing lines lie in the interior of the antipenumbra because the edge graph of $\bigcap_k h_k^+$, when "projected" via $\mathcal{L}$ into three-space, overlaps itself.

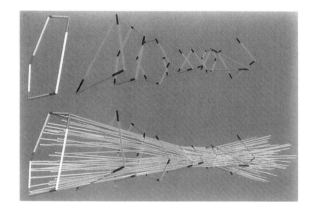

Figure 9: The eighty-two extremal stabbing lines of nine oriented polygons in 3D. The total edge complexity n is thirty-nine.

4 Extremal Swaths (Event Surfaces)

There are three types of extremal stabbing lines: vertex-vertex, or VV lines; vertex-edge-edge, or VEE lines; and quadruple edge, or 4E lines. Imagine "sliding" an extremal stabbing line (of any type) away from its initial position, by relaxing exactly one of the four edge constraints determining the line (Figure 10). The surface, or *swath*, swept out by the sliding line must either be planar (if the line remains tight on a vertex) or a regulus, whose three generator lines embed three polygon edges. In the terminology of [10], swaths are VE or EEE *event surfaces* important in the construction of aspect graphs, since they are loci at which qualitative changes in occlusion occur.

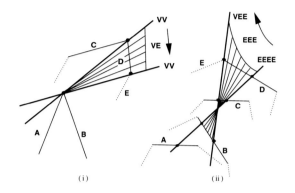

Figure 10: Sliding a stabbing line away from various extremal lines in 3D generates a VE plane (i) or a EEE quadratic surface (ii).

Figure 10-i depicts an extremal VV stabbing line tight on four edges A,B,C and D. Relaxing constraint C yields a VE (planar) swath tight on A, B, and D. Eventually, the sliding line encounters an obstacle (in this case, edge E), and terminates at a VV line tight on A,B,D, and E. Figure 10-ii depicts an extremal 4E stabbing line tight on the mutually skew edges A,B,C, and D; relaxing constraint A produces a EEE (regulus) swath tight on B, C, and D. The sliding line eventually encounters edge E and induces an extremal VEE line, terminating the swath.

Consider the same situations in the 5D space generated by the Plücker mapping (Figure 11). Extremal lines map to particular points in Plücker coordinates; namely, the intersections of the edges, or 1D-faces, of the polytope $\bigcap_k h_k^+$ with the Plücker surface. Since swaths are one-parameter line families, they correspond to *curves* in Plücker coordinates. These curves are the *traces* or intersections of the 2D-faces of $\bigcap_k h_k^+$ with the Plücker surface, and are therefore conics (in 5D, a polytope's 2D-faces are planar, and determined by the intersection of some three h_k). We call the 3D swaths corresponding to these 5D conic traces *extremal swaths*. All swaths have three generator lines, and consequently three generator edges, arising from the input polygons.

5 Internal and Penumbral Swaths

An object can be extremal (that is, lie on the boundary of the convex hull) in 5D, yet lie wholly inside the antipenumbra in three-space. Just as there are extremal stabbing lines that lie in the interior of the antipenumbra, so there are extremal swaths in the interior as well. We define a *penumbral* swath as an extremal swath that lies on the boundary of the antipenumbra (these are the red and green surfaces in Figure 4). All other extremal swaths are *internal*. Examining the 2D-faces of the polytope $\bigcap_k h_k^+$ yields all extremal swaths; however, we must distinguish between penumbral and internal swaths. This distinction can be made purely locally; that is, by examining only the swath's three generator edges and, in turn, their generator polygons. From only these (constant number of) objects, we show how to determine whether stabbing lines can exist on "both sides"

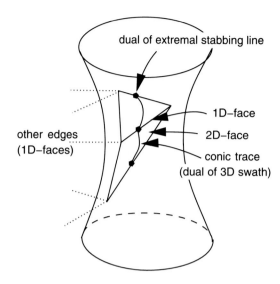

Figure 11: Traces (intersections) of extremal lines and swaths on the Plücker surface in 5D (higher-dimensional faces are not shown).

of the swath in question. If so, the swath cannot be penumbral, and is classified as internal.

5.1 Edge-Edge-Edge Swaths

Internal and penumbral EEE swaths can be distinguished as follows. Suppose three mutually skew generator edges A, B, and C give rise to an extremal EEE swath. Choose some line **L** incident on the generators respectively at points **a**, **b**, and **c** (Figure 12-i). At these points, erect three vectors $\mathbf{N}_a$, $\mathbf{N}_b$, and $\mathbf{N}_c$, perpendicular both to **L** and to the relevant generator edge, with their signed directions chosen so as to have a positive dot product with a vector pointing into the interior of the edge's generator polygon. (We refer to these vectors collectively as the $\mathbf{N}_i$.)

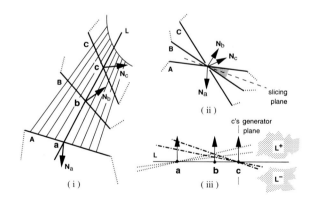

Figure 12: An internal EEE swath (i), viewed along **L** (ii) and transverse to **L** (iii). The $\mathbf{N}_i$ can be contained.

We say that three coplanar vectors can be *contained* if there exists a vector whose dot product with all three vectors is strictly positive. We claim that a swath is internal if and only if its corresponding $\mathbf{N}_i$ can be contained.

Suppose that the $\mathbf{N}_i$ can be contained (as in Figure 12). Consider any vector having a positive dot product with the $\mathbf{N}_i$ (such as one pointing into the gray region of Figure 12-ii). Next, "slice" the configuration with a plane containing both **L** and this vector, and view the swath in this plane (Figure 12-iii).

The trace (intersection) of the swath on this plane is simply the stabbing line **L**, which partitions the slicing plane into two regions $\mathbf{L}^+$ and $\mathbf{L}^-$ beyond the plane of C's generator polygon (Figure 12-iii). We can move **L** infinitesimally by keeping it tight on, say, point **a**. The interiors of the other two holes allow **L** to pivot in only one direction, thus generating stabbing lines into $\mathbf{L}^+$ (dotted). Analogously, pivoting about point **c** generates stabbing lines into $\mathbf{L}^-$ (dashed). Since, by construction, the swath admits stabbing lines on both sides, it cannot be penumbral.

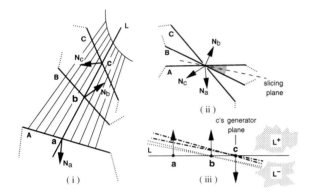

(i)   (ii)   (iii)

Figure 13: A penumbral EEE swath (i), viewed along **L** (ii) and transverse to **L** (iii). The $\mathbf{N}_i$ cannot be contained.

In contrast, the $\mathbf{N}_i$ of Figure 13-i cannot be contained. Thus, any vector (including one chosen from the gray region of Figure 13-ii) will have a negative dot product with at least one, and at most two, of the $\mathbf{N}_i$. Suppose it has a negative dot product with $\mathbf{N}_c$. Slice the configuration with a plane containing both **L** and one such vector (Figure 13-iii). Pivoting on point **b** generates stabbing lines into $\mathbf{L}^-$ (dotted), as does pivoting on point **c** (dashed). The configuration does not admit any stabbing lines into $\mathbf{L}^+$. Since this is true for any choice of slicing plane and (as we will show) for any choice of **L**, we conclude that the swath is penumbral; i.e., it separates a region of zero illumination from a region of partial illumination.

5.2   Vertex-Edge Swaths

Suppose the swath in question has type VE. Label the two generator edges defining the swath vertex **v** as A and B, the remaining edge C (not in the plane of A and B), the two relevant generator polygons P and Q, and the plane through C and **v** as S (Figure 14). Orient **S** so that Q (C's generator polygon) is above it (i.e., in $\mathbf{S}^+$); this is always possible, since Q is convex. Plane **S** divides the space beyond the plane of Q into two regions $\mathbf{S}^+$ and $\mathbf{S}^-$. If stabbing lines can exist in only one of these regions, the swath is penumbral. This occurs if and only if **S** is a *separating plane* of P and Q; that is, if and only if polygon P is entirely below **S**.

Suppose **S** separates polygons P and Q. Imagine choosing some stabbing line from the swath, and moving it so that it comes free from the swath vertex **v**, but remains tight on edge C (and remains a valid, though non-extremal, stabbing line). If **S** separates P and Q, the moving line's intersection with P can only lie below **S** (Figure 14-i); thus, beyond the plane of Q, all such stabbing lines must intersect $\mathbf{S}^+$. Similarly, should the stabbing line move off of C and into Q's interior, while remaining tight on **v**, it can only intersect $\mathbf{S}^+$. The swath admits only stabbing lines in $\mathbf{S}^+$, and is therefore penumbral.

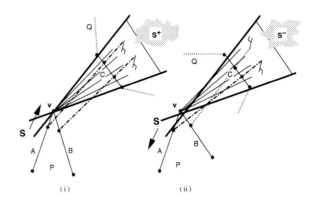

(i)   (ii)

Figure 14: Penumbral (i) and internal (ii) VE swaths.

Suppose, in contrast, that the plane **S** does not separate P and Q, i.e., that one or both of the edges A and B lie in $\mathbf{S}^+$ (Figure 14-ii). Again move a swath line so that it comes free from the swath vertex **v**, but stays tight on edge C. If the line (dashed) moves along A above (say) plane S, it will intersect the region $\mathbf{S}^-$ beyond the plane of Q. Similarly, motion along edge B below **S** produces stabbing lines (dotted) in $\mathbf{S}^+$. The swath admits stabbing lines into both $\mathbf{S}^-$ and $\mathbf{S}^+$, and therefore cannot be penumbral.

Note that the three-vector construction for EEE swaths is applicable in this (degenerate) setting as well, since **S** is a separating plane if and only if the normals erected along A,B, and C cannot be contained.

5.3   The Containment Function

The containment function is a criterion for distinguishing between penumbral and internal swaths. However, it applies only along a single stabbing line, not over an entire swath. Fortunately, evaluating the containment function anywhere along a swath produces the same result. To see why this is so, consider any configuration of three coplanar vectors $\mathbf{N}_a$, $\mathbf{N}_b$, and $\mathbf{N}_c$. Suppose that the configuration changes continuously from containable to non-containable (e.g., by rotation of vector $\mathbf{N}_c$), as in Figure 15. At either moment of transition (marked with dotted lines in the figure), $\mathbf{N}_c$ and one of $\mathbf{N}_a$ or $\mathbf{N}_b$ must be antiparallel.

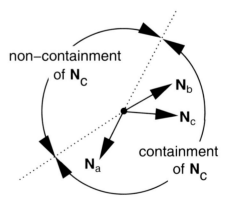

Figure 15: Directions of containment and non-containment for $\mathbf{N}_c$, for fixed $\mathbf{N}_a$ and $\mathbf{N}_b$. Transition directions are marked.

For this to occur in the EEE swath construction (Figure 13) two of the three generator edges must be coplanar. Similarly, in the VE swath construction (Figure 14), edge C and one of the edges A

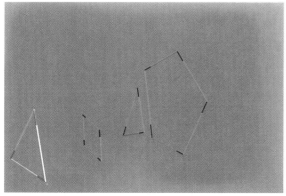

(i) A light source and three holes ($n = 15$).

(ii) VE (red), EEE (green) penumbral swaths.

Figure 16: The antipenumbra cast by a triangular light source through three convex holes ($n = 15$).

or B must be coplanar. But the generator edges are *fixed*; only the sliding line varies. Thus, even though sliding an extremal line along a swath generates a continuously changing vector configuration, the *containment* of the vectors is a constant function. If either of the EEE or VE degenerate cases occurs in practice, the containment function is indeterminate. We detect this while examining the polytope face structure, and use special-case processing to generate the correct swath.

6 Computing the Antipenumbra

We have assembled all of the computational machinery necessary for determining the antipenumbra. We make the following assumptions: the input is a list of m oriented polygons, $P_1 \ldots P_m$, given as linked lists of edges, the total number of edges being n. The first polygon P_1 is the light source, and all others are holes. The polygons are ordered in the sense that the negative halfspace determined by the plane of P_i contains all polygons P_j, $i < j \leq m$ (thus, an observer looking along a stabbing line would see the vertices of each polygon arranged in counterclockwise order).

The algorithm dualizes each directed input edge to a hyperplane in Plücker coordinates, then computes the common intersection of the resulting halfspaces, a 5D convex polytope. If there is no such intersection, or if the polytope has no intersection with the Plücker surface, the antipenumbra is vacuous. Otherwise, the face structure of the polytope is searched for traces of penumbral swaths resulting from intersections of its 1D-faces (edges) and 2D-faces (generically, triangles) with the Plücker surface (cf. Figure 11). These traces are linked into loops, each corresponding to a connected component of the antipenumbral boundary. There may be multiple loops since the intersection of the polytope boundary with the non-planar Plücker surface may have several components.

Each loop consists of polytope edges and triangles in alternation. Each edge intersection with the Plücker surface (a point in 5D) is the dual of an extremal stabbing line in 3D; each triangle intersection with the Plücker surface (a conic in 5D) is the dual of an extremal swath in 3D. Incidence of an edge and triangle on the polytope implies adjacency of the corresponding line and swath in 3D; stepping across a shared edge from one triangle to another on the polytope is equivalent to stepping across a shared extremal stabbing line (a "seam") between two extremal swaths in three-space. Thus the algorithm can "walk" from 2D-face to 2D-face on the polytope's surface, crossing the 1D-face incident to both at each

step. Each closed loop found in this manner in 5D is the dual (under the Plücker mapping) of the boundary of one connected component of the antipenumbra in three-space.

The algorithm can be described in pseudocode as:

> input directed edges E_k from polygons $P_1 \ldots P_m$
>
> convert directed edges to directed lines e_k
>
> transform e_k to Plücker halfspaces $h_k = \Pi(e_k)$
>
> compute 5D convex polytope $\bigcap_k h_k^+$
>
> identify 2D-face intersections of $\bigcap_k h_k^+$ with Plücker surface
>
> classify resulting extremal swaths as penumbral or internal
>
> for each connected component of the antipenumbra
>
> > traverse penumbral 2D-faces of $\bigcap_k h_k^+$
> >
> > > map each trace found to a 3D penumbral swath
> > >
> > > output swath loop as piecewise quadratic surface

7 Implementation

We have implemented the antipenumbra algorithm in C and FORTRAN-77 on a 20-MIP Silicon Graphics superworkstation. To compute the convex hull of n hyperplanes in 5D, we used a d-dimensional Delaunay simplicialization algorithm implemented by Allan Wilks at AT&T Bell Labs and Allen McIntosh at Bellcore, and a d-dimensional linear programming algorithm [22] implemented by Michael Hohmeyer at U.C. Berkeley.

Figure 16-i depicts a set of four input polygons with $n = 15$, and the leftmost polygon acting as a light source. The antipenumbra computation took about 2 CPU seconds. The polytope $\bigcap_k h_k^+$, formed from 15 halfspaces in 5D, has 80 facets, 186 2D-faces (triangles), and 200 1D-faces (edges). Of the 186 triangles, 78 induce dual traces on the Plücker surface, generating 78 extremal swaths in 3D. Of these 78 swaths, 62 are internal, and 16 are penumbral (Figure 16-ii); of these, 10 are planar VE swaths (red), and 6 are quadric EEE swaths (green). Of the 200 edges, 39 intersect the Plücker surface to yield extremal VV, VEE, or 4E stabbing lines (Figure 17-i). Note that the extremal stabbing lines form the "seams" of the antipenumbral boundary, as they demarcate junctions between adjacent VE and/or EEE swaths (Figure 17-ii).

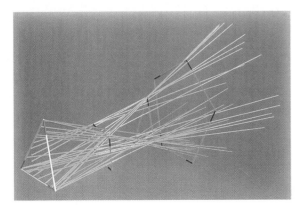

(i) The 39 extremal stabbing lines from Figure 16.

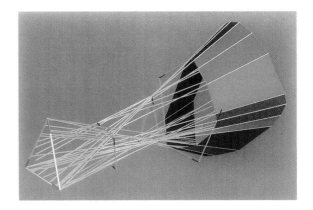

(ii) Extremal stabbing lines as penumbral "seams."

Figure 17: The relationship between extremal stabbing lines and penumbral swaths.

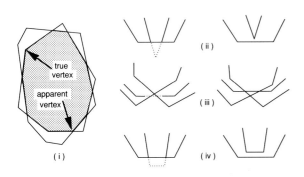

Figure 18: An observer's view of the light source (i). Crossing an extremal VE (ii), EEE (iii), or degenerate (iv) swath.

Figure 19: Curves of discontinuous illumination from the antipenumbra of Figure 16, intersected with a receiver plane.

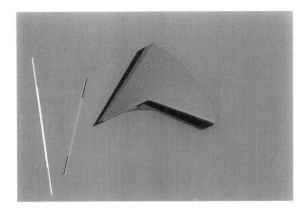

(i) The antipenumbra cast by a
light shining through two slits.

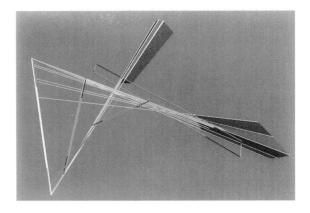

(ii) The third slit "clips" the
antipenumbra, yielding two pieces.

Figure 20: An area light source and three holes can yield a disconnected antipenumbra.

8 Illumination Discontinuities

Internal VE and EEE swaths, which were merely categorized and discarded by the antipenumbra algorithm, are generally surfaces along which discontinuities occur in the first or second spatial derivatives of illumination intensity. Imagine an observer inside an antipenumbral volume, looking back through the generating hole sequence to the light source. Since each intervening hole edge "clips" a halfplane away from the light source, the observer must see a convex polygonal region of the light (Figure 18-i). The region edges arise directly from hole edges. The region vertices arise either from hole vertices, or from apparent intersections among non-adjacent hole edges as seen by the observer.

As the observer moves, the apparent area of the light source (and therefore the illumination intensity at the observer location) changes smoothly, except when a swath (i.e., event surface) is encountered. Generically, this happens in one of two fundamental ways for polyhedral objects [11]. Either a hole vertex appears (disappears) from the region boundary (Figure 18-ii), or the observer's line of sight simultaneously intersects three edges, causing the appearance (disappearance) of an apparent boundary vertex (Figure 18-iii). In either case a qualitative change occurs in the effect of infinitesimal observer motion on the apparent area of the light source.

Imagine the observer's motion as "sweeping" an occluding halfplane, determined by a hole edge and the observer position, over the light source. In general, each sweep surface occludes or reveals an area that changes quadratically with the observer position (parallel edges, as in Figure 18-iv, can cause linear variation in apparent area). Along extremal swaths, the set of contributing edges changes, adding or removing linear or quadratic terms from the function relating the amount of visible light area to observer location. Consequently, extremal swaths are in general loci of first- or second-derivative discontinuities in illumination intensity. (In the terminology of [13], planar traces of extremal swaths are curves of D^1 or D^2 discontinuity.)

Zeroth-derivative discontinuities (i.e., abrupt changes in illumination value) can occur only in the presence of a point light source, or if the observer crosses the plane of an area light source. Neither of these circumstances occurs in the antipenumbra computation, since (1) all light sources and holes are areal, and (2) no portal plane can be traversed twice during any valid portal sequence through the spatial subdivision.

The internal swaths induced by the polygon configuration of Figure 16, intersected with a plane beyond the final hole to produce segments of lines and conics, are shown in Figure 19. The segments comprise a planar curve arrangement of complexity $O(n^2)$, each cell of which contains points having the same *aspect*, or qualitative view, of the light source. Of course, penumbral swaths also demarcate qualitative changes in occlusion, since by stepping across one, an observer would see the light source appear or disappear from view.

Finally, we show how an area light source and as few as three holes can produce a disconnected antipenumbra. First, a light source and two holes, all thin rectangular slits, are arranged so as to admit a fattened regulus of antipenumbral light (Figure 20-i). A third slit then partitions the fattened regulus into two disconnected components (Figure 20-ii).

Conclusion

We presented an $O(n^2)$ time algorithm that computes the antipenumbra cast by a convex light source through a sequence of convex holes in three dimensions, with total edge complexity n. We described the antipenumbra as a disconnected volume bounded by regions of quadric and planar surfaces, and showed that each swath, or portion of the antipenumbral boundary in three-space, arises from a conic segment on the intersection of a five-dimensional convex hull with a four-dimensional quadric surface, the Plücker quadric. The algorithm is related to the aspect graph computation, in that it generates surfaces that separate regions with qualitatively distinct views of the light source or the intervening holes. We identified both penumbral and internal swaths as surfaces along which the first derivative of illumination intensity changes discontinuously due to occlusion.

We demonstrated an implementation of the antipenumbra computation on several polygon sequences. The algorithm was motivated by a visibility scheme involving static, volume-based culling in three dimensions. Knowledge of the antipenumbra may also prove useful, however, in shadowing algorithms and meshing schemes that model illumination discontinuities.

Acknowledgments

Jim Winget, my mentor at Silicon Graphics, was an extraordinary motivator and facilitator of this work. My advisor Carlo Séquin has been a constant source of inspiration, encouragement, and valuable observations. The late Professor René de Vogelaere taught me about reguli and classical geometry. Ziv Gigus, John Airey, Jim Ruppert, and Efi Fogel made thoughtful comments on an early draft of this paper. Raimund Seidel and Michael Hohmeyer also contributed helpful insight and comments. Paul Haeberli provided aesthetic advice, and helped prepare the color figures for submission and publication. Finally, Silicon Graphics afforded me access to their considerable physical resources.

References

[1] P. Atherton, K. Weiler, and D. Greenberg. Polygon shadow generation. *Computer Graphics (Proc. SIGGRAPH '78)*, 12:275–281, 1978.

[2] B. Grünbaum. *Convex Polytopes*. Wiley-Interscience, New York, 1967.

[3] Daniel R. Baum, Stephen Mann, Kevin P. Smith, and James M. Winget. Making radiosity usable: Automatic preprocessing and meshing techniques for the generation of accurate radiosity solutions. *Computer Graphics (Proc. SIGGRAPH '91)*, 25(4):51–60, 1991.

[4] A.T. Campbell III and Donald S. Fussell. Adaptive mesh generation for global diffuse illumination. *Computer Graphics (Proc. SIGGRAPH '91)*, 24(4):155–164, 1990.

[5] Norman Chin and Steven Feiner. Fast object-precision shadow generation for area light sources using BSP trees. In *Proc. 1992 Symposium on Interactive 3D Graphics*, pages 21–30, 1992.

[6] Kenneth L. Clarkson and Peter W. Shor. Applications of random sampling in computational geometry II. *Discrete Computational Geometry*, pages 387–421, 1989.

[7] Frank C. Crow. Shadow algorithms for computer graphics. *Computer Graphics (Proc. SIGGRAPH '77)*, 11(2):242–248, 1977.

[8] H. Fuchs, Z. Kedem, and B. Naylor. On visible surface generation by a priori tree structures. *Computer Graphics (Proc. SIGGRAPH '80)*, 14(3):124–133, 1980.

[9] Thomas A. Funkhouser, Carlo H. Séquin, and Seth J. Teller. Management of large amounts of data in interactive building walkthroughs. In *Proc. 1992 Workshop on Interactive 3D Graphics*, pages 11–20, 1992.

[10] Ziv Gigus, John Canny, and Raimund Seidel. Efficiently computing and representing aspect graphs of polyhedral objects. *IEEE Transactions on Pattern Analysis and Machine Intelligence*, 13(6):542–551, 1991.

[11] Ziv Gigus and Jitendra Malik. Computing the aspect graph for line drawings of polyhedral objects. *IEEE Transactions on Pattern Analysis and Machine Intelligence*, 12(2):113–122, 1990.

[12] Pat Hanrahan and David Salzman. A rapid hierarchical radiosity algorithm. *Computer Graphics (Proc. SIGGRAPH '91)*, 25(4):197–206, 1991.

[13] Paul S. Heckbert. *Simulating Global Illumination Using Adaptive Meshing*. PhD thesis, Computer Sciences Department, University of California, Berkeley, June 1991.

[14] J.J. Koenderink and A.J. van Doorn. The internal representation of solid shape with respect to vision. *Biol. Cybern.*, 32:211–216, 1979.

[15] Tomoyuki Nishita and Eihachiro Nakamae. Half-tone representation of 3-D objects illuminated by area sources or polyhedron sources. In *Proc. IEEE COMPSAC, 1983*, pages 237–242, 1983.

[16] Tomoyuki Nishita and Eihachiro Nakamae. Continuous-tone representation of three-dimensional objects taking account of shadows and interreflection. *Computer Graphics (Proc. SIGGRAPH '85)*, 19(3):23–30, 1985.

[17] Joseph O'Rourke. *Art Gallery Theorems and Algorithms*. Oxford University Press, 1987.

[18] Marco Pellegrini. Stabbing and ray-shooting in 3-dimensional space. In *Proc. 6th ACM Symposium on Computational Geometry*, pages 177–186, 1990.

[19] Ken Perlin and Xue-Dong Wang. An efficient approximation for penumbra shadow. Technical Report 346, New York University Courant Institute of Mathematical Sciences, Computer Science Division, 1988.

[20] W.H Plantinga and C.R. Dyer. Visibility, occlusion, and the aspect graph. *Int. J. Computer Vision*, 5(2):137–160, 1990.

[21] David Salesin, Dani Lischinski, and Tony DeRose. Reconstructing illumination functions with selected discontinuities. In *Proc. 3rd Eurographics Workshop on Rendering*, 1992.

[22] Raimund Seidel. Linear programming and convex hulls made easy. In *Proc. 6th ACM Symposium on Computational Geometry*, pages 211–215, 1990.

[23] D.M.Y. Sommerville. *Analytical Geometry of Three Dimensions*. Cambridge University Press, 1959.

[24] Seth J. Teller and Michael E. Hohmeyer. Computing the lines piercing four lines. Technical Report UCB/CSD 91/665, Computer Science Department, U.C. Berkeley, 1991.

[25] Seth J. Teller and Michael E. Hohmeyer. Stabbing oriented convex polygons in randomized $O(n^2)$ time. Technical Report UCB/CSD 91/669, Computer Science Department, U.C. Berkeley, 1992.

[26] Seth J. Teller and Carlo H. Séquin. Visibility preprocessing for interactive walkthroughs. *Computer Graphics (Proc. SIGGRAPH '91)*, 25(4):61–69, 1991.

[27] Seth J. Teller and Carlo H. Séquin. Visibility computations in polyhedral three-dimensional environments. Technical Report UCB/CSD 92/680, Computer Science Department, U.C. Berkeley, 1992.

Topological Design of Sculptured Surfaces

Helaman Ferguson
Supercomputing Research
Center
Bowie, MD

Alyn Rockwood
Computer Science Dept.
Arizona State University
Tempe, AZ

Jordan Cox[†]
Dept. of Mech. Eng.
Purdue University
West Lafayette, IN

ABSTRACT

Topology is primal geometry. Our design philosophy embodies this principle. We report on a new surface design perspective based on a "marked" polygon for each object. The marked polygon captures the topology of the object surface. We construct multiply periodic mappings from polygon to sculptured surface. The mappings arise naturally from the topology and other design considerations. Hence we give a single domain global parameterization for surfaces with handles. Examples demonstrate the design of sculptured objects and their manufacture.

CR Categories: I.3.5 [Computer Graphics] Computational Geometry and Object Modeling - Geometric Algorithms; I.3.6 [Computer Graphics] Methodologies and Techniques - Interactive Techniques.
Additional Key Words and Phrases: Computer-aided design, sculptured surfaces, topology, marked polygon, automorphic functions, multiply periodic functions, boundary value problems.

1. Introduction

Creating shape excites many artistic and scientific minds. It is important to areas as diverse as sculpture, mathematics, cartoon animation, molecular modeling, architecture, mechanical design. It is also one of the most difficult to automate because it demands a comprehensive toolset to handle such needs as topology, geometry, analysis, and manufacture.

Traditional design methods (see [Far88, Hof89]) define the surface of an object as a quiltwork of many patches; topological issues are treated superficially during the design stage. For example, the methods of Coons and Bézier and the B-rep method of solid modeling define an object as a collection of patches (or faces) that match at

†Currently at the Dept of Mech. Eng., Brigham Young University, Provo, UT.

boundaries. The burden of maintaining topological integrity falls to the designer. In these methods, there is no single parameter space, there are many sets of separate coordinate functions. Control of the topology may be simple for some shapes, but it is difficult for topologically complex ones. Some "solid" modelling systems check topology after the design stage, e.g. via the Euler-Poincaré formulae [Hof89]. The check only determines when an invalid operation has occured, but does not participate in the design process.

This paper describes a design philosophy that includes surface topology as an integral part. Our interest in this subject came from a desire to automate the sculpture of mathematical concepts such as in Figures 1.1 and 1.2 (see [Fer89, Fer90, or Roc86]).

Figure 1.1. Automatically sculptured "Umbilic Torus NC." The continuous NC path was generated by a Peano-Hilbert surface filling curve. The torus itself is defined on a single domain.

Figure 1.2. Milling the "Umbilic Torus NC" on a three axis milling machine, ball end mill tangent to the torus surface defined globally over a single parametric patch.

Our approach decomposes the surface of an object into a polygon, using a series of virtual surface cuts. The virtual cuts are identified with oriented markings that bound the polygon. Such a marked polygon encodes the topology of the object. A mapping from the two dimensional interior of this polygon into three dimensional space is then constructed. The domain of the mapping is a the interior of the polygon; the image of the mapping is the surface of the object. The surface is a **single** topologically consistent patch.

As we investigated the problem, the value of the single polygon patch approach for analysis and manufacture was better appreciated. Even topologically simple objects benefit. The texture on the object in Figure 1 depends on a pattern that is continuous across the marked boundaries of the domain and drove the milling tool.

In his famous Erlangen lecture, [Fir82], Felix Klein described geometries by their associated mappings, especially groups of mappings. Objects within the geometries are related and classified by the transformations between them. Rigid body transformations preserve congruence, projective transformations preserve similarity, C^1 transformations preserve differentiability, C^0 preserves topological structure. For example, a cuboid with corners is C^0 to a sphere but not C^1; a sphere is not C^0 to a torus.

The most fundamental mappings are C^0, these preserve topology.

Topology is primal geometry. Our design philosophy embodies this principle.

This paper is organized as follows. Section 2 introduces the topological concepts mapping, domain, image, homeomorphism, immersion, embedding, and genus. Section 3 gives three examples from this design philosophy: a circle, a torus, and a genus three surface with many Bézier sub-patches over a single twelve-sided polygon. Section 4 reveals how to give a single polygon parameterization of a surface of arbitrary genus by constructing real analytic (smooth) multiply-periodic coordinate functions. Section 5 constructs an embedding of a double torus by solving boundary value problems.

2. Surface Topology

Figuratively, two objects are *homeomorphic* if one object can be re-formed into the other by a continuous deformation that does not tear the object nor make it self-intersect. For a readable exposition see [Nas83], for rigorous definitions see [Hoc61]. We keep to an intuitive level.

Consider a polygon in the plane. Think of the polygon as elastic material to be sewn up along the edges. Give each edge a direction and name each edge with a captial letter. We define, figuratively, a surface to be a `sewing up' of this polygon in space by stitching together the edges with the same capital letters. Assume there are no left-over edges and that the sewing is direct, without twisting or knotting the material. There are two possibilities: the sewn material may self-intersect or not. If there are self-intersections we call the spatial result an *immersion*. If there are none we call the resulting surface S an *embedding*. The embeddings bound natural objects.

There exists a set of directed virtual cuts on any surface S that induce a one-to-one correspondance from the surface with virtual cuts to its polygon with directed edges (see [Fir82, Sie88]). The polygon together with its directed and labelled edges is called the *marked polygon* of the surface. Note that a pairwise identification of two edges occurs from a single cut in the surface. This pair of edges is identified by the same letter, but differentiated by the superscripts. Figure 2.1 illustrates two cuts which convert a torus into a marked rectangle. It is also the topology used to create the "Umbilic Torus NC" of Figure 1.1.

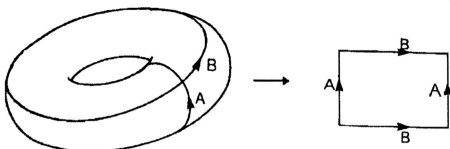

Figure 2.1. The torus and its fundamental polygon with formal word $ABA^{-1}B^{-1}$.

Move clockwise around the polygon and give the letter a "-1" superscript if its edge runs counter to the movement, otherwise the letter gets no superscript. The "word" that describes the torus in Figure 2.1 is $ABA^{-1}B^{-1}$. The word $ABAB^{-1}$, for which the direction of the third edge differs from the torus, represents the Klein bottle and is always an immersion. Immersions and embeddings are both possible for tori.

A surface is *orientable* if an inside and an outside can be distinguished, i.e. bounds a natural object. The sphere and torus are orientable; the Klein bottle is not. The following theorem classifies **all** orientable surfaces:

A closed, orientable surface has a marked polygon word either of the form AA^{-1} or $A_1B_1A_1^{-1}B_1^{-1} \dots A_gB_gA_g^{-1} B_g^{-1}$ (g > 0).

The first case is a sphere. The second can be thought of as gluing g tori together. The number g is the *genus* of the object. It counts the number of "donut holes." These are called *handles*. All objects of the same genus are topologically equivalent; they can be continuously deformed from one to another. A corollary to the above theorem is:

A closed, orientable surface (g>0) has a marked polygon with 4g sides.

Many cutting schemes are possible for objects of genus $g>1$. The textbook cuts [Fir82, Sre88] usually emanate from a central point and emphasize symmetries as in Figure 6. We have devised non-standard cuts that are better for some purposes. Consider the double torus ("Borus") shown in Figure 2.2.

All cuts begin at point A inside on the bottom of the lower handle. The first cut divides the bottom loop into two sleeves. The next one slits the sleeve orthogonally to the first along C. The next pair of cuts run from one sleeve corner to the other through along B and then D.

The example is easily generalized to a genus g object, $g>2$. The object is first deformed into an extended figure "8." All cuts are made from the same point. The even cuts traverse through each handle and return to the point. The odd set of cuts start from the point and pass through the antipodal point in the handle without intersecting any other cuts.

The next step in the marked polygon design process determines vector valued functions that define the surface. Consider the function $f\colon P \to S$, for P a polygon in $\mathbf{R}^2$, surface S in $\mathbf{R}^3$ and $f\colon (u, v) \to (x, y, z)$. Notice that pairwise related edges of the marked polygon must map so their directions coincide on the surface.

The function f is vector-valued with *coordinate functions* $f_j\colon \mathbf{R}^2 \to \mathbf{R}$, $j=1,2,3$, where $x = f_1(u,v)$, $y = f_2(u,v)$ and $z = f_3(u,v)$. These coordinate functions have the polygon as a single common domain.

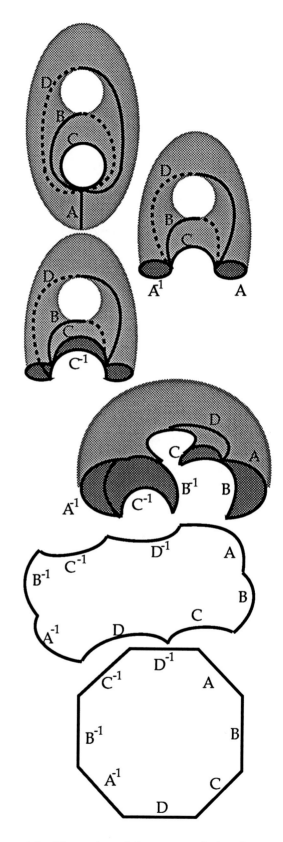

Figure 2.2. Illustration of the system of virtual cuts on a double torus as it is opened up to a stop sign shaped marked polygon with formal word $ACBDA^{-1}C^{-1}B^{-1}D^{-1}$.

3. The Circle, The Torus, and the Embedding by Many Bézier Patches.

3.1. The Circle. We now apply our design philosophy to the simplest posssible example which has all the essential elements of the general case -- a circle. The cut on a circle corresponds to a single point. The one dimensional polygon domain corresponds to a line segment. We take the line segment to be the interval (-1/2, 1/2]. Note that integer translations of this interval cover the real line. A polynomial mapping of the interval into the plane will image some kind of curve, which may cross itself (immersion) or be simple without self-intersection points (embedding). Two x and y coordinate polynomials which give a circle-like curve are $x(t) = 1-16t^2$ and $y(t)=t(1-4t^2)$. But polynomials are not periodic and the curve has a corner. Its tear-drop shape is in Figure 3.1. The coordinate functions should have period 1 since the distance from cut to cut on the (-1/2,1/2] interval is 1.

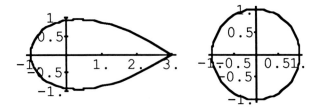

Figure 3.1. Left: A polynomial embedding of a circle. Note the corner at the cut point of the circle, because polynomials are not periodic. Right: A periodic embedding of a circle using the same polynomials in the periodizing transformation.

How does one make numerically computable periodic functions out of polynomials? For any polynomial $f(t)$, the rapidly convergent sum

$$F(t)= \sum_{k \in \mathbf{Z}} f(t+k)e^{-(t+k)^2}$$

is periodic: F has period 1, $F(t) = F(t+1)$, because the sum is over all integers $\mathbf{Z}$. Replace f by x in the sum to get a coordinate function $X(t)$ and f by y to get $Y(t)$. Then X and Y both have period 1. Normalizing X and Y appropriately and taking eleven terms in the sum gives the classical periodic cosine and sine functions within eleven decimal places, cf. Figure 3.1.

We recapitulate the features of this simple example: 1) we began with an idea of what we wanted to draw, a closed `circular' curve which can be cut open at one point. 2) we picked some qualitative guesses for the coordinate functions which could give an embedding. 3) We recognized the essential periodic nature of the curve and made our guesses periodic to get a smooth curve. Recognizing a period for a circle is the same idea as recognizing the topological genus or system of virtual cuts for a surface. The periods are roughly speaking distances between cuts.

3.2. The Torus. The next simplest case is the torus. The torus is a Cartesian product of two circles, so we could replicate our design philosophy in this similar

context: 1) We think of an inner tube shape, mark it with two virtual cuts so that the shape corresponds to a marked square. 2) We pick some qualitative bivariate polynomial guesses to give an embedding. 3) We recognize the torus as doubly periodic and convert our guesses into doubly periodic coordinate functions with a bivariate sum over all pairs of integers, $\mathbf{Z} \times \mathbf{Z}$.

This leads to the following parametric equations for a torus with major radius a and minor radius b: $(u,v) \rightarrow$ $((a+b\cos(2\pi v)) \cos(2\pi u), (a+b\cos(2\pi v)) \sin(2\pi u), b \sin(2\pi v))$. This maps the marked polygon (-1/2,1/2] x (-1/2,1/2] to the torus. This mapping is an embedding if $a>b>0$. Note that the coordinate functions in the vector are doubly periodic, i.e., invariant under replacing u by $u+1$ or v by $v+1$. Furthermore these doubly periodic functions are real analytic (smooth) and bounded.

3.3. Traditional method. It is possible to formulate the coordinate functions using traditional design methods, e.g. Bézier cross plots [Far88], which are piecewise polynomial. The single twelve sided polygon for the genus three surface in Figure 3.3 organizes the hundred or so Bézier patches in a coherent way.

In this case, the domain polygon is tessellated into four-sided regions which are associated with the domains of the polynomial patches; thus inducing a topological aspect into the design paradigm for conventional patch methods.

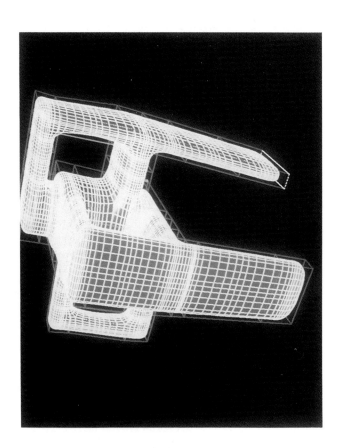

Figure 3.3. Genus 3 object from many Bézier patches coherently organized over a marked 12-gon.

4. Defining the Embedding with Multiply Periodic Functions.

Natural sculptured objects are always bounded by a surface, are closed, and have genus. For a surface to have genus amounts to having multiple periods. A simple closed curve in space is periodic and has periodic coordinate functions. Closed surfaces in space can be defined by coordinate functions that are multiply periodic. A rich class of multiply periodic functions are available in the classical literature [For51, Sie88]. In this literature multiply periodic functions are usually called automorphic functions because these functions are invarient under a group of automorphisms. A problem with the classical literature is that it tends to be preoccupied with **complex** analytic functions that do not give bounded embeddings. We circumvent this obstruction by constructing enough **real** analytic functions which are bounded. These real analytic (smooth) functions are the analogs of the classical doubly periodic real analytic functions of variables u and v, the finite Fourier series in $Sin(u)$, $Sin(v)$, $Cos(u)$, $Cos(v)$ encountered for the torus in Section 3.2. Another feature is that the multiple periods of interest for surfaces of genus greater than one are not additive. The periods are elements of a multiplicative and non-commutative group of transformations of the variables u and v.

Multiply periodic functions can be of any arbitrary differentiability class. In what follows, we solve the problem of defining a smooth embedding from the marked polygon to the surface of an object. It allows the embedding to be defined smoothly across the boundary marks of the domain, and thus the virtual cuts of the object. We realize this marked polygon in the hyperbolic disc with sides which are geodesics in the hyperbolic geometry. The multiple periods will be hyperbolic translations. All these hyperbolic translations form a multiplicative group. The hyperbolic translations tessellate the hyperbolic disc with copies of the marked polygon. Traversing the polygon from one tesselant to a neighbor is equivalent to re-entering the original polygon at another point of the boundary. A "periodizing" transformation is defined on the tesselated disc that takes functions, say polynomials, over the fundamental domain and blends them at the marks, making them seamless, i.e. infinitely smooth across the virtual cuts. This was done for taking the tear drop to the smooth circle in Section 3.1. This "multiple periodizing" transformation involves a sum over all of the elements of the group of hyperbolic translations. A different group will be defined for each genus.

4.1. The Hyperbolic Disc.
The natural geometry for the surfaces with handles which are of interest to us is a hyperbolic geometry. A surface with g handles can be cut with $2g$ cuts. The corresponding polygon has $4g$ sides and can be laid down in a hyperbolic geometry, [Mar83]. One model for this geometry, the Poincaré model, is given by imposing some geometric structure on the unit disc $\{z \mid zz^* < 1, z \in C\}$ where C is the usual complex number field and z^* is the complex conjugate. The points of this hyperbolic geometry are the points of the unit disc. The lines or geodesics of this hyperbolic geometry are given by arcs in the unit disc of circles perpendicular to the disc boundary at their endpoints. Lengths of arc segments, angles between intersecting arcs, and area of polygons bounded by arcs are all defined, [Sie66]. One-to-one, onto, analytic mappings of the disc to itself that preserve lengths and angles are given by linear fractional transformations of the form $z \rightarrow (az+b)/(b^*z+a^*)$ where a, b are complex numbers such that $aa^*-bb^*=1$. Among these are the hyperbolic translations we define for the periods of a sphere with finitely many handles.

4.2. The Single Marked Polygon Patch.
As described in Section 2, it is possible to mark a surface with exactly g handles in such a way that when the surface can be 'sewn up' from the interior of a polygon of exactly $4g$ sides, where opposite sides are identified and the sewing is done without twisting. We specify a particular such polygon with $4g$ circular arc sides in the hyperbolic disc. This special set of $4g$ circular arcs comprises the boundary of the what we will call the canonical $4g$-gon. It is symmetric about the origin. Adjoining arcs are constrained to meet a vertex with interior angles of exactly $\pi/2g$ radians. Hence, the sum of these $4g$ angles is exactly 2π. This ensures, by a theorem of Poincaré [Fir82], that a group of hyperbolic translations, Γ_g which we define below, of the $4g$-gon exactly covers the hyperbolic disc.

Each boundary circular arc is given by the inside arc of a circle of radius

$$r_g = \frac{\sin(\pi/4g)}{\sqrt{\cos(\pi/2g)}}$$

centered at integer multiples of $\pi/2g$ and radius $c_g = r_g \cot(\pi/4g)$. For genus two,

$$r_2 = \sqrt{\frac{\sqrt{2}-1}{2}} \text{ and } c_2 = \sqrt{\frac{\sqrt{2}+1}{2}}.$$

The radius of the excribed circle containing the eight vertices of the polygon is $2^{-1/4}$ and the radius of the inscribed circle is $(2^{1/2} - 1)^{1/2}$.

4.3. The Group Γ_g of Multiple Periods.
Define l_g and m_g by

$$l_g^2 = \tan \frac{\pi}{4} (1 - \frac{1}{g})$$

and

$$m_g = \frac{2l_g}{1 + l_g^2}.$$

Define the hyperbolic translation

$$T_g : z \rightarrow \frac{z - m_g}{1 - m_g z},$$

of infinite order, and the single rotation

$$R_g : z \rightarrow e^{\frac{\pi\sqrt{-1}}{2g}} \cdot z,$$

of order $4g$. Note that T_g and R_g do not commute. All of the elements of Γ_g are generated by the $4g$ fundamental hyperbolic translations

$$H_{g,k}=R_g^{-k} T_g R_g^{k}, \quad k=0,1,2,...,4g-1.$$

4.4. Enumeration of the Elements of Γ_g.

Every period or element of Γ_g is realized by a "word" in the symbols $H_{g,k}$ of the form $H_{g,k1}^{a1} ... H_{g,km}^{am}$, where the a_j are non-negative integers. The length of this word is given by the non-negative integer $a_1+...+a_m$. These words correspond to fractional linear transformations and there are relations among the words; some words are equal to other words that are spelled differently, this gives an equivalence class for a given word. A shortest word in a set of equivalent words is called a geodesic word. It is possible to write down finite state automata which generate all geodesic words in increasing order [Eps92]. It is important to enumerate algorithmically the geodesic words, in order of increasing word length, to efficiently compute a large class of multiply periodic functions.

For the case of the double torus and the group Γ_2, there are eight generators. Set $H_{2,k} = H_k$. The generators are H_0, H_1, H_2, H_3, H_4, H_5, H_6 and H_7, and the particular word $H_0H_5H_2H_7H_4H_1H_6H_3$ is equivalent to the identity word of zero length. The numbers of words of length 0, 1, 2, 3, 4, 5,... are 1, 8, 56, 392, 2736, 19096,... respectively. The generating function for this double torus case is $(1+2t+2t^2+2t^3+t^4)/(1-6t-6t^2-6t^3+t^4)$, [Can84, 92].

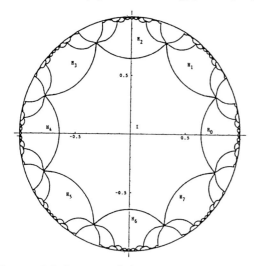

Figure 4.4. Images of the octagon for genus two in the hyperbolic disc under hyperbolic translations by the geodesic words of the group Γ_2. The center octagon is the identity surrounded by the alphabet of generators H_0, H_1, H_2, H_3, H_4, H_5, H_6, H_7, then words H_iH_j, then words $H_iH_jH_k$, ...

4.5. Multiply Periodic Functions for the Sphere with g handles, $g>1$.

A set of Γ_g multiply periodic basis functions is given by

$$F_{j,k}(z) = \sum_{H \in \Gamma_g} f_{j,k}(H \cdot z)$$

where

$$f_{j,k} = (1 - |z|^2)^j \operatorname{Re}(z^k)$$

or

$$f_{j,k} = (1 - |z|^2)^j \operatorname{Im}(z^k)$$

for $j=2,3,...$ and $k=0,1,2,...$. Note that the sum is over Γ_g; thus the need for the algorithm above to generate geodesic elements of this group in order. These series converge rapidly; for visual accuracy on the double torus fewer than $1+8+56+392=457$ terms suffice. See Figure 4.5 for an example basis function.

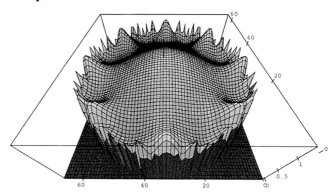

Figure 4.5. A multiply periodic basis function for the group Γ_g plotted over the marked octagon in the hyperbolic disc.

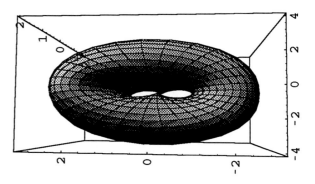

Figure 4.6. An infinitely smooth double torus definable on a single marked octagon.

5. Defining the Embedding by Solving Boundary Value Problems.

This approach to embedding homeomorphisms poses separate boundary value problems for the x, y, and z coordinate functions. The solution to these 2-dimensional boundary value problems models the specific coordinate function over the entire domain. The 3-tuples are formed by collecting the values of each coordinate function at specific parametric domain points. The parametric domain connects these 3-tuples to give the geometry of the desired object..

Each boundary value problem is constructed by selecting an appropriate differential operator which models the geometric shape of the coordinate function and then applying boundary conditions derived from the appropriate coordinate values of the markings on the actual object. Similar methods have been used to model surface patches (see [Blo90, Blo90c]). Since the markings represent the boundaries of the domain, see Figure 6, it is appropriate to define the boundary conditions for the boundary value problem to be the coordinates at these markings.

The development of the solutions to the boundary value problems can be accomplished through approximation techniques like finite element methods (see Lap82). For genus $g > 1$ objects the domain is $4g$-sided. These $4g$ sides require that the solution approximation technique include non-rectangles to "mesh" the domain. For this next example of a double torus, domain composition methods were used (see [Cox91a, Cox91b, Cox91c]). These methods allow overlaps in the finite elements. Thus the $4g$-sided domain can be meshed with overlaps.

The selection of the differential operator in the double torus example is based on a traditional potential problem. Potential problems (i.e. heat transfer, pressure, etc.) are modeled using Laplace or Poisson operators. The differential operator choice should be dictated by the shape of the object and the periodicity of the coordinate functions. The selection of the differential operator is important and further work on this topic is forthcoming. For this example the Laplace operator generally produces the required smoothness in the coordinate function. Most existing finite element packages provide Laplace or Poisson operators.

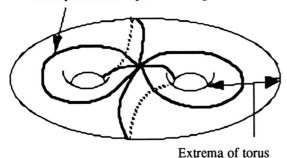

Figure 6. Topological form of a double torus where the embedding is constructed by solving three boundary value problems. Boundary conditions are determined from the coordinates along the four cycles or virtual cuts as marked. Internal constraints to force an embedding arise from the outer and inner radii.

Once the partial differential equation, the finite element mesh, and the complete set of boundary conditions are prescribed, there will exist a unique solution. However, it may not produce the desired coordinate function. Internal constraint conditions are added to the specification of the problem to achieve the desired results. These constraints specify some of the coordinate x,y, or z values in the interior of the solution surface. These can correspond to extrema of the object (i.e. the outer radius or inner radius of the double torus example.) Each of the coordinate boundary value problems will have different internal constraints. The

internal constraints can be applied using penalty functions. Figure 7 shows the z-coordinate function for a specific embedding and decomposition of the double torus. For example, Figure 7 shows a cross shaped flat area above the coordinate function indicating the location of the internal constraints. These constraints force the solution to be zero along the corresponding curve on the surface. These constraints prevent self-intersections in the double torus as the octagonal domain is embedded in space. The first subfigure of Figure 7 shows the double torus. The second subfigure shows the z-coordinate function as height over the octagonal domain. Both figures are contoured and rendered with a height related color map

A 3-tuple for the embedding is constructed from the x, y, and z coordinate values at the same domain point. All the 3-tuples of the embedding thus come from the three boundary value solutions representing the coordinate functions. If each of the coordinate functions are generated using equivalent finite element meshes in the domain, then the solutions at the nodes can be used directly as the 3-tuples that model the object. The connectivity of the elements in the domain will translate into appropriate connectivity in the object space. The double torus of Figure 7 is modeled by combining each of the elements in the three coordinate maps into elements covering the object. This is the image of the embedding from the octagonal domain into three dimensional space.

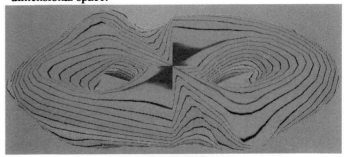

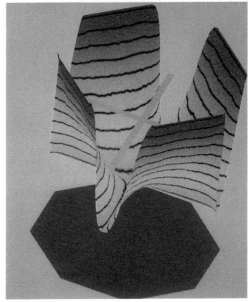

Figure 7. The double torus showing views of the z-coordinate function.

The surface of the double torus of Figure 7 has anomalous bumps and ridges. Changes in the partial differential operator affect bumpiness. For example, the "stiffness" of the surface could be increased, the order or form of the differential operator can be modified, or a body force applied to smooth the resulting object. Further investigation into these methods is ongoing. Another problem is the distortion of the grid on the octagonal domain to the image grid on the double torus. More research on partial differential operators and more development of methods of selecting internal constraints is invited to control the modeling of coordinate functions. It is significant to note that the genus of the object is preserved throughout while there is great flexibility in the shape and locations of the handles. This gives a spatial richness needed for geometric design.

6. Conclusion

Our approach is unique in its incorporation of topology as well as geometry into the design process. This leads to more comprehensive models for scientific visualization and manufacturing needs and is well-suited to a variety of representations of complex objects which arise naturally from the abstraction process in scientific research. A basic outstanding problem is to provide a good set of sufficient conditions (on the coordinate functions) to give an embedding of a sphere with handles. The techniques introduced here work in principle for any dimension. Future directions includes applying these ideas for volume domains and volume images with attached functions.

Acknowledgements

We appreciate Sareddy Madhukar of Spatial Technologies, Boulder, CO for help on Figure 3.3 and Dave Smittley of the Super computing Research Center Bowie, MD for help with Figure 4.5.

References

[Blo90]   Bloor, M. I. G., Wilson, M. J., "Using Partial Differential Equations To Generate Free-Form Surfaces", *Computer-Aided Design,* vol 22, number 1, May 1990.

[Blo89]   Bloor, M. I. G., Wilson, M. J., "Generating N-sided Patches with Partial Differential Equations", *Computer Graphics International,* Wyvil, B. (Editor), Springer-Verlag 1989.

[Can84]   Cannon, J., "The Combinatorial Structure of Cocompact Discrete Hyperbolic Groups," *Geometriae Dedicata*, vol 16, 1984, 123-148.

[Can92]   Cannon, J., Wagreich, P., "Growth Functions of Surface Groups", to appear in Math. Annalen, 1992.

[Cox91a] Cox, J., "Domain Composition Methods For Combining Geometric And Continuum Field Models", *PhD Thesis*, Purdue University, West Lafayette, IN, December 1991.

[Cox91b] Cox, J., Anderson, D., C., "Single Model Formulations That Link Engineering Analysis With Geometric Modeling", *Product Modeling for Computer-Aided Design and Manufacturing,* J. Turner, J. Pegna and M. Wozny (Editors), Elsiver Science Publishers B. V., North-Holland, New York, 1991.

[Cox91c] Cox, J., Charlesworth, W., W., Anderson, D. C., "Domain Composition Methods For Associating Geometric Modeling With Finite Element Modeling", *Proceedings of the ACM/SIGGRAPH Symposium on Solid Modeing Foundations and CAD/CAM Applications,* Austin, TX, June 5-7, 1991.

[Cox88]   Cox, J., Ferguson, H. R. P., Kohkonen, K., "Single Domain Methods For Modeling Objects In The Round For Engineering And Manufacturing Applications", *Advances in Design Automation*, ASME Design Automation Conference, Orlando, FL, Sept. 25-28, 1988.

[Eps92]   Epstein, D.B.A., J.W.Cannon, D.F.Holt, F.V.F. Levi, M.S.Paterson, W.P.Thurston, *Word Processing in Groups,* Jones and Bartlett, Boston, 1992.

[Far88]   Farin, G. E., *Curves and surfaces for Computer Aided Geometric Design*, Academic Press Inc., Boston, 1988.

[Fer89]   Ferguson, H., "Umbilic Torus NC," SIGGRAPH'89 Art Show, Boston, Mass., Leonardo, Journal of the International Society for the Arts, Sciences and Technology, Supplemental Issue, August 1989, page 117, 122.

[Fer90]   Ferguson, H., Two Theorems, Two Sculptures, Two Posters, *American Mathematical Monthly*, Volume 97, Number 7, August-September 1990, pages 589 - 610.

[Fer92]   Ferguson, H., "Algorithms for Scientific Visualization," Supercomputing Research Center Tech. report SRC-92-xxx, 1992.

[Fir82]   Firby, P. and C. Gardiner, *Surface Topology*, John Wylie & Sons, New York, 1982.

[For51]   Ford, L R., *Automorphic Functions*, Chelsea, New York 1951.

[Hof90]   Hoffmann, C., *Geometric Modeling*, Morgen Kaufman, New York, 1990.

[[Lap82] Lapidus, L., Pinder, G. F., *Numerical Solutions of Partial Differential Equations in Science and Engineering,* John Wiley & Sons, New York, 1982.

[Mar86]   Martin, G. E., *The Foundations of Geometry and the Non-Euclidean Plane*, Springer-Verlag, New York, Second Printing, 1986.

[Roc86]   Rockwood, Alyn, "The (5,3) Toroidal Knot," SIGGRAPH86 Art Show Catalog,August,1986.

[Sie88]   Siegel, C.L., *Topics in Complex Function Theory*, vol.1: "Elliptic Functions and Uniformization Theory"; vol.2, "Automorphic Functions and Abelian Integrals", Wylie Interscience, New York, 1988

Variational Surface Modeling

William Welch and Andrew Witkin
School of Computer Science
Carnegie Mellon University
Pittsburgh, PA 15213
{welch|witkin}@cs.cmu.edu

Abstract

We present a new approach to interactive modeling of free-form surfaces. Instead of a fixed mesh of control points, the model presented to the user is that of an infinitely malleable surface, with no fixed controls. The user is free to apply control points and curves which are then available as handles for direct manipulation. The complexity of the surface's shape may be increased by adding more control points and curves, without apparent limit. Within the constraints imposed by the controls, the shape of the surface is fully determined by one or more simple criteria, such as smoothness. Our method for solving the resulting constrained variational optimization problems rests on a surface representation scheme allowing nonuniform subdivision of B-spline surfaces. Automatic subdivision is used to ensure that constraints are met, and to enforce error bounds. Efficient numerical solutions are obtained by exploiting linearities in the problem formulation and the representation.

Keywords: surface design, constrained optimization, interaction techniques

1 Introduction

The most basic goal for interactive free-form surface design is to make it easy for the user to control the shape of the surface. Traditionally, the pursuit of this goal has taken the form of a search for the "right" surface representation, one whose degrees of freedom suffice as controls for direct manipulation by the user. The dominant approach to surface modeling, using a control mesh to manipulate a B-spline or other tensor product surface, clearly reflects this outlook.

The control mesh approach is appealing in large measure because the surface's response to control point displacements is intuitive: pulling or pushing a control point makes a local bump or dent whose shape is quite easily controlled by fine interactive positioning. Unfortunately, local bumps and dents are not the only features one wants to create. For example, almost anyone who has used a control mesh interface has had the frustrating experience of trying to make a conceptually simple change, but being forced in the end to precisely reposition many—even all—the control points to achieve the desired effect.

This sort of problem is bound to arise whenever the controls provided to the user are closely tied to the representation's degrees of freedom, since no fixed set of controls can be expected to anticipate all of the users' needs.

The work we will describe in this paper represents an effort to escape this kind of inflexibility by severing the tie between the controls and the representation. The model we envision presenting to the user is that of an infinitely malleable piecewise smooth surface, with no fixed controls or structure of its own, and with no prior limit on its complexity or ability to resolve detail. To this surface, the user may freely attach a variety of features, such as points and flexible curves, which then serve as handles for direct interactive manipulation of the surface.

Within the constraints imposed by these controls, surface behavior is governed not by the vagaries of the representation, but by one or more simply expressed criteria—that the surface should be as smooth as possible, should conform as closely as possible to a prototype shape, etc.

Our choice of this formulation is motivated by the desire to present a simple representation-independent facade to the user; however, maintaining the facade is anything but simple. Formally, our approach entails the specification of surfaces as solutions to constrained variational optimization problems, i.e. surfaces that extremize integrals subject to constraints. To realize our goal of forming and solving these problems quickly enough to achieve interactivity, yet accurately enough to provide useful surface models, we must address these key issues:

©1992   ACM-0-89791-479-1/92/007/0157 $01.50   157

- **Surface Representation.** We require a surface representation that is concise, yet capable of resolving varying degrees of detail with no inherent limit to surface complexity; that is capable of representing C^n surfaces (in practice we are usually content with C^2 continuity) and that supports efficient solution of the constrained optimization problems we wish to solve. On the other hand, since the representation is to be hidden from the user, we do not require the surface to respond in an intuitive or natural way to direct control-point manipulation.

- **Constrained Optimization** We must be able to accurately and efficiently impose and maintain a variety of constraints on the surface, including those requiring the surface to contain a curve, or requiring two surfaces to join along a specified trim curve. Such constraints raise special problems because the constraint equation involves an integral which must be extremized. Subject to the constraints, we must be able to extremize any of a variety of surface integrals—to create fair surfaces, minimize deviation from a specified rest shape, etc.

- **Automatic Refinement** To create surfaces that reflect the variational solution, without letting the limitations of the representation show through, the resolution of the surface representation must be automatically controlled. Ideally, subdivision should be driven by a measure of the error due to the surface approximation. As constraints are added, additional degrees of freedom must be provided to allow all constraints to be satisfied simultaneously without ill conditioning. Unlike point constraints, which can be met exactly, integral constraints require subdivision to bring their approximation error within a specified tolerance. Additional subdivision should be driven by estimates of the error with which the constrained variational minimum is approximated.

In this paper we report on our progress to date in pursuing the substantial research agenda that these requirements define. Following a discussion of background and related work, we will address each of the issues outlined above. First, the need to compactly represent arbitrarily detailed surfaces leads us to consider schemes for locally refinable representations. Although many have been developed, none meets all of our requirements. We describe a surface representation based on sums of tensor-product B-splines at varying levels of detail. Next we consider the constrained optimization problem itself. We give formulations for several quadratic objective functions, and discuss linear constraints for controlling arbitrary points and curves on the surface. We then turn to the problem of automatic surface refinement based on two kinds of approximation error: objective function error, and constraint

error. Finally, we describe a preliminary implementation and present results.

2 Background

2.1 Direct control of curve and surface points

The limitations of control meshes as interactive handles have been noted before. To address them, Fowler and Bartels[11, 12] present techniques that allow the user to directly manipulate arbitrary points on linear blend curves and surfaces: the curve/surface is constrained to interpolate the grabbed point. As the point is moved interactively, the change to the control points is minimized subject to the interpolation constraint. Parametric derivatives are also presented to the user for direct manipulation, to control surface orientation and curvature at a point. Moving beyond point constraints, Celniker and Welch[6] presented a technique for freezing the shape of the surface along an embedded curve, although the issues involved in having the surface track a moving control-curve were not addressed.

2.2 Nonuniform surface refinement

One of our key requirements is the ability to represent smooth surfaces with no *a priori* limit on the detail that can be resolved. Although a number of nonuniform refinement schemes have been developed, no existing one meets all of our needs. Most of these fail to provide C^2 continuity we require. In computer graphics, Bezier patches [8] have been most widely used for nonuniform refinement. In general, however, higher-order continuity between Bezier patches is not preserved if they are manipulated after subdivision, though [20] formulates adaptive Bezier patch refinement with G^1 continuity. Triangular patches, which support topologically irregular meshes, are widely used in finite element analysis, but have been restricted to first-order continuity. Recent developments[9] point to triangular B-spline patches as a way of constructing a surface with higher-order continuity across a triangular mesh, although a computationally efficient refinement scheme for such a representation has not yet been presented.

Forsey [10] presents a refinement scheme that uses a hierarchy of rectangular B-spline overlays to produce C^2 surfaces. Overlays can be added manually to add detail to the surface, and large- or small-scale changes to the surface shape can be made by manipulating control points at different levels. The hierarchic offset scheme may be well-suited to direct user manipulation of the control points, but it does not meet our need for a refinable substrate for constrained variational optimization. One of the fundamental advantages of conventional tensor product surfaces is linearity: surface points and derivatives are linear functions of the control points. Under Forsey's formulation linearity is lost because unit normals are used to compute offsets. We depend heavily on linearity in later sections; use of the hierarchic offset representation would have a devastating impact on performance.

2.3 Constrained optimization

Variational constrained optimization plays a central role in the formulation of so-called natural splines, piecewise cubic C^2 plane curves that interpolate their control points. The proof that natural splines minimize the integral of second derivative squared subject to the interpolation constraints frequently appears as a demonstration problem in the calculus of variations[22].

Surface models based on variational principals have been widely used in computer vision to solve surface reconstruction problems, in which a surface is fit to stereo measurements, noisy position data, surface orientations, shading information etc. [14, 15, 24]. Similar formulations have been employed in computer graphics for physically based modeling of deformable surfaces [23]. All of these are based on regular finite difference grids of fixed resolution.

Constrained optimization based on second-derivative norms has been used in fairing B-spline surfaces[18]. Moreton[19] minimizes variation of curvature to generate surfaces which skin networks of curves while seeking circular or straight-line cross-sections. Such schemes can give rise to very fair surfaces, but the nonlinearity of their fairness metrics prevents them from being used for interactive surface design.

Celniker [5] proposed a physically-based model for interactive free-form surface design, in which the surface is modeled using a C^1 mesh of triangular patches, and positions and normals may be controlled along patch boundaries. Interactivity is possible because the surface fairing problem is formulated as a minimization of a quadratic functional subject to linear constraints. Our approach is closely related in this respect, although we consider more general formulations for both surface functionals and shape control constraints.

3 Surface Representation

We require a representation for smoothly deformable surfaces, which has no *a priori* limit on the detail that can be resolved. Further, we require that points on such a surface be linear functions of its shape control parameters, yielding a more tractable control problem.

Tensor-product B-splines[8] conveniently represent C^n piecewise polynomial surfaces as control-point weighted sums of nonlinear shape functions, and they form the basis of our representation scheme. Unfortunately, the standard tensor-product construction does not allow detail to be nonuniformly added to the surface through local refinement. We instead represent such a locally refined region as a sum of the original surface and smaller, more finely parameterized surfaces. Surface patches at various levels are evaluated and summed to compute the nonuniform surface's value. This is related to Forsey's overlay scheme for B-spline surface refinement [10], but the formulation is much simpler because there is no notion of hierarchic offsets for overlays. The nonuniform surface is a simple sum of sparse, uniform surface layers, which may overlap in arbitrary ways. Further, the resulting surface shape remains a linear function of the control-points, leading to a tractable surface control problem.

A degree$-r$ tensor-product B-spline surface span is formulated as

$$\mathbf{w}(u,v) = \sum_{i}^{r+1} \sum_{j}^{r+1} N_i(u)N_j(v)P_{ij}, \qquad (1)$$

where $\mathbf{N}(t)$ is the vector of $r+1$ uniform B-spline basis functions evaluated at t, and $\mathbf{P}$ is an $(r+1) \times (r+1)$ array of control-points. A mesh of such spans will form a C^{r-1} composite surface if neighboring spans share r rows of control-points along their common boundary. A $U \times V$ array of control-points thus yields a $(U-r) \times (V-r)$-span composite surface.

It is easy to get lost in the sea of summations and indices when working with composite surfaces and formulas involving (1). To simplify notation in this and following sections, we take advantage of the fact that the X, Y, and Z dimensions of the surface in this representation scheme may be treated independently, and state our formulas in one dimension only. Further, we will represent the nth uniform surface layer w^n in terms of a $1 \times (U_nV_n)$ *control vector* $\mathbf{p}$, which is related to the $U_n \times V_n$ control-point matrix $\mathbf{P}$ by the structure-flattening constant $\mathbf{S}$:

$$P_{ij} = \sum_{k} S_{ijk}p_k,$$

where $S_{ijk} = 1$ if P_{ij} corresponds to p_k, and is 0 otherwise (S converts between a matrix and eg. its row-major representation). Then

$$b_k(u,v) = \sum_{i} \sum_{j} N_i(u)N_j(v)S_{ijk}$$

is a vector of basis functions, and its dot-product with the control vector yields the value of the surface at that point. A nonuniform surface w represented as the sum of n uniform surfaces at varying levels of refinement is then

$$\begin{aligned} w(u,v) &= \sum_{i}^{n} \mathbf{p}^i \cdot \mathbf{b}^i(u,v) \\ &= \mathbf{p}^T \mathbf{b}(u,v) \qquad (2) \end{aligned}$$

where $\mathbf{b}$ and $\mathbf{p}$ are concatenations of the individual layers' basis and control vectors into respective global vectors.

Note that although each level's parameterization spans the (u,v) domain of the base surface, its control-vector will in general be sparse, with nonzero entries corresponding to local refinements of the surface. In our implementation, we represent a particular layer of refinement as a sparse plugboard of control-points which exist independently of any spans which reference them. Whenever a new span is created within a particular level, it is connected to the appropriate subset of the control-points for that level. This implements the necessary control-point sharing between adjacent spans. New control-points are created within a layer the first time they are referenced by a span belonging to that layer. Thus, only the regions where refinement has actually taken place within a level are explicitly represented and evaluated.

It remains to ensure that the resulting sum of surfaces has the proper degree of parametric continuity. Although the summed surface is not formulated as a hierarchic offset surface as in [10], Forsey's technique for enforcing continuity over a composite offset surface is still applicable. For any patch belonging to a particular level of refinement, we constrain an r-wide band of control-points associated with the patch's boundary to be 0. This forces each patch's position and $r - 1$ derivatives to 0 at the patch boundaries, which is sufficient to guarantee that the summed surface is C^{r-1} regardless of the way in which patches in various layers overlap. When disjoint patches within a particular layer have grown to the extent that they meet at a common boundary, the constraints along that boundary may be discarded and the patches merged into one.

4   Constrained Optimization

We would like to control a surface by attaching points and curves to it, letting the surface interpolate between the controls in an appropriate way, so that the user need not completely specify the surface at every point. Exactly what characterizes desirable surface behavior depends on the application, though there is often the requirement that the surface prefer fair, graceful shapes. Regardless of their particulars, many such behaviors can be cast as minimum principles over the surface. One formulates a measure of "goodness" at each surface point, and then integrates this measure over the entire surface to get a single number which characterizes the desirability of the surface shape under that metric. We then search for surface shapes which optimize this quantity while still satisfying the geometric constraints specified by the user.

More formally, we seek shapes which extremize the integral of a surface metric subject to geometric constraints. Such shapes are not intrinsically linked to any particular surface representation scheme, but exist instead as the solutions to constrained variational optimization problems[22]. Our modeler must construct acceptable approximations to such infinite-dimensional variational surfaces using a finite number of control parameters. The approach taken is to approximate the ideal surface as a

piecewise polynomial surface using the nonuniform B-spline representation of the previous section.

In this section we describe techniques for computing the B-spline control-points which optimize surface shape while satisfying user-supplied geometric constraints. We first discuss a number of possible surface metrics (*objective functions*, in optimization parlance). We then formulate point and curve constraints for controlling the surface. Finally, we discuss techniques for solving the resulting constrained optimization problems at interactive speeds.

4.1   Surface Objective Functions

One might choose to extremize any number of functions over a surface to achieve fair shapes. One such function measures how much the surface is stretched and bent by looking at the differential area and curvature at each point[23]:

$$Q(\mathbf{w}) = \int_{\mathbf{w}} \|\mathbf{G}\|_\alpha^2 + \|\mathbf{B}\|_\beta^2, \qquad (3)$$

where $\mathbf{G}$ and $\mathbf{B}$ represent the first and second fundamental surface forms, and α and β weight the matrix norms. The α and β terms determine resistance to stretching and resistance to bending, respectively.

The vector and matrix norms in this function make it highly nonlinear, leading to a difficult nonlinear optimization problem. It is therefore common[23, 5, 24] to simplify this objective function by linearizing the matrix norms and $\mathbf{B}$ (this is the *thin plate under tension* model [21, 25]):

$$Q(\mathbf{w}) = \int_{\mathbf{w}} \sum_{i,j=1}^{2} \alpha_{ij} D_i \mathbf{w} D_j \mathbf{w} + \beta_{ij}(D_i D_j \mathbf{w})^2, \quad (4)$$

where $D_i \mathbf{w}$ represents the partial derivative of the surface $\mathbf{w}$ with respect to the ith parameter. The approximation is only accurate near the actual minimum (where higher order terms tend to 0) but it is still well-behaved away from the minimum, and the computational benefits are enormous: for a linear surface representation such as a tensor product B-spline, this simplified objective function is quadratic in the underlying surface degrees of freedom, and we can cast the optimization problem as a constrained least-squares minimization.

First, we formulate (4) in terms of the composite B-spline surface of equation(2):

$$Q(\mathbf{w}) = \int_{\mathbf{w}} \sum_{i,j=1}^{2} \left(\begin{array}{c} \alpha_{ij}\mathbf{p}^T D_i \mathbf{b} \ \mathbf{p}^T D_j \mathbf{b} \\ + \\ \beta_{ij}(\mathbf{p}^T D_i D_j \mathbf{b})^2 \end{array} \right).$$

Since the surface is linear in the control vector $\mathbf{p}$ it may be brought outside and the integration in (u, v) completed to yield a $\dim(\mathbf{p}) \times \dim(\mathbf{p})$ matrix $\mathbf{H}$:

$$
\begin{aligned}
Q(\mathbf{w}) &= \mathbf{p}^T \int_{\mathbf{w}} \sum_{i,j=1}^{2} \left(\begin{array}{c} \alpha_{ij} D_i \mathbf{b} \otimes D_j \mathbf{b} \\ + \\ \beta_{ij} D_i D_j \mathbf{b} \otimes D_i D_j \mathbf{b} \end{array} \right) \mathbf{p} \\
&= \mathbf{p}^T \mathbf{H} \mathbf{p}. \quad (5)
\end{aligned}
$$

(the symbol $\otimes$ signifies an outer product)

Minimizing (5) yields a value for the control vector $\mathbf{p}$ corresponding to the optimal approximation to the variational surface defined by (4), for the given surface refinement. This is the Rayleigh-Ritz method of approximating a continuum solution with a finite set of continuous linear functions[22]. Clearly a minimal solution to equation (5) is 0 — we must add constraints to keep the surface from collapsing to a point if things are to be at all interesting. As we will see in the next subsection, a variety of geometric constraints can be expressed as linear relations over the control vector. Then the optimization becomes a linearly constrained quadratic minimization, which can be efficiently solved using techniques described in Section 4.3.

But first, consider another possibility for the objective function. Suppose we measure the amount the surface has deformed from some prototype shape. In the absence of constraints, minimizing this deformation metric causes the surface to assume the prototype shape. When constraint handles are attached to such a surface and manipulated, the surface should gracefully deform from this shape.

One way of formulating such a shape attractor is to modify (4) to measure the change in stretch and bending from that of a rest shape $\hat{\mathbf{w}}$ [23, 18]. This yields

$$
Q(\mathbf{w}) = \int_{\mathbf{w}} \sum_{i,j=1}^{2} \left(\begin{array}{c} \alpha_{ij} D_i(\mathbf{w} - \hat{\mathbf{w}}) D_j(\mathbf{w} - \hat{\mathbf{w}}) \\ + \\ \beta_{ij}(D_i D_j(\mathbf{w} - \hat{\mathbf{w}}))^2 \end{array} \right),
$$

leading to

$$
Q(\mathbf{w}) = (\mathbf{p} - \hat{\mathbf{p}})^T \mathbf{H}(\mathbf{p} - \hat{\mathbf{p}}) \quad (6)
$$

where $\hat{\mathbf{p}}$ is the control vector corresponding to the prototype shape. We must then minimize (6) subject to constraints.

The curve manipulation techniques of [2, 11] can also be cast as a shape-attracting quadratic optimization. They minimize absolute control-point displacement subject to point constraints. That is, their deformation metric is simply $(\mathbf{p} - \hat{\mathbf{p}})^T (\mathbf{p} - \hat{\mathbf{p}})$, where $\hat{\mathbf{p}}$ is the control vector for the current shape. This is not a satisfactory objective function from the standpoint of representation-independent control because, as the authors noted, the local properties of the basis show through. Components of $\mathbf{p}$ which are not directly affected by constraints will always keep their original values, as this produces the minimum "deformation".

Thus, the size of the bump raised by pulling on such a surface depends on the level of refinement in the underlying representation.

4.2 Geometric Constraints

The user must be able to attach points and curves to the surface and use them to control the surface shape during sculpting. We implement these handles as geometric constraints which the surface must satisfy while optimizing its objective function. In this section, we discuss two broad classes of geometric constraints: finite-dimensional constraints, which control the surface shape at discrete points, and transfinite constraints, which control the surface shape along embedded curves or sub-regions of the surface.

Within each of these classes, we focus on constraint formulations which are *linear* in the surface control vector, as they lead to a constrained optimization problem which can be solved at interactive speeds. In general, such constraints involve surface features whose surface u, v coordinates remain fixed, so that the B-spline basis functions may be evaluated once to yield linear relationships among the components of the control vector. Thus, constraints involving sliding surface points of attachment are excluded in such formulations.

Within the class of linear constraints, we further restrict our focus to constraint formulations which do not couple the (independent) control vectors for each of the surface's spatial dimensions. Computing an independently constrained solution in each spatial dimension is significantly cheaper than computing a single coupled solution for all dimensions because the system matrices involved grow as the square of the size of the control vector, though for some applications the additional cost may be justified.

4.2.1 Finite-Dimensional Constraints

In sculpting a surface one might specify shape requirements which must hold at a set of discrete points on the surface. Surface point positions, point normal directions, and offset relationships between points are all examples of useful point constraints for controlling the surface. Each generates some fixed number of constraints, depending on the way in which the relationship is formulated.

For example, the constraint that a surface point $\mathbf{w}(u_0, v_0)$ remain fixed at a world-space point x can be written as

$$
\begin{aligned}
\mathbf{x} &= \mathbf{w}(u_0, v_0) \\
&= \mathbf{p}^T \mathbf{b}(u_0, v_0).
\end{aligned}
$$

This actually represents three independent constraints, one in each spatial dimension, and $\mathbf{b}(u_0, v_0)$ may be evaluated to yield linear constraints in their respective $\mathbf{p}$'s. Constraints to control various parametric derivatives of the surface, such as tangent vectors at a point, are similarly formulated [11].

4.2.2 Transfinite Constraints

A constraint which involves a one- or two-dimensional surface entity, such as an embedded curve or surface patch, must be formulated as an integral over the entity. For example, given a parametric (u, v) curve $\mathbf{c}(t) = (u(t), v(t))$, the constraint that the surface curve $\mathbf{C}(t) = (\mathbf{w} \circ \mathbf{c})(t)$ align itself with the space curve $\mathbf{D}(t)$ would be written:

$$\int_{\mathbf{C}} (\mathbf{C} - \mathbf{D})^2 = 0. \qquad (7)$$

Such a constraint statement is dimensionally infinite, and because our surface representation has only a finite number of control points the surface will in general not be able to exactly satisfy the constraint. We will instead constrain the discretized surface to optimally approximate the constraint in a least-squares sense.

Analogous to the objective functions of the previous section, we formulate a transfinite constraint as a quadratic function which achieves a global minimum when the constraint is satisfied[6].

Thus, equation (7) is at a minimum when its gradient with respect to the control vector is 0, and yields the discretized gradient constraints:

$$
\begin{aligned}
0 &= \frac{\partial \int (\mathbf{C} - \mathbf{D})^2}{\partial \mathbf{p}} \\
&= \int_{\mathbf{C}} (\mathbf{C} - \mathbf{D}) \frac{\partial \mathbf{C}}{\partial \mathbf{p}} \\
&= \int_{\mathbf{c}} ((\mathbf{w} \circ \mathbf{c}) - \mathbf{D}) \frac{\partial (\mathbf{w} \circ \mathbf{c})}{\partial \mathbf{p}}
\end{aligned}
$$

For our B-spline surface this becomes

$$
\begin{aligned}
0 = \; &\mathbf{p}^T \int_{\mathbf{c}} (\mathbf{b} \circ c)(t) \otimes (\mathbf{b} \circ c)(t) - \\
&\int_{\mathbf{c}} \mathbf{D}(\mathbf{b} \circ c)(t),
\end{aligned}
$$

The integration is completed independently of $\mathbf{p}$ (analytically, or numerically by point sampling), leading to a system of linear constraints in the control vector $\mathbf{p}$. The constraints clamp the surface in a shape which minimizes its least-square deviation from the control curve c. Unacceptably large deviations can be eliminated by refining the parts of the surface through which the curve passes.

The constraints generated by this gradient-clamping operation are not necessarily independent. The shape of the embedded curve in u, v determines number of independent constraint rows generated — an iso-paramteric line only produces $r+1$ independent constraint rows per span, while a zigzag stitch across a span might produce fully $(r + 1)^2$ independent rows, so that the space curve would completely control the shape of the underlying surface span. Thus, the presence of dependent constraint rows, while numerically inconvenient, is desirable because it means the surface can interpolate the constraint curve with some of its control points remaining undetermined. The surface is then free to change so as to minimize its objective function or to respond to other sculpting operators while still preserving the constraint.

As with any technique in which the question of linear independence arises, there are delicate numeric issues which must be considered. In particular, a u, v curve with very slight high-degree oscillations will give rise to nearly-dependent constraint rows for an interpolation constraint, and thus will lock down all degrees of freedom in the spans it passes through. When such a curve is attached to a space curve, the surface shape is completely determined by the space curve, and thus the surface can behave arbitrarily badly with respect to the objective function. Such constraint leverage can be reduced by adaptively refining the surface representation. Another technique, *reduced quadrature* [27], involves numerically evaluating the constraint integral by sampling as if the surface representation was of a lower order. Such undersampling leads to a dependent set of constraints, thereby eliminating some of the locking behavior associated with a higher-order integration.

4.3 Linearly Constrained Quadratic Optimization

Having formulated the surface approximation problem with a quadratic objective function and linear constraints, a vast body of optimization literature can be brought to bear. In particular, very efficient techniques exist for enforcing linear constraints in this context, and we discuss two we have used: one method using Lagrange multipliers to enforce a least-squares fit to the constraint matrix, the other using a penalty-based approach.

We seek solution methods for the linearly constrained quadratic optimization problem

$$
\begin{aligned}
\min_{\mathbf{p}} \; &\left\| \tfrac{1}{2}\mathbf{p}^T \mathbf{H} \mathbf{p} - \mathbf{p}^T \mathbf{f} \right\| \\
&\text{subject to } \mathbf{A}\mathbf{p} = \mathbf{b}
\end{aligned} \qquad (8)
$$

where $\mathbf{H}$ is the Hessian of the quadratic metric to be minimized, $\mathbf{f}$ is the gradient optimization term, and $\mathbf{A}\mathbf{p} = \mathbf{b}$ is the system of linear constraints to be satisfied (each row of $\mathbf{A}$ represents a single linear constraint, and the corresponding component of $\mathbf{b}$ is its value). Solution methods generally transform this to an unconstrained system

$$
\min_{\widehat{\mathbf{p}}} \; \left\| \frac{1}{2}\widehat{\mathbf{p}}^T \widehat{\mathbf{H}} \widehat{\mathbf{p}} - \widehat{\mathbf{p}}^T \widehat{\mathbf{f}} \right\|,
$$

whose solutions $\widehat{\mathbf{p}}$, when transformed back to $\mathbf{p}$'s, are guaranteed to satisfy the constraints. The unconstrained system is at a minimum when its derivatives are 0, thus we are led to solve the system

$$\widehat{\mathbf{H}}\widehat{\mathbf{p}} = \widehat{\mathbf{f}}$$

to find the minimizing $\widehat{\mathbf{p}}$, then transform it back to $\mathbf{p}$ to recover the constrained minimum solution.

We may make either of two transformations of the problem to an unconstrained optimization. For the first, we reformulate equation (8) by adding a single degree of freedom y_i (a Lagrange multiplier[22]) for each constraint row $\mathbf{A}_i$ and we then minimize the unconstrained

$$\min_{p} \left\| \frac{1}{2}\mathbf{p}^T\mathbf{H}\mathbf{p} - \mathbf{p}^T\mathbf{f} + (\mathbf{A}\mathbf{p} - \mathbf{b})^T\mathbf{y} \right\|.$$

Differentiating with respect to $\mathbf{p}$ then $\mathbf{y}$ leads to the augmented system

$$\begin{vmatrix} \mathbf{H} & \mathbf{A}^T \\ \mathbf{A} & 0 \end{vmatrix} \begin{vmatrix} \mathbf{p} \\ \mathbf{y} \end{vmatrix} = \begin{vmatrix} \mathbf{f} \\ \mathbf{b} \end{vmatrix}, \qquad (9)$$

which, though no longer positive-definite, does determine the unique minimum which satisfies the constraints provided the constraint matrix contains no dependent rows. This method has the advantage that it enforces the constraints exactly, in contrast with the penalty method below. This is at the expense of adding an additional variable y_i for each constraint to be enforced. Also, an initial reduction of the constraint matrix to a set of independent rows must be performed. Note that if a least-squares fit to the constraints is to be enforced, we must actually form the normal matrix $\mathbf{A}^T\mathbf{A}$, and take its independent rows as our constraints.

A second solution method associates a penalty term with each constraint, so that the minimization becomes

$$\min_{\hat{\mathbf{p}}} \left\| \begin{pmatrix} \mu\mathbf{A} \\ \mathbf{H} \end{pmatrix} \mathbf{p} - \begin{pmatrix} \mu\mathbf{b} \\ \mathbf{f} \end{pmatrix} \right\|, \qquad (10)$$

where μ is a large positive weight and the solution to the resulting unconstrained minimization approaches the true constrained minimum as $\mu \to \infty$. In computing a least-squares solution to (10), we can avoid the numerical conditioning problems associated with forming the constraint normal matrix $\mathbf{A}^T\mathbf{A}$ by instead performing a QR factorization[13] of the matrix in (10). Since μ must be chosen small enough to leave a well-conditioned problem, the solution to the penalty system can leave an unacceptably large constraint residual. This can be reduced by performing additional minimization steps on the residual using the same factored matrix[26].

An advantage to formulating the constrained minimization in this way is that no new variables are added to the system. This is offset, however, by the need to perform additional solver steps in refining the residual. A more important advantage to the formulation is that dependent constraint rows need not be eliminated prior to building and factoring the augmented matrix. This makes it straightforward to use factorization update techniques [3, 4] to incrementally update the factorization of the system matrix as surface constraints are added or deleted.

4.4 Automatic Refinement

We are using a piecewise polynomial surface with a finite number of control parameters to approximate an infinite-dimensional variational surface. To maintain a representation-independent facade, we must be able to control the error introduced by this approximation. We must be concerned with two kinds of approximation error. First, the discretized surface may be unable to satisfy all constraints simultaneously (*constraint error.*) Second, even if all constraints are met, the discretized surface may fail to achieve the variational minimum (*objective function error.*)

Of the two, objective function error is more difficult to handle because it cannot be measured directly[1]. How to estimate this kind of error *a priori* is an open research problem [27, 16]. More widely used are *a posteriori* methods in which an estimate is obtained by comparing higher-order solutions to lower-order ones. [1, 17, 7]

In contrast, constraint error can generally be measured directly, by calculating point-to-point or curve-to-curve distances. A straightforward refinement scheme is to compute the constraint error per surface span, refining those spans whose error exceeds a specified tolerance.

5 Results

An interactive free-form surface modeler implementing the techniques described in this paper has been developed at CMU. The modeler, which runs on Silicon Graphics Iris workstations, allows the user to interactively manipulate variational curves and surfaces, controlling and combining them through a variety of constraints and objective functions.

By default, surfaces minimize the fairness integral given in equation (4) subject to the constraints acting on them. At any time, the user may install a surface's current shape as its rest shape, or "melt" a previously remembered rest shape. We have found that additional objective function terms can be useful as interactive sculpting tools—for instance, terms which inflate or deflate the surface.

Basic surface control is provided by point constraints, which take the place of conventional control points. Ephemeral position constraints allow the user to grab and drag arbitrary points on the surface, while persistent constraints help define surface shape. Additional control is afforded by surface normal constraints.

Curve constraints have proven to be a far more powerful modeling tool. To create a surface or space curve, the user defines a sequence of surface or space points, from which an interpolating curve is constructed. Once created, curves become first-class variational objects that can be controlled by constraints. To use curves as surface controls, a surface curve is attached to a space curve, which may be manipulated by the user. This attachment can be established in either of two ways. First, a surface curve may be snapped to an independently created free-

---

[1]unless the error-free answer is available for comparison!

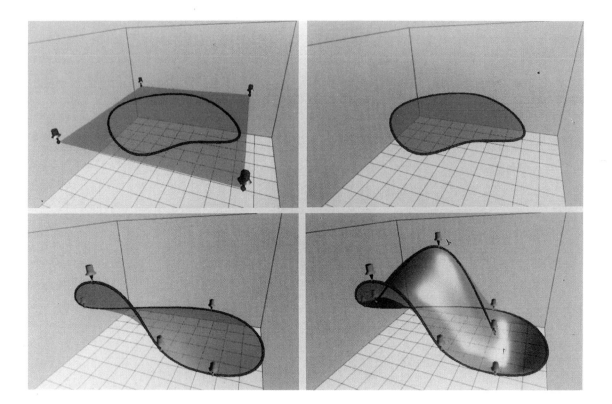

Figure 1: Surface modeling with curve constraints. Upper left: the user creates a surface curve on a sheet. The push-pins identify point constraints, which keep the surface from collapsing to a point. Upper right: the surface has been trimmed. The surface curve defining the boundary has been promoted to a space curve which can be independently controlled by the user. Lower left: Point constraints are applied to the space curve to modify its shape. The surface, which is now constrained to contain the space curve, deforms to follow the curve. Lower right: a second control curve is added and manipulated.

standing space curve, allowing the user to define literal wireframes, then fit surfaces onto them. Second, the user may inscribe control curves on the surface to which automatically created space curves are fit. Figure 1 shows the use of curve constraints. Additionally, the user may impose ribbon constraints that control surface orientation as well as position along the curve.

Curve constraints may also be used to join surface patches by snapping a pair of surface curves to a single space curve. The result is that the two surfaces are constrained to intersect along the space curve. The intersection curve may then be directly manipulated by the user. In this way, surface sheets may be assembled and trimmed against the joined curves to form boundary representations for solids (see figure 2). As a generalization of ribbon constraints, joined surfaces may be subjected to hinge constraints that independently control the surfaces' orientations along the intersection curve.

The modeler employs the refinable surface representation described in section 3. The user may refine the surface manually by selecting regions to be refined, or request automatic refinement based on constraint error. Currently, the system does not perform refinement based on objective function error. The use of automatic refinement is illustrated in figure 3.

References

[1] I. Babuska and W. C. Rheinboldt. Error estimates for adaptive finite element computations. *SIAM J. Numer. Anal.*, 15(4), 1978.

[2] Richard H. Bartels and John C. Beatty. A technique for the direct manipulation of spline curves. In *Proceedings, Graphics Interface*, 1989.

[3] Richard. H. Bartels and Gene Golub. The simplex method of linear programming using lu decomposition. *CACM*, 12(5), May 1969.

[4] Å ke Björck. A general updating algorithm for constrained linear least squares problems. *SIAM J. Sci. and Stat. Comp.*, 5(2), 1984.

[5] George Celniker and Dave Gossard. Deformable curve and surface finite-elements for free-form shape design. *Computer Graphics*, 25(4), July 1991. Proceedings SIGGRAPH '91.

[6] George Celniker and William Welch. Linear constraints for nonuniform b-spline surfaces. In *Proceedings, Symposium on Interactive 3D Graphics*, 1992.

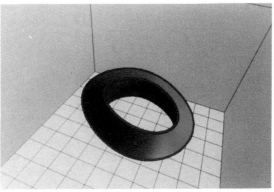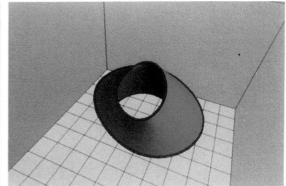

Figure 2: Left: A B-rep solid constructed using variational sheets joined by curve constraints. Intersection curves are formed by constraining curves on each surface to contain a common space curve. Surfaces are then trimmed to the intersection. Right: As the user reshapes the space curve, both adjoining faces follow, maintaining the intersection.

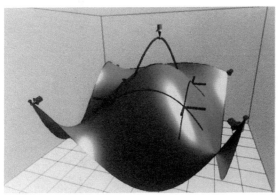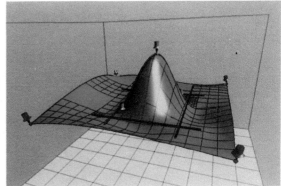

Figure 3: Left: A single bicubic span, subject to point and curve constraints, with large constraint error. Right: the same surface, following automatic refinement driven by constraint error. Error was measured per surface span. Spans exceeding the specified error tolerance were recursively refined.

[7] J. P. De. S. R. Gago, D. W. Kelly, and O. C. Zienkiewicz. A posteriori error analysis and adaptive processes in the finite element method: Part ii – adaptive mesh refinement. *Int. J. Numer. Methods Eng.*, 19:1621–1656, 1983.

[8] Gerald Farin. *Curves and Surfaces for Computer Aided Geometric Design*. Academic Press, Inc., 1990.

[9] Philip Fong and Hans-Peter Seidel. Control points for multivariate b-spline surfaces over arbitrary triangulations. *Computer Graphics Forum*, 10:309–317, 1991.

[10] D.R. Forsey and R.H. Bartels. Hierarchical b-spline refinement. *Computer Graphics*, 22(4), August 1988. Proceedings SIGGRAPH '88.

[11] Barry Fowler. Geometric manipulation of tensor-product surfaces. In *Proceedings, Symposium on Interactive 3D Graphics*, 1992. (to appear).

[12] Barry Fowler and Richard Bartels. Constraint-based curve manipulation. In *ACM Siggraph Course Notes, Topics in the Construction, Manipulation, and Assessment of Spline Surfaces*, 1991.

[13] Gene Golub and Charles Van Loan. *Matrix Computations*. Johns Hopkins University Press, 1989.

[14] W.E.L. Grimson. An implementation of a computational theory of surface orientation. *Computer Vision, Graphics, and Image Processing*, 22(1):39–69, 1983.

[15] B.K.P. Horn and M.J. Brooks. The variational approach to shape from shading. *Computer Vision, Graphics, and Image Processing*, 33:174–208, 1986.

[16] D. W. Kelly. The self-equilibration of residuals and upper bound eror estimates in the finite element method. In I. Babuska, editor, *Accuracy Estimates and Adaptive Refinements in Finite Element Computations*, pages 129–146. Wiley, 1986.

[17] D. W. Kelly, J. P. De. S. R. Gago, and O. C. Zienkiewicz. A posteriori error analysis and adaptive processes in the finite element method: Part i –

error analysis. *Int. J. Numer. Methods Eng.*, 19:1593–1619, 1983.

[18] N. J. Lott and D. I. Pullin. Method for fairing b-spline surfaces. *Computer-Aided Design*, 20(10), 1988.

[19] Henry Moreton and Carlo Séquin. Functional minimization for fair surface design. *In these proceedings*.

[20] Francis J. M. Schmitt, Brian A. Barsky, and Wen-Hui Du. An adaptive subdivision method for surface-fitting from sampled data. *Computer Graphics*, 20(4), 1986. Proceedings SIGGRAPH '86.

[21] D.G. Schweikert. An interpolation curve using a spline in tension. *Journal of Math and Phys.*, 45:312–317, 1966.

[22] Gilbert Strang. *Introduction to Applied Mathematics*. Wellesley-Cambridge Press, 1986.

[23] Demetri Terzopoulis, John Platt, Alan Barr, and Kurt Fleischer. Elastically deformable models. *Computer Graphics*, 21(4), July 1987. Proceedings of SIGGRAPH '87.

[24] D. Terzopoulos. Multi-level reconstruction of visual surfaces. *MIT Artificial Intelligence Memo Number 671*, April 1981.

[25] D. Terzopoulos. Regularization of inverse visual problems involving discontinuities. *IEEE Trans. Pattern Analysis and Machine Intelligence*, PAMI-8:413–424, 1986.

[26] Charles Van Loan. On the method of weighting for equality-constrained least-squares problems. *SIAM J. Numer. Anal.*, 22(5), 1985.

[27] O.C. Zienkiewicz and K. Morgan. *Finite Elements and Approximation*. John Wiley and Sons, 1983.

Functional Optimization for Fair Surface Design

Henry P. Moreton
Carlo H. Séquin

Computer Science Division
University of California, Berkeley

Abstract

This paper presents a simple-to-use mechanism for the creation of complex smoothly shaped surfaces of any genus or topological type. The surfaces are specified through interpolated geometric constraints consisting of positions and, optionally, surface normals and surface curvatures. From a designer's point of view, this is a very natural way to specify a desired shape, whether free-form or technical. Nonlinear optimization techniques are then used to minimize a fairness functional based on the variation of curvature. This functional produces very high quality surfaces with predictable, intuitive behavior, while generating, where possible, simple shapes, such as cylinders, spheres, or tori, which are commonly used in geometric modeling. While easy to use, this optimization-based approach is computationally quite demanding. With more efficient optimization algorithms and with the ever increasing processing power available on every desk-top, the techniques described here will provide the basis for a new class of practical interactive geometric modeling tools.

1 Introduction

In this paper we present a simple-to-use mechanism for the creation of complex, smoothly shaped models of any genus or topological type. The shapes are specified using interpolated geometric constraints. The resulting models accurately reflect these specifications and are free of unwanted wrinkles, bulges, and ripples. When the given constraints indicate and/or permit, the resulting surfaces take on the desirable shapes of spheres, cylinders, cones, and tori. Specification of a desired shape is straightforward, allowing simple or complex shapes to be described easily and compactly. For example, a "suitcase corner," the blend of three quarter cylinders of differing radii, is formed by specifying just six sets of constraints (Fig. 1).

A Klein bottle is specified with equal ease; only twelve point-tangent constraints are used to model the surface shown in Figure 2.

Authors' addresses:

Computer Science Division
Department of Electrical Engineering and Computer Science
University of California, Berkeley, CA 94720
H.P. Moreton, (510) 339-8715, moreton@cs.berkeley.edu
C.H. Séquin, (510) 642-5103, sequin@cs.berkeley.edu

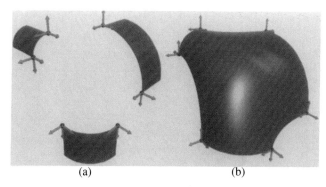

Figure 1. A suitcase corner. (a) illustrates the specification with normal and curvature constraints. (b) illustrates the resulting blend.

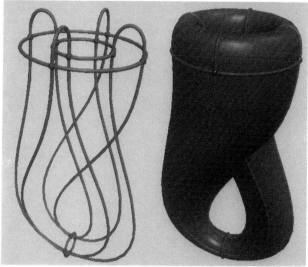

Figure 2. A Klein bottle defined by twelve constraint sets.

The work described here is the result of research into the fairness of curves and surfaces specified through geometric interpolatory constraints. These geometric constraints consist of points, surface normals, and surface curvatures. We use nonlinear optimization techniques to minimize a fairness functional subject to the given geometric constraints.

Once the geometric constraints are satisfied by construction, the techniques described here set the remaining surface parameters (degrees of freedom) to minimize our fairness functional while maintaining G^1 continuity by using a penalty function. The problem of creating surfaces with G^1 continuity is very difficult to solve satisfactorily. Most techniques use heuristics to set extra degrees of freedom and sufficient but not necessary constructions to guarantee G^1 continuity; however they typically produce unnecessary and undesirable "wrinkles". An extensive survey by members of the Graphics Group at the University of Washington [17] demonstrates these common flaws.

The curve and surface functionals that we have derived minimize the *variation* of curvature; thus we refer to the curves as *minimum variation curves* (MVC[1]) and to the surfaces as *minimum variation surfaces* (MVS). In the case of curves, the integral of the squared magnitude of the derivative of curvature is minimized

$$\int \left| \frac{d\vec{\kappa}}{ds} \right|^2 ds. \tag{1}$$

Note that this integral evaluates to zero for circular arcs and straight lines. For surfaces, the functional is the integral of the squared magnitude of the derivatives of normal curvature taken in the principle directions[2]

$$\int \frac{d\kappa_n}{d\hat{e}_1}^2 + \frac{d\kappa_n}{d\hat{e}_2}^2 dA.$$

Note that analogous to the MVC, the MVS functional evaluates to zero for cyclides: spheres, cones, cylinders, tori, and planes.

Section 2 reviews previous related work, discussing approaches, advantages, and shortcomings. Section 3 presents an overview of our approach outlining the steps taken to produce a surface model from specified constraints. Section 4 provides details of the representation of the surfaces, and a description of the optimization techniques used to compute them. Section 5 details the computation of the minimum energy networks used in our algorithm. Section 6 presents a comparison of our approach with other methods; it exhibits examples of complex surfaces created from simple, compact specifications.

2 Previous Work

The work described in this paper touches on several problems and thus several areas of study. First, we discuss work on creating a G^1 surface out of a collection of non-degenerate polynomial patches. Second, we reference work on functional minimization, constrained optimization, and finite element analysis, all applied to surface design. The last portion of this section reviews minimum energy networks.

2.1 G^1 Continuity

Peters [22] provides a good classification and review of G^1 interpolation techniques. All of the methods discussed are constructive, using heuristics to set those degrees of freedom that are not fixed by continuity constraints or set as side effects of the construction method. These methods rely on the computation of a network of curves that interpolate the data, subject to various continuity and connectivity constraints. Peters has done a great deal of work on the construction of geometrically continuous surfaces. His most recent work outlines a method for creating "C^k" surfaces. Relevant to this discussion, Peters [23] shows that a curve network maintaining G^2 continuity is sufficient and in general necessary for the construction of a G^1 surface. This result assumes that a single quintic polynomial patch is placed in each network opening, and that the opening boundaries are fixed. In addition, there are no restrictions on the order of (i.e., the number of edges joining) the network nodes.

Our work combines a solution to the G^1 continuity problem with the setting of the unconstrained degrees of freedom to form a fair G^1 continuous surface. No explicit G^1 construction is used; rather a suitable penalty function is incorporated into the objective function.

In related work, DeRose [10] presents the necessary and sufficient conditions for G^1 continuity between adjacent triangular and quadrilateral Bézier patches of equal degree. We use these results to formulate the penalty function that imposes G^1 continuity.

2.2 Optimization, Minimization, and Finite Element Analysis

In [32] Williams describes a system using finite difference methods for the computation of smooth surfaces. The system minimizes the total energy of a fictitious elastic plate. In [26] Pramila describes techniques for ship hull design that employ finite element analysis to minimize a quadratic functional approximating strain energy. Celniker and Gossard [6] present a free form design system that uses finite element analysis to simulate physical models. Interactive deformation is carried out by simulating forces applied to the subject model. Surfaces are represented by triangular patches meeting with C^1 continuity. Approximations are used to model deformations. As a result, surfaces converge on their theoretical shape after multiple elements are inserted between constraints. Rando and Roulier [28] propose several specialized geometrically based fairness functionals. These functionals are referred to as "flattening," "rounding," and "rolling." They apply these functionals to Bézier patches. Some of the Bézier control points are fixed in order to guarantee continuity, while others are varied to minimize the functionals. Hagen and Schulze [13] use the calculus of variations to fit generalized Coons patches to three-dimensional data. The resulting patches minimize a strain energy fairness criterion. The analysis uses simplifying approximations to limit the complexity of calculations. Most recently, Kallay and Ravani [15] discuss a method for determining "optimal" twist vectors for the surface formed by a rectangular mesh of cubic curves. In their work, twist vectors are computed to minimize a quadratic energy term.

Our work uses higher order patches and the full nonlinear expression for the functional to achieve the highest possible surface quality from the fewest underlying patches.

2.3 Minimum Energy Networks

Nielson [20] introduced the minimum norm network (MNN) using linear energy terms to produce a C^1 network and a resulting C^1 surface. Pottmann [25] presents a generalization of MNN to produce a C^2 surface. Most recently, we [19] describe an algorithm for the computation of a G^2 minimum energy network composed of curves minimizing (1) along the edges of the network. These MVC networks are of higher fairness and are usually closer to the corresponding minimum variation surface than networks computed heuristically or using linear energy terms.

3 Our Algorithm

We treat the problem of creating a surface interpolating a collection of geometric constraints as one of scattered data interpolation. The interpolation problem is broken into three steps (Fig. 3); 1) connectivity definition, 2) curve network computation, 3) patch blending. In accordance with the topological type of the desired surface, the geometric constraints are first connected into a network of straight edges. A curve is then placed at each edge of the network, and an optimized network is computed composed of minimum variation curves (MVC) subject to the specified geometric constraints and the additional constraint that the curve segments meet with second order geometric continuity, G^2, at the

---

1. Emery Jou coined this name/acronym.

2. It is our convention that a "hat", e.g. $\hat{e}$, indicates a unit vector.

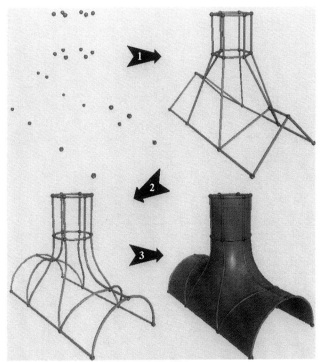

Figure 3. The construction of a blend of two pipes.

vertices. Finally, an interpolatory minimum variation surface (MVS) is computed, interpolating the MVC network with tangent continuity. In a first approach, the boundaries of the MVS patches are fixed, interpolating the previously constructed curve network. Alternatively, the surface calculation may use the MVC network as a starting point and modify its geometry during surface calculation. The latter approach yields even smoother surfaces, but at a substantially higher computational expense. The higher quality surfaces result because the curves of an MVC network resulting from a given constraint set do not always lie in the MVS resulting from the same set of constraints.

During the modeling process, the connectivity of the geometrical constraints is typically established as a natural outgrowth of the design process. The techniques described here are also amenable to true scattered data interpolation, in which case connectivity must first be derived with some other method, possibly based on some minimal triangulation on the data points.

Our system is based on triangular and quadrilateral patches. All constraints are located at corners of these patches. Additional vertices and edges may be added to the network so that is has only three and four sided openings. These additional vertices are not constraints and are appropriately positioned by the curve network computation and patch blending phases of the construction.

The computation of a curvature continuous (G^2) MVC network is cast as a nonlinear optimization or finite element problem. First an initial shape of the curve network is computed using heuristics based on the geometry of the network. The optimization then proceeds from this starting point using standard gradient descent techniques. The geometric constraints and the second order continuity of the curve network are maintained by construction. During each iteration, at each vertex of the network, the algorithm defines a surface normal, principle directions, and principle curvatures; all the curve segments are then constrained to remain consistent with them. Once the geometric and continuity constraints are satisfied, the gradient of the functional with respect to the remaining degrees of freedom is calculated, and the free parameters are iteratively adjusted to minimize the curvature variation functional overall.

Based on this MVC network, the computation of the MVS interpolatory surface is accomplished using constrained optimization. The geometric constraints are again imposed by constructions similar to those used in the calculation of the network. Patch-to-patch tangent continuity is imposed by means of a penalty function that is equal to zero when the patches composing the MVS meet with tangent continuity and proportionally greater than zero for any G^1 discontinuity. The use of penalty functions alone does not guarantee perfect tangent continuity. Exact tangent continuity may be achieved in a subsequent phase of optimization using Lagrange multipliers [8] or using the continuation method, a continuous reduction to zero of the weight of the curvature variation term in the functional. In practice, it is rarely necessary to resort to this second phase because the surfaces resulting from the first phase are of high quality and sufficiently close to tangent continuous. Mann and DeRose have shown this type of *approximate* tangent continuity to be sufficient and, in fact, desirable in some applications [9].

4 Representation and Computation

As described in section 3 the computation of an MVS satisfying a given set of constraints is broken into several steps. In this section we will focus on the last phase of the algorithm where surface patches are fit to a G^2 MVC network. The curves may remain fixed or they may be used simply as a starting point for optimization. The choice between fixed and variable curves is up to the designer and does not affect the algorithms described here. Section 5 provides the details of MVC network calculation.

The MVS is approximated by a quilt of parametric polynomial patches which interpolate the curve network, satisfy the geometric constraints, and meet with approximate tangent plane continuity. The surface functional is then minimized by varying the surface parameters that are not fixed by geometric constraints.

4.1 Bézier Patches

The curves of the network are represented by quintic Hermite polynomial segments; one segment replaces each edge of the network of constraints. Consequently, the patches making up the interpolatory surface are [bi-]quintic patches. Peters [23] has demonstrated that quintics are sufficient to achieve tangent continuity for all triangular/quadrilateral patch-patch combinations. One patch is used for each opening in the network. Though we have found single patches to have sufficient descriptive power, it is simple to subdivide network patches creating multiple patches per opening. The use of multiple patches improves the approximation of the theoretical MVS surface which in general has no closed form representation. Note that while Peters' construction requires that the curve network being interpolated has G^2 continuity, the interpolatory surface resulting from his construction is only G^1 across boundaries and at the vertices of the network. In contrast, our surfaces are constrained to meet with G^2 continuity at the vertices of the network (see section 4.8).

Even though the boundary curves are in the Hermite form, we have chosen to use Bézier patches because of their superior numerical characteristics and because the tangent continuity conditions we use are particularly concise when formulated in terms of Bézier coefficients. Also, Bézier patches are more amenable to rendering, and may be rendered directly by subroutines found in the graphics library of workstations such as the Silicon Graphics IRIS[®].

4.2 Fairness Functionals

Our choice of functional for minimization was prompted by the need for very high quality surfaces with predictable, intuitive behavior, and the desire to capture shapes commonly used in geometric modeling. The fairness of curves and surfaces has been studied extensively and has been shown to be closely related to how little and how smoothly a curve or surface bends. For an early and interesting reference see [2].

Work on the *fairness of curves* has traditionally focused on the minimization of *strain energy* or the arc length integral of the squared magnitude of curvature [18]

$$\int \vec{\kappa}^2 \, ds.$$

We use an alternative fairness metric based on the minimization of the arc length integral of the squared magnitude of the *derivative* of curvature

$$\int \frac{d\vec{\kappa}}{ds}^2 \, ds.$$

This new functional results in curves with noticeably smoother curvature plots, and it has the added benefit that circular arcs are formed when constraints permit, since according to this new functional they are optimally curved.

Traditional work on the *fairness of surfaces* also focuses on strain energy, minimizing the area integral of the sum of the principle curvatures squared [13, 16, 21, 32]

$$\int \kappa_1^2 + \kappa_2^2 \, dA.$$

Again, our approach minimizes the *variation* of curvature, rather than its magnitude. For surfaces, we minimize the area integral of the sum of the squared magnitudes of the derivatives of the normal curvatures taken in the principle directions:

$$\int \frac{d\kappa_n}{d\hat{e}_1}^2 + \frac{d\kappa_n}{d\hat{e}_2}^2 \, dA. \tag{2}$$

The *normal curvature* at a point on a surface in a direction specified by a surface tangent vector is determined from the intersection curve of the surface with the plane spanned by the surface normal and the given tangent vector. The principle directions, $\hat{e}_1$ and $\hat{e}_2$, and the principle curvatures, κ_1 and κ_2, at a point on a surface are the directions and magnitudes of the minimum and maximum of all possible normal curvatures at that point [11] (Fig. 4).

Like the MVC functional, the MVS functional has associated shapes that are optimal in the sense that the functional evaluates to zero. In the case of the MVS functional, the shapes belong to a special family of curved surfaces call cyclides [4, 27] that includes spheres, cylinders, cones, and tori. These all have *lines of principal curvature* where the associated normal curvature remains constant. Lines of principal curvature follow the paths of minimum and maximum normal curvature across a surface.

4.3 Parametric Functionals

The fairness functional for surfaces (2) is defined in terms of an area integral. To evaluate the functional and its gradient in the context of the parametric polynomial surfaces patches described in section 4.1, the functional must be converted to a compatible form. Here we outline the calculations necessary to evaluate the functional. The fairness functional is computed for each patch, and the value of the functional for the surface as a whole is the sum of the values for each patch. The area based definition

$$\int \frac{d\kappa_n}{d\hat{e}_1}^2 + \frac{d\kappa_n}{d\hat{e}_2}^2 \, dA$$

is converted to integrals of functions of the independent parameters

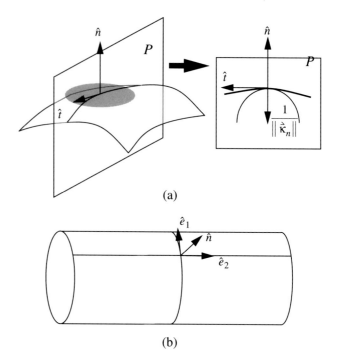

(a)

(b)

Figure 4. (a) Normal curvature is the curvature of the curve formed by the intersection of the surface and a plane containing the normal and tangent. (b) Principle directions and principle curvatures are the directions and magnitudes of the maximum and minimum normal curvature.

u and v in $\vec{S}(u, v)$. For quadrilateral patches, the bounds of the integrals are set to vary over the unit square, and the differential with respect to area is converted to differentials in u and v

$$\int_0^1 \int_0^1 \left(\frac{d\kappa_n}{d\hat{e}_1}^2 + \frac{d\kappa_n}{d\hat{e}_2}^2 \right) \| S_u \times S_v \| \, du \, dv$$

where

$$\| S_u \times S_v \| = \sqrt{EG - F^2},$$

and

$$E = \vec{S}_u \cdot \vec{S}_u \quad F = \vec{S}_u \cdot \vec{S}_v \quad G = \vec{S}_v \cdot \vec{S}_v. \tag{3}$$

The variables E, F, and G, are from the first fundamental form from differential geometry [11]. The principal curvatures κ_1 and κ_2 are the normal curvatures in the principle directions. Thus the problem of computing $d\kappa_n/d\hat{e}_1$ and $d\kappa_n/d\hat{e}_2$ becomes one of computing $d\kappa_1/d\hat{e}_1$ and $d\kappa_2/d\hat{e}_2$. First we find expressions for these in terms of derivatives taken in the parametric *directions*

$$\frac{d\kappa_1}{d\hat{e}_1} = \frac{d\kappa_1}{d\hat{u}} (\hat{e}_1 \cdot \hat{S}_u) + \frac{d\kappa_1}{d\hat{v}} (\hat{e}_1 \cdot \hat{S}_v)$$

$$\frac{d\kappa_2}{d\hat{e}_2} = \frac{d\kappa_2}{d\hat{u}} (\hat{e}_2 \cdot \hat{S}_u) + \frac{d\kappa_2}{d\hat{v}} (\hat{e}_2 \cdot \hat{S}_v)$$

where

$$\hat{S}_u = S_u / (\| S_u \|) \quad \hat{S}_v = S_v / \| S_v \|.$$

Next we define the derivatives of κ_1, κ_2 taken in the parametric *directions* using parametric derivatives:

$$\frac{d\kappa_i}{d\hat{u}} = \frac{d\kappa_i}{du} \frac{1}{\| \vec{S}_u \|} \quad \frac{d\kappa_i}{d\hat{v}} = \frac{d\kappa_i}{dv} \frac{1}{\| \vec{S}_v \|}.$$

Finally, the parametric derivatives of κ_1 and κ_2 are computed from an expression derived from the fact that the principle curvatures are the eigenvalues of the curvature tensor. The expression for the curvature tensor is

$$\begin{bmatrix} a_{11} & a_{21} \\ a_{12} & a_{22} \end{bmatrix},$$

where

$$a_{11} = \frac{fF - eG}{EG - F^2} \qquad a_{21} = \frac{eF - fE}{EG - F^2}$$

$$a_{12} = \frac{gF - fG}{EG - F^2} \qquad a_{22} = \frac{fF - gE}{EG - F^2}$$

$$e = \hat{n} \cdot \vec{S}_{uu} \quad f = \hat{n} \cdot \vec{S}_{uv} \quad g = \hat{n} \cdot \vec{S}_{vv}. \qquad (4)$$

E, F, and G are defined as in equation (3), e, f, and g are the terms of the second fundamental form from differential geometry [11]. Since κ_1 and κ_2 are the eigenvalues of the curvature tensor, we get the following expression:

$$\kappa_i = \frac{a_{11} + a_{22} \pm \sqrt{a_{11}^2 + 4a_{12}a_{21} - 2a_{11}a_{22} + a_{22}^2}}{2}.$$

This expression is in terms of the surface parameters u and v. Using the chain rule, it is simple to compute the required parametric derivatives, $d\kappa_i/du$, $d\kappa_i/dv$. Note that in computing the parametric derivatives of e, f, and g, it is helpful to have a simple way of computing $\hat{n}_u$ and $\hat{n}_v$:

$$\hat{n}_u = \kappa_1 (\vec{S}_u \cdot \hat{e}_1) \hat{e}_1 + \kappa_2 (\vec{S}_u \cdot \hat{e}_2) \hat{e}_2$$

$$\hat{n}_v = \kappa_1 (\vec{S}_v \cdot \hat{e}_1) \hat{e}_1 + \kappa_2 (\vec{S}_v \cdot \hat{e}_2) \hat{e}_2.$$

4.4 Numerical Integration

In section 4.3 we discussed a method for evaluating the quantity on the inside of the fairness integral (2). Because it is impractical to compute the integral analytically, we use numerical integration to evaluate the integral. Instead of using standard Gauss-Legendre quadrature, we use Lobatto quadrature [1]. Lobatto quadrature has approximately the same convergence and samples the *perimeter* of the integration domain:

$$\int_0^1 f(x)dx \approx w_1 f(0.0) + \sum_{i=2}^{n-1} w_i f(x_i) + w_n f(1.0)$$

We have found Lobatto's integration formula to be more effective than Gauss-Legendre quadrature for our application. As a default, we use ten integration points in each parametric direction, a satisfactory number for the modeling problems we have encountered so far. If the number of sample points is reduced, the surface might form a cusp or crease between sample points where the integrator will not "see" it.

The first ten sets of abscissas and weight factors for Lobatto's integration formula are tabulated in [1]. The computation of other sets of weights and abscissas requires finding the roots of the first derivative of a Legendre polynomial. Mathematica [33] may be used to generate larger tables. Because finding the roots of high order polynomials is difficult and prone to numerical errors, the results calculated for a new table should be checked for accuracy, e.g. verifying that the weights sum to 1. An alternative to computing higher order sets of weights and abscissas is to subdivide the domain and integrate over the subdomains.

4.5 Differentiation

During the optimization process, it is necessary to compute the gradient of the functional with respect to all the available degrees of freedom. When computing the curve network, analytical par-

tial derivatives are used in conjunction with numerical integration to compute the gradient. In the case of surfaces, the functional is of such complexity that it is impractical to compute the gradient in this fashion. Instead we use central differences [7] to approximate the partial derivatives. The standard central difference formula for computing the derivative of $f(a)$ with respect to a follows:

$$f'(a) = \frac{f(a+h) - f(a-h)}{2h}. \qquad (5)$$

In order to get accurate derivative estimates, it is necessary to choose the difference value h carefully. An optimum value of h balances the trade-off between the discretization error resulting from a large h and an increasing relative roundoff error resulting from too small a value for h. The analysis used to compute h is taken from [7]. First we find the approximate roundoff error in computing our functional. By computing the fairness functional, FF, in both single and double precision, we find the number of significant digits in the single precision calculation:

$$s_{single} = -\log_{10} \left| \frac{FF_{single} - FF_{double}}{FF_{double}} \right|.$$

The roundoff error R in (5) is approximately

$$R = \pm \frac{2FF \times 10^{-s_{single}}}{2h}.$$

The discretization error T is approximately

$$T = -\frac{1}{6} h^2.$$

To find the optimum h we must minimize

$$\frac{FF \times 10^{-s_{single}}}{h} + \frac{1}{6} h^2. \qquad (6)$$

To find the value of h for which (6) is a minimum, we differentiate with respect to h and find the positive root.

$$-\frac{FF \times 10^{-s_{single}}}{h^2} + \frac{h}{3} = 0 \qquad h = \sqrt[3]{3FF \times 10^{-s_{single}}}.$$

Currently our calculations are carried out in double precision. Because we can only directly compute $s_{single} \approx 5.1$, we presume a value of $s_{double} = 9$ by extrapolation. We recalculate h for each new value of the functional. For example, $FF = 10.0$ yields $h = 0.006$. Note that because the functional (FF) and its derivatives are computed on a patch by patch basis, the value of h is also set on a patch by patch basis.

4.6 Tangent Continuity

In [10] DeRose sets forth the necessary and sufficient conditions for G^1 continuity. The G^1 conditions take the form of a series of formulas, eq_i, all of which must be zero for G^1 continuity to exist. Using the notation of DeRose, $N_{F'}$, $N_{G'}$ and $N_{H'}$ refer to the degree of the cross-boundary tangent functions (F', G') and the degree of the tangent function (H') along the boundary (Fig. 5). For example, a pair of abutting bi-quintic patches have $N_{F'} = N_{G'} = 5, N_{H'} = 4$ and formulas

$$eq_m = \sum_{j+k+l=m} \left| F_j^*, G_k^*, H_l^* \right| = 0 \qquad (7)$$

$$m = 0 \ldots D \qquad D = N_{F'} + N_{G'} + N_{H'}$$

where

$$F_j^* = \binom{N_{F'}}{j} F'_j \qquad G_k^* = \binom{N_{G'}}{k} G'_k \qquad H_l^* = \binom{N_{H'}}{l} H'_l$$

where the F'_j, G'_k and H'_l are difference vectors as shown in Figure 5. The result per shared boundary, for our example of bi-quintic patches, is a set of fifteen equations, made up of one hundred distinct 3×3 determinants. The complexity of solving this

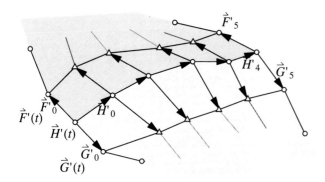

Figure 5. Difference vectors for a pair of bi-quintic patches.

system of equations has been outlined by a number of authors [14, 23, 29, 30]. This complexity arises because the corner interior control points (▲ Fig. 6) appear in the cross-boundary equations for multiple sides. This multiple appearance couples different patch-patch continuity equations and thereby creates a global system of equations with a very large number of variables. In the context of the optimization described here, it is impractical and unproductive to solve this explicitly.

We have described how the fairness functional is evaluated. We complete the objective function to be minimized by adding a penalty for lack of G^1 continuity. In formulating the penalty function, we square the terms from equation (7) yielding

$$\sum_{m=0}^{D} \left(\sum_{j+k+l=m} \left| F_j^*, G_k^*, H_l^* \right| \right)^2 . \qquad (8)$$

The penalty is computed for every patch-patch boundary and added to the fairness functional forming the objective function.

4.7 Initialization

The gradient descent scheme described in section 3 starts with an initial surface and iteratively refines that surface until the surface functional reaches a (local) minimum and an optimal surface is reached. In this section we discuss a method for finding a suitable initial surface. In terms of the desired optimization, the goal is to find an initial point in the proper "valley" of the solution space such that the desired surface is found as the minimal point in that valley. The optimization requires that initial values be provided for any parameters not explicitly set. The use of an optimized curve network initializes the control points on the perimeter of each patch. The interior control points are positioned

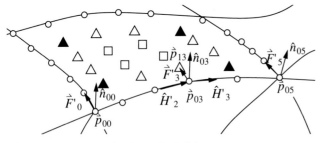

Figure 6. The control points of a Bézier patch are grouped as the 20 perimeter control points (○), the 12 adjacent control points (△, ▲), and the 4 central control points (□). As an example of initialization, $\vec{p}_{13}$ is computed by linearly interpolating the surface normal vectors at the corners and the magnitudes of the corresponding difference vectors.

so as to: 1) achieve approximate G^1 continuity and 2) set the high order derivatives at the patch corners equal to zero. The first step initializes the twelve control points adjacent to the perimeter (△, ▲), and the second step initializes the four points in the center of the patch (□) (Fig. 6). The heuristic used to position the control points adjacent to the perimeter linearly interpolates the normal vectors and the magnitudes of difference vectors. Figure 6 and equation (9) demonstrate the approach, with the calculation of $\vec{p}_{13}$:

$$\vec{p}_{13} = \vec{p}_{03} + \vec{F}'_3 \qquad \vec{F}'_3 = \left\| \vec{F}'_3 \right\| \hat{F}'_3$$

$$\hat{F}'_3 = \frac{\hat{H}'_2 \times \hat{n}_{03} + \hat{H}'_3 \times \hat{n}_{03}}{\left\| \hat{H}'_2 \times \hat{n}_{03} + \hat{H}'_3 \times \hat{n}_{03} \right\|}$$

$$\left\| \vec{F}'_3 \right\| = \frac{2}{5} \left\| \vec{F}'_0 \right\| + \frac{3}{5} \left\| \vec{F}'_5 \right\| \qquad (9)$$

$$\hat{n}_{03} = \frac{\frac{2}{5}\hat{n}_{00} + \frac{3}{5}\hat{n}_{05}}{\left\| \frac{2}{5}\hat{n}_{00} + \frac{3}{5}\hat{n}_{05} \right\|} .$$

Alternatively, one could also use the construction due to Peters [23].

4.8 G^2 Vertices

The order of the derivatives in the surface functional indicate a requirement for G^2 continuity. Rather than imposing G^2 cross boundary continuity at the cost of many more equations to evaluate, we construct the network of patches to meet with G^2 continuity at the vertices only, and we maintain this continuity by construction during the minimization process. Because of this, the elements used in these optimizations are classified as nonconforming elements, and the "patch test" [34] must be used to guarantee convergence. Intuitively, because of the nature of the fairness functional, G^2 continuity tends to "propagate" along the patch-patch boundaries. If the surface elements are subdivided into smaller and more numerous elements and G2 vertex continuity is maintained, the overall surface converges on G2 continuity. A comparison of surfaces with and without G^2 vertex continuity shows those with G^2 continuity to have superior overall curvature distribution.

The construction used to maintain G^2 vertex continuity of the surface is a simple extension of the construction used to maintain G^2 compatibility of the MVC network (section 5). An additional step is carried out after the principle directions and curvatures at the vertices of the network have been established. This extra step of the construction requires that the twist vector of each incident patch corner be compatible with the established curvature. The restriction on $\vec{S}_{uv}$ is derived from the formulas for mean and Gaussian curvature:

$$\text{Gaussian} = \kappa_1 \kappa_2 = \frac{eg - f^2}{EG - F^2}$$

and

$$\text{mean} = \frac{\kappa_1 + \kappa_2}{2} = \frac{1}{2} \frac{gE - 2fF + eG}{EG - F^2}$$

where e, f, g, E, F, G are defined as in equations (3) and (4). The twist vector must be adjusted to satisfy $f = \hat{n} \cdot \vec{S}_{uv}$. This is accomplished by forcing the tip of $\vec{S}_{uv}$ to lie in the plane perpendicular to $\hat{n}$, offset by distance f from the vertex

$$\vec{S}'_{uv} = \vec{S}_{uv} + (f - \hat{n} \cdot \vec{S}_{uv}) \hat{n} .$$

f can be computed from the values of κ_1, κ_2 and the first and second order derivatives of $\vec{S}(u, v)$.

5 MVC Network Computation

MVC networks are used to initialize the boundaries of the patches from which the surface is composed. Many of the techniques used in computing the network are used in the computation of an MVS where the initial shape of the curve network is allowed to change. In this section we outline the methods used to compute the G^2 curve network.

5.1 Network Representation and Continuity

The network of curves is defined via the second order parameters of a surface description at each vertex of the network and via a description of how each curve segment emerges from within the surfaces specified at its endpoints. Each surface is defined by the vertex position $\vec{p}$, a pair of conjugate directions, $\hat{w}_1, \hat{w}_2$, and the normal curvatures in those directions $\kappa_{w_1}, \kappa_{w_2}$. Conjugate directions are equivalent to principle directions in that, coupled with the associated curvatures, they fully characterize the curvature of a surface at a point [11]. Conjugate directions are more amenable to optimization because they do not have to be constrained to mutual orthogonality. The network is represented by quintic Hermite curves. These Hermite curves are defined by the positions and first two parametric derivatives at their endpoints. Each curve in the network is defined by the position $\vec{p}$, tangent direction $\hat{t}$, and three scalar parameters, m, α, c, at each endpoint. The mapping from these values to the parameters defining the corresponding Hermite curve is

$$\vec{P} = \vec{p} \qquad \vec{P}' = m^2 \hat{t} \qquad \vec{P}'' = m^4 \vec{\kappa} + \alpha m^2 \hat{t}$$

$$\vec{\kappa} = \kappa_n \hat{n} + c\hat{b} \qquad \hat{b} = \hat{n} \times \hat{t}$$

$$\kappa_n = \hat{t} \cdot \left[K \right] \cdot \hat{t}$$

$$\left[K \right] = \begin{bmatrix} \hat{w}_1 \\ \hat{w}_2 \\ \hat{n} \end{bmatrix}^{-1} \cdot \begin{bmatrix} \kappa_{w_1} & 0 & 0 \\ 0 & \kappa_{w_2} & 0 \\ 0 & 0 & 0 \end{bmatrix} \cdot \left(\begin{bmatrix} \hat{w}_1 \\ \hat{w}_2 \\ \hat{n} \end{bmatrix}^{-1} \right)^T \qquad \textbf{(10)}$$

Note that the curvature of the curve is the sum of two orthogonal components; κ_n, the component in the normal direction is a function of the surface at the vertex and the tangent direction of the curve at its end point; c, the component in the binormal direction is independent of the surface curvature at the vertex and represents the curvature of the curve "within the surface."

During the optimization process, those variables not fixed by constraints are iteratively adjusted to minimize the MVC functional (1). At each iteration step, $\hat{w}_1$ and $\hat{w}_2$ are renormalized, and $\hat{t}$ is projected onto the plane spanned by $\hat{w}_1, \hat{w}_2$ and also renormalized. It is this normalization step in combination with the construction outlined in equation (10) that guarantees G^2 continuity is maintained.

5.2 Network Initialization

The curve network must be initialized to some reasonable values before optimization can proceed. First a vertex normal vector is initialized, then the tangent vectors of the incident curves are computed, next the principle directions and curvatures are defined, and finally each curve's scalar coefficients are initialized.

The vertex normal is initialized as an average of the incident face normals weighted inversely proportional to the area of the incident face, i.e. the smaller the face the greater its influence on the vertex normal [5]. The tangent vectors of curves incident to a vertex are set to the direction of the incident chords projected onto the plane defined by the vertex position $\vec{p}_i$ and the normal $\hat{n}$ (Fig. 7).

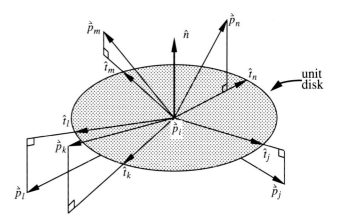

Figure 7. Tangent initialization. The projection of incident chords onto the plane defined by the normal.

Once vertex normal vectors and incident tangent directions have been computed, the principle curvatures and principle directions at a vertex are calculated. Both Calladine [5] and Todd and McLeod [31] describe approaches for estimating the curvature of polyhedral surfaces. Calladine's method only estimates Gaussian curvature. Todd and McLeod require that a pairing be established among the points neighboring a point; this is not possible at vertices of odd order. At even order vertices, it remains problematic since the results vary greatly depending on the pairing chosen; logically opposite curves are not always appropriate partners.

Our approach uses a least squares fit of sample tangent directions and normal curvatures to compute the principle directions and curvatures. The initialization of these values is very important to the speed of convergence. First consider the situation shown in Figure 7. A vertex is shown with a number of incident edges. For each edge we calculate the curvature implied by that edge emanating from the vertex. Starting with edge $\vec{p}_i, \vec{p}_n$ we reflect $\vec{p}_n$ through the normal and fit a circle through $p'_n, \vec{p}_i$ and $\vec{p}_n$. The radius of the resulting circle is the radius of curvature (Fig. 8). Repeating this procedure for each of the incident edges

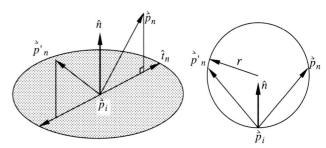

Figure 8. Calculating an approximate radius of curvature in the direction of $\hat{t}_n$.

provides a set of sample tangent directions and normal curvatures. This set is used to compute a least squares fit for the principle directions and principle curvatures of the surface at the vertex as follows.

We start with the expression for normal curvature expressed with respect to any convenient basis in the plane defined by the normal,

$$\kappa_n = \hat{t} \cdot \left[K \right] \cdot \hat{t}$$

$$\left[K \right] = \begin{bmatrix} \hat{e}_{1,x} & \hat{e}_{1,y} \\ -\hat{e}_{1,y} & \hat{e}_{1,x} \end{bmatrix}^{-1} \cdot \begin{bmatrix} \kappa_1 & 0 \\ 0 & \kappa_2 \end{bmatrix} \cdot \left(\begin{bmatrix} \hat{e}_{1,x} & \hat{e}_{1,y} \\ -\hat{e}_{1,y} & \hat{e}_{1,x} \end{bmatrix}^{-1} \right)^{T}$$

and extract the tangent components, to produce an over determined set of linear equations:

$$\begin{bmatrix} \hat{t}_{0,x}^2 & \hat{t}_{0,x}\hat{t}_{0,y} & \hat{t}_{0,y}^2 \\ \hat{t}_{1,x}^2 & \hat{t}_{1,x}\hat{t}_{1,y} & \hat{t}_{1,y}^2 \\ . & . & . \\ \hat{t}_{m,x}^2 & \hat{t}_{m,x}\hat{t}_{m,y} & \hat{t}_{m,y}^2 \end{bmatrix} \cdot \begin{bmatrix} \hat{e}_{1,x}^2 \kappa_{\hat{e}_1} + \hat{e}_{1,y}^2 \kappa_{\hat{e}_2} \\ 2\hat{e}_{1,x}\hat{e}_{1,y}(\kappa_{\hat{e}_1} - \kappa_{\hat{e}_2}) \\ \hat{e}_{1,x}^2 \kappa_{\hat{e}_2} + \hat{e}_{1,y}^2 \kappa_{\hat{e}_1} \end{bmatrix} = \begin{bmatrix} \kappa_{n,0} \\ \kappa_{n,1} \\ . \\ \kappa_{n,m} \end{bmatrix}$$

$$Ax = b. \qquad (11)$$

The general formula for computing the least squares solution to this type of system is $A^T A \bar{x} = A^T b$, where $\bar{x}$ is the least squares solution for "x" in equation (11). Having solved for $\bar{x}$ we have three equations and four unknowns

$$\begin{bmatrix} \hat{e}_{1,x}^2 \kappa_1 + \hat{e}_{1,y}^2 \kappa_2 \\ 2\hat{e}_{1,x}\hat{e}_{1,y}(\kappa_1 - \kappa_2) \\ \hat{e}_{1,x}^2 \kappa_2 + \hat{e}_{1,y}^2 \kappa_1 \end{bmatrix} = \begin{bmatrix} \bar{x}_0 \\ \bar{x}_1 \\ \bar{x}_2 \end{bmatrix}.$$

Adding the fact that $\hat{e}_{1,x}^2 + \hat{e}_{1,y}^2 = 1$, allows us to solve for the principle directions and principle curvatures.

To complete the initialization of the network, the scalars associated with each curve are set as follows: m is set to the chord length, and α, c are set to zero.

5.3 Optional Network Constraints

Since the quality of the network directly impacts the quality of the resulting surface, we present an optional heuristic constraint. A very successful method for improving network quality is to force pairs of curve segments incident to a common vertex of the network to join with G^2 continuity. Pairs of curves are made G^1 continuous by forcing them to share tangent vectors. G^2 continuity is imposed by forcing the curves to also share the bi-normal component, c, from (10).

During initialization, shared tangents are set to the average of the individual tangents computed by chord projection. Figure 9

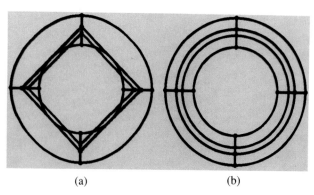

(a)   (b)

Figure 9. A network through points on a torus (a) with G^0 and (b) with G^2 continuous curves through vertices.

illustrates curve continuity applied to 16 regularly spaced points on the surface of a torus. Figure 9b illustrates the improvement to the network when G^2 continuity is imposed.

6 Examples: A Comparison of Functionals

In order to evaluate the quality and usefulness of MVS, we examine a few interpolation and design problems. Special rendering techniques are used to assist in the evaluation of the quality of these surfaces. Functional shading is used to examine the distribution of curvature. In this case, mean and Gaussian curvature are used to index into a color map. Lines of reflection are used to demonstrate G1 and G2 continuity [24]. They are generated by assuming that the surface is highly reflective and is place inside a large box with vertical lines drawn on its walls. The surface is then rendered using environment mapping [3, 12]. Generally, smooth surfaces have smooth lines of reflection. G2 (surface curvature) discontinuities appear as kinks or G1 discontinuities in the lines of reflection. G1 (surface tangent) discontinuities cause G^0 discontinuities in the lines of reflection.

6.1 Spheres

In Figure 10 we use functional shading to compare the MVS

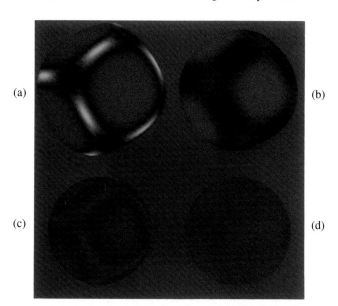

(a)   (b)

(c)   (d)

Figure 10. Surfaces are computed interpolating the 8 corners of a cube. These illustrate the differences among different methods. Pseudo-coloring according to mean and Gaussian curvature exposes the differences between objective functions. (a) - G^1 penalty, (b) - linearized strain energy, (c) - strain energy, (d) - MVS.

functional with three other functionals. In (a) only the G^1 penalty function was minimized when fitting a surface to the points of a cube. (b) illustrates the result of using a linearized approximation to strain energy; curvature distribution is improved. Next, (c) true strain energy is minimized producing a surface with fairly uniform curvature. Finally, in Fig. 10d an MVS surface fitted to the corners of a cube produces a very close approximation to a sphere.

6.2 Three Handles

Figure 11 illustrates the application of MVC to a more complicated example. Fig. 11a is the MVC network interpolated to create the G^1 MVS. (b) illustrates the surface rendered with lines of reflection. In the lower half of Figure 11, strain energy (c) and the

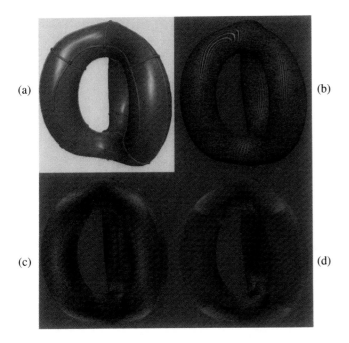

(a)   (b)

(c)   (d)

Figure 11. Three Handles. Minimization of strain energy is compared with the MVS starting with the same MVC network. (a) - the MVC network. (b) - the MVS rendered with lines of reflection indicating G^1, ~G^2 continuity. (c) - the surface minimizing strain energy. (d) - the MVS interpolating the same network of curves. (c) and (d) are rendered using functional shading to expose the differences in curvature distribution.

MVS functional (d) are compared. The differences are subtle, curvature varies more smoothly and is distributed more evenly over the MVS surface.

6.3 Tetrahedral Frame

As our last example, an MVS surface is fit to a tetrahedral frame, (Fig. 12). (a) illustrates the fitted surface with its MVC network. (b) shows the parameterization of individual patches demarcated by black borders. In (c) the surface is rendered with lines of reflection. Finally, (d) is a simple lighted rendering of the surface. This last example demonstrates the versatility and power of MVS to solve a very difficult interpolation problem.

7 Conclusions

Constructing a network of G^1 continuous surface patches is known to be a difficult task, and it is even harder to shape such a network into a satisfactory surface. The use of a general optimization procedure with suitable penalty functions greatly simplifies both tasks.

In this paper we have described a conceptually simple yet powerful technique for surface modeling. Nonlinear optimization is used to minimize a fairness functional while maintaining geometric and continuity constraints. The functional of choice is the variation of curvature. This choice has the advantage that it leads to regular shapes commonly used in geometric modeling; spheres, cylinders, and tori are formed in response to a compatible set of constraints. The minimization of our fairness functional also produces very fair free-form surfaces. This allows the designer to specify technical and artistic shapes in a very natural way for a given design problem.

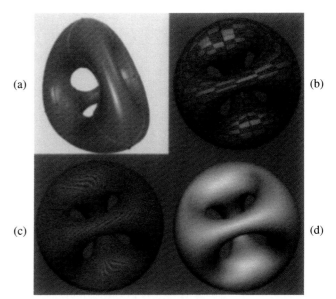

(a)   (b)

(c)   (d)

Figure 12. TetraThing. (a) - the interpolated MVC network. (b) - individual patches demarcated by black boundaries. (c) - lines of reflection indicating G^1, ~G^2 continuity. (d) - a simple shaded rendering.

Surfaces are represented by a patchwork of quintic polynomial Bézier patches. The use of quintic patches makes the satisfaction of geometric constraints simple, direct, and exact. The use of a quintic patch also tends to minimize the *number* of patches needed to solve a given problem. The use of Bézier patches eases numerical problems and simplifies communication with other modeling systems.

The techniques described here are computationally very expensive. They have only become practical because of the wide availability of very fast workstations. As computers increase in speed, these techniques will become even more attractive.

Acknowledgments

The authors thank Silicon Graphics Inc. for its generous support. We would also like to thank Tony DeRose and the reviewers for their many helpful comments on this paper.

References

1. Abramowitz, M. and Stegun, I.A. (editors), *Handbook of Mathematical Functions with Formulas, Graphs, and Mathematical Tables*, Dover, Inc., New York, N.Y. 1972.

2. Birkhoff, G.D., *Aesthetic Measure*, Harvard University, Cambridge, Mass., 1933.

3. Blinn, J.F., Newell, M.E., Texture and Reflection in Computer Generated Images, *Communications of the ACM* 19, 10 (Oct. 1976), 542-547.

4. Böhm, W., On Cyclides in Geometric Modeling, *Computer Aided Geometric Design* 7 (1990), 243-255.

5. Calladine, C.R., Gaussian Curvature and Shell Structures. In *The Mathematics of Surfaces*, Clarendon, Oxford, England, 1986, pp. 179-196.

6. Celniker, G. and Gossard, D., Deformable Curve and Surface Finite-Elements for Free-Form Shape Design, Proceedings of SIGGRAPH '91 (Las Vegas, Nevada, July 29-August 2, 1991). In *Computer Graphics* 25, 4 (July 1991), 257-266.

7. Conte, S.D. and de Boor, C. *Elementary Numerical Analysis, An Algorithmic Approach*, McGraw-Hill, New York, N.Y., 1980.

8. Courant, R. and Hilbert, D., *Methods of Mathematical Physics, Volume 1*, Wiley-InterScience, New York, N.Y., 1953.

9. DeRose, T.D. and Mann, S., An Approximately G1 Cubic Surface Interpolation. To appear in the Proceedings of the 1991 Biri Conference.

10. DeRose, T.D., Necessary and Sufficient Conditions for Tangent Plane Continuity of Bézier Surfaces, *Computer Aided Geometric Design* 7 (1990), 165-179.

11. Do Carmo, M.P., *Differential Geometry of Curves and Surfaces,* Prentice-Hall, Englewood Cliffs, New Jersey, 1976.

12. Greene, N., Environment Mapping and Other Applications of World Projections, *IEEE Computer Graphics and Applications* 6, 11 (Nov. 1986), 21-29.

13. Hagen, H. and Schulze, G., Automatic Smoothing with Geometric Surface Patches, *Computer Aided Geometric Design* 4, (1987), 231-236.

14. Jones, A.K., Nonrectangular Surface Patches with Curvature Continuity, *Computer Aided Design* 20, 6 (Jul./Aug. 1988), 325-335.

15. Kallay, M. and Ravani, B., Optimal Twist Vectors as a Tool for Interpolating a Network of Curves with a Minimum Energy Surface, *Computer Aided Geometric Design* 7, 6 (1990), 465-473.

16. Lott, N.J. and Pullin, D.L., Method for Fairing B-spline Surfaces, *Computer Aided Design* 20, 10 (Dec. 1988), 597-604.

17. Mann, S., Loop, C., Lounsbery, M., Meyers, D., Painter, J., DeRose, T., and Sloan, K., A Survey of Parametric Scattered Data Fitting Using Triangular Interpolants. In *Curve and Surface Modeling*, Hagen, H. (editor), SIAM.

18. Mehlum, E., Nonlinear Splines. In *Computer Aided Geometric Design*, R.E. Barnhill and R.F. Riesenfeld (editors), Academic, Orlando, Florida, 1974, pp. 173-207.

19. Moreton, H.P. and Séquin, C.H., Surface Design with Minimum Energy Networks. In *Proceeding of the Symposium on Solid Modeling Foundations and CAD/CAM Applications* (Austin, Tex., June 5-7). ACM, New York, N.Y., 1991, pp. 291-301.

20. Nielson, G.M., A Method for Interpolating Scattered Data Based Upon a Minimum Norm Network, *Mathematics of Computation* 40, 161 (1983), 253-271.

21. Nowacki, H. and Reese, D., Design and Fairing of Ship Surfaces. In *Surfaces in Computer Aided Geometric Design*, Barnhill, R.E. and Boehm, W. (editors), North-Holland, Amsterdam, The Netherlands 1983, pp. 121-134.

22. Peters, J., Local Smooth Surface Interpolation: A Classification, *Computer Aided Geometric Design* 7 (1990), 191-195.

23. Peters, J., Smooth Interpolation of a Mesh of Curves, *Constructive Approximation* 7 (1991), 221-247.

24. Poeschl, T., Detecting Surface Irregularities Using Isophotes, *Computer Aided Geometric Design*, 1 (1984), 163-168.

25. Pottmann, H., Scattered Data Interpolation Based upon Generalized Minimum Norm Networks, Preprint Nr. 1232, Technische Hochschule, Darmstadt, May 1989.

26. Pramila, A., Ship Hull Surface Using Finite Elements, *International Shipbuilding Progress* 25, 284 (1978), 97-107.

27. Pratt, M.J., Cyclides in Computer Aided Geometric Design, *Computer Aided Geometric Design* 7 (1990), 221-242.

28. Rando, T. and Roulier, J.A., Designing Faired Parametric Surfaces, *Computer Aided Design* 23, 7 (Sept. 1991), 492-497.

29. Sarraga, R.F., G^1 Interpolation of Generally Unrestricted Cubic Bézier Curves, *Computer Aided Geometric Design* 6, 2 (1987), 23-40.

30. Shirman, L. and Séquin, C.H., Local Surface Interpolation with Bézier Patches, *Computer Aided Geometric Design* 4 (1987), 279-295.

31. Todd P.H. and McLeod, R.J.Y., Numerical Estimation of the Curvature of Surfaces, *Computer Aided Design* 18, 1 (Jan./Feb. 1986), 33-37.

32. Williams, C.J.K., Use of Structural Analogy in Generation of Smooth Surfaces for Engineering Purposes, *Computer Aided Design* 19, 6 (Jul./Aug. 1987), 310-322.

33. Wolfram, S., *Mathematica, A System for Doing Mathematics by Computer*, *2nd ed.*, Addison-Wesley, Redwood City, California, 1991.

34. Zienkiewicz, O.C., *The Finite Element Method*, McGraw-Hill, London, England, 1977.

Direct Manipulation of Free-Form Deformations

William M Hsu[1]
Cambridge Research Lab
Digital Equipment Corporation

John F. Hughes[2] and **Henry Kaufman**[3]
Department of Computer Science
Brown University

Abstract

Free-form deformation (FFD) is a powerful modeling tool, but controlling the shape of an object under complex deformations is often difficult. The interface to FFD in most conventional systems simply represents the underlying mathematics directly; users describe deformations by manipulating control points. The difficulty in controlling shape precisely is largely due to the control points being extraneous to the object; the deformed object does not follow the control points exactly. In addition, the number of degrees of freedom presented to the user can be overwhelming. We present a method that allows a user to control a free-form deformation of an object by manipulating the object directly, leading to better control of the deformation and a more intuitive interface.

CR Categories: I.3.5 [Computer Graphics]: Computational Geometry and Object Modeling - Curve, Surface, Solid, and Object Representations; I.3.6 [Computer Graphics]: Methodology and Techniques - Interaction Techniques.

Additional Keywords: Direct manipulation, free-form deformations.

1 Introduction

Geometric modeling of complex objects is a difficult task. Sophisticated techniques for shaping and creating complex objects are generally awkward and tedious to use [8]. Free-form deformation [15] falls into this category. It is a powerful modeling technique that enables the deformation of objects by deforming the space around them, but using this technique is sometimes difficult. The deformations are defined by parametric functions (3D splines) whose values are determined

---

[1] One Kendall Square, Cambridge, MA 02139. email: hsu@crl.dec.com. phone: 617-621-6645

[2] Box 1910, Providence, RI 02912. email: jfh@cs.brown.edu. phone: 401-863-7638

[3] Current address: 3D Ltd. 4 Belinson Street, Tel-Aviv 63567, Israel

by the location of control points. Describing a free-form deformation (FFD) in conventional modeling systems is done by manipulating these control points, an interface that reflects the underlying mathematics of the modeling method. This type of interface can be confusing because the control point movement merely hints at the type of deformation the object will be subjected to. The following examples will help to clarify this.

Although the movement of the control points gives an indication of the resulting deformation, some shapes are not intuitive to form. As a first example, to create a bulge with a flat top one may think to align the control points to a plane, as shown in Figure 1a. However, it is actually necessary to position the control points as shown in Figure 1b to create the flat top. As a second example, Figures 6 and 7 show the prongs of a ring modeled with free-form deformations. Precise placement of the prongs is needed to ensure that they do not penetrate the gem stone.

Complex deformation operations often require a large number of control points resulting in screen clutter. They also tend to get buried within the model being deformed. As a result, it is virtually impossible to select or manipulate the control points efficiently.

Thus we can see four problems in manipulating deformations via control points.

1. Exact shape is difficult to achieve.

2. Exact placement of object points is difficult to achieve.

3. Users unfamiliar with splines do not understand the purpose of the control points and the results of their movement.

4. The control points become difficult to manipulate when occluded by the object being deformed, or when there are so many they clutter the screen.

One way to improve the usability of this technique is to move control points in groups, and then apply linear and non-linear transformations to them, similar to the group control point manipulation presented in [5] for spline surfaces. While helping the user move many control points at one time, this

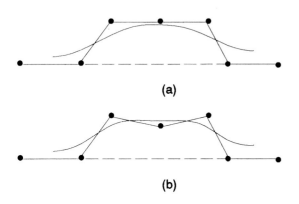

(a)

(b)

Figure 1: An FFD in the plane. The dashed line shows the original shape, and the solid line shows the shape after the deformation. (a) shows the result of a flat line of control points. (b) shows the control point configuration to create a flat top.

does nothing to alleviate the shape and placement problems. It is unclear which control points should be moved and how transformations will affect the object. The limited usefulness of this approach for spline surfaces was noted by [14]; the 3D volume of control points for FFDs (in contrast to the 2D mesh of control points for spline surfaces) exacerbates the difficulties of deciding how an aggregate move should be performed.

Another approach to an easier and more intuitive interface is the Extended Free-Form Deformation (EFFD) technique of [6]. With EFFDs, the user configures the initial lattice of control points to the approximate shape of the intended deformation, instead of starting with the FFD's parallelepiped of control points. EFFDs are quite effective for creating impressions, reliefs, and other fairly simple deformations that might otherwise be difficult to achieve with FFDs. However, the user must know the general shape of the deformation before starting to model, and the interface is still a direct representation of the underlying mathematics.

Both FFDs and EFFDs are based on the notion of deforming the underlying space in which an object lies. This has the advantage that it can be applied to any parametric or polygonal model, and is therefore not restricted to any class of objects. On the other hand, the control lattice used to manipulate the underlying space is not directly related to the object being deformed. Therefore, a control point that happens to be close to the surface of the object (which is, after all, the focus of the user's attention) may be far from the object surface after the deformation. Thus, these methods may surprise a user who does not understand the distinction between the object and the space in which it lies.

In this paper, we develop a direct manipulation technique which makes formation and placement of deformations easier. The essential idea is that the user selects (with some sort of pointer) a point on an object and then moves the pointer to a location where that object point should be.

Our technique computes the necessary alteration to the control points of the FFD spline that will induce this change. This alteration is generally under-determined; we use a least squares approach to select a particular alteration.

The rest of the paper is structured in 4 sections. Section 2 describes FFDs, and introduces B-spline FFDs. Section 3 describes a direct manipulation interface to B-spline FFDs, in which the user describes actions, and these actions are converted into control point displacements that will effect the actions. Section 4 discusses related work in direct manipulation interfaces, possible applications and directions for future research. Section 5 summarizes the results of the paper.

2 Free-Form Deformation

The FFD method deforms an object by first assigning to each of its points within the deformation lattice a set of local coordinates. The local coordinate system is defined by a parallelepiped-shaped lattice of control points with axes defined by the orthogonal vectors **s**, **t**, and **u**, as shown in Figure 2. All object points within this parallelepiped are assigned local coordinates through a mapping applied to their xyz-coordinates; we describe this mapping later.

Once the control points are moved, the new location of an object point is then determined by a weighted sum of the control points. The weights are functions of the local coordinates originally assigned to the point. Hence, a positional change of the control points changes the location of the object point.

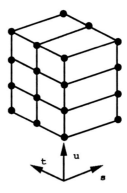

Figure 2: A lattice of control points. The s, t, and u vectors define the local coordinate system

In our implementation, the deformation function is a trivariate B-spline tensor product. We use the B-spline basis instead of the Bernstein polynomials used by Sederberg and Parry because of the local control properties of B-splines. Local control is desirable for both aesthetic value and for efficient computation with large control point lattices. We also prefer B-splines for its guaranteed continuity when any of its control points are moved, in contrast to, for example, Bézier splines.

In summary, then, the deformed position, q, of any arbitrary point with local coordinates, (s, t, u), is given by

$$\mathbf{q}_{i,j,k}(s, t, u) = \sum_{l,m,n=-3}^{0} \mathbf{P}_{i+l,j+m,k+n} B_l(s) B_m(t) B_n(u) \tag{1}$$

where $\mathbf{P}_{i,j,k}$ is the ith, j^{th}, k^{th} control point in the s, t, and u direction, respectively, and the Bs are the B-spline blending functions.

In our implementation of FFD we allow both direct manipulation of the object and manipulation of the control points. A drawback of using B-splines is that the image of the B-spline does not fill the convex hull of the control lattice, if the control lattice is evenly spaced and all control points have multiplicity one. We compensate for this by giving the outer control points of the lattice a multiplicity of three, which ensures that the image of the B-spline is the convex hull of the control lattice.[4] Phantom control points could be used as well; constraining their positions guarantees C^2 continuity along the borders. See [3] for more details.

Before the deformation is applied, object points must first be assigned local (s, t, u) coordinates, as already mentioned. When the control lattice is in its initial position, it defines an injective map from its domain to the convex hull of the lattice. Thus each point w within this hull is $\mathbf{q}(s_0, t_0, u_0)$ for some s_0, t_0, u_0 in the parameter space of the B-spline. The numbers s_0, t_0, u_0 are the local coordinates we assign. To compute them, we must invert the B-spline map. We first determine the spline segment $\bar{\mathbf{q}}_{i,j,k}$ that contains the object point. Then we compute s_0, t_0, and u_0 by explicitly solving the cubic equations $\bar{\mathbf{q}}_{i,j,k}(s_0, t_0, u_0) = \mathbf{w}$.[5] Note that the local coordinates need only be computed once for a given lattice, and not for each deformation calculation.

3 Direct Manipulation

In this section, we describe an interaction technique that converts a user action of the form "move *this* point of the object to *there*" and finds control point positions that will effect this action. We first describe the method in the case where the user wants to move a single *selected object point* to a new position, or *target point*. We then build upon this technique to describe how multiple selected points can be moved simultaneously. Although we demonstrate this method with the B-spline FFD, it can be used in conjunction with any other spline basis.

---

[4]If control points are not displayed at all, then all the control points in the lattice can be of multiplicity one, and the region deformed can be represented by the border of the B-spline image. This simplifies the deformation equation, and the latter portion of section 3.1 can be dismissed.

[5]General root finding is needed only for the outer two segments due to the tripling of control points at the borders. Otherwise, (s_0, t_0, u_0) can be found by the position of the object point in relation to the segments that contain it directly, as was done in the original FFD paper [15].

3.1 Single point constraint

As the user moves a target point our goal is to configure the control points such that the deformed location of the selected point matches the target point location. This problem is under-determined; there are many control-point configurations that will yield the same deformed location for the selected point. One obvious, but not very useful, solution is to simply translate all the control points by the target point's translation. Another solution is to choose the nearest control point and translate it until the target point reaches the desired location. A more natural solution is one that moves the control points the least (in the least-squares sense). The blending functions of Equation (1) assign weights to the control points for a given target point. The closer the control point is to the target point the greater the weight, or influence, the control point has. By using a least squares solution, control points are moved such that the resulting surface reaches its intended destination while the effect of the deformation smoothly tapers off. This effect provides predictable and physically intuitive behavior. We begin with some linear algebra.

Recall from Equation (1) that the deformed object point location, q, is a linear function of 64 control points, P, which can be written in matrix form as $\mathbf{q} = \mathbf{BP}$, where $\mathbf{B}$ is a single row matrix of the blending functions, and P is an 64×3 array whose rows are control point coordinates. (Henceforth we write coordinates of all points as row vectors.) A new location for the point q, $\mathbf{q}_{new}$, is then $\mathbf{q}_{new} = \mathbf{B}(\mathbf{P} + \Delta\mathbf{P})$, or

$$\Delta\mathbf{q} = \mathbf{B}\Delta\mathbf{P} \tag{2}$$

where $\Delta\mathbf{P}$ is the change in position of the control points and $\Delta\mathbf{q}$ is the change in position of the object point. We are given $\Delta\mathbf{q}$ (the difference between the target point and the selected point), and wish to find a value of $\Delta\mathbf{P}$ satisfying Equation 2. To do this we use the *pseudoinverse* (often referred to as the *generalized inverse*) $\mathbf{B}^+$ of $\mathbf{B}$.

Digression on Pseudoinverses Given a system of linear equations $\mathbf{y} = \mathbf{Bx}$, the pseudoinverse $\mathbf{B}^+$ is a matrix where $\mathbf{x}_0 = \mathbf{B}^+\mathbf{y}$ is the best solution, in the least squares sense, to the system of equations, (i.e., for which $\|\mathbf{Bx}_0 - \mathbf{y}\|$ is minimized and $\|\mathbf{x}_0\|$ is as small as possible [12]). The pseudoinverse is computed by first representing the $m \times n$ matrix $\mathbf{B}$ in the form $\mathbf{B} = \mathbf{CD}$, where $\mathbf{C}$ is $m \times k$ and $\mathbf{D}$ is $k \times n$, so that all three matrices $\mathbf{B}$, $\mathbf{C}$, and $\mathbf{D}$ have rank k. The general formula for the pseudoinverse $\mathbf{B}^+$ of $\mathbf{B}$ is then given by

$$\mathbf{B}^+ = \mathbf{C}^T(\mathbf{CC}^T)^{-1}(\mathbf{D}^T\mathbf{D})^{-1}\mathbf{D}^T \tag{3}$$

This formula can be used for both under-determined and over-determined systems of equations. When the problem is under-determined, as with the single target point constraint, only $(\mathbf{D}^T\mathbf{D})^{-1}\mathbf{D}^T$ is needed to compute the pseudoinverse, and $\mathbf{B} = \mathbf{D}$. Likewise, the pseudoinverse for the over-determined case is computed by $\mathbf{C}^T(\mathbf{CC}^T)^{-1}$. $(\mathbf{DD}^T)^{-1}$ reduces to $1/\|\mathbf{D}\|^2$, and the pseudoinverse of the single-row matrix $\mathbf{B}$ can now be found by the equation

$$B^+ = \frac{1}{\|B\|^2} B^T \qquad (4)$$

(end of digression).

Once the pseudoinverse of B is determined, the change in position of the control points based on the movement of the target point can be expressed as

$$\Delta P = B^+ \Delta q \qquad (5)$$

Because the pseudoinverse gives a least-squares solution, the change in control point positions is minimized.

This solution, however, applies only when all control points are allowed to move independently. Recall from Section 2 that in our implementation the control points on the outer border have a multiplicity of three, and therefore must be coincident. To formulate the pseudoinverse equation to reflect this constraint, a matrix, S, which selects the proper control point position is added to Equation (2), so that the deformed object point location is defined by

$$\Delta q = BS\Delta P \qquad (6)$$

The matrix S is the identity matrix, if all control points are allowed to move freely. Control points that must be coincident with one another have the one in their row shifted to the column that corresponds to the control point it must follow. For example, in the one-dimensional border case, if $P = [p_{-2} p_{-1} p_0 p_1]^T$, where p_{-2} and p_{-1} are required to be coincident with p_0 (i.e., p_0 has a multiplicity of three), then

$$S = \begin{bmatrix} 0 & 0 & 1 & 0 \\ 0 & 0 & 1 & 0 \\ 0 & 0 & 1 & 0 \\ 0 & 0 & 0 & 1 \end{bmatrix}$$

The equation for the pseudoinverse $(BS)^+$ is

$$(BS)^+ = (DS)^T (DSS^T D^T)^{-1} \qquad (7)$$

For efficiency, S can be compressed to a vector, and B^+ need be computed only once for a given target point.

3.2 Multiple target point constraints

The same technique is used to move several selected points to new targets simultaneously. Precise control over shaping objects becomes easier. When the multiple selected points are independent (i.e., when they share no control points), solving for control point position is a straightforward extension of the single target point method.

When selected points are influenced by the same control point, the system of equations must be designed so that each control point only appears once in the array P. The number of columns of B is the number of distinct control points affecting the selected points. The number of rows of B will be the number of target points. In a one-dimensional analog of this situation, if we want to move two selected points that

share three control points, then the dimension of B is 2×5 and P would list 5 control points. The blending functions in B are arranged in accordance to the listing of the control points. In this example, the equation becomes

$$\begin{bmatrix} q_0 \\ q_1 \end{bmatrix} = \begin{bmatrix} b_0^0 & b_1^0 & b_2^0 & b_3^0 & 0 \\ 0 & b_0^1 & b_1^1 & b_2^1 & b_3^1 \end{bmatrix} \begin{bmatrix} p_0 \\ p_1 \\ p_2 \\ p_3 \\ p_4 \end{bmatrix}$$

where q_0 is affected by control points 0-3 and q_1 is affected by control points 1-4, and b_j^i are the blending functions used to compute the location of the ith selected point.

Once again, the pseudoinverse of B is calculated using Equation 3 and the new control point locations are determined by Equation 5. Figures 3 to 5 show how multiple constraints can quickly effect a change in the shape of an object.

As more target points are added, the problem *can* become over-determined. For example, if a user tries to create a wavy surface with more undulations than is possible to generate with the given B-spline, then the pseudoinverse cannot provide a complete solution. The pseudoinverse has, however, the property of providing the solution with the least squared error, which is the best solution considering the given constraints. Furthermore, the failure to move the selected points to the target points can be quantified; large errors suggest to the user the need to use a B-spline with a finer mesh.

4 Discussion

4.1 Other direct manipulation techniques

Direct manipulation has long been used as a 3D modeling technique for polygonal meshes [13]. However, we find that coupling the free-form deformation technique with direct manipulation is a richer modeling tool with several advantages over polygonal and purely spline-based modeling methods. FFDs work independently of the underlying data structure of the object being deformed, and hence can be applied to any parametric or polygonal model. An implication of this is that FFDs are "resolution" independent. Complex objects can be modeled in real-time by rendering them in low resolution, which can later be rendered at high resolution using the same deformation description. Though a procedural language may provide similar capabilities for a polygonal modeler, some restrictions apply. For example, vertices moved by the user in one level of mesh refinement must have a corresponding, coincident vertex in every other level of refinement [1].

Since the FFD technique deforms the space within it, another advantage is that the same description can be used for several objects. The deformation is dependent on the relative position of the control points. The control points undergo rigid transformations and scaling without affecting the general shape of the deformation, which is useful when applying the same deformation definition to objects of different size. If more than one object lies within the deformation space, the deformation can be applied to all objects, preserving automatically their relative position and spacing.

Recent developments have been made in the direct manipulation of B-splines. Forsey and Bartels allow direct manipulation of hierarchical B-spline surfaces [9], but only at the B-spline joints, severely limiting the possible shapes that can be formed. The method was extended by Bartels and Beatty to manipulate spline curves at arbitrary points [2]. Their method is based on the Householder transformation, which computes a weighting function that relates positional changes in the target point to positional changes in the control points. In [10], Fowler and Bartels have extended the technique to include the manipulation of the first and second derivatives of the function at an arbitrary point as well.

Recently, [16] independently developed a system for direct manipulation of B-spline surfaces, based on their differential manipulation technique. This technique uses the Jacobian to "suggest" the direction of movement, and through least square projection uses the inverse of the Jacobian to solve for the position of the control points. Though this method for direct manipulation is similar to the method presented in this paper, it is applied only to B-spline surfaces. In contrast, the method described in this paper merely requires that the substrate in which the model lives (namely 3-space) be the image of a 3D spline; this is a property of the substrate and not of the model, and hence lets the technique apply to all polygonal models as well. Also, since our FFD technique is an "indirect" method of modeling, lattices of different size and resolution can be used on the same object to create a multitude of different curvatures.

4.2 Application

In addition to modeling static models, the direct manipulation technique can automate some forms of animated deformations. For instance, the technique can be used to simulate "Play-Doh®[6] physics," where objects deform when they are pressed against other objects, but without the complexities of simulating momentum transfer and non-rigid behavior. This level of simulation is useful to animators who want full object motion control, while still desiring automatic deformation in response to interpenetration or object collisions. In addition, this technique could be used to construct the final deformation lattices for Animated Free-Form Deformations (AFFD) [7]. In general, direct manipulation could be easily incorporated into EFFD (which AFFD is based upon) as a means for interactive shape control.

4.3 Future Research

Though the general technique for direct manipulation of free-form deformations has been implemented, further research is needed to provide a complete and robust user interface. Intuitive and easy to use techniques for moving aggregates

---

[6]Play-Doh is a registered trademark of Tonka Corporation. It is a soft modeling compound similar to clay.

of object points are needed. Some widgets we have developed are based on the idea of using a magnet or suction cup to move several points at a time [11]. It would be desirable for users (especially naive users) not to deal with control points at all. The proper metaphors for controlling the resolution of the lattice of control points and the spacing between the points must therefore be developed. Other aids, such as highlighting the area affected by the deformation can convey information that was previously conveyed by displaying control points. In general, a comprehensive metaphor needs to be developed to fully hide the details of the FFD technique and make the interface as transparent as possible. Creating a metaphor that is both believable and general enough to encompass all operations is a difficult task and will require further study [4]. We envision an environment where users will be able to sculpt objects using a Dataglove-like input device. The finger tips, digits, and palm of the hand will be tracked to offset selected points in a malleable object, with smooth valleys and hills attained by the FFD operation. Different elasticities can be assigned to the object by varying the resolution of the control-point lattice. Perhaps a metaphor of molten metal or glass may be appropriate, where a blow torch and cold air are used to heat and cool the object to give it different molding properties. By making modeling as natural as possible, or by imitating the ways it is done in the real world, a greater number of users can be reached and an increase in expressiveness in modeling attained.

With the technique described in this paper, there are occasions when the user can create over-constrained situations, and although the resulting solution has the minimum error it may not be what the user expects. A more gracious solution needs to be found, perhaps one that reconfigures the lattice of control points automatically, without disturbing the previous deformations.

5 Conclusion

With direct manipulation, using FFDs for modeling complex objects becomes more intuitive. Better control over the shape and placement of the deformation is gained. By eliminating the need to display control points (and its associated control lattice) the interface is more transparent, allowing the user to concentrate on his or her work. With the proper metaphor, users no longer need to understand splines in order to use this powerful modeling tool. By adding greater control over how an object is shaped, new modeling paradigms and environments can be explored.

6 Acknowledgments

The authors of this paper would like to thank the members of the Graphics Group at Brown for their helpful comments and support, especially Daniel C. Robbins for creating the gargoyle bust. This paper is based on the Master's thesis of the first author, whose attendance at Brown University was made possible by Digital Equipment Corporation's Graduate Engineering Education Program. Special thanks to Richard

Szeliski for his review and suggestions of this work, and to the other members of the Visualization group at DEC's Cambridge Research Lab for their review of this paper. This work was supported in part by grants from Digital Equipment Corporation, NSF, DARPA, IBM, NCR, Sun Microsystems, and HP.

References

[1] Allen, Jeff B., Wyvil, Brian, and Witten, Ian H. A Method for Direct Manipulation of Polygon Meshes. *Proceedings of Computer Graphics International '89*, pages 451–469, 1989.

[2] Bartels, Richard H. and Beatty, John C. A Technique for the Direct Manipulation of Spline Curves. *Proceedings of Graphics Interface '89*, June 1989.

[3] Bartels, Richard H., Beatty, John C., and Barsky, Brian A. *An Introduction to Splines for use in Computer Graphics and Geometric Modeling*. Morgan Kaufmann, 1987.

[4] Carroll, John M. and Thomas, John C. Metaphor and the Cognitive Representation of Computing Systems. *Trans Systems, Man, and Cybernetics*, 12(2):107–116, March/April 1982.

[5] Cobb, Elizabeth S. *Design of Sculptured Surfaces Using the B-spline Representation*. PhD thesis, University of Utah, June 1984.

[6] Coquillart, Sabine. Extended Free-Form Deformation: A Sculpting Tool for 3D Geometric Modeling. *Proceedings of SIGGRAPH '90*, In *Computer Graphics*, 24, 4, pages 187–196, August 1990.

[7] Coquillart, Sabine and Jancène, Pierre. Animated Free-Form Deformation: An Interactive Animation Technique. *Proceedings of SIGGRAPH '91*, In *Computer Graphics*, 25, 4, pages 23–26, July 1991.

[8] Csuri, Charles A. Art and Animation. *IEEE Computer Graphics and Applications*, pages 30–35, January 1991.

[9] Forsey, David R. and Bartels, Richard H. Hierarchical B-spline Refinemen. *Proceedings of SIGGRAPH '88*, In *Computer Graphics*, 22, 4, pages 205–212, August 1988.

[10] Fowler, Barry M. and Bartels, Richard H. Constraint Based Curve Manipulation. *SIGGRAPH '91 course 25 notes, Topics in the Construction, Manipulation, and Assessment of Spline Surfaces*, pages 4.0–4.16, July 1991.

[11] Hsu, William M. Direct Manipulation of Free-Form Deformations. Master's thesis, Brown University, March 1991.

[12] Noble, Ben and Daniel, James W. *Applied Linear Algebra*. Prentice-Hall, 2nd edition, 1977.

[13] Parent, Richard E. A System for Sculpting 3D Data. *Computer Graphics*, 11(2):138–147, August 1977.

[14] Riesenfield, Richard F. Design Tools for Shaping Spline Models. In Lyche and Schumaker, editors, *Mathematical Models in Computer Aided Geometric Design*, pages 499–519. Academic Press, 1989.

[15] Sederberg, Thomas W. and Parry, Scott R. Free-Form Deformation of Solid Geometric Models. *Proceedings of SIGGRAPH '86*, In *Computer Graphics*, 20, 4, pages 151–160, August 1986.

[16] Welch, William, Gleicher, Michael, and Witkin, Andrew. Manipulating Surfaces Differentially. Technical Report CS-91-175, CMU, September 1991.

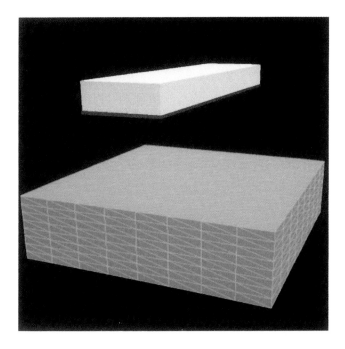

Figure 3: An example of multiple constraints. The red and white object is a deformation tool which projects all points which lie within it against the red plane.

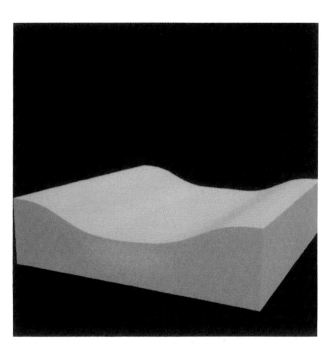

Figure 5: The results of the deformation at a higher resolution.

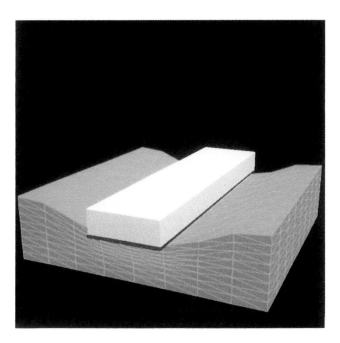

Figure 4: The deformation is created by positioning the control points according to the displacement of several of the vertices of the green object.

Figure 6: A ring with prongs shaped by free-form deformation.

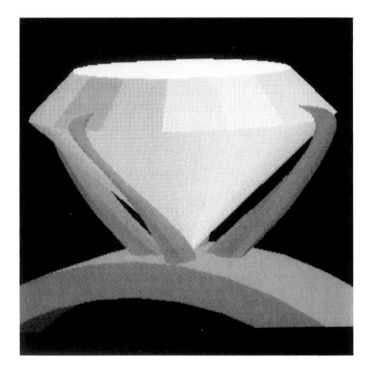

Figure 7: A close-up of the prongs in the ring.

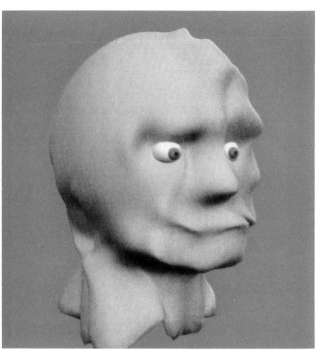

Figure 9: An intermediate stage of the gargoyle bust.

Figure 8: An elongated sphere is used as the foundation for a gargoyle bust. The resolution of the deformation lattice is 20x20x20.

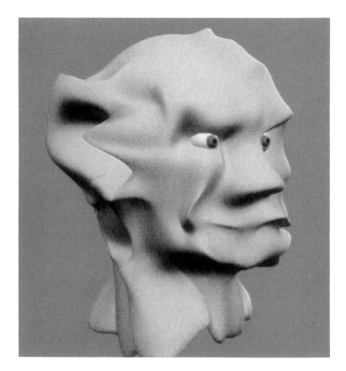

Figure 10: The resulting gargoyle bust. The entire model, except for the eyes, was modeled using the free-form deformation modeling technique with direct manipulation.

Surface Modeling with Oriented Particle Systems

Richard Szeliski[†] and David Tonnesen[‡]

[†]Digital Equipment Corp., Cambridge Research Lab, One Kendall Square, Bldg. 700, Cambridge, MA 02139
[‡]Dept. of Computer Science, University of Toronto, Toronto, Canada M5S 1A4

Abstract

Splines and deformable surface models are widely used in computer graphics to describe free-form surfaces. These methods require manual preprocessing to discretize the surface into patches and to specify their connectivity. We present a new model of elastic surfaces based on interacting particle systems, which, unlike previous techniques, can be used to split, join, or extend surfaces without the need for manual intervention. The particles we use have long-range attraction forces and short-range repulsion forces and follow Newtonian dynamics, much like recent computational models of fluids and solids. To enable our particles to model surface elements instead of point masses or volume elements, we add an orientation to each particle's state. We devise new interaction potentials for our *oriented particles* which favor locally planar or spherical arrangements. We also develop techniques for adding new particles automatically, which enables our surfaces to stretch and grow. We demonstrate the application of our new particle system to modeling surfaces in 3-D and the interpolation of 3-D point sets.

Keywords: Surface interpolation, particle systems, physically-based modeling, oriented particles, self-organizing systems, simulation.
CR Categories and Subject Descriptors: I.3.5 [Computer Graphics]: Computational Geometry and Object Modeling — *Curve, surface, solid, and object representations*; I.3.7 [Computer Graphics]: Three-Dimensional Graphics and Realism — *Animation*.

1 Introduction

The modeling of free-form surfaces is one of the central issues of computer graphics. Spline models [3, 8] and deformable surface models [25] have been very successful in creating and animating such surfaces. However, these methods either require the discretization of the surface into patches (for spline surfaces) or the specification of local connectivity (for spring-mass systems). These steps can involve a significant amount of manual preprocessing before the surface model can be used.

For shape design and rapid prototyping applications, we require a highly interactive system which does not force the designer to think about the underlying representation or be limited by its choice [18]. For example, we require the basic abilities to join several surfaces together, to split surfaces along arbitrary lines, or to extend existing surfaces, without specifying exact connectivity. For scientific visualization, data interpretation, and robotics applications, we require a modeling system that can interpolate a set of scattered 3-D data without knowing the topology of the surface. To construct such a system, we will keep the ideas of deformation energies from elastic surface models, but use interacting particles to build our surfaces.

Particle systems have been used in computer graphics by Reeves [16] and Sims [21] to model natural phenomena such as fire and waterfalls. In these models, particles move under the influence of force fields and constraints but do not interact with each other. More recent particle systems borrow ideas from molecular dynamics to model liquids and solids [12, 26, 29]. In these models, which have spherically symmetric potential fields, particles arrange themselves into volumes rather than surfaces.

In this paper, we develop *oriented particles*, which overcome this natural tendency to form solids and prefer to form surfaces instead. Each particle has a local coordinate frame which is updated during the simulation [17]. We design new interaction potentials which favor locally planar or locally spherical arrangements of particles. These interaction potentials are used in conjunction with more traditional long-range attraction forces and short-range repulsion forces which control the average inter-particle spacing.

Our new surface model thus shares characteristics of both deformable surface models and particle systems. Like traditional spline models, it can be used to model free-form surfaces and to smoothly interpolate sparse data. Like interacting particle models of solids and liquids, our surfaces can be split, joined, or extended without the need for reparameterization or manual intervention. We can thus use our new technique as a tool for modeling a wider range of surface shapes.

The remainder of the paper is organized as follows. In Section 2 we review traditional splines and deformable surface models, as well as particle systems and the potential functions traditionally used in molecular dynamics. In Section 3 we present our new oriented particle model and the new interaction potentials which favor locally planar and locally spherical arrangements. Section 4 presents the dynamics (equations of motion) associated with our interacting particle system and discusses numerical time integration and complexity issues. Section 5 discusses alternative rendering techniques for particles and surfaces. In Section 6 we present simple shaping operations for surfaces built out of particles. In Section 7 we show how to extend existing surfaces by adding new particles, and how to use this approach to automatically fit surfaces to 3-D point collections. In Section 8 we discuss applications of our system to geometric modeling.

2 Background

Our new surface modeling technique is based on two previously separate areas of computer graphics, namely deformable surface models and particle systems. Below, we present a brief review of these two fields.

2.1 Deformable Surface Models

Traditional spline techniques [3, 8] model an object's surface as a collection of piecewise-polynomial patches, with appropriate continuity constraints between the patches to achieve the desired degree of smoothness. Within a particular patch, the surface's shape can be expressed using a superposition of basis functions

$$\mathbf{s}(u_1, u_2) = \sum_i \mathbf{v}_i B_i(u_1, u_2) \tag{1}$$

where $\mathbf{s}(u_1, u_2)$ are the 3D coordinates of the surface as a function of the underlying parameters (u_1, u_2), $\mathbf{v}_i$ are the *control vertices*, and $B_i(u_1, u_2)$ are the piecewise polynomial *basis functions*. The surface shape can then be adjusted by interactively positioning the control vertices or by directly manipulating points on the surface [2].

Elastically deformable surface models [25] also start with a parametric representation for the surface $\mathbf{s}(u_1, u_2)$. To define the dynamics of the surface, Terzopoulos *et al.* [25] use weighted combinations of different tensor (stretching and bending) measures to define a simplified deformation energy which controls the elastic restoring forces for the surface. Additional forces to model gravity, external spring constraints, viscous drag, and collisions with impenetrable objects can then be added.

To simulate the deformable surface, these analytic equations are discretized using either finite element or finite difference methods. This results in a set of coupled differential equations governing the temporal evolution of the set of control points. Physically-based surface models can be thought of as adding temporal dynamics and elastic forces to an otherwise inert spline model. They can also be thought of as a collection of point masses connected with a set of finite-length springs [26].

Physically-based surface models have been used to model a wide variety of materials, including cloth [30, 6], membranes [25], and paper [24]. Viscoelasticity, plasticity, and fracture have been incorporated to widen the range of modeled phenomena [24].

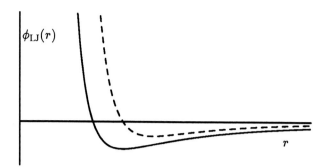

Figure 1: Lennard-Jones type function, $\phi_{\mathrm{LJ}}(r) = B/r^n - A/r^m$. The solid line shows the potential function $\phi_{\mathrm{LJ}}(r)$, and the dashed line shows the force function $f(r) = -\frac{d}{dr}\phi_{\mathrm{LJ}}(r)$.

The main drawback of both splines and deformable surface models is that the rough shape of the object must be known or specified in advance [27]. For spline models, this means discretizing the surface into a collection of patches with appropriate continuity conditions, which is generally a difficult problem [11]. For deformable surface models, we can bypass the patch formation stage by specifying the location and interconnectivity of the point masses in the finite element approximation. In either case, defining the model topology in advance remains a tedious process. Furthermore, it severely limits the flexibility of a given surface model.

2.2 Particle Systems

Particle systems consist of a large number of point masses (particles) moving under the influence of external forces such as gravity, vortex fields, and collisions with stationary obstacles. Each particle is represented by its position, velocity, acceleration, mass, and other attributes such as color. The ensemble of particles moves according to Newton's laws of motion. Particle systems built from non-interacting particles have been used to realistically model a range of natural phenomena including fire [16] and waterfalls [21]. Interacting (oriented) particles have been used to simulate flocks of "boids" [17].

Ideas from molecular dynamics have been used to develop models of deformable materials using collections of interacting particles [26, 12, 29]. In these models, long-range attraction forces and short-range repulsion forces control the dynamics of the system. Typically, these forces are derived from an intermolecular potential function such as the Lennard-Jones function ϕ_{LJ} shown in Figure 1. The force $\mathbf{f}_{ij}$ attracting a molecule to its neighbor is computed from the derivative of the potential function

$$\mathbf{f}_{ij} = -\nabla_{\mathbf{r}} \phi_{\mathrm{LJ}}(\|\mathbf{r}_{ij}\|), \tag{2}$$

where $\mathbf{r}_{ij} = \mathbf{p}_j - \mathbf{p}_i$ is the vector distance between molecules i and j (Figure 2).

Physical systems whose dynamics are governed by potential functions and damping will evolve towards lower energy states. When external forces are insignificant, molecules

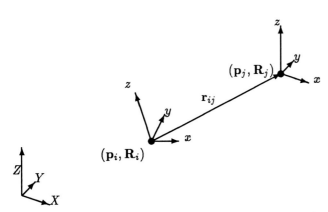

Figure 2: Global and local coordinate frames. The global interparticle distance $\mathbf{r}_{ij}$ is computed from the global coordinates $\mathbf{p}_i$ and $\mathbf{p}_j$ of particles i and j. The local distance $\mathbf{d}_{ij}$ is computed from $\mathbf{r}_{ij}$ and the rotation matrix $\mathbf{R}_i$.

will arrange themselves into closely packed structures to minimize their total energy. For circularly symmetric potential energy functions in 2-D, the molecules will arrange themselves into hexagonal orderings. In 3-D, the molecules will arrange themselves into hexagonally ordered 2-D layers, and therefore make good models of deformable solids [29]. When external forces become larger or internal particle forces smaller, the behavior resembles that of viscous fluids [26, 12]. More sophisticated models of molecular dynamics are used in simulations of physics and chemistry [10]; however, these are designed for high accuracy and are usually too slow for animation or modeling applications.

3 Oriented Particles

While particle systems are much more flexible than deformable surface models in arranging themselves into arbitrary shapes and topologies, they do suffer from one major drawback: in the absence of external forces and constraints, 3-D particle systems prefer to arrange themselves into solids rather than surfaces. To overcome this limitation, we introduce a new distributed model of surface shape which we call *oriented particles*, in which each particle represents a small surface element (which we could call a "surfel"). In addition to having a position, an oriented particle also has its own local coordinate frame, which adds three new degrees of freedom to each particle's state.

To force oriented particles to group themselves into surface-like arrangements, we devise a collection of new potential functions. These potential functions can be derived from the deformation energies of local triangular patches using finite element analysis [23].

Each oriented particle defines both a normal vector (z in Figure 2) and a local tangent plane to the surface (defined by the local x and y vectors). More formally, we write the state of each particle as $(\mathbf{p}_i, \mathbf{R}_i)$, where $\mathbf{p}_i$ is the particle's position and $\mathbf{R}_i$ is a 3×3 rotation matrix which defines the orientation of its local coordinate frame (relative to the global frame (X, Y, Z)). The third column of $\mathbf{R}_i$ is the local normal

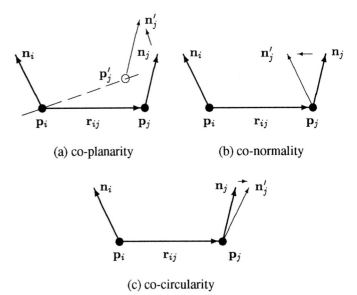

(a) co-planarity   (b) co-normality

(c) co-circularity

Figure 3: The three oriented particle interaction potentials. The open circles and thin arrows indicate a possible new position or orientation for the second particle which would lead to a null potential.

vector $\mathbf{n}_i$.

For surfaces whose rest (minimum energy) configurations are flat planes, we would expect neighboring particles to lie in each other's tangent planes. We can express this *co-planarity* condition as

$$\phi_P(\mathbf{n}_i, \mathbf{r}_{ij}) = (\mathbf{n}_i \cdot \mathbf{r}_{ij})^2 \psi(\|\mathbf{r}_{ij}\|), \qquad (3)$$

i.e., the energy is proportional to the dot product between the surface normal and the vector to the neighboring particle (Figure 3a). The weighting function $\psi(r)$ is a monotone decreasing function used to limit the range of inter-particle interactions.

The co-planarity condition does not control the "twist" in the surface between two particles. To limit this, we introduce a *co-normality* potential

$$\phi_N(\mathbf{n}_i, \mathbf{n}_j, \mathbf{r}_{ij}) = \|\mathbf{n}_i - \mathbf{n}_j\|^2 \psi(\|\mathbf{r}_{ij}\|), \qquad (4)$$

which attempts to line up neighboring normals, much like interacting magnetic dipoles (Figure 3b).

An alternative to surfaces which prefer zero curvature (local planarity) are surfaces which favor constant curvatures. This can be enforced with a *co-circularity* potential

$$\phi_C(\mathbf{n}_i, \mathbf{n}_j, \mathbf{r}_{ij}) = ((\mathbf{n}_i + \mathbf{n}_j) \cdot \mathbf{r}_{ij})^2 \psi(\|\mathbf{r}_{ij}\|) \qquad (5)$$

which is zero when normals are antisymmetrical with respect to the vector joining two particles (Figure 3c). This is the natural configuration for surface normals on a sphere.

The above potentials can also be written in term of a particle's *local coordinates*, e.g., by replacing the interparticle distance $\mathbf{r}_{ij}$ by

$$\mathbf{d}_{ij} = \mathbf{R}_i^{-1}\mathbf{r}_{ij} = \mathbf{R}_i^{-1}(\mathbf{p}_j - \mathbf{p}_i), \qquad (6)$$

which gives the coordinates of particle j in particle i's local coordinate frame. This not only simplifies certain potential equations such as (3), but also enables us to write use a weighting function $\psi(\mathbf{d}_{ij})$ which is not circularly symmetric, e.g., one which weights particles more if they are near a given particle's tangent plane. In practice, we use

$$\psi(x, y, z) = K \exp\left(-\frac{x^2 + y^2}{2a^2} - \frac{z^2}{2b^2}\right) \qquad (7)$$

with $b \leq a$.

To control the bending and stiffness characteristics of our deformable surface, we use a weighted sum of potential energies

$$E_{ij} = \alpha_{\mathrm{LJ}}\phi_{\mathrm{LJ}}(\|\mathbf{r}_{ij}\|) + \alpha_{\mathrm{P}}\phi_{\mathrm{P}}(\mathbf{n}_i, \mathbf{r}_{ij}) \qquad (8)$$
$$+ \alpha_{\mathrm{N}}\phi_{\mathrm{N}}(\mathbf{n}_i, \mathbf{n}_j, \mathbf{r}_{ij}) + \alpha_{\mathrm{C}}\phi_{\mathrm{C}}(\mathbf{n}_i, \mathbf{n}_j, \mathbf{r}_{ij}).$$

The first term controls the average inter-particle spacing, the next two terms control the surface's resistance to bending, and the last controls the surface's tendency towards uniform local curvature. The total internal energy of the system E_{int} is computed by summing the inter-particle energies

$$E_{\mathrm{int}} = \sum_i \sum_j E_{ij}.$$

4 Particle Dynamics

Having defined the internal energy associated with our system, we can derive its equations of motion. The variation of inter-particle potential with respect to the particle position and orientations gives rise to forces acting on the positions and torques acting on the orientations. The formulas for the inter-particle forces $\mathbf{f}_{ij}$ and torques $\boldsymbol{\tau}_{ij}$ are given in Appendix A. These forces and torques can be summed over all interacting particles to obtain

$$\mathbf{f}_i = \sum_{j \in \mathcal{N}_i} \mathbf{f}_{ij} + \mathbf{f}_{\mathrm{ext}}(\mathbf{p}_i) - \beta_0 \mathbf{v}_i, \qquad (9)$$

$$\boldsymbol{\tau}_i = \sum_{j \in \mathcal{N}_i} \boldsymbol{\tau}_{ij} - \beta_1 \boldsymbol{\omega}_i, \qquad (10)$$

where $\mathcal{N}_i$ are the neighbors of i (Section 4.2). Here, we have lumped all external forces such as gravity, user-defined control forces, and non-linear constraints into $\mathbf{f}_{\mathrm{ext}}$, and added velocity-dependent damping $\beta_0 \mathbf{v}_i$ and $\beta_1 \boldsymbol{\omega}_i$.

Using these forces and torques, we can write the standard Newtonian equations of motion

$$\begin{array}{llll} \mathbf{a}_i & = & \mathbf{f}_i/m_i & \boldsymbol{\alpha}_i & = & \mathbf{I}_i^{-1}\boldsymbol{\tau}_i \\ \mathbf{v}_i & = & \mathbf{a}_i & \boldsymbol{\omega}_i & = & \boldsymbol{\alpha}_i \\ \mathbf{p}_i & = & \mathbf{v}_i & \mathbf{q}_i & = & \boldsymbol{\omega}_i, \end{array}$$

where m_i is the particle's mass, and $\mathbf{I}_i$ is its rotational inertia (which for a circularly symmetric particle is diagonal). The equations for translational acceleration $\mathbf{a}$, velocity $\mathbf{v}$, and position $\mathbf{p}$ are the same as those commonly used in physically-based modeling and particle systems. The equations for rotational acceleration $\boldsymbol{\alpha}$, velocity $\boldsymbol{\omega}$, and orientation $\mathbf{q}$ are less commonly used. The rotational accelerations and velocities are vector quantities representing infinitesimal changes and can be added and scaled as regular vectors. The computation of the orientation (local coordinate frame) is more complex, and a variety of representations could be used. While we use the rotation matrix $\mathbf{R}$ to convert from local coordinates to global coordinates and vice versa, we use a unit quaternion $\mathbf{q}$ as the state to be updated. The unit quaternion

$$\mathbf{q} = (\mathbf{w}, s) \quad \text{with} \quad \begin{array}{rcl} \mathbf{w} & = & \mathbf{n}\sin(\theta/2) \\ s & = & \cos(\theta/2) \end{array}$$

represents a rotation of θ about the unit normal axis $\mathbf{n}$. To update this quaternion, we simply form a new unit quaternion from the current angular velocity $\boldsymbol{\omega}$ and the time step Δt, and use quaternion multiplication [20].

4.1 Numerical Time Integration

To simulate the dynamics of our particle system, we integrate the above system of differential equations through time. At each time step $t_{j+1} = t_j + \Delta t$ we sum all of the forces acting on each particle i and integrate over the time interval. The forces include the inter-particle forces, collision forces, gravity, and damping forces. We use Euler's method [15] to advance the current velocity and position over the time step. More sophisticated numerical integration techniques such as Runge-Kutta [15] or semi-implicit methods [25] could also be used, and would result in better convergence and larger timesteps, at the expense of a more complicated implementation.

4.2 Controlling Complexity

The straightforward evaluation of (9) and (10) to compute the forces and torques at all of the particles requires $O(N^2)$ computation. For large values of N, this can be prohibitively expensive. This computation has been shown to be reducible to $O(N \log N)$ time by hierarchical structuring of the data [1]. In our work, we use a *k-d tree* [19] to subdivide space sufficiently so that we can efficiently find all of a point's neighbors within some radius (e.g., $3\, r_0$, where r_0 is the natural inter-particle spacing). To further reduce computation, we perform this operation only occasionally and cache the list of neighbors for intermediate time steps.

5 Rendering

A variety of techniques have been developed for rendering particle systems, including light emitting points [16, 21] and iso-surfaces or "blobbies" [4, 28] for modeling volumes. For rendering oriented particles, simple icons such as axes (Figure 4a) or flat discs (Figure 4b) can be used to indicate the location and orientation of each particle. A more realistic

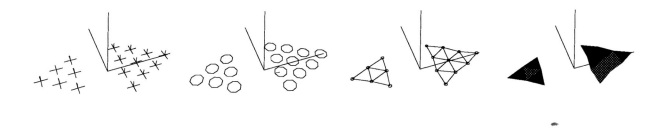

Figure 4: Rendering techniques for particle-based surfaces: (a) axes, (b) discs, (c) wireframe triangulation (d) flat-shaded triangulation.

looking surface display requires the generation of a triangulation over our set of particles, which can then be displayed as a wireframe (Figure 4c) or shaded surface (Figure 4d). For shaded rendering, Gouraud, Phong, or flat shading can be applied to each triangle. For a smoother looking surface, a cubic patch can be interpolated at each triangle (since we know the normals at each corner).

Because our particle system does not explicitly give us a triangulation of the surface, we have developed an algorithm for computing it. A commonly used technique for triangulating a surface in 2-D or a volume in 3-D is the Delaunay triangulation [5]. In 2-D, a triangle is part of the Delaunay triangulation if no other vertices are within the circle circumscribing the triangle. To extend this idea to 3-D, we check the smallest sphere circumscribing each triangle. This heuristic works well in practice when the surface is sufficiently sampled with respect to the curvature. The results of using our triangulation algorithm are shown in Figures 4c and 4d.

6   Basic modeling operations

This section describes some basic operations for interactively creating, editing, and shaping particle-based surfaces.

The most basic operations are adding, moving, and deleting single particles. We can form a simple surface patch by creating a number of particles in a plane and allowing the system dynamics to adjust the particles into a smooth surface. We can enlarge the surface by adding more particles (either inside or at the edges), shape the surface by moving particles around or changing their orientation, or trim the surface by deleting particles. All particle editing uses direct manipulation. Currently, we use a 2-D locator (mouse) to perform 3-D locating and manipulation, inferring the missing depth coordinate when necessary from the depths of nearby particles. Adding 3-D input devices for direct 3-D manipulation [18] would be of obvious benefit.

In addition to particle-based surfaces, our modeling system also contains user-definable solid objects such as planes, spheres, cylinders, and arbitrary polyhedra. These objects are used to shape particle-based surfaces, by acting as solid tools [14], as attracting surfaces, as "movers" which grab all of the particles inside them, or as large erasers. These geomet-

ric objects are positioned and oriented using the same direct manipulation techniques as are used with particles. Another possibility for direct particle or surface manipulation would be extended free-form deformations [7].

Using these tools, particle-based surfaces can be "cold welded" together by abutting their edges (Figure 5). Inter-particle forces pull the surfaces together and readjust the particle locations to obtain a seamless surface with uniform sampling density. We can "cut" a surface into two by separating it with a knife-like constraint surface (Figure 6). Here, we use the "heat" of the cutting tool to weaken the inter-particle bonds [29]. Or we can "crease" a surface by designating a line of particles to be *unoriented*, thereby locally disabling surface smoothness forces (co-planarity, etc.) without removing inter-particle spacing interactions (Figure 7).

7   Particle creation and 3-D interpolation

Our particle-based modeling system can be used to shape a wide variety of surfaces by interactively creating and manipulating particles. This modeling system becomes even more flexible and powerful if surface extension occurs automatically or semi-automatically. For example, we would like to stretch a surface and have new particles appear in the elongated region, or to fill small gaps in the surface, or extend the surface at its edges. Another useful capability would be a system which can fit a surface to an arbitrary collection of 3-D points. Below, we describe how our system can be extended to generate such behaviors.

The basic components of our particle-based surface extension algorithm are two heuristic rules controlling the addition of new particles. These rules are based on the assumption that the particles on the surface are in a near-equilibrium configuration with respect to the flatness, bending, and inter-particle spacing potentials.

The first (*stretching*) rule checks to see if two neighboring particles have a large enough opening between them to add a new particle. If two particles are separated by a distance d such that $d_{min} \leq d \leq d_{max}$, we create a candidate particle at the midpoint and check if there are no other particles within $1/2\, d_{min}$. Typically $d_{min} \approx 2.0\, r_0$ and $d_{max} \approx 2.5\, r_0$, where

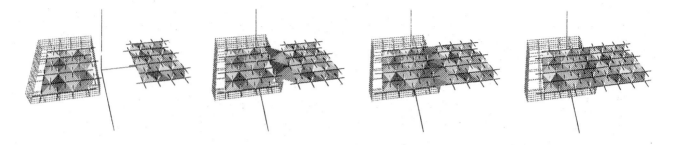

Figure 5: Welding two surfaces together. The two surfaces are brought together through interactive user manipulation, and join to become one seamless surface.

Figure 6: Cutting a surface into two. The movement of the knife edge pushes the particles in the two surfaces apart.

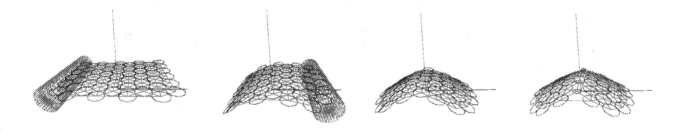

Figure 7: Putting a crease into a surface. The center row of particles is turned into unoriented particles which ignore smoothness forces.

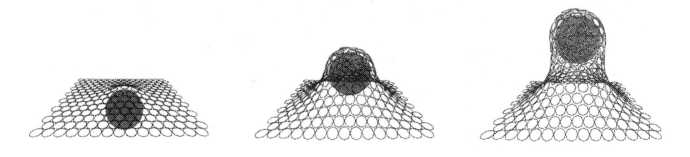

Figure 8: Particle creation during stretching. As the ball pushes up through the sheet, new particles are created in the gaps between pairs of particles.

r_0 is the natural inter-particle spacing. An example of this stretching rule in action is shown in Figure 8, where a ball pushing against a sheet stretches it to the point where new particles are added.

The second (*growing*) rule allows particles to be added in all directions with respect to a particle's local x-y plane. The rule is generalized to allow a minimum and maximum number of neighbors and to limit growth in regions of few neighboring particles, such as at the edge of a surface. The rule counts the number of immediate neighbors n_N to see if it falls within a valid range $n_{min} \leq n_N \leq n_{max}$. It also computes the angles between successive neighbors $\Delta\theta_i = \theta_{i+1} - \theta_i$ using the particle's local coordinate frame, and checks if these fall within a suitable range $\theta_{min} \leq \Delta\theta_i \leq \theta_{max}$. If these conditions are met, one or more particles are created in the gap. In general, a sheet at equilibrium will have interior particles with six neighbors spaced $60°$ apart while edge particles will have four neighbors with one pair of neighbors $180°$ apart.

With these two rules, we can automatically build a surface from collections of 3-D points. We create particles at each sample location and fix their positions and orientations. We then start filling in gaps by growing particles away from isolated points and edges. After a rough surface approximation is complete we can release the original sampled particles to smooth the final surface thereby eliminating excessive noise. If the set of data points is reasonably distributed, this approach will result in a smooth continuous closed surface (Figure 9). The fitted surface is not limited to a particular topology, unlike previous 3-D surface fitting models such as [25, 13].

We can also fit surfaces to data that does not originate from closed surfaces, such as stereo range data [9, 22]. Simply growing particles away from the sample points poses several problems. For example, if we allow growth in all directions, the surface may grow indefinitely at the edges, whereas if we limit the growth at edges, we may not be able to fill in certain gaps. Instead, we apply the stretching heuristic to effectively interpolate the surface between the sample points (Figure 10). When the surface being reconstructed has holes or gaps, we can control the size of gaps that are filled in by limiting the search range. This is evident in Figure 10, where the cheek and neck regions have few samples and were therefore not reconstructed. We could have easily filled in these regions by using a larger search range.

8 Geometric Modeling Applications

The particle-based surface models we have presented can be used in a wide range of geometric modeling and animation applications. These include applications which have been previously demonstrated with physically-based deformable surface models, such as cloth draping [30, 25, 6], plastic surface deformations [24], and tearing [24].

Using our surface model as an interactive design tool we can spray collections of points into space to form elastic sheets, shape them under interactive user control, and then freeze them into the desired final configuration. We can create any desired topology with this technique. For example, we can form a flat sheet into an object with a stem and then a handle (Figure 11). Forming such surface with traditional spline patches is a difficult problem that requires careful attention to patch continuities [11]. To make this example work, we add the concept of *heating* the surface near the tool [29] and only allowing the hot parts of the surface to deform and stretch. Without this modification, the extruded part of the surface has a tendency to "pinch off" similar to how soap bubbles pinch before breaking away. As another example, we can start with a sphere, and by pushing in the two ends, form it into a torus (Fig 12). New particles are created inside the torus due to stretching during the formation process, and some old sphere particles are deleted when trapped between the two shaping tools.

Another interesting application of our oriented particle systems is the interpolation and extrapolation of sparse 3-D data. This is a difficult problem when the topology or rough shape of the surface to be fitted is unknown. As described in the previous section, oriented particles provide a solution by extending the surface out from known data points. We believe that these techniques will be particularly useful in machine vision applications where it can be used to interpolate sparse position measurements available from stereo or tactile sensing [22].

9 Discussion

The particle-based surface model we have developed has a number of advantages over traditional spline-based and physically-based surface models. Particle-based surfaces are easy to shape, extend, join, and separate. By adjusting the relative strengths of various potential functions, the surface's resistance to stretching, bending, or variation in curvature can all be controlled. The topology of particle-based surfaces can easily be modified, as can the sampling density, and surfaces can be fitted to arbitrary collections of 3-D data points.

One limitation of particle-based surfaces is that it is harder to achieve exact analytic (mathematical) control over the shape of the surface. For example, the torus shaped from a sphere is not circularly symmetric, due to the discretization effects of the relatively small number of particles. This behavior could be remedied by adding additional constraints in the form of extra potentials, e.g., a circular symmetry potential for the torus. Particle-based surfaces also require more computation to simulate their dynamics than spline-based surfaces; the latter may therefore be more appropriate when shape flexibility is not paramount.

One could easily envision a hybrid system where spline or other parametric surfaces co-exist with particle-based surfaces, using each system's relative advantages where appropriate. For example, particle-based surface patches could be added to a constructive solid geometry (CSG) modeling system to perform fileting at part junctions.

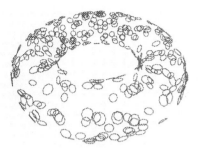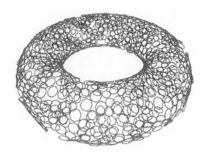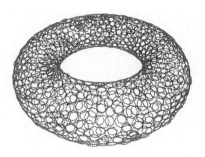

Figure 9: Surface interpolation through a collection of 3-D points. The surface extends outward from the seed points until it fills in the gaps and forms a complete surface.

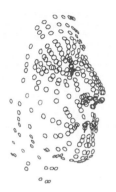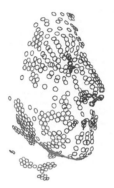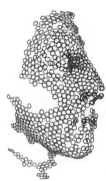

Figure 10: Interpolation of an open surface through a collection of 3-D points. Particles are added between control points until all gaps less than a specified size are filled in. Increasing the range would allow the sparse areas of the cheek and neck to filled in.

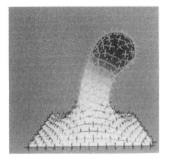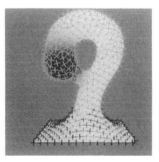

Figure 11: Forming a complex object. The initial surface is deformed upwards and then looped around. The new topology (a handle) is created automatically.

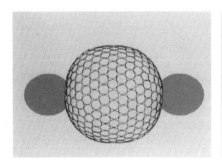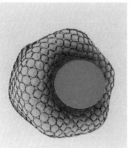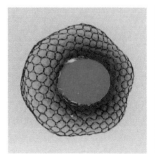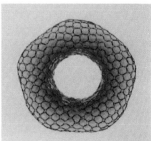

Figure 12: Deformation from sphere to torus using two spherical shaping tools. The final view is from the side, showing the toroidal shape.

In future work, we plan to apply particle-based surfaces to iso-surfaces in volumetric data sets. When combined with the stretching heuristic for particle creation and an inflation force, this model would behave in a manner similar to the geometrically deformed models (GDM) of [13]. We could extend this idea by tracking a volumetric data set through time by deforming the particle surface from one frame to the next.

In another application, we could distribute the particles over the surface of a CAD model and allow the particles to change position and orientation while remaining on the surface of the model, thereby creating a uniform triangulation of the surface. Figure 10 shows how this can be achieved, even without the presence of the CAD model surface to attract the particles. A curvature-dependent adaptive meshing of the surface could also be obtained by locally adjusting the preferred inter-particle spacing. This would be very useful for efficiently rendering parametric surfaces such as NURBS.

10 Conclusion

In this paper, we have developed a particle-based model of deformable surfaces. Our new model, which is based on oriented particles with new interaction potentials, has characteristics of both physically-based surface models and of particle systems. It can be used to model smooth, elastic, moldable surfaces, like traditional splines, and it allows for arbitrary interactions and topologies, like particle systems. A potential drawback of our technique is the lack of precise control over the mathematical form of the surface, which may be important in engineering applications.

Like previous deformable surface models, our new particle-based surfaces can simulate cloth, elastic and plastic films, and other deformable surfaces. The ability to grow new particles gives these model more fluid-like properties which extend the range of interactions. For example, the surfaces can be joined and cut at arbitrary locations. These characteristics make particle-based surfaces a powerful new tool for the interactive construction and modeling of free-form surfaces.

Oriented particles can also be used to automatically fit a surface to sparse 3-D data even when the topology of the surface is unknown. Both open and closed surfaces can be reconstructed, either with or without holes. The reconstructed model can be used as the starting point to interactively create a new shape and then animated within a virtual environment. Thus oriented particle systems provide a convenient interface between surface reconstruction in computer vision, free form modeling in computer graphics, and animation.

References

[1] Appel, Andrew. An Efficient Algorithm for Many-body Simulations. *SIAM J. Sci. Stat. Comput.*, 6(1), 1985.

[2] Bartels, Richard. H. and Beatty, John. C. A Technique for the Direct Manipulation of Spline Curves. In *Graphics Interface '89*, pages 33–39, June 1989.

[3] Bartels, Richard. H., Beatty, John. C., and Barsky, Brian. A. *An Introduction to Splines for use in Computer Graphics and Geeometric Modeling*. Morgan Kaufmann Publishers, Los Altos, California, 1987.

[4] Blinn, James F. A Generalization of Algebraic Surface Drawing. *ACM Transactions on Graphics*, 1(3):235–256, July 1982.

[5] Boissonat, J.-D. Representing 2D and 3D Shapes with the Delaunay Triangulation. In *Seventh International Conference on Pattern Recognition (ICPR'84)*, pages 745–748, Montreal, Canada, July 1984.

[6] Breen, David E., House, Donald H., and Getto, Phillip H. A Particle-Based Computational Model of Cloth Draping Behavior. In Patrikalakis, N. M., editor, *Scientific Visualization of Physical Phenomena*, pages 113–134. Springer-Verlag, New York, 1991.

[7] Coquillart, Sabine. Extended Free-Form Deformations: A Sculpturing Tool for 3D Geometric Modeling. *Computer Graphics (SIGGRAPH'90)*, 24(4):187–196, August 1990.

[8] Farin, Gerald. E. *Curves and Surfaces for Computer Aided Geometric Design: A Practical Guide*. Academic Press, Boston, Massachusetts, 2nd edition, 1990.

[9] Fua, Pascal and Sander, Peter. Reconstructing Surfaces from Unstructured 3D Points. In *Second European Conference on Computer Vision (ECCV'92)*, Sta. Margherita, Italy, May 1992. Springer-Verlag.

[10] Hockney, Roger W. and Eastwood, James W. *Computer Simulation using Particles*. McGraw-Hill Inc., New York, 1988.

[11] Loop, Charles and DeRose, Tony. Generalized B-spline Surfaces of Arbitrary Topology. *Computer Graphics (SIGGRAPH'90)*, 24(4):347–356, August 1990.

[12] Miller, Gavin and Pearce, Andrew. Globular Dynamics: A Connected Particle System for Animating Viscous Fluids. In *SIGGRAPH '89, Course 30 notes: Topics in Physically-based Modeling*, pages R1 – R23. SIGGRAPH, August 1989. Boston, Massachusetts.

[13] Miller, James V., Breen, David E., Lorensen, William E., O'Bara, Robert M., and Wozny, Michael J. Geometrically Deformed Models: A Method of Extracting Closed Geometric Models from Volume Data. *Computer Graphics (SIGGRAPH'91)*, 25(4):217–226, July 1991.

[14] Platt, John C. and Barr, Alan H. Constraint Methods for Flexible Models. *Computer Graphics (SIGGRAPH'88)*, 22(4):279–288, August 1988.

[15] Press, William H., Flannery, Brian P., Teukolsky, Saul A., and Vetterling, William T. *Numerical Recipes in C: The Art of Scientific Computing*. Cambridge University Press, Cambridge, England, 1988.

[16] Reeves, William. T. Particle Systems—A Technique for Modeling a Class of Fuzzy Objects. *ACM Transactions of Graphics*, 2(2):91–108, April 1983.

[17] Reynolds, Craig. W. Flocks, Herds, and Schools: A Distributed Behavioral Model. *Computer Graphics (SIGGRAPH'87)*, 21(4):25–34, July 1987.

[18] Sachs, Emanuel, Roberts, Andrew, and Stoops, David. 3-Draw: A Tool for Designing 3D Shapes. *IEEE Computer Graphics & Applications*, 11(6):18–26, November 1991.

[19] Samet, Hanan. *The Design and Analysis of Spatial Data Structures*. Addison-Wesley, Reading, Massachusetts, 1989.

[20] Shoemake, Ken. Animating Rotation with Quaternion Curves. *Computer Graphics (SIGGRAPH'85)*, 19(3):245–2540, July 1985.

[21] Sims, Karl. Particle Animation and Rendering Using Data Parallel Computation. *Computer Graphics (SIGGRAPH'90)*, 24(4):405–413, August 1990.

[22] Szeliski, Richard. Shape from Rotation. In *IEEE Computer Society Conference on Computer Vision and Pattern Recognition (CVPR'91)*, pages 625–630, Maui, Hawaii, June 1991. IEEE Computer Society Press.

[23] Szeliski, Richard and Tonnesen, David. Surface Modeling with Oriented Particle Systems. Technical Report 91/14, Digital Equipment Corporation, Cambridge Research Lab, December 1991.

[24] Terzopoulos, Demetri and Fleischer, Kurt. Modeling Inelastic Deformations: Visoelasticity, Plasticity, Fracture. *Computer Graphics (SIGGRAPH'88)*, 22(4):269–278, August 1988.

[25] Terzopoulos, Demetri, Platt, John, Barr, Alan, and Fleischer, Kurt. Elastically deformable models. *Computer Graphics (SIGGRAPH'87)*, 21(4):205–214, July 1987.

[26] Terzopoulos, Demetri, Platt, John, and Fleischer, Kurt. From Goop to Glop: Heating and Melting Deformable Models. In *Proceedings Graphics Interface*, pages 219–226. Graphics Interface, June 1989.

[27] Terzopoulos, Demetri, Witkin, Andrew, and Kass, Michael. Symmetry-Seeking Models and 3D Object Reconstruction. *International Journal of Computer Vision*, 1(3):211–221, October 1987.

[28] Tonnesen, David. Ray-tracing Implicit Surfaces Resulting from the Summation of Bounded Polynomial Functions. Technical Report TR-89003, Rensselaer Design Research Center, Rensselaer Polytechnic Institute, Troy, New York, 1989.

[29] Tonnesen, David. Modeling Liquids and Solids using Thermal Particles. In *Graphics Interface '91*, pages 255–262, 1991.

[30] Weil, Jerry. The Synthesis of Cloth Objects. *Computer Graphics (SIGGRAPH'86)*, 20(4):49–54, August 1986.

A Computation of internal forces

To compute the internal inter-particle forces and torques, we compute the variation of inter-particle potentials with respect to particle positions and orientations. We can compute these forces and torques using the equations

$$\mathbf{f} = -\nabla_{\mathbf{p}}\phi \quad \text{and} \quad \nabla_{\mathbf{p}}(\mathbf{p} \cdot \mathbf{v}) = \mathbf{v}$$
$$\boldsymbol{\tau} = -\nabla_{\boldsymbol{\omega}}\phi \quad \text{and} \quad \nabla_{\boldsymbol{\omega}}(\mathbf{n} \cdot \mathbf{v}) = \mathbf{n} \times \mathbf{v}$$

where $\boldsymbol{\omega}$ is the incremental change in orientation $\mathbf{R}$, i.e., $\dot{\mathbf{n}} = \mathbf{n} \times \boldsymbol{\omega}$.

Applying these equations to the four internal potentials, we obtain

$$\mathbf{f}_{\text{LJ}}(\mathbf{r}_{ij}) = -\hat{\mathbf{r}}_{ij}\, \phi'_{\text{LJ}}(\|\mathbf{r}_{ij}\|)$$
$$\mathbf{f}_{\text{P}}(\mathbf{n}_i, \mathbf{r}_{ij}) = -\mathbf{n}_i(\mathbf{n}_i \cdot \mathbf{r}_{ij})\,\psi(\|\mathbf{r}_{ij}\|)$$
$$\qquad - \hat{\mathbf{r}}_{ij}(\mathbf{n}_i \cdot \mathbf{r}_{ij})^2\,\psi'(\|\mathbf{r}_{ij}\|)$$
$$\boldsymbol{\tau}_{\text{P}}(\mathbf{n}_i, \mathbf{r}_{ij}) = \mathbf{r}_{ij} \times \mathbf{n}_i(\mathbf{n}_i \cdot \mathbf{r}_{ij})\,\psi(\|\mathbf{r}_{ij}\|) = \mathbf{r}_{ij} \times \mathbf{f}_{\text{P}}$$
$$\mathbf{f}_{\text{N}}(\mathbf{n}_i, \mathbf{n}_j, \mathbf{r}_{ij}) = -\hat{\mathbf{r}}_{ij}\|\mathbf{n}_i - \mathbf{n}_j\|^2\,\psi'(\|\mathbf{r}_{ij}\|)$$
$$\boldsymbol{\tau}_{\text{N}}(\mathbf{n}_i, \mathbf{n}_j, \mathbf{r}_{ij}) = \mathbf{n}_i \times \mathbf{n}_j\,\psi(\|\mathbf{r}_{ij}\|)$$
$$\mathbf{f}_{\text{C}}(\mathbf{n}_i, \mathbf{n}_j, \mathbf{r}_{ij}) = -\mathbf{n}_i((\mathbf{n}_i + \mathbf{n}_j) \cdot \mathbf{r}_{ij})\,\psi(\|\mathbf{r}_{ij}\|)$$
$$\qquad - \hat{\mathbf{r}}_{ij}((\mathbf{n}_i + \mathbf{n}_j) \cdot \mathbf{r}_{ij})^2\,\psi'(\|\mathbf{r}_{ij}\|)$$
$$\boldsymbol{\tau}_{\text{C}}(\mathbf{n}_i, \mathbf{n}_j, \mathbf{r}_{ij}) = \mathbf{r}_{ij} \times \mathbf{f}_{\text{C}}$$

where $\hat{\mathbf{r}}_{ij}$ is the unit vector along $\mathbf{r}_{ij}$. These forces have the following simple physical interpretations.

The co-planarity potential gives rise to a force parallel to the particle normal and proportional to the distance between the neighboring particle and the local tangent plane. The second term in the force, which can often be ignored, arises from the gradient of the spatial weighting function. The cross product of this force with the inter-particle vector produces a torque on the particle. The co-normality potential produces a torque proportional to the cross-product of the two particle normals, which acts to lign up the normals. The co-circularity force is similar to the co-planarity force, except that the local tangent plane is defined from the average of the two normal vectors.

To compute the total inter-particle force and torque from all three potentials, we use the formulas

$$\mathbf{f}_i = \sum_{j \in \mathcal{N}_i} 2\alpha_{\text{LJ}}\mathbf{f}_{\text{LJ}}(\mathbf{r}_{ij}) + \alpha_{\text{P}}(\mathbf{f}_{\text{P}}(\mathbf{n}_i, \mathbf{r}_{ij}) - \mathbf{f}_{\text{P}}(\mathbf{n}_j, \mathbf{r}_{ji}))$$
$$+ 2\alpha_{\text{N}}\mathbf{f}_{\text{P}}(\mathbf{n}_i, \mathbf{n}_j, \mathbf{r}_{ij}) + 2\alpha_{\text{C}}\mathbf{f}_{\text{C}}(\mathbf{n}_i, \mathbf{n}_j, \mathbf{r}_{ij})$$
$$\boldsymbol{\tau}_i = \sum_{j \in \mathcal{N}_i} \alpha_{\text{P}}\boldsymbol{\tau}_{\text{P}}(\mathbf{n}_i, \mathbf{r}_{ij})$$
$$+ 2\alpha_{\text{N}}\boldsymbol{\tau}_{\text{P}}(\mathbf{n}_i, \mathbf{n}_j, \mathbf{r}_{ij}) + 2\alpha_{\text{C}}\boldsymbol{\tau}_{\text{C}}(\mathbf{n}_i, \mathbf{n}_j, \mathbf{r}_{ij})$$

High Resolution Virtual Reality

Michael Deering
Sun Microsystems Computer Corporation[†]

ABSTRACT

An important component of many virtual reality systems is head-tracked stereo display. The head-tracker enables the image rendering system to produce images from a viewpoint location that dynamically tracks the viewers head movement, creating a convincing 3D illusion. A viewer can achieve intricate hand/eye coordination on virtual objects if virtual and physical objects can be registered to within a fraction of a centimeter. Computer graphics has traditionally been concerned with forming the correct image on a screen. When this goal is expanded to forming the correct pair of images on the viewers retinas, a number of additional physical factors must be taken into account. This paper presents the general steps that must be taken to achieve accurate high resolution head-tracked stereo display on a workstation CRT: the need for predictive head-tracking, the dynamic optical location of the viewers eyepoints, physically accurate stereo perspective viewing matrices, and corrections for refractive and curvature distortions of glass CRTs. Employing these steps, a system is described that achieves sub-centimeter virtual to physical registration.

CR Categories and Subject Descriptors: I.3.3 [Computer Graphics]: Picture/Image Generation - *Display algorithms*; I.3.7 [Computer Graphics]: Three Dimensional Graphics and Realism.

Additional Keywords and Phrases: Stereoscopic Display, Virtual Reality, Head-Tracking.

1 INTRODUCTION

Computer graphics traditionally deals with the formation of an image on a screen in a manner visually faithful to the formation of an image by a camera. However, the human visual system evolved not for viewing photographs, but for close range binocular (stereo)

[†]2550 Garcia Avenue
Mountain View, CA 94043-1100
michael.deering@Eng,Sun.COM

viewing of 3D objects, with unrestricted head motion. Holograms and holographic stereograms support this, providing proper perspective and motion parallax effects [1][6]. Unfortunately, technology does not yet allow these forms of display to be created in real-time. An alternate technique for emulating close range examination of a physical object by a user is employed by many virtual reality systems. If a 3D stereo image display system is augmented by a head-tracking device, the synthetic viewpoint of the rendering process can be made to correspond to the actual dynamic physical viewpoint of the user [18][19][9][2][3][14]. In principle, such a system dynamically computes a stereo pair of images that has the same appearance as a hologram: the virtual object appears to remain stationary when the viewer tilts his head, or moves his head look around its side or over its top.

Making a head-tracked stereo display system work in practice involves achieving an accurate mapping of the mathematical viewing pyramid onto the real world of physical CRTs and biological heads and eyeballs. But how accurate must this mapping be? In the case of the head mounted displays that are used in today's virtual reality systems — whose image resolution is typically below the threshold of legal blindness — the mathematical-to-physical mapping can be quite loose. But many potential applications of virtual reality will require highly accuracy co-siting of physical and virtual objects. For example, for a surgeon viewing 3D CAT scan data overlaid on a patient during surgery, the positions of the virtual and real objects must coincide within a fraction of an inch. In electronics and mechanical repair it might be desirable to overlay diagnostic and schematic information directly on physical components having dimensions of the order of fractions of an inch. With accurate physical/virtual correspondent, direct interactive sculpting of objects is possible using tools such as the virtual lathe shown in Figures 1 and 7.

This paper describes the general steps required for head-tracked stereo display on a workstation stereo CRT, and the corrections necessary to achieve accurate visual correspondent of physical and virtual objects. The system used for these investigations comprises a graphics workstation augmented by a stereo CRT, stereo shuttered glasses, a 3D 6-axis head-tracker and a 3D 6-axis mouse. The system is pictured in Figure 1.

2 STEREO VIEWING MODELS

A stereo 3D display pipeline is specified by two 4x4 perspective viewing matrices (effectively, one monocular pipeline for each eye). These matrices implicitly contain information about the overall physical configuration of the viewing.

Previous work in stereo computer graphics concentrated on the generation of a stereo pairs for viewing in environments where the viewers position was not well controlled [16][17][7][8]. For viewing stereo imagery in environments such as a film theater there is no single correct view projection. Various viewing matrix formulations have been used by different authors reflecting different viewing compromises. Some workers have taken the left and right viewpoints as corresponding to a rotation about a single point in space, an approach that is correct only for objects at infinity (orthographic display). The correct approach is to take the left and right viewpoints to be offset parallel to the image plane. Each resulting matrix includes a skew component.

Figure 1: Photograph of system setup.

The physical configuration of the viewing is determined by the location of the CRT video raster in 3-space and the (dynamic) location of each of the viewers eyes. When these parameters are known, the viewing matrices are unique to within a scale factor. The viewing matrix for each eye corresponds to a pyramid whose tip is at the users eye and whose base is defined by the four corners of the display window within the visible raster of the CRT. The front and back clipping planes are parallel to the plane of the CRT faceplate (assumed for the moment to be perfectly flat).

Traditional 3D computer graphics viewing models — such as that of the PHIGS standard — involve an abstract camera located in the virtual world and a physical user viewing the scene on a display device in the physical world. A PHIGS application has complete control of the virtual position, orientation, and field of view of the camera. However the application has no access to information about the physical world such as the location of the viewer or the position in space of the display window.

For a virtual reality system with a head-tracked stereo screen display, a viewing model abstraction is needed that promotes the coordinates of the physical world to the status of a first class coordinate system — physical coordinates (PC). In our system, an application specifies the relationship between physical coordinates and virtual coordinates (VC, PHIGS "world coordinates") by a matrix M. The relative position, orientation, and scale implied by the matrix specify how the virtual and physical worlds are to be superimposed. (This scale factor is denoted g.) The physical configuration of the stereo display device and the sensed real-time location of the viewers eyes contribute the rest of the information necessary to compute the final 4x4 viewing matrices to be handed to the rendering system.

Each display device has a physical coordinate system registered to its display surface: "display plate coordinates" (DPC) illustrated in Figure 2. DPC has its origin at the lower left hand corner of the visible raster. The x axis proceeds horizontally to the right. The y axis proceeds vertically upwards. The z axis is normal to the display surface, with positive coordinates out towards the viewer. A window on the display is defined by specifying its lower left hand and upper right hand corners as two DPC points L and H on the $z=0$ plane. Each eye has a separate coordinate in DPC space; a single eyepoint is denoted E. The front and back clipping planes are at distance F and B along the z axis [4].

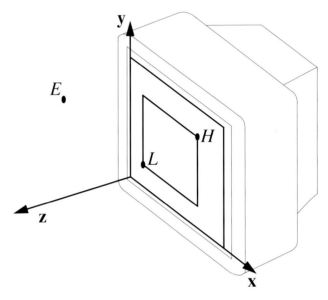

Figure 2: "Display plate coordinates".

The view matrix for a single eye — expressed in column vector matrix format — that maps visible points in DPC into the extended unit cube of [-1 +1] [-1 +1] [-1 +1], is as follows:

$$P =$$

$$\begin{bmatrix} \dfrac{2 \cdot E_z}{H_x - L_x} & 0 & \dfrac{H_x + L_x - 2 \cdot E_x}{H_x - L_x} & \dfrac{-E_z \cdot (H_x + L_x)}{H_x - L_x} \\[2ex] 0 & \dfrac{2 \cdot E_z}{H_y - L_y} & \dfrac{H_y + L_y - 2 \cdot E_y}{H_y - L_y} & \dfrac{-E_z \cdot (H_y + L_y)}{H_y - L_y} \\[2ex] 0 & 0 & \dfrac{B + F - 2 \cdot E_z}{B - F} & B - E_z - B \cdot \dfrac{B + F - 2 \cdot E_z}{B - F} \\[2ex] 0 & 0 & -1 & E_z \end{bmatrix}$$

To relate these matrices to traditional computer graphics models, in the case that only a single display device is present, PC and DPC can be chosen to coincide. In this case, $\frac{1}{g}M$ corresponds to the PHIGS "view orientation matrix" and gP to the PHIGS "view mapping matrix", except that PHIGS requires P to be in [0 1] unit cube form.

The equations above apply to display devices including stereo CRTs, projection stereo displays and stereo LCD panels. Notice that intraocular distance — the distance between the viewers eyes — is not directly represented in this equation. In a head-tracking display system, parallax on the display surface is not necessary horizontal. If a viewer observes the display with his eyes oriented vertically, than the parallax at the screen will be completely vertical. The amount of parallax at the screen is not constant even for a given head distance and object location: a viewer with his head turned 30° to one side of the screen has parallax at the screen surface that is less than when he squarely faces the screen.

If two fixed eye positions are substituted into the equation above, than the equation of [7] results. Both [7] and [12] start with a compatible model, but introduce modifications that directly control the maximum amount of parallax in the image to lessen viewer discomfort. A number of techniques can satisfy the important application goal of ensuring that a user can comfortably converge the stereo pair. Accomplishing this objective by deforming the matrix P will cause the viewing matrices to diverge from the real physical projection, and preclude our physical and virtual object correlation goal. Our approach was to get the projection geometry completely correct for arbitrary viewer head position, and deal with convergence as a separably issue, and is discussed in section 10.

3 EYEPOINT

In traditional computer graphics, the viewing projection point is referred to as the "eyepoint" or "viewpoint" and is intended to correspond to the viewers eye. However, for the purpose of accurate display, this location must be identified much more precisely physiologically.

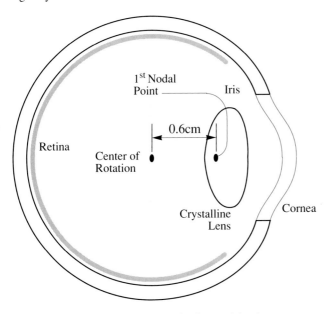

Figure 3: The human eye and its first nodal point.

Optically, in general the "viewpoint" of a lens system is the first nodal point. As seen in Figure 3, the human eye can be modeled as a compound lens system with two lenses. The first nodal point of this system lies inside the second lens, approximately 0.6 cm from the center of the eye. For a discussion of nodal points and human eye models, see [13], chapter 9. Bespectacled viewers — such as the author — may require a more complex model.

Because the real "eyepoint" does not lie at the center of rotation of the eye, the exact location of the eyepoint changes slightly depending on the direction of the viewers gaze. As the eye can readily rotate ±45° or more from center during normal viewing, this represents a potential displacement of eyepoint location of about ±0.4 cm. In stereo viewing the gaze direction is eye specific: the closer the object the larger the angle between gaze directions (the

angle of convergence). Error in the distance between the two eyepoints is more critical than in the absolute eye point locations: the former incudes perceived depth errors. This error is potentially most damaging at vary close distances: in applications having minimum object distances greater than several feet, the eyepoint locations can be assumed to be fixed relative to the head (as was assumed in [19]).

Near-perfect compensation for eyepoint location could be achieved by using eye-tracking hardware to acquire information about the direction of gaze of each of the viewers eyes, in addition to his head position and orientation. This is a promising long term solution, since gaze direction information can be exploited for other purposes such as identifying the region of screen space — corresponding to the fovial portion of the retina — that deserves to be rendered with high spatial detail.

In the absence of directly-acquired gaze direction information, errors due to uncertainty in eye nodal point location can be minimized by guessing the likely direction of gaze. The obvious guess is the center of the stereo window. When a 3D mouse is in use, a better guess is that the viewers gaze is in the direction of its "hot spot", as it is likely that the tightest accuracy requirement reflects "touching" the mouse to a virtual object. At the mouse tip, this assumption perfectly compensates for errors due to rotation of the eyes.

4 HEAD TRACKING

Many different technologies have been employed to acquire dynamic viewer head position and orientation information. At present no single technology is superior for all applications. Devices based on magnetic fields tend to have problems with lag and spatial nonlinearities. Devices based on ultrasound have line of sight limitations and limited orientational accuracy. The prototype system described in this paper employed an ultrasonic tracking device. None of the mathematics of this paper depend on the tracking technology used.

Head-tracking location and orientation data is used to derive the rotational centers of the viewers eyes moment to moment, using fixed (head coordinate) vectors from the location of the head tracker to the viewers eyes. The nominal human intraocular distance of 6.3 cm can vary between individuals by as much as ±2.6 cm; it is therefore important that these vectors be viewer specific. The vectors must also account for the registration of the head tracking device to the viewers head. In the case of our system, this means accounting for how the head tracking stereo glasses sit on a particular individual's face relative to his eyes. Errors in intraocular distance on the order of a fraction of a centimeter can change the stereo perception of depth by an amount several times greater.

Our goal in head-tracked synthetic stereo imagery is for the viewer to perceive computer generated objects as solid, rigid, three dimensional physical objects. In common with monocular systems, it is necessary to have a display frame rate sufficient for motion fusion. With stereo imagery there is the additional phenomenon of *induced stereo movement* [20], where objects displayed at a low frame rate appear to deform and twist.

An even more important issue is perceived lag. Perceived lag is caused by the visual difference between the stereo image generated by the system, and the physically correct image given the viewers true head position at the time of perception. A number of factors contribute to this lag: errors in head position due to the tracking device; the latency of the head-tracking device; and the latency of the image generation hardware. Just as for motion fusion, there appears to be a (soft) maximum degree of perceived lag beyond which the illusion begins to break up. The visual effect is for the virtual object to "distort and jump". While much more detailed formal physiological studies of this issue remain to be performed, initial empirical results are similar to that for motion fusion, e.g., perceived lags should be no more than 50-100 ms.

The effect of latency can be reduced by using, instead of the directly sensed location of the viewers head, a forward prediction of where the viewers head is likely to be when rendering and display of the next frame is completed. Prediction works best when limited to a few hundreds of milliseconds: the overshoot resulting from longer-term prediction is more visually objectionable than the lag.

The simplest prediction method is linear interpolation, where the two most recent samples of position are interpolated in a straight line. This works reasonably well when the rendering-to-display latency is less than about 100 ms, however, this technique overshoots during rapid deceleration. Higher order interpolators based on Kalman filtering have been used [10][5]. Use of such filters involves a trade-off between lag reduction with the potential of further amplifying sensor noise.

It is important to correctly choose the parameters to be predicted. If the two eye nodal points are independently extrapolated, than intraocular distance is not necessary be maintained, resulting in distortion of depth. A better alternative is to extrapolate the location and orientation of the head, compute the eyeball centers from the predicted head location, and than derive the eye nodal points. The head-location prediction strategy may have to take the characteristics of the particular head tracking device into account. Improved prediction might be possible if a head-tracking device were to provide velocity and/or acceleration data in addition to position and orientation data.

At low head velocities — below about 4 cm/s — the visual advantage due to forward head prediction is small, while the potential for amplifying sensor jitter is large. Thus, depending on the specifics of the sensors used, a filter to ramp down the contribution of the head prediction function at small velocities generally reduces jitter of the virtual objects image when the viewer is trying to hold their head still or making vary fine head movements.

An image on a CRT is not flashed instantaneously on the screen, but takes almost a frame time to be fully scanned out. Furthermore, for field sequential stereoscopic displays, the left and right images are offset in time by one field. At a 120 Hz field rate, this corresponds to an 8.3 ms temporal offset between the two eyes views. Fortunately, the actual perception of the displayed image is also not instantaneous. The human visual system takes several tens of milliseconds to perceive a stereo pair, and apparently is not sensitive to small temporal errors [11]. This does not put a lower limit on perceivable temporal effects, as high head velocities can cause visual blur of virtual objects whose physical counterpart retinal images would have been stabilized.

The head position prediction algorithm currently used by our system is linear interpolation with low velocity and low frame rate ramp down. We are actively experimenting with a number of different sensing technologies and higher order prediction algorithms.

5 THE "IMAGE PLANE" OF A CRT

The classic viewing projection used in computer graphics assumes that the light-emitting image plane is planar. However the phosphor screen of a typical CRT is by design a section of a sphere or of a cylinder. Also, the phosphor screen is viewed through a thick glass faceplate that has an index of refraction significantly higher than that of air. In conventional computer graphics the inaccuracies produced by ignoring these effects are imperceptible. But for high resolution stereo, the errors produced are significant enough to require correction. (The corresponding problem for head mounted displays are the distortions caused by the wide field of view lenses placed in front of the viewer's eyes. [15] presents an accurate model of the distortion function of a commonly used lens, showing it to be quite nonlinear, and not amenable to any computationally simple correction function.)

As will be shown, CRT glass induced errors are viewpoint dependent and nonlinear. To exploit conventional rendering accelerators, we implement the correction by modifying the viewing matrix equation P (of section 2) by adjusting the values of L and H. This correction is approximate, but very effective: at present, more accurate correction would impose a prohibitive computational load.

One approach to improve the correction for this effect would be to model the CRT surface as multiple flat "patches" positioned and tilted to approximate the spherical or cylindrical shape of the actual screen. Each patch would than be rendered separately with a patch-specific viewing matrix. This "piecewise" approximation would take longer to render than a single patch, although with effective use of bounding box data structures the rendering time increase need not grow as rapidly as the number of patches.

Another approach at higher accuracy correction takes into account direction of view information. Most of the distortions discussed in this paper are only visible to the fovea, that is within an angle of $2°$-$6°$ of the gaze direction. If angle of view information is available — either directly as a result of eye tracking, or indirectly through the "hot spot" assumption — than the correction can be biased to be correct at the point of view, but representable as a single 4x4 viewing matrix.

Phosphor image refraction by faceplate glass

Every direct-view CRT display has a glass faceplate that intervenes between the image formed on the phosphor and the eye of the viewer. In addition to its obvious function of enclosing the vacuum within the tube, the faceplate provides implosion protection, antiglare and contrast-improvement functions. For a 21 inch CRT the faceplate is about 2 cm thick and has an index of refraction in the range of 1.5 to 1.6. At an angle of view $60°$ normal to the plane of the CRT glass, Snell's law dictates that the glass will bend the light from the phosphor by $25°$ at the glass/air interface ([4] pp. 756). This effect introduces an apparent positional error of up to 2 cm, depending on eyepoint location. Figure 4 shows the geometry of the ray paths. (Point O is the projection of point E onto the xy plane.) Approximating the calculation of the incident angle θ, the refraction distortion function of a point S when viewed from the eyepoint E is:

$$\text{ref}(S) = S + h \cdot (\tan\theta - \tan\phi) \cdot \frac{S - O}{f}, \qquad \phi = \sin^{-1}(\frac{\sin\theta}{n_g})$$

$$\theta \approx \tan^{-1}\frac{f}{E_z}, \qquad f = \sqrt{(S_x - E_x)^2 + (S_y - E_y)^2}$$

Effect of curvature of CRT screen

As explained above, the actual image raster of a modern CRT is a sections of a sphere or a cylinder. Modern CRTs of the so-called "flat-square-tube" (FST) variety have a radius of curvature of about 2 m. The curvature is more severe for less flat CRTs. This curvature causes the actual image to deviate from a plane by as much as 1 cm across its faceplate. (Certain CRTs are truly flat, but none of those are presently manufactured with horizontal scan rates sufficient for high resolution 120 Hz stereo.)

At a view angle of $60°$, and a head position to one side of the CRT and 50 cm away, this curvature represents a potential positional error on the order of 1.8 cm in position. Figure 5 depicts the geometry of the ray paths. Point C is the tangent to the sphere in display plate

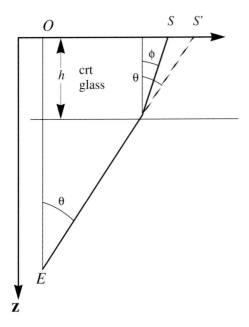

Figure 4: Effect of refraction of CRT front glass. Viewed from point E, the pixel at point S on phosphor appears to come from point S'.

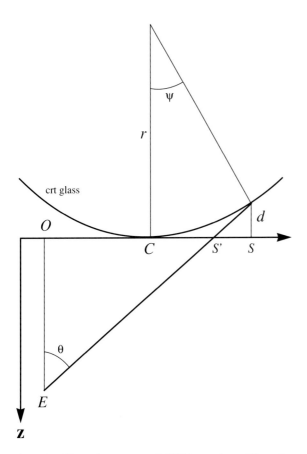

Figure 5: Effect of curvature of CRT front glass. Viewed from point E, the pixel at point S on the phosphor appears to come from point S'.

coordinates. The screen curvature distortion function for a CRT with spherical section of effective radius r is:

$$sph(S) = S - d \cdot \tan\theta \cdot \frac{S-O}{f}, \qquad d = r \cdot (1.0 - \cos\psi)$$

$$\psi = \sin^{-1}\frac{\sqrt{(S_x - C_x)^2 + (S_y - C_y)^2}}{r}$$

Combining the corrections

These two distortions apply in opposite directions: the glass tends to magnify the image; the curvature minifies. But they by no means cancel out. The effects do interact: to be completely accurate the refraction incident angle must be measured relative to the normal of the curving glass. Including this, the combined refraction and curvature distortion function is:

$$dis(S) =$$
$$S + (h \cdot (\tan\theta' - \tan\phi') - r \cdot (1.0 - \cos\psi) \cdot \tan\theta) \cdot \frac{S-O}{f}$$

$$\phi' = \sin^{-1}(\frac{\sin\theta'}{n_g}), \qquad \theta' = \cos^{-1}\frac{\vec{v} \bullet \vec{\eta}}{|\vec{v}| \cdot |\vec{\eta}|}$$

$$\vec{v} = \langle E_x - S_x, E_y - S_y, -E_z \rangle$$

$$\vec{\eta} = \langle S_x - C_x, S_y - C_y, \sqrt{r^2 - (S_x - C_x)^2 - (S_y - C_y)^2} \rangle$$

This distortion function can be used in a number of ways to help correct the screen image. A simple use is to linearly approximate a corrected display. The idea is just to adjust the 3D location of two corners of the display area. This yields a final modification to the L and H values to be input to the viewing equation:

$$L' = dis(L), \qquad H' = dis(H)$$

or to bias the correction for a hot spot Q:

$$L = L + Q - dis(Q), \qquad H' = H + Q - dis(Q)$$

6 LIGHTING

While it does not change the location of pixels, making the light source directions and colors in the virtual world roughly match those in the physical world enhances the illusion of the virtual object inhabiting our world. In one experiment we put a blinking green spotlight in both worlds; the illusion was so natural that even many graphics experts didn't understand why there was a blinking light until we disabled one of them.

As may be expected, additional sensory inputs to the viewer amplify the illusion of reality. For our virtual lathe, we dynamically varied the grinding sound by the amount of material being cut away at any instant.

7 HARDWARE CONFIGURATION

The hardware in our system consisted of a standard 3D graphics workstation augmented with off the shelf stereo and 3D tracking peripherals:

Sun SPARCstation™ 2GT	3D graphics workstation
Hitachi 21" Color CRT monitor	CM2187M (85 KHz horizontal) 960 x 680 @ 108 Hz
Logitech 3D mouse and head-tracker	specified positional accuracy ±.0635 cm, angular ±1/20°
StereoGraphics CrystalEyes VR™	stereo LCD shutter glasses with integral Logitech head-tracker

8 EXPERIMENTAL RESULTS

Figures 6, 7, and 8 are (divergent) stereo pairs from the system in operation. The operational accuracy of the system is presented empirically in Figure 6. The photograph is of two metric rulers; one physical, one virtual. The physical ruler was placed directly below the virtual ruler. This photograph was taken at an angle of about 35° from normal to the screen. In stereo, the virtual ruler appears to stick out of the screen at the same angle and horizontal location as its physical counterpart. Even viewed monocularly, it can be seen that the real and synthetic images are closely aligned to within a fraction of a centimeter. The CRT correction was based on the hot spot assumption. The penny was included not only for scale, but to show where the front of the CRT glass was, relative to the caret cursor on the inner surface. All three image pairs are extreme close-ups, and represent only a small portion of the usable area of the screen.

An emulation of a lathe is shown in Figure 7. The tip of the (physical) plastic rod is the 3D mouse hot spot. Wherever in space it is touched to the stock, virtual material is cut away accompanied by virtual sparks and a grinding sound. Precise shape cutting would not be possible here without accurate registration between the viewers retinal image of the virtual material being cut and the retinal image physical tip of the 3D mouse.

Figure 8 shows a drawing application where a thin tube of virtual material is laid down wherever the 3D mouse has been; here a knot has been drawn.

An earlier version of our system has been tried on several thousand different individuals during 3 minute demonstrations. Almost universally, individuals with normal stereo vision reported good stereo perception. Most first time users who attempted to were able to successfully tie a knot with the drawing package.

In the system of [17], knot tying was also possible. They reported that: "... only an experienced viewer could reliably and comfortably see the proper depth...". They went on to speculate that this was due to pure stereo missing important depth cues: shadows, textures, perspective, and motion parallax. While our system adds motion parallax, we found that high quality results could be obtained even from a fixed viewpoint, so long as that viewpoint had the absolutely correct perspective image pairs computed.

This paper details several techniques for improving the accuracy of visual registration of the virtual and physical worlds. How much did each technique contribute? Are all of them necessary? Are there other sources of error not covered? The visual effect of many of the errors is frustratingly similar. For example, errors in registering the tracker to display plate coordinates look vary much like errors in the head to eyepoint vectors. However, once the complete system was functioning and calibrated, it became possible to observe the contribution of the correction steps by disabling them one by one. Investigations of these observations can both explain and validate their effect. The specific error amounts described in each section were arrived at in this manner.

The visual registration of the virtual and physical worlds is limited by the accuracy of the head-tracking technology, and the accuracy and stability of the calibration measurements of the physical setup.

The specified accuracy of the tracking subsystem is 200 dpi, e.g. a potential spatial error of ±1/400 of an inch (±.0635 cm). The orientational accuracy is specified as ±1/20°. The calibration of the sensors to the viewers eyes and the CRT phosphor was done with fairly crude techniques, probably only accurate to within 0.5 cm. The overall system accuracy varies with head position, but for a large region, centimeter virtual to physical registration accuracies are obtained. The error becomes larger at extreme angles to the CRT glass, and wherever the 3D tracking device delivers measurements substantially below its rated accuracy.

9 OTHER APPLICATIONS

The technology described in this paper can be applied to other 3D display configurations besides real-time projected geometry. If sixteen or so images have been precomputed (or sixteen real photographs taken and digitized), than a form of lenticular lens emulation display is possible. The idea is to compute the predicted eye nodal points as before, but now use them to select which two of the sixteen existing images will be displayed as a stereo image during the next frame. We have tried this approach on our system with satisfactory results. Such a system assumes that the viewers head is upright, and allows only for vary limited side to side head motion, just as is true for a physical lenticular lens display.

Unlike a real lenticular lens system, there is no need to stop at sixteen side-to-side samples. As a refinement to the system described in [3], a general precomputed head-tracked display could always use the eyes predicted nodal point to select the image with the closest precomputed (or pre-photographed) viewpoint. If hundreds of viewpoints have been densely sampled over a reasonably large 3D range, one once again achieves a full hologram-like effect; visually the overall display is vary similar to a holographic stereogram. (And just as has been found with holographic stereograms, the viewpoints need not be sampled as frequently in the vertical direction, reducing the number of samples needed.) A space optimization could employ image compression technology to pre-compress the sampled images, than decompress the two selected images. If sufficient compression is achieved, moving displays are possible by temporal viewpoint sampling.

The techniques described here apply not only to live stereo displays. The head tracker can be attached to a video, film, or still camera. With proper lens first nodal point location, the camera can be placed anywhere within the tracking region and registered images of synthetic and real objects can be captured live. The stereo images in this paper were photographed this way. For video or movie filming, so long as the camera field of view is wide enough to include some of the physical world beyond the CRT, and the camera is moved about while recording, significant amounts of shape from motion can be perceived by later viewers.

10 LIMITATIONS

Just as vector refresh displays in the early days of computer graphics were limited in object display complexity to that which could be redrawn at an acceptable frame rate, so too are the sort of virtual display systems described in this paper.

The display techniques here implicitly assume a single viewer at a time; additional viewers would be presented with incorrect image pairs. The viewer is currently constrained to wear a pair of special glasses and stay within the working range of the 3D tracking technology. At practical viewing distances, the viewers field of view of a stereo CRT is limited to 20° to 60°. Projection stereo displays (perhaps multiple thereof) can support wider fields of view.

Current stereo CRT phosphors have long secondary decays; this results in distracting "ghosting" of one eyes image into the other. Improved phosphors are in development.

The depth of field (focus) of the virtual object is *always* at the CRT surface (unless additional optics are employed), while the stereo cues are indicating that the focus should be at a different distance. When the apparent stereo location of an object is significantly displaced from the CRT surface, the mismatch in accommodation cues can make it uncomfortable to impossible for a viewer to converge the display image. Getting other visual depth cues right can greatly extend the displacement range: we have had a much greater percentage of users drawing 3D doodles inches in front of their noses than experts familiar with other stereo display systems thought possible. The amount of CRT to virtual object distance acceptable varies greatly from one individual to another. In general for CRTs a conservative approach is to keep it within plus or minus ten centimeter of the physical display surface. This can be achieved by scaling, clipping planes, or in extremes even nonuniform object scaling, in place of the direct parallax control of [7] and [12]. In the future, systems including gaze tracking and computer controlled active optics may allow stereo images to be synthesized with proper optical depth of field.

11 CONCLUSIONS

3D synthetic image rendering can be extended beyond the confines of the frame buffer to encompass the physical and optical details of the path to the viewers retina. These techniques allow computer generated worlds to be superimposed onto the physical world with registration accuracy better than a centimeter. Such registration allows users to use their normal binocular vision to accurately judge distances to virtual objects, and allows virtual and physical objects to be intermixed. The ability of users to move their heads enables even naive users to rapidly perceive the spatial relationships of complex 3D shapes in a natural way. These techniques further blur the distinction between the physical and computer worlds.

ACKNOWLEDGEMENTS

Many thanks to Salem Abi-Azzi and Laon Shirman combing through the math, and to Mike Lavelle, Scott Nelson, Greg Schechter, and most especially Charles Poynton and Will Shelton for combing through the English.

REFERENCES

1. **Benton, Stephen.** Survey of Holographic Stereograms. Processing and Display of Three-Dimensional Data. In *Proceedings of the SPIE* 367 (1982), 15-19.

2. **Diamond, R., A. Wynn, K. Thomsen,** and **J. Turner.** Three dimensional perception for one-eyed guys, or the use of dynamic parallax. In *Computational Crystallography*, 286-293, ed. David Sayre, Clarendon Press, Oxford, 1982.

3. **Fisher, Scott.** Viewpoint dependent imaging: an interactive stereoscopic display. Processing and Display of Three-Dimensional Data. In *Proceedings of the SPIE* 367 (1982), 41-45.

4. **Foley, James, Andries van Dam, Steven Feiner,** and **John Hughes.** *Computer Graphics: Principles and Practice*, 2nd ed., Addison-Wesley, 1990.

5. **Friedmann, Martin, Tad Starner,** and **Alex Pentland.** Device Synchronization Using an Optimal Linear Filter. In *Proceedings of the ACM Symposium on Interactive 3D Graphics* (Cambridge, Massachusetts, March 29 - April 1, 1992), 57-62.

6. **Haines, Kenneth,** and **Debby Haines.** Computer Graphics for Holography. In *IEEE Computer Graphics and Applications* 12, 1 (January 1992), 37-46.

7. **Hibbard, Eric** *et al.* On the Theory and Application of Stereographics in Scientific Visualization. EUROGRAPHICS '91 (Vienna, Austria, September 2-6, 1991). In *Eurographics '91: State of the Art Reports* (1991), 1-21.

8. **Hodges, Larry.** Basic Principles of stereographic Software Development. Stereoscopic Displays and Applications. In *Proceedings of the SPIE* 1457 (1991), 9-17.

9. **Kubitz, W.** and **W. Poppelbaum.** Stereomatrix Interactive Three-Dimensional Computer Display. In *Proceedings of the SID* 14, 3 (Third Quarter 1973) 94-98.

10. **Liang, Jiandong, Chris Shaw,** and **Mark Green.** On Temporal-Spatial Realism in the Virtual Reality Environment. In *Proceedings of the ACM Symposium on User Interface Software and Technology* (Hilton Head, South Carolina, November 11-13, 1991), 19-25.

11. **Lipton, Lenny.** Temporal Artifacts in Field-Sequential Stereoscopic Displays. Proceedings of SID '91 (Anaheim, California, May 6-10, 1991). In *Proceedings of the SID* 22 (May 1991), 834-835.

12. **Lipton, Lenny.** *The CrystalEyes Handbook*. StereoGraphics Corporation, 1991.

13. **Ogle, Kenneth.** *Optics.* Charles C. Thomas, Publisher, Springfield, Illinois, 1968.

14. **Paley, W. Bradford.** Head-Tracking Stereo Display: Experiments and Applications. Stereoscopic Displays and Applications III (San Jose, California, February 12-13, 1992.). In *Proceedings of the SPIE* 1669, 1992.

15. **Robinett, Warren,** and **Jannick Rolland.** A Computational Model for the Stereoscopic Optics of a Head-Mounted Display. In *Presence* 1, 1 (Winter 1992), 45-62.

16. **Roese, John,** and **Lawrence McCleary.** Stereoscopic Computer Graphics for Simulation and Modeling. Proceedings of SIGGRAPH '79 (Chicago, Illinois, August 8-10, 1979). In *Computer Graphics* 13, 2 (August 1979), 41-47.

17. **Schmandt, Christopher.** Spatial Input/Display Correspondence in a Stereoscopic Computer Graphic Work Station. Proceedings of SIGGRAPH '83 (Detroit, Michigan, July 25-29, 1983). In *Computer Graphics* 17, 3 (July 1983), 253-261.

18. **Sutherland, Ivan.** The Ultimate Display. In *Proceedings of the IFIPS Conference* 2 (1965), 506-508.

19. **Sutherland, Ivan.** A Head Mounted Three Dimensional Display. In *Fall Joint Computer Conference*, AFIPS Conference Proceedings 33 (1968), 757-764.

20. **Tyler, William.** Induced Stereomovement. *Vision Res.* 14 (1974), 609-613.

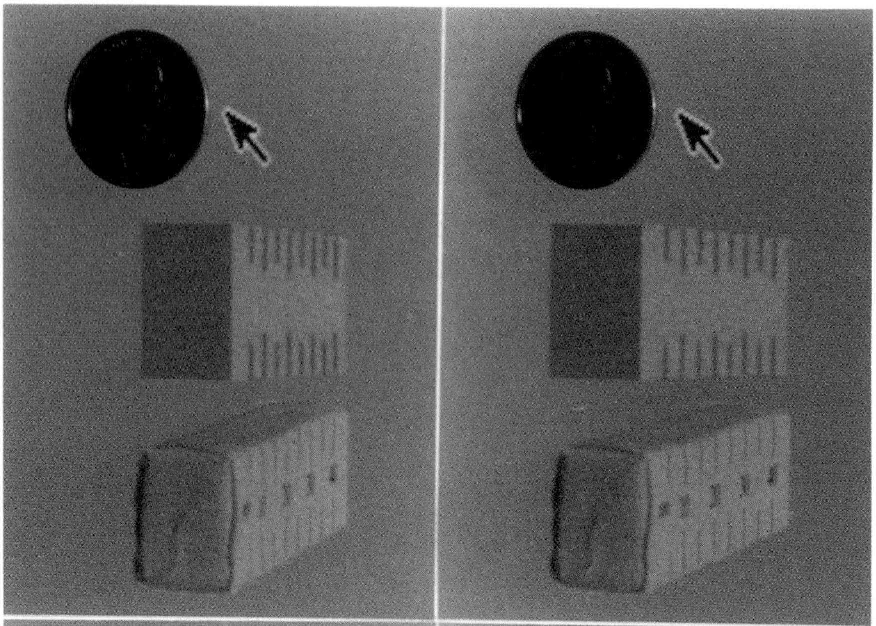

Figure 6: Stereogram of physical and virtual rulers in correspondent.

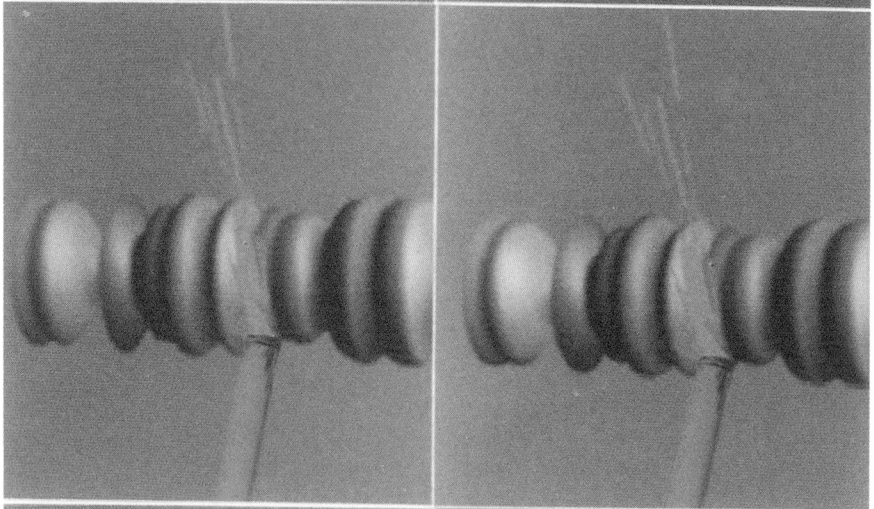

Figure 7: Stereogram of virtual lathe. The tip of the plastic rod is registered to the virtual cutting tip.

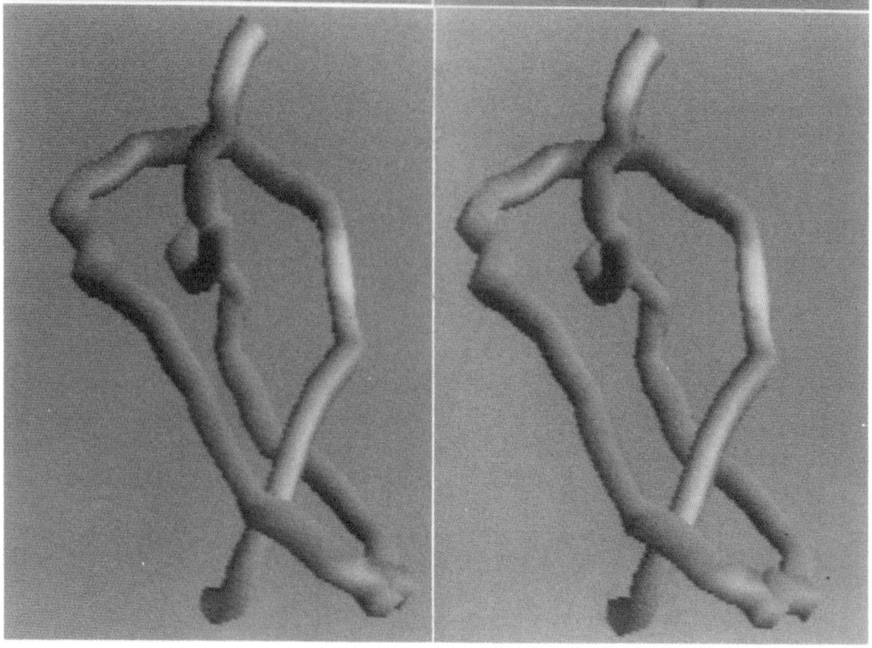

Figure 8: Stereogram of 3D drawing example: a freehand knot.

Merging Virtual Objects with the Real World:

Seeing Ultrasound Imagery within the Patient

Michael Bajura, Henry Fuchs, and Ryutarou Ohbuchi

Department of Computer Science
University of North Carolina
Chapel Hill, NC 27599-3175

Abstract

We describe initial results which show "live" ultrasound echography data visualized within a pregnant human subject. The visualization is achieved by using a small video camera mounted in front of a conventional head-mounted display worn by an observer. The camera's video images are composited with computer-generated ones that contain one or more 2D ultrasound images properly transformed to the observer's current viewing position. As the observer walks around the subject, the ultrasound images appear stationary in 3-space within the subject. This kind of enhancement of the observer's vision may have many other applications, e.g., image guided surgical procedures and on location 3D interactive architecture preview.

CR Categories: I.3.7 [Three-Dimensional Graphics and Realism] Virtual Reality, I.3.1 [Hardware architecture]: Three-dimensional displays, I.3.6 [Methodology and Techniques]: Interaction techniques, J.3 [Life and Medical Sciences]: Medical information systems.

Additional Keywords and Phrases: Virtual reality, see-through head-mounted display, ultrasound echography, 3D medical imaging

1. Introduction

We have been working toward an 'ultimate' 3D ultrasound system which acquires and displays 3D volume data in real time. Real-time display can be crucial for applications such as cardiac diagnosis which need to detect certain kinetic features. Our 'ultimate' system design requires advances in both 3D volume data *acquisition* and 3D volume data *display*. Our collaborators, Dr. Olaf von Ramm's group at Duke University, are working toward real-time 3D volume data acquisition [Smith 1991; von Ramm 1991]. At UNC-Chapel Hill, we have been conducting research on real-time 3D volume data visualization.

Our research efforts at UNC have been focused in three areas: 1) algorithms for acquiring and rendering real-time ultrasound data, 2) creating a working virtual environment which acquires and displays 3D ultrasound data in real time, and 3) recovering structural information for volume rendering specifically from ultrasound data, which has unique image processing requirements. This third area is presented in [Lin 1991] and is not covered here.

Section 2 of this paper reviews previous work in 3D ultrasound and Section 3 discusses our research on processing, rendering, and displaying echographic data without a head-mounted display. Since the only real-time volume data scanners available today are 2D ultrasound scanners, we try to approximate our 'ultimate' system by incrementally visualizing a 3D volume dataset reconstructed from a never-ending sequence of 2D data slices [Ohbuchi 1990; 1991]. This is difficult because the volume consisting of multiple 2D slices needs to be visualized incrementally as the 2D slices are acquired. This incremental method has been successfully used in off line experiments with a 3-degree-of-freedom (DOF) mechanical arm tracker and is extendible to 6 degrees of freedom, e.g., a 3D translation and a 3D rotation, at greater computational cost.

Sections 4 and 5 present our research on video see-through head-mounted display (HMD) techniques involving the merging of computer generated images with real-world images. Our video see-through HMD system displays ultrasound echography image data in the context of real (3D) objects. This is part of our continuing see-through HMD research, which includes both optical see-through HMD and video see-through HMD. Even though we concentrate here on medical ultrasound imaging, applications of this display technology are not limited to it (see Section 6.2).

2. Previous Research in 3D Ultrasound

The advantages of ultrasound echography are that it is relatively safe compared with other imaging modalities and that images are generated in real time [Wells 1977]. This makes it the preferred imaging technique for fetal examination, cardiac study, and guided surgical procedures such as fine-needle aspiration biopsy of breast tumors [Fornage 1990]. Ultrasound echography offers the best real-time performance in 3D data acquisition, although slower imaging modalities such as MRI are improving.

The drawbacks of ultrasound imaging include a low signal to noise ratio and poor spatial resolution. Ultrasound images exhibit "speckle" which appears as grainy areas in images. Speckle arises from coherent sound interference effects from tissue substructure. Information such as blood flow can be derived from speckle but in

©1992   ACM-0-89791-479-1/92/007/0203 $01.50

general speckle is hard to utilize [Thijssen 1990]. Other problems with ultrasound imaging include attenuation that increases with frequency, phase aberration due to tissue inhomogeneity, and reflection and refraction artifacts [Harris 1990] .

2.1 3D Ultrasound Image Acquisition

Just as ultrasound echography has evolved from 1D data acquisition to 2D data acquisition, work is in progress to advance to 3D data acquisition. Dr. Olaf von Ramm's group at Duke University is developing a 3D scanner which will acquire 3D data in real time [Shattuck 1984; Smith 1991; von Ramm 1991]. The 3D scanner uses a 2D phased array transducer to sweep out an imaging volume. A parallel processing technique called *Explososcan* is used on return echoes to boost the data acquisition rate.

Since such a real-time 3D medical ultrasound scanning system is not yet available, prior studies on 3D ultrasound imaging known to the authors have tried to reconstruct 3D data from imaging primitives of a lesser dimension (usually 2D images). To reconstruct a 3D image from images of a lesser dimension, the location and orientation of the imaging primitives must be known. Coordinate values are explicitly tracked either acoustically [Brinkley 1978; King 1990; Moritz 1983], mechanically [Geiser 1982a; Geiser 1982b; Hottier 1989; McCann 1988; Ohbuchi 1990; Raichelen 1986; Stickels 1984], or optically [Mills 1990]. In other systems, a human or a machine makes scans at predetermined locations and/or orientations [Collet Billon 1990; Ghosh 1982; Itoh 1979; Lalouche 1989; Matsumoto 1981; Nakamura 1984; Tomographic Technologies 1991].

A particularly interesting system under development at Philips Paris Research Laboratory is one of the closest yet to a real-time 3D ultrasound scanner [Collet Billon 1990]. It is a follow on to earlier work which featured a manually guided scanner with mechanical tracking [Hottier 1990]. This near real-time 3D scanner is a mechanical sector scanner, in which a conventional 2D sector scanhead with an annular array transducer is rotated by a stepper motor to get a third scanning dimension. In a period of 3 to 5 seconds, 50 to 100 slices of 2D sector scan images are acquired. Currently the annular array transducer in this system provides better spatial resolution, but less temporal resolution, than the real-time 3D phased array system by von Ramm et al., mentioned above. A commercial product, the *Echo-CT* system by Tomographic Technologies, GMBH, uses the linear translation of a transducer inside a tube inserted into the esophagus to acquire parallel slices of the heart. Image acquisition is gated by respiration and an EKG to reduce registration problems [Tomographic Technologies 1991].

2.2 3D Ultrasound Image Display

One should note that 3D image data can be presented not only in visual form, but also as a set of calculated values, e.g., a ventricular volume. The visual form can be classified further by the rendering primitives used, which can be either geometric (e.g., polygons) or image-based (e.g., voxels). Many early studies focused on non-invasively estimating of the volume of the heart chamber [Brinkley 1978; Ghosh 1982; Raichelen 1986; Stickels 1984]. Typically, 2D echography (2DE) images were stored on video tape and manually processed off-line. Since visual presentation was of secondary interest, wire frames or a stack of contours were often used to render

An interesting extension to 2D display is a system that tracks the location and orientation of 2D image slices with 6 DOF [King 1990]. On each 2D displayed image, the system overlays lines indicating the intersection of the current image with other 2D images already acquired. The authors claim that these lines help the viewer understand the relationship of the 2D image slices in 3D space. Other studies reconstructed 3D grey level images preserving grey scale, which can be crucial to tissue characterization [Collet Billon 1990; Hottier 1989; Lalouche 1989; McCann 1988; Nakamura 1984; Pini 1990; Tomographic Technologies 1991]. [Lalouche 1989] is a mammogram study using a special 2DE scanner that can acquire and store 45 consecutive parallel slices at 1 mm intervals. A volume is reconstructed by cubic-spline interpolation and then volume rendered. [McCann 1988] performed gated acquisition of a heart's image over a cardiac cycle by storing 2DE images on video tape and then reconstructing and volume rendering them. 'Repetitive low-pass filtering' was used during reconstruction to fill the spaces between radial slices, which suppressed aliasing artifacts. [Tomographic Technologies 1991] provides flexible re-slicing by up to 6 planes as well other imaging modes. [Collet Billon 1990] uses two visualization techniques: re-slicing by an arbitrary plane and volume rendering. The former allows faster but only 2D viewing on a current workstation. The latter allows 3D viewing but often involves cumbersome manual segmentation. The reconstruction algorithm uses straightforward low pass filtering.

3. Incremental Volume Visualization

We have been experimenting with volume rendering as one alternative for visualizing dynamic ultrasound volume data. Standard volume rendering techniques which rely heavily on preprocessing do not apply well to dynamic data which must be visualized in real time [Levoy 1988; Sabella 1988; Upson 1988]. We review here an incremental , interactive, 3D ultrasound visualization technique which visualizes a 3D volume as it is incrementally updated by a sequence of registered 2D ultrasound images [Ohbuchi 1990; 1991].

Our target function is sampled at irregular points and may change over time. Instead of directly visualizing samples from this target, we reconstruct a regular 3D volume from this time series of spatially irregular sample points. This places a limit on storage and computation requirements which would grow without bound if we retained all the past sample points. The reconstructed volume is then rendered with an incremental volume-rendering technique.

The reconstruction is a 4D convolution process. A 3D Gaussian kernel is used for spatial reconstruction followed by a temporal reconstruction based on simple auto regressive moving average (ARMA) filtering [Haddad 1991]. Time stamps are assigned to each 3D voxel, which are updated during reconstruction. The time stamp difference between a reconstructed voxel and an incoming sample is used to compute coefficients for the ARMA filter. The 3D Gaussian filter is loosely matched to the point spread function of the ultrasound transducer and is a good choice because it minimizes the product of spatial bandwidth and spatial frequency bandwidth [Hildreth 1983; Leipnik 1960].

An image-order, ray-casting algorithm based on [Levoy 1988] renders the final images incrementally. Rendering is incremental and fast only if the viewpoint is fixed and if the updated volume is relatively small. Shading and ray sampling are done only for voxels proximate to incoming data. The ray samples are stored

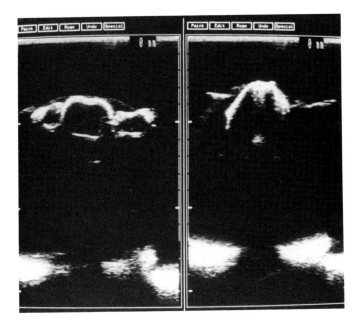

Figure 1. Two of 90 2D ultrasound echography images of a plastic toy doll phantom which was scanned in a water tank. The scans shown are at the torso (left) and at the head (right). The clouds at the bottom of the scans are artifacts due to reflections from the bottom of the water tank.

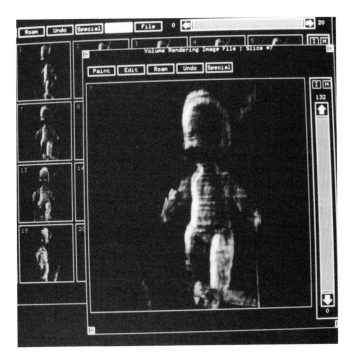

Figure 2. Reconstructed and rendered image of the toy doll phantom using incremental volume visualization.

in a 3D array in screen space called a "ray cache" for later use. The ray cache is hierarchical so that a small partial update of the ray cache can be composited quickly ($O(log(n))$) [Ohbuchi 1991]. The hierarchical ray cache also allows fast rendering of polygons properly composited with volume data, which can enhance the volume visualization [Levoy 1990; Miyazawa 1991]. This incremental volume rendering algorithm is not restricted to ultrasound and is applicable to other problems which update volume data incrementally, e.g., interactive volume modeling by sculpting [Galyean 1991].

To test this visualization technique, we acquired a series of 2D images with a manually guided conventional 2DE scanhead attached to a mechanical tracking arm with 3 DOF (two translations and one rotation). As we scanned various targets in a water tank, their images and their corresponding geometry were stored off-line. We then ran the incremental volume visualization algorithm on a DECstation 5000 with 256 MB of memory using this data. With a reconstruction buffer size of $150 \times 150 \times 300$ and an image size of 256×256, it took 15–20 seconds to reconstruct and render a typical image after insertion of a 2D data slice. This time varied with reconstruction, shading, and viewing parameters.

Figure 1 shows 2 out of 90 2D images of a plastic toy doll phantom which is visualized in Figure 2. The 2D images were produced by an ATL Mark-4 Scanner with a 3.5 MHz linear scanhead. The 2D images overlap but are roughly parallel at approximately 2 mm intervals.

4. Virtual Environment Ultrasound Imaging

Various medical ultrasound imaging applications require a registration of ultrasound images with anatomical references, e.g., in performing a fine needle aspiration biopsy of a suspected breast tumor [Fornage 1990]. A virtual environment which displays images acquired by ultrasound equipment in place within a patient's anatomy could facilitate such an application. We have developed an experimental system that displays multiple 2D medical ultrasound images overlaid on real-world images. In January 1992, after months of development with test objects in water tanks, we performed our first experiment with a human subject.

Our virtual environment ultrasound imaging system works as follows (note that this is a different system than our older one described in the previous section): as each echography image is acquired by an ultrasound scanner, its position and orientation in 3D world space are tracked with 6 degrees of freedom (DOF). Simultaneously the position and orientation of a HMD are also tracked with 6 DOF. Using this geometry, an image-generation system generates 3D renderings of the 2D ultrasound images. These images are video mixed with real-world images from a miniature TV camera mounted on the HMD. The resulting composite image shows the 2D ultrasound data registered in its true 3D location.

Figure 3 is a block diagram of our system's hardware. There are three major components: 1) an image-acquisition and tracking system, which consists of an ultrasound scanner and a Polhemus tracking system, 2) an image-generation system, which is our Pixel-Planes 5 graphics multicomputer, and 3) a HMD which includes a portable TV camera, a video mixer, and a VPL EyePhone. Each component is described in more detail in Sections 4.1–4.3.

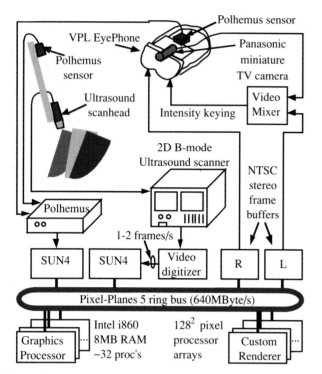

Figure 3. Hardware block diagram for the virtual environment ultrasound system.

4.1 Image Acquisition and Tracking

Two dimensional ultrasound images are generated by an IREX System III echography scanner with a 16 mm aperture 2.5 MHz phased array transducer. These images are digitized by a SUN 4 with a Matrox MVP/S real-time video digitizer and transferred to our Pixel-Planes 5 graphics multicomputer [Fuchs 1989]. The SUN 4 operates as a 2DE image server for requests from the Pixel-Planes 5 system. Images are distributed among the Graphics Processors (GPs) on a round-robin scan-line by scan-line basis. Due to the bandwidth limitations of the SUN 4 VME bus, transfer of the $512 \times 480 \times 8$ bits/pixel images is limited to 2 Hz.

A Polhemus system with one source and two receivers is used for tracking [Polhemus 1980]. One receiver tracks the HMD. The other tracks the ultrasound transducer. The Polhemus system is mounted in non ferrous materials away from magnetic interference sources such as the ultrasound transducer, HMD, and other lab equipment. A calibration procedure is used to relate both the ultrasound transducer to its Polhemus receiver and the HMD TV camera to its Polhemus receiver mounted on the HMD. This calibration procedure is described in Section 4.4.

4.2 Image Generation

Images are generated by the Pixel-Planes 5 system based on geometry information from the tracking system. Pixel-Planes 5 runs a custom PHIGS implementation which incorporates a facility to update display structures asynchronously from the display process. This separates the interactive virtual environment update rate from the 2D ultrasound image data acquisition rate. Images in the virtual

environment are registered to the real world within the update-rate limit of the tracking and display system and not within the acquisition-rate limit of the image-acquisition system.

Pixels from the 2D ultrasound images are rendered as small, unshaded sphere primitives in the virtual environment. The 2D ultrasound images appear as space-filling slices registered in their correct 3D position. The ultrasound images are distributed among the GPs where they are clipped to remove unnecessary margins and transformed into sphere primitives, which are then sent to the Renderer boards for direct rasterization. Pixel-Planes 5 renders spheres very rapidly, even faster than it renders triangles, over 2 million per second [Fuchs 1985; 1989]. Final images are assembled in double buffered NTSC frame buffers for display on the HMD. To reduce the number of sphere primitives displayed, the ultrasound images are filtered and subsampled at every 4th pixel. Due to the low resolution of the HMD and inherent bandwidth limitation of the ultrasound scanner, this subsampling does not result in a substantial loss of image quality. An option to threshold lower intensity pixels in 2D ultrasound images prior to 3D rendering can suppress lower intensity pixels from being displayed.

4.3 Video See-Through HMD

A video see-through HMD system combines real-world images captured by head-mounted TV cameras with synthetic images generated to correspond with the real-world images. The important issues are tracking the real-world cameras accurately and generating the correct synthetic images to model the views of the cameras. Correct stereo modeling adds concerns about matching a pair of cameras to each other as well as tracking and modeling them. [Robinett 1991] discusses stereo HMD in detail and includes an analysis of the VPL EyePhone.

A Panasonic GP-KS102 camera provides monocular see-through capability for the left eye in our current system. Images from this camera are mixed with synthetic images from the Pixel-Planes 5 system using the luminance (brightness) keying feature on a Grass Valley Group Model 100 video mixer. With luminance keying, the pixels in the output image are selected from either the real-world image or the synthetic image, depending on the luminance of pixels in the synthetic image. The combined image for the left eye and a synthetic image only for the right eye are displayed on a VPL EyePhone.

4.4 Calibration

Two transformations, a "transducer transformation" and a "camera transformation," are needed to calibrate our test system. The transducer transformation relates the position and orientation of the Polhemus tracker attached to the ultrasound transducer to the position and scale of 2D ultrasound image pixels in 3D space. The camera transformation relates the position and orientation of the head-mounted Polhemus tracker to the HMD TV camera position, orientation, and field of view.

Both transformations are calculated by first locating a calibration jig in both the lab (real) and tracker (virtual) 3D coordinate systems. This is accomplished by performing rigid body rotations with the transducer tracker about axes which are to be fixed in both the real and virtual coordinate systems. Two samples from the tracker, each consisting of both a position and an orientation, are sufficient to fix each calibration axis. The transducer transformation is computed by taking an ultrasound image of a target of known geometry placed at a known position on the calibration jig. By finding the pixel coordinates of point targets in the ultrasound image, the world coordinates of pixels in the ultrasound image can be found. From this relationship and the location of the Polhemus tracker attached to the ultrasound transducer at the time the target was imaged, the transducer transformation is derived. Similarly, the camera transformation is found by placing the HMD TV camera at known positions and orientations relative to the calibration jig. The field of view of the TV camera is known from camera specifications. Manual adjustments are used to improve the camera transformation.

5. Experimental Results

In January 1992 we conducted an experiment with a live human subject using the method described above. We scanned the abdomen of a volunteer who was 38 weeks pregnant. An ultrasound technician from the Department of Obstetrics & Gynecology of the UNC Hospitals performed the ultrasound scanning.

Figure 4 is a scene from the experiment. A person looks on with modified VPL EyePhone with the miniature video camera mounted on top and in front. Figure 5 shows the left eye view from the HMD, a composition of synthetic and real images. Figure 6 is another view from the left eye of the HMD wearer which shows several 2D ultrasound images in place within the subject's abdomen.

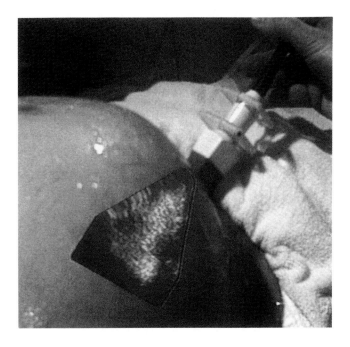

Figure 5. A video image presented to the left eye of the HMD showing a view of the subject's abdomen with a 2D ultrasound image superimposed and registered. Note the ultrasound transducer registered with the image acquired by it. The 2D image is from the antero-inferior view.

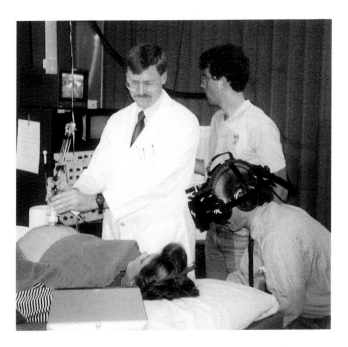

Figure 4. An ultrasound technician scans a subject while another person looks on with the video see-through head-mounted display (HMD). Note the miniature video camera attached to the front of the VPL EyePhone HMD.

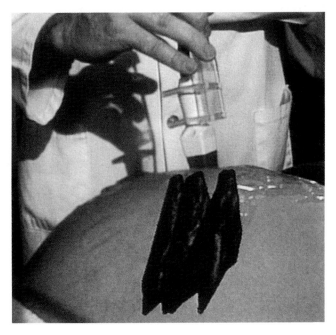

Figure 6. Another video image presented to the HMD showing several 2D image slices in 3D space within the patient's abdomen. The image slices are from the anterior view.

6. Conclusions and Future Directions

The results presented so far are the initial steps in the first application of what we hope will be a flourishing area of computer graphics and visualization.

6.1 Remaining Technical Problems

1) Conflicting visual cues: Our experiment (Figures 5 and 6) showed that simply overlaying synthetic images on real ones is not sufficient. To the user, the ultrasound images did not appear to be *inside* the subject, so much as pasted on *top* of her. To overcome this problem, we now provide additional cues to the user by making a virtual hole in the subject (Figure 7) by digitizing points on the abdomenal surface and constructing a shaded polygonal pit. The pit provides occlusion cues by obscuring the abdomenal surface along the inside walls of the pit. Shading the pit provides an additional cue. Unfortunately, this does not completely solve the problem; the pit hides *everything* in the real image that is in the same location (in 2D) as the pit, including real objects that are closer in 3D than the pit. (Note in Figure 7, the edge of the transducer is hidden behind the pit representation even though it should appear in front of it.)

To solve this problem, the systems needs to know depth information for both the real and synthetic objects visible from the HMD user's viewpoint. This would make it possible to present correct occlusion cues by combining the live and synthetic images with a Z-buffer like algorithm. An ideal implementation of this would require real-time range finding from the viewpoint of the HMD user - a significant technical challenge. Graphics architectures that provide real-time depth-based image composition are already under development [Molnar 1992].

Another remaining problem is the visualization of internal 3D structure in data captured by the ultrasound scanner. Neither our incremental volume rendering algorithm (Section 3) nor multiple explicit image slices in 3-space (Figure 6) solve this problem well. A combination of multiple visualization methods will probably be necessary in the future. We suspect that this problem is difficult because the human visual system is not accustomed to seeing structure within opaque objects, and so our development cannot be guided by the "gold standard" of reality that has been used so effectively in guiding other 3D rendering investigations.

2) System lag: Lag in image generation and tracking is noticeable in all head-mounted displays; but it is dramatically accentuated with see-through HMD. The "live video" of the observer's surroundings moves appropriately during any head movement but the synthetic image overlay lags behind. This is currently one of our system's major problems which prevents it from giving the user a convincing experience of seeing synthetic objects or images hanging in 3-space. A possible solution may be to delay the live video images so that their delay matches that of the synthetic images. This will align the real and synthetic images, but won't eliminate the lag itself. We are also considering predictive tracking as a way to reduce the effect of the lag [Liang 1991]. Developers of some multi-million dollar flight simulators have studied predictive trackingfor many years, but unfortunately for us, they have not, to our knowledge, published details of their methods and their methods' effectiveness. For the immediate future, we are planning to move to our locally-developed "ceiling tracker" [Ward 1992] and use predictive tracking.

3) Tracking system range and stability: Even though we are using the most popular and probably most effective commercially available tracking system from Polhemus, we are constantly plagued by limitations in tracking volume and tracking stability [Liang 1991]. The observer often steps inadvertently out of tracker range, and even while keeping very still the observer must cope with objects in the synthetic image "swimming" in place. We are eagerly awaiting the next generation of tracking systems from Polhemus and other manufacturers that are said to overcomemost of these problems. Even more capable tracking systems will be needed in order to satisfy the many applications in which the observer must move about in the real world instead of a laboratory, operating room or other controlled environment. Many schemes have been casually proposed over the years, but we know of no device that has been built and demonstrated. Even the room-size tracker we built and demonstrated for a week at SIGGRAPH'91 still needs special ceiling panels with infrared LEDs [Ward 1992].

4) Head-mounted display system resolution: For many of the applications envisioned, the image quality of current head-mounted video displays is totally inadequate. In a see-through application, a user is even more sensitive to the limitations of his head-mounted display than in a conventional non-see-through application because he is painfully aware of the visual details he's missing.

5) More powerful display engines: Even with all the above problems solved, the synthetic images we would like to see, for example, real-time volume visualization of real-time volume data, would still take too long to be created. Much more powerful image

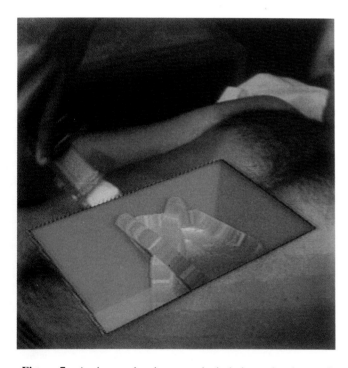

Figure 7. An image showing a synthetic hole rendered around ultrasound images in an attempt to avoid conflicting visual cues. Note the depth cues provided by occlusion of the image slices by the pit walls and shading of the pit. Also note the incorrect obscuration of the ultrasound transducer by the pit wall. (RT3200 Advantage II ultrasound scanner courtesy of General Electric Medical Systems.)

generation systems are needed if we are to be able to visualize usefully detailed 3D imagery.

6.2 Other Applications

1) Vision in surgery: In neurosurgery, ultrasound is already used to image nearby arteries that should be avoided by an impending surgical incision.

2) Burning buildings: With close-range, millimeter wavelength radar, rescuers may be able to "see through" the smoke in the interior of burning buildings.

3) Building geometry: Geometry or other structural data could be added to a "live" scene. In the above "burning building" scenario, parts of a building plan could be superimposed onto the visual scene, such as the location of stairways, hallways, or the best exits out of the building.

4) Service information: Information could be displayed to a service technician working on complicated machinery such as a jet engine. Even simpler head-mounted displays, ones without head tracking, already provide information to users on site and avoid using a large cumbersome video screens. Adding head tracking would allow 3D superimposition to show, for instance, the location of special parts within an engine, or the easiest path for removal or insertion of a subassembly.

5) Architecture on site: Portable systems could allow builders and architects to preview buildings on site before construction or visualize additions to existing architecture.

With the work presented here and the identification of problems and possibilities for further research, we hope to encourage applications not only of "virtual environments" (imaginary worlds), but also applications that involve an "enhancement of vision" in our real world.

Acknowledgments

We would like to thank the following people: David Chen and Andrew Brandt for experimental assistance; General Electric Medical Systems (and especially R. Scott Ray) for the loan of an ultrasound scanner; Stefan Gottschalk for much assistance with video acquisition, editing, and printing; Professor Olaf von Ramm (Duke University) for donation of the IREX ultrasound scanner; ultrasound technician George Blanchard, RDMS, for scanning the subject; David Harrison and John Hughes for video and laboratory setup; Andrei State for experimental assistance; John Thomas for fabrication of a custom camera mount; Terry Yoo for video tape editing; Vern Katz, MD, for assistance with multiple ultrasound machines and scanning experiments; Nancy Chescheir, MD, for loan of an ultrasound machine and arrangements with the ultrasound technician; Warren Newton, MD, and Melanie Mintzer, MD, for finding our subject; Warren Robinett and Rich Holloway, for consultation with HMD optics and software; Professor Stephen Pizer and Charlie Kurak for consultation on the difficulty of enhancing ultrasound images; David Adam (Duke University) for instruction in the use of the IREX scanner; and our subject and her husband for their time and patience.

This research is partially supported by DARPA ISTO contract DAEA 18-90-C-0044, NSF ERC grant CDR-86-22201, DARPA ISTO contract 7510, NSF grant MIP-9000894, NSF cooperative agreement ASC-8920219, and NIH MIP grant PO 1 CA 47982, and by Digital Equipment Corporation.

References

[Brinkley 1978] Brinkley, J. F., Moritz, W.E., and Baker, D.W. "Ultrasonic Three-Dimensional Imaging and Volume From a Series of Arbitrary Sector Scans." *Ultrasound in Med. & Biol.*, **4**, pp317-327.

[Collet Billon 1990] Collet Billon, A., *Philips Paris Research Lab.* Personal Communication.

[Fornage 1990] Fornage, B. D., Sneige, N., Faroux, M.J., and Andry, E. "Sonographic appearance and ultrasound guided fine-needle aspiration biopsy of brest carcinomas smaller than 1 cm^3." *Journal of Ultrasound in Medicine*, **9**, pp559-568.

[Fuchs 1985] Fuchs, H., GoldFeather, J., Hultiquist, J.P., Spach, S., Austin, J., Brooks, Jr., F.P., Eyles, J., and Poulton, J. "Fast Spheres, Textures, Transparencies, and Image Enhancements in Pixel Planes." *Computer Graphics (Proceedings of SIGGRAPH'85)*, **19**(3), pp111-120.

[Fuchs 1989] Fuchs, H., Poulton, J., Eyles, J., Greer, T., Goldfeather, J., Ellsworth, D., Molnar, S., and Israel, L. "Pixel Planes 5: A Heterogeneous Multiprocessor Graphics System Using Processor-Enhanced Memories." *Computer Graphics (Proceedings of SIGGRAPH'89)*, **23**(3), pp79-88.

[Galyean 1991] Galyean, T. A., and Hughes, J.F. "Sculpting: An Interactive Volumetric Modeling Technique." *Computer Graphics (Proceedings of SIGGRAPH'89)*, **25**(4), pp267-274.

[Geiser 1982a] Geiser, E. A., Ariet, M., Conetta, D.A., Lupkiewicz, S.M., Christie, L.G., and Conti, C.R. "Dynamic three-dimensional echocardiographic reconstruction of the intact human left ventricle: Technique and initial observations in patients." *American Heart Journal*, **103**(6), pp1056-1065.

[Geiser 1982b] Geiser, E. A., Christie, L.G., Conetta, D.A., Conti, C.R., and Gossman, G.S. "Mechanical Arm for Spatial Registration of Two-Dimensional Echographic Sections." *Cathet. Cariovasc. Diagn.*, **8**, pp89-101.

[Ghosh 1982] Ghosh, A., Nanda, C.N., and Maurer, G. "Three-Dimensional Reconstruction of Echo-Cardiographics Images Using The Rotation Method." *Ultrasound in Med. & Biol.*, **8**(6), pp655-661.

[Haddad 1991] Haddad, R. A., and Parsons, T.W. *Digital Signal Processing, Theory, Applications, and Hardware.* New York, Computer Science Press.

[Harris 1990] Harris, R. A., Follett, D.H., Halliwell, M, and Wells, P.N.T. "Ultimate limits in ultrasonic imaging resolution." *Ultrasound in Medicine and Biology*, **17**(6), pp547-558.

[Hildreth 1983] Hildreth, E. C. "The Detection of Intensity Changes by Computer and Biological Vision Systems." *Computer Vision, Graphics, and Image Processing*, **22**, pp1-27.

[Hottier 1989] Hottier, F., *Philips Paris Research Lab.* Personal Communication.

[Hottier 1990] Hottier, F., Collet Billon, A. *3D Echography: Status and Perspective.* 3D Imaging in Medicine. Springer-Verlag. pp21-41.

[Itoh 1979] Itoh, M., and Yokoi, H. "A computer-aided three-dimensional display system for ultrasonic diagnosis of a breast tumor." *Ultrasonics*, , pp261-268.

[King 1990] King, D. L., King Jr., D.L., and Shao, M.Y. "Three-Dimensional Spatial Registration and Interactive Display of

Position and Orientation of Real-Time Ultrasound Images." *Journal of Ultrasound Med*, **9**, pp525-532.

[Lalouche 1989] Lalouche, R. C., Bickmore, D., Tessler, F., Mankovich, H.K., and Kangaraloo, H. "Three-dimensional reconstruction of ultrasound images." *SPIE'89, Medical Imaging*, pp59-66.

[Leipnik 1960] Leipnik, R. "The extended entropy uncertainty principle." *Info. Control*, **3**, pp18-25.

[Levoy 1988] Levoy, M. "Display of Surface from Volume Data." *IEEE CG&A*, **8**(5), pp29-37.

[Levoy 1990] Levoy, M. "A Hybrid Ray Tracer for Rendering Polygon and Volume Data." *IEEE CG&A*, **10**(2), pp33-40.

[Liang 1991] Liang, J., Shaw, C., and Green, M. "On Temporal-Spatial Realism in the Virtual Reality Environment." *User Interface Software and Technology, 1991*, Hilton Head, SC., U.S.A., pp19-25.

[Lin 1991] Lin, W., Pizer, S.M., and Johnson, V.E. "Surface Estimation in Ultrasound Images." *Information Processing in Medical Imaging 1991*, Wye, U.K., Springer-Verlag, Heidelberg, pp285-299.

[Matsumoto 1981] Matsumoto, M., Inoue, M., Tamura, S., Tanaka, K., and Abe, H. "Three-Dimensional Echocardiography for Spatial Visualization and Volume Calculation of Cardiac Structures." *J. Clin. Ultrasound*, **9**, pp157-165.

[McCann 1988] McCann, H. A., Sharp, J.S., Kinter, T.M., McEwan, C.N., Barillot, C., and Greenleaf, J.F. "Multidimensional Ultrasonic Imaging for Cardiology." *Proc.IEEE*, **76**(9), pp1063-1073.

[Mills 1990] Mills, P. H., and Fuchs, H. "3D Ultrasound Display Using Optical Tracking." *First Conference on Visualization for Biomedical Computing*, Atlanta, GA, IEEE, pp490-497.

[Miyazawa 1991] Miyazawa, T. "A high-speed integrated rendering for interpreting multiple variable 3D data." *SPIE*, **1459**(5),

[Molnar 1992] Molnar, S., Eyles, J., and Poulton, J. "PixelFlow: High-Speed Rendering Using Image Composition." *Computer Graphics (Proceedings of SIGGRAPH'92)*, ((In this issue)),

[Moritz 1983] Moritz, W. E., Pearlman, A.S., McCabe, D.H., Medema, D.K., Ainsworth, M.E., and Boles, M.S. "An Ultrasonic Techinque for Imaging the Ventricle in Three Dimensions and Calculating Its Volume." *IEEE Trans. Biom. Eng.*, **BME-30**(8), pp482-492.

[Nakamura 1984] Nakamura, S. "Three-Dimensional Digital Display of Ultrasonograms." *IEEE CG&A*, **4**(5), pp36-45.

[Ohbuchi 1990] Ohbuchi, R., and Fuchs, H. "Incremental 3D Ultrasound Imaging from a 2D Scanner." *First Conference on Visualization in Biomedical Computing*, Atlanta, GA, IEEE, pp360-367.

[Ohbuchi 1991] Ohbuchi, R., and Fuchs, H. "Incremental Volume Rendering Algorithm for Interactive 3D Ultrasound Imaging." *Information Processing in Medical Imaging 1991 (Lecture Notes in Computer Science, Springer-Verlag)*, Wye, UK, Springer-Verlag, pp486-500.

[Pini 1990] Pini, R., Monnini, E., Masotti, L., Novins, K. L., Greenberg, D. P., Greppi, B., Cerofolini, M., and Devereux, R. B. "Echocardiographic Three-Dimensional Visualization of the Heart." *3D Imaging in Medicine*, Travemünde, Germany, **F 60**, Springer-Verlag, pp263-274.

[Polhemus 1980] Polhemus. *3Space Isotrak User's Manual*.

[Raichelen 1986] Raichelen, J. S., Trivedi, S.S., Herman, G.T., Sutton, M.G., and Reichek, N. "Dynamic Three Dimensional Reconstruction of the Left Ventricle From Two-Dimensional Echocardiograms." *Journal. Amer. Coll. of Cardiology*, **8**(2), pp364-370.

[Robinett 1991] Robinett, W., and Rolland, J.P. "A Computational Model for the Stereoscopic Optics of a Head-Mounted Display." *Presence*, **1**(1), pp45-62.

[Sabella 1988] Sabella, P. "A Rendering Algorithm for Visualizing 3D Scalar Fields." *Computer Graphics (Proceedings of SIGGRAPH'88)*, **22**(4), pp51-58.

[Shattuck 1984] Shattuck, D. P., Weishenker, M.D., Smith, S.W., and von Ramm, O.T. "Explososcan: A Parallel Processing Technique for High Speed Ultrasound Imaging with Linear Phased Arrays." *JASA*, **75**(4), pp1273-1282.

[Smith 1991] Smith, S. W., Pavy, Jr., S.G., and von Ramm, O.T. "High-Speed Ultrasound Volumetric Imaging System - Part I: Transducer Design and Beam Steering." *IEEE Transaction on Ultrasonics, Ferroelectrics, and Frequency Control*, **38**(2), pp100-108.

[Stickels 1984] Stickels, K. R., and Wann, L.S. "An Analysis of Three-Dimensional Reconstructive Echocardiography." *Ultrasound in Med. & Biol.*, **10**(5), pp575-580.

[Thijssen 1990] Thijssen, J. M., and Oosterveld, B.J. "Texture in Tissue Echograms, Speckle or Information ?" *Journal of Ultrasound in Medicine*, **9**, pp215-229.

[Tomographic Technologies 1991] Tomographic Technologies, G. *Echo-CT*.

[Upson 1988] Upson, C., and Keeler, M. "VBUFFER: Visible Volume Rendering." *ACM Computer Graphics (Proceedings of SIGGRAPH'88)*, **22**(4), pp59-64.

[von Ramm 1991] von Ramm, O. T., Smith, S.W., and Pavy, Jr., H.G. "High-Speed Ultrasound Volumetric Imaging System - Part II: Parallel Processing and Image Display." *IEEE Transaction on Ultrasonics, Ferroelectrics, and Frequency Control*, **38**(2), pp109-115.

[Ward 1992] Ward, M., Azuma, R., Bennett, R., Gottschalk, S., and Fuchs, H. "A Demonstrated Optical Tracker with Scalable Work Area for Head-Mounted Display Systems." *1992 Symposium on Interactive 3D Graphics*, Cambridge, MA., ACM, pp43-52.

[Wells 1977] Wells, P. N. T. *Biomedical ultrasonics*. London, Academic Press.

Sound Rendering

Tapio Takala* and James Hahn†

*Helsinki University of Technology
02150 Espoo, Finland

†The George Washington University
Washington, DC 20052

Abstract

We present a general methodology to produce synchronized soundtracks for animations. A sound world is modeled by associating a characteristic sound for each object in a scene. These sounds can be generated from a behavioral or physically-based simulation. Collision sounds can be computed from vibrational response of elastic bodies to the collision impulse. Alternatively, stereotypic recorded sound effects can be associated with each interaction of objects. Sounds may also be generated procedurally. The sound world is described with a sound event file, and is rendered in two passes. First the propagation paths from 3D objects to each microphone are analyzed and used to calculate sound transformations according to the acoustic environment. These effects are convolutions, encoded into two essential parameters, delay and attenuation of each sound. Time-dependency of these two parameters is represented with keyframes, thus being completely independent of the original 3D animation script. In the second pass the sounds associated with objects are instantiated, modulated by interpolated key parameters, and summed up to the final soundtrack. The advantage of a modular architecture is that the same methods can be used for all types of animations, keyframed, physically-based and behavioral. We also discuss the differences of sound and light, and the remarkable similarities in their rendering processes.

CR Categories and Subject Descriptors: I.3.7 [**Computer Graphics**]: Animation.

Additional keywords: audio, multimedia, soundtrack, physically-based modeling, virtual reality.

1 Introduction

In traditional hand-drawn animation, sound effects and their synchronization to the motion are of utmost importance. Often the whole story is first composed as a musical bar sheet, on which the movements are designed based on key events [17]. Sounds are usually dubbed onto the action after the motions are generated but this is a tedious manual process and requires expertise to synchronize correctly. In computer animation, similar techniques have been used in key-framing and rotoscoping. However, most of the computer animations produced have emphasized the motion itself and have added sound during post-production. The major reason is that there does not yet exist a general framework for sound synchronization. This is especially true in behavioral or physically-based motion control where the lack of absolute control have made the motion-to-sound synchronization difficult. A notable exception from the mainstream is the film "More Bells and Whistles" [9]. There, both music and animation were designed as a single score, which served as a synchronizing controller for both MIDI-driven music synthesizers and animated synthetic actors.

Video games and multimedia installations [22] have also relied on synchronized sound. Sound as another dimension of interaction has been utilized in user interfaces to symbolize objects and to draw attention to alerts [6, 2]. In scientific visualization, sound can be used to characterize objects' attributes and to emphasize timing of events [10]. Simulations of sound wave propagation have been done to analyze room acoustics or dummy head models [21], and special hardware built to perform these effects in real time [5], but to our knowledge none of these has been combined with animated graphics except for visualizing the acoustical parameters [15].

1.1 The Nature of Sound

As waves, both light and sound behave similarly in many ways. Both propagate as wavefronts, spreading in all directions according to the Huygens' principle. They reflect and refract whenever there are discontinuities in the medium, and obstacle edges cause diffraction. However, their different propagation speeds and wavelengths cause essential practical differences. Light travels instantaneously without noticeable delay, and its wave nature only appears when it interacts with structures of microscopic size. On the other hand, the speed of sound easily causes delays perceived as echo or reverberation. There is considerable diffraction, too, because the wavelength is of human proportions – the sound propagates around the edges of objects. For these reasons, sound propagation cannot be accurately traced using simple ray optics.

The human sensory organs for light and sound are sensitive to different characteristics. The eye has good spatial resolution, whereas the ear integrates signals from all directions. Light is sensed as a color spectrum integrated over a period of time, and not as individual waveforms. Sound instead is perceived in time rather than as a stationary spectrum in frequency domain.

1.2 Sound Signals and Convolutions

Sound is a one-dimensional signal that can be represented as an intensity regularly sampled in time. Out of possible representations this appears to be the most general and suitable for our purposes. The concepts of pitch and note length are akin to traditional music but are unable to describe speech or noise. A spectral distribution (Fourier transform) with phase and amplitude of each component is theoretically complete, but is intuitively difficult for other than stationary waveforms, and is not at all suitable for time-dependent effects like echo. Similar arguments apply to other integral representations, like Laplace transform for example.

As an object generates sound in a three-dimensional environment, it acts like a light source in image rendering. Its signal is propagated in all directions, reflected and refracted by other objects and participating media, and finally caught by a receiver. The received signal is an integral of signals via multiple simultaneous paths from the emitter to the receiver. To compute this integral, each possible path can be independently traced through the environment, its effects on the sound signal calculated, and the results composed as a convolution of the original sound:

$$received(t) = \int_0^\infty w(t,\tau) \cdot emitted(t - \tau)\, d\tau$$

where $w(t,\tau)$ is the amount of signal received through all paths with delay τ.

The convolution weighting function $w(t,\tau)$ corresponds to the paths of different lengths causing different delays and attenuations for the same signal. Generally it is time-dependent, continuous and semi-infinite. For computational purposes it has to be discretized into a finite number of samples. The script format we are going to present is a possible way to do this, emphasizing the role of moving objects as the cause of time-dependencies in convolution.

1.3 Outline of the Paper

In this paper we present a structured methodology for generation, representation, and synchronization of sounds in computer animation. In section 2, we will outline the overall system structure as a pipeline with sound signals flowing through it. This is followed by a detailed description of each module of the system. First, (section 3) we describe how natural sounds may be generated by physical phenomena and how characteristic sounds are attached to geometric objects in three-dimensional space (section 4). Next, we show how the modulation of signals due to their propagation in an environment can be represented as convolutions (section 5). The final process is the rendering of key-framed sounds by resampling the original signals (section 6). Examples of various effects are also presented.

2   Sound Rendering Pipeline

The basic idea in our approach is that sounds are treated as one-dimensional data objects associated with geometric objects of a three-dimensional world. Each sound is a time-dependent signal. Much like a graphical texture map, it is located on a geometric object, but extends in time instead of spatial dimensions. It may be bounded or semi-infinite. In the latter case it can be either a repeated waveform or a fractal-like continuously changing noise pattern.

We call *sound rendering* the process of forming the composite soundtrack from component sound objects. This is due to its methodological similarity to image rendering and texture mapping and its close connections to the same geometric data. To keep the process manageable, we have divided it into a pipeline of processes, as shown by the overall system architecture in figure 1. First process (I) is the generation of the prototype sounds that are characteristic of each object and its interaction with others. These can be either based on modal analysis of elastic body vibrations, or they can be user-defined (recorded or synthesized). In the next process (II), the prototype sounds are instantiated and attached to moving three-dimensional objects, based on the same physical or behavioral simulation that controls motion. Following that, (III) the modulatory effects of the three-dimensional environment are computed as transformations from sounds on the objects to sounds at a microphone. These time-dependent sound transformations are represented independently of the original object sounds, and are finally (IV) applied to the sounds in the last process. Thus just a reference of prototype sound goes through processes II and III, and the samples are actually used only in process IV.

The sounds produced by objects may be endogenous like barking, yelling or talking. Such prototypes can be digitally recorded, analogous to using digitized photographic images as textures. Alternatively they may be synthesized by behavioral models, like the buzz of a bee determined by the way it flies. Other, more physically-based sounds emanate from vibrations of bodies, caused by interactive

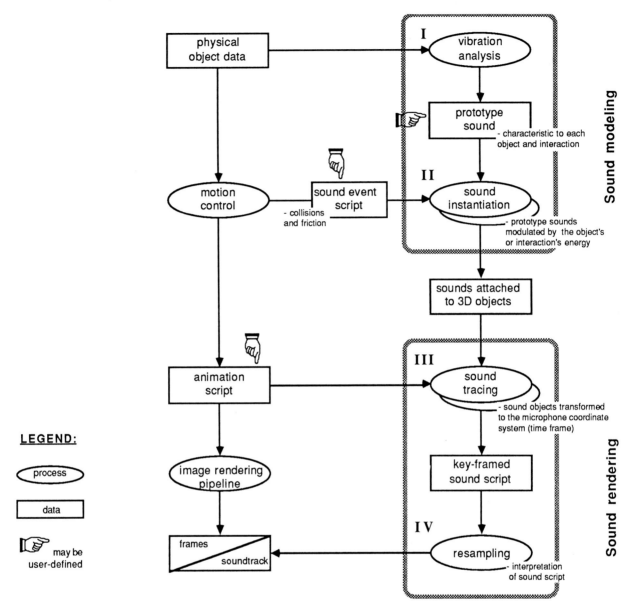

Figure 1: Parallel pipelines for image and sound rendering.

forces between objects and their environment. Examples of these are collisions, friction, and turbulent air flow around an object. Spectral composition may be used for these sounds, as has been used for textures [12].

In our system, we separate a sound and its association to objects. The characteristic potential sound is represented as a sampled signal or procedure, whereas its instantiation is described in a *sound script*. The script describes when and how a characteristic sound is actually generated, determined by certain events in the animation, like physically calculated collisions. Attachment of prototype sounds to objects located in space-time is comparable to the geometric mapping of textures to object's surfaces.

For an animation, the sounds are recorded by virtual microphones usually attached to a virtual camera. A sound may undergo various modulations during its course from a geometric object to the microphone, through the simulated environment. It is attenuated due to the dispersion of energy in space, and is delayed by the traveling time along a sound path. The emission of sound from an object may vary by direction, and it may be reflected, refracted or obscured by other objects, much as light waves are. The sound's spectrum (sound color or timbre) may be modified in these interactions, as well as due to the participating medium. Finally, the intensity of a sound heard by a microphone may vary due to its directional sensitivity. These processes correspond to the mapping of textures from geometric objects to the image plane. This is why we use the terms *object space* and *image space* for the time-frames of sounds as well as for the corresponding geometric coordinate systems.

Since sound signals are additive, all the effects described above are computed in a resampling process independently for each emitted sound, and summed up (mixed) to make a complete soundtrack. In stereo, this will be done separately for each channel.

We have implemented an experimental sound renderer as a collection of software modules that can be pipelined together. Our implementation is written in C language and currently runs on a Macintosh IIci. For this equipment the sound intensities are represented with only 8-bit sample resolution, causing noticeable digitization noise. For higher quality sounds, we have used AIFF files with 16-bit resolution, from which the sounds are reproduced with Silicon Graphics Indigo. As an alternative, we have also considered a MIDI-based interface to a high-quality music synthesizer, with object sounds selected from its library and modulated in real time. However, it has appeared rather difficult to find suitable MIDI-driven components to produce all the effects needed.

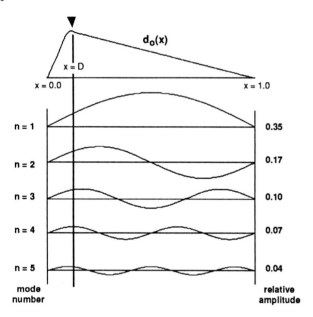

Figure 2: Vibration modes of a guitar string.

3 Sound Synthesis

Sound can be synthesized from physical principles in the same way as physically-based motion control generates motion [1, 16]. However, this is a much more difficult problem, because many material factors involved are poorly known. In this sense it is analogous to determining color of a material based on its physical properties [8]. Some heuristics can be used to simplify the process for certain classes of sounds.

3.1 Vibration of Bodies

Many sounds are generated when objects vibrate after being struck. The process is difficult to model for arbitrary objects without using complex finite-element models [14]. One way to attack this problem is to calculate the natural vibration modes of a body, and to approximate a complex vibration as a weighted sum of them [11]. Though not strictly correct for transient vibrations, this approach can be developed to give subjectively quite acceptable results. Crucial in it is the ability to calculate the appropriate weight for each mode, based on the body's deformation at a collision. This is generally a complex problem. In the following we demonstrate it with a simple example.

In thin bars or strings of musical instruments, the natural harmonics are standing waves with displacements along the string given as $d_n(x) = w_n \sin(n\pi x)$. The vibration modes are orthogonal, so assuming the initial rest position of the string as $d_0(x)$, the weighting factor of each mode is the integral

$$w_n = \int_0^1 d_0(x) \cdot d_n(x) \, dx$$

For example, we assumed the initial displacement to be triangular, as when stretching a guitar string with a pick (figure 2). Then

$$d_0(x) = \frac{x}{D} \text{ for } x \le D, \quad d_0(x) = \frac{1-x}{1-D} \text{ for } x \ge D$$

and the weights will be

$$w_n(D) = \left(\frac{1}{D} + \frac{1}{1-D}\right)\left(\frac{1}{n\pi}\right)^2 \sin(n\pi D) \ .$$

The sum of the weighted components is multiplied by an exponential decay function, with damping factor proportional to the frequency. This gives a waveform corresponding to the displacement of string at the point where it was struck, which can be used as a prototype collision sound for the string. Each stroke of the string will then generate an instance of that sound, with amplitude proportional to the magnitude of the collision impulse.

3.2 Friction and Turbulence Noise

Sounds generated by two objects rubbing against each other is a poorly understood process caused by microscopic surface features of the materials of the two objects. We have chosen to represent the process as a combination of two factors. First, the surface features cause both of the objects to vibrate in the same way as a phonograph needle vibrates when dragged in the groove of a record disk. The waveform of the sound generated is similar to the shape of surface imperfections of the objects. The so-called 1/f-noise [19, 20] could be used to model this phenomenon for rough surfaces. Another type of frictional noise we have simulated is generated by an object which alternates between sliding and sticking on a surface. This kind of interaction happens, for example, between a violin string and the bow. The resulting sound signal is approximated as a sawtooth waveform. Variation in the coefficients of friction can be modeled by adding some randomness to the wavelength, introducing noise to the sound.

Objects that disturb the air by causing turbulence also generate sounds. Modeling the frequency components of this phenomenon is difficult and outside the scope of this paper. We simply represent this as white noise modulated by the velocity of the object through the air and by the amount of air that it disturbs (a purely geometric factor with experimental values).

3.3 Other Procedural Sounds

Other subjectively interesting sounds can be generated with procedures that are not physically-based but model the behavior of an object. For example, we have synthesized the sound of an ambulance siren as a single tone frequency-modulated by a slow sine wave (figures 4 and 7).

The insect-like sound for behaviorally animated bees (figure 9), was generated as a constant wave-form with a noisy but narrowly tuned wave-length. Each bee of a swarm has a distinct base frequency that slowly drifts around a preselected mean frequency, either randomly or according to the bee's velocity.

4   Attaching Sounds to Objects

In hand-drawn animation, all important events, like the bounce of a hit in figure 3, are located at frame times. These key frames can be used to synchronize sound effects. For example, we can mark the starting times of each recorded sound effect and use a sequencer and mixer to put them all together.

In addition to the starting time, we can also specify the sound's amplitude any time along its duration. Between these key values the amplitude can be interpolated (lower part of figure 3).

What we have described are *sound threads*. These are sequences of key values extending over the sound's lifetime for each sound event. They can be put in an interface file as a sound script, described in detail in section 6.

The key events of a script can be either defined by the animator, like in the example above, or automatically computed by a behavioral or physically-based motion control. For example, we have used the impulse after a collision calculated by a physically-based motion control for rigid bodies [7] to define the script (figure 8 shows a frame from the animation). For each object involved in a collision, a sound thread is started at the time of collision with an amplitude proportional to the impulse. With this method we can automatically produce accurately synchronized sound effects for complex situations that would be very difficult to achieve by other means.

Some sounds, like the turbulent wind noise, have infinite extent. They are represented in the script as threads extending throughout the duration of an animation scene.

5   Sound Propagation

In the following, we overview various effects of the acoustical environment and demonstrate how they can be incorporated into the system. The purpose is not to make detailed modeling of acoustics, but to show that each effect can be encoded as a transformation in the sound rendering script.

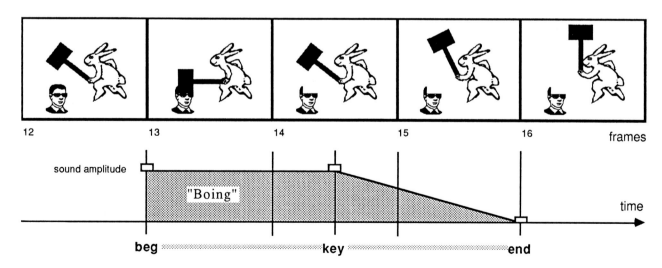

Figure 3: Keyframed sound thread for a hand-drawn animation.

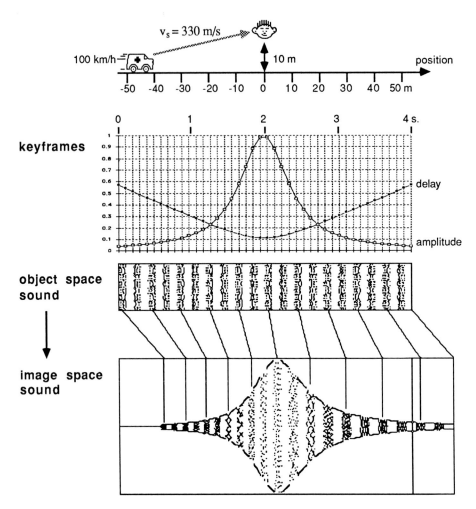

Figure 4: Key-framed values of amplitude and delay for a moving sound source,
and the corresponding mapping of sound signal from object to image space.

5.1 Effects of Distance and Direction

The simplest acoustic effect is due to the dispersion of sound waves into the environment. Assuming no other attenuation, the intensity decays proportionally to the square of the distance travelled, and the signal is delayed by a time proportional to the same distance. Denoting sound velocity by v_s, we have for amplitude and delay

$$A(d) = A_0 \cdot \left(\frac{d_0}{d}\right)^2 , \qquad \tau(d) = \frac{d}{v_s} ,$$

where d is the distance traveled, and A_0 is the sound intensity at a certain reference distance d_0. The effect of delay should be taken into account if the scene dimensions are of macroscopic magnitude, comparable to the sound speed. A delay of less than 50 ms is already clearly noticeable, corresponding to a distance of 15 m in atmosphere with a sound velocity of approximately 330 m/s.

Figure 4 illustrates sound animation of an ambulance passing a standing listener. The image space sound envelope shows the amplitude variation due to the 1:5 ratio in minimum and maximum distance between source and receiver of sound. Driving speed of 100 km/h gives a noticeable Doppler effect, with a deviation in pitch roughly corresponding to two halftones up and down from the car's original sound. When the car moves from the left field of view to the right, it gives a stereophonic illusion of movement.

The emission of sound may be directional. However, usually some sound is emitted in all directions. There seldom are as abrupt edges in its directional distribution as there are in directed light sources with flaps. Thus a spherical harmonics approximation [13] is appropriate.

Similarly, the microphone's directional sensitivity can be described with a spherical harmonic function. A representation sufficient in practice is given by the formula

$$S(\mu) = C + (1 + \cos \mu)^k$$

where μ is the angle between the microphone's principal axis and the incoming sound wave. Value k=0 defines an omnidirectional shape, and k=1 produces the typical cardioid sensitivity shape (figure 5). Lateral stereophonic hearing, due to differences in directional sensitivity of left and right ears, can be easily simulated with two microphones attached to opposite directions on a camera. With the sensitivity parameter k=1, the sum of left and right channels will be omnidirectional. Both sensitivities can be multiplied by a forward directed shape function, if rear attenuation is desired.

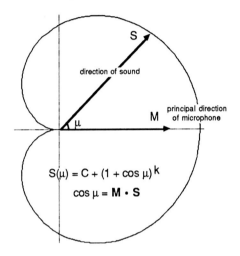

Figure 5: Microphone sensitivity shape (with k=1, C=0).

The total modulation of sound intensity is now the product of all directional functions in addition to the attenuation by distance.

$$A(d) = A_0 \cdot \left(\frac{d_0}{d}\right)^2 \cdot S(\sigma) \cdot S(\mu)$$

where σ and μ are the angles between the sound ray and the principal directions of sound source and microphone, respectively.

5.4 Sound Tracing in an Acoustic Environment

A common effect in acoustic environments is reverberation. It is caused by reflective objects in the scene acting as secondary sound sources. Algorithmically, this means making multiple instances of sound threads, with different delay and amplitude corresponding to each path through the environment. Generally this transformation would be a convolution of the signal with a continuous weighting function. In practical calculations, the weighting function is discretized to a finite number of samples. Reverberation is thus modeled with multiple echoes. In our approach each echo generates a separate thread for the sound renderer.

Because the sound wavelength is comparable to the geometric features of the objects, reflections are usually very diffuse. Specular reflection is soft, and refraction can in most cases be neglected. Due to diffraction, sound waves can propagate around a corner. Thus an obstacle occluding

visibility does not completely cut off a direct sound, but only gives a smooth damping.

Based on these arguments and the fact that the purpose of sound in animation is rather illustrative than exact acoustical analysis, we use a heuristically simplified sound tracing model to calculate the effects of interfering objects. The basic idea is to find all major paths of sound from a source to the microphone. Each of them is represented as a separate sound thread with delay and attenuation corresponding to the path length and reflectivity coefficients.

As in radiosity calculation, each reflecting surface is considered a secondary diffuse point source receiving energy proportional to its area and the cosine of the angle between its normal and sound source direction. To calculate the amount of re-radiated sound we use the same reflection formula as is traditionally used for shading, consisting of a diffuse radiation in all directions, and a Phong-like specular term. The ambient sound in an environment is not modeled as a separate term for each object, but as a global background sound at each microphone.

Due to diffraction, the shadowing effect of objects obscuring a sound path (the form factor) is more approximate than with radiosity. In this paper we do not attempt to make a detailed geometric analysis, but use a rule of thumb. Attenuation is approximated with a form factor proportional to the amount of occlusion.

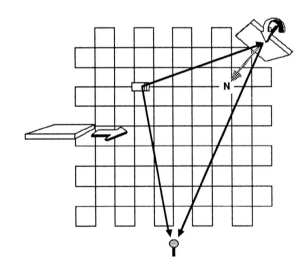

Figure 6: Principle of sound tracing.

A frame from an animation to demonstrate these effects is shown in figure 6. A standing car is producing continuous sound, which is received through two paths, directly and reflected by a wall. As the wall rotates, the echo is strongest when it is in an ideal mirroring position, and disappears when the tangent plane of the wall separates the car and the listener. As another wall moves by, it obscures visibility of the car first and then the mirror, damping each sound for a period.

6 Representation and Processing of Sound Scripts

The sound script defines how a prototype sound signal will be instantiated, and how it is transformed by the acoustic environment. This process will be best understood by an analogy with the mapping of a texture from texture to image space.

In a sound script all acoustic effects of the three-dimensional world are encoded in a geometry-free form. An advantage of making this transformation a separate process is that all the complex effects can be precomputed and combined in the same way as a sequence of geometric transformations can be concatenated into a single transformation matrix. Then each object sound can be rendered and checked separately, before mixing (overlaying) all sounds together. Another benefit is that this part of the sound renderer can be used for any key-framed animation, without necessarily having a three-dimensional model.

In this section we first describe how a sound script is used to describe transformations of sounds from prototypes to the soundtrack. Then the resampling algorithms interpreting the script and performing the transformation for each sound are discussed.

6.1 Representing Sound Transformations by Key-Framing

For describing a sound signal we have two independent coordinates, time and intensity, each of which can be transformed. For intensity, only scaling (amplitude modulation) is usually acceptable, since any non-linearity is perceived as distortion. Simple translation in time defines when a sound begins or how much it is delayed, whereas modifying the time scale causes change in pitch (frequency modulation). An arbitrary monotonic mapping – excluding reversal of time, which would be rather unnatural – can be approximated by interpolating specified key values of sound *attenuation* and *delay* (corresponding to the amplitude and phase angle of stationary signals).

Our script format for sound transformations consists of threads of values for attenuation and delay, one thread for each instantiated object sound. Each line of a script file contains the following information:

- keyword (start, in-between key, or end of a thread)

- ID (number) of a thread

- time stamp of the key

- attenuation and delay (for each stereo channel).

The file may be sorted by thread ID and or time stamp, depending on the resampling algorithm that calculates the soundtrack.

Key values may be specified at any points of time. In between the values are interpolated. Since the ear's resolution of intensity is not very high, we have found that linear interpolation is usually sufficient for amplitude values. However, the ear is very sensitive to abrupt changes in pitch. Thus, in order to keep the delay's rate of change (pitch level) continuous, either higher order interpolation or dense spacing of keys is needed. For simplicity, we have used the latter solution, specifying keys at each frame of an animation.

6.2 Resampling Algorithm

Just as in texture mapping, a sound transformation can be computed with an algorithm doing resampling either in sound object space or sound image space.

With an object space algorithm, each sample of a prototype sound is multiplied by the corresponding interpolated amplitude, and is written to a sound image buffer translated in time according to the corresponding interpolated delay (figure 4). A major problem with this approach is that gaps may be left in image space if the signal is expanded.

An image space algorithm determines the value for each image buffer position by sampling in object space at a point determined by the inverse transformation. The inverse mapping cannot be directly computed in our case, because the mapping of time (the delay) is defined in object space. We solve this problem by mapping the key positions from object space to image space, and interpolating the mapping parameters linearly. The interpolated delay gives the inverse mapping for each sample.

The same aliasing problems arise in sound transformations and sampling, just as they do in texture mapping, and could be solved similarly [4].

7 Conclusions

Sound rendering is a novel approach allowing the motion to define the sound, as opposed to the traditional way of starting with a soundtrack. This allows all types of motion control schemes to synchronize sound. With a physically-based motion control the sound events can be automatically produced, even if the objects' prototype sounds are not physically defined. With keyframed motion, the sound parameters can be keyframed as well. If the motion is three-dimensional, physically-based simulation of sound propagation can determine many acoustical parameters in a natural way.

In this work we have defined a modular sonic extension of the image rendering pipeline. Analogies have been drawn between sound and texture. Both are transformed from object to image space using similar algorithms with similar aliasing problems. We have simulated acoustical effects by sound tracing, analogous to forward ray-tracing and radiosity. With this analogy, the sound transformations correspond to shaders in a shade tree during its traversal from a source to a camera [3, 18]. We have applied the technique to generate sounds for a complex animation using keyframing, behavioral, and physically-based motion controls that illustrates its generality and flexibility.

One area we are currently working on is more rigorous physically-based modeling of sound-causing phenomena and sound propagation in acoustical environments. In this paper we have only given hints on how to approach the problem heuristically.

8 Acknowledgements

This work has been made possible in part by Helsinki University of Technology, who provided support for Tapio Takala's sabbatical to the George Washington University.

This work was also partly supported by funding from NASA (NCC 5-43) and NRL (NAVY N00014-91-K-203).

We would like to thank the students in the Computer Graphics and User Interface Group at George Washington University for their assistance. Special thanks go to Larry Gritz, Daria Bergen, and Rudy Darken for providing the image from "Graphic Violence".

We would also like to thank the reviewers for their enthusiastic comments and many useful suggestions.

References

[1] Barzel, R, A.Barr. Modeling with Dynamic Constraints. Proc. SIGGRAPH'88, ACM Computer Graphics, Vol.22, No.3, pp.178-188.

[2] Blattner, Meera, D.Sumikawa, R.Greenberg. Earcons and Icons: Their Structure and Common Design Principles. Human-Computer Interaction, Vol.4, No.1, 1989, pp.11-44. Also reprinted in: E.Glinert (ed.), Visual Programming Environments – Applications and Issues, IEEE Computer Society Press 1990, pp.582-606.

[3] Cook, Robert. Shade Trees. Proc. SIGGRAPH'84, ACM Computer Graphics, Vol.18, No.3, pp.195-206.

[4] Feibush, E.A., M.Levoy, R.Cook. Synthetic Texturing Using Digital Filters. Proc. SIGGRAPH'80, ACM Computer Graphics, Vol.14, No.3, pp.294-301.

[5] Foster, S, E.Wenzel. Virtual Acoustic Environments: TheConvolvotron. [multimedia installation] SIGGRAPH'91 Virtual reality and hypermedia show (August 1991).

[6] Gaver, William. The SonicFinder: An Interface That Uses Auditory Icons. Human-Computer Interaction, Vol.4, No.1, 1989, pp.67-94. Also reprinted in: E.Glinert (ed.), Visual Programming Environments – Applications and Issues, IEEE Computer Society Press 1990, pp.561-581.

[7] Hahn, James. Realistic Animation of Rigid Bodies. Proc. SIGGRAPH'88, ACM Computer Graphics, Vol.22, No.3, pp.299-308

[8] He, Xiao, K.Torrance, F.Sillion, D.Greenberg. A Comprehensive Physical Model for Light Reflection. Proc. SIGGRAPH'91, ACM Computer Graphics, Vol.25, No.3, pp.175-186.

[9] Lytle, Wayne. More Bells and Whistles. [video] in SIGGRAPH'90 film show. Also described in Computer, Vol.24, No.7, July 1991, p.4 and cover.

[10] NCSA Visualization Group and CERL Sound Group. Using Sound to Extract Meaning from Complex Data. [video] SIGGRAPH'91 Screening Room, Visualization & Technical series (August 1991).

[11] Pentland, Alex, J.Williams. Good Vibrations: Modal Dynamics for Graphics and Animation. Proc. SIGGRAPH'89, ACM Computer Graphics, Vol.23, No.3, pp.215-222.

[12] Perlin, K. An Image Synthesizer. Proc. SIGGRAPH'85, ACM Computer Graphics, Vol.19, No.3, pp.287-296.

[13] Sillion, François., J.Arvo, S.Westin, D.Greenberg. A Global Illumination Solution for General Reflectance Distributions. Proc. SIGGRAPH'91, ACM Computer Graphics, Vol.25, No.3, pp.187-196.

[14] Smith, J.W. Vibration of Structures - Applications in Civil Engineering Design. Chapman & Hall 1988

[15] Stettner, Adam, D.Greenberg. Computer Graphics Visualization for Acoustic Simulation. Proc. SIGGRAPH'89, ACM Computer Graphics, Vol.23, No.3, pp.195-206.

[16] Terzopoulos, Dimitri, J.Platt , A.Barr, K.Fleischer. Elastically Deformable Models. Proc. SIGGRAPH'87, ACM Computer Graphics, Vol.21, No.3, pp.205-214.

[17] Thomas, Frank, O.Johnston. Disney Animation – The Illusion of Life, chapter 11. Abbeville Press 1981.

[18] Upstill, Steve. The RenderMan Companion. Pixar/Addison-Wesley, 1989.

[19] Voss, Richard and J.Clarke. "1/f noise" in Music: Music from 1/f Noise. J. Acoust. Soc. Am. 63 (1), January 1978, pp.258-263.

[20] Voss, Richard. Fractals in Nature: Characterization, Measurement, and Simulation. SIGGRAPH'87 Course Notes.

[21] Wightman, Frederick, D.Kistler. Headphone Simulation of Free-Field Listening. I: Stimulus Synthesis. J. Acoust. Soc. Am. 85 (2), February 1989, pp.858-867.

[22] Wyshynski Susan, The Vivid Group. The Mandala VR System. [multimedia installation] in SIGGRAPH'91 virtual reality and hypermedia show (August 1991).

Figures 7: Frame from a key-framed animation.

Figure 8: Frame from a physically based animation.

Figure 9: Frame from a behavioral animation.

An Algorithm With Linear Complexity
For Interactive, Physically-based Modeling of Large Proteins

Mark C. Surles
Department of Computer Science
University of North Carolina at Chapel Hill
Chapel Hill, NC   27599-3175

Abstract

Physically-based modeling applications usually require batch processing for each frame of an animation or simulation. This paper describes a graphics modeling system, called *Sculpt,* that maintains physically-valid protein properties while a user interactively moves atoms. *Sculpt* models stiff properties such as bond lengths and angles as rigid constraints and models weak properties such as non-bonded interactions as potential energies. *Sculpt* continually satisfies the constraints and maintains a local energy minimum throughout user interaction. On a Silicon Graphics 240-GTX, *Sculpt* maintains 1.9 updates per second on a molecular model with 355 atoms (1065 variables, 1027 constraints, and 3465 potential energies). Performance decreases *linearly* with increased problem size.

This paper presents a Lagrange multiplier method with linear computational complexity that finds a constrained minimum for articulated figures with many more joints in their spines than in any limb (e.g. reptiles, mammals, and proteins). The method computes the Jacobian matrix of the constraints and solves a system of linear equations that results from multiplying the Jacobian by its transpose. The paper proves that a sort of the Jacobian yields a band-diagonal pattern of nonzeros. The pattern does not change during a modeling session, so the sort can run during a pre-processing step. Multiplication and solution of band-diagonal matrices require computation that increases linearly with problem size. Previous applications of Lagrange multipliers to constrained, physically-based modeling did not take advantage of the constraint connectivity in the spine. They either required many iterations of a linear algorithm or few iterations of a quadratic algorithm for each frame of a simulation. This application finds a constrained minimum with a linear algorithm in a few iterations. Additionally, most of the algorithm's steps execute in parallel for increased performance.

CR Categories and Subject Descriptors: **I.3.6** **[Computer Graphics]:** Methodology and Techniques; **J.2** **[Computer Applications]:** Physical Sciences.

Additional Keywords and Phrases: Constraint systems, Lagrange multiplier method, molecular modeling.

1. Introduction

Two factors hinder large, interactive applications of physically-based modeling—model complexity and algorithm complexity. Most physically-based modeling applications in computer graphics simulate Newtonian dynamics of complex models to generate realistic motions and shapes. The complexity of the models requires batch processing to evaluate their properties for each frame in an animation. For example, Platt models surface tensors and finite elements to create incompressible Jello and compressible clay [15], and Terzopoulos models fracture and elasticity to simulate tearing paper [21].

The algorithms that generate frames in physically-based modeling animations usually require a few iterations with quadratic (or higher) computational complexity or numerous iterations with linear complexity. Linear algorithms such as those that explicitly integrate differential equations of motion usually require many iterations with small time steps for each frame in a simulation. Algorithms that constrain stiff model components (e.g. stiff springs) allow larger time steps, but require more operations per iteration to satisfy the constraints [14]. One physically-based modeling algorithm that maintains constraints among arbitrary objects requires only a few iterations per screen update, but the computation in each iteration increases quadratically with the number of constraints [24, 25]. Algorithm and model complexities limit the size of models that run interactively on current graphics workstations.

I show an algorithm and system that interactively models large proteins with physically-based modeling. The system, called *Sculpt,* maintains rigid bond lengths and angles and minimizes potential energy while a user interactively moves atoms. *Sculpt* lets a user tug atoms in an existing model into new conformations (e.g. twist a sequence of bonded atoms into a helix) while automatically maintaining physically-valid protein geometry. The computation in *Sculpt* increases linearly with protein size. On a Silicon Graphics 240-GTX, *Sculpt* maintains 1.9 updates per second on a model with 1065 variables, 1027 constraints, and 3465 energy functions. Chemists have used *Sculpt* to create new protein conformations and examine interactions within protein interiors [19].

An algorithm in *Sculpt* with linear computational complexity in problem size satisfies a set of connectivity constraints and minimizes the ensemble model energy. The algorithm is applicable to articulated figures that have many more joints in the spine than in any limb. The algorithm assumes the atom positions at a local energy minima are more important than the

© 1992   ACM-0-89791-479-1/92/007/0221 $01.50

trajectory for reaching them. This assumption lets the algorithm minimize strain energy in the model rather than simulate model dynamics. The time steps in the algorithm are large enough for interactive physically-based modeling of large models. Most of the algorithm's steps can execute in parallel for additional performance. This paper concentrates on the constrained minimization algorithm and the class of problems for which the algorithm runs with linear complexity.

Two issues in this application are important to the computer graphics community. First, the algorithm that finds a constrained minimum is not protein specific. Proteins, to a first approximation, are articulated figures with many more joints in their backbone than in any limb. The constrained minimization algorithm is applicable to any articulated figure with this property (e.g. vertebrates such as reptiles, fish, and most mammals). Second, *Sculpt* significantly expands the benefits of interactive graphics in biochemistry by maintaining physical-realism during interactive modeling. Biochemists use interactive graphics to study three-dimensional molecular structures and visualize results from supercomputer molecular dynamics simulations. However, commercial interactive modeling systems [3, 16, 22] restrict modeling operations to simple geometric transformations that do not maintain a physically-valid model. Returning a model to a physically-valid configuration is left to the user.

Sections 2 and 3 describe the driving problem and the *Sculpt* interface. Section 4 details specific articulated bodies for which the Lagrange multiplier method in Section 5 runs with linear complexity. Section 6 shows a pre-processing step that lets subsequent constrained minimizations run with linear computational complexity. Section 7 outlines parallel components of the algorithm. Section 8 describes some application-specific complications, and Section 9 presents performance results.

2. Problem description

Chemists build and change molecular models with interactive graphics systems. Commercial molecular modeling systems only model a small set of protein properties in order to preserve interactive performance. In these systems, simple changes often leave the model in a physically-invalid configuration. Chemists spend much of their modeling effort returning the model to a physically-valid configuration. The driving problem in this research is to create an interactive protein modeling system that relieves the chemist of the repair process by maintaining a physically-valid model throughout a modeling session. Protein modeling was picked as a starting point before generalizing to other molecules. This section describes relevant protein properties and commercial interactive modeling systems for proteins.

A protein, to a first approximation, contains fixed bond lengths, bond angles, and planar segments. Figure 1 shows three sequential segments in a protein with vectors representing bonds between atoms and gray areas denoting planar regions. The only degrees of freedom in the figure are rotations between the planar segments (shown with arrows about the N-C_α and C_α-C bonds). A linear sequence of the segments comprise the protein *backbone*. Attached to the atom (C_α) between each segment are *sidechains* (not shown) with additional fixed length and angle properties. The number of atoms in the sidechain is small relative to the backbone (up to eighteen atoms versus hundreds to thousands of atoms).

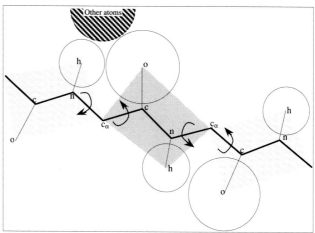

Figure 1: Three planar segments in the backbone.

Proteins also contain attractions and repulsions between non-bonded atoms (points without connecting vectors). Attractions hold nearby atoms together, whereas repulsions maintain a minimal separation defined by the atom's electron shells. Figure 1 shows near-ideal separation between *H* and *O* atoms with adjacent circles. If two circles overlap, their atoms repel each other; otherwise, they attract.

Molecular modeling systems [3, 16, 22] usually restrict modeling operations to rotations about the N-C_α and C_α-C bonds so that bond lengths and angles between segments remain correct. Adjusting an interior segment with this restriction often requires numerous rotations (an inverse-kinematics problem with hundreds of joints), since even a small rotation moves all the atoms further along the backbone. Additionally, interactive systems do not maintain proper non-bonded atom separations during a modeling session. A user must return a protein to valid geometry by either laborious manual adjustments using these rotations or batch energy minimization. Batch minimization automates model repair but often changes the model differently than desired.

Modal dynamics allows interactive, physically-based model deformations by linearly interpolating independent, principal normal (or vibrational) modes of an object [13]. Modal dynamics requires a batch pre-processing step that determines the principal axes of change in a given model. As the deformed model differs more from the original model, the results of the normal-mode analysis become less accurate. After the model changes a specified amount, a new normal-mode analysis must determine the modes for the new structure. Modal dynamics is not a good choice for this molecular modeling problem since a user may significantly change the protein structure during a modeling session. Running a new modal analysis of a medium-size protein in the middle of a session requires too much time for an interactive application.

3. The *Sculpt* system

Sculpt lets a user move any atom by first attaching a simulated spring between it and the cursor and then dragging the cursor in the desired direction. Throughout the dragging process, *Sculpt* polls the cursor position and adds the strain energy of that spring to the energy in the protein. *Sculpt* then finds a local minimum of the new total energy that also maintains rigid bond lengths, angles, and planar segments. Lastly, *Sculpt* displays the results.

Figures 2a and 2b show photographs of the *Sculpt* display using the medium-size protein, Felix [8]. Depth-cued vectors represent bonds between atoms; cyan denotes the central backbone, and tan denotes sidechains (shown in 2b) connected to the backbone. Figure 2a shows that the backbone winds through four helices. Each gold coil illustrates a spring inserted by the user that pulls an atom towards the three-dimensional position denoted with the thumbtack. The model contains 760 atoms, 2205 constraints (bond length, angle, and others), and approximately 8029 energy functions (attraction, repulsion, and others).

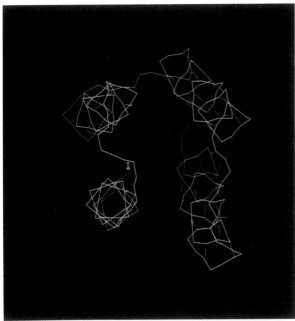

Figure 2a: Bonds in a protein backbone.

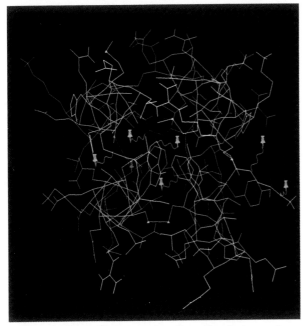

Figure 2b: Photograph of a *Sculpt* session.

Sculpt models stiff properties (bond lengths and angles) with constraints and weak and multi-value properties with energy functions. For example, certain dihedral angles are three orders-of-magnitude weaker than bond lengths. *Sculpt* models these dihedral angles with springs with an ideal value equal to the ideal angle and models bond lengths with constraints fixed to their ideal values. Assume the list of independent variables (e.g. atom positions) are represented by the column vector, x. *Sculpt* continuously maintains a local minimum of the total energy, denoted $e(x)$, while maintaining a set of constraint functions, $c(x) = 0$. The next section describes the specific contents of the energy and constraint functions.

4. Model parameters

The algorithm in Section 5 finds a constrained minimum with linear computational complexity for articulated figures containing particular properties. This section presents a detailed parameterization of the properties and lists restrictions on the topology of the constraints. The most important restriction is that only a fixed number of constraints among arbitrary variables are allowed; the number of constraints defined on topologically-near variables is not restricted. The model parameters are used extensively in the algorithm analysis of Section 6. This section concludes with a discussion of articulated figures that have these properties.

4.1. Connectivity restrictions

Figure 3 shows a graph of the bond topology in a protein (lengths and angles are not drawn to scale). Nodes represent model variables (a three-dimensional coordinate for each atom). The total number of variables, n, equals three times the number of nodes. The nodes are numbered by a depth-first traversal beginning at the left.

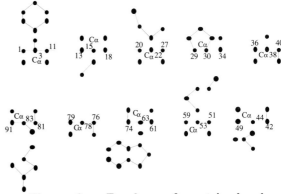

Figure 3: Topology of protein bonds.

k_{branch} specifies the maximum number of arcs connected to a node. In proteins the number is four, the maximum number of atoms that bond to a carbon.

k_{side} specifies the maximum number of nodes in any limb (sidechain) attached to the backbone. In proteins this is fifteen, the number of sidechain atoms in the largest amino acid, tryptophan. The maximum separation in node indices along any arc is k_{side} which occurs between the C_α and the next backbone node.

4.2. Constraint functions

In general, constraints are defined on nodes connected by a fixed number of arcs. For example, a distance constraint is defined on each pair of connected nodes. Angle and dihedral angle constraints are defined on nodes connected by two and three arcs, respectively. Each constraint function, $c_i(\boldsymbol{x})$, has an ideal value, $\bar{c}_i$, and is represented as $c_i(\boldsymbol{x}) - \bar{c}_i = 0$. At program initialization all constraints must be satisfied. In the protein application, all the constraints are specified at program initialization. Constraints that meet these criteria can be added or removed during a session with some loss of interactivity.

$\boldsymbol{k_{domain}}$ specifies the maximum dimension of any constraint function's domain. This gives the maximum number of variables referenced by a constraint. In *Sculpt* the dihedral angle function references the most variables—twelve, four atoms each with three variables. This constant and the requirement that constraints, in general, are defined on connected nodes restrict constraint functions to nodes in close topological proximity. Assume during the subsequent analysis that a constraint function *cannot* reference nodes arbitrarily separated in the topology graph; local loops, however, are allowed. Section 6.4 shows that the linear complexity analysis remains valid given a fixed number (independent of n) of constraints defined on arbitrary nodes.

$\boldsymbol{k_{cv}}$ specifies the maximum number of constraints defined on a given variable. This constant is a function of k_{branch} and k_{domain}. Consider the number of constraints that can reference a particular node in a protein. At most k_{branch} length functions contain the same atom. Each of the connected atoms connect to at most $k_{branch} - 1$ other atoms, giving a maximum of $k_{branch}(k_{branch} - 1)$ angle functions that reference the initial atom. A similar argument follows for dihedral angle functions.

$\boldsymbol{f_c}$ specifies the total number of constraint functions. An upper bound on this number is the number of variables times the maximum number of constraints per variable, $k_{cv}n$.

$\boldsymbol{k_{span}}$ defines the maximum separation between the lowest and the highest variable indices in a constraint. This constant is a function of k_{domain} and k_{side}. In proteins, this constant is derived by examining a dihedral angle function defined on atoms before and after the largest sidechain.

$\boldsymbol{c(x)}$ is a column vector that contains all the constraint functions in a model. Row i in $\boldsymbol{c(x)}$ represents the constraint function, $c_i(\boldsymbol{x})$, minus its constrained value, $\bar{c}_i$, as follows:

$$\mathbf{c}(\mathbf{x}) = \begin{bmatrix} c_1(\mathbf{x}) - \bar{c}_1 \\ c_2(\mathbf{x}) - \bar{c}_2 \\ \vdots \\ c_{f_c}(\mathbf{x}) - \bar{c}_{f_c} \end{bmatrix} = \begin{bmatrix} 0 \\ 0 \\ \vdots \\ 0 \end{bmatrix}$$

4.3. Energy functions

$e(\boldsymbol{x})$ equals the sum of all the energy functions in the model. Energy functions model weak and multi-value properties. In *Sculpt* some energy functions are defined throughout a modeling session (e.g. a weak bond length between two atoms) and some are defined only when atoms are within a given neighborhood of each other. The latter functions model attractions and repulsions among nearby, non-bonded atoms (detailed in Section 8).

Most of the previous restrictions on constraints are not placed on energy functions. For example, an arbitrary number of energy functions can reference arbitrary nodes and can be added and removed during a modeling session without significant loss in interactivity. The only restriction on energy functions is that the number of energy functions, f_e, increases at most linearly with the number of variables. $k_{cv}n$ bounds the

number of energy functions if the k_{cv} constant is increased to account for length, angle, and dihedral angle energy functions. Section 8 shows that the number of non-bonded interactions also meets this criterion.

4.4. Similar applications

Many articulated bodies such as mammals, reptiles, and fish have limbs with few joints attached to spines with numerous joints. A human skeleton marginally fits this characterization due to the large number of bones in the hands and feet. A human skeleton does meet the model restrictions if the hands and feet are approximated with fewer bones. Since an energy function can reference arbitrary variables, operations such as *clap hands* and *pat knee with hand* can place a spring between the two bones.

In order to keep the constrained minimization algorithm and modeling system general, *Sculpt* does not take advantage of specific protein properties to reduce variables and improve performance. For example, a protein is modeled as a set of points with length and angle constraints rather than a set of rigid segments connected with free rotations between them. A planar segment in Figure 1 remains rigid by constraining the lengths, angles, and dihedral angles among its atoms.

5. Finding a locally constrained minimum

This section presents an algorithm that finds a local solution to the following problem:

$$\begin{array}{ll} \text{minimize} & e(\boldsymbol{x}) \\ \text{such that} & \boldsymbol{c(x)} = \boldsymbol{0}. \end{array}$$

Minimizing an arbitrary function subject to arbitrary constraints is an open research problem. Different constrained minimization algorithms work better for problems with different properties. Some common classes of properties include the following: linear, quadratic, or nonlinear energy function; linear or nonlinear constraints; equality and/or inequality constraints; smooth and continuous functions in zero or more derivatives; starting value of variables satisfies (or does not satisfy) the constraints. The class of problems in this research has the following properties:

1. nonlinear energy and constraint functions;
2. equality constraints;
3. continuous functions through the second derivative;
4. initial variables satisfy or nearly satisfy constraints.

Additionally, a local minimum is usually very close to the starting point. A new constrained minimization runs each time a user tugs an atom. The only difference in the total energy from the previous invocation is energy from a user spring and near-neighbor interactions resulting from prior atom movements. Neither case changes the total system energy very much. A small change in the total energy typically shifts the minimum only slightly. This property lets the following algorithm converge usually in one or two iterations.

Sculpt finds a local constrained minimum with the augmented Lagrange method. This method is based on the first-order necessary conditions of a local solution. This section first states the necessary conditions and the augmented Lagrange method and then presents the particular implementation of the method used in *Sculpt*.

5.1. Notation

The gradient operator, ∇, is a column vector of partial derivatives. In particular, the gradient of the energy function, $\nabla e(x)$, is defined as follows:

$$\nabla e(\mathbf{x}) = \left[\begin{array}{cccc} \dfrac{\partial e}{\partial x_1} & \dfrac{\partial e}{\partial x_2} & \cdots & \dfrac{\partial e}{\partial x_n} \end{array} \right]^{\mathrm{T}}, T \text{ denotes the transpose.}$$

The gradient of the constraints, $\nabla c(x)$, is called the *Jacobian matrix*. Element *(i,j)* of the Jacobian represents the partial derivative with respect to variable x_i of constraint j. Sometimes this is denoted by $\boldsymbol{J}$ for notational clarity.

5.2. Necessary conditions

First-order, necessary conditions require that a locally constrained minimum, x^*, satisfy two conditions [6, p. 200]:

1. $c(x^*) = 0$ constraints are satisfied
2. $\nabla e(x^*) = \nabla c(x^*)\lambda^*$ energy gradient is a linear combination of constraint
   $= \Sigma_i \nabla c_i(x^*)\lambda_i^*$ gradients

There is one scalar, called a *Lagrange multiplier*, λ_i, for each constraint. The vector λ^* denotes the vector of Lagrange multipliers at the minimum, x^*. Figure 4 illustrates these conditions with a two-dimensional energy function and one constraint. At the point x the gradient of the energy is not a linear combination of the constraint gradients. A step in the direction d reduces the energy and maintains the constraints. At the local minimum, x^*, the conditions are satisfied and no descent direction remains that satisfies the constraints.

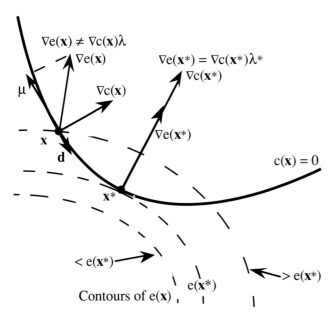

Figure 4: Example of first-order necessary conditions at a constrained minimum.

5.3. Augmented Lagrange function

Algorithms that find a locally constrained minimum using Lagrange multipliers seek a vector (x^*,λ^*) that satisfies the first-order necessary conditions. No direct, general solution exists because these conditions give $n+f_c$ nonlinear equations with $n+f_c$ unknowns for problems with n variables and f_c constraints. Rather than solving these equations directly, I find a saddlepoint of another function, called the *augmented*

Lagrange function, that contains no constraints. Finding an unconstrained saddlepoint is easier than solving the nonlinear equations associated with a constrained minimum.

A solution (x^*,λ^*) of the following minimax problem, for sufficiently large p, is also a solution to the constrained minimization problem [9]:

$$\min_{\mathbf{x}} \max_{\lambda} \mathrm{L}(\mathbf{x}, \lambda, \mathrm{p}) = \min_{\mathbf{x}} \max_{\lambda} e(\mathbf{x}) - \lambda^{\mathrm{T}} c(\mathbf{x}) + \tfrac{\mathrm{p}}{2} c(\mathbf{x})^{\mathrm{T}} c(\mathbf{x}).$$

The solution of the minimax problem is a saddlepoint of the augmented Lagrange function, $L(x,\lambda,p)$. The gradient of a function evaluated at a saddlepoint is zero. In this case, the gradient with respect to λ set to zero gives necessary condition (1). The gradient with respect to x set to zero gives $\nabla e(x) - \nabla c(x)\lambda + p\nabla c(x)c(x) = 0$. Rearranging this equation gives necessary condition (2) plus an extra term, called the *penalty*. Notice the penalty is zero when the constraints are satisfied. For penalties greater than some finite value, a point x minimizes $L(x,\lambda^*,p)$ if and only if it is a constrained minimum of the original problem [7, p. 226]. Additionally, a sequence x^i that minimizes $L(x,\lambda^i,p)$, for a sequence of multipliers that converge to λ^*, converges to x^* [9, p. 308].

5.4. Algorithm

Numerous iterative algorithms can find a saddlepoint of a function [12]. The method of steepest descent follows the negative gradient with respect to x to find the minimum and the gradient with respect to λ to find the maximum. The steepest descent evaluates the gradient during each iteration but usually requires numerous iterations. Newton's method finds a zero of an equation (in this case, the gradient of the Lagrange function) using its value and derivative. The derivative of the Lagrange gradient is actually the second derivative of the Lagrange function, a matrix $(n+f_c) \times (n+f_c)$ in dimension. Newton's method should converge rapidly, since we assume the solution is near. However, solving a system of $n+f_c$ equations destroys interactive performance.

The algorithm used in *Sculpt* blends these two approaches (see Figure 5). First, estimate the optimal Lagrange multipliers using the current value of the variables. Second, compute a penalty. Third, minimize the Lagrange function with respect to x using the estimated Lagrange multipliers. Fourth, repeat the algorithm until sufficiently close to the constrained minimum. The method is first presented in Gill [7, p. 227]; Witkin presents a similar algorithm for constrained dynamics [24].

     0. Given initial x
     1. Estimate the Lagrange multipliers, λ
     2. Determine a penalty term, p
     3. $x^{new} \leftarrow \underset{x}{\text{minimize}} \; L(x; \lambda, p)$
     4. $x \leftarrow x^{new}$; Goto step 1

Figure 5: The constrained minimization algorithm.

5.4.1. Estimate Lagrange multipliers

The first-order multiplier method [7, p. 248] estimates the Lagrange multipliers. Given the current variables, x, this method finds the Lagrange multipliers that *best* satisfy necessary condition (2). The algorithm estimates the ideal Lagrange multipliers at each iteration by solving the following system of equations for λ: $[\nabla c(x)]\lambda = \nabla e(x)$.

The dimension of the Jacobian matrix, $\nabla c(x)$, is $n \times f_c$, and the Lagrange multiplier vector has dimension $f_c \times 1$. Since the number of constraints is typically less than the number of variables, this system of equations is overconstrained (note, λ is overconstrained, not the free variables, x). *Sculpt* finds a least-squares approximation to the system of equations by multiplying both sides of the equality by the transpose of the matrix and solving for λ: $[\nabla c(x)^T \nabla c(x)]\lambda = \nabla c(x)^T \nabla e(x)$.

5.4.2. Determine a penalty term

The penalty, p, pulls the solution towards one that satisfies the constraints. The previous step estimates the Lagrange multipliers using a first-order approximation of the constraints. Since the constraints are nonlinear, this approximation lets the solution drift from the constraints. The penalty keeps this from moving beyond some limit. The penalty is set to the error in the least-squares approximation (i.e. $p \leftarrow \|\nabla e(x) - \nabla c(x)\lambda\|$).

5.4.3. Minimize augmented Lagrange function

This step minimizes the augmented Lagrangian with respect to x using the multipliers and penalty term from previous steps. The steepest descent method, in practice, converges in one or two iterations since the starting point is close to a minimum. The steepest descent method requires the negative gradient of the Lagrange function: $-\nabla e(x) + \nabla c(x)\lambda - p\nabla c(x)c(x)$.

5.4.4. Exit or repeat

If the previous step changes x more than a user-defined threshold, the algorithm repeats with the new value of x. Since the starting point is usually close to the local minimum, only one or two iterations typically run. Users occasionally decrease the threshold near the end of a modeling session so the model will settle closer to the local minimum.

6. Algorithm analysis

The step that estimates the Lagrange multipliers requires multiplying the $f_c \times n$ Jacobian transpose by the $n \times f_c$ Jacobian and solving the $f_c \times f_c$ system of linear equations. In a general problem, the multiplication requires $O(f_c^2 n)$ operations and the solution of linear equations requires $O(f_c^3)$ operations. Since the number of constraints increases linearly with the problem size (i.e. $f_c = O(n)$), the Lagrange multiplier estimate requires $O(n^3)$ steps in a general problem.

Constraint properties in this application let the estimation of Lagrange multipliers run in $O(n)$ operations. A pre-processing step that sorts rows in the Jacobian transpose gives a matrix with nonzeros within a constant bandwidth, independent of problem size, from the diagonal. Multiplication and solution of matrices with this structure require $O(n)$ operations. This section explains the sort and analyzes the complexity of the minimization algorithm. Figure 6 summarizes the computational complexity of each step. The Jacobian is represented with J in the following discussion.

6.1. Matrix properties

Sculpt stores two matrices, the transpose of the Jacobian (J^T) and its product with the Jacobian ($J^T J$). Both matrices are very sparse (typically more than ninety-five percent of the entries

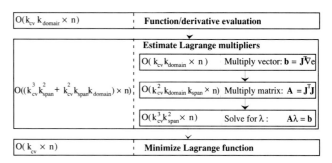

Figure 6: Computational complexity of algorithm.

are zero). Algorithms and data structures that exploit the sparsity drastically reduce the computational and memory requirements.

6.1.1. Contents of matrices

Jacobian transpose, J^T. The Jacobian transpose contains f_c rows and n columns. Element (i,j) holds the first partial derivative of constraint i with respect to variable j. Most of the entries in each row are zero since each constraint only references a small number of variables (much smaller than the total number of variables). For example, an average row in a model with 300 atoms is 94.7 percent zero; the percentage increases with more atoms. *Sculpt* stores a linked list for each constraint in the Jacobian transpose. A linked list contains a node for each variable referenced by its constraint. Each node in the list has pointers to the next nonzero element in the row and in the column [10, p. 300].

Matrix product, $A \equiv J^T J$. Nonzero elements in this matrix are related to nonzero elements in the Jacobian transpose. Matrix multiplication defines an element $a_{r,c}$ in A as the inner product of row r in the left matrix and column c in the right matrix (i.e. $a_{r,c} \equiv \sum_k J_{r,k}^T J_{k,c}$). Column c in a matrix is also row c in its matrix transpose. Rewriting the definition of $a_{r,c}$ using this information gives $a_{r,c} = \sum_k J_{r,k}^T J_{c,k}^T$. The element is nonzero only when rows r and c in the Jacobian transpose contain a nonzero entry in the same column (i.e. when constraints r and c reference the same variable).

At program initialization *Sculpt* determines the nonzero elements of A by comparing each row in the Jacobian transpose with the other rows for common, nonzero columns. Since rows (constraints) are not added or removed during an interactive session, the sparsity patterns of J^T and A remain constant.

6.1.2. Sparsity pattern using a sort

Matrix A is a band-diagonal matrix when the rows of the Jacobian transpose are sorted, relative to the smallest nonzero column index, before determining the nonzero elements in A. All the nonzero elements in a band-diagonal matrix are within a constant distance (bandwidth) from the diagonal (Figure 7 shows a band-diagonal matrix with bandwidth b). The bandwidth of a matrix depends on the maximum separation of nonzero column indices. The bandwidth of A is found by considering an arbitrary row i. Column j in row i is nonzero if and only if constraints i and j reference the same variable. The worst-case structure of the sorted Jacobian transpose shows the maximum separation between i and j.

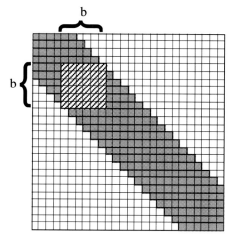

Figure 7: A band-diagonal matrix with bandwidth b. White squares represent zeros.

Assume constraint i references variables L and $L+k_{span}$, the maximum separation of variable indices allowed in one constraint. Figure 8 shows the worst-case separation of nonzero elements around constraint i in the sorted Jacobian transpose. One constraint references variables L and $L-k_{span}$, and one references $L+k_{span}$ and $L+2k_{span}$. At most k_{cv} constraints reference each of the variables between $L-k_{span}$ and $L+k_{span}$. Therefore, the smallest-numbered constraint that can reference a variable in constraint i is $i-k_{cv}k_{span}$ and the largest is $i+k_{cv}k_{span}$.

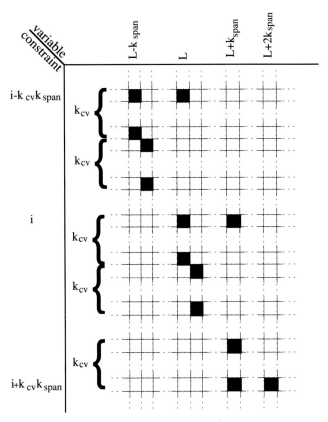

Figure 8: Worst-case structure of sorted Jacobian transpose around constraint i.

An arbitrary row in matrix A, therefore, contains nonzero elements at most $k_{cv}k_{span}$ columns before and $k_{cv}k_{span}$ columns after the diagonal element. The bandwidth, b, of matrix A is $k_{cv}k_{span}$. The positions of nonzero elements in the Jacobian transpose and A do not change since constraints are not added or removed during an interactive modeling session. Therefore, only one sort at or before program initialization is necessary.

6.2. Matrix algorithms

Matrix-vector multiplication, $b \leftarrow J^T \nabla e$. This step multiplies each of the f_c rows in the Jacobian transpose by a vector. Since each row contains at most k_{domain} nonzero elements, the entire multiplication requires $O(k_{domain}f_c) = O(k_{domain}k_{cv}n)$ operations.

Matrix-matrix multiplication, $A \leftarrow J^T J$. The bandwidth limits the number of nonzero elements in A to twice the bandwidth times the number of rows. Computing the value of a given element, (r,c), requires multiplying rows r and c of the Jacobian transpose. This requires $O(k_{domain})$ operations since a row in the Jacobian transpose contains at most k_{domain} nonzero elements. The entire multiplication requires $O(k_{domain}bf_c)$ operations. Substituting for b and f_c gives $O(k_{domain}k_{span}k_{cv}^2 n)$ operations.

Linear equation solution, $A\lambda = b$. Gaussian elimination reduces the band-diagonal matrix in $O(b^2 f_c)$ operations. Figure 7 highlights one block of a band-diagonal matrix. Consider the operations necessary to eliminate the elements under the diagonal in the left-most column of the highlighted block. This requires eliminating the value in the $b-1$ rows following the first row in the block. Each row elimination requires multiplying and adding b elements in the row. Therefore, eliminating the column elements below a diagonal element requires $O(b^2)$ operations. This elimination is then repeated for each diagonal element. Substituting gives the following complexity: $O(b^2 f_c) = O(k_{cv}^3 k_{span}^2 n)$.

6.3. Vector operations

Function and derivative evaluation. Evaluating the partial derivative of a function with respect to each of its variables requires $O(k_{domain})$ operations. This is done for the constraints and the energy functions, resulting in $O(k_{domain}(f_c+f_e)) = O(k_{domain}k_{cv}n)$ operations.

Lagrange function minimization. *Sculpt* finds a minimum over x of the Lagrange function with the steepest descent method by following the negative gradient with respect to x: $-\nabla e + J\lambda - pJc$. Both vector additions require $O(n)$ operations. Both matrix-vector multiplications multiply each of the n rows in the Jacobian matrix by a vector. A row in the Jacobian matrix contains partial derivatives of all the constraints with respect to a particular variable. Each row contains at most k_{cv} nonzero entries since at most k_{cv} constraints reference the same variable. The entire matrix-vector multiplication (and also the Lagrange minimization step), therefore, requires $O(k_{cv}n)$ operations.

6.4. Summary of analysis and generalizations

The analysis shows the computational complexity of an iteration in the constrained minimization algorithm increases linearly with problem size for a class of articulated figures. The values of the proportionality constants listed for the protein application are very conservative and fit many applications.

The parameter that varies the most among applications is the maximum number of joints (nodes) in a limb. The bandwidth increases with both this parameter and the number of variables referenced by a constraint in the topology graph.

The matrix properties are actually invariant to the variable numbering and the row sort. I use these to show that the articulated figures yield a matrix with the same properties as a band-diagonal matrix. This analysis applies to applications with the same constraint topology that use a different numbering scheme. Sparse matrix packages (e.g. [5]) employ a similar sort during a pre-processing step that tries to align the nonzeros near the diagonal. Also, the fixed-width band along the diagonal shows a worst-case scenario. In practice some rows span the maximum bandwidth while most do not. Using this information can reduce the average computation.

The algorithm still has linear computational complexity when the model contains a fixed number of constraints defined on arbitrary nodes. Consider a distance constraint, i, defined between two arbitrary nodes. The constraint can reference variables in k_{cv} other constraints that may be arbitrarily separated from i. The nonzeros in this matrix are either within the original bandwidth or at a few stray places such as (i,j) and (j,i), where constraint j references a variable in i. The order of Gaussian elimination's computational complexity does not change, since only elements in the column under these stray elements are filled. Similarly, the complexity remains linear when there is some constant number of constraints defined among arbitrary atoms; an unbounded number of these constraints, however, yields a general matrix which requires $O(f_c^3)$ operations to solve.

At the loss of some interactivity, *Sculpt* can add or remove a constraint that satisfies the other criteria. *Sculpt* removes a constraint by removing its row in the Jacobian transpose and its row and column in the matrix product. *Sculpt* adds a constraint with an in-order row insertion in the Jacobian transpose and adds a row and a column in the matrix product. *Sculpt* then searches the Jacobian transpose for nonzero elements in the same columns that the new constraint references to determine the new nonzeros in the matrix product.

7. Parallel and concurrent processing

The constrained minimization algorithm contains computationally-intensive steps that can execute concurrently and in parallel. Figure 9 presents steps that can run in parallel (apply one algorithm to data in parallel) and concurrently (simultaneous algorithms). Boxes with round corners represent independent steps in the minimization. The vertical axis shows data dependencies; a stage cannot begin until the previous stage completes. The horizontal axis shows parallel processing within a step and concurrent processing between steps. Algorithms beside one another (in Stages 2 and 4) can execute concurrently. Square boxes within an algorithm represent processing elements that can execute in parallel.

Vector and function operations. Stage 1 evaluates the constraint and energy functions and their derivatives in parallel. Writing the constraint value and constraint gradient does not require synchronization since *Sculpt* stores constraint values in separate array elements and constraint gradients in separate rows of the Jacobian transpose. Synchronization is necessary when energy gradients are stored because *Sculpt* stores the sum of all the energy gradients. Since energy functions can reference the same variable, simultaneously

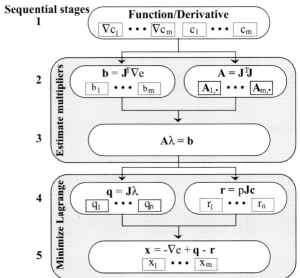

Figure 9: Algorithm concurrency (adjacent boxes with round corners) and data parallelism (square boxes) in algorithm.

updating the sum can cause errors. *Sculpt* adjusts for this by computing the energy gradients on a small number (four or eight) of processors that each holds a local copy of the sum. When all the processors complete, a final step combines the local copies. Stage 5 performs a vector addition, and Stages 2 and 4 calculate a matrix-vector multiplication. Separate processors can compute elements of the resulting vector in parallel.

Linear equation solution. Parallel execution of Gaussian elimination can reduce the constant of proportionality but not the linear order of complexity. Before reducing any row, all prior rows must be reduced. Consider a tri-diagonal matrix—a band-diagonal matrix with one band of nonzeros above and below the diagonal. Eliminating the rows below the diagonal element (i,i) affects the next row, $i+1$. This prevents processing row $i+1$ until completion of row i. Therefore, processing row *1* must complete before beginning row *2*, which must complete before beginning row *3*, etc.

8. Near-neighbor interactions

Modeling proteins also requires computing attractions and repulsions among nearby atoms. For each atom, *Sculpt* determines the atoms within a given distance, r_{neigh}, and evaluates the van der Waals attractive/repulsive energy function [17] between them (the energy becomes infinitesimal beyond six or seven Ångstroms). Only a finite number of atoms fit within this neighborhood because each atom's electron shell occupies a nonzero volume [11]. A *very* conservative bound on this number is r_{neigh}^3, the neighborhood volume divided by the volume of the smallest atom, hydrogen, with a radius of one Ångstrom.

Sculpt uses an algorithm described in [2] to determine neighbor lists. First, uniformly subdivide space into cubes with r_{neigh} on each side. Second, deposit each atom into the cube that contains its three-dimensional position. Third, set the neighbor list for each atom to the atoms in its cube and adjacent cubes. The algorithm takes $O(n)$ steps and runs before Stage 1 in Figure 9.

Model	Model statistics				Without near-neighbor interactions		With near-neighbor interactions using four processors		
	Atoms	Variables	Constraints	Energies	1 processor	4 processors	Same list	New list	Interactions
(1)	760	2280	2205	428	1.405	0.954	1.228	1.603	7601
(2)	355	1065	1027	198	0.586	0.396	0.514	0.689	3267
(3)	99	297	282	43	0.147	0.105	0.126	0.169	745
(4)	36	108	96	18	0.045	0.048	0.047	0.054	198

Figure 10: Seconds per update with four models using a Silicon Graphics 240-GTX.

9. Implementation and performance

Sculpt runs on a Silicon Graphics 240-GTXB [1]. This machine contains four general-purpose, MIPS R3000 processors that run at 25 MHz. Figures 10 and 11 show performance results with four protein models. The performance (seconds per update) includes the time to receive a user tug, run an iteration of the constrained minimization, and re-display the screen. All calculations use double-precision floating-point arithmetic. The data on near-neighbor interactions show the performance with and without a new neighbor list determined on each iteration (most batch molecular modeling systems create a new list every few iterations). The *Interactions* column lists the average number of interactions per iteration.

The models include (1) the medium-size protein in Figure 2, (2) two of the four helices from that model, (3) a segment of ten residues, and (4) a small segment with four residues. The variable field equals the number of atoms times three (a three-dimensional coordinate). All data sets model bond lengths, bond angles, and single-value dihedral angles with constraints and model multi-value dihedral angles with energy functions. Data sets (1) and (2) also contain hydrogen bonds (a weak attraction between nearby atoms, far along the backbone) modeled with length and angle springs.

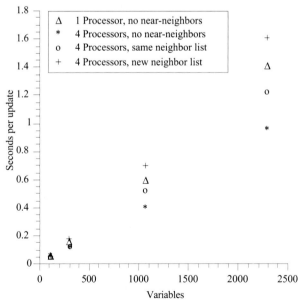

Figure 11: Plot showing linear increase in computation with model size.

Sculpt contains display, user interface, and minimization modules written in C++ [18]. Only five percent of the total code is specific to molecular modeling. That code evaluates the near-neighbor potential energy given a list of neighboring atoms and parses optional, protein-specific input.

The input file specifies a protein as a list of three-dimensional points with functions defined among them. Figure 12 shows the input for one amino acid residue. Beside each point are optional fields specifying protein-specific information used in near-neighbor calculations. A sequence of functions appears after the list of points. Each function contains the points that define it, the ideal value, and energy constant. This format lets a chemist choose their energy model and parameters (e.g. from [4] or [23]). The energy constant is ignored if, at program initialization, a user constrains them to their ideal value.

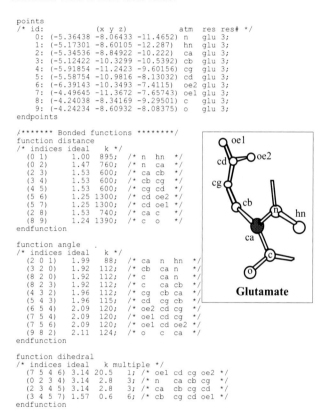

Figure 12: Input file specifying atom positions and topology for a glutamate residue.

The update rates, though far from those needed for smooth interaction, allow productive new research in biochemistry. Professors David and Jane Richardson, collaborators from Duke University's Department of Biochemistry, use a preliminary version of *Sculpt* for *de novo* design of proteins. They believe *Sculpt* improves productivity and understanding over previous molecular modeling systems [19, 20]. Maintaining a physically-valid model throughout a modeling session relieves the user from the time-consuming task of returning the model to a physically-valid state. Immediately viewing the effect of an atom movement provides better awareness of intricate interactions among atoms.

10. Future Work

With faster machines, *Sculpt* could model long-distance electrostatic interactions at interactive rates. These interactions are commonly modeled between atoms within a ten Ångstrom neighborhood (approximately sixty-five percent longer than the current radius). The number of atoms in the neighborhood is still bounded, so the linear complexity remains valid. However, the larger radius yields substantially more interactions which destroys interactivity on a 240-GTX.

The number of functions and variables limits *Sculpt's* interactive performance on current graphics workstations to medium-size proteins. An area for future research is to reduce the number of functions and variables by using rigid and deformable bodies. A rigid object with few variables could replace large segments of a model that a user does not want to change. For example, a user could twist a backbone into a helix and then freeze the helix by replacing its atoms and bonds with a cylinder of rigid shape but movable position.

The bottleneck in the minimization algorithm is the solution of linear equations. With four processors, approximately fifty percent of the time in model (1) is used to solve the linear equations. Two approaches can significantly reduce this bottleneck. First, an iterative method, such as Gauss-Seidel or Conjugate Gradient [12], should converge to a solution faster than direct Gaussian elimination. Iterative methods can reduce the average computation but cannot reduce the linear complexity. Second, the constrained minimization can use a different Lagrange multiplier estimation that does not require solving a system of equations. A zero-order method estimates the Lagrange multipliers using previous values of the constraints rather than the first-order information contained in the Jacobian [7]. A zero-order estimator, in practice, does not make as accurate a prediction as the first-order method, so the constrained minimization algorithm requires more iterations. However, the estimation can execute in parallel. A constrained minimizer using a zero-order estimator may run significantly faster on a massively-parallel machine than the current implementation.

Acknowledgements

Professors David and Jane Richardson of Duke University conceived the idea of interactively sculpting proteins. I thank them for continued guidance and encouragement. I thank Professor Frederick Brooks for useful critiques about the research and the manuscript. This work is supported by NIH National Center for Research Resources grant RR-02170.

References

1. Akeley, K. and Jermoluk, T. High-Performance Polygon Rendering. *Computer Graphics. 22*, 4 (1988), 239-246.

2. Bentley, J. L. and Friedman, J. H. Data Structures for Range Searching. *Computing Surveys. 11*, 4 (1979), 397-409.

3. *Insight.* Biosym Technologies Inc., 1991.

4. Brooks, B. R., Bruccoleri, R. E., Olafson, B. D., States, D. J., Swaminathan, S. and Karplus, M. CHARMM: A Program for Macromolecular Energy, Minimization, and Dynamics Calculations. *Journal of Computational Chemistry. 4*, 2 (1983), 187-217.

5. Duff, I. S., Erisman, A. M. and Reid, J. K. *Direct Methods for Sparse Matrices.* Clarendon Press, Oxford, 1986.

6. Fletcher, R. *Practical Methods of Optimization.* John Wiley and Sons, 1987.

7. Gill, P., Murray, W. and Wright, M. *Practical Optimization.* Academic Press, 1981.

8. Hecht, M. H., Richardson, J. S., Richardson, D. C. and Ogden, R. C. De Novo Design, Expression, and Characterization of Felix: A Four-Helix Bundle Protein of Native-Like Sequence. *Science. 249*, 4964 (1990), 884-891.

9. Hestenes, M. R. *Optimization Theory, The Finite Dimensional Case.* John Wiley and Sons, New York, 1975.

10. Knuth, D. E. *Fundamental Algorithms, The Art of Computer Programming.* Addison-Wesley, 1973.

11. Levinthal, C. Molecular Model-building by Computer. *Scientific American. 214*, 6 (1966).

12. Luenberger, D. G. *Introduction to Linear and Nonlinear Programming.* Addison-Wesley, 1973.

13. Pentland, A. and Williams, J. Good Vibrations: Modal Dynamics for Graphics and Animation. *Computer Graphics. 23*, 3 (1989), 215-222.

14. Platt, J. *Constraint Methods for Neural Networks and Computer Graphics.* Ph.D. Dissertation, California Institute of Technology, 1989.

15. Platt, J. and Barr, A. Constraint Methods for Flexible Models. *Computer Graphics. 22*, 4 (1988), 279-288.

16. *Quanta.* Polygen Corporation, 1991.

17. Schulz, G. E. and Schirmer, R. H. *Principles of Protein Structure.* Springer-Verlag, New York, 1979.

18. Stroustrup, B. *The C++ Programming Language.* Addison-Wesley, 1986.

19. Surles, M. Interactive Modeling Enhanced with Constraints and Physics—With Applications in Molecular Modeling. *Symposium on Interactive 3D Graphics. 26*, 2 (1992), 175-182.

20. Surles, M. *Techniques For Interactive Manipulation of Graphical Protein Models.* Ph.D. Dissertation, University of North Carolina at Chapel Hill, 1992.

21. Terzopoulos, D. and Fleischer, K. Modeling Inelastic Deformation: Viscoelasticity, Plasticity, Fracture. *Computer Graphics. 22*, 4 (1988), 269-278.

22. *Sybyl.* Tripos Associates, 1988.

23. Weiner, S. J., Kollman, P. A., Case, D. A., Singh, C., Ghio, C., Alagona, G., Profeta, S. and Weiner, P. A New Force Field for Molecular Mechanical Simulation of Nucleic Acids and Proteins. *Journal of the American Chemical Society. 106*, (1984), 765-784.

24. Witkin, A., Gleicher, M. and Welch, W. Interactive Dynamics. *Symposium on Interactive 3D Graphics. 24*, 2 (1990), 11-21.

25. Witkin, A. and Welch, W. Fast Animation and Control of Nonrigid Structures. *Computer Graphics. 24*, 4 (1990), 243-252.

PixelFlow: High-Speed Rendering Using Image Composition

Steven Molnar, John Eyles, John Poulton

Department of Computer Science
University of North Carolina
Chapel Hill, NC 27599-3175

ABSTRACT

We describe PixelFlow, an architecture for high-speed image generation that overcomes the transformation- and frame-buffer–access bottlenecks of conventional hardware rendering architectures. PixelFlow uses the technique of image composition: it distributes the rendering task over an array of identical renderers, each of which computes a full-screen image of a fraction of the primitives. A high-performance image-composition network composites these images in real time to produce an image of the entire scene.

Image-composition architectures offer performance that scales linearly with the number of renderers; there is no fundamental limit to the maximum performance achievable using this approach. A single PixelFlow renderer rasterizes up to 1.4 million triangles per second, and an *n*-renderer system can rasterize at up to *n* times this basic rate.

PixelFlow performs antialiasing by supersampling. It supports deferred shading with separate hardware shaders that operate on composited images containing intermediate pixel data. PixelFlow shaders compute complex shading algorithms and procedural and image-based textures in real-time. The shading rate is independent of scene complexity. A PixelFlow system can be coupled to a parallel supercomputer to serve as an immediate-mode graphics server, or it can maintain a display list for retained-mode rendering.

The PixelFlow design has been simulated extensively at high level. Custom chip design is underway. We anticipate a working system by late 1993.

CR Categories and Subject Descriptors: C.1.2 [Processor Architectures]: Multiprocessors; C.5.4 [Computer System Implementation]: VLSI Systems; I.3.1 [Computer Graphics]: Hardware Architecture; I.3.3 [Computer Graphics]: Picture/Image Generation; I.3.7 [Computer Graphics]: Three-Dimensional Graphics and Realism.

Additional Keywords and Phrases: antialiasing, compositing, deferred shading, rendering, scalable.

1 INTRODUCTION

Graphics applications such as flight and vehicle simulation, computer-aided design, scientific visualization, and virtual reality demand high-quality rendering, high polygon rates, and high frame rates. Existing commercial systems render at peak rates up to 2 million polygons per second (*e.g.*, Silicon Graphics' SkyWriter and Hewlett-Packard's VRX). If antialiasing or realistic shading or texturing is required, however, their performance falls by an order of magnitude.

To support demanding applications, future graphics systems must generate high-resolution images of datasets containing hundreds of thousands or millions of primitives, with realistic rendering techniques such as Phong shading, antialiasing, and texturing, at high frame rates (≥ 30 Hz) and with low latency.

Attempts to achieve high performance levels encounter two bottlenecks: inadequate floating-point performance for geometry processing and insufficient memory bandwidth to the frame buffer [FOLE90]. For example, to render a scene with 100,000 polygons updated at 30 Hz, geometry processing requires approximately 350 million floating-point operations per second, and rasterization requires approximately 750 million integer operations and 450 million frame-buffer accesses.[1] Parallel solutions are mandatory.

Most current high-performance architectures use object-parallelism for geometry processing; they distribute primitives over a parallel array of floating-point processors, which perform transformation, clipping, and perspective division [ELLS90; MART90; SGI90].

The same systems use pixel-parallelism for rasterization; frame-buffer memory is divided into several interleaved partitions, each with its own rasterization processor. [AKEL88; APGA88; POTM89]. This multiplies the effective frame-buffer bandwidth by the number of partitions, but does not reduce the number of primitives each processor must handle, since most primitives contribute to most partitions [FUCH79]. Because of this limitation, and the bandwidth limitations of commercial VRAMs, this approach does not scale much beyond today's rates of a few million polygons per second.

---

[1] Assumes 50-pixel Gouraud-shaded connected triangles; 3/4 of pixels initially visible; includes screen clear for 1280x1024 display.

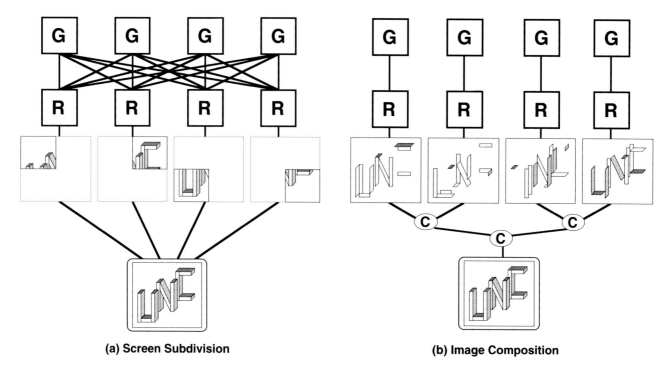

(a) Screen Subdivision   **(b) Image Composition**

Figure 1: Rasterization methods that combine both pixel-and object-parallel rasterization (G = geometry processor, R = rasterizer, and C = pixel compositor).

To achieve higher rendering performance, object-parallelism must be applied throughout the rendering process—in rasterization, as well as in geometry processing. There appear to be two ways to achieve this: *screen subdivision* and *image composition*. The two schemes are shown conceptually in Figure 1.

In the screen-subdivision approach (introduced in [FUCH77] and [PARK80]), the screen is divided into disjoint regions of contiguous pixels, and a rasterization processor is provided for each region (Figure 1a). The processors simultaneously rasterize primitives that fall into different screen regions. These sub-images are concatenated to form a full-screen image. Several systems of this type have been described [GARD81; GHAR88] and one built [FUCH89].

This approach is a natural advance from a simple rendering system in which a single geometry processor feeds a single rasterizer. Its main additional requirement is a global routing network to transfer primitives from geometry processors to the appropriate rasterizer. Since the mapping of primitives to rasterizers varies with the viewing transformation, every primitive in the database must be transferred over the network every frame. The network bandwidth is therefore high, and increases linearly with the rendering rate, so the approach does not scale indefinitely.

A second limitation, also due to the global routing network, is the software complexity required to sort primitives by screen region and to route them to rasterizers at the appropriate time. Finally, the architecture is subject to load imbalances when primitives clump into a few screen regions. System performance can decrease significantly in this case.

In the image-composition approach, rasterization processors are associated with a portion of the primitives, rather than with a portion of the screen (Figure 1b). Each rasterizer computes a full-screen image of its portion of the primitives, and these images are composited, based on visibility, to form a final image.

In an image-composition architecture, geometry processors and rasterizers can be paired into self-contained units, so the global routing network for primitives disappears. Instead, an image-composition network is required to composite output pixels from the rasterizers to form the final image. This network can be arranged as a binary tree or a pipeline; in either case, all traffic is local, with fixed bandwidth determined by frame rate and screen size. This gives the architecture its property of linear scalability.[2]

The remainder of this paper explores the opportunities and limitations of the image-composition approach. Section 2 discusses image-composition architectures in general. Section 3 introduces PixelFlow, an image-composition architecture that achieves linearly scalable rendering performance and supports high-quality rendering. Sections 4 and 5 describe its major hardware and software components. Section 6 discusses performance issues and presents simulated performance results.

2 IMAGE COMPOSITION ARCHITECTURES

Image composition has been used in various forms for many years, particularly in the video industry (*e.g.,* video overlays and chroma-key) and the computer graphics community (*e.g.,* for off-line compositing of rendered images).

---

[2]A third method, closely related to image composition, is to provide separate rendering pipelines for multiple image frames. This technique, used in SGI's SkyWriter, multiplies a system's rendering rate and frame rate by the number of rendering pipelines, but does not improve its latency over that of a single pipeline.

Several graphics architectures based on image composition have been proposed. Processor-per-primitive graphics systems are a simple type of image-composition architecture. [BUNK89] describes one such system, General Electric's 1967 NASA II flight simulator. In the NASA II system, polygons (faces) in the database were assigned to individual processors (face cards). Each face card rendered an image of its respective face, and the results were composited using a static priority scheme.

Later researchers proposed using z-values to determine the image priority at individual pixels [DEME80; FUSS82]. [WEIN81] proposed an antialiasing scheme for a processor-per-primitive system. [DEER88] and [SCHN88] proposed deferred shading as a way to support high-quality shading in a processor-per-primitive system. [ELLI91] describes a processor-per-primitive system specialized for CSG rendering, which was built at Duke University and UNC.

A few image-composition architectures with multi-primitive renderers have been proposed: [SHAW88] described a simplified version of Duff's compositing algorithm [DUFF85] cast in VLSI to create a multi-renderer system that performs antialiasing. [MOLN88] proposed a simple z-buffer image-composition scheme to achieve linearly scalable rendering performance; this idea was expanded into a dissertation on image-composition architectures [MOLN91b], which also describes an early version of the PixelFlow architecture.

2.1 Advantages and Disadvantages

Image-composition offers two potential advantages over other architectural approaches: linear scalability and a simple programming model. An arbitrary number of renderers can be added to the system, since the image-composition network has only local traffic with fixed bandwidth determined by screen size and frame rate. Also, since renderers compute their sub-images independently, they can operate with little synchronization. This makes the parallel nature of the system largely transparent to the programmer.

Image-composition architectures have several disadvantages, however. First, the image-composition network must support very high bandwidth communication between renderers. Even though the bandwidth is fixed, the network must transfer every pixel during every frame, and each pixel must include visibility information and color (and possibly even more data, if deferred shading is used). Second, pixels must be reduced to a common format for compositing, so the visibility algorithm is more restrictive than in some other approaches. Finally, up to a frame of pixel storage is required per renderer, if an entire frame is buffered before being composited; fortunately, this storage requirement can be reduced, as we will see in Section 3.

2.2 Antialiasing

Aliasing artifacts, once ubiquitous in interactive systems, are tolerated less and less each year. Future real-time systems must provide ways to reduce or eliminate these artifacts. There appear to be two ways to combat aliasing in image-composition systems: supersampling, and A-buffer algorithms [MOLN91b]. In the supersampling approach, the image is generated and composited multiple times, once for each sample in a filter kernel. The compositors perform a simple z comparison for each subpixel; then subpixels are blended together after composition to form a final image. In the A-buffer approach, each pixel is represented by a variable-length packet describing all surfaces potentially visible at the pixel. Compositors merge packets together based on visibility and coverage information. The output of the network describes all of the surfaces contributing to each pixel, and this information is used to compute the pixel's final color.

In comparing the two approaches, the critical factors are image quality, image-composition bandwidth, and hardware complexity. Supersampling produces good results, provided that sufficient samples are taken per pixel. Unfortunately, the number of samples directly affects the bandwidth required of the image-composition network; however, we have produced reasonable-quality images with as few as 5 samples per pixel by choosing sample locations and weights carefully [MOLN91a].

Only the simplest A-buffer methods are feasible in current real-time systems. These methods generally sample color and z values at pixel centers only, while calculating pixel coverage at higher resolution. This can lead to artifacts. To avoid these artifacts, additional information must be added to the surface descriptors; the result is that the two approaches require comparable bandwidth. In terms of hardware complexity, A-buffer renderers and compositors are fairly complex, while the z-depth compositors for supersampling are very simple. The A-buffer approach supports true transparency, however, which is problematic in the supersampling approach.

2.3 Deferred Shading

Image-composition architectures can take special advantage of *deferred shading*, a general method for reducing the calculations required for complex shading models by factoring them out of the rasterization step [DEER88; ELLS91]. Many shading calculations depend only on geometric and intrinsic attributes, such as surface-normal vectors and surface color. If these attributes are calculated and stored during rasterization, shading can be deferred until the entire scene has been rasterized, and applied only to the surfaces that are visible.

To defer shading in an image-composition system, rasterizers compute generic pixel attributes and composite these, rather than pixel colors. A separate hardware unit performs shading *after* pixels have been composited. In this manner, shading is performed just once per pixel, no matter how many surfaces contribute to it and how many rasterizers are in the system. Deferred shading does increase image-composition bandwidth, however, since the number of bits per pixel is generally higher.

Deferred shading also separates performance concerns between the rendering and shading portions of the machine. Renderers can be built to rasterize as fast as possible, and the number of renderers can be chosen to achieve a given polygon rate. Shading performance is independent of the rasterizing performance of the system, but most be high enough to support the desired shading model.

3 PIXELFLOW ARCHITECTURAL OVERVIEW

PixelFlow is an experimental graphics system designed to demonstrate the advantages of image-composition architectures and to provide a research platform for real-time 3D graphics algorithms and applications. In this section we describe its major architectural features and the rationale under which they were chosen. Section 4 provides details of system components.

Supersampling antialiasing. PixelFlow uses the supersampling approach because it is general, the compositor hardware is simple, and therefore fast, and it can be tuned to trade speed for image quality. This leads to renderers based on z-buffer rasterizers and a z-based image-composition network. Unfortunately, this requires screen-door or multi-pass algorithms to support transparency.

Pipelined image-composition network. Generating Gouraud-shaded, supersampled, high-resolution images at 30 Hz frame rates requires composition-network bandwidth of at least 1280x1024 pixels • 5 samples/pixel • 48 bits/sample • 30 frames/second = 9.4 Gbits/second. Deferred shading algorithms require 2 to 3 times this amount.

Packaging considerations favor a pipeline image-composition network. The image-composition network can be distributed across the system by including a compositor on each board and daisy-chaining connections between boards.

Logic-enhanced memory rasterizer. The renderer should a single-board design, must provide a way to scan out pixels at the bandwidth required, and should implement the compositor function at relatively low cost in board area, power, and dollars. These considerations mainly affect the design of the rasterizer.

The logic-enhanced memory approach used in Pixel-Planes 5 allows a powerful rasterizer and high-bandwidth compositor to be built in a single, compact package. In PixelFlow, we use a similar logic-enhanced memory approach. A rasterizer built with new PixelFlow enhanced-memory chips (EMCs) can render in excess of one million triangles per second and provide image-composition bandwidth exceeding 30 Gbits/second using 64 custom memory chips and one custom controller on about 50 square inches of board area.

Region-based rendering scheme. The compactness of this approach is obtained at the cost of introducing screen subdivision at the level of the individual renderers. As in Pixel-Planes 5, each rasterizer contains only 128x128 pixel processors, and must generate a full-screen image in multiple steps. The advantage is that an entire screen's worth of pixel memory is not required. Unfortunately, this implementation incurs the load-balancing problems of screen subdivision, but these difficulties are greatly reduced by providing several region's worth of buffering within the PixelFlow EMCs.

The required image-composition bandwidth is achieved in two ways. First, the network operates bit-serially, but in parallel on 256 pixels, each with its own single-wire channel. Bit-serial z-comparison simplifies the compositors and thereby allows them to operate at high speed. Second, the network consists entirely of point-to-point communication between identical custom chips on neighboring boards, so low voltage swings and source termination can be used to save power and provide the necessary speed (132 MHz) [KNIG88].

Separate shaders for deferred shading. Deferred shading algorithms, such as Phong shading and procedural and image-based textures, are implemented on separate hardware *shaders* that reside just ahead of the frame buffer. Regions of pixels, containing attributes such as intrinsic color, surface normals, and texture coordinates are rasterized on the renderers, composited on the image-composition network, and loaded into the shaders. Shaders operate on entire regions in parallel, to convert raw pixel attributes into final RGB values, blend multiple samples together for antialiasing, and forward final color values to the frame buffer.

Regions are assigned to shaders in round-robin fashion. The number of shaders required depends on the shading algorithm only, not on the number of primitives, since deferred shading is employed.

The SIMD rasterizer used in the renderer is an ideal processor for deferred shading, since shading calculations can be performed for all pixels simultaneously. Therefore, the shaders can simply be designated renderers, with a slight enhancement of the compositor hardware on the EMC to allow bidirectional data transfers between the image-composition network and EMC memory. Shaders can be augmented with additional hardware to allow them to compute image-based textures in addition to procedural textures.

4   PIXELFLOW HARDWARE

A PixelFlow system is composed of one or more card cages, each containing up to 20 circuit boards. The backplane contains wiring for the image-composition network and clock and power distribution. The system is modular and can be configured with any number of card cages. Each board has a high-speed link connecting it to a host computer. Figure 2 shows a block diagram of a PixelFlow system.

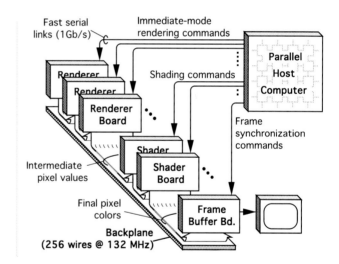

Figure 2:   Block diagram of a PixelFlow system.

Renderers operate by sequentially processing 128x128-pixel regions of the screen. They scan out the region's rasterized pixels over the image-composition network in synchrony with the other renderers. Shaders load pixels from the image-composition network, perform texturing and shading, blend subpixel samples, and forward pixel values to the frame buffer.

The system is designed to be used in one of two basic modes:

1) *Immediate Mode.* PixelFlow is hosted by a parallel computer, with each link connected to a separate compute node in the host. The host (*e.g.*, an Intel Touchstone) runs an application and generates immediate-mode primitives, which are transmitted to renderers over the links.

2) *Retained Mode.* PixelFlow is hosted by a workstation; the high-speed links are bussed together and connected to the host via a single interface. The host distributes a display

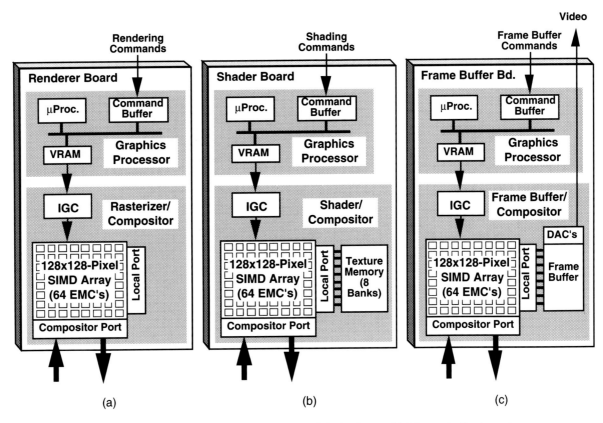

Figure 3: Block diagrams of (a) renderer, (b) shader, and (c) frame-buffer boards.

list over the renderers and loads a shading model into the shaders. On each frame, the host broadcasts editing commands and viewing parameters to the renderers, each of which then computes an image of its fraction of the dataset.

Each of the primary board types (renderers, shaders, and frame buffers) includes a core consisting of a geometry processor and a rasterizer built from the new EMC chips. These core elements have different function on the three board types, and shaders and frame buffers contain additional components (Figure 3).

4.1 Image-Composition Network

The image-composition network is a wide (256-bit), high-speed (132 MHz) special-purpose communication network for rapidly moving pixel data between boards. It is distributed across the EMCs on each board, with each EMC implementing a 4-bit-wide slice (4 input pins and 4 output pins). Compositors on the EMCs synchronously transmit data unidirectionally to the compositors on the downstream board.

Compositor modes. The basic unit of operation is the transfer of one 128x128-pixel region of pixel data; the amount of data transferred per pixel is preset according to the specific algorithm. The compositors operate in one of four modes, as shown in Figure 4.

4.2 Renderer

The renderer block diagram is shown in Figure 3a. Its major components are:

Geometry processor. The geometry processor is a fast floating-point processor that retains a portion of a distributed display list (retained mode) or receives a fraction of the primitives from the host on each frame (immediate mode). It transforms its portion of the primitives into screen coordinates, sorts them by screen region, and passes them to the rasterizer. It contains 8 MBytes of VRAM memory, serving both as main memory and as a large FIFO queue for buffering commands to the rasterizer. A DMA engine controls the flow of commands from the VRAMs' serial port to the rasterizer, maintaining separate queues of commands for rasterization and for transfers over the image-composition network.

Rasterizer. The rasterizer is a 128x128 SIMD processor array implemented with 64 PixelFlow EMCs driven by instructions and data broadcast from an Image Generation Controller (IGC) ASIC.

The PixelFlow EMC (Figure 5) is similar to our previous designs [EYLE88; POUL85]. A *linear expression evaluator* computes values of the bilinear expression $Ax+By+C$ at every pixel processor in parallel (x,y is the pixel processor's screen location and A, B, and C are user-specified). Each pixel has a small local ALU that performs arithmetic and logical operations on local memory and on the local value of the bilinear expression. Operation of the pixel processors is SIMD (single-instruction-multiple-data), and all processors operate on data items at the same address. Each pixel processor includes an *enable* register which qualifies writes to memory, so that a subset of the processors can be disabled for certain operations (*e.g.* painting a scan-converted polygon).

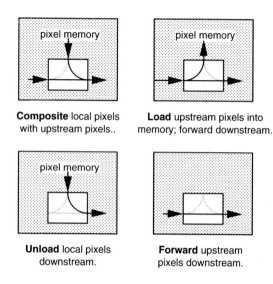

Composite local pixels with upstream pixels..

Load upstream pixels into memory; forward downstream.

Unload local pixels downstream.

Forward upstream pixels downstream.

Figure 4: Compositor operating modes.

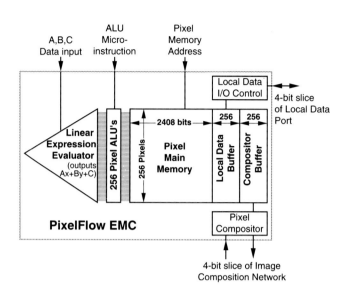

Figure 5: Block diagram of PixelFlow Enhanced Memory Chip.

Several features distinguish the PixelFlow EMC from our previous designs:

- **Higher clock speed.** The new EMC, fabricated on a 0.8μ CMOS process, operates at 66 MHz for image-generation operations; its image-composition port transmits data at 132 MHz.

- **8-bit processors.** The pixel processors, linear expression evaluator, and memory bus for each pixel are eight bits wide, rather than bit-serial. This increases the performance for many operations by nearly a factor of eight.

- **Fast multiply hardware.** Pixel processors include hardware support for multiplies, allowing 16-bit multiplies to be performed in less than a microsecond—a total of 19 billion multiplies per second for a 128x128-pixel array. This feature accelerates multiply-intensive shading calculations.

- **2048+ bits per pixel.** The memory design uses a 1-transistor dynamic memory cell [SPEC91], rather than the 6-transistor static memory cell used previously. Memory per pixel can be increased to 2048 bits, plus two 256-bit communication buffers.

- **Compositor and local-access ports.** The PixelFlow EMC contains two communication ports, one for the image-composition network, and one for communicating with texture memory or a frame buffer. Each port contains a 256-bit buffer of pixel memory that can be read or written by the pixel ALU or decoupled from it during port operation. The local-port connects to external texture memory (on a shader board) or a VRAM frame store (on a frame-buffer board) through a custom datapath ASIC.

The IGC is a single custom ASIC which controls the rasterizer array. It converts floating-point A, B, and C coefficients into byte-serial, fixed-point form; it sequences EMC operations by broadcasting data, control, and address information to the EMC array; and it controls the compositor ports on the EMCs.

The IGC contains a subpixel offset register that allows the multiple samples of the supersampling filter kernel to be computed from the same set of rasterization commands, by repeatedly reading these commands from VRAM memory. This improves system performance when supersampling, since additional samples are rasterized without increasing the load on the geometry processor. As a result, a single i860XP geometry processor can keep up with the rasterizer when supersampling with 6 or more samples per pixel.

4.3 Shader

The shader (Figure 3b), like the renderer, contains a geometry processor, rasterizer, and compositor. The shader's geometry processor is merely a control processor which passes shading commands to the rasterizer. The rasterizer is used as a SIMD shading processor, computing lighting and shading models for all pixels in a region in parallel. The compositors are used to load composited regions and unload fully-shaded pixels.

The local communication port of the EMCs is connected to external memory that contains image-based textures (such as Mip-maps). Multiple banks of texture memory, each holding an identical copy of the texture data, are required to match the performance of the shader to that of the image-composition network. The shader supports general table-lookup operations, so it can perform related functions such as bump mapping, environment mapping, and image warping. The shader can be loaded with an image, from which it computes a Mip-map that can then be loaded into texture memory. These algorithms will be described in a future publication.

4.4 Frame Buffer

The frame buffer (Figure 3c) closely resembles the shader, but in place of texture storage, it contains a separate double-buffered VRAM frame buffer. The frame buffer board is itself a complete, fairly powerful, self-contained graphics system, since it also contains the core elements (geometry processor and rasterizer).

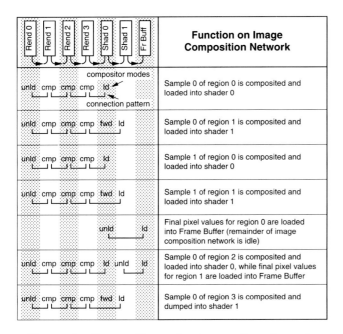

	Function on Image Composition Network
compositor modes unld cmp cmp cmp ld connection pattern	Sample 0 of region 0 is composited and loaded into shader 0
unld cmp cmp cmp fwd ld	Sample 0 of region 1 is composited and loaded into shader 1
unld cmp cmp cmp ld	Sample 1 of region 0 is composited and loaded into shader 0
unld cmp cmp cmp fwd ld	Sample 1 of region 1 is composited and loaded into shader 1
unld ld	Final pixel values for region 0 are loaded into Frame Buffer (remainder of image composition network is idle)
unld cmp cmp cmp ld unld ld	Sample 0 of region 2 is composited and loaded into shader 0, while final pixel values for region 1 are loaded into Frame Buffer
unld cmp cmp cmp fwd ld	Sample 0 of region 3 is composited and dumped into shader 1

Figure 6: Composition network operations for a 4-renderer, 2-shader system computing an image with 2-sample-per-pixel antialiasing.

5   SOFTWARE

PixelFlow software consists of two parts: rendering software, which transforms primitives and produces rasterization/shading commands for the rasterizer, and control software, which sequences region-by-region operations. Both sets of software run on the geometry processor of each system board.

Geometric transformations are performed using standard algorithms, and rasterization and shading are performed using the algorithms developed for Pixel-Planes 4 and 5 [FUCH85; FUCH89].

The basic control algorithm to compute an image contains four steps:

1)   The geometry processor on each renderer transforms its portion of the primitives and sorts them by 128x128-pixel regions on the screen.

2)   The rasterizer computes pixel values for all primitives in a region and for one sample of the antialiasing kernel.

3)   When all renderers have finished step (2), the region is composited over the image-composition network and deposited into one of the shaders.

4)   Steps (2) and (3) are repeated for each sample and for each region on the screen. These steps can be pipelined (i.e. one region/sample is rasterized while the previous one is composited).

Transfers over the image-composition network are the only operations that require tight synchronization between boards. A hardware token chain determines when all of the boards are ready to begin each transfer. Figure 6 shows the sequence of composition network operations in a 4-renderer, 2-shader system computing an image with 2-sample-per-pixel antialiasing.

The large amount of pixel memory on the EMCs allows several regions of pixels to be buffered before they are composited. This is important for load balancing, since different numbers of primitives may fall into a given region on different renderers (see Section 6). To take full advantage of this buffering, regions are processed in a scattered pattern, since neighboring regions tend to have similar over- or underloads; successive samples of a given region are never handled sequentially.

6   PERFORMANCE

The performance of a PixelFlow system is governed by four basic parameters:

- **Image-Composition Network bandwidth.** Gross bandwidth = 256 bits • 132 MHz = 33.8 GBits/sec. Net bandwidth (assuming 10% synchronization overhead) = 30 GBits/sec.

- **Geometry processor performance.** A single i860XP microprocessor can process approximately 150,000 triangles per second, independent of the number of samples per pixel.

- **Rasterizer performance.** A 64-EMC rasterizer can process approximately 1.4 million Gouraud-shaded triangles per second and 0.8 million Phong-shaded, textured triangles per second, but this rate must be divided by the number of samples per pixel.

- **Shader Performance.** A single shader can Phong-shade and compute procedural textures for approximately 10,000 128x128-pixel regions per second. It can compute Mipmap textures for approximately 3,700 regions per second.

The following expression can be used to estimate system performance given the performance above:

$$T_{frame} = \sum_{i=1}^{N_{regions}} \max\left(T_{rend_i}, T_{comp}, T_{shade} / N_{shaders} \right)$$

where

T_{rend_i} = $\max(T_{geom_i}, T_{rast_i})$ (the rendering time for $Region_i$)

T_{comp} = compositing time for a region (128^2 pixels • bits per pixel / 30 GBits/sec)

T_{shade} = time to shade a region (approx. 270 μsec for Phong shading and texturing)

If antialiasing is done, the summation is over all regions and over all antialiasing samples.

This equation says that the frame time is given by the sum of the times required to compute each region, and that each region time is given by the maximum of the geometry processing/rasterization time, image composition time, and shading time for the region. Both T_{comp} and T_{shade} are constants, for a given rendering algorithm. T_{rend_i} varies depending on the number of renderers, the number of primitives, and their distribution over the renderers and over the screen.

T_{comp} provides an upper bound on frame rate, as shown in Figure 7 for several rendering algorithms and system configurations.

Bits per pixel	Samples	Screen	Frame/sec
64 (Gouraud)	16	1280x1024	22
96 (Phong)	1	1280x1024	>100
96 (Phong)	5	1280x1024	48
192 (Phong, textured)	5	1280x1024	24
192 (Phong, textured)	16	640x512	29

Figure 7: Peak performance dictated by composition-network bandwidth under varying conditions.

Actual system performance can be lower than predicted by this equation because of several factors: First, primitives may cross region boundaries and require processing in multiple regions. This increases the rasterization load by approximately 20% for 100-pixel polygons. Second, primitives may clump in different screen regions on different renderers. This increases the rasterization time on certain renderers relative to others. The extra buffering on the EMCs reduces this effect, but does not eliminate it entirely. For severely clumped images, system performance can be reduced from 20-60%. Finally, rasterization and compositing are pipelined, so that one region is rasterized while the previous one is composited. This requires a few idle region times at the start and end of a frame (approximately 5–10% overhead).

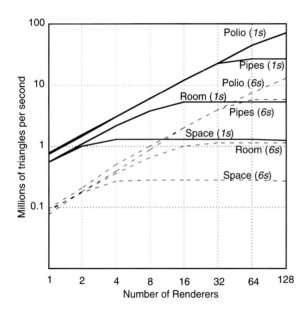

Figure 8: Simulated performance for various system configurations.

Because these factors are scene dependent, they cannot be modelled analytically. We have written a timing simulator for PixelFlow that models these effects and have used it to compute performance for a variety of images and rendering algorithms. Figure 8 shows simulated performance for the four sample

databases shown in Figure 9. Simulations were run with 1 to 128 renderers and 4 shaders. Two curves are shown for each dataset: one for a supersampled image with 6 samples per pixel (*6s*), and one for a "fully-aliased" image with one sample per pixel (*1s*). For the *6s* case, we assumed the geometry processor is a 66-MHz i860XP; for the *1s* case, we assumed that a sufficiently powerful geometry processor is available so that renderer performance is rasterizer-limited.

These simulated results show the behavior predicted by the equation above. System performance scales linearly with the number of renderers until a knee is reached, where compositing time dominates rasterization time (shading time is not a limiting factor for any of these datasets). The space station dataset, in particular, is very small (3,784 primitives), so this knee is reached at only 4 renderers. Only the polio dataset is large enough to show linear scalability to 128 renderers.

7 CONCLUSIONS

We have introduced PixelFlow, a new architecture for high-speed image generation, and one of the first to use real-time image composition with multi-primitive renderers. Its combination of million-triangle-per-second renderers and high-performance compositing network give it linearly scalable performance to tens of millions of polygons per second— far above the performance of current systems.

All of the components of PixelFlow are programmable: its geometry processors are conventional microprocessors; its rasterizers are programmable SIMD processors; its image-composition network is a general pixel datapath. In addition to standard rendering algorithms, such as Gouraud- and Phong-shading of polygonal primitives, PixelFlow can render primitives such as spheres, quadrics, and volume data with high-quality shading methods, such as local light sources, procedural and image-based texturing, and environment mapping.

A PixelFlow system can be configured in a variety of ways. Hosted by a single workstation, it can render PHIGS-type retained-mode datasets. Coupled to a parallel supercomputer, it can serve as a visualization subsystem for immediate-mode rendering. Using PixelFlow silicon, a million-triangle-per-second rasterizer could be built on a small circuit board.

At the time this paper was written, logic design for the custom chips was nearly complete. We anticipate completing circuit design for the system by mid-1993 and completing a prototype system by late 1993.

ACKNOWLEDGEMENTS

We acknowledge the following people for their suggestions and contributions to this work: Henry Fuchs, Turner Whitted, Anselmo Lastra, Jon Leech, Brice Tebbs, Trey Greer, Lee Westover, and the entire Pixel-Planes team.

This research is supported in part by the Defense Advanced Research Projects Agency, DARPA ISTO Order No. 7510, and the National Science Foundation, Grant No. MIP-9000894.

(a) Space station and space shuttle, Phong-shaded, 6,549 triangles (Don Eyles, Charles Stark Draper Labs).

(b) Radiosity-shaded room interior with procedural textures, 53,514 triangles (F.P. Brooks, A. Varshney, UNC).

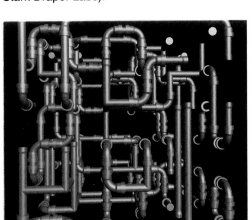

(c) Procedurally generated pipes model, Phong-shaded, 137,747 triangles (Lee Westover, Sun Microsystems).

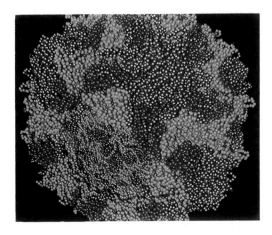

(d) Poliovirus molecule, Phong-shaded, 389,819 triangles (J. Hogle, M. Chow, D. Filman, Scripps Institute).

Figure 9: Four sample datasets used for timing simulation.

REFERENCES

AKEL88 Akeley, K. and T. Jermoluk, "High-Performance Polygon Rendering," *SIGGRAPH '88*, Vol. 22, No. 4, pp. 239–246.

APGA88 Apgar, B., B. Bersack, and A. Mammen, "A Display System for the Stellar Graphics Supercomputer Model GS1000," *SIGGRAPH '88*, Vol. 22, No. 4, pp. 255–262.

BUNK89 Bunker, M. and R. Economy, "Evolution of GE CIG Systems," *SCSD Document*, General Electric Company, Daytona Beach, FL 32015, 1989.

DEER88 Deering, M., S. Winner, B. Schediwy, C. Duffy, and N. Hunt, "The Triangle Processor and Normal Vector Shader: A VLSI System for High Performance Graphics," *SIGGRAPH '88*, Vol. 22, No. 4, pp. 21–30.

DEME80 Demetrescu, S., *A VLSI-Based Real-Time Hidden-Surface Elimination Display System*, Master's Thesis, Dept. of Computer Science, California Institute of Technology, 1980.

DUFF85 Duff, T., "Compositing 3D Rendered Images," *SIGGRAPH '85*, Vol. 19, No. 3, July 1985, pp. 41–44.

ELLI91 Ellis, J., G. Kedem, T. Lyerly, D. Thielman, R. Marisa, J. Menon, H. Voelcker, "The Raycasting Engine and Ray Representation: A Technical Summary," *Proc. of the Intl. Jornal of Computational Geometry and Applications*, 1991.

ELLS90 Ellsworth, D.E., H. Good, and B. Tebbs, "Distributing Display Lists on a Multicomputer," *Computer Graphics* (Proceedings of the 1990 Symposium on Interactive 3D Graphics), Vol. 24, No. 2, March 1990, p.147–154.

ELLS91   Ellsworth, D.E. "Parallel Architectures and Algorithms for Real-Time Synthesis of High-Quality Images Using Deferred Shading," Workshop on Algorithms and Parallel VLSI Architectures, Pont-à-Mousson, France, June 12, 1990.

EYLE88   Eyles, J., J. Austin, H. Fuchs, T. Greer, and J. Poulton, "Pixel-Planes 4: A Summary," *Adv. in Computer Graphics Hardware II* (1987 Eurographics Workshop on Graphics Hardware), Eurographics Seminars, 1988, pp. 183-208.

FOLE90   Foley, J.D., A. van Dam, S.K. Feiner, and J.F. Hughes, *Computer Graphics: Principles and Practice*, Addison-Wesley, Reading, MA, 1990. (especially Chapter 18, "Advanced Raster Graphics Architecture")

FUCH77   Fuchs, H., "Distributing a Visible Surface Algorithm over Multiple Processors," *Proceedings of the ACM Annual Conference*, pp. 449–451.

FUCH79   Fuchs, H. and B. Johnson, prepublication draft of "An Expandable Multiprocessor Architecture for Video Graphics," *Proceedings of the 6th ACM-IEEE Symposium on Computer Architecture*, April, 1979, pp. 58–67.

FUCH85   Fuchs, H., J. Goldfeather, J. Hultquist, S. Spach, J. Austin, F. Brooks, J. Eyles, and J. Poulton, "Fast Spheres, Shadows, Textures, Transparencies, and Image Enhancements in Pixel-planes," *SIGGRAPH '85*, Vol. 19, No. 3, pp. 111-120.

FUCH89   Fuchs, H., J. Poulton, J. Eyles, T. Greer, J. Goldfeather, D. Ellsworth, S. Molnar, G. Turk, B. Tebbs, and L. Israel, "Pixel-Planes 5: A Heterogeneous Multiprocessor Graphics System Using Processor-Enhanced Memories," *SIGGRAPH '89*, Vol. 23, No. 3, pp. 79–88.

FUSS82   Fussel, D. and B. D. Rathi, "A VLSI-Oriented Architecture for Real-Time Raster Display of Shaded Polygons." *Graphics Interface '82*, 1982, pp. 373–380.

GARD81   Gardner, G.Y., E.P. Berlin, Jr., and B.M. Gelman, "A Real-Time Computer Image Generation System using Textured Curved Surfaces," *Proceedings of IMAGE II*, 1981, pp. 59–76.

GHAR88   Gharachorloo, N., S. Gupta, E. Hokenek, P. Balasubramanian, B. Bogholtz, C. Mathieu, and C. Zoulas, "Subnanosecond Pixel Rendering with Million Transistor Chips," *SIGGRAPH 88*, Vol. 22, No. 4, pp. 41–49.

KNIG88   Knight, T. and A. Krimm, "A Self-Terminating Low-Voltage Swing CMOS Output Driver," *IEEE Journal of Solid-State Circuits*, Vol. 23, No. 2, April 1988, pp. 457–464.

MART90   Martin, P., and H. Baeverstad, "TurboVRX: A High-Performance Graphics Workstation Architecture," *Proc. of AUSGRAPH 90*, September 1990, pp. 107-117.

MOLN88   Molnar, S.E., "Combining Z-buffer Engines for Higher-Speed Rendering," *Advances in Computer Graphics Hardware III*, Eurographics Seminars, 1988, pp. 171–182.

MOLN91a   Molnar, S.E., "Efficient Supersampling Antialiasing for High-Performance Architectures," Technical Report TR-91-023, Dept. of Computer Science, UNC-Chapel Hill, 1991.

MOLN91b   Molnar, S.E., "Image Composition Architectures for Real-Time Image Generation," Ph.D. dissertation, also available as UNC-Computer Science Technical Report TR91-046, 1991.

PARK80   Park, F., "Simulation and Expected Performance Analysis of Multiple Processor Z-Buffer Systems," *SIGGRAPH '80*, Vol. 14, No. 3, pp. 48–56.

POTM89   Potmesil, M., and E. Hoffert, "The Pixel Machine: A Parallel Image Computer," *SIGGRAPH '89*, Vol. 23, No. 3, pp. 69-78.

POUL85   Poulton, J., H. Fuchs, and A. Paeth, "Pixel-planes graphic engine," Section 9.5 in *Principles of CMOS VLSI Design: A System Perspective*, by Neil Weste and Kamran Eshrahian, Addison-Wesley, New York, 1985, pp. 448-480.

SGI90   Silicon Graphics Computer Systems, *Vision Graphics System Architecture*, Mountain View, CA 94039-7311, February 1990.

SHAW88   Shaw, C.D., M. Green, and J. Schaeffer, "A VLSI Architecture for Image Composition," *Advances in Computer Graphics Hardware III,*, Eurographics Seminars, 1988, pp. 183–199.

SPEC91   Speck, D., "The Mosaic Fast 512K Scalable CMOS DRAM," *Proceedings of the 1991 University of California at Santa Cruz Conference on Advanced Research in VLSI*, 1991, pp. 229–244.

SCHN88   Schneider, B.O. and U. Claussen, "PROOF: An Architecture for Rendering in Object-Space," *Advances in Computer Graphics Hardware III*, Eurographics Seminars, 1988, pp. 121–140.

WEIN81   Weinberg, R., "Parallel Processing Image Synthesis and Anti-Aliasing," *SIGGRAPH '81*, Vol. 15, No. 3, pp. 55–61.

A Scalable Hardware Render Accelerator using a Modified Scanline Algorithm

Michael Kelley   Stephanie Winner   Kirk Gould

Apple Computer, Inc.
20525 Mariani Avenue
Cupertino, CA 95014

1. ABSTRACT

A hardware accelerator for 3D rendering, based on a modified scanline algorithm, is presented. The accelerator renders multiple scanlines in parallel with high efficiency, and is optimized for integration into systems that support high speed data streams (such as video). The architecture has a very high performance/cost ratio, but maintains a low entry cost and a high degree of scalability — key issues for incorporation in personal computers. The performance of both the general algorithm and the prototype implementation is analyzed.

CR Categories and Subject Descriptors: B.2.1 [Arithmetic and Logic Structures]: Design Styles - parallel; **I.3.1** [Computer Graphics]: Hardware Architecture - raster display devices; **I.3.3** [Computer Graphics]: Picture/Image Generation - display algorithms; **I.3.7** [Computer Graphics]: Three-Dimensional Graphics and Realism - visible surface algorithms

General Terms: algorithms, architecture, parallel

Additional Key Words and Phrases: scanline, data sharing, low bandwidth, low cost

2. INTRODUCTION

Advances in CPU technology have given personal computers the compute power necessary to run 3D applications. However, interactive applications require faster rendering than can be achieved by the CPU alone — today's 3D workstations also include sophisticated rendering hardware [1, 2, 11, 14]. The goal of our project is to provide similar functionality in a personal computer.

We began by determining what differences, if any, there were between the requirements of 3D acceleration in a workstation and a personal computer. We identified some key features required for a personal computer:

- *Low cost*. The accelerator must have a very low entry cost.

- *Modularity*. It should be possible to add the accelerator to a system as an option.

- *High performance*. An intuitive, direct manipulation user interface requires a high frame rate and high speed hit testing.

- *Visual realism*. Although schematic representations such as wireframe are useful, naive users are more comfortable with "realistic" shaded images with shadows.

Existing workstations meet some of these requirements, but not all. High end workstations deliver high performance shaded rendering, but prices are stratospheric by personal computer standards. Recent entry level workstations have reduced this cost, but at the expense of lower speed, particularly for high quality rendering modes. And even these systems are many times the entry price of a typical personal computer. Finally, because the graphics accelerator in these systems is tightly coupled to the system frame buffer, providing the accelerator as an option, e.g. a plug-in card, is difficult — typically a local frame buffer must be added to the accelerator, increasing cost.

The architecture described in this paper has been optimized for a personal computer graphics system. It uses a modified scanline rendering algorithm to greatly reduce cost by combining the rasterization hardware and scanline RAM on chip. The architecture emphasizes shaded rendering, and new rendering features (e.g. CSG, antialiasing) can be added with little cost increase. The design is highly scalable because performance and functionality are limited by ASIC complexity (which is rapidly increasing), and because the architecture efficiently supports parallelism — a parallel implementation is described which can rasterize 880K triangles per second.

This paper primarily discusses rasterization, as standard techniques are used for transformation, clipping and shading [e.g. 4, 6]. We plan to use general purpose RISC or DSP devices to accelerate these tasks [2, 11].

3. BACKGROUND AND PREVIOUS WORK

3.1 Screen Z-Buffer Algorithm

The screen Z-buffer algorithm was one of the first shaded hidden surface removal algorithms, and was used by both software and hardware implementations [3, 8]. Its advantage is simplicity — each object to be rendered can be transformed and rasterized independently, allowing an arbitrarily large number of objects to be rendered (given enough patience). Hardware implementations of this algorithm have been very successful; in fact, it is the method used in virtually all 3D workstations [1, 2, 11].

However, the screen Z-buffer algorithm has disadvantages which make it less suitable for personal computers. The most obvious of these is memory use — the algorithm requires storing a Z value for every pixel on the screen. Storing a 24 bit Z for a 1Kx1K screen uses 3M bytes of memory, an appreciable amount in an entry level computer. More importantly, this memory must be very high performance — pixel shading speed is directly proportional to the sustained bandwidth to the RAM. For example, rendering one million 100 pixel triangles/second requires[1]:

1M tri/s x 100 pixel/tri = 100M pixel/s
100M pixel/s x 3 Z bytes/pixel x 1.5 = 450 MB/s

In practice, these very high bandwidths are achieved with wide, fast RAM [1], often coupled with sophisticated caching and prefetching. Although it's reasonable to add these costs to a dedicated workstation, they make it impractical to add high performance graphics to a low cost personal computer.

More abstractly, these disadvantages of the screen Z-buffer algorithm are caused because it stores the state of the rendering calculation for each pixel individually; effectively, the state information necessary to render one pixel is replicated for every pixel on the screen. As a result, rendering algorithms which require additional information per pixel (e.g. CSG, shadows, antialiasing) are expensive to implement; for example, the system described in [10] has over 150 bits per pixel.

3.2 Scanline Z-buffer algorithm

To find a more cost effective implementation of these rendering algorithms, we adopted the same solution used by many software renderers, the scanline Z-buffer algorithm [12]. In comparison to the screen Z-buffer algorithm, where the state information necessary for rendering a pixel is stored for every pixel on the screen, the scanline algorithm presorts the object database in screen space [15], and renders each scanline individually — only one scanline of pixel state information is kept. The difference between the two methods is substantial: for a 1Kx1K screen, the screen Z-buffer algorithm uses 3M bytes for Z, whereas the scanline algorithm uses only 3K bytes [9].

Additional information on scanline algorithms can be found in [6].

4. OVERVIEW OF THE PROTOTYPE

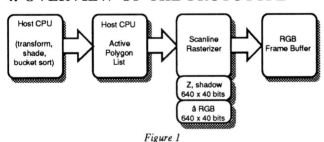

Figure 1

The prototype (shown above) is based on a Macintosh® Quadra™ personal computer; the scanline rasterizer is implemented as a Processor Direct expansion card. The host

68040 is used for transformation, shading, and active list maintenance; faster prototypes, using more powerful floating point engines, are also being developed.

The scanline rasterizer performs Gouraud shading, hidden surface removal via a 32 bit Z-buffer, shadow volumes [7] and alpha blending (with 10 bits of accuracy). The rasterizer is implemented as two 0.8μm ICs (Figure 10, at the end of the paper), designed with silicon compilation tools; the chips operate at 40MHz. The first chip intersects polygons transferred from the active polygon list with the current scanline, generating a series of horizontal spans. The second chip rasterizes the resulting spans, doing hidden surface removal, shadow plane tests and alpha blending. Multiple chip sets can be connected in parallel with virtually no glue logic, providing very high performance with low chip count (sections **7** and **8** discuss parallel rasterization).

The following pseudo-code shows the basic rendering algorithm of the prototype:

```
RenderFrame()
{
  /* First pass: transform, shade, sort */
  foreach (Poly)
  {
    Transform (Poly);
    if ( ! Cull (Poly))
    {
      Shade (Poly);
      BucketSort (Poly);
    }
  }

  /* Second pass: rasterize */
  foreach (Scanline)
  {
    AddNewPolys (BucketedPolys[Scanline]);
    Rasterize (ActiveList, Scanline);
    RemoveFinishedPolys (ActiveList, Scanline);
  }
}
```

Rendering begins when the host CPU traverses the 3D database, generating transformed, projected, clipped and shaded polygons. The polygons are then bucket sorted by the number of the first scanline on which they first become active. Once the main database traversal is complete, the host traverses the bucket sorted list in screen Y order, maintaining an active polygon list which is transferred into the rasterizer to drive rendering.

5. DISADVANTAGES OF THE SCANLINE ALGORITHM

5.1 Database sorting

Computationally, the penalty for the two pass algorithm is relatively minor [5]. Because the second pass is driven by the bucket sorted list, only a single traversal of the database hierarchy is required. The computational overhead of the bucket sort itself is low compared with transformation, clipping and shading, and is principally a problem of efficient memory management.

A more substantial penalty is the memory used to store the bucket sorted polygons; in the prototype, 40 bytes are required for each transformed, shaded triangle. However, this is offset by the other memory savings of the scanline algorithm; for

---

[1] This assumes 50% of pixels are visible; section 8.4 discusses this in more detail.

example, the 3 megabytes saved by not using a Z-buffer would be enough to store 75K triangles (a large interactive database for a personal computer). In practice, culling and the use of more efficient primitives (e.g. quadrilaterals) further reduce memory use.

5.2 Loss of concurrent scan conversion

Because bucket sorting must complete before scan conversion begins, a simple implementation of the scanline algorithm can cause poor utilization of the graphics subsystem. For example, if the first pass (transform, clip, shade) and the second pass (rasterize) require the same length of time, the hardware will never exceed 50% utilization. This compares poorly to a classical graphics pipeline model, where a well-balanced pipeline can achieve 100% utilization.

One solution to this problem is to double buffer the bucket sorted polygon list; this allows the two passes of the algorithm to run simultaneously, permitting 100% efficiency. Unfortunately this does *not* reduce latency; a direct manipulation interface which requires user feedback every frame will have to flush both buffers, negating the advantage. However, for tasks where latency is less critical (e.g. rotating an object for viewing), double buffering is effective.

A more general solution to this problem is to shorten the time required for first pass processing, which provides more time for rasterization and increases utilization. For polygons, postponing clipping, normal normalization and lighting to the second pass reduces first pass computation by approximately 50% [1][2]; the savings increase as the lighting model becomes more complex. Curved surfaces can be transformed without tesselation, postponing virtually all computation until the object becomes active during the second pass, at which point the object can be decomposed into renderable primitives. This technique also reduces memory use for the bucket sort.

5.3 Poor wireframe performance

Although scanline algorithms are efficient for shaded primitives, there is a substantial performance loss for wireframe rendering — in the prototype, wireframe performance will be roughly equal to shaded performance, as opposed to the 5X - 10X ratio commonly encountered in workstations. Because of our emphasis on shaded rendering, this was considered acceptable.

6. ADVANTAGES OF THE SCANLINE ALGORITHM

6.1 On-chip rasterization

A key implementation advantage of the scanline algorithm is that the Z and αRGB memory used for pixel rendering can be placed on the same chip as the rasterization hardware. For example, the prototype stores 32 bits for Z, 8 for shadows, and 10 for each of αRGB, a total of 80 bits per pixel — a 640 pixel scanline requires 51K bits of RAM. In the prototype, this scanline RAM uses only 25% of the rasterizer chip's area.

By placing the rasterization hardware on-chip with the RAM, very high rasterization speeds can be achieved without high off-chip bandwidth — the prototype rasterizer runs at 40M alpha-blended Z-buffered pixels per second, using 720M bytes/s of on-chip RAM bandwidth. Because chip I/O is not in the critical path, speed is limited only by core logic and RAM performance, allowing rapid performance increase as chip technology advances.

6.2 Raster output and modularity

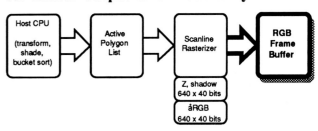

Figure 2

As scanlines complete, they are transferred from the rasterizer into the frame buffer (Figure 2). To the system, these transfers appear as a video-like high speed raster — this similarity allows easy integration into future video-capable personal computers.

Because the dataflow from rasterizer to frame buffer is unidirectional, the rasterizer does not require a tightly coupled low latency frame buffer interface. This makes it possible to add a scanline rendering accelerator to a system as an option (i.e. a card) without the cost of a local frame buffer.

6.3 High resolution rendering and antialiasing

For an NxN image, the memory requirements of the scanline Z-buffer algorithm are proportional to N, whereas the memory requirements of the screen algorithm are proportional to N^2.[3] This allows scanline algorithms to render large (e.g. 8Kx8K) images with high efficiency.

Unfortunately, when the scanline buffer is stored on-chip, scanline width is limited by RAM size — for example, the prototype has a maximum width of 640 pixels. This limitation can be removed by rendering wider scanlines in segments. For each scanline, the active object list is traversed multiple times, the first time rasterizing pixels 0 to 639, the second time 640 to 1279, etc. The resulting segments abut left to right, and are indistinguishable from the result had the entire scanline been rendered in a single pass. Only a single traversal of the main database is required, avoiding the redundant transformation and clipping which are caused by a tiling algorithm.

Because the scanline algorithm generates the image in scanline order, traditional super-sampled antialiasing techniques can be implemented with an accumulation buffer of only a few scanlines; in particular, hosts with video support may already include such hardware for window re-sizing and filtering. More advanced antialiasing algorithms (e.g. A-buffer) could be

---

[2] From Akeley's paper, 23 of 46.5 Mflops = 50%. These figures are for a single light source at infinity.

[3] Screen algorithms can render high resolution images by tiling, but with a substantial performance penalty for performing multiple database traversals.

implemented; because only one scanline is rendered at a time, the limiting factor is complexity, rather than RAM.

7. MODIFYING THE SCANLINE ALGORITHM FOR PARALLELISM

Thus far has we have discussed the pros and cons of the traditional scanline algorithm. However, a goal of the project was to develop an algorithm with a highly scalable implementation; in particular, our goal was to devise an algorithm where performance could be increased by rendering multiple scanlines in parallel.

7.1 Previous solutions: Screen partitioning

One solution to this problem [13] is to partition the screen into a number of relatively large contiguous regions, and render each region with an unmodified scanline algorithm. When complete, the regions are tiled together to produce a complete frame. While simple to implement, this divide-and-conquer solution suffers from poor load balancing — an image whose complexity is unevenly distributed across the screen will not be efficiently parallelized. Adaptive partitioning of the screen can improve load balancing, but the setup overhead for a region limits efficiency if fine subdivision of the screen is attempted. Also, this algorithm is expensive: active list hardware, memory, and rasterization hardware are all replicated.

Instead, we wanted a solution that renders multiple *adjacent* scanlines simultaneously. This largely solves the load balancing problem, as adjacent scanlines usually have similar complexity. Also, it has the potential to exploit scanline coherence by maintaining a single active polygon list which is shared by multiple rasterizers, each working on a separate scanline.

7.2 Scanline coherence vs parallelism

Unfortunately, the typical implementation of the scanline algorithm makes this difficult. To increase performance, scanline renderers exploit coherence by converting the interpolation calculation of the edge parameters at the current scanline into a forward differencing calculation in Y [6, 15]:

Y_{top}, Y_{bottom} = top and bottom of edge

$P_{top[n]}, P_{bottom[n]}$ = parameter n at top, bottom

H_{inv} = inverse of height of edge

$\Delta P_{[n]}$ = change/scanline of parameter [n]

$P_{[n]}$ = interpolated value of parameter [n]

$H_{inv} = 1 / (Y_{bottom} - Y_{top})$

$\Delta P_{[n]} = H_{inv} \times (P_{bottom[n]} - P_{top[n]})$

$P_{0[n]} = P_{top[n]}$

$P_{i+1[n]} = P_{i[n]} + \Delta P_{[n]}$

(The initialization function $P_{0[n]}$ has been simplified for clarity; the actual subpixel accurate function is more complex.) Rendering multiple scanlines in parallel requires parallelizing this forward differencing calculation, which is possible but awkward; in particular, the calculation of $P_{0[n]}$ and the end-of-edge test must be replicated for every interpolator.

7.3 Direct evaluation vs forward differencing

A different approach to the problem is to abandon the forward differencing solution and directly evaluate the interception calculation of the object edge and the scanline:

w_y = interpolation weight at Y

$w_y = (Y - Y_{top}) / (Y_{bottom} - Y_{top})$

$P_{y[n]} = (P_{top[n]} \times (1 - w_y)) + (P_{bottom[n]} \times w_y)$

Direct evaluation is computationally more expensive than forward differencing (for each scanline, an additional divide and two multiplies per parameter). However, because the cost of computation on an ASIC is declining so rapidly, we felt comfortable adopting a computationally intensive solution, as it provides advantages in the following, more problematic areas.

7.3.1 Simplified setup

The most obvious advantage of direct evaluation is that it greatly simplifies the setup procedure for an active object — the calculation of H_{inv}, $\Delta P_{[n]}$ and $P_{0[n]}$[4] is completely avoided. With direct evaluation, the object is simply inserted into the active object list; no other processing is necessary.

7.3.2 Reduced active list memory and bandwidth

To forward difference a parameter $P_{[n]}$ of N bits requires storage of $\Delta P_{[n]}$, typically 2N bits[5], and the current parameter value $P_{i[n]}$, also 2N bits, for a total of 4N bits. Using direct evaluation, only $P_{top[n]}$ and $P_{bottom[n]}$ are stored, a total of 2N bits, providing a 50% memory saving.

More important, however, is the reduction of memory bandwidth. To directly evaluate a parameter, $P_{top[n]}$ and $P_{bottom[n]}$ are read for a total of 2N bits of bandwidth. For forward differencing, $\Delta P_{[n]}$ and $P_{i[n]}$ are read, and then $P_{i+1[n]}$ is written back, a total of 6N bits or three times the bandwidth of direct evaluation. As shown later, active list bandwidth is directly proportional to rasterization speed; the reduction from direct evaluation allows much higher performance.

Also, because direct evaluation does not require writing back $P_{i+1[n]}$, the dataflow is unidirectional, substantially simplifying system design. For example, high latency bursting memory such as VRAM can be used for active polygon storage, reducing cost.

7.3.3 Data sharing for parallelism

The most important advantage of direct evaluation is that the data in the active object list no longer reflects the state of any particular scanline — the same data can be used to render multiple scanlines in parallel. In fact, the prototype is designed to transfer data from the active object list to multiple rasterizers simultaneously:

---

[4] Direct evaluation is intrinsically sub-pixel accurate, so sub-pixel alignment does not have to be specially treated.

[5] The extra N bits are fractional guard bits. The number of guard bits is actually $\log_2$(max number of iterations), i.e. forward differencing an 8 bit value across an 8K screen requires 15 guard bits.

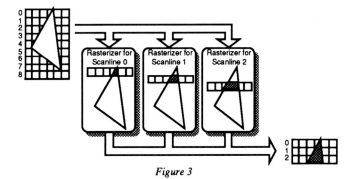

Figure 3

In this example, the triangle description is transferred into all three rasterizers simultaneously. Each rasterizer intercepts the triangle with its target scanline, and renders the resulting horizontal span. All three rasterizers then output their scanlines, generating a three scanline strip of the final image.

Because the data is shared by all rasterizers, efficiency is high: bandwidth is wasted only when an object does not intersect all of the scanlines being rendered. In this example, the triangle description is transferred only twice to render scanlines 0 to 5 (each transfer renders three scanlines), yielding an ideal $6/2 = 3X$ increase in rasterization speed over a single rasterizer.[6] However, when rendering scanlines 6 to 8, the triangle intersects only two of the three rasterizers, leaving one idle. Therefore, a frame that would have required 8 triangle transfers in a single rasterizer design requires 3 transfers, for a speed increase of $8/3 = 2.7X$, and a rasterizer utilization efficiency of $(8/3) \times (1/3) = 8/9 = 89\%$.

In practice, rather than allowing the decrease in utilization to reduce rasterization speed, the input data bandwidth is increased. Because the rasterizers can discard a triangle that doesn't intersect the scanline much faster than rendering it, increasing input bandwidth to compensate for the unnecessary triangle transfers permits all rasterizers to run at full speed (an input FIFO on the rasterizer is used to smooth the dataflow). Therefore, the efficiency of a given number of parallel scanline rasterizers can be characterized by the increase in input bandwidth necessary to keep all rasterizers fully utilized:

N_{par} = number of parallel scanlines
H_{avg} = average height of an active object
B_{par} = bandwidth increase over a single rasterizer

$B_{par} = (N_{par} - 1) / H_{avg}$

For the example above, with three parallel rasterizers and an average object height of eight scanlines:

$B_{par} = (3 - 1) / 8$
$= 25\%$ increase

In other words, a 25% increase in active list bandwidth over a single rasterizer would be enough to keep three rasterizers fully utilized.

---

[6] For this example, we assume performance is limited by active list bandwidth. More complete performance analysis is in the following section.

8. PERFORMANCE ANALYSIS

8.1 Rasterization performance

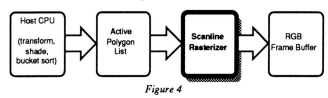

Figure 4

Rasterization performance can be characterized by two values:

P_{int} = primitive-scanline intersections/s
P_{raster} = rasterization speed (pixels/s)

The prototype hardware intersects a triangle with the current scanline in 14 clocks, yielding a P_{int} of:

P_{int} = 40 MHz / 14 clocks/intersection
$= 2.86M$ intersections/s

Rasterization speed is one pixel per clock, or:

$P_{raster} = 40M$ pixels/s

From this, rasterization performance can be approximated by the formula:

A_{avg} = average pixels per primitive
P_{prim} = primitives/second
$= \min((P_{int} / H_{avg}), (P_{raster} / A_{avg}))$
P_{pixel} = rendered pixels/second
$= A_{avg} \times P_{prim}$

For example, a 100 pixel triangle:

H_{avg} = 13 scanlines
A_{avg} = 100 pixels
$P_{prim} = \min (2.86M / 13, 40M / 100)$
$= 220K$ triangles/s
$P_{pixel} = 100 \times 220K = 22M$ pixels/s

8.2 Active list bandwidth

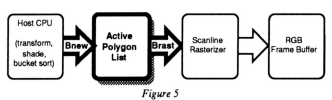

Figure 5

A key factor for system performance is B_{rast} (shown in Figure 5), the bandwidth used to transfer polygons from the active list to the rasterizer(s). For a single rasterizer this can be computed as:

S_{prim} = size of primitive
$B_{rast} = P_{prim} \times S_{prim} \times H_{avg}$

For the example given earlier, a triangle requires 40 bytes; the resulting rasterizer input bandwidth is:

$B_{rast} = 220K$ tri/s $\times$ 40 bytes $\times$ 13 scanlines/tri
$= 114$ MB/s

In addition, new primitives must be added to the active object list as they first become active:

$$B_{new} = P_{prim} \times S_{prim}$$

So total active list bandwidth for a single rasterizer system is:

$$B_{total} = B_{new} + B_{rast}$$
$$B_{total} = P_{prim} \times S_{prim} + P_{prim} \times S_{prim} \times H_{avg}$$
$$B_{total} = P_{prim} \times S_{prim} \times (1 + H_{avg})$$

For the previous example:

$$B_{total} = 220K \times 40 \times (1 + 13)$$
$$= 123M \text{ bytes/s}$$

8.3 Parallelism

Rewriting the equations for active list bandwidth to include N_{par} and B_{par} from section **7.3.3** yields ($\sum$ is used to indicate the sum of parallel rasterizers):

N_{par} = number of parallel scanlines
B_{par} = bandwidth increase over a single rasterizer

$$P_{\sum prim} = N_{par} \times P_{prim}$$
$$P_{\sum pixel} = A_{avg} \times P_{\sum prim}$$
$$B_{\sum rast} = (B_{par} + 1) \times P_{prim} \times S_{prim} \times H_{avg}$$
$$= (N_{par} + H_{avg} - 1) \times P_{prim} \times S_{prim}$$
$$B_{\sum new} = P_{\sum prim} \times S_{prim}$$
$$= N_{par} \times P_{prim} \times S_{prim}$$
$$B_{\sum total} = B_{\sum new} + B_{\sum rast}$$
$$= P_{prim} \times S_{prim} \times (2N_{par} + H_{avg} - 1)$$

Figure 6 graphs $B_{\sum total}$, showing the relatively gradual increase in bandwidth necessary to drive parallel rasterizers:

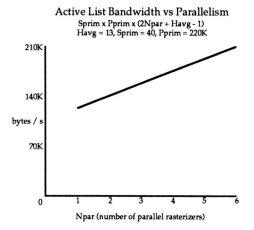

Active List Bandwidth vs Parallelism
Sprim x Pprim x (2Npar + Havg - 1)
Havg = 13, Sprim = 40, Pprim = 220K

Figure 6

This gradual increase is responsible for a rapid improvement in the performance/bandwidth ratio ($P_{\sum prim}/B_{\sum total}$) as parallelism is increased:

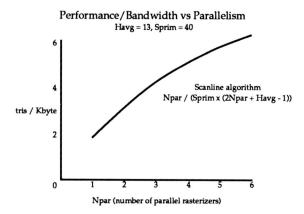

Performance/Bandwidth vs Parallelism
Havg = 13, Sprim = 40

Scanline algorithm
Npar / (Sprim x (2Npar + Havg - 1))

Figure 7

Repeating the previous example from **8.2**, but with four parallel rasterizers:

$$P_{\sum prim} = 4 \times 220K = 880K \text{ triangles/s}$$
$$P_{\sum pixel} = 100 \times 880K = 88M \text{ pixels/s}$$
$$B_{\sum rast} = (4 + 13 - 1) \times 220K \times 40 = 141M \text{ bytes/s}$$
$$B_{\sum new} = 4 \times 220K \times 40 = 35M \text{ bytes/s}$$
$$B_{\sum total} = 35M + 141M = 176M \text{ bytes/s}$$

Figure 8 shows the total system dataflow, adding the assumption of 30 fps update of a 1M pixel frame buffer:

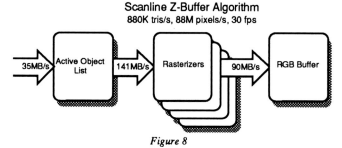

Scanline Z-Buffer Algorithm
880K tris/s, 88M pixels/s, 30 fps

35MB/s — Active Object List — 141MB/s — Rasterizers — 90MB/s — RGB Buffer

Figure 8

Note that the bandwidth is distributed and unidirectional, allowing an inexpensive high latency dataflow design. For this example, a 4X increase in rasterization performance required a 176M/123M = 43% increase in total active object list bandwidth.

8.4 Comparison to screen Z-buffer

For comparison, we can analyze the bandwidth that would be required to achieve this performance using a screen Z-buffer algorithm. The combined Z-buffer/frame buffer bandwidth necessary can be calculated by:

V = % of pixels visible
α = % of pixels with alpha blending
B_z = Z bytes/pixel
B_{argb} = αRGB bytes/pixel
$$B_{zbuf} = P_{pixel} \times (B_z + V \times (B_z + B_{argb} + \alpha \times B_{argb}))$$

Assuming 50% of the pixels are visible[7], 50% are blended, and 32 bits for Z and αRGB , this would be:

---

[7] E.g. at 30 fps, 88M/30 = 2.9M pixels/frame x 50% = 1.5M "visible" pixels. Of these, only 1M are actually visible; the others are subsequently overwritten (or blended) as rendering continues.

$$B_{zbuf} = 88M \times (4 + 50\% \times (4 + 4 + 50\% \times 4))$$
$$= 792M \text{ bytes/s}$$

Which is 4.5X the active list bandwidth of the scanline algorithm. A diagram of system dataflow for the screen Z-buffer algorithm shows this more clearly:

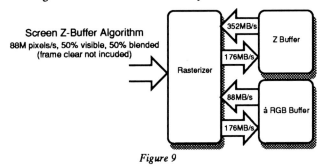

Screen Z-Buffer Algorithm
88M pixels/s, 50% visible, 50% blended
(frame clear not incuded)

Figure 9

Here, high performance bidirectional (i.e. low latency) bandwidth is required for both the Z and αRGB buffers, increasing cost.

9. MEASURED PERFORMANCE

Figure 11 (at the end of the paper), shows a test image rendered on the prototype hardware. The image has 18 torusus, each composed of 1020 triangles; 9468 tris are rendered after culling. Rendering the scene requires a total of 2.06 MBytes of input data to the rasterizer. The current prototype (which is primarily a test vehicle) is limited by the 68040 host to between 5K and 10K triangles/s; however, we were able to evaluate the performance of the rasterization silicon itself by reducing the rasterizer clock until rasterization became the system bottleneck.

With the clock reduced to 1MHz, Figure 11 requires 1.5 seconds to render on a single rasterizer. Extrapolating performance to the full 40MHz clock rate:

$$Framerate = 1 \text{ frame} / 1.5s \times (40MHz/1MHz)$$
$$= 26.7 \text{ frames/s}$$

$$Pprim = 9468 \text{ tris} \times 26.7 \text{ frames/s}$$
$$= 252K \text{ tris/s}$$

The input bandwidth required for this performance is[8]:

$$B_{rast} = 2.06 \text{ MBytes/frame} \times 26.7 \text{ frames/s}$$
$$= 54.9 \text{ MBytes/s}$$

A higher performance, RISC-based prototype is being developed which will provide system performance that better matches rasterization capability.

10. OTHER ISSUES

10.1 Latency

For the examples presented here, the delay from start of database traversal to screen update (i.e. swap buffers) is the same for the screen and scanline algorithms. However, if double buffering is *not* being used (for example, a very large database is being drawn on the screen while the user watches), a

screen algorithm would be perceived as having lower latency, as the screen update would begin sooner. This wasn't considered a serious disadvantage, however, as our target is interactive applications running at high frame rates, necessitating a double buffered display.

10.2 Hit testing

The scanline algorithm has advantages for direct manipulation applications with an interaction loop like:

```
while (FOREVER)
{
  DrawDatabase();
  GetMouse (&x, &y);
  SelectedObject = HitTestDatabase (x, y);
  UpdateDatabase (SelectedObject);
}
```

For this interaction model, the Y-sorted object activation list created during DrawDatabase() can be used to dramatically accelerate HitTestDatabase() by providing a list of only those objects visible on scanline y. This is an improvement over the classic screen Z-buffer model, where HitTestDatabase() requires a second traversal of the database and hit testing of every primitive.

11. ACKNOWLEDGEMENTS

Lee Mighdoll was a major contributor to the early stages of this project.

This research was performed in the Systems Technology Research Group of Apple Computer, Inc. Thanks to Frank Crow, Brian Heaney, Jill Huchital, David Jevans, Al Kossow, Lee Mighdoll and Libby Patterson for their reviews.

12. REFERENCES

1. Akeley, Kurt and T. Jermoluk, "High-Performance Polygon Rendering", Computer Graphics, Vol. 22, No. 4, August 1988, 239-246

2. Apgar, Brian, B. Bersack and A. Mammen, "A Display System for the Stellar Graphics Supercomputer Model GS1000", Computer Graphics, Vol. 22, No. 4, August 1988, 255-262

3. Catmull, E., "A Subdivision Algorithm for Computer Display of Curved Surfaces", UTEC-CSc-74-133, Computer Science Department, University of Utah, Salt Lake City, UT, December 1974

4. Clark, James, "The Geometry Engine: A VLSI Geometry System for Graphics", Computer Graphics, Vol. 16, No. 3, July 1982, 127-133

5. Deering, Michael, S. Winner, B. Schediwy, C. Duffy and N. Hunt, "The Triangle Processor and Normal Vector Shader: A VLSI System for High Performance Graphics", Computer Graphics, Vol. 22, No. 4, August 1988, 21-30

6. Foley, James, A. van Dam, S. Feiner and J. Hughes, "Computer Graphics Principles and Practice, 2nd Edition", Addison-Wesley, 1990, 96-99 (basic scan conversion), 201-283 (transformation), 680-685 (scanline algorithms), 885-887 (scanline rasterization)

7. Fournier, Alain and D. Fussell, "On the Power of the Frame Buffer", Transactions on Graphics, Vol. 7, No. 2, April 1988, 103-128

---

[8] For this image, input bandwidth is reduced approximately 30% by shared vertex data.

8. Fuchs, Henry and J. Poulton, "Pixel-Planes: A VLSI-Oriented Design for a Raster Graphics Engine", Computer Graphics, Vol. 15, No. 3, August 1981, 80-81

9. Gharachorloo, Nader, S. Gupta, R. Sproull and I. Sutherland, "A Characterization of Ten Rasterization Techniques", Computer Graphics, Vol. 23, No. 3, July 1989, 355-368

10. Haeberli, Paul and K. Akeley, "The Accumulation Buffer: Hardware Support for High-Quality Rendering", Computer Graphics, Vol. 24, No. 4, August 1990, 309-318

11. Kirk, David and D. Voorhies, "The Rendering Architecture of the DN10000VS", Computer Graphics, Vol. 24, No. 4, August 1990, 299-307

12. Myers, A. J., "An Efficient Visible Surface Program", Report to the National Science Foundation, Computer Graphics Research Group, Ohio State University, Columbus, OH, July 1975

13. Niimi, Haruo, Y. Imai, M. Murakami, S. Tomita and H. Hagiwara, "A Parallel Processor System for Three-Dimensional Color Graphics", Computer Graphics, Vol. 18, No. 3, July 1984, 67-76

14. Rhoden, Desi and C. Wilcox, "Hardware Acceleration for Window Systems", Computer Graphics, Vol. 23, No. 3, July 1989, 61-67

15. Watkins, G. "A Real-Time Visible Surface Algorithm", Computer Science Department, University of Utah, UTECH-CSC-70-101, June 1970

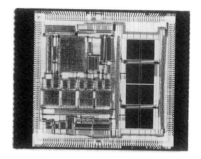

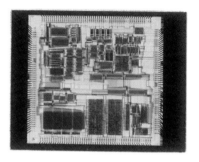

Figure 10

Rasterizer chips

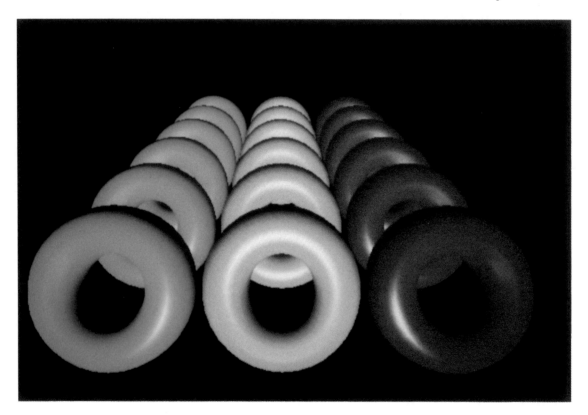

Figure 11

9468 triangle image rendered on prototype

Fast Shadows and Lighting Effects Using Texture Mapping

Mark Segal
Carl Korobkin
Rolf van Widenfelt
Jim Foran
Paul Haeberli
Silicon Graphics Computer Systems*

Abstract

Generating images of texture mapped geometry requires projecting surfaces onto a two-dimensional screen. If this projection involves perspective, then a division must be performed at each pixel of the projected surface in order to correctly calculate texture map coordinates.

We show how a simple extension to perspective-correct texture mapping can be used to create various lighting effects. These include arbitrary projection of two-dimensional images onto geometry, realistic spotlights, and generation of shadows using shadow maps[10]. These effects are obtained in real time using hardware that performs correct texture mapping.

CR Categories and Subject Descriptors: I.3.3 **[Computer Graphics]**: Picture/Image Generation; I.3.7 **[Computer Graphics]**: Three-Dimensional Graphics and Realism - *color, shading, shadowing, and texture*

Additional Key Words and Phrases: lighting, texture mapping

1 Introduction

Producing an image of a three-dimensional scene requires finding the projection of that scene onto a two-dimensional screen. In the case of a scene consisting of texture mapped surfaces, this involves not only determining where the projected points of the surfaces should appear on the screen, but also which portions of the texture image should be associated with the projected points.

If the image of the three-dimensional scene is to appear realistic, then the projection from three to two dimensions must be a perspective projection. Typically, a complex scene is converted to polygons before projection. The projected vertices of these polygons determine boundary edges of projected polygons.

Scan conversion uses iteration to enumerate pixels on the screen that are covered by each polygon. This iteration in the plane of projection introduces a homogeneous variation into the parameters that index the texture of a projected polygon. We call these parameters *texture coordinates*. If the homogeneous variation is ignored in favor of a simpler linear iteration, incorrect images are produced

*2011 N. Shoreline Blvd., Mountain View, CA 94043

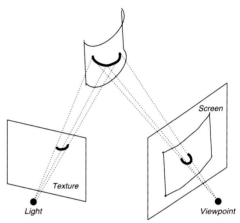

Figure 1. Viewing a projected texture.

that can lead to objectionable effects such as texture "swimming" during scene animation[5]. Correct interpolation of texture coordinates requires each to be divided by a common denominator for each pixel of a projected texture mapped polygon[6].

We examine the general situation in which a texture is mapped onto a surface via a projection, after which the surface is projected onto a two dimensional viewing screen. This is like projecting a slide of some scene onto an arbitrarily oriented surface, which is then viewed from some viewpoint (see Figure 1). It turns out that handling this situation during texture coordinate iteration is essentially no different from the more usual case in which a texture is mapped linearly onto a polygon. We use *projective textures* to simulate spotlights and generate shadows using a method that is well-suited to graphics hardware that performs divisions to obtain correct texture coordinates.

2 Mathematical Preliminaries

To aid in describing the iteration process, we introduce four coordinate systems. The *clip* coordinate system is a homogeneous representation of three-dimensional space, with x, y, z, and w coordinates. The origin of this coordinate system is the viewpoint. We use the term clip coordinate system because it is this system in which clipping is often carried out. The *screen* coordinate system represents the two-dimensional screen with two coordinates. These are obtained from clip coordinates by dividing x and y by w, so that screen coordinates are given by $x^s = x/w$ and $y^s = y/w$ (the s superscript indicates screen coordinates). The *light* coordinate system is a second homogeneous coordinate system with coordinates x^l, y^l,

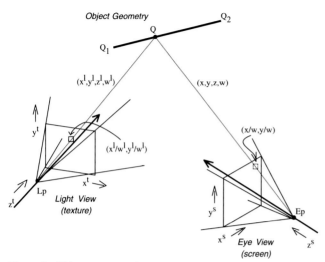

Figure 2. Object geometry in the light and clip coordinate systems.

z^l, and w^l; the origin of this system is at the light source. Finally, the *texture* coordinate system corresponds to a texture, which may represent a slide through which the light shines. Texture coordinates are given by $x^t = x^l/w^l$ and $y^t = y^l/w^l$ (we shall also find a use for $z^t = z^l/w^l$). Given (x^s, y^s), a point on a scan-converted polygon, our goal is to find its corresponding texture coordinates, (x^t, y^t).

Figure 2 shows a line segment in the clip coordinate system and its projection onto the two-dimensional screen. This line segment represents a span between two edges of a polygon. In clip coordinates, the endpoints of the line segment are given by

$$\mathbf{Q}_1 = (x_1, y_1, z_1, w_1) \qquad \text{and} \qquad \mathbf{Q}_2 = (x_2, y_2, z_2, w_2).$$

A point $\mathbf{Q}$ along the line segment can be written in clip coordinates as

$$\mathbf{Q} = (1 - t)\mathbf{Q}_1 + t\mathbf{Q}_2 \qquad (1)$$

for some $t \in [0, 1]$. In screen coordinates, we write the corresponding projected point as

$$\mathbf{Q}^s = (1 - t^s)\mathbf{Q}_1^s + t^s \mathbf{Q}_2^s \qquad (2)$$

where $\mathbf{Q}_1^s = \mathbf{Q}_1/w_1$ and $\mathbf{Q}_2^s = \mathbf{Q}_2/w_2$.

To find the light coordinates of $\mathbf{Q}$ given $\mathbf{Q}^s$, we must find the value of t corresponding to t^s (in general $t \neq t^s$). This is accomplished by noting that

$$\mathbf{Q}^s = (1 - t^s)\mathbf{Q}_1/w_1 + t^s \mathbf{Q}_2/w_2 = \frac{(1 - t)\mathbf{Q}_1 + t\mathbf{Q}_2}{(1 - t)w_1 + tw_2} \qquad (3)$$

and solving for t. This is most easily achieved by choosing a and b such that $1 - t^s = a/(a + b)$ and $t^s = b/(a + b)$; we also choose A and B such that $(1 - t) = A/(A + B)$ and $t = B/(A + B)$. Equation 3 becomes

$$\mathbf{Q}^s = \frac{a\mathbf{Q}_1/w_1 + b\mathbf{Q}_2/w_2}{(a + b)} = \frac{A\mathbf{Q}_1 + B\mathbf{Q}_2}{Aw_1 + Bw_2}. \qquad (4)$$

It is easily verified that $A = aw_2$ and $B = bw_1$ satisfy this equation, allowing us to obtain t and thus $\mathbf{Q}$.

Because the relationship between light coordinates and clip coordinates is affine (linear plus translation), there is a homogeneous matrix M that relates them:

$$\mathbf{Q}^l = M\mathbf{Q} = \frac{A}{A + B}\mathbf{Q}_1^l + \frac{B}{A + B}\mathbf{Q}_2^l \qquad (5)$$

where $\mathbf{Q}_1^l = (x_1^l, y_1^l, z_1^l, w_1^l)$ and $\mathbf{Q}_2^l = (x_2^l, y_2^l, z_2^l, w_2^l)$ are the light coordinates of the points given by $\mathbf{Q}_1$ and $\mathbf{Q}_2$ in clip coordinates.

We finally obtain

$$\begin{aligned} \mathbf{Q}^t &= \mathbf{Q}^l/w^l \\ &= \frac{A\mathbf{Q}_1^l + B\mathbf{Q}_2^l}{Aw_1^l + Bw_2^l} \\ &= \frac{a\mathbf{Q}_1^l/w_1 + b\mathbf{Q}_2^l/w_2}{a(w_1^l/w_1) + b(w_2^l/w_2)}. \end{aligned} \qquad (6)$$

Equation 6 gives the texture coordinates corresponding to a linearly interpolated point along a line segment in screen coordinates. To obtain these coordinates at a pixel, we must linearly interpolate x^l/w, y^l/w, and w^l/w, and divide at each pixel to obtain

$$x^l/w^l = \frac{x^l/w}{w^l/w} \qquad \text{and} \qquad y^l/w^l = \frac{y^l/w}{w^l/w}. \qquad (7)$$

(For an alternate derivation of this result, see [6].)

If w^l is constant across a polygon, then Equation 7 becomes

$$s = \frac{s/w}{1/w} \qquad \text{and} \qquad t = \frac{t/w}{1/w}, \qquad (8)$$

where we have set $s = x^l/w^l$ and $t = y^l/w^l$. Equation 8 governs the iteration of texture coordinates that have simply been assigned to polygon vertices. It still implies a division for each pixel contained in a polygon. The more general situation of a projected texture implied by Equation 7 requires only that the divisor be w^l/w instead of $1/w$.

3   Applications

To make the various coordinates in the following examples concrete, we introduce one more coordinate system: the *world* coordinate system. This is the coordinate system in which the three-dimensional model of the scene is described. There are thus two transformation matrices of interest: M_c transforms world coordinates to clip coordinates, and M_l transforms world coordinates to light coordinates. Iteration proceeds across projected polygon line segments according to equation 6 to obtain texture coordinates (x^t, y^t) for each pixel on the screen.

3.1   Slide Projector

One application of projective texture mapping consists of viewing the projection of a slide or movie on an arbitrary surface[9][2]. In this case, the texture represents the slide or movie. We describe a multi-pass drawing algorithm to simulate film projection.

Each pass entails scan-converting every polygon in the scene. Scan-conversion yields a series of screen points and corresponding texture points for each polygon. Associated with each screen point is a color and z-value, denoted c and z, respectively. Associated with each corresponding texture point is a color and z-value, denoted c_τ and z_τ. These values are used to modify corresponding values in a framebuffer of pixels. Each pixel, denoted p, also has an associated color and z-value, denoted c_p and z_p.

A color consists of several indepenedent components (e.g. red, green, and blue). Addition or multiplication of two colors indicates addition or multiplication of each corresponding pair of components (each component may be taken to lie in the range $[0, 1]$).

Assume that z_p is initialized to some large value for all p, and that c_p is initialized to some fixed ambient scene color for all p. The slide projection algorithm consists of three passes; for each scan-converted point in each pass, these actions are performed:

Pass 1 If $z < z_p$, then $z_p \leftarrow z$ *(hidden surface removal)*

Pass 2 If $z = z_p$, then $c_p \leftarrow c_p + c_\tau$ *(illumination)*

Pass 3 Set $c_p = c \cdot c_p$ *(final rendering)*

Pass 1 is a z-buffering step that sets z_p for each pixel. Pass 2 increases the brightness of each pixel according to the projected spotlight shape; the test ensures that portions of the scene visible from the eye point are brightened by the texture image only once (occlusions are not considered). The effects of multiple film projections may be incorporated by repeating Pass 2 several times, modifying M_l and the light coordinates appropriately on each pass. Pass 3 draws the scene, modulating the color of each pixel by the corresponding color of the projected texture image. Effects of standard (i.e. non-projective) texture mapping may be incorporated in this pass. Current Silicon Graphics hardware is capable of performing each pass at approximately 10^5 polygons per second.

Figure 3 shows a slide projected onto a scene. The left image shows the texture map; the right image shows the scene illuminated by both ambient light and the projected slide. The projected image may also be made to have a particular focal plane by rendering the scene several times and using an accumulation buffer as described in [4].

The same configuration can transform an image cast on one projection plane into a distinct projection plane. Consider, for instance, a photograph of a building's facade taken from some position. The effect of viewing the facade from arbitrary positions can be achieved by projecting the photograph back onto the building's facade and then viewing the scene from a different vantage point. This effect is useful in walk-throughs or fly-bys; texture mapping can be used to simulate buildings and distant scenery viewed from any viewpoint[1][7].

3.2 Spotlights

A similar technique can be used to simulate the effects of spotlight illumination on a scene. In this case the texture represents an intensity map of a cross-section of the spotlight's beam. That is, it is as if an opaque screen were placed in front of a spotlight and the intensity at each point on the screen recorded. Any conceivable spot shape may be accommodated. In addition, distortion effects, such as those attributed to a shield or a lens, may be incorporated into the texture map image.

Angular attenuation of illumination is incorporated into the intensity texture map of the spot source. Attenuation due to distance may be approximated by applying a function of the depth values $z^t = z^l/w^l$ iterated along with the texture coordinates (x^t, y^t) at each pixel in the image.

This method of illuminating a scene with a spotlight is useful for many real-time simulation applications, such as aircraft landing lights, directable aircraft taxi lights, and automotive headlights.

3.3 Fast, Accurate Shadows

Another application of this technique is to produce shadows cast from any number of point light sources. We follow the method described by Williams[10], but in a way that exploits available texture mapping hardware.

First, an image of the scene is rendered from the viewpoint of the light source. The purpose of this rendering is to obtain depth values in light coordinates for the scene with hidden surfaces removed. The depth values are the values of z^l/w^l at each pixel in the image. The array of z^t values corresponding to the hidden surface-removed image are then placed into a texture map, which will be used as a *shadow map*[10][8]. We refer to a value in this texture map as z_τ.

The generated texture map is used in a three-pass rendering process. This process uses an additional framebuffer value α_p in the range $[0, 1]$. The initial conditions are the same as those for the slide projector algorithm.

Pass 1 If $z < z_p$, then $z_p \leftarrow z, c_p \leftarrow c$ *(hidden surface removal)*

Pass 2 If $z_\tau = z^t$, then $\alpha_p \leftarrow 1$; else $\alpha_p \leftarrow 0$ *(shadow testing)*

Pass 3 $c_p \leftarrow c_p + (c$ modulated by $\alpha_p)$ *(final rendering)*

Pass 1 produces a hidden surface-removed image of the scene using only ambient illumination. If the two values in the comparison in Pass 2 are equal, then the point represented by p is visible from the light and so is not in shadow; otherwise, it is in shadow. Pass 3, drawn with full illumination, brightens portions of the scene that are not in shadow.

In practice, the comparison in Pass 2 is replaced with $z_\tau > z^t + \epsilon$, where ϵ is a bias. See [8] for factors governing the selection of ϵ.

This technique requires that the mechanism for setting α_p be based on the result of a comparison between a value stored in the texture map and the iterated z^t. For accuracy, it also requires that the texture map be capable of representing large z_τ. Our latest hardware posseses these capabilites, and can perform each of the above passes at the rate of at least 10^5 polygons per second.

Correct illumination from multiple colored lights may be produced by performing multiple passes. The shadow effect may also be combined with the spotlight effect described above, as shown in Figure 4. The left image in this figure is the shadow map. The center image is the spotlight intensity map. The right image shows the effects of incorporating both spotlight and shadow effects into a scene.

This technique differs from the hardware implementation described in [3]. It uses existing texture mapping hardware to create shadows, instead of drawing extruded shadow volumes for each polygon in the scene. In addition, percentage closer filtering [8] is easily supported.

4 Conclusions

Projecting a texture image onto a scene from some light source is no more expensive to compute than simple texture mapping in which texture coordinates are assigned to polygon vertices. Both require a single division per-pixel for each texture coordinate; accounting for the texture projection simply modifies the divisor.

Viewing a texture projected onto a three-dimensional scene is a useful technique for simulating a number of effects, including projecting images, spotlight illumination, and shadows. If hardware is available to perform texture mapping and the per-pixel division it requires, then these effects can be obtained with no performance penalty.

Acknowledgements

Many thanks to Derrick Burns for help with the texture coordinate iteration equations. Thanks also to Tom Davis for useful discus-

Figure 3. Simulating a slide projector.

Figure 4. Generating shadows using a shadow map.

sions. Dan Baum provided helpful suggestions for the spotlight implementation. Software Systems provided some of the textures used in Figure 3.

References

[1] Robert N. Devich and Frederick M. Weinhaus. Image perspective transformations. *SPIE*, 238, 1980.

[2] Julie O'B. Dorsey, Francois X. Sillion, and Donald P. Greenberg. Design and simulation of opera lighting and projection effects. In *Proceedings of SIGGRAPH '91*, pages 41–50, 1991.

[3] Henry Fuchs, Jack Goldfeather, and Jeff P. Hultquist, et al. Fast spheres, shadows, textures, transparencies, and image enhancements in pixels-planes. In *Proceedings of SIGGRAPH '85*, pages 111–120, 1985.

[4] Paul Haeberli and Kurt Akeley. The accumulation buffer: Hardware support for high-quality rendering. In *Proceedings of SIGGRAPH '90*, pages 309–318, 1990.

[5] Paul S. Heckbert. Fundamentals of texture mapping and image warping. Master's thesis, UC Berkeley, June 1989.

[6] Paul S. Heckbert and Henry P. Moreton. Interpolation for polygon texture mapping and shading. In David F. Rogers and Rae A. Earnshaw, editors, *State of the Art in Computer Graphics: Visualization and Modeling*, pages 101–111. Springer-Verlag, 1991.

[7] Kazufumi Kaneda, Eihachiro Nakamae, Tomoyuki Nishita, Hideo Tanaka, and Takao Noguchi. Three dimensional terrain modeling and display for environmental assessment. In *Proceedings of SIGGRAPH '89*, pages 207–214, 1989.

[8] William T. Reeves, David H. Salesin, and Robert L. Cook. Rendering antialiased shadows with depth maps. In *Proceedings of SIGGRAPH '87*, pages 283–291, 1987.

[9] Steve Upstill. *The RenderMan Companion*, pages 371–374. Addison Wesley, 1990.

[10] Lance Williams. Casting curved shadows on curved surfaces. In *Proceedings of SIGGRAPH '78*, pages 270–274, 1978.

A Fast and Accurate Light Reflection Model

Xiao D. He   Patrick O. Heynen   Richard L. Phillips*

Kenneth E. Torrance   David H. Salesin

Donald P. Greenberg

Program of Computer Graphics
Cornell University
Ithaca, New York 14853

*Los Alamos National Laboratory
Los Alamos, New Mexico 87545

Abstract

This multimedia paper elaborates on the comprehensive physically-based light reflection model introduced by He *et al.* [1]. To explain the model more fully, the paper gives an overview of the light reflection process at a surface, and employs an interactive graphical tool to demonstrate the reflection model's directional behavior. To make the model more practical, the paper describes an accurate approximation of the reflection model, based on a spline surface, that is much faster to compute. The paper concludes with two animated sequences, which demonstrate some features of light reflection that are accounted for by the model. The full paper demonstrates the potential of interactive multimedia. It is written using MediaView [2], a system for authoring documents that include graphics, sound, video, and computer animation.

CR Categories and Subject Descriptors: I.3.7 [Computer Graphics]: Three-Dimensional Graphics and Realism; I.3.3 [Computer Graphics]: Picture/Image Generation; J.2 [Physical Sciences and Engineering]: Physics.

Additional Key Words: reflectance model, multimedia.

1 Introduction

For photorealistic image generation it is essential to use a comprehensive light reflection model that provides a smooth transition from specular to diffuse behavior. In addition, to ensure accuracy the model must be physically based.

For these reasons, a new general light reflection model was presented by He *et al.* at SIGGRAPH '91 [1]. The model is based on physical optics and describes specular, directional diffuse, and uniform diffuse reflections off a surface. The reflected light pattern depends on wavelength, incidence angle, two surface roughness parameters, and the surface refractive index. The model applies to a wide range of materials and surface finishes, and has been experimentally verified.

However, the model also has some disadvantages. It contains an infinite summation term that converges very slowly. In addition, because the model is complex, it is difficult to understand.

In this multimedia paper we address both of these issues. To help explain the light reflection model, the paper gives a graphical overview of the light reflection process at a surface, and employs an interactive graphical tool to demonstrate the model's directional behavior. This tool allows the viewer to observe the effects on the various terms of the light distribution function as parameters are changed.

To make the model practical, the paper describes how the infinite summation term can be closely approximated by a spline surface and stored as a small lookup table of control points. This approximation allows very fast computation of the full BRDF, as demonstrated by the interactive sessions themselves.

Finally, the multimedia paper includes two animation sequences, which demonstrate some features of light reflection that are accounted for by the physically-based model and were not accounted for by previous models.

The full paper was written using the MediaView system, developed by Richard Phillips [2]. In this extended abstract, we attempt to give the flavor of the full multimedia document by using a sequence of illustrations from its interactive tools and animations.

2 Understanding the physically-based model

The bidirectional reflectance distribution function (BRDF) depends on a number of geometrical and physical parameters [1]. The geometrical parameters include, among other things, the polar angle of incidence θ and the solid angle of the incident beam $d\omega$. The physical parameters include the wavelength of the light λ, as well as some physical parameters of the surface—its "roughness," given by σ and τ, which specify the height and width of small statistical peaks on the surface; and its index of refraction $\bar{n}$, which is a function of λ.

The full BRDF can be divided into three major reflection components—specular, directional diffuse, and uniform diffuse—which in turn can be broken into smaller terms, such as Fresnel reflectivity, effective roughness, and surface masking and shadowing. Each of these terms can be written as a function of the various geometrical and physical parameters of the reflecting surface and the illuminating light.

In the multimedia paper, the reader learns about the behavior of the full BRDF by studying the effect of these various parameters on each of the model's terms. The user interacts with the model by varying the positions of sliders on the menu shown in Figure 2. To vary the index of refraction $\bar{n}$, the user changes the material "type" (e.g., aluminum is selected in Figure 2). In addition, by touching

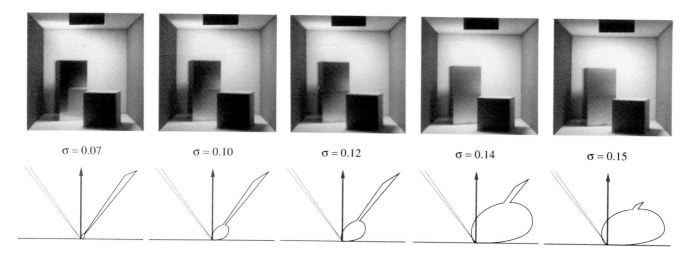

| $\sigma = 0.07$ | $\sigma = 0.10$ | $\sigma = 0.12$ | $\sigma = 0.14$ | $\sigma = 0.15$ |

Figure 1: Effect of surface roughness σ (in μm) on light reflection

the "Play" button, the user can watch a "prerecorded" demonstration of this interaction, which is played back along with an audio track explaining the parameter effects.

The graphical style of this interactive tool is illustrated in the bottom row of Figure 1, which shows a sequence of polar plots of the full BRDF for aluminum as the surface roughness parameter (σ) is increased.

3 A fast approximation

In order to make the light reflection model computationally tractable, we describe how it can be approximated by a spline surface. This surface can be computed once for all materials and stored as a two-dimensional lookup table of control points. A table of 80×80 points allows any material's reflection function to be approximated to within a relative error of 1%. Using this spline approximation gives a two- to three-orders-of-magnitude speedup over computing the summation directly to within 1% error.

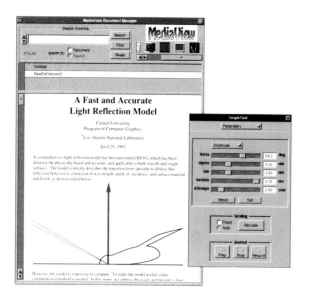

Figure 2: Control panel and document

4 Animated sequences

To demonstrate some features of the physically-based light reflection model that are not accounted for by previous models, the paper uses two animated sequences.

The first animation shows the transition of reflections on the faces of a roughened aluminum box as the surface roughness (σ) increases. Five frames of this sequence are shown in the top row of Figure 1. Above each frame is shown a schematic diagram of the BRDF for that value of σ.

The second animation shows the emergence of specular reflection off a gallery floor as the camera moves to grazing angles. Three frames of this sequence are shown in Figure 3.

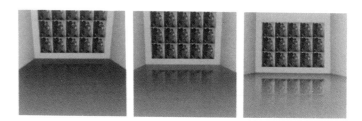

Figure 3: Emergence of specular reflection

Acknowledgments

This work was supported by the NSF grant, "Interactive Computer Graphics Input and Display Techniques" (CCR-8617880), by the NSF/DARPA Science and Technology Center for Computer Graphics and Scientific Visualization (ASC-8920219), and by generous donations of equipment from Hewlett-Packard and NeXT.

References

[1] Xiao D. He, Kenneth E. Torrance, François X. Sillion, and Donald P. Greenberg. A comprehensive physical model for light reflection. *Computer Graphics* 25(4): 175–86, 1991.

[2] Richard L. Phillips. A general multimedia publishing system. *Communications of the ACM* 34(7), 1991.

Predicting Reflectance Functions from Complex Surfaces

Stephen H. Westin
James R. Arvo
Kenneth E. Torrance

Program of Computer Graphics
Cornell University
Ithaca, New York 14853

Abstract

We describe a physically-based Monte Carlo technique for approximating bidirectional reflectance distribution functions (BRDFs) for a large class of geometries by directly simulating optical scattering. The technique is more general than previous analytical models: it removes most restrictions on surface microgeometry. Three main points are described: a new representation of the BRDF, a Monte Carlo technique to estimate the coefficients of the representation, and the means of creating a milliscale BRDF from microscale scattering events. These allow the prediction of scattering from essentially arbitrary roughness geometries. The BRDF is concisely represented by a matrix of spherical harmonic coefficients; the matrix is directly estimated from a geometric optics simulation, enforcing exact reciprocity. The method applies to roughness scales that are large with respect to the wavelength of light and small with respect to the spatial density at which the BRDF is sampled across the surface; examples include brushed metal and textiles. The method is validated by comparing with an existing scattering model and sample images are generated with a physically-based global illumination algorithm.

CR Categories and Subject Descriptors: I.3.7 [Computer Graphics]: Three-Dimensional Graphics and Realism.
Additional Key Words: spherical harmonics, Monte Carlo, anisotropic reflection, BRDF

1 Introduction

Since the earliest days of computer graphics, experimenters have recognized that the realism of an image is limited by the sophistication of the model of local light scattering [3, 12]. Non-physically-based local lighting models, such as that of Phong [12], although computationally simple, exclude many important physical effects and lack the energy consistency needed for global illumination calculations. Physically-based models [2, 5, 15] reproduce many effects better, but cannot

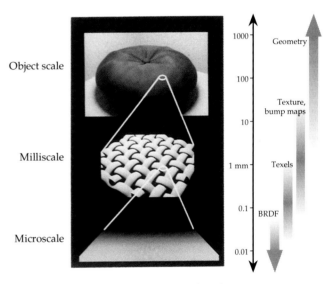

Figure 1: Applicability of Techniques

model many surfaces, such as those with anisotropic roughness. Models that deal with anisotropic surfaces [8, 11] fail to assure physical consistency.

This paper presents a new method of creating local scattering models. The method has three main components: a concise, general representation of the BRDF, a technique to estimate the coefficients of the representation, and a means of using scattering at one scale to create a BRDF for a larger scale. The representation used makes it easy to enforce the basic physical property of scattering reciprocity, and its approximation does not require discretizing scattering directions as in the work of Kajiya [8] and Cabral et al. [1].

The method can predict scattering from any geometry that can be ray-traced: polygons, spheres, parametric patches, and even volume densities. Previous numerical techniques were limited to height fields, and analytical methods have been developed only for specific classes of surface geometry. The new method accurately models both isotropic and anisotropic surfaces such as brushed metals, velvet, and woven textiles.

Figure 1 shows several representations used in realistic rendering, along with approximate scale ranges where each is applicable. At the smallest scale (size ≪ 1 mm), which we call *microscale*, the BRDF accurately captures the appearance of a surface. As individual surface features become larger than one pixel, texture maps, bump maps, and texels can be used to show surface features. At the largest scale, *object scale*, the geometry must be modeled explicitly, for example with polygons or parametric patches.

The applicability of each representation ultimately depends on the context: the upper limit of applicable scale is determined by the frequency of sampling across a surface, and the lower limit is determined by the integration area for each sample; this is often the surface area represented by a pixel. When rendering, say, an interior scene, objects as small as a pencil must be modeled at object scale; when simulating the view from orbit, however, objects as large as trees and buildings can be modeled within the BRDF, so we can think of them as microscale geometry, or *microgeometry*. The advent of global illumination methods (e.g. [6, 18]) has created another concept of scale: these methods generally use a coarser characterization of scattering for indirect illumination, but demand careful attention to energy consistency and physical accuracy.

The method of this paper is applicable wherever the BRDF is an adequate model of surface geometry. It uses an analytical BRDF model for scattering at one scale of roughness, the *microscale*, simulating geometric optical scattering at a larger scale, the *milliscale*. Milliscale scattering embodies large-scale roughness effects (roughness size $\gg$ wavelength of light, λ), and any smooth surface effects (roughness size $\approx \lambda$ or $< \lambda$) are modeled by the microscale BRDF, which can include wave optics effects.

The next three sections present the heart of the technique: the BRDF representation, the Monte Carlo estimator, and the means of estimating a milliscale BRDF from the microscale description of surface roughness.

2 Wheels Within Wheels: Representing the BRDF with Spherical Harmonics

A general scattering function for unpolarized light is a function of four variables, $\rho_{bd}(\theta_i, \phi_i, \theta_r, \phi_r) : S^2 \times S^2 \mapsto \mathcal{R}$, where S^2 is the unit sphere, θ_i, ϕ_i are the elevation and azimuth angles of incidence, and θ_r, ϕ_r are the corresponding angles of reflection (Figure 2). For a BRDF, ρ_{bd} is zero whenever θ_i or $\theta_r > \frac{\pi}{2}$. The BRDF can take on highly arbitrary shapes [5, 16], so a very general method is needed to represent it. Fortunately, a BRDF

is generally smooth, making it a good candidate for representation by smooth orthogonal functions. Previous authors have used spherical harmonics to represent scattering functions [1, 9, 13], since they form a complete basis set of smooth functions over the sphere. Kajiya [9] used spherical harmonics to derive an analytical scattering function; Cabral et al. [1] and Sillion et al. [13] used them as a numerical approximation to the BRDF. The representation used in this paper is an extension of Sillion's technique; it provides an accurate, concise embodiment of the general BRDF.

2.1 Overview of Spherical Harmonics

Any square-integrable function over the sphere can be exactly represented by an infinite sum of spherical harmonic basis functions, $Y_{lm}(\theta, \phi)$, of varying order, l, and degree, m:

$$f(\theta, \phi) = \sum_{l=0}^{\infty} \sum_{m=-l}^{l} C_{lm} Y_{lm}(\theta, \phi). \tag{1}$$

As with a Fourier representation, we can approximate f by truncating the series to a finite number of terms. For convenience, we organize this finite collection of basis functions into a vector by the convention of encoding both order and degree with a single subscript. Thus

$$f(\theta, \phi) \approx \sum_{k=0}^{n} C_k Y_k(\theta, \phi) = \mathbf{C} \cdot \mathbf{Y}(\theta, \phi). \tag{2}$$

Each coefficient C_k is defined by the inner product of $f(\theta, \phi)$ with the corresponding spherical harmonic basis function:

$$\begin{aligned} C_k &= \int_0^{2\pi} \int_0^{\pi} f(\theta, \phi) Y_k(\theta, \phi) \sin \theta \, d\theta \, d\phi \\ &= \langle Y_k | f \rangle. \end{aligned} \tag{3}$$

This follows directly from the orthogonality of the basis functions [17].

2.2 Representing the BRDF

If we fix the incident direction (θ_i, ϕ_i), the BRDF is a function of two variables, (θ_r, ϕ_r), and the representation in Equation 2 suffices. To account for variation of the BRDF with incident direction, the coefficient vector $\mathbf{C}$ in Equation 2 can be thought of as a function of the incident direction. If a surface has isotropic roughness, as assumed in [1] and [13], the scattering function ρ_{bd} is independent of rotation about the surface normal. In this case,

$$\rho_{bd}(\theta_i, \phi_i, \theta_r, \phi_r) = \rho_{bd}(\theta_i, 0, \theta_r, \phi_r - \phi_i). \tag{4}$$

Each coefficient C_k is a function of θ_i alone, which can be calculated for a number of selected values of θ_i and interpolated for all θ_i [1, 13]. In general, however, a BRDF is a function of ϕ_i as well as of $(\theta_i, \theta_r, \phi_r)$, so a richer representation is needed.

2.3 Extension to Anisotropic Surfaces

For an anisotropic surface both θ_i and ϕ_i must be considered, and none of the previous representations suffices [1, 13]. Each coefficient C_k in Equation 2 is thus a function of θ_i and ϕ_i:

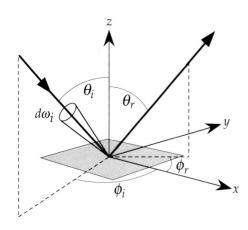

Figure 2: Scattering Angles

Nomenclature

C_k	Spherical harmonics coefficient for basis function Y_k
$\mathbf{C}$	Vector of coefficients
E_i	Incident energy flux density (irradiance)
E_r	Reflected energy flux density
G_k	Estimator of C_k
I_i	Incident radiance
I_r	Reflected radiance
$\mathbf{M}$	Exact matrix of coefficients to represent ρ_{bd}
$\widetilde{\mathbf{M}}$	Monte Carlo approximation of $\mathbf{M}$
m_{jk}	Element at row j, column k of matrix $\mathbf{M}$
N_b	Number of exit rays resulting from one incident ray
N_i	Number of incident ray directions
N_p	Number of sample points on surface of specimen
$p(\theta_i, \phi_i, \theta_r, \phi_r)$	Probability density function of scattering from (θ_i, ϕ_i) to (θ_r, ϕ_r)
$R(\theta_i, \phi_i, \theta_r, \phi_r)$	Attenuation of a single ray incident from (θ_i, ϕ_i) and reflected to (θ_r, ϕ_r)
$Y_k(\theta, \phi)$	Spherical harmonics basis function
$\mathbf{Y}$	Vector of basis functions
θ	Elevation angle: $\theta = 0$ at surface normal
ϕ	Azimuth angle: $\phi = 0$ at x axis
$\rho_{bd}(\theta_i, \phi_i, \theta_r, \phi_r)$	Milliscale bidirectional reflectance distribution function (BRDF)
$\hat{\rho}_{bd}(\theta_i, \phi_i, \theta_r, \phi_r)$	Microscale bidirectional reflectance distribution function (BRDF)
$\hat{\rho}_s(\theta_i, \phi_i)$	Microscale specular reflectivity
$d\omega_i$	Differential solid angle of incident energy
$d\omega_r$	Differential solid angle of reflected energy
$\langle a \mid b \rangle$	Inner product of two functions: $\int a(t)b(t)dt$
$\langle \xi \rangle$	Expected value of random variable ξ

$$\rho_{bd}(\theta_i, \phi_i, \theta_r, \phi_r) \approx \sum_{k=0}^{n} C_k(\theta_i, \phi_i) Y_k(\theta_r, \phi_r). \tag{5}$$

Each coefficient function, $C_k(\theta_i, \phi_i)$, is defined by the inner product of $\rho_{bd}(\theta_i, \phi_i, \cdot, \cdot)$ with the corresponding spherical harmonic basis function:

$$C_k(\theta_i, \phi_i) = \langle \rho_{bd} \mid Y_k \rangle_{refl} \tag{6}$$

where the subscript "refl" denotes integration over the reflected hemisphere. Reciprocity makes the dependence of ρ_{bd} on (θ_i, ϕ_i) exactly like its dependence on (θ_r, ϕ_r). Since spherical harmonics concisely represent the latter dependence, we also use them to represent the dependence on (θ_i, ϕ_i), expressing each coefficient function in terms of spherical harmonics. Each element of our vector $\mathbf{C}$ of coefficients is now represented in turn by a vector of coefficients, giving us a matrix $\mathbf{M}$ to represent the BRDF. Each element of the matrix $\mathbf{M}$ is given by

$$m_{jk} = \left\langle Y_j \mid \langle \rho_{bd} \mid Y_k \rangle_{refl} \right\rangle_{in} \tag{7}$$

where the subscripts "in" and "refl" denote integration over the incident and reflected hemispheres, respectively. Evaluation of the BRDF becomes

$$\begin{aligned}
\rho_{bd}(\theta_i, \phi_i, \theta_r, \phi_r) &\approx \sum_{j=0}^{N} \sum_{k=0}^{N} Y_j(\theta_i, \phi_i) m_{jk} Y_k(\theta_r, \phi_r) \\
&= \mathbf{Y}^T(\theta_i, \phi_i) \mathbf{M} \mathbf{Y}(\theta_r, \phi_r), \tag{8}
\end{aligned}$$

where $\mathbf{Y}(\theta, \phi)$ is the column vector of basis functions evaluated at (θ, ϕ).

2.4 Reciprocity

An important physical constraint on the BRDF is *reciprocity*, which states that

$$\rho_{bd}(\theta_i, \phi_i, \theta_r, \phi_r) = \rho_{bd}(\theta_r, \phi_r, \theta_i, \phi_i) \tag{9}$$

for all angles of incidence and reflection [14]. If the matrix $\mathbf{M}$ is symmetric, then

$$\mathbf{Y}^T(\theta_i, \phi_i) \mathbf{M} \mathbf{Y}(\theta_r, \phi_r) = \mathbf{Y}^T(\theta_r, \phi_r) \mathbf{M} \mathbf{Y}(\theta_i, \phi_i) \tag{10}$$

and the approximation in Equation 8 satisfies Equation 9. By assuring that we compute a symmetric matrix $\mathbf{M}$, we can enforce exact reciprocity; previous approaches [1, 8, 11, 13] afforded, at best, approximate reciprocity.

2.5 Storage Reduction and Filtering

The matrix $\mathbf{M}$ can be quite large; tens of thousands of elements are typical. Since our BRDF representation, like that of [13], is based on spherical harmonics, we can adapt two techniques from that work to reduce the number of coefficients (and corresponding basis functions) needed: the first technique causes half the coefficients to vanish, and the second reduces the high-frequency content of the BRDF, reducing the number of coefficients needed to achieve an acceptably accurate approximation. Since we deal only with scattering to one hemisphere, we can complete the other hemisphere with an arbitrary function. We chose a function which reduces the size of the representation: $\rho_{bd}(\theta_i, \phi_i, \pi - \theta_r, \phi_r) = -\rho_{bd}(\theta_i, \phi_i, \theta_r, \phi_r)$; this causes half of the coefficients (those with $l + m$ even in the real form of spherical harmonics) to be zero; they can be omitted from the representation, reducing the matrix size by $\frac{3}{4}$. To economize further, we represent $\rho_{bd} \cos \theta_i \cos \theta_r$ instead of ρ_{bd}; Multiplication by $\cos \theta_i$, together with the completion described above, forces C^1 continuity at the equator and drastically reduces ringing. To maintain symmetry of the matrix $\mathbf{M}$, we also multiply by $\cos \theta_r$. Representing $\rho_{bd} \cos \theta_i \cos \theta_r$ assures that Equation 9 is still satisfied. We omit this implementation detail from the following discussion.

As with a Fourier representation of a function, simply truncating all coefficients with index $l > l_{max}$ will cause ringing in the approximation, called the Gibbs phenomenon. To reduce this, we attenuate higher frequencies, as did Cabral et al. [1], by progressively reducing the magnitude of coefficients with $l_{filter} < l \leq l_{max}$, where l_{filter} is an empirically-determined threshold. The magnitude is reduced according to a half-Gaussian with empirically-determined width.

3 Monte Carlo Estimation of the Coefficient Matrix

If we bombard a specimen with incident rays from an arbitrary direction $U = (\theta_i, \phi_i)$, the BRDF can be expressed as

$$\rho_{bd}(U, V) = \frac{p(U, V) \langle R(U, V) \rangle}{\cos \theta_r} \qquad (11)$$

where a ray from direction U will scatter into $V = (\theta_r, \phi_r)$ with a probability density $p(U, V)$, and $\langle R(U, V) \rangle$ is the mean attenuation of all rays incident from direction U and scattered in direction V.

In order to obtain a spherical harmonics coefficient, we must integrate the product $\rho_{bd} Y_k$ over the hemisphere.

$$\begin{aligned} C_k(U) &= \int_{S^2} \rho_{bd}(U, V) Y_k(V) dV \\ &= \int_{S^2} \langle g_k(U, V) \rangle p(U, V) dV \end{aligned} \qquad (12)$$

where

$$g_k(U, V) = \frac{R(U, V)}{\cos \theta_r} Y_k(V). \qquad (13)$$

Unfortunately we have no analytical expression for p or R; we can, however, use a Monte Carlo simulation to estimate the integral in Equation 12. The integral can be interpreted as the expected value of $g(U, V)$, where V is a random variable with probability density function $p(U, V)$. If we define

$$G_k(U) = \frac{1}{N} \sum_{n=1}^{N} g_k(U, V_n) \qquad (14)$$

where V_n are random samples distributed according to p, then the expected value of G_k is $C_k(U)$; G_k is said to be an *estimator* of the integral [10]. The rays departing from the specimen in direction V will have mean attenuation $\langle R(U, V) \rangle$; this attenuation must be multiplied by $Y_k(V) / \cos \theta_r$ to give the expected value g for the estimator.

This leaves another integration, that with respect to U:

$$m_{jk} = \int_{S^2} C_k(U) Y_j(U) dU. \qquad (15)$$

This integration can also be handled via Monte Carlo, this time as *quadrature*, a discrete approximation to an integral. This is handled similarly, with the estimator

$$\widetilde{m}_{jk} = \frac{1}{N} \sum_{n=1}^{N} C_j(U_n) Y_j(U_n) \qquad (16)$$

where the U_n are uniformly distributed over the incident hemisphere. These two sampling processes, each approximating an integral in two dimensions, can be combined into one process to approximate the four-dimensional integral desired.

$$\widetilde{m}_{jk} = \frac{1}{N} \sum_{n=1}^{N} g_k(U_n, V_n) Y_j(U_n) \qquad (17)$$

where the U_n are distributed uniformly and the V_n are distributed according to p. $\widetilde{m}_{jk}$ is an unbiased estimator of m_{jk}.

The simulation yields $\widetilde{\mathbf{M}}$, an approximation to the symmetric matrix $\mathbf{M}$, and does not guarantee symmetry, so reciprocity of the BRDF is not guaranteed. We average the upper triangle and the lower triangle of $\widetilde{\mathbf{M}}$ to obtain a symmetric matrix $\frac{1}{2}(\widetilde{\mathbf{M}} + \widetilde{\mathbf{M}}^T)$ which is used to compute ρ_{bd}. The two triangles are independent unbiased estimates of the BRDF; by averaging them to obtain a symmetric matrix, we also reduce the variance of our estimate of $\mathbf{M}$.

4 From Microscale to Milliscale

The BRDF can be used to model features ranging from microscale to milliscale for visible light, as shown in Figure 1. This section explains how to use microscale scattering events to calculate a milliscale BRDF. The section starts with basic BRDF definitions, describes the individual microscale scattering events, then explains how individual Monte Carlo events are incorporated into the milliscale model to obtain an aggregate BRDF.

At the microscale, arbitrary reflection models may be employed, including ideal specular, ideal diffuse, and directional diffuse models. One illustrative case is where the microgeometry is composed of planar ideal specular surfaces; this is equivalent to geometric optics models based on microfacets, such as the Torrance-Sparrow model [15].

We use ray tracing to model scattering events, as suggested by Cabral et al. [1]. The ray tracer must be carefully designed to assure physically accurate results. Each ray has a certain amount of energy associated with it; microscale reflection will attenuate this energy and perhaps divide it among multiple rays at each bounce. All calculations involve energy flux density until a ray finally exits the model; then the energy is converted to radiance, the proper quantity for the BRDF, by dividing by $\cos \theta_r$. The radiance distribution is averaged over the specimen surface to create a milliscale BRDF.

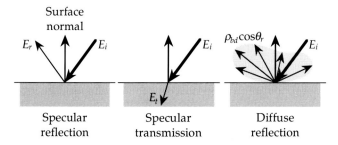

Figure 3: Local Scattering Modes

4.1 Incident Energy and the BRDF

We are estimating the BRDF ρ_{bd}, which is expressed at a given wavelength as

$$\rho_{bd}(\theta_r, \phi_r, \theta_i, \phi_i) = \frac{dI_r(\theta_r, \phi_r)}{dE_i(\theta_i, \phi_i)} \qquad (18)$$

where dI_r is the reflected radiance and dE_i is the incident energy flux density, the incident energy per unit time per unit area. This equation holds at both micro- and milliscales. It becomes simpler to evaluate if we hold the denominator (incident energy flux density) constant and vary the incident angles θ_i, ϕ_i. Then

$$\rho_{bd}(\theta_r, \phi_r, \theta_i, \phi_i) = \frac{dI_r(\theta_r, \phi_r)}{dE_i} \qquad (19)$$

where dE_i is the (constant) incident energy flux density.

Incident radiance I_i is defined as the incident energy flux density per unit projected area per unit solid angle

$$I_i = \frac{dE_i}{\cos \theta_i d\omega_i}. \qquad (20)$$

Thus

$$dE_i(\theta_i, \phi_i) = I_i(\theta_i, \phi_i) \cos \theta_i d\omega_i. \qquad (21)$$

The factor $\cos \theta_i$ converts receiving area to projected area, accounting for the dependence of projected surface area on θ_i.

The method allows different local scattering modes, three of which are shown in Figure 3. The next three sections describe how these modes are modeled.

4.2 Specular Reflection

The BRDF at the microscale may contain an ideal specular component $\hat{\rho}_s$. Whenever a ray hits such a microfacet, we model the transfer by spawning a ray in the specular direction as in classical ray-tracing [19]. The energy flux density of this ray is determined by the equation

$$dE_r = \hat{\rho}_s(\theta_i) dE_i \qquad (22)$$

where dE_i is the flux density of the incident ray, θ_i is the incident elevation with respect to the local facet, and $\hat{\rho}_s$ is the microscale specular reflection coefficient for the facet.

4.3 Specular Transmission

The method may be used to model microgeometries that include transparent materials. Whenever a ray encounters a smooth interface between media of different refractive indices, we must calculate the energy transfer through the interface. Neither energy flux density nor radiance is preserved at the interface [4], since solid angles are altered, but the distribution of transmitted rays accounts for this. We also must model any attenuation of the ray as it passes through a transparent medium; for a uniform medium, the ray is attenuated by $e^{-\kappa s}$ where s is the path distance and κ is an extinction coefficient determined by the material.

4.4 Directional-Diffuse Reflection

The most complex transfer takes place when a ray strikes a facet that shows directional-diffuse scattering. When a ray hits such a facet, we send out n rays to the hemisphere above the facet and weight them according to $\hat{\rho}_{bd}$; this serves as a discrete approximation of scattering according to the ideal-diffuse and directional-diffuse parts of the BRDF. The total energy transfer is determined by

$$\begin{aligned} dE_r(\theta_r, \phi_r) &= dI_r d\omega_r \cos \theta_r \\ &= dE_i \hat{\rho}_{bd}(\theta_i, \phi_i, \theta_r, \phi_r) d\omega_r \cos \theta_r \end{aligned} \qquad (23)$$

where dE_r is the reflected energy flux density in a particular direction, $\hat{\rho}_{bd}$ is the diffuse part (including directional-diffuse) of the microscale BRDF, and $d\omega_r$ is the solid angle of reflection. The angles (θ_r, ϕ_r) give the reflection direction with respect to the local facet. We multiply by $d\omega_r \cos \theta_r$ to convert the radiance given by $\hat{\rho}_{bd}$ to energy flux density for the next scattering event.

In our implementation reflected rays are cast randomly into the hemisphere above the local (microscale) surface; they are distributed uniformly over this hemisphere, so each ray represents a solid angle of

$$d\omega_r = \frac{2\pi}{n} \qquad (24)$$

where 2π is the total solid angle of the hemisphere and n is the number of reflected rays shot.

4.5 Integrating Over Milligeometry

We have described the possible microscale events of a single ray striking a point on the surface, but we must integrate over the specimen to obtain the aggregate BRDF. Just as the Monte Carlo integration was extended in Section 3 to accomodate the two dimensions of the incident hemisphere, it can be extended further to integrate over a two-dimensional specimen surface. We can keep the incident energy flux density constant by keeping both the total incident flux and the receiving surface area constant. We do this by shooting a constant number of rays (energy flux) and by distributing them over a constant surface area. The simplest way to do this is to select a fixed region of the surface, as shown in Figure 4, and to distribute the samples uniformly over this region at each incident angle. The direction of each ray is determined by the incident angles (θ_i, ϕ_i) with respect to the mean surface; its origin will be calculated so that the ray will strike the notional plane of the surface, shown in Figure 4 in red, at the chosen sample point.

Figure 4: Target Area

The surface region chosen should be

- large with respect to the lateral geometric features of the surface, to assure a good statistical average of large-scale scattering;

- large with respect to the *vertical thickness* of the surface geometry; and

- a subset of the total surface geometry, since geometry outside the nominal surface region will be important at high incident angles.

When a ray leaves the specimen area, we update the approximate matrix $\widetilde{\mathbf{M}}$ by adding $\mathbf{Y}(U)\mathbf{Y}^T(V)R/\cos\theta_r$. This matrix represents the BRDF ρ_{bd}. We integrate over the portion of the surface that is visible from the reflection direction (ϕ_r, θ_r), projected onto the mean surface.

4.6 Efficiency Considerations

We can reduce the computation needed to maintain the matrix $\widetilde{\mathbf{M}}$ by holding the incident direction U constant for several reflected directions V, updating the matrix only once for each distinct U. This happens automatically when several randomly distributed rays are spawned at each intersection, as in directional-diffuse scattering. In addition, we choose several target points on the surface for each U, further amortizing the cost of updating the matrix. Updating the matrix then becomes a triple sum

$$\widetilde{\mathbf{M}} = \frac{1}{N_i N_p N_b} \sum_{n=1}^{N_i} \mathbf{Y}(U_n) \left\{ \sum_{m=1}^{N_p} \sum_{l=1}^{N_b} \mathbf{Y}^T(V_{ml}) \frac{R_{nml}}{\cos\theta_r} \right\} \quad (25)$$

where R_{nml} is the attenuation of a ray from incident direction U_n reflected in direction V_l from target point P_m on the surface. N_i is the number of incident directions used, N_p is the number of sample positions across the specimen for each incident direction, and N_b is the number of exit rays resulting from a single incident ray. This approach reduces the number of evaluations of the spherical harmonics basis functions; for $N_i N_p N_b$ samples to update the matrix, $\mathbf{Y}(U)$ is evaluated only N_i times, while $\mathbf{Y}^T(V)$ is evaluated $N_i N_p N_b$ times. The greatest savings, however, comes in matrix adds; we need only perform N_i matrix additions; the other updates simply add vectors and require far less computation.

4.7 Convergence Measure

Since the exact matrix $\mathbf{M}$ is symmetric, we can use the asymmetry of our estimate as a measure of convergence in approximating the true BRDF. We calculate the error Q as

$$Q = \left\| \widetilde{\mathbf{M}} - \widetilde{\mathbf{M}}^T \right\| \quad (26)$$

where

$$\|\mathbf{A}\| = \frac{1}{N^2} \sum_{j=1}^{J} \sum_{k=1}^{J} |\mathbf{A}_{ij}| \quad (27)$$

where J is the size of the matrix $\mathbf{A}$. This is perhaps not as informative as a direct estimate of the variance of each coefficient, but is much cheaper to compute and tends to decline as $\frac{1}{\sqrt{N}}$, which suggests that it is directly proportional to the variance.

5 Results

We now show several applications of the technique. We obtain BRDF's for surfaces textured at milliscale. At the microscale, the BRDF can be ideal specular, ideal diffuse, or an analytical BRDF that includes wave optics effects. The technique can also be used recursively by using the results of one simulation as the microscale BRDF in another simulation.

All images shown in this section were generated by Monte Carlo ray tracing; the grainy texture of the images is caused by the Monte Carlo integration used to compute global illumination. Other global illumination and rendering techniques might have been used, such as that of Sillion et al. [13].

We first consider a flat Gaussian-rough surface for which, at the microscale, the surface is an ideal specular reflector. We can compare the results of the new method with the results of an existing analytical model for such a surface [5], thus giving some verification of the new technique.

5.1 Initial Verification: An Isotropic Surface

Wave optics effects were not included, except for the Fresnel coefficient for each microfacet. Reflection is governed by geometric optics; shadowing and masking effects of the surface are included because of the occlusion calculations in the ray tracer.

Gaussian height fields were generated by FFT filtering of white noise, and the resulting points were connected by triangles, each of which was modeled as a mirror. To integrate over a specimen large compared to the roughness height, an area of 8×8 millimeters was used. To assure adequate representation of the surface, a total of 524,288 polygons was used. The model was created in four sections of 131,072 polygons, each generated with a different random number seed, to represent a square patch of surface 4mm wide. The roughness length parameters of the surface were $\sigma = 10\mu m$ vertically and $\tau = 65\mu m$ horizontally (Figure 5). The specimen patch actually used was 3.13mm wide in the center of the geometric model; this assured that all incident rays would intersect the "sides" of the patch at least 2σ away from the notional plane.

Incident ray angles were restricted to $88°$ to keep the effective roughness greater than 460 nm, the shortest wavelength employed. This keeps behavior in the regime where geometric optics is valid; were the wavelength to approach the size

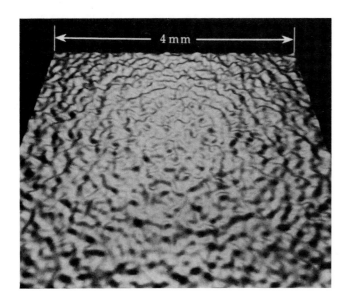

Figure 5: Gaussian Surface

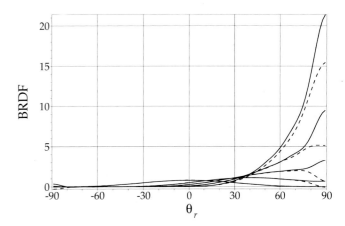

Figure 6: Comparison with Previous Model

of surface features, wave-related effects would begin to affect the scattering. Results are plotted as solid lines in Figure 6 for incident angles $\theta_i = 0°, 30°, 45°, 60°, 75°$. Dashed lines show results from the model of He [5], which assumes a Gaussian rough surface and allows for wave optics effects. The He model is shown in the limit of large surface roughness, $\sigma \gg \lambda$, where wave optics effects should be negligible. The simulation agrees quite well with the analytical model for reflection angles less than about $80°$; the divergence at greater angles is disturbing, but not very significant in terms of energy values. Recall that the BRDF ρ_{bd} gives a radiance value dI_r; the energy dE_r scattered in any reflected direction (θ_r, ϕ_r) is proportional to $dI_r \cos \theta_r$, reducing the effect of the error at high angles of reflection. We believe that the error results because we approximate $\rho_{bd} \cos \theta_r$. If we assume that error in approximating this function is roughly constant over the hemisphere, dividing by $\cos \theta_r$ to recover ρ_{bd} will magnify the error near the horizon (i.e. as $\theta_r \to \frac{\pi}{2}$).

5.2 Simple Anisotropy

We can use the method to create an anisotropic milliscale BRDF by using an isotropic analytical microscale BRDF model; we rely on He's analytical model for microgeometric effects, and use the new technique to model larger-scale anisotropy. Figure 7 shows, at the top, a model of parallel cylinders of slightly rough aluminum. In the left side of the figure, the cylinders are oriented with axes perpendicular to the screen; in the right side the axes are parallel to the screen. The bottom half of the figure shows a similar scene, but with two flat plates replacing the arrays of cylinders. Both plates use a BRDF generated from parallel cylinders like those in the top half of the figure. In the left half of the figure, the axis of anisotropy was oriented perpendicular to the screen; in the right half, it is oriented left-right.

The scattering patterns are similar; when viewed from a distance, the images look the same. The microscale BRDF is important for generating the upper images; the milliscale BRDF is used for the lower figures. Note how the surface orientation affects the appearance, revealing the anisotropic behavior of the reflected light. This is further illustrated in

Figure 8, where the same object is rendered with two BRDFs for brushed aluminum, one isotropic and one anisotropic.

Figures 9 and 10 show an aluminum automotive wheel and an aluminum teapot created using this anisotropic BRDF. The polishing scratches were oriented as from rotation, about the vertical axis of the teapot and about the hub of the wheel. The energy-consistency of the BRDF, not guaranteed by previous approaches, allows an accurate global illumination solution.

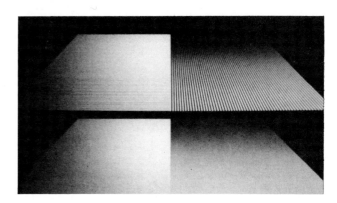

Figure 7: Parallel Cylinder Model of Anisotropic Surface

Figure 8: Isotropic and Anisotropic Aluminum

Figure 10: Anisotropic Aluminum Teapot

Figure 12: Velvet Doughnut

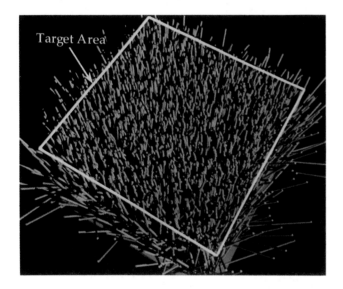

Figure 11: Microscale Geometry for Velvet

Figure 13: Microscale Structure of Cloth Model

5.3 Velvet

A more complex microgeometry is that of velvet: it consists of many roughly parallel specular fibers extending from a fabric base. This was modeled as a forest of narrow cylinders, with the angle of each cylinder perturbed randomly (Figure 11). The target area for incident rays is shown at the top of the fibers. The fibers are shown as ideal diffuse for clarity; in the BRDF simulation, the fibers were transparent ideal-specular plastic. Whenever a ray intersected a fiber, it was either reflected (with probability equal to the Fresnel reflectivity) or transmitted; when it intersected the base plane, it was absorbed. Figure 12 shows an image made using the resulting BRDF.

5.4 Woven Cloth

The method can also be used recursively to model several scales of roughness; this is demonstrated by modelling woven cloth as shown in Figure 1. At the milliscale, the

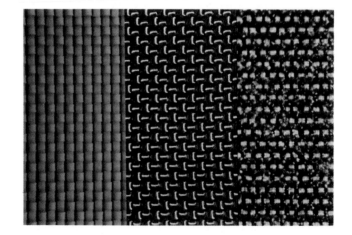

Figure 14: Cloth Microscale Geometry and Real Cloth

Figure 9: Anisotropic Aluminum Wheel

Figure 15: Nylon Cushion

weave pattern of the cloth was modeled as shown in Figure 13, and an anisotropic BRDF was used to model the scattering from individual fibers in the threads. The scattering from the surface of each thread (microgeometry) was modeled by the same geometry used in Section 5.2, but using a Fresnel reflectance function to simulate black synthetic fibers. Figure 14 has three parts: on the left, the cloth microgeometry is shown with an ideal-diffuse BRDF; in the center, it is shown with the thread BRDF, and on the right is a magnified photograph of actual cloth. Figure 15 shows a cushion upholstered in black nylon, rendered using the BRDF obtained from this process.

6 Conclusion

Three main points are described in this paper: a new representation of the BRDF, a Monte Carlo technique to estimate the coefficients of the representation, and the means of creating a milliscale BRDF from microscale scattering events. These allow the prediction of scattering for essentially arbitrary geometries. BRDFs for complex surfaces can be simulated hierarchically by using the result of one simulation in generating the BRDF for the next larger scale.

The new representation is concise and well-suited for use in rendering and global illumination calculations. The technique of [13] can be easily extended to accommodate the new representation. Its ease of evaluation suits it for other global illumination methods such as stochastic ray tracing [7, 18] as well.

The Monte Carlo integration used here enables us to model the scattering of many surfaces which have hitherto been impossible to model in computer graphics, producing accurate models for anisotropic surfaces and surfaces with transparent elements.

7 Acknowledgements

The authors would like to thank the Hewlett-Packard Company for donating the Apollo and HP workstations used in this work. Stephen Westin was supported by a fellowship funded by Ford Motor Company. Thanks to Xiao-Dong He for valuable discussions of the physical process of scattering, and to Don Greenberg and Roy Hall for careful reading and criticism of the manuscript. Special thanks to Julie and Kurk Dorsey and to Harold Zatz for their help in assembling the manuscript. Suzanne Smits assisted ably and patiently with the illustrations. Thanks also to Ben Trumbore, Jim Ferwerda, and Hurf Sheldon for maintaining an excellent software and hardware environment. Geometric models were graciously provided by Sabine Coquillart of INRIA for the cushion in Figures 1 and 15, and by Ford Motor Company Design Staff for the wheel in Figure 9.

References

[1] Cabral, B., Max, N., and Springmeyer, R., Bidirectional reflection functions from surface bump maps. In *Proceedings of SIGGRAPH '87*(July 27-31, 1987, Anaheim, California), *Computer Graphics* 21, 4 (July 1990), 273-281.

[2] Cook, R. L, and Torrance, K. E. A reflectance model for computer graphics, *ACM Transactions on Graphics* 1, 1 (January 1982), 7-24.

[3] Gouraud, H. Continuous shading for curved surfaces. *IEEE Transactions on Computers* 20, 6 (June 1971), 623-628.

[4] Hecht, E., and Zajac, A. *Optics*. Addison-Wesley, 1974.

[5] He, X. D., Torrance, K. E., Sillion, F. X., and Greenberg, D. P. A comprehensive physical model for light reflection. In *Proceedings of SIGGRAPH '91*(July 28-August 2, 1991, Las Vegas, Nevada), *Computer Graphics* 25, 4 (July 1991), 175-186.

[6] Goral, C. M., Torrance, K. E., Greenberg, D. P., and Battaile, B. Modeling the interaction of light between diffuse surfaces. In *Proceedings of SIGGRAPH '84*(July 23-27, 1984, Minneapolis, Minnesota), *Computer Graphics* 18, 3 (July 1984), 213-222.

[7] Kajiya, J. The rendering equation. In *Proceedings of SIGGRAPH '86*(August 18-22, 1986, Dallas, Texas), *Computer Graphics* 20, 4 (August 1986), 143-150.

[8] Kajiya, J. Anisotropic reflectance models. In *Proceedings of SIGGRAPH '85*(July 22-26, 1985, San Francisco, California), *Computer Graphics* 19, 4 (July 1985), 15-21.

[9] Kajiya, J., and Von Herzen, B. Ray tracing volume densities. In *Proceedings of SIGGRAPH '84*(July 23-27, 1984, Minneapolis, Minnesota), *Computer Graphics* 18, 3 (July 1984), 165-174.

[10] Kalos, M, H., and Whitlock, P. A. *Monte Carlo Methods*. John Wiley & Sons, 1986.

[11] Poulin, P., and Fournier, A. A model for anisotropic reflection. In *Proceedings of SIGGRAPH '90* (August 6-10, 1990, Dallas, Texas), *Computer Graphics* 24, 4 (August 1990), 273-282.

[12] Phong, B-T. Illumination for computer generated pictures., *Communications of the ACM* 18, 6 (June 1975), 311-317.

[13] Sillion, F. X., Arvo, J., Westin, S. H., and Greenberg, D. P. A global illumination solution for general reflectance distributions. In *Proceedings of SIGGRAPH '91* (July 28-August 2, 1991, Las Vegas, Nevada), *Computer Graphics* 25, 4 (July 1991), 187-196.

[14] Siegel, R., and Howell, J. R. *Thermal Radiation Heat Transfer*. Hemisphere Publishing, New York, 1981.

[15] Torrance, K. E. and Sparrow, E. M. Theory for off-specular reflection from roughened surfaces. In *Journal of the Optical Society of America* 57, 9 (September 1967) 1105-1114.

[16] Torrance, K. E. and Sparrow, E. M. Off-specular peaks in the directional distribution of reflected thermal radiation. In *Journal of Heat Transfer* (May 1966) 223-230.

[17] Wallace, P. R. *Mathematical Analysis of Physical Problems*. Dover Publications, Mineola, N. Y. 1984.

[18] Ward, G. J., Rubinstein, F. M. and Clear, R. D. A ray tracing solution for diffuse interreflection. In *Proceedings of SIGGRAPH '88* (August 1-5, 1988, Atlanta, Georgia), *Computer Graphics* 24, 4 (August 1988), 85-92.

[19] Whitted, T. An improved illumination model for shaded display. In *Communications of the ACM* 23, 6 (June 1980) 343-349.

Measuring and Modeling Anisotropic Reflection

Gregory J. Ward
Lighting Systems Research Group
Lawrence Berkeley Laboratory

ABSTRACT

A new device for measuring the spatial reflectance distributions of surfaces is introduced, along with a new mathematical model of anisotropic reflectance. The reflectance model presented is both simple and accurate, permitting efficient reflectance data reduction and reproduction. The validity of the model is substantiated with comparisons to complete measurements of surface reflectance functions gathered with the novel reflectometry device. This new device uses imaging technology to capture the entire hemisphere of reflected directions simultaneously, which greatly accelerates the reflectance data gathering process, making it possible to measure dozens of surfaces in the time that it used to take to do one. Example measurements and simulations are shown, and a table of fitted parameters for several surfaces is presented.

General Terms: algorithms, measurement, theory, verification. **CR Categories and Descriptors:** I.3.7 Three-dimensional graphics and realism, I.6.4 Model validation and analysis. **Additional Keywords and Phrases:** reflectance, Monte Carlo, raytracing, shading.

1. Introduction

Numerous empirical and theoretical models for the local reflection of light from surfaces have been introduced over the past 20 years. Empirical and theoretical models have the same goal of reproducing real reflectance functions, but the respective approaches are very different.

An empirical model is simply a formula with adjustable parameters designed to fit a certain class of reflectance functions. Little attention is paid to the physical derivation of the model, or the physical significance of its parameters. A good example of an empirical model is the one developed by Sandford [Sandford85]. This is a four parameter model of isotropic reflection, where the parameters must be fit to a specific set of reflectance measurements. While two of these parameters correspond roughly to measurable quantities such as total reflectance and specularity, the other two parameters have no physical significance and are merely shape variables that make the specular lobe of the model more closely match the data.

In contrast to an empirical model, a theoretical model attempts to get closer to the true distribution by starting from physical theory. A good example of a theoretical model is the one derived recently by He et al [He91]. This is also a four parameter isotropic model, but all four parameters have some physical meaning and can in principle be measured separately from the surface reflectance distribution. In practice, however, it is usually necessary to fit even a theoretical model to measurements of reflectance because the physical parameters involved are difficult to measure. This is the case in the He-Torrance model, since measurements of the requisite surface height variance and auto-correlation distance variables are impractical for most surfaces. Thus, the physical derivation of such a model serves primarily to inspire greater confidence, and is not necessarily a practical advantage when it comes to fitting measured data. As in all scientific disciplines, if the theory does not fit the data, then the theory must be discarded, not the data.

But where is the data? There is almost no published data on surface reflectance as a function of angle, and what little data is available is in the form of plane measurements of isotropic surfaces with no rotational variance in their reflectance functions. Thus, we have little to compare our reflectance models to, and no real assurance that they are valid. This means that we may once again be falling back on the "if it looks reasonable then it's OK" philosophy that has misdirected computer graphics so often in the past.

Why is the oldest specular model, the one introduced by Phong in 1975 [Phong75], still the most widely used to this day? This model is neither theoretically plausible nor empirically correct. Any renderings that use the straight Phong model are most likely wrong because the model is not physical, and more light may be emitted than is received (for example). The sole virtue of the Phong model is its mathematical simplicity.

Simplicity is indispensable in computer graphics. Simplicity is what permits fast renderings and hardware implementations. Without it, a reflectance model is little more than a novelty. Even a relatively straightforward model such as the one developed by Torrance and Sparrow [Torrance67] and tailored for rendering applications by Blinn [Blinn77] and later Cook [Cook82] has been underutilized in computer graphics due to its moderately complex form. More recent introductions by Poulin and Fournier [Poulin90] as well as He et al [He91] are even more complex. What is really needed for computer graphics is a simple reflectance model that works reasonably well for most materials.

Our goal in this paper is not to present the ultimate mathematical model of reflectance, but to provide a simple formula that is physically valid and fits measured reflectance data. Here we will present both a new method for measuring isotropic and anisotropic reflectance distributions and a mathematical model that fits these data with both accuracy and simplicity.

2. Definition of the BRDF

The interaction of light with a surface can be expressed as a single function, called the *bidirectional reflectance distribution function*, or BRDF for short [Nicodemus77]. This is a function of four angles, two incident and two reflected, as well as the wavelength and polarization of the incident radiation. For the sake of simplicity, we will leave wavelength and polarization out of our equations, but keep in mind that they are contained implicitly in the function ρ_{bd}, which is defined in terms of incident and reflected radiance by the following integral:

$$L_r(\theta_r, \phi_r) = \int_0^{2\pi} \int_0^{\pi/2} L_i(\theta_i, \phi_i)\, \rho_{bd}(\theta_i, \phi_i; \theta_r, \phi_r)\, \cos\theta_i\, \sin\theta_i\, d\theta_i\, d\phi_i \qquad (1)$$

where: ϕ is the azimuthal angle measured about the surface normal

     $L_r(\theta_r, \phi_r)$ is the reflected radiance (watts/steradian/meter^2)

     $L_i(\theta_i, \phi_i)$ is the incident radiance

     $\rho_{bd}(\theta_i, \phi_i; \theta_r, \phi_r)$ is the BRDF (steradian^{-1})

Author's address: 1 Cyclotron Rd., 90-3111, Berkeley, CA 94720.
E-mail: GJWard@lbl.gov

1992   ACM-0-89791-479-1/92/007/0265

The function ρ_{bd} is *bidirectional* because the incident and reflected directions can be reversed and the function will return the same value. This arises from the fact that the physics of light is the same run backwards as forwards, which is why light-backwards ray tracing works [Whitted80].

3. Measuring the BRDF of a Surface

A device for measuring BRDFs is called a *gonioreflectometer*. The usual design for such a device incorporates a single photometer that is made to move in relation to a surface sample, which itself moves in relation to a light source, all under the control of a computer. Because BRDFs are in general a function of four angles, two incident and two reflected, such a device must have four degrees of mechanical freedom to measure the complete function. This requires substantial complexity in the apparatus and long periods of time to measure a single surface. A typical gonioreflectometer arrangement, designed by Murray-Coleman and Smith [Murray-Coleman90], is shown in Figure 1.

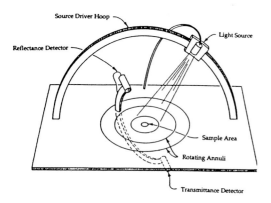

Figure 1. A conventional gonioreflectometer with movable light source and photometer.

As an alternative to building such a gonioreflectometer, there are several labs in North America where one can send a surface sample for BRDF characterization. For a few hundred dollars, one can get a three plane measurement of an isotropic material at four or five angles of incidence. (An isotropic material has a BRDF that is independent of rotation about the the normal. Therefore, only one ϕ_i direction is sampled.) Unfortunately, a comprehensive BRDF measurement of an anisotropic surface typically costs a few *thousand* dollars. (An anisotropic material reflects light differently at different angles of rotation, thus multiple ϕ_i directions must be sampled.) Because of the difficulty and expense of the BRDF measurements themselves, only the very richest research programs can afford their own data. This data is essential, however, for the correct modeling of surface reflectance.

3.1. An Imaging Gonioreflectometer

The Lighting Systems Research Group at Lawrence Berkeley Laboratory has developed a relatively simple device for measuring BRDFs that uses imaging technology to obtain results more quickly and at a lower cost than conventional methods. This *imaging gonioreflectometer* has been developed over the past three years and represents an important advance towards the more practical characterization of BRDFs for lighting simulation and computer graphics. It is our hope that other laboratories and research institutions will construct their own versions of this apparatus and thereby make BRDF measurement a more common and economical practice.

The basic arrangement of the LBL imaging gonioreflectometer is shown in Figure 2†. The key optical elements are a half-silvered hemisphere or hemi-ellipsoid and a charge-coupled device (CCD) camera with a fisheye lens. Combined, these elements take care of the two degrees of freedom handled by a mechanically controlled photometer in a conventional gonioreflectometer. Light reflected off the sample surface in

---

†A U.S. patent is pending on the imaging gonioreflectometer. If granted, the patent will restrict other patents on similar devices, but will not otherwise limit the free availability of the invention since it was developed under Department of Energy funding.

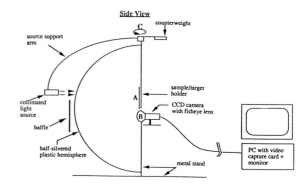

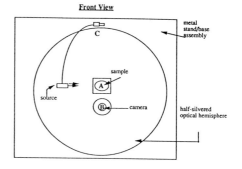

Figure 2. The LBL imaging gonioreflectometer.

holder A is collected by the hemispherical mirror and reflected back into the fisheye lens and onto the CCD array B. By focusing the lens at one half the hemisphere radius, a near perfect imaging of the reflected angles takes place. (See ray diagram in Figure 3.) Because of this highly efficient collector arrangement, the light source does not have to be very bright to obtain a good measurement, and can thus be optimized for collimation to get the best possible angular resolution. In our device, a 3-watt quartz-halogen lamp is used with an optically precise parabolic reflector to produce a well collimated beam. White light is preferable for photopic measurements, although an array of colored filters may be used to measure the spectral dependence of the BRDF. The hemisphere is half-silvered to allow the light beam to illuminate the sample, and an exterior baffle shields the camera from stray radiation. This unique arrangement of light source and optics allows retroreflection (light reflected back towards the light source) and transmission to be measured as well.

The incident θ_i and ϕ_i angles are controlled mechanically by pivoting the light source arm at point C and the sample holder at point A, respectively. In our current prototype, the light source is moved by a computer-controlled motor during data collection, and the sample is rotated manually. Because the hemisphere of reflected directions is captured in a single image, data collection proceeds quite rapidly and a complete BRDF can be recorded in a few minutes, including time for manual rotation of the sample.

3.2. Calibration and Data Reduction

All measurements are made relative to a standard diffuse sample and a background measurement. The background measurement is made with the source on but without any sample in the holder (using the dark room behind to simulate a black body), and is subtracted from the other measurements to reduce the effects of stray and ambient light. The standard sample measurement is used as a basis for obtaining absolute reflectance values using the following simple equation at each image point:

$$\rho_{bd} = \frac{v_{measured} - v_{background}}{v_{standard} - v_{background}} \cdot \frac{\rho_{standard}}{\pi} \qquad (2)$$

where:

$\rho_{standard}$ is the total diffuse reflectance of the standard sample

The ability to measure absolute BRDF values directly is an important feature of the imaging gonioreflectometer. Most other devices rely on auxiliary measurements of directional reflectance (ie. total reflectance for

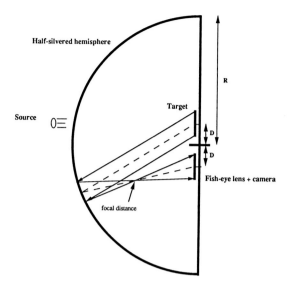

Figure 3. Imaging gonioreflectometer geometry. Light reflected by the sample in a specific direction is focused by the hemisphere or hemi-ellipsoid through a fisheye lens onto a CCD imaging array.

light incident at some (θ_i, ϕ_i)) and numerical integration to arrive at absolute quantities.

Recovering the reflected angles from pixel locations in the captured image is accomplished in two steps. The first step is to determine the mapping from image point locations to the lens incident direction. This is a function of the particular fisheye lens used, the camera, and the video capture board. Since this mapping varies so much from one implementation to the next and is easily measured, we will not discuss it any further here. The second step is to compute the target reflection angles from these camera incident angles. Figure 3 shows the geometry involved, and after a bit of trigonometry one can derive the following approximation:

$$r_c = D \sin\phi_c \sin\theta_c + \sqrt{D^2 \sin^2\phi_c \sin^2\theta_c + R^2 - D^2}$$

$$\theta_r = \cos^{-1}\left[\frac{r_c \cos\theta_c}{\sqrt{r_c^2 \cos^2\phi_c \sin^2\theta_c + (r_c \sin\phi_c \sin\theta_c - 2D)^2 + r_c^2 \cos^2\theta_c}} \right] \quad (3)$$

$$\phi_r = \tan^{-1}\left[r_c \sin\phi_c \sin\theta_c - 2Dr_c \cos\phi_c \sin\theta_c \right]$$

where:

θ_r is polar angle relative to target

ϕ_r is azimuthal angle relative to target, right is 0°

θ_c is polar angle relative to camera

ϕ_c is azimuthal camera angle, right is 0°

R is radius of sphere or approximate radius of ellipsoid

D is one half the separation between target and camera centers

r_c is an intermediate result which is the distance from camera to reflector

notes:

The arctangent in the above equation should be computed using the signs of the numerator and denominator to get a range of 360°. Many math libraries provide a function named atan2 for this purpose.

The above equations are a good approximation both for hemispherical and hemi-ellipsoidal reflectors as long as D is small in relation to R.

Figure 4. An image captured by the gonioreflectometer from an unfinished aluminum sample.

The image captured by our gonioreflectometer for a piece of unfinished aluminum illuminated at $(\theta_i, \phi_i) = (30°, 0°)$ is shown in Figure 4. Although the image was reduced before data reduction to a resolution of 108 by 80 pixels, there is still much more information than is needed for an accurate lighting simulation. Also, since two or more f-stops may be used to capture the full dynamic range of the BRDF, there is often redundant information where the useful ranges of exposures overlap. We therefore apply a program to eliminate crowding of data points and insure that the peak is recorded at a high enough angular resolution while the rest of the usable distribution is recorded at a uniform density. A data fitting program can then be used to match the reduced data set to a specific reflectance model.

3.3. Measurement Limitations

Our current implementation of the imaging gonioreflectometer has two main limitations in its measurement abilities. First, we are limited in our ability to measure the reflectance function near grazing angles, due to the size and shape of our reflecting hemisphere and the size of our sample. Our present hemisphere is formed from acrylic plastic and its optical properties are less than perfect, especially near the edges. It should be possible to partially overcome this limitation by placing the sample at right angles to its current configuration and illuminating it through the target holder, but this has not yet been tried. The ultimate solution would be to go to a larger, more precise hemisphere and a larger sample target.

The second limitation is our inability to measure more polished surfaces with sharp specular peaks. Again, the optical precision of our hemisphere is a problem, but so is the finite collimation of our light source. A highly uniform, collimated light source is required for the measurement of polished surfaces. That is why many commercial gonioreflectometers employ a laser, despite the laser's inability to yield spectrally balanced measurements. By using an incandescent source with an even smaller filament, it should be possible to measure more polished surfaces without resorting to a laser.

Note that the BRDF of a perfectly smooth surface is not directly measurable by *any* gonioreflectometer, since it is a Dirac delta function with an infinite value at a single point. Measuring such a BRDF of such a surface is not required however, since the physics of smooth surfaces are well understood and measurements of total reflectance are adequate for their characterization.

4. Modeling Anisotropic Reflectance

Armed with a device that can measure anisotropic reflectance functions economically, we need a mathematical model that can be fit to our newfound data. Using the data directly is impractical because it requires too much memory, and oftentimes the data is noisy and not complete enough to cover the entire domain of the BRDF. We could represent the BRDF as a sum of 100 or so terms in a spherical harmonic series, but this would also be expensive in terms of computation time and of memory [Cabral87][Sillion91]. We would prefer a model that fits the data with as few parameters as possible. Ideally, these parameters would be either physically derived or meaningful so that they could be set manually in the absence of any data at all.

Many models have been suggested for isotropic reflection, but only a few models have been published for the more general anisotropic case. Kajiya published a fairly robust method for deriving BRDFs of metals from surface microstructure [Kajiya85]. However, his approach is not amenable to fitting measured reflectance data because the parameter space is too large (ie. all possible surface microstructures) and the BRDFs take too long to compute. Poulin and Fournier developed a model based on cylindrical scratches that is better suited [Poulin90], but their model is restricted to a specific microstructure with cross-sectional uniformity, and its evaluation is still somewhat expensive.

Our goal is to fit our measured reflectance data with the simplest empirical formula that will do the job. If we can develop a model with physically meaningful parameters without adding undue complexity, so much the better.

4.1. The Isotropic Gaussian Model

The Gaussian distribution has shown up repeatedly in theoretical formulations of reflectance [Beckmann63][Torrance67][Cook82], and it arises from certain minimal assumptions about the statistics of a surface height function. It is usually preceded by a Fresnel coefficient and geometrical attenuation factors, and often by an arbitrary constant. Since the geometric attenuation factors are typically difficult to integrate and tend to counteract the Fresnel factor anyway, we have replaced all of these coefficients with a single normalization factor that simply insures the distribution will integrate easily and predictably over the hemisphere.

$$\rho_{bd,iso}(\theta_i,\phi_i;\theta_r,\phi_r) = \frac{\rho_d}{\pi} +$$
$$\rho_s \cdot \frac{1}{\sqrt{\cos\theta_i \cos\theta_r}} \cdot \frac{\exp[-\tan^2\delta/\alpha^2]}{4\pi\alpha^2} \qquad (4)$$

where:

ρ_d is the diffuse reflectance

ρ_s is the specular reflectance

δ is the angle between vectors $\hat{n}$ and $\hat{h}$ shown in Figure 5

α is the standard deviation (RMS) of the surface slope

notes:

The ρ values may have some spectral dependence, and this dependence may vary as a function of angle so long as $\rho_d + \rho_s$ (the total reflectance) is less than 1. Thus, Fresnel effects may be modeled if desired.

The normalization factor, $\frac{1}{4\pi\alpha^2}$, is accurate as long as α is not much greater than 0.2, when the surface becomes mostly diffuse.

The main difference between this isotropic Gaussian reflectance model and that of Phong is its physical validity. For example, most Phong implementations do not have the necessary bidirectional characteristics to constitute a valid BRDF model. It is clear by inspection that the above formula is symmetric with respect to its incident and reflected angles. Without this symmetry, a BRDF model cannot possibly be physical because the simulated surface reflects light differently in one direction than the other, which is forbidden by natural law. Also, without proper normalization, a reflectance model does not yield correct energy balance and thus cannot produce physically meaningful results. Even

the model introduced recently by He et al [He91] with its rigorous physical derivation does not seem to pay close enough attention to normalization. Specifically, the so-called ambient term in the He-Torrance model is added without regard to the overall reflectance of the material, which by nature of the model is very difficult to compute. Comparisons were not made in He's paper between the reflectance model and absolute BRDF measurements (the data was scaled to match the function), thus normalization was not even demonstrated empirically. The fact that normalization was not adequately treated in He's otherwise impeccable derivation shows just how much normalization is overlooked and undervalued in reflectance modeling. The simplicity of the model presented here is what allows us to incorporate built-in normalization and has other desirable features as well, such as permitting quick evaluation for data reduction and Monte Carlo sampling.

4.2. The Anisotropic (Elliptical) Gaussian Model

It is relatively simple to extend the Gaussian reflectance model to surfaces with two perpendicular (uncorrelated) slope distributions, α_x and α_y. The normalized distribution is as follows:

$$\rho_{bd}(\theta_i,\phi_i;\theta_r,\phi_r) = \frac{\rho_d}{\pi} +$$
$$\rho_s \cdot \frac{1}{\sqrt{\cos\theta_i \cos\theta_r}} \cdot \frac{\exp[-\tan^2\delta\,(\cos^2\phi/\alpha_x^2 + \sin^2\phi/\alpha_y^2)]}{4\pi\alpha_x\alpha_y} \qquad (5a)$$

where:

ρ_d is the diffuse reflectance

ρ_s is the specular reflectance

α_x is the standard deviation of the surface slope in the $\hat{x}$ direction

α_y is the standard deviation of the surface slope in the $\hat{y}$ direction

δ is the angle between the half vector, $\hat{h}$ and the surface normal, $\hat{n}$.

ϕ is the azimuth angle of the half vector projected into the surface plane.

A computationally convenient approximation for ρ_{bd} is:

$$\rho_{bd}(\theta_i,\phi_i;\theta_r,\phi_r) = \frac{\rho_d}{\pi} +$$
$$\rho_s \cdot \frac{1}{\sqrt{\cos\theta_i \cos\theta_r}} \cdot \frac{1}{4\pi\alpha_x\alpha_y} \exp\left[-2\,\frac{\left[\frac{\hat{h}\cdot\hat{x}}{\alpha_x}\right]^2 + \left[\frac{\hat{h}\cdot\hat{y}}{\alpha_y}\right]^2}{1 + \hat{h}\cdot\hat{n}}\right] \qquad (5b)$$

where:

$$\hat{h}\cdot\hat{x} = \frac{\sin\theta_r\cos\phi_r + \sin\theta_i\cos\phi_i}{||\vec{h}||}$$

$$\hat{h}\cdot\hat{y} = \frac{\sin\theta_r\sin\phi_r + \sin\theta_i\sin\phi_i}{||\vec{h}||}$$

$$\hat{h}\cdot\hat{n} = \frac{\cos\theta_r + \cos\theta_i}{||\vec{h}||}$$

$$||\vec{h}|| = \left[2 + 2\sin\theta_r\sin\theta_i(\cos\phi_r\cos\phi_i + \sin\phi_r\sin\phi_i) + 2\cos\theta_r\cos\theta_i\right]^{½}$$

For vector calculations, the following substitutions are used:

$$\vec{h} = \hat{d}_r + \hat{d}_i$$

$$\hat{h} = \frac{\vec{h}}{||\vec{h}||}$$

$$\cos\theta_r = \hat{d}_r\cdot\hat{n}$$

$$\cos\theta_i = \hat{d}_i\cdot\hat{n}$$

where:

$\hat{d}_r$ is the reflected ray direction (away from surface)

$\hat{d}_i$ is the incident ray direction (away from surface)

$\hat{x}$ is a unit vector in the surface plane

$\hat{y}$ is a unit vector in the surface plane perpendicular to $\hat{x}$

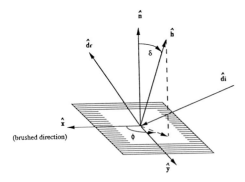

Figure 5. Angles and vectors used in reflection equations. The incident light arrives along vector $\hat{d}_i$ and is measured or simulated in direction $\hat{d}_r$. The polar angle between the half vector $\hat{h}$ and the surface normal $\hat{n}$ is δ. The azimuthal angle of $\hat{h}$ from the direction $\hat{x}$ is ϕ.

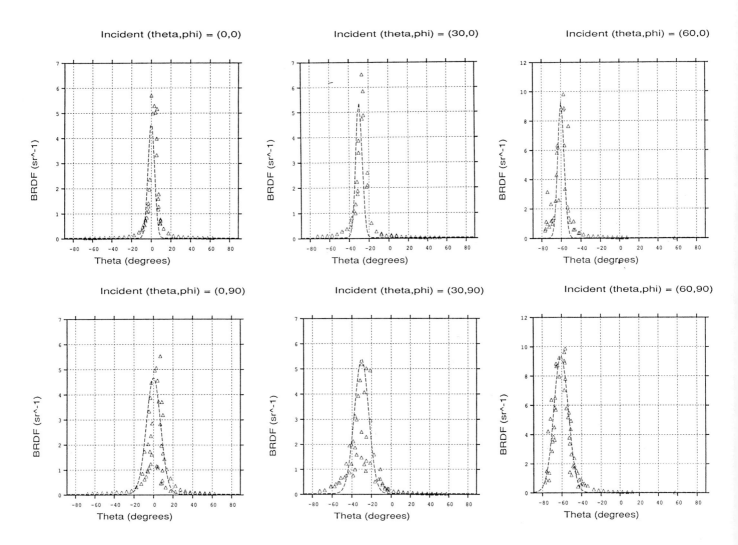

Figure 6. Measured data and elliptical Gaussian fit for unfinished aluminum. Unfinished aluminum exhibits anisotropy from rolling during its manufacture.

As in the isotropic case, the normalization of the above anisotropic model is such that the total surface reflectance will equal the diffuse reflectance coefficient, ρ_d, plus the "rough specular" or "directional-diffuse" coefficient, ρ_s. The two other model parameters, α_x and α_y, represent the standard deviation of the surface slope in each of two perpendicular directions. Thus, all four of the model's parameters have physical meaning and can be set independently of measured data to produce a valid reflectance function. As long as the total reflectance, $\rho_d + \rho_s$, is less than 1 and the two α's are not too large, Equation 5 will yield a physically valid reflectance function.

The elliptical nature of our model arises from the two perpendicular slope distributions, and is apparent in the exponent of Equation 5a. A similar elliptical reflectance model was developed by Ohira and described by Yokoi and Toriwaki [Yokoi88], but this model was derived from that of Phong and likewise lacks physical meaning. By starting with a valid, normalized function, it is much easier to fit the model parameters to physical measurements as well as other specifications such as appearance.

Our simple four parameter model fits well the data we have gathered from anisotropic surfaces such as varnished wood and unfinished (rolled) or brushed metals. Because of its simplicity, it is easy to apply a least squares error minimization method to fit a set of parameters to measured data automatically. Automatic data fitting is essential to the economic modeling of surface reflectance for any significant database of materials. Figure 6 shows an example fit to the BRDF of an unfinished aluminum sample. Although the full hemisphere of reflected data was measured at 21 incident angles, it is difficult to visualize the 21 corresponding 3-dimensional point plots. We therefore present here only a slice of the data in the incident plane at 6 angles. The results section (6) lists the fitted parameters for this material as well as some other example surfaces.

5. Rendering Anisotropic Surfaces

The challenge to applying a new reflectance model to computer graphics is to approximate the luminance equation (1) in a manner that is unbiased and has low variance [Kajiya86]. Unfortunately, unbiased techniques (ie. pure Monte Carlo) tend to have high variance, while low variance approaches (ie. closed-form approximations) tend to be biased. To satisfy these conflicting requirements, we use a hybrid deterministic and stochastic ray tracing technique [Cook84][Cook86]. A strictly deterministic calculation of the highlight contribution of sources, similar to the widely used Whitted approximation [Whitted80], fails to pick up indirect semispecular contributions as demonstrated in Figure 7a. (Note that the crescent shape of the highlight is due to longitudinal anisotropy and not the light source.) Conversely, relying solely on stochastic sampling causes the highlights from sources to show high variance in the form of excessive noise, even with 16 samples per pixel (Figure 7b). By combining the two techniques, using a deterministic solution for source contributions and a stochastic sampling for indirect contributions, we get a clean result without compromising accuracy. Figure 7c was calculated using the hybrid technique and the same number of samples as Figure 7b. Both figures took approximately the same time to compute. (Figure 7a took less time since no sampling was required.)

The hybrid approach described reduces to the following equation:

$$L(\theta_r, \phi_r) = I \frac{\rho_d}{\pi} + L_s \rho_s + \sum_{i=1}^{N} L_i \omega_i \cos\theta_i \rho_{bd}(\theta_i, \phi_i; \theta_r, \phi_r) \qquad (6)$$

where:

I is the indirect irradiance at this point (a constant ambient level or the result of a diffuse interreflection or radiosity calculation)

L_s is the radiance value in the Monte Carlo sample direction given in Equation 7 below

L_i is the radiance of light source i

ω_i is the solid angle (in steradians) of light source i

N is the number of light sources

ρ_{bd} is the elliptical Gaussian function defined in Equation 5

In applying this technique, it is very important not to bias the sample by overcounting the specular component. Bias is easily avoided by associating a flag with the stochastically sampled specular ray. If the ray hits a light source whose contribution is being included in a closed form calculation, then the ray is not counted. Few rays are wasted in this way, since light sources occupy a small amount of the visual space in most scenes.

5.1. Stochastic Sampling of Elliptical Gaussian

Because of its simplicity, the elliptical Gaussian model adapts easily to stochastic sampling techniques. Using standard Monte Carlo integral conversion methods [Rubenstein81], we can write the following formulas for obtaining uniformly weighted sample directions for each L_s ray in Equation 6:

$$\delta = \left[\frac{-\log(u_1)}{\cos^2\phi/\alpha_x^2 + \sin^2\phi/\alpha_y^2} \right]^{\frac{1}{2}} \qquad (7a)$$

$$\phi = \tan^{-1}\left[\frac{\alpha_y}{\alpha_x} \tan(2\pi u_2) \right] \qquad (7b)$$

where:

δ, ϕ are the angles shown in Figure 5

u_1, u_2 are uniform random variables in the range (0,1]

notes:

The tangent and arctangent in the Equation 7a should be computed carefully so as to keep the angle in its starting quadrant.

Uniformly weighted sample rays sent according to the above distribution will correctly reproduce the specified highlight. This is much more efficient than either distributing the samples evenly and then weighting the result, or using other techniques, such as rejection sampling, to arrive at the correct scattering. Readers familiar with Monte Carlo sampling techniques will immediately appreciate the advantage of having a formula for the sample point locations -- something that is impossible with more complicated reflectance models such as He-Torrance.

6. Results

Figure 8a shows a photograph of a child's varnished wood chair with a small desk lamp immediately behind and above it. This arrangement results in a large anisotropic highlight in the seat of the chair. Figure 8b shows the closest simulation possible using a deterministic isotropic reflectance model. Figure 8c shows a hybrid simulation with the elliptical Gaussian model. Notice how the hybrid rendering technique reproduces not only the highlight from the light source, but also the semispecular reflection from the back wall in the seat of the chair.

Figure 9 shows a table with anisotropic reflections in the wood varnish and the two candle holders. The lid of the silver box shown is also anisotropic, and demonstrates the use of local control to affect the reflectance properties of an anisotropic surface. A wave function determines the orientation of the brushed direction in the box lid, producing characteristic highlights. There are four low level light sources in the scene, the two candles on the table, an overhead light source above and to the right, and the moon shining in through a window.

Figure 7a, 7b, 7c. Alternative rendering techniques for anisotropic reflection. 7a on the left shows deterministic technique with no sampling. 7b center shows strict Monte Carlo sampling approach. 7c on the right shows hybrid deterministic and stochastic method.

Figure 8a, 8b, 8c. Varnished wood comparison. 8a on the left shows a photograph of a child's chair. 8b center shows a simulation of the chair using the isotropic Gaussian model given in Section 4.1 with a strictly deterministic calculation. (This is similar to the appearance one might obtain using a normalized Phong reflectance model.) 8c on the right shows a hybrid deterministic and stochastic simulation of the chair using the elliptical Gaussian model from Section 4.2.

Figure 9. A table scene with anisotropic reflection in metallic and varnished wood surfaces.

The following table gives a short list of surfaces and their elliptical Gaussian fits. Color was not measured for any of the surfaces. The materials in the second half of the table are isotropic, so the two α values are the same, and Equation (4) can be used.

Material	ρ_d	ρ_s	α_x	α_y
rolled brass	.10	.33	.050	.16
rolled aluminum	.1	.21	.04	.09
lightly brushed aluminum	.15	.19	.088	.13
varnished plywood	.33	.025	.04	.11
enamel finished metal	.25	.047	.080	.096
painted cardboard box	.19	.043	.076	.085
white ceramic tile	.70	.050	.071	.071
glossy grey paper	.29	.083	.082	.082
ivory computer plastic	.45	.043	.13	.13
plastic laminate	.67	.070	.092	.092

We have also measured the reflectance functions of various painted surfaces. We found the "flat" Latex paint we tested to be very nearly diffuse, at least for incident angles up to 60°. Therefore, we present only the results from our measurements of "semi-gloss" and "gloss" Latex. Our ρ_d was around 0.45 for both the semi-gloss and the gloss paints. The value for ρ_s of the semi-gloss Latex was around 0.048 for all surfaces, and the gloss Latex had a slightly higher average of 0.059. Although ρ_d changes dramatically with the color of paint, the value for ρ_s remains fairly constant since it is determined by the index of refraction of the paint base. The values for α_x and α_y are also unaffected by paint color, but since they depend on the exact microstructure of the painted surface, they vary with the application method and the underlying material, as shown in the following two tables.

(α_x, α_y) for Latex Semi-Gloss, $\rho_s \approx 0.048$		
	brushed	rolled	sprayed
metal	(.037, .064)	(.045, .068)	(.041, .055)
sheetrock	(.078, .12)	(.083, .12)	(.096, .11)
wood	(.097, .24)	(.12, .26)	(.099, .26)

(α_x, α_y) for Latex Gloss, $\rho_s \approx 0.059$		
	brushed	rolled	sprayed
metal	(.037, .063)	(.054, .080)	(.038, .054)
sheetrock	(.10, .10)	(.12, .12)	(.10, .10)
wood	(.13, .22)	(.13, .20)	(.12, .17)

7. Conclusion

We have presented an economical new device for measuring BRDFs, and a simple reflectance model that fits a large class of materials. The imaging gonioreflectometer presented here is a working prototype, but improvements are necessary for the measurement of grazing angles and smoother materials. Likewise, the elliptical Gaussian model presented is fast and accurate for many surfaces, but there are still many materials that do not fit our function. In conclusion, although the initial efforts are promising, we hope that this work will stimulate further investigation of empirical shading models. After all, good science requires both theory and data -- one is of little use without the other.

8. Acknowledgements

This work was supported in part by a grant from Apple Computer Corporation, and by the Assistant Secretary for Conservation and Renewable Energy, Office of Building Technologies, Buildings Equipment Division of the U.S. Department of Energy under Contract No. DE-AC03-76SF00098.

Ken Turkowski of Apple's Advanced Technology Division was jointly responsible for supervision of this project. Francis Rubinstein, Rudy Verderber and Sam Berman each gave invaluable support, and Robert Clear had a direct hand in overseeing the calibration and validation of the camera and reflectometer equipment. Thanks also to Stephen Spencer and Kevin Simon of Ohio State University for discovering a problem with our original reflectance formula.

Anat Grynberg participated in the initial design and construction of the imaging gonioreflectometer, and Lisa Stewart made numerous equipment modifications during the calibration stage and took most of the BRDF measurements used in this paper.

Carol Stieger did the tole painting on the real and simulated versions of the child's chair.

9. References

[Beckmann63]
Beckmann, Petr, Andre Spizzichino, *The Scattering of Electromagnetic Waves from Rough Surfaces*, Pergamon Press, NY, 1963.

[Blinn77]
Blinn, James F., "Models of Light Reflection for Computer Synthesized Pictures," *Computer Graphics*, Vol. 11, No. 2, July 1977.

[Cabral87]
Cabral, Brian, Nelson Max, Rebecca Springmeyer, "Bidirectional Reflection from Surface Bump Maps," *Computer Graphics*, Vol. 21, No. 4, July 1987.

[Cook82]
Cook, Robert L., Kenneth E. Torrance, "A Reflectance Model for Computer Graphics," *Computer Graphics*, Vol. 15, No. 3, August 1981.

[Cook84]
Cook, Robert L., Thomas Porter, Loren Carpenter, "Distributed Ray Tracing," *Computer Graphics*, Vol. 18, No. 3, July 1984.

[Cook86]
Cook, Robert L., "Stochastic Sampling in Computer Graphics," *ACM Transactions on Graphics*, Vol. 5, No. 1, January 1986.

[He91]
He, X., K.E. Torrance, F.X. Sillion, D.P. Greenberg, "A Comprehensive Physical Model for Light Reflection," *Computer Graphics*, Vol. 25, No. 4, July 1991.

[Kajiya85]
Kajiya, James T., "Anisotropic Reflection Models," *Computer Graphics*, Vol. 19, No. 3, July 1985.

[Kajiya86]
Kajiya, James T., "The Rendering Equation," *Computer Graphics*, Vol. 20, No. 4, August 1986.

[Murray-Coleman90]
Murray-Coleman, J.F., A.M. Smith, "The Automated Measurement of BRDFs and their Application to Luminaire Modeling," *Journal of the Illuminating Engineering Society*, Winter 1990.

[Nicodemus77]
Nicodemus, F.E., J.C. Richmond, J.J. Hsia, *Geometrical Considerations and Nomenclature for Reflectance*, U.S. Department of Commerce, National Bureau of Standards, October 1977.

[Phong75]
Phong, B., "Illumination for Computer Generated Pictures," *Communications of the ACM*, Vol. 18, No. 6, June 1975.

[Poulin90]
Poulin, Pierre, Alain Fournier, "A Model for Anisotropic Reflection," *Computer Graphics*, Vol. 24, No. 4, August 1990.

[Rubenstein81]
Rubenstein, R.Y., *Simulation and the Monte Carlo Method*, J. Wiley, New York, 1981.

[Sandford85]
Sandford, Brian P., David C. Robertson, "Infrared Reflectance Properties of Aircraft Paints," *Proceedings IRIS Targets, Backgrounds, and Discrimination*, 1985.

[Sillion91]
Sillion, Francois, James Arvo, Donald Greenberg, "A Global Illumination Solution for General Reflectance Distributions," *Computer Graphics*, Vol. 25, No. 4, July 1991.

[Torrance67]
Torrance, K.E., E.M. Sparrow, "Theory for Off-Specular Reflection from Roughened Surfaces," *Journal of the Optical Society of America*, Vol. 57, No. 9, September 1967.

[Whitted80]
Whitted, Turner, "An Improved Illumination Model for Shaded Display," *Communications of the ACM*, Vol. 23, No. 6, June 1980, pp. 343-349.

[Yokoi88]
Yokoi, Shigeki, Jun-ichiro Toriwaki, "Realistic Expression of Solids with Feeling of Materials," *JARECT*, Vol. 18, 1988.

An Importance-Driven Radiosity Algorithm

Brian E. Smits
James R. Arvo
David H. Salesin

Program of Computer Graphics
Cornell University
Ithaca, NY 14853

Abstract

We present a new radiosity algorithm for efficiently computing global solutions with respect to a constrained set of views. Radiosities of directly visible surfaces are computed to high accuracy, while those of surfaces having only an indirect effect are computed to an accuracy commensurate with their contribution. The algorithm uses an adaptive subdivision scheme that is guided by the interplay between two closely related transport processes: one propagating power from the light sources, and the other propagating *importance* from the visible surfaces. By simultaneously refining approximate solutions to the dual transport equations, computation is significantly reduced in areas that contribute little to the region of interest. This approach is very effective for complex environments in which only a small fraction is visible at any time. Our statistics show dramatic speedups over the fastest previous radiosity algorithms for diffuse environments with details at a wide range of scales.

CR Categories and Subject Descriptors: I.3.7 [Computer Graphics]: Three-Dimensional Graphics and Realism.

Additional Key Words: importance functions, adaptive meshing, hierarchical radiosity, adjoint transport equation, global illumination, view-dependence.

1 Introduction

View-independent global radiosity algorithms have two major drawbacks: they oversolve globally and undersolve locally. The algorithms oversolve globally in that they attempt to compute radiosities to a uniform precision throughout the environment—even on surfaces hidden from all useful points of view. They undersolve locally in that a single global radiosity solution is seldom adequate under close inspection—local effects such as shadowing and color bleeding among small objects are often lost when the radiosity of the entire environment has to be computed to a uniform precision. Thus, the utility of a purely view-independent solution diminishes as the environment complexity or the required accuracy increases.

To address this problem, several adaptive meshing schemes have been devised to increase the level of approximation where signifi-

cant intensity gradients occur [3, 4, 6]. These algorithms can achieve good results with fewer surface elements. For complex environments, however, the cost of creating a fine mesh to capture every illumination detail, whether visible or not, may still be far too high.

In practice, radiosity implementations often rely on some form of additional intervention by the user in order to handle complex scenes. For example, in order to keep the total number of surface elements small, the user may need to supply meshing hints based on the anticipated set of views. This approach has the advantage of saving work in areas that are unimportant to the final image. However, it also tends to sacrifice global accuracy, as there is no obvious way for the user to predict the level of meshing required for distant objects to have their proper effects on the visible parts of the scene.

The converse of this problem arises during the solution process: which of the vast number of interactions in a complex environment are significant enough to evaluate? Consider, for example, computing a radiosity solution for a large building. In principle, light leaving a small surface on one floor could reach any other floor by some circuitous path of stairwells and corridors. A radiosity algorithm that accurately computed all such interactions would be highly impractical.

Hanrahan, Salzman, and Aupperle [12] have recently proposed a brightness-weighted hierarchical radiosity algorithm that goes a long way toward resolving this difficulty. The hierarchical algorithm focuses effort on the significant energy transfers, quickly approximating the insignificant interactions. However, because the algorithm is still view-independent, it does more work than necessary in complex environments when only a single view or set of views is required. Indeed, it is not difficult to construct models for which even this rapid algorithm is impractically slow.

One way to make radiosity practical for complex environments is to incorporate a notion of view-dependence. For instance, we might first use some form of visibility preprocessing to determine the surfaces that are directly visible [1, 19]. To compute the radiosities of these surfaces, all surfaces contributing energy must be taken into account. But these contributing surfaces, in turn, receive energy from surfaces that are still further away. However, in general the effect of distant interactions will be less important to the visible scene. In short, to make effective use of view-dependence it is necessary to consider *all* potential interactions among surfaces, but to compute each interaction only to an appropriate level of accuracy.

In this paper, we describe such an algorithm: an extension to hierarchical radiosity that refines the interactions contributing the most

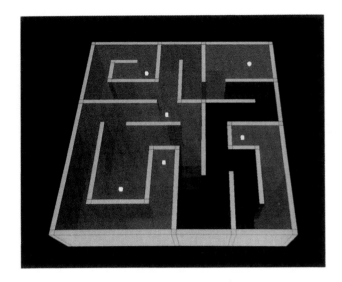

Figure 1: A radiosity solution for a labyrinth.

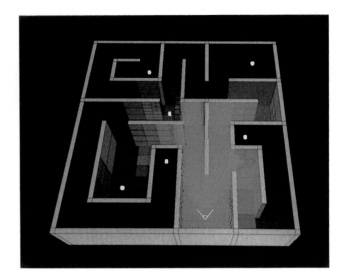

Figure 2: An importance solution for the same model.

error to the view-dependent solution. The algorithm makes use of *importance functions*, which have been studied extensively in neutron transport theory [15, 16]. In our context, importance functions describe how the radiosity originating at a given patch influences the visible surfaces. The algorithm we propose combines estimates of importance and radiosity to drive the global solution, allowing it to exploit view-dependent information as part of an adaptive refinement scheme.

2   Importance

Illumination algorithms can be divided into two categories: those that simulate the propagation of all light throughout an environment, typified by radiosity algorithms; and those that simulate only the light reaching the eye, typified by ray tracing. These two strategies are in some sense dual: the former simulate the process of photons emanating from sources of light, while the latter trace rays that emanate from the eye, but behave very much like photons in every other respect. The two strategies have advantages for modeling different modes of light scattering. Indeed, the many bidirectional ray tracing and multi-pass radiosity methods suggested in the last few years [2, 5, 13, 17, 18, 20] exploit the complementary nature of these two processes.

An analogous duality appears in neutron transport theory, where equations similar to those of radiative transfer are used to predict neutron flux [8]. If only the flux impinging on a small receiver is required, it is typically the *adjoint* of the original transport equation that is solved, in effect reversing the direction of neutron migration back toward the source. This strategy is closely related to the various ray tracing approaches for global illumination [14, 22].

The efficiency of these "backward" methods depends on the ability to quickly find paths leading back to the source. But determining these paths is equivalent to solving the transport equation in the forward direction. Thus, solving the transport equation in one direction would seem to require its prior solution in the other direction. However, through variational methods, nuclear engineers have been able to use this interdependence to advantage. These methods allow approximate solutions to the two transport equations to be combined, yielding an overall solution with higher accuracy than either component alone [8, 16].

The effectiveness of these techniques suggest that in the realm of global illumination it may also be possible to exploit the dual nature of light transport more effectively than has previously been recognized. Rather than using these dual processes in multiple passes to simulate different light scattering modes, we can instead use the two processes together—solving them simultaneously—in order to produce an accurate result more quickly.

As an illustration of our approach, consider the labyrinth model depicted in Figure 1. The model is illuminated by several light sources, shown in white. The radiosity solution due to these lights is shown in red. In an analogous fashion, the camera can also "illuminate" the scene with a new quantity, "importance." Figure 2 depicts the importance solution due to the camera in green.

Our algorithm uses radiosity and importance together to accelerate the radiosity solution for the visible scene. It does this by refining estimates of the transport equations most where the interaction of radiosity and importance is highest. Thus, in Figure 3 the algorithm uses the finest mesh for the parts of the scene that are yellow, somewhat less meshing for the parts that are orange, and even less for the parts that are red, green, or black—i.e., in regions of little importance, little brightness, or little of either.

The remainder of this section shows how the duality of radiosity and importance can be established more formally, and develops some mathematical tools for using these quantities together to drive a hierarchical algorithm.

2.1   Duality of radiosity and importance

Suppose we have a linear operator $\mathbf{L}$ governing some transport process, and a *source* term S. Then the transport equation and its adjoint can be written as follows:

$$\mathbf{L}\Phi = S \tag{1}$$
$$\mathbf{L}^*\Psi = R \tag{2}$$

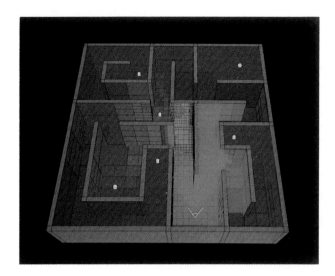

Figure 3: The radiosity and importance solutions together.

where * is the adjoint operator, and R is a *receiver*, dual to the source. In the context of radiosity, Φ is a vector of radiosities, S a vector of emittances, and $\mathbf{L}$ a discrete approximation to the continuous transport operator. Because $\mathbf{L}$ is a matrix of real numbers, $\mathbf{L}^* = \mathbf{L}^T$.

In the adjoint equation (2), the vector Ψ is the *importance* vector dual to Φ. To understand the significance of R and Ψ, suppose that we wish to compute a scalar function of the radiosity solution $v(\Phi)$, rather than the entire solution Φ. For example, the function v might compute the average radiosity visible through a certain aperture, such as a pixel or the entire image plane. Since any linear function of Φ can be expressed as an inner product, we can write $v(\Phi)$ as the product $R^T\Phi$, where R_i gives the contribution of Φ_i to the scalar function v. We can then use equations (1) and (2) together to derive an alternate formulation of $v(\Phi)$ with respect to Ψ:

$$v(\Phi) = R^T\Phi = (\mathbf{L}^T\Psi)^T\Phi = \Psi^T\mathbf{L}\Phi = \Psi^T S. \qquad (3)$$

Thus, each element Ψ_j of the importance vector Ψ gives the contribution made by a unit of emittance at patch j to the scalar function $v(\Phi)$. In other words, if v is chosen for a particular view, then Ψ_j gives *the fraction of radiosity emitted at patch j that ultimately reaches the eye*.

Note that since the vector R plays a role dual to S in equations (1) and (2), we can think of R as describing the initial "emittance of importance." In this sense, we can think of every patch j as having associated with it both a steady-state radiosity Φ_j coming from all patches in the environment but originating at the lights S, and also a steady-state importance Ψ_j coming from all patches but originating at R, determined by the eye (Figure 4).

While radiosity and importance are similar in many respects, the two quantities are not exactly the same. Radiosity is a flux density, measured in watts per meter-squared, whereas importance is defined as a fraction, and is therefore a dimensionless quantity. This distinction has ramifications when we distribute the two quantities in a hierarchical system, as described in Section 2.3.

2.2 Importance-driven refinement

For most transport equations, we must use a discrete approximation to the exact transport operator. The global illumination problem is no exception; the matrix approximation of $\mathbf{L}$ generally contains imprecise form-factor estimates and other assumptions that introduce error. However, the approximate matrix can be expressed as a perturbation of the exact operator, and refined using estimates of radiosity and importance, as follows.

Let $\widetilde{\mathbf{L}}$ be an approximation to $\mathbf{L}$, with $\widetilde{\mathbf{L}} = \mathbf{L} + \Delta\mathbf{L}$, and let $\widetilde{\Phi}$ be the solution to the corresponding transport equation, which is an approximation to the exact radiosity vector Φ. Assuming exact emittances S, the approximate radiosity transport equation can be written as

$$\widetilde{\mathbf{L}}\widetilde{\Phi} = S, \qquad (4)$$

which is equivalent to

$$\mathbf{L}\widetilde{\Phi} = S - \Delta\mathbf{L}\widetilde{\Phi}. \qquad (5)$$

Thus, we can rewrite the approximate transport equation with exact emittances S in terms of an exact transport operator with perturbed emittances $S - \Delta\mathbf{L}\widetilde{\Phi}$.

Since the importance of a patch describes the fraction of emitted radiosity that reaches the eye, we can now derive an expression for how the error in the emittances affects the view-dependent function v. Writing the visible error as $v(\Phi - \widetilde{\Phi})$ and using equations (3) and (5), we have:

$$\begin{aligned}
v(\Phi - \widetilde{\Phi}) &= R^T\Phi - R^T\widetilde{\Phi} \\
&= \Psi^T S - \Psi^T\mathbf{L}\widetilde{\Phi} \\
&= \Psi^T S - \Psi^T(S - \Delta\mathbf{L}\widetilde{\Phi}) \\
&= \Psi^T\Delta\mathbf{L}\widetilde{\Phi}. \qquad (6)
\end{aligned}$$

Thus, the quantity $\Psi^T\Delta\mathbf{L}\widetilde{\Phi}$ is the error that the approximations to $\mathbf{L}$ and Φ contribute to the view-dependent function.

Unfortunately, in practice it is not possible to compute the importance vector Ψ exactly, since computing the global importance solution is as difficult as computing the global radiosity solution. However, we can compute an approximation $\widetilde{\Psi}$ to the exact importance vector Ψ, and refine it as we refine $\widetilde{\mathbf{L}}$ and $\widetilde{\Phi}$. In this case, we can use

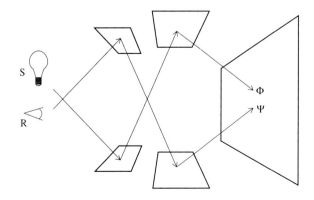

Figure 4: The duality of radiosity and importance.

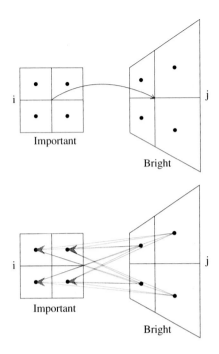

Figure 5: Transporting radiosity and importance in a hierarchy.

the quantity $\widetilde{\Psi}^T \Delta \mathbf{L} \widetilde{\Phi}$ as a close approximation to the actual error $\Psi^T \Delta \mathbf{L} \widetilde{\Phi}$.

To incorporate this insight into a hierarchical radiosity algorithm we begin by considering the interaction between two patches i and j. In general, computation of the energy transfer between any two patches will be approximate, due to the approximations inherent in the discrete operator $\widetilde{\mathbf{L}}$. Let δ_{ij} denote the product $|\widetilde{\Psi}_i \Delta \mathbf{L}_{ij} \widetilde{\Phi}_j|$. The quantity δ_{ij} approximates the error contributed by the interaction of patch i and j to the view-dependent function v. By reducing δ_{ij} over all pairs (i, j), we can make the magnitude of the overall error $\widetilde{\Psi}^T \Delta \mathbf{L} \widetilde{\Phi}$ arbitrarily small.

We reduce the error in an interaction by subdividing one of the two patches involved and computing new interactions for the refined system. The net effect of this refinement is that transfers of radiosity from bright patches and transfers of importance from important patches will generally be treated with greater accuracy at a lower level in the hierarchy.

Figure 5 illustrates this idea for two patches i and j with high importance and high radiosity, respectively. The diagram on the top shows a single link from patch i to patch j. The link carries radiosity from i to j, in the direction of the arrow, and importance from j to i, against the arrow. Since the effect of these interactions on the error is not great, they take place at a high level in the hierarchy. On the other hand, the diagram on the bottom shows the transfer of radiosity from j to i and of importance from i to j. These transfers, which have greater potential effect on the error, take place at a more refined level of the hierarchy. In this way the algorithm can put the most work into refining the parts of the transport process where the impact of error is greatest.

Because of the duality of radiosity and importance, the same error

criterion $|\widetilde{\Psi}_i \Delta \mathbf{L}_{ij} \widetilde{\Phi}_j|$ used to refine radiosity can be used to refine the importance solution as well. Moreover, since estimates of importance are used to drive the radiosity solution and *vice versa*, we need to refine both solutions to the same level of accuracy. Therefore, the hierarchical system used for radiosity is also appropriately refined for importance, so a single hierarchical system suffices for both.

2.3 Radiosity and importance transport

While managing radiosity in a hierarchical system is well-understood [6, 12], importance is new and subtly different. For completeness, we discuss the equations governing both importance and radiosity here.

Until now, we have described the linear operator $\mathbf{L}$ only as a general matrix. For the radiosity transport equation, the operator $\mathbf{L}$ can be expressed as follows:

$$\mathbf{L} = \begin{bmatrix} 1 - \rho_1 F_{11} & -\rho_1 F_{12} & \cdots & -\rho_1 F_{1n} \\ -\rho_2 F_{21} & 1 - \rho_2 F_{22} & \cdots & -\rho_2 F_{2n} \\ \vdots & \vdots & \ddots & \vdots \\ -\rho_n F_{n1} & -\rho_n F_{n2} & \cdots & 1 - \rho_n F_{nn} \end{bmatrix}, \quad (7)$$

where ρ_i is the *reflectance* of patch i, and F_{ij} is the *form factor* from patch i to patch j [10].

The form factor F_{ij} expresses the fraction of power leaving patch i that arrives at patch j. The form factor between two unoccluded differential patches di and dj is given by

$$F_{di,dj} = \frac{\cos \theta_i \cos \theta_j}{\pi r^2} dA_j, \quad (8)$$

where θ_i and θ_j relate the normal vectors of di and dj to the vector joining the two patches, r is the distance between the patches, and dA_j is the differential area of dj.

The form factor from a differential patch di to a finite-area patch j is given by

$$F_{di,j} = \int_{A_j} \left[\frac{\cos \theta_i \cos \theta_j}{\pi r^2} \right] dA_j, \quad (9)$$

where A_j is the area of patch j. The form factor between two finite-area patches i and j is the average of this quantity over all of patch i:

$$F_{ij} = \frac{1}{A_i} \int_{A_i} \int_{A_j} \left[\frac{\cos \theta_i \cos \theta_j}{\pi r^2} \right] dA_j \, dA_i. \quad (10)$$

This double integral can be approximated by the single-integral formulation (9), assuming the two patches are "well-separated" [10].

It is easy to check from equation (10) that the following reciprocity relationship holds between the form factors F_{ij} and F_{ji}:

$$A_i F_{ij} = A_j F_{ji}. \quad (11)$$

We can rewrite equations (1) and (2) in terms of the radiosity and importance arriving at a single patch i from every other patch j to give the familiar radiosity formulation, along with an analogous formulation for importance:

$$\Phi_i = S_i + \rho_i \sum_j \Phi_j F_{ij}, \quad (12)$$

$$\Psi_i = R_i + \sum_j \rho_j \Psi_j F_{ji}. \tag{13}$$

Since $\mathbf{L}$ is used for radiosity and $\mathbf{L}^\mathsf{T}$ is used for importance, the two equations differ only in the indices of the reflectance ρ and the form factor F.

We now examine how radiosity and importance can be distributed up and down a hierarchical system. Let i be a child patch, and I its parent in the patch hierarchy. We will assume that reflectance, as well as emittance of radiosity and importance, is constant over every patch.

When the patches are well-separated, equations (9) and (11) imply the following form-factor relationships:

$$F_{ij} \approx F_{Ij}, \tag{14}$$

$$F_{ji} \approx \frac{A_i}{A_I} F_{jI}. \tag{15}$$

Substituting these equations into (12) and (13) allows us to express the radiosity and importance of a child patch in terms of those of its parent, as follows:

$$\Phi_i \approx \Phi_I, \tag{16}$$

$$\Psi_i \approx \frac{A_i}{A_I} \Psi_I. \tag{17}$$

Thus, radiosity does not change when pushed down from a parent to its children, while importance is distributed according to the proportional area of each child.

We also need to be able to solve for the radiosity and importance of a parent patch from those of its children. To derive these relationships, first note that equations (10) and (11) allow us to express the form factors for a parent patch in terms of those of its children:

$$F_{Ij} = \frac{1}{A_I} \sum_{i \in I} F_{ij} A_i, \tag{18}$$

$$F_{jI} = \sum_{i \in I} F_{ji}. \tag{19}$$

Substituting these equations into (12) and (13) gives:

$$\Phi_I = \frac{1}{A_I} \sum_{i \in I} A_i \Phi_i, \tag{20}$$

$$\Psi_I = \sum_{i \in I} \Psi_i. \tag{21}$$

Thus, radiosities must be averaged according to area when pulled up the hierarchy, whereas importances are simply summed.

3 Algorithm

The view-dependent radiosity algorithm we describe here is very similar to the brightness-weighted hierarchical algorithm proposed by Hanrahan, *et al.*, with the crucial difference that in the view-dependent algorithm, importance as well as radiosity plays a role in refining interactions.

The algorithm iteratively computes an accurate radiosity solution for visible patches by refining the interactions between any two patches i and j whose estimated error $|\widetilde{\Psi}_i \Delta \mathbf{L}_{ij} \widetilde{\Phi}_j|$ exceeds a given tolerance ϵ.

3.1 Overview

The algorithm takes as input the initial emittance of radiosity S and importance R for each patch, along with an initial set of interactions $\mathcal{I}$ among the patches. The set $\mathcal{I}$ contains a link between every pair of patches that are not completely occluded from one another. Each link carries radiosity in one direction and importance in the other. The set $\mathcal{I}$ can be computed once for each model and stored along with it.

The algorithm refines the initial set of interactions $\mathcal{I}$ by transforming this single-level network into a hierarchy of interactions. At each iteration of the outermost loop, the algorithm solves for both radiosity and importance using the current set $\mathcal{I}$. These solutions, in turn, are used to guide a refinement step, which improves the accuracy of the radiosities and importances with respect to a particular view, by adding more links to $\mathcal{I}$. The iteration continues until a preset error tolerance F_ϵ is met.

The basic algorithm can be described in pseudocode as follows:

> $\underline{ImportanceDrivenRadiosity(S, R, \mathcal{I})}$
> $(\widetilde{\Phi}, \widetilde{\Psi}) \leftarrow (S, R)$
> **for** ϵ decreasing from ∞ to F_ϵ **do**
> $SolveDualSystems(\widetilde{\Phi}, \widetilde{\Psi}, S, R, \mathcal{I})$
>   **for** each interaction $j \to i$ of $\mathcal{I}$ **do**
> $RefineInteraction(j \to i, \mathcal{I}, \epsilon)$
>   **end for**
> **end for**

The following sections describe the steps of this refinement process in more detail.

3.2 Solving for radiosity and importance

For a given hierarchical system, $\widetilde{\Phi}$ and $\widetilde{\Psi}$ are found by iteratively solving two systems of linear equations. Each iteration involves gathering radiosity and shooting importance between every linked pair of patches. Radiosity and importance are then distributed up and down the hierarchy so that every patch receives the appropriate contributions from its ancestors and descendants. This process is repeated until convergence—that is, until the difference between the radiosities and importances from one iteration to the next becomes smaller than some tolerance:

> $\underline{SolveDualSystems(\widetilde{\Phi}, \widetilde{\Psi}, S, R, \mathcal{I})}$
> **repeat**
> $GatherAndShoot(\widetilde{\Phi}, \widetilde{\Psi}, \mathcal{I})$
>   **for** each top-level patch p **do**
> $SweepRadiosity(\widetilde{\Phi}, S, p, 0)$
> $SweepImportance(\widetilde{\Psi}, R, p, 0)$
>   **end for**
> **until** convergence of $\widetilde{\Phi}$ and $\widetilde{\Psi}$

Gathering radiosity and shooting importance is implemented as follows:

GatherAndShoot$(\widetilde{\Phi}, \widetilde{\Psi}, \mathcal{I})$

$(\widetilde{\Phi}', \widetilde{\Psi}') \leftarrow (0, 0)$

for each patch i **do**

    for each interaction $j \rightarrow i$ of $\mathcal{I}$ **do**

        $\widetilde{\Phi}'_i \leftarrow \widetilde{\Phi}'_i + \rho_i \widetilde{F}_{ij} \widetilde{\Phi}_j$

        $\widetilde{\Psi}'_j \leftarrow \widetilde{\Psi}'_j + \rho_i \widetilde{F}_{ij} \widetilde{\Psi}_i$

    end for

end for

$(\widetilde{\Phi}, \widetilde{\Psi}) \leftarrow (\widetilde{\Phi}', \widetilde{\Psi}')$

For each interaction between two patches $j \rightarrow i$, radiosity is "gathered" from j to i, and importance is "shot" from i to j. Because the importance matrix is the transpose of the radiosity matrix, the same matrix entry $\rho_i \widetilde{F}_{ij}$ appears in both these operations. Here $\widetilde{F}_{ij}$ denotes an estimate of the actual form factor F_{ij}.

Once radiosity and importance have been transferred between linked patches, the two quantities are distributed up and down the hierarchy so that every patch receives the appropriate contributions from its parents and children:

SweepRadiosity$(\widetilde{\Phi}, S, i, \phi_{\text{down}})$

if i is a leaf **then**

    $\phi_{\text{up}} \leftarrow S_i + \widetilde{\Phi}_i + \phi_{\text{down}}$

else

    $\phi_{\text{up}} \leftarrow 0$

    for each child i' of i **do**

        $x \leftarrow$ *SweepRadiosity*$(\widetilde{\Phi}, S, i', \widetilde{\Phi}_i + \phi_{\text{down}})$

        $\phi_{\text{up}} \leftarrow \phi_{\text{up}} + x * A_{i'} / A_i$

    end for

end if

$\widetilde{\Phi}_i \leftarrow \phi_{\text{up}}$

return ϕ_{up}

SweepImportance$(\widetilde{\Psi}, R, i, \psi_{\text{down}})$

if i is a leaf **then**

    $\psi_{\text{up}} \leftarrow R_i + \widetilde{\Psi}_i + \psi_{\text{down}}$

else

    $\psi_{\text{up}} \leftarrow 0$

    for each child i' of i **do**

        $x \leftarrow (\widetilde{\Psi}_i + \psi_{\text{down}}) * A_{i'} / A_i$

        $\psi_{\text{up}} \leftarrow \psi_{\text{up}} + $ *SweepImportance*$(\widetilde{\Psi}, R, i', x)$

    end for

end if

$\widetilde{\Psi}_i \leftarrow \psi_{\text{up}}$

return ψ_{up}

The two quantities are distributed in slightly different ways, as discussed in Section 2.3. The radiosity ϕ of a child patch i is the sum of its emitted radiosity S_i, the radiosity it receives directly, and the radiosity of its parent ϕ_{down}. The importance of a child patch i is the sum of its emitted importance R_i, the importance it receives directly, and an area-weighted fraction of the importance of its parent ψ_{down}.

When pulling radiosity and importance back up the hierarchy the situation is reversed. The radiosity of a parent patch is the area-weighted average of the radiosities of its children, whereas its importance is the sum of the importances of its children.

3.3 Refining the interactions

We refine any interactions whose estimated error $|\widetilde{\Psi}_i \rho_i F_{\text{err}} \widetilde{\Phi}_j|$ exceeds the tolerance ϵ. For F_{err}, we use an upper bound on the error in the form factor, computed by taking the difference between upper and lower bounds F_{ij}^+ and F_{ij}^- on the actual form factor F_{ij}, as described in the next section. If the error in the interaction exceeds the tolerance ϵ, the interaction is refined by subdividing the patch p with greater area and creating new links directly from the children of p to the other patch:

RefineInteraction$(j \rightarrow i, \mathcal{I}, \epsilon)$

$F_{\text{err}} \leftarrow F_{ij}^+ - F_{ij}^-$

if $\widetilde{\Psi}_i \rho_i F_{\text{err}} \widetilde{\Phi}_j > \epsilon$ **then**

    SubdivideAndRefine$(p, j \rightarrow i, \epsilon)$

    $\mathcal{I} \leftarrow \mathcal{I} \cup \{$new links created through subdivision$\}$

end if

The procedure *SubdivideAndRefine* is essentially the same as the refinement routine described by Hanrahan, *et al.*With importance-driven refinement, however, the minimum patch-size criterion that guarantees termination is rarely necessary, since the importance of a patch always decreases with its area.

3.4 Estimating the form factors

We estimate the form factor F_{ij} from patch i to patch j by taking a number of samples across patch i and averaging the point-to-disk form factors [21] over all samples.

Care is needed in estimating upper and lower bounds on F_{ij}, since the assumptions required by point-to-disk form factors may not always hold. We choose samples on both patch i and j and compute double-differential form factors, using equation (8). We set the upper and lower bounds F_{ij}^+ and F_{ij}^- to $A_j \max \{F_{di,dj}\}$ and $A_j \min \{F_{di,dj}\}$, respectively. These "bounds" are not necessarily strict if the samples are poorly chosen; however, they seem to work well in practice. Note that if any of the double-differential form factors encounters an occluding object, then the lower bound F_{ij}^- is 0, and the estimated form-factor error is set to the upper bound F_{ij}^+.

3.5 Assigning initial importance

The vector R determines the initial emitters of importance. Different choices of R allow us to use importance in different ways.

Typically, for a single, static view, we define an infinitesimal patch for the "camera" and make it the sole emitter of importance. In this case, we also ensure that an initial link between the camera and the rest of the environment is set up only if it falls within the camera's viewing frustum. This choice of R has the same effect as assigning an initial importance to each patch according to its visible projected area.

There is nothing, however, that limits us to a single, static view. For example, importance could be used to speed the radiosity solution for an animation or walk-through of an environment by making every patch that is visible at any time an emitter of importance. Similarly, importance could be used when the scene is visible from more than a single viewpoint, such as in stereoscopic views or in stage design applications [9].

Finally, for some applications it may not be necessary for everything visible to be important. For example, perhaps we would like to study a particular object from all angles, such as a sculpture in a museum. If we are unconcerned about the environment itself except in how it contributes to the illumination of this object, we could make the object itself the sole emitter of importance.

Note that in all cases, the overall magnitude of R is arbitrary. However, the error tolerance F_ϵ must be scaled appropriately.

4 Reconstruction and display

The algorithm described in this paper addresses only the global illumination problem—i.e., how to determine the radiosities of visible surfaces to within a certain accuracy.

However, producing an accurate global radiosity solution does not guarantee a high-quality picture. Indeed, the reconstruction and display of a radiosity solution is a tricky problem for any algorithm that assumes constant radiosities over a patch [11], and a hierarchical algorithm is no exception. Annoying artifacts become apparent if each patch is displayed with a single constant intensity, as the eye is extremely sensitive to such discontinuities.

Artifacts due to poor reconstruction are in fact even more noticeable for hierarchical algorithms than for standard adaptive subdivision schemes. Since constant radiosities are distributed over patches of different sizes at many different levels of the hierarchy, the straightforward approach of pushing constant radiosities down to the leaves and Gouraud-shading these smallest elements leaves the boundaries between higher-level patches readily apparent.

In order to avoid these artifacts, we can take advantage of view-dependence by adding extra meshing to visible surfaces as part of the reconstruction process, once the importance-weighted global solution has been computed. In our implementation, we force subdivision of all visible surfaces down to a fixed projected-area threshold, and push all interactions down to these leaves.

Displaying these smaller patches with Gouraud shading produces results comparable to a standard Gouraud-shaded adaptive subdivision solution. In order to eliminate Mach banding and z-buffer artifacts, we use ray casting with a modified form of supersampling. For each ray–surface intersection, we choose 16 Gaussian-jittered samples in the (u, v)-coordinates of the intersected surface. The 16 radiosities from the patches at the bottom of the hierarchy are then averaged together to give the intensity of the pixel.

5 Results

Figures 6 and 7 show a small maze sitting on a table. The images were computed using importance-driven refinement. Figure 6 is flat-shaded to show the meshing produced by the algorithm, while Figure 7 is displayed using the reconstruction algorithm described in Section 4. Note the color bleeding from the red wall of the maze to the wall behind it. This effect is most pronounced on the top of the wall, as the bottom half of the wall is illuminated mostly by light reflected from the maze floor.

The next pair, Figures 8 and 9, show the same computed solution, but displayed from further back. Figure 8 shows the radiosity of each patch, while Figure 9 depicts the importance of each patch, divided by its area. In the latter image, the visible parts of the scene show up very clearly as white because all wavelengths of light emitted from these surfaces are equally important to the camera. The other surfaces in the room also have importance, but to a lesser degree. The color of each surface gives the fraction of light emitted at a particular wavelength that finds its way to the camera. Due to the red and blue walls, red light is more important on the left side of the floor and back wall, while blue light is more important on the right. Note how the algorithm has done less meshing in areas with little importance.

Figures 10 and 11 show the radiosity and importance of the same solution—displayed from even further back, showing the whole environment. From this vantage point, the meshing done on the table is extremely fine. A view-independent algorithm would have great difficulty solving the entire environment to such high precision. Note that no meshing at all has taken place in the room at the lower left, which contains a complex block sculpture, since the importance of the room and everything inside it is negligible. Note also that the wall illuminated by the bright light in the center does have some importance, and is therefore refined to a certain extent. The importance of indirect interactions such as these would be very difficult for a user to anticipate in giving meshing hints to a conventional algorithm.

Some quantitative measurements of our tests are summarized in Table 1. All tests were run on an HP 720, a 55 MIPS machine with 64 megabytes of physical memory.

Figures 12 and 13 compare brightness-weighted refinement (B-only) to brightness-and-importance-weighted refinement (BI). In running the test, we refined the B-only solution as much as possible before running out of physical memory. We then ran a BI algorithm on the same environment until the solution appeared to be at a similar or slightly higher level of refinement. For this environment of moderate complexity (1002 initial polygons), the B-only solution was 45 times slower, requiring 16 times the total number of patches, and 22 times the total number of links. We expect that for environments of greater complexity, the speedups would be even more dramatic.

We have also tried to compare timings for the more refined solution of Figure 6 with a B-only solution of comparable accuracy. However, the extraordinary memory requirements for a high-accuracy global solution makes this comparison difficult. We let the B-only solution run for about 40 hours, at which point the virtual memory size was well over 100 megabytes. With 19 times the number of patches, 35 times the number of links, and 30 times the number of CPU-minutes as the BI solution, the B-only algorithm still had not achieved a solution close to the same level of accuracy.

As an additional test, the camera was moved inside the small maze on the table, in the same position with respect to the small maze as it was with respect to the large maze in Figure 13. The BI solution was more accurate than B-only and took only 0.5% of the time to compute.

Figure 6: A view-dependent radiosity solution.

Figure 7: The same solution after reconstruction.

Figure 8: The radiosity solution of Figure 6, seen from further back.

Figure 9: The importance solution for Figure 6.

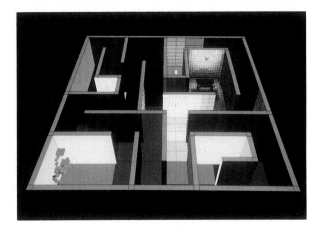

Figure 10: The radiosity solution from even further back.

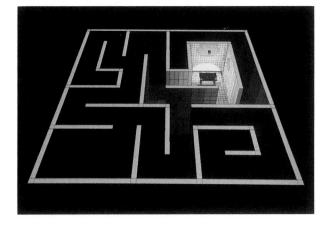

Figure 11: The importance solution from even further back.

	Maze on table Medium accuracy			Maze on table High accuracy			Inside maze Medium accuracy		
	B-only	*BI*	Gain	*B-only*	*BI*	Gain	*B-only*	*BI*	Gain
Total patches	46778	2983	16×	163053+	8779	≫ 19×	46778	1299	36×
Total links	585308	27055	22×	2803112+	79192	≫ 35×	585308	19288	30×
Time (minutes)	585	13	45×	2337+	76	≫ 30×	585	3	195×

Table 1: *B-only* versus *BI* refinement. Statistics for three test cases.

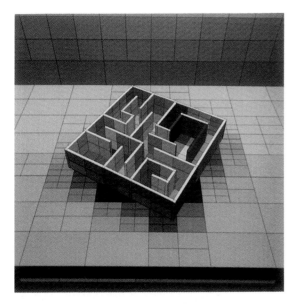

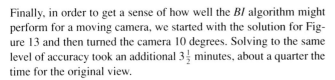

Figure 12: A *B-only* solution.

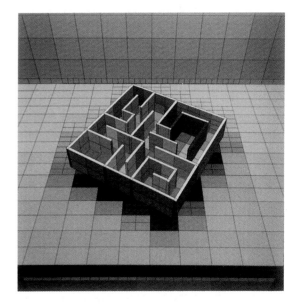

Figure 13: A comparable *BI* solution.

Finally, in order to get a sense of how well the *BI* algorithm might perform for a moving camera, we started with the solution for Figure 13 and then turned the camera 10 degrees. Solving to the same level of accuracy took an additional $3\frac{1}{2}$ minutes, about a quarter the time for the original view.

The initial-linking time, which is identical for *BI* and *B-only* refinement, is not included in the statistics in Table 1. For the 1002-polygon environment used in these tests, initial linking took 75 minutes and produced 18314 links. Note, however, that since initial linking is independent of the level of refinement, material characteristics, or view, it can performed once and stored along with the model. Our current implementation of initial linking uses a brute-force algorithm that checks every pair of patches to determine visibility; however, this step could be easily optimized using a more sophisticated visibility testing scheme.

6 Conclusions and future work

We have described a hierarchical radiosity algorithm that substantially reduces the computation required for an accurate global solution with respect to a particular view. The algorithm works by refining interactions according to the error each interaction introduces to the visible portions of a global solution. Our results show dramatic speedups, even for scenes of moderate complexity. We expect

that for a truly complex environment these speedups would be even greater.

There are many aspects of the algorithm that require further research:

Walk-throughs. One way to handle an animated sequence is to make every patch that becomes visible an emitter of importance, as described in Section 3.5. Another approach would be to update importances incrementally as the animation progressed. Because there is a great deal of coherence from one frame to the next in most animations, the importance-driven solution for one frame is likely to be a very good starting point for the computation of the next. Indeed, for many walk-through applications, computing a series of view-dependent solutions may actually be faster than computing a single view-independent solution, especially if high accuracy is required. The one essential change is to add a mechanism for pruning links from the hierarchy that are no longer sufficiently important.

Error analysis. It is easy to get a trivial upper bound on the overall error in the view-dependent radiosity solution by summing the error over all the links: if the system has N links, each refined to a tolerance of ϵ, then an overall bound is given by $N\epsilon$. However, this analysis is clearly too coarse, as we have no guarantee that N grows more slowly than ϵ shrinks. In addition, a rigorous error bound requires a bound on the difference between the estimated error at each link $\widetilde{\Psi}^T \Delta L \widetilde{\Phi}$ and the actual error $\Psi^T \Delta L \widetilde{\Phi}$. Currently, we have no guarantee that this difference will always be small.

Clustering. A major advantage of using a hierarchical approach is that it reduces the total number of interactions between patches from $O(n^2)$ to $O(n+m)$, where n is the total number of patches after subdivision, and m is the number of initial, top-level patches. Still, when m is large, which is often the case for complex environments, the number of initial interactions may be too large to be practical. In this case, we would like to group patches into higher-level clusters in order to reduce the initial interactions. This problem was mentioned by Hanrahan, *et al.* in the description of their brightness-weighted hierarchical algorithm; however, resolving this problem becomes even more crucial in an importance-driven algorithm, since the latter is better able to handle complex environments in every other respect.

Acknowledgments

We would like to thank Donald Greenberg for helpful discussions during the development of these ideas, and Eric Haines, John Wallace and Harold Zatz for reviewing the manuscript. Thanks to Suzanne Smits for creating the models, and to Susan Verba for suggesting a maze. This work was supported by the NSF grant, "Interactive Computer Graphics Input and Display Techniques" (CCR-8617880), by the NSF/DARPA Science and Technology Center for Computer Graphics and Scientific Visualization (ASC-8920219), and by generous donations of equipment from Hewlett-Packard. Brian Smits is supported by a National Science Foundation Graduate Fellowship.

References

[1] Airey, John M., John H. Rohlf, and Frederick P. Brooks Jr. Towards image realism with interactive update rates in complex virtual building environments. *Computer Graphics* (Special Issue on 1990 Symposium on Interactive 3D Graphics) 24(2): 41–50, 1990.

[2] Arvo, James. Backward ray tracing. In the SIGGRAPH '86 "Developments in Ray Tracing" course notes, 1986.

[3] Baum, Daniel R., Stephen Mann, Kevin P. Smith, and James M. Winget. Making radiosity usable: automatic preprocessing and meshing techniques for the generation of accurate radiosity solutions. *Computer Graphics* 25(4): 51–60, 1991.

[4] Campbell, III, A. T. and Donald Fussell. Adaptive mesh generation for global diffuse illumination. *Computer Graphics* 24(4): 155–64, 1990.

[5] Chen, Shenchang Eric, Holly E. Rushmeier, Gavin Miller, and Douglass Turner. A progressive multi-pass method for global illumination. *Computer Graphics* 25(4): 165–74, 1991.

[6] Cohen, Michael F., Donald P. Greenberg, David S. Immel, and Philip J. Brock. An efficient radiosity approach for realistic image synthesis. *IEEE Computer Graphics and Applications* 6(2): 26–35, 1986.

[7] Cohen, Michael F., Shenchang Eric Chen, John R. Wallace, and Donald P. Greenberg. A progressive refinement approach to fast radiosity image generation. *Computer Graphics* 22(4): 75–84, 1988.

[8] Davison, B. *Neutron Transport Theory.* Oxford University Press, London, 1957.

[9] Dorsey, Julie O'B., François X. Sillion, and Donald P. Greenberg. Design and simulation of opera lighting and projection effects. *Computer Graphics* 25(4): 41–50, 1991.

[10] Goral, Cindy M., Kenneth E. Torrance, Donald P. Greenberg, and Bennett Battaile. Modeling the interaction of light between diffuse surfaces. *Computer Graphics* 18(3): 213–22, 1984.

[11] Haines, Eric. Ronchamp: a case study for radiosity. In the SIGGRAPH '91 "Frontiers in Rendering" course notes, §3:1–28, 1991.

[12] Hanrahan, Pat, David Salzman, and Larry Aupperle. A rapid hierarchical radiosity algorithm. *Computer Graphics* 25(4): 197–206, 1991.

[13] Heckbert, Paul S. Adaptive radiosity textures for bidirectional ray tracing. *Computer Graphics* 24(4): 145–54, 1990.

[14] Kajiya, J. T. The rendering equation. *Computer Graphics* 20(4): 143–50, 1986.

[15] Kalos, M. H., and Paula A. Whitlock. *Monte Carlo Methods, Volume I: Basics.* J. Wiley, New York, 1986.

[16] Lewins, Jeffery. *Importance, The Adjoint Function: The Physical Basis of Variational and Perturbation Theory in Transport and Diffusion Problems.* Pergamon Press, New York, 1965.

[17] Sillion, François and Claude Puech. A general two-pass method integrating specular and diffuse reflection. *Computer Graphics* 23(4): 335–44, 1989.

[18] Sillion, François X., James R. Arvo, Stephen H. Westin, and Donald P. Greenberg. A global illumination solution for general reflectance distributions. *Computer Graphics* 25(4): 187–96, 1991.

[19] Teller, Seth J. and Carlo H. Séquin. Visibility preprocessing for interactive walkthroughs. *Computer Graphics* 25(4): 61–9, 1991.

[20] Wallace, John R., Michael F. Cohen, and Donald P. Greenberg. A two-pass solution to the rendering equation: a synthesis of ray tracing and radiosity methods. *Computer Graphics* 21(4): 311–20, 1987.

[21] Wallace, John R., Kells A. Elmquist, Eric A. Haines. A ray tracing algorithm for progressive radiosity. *Computer Graphics* 23(3): 315–24, 1989.

[22] Ward, Gregory J., Francis M. Rubenstein, and Robert D. Clear. A ray-tracing solution for diffuse interreflection. *Computer Graphics* 22(4): 85–92, 1988.

Illumination from Curved Reflectors

Don Mitchell †

Pat Hanrahan ‡

† AT&T Bell Laboratories
‡ † Princeton University

Abstract

A technique is presented to compute the reflected illumination from curved mirror surfaces onto other surfaces. In accordance with Fermat's principle, this is equivalent to finding extremal paths from the light source to the visible surface via the mirrors. Once pathways of illumination are found, irradiance is computed from the Gaussian curvature of the geometrical wavefront. Techniques from optics, differential geometry and interval analysis are applied to this problem in global illumination.

CR Categories and Subject Descriptions: I.3.3 [**Computer Graphics**]: Picture/Image Generation; I.3.7 [**Computer Graphics**]: Three-Dimensional Graphics and Realism

General Terms: Algorithms

Additional Keywords and Phrases: Automatic Differentiation, Caustics, Differential Geometry, Geometrical Optics, Global Illumination, Interval Arithmetic, Ray Tracing, Wavefronts

1. Introduction

Ray tracing provides a straightforward means for synthesizing realistic images on the computer. A scene is first modeled, usually by a collection of implicit or parametric surfaces. For each point in an image, a visual ray is traced from the eye into the scene. The visible (i.e., closest) surface intersection is found by geometrical and numerical methods, and the radiance at that visible point is calculated according to some shading model.

Whitted's shading model extends the notion of visibility by simulating reflecting and refracting surfaces [Whitted80]. A visual ray that encounters a reflective surface is bounced off and continues in the direction of reflection (see Figure 1). Eventually, it will encounter a non-reflecting surface, and the shading calculation is performed.

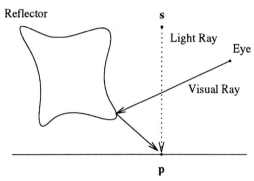

Figure 1. Reflected Visual Rays

This model simulates the effect of seeing the scene reflected in a mirror or refracted through glass, but it does not extend the notion of illumination. Once a visual ray arrives at a point **p**, the shading calculation is limited to the direct component of illumination—just the effect of light traveling directly from the light at **s**. Shading occurs in two steps, first the irradiance at **p** is computed, and next the reflected radiance in the direction of the visual ray is determined, based on the bidirectional reflectance of the surface.

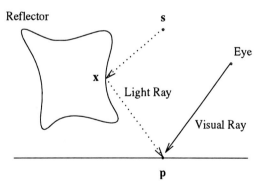

Figure 2. Reflected Illumination

Figure 2 illustrates a much more difficult task; to illuminate a visible point with reflected light. There are two problems involved. The first is finding the proper direction (or directions) in which to cast light rays, so that they arrive at the visible point **p**. The second problem is to compute the proper irradiance, given that the light may reflect off a curved surface and converge or diverge.

Two approaches have been used previously to simulate specularly reflected and refracted illumination. If the reflectors and refractors are polyhedral, illumination can be computed by *backward beam tracing* [Shinya87, Shinya89, Watt90]. For each face of a reflector visible from the light source, the subtended solid angle is traced outward until it reaches a non-specular surface, where radiant power is deposited.

For curved specular surfaces, *backward ray tracing* (also called light-ray or illumination-ray tracing) provides an approximate solution [Arvo86, Heckbert90, Shirley90]. In this method, rays are cast stochastically from the light source, like individual photons, reflecting through the scene until striking a non-specular surface. Shirley has produced some of the most impressive photorealistic images to date with this method (e.g., Figure 7 in [Shirley90]).

The primary difficulties with backward ray tracing involve sampling and estimating the distribution of radiant power (irradiance). Illumination rays arrive at their final destinations in a nonuniform pattern; and if they gave us samples of irradiance, we would have some difficulty with nonuniform interpolation. However, the problem is worse, because illumination rays just give samples of radiant power. We must estimate the *distribution* of radiant power from photon locations and density. This problem has been discussed by Heckbert [Heckbert90]. Chen et al. [Chen91] describe a nice resampling method, but even this method is fraught with difficulties. This is a troublesome problem which has not been completely solved. The method we propose will compute irradiance values at locations of our choosing, and thus avoids both of these problems.

2. Geometrical Optics

The shading models of image synthesis are based on the principles of *geometrical optics,* where wave-like behavior of light is assumed to occur only on an invisibly small scale. In this scheme, light emitted from some point in some direction travels along a curve or "ray" $C(t)$ through space. We define the *optical path length* from one point on a ray to another as the geometric path length weighted by the refractive index of the media:

$$S(t) = \int_C \eta \, dt$$

A surface of constant S (relative to some source point) is called a geometrical *wavefront,* which is always perpendicular to the light rays passing through it [Born80].

In homogeneous media, light rays are rectilinear; and if there are regions of constant refractive index separated by smooth boundaries, then rays will travel along piecewise straight paths—reflecting or refracting at boundaries. In a medium with smoothly varying refractive index, rays would be curved. In all of these settings, *Fermat's Principle* is obeyed, which stipulates that light travels along paths of stationary optical length. That is, the optical path length is a local maximum or local minimum with respect to any small variation in the path.

Given a stationary path, the important question is how much light propagates along it. In optics, *intensity, I,* is defined to be the radiant power per wavefront area at any point along a ray. The irradiance of a surface is then $E = I \cos\theta$, where θ is the angle between the ray and the surface normal. In the case of direct illumination from a point source, rays emanate radially, and the wavefronts are spherical. At a distance d, the wavefront intensity is simply $I = P/(4\pi d^2)$, where P is the total power of the source. However, once the ray has reflected off a curved surface, the shape of the wavefront is no longer as simple.

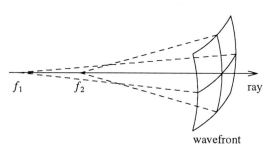

f_1 f_2 ray

wavefront

Figure 3. Wavefront and Principle Radii

Figure 3 illustrates the general situation in the neighborhood of a point on a rectilinear ray. A plane containing the ray will intersect the wavefront on a curve with some radius of curvature. From elementary differential geometry, we know there will be some orientation of the plane giving a curve with maximum radius of curvature r_1, and another orientation will give a minimum radius r_2. Furthermore, the planes associated with these *principle radii of curvature* will always be orthogonal. The circles of curvature are centered at points f_1 and f_2, on the ray. Let dA be an element of area on this wavefront. All the rays passing through dA will intersect some subsequent wavefront in an area dA'. Let $d\theta_1$ and $d\theta_2$ be the elements of angle subtended at the centers of curvature by these areas. By conservation of energy, we know the following *intensity law* must hold true:

$$\frac{I'}{I} = \frac{dA}{dA'} = \frac{r_1 r_2 d\theta_1 d\theta_2}{r_1' r_2' d\theta_1 d\theta_2} = \frac{r_1 r_2}{r_1' r_2'}$$

This shows the important fact that the intensity along the ray is proportional to the Gaussian curvature of the wavefront $1/(r_1 r_2)$.

3. Fermat Paths

A first step in computing the reflected illumination, as pictured in Figure 2, would be to find the stationary paths from the point **s** to **p**. In general, this would be a difficult problem of variational calculus; but in the case we are considering, it reduces to a simple optimization problem.

Figure 2 pictures a "one-bounce" path from the light **s** to **p** via a reflection at **x**. The total optical path length is a simple function of **x**.

$$d(\mathbf{x}) = \sqrt{(\mathbf{s} - \mathbf{x})^2} + \sqrt{(\mathbf{p} - \mathbf{x})^2}$$

If the mirror surface is defined implicitly by $g(\mathbf{x}) = 0$, then the optimization of $d(\mathbf{x})$ subject to the contraint that all points lie on g can be accomplished by the method of *Lagrange multipliers*. This will give a system of four equations in four variables.

$$\nabla d(\mathbf{x}) + \lambda \nabla g(\mathbf{x})) = 0$$
$$g(\mathbf{x}) = 0$$

The solutions of these non-linear equations will yield paths of locally extremal length.

Recall from analytic geometry that the loci of points whose sum of distances to two points is constant form an ellipsoid. Varying the total distance yields a family of confocal ellipsoids whose foci are **s** and **p**. Recall also that the gradient of an implicit function evaluated on a surface is in the direction of the normal to the surface. Thus, the system of equations produced by the method of Lagrange multipliers have the simple geometric interpretation that the extremal points must not only lie on the implicit surface g, but also that the ellipsoid, and the surface must be tangent at those points (see Figure 4). Therefore, we seek those ellipsoids in the family of confocal ellipsoids that are tangent to the surface.

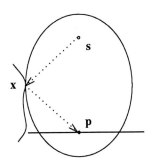

Figure 4. Osculating Ellipsoid

If the light is at infinity, we can use a simpler formula for optical path length.

$$d(\mathbf{x}) = \sqrt{(\mathbf{p} - \mathbf{x})^2} - (\mathbf{s} \cdot \mathbf{x})$$

where in this case $\mathbf{s}$ is a unit vector in the direction of the light source. The surfaces of varying d define a family of confocal paraboloids about the visible point $\mathbf{p}$. The extrema paths are where these parabolods are tangent to the surface.

The case of one-bounce refraction is similar to reflection. If the light and the visible point are on different sides of a smooth boundary between two transparent media, the optical path length becomes:

$$d(\mathbf{x}) = \eta_1 \sqrt{(\mathbf{s} - \mathbf{x})^2} + \eta_2 \sqrt{(\mathbf{p} - \mathbf{x})^2}$$

where η_1 and η_2 are the respective refractive indices. Surfaces of constant d are confocal *Cartesian ovals*. A Cartesian oval has the appearance of an egg-shaped ellipsoid and is a quartic surface. The mathematics of these surfaces are discussed in [Stravroudis72].

If the curved mirror is defined by a parametric surface $\mathbf{x}(u,v)$, then the tangency conditions are equivalent to stating that the parametric derivatives of the surface are perpendicular to the normal of the ellipsoid.

$$\mathbf{x}_u(u,v) \cdot \nabla d(u,v) = 0$$
$$\mathbf{x}_v(u,v) \cdot \nabla d(u,v) = 0$$

where $\mathbf{x}_u$ and $\mathbf{x}_v$ are the derivatives in the u and v directions, respectively, and $d(u,v)$ is the distance function evaluated at points on the surface. This leads to a system of two equations in two unknowns. In this paper, we will focus on the problem of the implicitly defined reflecting surface. Such surfaces are harder to deal with because they require a higher dimensional system of equations. However, they are typically easier to ray trace.

The more general case of paths with N bounces can be formulated as a system of $4N$ equations. $\mathbf{x}_0 = \mathbf{s}$ and $\mathbf{x}_{N+1} = \mathbf{p}$; however, only $\mathbf{x}_1$ through $\mathbf{x}_N$ are variables in the optimization problem. The total optical path length for multiple reflections is then:

$$d(\mathbf{x}_0, \cdots \mathbf{x}_{N+1}) = \sum_{i=0}^{N} \eta_i \sqrt{(\mathbf{x}_i - \mathbf{x}_{i+1})^2}$$

The implicit mirror surfaces are denoted by $g_i(\mathbf{x}_i) = 0$, and the so the system of equations to be solved are (for i from 1 to N):

$$\nabla_i d(\mathbf{x}_0, \cdots \mathbf{x}_{N+1}) + \lambda_i \nabla_i g_i(\mathbf{x}_i) = 0$$
$$g_i(\mathbf{x}_i) = 0$$

The gradient equations represent the condition that an ellipsoid with foci at $\mathbf{x}_{i-1}$ and $\mathbf{x}_{i+1}$ must kiss the mirror surface $g_i(\mathbf{x}_i) = 0$. Notice that the $\nabla_i d$ contains only three terms, and hence the system of $4N$ equations is sparse.

There exist many special purpose methods for solving the above systems of equations for particular classes of surfaces. For example, finding the ellipsoid tangent to a plane or to a sphere is very easy. In Section 5, however, we present numerical methods based on interval techniques that work for general implicit surfaces.

Once a path is determined, it is still necessary to check that no intervening surface blocks light traveling along it. This is easily done with the ray tracing occlusion tests. This is just the obvious generalization of Appel's shadow-probe method [Appel68].

4. Wavefront Tracing

Once a path from the light source to the receiver has been determined, the intensity of the incoming ray must be computed. As was discussed in Section 2, the intensity at a point along a ray path is proportional to the Gaussian curvature of the wavefront associated with that point. This intensity law suggests an algorithm where we keep track of the Gaussian curvature as the ray interacts with surfaces on its way to the receiver. The implementation requires (i) tools to analyze the differential geometry of wavefronts and surfaces, and (ii) functions that transform the wavefront as it is transferred through homogeneous media and as it reflects and refracts from a surface. Methods for performing (i) are derived from classical differential geometry (For example [Struik61]); methods for performing (ii) are derived from classical geometrical optics (For example [Stavroudis72]). More details (particularly the derivations) of the results used this section are available in the quoted references.

The local properties of a surface can be derived by computing its derivatives in different directions. A unit tangent in a direction $d\mathbf{x}$ is equal to

$$\mathbf{t} = \frac{d\mathbf{x}}{ds}$$

where $ds^2 = d\mathbf{x} \cdot d\mathbf{x}$ is the differential arc length. Differentiating $\mathbf{t}$ again yields

$$\frac{d\mathbf{t}}{ds} = \kappa_n \mathbf{n} + \kappa_g (\mathbf{n} \times \mathbf{t})$$

The normal curvature κ_n is the component of curvature in the direction $\mathbf{n}$.

$$\kappa_n = \mathbf{n} \cdot \frac{d\mathbf{t}}{ds} = -\frac{d\mathbf{x}}{ds} \cdot \frac{d\mathbf{n}}{ds} = -\frac{d\mathbf{x} \cdot d\mathbf{n}}{d\mathbf{x} \cdot d\mathbf{x}}$$

where we use the fact that $\mathbf{t} \cdot \mathbf{n} = 0$ and hence $\mathbf{t}' \cdot \mathbf{n} = -\mathbf{t} \cdot \mathbf{n}'$. In the remainder of this paper whenever curvature is mentioned it will mean the normal curvature. For this reason from this point on the subscript n will be dropped.

The curvature is defined for all directions tangent to the surface. The radius of curvature, which is equal to the reciprocal of curvature, is the radius of the osculating circle attached to a curve created by cutting the surface with a normal plane, that is, a plane containing $\mathbf{n}$ and $\mathbf{t}$. Note that if a plane cuts the surface in a convex curve, the curvature will be *negative,* whereas if the curve is concave, the curvature will be *positive.* A classic result in differential geometry is that the curvature attains a minimum and a maximum value along two perpendicular directions called the *lines of curvature,* or *principal directions.* These extrema, or *principal curvatures,* are denoted by κ_1 and κ_2. The Gaussian curvature K equals $\kappa_1\kappa_2$. If the Gaussian curvature is positive, then κ_1 and κ_2 have the same sign, and hence the surface is locally strictly convex or concave. However, if the Gaussian curvature is negative, then locally the surface is saddle-shaped, being convex along one line of curvature and concave along another.

Given two principal directions $\mathbf{u}_1$ and $\mathbf{u}_2$, the curvature in two other perpendicular directions

$$\mathbf{u} = \cos\theta\,\mathbf{u}_1 - \sin\theta\,\mathbf{u}_2$$
$$\mathbf{v} = \sin\theta\,\mathbf{u}_1 + \cos\theta\,\mathbf{u}_2$$

is given by Euler's Formula (which is easily derived from the definition of curvature).

$$\kappa_u = \kappa_1\cos^2\theta + \kappa_2\sin^2\theta$$
$$\kappa_v = \kappa_1\sin^2\theta + \kappa_2\cos^2\theta$$
$$\kappa_{uv} = (\kappa_1 - \kappa_2)\cos\theta\sin\theta$$

where κ_u and κ_v are the curvatures in the directions $\mathbf{u}$ and $\mathbf{v}$, respectively. These equations can be inverted to find the principal curvatures, given the curvatures in any two other orthogonal directions.

$$\tan 2\theta = 2\kappa_{uv}/(\kappa_v - \kappa_u)$$
$$\kappa_1 = \kappa_u\cos^2\theta + 2\kappa_{uv}\cos\theta\sin\theta + \kappa_v\sin^2\theta$$
$$\kappa_2 = \kappa_u\sin^2\theta - 2\kappa_{uv}\cos\theta\sin\theta + \kappa_u\cos^2\theta$$

This last formula will be used to derive the principal curvatures after a wavefront interacts with a surface.

Formulas for curvature are usually stated in terms of derivatives of parametric surfaces (see e.g. [Struik61]). In our implementation we wish to compute the curvature of an implicit surface, so we derive the curvature formula in this case. (Curiously, in our scan of the literature, we were not able to find a reference to these formulae.) Recall the formula for curvature,

$$\kappa = -\frac{d\mathbf{x}\cdot d\mathbf{n}}{d\mathbf{x}\cdot d\mathbf{x}}$$

This requires the evaluation of $d\mathbf{n}$, the derivative of the unit normal vector in the direction $d\mathbf{x}$. For an implicit surface $f(x,y,z)$,

$$\mathbf{n} = \frac{\mathbf{g}}{(\mathbf{g}\cdot\mathbf{g})^{1/2}}$$

where

$$\mathbf{g} = \nabla f$$

and

$$\mathbf{g}\cdot\mathbf{g} = (f_x^2 + f_y^2 + f_z^2)$$

From this we can calculate

$$d\mathbf{n} = \frac{d\mathbf{g}}{(\mathbf{g}\cdot\mathbf{g})^{1/2}} - \frac{\mathbf{g}(\mathbf{g}\cdot d\mathbf{g})}{(\mathbf{g}\cdot\mathbf{g})^{3/2}} = \frac{((\mathbf{g}\cdot\mathbf{g})\mathbf{I} - (\mathbf{g}\mathbf{g}^T))\,d\mathbf{g}}{(\mathbf{g}\cdot\mathbf{g})^{3/2}}$$

where

$$\mathbf{g}\mathbf{g}^T = \begin{bmatrix} f_x f_x & f_x f_y & f_x f_z \\ f_y f_x & f_y f_y & f_y f_z \\ f_z f_x & f_z f_y & f_z f_z \end{bmatrix}$$

and $\mathbf{I}$ is the identity matrix. The derivative of $\mathbf{g}$ is

$$d\mathbf{g} = \mathbf{H}\,d\mathbf{x}$$

where H is the Hessian and equals

$$H = \begin{bmatrix} f_{xx} & f_{xy} & f_{xz} \\ f_{yx} & f_{yy} & f_{yz} \\ f_{zx} & f_{zy} & f_{zz} \end{bmatrix}$$

Thus, we arrive at a formula for the curvature that involves the 1st and 2nd partial derivatives of the surface. In Section 5.1 we discuss a method for efficiently computing these derivatives at a point using automatic differentiation. In Plate 1, colors code the Gaussian curvature of a quartic surface computed using these techniques. Similar illustrations have been produced by [Forrest79] and [Dill81] for parametric surfaces.

Plate 1. Gaussian Curvature

We now return to the task of tracing a wavefront along a ray path. The above characterization of the local surface geometry in terms of principal curvature leads to a nice representation of the wavefront at a point:

```
typedef struct {
    Vector3 u, v, n;
    float κ_u, κ_v;
} Wavefront;
```

The initial wavefront for a point light source is spherical; this implies that both radii of curvature are equal to the radius of the sphere and that there are no distinguished principal directions (that is, any directions may be used). The initial wavefront for a distant light source is a plane; this implies that both radii of curvature are 0, and once again there are no unique principal directions.

The wavefront is now traced through the system. This involves three operations:

- Transfer
- Reflection
- Refraction

The equations describing the evolution of the wavefront for each of these situations were originally derived in 1906 by Gullstrand [Gullstrand06], and more recently using modern notation by Kneisly [Kneisly64] and Stavroudis [Stavroudis72].

The equations of transfer are simplest:

$$\kappa_u' = \frac{\kappa_u}{1 - d\kappa_u}$$

$$\kappa_v' = \frac{\kappa_v}{1 - d\kappa_v}$$

where d is the distance the wavefront moves. Noting that $\kappa = 1/r$, where r is the radius of curvature, these equations also can be written in the form:

$$\frac{1}{r_u'} = \frac{1}{r_u - d}$$

$$\frac{1}{r_v'} = \frac{1}{r_v - d}$$

which simply states that the radius of curvature of the wavefront changes by an amount equal to the distance travelled. Remember that for a converging wavefront the radius of curvature is positive. Inspecting the above equations, we note that when a converging wavefront moves a distance equal to original radius of curvature, the denominator goes to 0, and hence the intensity goes to infinity. These positions of extremely high intensity are the caustics of the wavefront.

The equations for refraction and reflection are more complicated and involve the following three steps:

1) Recall the equations giving the directions of the reflected and refracted ray:

$$\mathbf{n}^{(r)} = \mathbf{n}^{(i)} + 2\cos i\ \mathbf{n}^{(s)}$$

$$\mathbf{n}^{(t)} = \eta\ \mathbf{n}^{(i)} + \gamma\ \mathbf{n}^{(s)}$$

In these equations $\mathbf{n}^{(i)}$ and $\mathbf{n}^{(s)}$ are the normals to the incident wavefront and surface, respectively; $\mathbf{n}^{(r)}$ and $\mathbf{n}^{(t)}$ are the normals to the reflected and transmitted (refracted) wavefronts. η is the ratio of the indices of refraction in the two media, η_1/η_2, and $\gamma = \eta\cos i + \cos t$ (i is the angle of incidence and t is the angle of refraction) [Stavroudis72].

2) The direction $\mathbf{u} = \mathbf{n}^{(i)} \times \mathbf{n}^{(s)}$ is tangent both to the incident wavefront and to the surface (since it is perpendicular to both normals). The curvatures of the incident wavefront in the direction $\mathbf{u}$ can be computed by rotating the principal curvatures using the angle between $\mathbf{u}$ and the line of curvatures and Euler's Formula. The curvatures of the surface in this direction can be computed using the curvature tensor of the surface.

3) The curvatures of the new wavefronts can be computed by taking the directional derivatives of $\mathbf{n}^{(r)}$ and $\mathbf{n}^{(t)}$ in the direction $\mathbf{u}$. These derivatives can be computed directly from the formulae for the reflected and refracted vectors and the directional derivatives of the normals on the incident wavefront and the surface. This calculation can be found on pp. 149-157 of [Stavroudis72]; only the results are stated here.

For reflection:

$$\kappa_u^{(r)} = \kappa_u^{(i)} + 2\cos i\kappa_u^{(s)}$$

$$\kappa_{uv}^{(r)} = -\kappa_{uv}^{(i)} - 2\kappa_{uv}^{(s)}$$

$$\kappa_v^{(r)} = \kappa_v^{(i)} + (2/\cos i)\kappa_v^{(s)}$$

For refraction:

$$\kappa_u^{(t)} = \eta\kappa_u^{(i)} + \gamma\kappa_u^{(s)}$$

$$\kappa_{uv}^{(t)} = \eta\kappa_{uv}^{(i)} + \gamma(\cos i/\cos t)\kappa_{uv}^{(s)}$$

$$\kappa_v^{(t)} = \eta\kappa_v^{(i)} + \gamma(\cos i/\cos t)^2\kappa_v^{(s)}$$

Remember that the curvature of a plane is 0. Therefore, the curvatures of an outgoing wavefront reflected from a planar surface will be the same as the incoming wavefront (the fact the κ_{uv} switches sign is a result of the change in orientation of the coordinate system due to the reflection). This is as expected, since a perfectly reflected wave does not change its shape. Note also that a planar wavefront incident onto a reflecting surface essentially inherits the curvature of the surface. Thus if the surface is convex, the reflected wavefront will be diverging; whereas if the surface is concave, the wavefront will be converging, eventually forming a caustic.

Once we know the curvatures of the outgoing wavefront in the $\mathbf{u}$ direction, we can compute the directions of principal curvatures using Euler's Formula, converting to our canonical wavefront representation. This process is then repeated for the next surface that the wavefront is incident upon.

The outgoing intensity of reflected and refracted light should also be multiplied by the corresponding Fresnel coefficients to account for the changes in the magnitudes of reflected vs. refracted light as a function of the angle of incidence.

5. Numerical Techniques

Solving systems of nonlinear equations like the ones in section 3 can be a difficult numerical problem; and in graphics, there is a desire to include a diverse selection of implicit surfaces $g(\mathbf{x}) = 0$. The combination of two interesting techniques make this practical: *automatic differentiation* and *interval arithmetic*.

5.1. Automatic Differentiation

Imagine that we want to evaluate a function $f(x_0)$ at some point and also the derivative $f_x(x_0)$. We could symbolically differentiate f, but this can result in a large expression that is computationally expensive to evaluate. We could compute a finite-difference approximation to the derivative, but this yields poor numerical accuracy.

An alternative is to compute with pairs of numbers representing values of f and f_x at a point [Rall81]. For constant $f = c$, this pair will be $(c, 0)$, and for $f = x$, the value/derivative pair is simply $(x_0, 1)$. Starting from there, a formula for f can be evaluated by performing operations on these pairs of numbers. The pairs are combined according to familiar rules of differentiation, such as the following rules for multiplication and square root:

$$(g(x_0), g_x(x_0)) * (f(x_0), f_x(x_0))$$
$$\rightarrow (g(x_0)f(x_0), g(x_0)f_x(x_0) + f(x_0)g_x(x_0))$$

$$\sqrt{(f(x_0), f_x(x_0))}$$
$$\rightarrow (\sqrt{f(x_0)}, \frac{(f_x)(x_0)}{2\sqrt{f(x_0)}})$$

This method can be easily extended to evaluate partial derivatives with respect to different variables. It also can be extended to simultaneously compute higher order derivatives.

5.2. Interval Arithmetic

An alternative system of arithmetic can be defined, based on *interval numbers*. A number of powerful numerical techniques are based on interval arithmetic [Moore79], and some of these techniques have been applied to problems in computer graphics [Murdur84,Toth85,Mitchell90]. An interval number corresponds to a range of real values and can be represented by a pair of numbers $[a, b]$, the lower and upper bounds of the interval. Given interval numbers X and Y, we would like to compute interval values of expressions such as $X + Y$ or function values $f(X)$. Ideally, these values should be exact bounds, the range of lowest to highest values of $f(x)$ for all $x \in X$. Often it is not possible to find the exact bound, but it may still be very useful to know an interval value guaranteed to contain the exact bound.

It is straightforward to define interval extensions of basic arithmetic operations:

$$[a,b] + [c,d] = [a + c, b + d] \tag{1a}$$

$$[a,b] - [c,d] = [a - d, b - c] \tag{1b}$$

$$[a,b] * [c,d] = \\ [\min(ac,ad,bc,bd), \\ \max(ac,ad,bc,bd)] \tag{1c}$$

and if $0 \notin [c,d]$

$$[a,b] / [c,d] = [a,b] * [1/d,1/c] \tag{1d}$$

Given a rational function $r(x)$, the *natural interval extension* can be defined by evaluating the expression $r(X)$ for an interval argument $X = [x_0, x_1]$ and using the interval-arithmetic operations in (1). Interval extensions of familiar functions like cosine or square root can also be defined and included in expressions. The resulting interval value of $r(X)$ is guaranteed to contain the exact bound of the real-valued $r(x)$ over the interval X. The tightness of the bound may depend on how $r(X)$ is expressed. For example, interval arithmetic is *subdistributive*: $X(Y + Z) \subseteq XY + XZ$. One of the most important properties of the natural interval extension is *inclusion monotonicity*:

$$X' \subset X, \quad \text{implies} \quad r(X') \subseteq r(X)$$

This means that as the interval X becomes more narrow, the interval $r(X)$ will converge to its real restriction.

5.3. Solving Nonlinear Systems

A robust and general method of solving nonlinear systems combines automatic differentiation with interval arithmetic. Suppose we are attempting to solve a system of N equations in N unknowns, $\mathbf{f}(\mathbf{x}) = 0$. Ordinary Newton's method does not provide a reliable way to locate every solution within a given region, but interval extensions have been developed which do [Moore79]. The most straightforward interval Newton's method is the sequence beginning with some interval vector $\mathbf{X}_0$:

$$\mathbf{X}_{k+1} = N(\mathbf{X}_k) \cap \mathbf{X}_k$$

where

$$N(\mathbf{X}) = m(\mathbf{X}) - [F'(\mathbf{X})]^{-1} f(m(\mathbf{X}))$$

Here, $m(\mathbf{X})$ is an ordinary vector made up of midpoint values of the $\mathbf{X}$ components, and $F'(\mathbf{X})^{-1}$ is the interval Jacobian of the system of equations at $\mathbf{X}$. The intersection $N(\mathbf{X}_k) \cap \mathbf{X}_k$ constrains the new interval to be within the original and is a common precaution against effects of finite-precision machine arithmetic.

A problem with Newton-step operator $N(\mathbf{X})$ is that it involves the inversion of an interval matrix. Krawczyk developed an alternative Newton-like method using an operator which is cheaper to compute. This operator only requires inversion of an ordinary (non-interval) matrix:

$$K(\mathbf{X}) = m(\mathbf{X}) - [m(F'(\mathbf{X}))]^{-1} f(m(\mathbf{X})) \\ + \{I - [m(F'(\mathbf{X}))]^{-1} F'(\mathbf{X})\}(\mathbf{X} - m(\mathbf{X}))$$

Moore and others have proven a number of theorems about the convergence of these Newton-like methods which are used to construct a sound method for isolating and refining solution estimates [Moore79,Rall81].

Theorem 1 (NonExistance I) *If* $0 \notin \mathbf{F}(\mathbf{X})$, *there is no solution of* $\mathbf{f}(\mathbf{x}) = 0$ *in X.*

Theorem 2 (NonExistance II) *If* $K(\mathbf{X}) \cap \mathbf{X} = \varnothing$, *there are no roots in* $\mathbf{X}$.

Theorem 3 (Convergence). *If* $K(\mathbf{X}) \subseteq \mathbf{X}$ *and* $\|I - [m(F'(\mathbf{X}))]^{-1} F'(\mathbf{X})\| < 1$, *there is a unique root in* $\mathbf{X}$ *and a number of iterative methods will converge to it.*

The algorithm for finding all solutions is then quite simple. Given an interval X, these three theorems are automatically tested. The interval is discarded if it is known to have no solutions within it. Some Newton-like iterative method is applied if Theorem 3 guarantees convergence. Otherwise, the interval is subdivided and the procedure applied recursively. Subdivision must terminate when the limits of machine-arithmetic are reached (i.e., when the width of X is less than some ε_x).

In our problem of reflected illumination, the systems given in Section 3 must be solved. Since the equations involve ∇g and ∇d, the interval Newton method will require values of the second derivatives of g and d. The process of finding solutions must begin with an initial interval value for the variables x,y,z,λ. The first three dimensions are initialized to a box tightly enclosing the implicit surface $g(\mathbf{x}) = 0$.

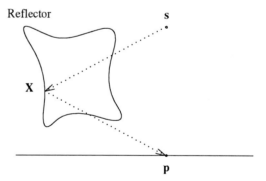

Figure 5. Back-Facing Reflection Points

As Figure 5 shows, we wish to exclude points on the mirror where the osculating ellipsoid touches a back-facing surface, since the body of the mirror itself would block the light's paths. These points are eliminated automatically by choosing the initial λ interval to be $[0, \lambda_{max}]$. This will only allow points where the mirror's normal points in the opposite direction of the normal on the osculating ellipsoid. A nice property of the interval root-finding methods is that they do not expend resources searching outside the initial interval, so no time is wasted on back-facing reflection points.

It's important to note that more than one stationary path may exist from a given **p** to the light source. Figure 6 shows the paths at a series of points in a two-dimensional scene. Rays from the light (in the upper right) to the surface are omitted to avoid cluttering the image. Regions containing one path and a region containing three paths are separated by a caustic surface. In the regions containing three stationary paths, notice that the middle pathway is a local maximum. A common misconception is that Fermat's principle requires paths to be of minimum length.

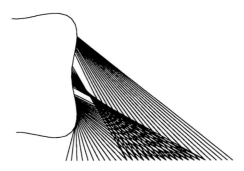

Figure 6. Examples of Stationary Paths of Illumination

6. Implementing Multiple Extensions of a Function

Our ray tracer can accept an expression for an implicit surface in a simple symbolic form, and then construct and solve the system of equations described above. To accomplish this, expressions $g(\mathbf{x})$ are represented by sequences of codes for a push-down stack machine. For example, the function for a unit sphere,

$$g(\mathbf{x}) = x^2 + y^2 + z^2 - 1 = 0,$$

is defined as:

```
Bytecode sphere[] = {
        LDX, SQR, LDY, SQR, LDZ, SQR,
        ADD, ADD,
        NUM, 1.0, SUB,
        RET,
};
```

The LDX instruction pushes the value of x onto the stack. ADD pops two values and pushes the sum, etc. A slightly more interesting surface, shaped like a rounded cube with the faces dented inward, is given by this quartic formula,

$$g(\mathbf{x}) = x^4 + y^4 + z^4 - x^2 - y^2 - z^2 = 0,$$

is defined as:

```
Bytecode cuboid[] = {
        LDX,SQR,SQR,
        LDY,SQR,SQR,
        LDZ,SQR,SQR,
        ADD,ADD,
        LDX,SQR,LDY,SQR,LDZ,SQR,ADD,ADD,
        SUB,
        RET,
}
```

These stack-machine codes are evaluated by a collection of six stack-machine interpreters in the ray tracer. Each of these interpreters takes a code sequence and argument **x**.

The first group of interpreters operate on real numbers. The simplest interpreter evaluates the code with ordinary floating-point arithmetic and returns the scalar value $g(\mathbf{x})$. This stack machine is used primarily during root refinement by ordinary Newton's method (when the interval methods have proven convergence within an interval). A second stack machine used automatic differentiation to compute $g(\mathbf{x})$ and a corresponding value of ∇g. This is used primarily to find surface normal vectors for the shading calculation. A third machine computes the Hessian, and is used in wavefront-curvature calculations.

The second group of interpreters operate on intervals. A first machine in this group computes an interval extension of g and an interval extension of the directional derivative $\partial g / \partial t$ along a ray. This stack machine is used by the ray/surface intersection routines as described in [Mitchell90]. A second machine computes interval extensions of g and its gradient ∇g, and a third machine computes these as well as an interval extension of the Hessian matrix for g. These two machines are used to compute the Krawczyk operator (8) during the root isolation phase.

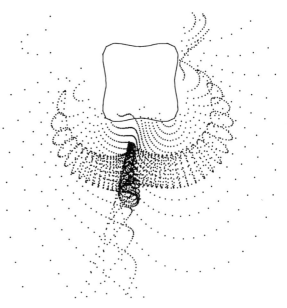

Figure 7. Spot Diagram of Rays Reflected off Cuboid

7. Results

A basic ray tracer augmented with the reflection-illumination techniques described above was implemented in 3400 lines of C code. Two 512×512 images were rendered of a reflective copper-colored cuboid defined by:

$$g(\mathbf{x}) = x^4 + y^4 + z^4 - x^2 - y^2 - z^2 = 0$$

This surface is a good test of our method, because it has regions of concave, convex, and saddle-shaped curvature. The light source is a point at infinity behind the viewer and slightly to their right. In Plate 2, the wavefront intensity is not used, so the brightness of the reflection is simply a function of how many virtual light sources illuminate each visible point. Plate 3 is the same image, using the intensity laws developed in Section 4. Note that some reflections seen in Plate 2 have vanished because they make an insignificant contribution to the intensity. Interesting structure in the reflection includes the bright focal point below the concave side and the bright edges of the caustic structure—a singularity in intensity that occurs at the boundaries between regions having different numbers of virtual lights. These plates (as well as Figure 6) further demonstrate that the table top is divided into distinct regions according to how many virtual lights (i.e, stationary paths to the light source) are present.

Figure 7 shows a *spot diagram* of this system. This is the pattern of dots formed by casting light rays toward the reflector and recording where they hit the table. In this case, the light was not at infinity, so the shape of the caustic is slightly different, but the topology is essentially the same. Not only does this help verify the correctness of the geometry and intensity calculation, but it is an excellent demonstration of why backward ray tracing has difficulty deriving a smooth and correct irradiance value from a nonuniform pattern of radiant-power samples.

Plate 3 was computed on an 8-processor Silicon Graphics IRIS (model 480) in about 10 hours.

Plate 3. Illumination with Intensity Law

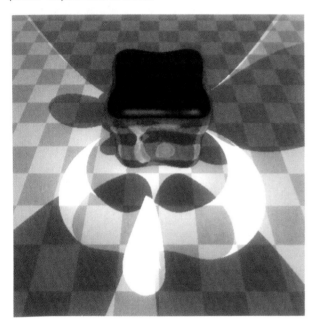

Plate 2. Illumination from Virtual Lights

8. Discussion

Our algorithm is based on two key ideas. First, Fermat's Principle—that light travels along extremal paths—allows us to formulate the path calculation as a multidimensional non-linear optimization problem, which we can solve robustly using interval techniques. Second, the intensity law states that the incident irradiance at a point is proportional to the Gaussian curvature of the wavefront at that point. Gaussian curvature is computed by keeping track of the local geometry of the wavefront as it propagates along a Fermat path. The combination of the two techniques allows us to calculate directly the illumination via virtual lights at any point in the scene.

The intensity law has been used in the two-pass rendering algorithms developed by Shinya and Takahashi [Shinya87,Shinya89] and by Watt [Watt90]. What is novel about our approach is that we avoid the second pass, and hence the problem of resampling the light rays by the eye rays. We also formulate the intensity calculation in a way suitable for ray tracing programs. Shinya and Takahashi's formulation requires the notion of paraxial rays, and Watt's formulation only works for polygonal beams. We also discuss how to compute curvatures for general implicit functions.

Profiling our program, we find that the majority of the time is spent solving for path extrema. The time involved is significant,

but we take solace in a observation by Turner Whitted that his first ray tracer spent the majority of its time in the line-surface intersection calculation. We believe that cost of solving for ellipse-surface tangency has roughly the same complexity as line-surface intersection, and, hence, can be speeded up significantly.

An important application of this technique that we have yet to explore is the calculation of extended form factors [Sparrow62]. A form factor between two surface elements is defined to be the percentage of light leaving one element that impinges directly on the other. An extended form factor includes light traveling via intermediate specular surfaces. Fermat path tracing finds all the paths between the two surface elements explicitly. Previous techniques compute extended form factors by distributing rays over the hemisphere above a surface [Wallace87,Sillion89]. Since this involves sampling the hemisphere, it may miss important modes of light transport. Also, the wavefront intensity correction must be performed if the path involves interactions with curved surfaces. To the authors' knowledge, this has not been done in existing systems.

Finally, we have discussed the local geometry of wavefronts, but have ignored their global geometry. This distinction roughly corresponds to that of sampling visibility at a point vs. over an area. The key feature of wavefronts are their singularities, or caustics, where the intensity goes to infinity and bright burning spots are formed. Although caustics at first seem to be a problem (since they cause a potentially nasty divide by zero), they can also be used to advantage. Caustics separate "ray-space" into topologically uniform regions---for example, where there are one vs. three virtual light sources. Within topologically uniform regions we can compute paths incrementally using Newton's method, since there is no need to go through a root isolation phase, since we already know a neighboring path. This observation has the potential for speeding up the program enormously. Also, the shapes of the caustics themselves are very interesting. There is a one-to-one correspondence between the types of caustics and the types of singularities, or catastrophes, produced by a function and its gradient map [Berry80]. Producing mathematical visualizations of such functions would be extremely interesting to mathematical physicists.

9. References

[Appel68]   Appel, A. Some techniques for shading machine renderings of solids. *AFIPS 1968 Spring Joint Computer Conf.* 32 (1968), 37-45.

[Arvo86]   Arvo, J. Backward ray tracing. *Developments in Ray Tracing* SIGGRAPH Course Notes, 12 (1986).

[Berry80]   Berry, M. V., Upstill, C., Catastrophe Optics: Morphologies of Caustics and their Diffraction Patterns, *Progress in Optics* XVIII, (1980), 259-346.

[Born80]   Born, M. and Wolf, E., *Principles of Optics.* Pergamon, 1980.

[Chen91]   Chen, S. E., Rushmeier, H. E., Miller, G., Turner, D., A Progressive Multi-Pass Method for Global Illumination *Computer Graphics* 25, 4 (1991), 165-174.

[Dill81]   Dill, John C., An Application of Color Graphics to the Display of Surface Curvature *Computer Graphics* 15, 3 (1981), 153-161.

[Forrest79]   Forrest, A. R., On the Rendering of Surfaces. *Computer Graphics* 13, 2 (1979), 253-259.

[Gullstrand06]   Gullstrand, A. Die reelle optische Abbildung. *Sv. Vetensk. Handl.* 41, (1906), 1-119.

[Heckbert90]   Heckbert, P. Adaptive Radiosity Textures for Bidrectional Ray Tracing. *Computer Graphics,* 24, 4 (August 1990), 145-154.

[Kneisly64]   Kneisly, J. A. III, Local curvature of wavefronts in an optical system. *J. Opt. Soc. Amer.* 54, (1964), 229-235.

[Mitchell90]   Mitchell, D. P. Robust ray intersection with interval arithmetic. *Graphics Interface 90,* (May 1990) 68-74.

[Moore79]   Moore, R. E., *Methods and applications of interval analysis.* SIAM, 1979.

[Murdur84]   Murdur, S. P., Koparkar, P. A., Interval methods for processing geometric objects. *IEEE Computer Graphics and Applications,* 4,2 (February 1984), 7-17.

[Rall81]   Rall, Louis B., *Automatic Differentiation: Techniques and Applications.* Springer-Verlag, 1981.

[Shinya87]   Shinya, M., Takahashi, T, Naito, S. Principles and applications of pencil tracing. *Computer Graphics,* 21, 4 (July 1987), 45-54.

[Shinya89]   Shinya, M., Saito, T., Takahashi, T. Rendering techniques for transparent objects. *Proc. Graphics Interface '89,* (1989) 173-182.

[Shirley90]   Shirley, P. A ray tracing method for illumination calculation in diffuse-specular scenes. *Proc. Graphics Interface '90,* (1990) 205-212.

[Sillion89]   Sillion, F., Puech, C., A General Two-Pass Method Integrating Specular and Diffuse Reflection. *Computer Graphics* 23, 3 (1989), 335-344.

[Sparrow62]   Sparrow, E. J., Eckert, E. R. G., Jonsson, V. K., An Enclosure Theory for Radiative Exchange Between Specularly and Diffusely Reflecting Surfaces. *Journal of Heat Transfer* 84C,4, (1962).

[Stavroudis72]   Stavroudis, O. N. *The Optics of Rays, Wavefronts, and Caustics,* Academic, 1972.

[Struik61]   Struik, Dirk J., *Lectures on Classical Differential Geometry* 2nd. Edition, Dover Publications, New York, 1961.

[Toth85]   Toth, D. L. On ray tracing parametric surfaces. *Computer Graphics,* 19, 3 (July 1985), 171-179.

[Wallace87]   Wallace, J., Cohen, M. F., Greenberg, D. P., A Two-Pass Solution to the Rendering Equation: A Synthesis of Radiosity and Ray Tracing Methods. *Computer Graphics* 21, 4, (1987), 311-320.

[Watt90]   Watt, M. Light-water interaction using backward beam tracing. *Computer Graphics,* 24, 4 (August 1990) 377-385.

[Whitted80]   Whitted, T. An improved illumination model for shaded display. *Comm. ACM,* 23, 6 (June 1980), 343-349.

Interactive Spacetime Control for Animation

Michael F. Cohen*
Department of Computer Science
University of Utah
Salt Lake City, Utah 84112

Abstract

This paper describes new techniques to design physically based, goal directed motion of synthetic creatures. More specifically, it concentrates on developing an interactive framework for specifying constraints and objectives for the motion, and for *guiding* the numerical solution of the optimization problem thus defined.

The ability to define, modify and guide constrained spacetime problems is provided through an interactive user interface. Innovations that are introduced include, (1) the subdivision of spacetime into discrete pieces, or *Spacetime Windows*, over which subproblems can be formulated and solved, (2) the use of cubic B-spline approximation techniques to define a C^2 function for the creature's time dependent degrees of freedom, (3) the use of both symbolic and numerical processes to construct and solve the constrained optimization problem, and (4) the ability to specify inequality and conditional constraints.

Creatures, in the context of this work, consist of rigid links connected by joints defining a set of generalized degrees of freedom. Hybrid symbolic and numeric techniques to solve the resulting complex constrained optimization problems are made possible by the special structure of physically based models of such creatures, and by the recent development of symbolic algebraic languages. A graphical user interface process handles communication between the user and two other processes; one devoted to symbolic differentiation and manipulation of the constraints and objectives, and one that performs the iterative numerical solution of the optimization problem. The user interface itself provides both high and low level definition of, interaction with, and inspection of, the optimization process and the resulting animation. Implementation issues and experiments with the Spacetime Windows system are discussed.

CR Categories: I.3.7: [Computer Graphics] Three-Dimensional Graphics and Realism; I.6.3 [Simulation and Modeling] Applications; G.1.6 [Constrained Optimization]

Additional Keywords: Animation, Design, Spacetime.

* Current Address: Dept. of Computer Science, Princeton University, 35 Olden St, Princeton, NJ 08544

1 Introduction

Computers have been used to assist in the creation of animated sequences for more than a decade, yet the resulting animation still cannot reproduce the lifelike qualities imparted to creatures through traditional hand animation. There has been some success in creating realistic motion of inanimate objects such as chains and machines by simulating physical laws. The lifelike motion of animate creatures is, however, driven both by physics and by internal motivations (or *actuated systems* [32]), and thus cannot be captured by a direct application of Newton's laws of motion.

The goal of this research is to provide the ability to interactively design the motion of simulated creatures which appears correct, and satisfies goals and objectives set by the user. Thus the laws of physics provide possible constraints on the motion rather than the primary driving force for simulation. The motion of the creatures is derived through a user guided optimization process that minimizes an objective function subject to physical and other user-defined constraints. The use of *spacetime constraints* and *optimal control* introduced to computer animation by Witkin and Kass [36] and Brotman and Netravali [6] is enhanced and embedded into an interactive framework.

Interactive constraint and objective definition, symbolic and numerical optimization capabilities, and graphical feedback are provided in the *Spacetime Windows* system. The Spacetime Windows system consists of three separate processes, a graphical user interface, a symbolic manipulation process, and a spacetime numerical optimization system. Animations are designed in an iterative fashion through the creation and manipulation of symbolic constraints and objectives, providing "sketches" of the proposed animation, and by focusing the optimization on subsets (windows) of spacetime during the numerical optimization process.

The remainder of the paper is organized as follows. After a brief review of computer animation methods, the Spacetime Windows system and its implementation are described. This is followed by some example animation segments, and a discussion of areas for future research.

2 Previous Work in Computer Animation

In the past decade, two main approaches have evolved for creating motion of synthetic figures. The first approach recreates and enhances the kinematic tools used by traditional animators to relieve some of the tedious and time consuming tasks of hand animation. The second path simulates the physical laws that govern motion in the real world. Although each of the two methodologies has produced some beautiful computer generated motion, they both have serious limitations. Traditional animation methods provide great *control* to the artist, but do not provide any tools for *automatically* creating realistic motion. Dynamic simulation, on the other hand, generates physically correct motion (within limits) but it does not provide sufficient control for an artist or scientist to create desired motion [22]. More recent work, and the focus of the work reported here, has concentrated on adding control within a dynamic framework.

2.1 Kinematics and Dynamics

Not surprisingly, the most successful computer animation to date has relied heavily on the abilities of the animator. Films such as "Tony de Peltrie" and "Luxo Jr" brought creatures convincingly to life. The primary role of the computer was to render images and perform interpolation tasks, thus allowing the artist/animator to concentrate explicitly on the creation of key frames. A more powerful technique involves the use of *inverse kinematics* permitting direct specification of end point positions (e.g., a hand or foot) [15; 20; 29; 28].

Dynamics has been the focus of the work of a number of researchers attempting to automatically generate realistic motion [1; 2; 4; 16; 18; 19; 21; 24; 23; 27; 34]. The motion of chains, waves, spacecraft, automobiles and other inanimate objects has been successfully simulated. The reason for this success is the objects' response to *external* forces in accordance with physical principles. The objects are, however, not under the control of the animator after initial conditions are specified.

How to return some level of control to the animator is one of the most difficult issues in dynamic simulation. In [18; 19], constraints are included to allow the concurrent explicit control of some degrees of freedom while allowing others to react in a correct dynamic fashion. Witkin and Welch take this concept one step further and generate kinematic constraints from higher level control specifications and apply them to non-rigid bodies [37]. Wilhelms explores similar directions for adding control within a dynamic system [34], but does not include goal directed motion in an integrated fashion.

2.2 Constraints and Control

Various types and levels of control have been added to dynamic systems to achieve control over the motion of simulated creatures. Bruderlin and Calvert [7] create convincing walking motion of human figures through the use of a hybrid hierarchical control process that incorporates an approximate dynamic model. Raibert and his colleagues produce running motion of a variety of simulated (and real) creatures [32]. Control algorithms are used to regulate speed, gait, and to maintain balance. This control is exerted at each time interval based on the current state of the creature. Motion sequences are then created as in dynamic systems by integrating forward through time. Each of these systems has been extremely successful over their limited domain of applicability.

Ading constraints to modeling systems is not new and has resulted in animation sequences. Barr and others use constraints to construct static assemblies of rigid bodies, e.g., a cable tower [35; 4; 30]. The process of solving the constraints leads to a series of configurations for the constrained objects, thus creating an animation as a byproduct of the solution process.

2.3 Spacetime Constraints and Control

In contrast to systems that *simulate* motion by stepping forward through time, animation *design* involves planning en-

tire sequences of motion as a single unit. Scenes are designed to have particular events occur at specified times. Thus, one would like a system that provides control over the total animation while incorporating dynamics principles.

Witkin and Kass describe a spacetime constraint system [36] in which constraints and objectives are defined over *Spacetime*, referring to the set of all forces and positions of all of a creature's degrees of freedom (DOF) from the beginning to the end of an animation sequence. Brotman and Netravali [6] achieved a similar result through the use of Optimal Control methodologies. In each case, the animation is derived through an optimization of the objective subject to the constraints. This integration of user-defined constraints and physical constraints answers many of the difficulties of earlier systems.

The work reported in these papers demonstrates impressive results, but suffers from a number of restrictions. The first restriction is that the complexity growth of the problem limits the length of animation sequences. The second restriction is that creatures must have full knowledge of the future to optimize their actions. This is not dissimilar to the first restriction, in that all the motion is based on a single set of constraints and a single objective. The non-interactive nature of the specification and, more importantly, the numerical process also make it difficult to integrate these techniques into an animation design system. In addition, given the highly non-linear nature of the constraints and objectives, the available numerical methods often do not converge to acceptable solutions.

3 Spacetime Windows

The Spacetime Windows system, described below, includes a number of features designed to remove the restrictions of earlier systems and to enable the use of spacetime constraints in an interactive framework. The ability to interactively specify and modify constraints and objectives, and to define and iterate on solutions to subproblems provides the animator with tools to examine and thus *guide* the optimization process. The sensitivity of highly non-linear constrained optimization to starting values and solution algorithms can thus be controlled to a great extent by the user. Given visual and numeric feedback about the progress of the convergence towards a desired solution, the user is able to add new constraints, raise or lower the weight of previous constraints, or modify intermediate solutions. This is followed by further iterations until the animation is deemed satisfactory by the user. The ill-defined "design" process is thus left largely in the control of the animator.

A primary concept used to realize these goals is the ability to focus attention on overlapping pieces of spacetime, or *spacetime windows*. A window is defined over a subset of the creature's degrees of freedom, and across a subset of the time from the beginning to the end of the animation. Then, an iterative optimization process is run to find a set of functions of the DOF across the window, that minimize an objective while maintaining a set of weighted constraints. The solution for each spacetime window represents a partial solution of the entire animation. The solutions within windows are combined through continuity conditions with the spacetime outside of the window, and by overlapping subsequent windows in space and time. Spacetime windows also provide the facility to refine specific intervals of time or the motion of specific DOF.

This approach addresses problems inherent in Witkin and Kass' work. First, computational complexity is mitigated since each window represents an independent subproblem. In addition to keeping the iteration times of the optimization to a few seconds, the subproblem defined across a space-

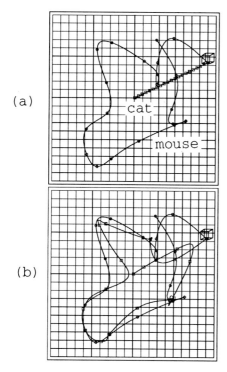

Figure 1: Cat and Mouse

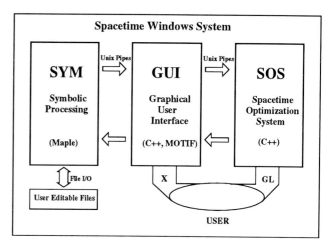

Figure 2: The Spacetime Windows System

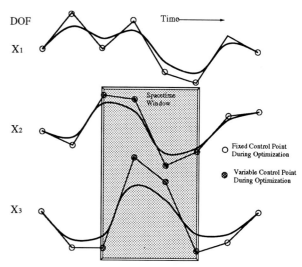

Figure 3: Spacetime

time window is generally more numerically stable, producing more robust convergence towards a solution. The use of spacetime windows also provides the semantics to simulate creatures with a limited knowledge of the future. For example, if a simulated cat is constrained to catch a mouse with minimum energy, in a full spacetime optimization, the cat would optimize its actions by simply moving in a straight line to where the mouse will be and then waiting for it to run into its mouth (Figure 1a). By optimizing over individual smaller spacetime windows overlapping in time, the cat's path is only influenced by local regions in spacetime (Figure 1b), resulting in a more realistic "chasing" action.

3.1   System Overview

An overview of the Spacetime Windows system is given in Figure 2. Three separate processes communicate via standard UNIX pipes and thus may reside on separate processors across a network. The graphical user interface (GUI) is written in C++ on top of X-windows/MOTIF. The user interface handles all communication between the user and the system and between processes, thus performing syncronization responsibilities. A symbolic manipulation process (SYM) is written on top of the symbolic algebra package, Maple [8]. SYM is responsible for symbolic simplification of the differential equations that describe the constraints and objective. It is also responsible for symbolic differentiation of these equations with respect to the DOF. The spacetime optimization system (SOS) parses the symbolic equations and their derivatives, evaluates the expressions at specific points in time, performs optimization steps and graphically reports results.

3.2   Spacetime

Spacetime refers to the set of all DOF over the entire animation sequence. In the context of figure animation, the "space" in spacetime refers to the DOF, or generalized coordinates that define a creature's position, e.g., the global position (X, Y, Z) of the creature in space, or the angle of an elbow or knee. The value of each DOF varies across time and is thus represented as a function of time, t (Figure 3). The set of DOF functions, (or simply DOF), will be denoted by $\mathbf{X}$, with reference to a particular DOF as X_j. Constraints or the objective imposed on the DOF may be any second order differential function of the DOF, $\mathcal{C}(\mathbf{X}, \dot{\mathbf{X}}, \ddot{\mathbf{X}}, t)$ and are thus *differential functionals* (differential functions of functions). The set of constraints are denoted $\mathcal{C}$, with a particular constraint $\mathcal{C}_{\mathbf{i}}$, and the objective, R.

Constraints may be expressions that should be true at a particular point in time, (e.g., the ball should be at a particular position at a particular time), or may express a relationship that should be true at all time or over a limited range of times, (e.g., the force on the ball in the vertical direction plus the force of gravity equals its vertical acceleration). Constraints that exist over time are discretized in time into a set of *constraint instances*, **C**, with a particular instance $C_{i,l}$, now a function of scalar values for the DOF and their first two derivatives at specific times.

Similarly, the DOF functions, are approximated from a set of discrete control points, **S**, that at a particular iteration have values, $\mathbf{S_k}$. The optimization problem can then be approximated as finding a set of values for **S** that minimize R subject to the constraint instances, **C**.

3.3 B-Spline Approximation

For the numerical evaluation of the constraints and the objective it is necessary to evaluate the DOF and their first two derivatives at specific points in time. First and second derivatives of the constraint instances with respect to the control points must also be evaluated for the numerical optimization. For these values to be defined at all times the **X** must be at least C^2. Earlier work relied on the use of finite difference techniques for the derivatives [36], but these are well defined only at the discrete time values used in the discretization. Here, cubic B-spline curves [3] have been chosen to represent the DOF. Uniform cubic B-spline curves are approximated by a set of control points that are blended together by a set of cubic B-spline blending functions. The blending functions in turn are derived from a set of knot values over the parameter of time. The B-spline curve is then defined by:

$$X_j(t) = \sum_{l=-2}^{N_j+2} S_{j,l} B_l(t)$$

where the B-splines, B_j, are non-zero over four spans between knot values, and $S_{j,l}$ are the values of the jth DOF's control points. Issues such as how to deal with end conditions, and much greater detail on this topic can be found in the extensive literature on B-splines [12; 3; 25].

The time derivatives of the DOF, $\dot{X}_j(t)$, are obtained from the time derivatives of the B-spline:

$$\dot{X}_j(t) = \sum_{l=-2}^{N_j+2} S_{j,l} \dot{B}_l(t) \quad and \quad \ddot{X}_j(t) = \sum_{l=-2}^{N_j+2} S_{j,l} \ddot{B}_l(t)$$

The derivatives of the DOF with respect to the control point are simply the B-spline itself and zero:

$$\frac{\partial X_j(t)}{\partial S_{j,l}} = B_l(t) \quad and \quad \frac{\partial^2 X_j(t)}{\partial S_{j,l}^2} = 0$$

Finally, the derivatives of the constraint instances (or objective integrand) with respect to the control points can be found with the chain rule:

$$\frac{\partial C_i(\mathbf{X}.\dot{\mathbf{X}}, \ddot{\mathbf{X}})}{\partial S_{j,l}} = \frac{\partial C_i}{\partial X_j}\frac{\partial X_j}{\partial S_{j,l}} + \frac{\partial C_i}{\partial \dot{X}_j}\frac{\partial \dot{X}_j}{\partial S_{j,l}} + \frac{\partial C_i}{\partial \ddot{X}_j}\frac{\partial \ddot{X}_j}{\partial S_{j,l}}$$

The partial derivatives of the constraints with respect to the DOF are solved analytically in SYM, and evaluated numerically for each instance of the constraint. The derivatives of the DOF with respect to the control points are independent of the value of the control points themselves, and are thus only a function of time and the knot vector.

The fact that B-splines are non-zero over a limited range of parameter (i.e., time) values creates a desired locality between changes in control point values and the shape of the resulting curve. This leads to a sparse Hessian matrix used in the numerical stage of the optimization. Particular DOF with rapidly changing values over a particular region can be refined [5; 9].

3.4 Constraints and Objective

Two classes of constraints are those provided directly by the user, and those derived from a physical description of the creature and its environment. A typical user constraint may be that the *foot* must be in a particular position at a particular time, or that a *hand* and *ball* must coincide during a specified time interval. Constraints can also be specified as inequality constraints, or as conditional constraints (i.e., enforced only during times when some condition is met). Physical constraints arise from the equations of motion for a particular creature. The simplest example is that of a point mass for which a direct application of Newton's second law applies. Constraints may take the form of any second order differential equation of the DOF. They may contain references to constants that can be set and changed by the user during the animation design process. Constraints themselves can also be added, deleted or modified. Equations of motion for the linkages are automatically derived through a lisp code [11] from a Denavit-Hartenberg description of the linkage [10]. The lisp code generates the symbolic equations of motion through a Newton-Euler formulation, that results in equating generalized forces and torques with differential expressions of the DOF. These forces become symbols for the corresponding expressions and can then be used as subexpressions in other constraints and the objective.

The objective is defined as a sum of integrals of the squares of *sub-objectives*. Sub-objectives are simply expressions with the same syntax as those for constraints. For example, if one wants to minimize the torque at the elbow, the expression for the torque is added to the set of sub-objectives.

3.5 Subexpressions

Forces are eliminated as explicit DOF (and thus the corresponding control points are not required) by symbolic substitution of the force's subexpression for all references to the force in any constraint or sub-objective. This *symbolic* solution for the physical constraints eliminates a large number of constraint instances that were required in previous work to hold the value of a force equal to its corresponding differential expression.

In addition to subexpressions for forces derived from the equations of motion, user defined subexpressions are of great utility. For example, the location of an end-effector (e.g., the hand at the end of an arm, $(HandX, HandY, HandZ)$) can be specified as a set of subexpressions derived from the Denavit-Hartenberg notation. These can then be used to hold the ball in the hand,

$$HandX[0,T] - BX[0,T],$$

(and likewise for $HandY$ and $HandZ$). The use of subexpressions simplifies the numerical optimization problem by reducing both the number of DOF and constraint instances. Derivatives of expressions containing subexpressions are generated symbolically with the chain rule.

3.6 Non-linear Constrained Optimization

General non-linear constrained optimization remains an unsolved problem [17; 13; 14; 26; 31]. The procedures that are currently used to solve general optimization problems are often described as an "art". The art of selecting appropriate algorithms, starting values, and parameters of the numerical process relies on experience and an understanding of the problem being solved. The animator's understanding of the desired motion, plus an intuitive understanding of what defines "correct" motion is brought to use through interactive monitoring and guidance of the numerical process. The user interface to the iterative process is discussed in section 4.

3.6.1 Minimization of the Lagrangian

It is easily shown that in the case of an unconstrained minimization problem, a local minimum will occur only at points where all partial derivatives of the objective with respect to the control points vanish. Similarly, in the constrained problem, the gradient of the objective must be equal to some linear combination of the constraint gradients for the solution to represent a constrained minimum. This leads to the formulation of the Langrangian of the constrained problem, that represents an equivalent unconstrained problem, and can thus be minimized using methods for unconstrained problems.

Given the objective, R, and the set of constraint instances, C_i, with control points, $\mathbf{S}$, the Lagrangian is given by:

$$L(\mathbf{S}, \lambda) = R(\mathbf{S}) + \sum_{i=1}^{m} \lambda_i C_i(\mathbf{S})$$

where the λ_i are referred to as Lagrange multipliers and correspond roughly to the influence of the constraints on the objective.

Just as the unconstrained problem has a mininum when all partial derivatives are zero, the augmented problem also has a minimum when all partial derivatives of L with respect to the S_j and λ_i are zero. Given n control points and m constraint instances, a set of $n + m$ homogeneous equations can be formed by taking the partial derivatives of L with respect to each of the elements of $\mathbf{S}$ and of λ, and setting them equal to zero. It should be noted that the partial derivatives of L with respect to the Lagrange multipliers are simply the constraints themselves, and thus setting them equal to zero solves the constraints implicitly.

3.6.2 Sequential Quadratic Programming

By applying a combination of Lagrange's method and Newton's method to the constrained objective, one can formulate a sequence of quadratic subproblems that lead towards a solution to the constrained optimization. To understand the method, we begin with the gradient of the Lagrangian at a local optimum $(\mathbf{S}_*, \lambda_*)$:

$$\nabla L(\mathbf{S}_*, \lambda_*) = 0$$

that must be zero as stated in the previous section.

Consider a sequence of iterations beginning with an initial guess for $\mathbf{S}$ and the multipliers, λ, $(\mathbf{S_0}, \lambda_0)$, (the subscripts, k, are used here to indicate the iteration number.) Expanding the $(k + 1)^{st}$ iteration into a first order Taylor series around the kth iteration and setting it equal to zero results in:

$$\nabla L(\mathbf{S_{k+1}}, \lambda_{k+1})^T \approx \nabla L(\mathbf{S_k} + \partial \mathbf{S}, \lambda_k + \partial \lambda)^T$$

$$\approx \nabla L_k^T + \nabla^2 L_k (\partial \mathbf{S_k}, \partial \lambda_k)^T = \mathbf{0}$$

where:

$$\nabla^2 L = \begin{bmatrix} \nabla^2_{ss} L & \nabla^2_{s\lambda} L \\ \nabla^2_{s\lambda} L & \nabla^2_{\lambda\lambda} L \end{bmatrix} = \begin{bmatrix} \nabla^2 R + \lambda^T \nabla^2 C & \nabla C^T \\ \nabla C & 0 \end{bmatrix}$$

Using Newton's method, one can now construct a linearized system around the current guess for the animation,

and equate the Hessian of the Lagrangian times a step, $(\partial S_k, \partial \lambda_k)$, with the gradient of the Lagrangian.

$$\nabla^2 L_k \begin{bmatrix} \partial S_k \\ \partial \lambda_k \end{bmatrix} = \nabla L_k^T$$

or

$$\begin{bmatrix} \nabla^2 R_k + \lambda_k^T \nabla^2 C_k & \nabla C_k^T \\ \nabla C_k & 0 \end{bmatrix} \begin{bmatrix} \partial S_k \\ \partial \lambda_k \end{bmatrix} = \begin{bmatrix} -\nabla R_k^T - \nabla C_k^T \lambda_k \\ -C_k \end{bmatrix}$$

Since $\partial \lambda_k = \lambda_{k+1} - \lambda_k$, one can solve for changes in state $\mathbf{S}$, and directly for the next set of Lagrange multipliers, λ_{k+1} :

$$\begin{bmatrix} \nabla^2 R_k + \lambda_k^T \nabla^2 C_k & \nabla C_k^T \\ \nabla C_k & 0 \end{bmatrix} \begin{bmatrix} \partial S_k \\ \lambda_{k+1} \end{bmatrix} = \begin{bmatrix} -\nabla R_k^T \\ -C_k \end{bmatrix}$$

This defines a sequence of quadratic subproblems, thus the name Sequential Quadratic Programming, also known as Lagrange-Newton equations. Each step performs a minimization of the Lagrangian subject to a linearized set of constraints.

3.6.3 Linear Equation Solution and Line Search

Each of the terms of the Hessian and the gradient in the above formulation is determined once analytically through symbolic differentiation of the constraints and the objective. Numeric values are then derived from the current guess for the control points and Lagrange multipliers. The B-spline formulation for the DOF ensures the sparsity of the Hessian of the Lagrangian. Finally, a solution of the linearized system of equations above is obtained using a conjugate gradient method for sparse systems [31]. If the above linear system is rephrased simply as $\nabla^2 L \cdot dS = -\nabla L$, then the conjugate gradient process itself solves for dS by performing a least squares minimization of $(\nabla^2 L \cdot dS + \nabla L)^2$,

Problems may arise if the current guess is far from the solution and the constraints are highly non-linear. A final modification to the above procedure uses the solution for ∂S_k as a step direction and seeks a scalar, α_k that minimizes a *merit function* along a line $S_k + \alpha_k \partial S_k$ [26]. The merit function is taken to be a weighted sum of the constraint violations and the objective function.

4 User Interaction with the Optimization Process

The graphical user interface is designed to provide control over constraint and objective specifications, and the progress and inspection of the optimization process. The GUI (Figure 4) is implemented with X-Windows/MOTIF and thus can be run on a variety of workstations. The interface is layed out in the following seven blocks of interaction widgets (from top to bottom):

1. Menu Bar: controls I/O such as input files to SYM, or output of numerical values for visual inspection.

2. Degrees Of Freedom: permits creation and inspection of DOF, the setting of DOF parameters such as bounds on the values, and inclusion and exclusion of specific DOF from the current spacetime window. Individual DOF motion curves (timelines) can be *filtered* or *shaken* to help move a solution towards or away from local minima. Display of the DOF value, and its first or second derivative through time is also supported as an introspection tool into the optimization process.

3. Equations: permits creation, and modification of constraints, objectives, and sub-expressions. This includes the definition and modification of the expression itself, the weighting of constraints and objectives, setting of the time scope of equations and displaying the equation values as a function of time.

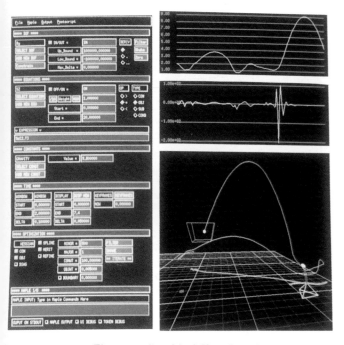

Figure 4: Graphical User Interface

4. Constants: permits creation of constants, and display and modification of their values.

5. Time: controls the time boundaries and discretization of the current spacetime window, the start, end, and frametime for animation display. It also invokes a keyframing system for input of initial and intermediate "sketches" for the animation.

6. Optimization: accepts commands that control the various options for the numerical process itself. This includes the relative weights within the merit function and the Hessian. An option to *refine* portions of the animation is selected here. Processes can also be invoked to *filter* or *shake* all DOF or invoke iterations of the optimization itself.

7. Maple: allows direct input to SYM. This feature allows user definable extensions for high level input, and direct querying of the internal data structures for debugging. A series of toggles are also created to set debug flags.

Input to the system consists of code acceptable to SYM, derived from three sources: direct user edited input, log files or interactive input generated from the GUI, and equations of motion generated directly from a creature's description. The ability to interleave automatic, hand edited and GUI generated code provides both high and low level interaction, and supports a high degree of code reusability.

4.1 Keyframes

In general, the specification of constraints will lead to highly underconstrained systems of equations. The use of an objective function in the context of constrained optimization may provide a unique "best" solution. However, given the highly non-linear nature of many physical and other constraints, numerous local minima are likely to occur. A physical example (that is explored in the following section) is an arm throwing a ball into a basket. The same set of constraints and objective may lead to drastically differing actions, such as an underhand toss or an overhand throw. Given the it-

erative nature of the optimization process itself, the choice of starting values for the control points has a great impact on convergence and the particular solution that is found. A keyframing system is thus provided to allow the user to "sketch" potential solutions, thus completing the specification of the animator's *intention*.

4.2 Spacetime Windows and Refinement

As indicated in the "cat and mouse" example, the use of spacetime windows increases the semantics that one can impart to the constraint specification. A more common use of spacetime windows, however, is to reduce the complexity of individual iterations of the optimization, and to *refine* portions of the animation. Just as an animator in a more traditional animation system would concentrate efforts on a single task performed by a simulated creature, the user here would focus attention on an interval of spacetime in the animation. The B-spline formulation ensures continuity across time boundaries of the window when constraints are enforced one knot value in time outside the time boundaries.

As the animation begins to converge to a satisfactory solution, minor constraint violations can be quickly satisfied by creating a spacetime window containing only one or a few DOF. In addition, intervals in which DOF values change rapidly can be refined by inserting new control points [9] before further iterations.

4.3 Weighting, Damping, Filtering and Shaking

The highly non-linear constraints in this work lead to large numbers of local minima, and to erratic behavior due to the cyclic nature of the trigonometric functions of the rotational DOF in the constraints. These characteristics of the problem require attention and are addressed by tools placed in the control of the user to guide the animation design process.

In general, it is immediately clear to the animator what is not correct with the current iteration. Since the solution process involves minimizing the constraint violations, changing the weight of a particular constraint will change the effect of that constraint on subsequent iterations. Large constraint gradients can sometimes lead to large absolute jumps in the DOF functions between iterations. The user is thus provided interactive support for damping the absolute changes to specified DOF during any particular iteration, and for smoothing individual DOF functions. The opposite problem of getting stuck in local minima can be overcome by *shaking* the current iterative solution. This idea has been used extensively in optimization and is generally referred to as "simulated annealing" [31]. The timing and amplitude of these shakes is also left in the user's hands.

4.4 Graphical Feedback

The final piece of the user interface is the graphical feedback provided to the animation designer. A fundamental claim of this work is that giving the designer a view of the iterative solutions of the animation will allow the animator to evaluate the motion and direct the addition, removal, and modification of constraints, objectives, and optimization parameters, and thus lead more quickly to better animations. To this end, graphical response from the optimization system is provided. To produce real-time motion, the graphical routines are implemented in *GL*, that is available on Silicon Graphics and IBM RS6000 workstations.

Three windows for feedback are provided for viewing DOF values, expression values, and the animation itself. The display of DOF function values has been found very useful to confirm motion, and to understand the effects of such operations as filtering, shaking, and keyframing. Display of expression values over time provides a rapid means to examine constraint violations, and suggest changing the weight of particular constraints and objectives when desired. The most important visual feedback for the animation designer is the animation itself resulting from each successive iteration.

5   Results

A series of experiments have been conducted with the Spacetime Windows system. They include animating a variety of simple creatures ranging from a 2D point mass to jumping and ball throwing linkages. The simpler creatures provide a didactic format to understand the internal numerical features, while the more complex figures provide a better format for discussing the user interface and how an animator might use the system in a real setting. Experiments with an arm and ball and a planar acrobat are described below.

Computational times given consist of both system and user time, and include the formulation of the Lagrangian problem, matrix solution, and line search minimization. All tests were run on an IBM RS6000 model 530 workstation, with 48 Mb RAM.

5.1   Three-Link Arm and a Ball

A three-link arm with a fixed shoulder position was animated. The arm's motion was confined to the plane, thus three generalized spatial DOF define its position, $SHOULDER$, $ELBOW$, and $WRIST$. Associated forces in this case consist of the torques exerted at each joint. The addition of a ball (point mass) adds two more spatial DOF and associated forces.

Throwing a Ball

Animating an arm throwing a ball requires a variety of constraint and objective choices. Physical constraints make the ball fly in a "natural" way (i.e., obey physical laws). Other constraints hold the ball in the hand until released and specify a goal point for the ball to fly to. The free-flight and ball-in-hand constraints must overlap in time by a short span (0.1 sec.), otherwise the ball could stay with the hand and simply jump to a new position to begin its flight. A short overlap in the time extent of the constraints creates a short interval when the hand must move along the parabolic path of natural free flight as it releases the ball. Two further constraint sets (one for each DOF) specify the starting and ending positions and velocity of the arm. Objectives that were used include minimizing the torques at the joints and the related, simpler objective without inertial force terms.

Animating such a sequence with the Spacetime Windows system illustrates many of the features previously described. Windows, refinement, and keyframes were used in combination to achieve a desired animation. Given a single spacetime window over the animation span with the constraints and objective described above and a starting position with the hand stretched out, the optimization quickly converged to an underhand toss in which the arm raises from the specified downward hanging starting position, and flicks the wrist to toss the ball to its goal (Figure 5 a). Aside from minor discrepancies between the ball and hand position (specified by subexpressions), all the constraints were met. However, although this may have represented a local minimum in the complex space of all possible ball throws, it may not have represented the animator's intention.

Influence of Keyframes: Setting a few keyframes that roughly approximate an overhand throw caused the animation to converge to an overhand toss instead (Figure 5 b). This integration of a simple "sketching" system greatly aids the optimization search. A quite different result again was obtained by simply changing the X value of the goal point for the throw leading to a more rigorous overhand throw (Figure 5 c). The full animation resulted in 70 constraint instances and 135 control points, with iterations taking approximately 13 seconds.

Windows and Refinement: Although the ball was constrained to be in the hand until release, the ball was not held tightly in the hand, particularly near the time of release. This was in part due to the fact that the hand position was a function of three *generalized* coordinates, while the ball was a function of two *global* coordinates. In general, there will not be a set of control points for the joint angles and ball position that exactly satisfy the constraint for the ball to be in the hand. Creating a smaller spacetime window around the time of release and refining the B-spline curve for the ball position quickly pulled the ball into a tighter agreement with the hand position. Finally, by removing all the DOF except the ball position from the spacetime window, very fast iterations further refined this process.

5.2   A Basketball Player

A more complex creature was created by adding a movable base to the arm above. The base was given three DOF, to move in the XZ plane, and rotate above the vertical axis. Thus the arm as a whole could move about the ground plane and rotate to throw the ball anywhere in the three dimensions (a third DOF for the ball was added).

A similar set of experiments was conducted with this new creature. The variations of throws was now greater. For example, it would settle into a throw in which it would twist the base rapidly to throw sideways, rather than turn and then throw straight. The use of a few keyframes would push the solution to one that was desired.

Playing Catch with Itself: A final sequence that was animated included the creature throwing the ball towards a goal point, then moving quickly to get in position to catch its own throw, and finally to throw the ball into a basket (Figures 6,8). The catch required a similar set of overlapping constraints to have the hand move with the ball's trajectory for a short stretch before the ball was free to follow the hand's motion. The complete sequence included a series of spacetime windows and refinements. The full spacetime took approximately 20 seconds per iteration. As before, smaller spacetime windows were useful to tighten the animation particularly at the time of the throw and catch.

5.3   Acrobat

A final creature was constructed of two links with four DOF, the two rotations at the $FOOT$ and $WAIST$ and two spatial motion DOF, X and Y to allow rigid body motion in the vertical plane. This creature is similar to the "jumping Luxo lamp" of the work in [36; 33]. Animations were created to simulate a series of jumps. In this case, jumping was specified in much the same way as throwing a ball was defined. The foot was constrained to stay in fixed positions for short time intervals. Physically based free flight was required during the inbetween intervals, but also overlapping each fixed position interval by 0.1 seconds. This insured that the body gained upward momentum to carry it into flight and brought itself to rest at the end of the jumps by continuing the motion of the creature's center of gravity for a short interval after landing. As in the case of the throw, multiple very different solutions formed in local minima of the constrained objective. Keyframed motion "sketches" moved the solutions between them.

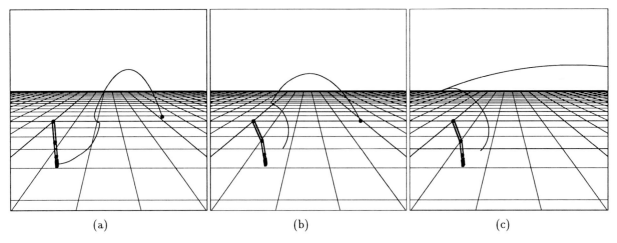

(a)   (b)   (c)

Figure 5: Throwing a Ball

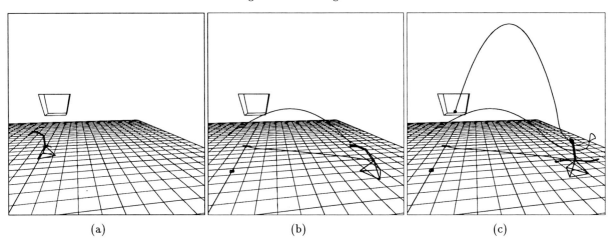

(a)   (b)   (c)

Figure 6: A Basketball Player

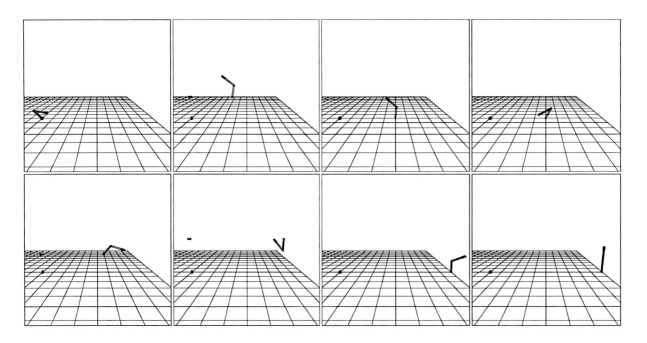

Figure 7: An Acrobat

Figure 8: Basketball Player

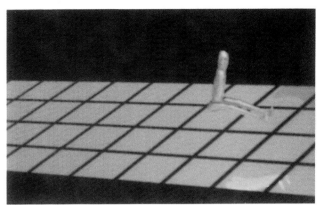

Figure 9: Acrobat

A Jump and a Flip: A "flip" jump was specified simply by constraining the final rotation of the foot to be $2*\pi$ at the end. Putting these two types of jumps in sequence created a short acrobatic routine illustrated in Figures 7 and 9. Once again, a series of small spacetime windows was found very helpful to complete the animation. In particular, a tendency for the foot to leave the ground early was overcome by focusing a small spacetime window on the foot over a short time interval. The double jump required 158 constraint instances, 212 control points, and approximately 13 seconds per iteration if the animation was placed into a single spacetime window. Smaller subproblems iterated in 3 to 5 seconds.

6   Conclusion

This paper has presented a new methodology for interactively guiding the motion of linked figures through the use of spacetime constraints. A *Spacetime Windows* system is described that provides the means to define physically based constraints as well as user defined constraints and objectives. A numerical optimization process based on a sequential quadratic programming paradigm was discussed that iteratively moves an animation towards a constrained minimum of the objective. The integration of three separate processes, a symbolic processor, a numerical processor, and a graphical user interface, allow for runtime modification and examination of the evolving motion design. Graphical feedback of the progress of the animation at each iteration enables interactive modification of the constraints and objectives as well as parameters of the numerical optimization.

The ability to select portions or *windows* of spacetime on which to focus current iterations, has been demonstrated as a way to reduce computational complexity at each iteration and allow the user to concentrate efforts on particularly difficult portions of the animation. It also expands the semantics of spacetime constraints by limiting a creature's knowledge of the future. The use of cubic B-spline curves to approximate the changing values of the degrees of freedom through time results in a formulation that provides local (in time) control, and a natural damping effect due to the variation diminishing property of B-spline curves. The B-spline curves also provide a basis for refining individual DOF. Additional features of the system include inequality and conditional constraints, symbolic reduction of the degrees of freedom at runtime and the use of symbolic subexpressions to reduce the computational and user interface complexity.

A set of experiments has been discussed with resulting animations described. The experimentation illustrated many of the strengths of the approach.

6.1   Limitations and Future Work

The experimentation also exposed some difficulties in using the system and indicated a series of features that would be desirable in future systems. The generality of the system allows a wide range of constraint and objective specification through a general language based interface to the symbolic process. However, a higher level specification interface will be required for a production animation system. The language interface already developed should provide the framework for such extensions.

Automatic extraction of common subexpressions within the equations of motion has not yet been implemented and should reduce the complexity of the Hessian evaluation. Some common subexpressions could also be precompiled to add efficiency without reducing generality.

6.2   Computer Animation

Designing the motion of simulated creatures requires geometric and kinematic specification. Actions that are governed primarily by physical principles require physical equations of motion. Goal oriented motion requires careful explicit animation or a use of constrained optimization techniques. All this must finally be embedded within a user interface with real time graphical feedback for a user to evaluate and modify the design. Solutions to the problems involved in computer animation thus must draw on a wide range of technology. It is hoped that the Spacetime Windows system presented here will provide new insights into ways to integrate computer animation techniques to give animators the tools they require.

Acknowledgements

The research reported in this paper was supported in part by grant CCR-8922312 from the National Science Foundation, and in part by a fellowship from Apple Computer Corporation. Hank Driskill is responsible for generating the raster images using the Alpha_1 system and is, with others, responsible for the lisp code that generates the symbolic equations of motion from a linkage description. He and Prof. Gary Ridsdale also participated in early discussions and implementations of the system. Special thanks to Robert Mecklenberg for systems help, and to Jutta Joesch, Mike Blum, and Elaine Cohen for suggestions on editing the writing. Robert McDermott and James Rose were instrumental in planning and editing the videotape.

References

[1] ARMSTRONG, B., AND GREEN, M. The dynamics of articulated rigid bodies for purposes of animation. In *Proceedings of Graphics Interface* (May 1986), Computer Graphics Society, pp. 407–415.

[2] BARAFF, D. Analytical models for dynamic simulation of non-penetrating rigid bodies. *ACM Computer Graphics 23*, 3 (July 1989), 223–232.

[3] BARTELS, R. H., BEATTY, J. C., AND BARSKY, B. A. *An Introduction to Splines for Use in Computer Graphics and Geometric Modeling.* Morgan Kaufmann, 1979.

[4] BARZEL, R., AND BARR, A. H. A modeling system based on dynamic constraints. In *Proceedings of SIGGRAPH'88 (Atlanta, Georgia, August 1–5, 1988)* (August 1988), ACM, pp. 179–188.

[5] BOEHM, W. Inserting new knots into b-spline curves. *IPC Business Press 12*, 4 (July 1980), 199–201.

[6] BROTMAN, L. S., AND NETRAVALI, A. N. Motion interpolation by optimal control. In *Proceedings of SIGGRAPH'88 (Atlanta, Georgia, August 1–5, 1988)* (Aug. 1988), vol. 22, ACM, pp. 309–315.

[7] BRUDERLIN, A., AND CALVERT, T. Goal-directed, dynamic animation of human walking. *ACM Computer Graphics 23*, 3 (July 1989), 233–422.

[8] CHAR, B. W., GEDDES, K. O., GONNET, G. H., MONAGAN, M. B., AND WATT, S. M. *MAPLE Reference Manual, Fifth edition.* Waterloo Maple Publishing, Waterloo, Ontario, 1988.

[9] COHEN, E., LYCHE, T., AND RIESENFELD, R. Discrete b-splines and subdivision techniques in computer-aided geometric design and computer graphics. *Computer Graphics and Image Processing 14*, 2 (October 1980), 87–111.

[10] CRAIG, J. J. *Introduction to Robotics.* Addison-Wesley, Reading, MA, 1986.

[11] DRISKILL, H. Symbolic kinematic and dynamic equations of motion. *LISP code* (1990).

[12] FAUX, I., AND PRATT, M. *Computational Geometry for Design and Manufacture.* Ellis Horwood Limited, 1979.

[13] FLETCHER, R. *Practical Methods of Optimization, Vol. 1 and 2.* John Wiley and Sons, 1980.

[14] GILL, P. E., AND MURRAY, W. *Numerical Methods for Constrained Optimization.* Academic Press, 1974.

[15] GIRARD, M. Interactive design of 3d computer-animated legged animal motion. *IEEE Computer Graphics and Applications 7*, 6 (June 1987), 39–51.

[16] HAHN, J. Realistic animation of rigid bodies. In *Proceedings of SIGGRAPH'88 (Atlanta, Georgia, August 1–5, 1988)* (August 1988), ACM, pp. 299–308.

[17] HIMMELBLAU, D. M. *Applied Nonlinear Programming.* McGraw-Hill, New York, 1972.

[18] ISAACS, P. M., AND COHEN, M. F. Controlling dynamic simulation with kinematic constraints, behavior functions, and inverse dynamics. In *Proceedings of SIGGRAPH'87 (Anaheim, California, July 27–31, 1987)* (July 1987), ACM, pp. 215–224.

[19] ISAACS, P. M., AND COHEN, M. F. Mixed methods for kinematic constraints in dynamic figure animation. *The Visual Computer 4* (1988).

[20] KOREIN, J. U., AND BADLER, N. I. Techniques for generating goal-directed motion of articulated structures. *IEEE Computer Graphics and Applications 2*, 6 (Nov. 1982), 71–81.

[21] LEE, P., WEI, S., ZHAO, J., AND BADLER, N. I. Strength guided motion. In *Proceedings of SIGGRAPH'90 (Dallas, Texas, August 6–10, 1990)* (August 1990), ACM, pp. 253–262.

[22] MAGNENAT-THALMANN, AND THALMANN. *Computer Animation: Theory and Practice.* Springer Verlag, 1985.

[23] MCKENNA, M., AND ZELTZER, D. Dynamic simulation of autonomous legged locomotion. In *Proceedings of SIGGRAPH'90 (Dallas, Texas, August 6–10, 1990)* (August 1990), ACM, pp. 29–38.

[24] MILLER, G. S. P. The motion dynamics of snakes and worms. In *Proceedings of SIGGRAPH'88 (Atlanta, Georgia, August 1–5, 1988)* (August 1988), ACM, pp. 169–173.

[25] MORTENSON, M. E. *Geometric Modeling.* John Wiley and Sons, New York, 1985.

[26] PAPALAMBROS, P. Y., AND WILDE, D. J. *Principles of Optimal Design.* Cambridge University Press, Cambridge, England, 1988.

[27] PENTLAND, A., AND WILLIAMS, J. Good vibrations: Modal dynamics for graphics and animation. In *Proceedings of SIGGRAPH'89 (Boston, Mass., July 31–Aug 4, 1989)* (July 1989), ACM, pp. 215–222.

[28] PHILLIPS, C. B., AND BADLER, N. I. Interactive behaviors for bipedal articulated figures. vol. 25, ACM, pp. 359–362.

[29] PHILLIPS, C. B., ZHAO, J., AND BADLER, N. I. Interactive real-time articulated figure manipulation using multiple kinematic constraints. In *Proceedings of Symposium on Interactive 3D Graphics (Snowbird, Utah, March, 1990)* (Mar. 1990), vol. 24, ACM, pp. 245–250.

[30] PLATT, J., AND BARR, A. H. Constraint methods for flexible models. In *Proceedings of SIGGRAPH'88 (Atlanta, Georgia, August 1–5, 1988)* (August 1988), ACM, pp. 279–288.

[31] PRESS, W. H., AND FLANNERY, B. *Numerical Recipes: The Art of Scientific Computing.* Cambridge University Press, 1986.

[32] RAIBERT, M. H., AND HODGINS, J. K. Animation of dynamic legged locomotion. *siggraph91 4*, 25 (1991), 349–358.

[33] VAN DE PANNE, M., FIUME, E., AND VRANESIC, Z. Reusable motion synthesis using state-space controllers. In *Proceedings of SIGGRAPH'90 (Dallas, Texas, August 6–10, 1990)* (August 1990), ACM, pp. 225–234.

[34] WILHELMS, J. Using dynamic analysis for realistic animation of articulated bodies. *IEEE Computer Graphics and Applications 7*, 6 (June 1987), 12–27.

[35] WITKIN, A., FLEISCHER, K., AND BARR, A. Energy constraints on parameterized models. In *Proceedings of SIGGRAPH'87 (Anaheim, California, July 27–31, 1987)* (July 1987), vol. 21, ACM, pp. 225–232.

[36] WITKIN, A., AND KASS, M. Spacetime constraints. In *Proceedings of SIGGRAPH'88 (Atlanta, Georgia, August 1–5, 1988)* (July 1988), ACM, pp. 159–168.

[37] WITKIN, A., AND WELCH, W. Fast animation and control of nonrigid structures. In *Proceedings of SIGGRAPH'90 (Dallas, Texas, August 6–10, 1990)* (August 1990), ACM, pp. 243–252.

Dynamic Simulation of
Non-penetrating Flexible Bodies

David Baraff

Program of Computer Graphics
Cornell University
Ithaca, NY 14853

Andrew Witkin

School of Computer Science
Carnegie Mellon University
Pittsburgh, PA 15213

Abstract

A model for the dynamic simulation of flexible bodies subject to non-penetration constraints is presented. Flexible bodies are described in terms of global deformations of a rest shape. The dynamical behavior of these bodies that most closely matches the behavior of ideal continuum bodies is derived, and subsumes the results of earlier Lagrangian dynamics-based models. The dynamics derived for the flexible-body model allows the unification of previous work on flexible body simulation and previous work on non-penetrating rigid body simulation. The non-penetration constraints for a system of bodies that contact at multiple points are maintained by analytically calculated contact forces. An implementation for first- and second-order polynomially deformable bodies is described. The simulation of second-order or higher deformations currently involves a polyhedral boundary approximation for collision detection purposes.

1. Introduction

In this paper we present a new formulation for the dynamics of flexible bodies that covers collisions and continuous contact as well as free motion. The model, which draws on the flexible-body model proposed by Witkin and Welch[9] and on the analytical contact force model for rigid bodies presented by Baraff[1,2], centers on the idea that flexible body simulation can be greatly simplified through the introduction of a suitable geometric approximation. By restricting the body's changes of shape to those that can be represented by a global parametric deformation, we solve two problems that plague conventional local formulations: first, the dimensionality of the simulation is reduced, and second, the severe numerical problems to which local interactions can give rise are eliminated.

Because it is restricted by the geometric approximation, the flexible body's behavior generally exhibits error when compared to the behavior of an ideal continuum body under like conditions. Whether this approximation error is acceptable depends on factors such as the materials and forces being modeled, and the purpose of the simulation. In any case, once an approximation has been adopted it is clearly desirable to minimize the resulting error.

Our formulation is derived from the criterion of minimal approximation error. Following a brief discussion of local models and the problems they introduce, we will review the global model of Witkin and Welch, and show that their formulation for free body motion is in fact the minimal error solution. Then we will consider the problem of collision-response for flexible bodies. Collisions between

rigid bodies are generally modeled as instantaneous events through the use of impulses. In the case of flexible bodies, this would be inappropriate, since we are interested in seeing them compress and rebound. The minimal error criterion leads us to a two-phase model in which an initial impulse prevents inter-penetration, followed by a non-impulsive phase of continuous contact in which the body compresses due to its own momentum, then rebounds due to the buildup of internal strain energy. Finally, we extend Baraff's analytic contact force model to flexible bodies, discuss implementation issues for polynomial deformations, and present simulation results.

1.1 Local models and the problem of stiffness

Traditional models for flexible bodies, including finite difference, finite element, and mass-and-spring lattice models, approximate the deviation of a continuum body from its rest shape in terms of displacements at a finite number of points called *nodal points*. Given a sufficient density of nodal points, these formulations can represent essentially any deformation. At the other end of the spectrum, continuum bodies whose deformations are considered small enough to be neglected can be approximated as rigid bodies, which are free only to translate and rotate.

Obviously, the rigid body formulation cannot be applied to bodies whose deformation we do not *want* to neglect. This is unfortunate because nodal formulations tend to give rise to stiff differential equations which are difficult to solve numerically. The basic problem is that nodal formulations model global phenomena—for example, acceleration of the whole body due to a point force—only via local interactions among adjacent nodes. The compression waves that translate these local interactions into large-scale effects involve deformations that are generally far too small and fast to play a significant role in computer animation, the more so as the mechanical stiffness of the flexible body is increased. Even so, if ordinary numerical methods are used, it is these high-speed effects rather than the phenomena of primary interest that dictate the size of the time steps, with potentially disastrous effects on performance[7]. Where it applies, the rigid body approximation sweeps these problems away by eliminating local interactions altogether: the only degrees of freedom a rigid body has are the global ones that govern its position and orientation.

Modeling of flexible body collisions and contact raises additional problems for the nodal formulation. In particular, collisions are difficult to handle because they usually involve extremely large transient forces and accelerations which, like any others, must operate strictly through local interactions. Hence the usual stiffness problem is exacerbated. Things are made still worse if penalty methods[1,3] (another local model) are used to enforce non-penetration constraints, since these introduce stiffness problems of their own.

1.2 Global models

Witkin and Welch[9] present a flexible-body model that represents a compromise between the extremes of the nodal and rigid formulations. Changes in the body's shape are approximated neither by nodal displacements nor by rigid body transformations, but by global deformations that apply a parametric "space warp" to all points in the body. This global formulation constrains the range of deformations that the body can undergo to those that can be represented by the chosen deformation function. However, because the shape parameters are global in their effect, the stiffness problems due to local interactions are eliminated, as in the rigid case. In a different flexible-body formulation, Pentland and Williams[6] achieve much the same goal by linearizing the dynamic model, then using modal analysis to eliminate high-frequency vibrations. We prefer the formulation used in Witkin and Welch primarily because, as we will see in the next section, it minimizes the error due to the geometric approximation, whereas the consequences of the dynamics-based approximations of Pentland and Williams are more difficult to assess.

1.3 Collision and contact

Baraff[1,2] presents an analytical method for computing contact forces between configurations of rigid bodies. Contact forces are computed by solving simultaneous equations that reflect all of the forces acting on all of the bodies. Thus, an external force acting on one body has an immediate effect on any contacting bodies. The formulation of the contact forces as a global problem eliminates the stiffness problems encountered by the penalty method for contact forces. To complete our global formulation, we will adapt this method to deal with flexible bodies.

2. Global Deformations

In this section, we will define the basic global formulation for flexible bodies used throughout this paper. As stated in the introduction, rather than describe the shape of a deformed body in terms of some number of nodal points, a body's shape is described in terms of a global deformation function D_q, where q is a vector of parameters that controls the deformation. The function D_q maps $\mathbf{R}^3$ onto itself; D_q describes the deformed shape of a body by mapping each point p of the body's rest shape to the point $D_q(p)$.

2.1 The dynamics of global deformations

Our goal in deriving the dynamical behavior of our flexible-body model is to relate the forces acting on a body to the acceleration of the control parameters q, in a generalization of the familiar equation $f = ma$. That is, given the control parameters q, and the first derivative $\dot{q}$, we want to express $\ddot{q}$ in terms of q, $\dot{q}$, and any forces acting on the body. We want the motion prescribed by this $\ddot{q}$ to have the minimum possible deviation from the motion of an ideal continuum body. The expression for $\ddot{q}$ derived in this paper that minimizes the deviation matches the expression derived by the earlier work of Witkin and Welch[9] using Lagrangian dynamics; thus, we show that the Lagrangian dynamics formulation satisfies our minimal approximation error criterion. The model of collision-response derived in section 3.2 is also based on a minimum error criterion.

In the derivations in this paper, bodies are parameterized by a coordinate p in body space, which ranges over some fixed volume. The density of the body at any point p in body space is denoted as $\rho(p)$. If we let $q(t)$ describe the *state* of the body as a function of time, then at time t, $D_{q(t)}$ specifies how the body is mapped from body space into world space. Specifically, at time t the deformed body has density $\rho(p)$ at the world space point $D_{q(t)}(p)$.

In an ideal continuum body, the acceleration at any point is given by the standard equation $f = ma$. An ideal continuum body is therefore completely unconstrained in its motion, and can be deformed into any arbitrary shape, by appropriate forces. In contrast, global deformations represent a constraint, limiting the allowable deformations, and thus the motion, of a body. Because of this constraint, the acceleration a of a point with mass m, in response to a force f, will not in general satisfy $a = f/m$. The best we can do is to minimize the deviation of the actual acceleration a, from the ideal acceleration f/m. To measure the total acceleration deviation for the entire body, we will integrate the acceleration deviation at each point over the entire volume of the body.

Let the net force in world space acting on a body be described as a vector-valued function $f(p)$ over the body. The force function f includes external forces such as gravity, internal forces due to deformation, and forces due to contact. If we let $a(p)$ denote the acceleration at each point of the body, then $a(p)$ would be "ideal" if it always satisfied $a(p) = f(p)/\rho(p)$, or equivalently, $a(p) - f(p)/\rho(p) = 0$. We will measure the net acceleration error E from this ideal acceleration for the entire body by writing

$$E = \tfrac{1}{2} \int \rho(p)|a(p) - f(p)/\rho(p)|^2 \, dV \qquad (1)$$

where p ranges over the volume of the body in world space. The deviation is mass-weighted, since the error contributed by an acceleration deviation in some region of the body should grow linearly with the density in that region. Using E, we can relate the acceleration of the control parameters to the net force function f by requiring that $\ddot{q}$ be chosen so as to minimize E.

However, the error E defined by equation (1) is the same as a quantity named by Gauss as the "constraint" of a system. Gauss formulated a principle called the *principle of least constraint* that asserts that the motion of a system subject to constraints always minimizes the "constraint", namely equation (1). The principle of least constraint yields the same result for constrained motion as is given by Lagrange's equation of motion[5]; thus, our notion of motion satisfying a minimal error criterion is equivalent to treating bodies as mechanical systems and defining their motion in terms of the very well known Lagrangian dynamics.

2.2 Linear deformations

The previous section describes the dynamics when the deformation function $D_{q(t)}$ is arbitrary. For the remainder of this paper, we will limit ourselves to deformations $D_{q(t)}(p)$ that depend linearly on q, but may vary non-linearly with respect to p. Rather than describe the state in terms of a vector $q(t)$, we will switch notation and define the state as a matrix $R(t)$; correspondingly, $D_{R(t)}$ denotes the deformation function specified by $R(t)$. The fact that the deformation $D_{R(t)}$ is linear with respect to $R(t)$ means that $D_{R(t)}$ must have the form

$$D_{R(t)}(p) = R(t)Z(p) \qquad (2)$$

where $Z(p)$ is a vector-valued function that does not depend on either t, or R. This restriction greatly simplifies some of the dynamics equations, while still allowing much latitude in the choice of the deformation function D. Note the $Z(p)$ need not be a linear function of p. A deformation that is quadratic in the undeformed coordinates could be specified by

$$Z(p) = [p_x^2, p_y^2, p_z^2, p_x p_y, p_x p_z, p_y p_z, p_x, p_y, p_z, 1]^T \qquad (3)$$

with $R(t)$ a 3×10 matrix. Clearly, polynomial deformations of any order can be expressed in terms of deformations that are linear with respect to the state. Second-order polynomial deformations in particular are fairly liberal in terms of the allowable deformations of a body. Section 4 will discuss the details of implementing first- and second-order polynomial deformation functions.

From the previous section, we know that we can use Lagrangian dynamics to relate $\ddot{R}(t)$ to $R(t)$, $\dot{R}(t)$, and the force $f(p)$ with minimal error. Witkin and Welch[9] derive the relation

$$\ddot{R}(t) = Q(t)M^{-1} \qquad (4)$$

where M is a constant square matrix and $Q(t)$ is a matrix of the generalized net force acting on the body. The matrix M is defined by

$$M = \int \rho(p)Z(p)Z(p)^T \, dV \qquad (5)$$

which yields a square matrix of size n, where n is the dimension of the column vector $Z(p)$. Additionally, M is both symmetric and positive definite. The matrix $Q(t)$ has dimension $3 \times n$. Generalized force Q is related to force in $\mathbf{R}^3$ as follows: a force f in $\mathbf{R}^3$ acting on the point $D_{R(t)}(p)$ in world space yields the matrix of generalized force $fZ(p)^T$. Note that both f and $Z(p)$ are column vectors, so that the outer product $fZ(p)^T$ yields a $3 \times n$ matrix.

For bodies with a complicated rest shape, the integral of equation (5) is difficult to calculate analytically. Since M is constant however, it can be calculated off-line of the simulation process by numerical techniques; currently, we use Monte-Carlo integration to precompute M. Thus, all that is required to simulate the motion of these flexible bodies is the solution of equation (4). This is done by converting equation (4) to the coupled first-order ordinary differential equation

$$\frac{\mathrm{d}}{\mathrm{dt}} \left(\begin{array}{c} R(t) \\ \dot{R}(t) \end{array} \right) = \left(\begin{array}{c} \dot{R}(t) \\ Q(t)M^{-1} \end{array} \right). \qquad (6)$$

The remaining task is to evaluate the generalized force $Q(t)$, which subsumes external forces, internal forces, and any contact forces acting on the body. External forces are by definition forces that are known to us at time t, such as gravity, or viscous damping. In the next section, we show how internal forces due to deformation may be calculated. Section 3 discusses the computation of the contact forces included in $Q(t)$.

2.3 Potential energy functions of linear deformations

The internal forces that act to restore a flexible body to its rest shape are specified in terms of the derivative $\partial V/\partial R$ of a potential energy function V[9]. For most physical bodies, potential energy functions can be described in terms of the *metric tensor* of a body. (Internal damping forces are calculated similarly in terms of the metric tensor and its time derivative.) For affine deformations, the metric tensor (and its time derivative), at any instant of time, are constant over the volume of a body; thus, evaluating integrals of the metric tensor over the body volume is trivial. However, for non-affine deformations, the metric tensor can vary over the volume of a body; if the body's shape is complex, the integrals needed to compute $\partial V/\partial R$ can be difficult to evaluate.

Our choices are to either calculate the integrals analytically, or use a numerical approximation. For polynomial deformations, integrals involving the metric tensor can be expressed as a linear combination of integrals that are independent of $R(t)$. These integrals are weighted by functions of $R(t)$ and summed to compute $\partial V/\partial R$. Internal damping forces are computed similarly as a linear combination of precomputed integrals, weighted by functions of both $R(t)$ and $\dot{R}(t)$. However, even for the second-order polynomial deformations we have implemented, the necessary expansion of precalculated integrals is quite large. An alternate technique is to simply approximate the integrals by evaluating the integrand at some finite number of points scattered throughout the body. This has the virtue of being trivial to implement, and may also be more general in dealing with complex energy functions that allow for

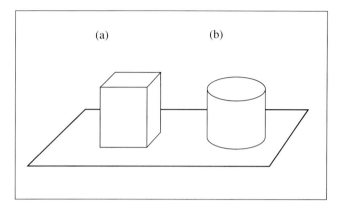

Figure 1: (a) Non-penetration is enforced by preventing only the four contacting vertices from moving below the plane. (b) The entire lower rim of the cylinder must be prevented from moving below the plane.

plasticity or fracture[8]. For second-order polynomial deformations, a small number of sample points (on the order of fifty) yields adequate results.

3. Non-penetration Constraints

The derivation for the contact forces between flexible bodies that prevent inter-penetration closely parallels the derivation of contact forces between rigid bodies in Baraff[1,2]. The most notable difference arises when considering collisions between bodies, and is detailed in section 3.2.

3.1 Contact geometry restrictions

In considering contact between bodies, we will make the assumption that contact between bodies can be described in terms of finitely many contact points. That is, we will restrict ourselves to configurations in which inter-penetration can be prevented globally by enforcing a finite number of local constraints. As an example, consider figure 1. If all the bodies involved are rigid, then in figure 1a, inter-penetration is prevented globally between the cube and the plane by enforcing the four local constraints that each vertex of the cube in contact with the plane remain on or above the plane. However, to prevent the cylinder in figure 1b from dipping below the plane and inter-penetrating, while still allowing it to tip over arbitrarily, we must constrain *each* of the infinitely many boundary points on the lower cylinder to remain on or above the plane.

Thus, we do not allow configurations such as figure 1b. For bodies whose deformations are affine functions of the material coordinates (as well as rigid bodies), polyhedral contact regions are allowed (figure 2a). However, for all other deformations, configurations such as figure 1a cannot be allowed. A deformation which caused the contact face of the cube to curve could result in inter-penetration even if the vertices of the face were prevented from inter-penetrating the plane (figure 2b). Section 4.2 describes a geometric polyhedral boundary discretization that permits the simulation of configurations with one- or two-dimensional polygonal contact regions when arbitrary deformation functions are allowed. This approximation is somewhat unsatisfactory; a non-discretized method for dealing with situations like figure 2b would be preferable.

3.2 Colliding contact

Having described the geometry of contact, we can now consider the dynamics of contact. When bodies initially come into contact at a point p_c, we say a collision has occurred. In order to maintain the non-penetration constraint between the two bodies, at least one

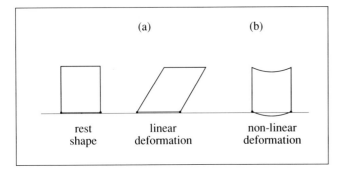

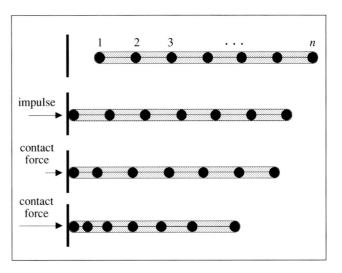

Figure 2: (a) Affine deformations allow polyhedral contact regions, because inter-penetration can be prevented with finitely many local constraints. (b) For non-linear deformations, preventing the vertices from moving below the plane does not necessarily prevent inter-penetration.

Figure 3: A discretized rod collides with an immovable obstacle. Mass 1's velocity changes instantaneously to zero upon impacting the obstacle. As mass 2 approaches mass 1, an internal force between the two acts, pushing mass 1 leftwards. A contact force acts rightwards on mass 1 to prevent inter-penetration.

of the two contact surfaces must undergo a velocity discontinuity at the contact point. Otherwise, some amount of inter-penetration would occur in the vicinity of the contact point. Since rigid bodies cannot deform at all, in the case of a collision between two rigid bodies, every point on the rigid body experiences a velocity discontinuity. This implies an abrupt change in momentum, which can only be accomplished by an impulse. Collisions can be quantified in terms of the energy lost: a collision can be completely elastic, meaning no energy is lost, or completely inelastic, meaning that the kinetic energy of both bodies is completely dissipated (measured with respect to a center of mass coordinate system). For rigid body collisions, this energy loss is instantaneous. Immediately after a collision, bodies bounce apart with a velocity that depends on the elasticity of the collision.

In contrast, the collision process for flexible bodies takes some non-zero amount of time. During that time, the colliding bodies remain in contact with each other. To derive a collision-response model for our flexible bodies, we will use a variational principle. To motivate such a derivation, let us consider the case of a one-dimensional rod colliding with a fixed obstacle. The rod is discretized into n mass points. Since this example is one-dimensional, each mass point may undergo displacement either left or right. The mass points are numbered left to right, from 1 to n (figure 3).

When the first mass point collides with the fixed obstacle, its velocity must discontinuously change to zero, to prevent inter-penetration. However, the velocity of the other mass points of the rod are unchanged. In particular, as the second mass point continues with its original velocity, the distance between the first and second mass point decreases. As this distance decreases, an internal force acts to repel the two mass points. This has the effect of deaccelerating the second mass point, which means that the distance between the second and third mass point decreases; clearly, this effect propagates throughout the entire rod. While this is happening, the fixed obstacle has been exerting a (non-impulsive) contact force on the first mass point, to prevent the repulsive internal force from accelerating the first mass point leftwards. After some finite period of contact, the internal forces cause the rod to bounce away from the obstacle. If there is no damping, the only energy lost will be due to the dissipation of the kinetic energy of the first mass point. However, in the limit as n goes to infinity, the mass of this point, and thus its initial kinetic energy, both go to zero. Even though a velocity discontinuity occurs (at the left end of the bar), the actual change in momentum is zero, and thus no energy is lost. If we wish to model collisions with some amount of inelasticity, we must impose damping forces on the body that dissipate energy during the collision.

The collision-response model for our constrained flexible bodies is based on this analysis. As in the rigid body case, we will need

to apply an impulse at the contact point to prevent immediate inter-penetration. This means that some kinetic energy must be lost, and we cannot attain a perfectly elastic collision. This is a consequence of limiting the allowable deformations of the body. After the impulse has been applied, the bodies will no longer be colliding, and a non-impulsive force (described in the next section) will act at the contact point to prevent inter-penetration.[1]

As in section 2.1, we use an error measure to compare the collision-response of our flexible-body model with the collision-response of an ideal continuum body. To measure the net collision-response, we generalize equation (1) to obtain a new error measure E' given by

$$E' = \tfrac{1}{2} \int \rho(p) |\Delta v(p)|^2 \, dV \qquad (7)$$

where $\Delta v(p)$ is the change in velocity in response to an impulse. For an ideal continuum body, $\Delta v(p)$ is zero everywhere except at the point of collision and E' is zero. For our flexible-body model, E' measures the deviation between the actual change in velocity, $\Delta v(p)$, and the ideal change in velocity, which is zero. The correct instantaneous change $\Delta \dot{R}(t)$ in the state velocity $\dot{R}(t)$ is the one which minimizes E', subject to the kinematic constraints of the collision.

From the description of the collision in figure 3, it seems intuitive that the correct course of action is to apply an impulse between two colliding bodies at the point of contact, such that they just come to rest (relative to each other) at the contact point. In the absence of friction, the impulse should act normal to the contact surfaces. A standard constrained-minimization principle applied to equation (7) shows that the change in velocity $\Delta \dot{R}(t)$ from such an impulse is in fact exactly the $\Delta \dot{R}(t)$ which minimizes E', subject to the kinematic constraints of the collision.

The actual computation of the impulse is trivial. For simplicity, let us consider a collision between a flexible body A and an immovable, undeformable obstacle B with a well defined surface normal at the contact point p_c. The vector $\hat{n}$ denotes the outwards pointing

---

[1]In general, the energy loss can be decreased by altering the deformation function D so that it allows the body more degrees of freedom. The limiting case, when D can represent any deformation, is the same as the limiting case for the discretized bar of figure 3 when n goes to infinity. Obviously, neither case can be simulated without an infinite amount of computation.

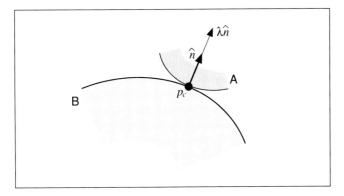

Figure 4: Impact between a flexible body A and an immovable undeformable body B.

unit surface normal of B at the contact point p_c (figure 4). The generalization to the case when B is an ordinary rigid or deformable body is straightforward. As is the case for generalized forces, an impulse f in $\mathbf{R}^3$ acting on a body at the point $D_{R(t)}(p)$ produces a generalized impulse $Q = fZ(p)^T$. A flexible body's state velocity $\dot{R}(t)$ changes discontinuously to $\dot{R}(t) + QM^{-1}$ when subject to a generalized impulse Q.

To calculate the required impulse, let $p_c = D_{R(t)}(p)$. We know that the impulse occurs at p_c, and has direction $\hat{n}$ for a frictionless impact. Thus, we can express the impulse as $\lambda\hat{n}$, where λ is an unknown scalar. The velocity of the contact point on the moving body before the collision is

$$\frac{\mathrm{d}}{\mathrm{d}t}D_{R(t)}(p) = \dot{R}(t)Z(p). \qquad (8)$$

After the collision, the velocity of the contact point is $(\dot{R}(t) + QM^{-1})Z(p)$. Since body B is fixed, the velocity of the contact point in the $\hat{n}$ direction after the collision must be zero; that is, we require

$$\hat{n} \cdot (\dot{R}(t) + QM^{-1})Z(p) = 0. \qquad (9)$$

Substituting $Q = (\lambda\hat{n})Z(p)^T$, we have the constraint

$$\hat{n} \cdot (\dot{R}(t) + \lambda\hat{n}Z(p)^T M^{-1})Z(p) = 0 \qquad (10)$$

which yields

$$\lambda = \frac{-\hat{n} \cdot \dot{R}(t)Z(p)}{\hat{n} \cdot \hat{n}Z(p)^T M^{-1}Z(p)} = \frac{-\hat{n} \cdot \dot{R}(t)Z(p)}{Z(p)^T M^{-1}Z(p)} \qquad (11)$$

since $\hat{n}$ has unit length. Since M is positive definite, the denominator of equation (11) is non-zero and positive. Moreover, since $\hat{n} \cdot \dot{R}(t)Z(p)$ is the initial approach speed in the normal direction (which is negative), λ is positive as one would expect from figure 4. For collisions involving more than one contact point, the collisions at the contact point can be considered as a sequence of collisions, slightly staggered in time. If collisions involving multiple contact points are modeled as occurring simultaneously, the approach taken by Baraff[1] can be used.

3.3 Resting contact

The derivation for the resting contact forces between flexible bodies is almost the same as the derivation for resting contact forces between rigid bodies. The non-penetration constraints for rigid bodies described in Baraff[2] are restricted to handle situations with only finitely many contact points, as described in section 3.1. Since we are restricted to situations in which inter-penetration can be prevented by considering only finitely many contact points, we can

index the contact points from 1 to n. At each contact point between two bodies A and B, we will write down a constraint of the form

$$\ddot{\chi}_i(t_0) \geq 0 \qquad (12)$$

where $\chi_i(t)$ is a measure of the separation between A and B in the normal direction at time t. Since $\chi_i(t)$ is a spatial measure, $\ddot{\chi}_i(t)$ measures the relative normal acceleration between A and B. In particular, if $\ddot{\chi}_i(t_0) < 0$, then the bodies are accelerating so as to inter-penetrate at the ith contact point. Conversely, if $\ddot{\chi}_i(t_0) > 0$, then the bodies are accelerating apart, and contact will be broken at the ith contact point immediately after time t_0. If $\ddot{\chi}_i(t_0) = 0$, then contact is not broken at the ith contact point. Thus, to prevent inter-penetration, we must enforce equation (12).

The relation $\ddot{\chi}_i(t) \geq 0$ is maintained at each contact point by a time-varying contact force, acting normal to the contact surface. As in the case of colliding contact, we need to calculate the magnitudes of these contact forces. Because $\ddot{\chi}_i(t_0)$ measures acceleration, $\ddot{\chi}_i(t_0)$ depends linearly upon all the forces acting on bodies A and B. The contact force at each contact point is required to be repulsive and conservative; that is, it must not add energy to the system of bodies. Since the normal force at one contact may affect the acceleration of one or both of the bodies at another contact, satisfying $\ddot{\chi}_i(t) \geq 0$ at all of the contact points involves satisfying a system of simultaneous linear inequalities. The constraint that the contact forces act conservatively can be expressed in terms of a quadratic constraint on the contact forces. Contact forces satisfying these constraints can be computed by quadratic programming[1,2].

Exactly the same formulation is used to prevent inter-penetration between flexible bodies. The expression derived for $\ddot{\chi}_i(t_0)$ in Baraff[2] requires the spatial and temporal derivatives of functions describing the contact surfaces. Suppose we express the undeformed rest shape of our contact surface in body space in terms of a real-valued function $F_0(p)$; that is, a point p_b in body space is on the undeformed surface if and only if $F_0(p_b) = 0$. Then the deformed contact surface at time t consists of those points p in world space for which

$$F(p, t) = F_0(D_{R(t)}^{-1}(p)) = 0. \qquad (13)$$

Deriving expressions for the various derivatives of $F(p, t)$ necessary to symbolically evaluate $\ddot{\chi}_i(t_0)$ becomes mostly an exercise in applying the chain rule of calculus. For any deformation function $D_{R(t)}(p) = R(t)Z(p)$, $\ddot{\chi}_i(t_0)$ is a linear function of $\ddot{R}(t_0)$, so $\ddot{\chi}_i(t_0)$ depends linearly upon the contact forces. The contact forces can be extended to include friction as described by Baraff[3].

4. Implementing Polynomial Deformations

We have implemented flexible bodies for the cases of first- and second-order polynomial deformations. There is no difficulty in performing simulations that involve bodies with a mix of differing deformation functions. Simulations can also mix rigid and deformable bodies. In this section, we will discuss a number of implementation details.

4.1 Collision detection

Currently, our bodies are limited to unions of convex primitives, where a primitive is either a polyhedron or a convex closed curved surface. When deformations are limited to first-order deformations, convexity is conserved under deformation. Thus, the collision detection method described in Baraff[2] can be used without alteration. Additionally, when flexible bodies are determined to contact at some point p_c in world space, it is necessary to compute p_c in the body space of both of the bodies; that is, $D_{R(t)}^{-1}(p_c)$ must be computed for each body. This is trivial for first-order deformations since $D_{R(t)}$ is simply an affine transformation whose inverse is easily computed.

Since polygons in body space are mapped into polygons in world space, one- or two-dimensional contact regions are allowed, as described in section 3.1.

Matters are more complicated for second-order or higher deformations. Computing $D_{R(t)}^{-1}(p_c)$ is not a severe problem. A coarse mesh of control points with known body space coordinates can be transformed into world space for each body. Given a point p_c in world space, the body space coordinates of the control points closest to p_c in world space can be interpolated to provide a rough estimate of $D_{R(t)}^{-1}(p_c)$. Starting with this estimate, $D_{R(t)}^{-1}(p_c)$ can be computed numerically using iterative techniques[4]. However, the initial determination of the contact points in world space is a difficult problem. Even given a suitable collision detection algorithm, our simulations would be severely restricted because of the contact geometry restrictions of section 3.1. It is our hope to eventually deal with these problems; for now however, we will describe an approximation method that removes the contact geometry restriction and lets us use previously developed collision detection algorithms.

4.2 Polyhedral approximation

Our approximation method consists of discretizing contact surfaces into a triangular mesh. The undeformed contact surface of the body is decomposed into some number of triangular patches that completely cover the surface. In body space, a given triangular patch can be described as the triple of vertices (p_0, p_1, p_2). At time t, this triangle is transformed into world space as the triangle $(D_{R(t)}(p_0), D_{R(t)}(p_1), D_{R(t)}(p_2))$. When performing collision detection and enforcing non-penetration constraints, the contact surface is considered to be the collection of these transformed triangles. The use of a coherence based culling step results in a collision detection algorithm that is nearly linear in the number of polygons[3].

The non-penetration constraints are written in terms of the deformed triangles. Each triangle is treated as a plane in solving for contact forces. Since the plane equation for each triangle can be written in terms of the vertices, the derivatives needed for section 3.3 can be computed in terms of the derivatives of $D_{R(t)}(p_0)$, $D_{R(t)}(p_1)$ and $D_{R(t)}(p_2)$. Since the contact surfaces always remain planar, the contact geometry restriction of finitely many contact points is not an issue. As in the first-order case, the non-penetration constraint can be formulated in terms of finitely many constraints, even if one- or two-dimensional contact regions result.

If the results of a simulation are displayed using the actual deformed shape of a body, instead of the polyhedral approximation used for the dynamics computations, visual anomalies can occur. If the discretization of the polyhedral mesh is very low compared to the curvature of the body, bodies may appear to inter-penetrate somewhat. We have found however that a fairly coarse mesh produces quite reasonable results for second-order deformations. Presumably, higher-order deformations would require finer meshes to avoid visual artifacts. Figure 5 shows a deformed rectangular block; for display purposes, the block was meshed sufficiently to appear as a smooth curved surface. For simulation purposes, the (deformed) block was subdivided into a $3 \times 3 \times 5$ cubic mesh, after which each exterior square face was split into two triangles (for a total of 156 triangles). This was sufficient to remove any suggestion of inter-penetration throughout the entire simulation.

5. Conclusions

We have demonstrated a new technique for simulating flexible bodies subject to non-penetration constraints. We have implemented both first- and second-order polynomial deformable bodies. The use of second-order deformations requires a polyhedral approximation for collision detection purposes. The model presented unifies previous work on deformable bodies, non-penetration constraints, and friction.

Acknowledgements

Research at Cornell University was supported in part by an AT&T Bell Laboratories PhD Fellowship, and grants from the NSF. Research at Carnegie Mellon University was supported in part by a grant from Apple Computer, Inc. Simulations were performed on equipment generously donated by the Hewlett Packard Corporation and the Digital Equipment Corporation. We would like to thank Gene Baraff for several helpful conversations concerning variational principles.

References

[1] D. Baraff. Analytical methods for dynamic simulation of non-penetrating rigid bodies. In *Computer Graphics (Proc. SIGGRAPH)*, volume 23, pages 223–232. ACM, July 1989.

[2] D. Baraff. Curved surfaces and coherence for non-penetrating rigid body simulation. In *Computer Graphics (Proc. SIGGRAPH)*, volume 24, pages 19–28. ACM, August 1990.

[3] D. Baraff. *Dynamic Simulation of Non-penetrating Rigid Bodies*. PhD thesis, Cornell University, May 1992.

[4] J.E. Dennis, Jr. and R.B. Schnabel. *Numerical Methods for Unconstrained Optimization and Nonlinear Equations*. Prentice Hall, Inc., 1983.

[5] C. Lanczos. *The Variational Principles of Mechanics*. Dover Publications, Inc., 1970.

[6] A. Pentland and J. Williams. Good vibrations: Modal dynamics for graphics and animation. In *Computer Graphics (Proc. SIGGRAPH)*, volume 23, pages 215–222. ACM, July 1989.

[7] W.H. Press, B.P. Flannery, S.A. Teukolsky, and W.T. Vetterling. *Numerical Recipes*. Cambridge University Press, 1986.

[8] D. Terzopoulos and K. Fleischer. Modeling inelastic deformation: Viscoelasticity, plasticity, fracture. In *Computer Graphics (Proc. SIGGRAPH)*, volume 22, pages 269–278. ACM, August 1988.

[9] A. Witkin and W. Welch. Fast animation and control of non-rigid structures. In *Computer Graphics (Proc. SIGGRAPH)*, volume 24, pages 243–252. ACM, August 1990.

Figure 5: Quadratically deformable block falling down stairs.

Dynamic Deformation of Solid Primitives with Constraints

Dimitri Metaxas and **Demetri Terzopoulos**[1]

Department of Computer Science, University of Toronto, Toronto, Ontario, M5S 1A4

Keywords: *Physics-Based Modeling and Animation, Deformable Models, Constraints, Solid Primitives, Finite Elements*

Abstract: *This paper develops a systematic approach to deriving dynamic models from parametrically defined solid primitives, global geometric deformations and local finite-element deformations. Even though their kinematics is stylized by the particular solid primitive used, the models behave in a physically correct way with prescribed mass distributions and elasticities. We also propose efficient constraint methods for connecting these new dynamic primitives together to make articulated models. Our techniques make it possible to build and animate constrained, nonrigid, unibody or multibody objects in simulated physical environments at interactive rates.*

1 Introduction

The graphics literature is replete with solid object representations. Unfortunately, it is not particularly easy to synthesize realistic animation through direct application of the geometric representations of solid modeling [5], and the problems are exacerbated when animate objects can deform. Physics-based animation has begun to overcome some of the difficulties.

We propose a systematic approach for creating dynamic solid models capable of realistic physical behaviors starting from common solid primitives such as spheres, cylinders, cones, or superquadrics. Such primitives can "deform" kinematically in simple ways; for example, a cylinder deforms as its radius or length is changed. To gain additional modeling power we allow the primitives to undergo parameterized global deformations (bends, tapers, twists, shears, etc.) of the sort proposed in [2]. To further enhance the geometric flexibility, we permit local free-form deformations. Our local deformations are similar in spirit to the FFDs of [12], but rather than being ambient space warps [12, 10], they are incorporated directly into the solid primitive as finite element shape functions.

Through the application of Lagrangian mechanics and the finite element method our models inherit *generalized coordinates* that comprise the geometric parameters of the solid primitive, the global and local deformation parameters, and the six degrees of freedom of rigid-body motion. Lagrange equations govern the dynamics, dictating the evolution of the generalized coordinates in response to forces. Thus our models exhibit correct mechanical behaviors and their various geometric parameters assume well-defined physical meanings

---

[1] Fellow, Canadian Institute for Advanced Research
E-mail addresses: dm@cs.toronto.edu; dt@cs.toronto.edu

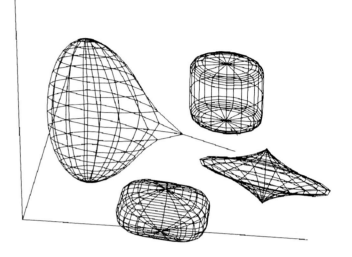

Figure 1: Interaction with deformable superquadrics.

in relation to prescribed mass distributions, elasticities, and energy dissipation rates.

For example, Fig. 1 shows several deformable superquadrics. A superellipsoid [1] is deforming in response to the traction from a linear spring attached to its surface and pulled interactively. In general, the models are abstract viscoelastic solids. It is possible, for instance, to mold a supersphere into any of the deformable superquadrics shown in the figure, not only through manual parameter adjustment but, more interestingly, by applying forces.

A distinguishing feature of our approach is that it marries the parameterized and free-form modeling paradigms within a single physical model. Roughly speaking, we successfully combine locally deformable models [14, 9] with globally deformable models [8, 16]. More precisely, the method applies generally across all geometric primitives and deformations, so long as their equations are differentiable. The coupling of rigid-body and deformation dynamics is similar to that described in [15], but our formulation accommodates global deformations defined by fully nonlinear parametric equations. Hence, our models are more general than the restrictive, linearly deformable ones in [16] and quadratically deformable ones in [8, 10].

Our dynamic deformable models raise interesting challenges related to the application of constraints to construct composite models and control animation. We describe a method for computing generalized constraint forces between our models which is based on Baumgarte's constraint stabilization technique [4, 18]. As in [17, 3], our algorithm may be used to assemble complex objects satisfying constraints from initially mispositioned and misshaped parts, and it enables us to construct and animate articulated objects composed of rigid or nonrigid components.

The remainder of this paper describes our general formulation and presents some results. Space limitations preclude a complete elaboration of the mathematics. We refer the reader to [13, 7] for further details.

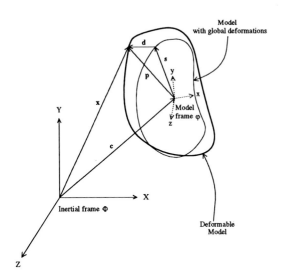

Figure 2: Geometry of deformable model.

2 Geometry

Consider a solid model whose intrinsic (material) coordinates are $u = (u, v, w)$. Referring to Fig. 2, $\mathbf{x}(u, t) = (x_1(u, t), x_2(u, t), x_3(u, t))^\top$, where $^\top$ denotes transposition, gives the positions of points on the model relative to the fixed reference frame Φ. We can write

$$\mathbf{x} = \mathbf{c} + \mathbf{R}\mathbf{p}, \qquad (1)$$

where $\mathbf{p}(u, t)$ denotes the positions of points relative to the noninertial, model-centered frame ϕ whose instantaneous position is $\mathbf{c}(t)$ and orientation relative to Φ is given by the rotation matrix $\mathbf{R}(t)$. We further express

$$\mathbf{p} = \mathbf{s} + \mathbf{d}, \qquad (2)$$

the sum of a reference shape $\mathbf{s}(u, t)$ and a displacement function $\mathbf{d}(u, t)$. We define the reference shape as

$$\mathbf{s} = \mathbf{T}(\mathbf{e}(u; a_1, a_2, \ldots); b_1, b_2, \ldots). \qquad (3)$$

Here, a geometric primitive $\mathbf{e}$, defined parametrically in u and parameterized by the variables a_i, is subjected to the *global deformation* $\mathbf{T}$ which depends on the parameters b_i. Although generally nonlinear, $\mathbf{e}$ and $\mathbf{T}$ are assumed to be differentiable (so that we may compute the Jacobian of $\mathbf{s}$) and $\mathbf{T}$ may be a composite sequence of primitive deformation functions. We define the vector of global deformation parameters

$$\mathbf{q}_s = (a_1, a_2, \ldots, b_1, b_2, \ldots)^\top. \qquad (4)$$

Next, we express the displacement as a linear combination of basis functions $\mathbf{b}_i(u)$. The basis functions can be local or global; however, finite element shape functions [6] are the natural choice for representing *local deformations*

$$\mathbf{d} = \mathbf{S}\mathbf{q}_d. \qquad (5)$$

Here $\mathbf{S}$ is a shape matrix whose entries are the shape functions and

$$\mathbf{q}_d = (\ldots, \mathbf{q}_i, \ldots)^\top \qquad (6)$$

is the vector of local deformation parameters. Typically, finite elements have nodes at their vertices, and the parameter $\mathbf{q}_i$ denotes a displacement vector associated with node i of the model.

In [13, 7] we provide the formulas for a superquadric ellipsoid $\mathbf{e}$ with tapering, bending, shearing, and twisting deformations (see also [2]).

3 Kinematics and Dynamics

To convert the above geometric representation into a physical model that responds dynamically to forces, we first consider the kinematics implied by the geometry and then introduce mass, damping, and elasticity into the model to derive its mechanics.

The velocity of points on the model is given by,

$$\dot{\mathbf{x}} = \dot{\mathbf{c}} + \dot{\mathbf{R}}\mathbf{p} + \mathbf{R}\dot{\mathbf{p}} = \dot{\mathbf{c}} + \mathbf{B}\dot{\boldsymbol{\theta}} + \mathbf{R}\dot{\mathbf{s}} + \mathbf{R}\mathbf{S}\dot{\mathbf{q}}_d, \qquad (7)$$

where $\boldsymbol{\theta} = (\ldots, \theta_i, \ldots)^\top$ is a vector of rotational coordinates and $\mathbf{B} = [\ldots \partial(\mathbf{R}\mathbf{p})/\partial\theta_i \ldots]$. Now, $\dot{\mathbf{s}} = [\partial\mathbf{s}/\partial\mathbf{q}_s]\dot{\mathbf{q}}_s = \mathbf{J}\dot{\mathbf{q}}_s$, where $\mathbf{J}$ is the Jacobian of the reference shape with respect to the global deformation parameter vector. We can therefore write the model kinematics compactly as

$$\mathbf{x} = \mathbf{c} + \mathbf{R}(\mathbf{s} + \mathbf{d}) = \mathbf{h}(\mathbf{q}), \qquad (8)$$

$$\dot{\mathbf{x}} = [\mathbf{I} \ \mathbf{B} \ \mathbf{R}\mathbf{J} \ \mathbf{R}\mathbf{S}]\dot{\mathbf{q}} = \mathbf{L}\dot{\mathbf{q}}, \qquad (9)$$

where

$$\mathbf{q} = (\mathbf{q}_c^\top, \mathbf{q}_\theta^\top, \mathbf{q}_s^\top, \mathbf{q}_d^\top)^\top, \qquad (10)$$

with $\mathbf{q}_c = \mathbf{c}$ and $\mathbf{q}_\theta = \boldsymbol{\theta}$ serving as the vector of generalized coordinates for the dynamic model.

To specify the dynamics, we introduce a mass distribution $\mu(u)$ over the model and assume that the material is subject to frictional damping. We also assume that the material may deform elastically or viscoelastically [14]. From Lagrangian mechanics we obtain order-second equations of motion which take the form

$$\mathbf{M}\ddot{\mathbf{q}} + \mathbf{D}\dot{\mathbf{q}} + \mathbf{K}\mathbf{q} = \mathbf{g}_q + \mathbf{f}_q. \qquad (11)$$

The mass matrix $\mathbf{M} = \int \mu \mathbf{L}^\top \mathbf{L} \, du$. The stiffness matrix $\mathbf{K}$ may be obtained from a deformation strain energy $(\mathbf{q}^\top \mathbf{K}\mathbf{q})/2$. The Raleigh damping matrix $\mathbf{D} = \alpha\mathbf{M} + \beta\mathbf{K}$. The generalized inertial forces $\mathbf{g}_q = -\int \mu \mathbf{L}^\top \dot{\mathbf{L}}\dot{\mathbf{q}} \, du$ include generalized centrifugal, Coriolis, and transverse forces due to the dynamic coupling between $\mathbf{q}\theta$, $\mathbf{q}_s$, and $\mathbf{q}_d$. Finally, $\mathbf{f}_\mathbf{q} = \mathbf{L}^\top \mathbf{f}$ are generalized external forces associated with the components of $\mathbf{q}$, where $\mathbf{f}(u, t)$ is the force distribution applied to the model. See [13, 7] for explicit formulas for the above matrices and vectors.

4 Constrained Nonrigid Motion

We can extend (11) to account for the motions of composite models with interconnected deformable parts. Shabana [11] describes the well-known Lagrange multiplier method for multibody objects. We form a composite generalized coordinate vector $\mathbf{q}$ and force vectors $\mathbf{g}_\mathbf{q}$ and $\mathbf{f}_\mathbf{q}$ for an n-part model by concatenating the $\mathbf{q}_i$, $\mathbf{g}_{\mathbf{q}_i}$, and $\mathbf{f}_{\mathbf{q}_i}$ associated with each part $i = 1, \ldots, n$. Similarly, the composite matrices M, D, and K for the n-part model are block diagonal matrices with submatrices $\mathbf{M}_i$, $\mathbf{D}_i$, and $\mathbf{K}_i$, respectively, for each part i. The method solves the composite equations of motion $\mathbf{M}\ddot{\mathbf{q}} + \mathbf{D}\dot{\mathbf{q}} + \mathbf{K}\mathbf{q} = \mathbf{g}_\mathbf{q} + \mathbf{f}_\mathbf{q} - \mathbf{C}_\mathbf{q}^\top\boldsymbol{\lambda}$. The generalized constraint forces $\mathbf{f}_{g_c} = -\mathbf{C}_\mathbf{q}^\top\boldsymbol{\lambda}$ acting on the parts stem from the holonomic constraint equations

$$\mathbf{C}(\mathbf{q}, t) = \mathbf{0}; \qquad (12)$$

i.e., $\mathbf{C} = [\mathbf{C}_1^\top, \mathbf{C}_2^\top, \ldots, \mathbf{C}_k^\top]^\top$ expresses k constraints among the n parts of the model. The term $\mathbf{C}_\mathbf{q}^\top$ is the transpose of the constraint Jacobian matrix and $\boldsymbol{\lambda} = (\boldsymbol{\lambda}_1^\top, \ldots, \boldsymbol{\lambda}_n^\top)^\top$ is a vector of Lagrange multipliers that must be determined.

To obtain an equal number of equations and unknowns, we differentiate (12) twice with respect to time, yielding

$$\boldsymbol{\gamma} = \mathbf{C}_\mathbf{q}\ddot{\mathbf{q}} = -\mathbf{C}_{tt} - (\mathbf{C}_\mathbf{q}\dot{\mathbf{q}})_\mathbf{q}\dot{\mathbf{q}} - 2\mathbf{C}_{\mathbf{q}_t}\dot{\mathbf{q}}. \qquad (13)$$

We obtain the augmented equations of motion

$$
\begin{bmatrix} \mathbf{M} & \mathbf{C_q^T} \\ \mathbf{C_q} & \mathbf{0} \end{bmatrix} \begin{bmatrix} \ddot{\mathbf{q}} \\ \boldsymbol{\lambda} \end{bmatrix} = \begin{bmatrix} -\mathbf{D}\dot{\mathbf{q}} - \mathbf{Kq} + \mathbf{g_q} + \mathbf{f_q} \\ \boldsymbol{\gamma} \end{bmatrix}. \quad (14)
$$

In principle, these equations may be integrated from initial conditions $\mathbf{q}(0)$ and $\dot{\mathbf{q}}(0)$ satisfying $\mathbf{C}(\mathbf{q}(0), 0) = \mathbf{0}$ and $\dot{\mathbf{C}}(\mathbf{q}(0), 0) = \mathbf{0}$. At each time step, we solve (14) for $\ddot{\mathbf{q}}$ and $\boldsymbol{\lambda}$ with known $\mathbf{q}$ and $\dot{\mathbf{q}}$, and then we integrate $\ddot{\mathbf{q}}$ and $\dot{\mathbf{q}}$ from t to $t + \Delta t$ to obtain $\dot{\mathbf{q}}$ and $\mathbf{q}$ (e.g., using the simple Euler method $\dot{\mathbf{q}}^{(t+\Delta t)} = \dot{\mathbf{q}}^{(t)} + \Delta t \, \ddot{\mathbf{q}}^{(t)}; \, \mathbf{q}^{(t+\Delta t)} = \mathbf{q}^{(t)} + \Delta t \, \dot{\mathbf{q}}^{(t+\Delta t)}$).

There are two practical problems in applying (14) to animation. First, the various parameters of the parts may not be set initially so that the constraints are satisfied (i.e., $\mathbf{C}(\mathbf{q}, 0) \neq \mathbf{0}$). Second, even if the constraints may be satisfied at a given time step of the animation (i.e., $\mathbf{C}(\mathbf{q}, t) = \mathbf{0}$), they may not be satisfied at the next time step (i.e., $\mathbf{C}(\mathbf{q}, t + \Delta t) \neq \mathbf{0}$) because of numerical errors, etc.

The constraint stabilization method of Baumgarte [4, 18] remedies these problems. The constraint equation $\mathbf{C} = \mathbf{0}$ is replaced in (14) by the damped second-order equation $\ddot{\mathbf{C}} + 2\alpha\dot{\mathbf{C}} + \beta^2\mathbf{C} = \mathbf{0}$, where α and β are stabilization factors. This replaces the lower entry of the vector on the rhs of (14) to $\boldsymbol{\gamma} - 2\alpha\dot{\mathbf{C}} - \beta^2\mathbf{C}$. Fast stabilization means choosing $\beta = \alpha$ to obtain the critically damped solution $\mathbf{C}(\mathbf{q}, 0)e^{-\alpha t}$ which, for given α, has the quickest asymptotic decay towards constraint satisfaction $\mathbf{C} = \mathbf{0}$. Baumgarte constraint stabilization and its variations are also applied in [3, 9, 16].

The Lagrange multiplier method is very general, but it is potentially expensive for our deformable models since the matrix in (14) is large. We have devised a fast specialized method to solve for the unknown constraint forces $\mathbf{f}_{g_c}$ arising from point-to-point constraints. The method involves the solution of a linear system whose size is on the order of the number of constraints, which is usually small. In this sense, it is similar to the dynamic constraint technique of [3], but it is suitable for nonrigid parts. The details are in [7].

5   Animation Examples

The partitioning of complex nonrigid behavior into rigid-body motions, global deformations, and local deformations leads to numerically well-conditioned discrete equations and stable simulation algorithms based on explicit numerical integration methods. We represent the rotation component of the models using quaternions, which facilitates the integration of $\mathbf{q}_\theta$. We do not assemble and factorize a finite element stiffness matrix as is common practice in finite element analysis, but instead compute $\mathbf{Kq}_d$ efficiently in an element-by-element fashion. For greater efficiency, we can lump masses to obtain a diagonal $\mathbf{M}$, and we may assume mass-proportional damping, i.e. $\mathbf{D} = \nu\mathbf{M}$ where ν is the damping coefficient [6].

The following animation examples involve deformable superquadric primitives that interact with one another and their simulated physical environments through point-to-point constraints, collisions, gravity, and friction against impenetrable surfaces. To attain animation rates of several frames per second (on an SGI 4D-35TG), we have implemented dynamic "shells" where the material domain is restricted to a membrane surface $\mathbf{u} = (u, v, 1)$ and the interior mass density $\mu(\mathbf{u}) = 0$ for $0 \leq w < 1$. We triangulate the surface of the model into linear elastic elements (see [13] for the details).

Fig. 3 shows several frames from an animation of multiple "balloon pendulums" suspended in gravity by inextensible strings. The simulation starts from the initial configuration shown in Fig. 3(a), and the balloons swing, collide, and deform until the kinetic energy is dissipated. The inelastic

collisions are implemented using reaction constraints [9] between multiple deformable bodies.

Fig. 4 shows the construction and animation of a minimalist dragonfly from its deformable body parts (Fig. 4(a)) and 4 point-to-point constraints. The dragonfly self-assembles [17, 3] and it "works," inasmuch as internal forces open and flap the wings (Fig. 4(b)). An impenetrable plane appears out of nowhere and swats the dragonfly in the rear (Fig. 4(c)). The body parts deform in response to the blow, but they remain joined by the constraints (Fig. 4(d)).

Fig. 5 illustrates the self-assembly and animation of a snowman. Twelve point-to-point constraints assemble and hold the deformable superquadric body parts together (Fig. 5(a–b)). When gravity is turned on, the assembled snowman drops to the impenetrable floor and locomotes along a prespecified path through controlled bouncing (Fig. 5(b–d)).

Fig. 6 illustrates a simple "circus stunt," in which two deformable superquadric balls interact with a pivoting springboard mounted on immobile planes. The simulation starts from Fig. 6(a) with the yellow ball dropping downward. Fig. 6(b) shows the motion tracks.

The figures have demonstrated a rather sophisticated family of parameterized models—deformable superquadrics with global twisting, bending, tapering, and shearing deformations, and local membrane deformations. We emphasize in closing, however, that our approach is generally applicable to a wide variety of parameterized models, global deformations, and finite element basis functions.

References

[1] Barr, A., (1981) "Superquadrics and angle preserving transformations," *IEEE Computer Graphics and Applications*, **1**(1), 11-23.

[2] Barr, A., (1984) "Global and local deformations of solid primitives," *Computer Graphics*, **18**(3), 21–30.

[3] Barzel, R., and Barr, A., (1988) "A modeling system based on dynamic constraints," *Computer Graphics*, **22**(4), 179-188.

[4] Baumgarte, J., (1972) "Stabilization of constraints and integrals of motion in dynamical systems," *Comp. Meth. in Appl. Mech. and Eng.*, **1**, 1–16.

[5] Hoffmann, C.M., (1989) *Geometric and solid modeling*, Morgan-Kaufman, Palo Alto.

[6] Kardestuncer, H., (ed.), (1987) *Finite element handbook*, McGraw–Hill, New York.

[7] Metaxas, D., and Terzopoulos, D., (1992) "Shape and nonrigid motion estimation from synthesis," *IEEE Transactions on Pattern Analysis and Machine Intelligence*, to appear.

[8] Pentland, A., and Williams, J., (1989) "Good vibrations: Modal dynamics for graphics and animation," *Computer Graphics*, **23**(3), 215–222.

[9] Platt, J., (1989) "Constraint methods for neural networks and computer graphics," PhD Thesis, Dept. of Computer Science, California Institute of Technology, Pasadena, CA (Caltech-CS-TR-89-07).

[10] Sclaroff, S., and Pentland, A., (1991) "Generalized implicit functions for computer graphics," *Computer Graphics*, **25**(4), 247–250.

[11] Shabana, A., (1989) *Dynamics of multibody systems*, Wiley, New York.

[12] Sederberg, T.W., and Parry, S.R., (1989) "Free-form deformation of solid geometric primitives," *Computer Graphics*, **20**(4), 151–160.

[13] Terzopoulos, D., and Metaxas, D., (1991) "Dynamic 3D models with local and global deformations: Deformable superquadrics," *IEEE Transactions on Pattern Analysis and Machine Intelligence*, **13**(7), 703–713.

[14] Terzopoulos, D., and Fleischer, K., (1988) "Deformable models," *The Visual Computer*, **4**(6), 306–331.

[15] Terzopoulos, D., and Witkin, A., (1988) "Physically-based models with rigid and deformable components," *IEEE Computer Graphics and Applications*, **8**(6), 41–51.

[16] Witkin, A., and Welch, W., (1990) "Fast animation and control of nonrigid structures," *Computer Graphics*, **24**(3), 243–252.

[17] Witkin, A., Fleischer, K., and Barr, A., (1987) "Energy constraints on parameterized models," *Computer Graphics*, **21**(4), 225–232.

[18] Wittenburg, J., (1977) *Dynamics of systems of rigid bodies*, Tubner, Stuttgart.

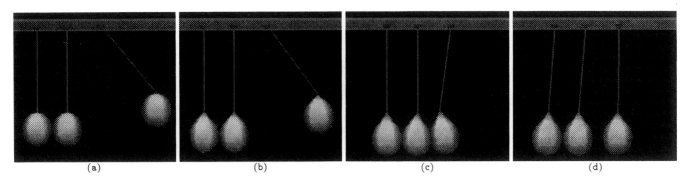

Figure 3: Balloon multi-pendulum. Initial state (a). Swinging and colliding (b–d).

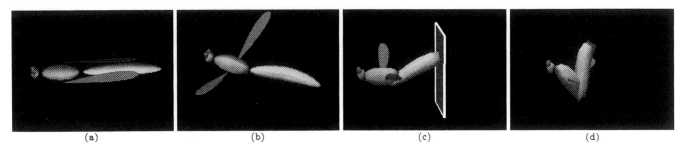

Figure 4: Dragonfly. Self-assembly (a). Flight (b). Swatting (c). Swatted fly (b).

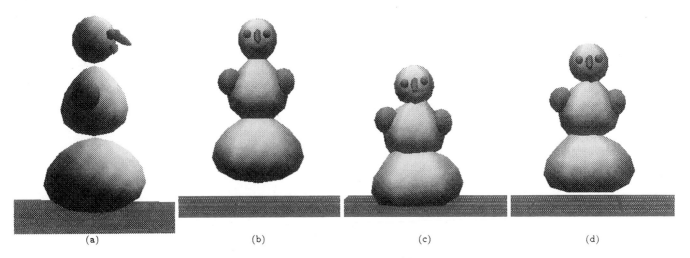

Figure 5: Yellow snowman. Self-assembly (a). Hopping (b–d).

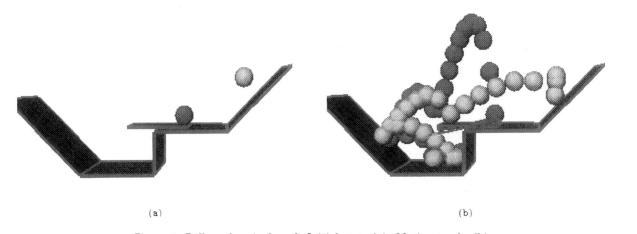

Figure 6: Balls and springboard. Initial state (a). Motion tracks (b).

Smooth Interpolation of Orientations
with Angular Velocity Constraints
using Quaternions

Alan H. Barr[†], Bena Currin[†], Steven Gabriel[††], John F. Hughes[†††]

California Institute of Technology[†]
Sage Design[††]
Brown University[†††]

Abstract

In this paper we present methods to smoothly interpolate orientations, given N rotational keyframes of an object along a trajectory. The methods allow the user to impose constraints on the rotational path, such as the angular velocity at the endpoints of the trajectory.

We convert the rotations to quaternions, and then spline in that non-Euclidean space. Analogous to the mathematical foundations of flat-space spline curves, we minimize the net "tangential acceleration" of the quaternion path. We replace the flat-space quantities with curved-space quantities, and numerically solve the resulting equation with finite difference and optimization methods.

1 Introduction

The problem of using spline curves to smoothly interpolate mathematical quantities in flat Euclidean spaces is a well-studied problem in computer graphics [BARTELS ET AL 87], [KOCHANEK&BARTELS 84]. Many quantities important to computer graphics, however, such as rotations, lie in non-Euclidean spaces. In 1985, a method to interpolate rotations using quaternion curves was presented to the computer graphics community [SHOEMAKE 85]; beyond this, there has been relatively little work in computer graphics to smoothly interpolate quantities in non-Euclidean, curved spaces [GABRIEL&KAJIYA 85]. In that paper, Kajiya and Gabriel developed a foundation for an "intrinsic" differential geometric formulation for comput-

ing spline paths on curved manifolds, and applied their results to quaternion paths.

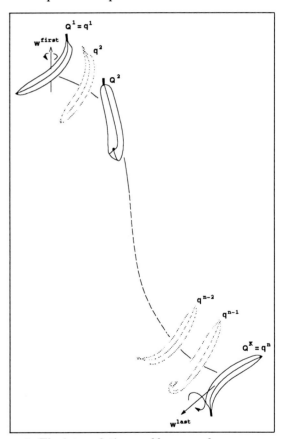

Figure 1. The interpolation problem we solve:

Given K keyframe quaternions, (capital) $\mathbf{Q}^i$, $i = 1, 2, \cdots, K$, at keyframe times $t_i = p_i\,h$, what are the n optimal interpolated quaternions $\mathbf{q}^{(p)}$, $p = 1, 2, \cdots, n$ at equally spaced times $\tau_p = h\,(p-1)$, that pass through the keyframe quaternions? $\mathbf{q}^{(p)} = \mathbf{Q}^i$ and $t_i = \tau_p$, when $p = p_i$. Optionally, find the n rotations (plus two extra keyframe rotations) when given angular velocities ω^{first} and ω^{last} of the first and last rotation along the path.

Splining in non-Euclidean Spaces

This paper presents a simpler version of the Gabriel/Kajiya approach to splining on arbitrary manifolds. Our approach uses extrinsic coordinates and constraints (rather than intrinsic methods, Christoffel symbols and coordinate patches), and generalizes to other manifolds that are embedded in Euclidean space.[1] The problem of computing spline curves on curved manifolds is of increasing importance to computer graphics, and we predict many future generalizations.

There are several reasons why someone would choose to use our interpolation techniques:

- The paths we generate through rotation space are very smooth.
- Our techniques allow the user to specify arbitrarily large initial and final angular velocities of a rotating body; by assigning large angular velocities, a user can make an object tumble several full turns between successive keypoints.
- It is fairly easy to add additional constraints.
- The techniques generalize to interpolations of other quantities in non-Euclidean spaces.
- The techniques are fast enough to experiment with, taking a few minutes per interpolation.

Of course, we cannot claim to have solved all problems of interpolating rotations and orientations. Through our choice of representation, we will have the classic advantages and disadvantages of using unit quaternions to represent rotations.[2] Also implicit in our approach is the assumption that the geometry of the space of orientations has a certain homogeneity, and that we can mathematically specify all of the constraints that we wish to apply.[3]

We find a path that minimizes a measure of net bending. We implement this, however, using a finite difference technique, so that we end up with a sequence of points on the path, rather than a continuous path. To produce a continuous path, we use Shoemake's *slerping* to interpolate between these points.

In section 2, we provide a brief discussion of quaternions, and present intuitive mathematical background to motivate the differences between interpolating in flat space and curved spaces; in section 3 we sketch the overall algorithm; in section 4 we present the constrained

---

[1] Whitney's original embedding theorem tells us that every M dimensional manifold can be embedded in a $2M+1$ dimensional Euclidean space.

[2] The main advantage is that quaternion constraints are simple to enforce (constructing a four dimensional unit vector); the main disadvantage is *double representation*: there are two unit quaternions that represent each rotation.

[3] For tumbling bodies this is reasonable, but it is not completely true for camera orientations: certain orientations (ones with no "tilt" around line of sight of the camera) are far preferable to others. We would need to determine the appropriate constraints to minimize the net tilting.

optimization problem; section 5 speaks briefly about numerical derivatives on manifolds; section 6 presents methods to solve the problem, while section 7 presents our results.

2 Mathematical Background

Shoemake's paper on quaternions provides a good introduction to the mathematics of quaternions and their relationship to rotations. For our results, we need three basic facts about quaternions:

- The set of unit-length quaternions (i.e., expressions of the form $\mathbf{q} = a + b\mathbf{i} + c\mathbf{j} + d\mathbf{k}$ with $a^2 + b^2 + c^2 + d^2 = 1$) corresponds to the unit 3-sphere in 4-dimensions. The quaternion $a + b\mathbf{i} + c\mathbf{j} + d\mathbf{k}$ corresponds to the point (a, b, c, d). The same quaternion is denoted by $\mathbf{q} = \begin{pmatrix} s \\ \mathbf{v} \end{pmatrix}$, where $s = a$ and $\mathbf{v} = (b, c, d)$.
- There is a natural map that takes a unit quaternion and produces a rotation: the quaternion $a + b\mathbf{i} + c\mathbf{j} + d\mathbf{k}$ corresponds to a rotation of $2\cos^{-1}(a)$ about the axis (b, c, d) in 3-space. If $(b, c, d) = (0, 0, 0)$ the rotation angle is $2\cos^{-1}(\pm 1) = 0$, and the rotation is the identity.
- The map from unit quaternions to rotations is 2-to-1. For every rotation, two quaternions, $+\mathbf{q}$ and $-\mathbf{q}$, lying at antipodal ends of a hypersphere, correspond to it.

Advantages of quaternions. There are several reasons to use quaternions to describe rotations. First, the quaternion space has the same local topology and geometry as the set of rotations (this is *not* true of the space of Euler angles, for example, but is true of the 3×3 orthogonal matrices of determinant 1). Second, the number of coordinates used in describing a quaternion is small (4 numbers, in contrast to the 9 in a 3×3 matrix). Third, the number of constraints on these coordinates is small: the only constraint on a quaternion representing a rotation is that it have unit length; a 3×3 matrix must satisfy six equations to represent a rotation. Finally, the extrinsic equations for quaternions turn out to be fairly simple.

Disadvantages of quaternions. The main disadvantage of using quaternions is that their 2-to-1 nature necessitates a preprocessing step, to choose whether the plus or minus keyframe quaternion is the appropriate one to use.

Euclidean and non-Euclidean-space splines. Since the 3-sphere is a non-Euclidean space, we discuss interpolation methods for Euclidean spaces, and then motivate and describe a generalization to non-Euclidean spaces. We will informally refer to them as "flat" spaces and "curved" spaces respectively.

2.1 Flat-space interpolation

The Hermite formulation expresses a spline curve as a parametric cubic curve $\gamma(t)$ that starts and ends at two given points[4], $\gamma(0) = P^0$ and $\gamma(1) = P^1$, and has given velocities there, i.e., $\gamma'(0) = R^0$ and $\gamma'(1) = R^1$. Given these boundary conditions (i.e., P^0, P^1, R^0, and R^1), we can find a unique cubic path that satisfies them. But why is a cubic the right curve to use?

One answer is given by reformulating the problem to ask "Among all curves starting at P^0 with velocity R^0 and ending at P^1 with velocity R^1, what curve bends the least?" We approximate the least square measure of curvature by minimizing the net squared length of the acceleration vector, γ''. Thus we seek to minimize

$$\mathcal{E} = \int_0^1 \gamma''(t) \cdot \gamma''(t) dt \qquad (1)$$

over all paths γ that satisfy the boundary conditions. The Euler-Lagrange equations [ZWILLINGER 89] provide a necessary condition for γ to be a minimum. Writing out these conditions gives $\gamma'''' = 0$, which means that each component of $\gamma(t)$ must be a cubic function of t.

A physical implementation of splines in a flat space. The word "spline" originally referred to a thin strip of wood or metal that was constrained by pins to form smooth curves for drafting or shipbuilding. For drafting, the pins were placed onto a flat surface; for shipbuilding, rigid posts were inserted into the earth, and wooden flexible planks were threaded between them. In each case, the splines flexed to meet the positional constraints imposed by the pins or posts. The spline took on curved shapes in its attempt to achieve a low-energy state, governed by equation (1).

2.2 Flat space splines versus curved-space splines.

We would like to carry out an analogous computation in a curved space: we define a "bending" measure of a curve, and then determine which curves minimize the measure. Unfortunately, the ordinary second derivative of a path is no longer the right way to measure net "bending." We can understand this by considering the problems that arise even for surfaces in 3-space.

If γ is a path on a surface M in 3-space, then γ can be thought of as a path in 3-space as well. As such, at each time t the path has a velocity vector $\gamma'(t)$ and an acceleration vector $\gamma''(t)$. Because γ lies within the

[4]We use superscripts to indicate different vectors, and subscripts to denote x, y, z, etc components of vectors.

surface, its velocity vector will always be tangent to the surface. Its acceleration vector, however, does not have to lie within the surface. It is likely to have components normal to the surface, as well as components tangential to the surface.

In Figure 2 we see a pair of curves on a surface. The midpoint of the upper curve has an acceleration vector **a** that points both out from the surface and up a little. We see that the acceleration vector **a** is not parallel to the surface normal N; the "non-N part" of vector **a** (the *tangential acceleration* or *covariant acceleration*) is labeled S in the drawing. The acceleration vector of the lower curve actually coincides with the normal vector to the surface, and hence its tangential acceleration is zero.

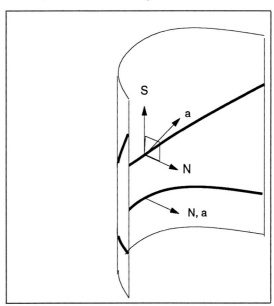

Figure 2. Two curves on a curved surface. The upper curve has an acceleration vector **a**, that does not lie in the surface. The vector **N** is the normal vector to the surface, along the path. The tangential part of the acceleration is the vector **S** = **a** \ **N** (described in section 2.3). The lower curve's acceleration is parallel to **N**, hence it has zero tangential acceleration.

A physical analogy. Imagine driving in a small circle in a hilly region. You feel two sorts of acceleration: you bounce up and down in your seat as you go over bumps, and you are pushed against your car door because you are turning in a tight circle. The first is acceleration in the direction normal to the surface of the earth; the second is the tangential acceleration. Note that if you want to take a drive, any path you take is likely to have some net tangential acceleration. But to make the trip as comfortable as possible, minimizing tangential acceleration is desirable.

Normal acceleration is inevitable. By contrast, the normal component of the acceleration is a necessary evil. Imagine trying to get from one place on a sphere to another in a way that minimizes total acceleration. If you travel along a great circle at a constant speed, the only acceleration will be normal. If you try to adjust your path so that you undergo *no* acceleration, you will have to be traveling in a straight line in 3-space, and hence will have to leave the surface of the sphere. This gets rid of the normal acceleration, but at the cost of violating the requirement that γ be a path *on* the surface.

Another physical example. Let us consider making a physical spline onto a spherical globe. Instead of placing pins into a flat drafting surface, we push the pins into the globe itself. We thread a semi-rigid elastic strip through the pins, making sure that the strip stays on the globe while being constrained by the pins. Since the strip needs to stay on the globe, we do not penalize it for bending to stay on the globe.

These examples motivate why we do not penalize acceleration normal to the surface, while penalizing acceleration within the surface, for constructing splines on curved surfaces. In generalizing Equation 1 to curved spaces, Kajiya and Gabriel therefore replaced the squared length of the acceleration vector with the squared length of the tangential acceleration. This is the starting point for our solution: we will seek a path in quaternion space, i.e., a path on the unit 3-sphere in 4-space, that minimizes the total squared tangential acceleration.

2.3 A formula for tangential acceleration

Given two n dimensional vectors $\mathbf{a}$ and $\mathbf{b}$, we wish to project away and remove all portions of $\mathbf{b}$ found in vector $\mathbf{a}$. The notation we use for this is $\mathbf{a} \setminus \mathbf{b}$ (read as vector $\mathbf{a}$ "without" vector $\mathbf{b}$). By definition,

$$\mathbf{a} \setminus \mathbf{b} = \mathbf{a} - \alpha \mathbf{b}, \text{ such that}$$
$$(\mathbf{a} \setminus \mathbf{b}) \cdot \mathbf{b} = 0$$
$$\text{which implies that } \alpha = \frac{(\mathbf{a} \cdot \mathbf{b})}{(\mathbf{b} \cdot \mathbf{b})}$$

If the surface M is a unit sphere, then the unit normal at the point (a, b, c) is (a, b, c). So for a path γ on the unit sphere, the total acceleration at time t is $\gamma''(t)$; its normal vector is $\gamma(t)$ itself, and the tangential acceleration $\mathbf{S}(t)$ is given by

$$\mathbf{S}(t) = \gamma''(t) \setminus \gamma(t).$$

For other applications, the formula for tangential acceleration of a curve on an arbitrary implicitly defined surface $f(x) = 0$ is

$$\mathbf{S}(t) = \gamma''(t) \setminus \mathbf{N}, \text{ where}$$
$$\mathbf{N} = \nabla f.$$

2.4 Physical meaning of paths on the quaternion sphere

We have already noted that each unit quaternion corresponds to a rotation. If we think of this rotation acting on a rigid body in a "home" coordinate system, then we can say that each quaternion corresponds to an orientation of the rigid body. Therefore a path in the quaternion sphere represents a continuously changing orientation. The derivative of the path at a particular instant represents the rate of change of orientation of the body, essentially its *angular velocity*. Thus to specify the endpoints and end tangents of a quaternion curve means to specify the initial and final orientations of a rigid body and its angular velocities at those points.

3 Algorithm Description

We provide a sketch of the overall algorithm in figure 3, using the curved-space results of the previous sections. In the subsequent few sections, we develop the mathematics for step 2. The implementation for step 2 is found in section 6.

---

1. Preprocess orientations into keyframe quaternions, $\mathbf{Q}^i$ as shown in Appendix A

2. Use constrained optimization techniques as described in section 6 to compute quaternions interpolated between the keyframes.

3. Optionally slerp between the interpolated quaternions to get a continuous representation.

4. Convert the quaternions back into rotation matrices (or other desired form).

Figure 3. The steps of the algorithm.

4 Mathematical Formulations

In this section, for our constrained optimization problem, we consider some of the merits of using a continuous derivative versus using discrete derivatives. Ultimately we will choose the discrete approach, because it is simpler. The reader should not infer that continuous approaches are not worthy of further investigation, however.

4.1 Continuous derivative approach

The problem statement for the continuous version without angular velocity constraints is: given K keyframe quaternions, $\mathbf{Q}^1$, $\mathbf{Q}^2$, $\cdots$, $\mathbf{Q}^K$, at times t_1, t_2, $\cdots$, t_K, what is the unit quaternion curve $\boldsymbol{\gamma}(t)$ of minimal net least square tangential acceleration that passes through the points?

We are looking for the unknown (four dimensional) unit magnitude quaternion function $\boldsymbol{\gamma}(t)$ which minimizes $\mathcal{E}$, the net square magnitude of the tangential acceleration. Without loss of generality,[5] we stipulate that $t_1 = 0$. Thus we minimize

$$\mathcal{E} = \int_0^{t_K} \left| \boldsymbol{\gamma}''(t) \setminus \boldsymbol{\gamma}(t) \right|^2 \, dt$$

subject to the constraints

$$\textbf{boundary values}: \quad \boldsymbol{\gamma}(t_i) = \mathbf{Q}^i, \quad i = 1, 2, \cdots, K.$$
$$\textbf{magnitudes}: \quad |\boldsymbol{\gamma}(t)| = 1, \quad 0 \le t \le t_K$$

The boundary value constraints ensure that the quaternion path passes through the keyframe quaternions; the unit magnitude constraint keeps the quaternion on the unit 3-sphere. t_K and 0 are the (prescribed) values of t at the endpoints of the quaternion path.

This constrained optimization problem is a calculus of variations problem, which produces an Euler-Lagrange ordinary differential equation formulation with constraints [ZWILLINGER]. It is an extrinsic form of the Gabriel/Kajiya equation. The authors have derived this equation, but feel it would needlessly clutter the presentation. The approach involves the solution of a K-point ODE boundary value problem with constraints; we leave the pursuit of this approach as future work.

4.2 Discrete derivative approach

If we do not wish to solve K-point boundary value problems, we can make discrete approximations to convert the calculus of variations problem into a calculus problem. Instead of solving for an unknown function $\boldsymbol{\gamma}(t)$, we solve for n fixed quaternions $\mathbf{q}^{(p)}$, $p = 1, 2, \cdots, n$. We retain the constraints that each $\mathbf{q}^{(p)}$ is a (four dimensional) unit vector, and that the appropriate $\mathbf{q}^{(p_i)}$s coincide with our keyframe quaternions $\mathbf{Q}^i$, $i = 1, 2, \cdots, K$.

We replace the continuous derivatives $\boldsymbol{\gamma}(t)''$ in the $\mathcal{E}$ equation with a numerical approximation, shown in section 4.3; we denote the discrete derivative approximation with $(\mathbf{q}^{(p)})''$, and compute them from the $\mathbf{q}^{(p)}$s. In addition, we replace the integral with a discrete approximation, the sum of about n equally spaced values, times the stepsize, $h = t_K/(n-1)$.

---
[5] The reader can shift the arguments of the function to reduce a $t_1 \ne 0$ problem to a $t_1 = 0$ problem.

Thus, we minimize the function

$$E(\mathbf{q}) = h \sum_{p=p_{\min}}^{p_{\max}} \left| (\mathbf{q}^{(p)})'' \setminus \mathbf{q}^{(p)} \right|^2$$

subject to the constraints that

$$\textbf{boundary values}: \quad \mathbf{q}^{(p_i)} = \mathbf{Q}^i, \quad i = 1, 2, \cdots, K$$
$$\textbf{magnitudes}: \quad |\mathbf{q}^{(p)}| = 1, \quad p = 1, 2, \cdots, n.$$

The p_i are those values of p where we wish the interpolated quaternions $\mathbf{q}^{(p)}$ to coincide with the keyframe quaternions $\mathbf{Q}^i$. $p_1 = 1$, and $p_K = n$; $p_{\min} = 1$ or 2 and $p_{\max} = n$ or $n - 1$. They are chosen so that $(\mathbf{q}^{(p)})''$ can be computed in each term in the sum. (This is equivalent to having a weighting factor in the sum).

4.3 Discrete second derivatives

A simple discrete version of the second derivative is the *three-point* formula:

$$(\mathbf{q}^{(p)})'' = \frac{\mathbf{q}^{(p+1)} - 2\mathbf{q}^{(p)} + \mathbf{q}^{(p-1)}}{h^2}$$

We now have a calculus problem: find the n quaternions $\mathbf{q}^{(p)}$ that minimize the scalar function $E(\mathbf{q})$ subject to the above constraints. Without the angular velocity constraints we let $p_{\min} = 2$ and $p_{\max} = n - 1$.

4.4 Angular velocity constraints

Sometimes, we may wish to stipulate that angular velocities $\boldsymbol{\omega}^{\text{first}}$ and $\boldsymbol{\omega}^{\text{last}}$ apply to the first and last rotations along the path.

We can stipulate that the angular velocity is constant over the time interval $-h \le t \le 0$ and $t_K \le t \le t_K + h$. We reduce the problem with angular velocity constraints into the previous case, creating new quaternions and new constraints $\mathbf{q}^{(0)} = \mathbf{Q}^0$ and $\mathbf{q}^{(n+1)} = \mathbf{Q}^{K+1}$. To compute $\mathbf{Q}^0$, let

$$\begin{aligned} \boldsymbol{\omega} &= \boldsymbol{\omega}^{\text{first}}, \\ \theta &= h\,|\boldsymbol{\omega}| \\ \hat{\boldsymbol{\omega}} &= \boldsymbol{\omega}/|\boldsymbol{\omega}| \\ \mathbf{Q}^0 &= \begin{pmatrix} \cos(\theta/2) \\ -\sin(\theta/2)\,\hat{\boldsymbol{\omega}} \end{pmatrix} \mathbf{Q}^1 \end{aligned}$$

To compute $\mathbf{Q}^{K+1}$, let

$$\begin{aligned} \boldsymbol{\omega} &= \boldsymbol{\omega}^{\text{last}}, \\ \theta &= h\,|\boldsymbol{\omega}| \\ \hat{\boldsymbol{\omega}} &= \boldsymbol{\omega}/|\boldsymbol{\omega}| \\ \mathbf{Q}^{K+1} &= \begin{pmatrix} \cos(\theta/2) \\ \sin(\theta/2)\,\hat{\boldsymbol{\omega}} \end{pmatrix} \mathbf{Q}^K \end{aligned}$$

Thus, the method involving angular velocity constraints is merely a renumbered version of the previous method. We let $p_{\min} = 1$ and $p_{\max} = n$, to add the two points. These points are the two smaller dots in figure 8.

5 Numerical derivatives on the 3-sphere

There are three problems that typically arise when using numerical methods to approximate derivatives on a manifold. First, some derivative formulas are not centered – they approximate the derivative, but not at the specified point. Secondly, there is a *numerical accuracy* problem – numerical approximations of the derivative typically will not lie in the tangent plane. Finally, there can be an *aliasing* problem, particularly for paths which circumnavigate the sphere or travel in tight loops. The aliasing problem greatly accentuates the numerical accuracy problem.

We compute our numerical derivatives using the centered three point formula for the second derivative shown in section 4.3. To solve the aliasing problem, we must choose n, the number of samples of $q^{(p)}$ to be large enough so that aliasing effects are not significant. To reduce aliasing, we suggest maintaining enough interpolation points so that adjacent $q^{(p)}$s do not travel more than $\pm 1/4$ way around the sphere, which can be tested via the condition $q^{(p)} \cdot q^{(p+1)} > 0$. For instance, between antipodal keyframe quaternions, two or more intervening interpolation points are needed.

For the angular velocity constraint, a similar condition suggests maintaining

$$|\theta| < \pi/2.$$

This implies that we need $n > \frac{2}{\pi}|d| \, t_{\max}$ steps, where $|d|$ is the magnitude of the larger of the two angular velocities.

6 Implementing the discrete derivative method

The most reliable way to implement the algorithm, whether or not angular velocity constraints are used, is to use a constrained optimization package for sparse systems, such as the MINOS package [MURTAGH&SAUNDERS 83]. Any method which solves for the $q^{(p)}$ can be used, as long as it minimizes $E(q)$, subject to the constraints. By using first and second derivatives of the energy function $E(q)$, you can speed up the solutions significantly.

An advantage of this approach is that the packaged algorithms implement a robust convergence test, to determine when the optimal solution is found.

6.1 Augmented Lagrangian constraints

If the implementer does not wish to use prepackaged algorithms, a practical approach is to implement a variation of the Lagrangian methods in [PLATT 88], using first-derivative information. (We leave the implementation of faster methods, with quadratic convergence, as future work.)

First, you need the constraint function which keeps the p-th quaternion on the unit sphere

$$g_p(\mathbf{q}) = \mathbf{q}^{(p)} \cdot \mathbf{q}^{(p)} - 1$$

Then construct a total energy $F(\mathbf{q})$ by adding the constraint and penalty terms

$$F(\mathbf{q}) = E(\mathbf{q}) + \sum_{p=p_{\min}}^{p_{\max}} \lambda_p \, g_p(\mathbf{q}) + c \, (g_p(\mathbf{q}))^2$$

and take its derivative with respect to $q_\ell^{(r)}$ and with respect to λ_r

$$\frac{\partial}{\partial q_\ell^{(r)}} F(\mathbf{q}) = \frac{\partial}{\partial q_\ell^{(r)}} E(\mathbf{q}) + 2 \sum_{p=1}^{n} (\lambda_p + c) \, q_\ell^{(r)}, \text{ where}$$

$$\frac{\partial}{\partial q_\ell^{(r)}} E(\mathbf{q}) = \frac{(q'' \setminus q)_\ell^{(r-1)}}{h^2} - \frac{2 \, (q'' \setminus q)_\ell^{(r)}}{h^2} - \frac{q_j^{(r)} q_j^{(r)''} (q'' \setminus q)_\ell^{(r)}}{q_k^{(r)^2}} + \frac{(q'' \setminus q)_\ell^{(r+1)}}{h^2}$$

If $r \in [p_{\min} + 1, p_{\max} - 1]$, the above equation is valid. If $r = p_{\min} - 1$, only the $r + 1$ term applies and the others are deleted; if $r = p_{\min}$, the $r + 1$ and r terms apply, but the first term is deleted; if $r = p_{\max} + 1$, only the first term applies, while if $r = p_{\max}$, the first three terms apply.

Then, set up the differential equations

$$\frac{d}{ds} q_\ell^{(r)} = -\frac{\partial}{\partial q_\ell^{(r)}} F(\mathbf{q}), \quad r \neq p_i$$
$$\frac{d}{ds} q_\ell^{(r)} = 0, \quad r = p_i$$
$$\frac{d}{ds} \lambda_r = +g_r(\mathbf{q})$$

and set up appropriate initial conditions:

$$q_\ell^{(r)}(0) = Q_\ell^i \quad r = p_i, \quad i = 1, \cdots, K, \quad \ell = 0, 1, 2, 3.$$
$q_\ell^{(r)}(0) = $ interpolated values between the Q_ℓ^is, either flat-space or results from previous runs with smaller numbers of points. Better initial conditions significantly improve the speed of this method
$$\lambda_p = 1$$

Numerically solve the differential equations with an automatic step-size method (such as Adams method), until you reach sufficiently constant values. This heuristic "stop" condition is why we advocate using packaged optimization algorithms, which have robust stop conditions.

It is recommended that the program be structured so that output from a smaller number of interpolated points can be used to set up the initial conditions for a run with a larger number of interpolated points.[6]

---

[6]You can also transform the variables in the differential equation via $s = 1 + 1/(\sigma - 1)$, essentially scaling the right hand side by $1/(1 - \sigma^2)$. The solution will then be found at $\sigma = 1$, rather than at $s = \infty$; you can iterate, numerically integrating the transformed differential equation repeatedly from 0 to 0.999 until the termination condition is reached.

7 Results

In the following figures, we show quaternion points visualized in three dimensions: we chose quaternions with the **k** component set to zero. Internally, of course, the implementation is fully four dimensional. We implemented augmented Lagrangian constraints, as well as a prepackaged version. The two methods agreed within the prescribed tolerances.

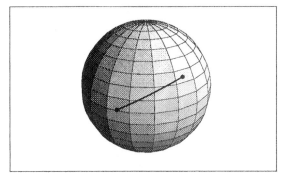

Figure 4a. Two keyframe rotations, without angular velocity constraints (shown as dots) on the interpolated path.

Figure 4b. The corresponding rotational path of the object. The two yellow objects are the two keyframe rotations, while the green images are the interpolated values. For clarity, we draw only a subset of the interpolated values.

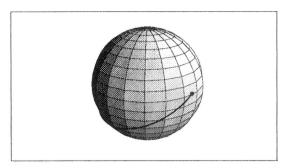

Figure 5a. We go half-way around the quaternion sphere for the same initial and final rotation, by choosing the antipodal point, $-\mathbf{Q}^1$. We rotate more fully around in space.

Figure 5b. The rotational path of the object in 5a.

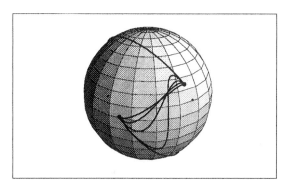

Figure 6a. Here we specify asymmetric angular velocity constraints, doubling until the path goes around the sphere.

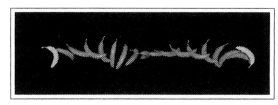

Figure 6b. The object rotates twice around.

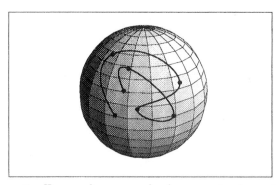

Figure 7a. Here we have seven keyframe quaternion points; there are 199 interpolated points.

Figure 7b. The seven keyframe rotations are clearly visible.

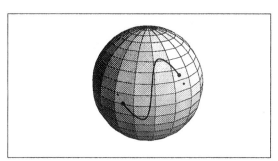

Figure 8. Symmetric angular velocity constraints are applied to the same endpoints in 4a. Note the two extra points, $\mathbf{Q}^0$ and $\mathbf{Q}^{K+1}$, drawn with smaller dots off of the curve.

Notes. In the figures, the keyframe quaternions are drawn with larger dots, while the keyframe quaternions from the angular velocity constraints are drawn with smaller dots. Note the qualitative similarity with flat-space splines. The banana rotates more in figure 5b than in 4b, due to the antipodal representation of the left rotation. Since the algorithm finds local minima, a different solution with a different number of loops might turn out to be the absolute minimum. The method, for large numbers of points, prefers good initial conditions, such as those produced by the algorithm with fewer points.

For figures 7a and 7b, 32 interpolation points are used in each interval, for a total of 199 points. The schedule of increasing points in each interval was $5 \Rightarrow 8 \Rightarrow 16 \Rightarrow 32$. The total computation time on an HP 700 was less than four minutes.

8   Conclusions

We have presented a new technique to smoothly interpolate rotations using quaternions. The method uses an extrinsic version of Kajiya and Gabriel's bend-minimization to characterize a spline in the quaternion 3-sphere; such splines are natural generalizations of splines in Euclidean space, and are particularly amenable to solution on the 3-sphere. We use a numerical method to determine several points between the key orientations; Shoemake's slerping can be applied to the points; the resulting splines are smooth, and have the desirable property that they pass through their control points exactly.

Our preliminary results are favorable, but there is much that can still be done to improve on this technique. We believe that splining in curved spaces will be of increasing importance to computer graphics, and predict many future generalizations.

Acknowledgements

The authors wish to thank Mark Montague, John Snyder, David Laidlaw, and Jeff Goldsmith at the Caltech graphics lab, as well as the Siggraph reviewers, for numerous helpful suggestions. The banana database is a generative model made by John Snyder and Jed Lengyel. This research was supported by the NSF/DARPA STC for Computer Graphics and Scientific Visualization, and by grants from HP, IBM, DEC and NCR to the university laboratories.

References

[1] R. Bartels, J. Beatty, and B. Barsky. *An Introduction to Splines for Use in Computer Graphics and Geometric Modeling.* Morgan Kaufmann, Los Angeles, 1987.

[2] S. Gabriel and J. Kajiya. Spline interpolation in curved space. In "State of the Art Image Synthesis," Course notes for SIGGRAPH '85, 1985.

[3] W. R. Hamilton. *Lectures on Quaternions.* Hodges and Smith, Dublin, 1853.

[4] D. Kochanek and R. Bartels. Interpolating splines with local tension, continuity, and bias control. *Computer Graphics*, 18(3):33–41, July 1984.

[5] R. S. Millman and G. D. Parker. *Elements of Differential Geometry.* Prentice-Hall, Englewood Cliffs, NJ, 1977.

[6] B. A. Murtagh and M. A. Saunder. MINOS 5.0 user's guide. Technical Report SOL 83-20, Dept. of Operations Research, Stanford University, 1983.

[7] Ltd Numerical Algorithms Group. NAG Fortran library routine document, 1988.

[8] J. Platt. Constraint methods for flexible models. *Computer Graphics*, 22(4):279–288, July 1988.

[9] W.H. Press, B.P. Flannery, S.A. Teukolskym, and W.T. Vetterling. *Numerical Recipes in C...* Cambridge Univ. Press, Cambridge, England, 1988.

[10] K. Shoemake. Animating rotation with quaternion curves. *Computer Graphics*, 19(3):245–254, July 1985.

[11] M. Spivak. *A Comprehensive Introduction to Differential Geometry.* Publish or Perish, Inc., Boston, 1970.

[12] D. Zwillinger. *Handbook of Differential Equations.* Academic Press, San Diego, 1989.

Appendix A: Preprocessing Step to Create Spin

First, convert the K rotation matrices into K quaternions (see Shoemake or other quaternion reference for details). Then choose the desired spinning behavior of the objects between the quaternions. Sometimes, the object is desired to undergo an odd number of full spins around on an interval (usually once). These will be the "odd" intervals (and the other intervals are regarded as "even," which usually do not spin around). Multiplying a quaternion by -1 does not change the orientation it represents, but it does change whether or not an even or odd number of full-spins around the object takes place. The dot product of adjacent keyframe quaternions should be greater than or equal to zero for the even intervals, and less than zero for the odd ones. Multiply the quaternion by by -1 to change the interval from one state to the other.

CONDOR: Constraint-Based Dataflow

Michael Kass

Apple Computer
Advanced Technology Group
20525 Mariani Ave., Cupertino, CA 95014

ABSTRACT

CONDOR is an interactive constraint-based dataflow programming environment which is particularly suited to problems that arise in computer graphics. In addition to traditional dataflow functions, CONDOR dataflow elements can perform efficient derivative evaluation and interval arithmetic. As a result, CONDOR is able to support constraints, dynamics, surface trimming, collision testing, and a variety of other computations which are difficult or impossible to implement in traditional dataflow systems. CONDOR includes a graphical interface in which mathematical functions are represented as boxes with vector or scalar inputs and outputs. The functions can be composed by interactively connecting together their inputs and outputs. CONDOR performance is sufficiently fast to make it suitable for creating shaders, parametric surfaces, and complex constrained models.

Keywords: Optimization, Dataflow, Constraints, Graphical Programming.

I. INTRODUCTION

CONDOR (**CON**straints **D**ynamics **O**bjects and **R**elationships) is an experimental interactive dataflow programming environment particularly suited to computer graphics problems. It consists of three parts. The first is a compiler which turns textual specifications of mathematical functions into efficient C++ implementations of corresponding dataflow elements. The second is a graphical user interface which allows these functions to be interactively composed and manipulated to express complex mathematical relationships. The third is a set of utilities which perform specialized operations on dataflow networks such as optimization, surface trimming and rendering. Together, they form a powerful tool for exploring a wide range of computations that arise in computer graphics.

Dataflow architectures[1] have some well known weaknesses which have limited their use for general computation. Among other things, flow of control is usually awkward if not impossible to express, and operations with side effects can pose severe difficulties because the order of evaluation is hard to specify. Nonetheless, dataflow architectures have been widely used in computer graphics (e.g. [2; 3]) largely because a wide variety of important computer graphics problems can be easily cast in dataflow form. Most shaders, for example[4], are easily put in dataflow form because they rarely use side effects or intricate flow of control. Parametric surfaces and spatial deformations are also very suitable for dataflow representation because they are usually expressed by pure mathematical mappings from one space to another. The standard "graphics pipeline" found in many workstations consists of a series of operations which are easily expressed in dataflow form.

For computer graphics, an important limitation of traditional dataflow systems is that they often fail to provide sufficient metadata, particularly information about how an output depends on inputs. CONDOR addresses this limitation by providing two valuable and unusual types of metadata which greatly expand its range of usefulness. The first is sparse derivative information and the second is interval information. CONDOR can rapidly determine which inputs an output port depends on, and what its derivatives are with respect to those inputs. In addition, if bounds are placed on the inputs, CONDOR can evaluate a bound on the output using interval arithmetic[5].

The availability of metadata makes it possible to implement a number of efficient numerical algorithms within CONDOR and apply them to a variety of computer graphics problems. The derivative evaluation has been designed to be suitable for optimization and the solution of ordinary and partial differential equations. The interval arithmetic has been designed for surface intersection and trimming calculations, as well as ray-surface intersections, tesselation of implicit surfaces and problems which require guaranteed root finding.

Thus far, the most extensive use of CONDOR's derivative evaluation has been in optimization. Problems suitable for optimization arise very frequently in the course of computer-graphics modeling and animation, so having a computer graphics systems with built-in optimization capabilities can be of great value. An important set of optimization problems in computer graphics involve inverse problems such as computing the joint angles necessary to place the foot of a figure on the ground (inverse kinematics). Some involve real-world data, such as the problem of computing the camera parameters for live video from the positions of a few reference points. Many are geometrical in nature and involve some type of shape optimization or constraint solving[6]. A very difficult set arises from trying to create physically-based character animation[7].

The most extensive use of CONDOR's interval arithmetic capability has been to compute intersection points of parametric surfaces for use in trimming operations. Interval arithmetic makes it possible to provide strong guarantees about the intersection points of extremely general parametric surfaces. There is no need to be limited to piecewise tensor product rational polynomials or some other set of primitives. Interval arithmetic can directly handle trigonometric functions and many other transcendentals. A variety of recent graphics algorithms make use of interval techniques (e.g. [8; 9; 10]).

The compiler built for CONDOR automatically generates code necessary for computing the derivative and interval arithmetic metadata. In addition, it generates very efficient code for the basic dataflow function evaluation. Experience with CONDOR has made it clear that this, even apart from the metadata, is a valuable capability. By wiring together dataflow elements in CONDOR, functions can be constructed and modified interactively, yet they can be evaluated very efficiently. Example of the use of this capability in CONDOR include interactively creating and modifying parametric surfaces, warping images, and constructing surface shaders for rendering purposes.

Section II. details the motivation and design goals of CONDOR and a general outline of how they were addressed. Section III. compares and contrasts CONDOR with prior work in light of those goals. Next, sections IV. through VII. discuss the details of the compiler, the function and metadata evaluation, the user interface, and the utilities. Finally section VIII. goes through a series of examples showing the ordinary dataflow capabilities of CONDOR as well as those based on its optimization and interval arithmetic metadata.

II. APPROACH

CONDOR was primarily intended as an interactive research testbed for computer graphics modeling, animation and rendering. Its main design goal was to approach the performance of hand-crafted code while providing an interactive programming environment to explore a wide variety of computer graphics computations. The idea was to create an exploratory system with performance sufficient for practical problems, so there would rarely be a need to re-implement CONDOR computations with special purpose code to achieve satisfactory performance.

The performance requirements for CONDOR dictated the use of a very efficient programming language supporting high speed floating point calculation. This effectively ruled out languages such as Lisp and Smalltalk for the function and metadata evaluation despite their merits for supporting ease of modification. In the end, C++ was chosen as the language for the run-time system because it allowed careful control of performance while providing the amenities of an object-oriented language.

In order to provide most of the flexibility of an interpreter while limiting the associated speed penalty, CONDOR relies on dynamic composition of compiled functions to compute dataflow outputs and metadata. Each dataflow element is associated with compiled functions which compute its output, its interval bounds and its derivatives. CONDOR uses a compiler to generate these functions to avoid the labor and potential for error inherent in creating them by hand. In some cases, the compiler can create code which is more efficient than code written by hand because of its symbolic mathematics, exhaustive common-subexpression elimination and loop unwinding.

When dataflow elements are wired together, CONDOR creates an expression tree which is used to control function and metadata evaluation. Storage is pre-allocated for intermediate results, so the tree can be traversed with minimum overhead. When computing the dataflow function or its interval bounds, evaluation consists of little more than a series of calls to compiled functions given by a set of pointers in the expression tree. As long as a dataflow element does substantial computation inside its compiled function, the overhead in following pointers in the expression tree is a small part of the total running time.

Evaluation of derivative information is somewhat different from the other evaluations. There are two general approaches available for computing derivatives of dataflow elements: numerical and symbolic differentiation. Numerical differentiation is much easier to code, but the results are less reliable than symbolic differentiation because the function has to be evaluated at nearby points. If the points are too far apart, the derivative estimate is poor. If the points are too close, numerical precision may limit the accuracy of the result. In addition, numerical differentiation can waste time evaluating derivatives which are always zero, but symbolic differentiation methods can detect such cases and thereby achieve important efficiency gains. For these reasons, CONDOR computes first derivatives of dataflow elements using compiled functions that evaluate their symbolic derivatives. First derivatives of expression trees are computed using the chain rule. Since the chain rule becomes somewhat unwieldy for second derivatives, CONDOR relies on numerical second derivatives calculated from symbolic first derivatives. This appears to be a good compromise. The symbolic first derivatives provide most of the valuable information about sparsity and the numerical second derivatives keep the complexity of the entire system to a manageable level.

The CONDOR compiler takes mathematical descriptions of dataflow elements and creates the set of functions necessary to support function and metadata evaluation. The compiler is written in Lisp and uses Mathematica[11] to do the required symbolic differentiation and simplification. The output of the compiler is very efficient, streamlined C++ code which is linked in with the CONDOR application. Note that neither Lisp nor Mathematica is called at run time. They are used only to generate C++ code. At run-time, all the code is C++, so the run-time speed is unaffected by the performance of either Lisp or Mathematica. While this odd assortment of programming languages may seem a little baroque,[1] each language is used in the domain for which it was designed: C++ for speed, Mathematica for symbolic mathematics, and Lisp for traversing and manipulating lists.

Connecting together dataflow elements into expression trees requires some kind of interface: CONDOR provides an object oriented C++ interface for programs and a graphical user interface. While it is probably possible to build similar capabilities into an interactive textual interface, the direct manipulation of the graphical interface lends an intangible satisfying element to the use of the system and makes certain types of operations particularly easy. In the user interface, dataflow elements are depicted by rectangles, so the the dataflow elements have come to be known as function blocks.

Having used the graphical interface to specify a dataflow computation, the user can interactively invoke several utilities which operate on these functions. One of the most useful of these is the optimizer. With the efficient derivative evaluation supplied by CONDOR, any of a wide variety of optimization algorithms can be used. The one currently implemented is a Newton's method with step-size control[12]. The gradient and sparse Hessian matrix provide a local quadratic approximation to the objective function. Based on this information, the optimizer computes a minimum of the quadratic approximation (safeguarded with step-size control) by using sparse LU decomposition and then moves towards the minimum. After each step, it re-evaluates the gradient and Hessian to construct a new quadratic approximation to the objective function. Iteration continues until some termination condition is met.

The CONDOR graphical user interface provides special mechanisms for the user to specify that a given dataflow function is to represent a parametric curve, surface, or shader. These curves and surfaces can be rendered interactively with a Z-buffer, or tesselated and written out to files in formats suitable for other renderers. In addition, parametric surfaces can be trimmed against each other using the interval bounds.

---

1. It is.

CONDOR is a system still under active development. The basic function and metadata evaluation has been stable for some time, but new utilities and features are constantly being added. Building the new utilities into CONDOR means that they immediately benefit from the efficient function and metadata evaluation, the graphical user interface and the interactive visualization capabilities of the system.

III. PRIOR WORK

In terms of motivation and general approach, CONDOR is most properly viewed as an evolutionary descendent of the math compiler described in [7] combined with some of the modeling capabilities of [3]. The design of CONDOR benefits enormously from experience with each of these systems.

Like the math compiler described in [7], CONDOR solves optimization problems posed graphically by wiring together visual representations of mathematical functions. Evolutionary improvements in CONDOR include the use of a direct L-U matrix solver instead of a conjugate gradient solver and a different method of handling sparse matrices which avoids a long pre-processing step before commencing optimization. The direct matrix solution and the fact that it is written in C++ instead of Lisp gives CONDOR substantially better performance. For banded systems, the direct matrix solution is the difference between O(n) and O(n^2) computation. In addition, CONDOR's graphical interface provides a variety of improvements such as the ability to change arbitrarily between vector and scalar representations, to create dataflow elements with variable numbers of inputs, and to create hierarchies of dataflow elements. More significantly, CONDOR adds interval arithmetic to the metadata and combines optimization with integrated modeling and visualization capabilities.

Like the modeling testbed described in [3], CONDOR provides facilities which allow a user to specify deformed parametric surfaces graphically[13]. Unlike the testbed, the same type of graphical programming can be used in CONDOR to specify shading calculations and motion paths as well. The uniformity of representation in CONDOR makes it possible, for example, to optimize and thereby constrain any parameter which appears in the computation, whether related to rendering, modeling, or animation path.

The graphical interface of CONDOR has many similarities with other graphical programming environments such as Fabrik[14], ConMan[2] and even the early animation system EOM[15] From a system-level perspective, the chief differences have to do with CONDOR's metadata capabilities. In addition, Fabrik suffers in performance because it is written in Smalltalk, while ConMan's performance is limited for small-grain computations by the speed of UNIX pipes.

The value of flexible yet high-performance calculations for shading has been well established since Cook's work on shade trees[16]. Since then, there have been a variety of attempts to create rapid interactive environments for constructing shaders. Abram and Whitted describe a graphical programming system[17] designed for just such a purpose. While CONDOR has not been specifically tailored to the demands of constructing shade trees, it does have substantial capabilities in this regard, and it derives a great deal of additional power from being able to use the same operations and graphical language to express geometry, constraints, motion and shading.

IV. CONDOR COMPILER

The CONDOR compiler is designed to convert concise mathematical descriptions of function blocks into definitions of very efficient C++ objects that compute the functions and associated metadata. The compiler is implemented in Common Lisp[18] and runs on Silicon Graphics 4D workstations. It uses a Unix pipe interface to Mathematica in order to compute symbolic derivatives.

The compiler parses the Mathematica output into a Lisp list which represents an expression tree. Before doing final code generation, the compiler does exhaustive common-subexpression elimination by putting the expression tree and all its subexpressions in a hash table. Any expression entered into the hash table more than once is flagged as a common subexpression. Common subexpressions which occur only inside of a single larger common subexpression are eliminated. The remaining common-subexpressions are used to generate assignment statements which precede the evaluation of the function or its derivatives.

The following is an example of the definition used for a cubic Catmull-Rom spline.

```
(defoptimize
    :name "CRSpline"
    :initially
      (string-append
        "MAT = {{-1,3,-3,1},{2,-5,4,-1},{-1,0,1,0},{0,2,0,0}}/2;"
        "U={u^3,u^2,u,1};  P = {a,b,c,d};  Y = U.MAT.P")·
    :inputs '(|u| |a| |b| |c| |d|)
    :outputs '((|Y| "Y") (|Yu| "D[Y,u]")(|Yuu| "D[D[Y,u],u]")))
```

The argument following ":initially" in the definition is a string sent to Mathematica before evaluating anything else. The syntax is a strange mixture of Lisp and Mathematica, but it specifies that the inputs to the function box are the spline parameter u and the four knot points a, b, c and d, while the outputs are the position Y of the spline, its derivative Yu with respect to the spline parameter u, and its second derivative Yuu. From this definition, the compiler generates a C++ class definition, a constructor, a structure describing the number and names of the inputs and outputs, a function to compute the value of each of the outputs, an interval arithmetic function, and a function for each output that computes the gradient of the output with respect to each of the inputs. The full output of the compiler from this definition amounts to 134 lines of C++ code. While the full output is too long to reproduce here, the following is the part of the compiler output which computes the gradient of Yu with respect to the inputs u, a, b, c and d.

```
void  CRSplineDeriv1(Real* in, Real* out)
{
  Real u, a, b, c, d;
  u = in[0];
  a = in[1];
  b = in[2];
  c = in[3];
  d = in[4];
{
  Real comsub1;
  comsub1 = u*u;
  out[0] = b*(-5 + 9*u) + d*(-1 + 3*u) + a*(2 - 3*u) + c*(4 - 9*u);
  out[1] = 2*u + comsub1*-3/2 -1/2;
  out[2] = -5*u + comsub1*9/2;
  out[3] = 4*u + comsub1*-9/2 + 1/2;
  out[4] = -u + comsub1*3/2;
}}
```

Note that the compiler effectively unwinds the implied loops in the matrix multiplication because everything is reduced to a single expression tree. Also note that the zeros in the matrix drop out of the expression due to the symbolic algebra -- this is an optimization that programmers are unlikely to do by hand. In addition to generating the C++ code for the new object, the compiler modifies the "make" file for the application, adds the new object to the application menu and adds the new object to a table, so it can be saved and retrieved. All that remains in order to be able to use the new object is to compile and link the application. In future, some form of dynamic linking will be used, but at present, the entire application has to be relinked.

V. FUNCTION AND METADATA EVALUATION

CONDOR uses a function evaluation scheme based on a dataflow model[1]. Values can be regarded as flowing from inputs of function boxes to their outputs and then propagating to connected inputs. For efficiency considerations, CONDOR uses a "Pull" version of dataflow evaluation with caching. If a function block is asked to evaluate its output, it first evaluates all of its inputs, then evaluates the appropriate function of its inputs and passes on the value. This should be contrasted with the "Push" model in which changed input values automatically propagate through the tree. The result of the "Pull" model is a depth-first evaluation of the expression tree. To prevent excess function evaluations, each function block caches the last set of output values it has computed and can return them without further computation if its inputs have not changed. Anytime a value is changed in the network, a cache-invalidate signal is "Pushed" through the graph, informing affected function-blocks that they will have to recompute their outputs the next time they are evaluated. Cache-invalidate signals need not be propagated past function blocks with caches that are already invalid. This method of pulling values with caching appears to prevent unnecessary function evaluations in most cases of interest. It prevents, for example, excess matrix multiplies when rendering models of standard articulated figures. The caches end up implementing the storage traditionally implemented in a transformation matrix stack.

Interval calculations are done with a small modification of the basic function evaluation where all the inputs and outputs are replaced with intervals. Using C++ overloading, ordinary mathematical functions are extended to interval arguments. For example the operator + is overloaded so that if x is the interval ($xmin$, $xmax$) and y is the interval ($ymin$, $ymax$) then x+y evaluates to the interval ($xmin+ymin$, $xmax+ymax$). The interval function for each operator has the property that if the inputs of the ordinary function lie within the input intervals, then the outputs of the ordinary function must lie within the output intervals. Interval functions are composed and cached in exactly the same way as ordinary functions.

Like the ordinary and interval-function evaluation, derivative evaluation is performed by depth-first pulling. Before it can start, a table of all changeable input variables is constructed. Each function block in turn is asked to supply a list of its inputs which are neither frozen nor connected to the output of another function block. These are given global indices and constitute the state variables of the optimization or differential equation.

Once state variables have been identified, the basic derivative operation provided by CONDOR is the evaluation of the gradient of any output. For efficiency, CONDOR uses a sparse representation of gradient vectors, maintaining a linked list of the non-zero components. Derivatives within a function block are evaluated using code generated by the compiler, and these derivatives are composed recursively using the chain rule.

Second derivatives are estimated from first derivatives by finite-differencing. When a complete sparse Hessian matrix is needed, it is constructed from the sparse gradients by finite-differencing and is represented by a data structure containing a list of the non-zero elements of each row. Function blocks which numerically integrate their inputs evaluate the sparse Hessian for each element of the sum and add them together. This frequently results in a banded or otherwise regular pattern of sparsity.

The visualization function boxes work somewhat differently from the others because they inherently involve the side effect of displaying something on the screen. When the "Draw" or "Render" command is executed, the visualization boxes pull the required data through the dataflow diagram and display the results. The Circle box, for example, pulls its radius and position through the dataflow tree and then displays a corresponding circle in the visualization window when the "Draw" command is exe-

cuted. Parametric curves and surfaces require a slightly different treatment. In CONDOR, they are represented with split nodes -- one which generates the parameters, and one which accepts the position and possibly color of a curve or surface point. When asked to "Draw" or "Render," the split nodes do a series of evaluations through the dataflow tree to tesselate and display the curve or surface. To evaluate each point on the curve or surface, they set the parameters (pushing a cache-invalidate signal) and then pull the position and/or color information through the tree.

VI. CONDOR USER INTERFACE

CONDOR provides a graphical user interface designed in the Macintosh tradition of pull-down menus, noun-verb interaction and direct manipulation. To facilitate its use with both high-performance graphics supercomputers and personal computers, the user interface was built using InterViews[19], a portable, public domain, C++ object-oriented user-interface toolkit using X-windows. InterViews was ported to use the Macintosh Toolbox when running on Macintoshes and the Silicon Graphics GL when running on Silicon Graphics workstations. The resulting performance is acceptable on both high-end Apple Macintosh computers and SGI IRIS 4D graphics workstations. In addition, a native Macintosh implementation of most of the CONDOR functionality has been embedded in Graphite, an experimental modeler in use in the Apple Computer Advanced Technology Group.

Fig. 1 shows a sample screen-image of CONDOR in use. The user has created and wired together five adder and multiplier function blocks to specify a simple optimization problem. New boxes are selected from the menus and wired together by clicking and dragging.

Each function block appears with its inputs on the bottom and its outputs on the top. Computed values flow from the output of one function box to the input of another along connections displayed as splines. Any input which is not connected to the output of another box contains a numeric value which the user can set. During the course of an optimization or a differential equation, the values can be changed unless the user freezes them by selecting the inputs and then choosing the "Freeze" command from the edit menu. Frozen inputs are displayed in blue and are regarded as constants for optimization and differential equations.

A function to be optimized can be selected by picking an output and choosing the "Minimize" command from the Edit menu. Any output selected for minimization is drawn in green. For convenience, several outputs can be selected for minimization at once. As far as the optimizer is concerned, this means that the objective function is the sum of the outputs that have been selected.

Fig. 2 shows a small subset of the different boxes that CONDOR supports. Additional boxes can be created very easily with the compiler. Inputs or outputs labelled with numbers in brackets are vectors. Creating a connection between a vector input and a vector output connects each component together. The user interface does not allow connections between inputs and outputs of different vector lengths. No distinction is made between scalars and vectors of length one. Note the adder box at the bottom of the figure. Adders and many other function boxes can be created with vector inputs of any length. This adder has its second input displayed as a sequence of three scalars (b0, b1, and b2) because the user selected the second input and chose the "To Scalar" command from the Edit menu. All vector inputs and outputs can be freely changed back and forth to scalars for convenience.

The box labelled CRSpline is the Catmull-Rom spline defined in section IV. The Dot box is a dot product which is available with variable numbers of inputs.

The Circle, Curve and Surf boxes are special boxes for visualization or rendering purposes. When the "Draw" command is executed, the Circle box draws a circle in a separate drawing window at the position given by its vector x input with a radius given by its r input. The Curve object is used to draw a parametric curve in the drawing window. It is represented visually by two blocks, one which generates values of the parameter u and one which accepts position values. To specify a curve, the user wires up a diagram which computes x as a function of u. Parametric surfaces are handled similarly with the Surf object except that one block generates u,v values while the other block accepts positions in three dimensions and an associated color. Surf objects are tesselated, Gouraud shaded and Z-buffered when drawn.

The Time box outputs a special global value which is controlled by the VCR buttons just below the menu bar. Combined with the visualization capabilities of the drawing objects, it provides a means of creating animation. When the VCR play button ">" is pressed, CONDOR displays an animation by sequentially changing the value of the time variable and drawing the results. Complex scenes can be computed frame by frame and written to files or directly to single-frame animation equipment by using the "Animate" command.

The Mouse box outputs the position and button state of the mouse. This is particularly useful when CONDOR is in a continuous optimization or display loop. As the mouse is moved, the objective function can be changed interactively. In addition, if CONDOR is told to minimize the product of an objective function and a mouse button, then the mouse button effectively turns the objective function on and off.

The Compound box is used for creating hierarchies of boxes. In order to use this facility, the user creates a compound box, opens it up and creates input and output boxes. Any series of other boxes can be connected between the inputs and outputs. When the compound box is closed, it appears again as a single box with the corresponding inputs and outputs. For convenience, it can be relabelled with a more meaningful name.

The Wire box is used to send a value from one part of a diagram to another without a connecting spline. Some have suggested that a better name would be "Wireless." It is designed to mimic the convention for connecting signals across long distances in electrical circuit diagrams by naming them at both ends. Wires can be given labels which denote the values they carry.

Binders are function boxes which simulate the parameter binding that occurs when subroutines are called in conventional computer languages. They save certain inputs of other boxes, change them to new values, evaluate the outputs and then restore the original input values. Their main value is that they allow arbitrary portions of a diagram to be used for multiple purposes. The binder in the diagram computes the value of the Yu output of the CRSpline box with only the b input changed.

The Selector box contains a potentially very long vector of values. Its outputs a,b,c and d are a sequence of values taken from the vector starting at an index given by the integer portion of the time input. For the selector shown in the figure, the values themselves are vectors of length five. The t output of the Selector computes the fractional portion of the time input. Selector boxes are particularly useful for supplying spline knots and neighborhoods of samples for finite-difference problems.

CONDOR supplies a collection of other general function blocks and a large set of problem-specific blocks which are easily constructed with the compiler. The collection is a rapidly expanding moving target as can be expected with an experimental system. Compiler definitions for some of the other function blocks used in the examples can be found in Appendix 1.

VII. CONDOR UTILITIES

Dataflow function composition is useful in many contexts, but it has important limitations for general purpose programming. Recognizing these limitations, CONDOR provides an expanding set of utilities which perform useful operations on functions specified by the dataflow diagrams. The utilities make widespread use of the function and metadata evaluation supplied by CONDOR.

The CONDOR optimizer is the utility responsible for computing the solutions of optimization problems posed with the user interface. Given the state vector, the gradient and the Hessian matrix, a variety of optimization methods are possible[12]. The currently implemented optimizer uses Newton's method with stepsize control. In order to solve the required linear system, the optimizer uses a public domain sparse LU decomposition algorithm from the ACM collected algorithms[20]. The CONDOR optimizer attempts to converge to the nearest local minimum from any given starting point. It does not do global optimization. The user has to pick a suitable starting point for the optimization and cast the problem in such a way that the nearest local minimum will be of value.

The CONDOR ODE solver is in an early stage of development, providing an explicit Runge Kutta integrator and an implicit Euler integrator[21]. Since it has not yet been fully integrated into the user interface, its use has been limited so far. ODEs of physical systems with energy functions are the easiest to handle because their energy functions can be specified the same way as objective functions for optimization. General dissipation terms require extensions to the interface which have not yet been completed.

PDEs are currently handled in CONDOR by using the finite difference or finite element method to express a residual. The residual is then squared and minimized with the optimizer. If the optimizer reduces the residual to zero, the PDE is solved. Sometime in the future, a solver aimed directly at PDEs may be added.

The CONDOR surface trimmer uses interval arithmetic to find intersection points between two parametric surfaces. For any u,v rectangle on a parametric surface, interval arithmetic provides a guaranteed 3D axis-aligned bounding box. It can be thought of as providing a mapping [(umin, umax), (vmin, vmax)] --> [(xmin, xmax), (ymin, ymax), (zmin, zmax)]. To compute intersection points, the surface trimmer begins by finding the bounding boxes corresponding to the whole parameter spaces of the two surfaces. If the bounding boxes do not intersect, then the surfaces do not intersect and the algorithm terminates. If the bounding boxes do intersect, both of the parameter spaces are subdivided in quadtrees. As the parameter-space regions are subdivided, their bounding boxes get smaller and smaller. In regions where the bounding boxes from the two surfaces overlap, the algorithm subdivides until the bounding boxes are smaller than a tolerance. The algorithm can then provide a set of points where the surfaces are guaranteed to intersect within a tolerance, and connected regions of parameter space in which the trimming curve might lie. The surface trimmer connects the intersection points into a trimming curve and triangulates the parameter-space region in such a way that pieces from the two parameter spaces can be joined without cracks. Details of the algorithm can be found in[22].

Other utilities based on interval arithmetic are planned. The CONDOR interval arithmetic capability makes it particularly suited to geometric problems where point sampling gives insufficient information. In triangulating parametric or implicit surfaces, for example, interval arithmetic provides a way to guarantee that small features are not missed. Similarly, interval arithmetic can provide direct guaranteed ray-object intersections for analytic surfaces. Other have used Lipschitz bounds for similar purposes[23; 24], but in most cases, interval arithmetic provides a suitable alternative.

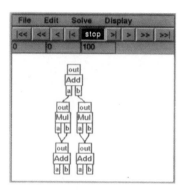

Fig. 1: A quadratic minimization specified with CONDOR.

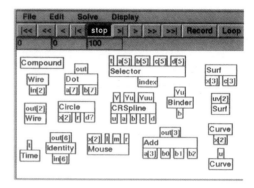

Fig. 2: A selection of different function blocks.

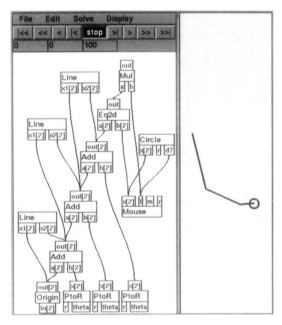

Fig. 3: CONDOR used to compute interactive 2D inverse

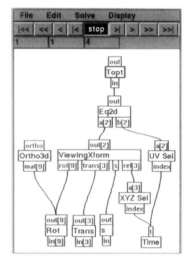

Fig. 4: Recovery of camera parameters from the screen positions of four known points.

VIII. EXAMPLES

The first example of the use of CONDOR is the trivial quadratic optimization in Fig. 1. Since two of the inputs to the adders are frozen, the optimization has only two state variables. Since the optimization function is the sum of two squares, the minimum clearly happens at $f = 0$, which occurs when each of the state variables is the negative of the nearby frozen constant. Without step-size control, CONDOR solves this problem in a single iteration -- as it does any positive-definite quadratic form. With the default step-size control, CONDOR is more conservative, but still converges to machine precision within about 3 iterations.

Fig. 3 shows CONDOR being used to solve a simple 2D inverse kinematics problem. A three-jointed arm is constructed from three PtoR (Polar to Rectangular) boxes, each of which represents a single link of the arm. The links are positioned relative to each other with the Add boxes and drawn using the Line boxes. The EQ2d box computes the squared distance from the mouse to the position of the tip of the arm. When the left mouse button is pressed, this distance is minimized, so the tip of the arm follows the motion of the mouse. CONDOR easily keeps up with interactive speed on simple examples such as this.

Fig. 4 shows CONDOR applied to a problem which occured while trying to rotoscope some movement automatically for the purpose of facial animation[25]. A performer moves around with a series of ultraviolet reflective spots on his face and a set of four spots on a piece of cardboard rigidly connected to his head. When video-taped in ultraviolet light, the spots are very easy to track automatically. For the purpose of the full facial animation, the positions of all the dots are used, but here we consider the problem of computing the transformation from the head coordinate system to the camera screen based on the screen-space projections of the four dots on the piece of cardboard. This problem has been previously addressed with optimization by means of special-purpose code[26; 27]. The point of Fig. 4 is to show that it can be posed and computed easily with CONDOR.

In this problem, we are given the 3D positions of four dots in a reference frame fixed on the piece of cardboard. For convenience, we can chose the reference frame so that the four points form a unit square centered on the origin in the x-y plane. We are also given the 2D positions of these same dots in the image plane. What we would like to find is the set of camera parameters which correspond to this projection. There are seven relevant camera parameters (3 rotation, 3 translation and the field-of view of the camera) and eight measured pieces of data (the x,y positions of the 4 dots), so there is hope of being able to recover the camera transformation.

The expression of this problem in CONDOR initially seems odd to many people, because at the bottom of Fig. 4 we start with the unknowns: the rotation matrix, the translation vector and the field of view, s. This is in contrast to more familiar methods of solving problems where one typically starts with the knowns. The boxes at the bottom represent hypothesized values for the rotation, translation and field of view. We then express a set of constraints on these hypothesized values and let the optimizer solve for them.

There are two selectors which contain data for the optimization. The first, labelled "XYZ Sel," holds the positions of the points in the reference frame on the piece of cardboard. The second, labelled "UV Sel," holds the positions of the observed points on the camera screen. The data in both of these selectors is frozen because it is given in the problem specification. This is denoted in the diagram by the blue color of the selector outputs. The boxes labelled "Viewing Xform" compute the transformation of the known 3D points given the hypothesized camera parameters. The points transformed into 2D are then subtracted from the measured 2D points and the result squared by the Eq2d function block. The TOpt box sums the result over the four points. The TOpt box achieves its minimum value of zero if and only if the hypothesized transformation of the 3D points brings them into the measured 2D positions. There is one further constraint on the problem which is that the rotation matrix should be orthogonal. This is handled by the Ortho3d function block which computes the function $|A A^T - I|^2$ which vanishes if and only if the matrix is orthogonal.

When given a starting point without an incorrect reflection, CONDOR solves the problem of Fig. 4 to nearly three digits accuracy in twenty to thirty Newton iterations, each taking substantially less than a second on a Personal IRIS. As stated, this problem involves a 13 by 13 full Hessian matrix and some difficult non-linearities due to the perspective projection. Given that, the performance is fairly reasonable. There are much more efficent ways of solving the same problem which involve much smaller matrices (e.g. using quaternions for the rotation) -- this was chosen for pedagogical purposes.

Fig. 5a shows an example based on a variational problem: the minimization of the energy of a natural spline. The selector box contains a set of 100 samples of a curve in the plane. Successive points along that curve are used to approximate the second derivative by the formula dxx = (a+b-2c)/h^2. The dot box computes the dot product of the second derivative approximation with itself. This yields the sum of the squares of the second derivatives of the x and y component of the curve. The TOpt box computes the integral of this quantity over time, the parameter of the curve. The user has frozen five points in the selector box with particular values input by hand. The result is a specification of the first-principle from which splines are typically derived. It is well known that the solution of this optimization involves piecewise cubics whose coefficients can be computed from a banded linear system. Faced with this problem, CONDOR constructs a related banded linear system for the raw optimization problem. It solves the system in a fraction of a second on a Silicon Graphics Personal IRIS and requires only a few iterations for convergence.

The function boxes on the right half of Fig. 5a concern the generation of the drawing. The five Circle blocks display the knot points while the Curve boxes draw the curve. The box labelled "Binder" is a Binder function box which points to one of the outputs of the Selector box as a function of time. This allows the drawing and optimization functions to be applied to the same set of data.

The optimization of Fig. 5a is interesting, but the answer exists in closed form. Such is not the case for the closely related optimization of Fig. 5b. In addition to the standard bending energy of a natural spline, CONDOR has been asked to minimize the integral along the curve of a *1/r* repulsion force located at a point given by an Identity box labelled "Repulsor." This time the solution can no longer be expressed as a piecewise cubic, but CONDOR still solves it in a fraction of a second using a similar, but different banded matrix. The ability to experiment rapidly with a variety of curve and surface optimization may well produce important new classes of functions for computer-aided geometrical design. The optimization of Fig. 5b is closely related to some valuable computations in computer vision[28].

Fig. 6 shows CONDOR applied to a spacetime constraint problem[7]. In this problem, we attempt to compute a physically valid motion for a damped spring which is constrained to be at two different places at two different points in time. If the two constrained points were at the very beginning, then this problem could be solved by integrating the differential equation with a standard ODE solver[21]. In this case, however, they are approximately one fourth and one half of the way into the motion, so the problem is most easily posed as an optimization. In Fig. 6a, the displacement of the damped spring is represented by a set of samples, and the constraints are expressed in terms of finite differences. In Fig. 6b, the displacements are represented by a Catmull-Rom spline curve -- effectively using the finite element method. Both minimize the integral along the curve of $(F-ma)^2$. At the minimum, F=ma everywhere along the curve. Both examples converge in a matter of seconds to the same answer, Fig. 6a with one hundred samples on the curve, and Fig. 6b with twenty-five spline segments.

Fig. 7 is an example of CONDOR being used to create a shade tree and connect it to a parametric surface. Roughly speaking, the left side of the dataflow diagram is responsible for modeling and the right side for shading. The u and v parameters of the surface go into a Torus node which computes the positions, tangents and normals of the torus. The torus is then twisted by sending its positions and normals through a Barr[13] Twist transformation and translated by sending the points through an adder. On the right side of the diagram, the *u* and *v* parameters are first remapped using a sinusoidal function of *v* (the PtoR function block computes a polar to rectangular coordinate transform) and then sent to an Image function block. The Image function block takes in a point on an RGB image and outputs a bilinearly interpolated color vector. The resulting color is used by the Phong box which relies on the transformed normals from the twist transformation. The picture was tesselated into 50,000 triangles and displayed in less than 10 seconds on a Personal IRIS. Quite complex shaders and geometry can be constructed at interactive speed.

Fig. 8 shows a simple example using the interval-arithmetic based surface trimming algorithm implemented inside CONDOR[22]. Two intersecting spheres have been trimmed against each other, leaving a sphere with a "bite" taken out. Fig. 8a shows the result of trimming with a fine subdivision. While a very similar image could have been created using ray tracing with CSG, this image was created by triangulating both surfaces. Fig. 8b shows the result with a much coarser subdivision which makes it more evident that the surfaces are triangulated. The triangulations were computed by recursively subdividing the parameter spaces of the two spheres and testing for intersections with interval arithmetic. The algorithm first does a breadth-first subdivision of the parameter spaces and then finds a series of points on the intersection curves by depth-first subdivision. The points are linked together into trimming curves and then the connected regions of the parameter spaces are triangulated. The triangulations of the two pieces share all vertices along the trimming curve, so no cracking can arise. Fig. 8c shows the quadtree subdivision of parameter space used to compute and triangulate the trimmed regions.

IX. CONCLUSION

CONDOR was designed to provide a high-performance exploratory environment for a variety of computer graphics computations. Despite being a fairly general tool, its performance is good enough to make it practical for problems of substantial complexity. For example, it achieves linear-time asymptotic performance on an important class of optimization problems that involve curves or functions of time. For geometry and rendering calculations, the efficiency of the compiler and the function composition make it a powerful interactive tool. The ability to combine these capabilities in a uniform dataflow representation means that geometry, rendering and animation computations can influence each other. This is in contrast to most computer graphics software in which modeling, rendering, and animation are regarded as very separate computations.

Acknowledgements

Special thanks to Andrew Witkin for his role in developing some of the problems which motivated CONDOR and many of the ideas for solving them. Thanks to Pete Litwinowicz and Roger Spreen for porting InterViews and helping debug problems. Roger Spreen also implemented the linear system code used by CONDOR and helped with an early version of the user interface. Michael Gleicher implemented the interval arithmetic operator overloading and the trimming code. Steven Rubin wrote the Macintosh modeler Graphite and ported the function and metadata evaluation of CONDOR to run within Graphite. Thanks to Lance Williams, Larry Tesler and Frank Ludolph for helpful advice and suggestions. Thanks to Frank Crow, Rick Le Faivre, Dave Nagel and the Advanced Technology Group at Apple Computer for supporting this work.

Trademarks: Macintosh is a trademark of Apple Computer Inc. Mathematica is a trademark of Wolfram Research Inc. UNIX is a trademark of AT&T. IRIS is a trademark of Silicon Graphics Inc.

APPENDIX 1

The following are compiler definitions of some of the function boxes used in the examples.

```
(defoptimize
  :name "Viewing Xform"
  :inputs '((|rot| :dims (3 3)) (|transl| :dims (3))
           |s| (|refl| :dims (3)))
  :initially
    (string-append
      "srow = {s,s,1};"
      "Mat = {srow,srow,srow}*Append[rot,trans];"
      "OutVec = Append[ref,1].Mat")
  :outputs '(((|out| :dims (2)) "{OutVec[[1]]/OutVec[[3]],
OutVec[[2]]/OutVec[[3]]}")) )

(defoptimize
  :name "Torus"
  :inputs '(|a| |b| |u| |v| )
  :initially
    (string-append
      "P = {(a + b Cos[u*2*Pi]) Cos[v*2*Pi],"
      "-(a + b Cos[u*2*Pi]) Sin[v*2*Pi],"
      "b Sin[u*2*Pi]};"
      "Tu = D[P,u];"
      "Tv = D[P,v];"
      "C = Cross[Tu,Tv];"
      "Norm = Divide[C,(Sqrt[C.C])];")
  :outputs '(((|X| :dims (3)) "P")
             ((|Tu| :dims (3)) "Tu")
             ((|Tv| :dims (3)) "Tv")
             ((|N| :dims (3)) "Norm")) )

(defoptimize
  :name "Twist"
  :inputs '( (|p| :dims (3)) (|n| :dims (3)) |k|)
  :initially
    (string-append
      "x = p[[1]]; y=p[[2]]; z=p[[3]];"
      "newp = {x,z Sin[k x] + y Cos[k x],z Cos[k x] - y Sin[k x]};"
      "Jac = {D[newp,p[[1]]],D[newp,p[[2]]],D[newp,p[[3]]]};"
      "newn = TrigReduce[Transpose[Inverse[TrigReduce[Jac]]]].n")
  :outputs '(((|p| :dims (3)) "newp") ((|n| :dims (3)) "newn")))
```

REFERENCES

[1]   Davis, A. and Keller, R., "Data flow Program Graphs," *IEEE Computer*, Feb. 1982, p. 26-241

[2]   Haeberli, P., "ConMan: A Visual Programming Language for Interactive Graphics," Proc. of Siggraph '88, p. 103-111.

[3]   Fleischer, K. and Witkin, A., "A Modeling Testbed," *Proc. of Graphics Interface '88*, Edmonton, Alberta, 1988

[4]   Perlin, K. "An Image Synthesizer," *Computer Graphics* 19 (3) Proc. Siggraph '85, 1985 p. 287-296.

[5]   Alefeld, G. and Herzberger, J, "Introduction To Interval Computations," Academic Press, 1983.

[6]   Witkin, A, Fleischer, K., and Barr, A., "Energy Constraints On Parameterized Models," Proc. Siggraph '87, Anaheim, California, 1987.

[7]   Witkin, A. and Kass, M., "Spacetime Constraints," Proc. Siggraph '88, p. 159-168.

[8]   Snyder, J., "Interval Analysis for Computer Graphics," *Proc. Siggraph '92.*

[9]   Duff, T., "Interval Arithmetic and Recursive Subdivision for Implicit Functions and Constructive Solid Geometry," *Proc. Siggraph '92.*

[10] Mitchel, D. and Hanrahan, P.,"Illumination from Curved Reflectors," *Proc. Siggraph '92.*

[11] Wolfram, S., *Mathematica: A System for Doing Mathematics by Computer, Addison-Wesley*, Redwood City, California, 1988.

[12] Gill, E., Murray, W. and Wright, M., *Practical Optimization*, Academic Press, New York, 1981.

[13] Barr, A., "Global and local deformations of solid primitives," *Proc. Siggraph '84* p. 21-29.

[14] Ingalls, D. et al, "Fabrik: A Visual Programming Environment," Proc. OOPSLA '88, September 25-30, 1988, p. 176-190.

[15] Pangaro, P., Steinberg, S., Davis, J. and McCann, B., "EOM: a Graphically Scripted, Simulation-Based Animation System," Architecture Machine Group, Massachusetts Institute of Technology, August 1977.

[16] Cook, R., "Shade Trees," *Proc. Siggraph '84*, p. 223-230, 1984.

[17] Abram, G., and Whitted, T., "Building Block Shaders," *Proc. Siggraph '90*, 1990,p. 283-288.

[18] Steele, G. et. al., *Common Lisp the Language*, Digital Press, Bedford, Massachusetts, 1984.

[19] Linton, M., Calder, P., and Vlissides, J., "The Design and Implementation of InterViews," *Proceedings of the USENIX C++ Workshop,*, November 1987.

[20] Sherman, A., Algorithm 533: "NSPIV, A Fortran Subroutine for Sparse Gaussian Elimination With Partial Pivoting," ACM TOMS, Vol. 4, No. 4, December, 1978, p. 391-398.

[21] Press, W. et. al., *Numerical Recipes*, Cambridge University Press, Cambridge, England, 1986

[22] Gleicher, M, and Kass, M, "An Interval Refinement Technique for Surface Intersection," Graphics Interface '92, to appear.

[23] Von Herzen, B. and Barr, A., "Accurate Triangulations of Deformed, Intersecting Surfaces," Computer Graphics 21 (4) Proc. Siggraph '87, 1987 p. 103-110.

[24] Von Herzen, B., Barr, A., and Zatz, H., "Geometric Collisions for Time-Dependent Parametric Surfaces," *Computer Graphics* 24 (4) Proc. Siggraph '90, 1990 p. 39 - 48.

[25] Williams, L., "Performance-Driven Facial Animation," Proc. Siggraph '90, 1990, p. 235-242.

[26] Lowe, D., "Solving for the Parameters of Object Models from Image Descriptions," *Proc. Image Understanding Workshop*, April 1980, p. 121-127.

[27] Gennery, D., "Stero Camera Calibration," *Proc. Image Understanding Workshop*, April 1980, p. 201-208.

[28] Kass, M., Witkin, A., and Terzopoulos, D., "Snakes: Active Contour Models," *International Journal of Computer Vision*, 1988, p. 321-331

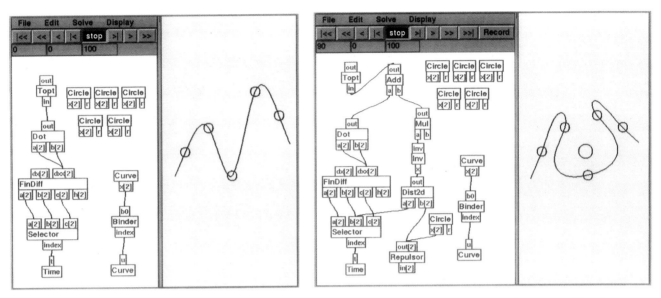

Fig. 5: Minimization of the energy corresponding to (a) a natural spline and (b) a natural spline experiencing a1/r repulsive force.

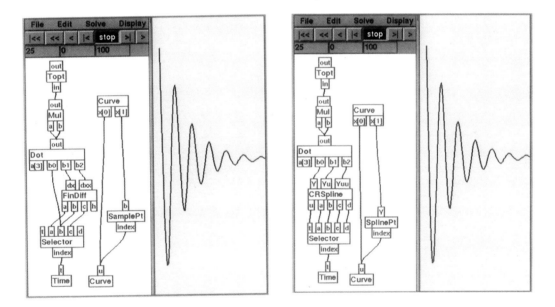

Fig. 6: Spacetime constraint problem for a damped spring solved with (a) finite differences and (b) finite elements.

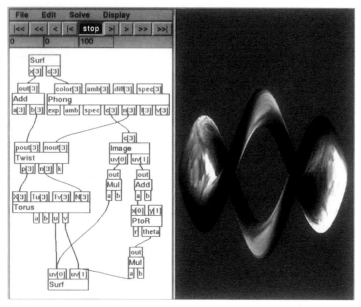

Fig. 7: CONDOR used for rendering and modeling a twisted torus.

Fig. 8: Two spheres trimmed against each other.   (a) Fine tesselation. (b) Coarse tesselation.

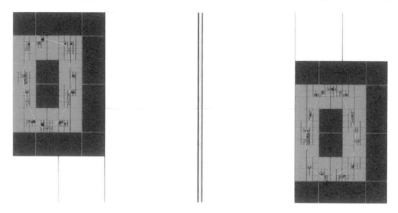

Fig. 8c: Parametric subdivision corresponding to the coarse tesselation.

Through-the-Lens Camera Control

Michael Gleicher and Andrew Witkin
School of Computer Science
Carnegie Mellon University
Pittsburgh, PA
{gleicher|witkin}@cs.cmu.edu

Abstract

In this paper we introduce *through-the-lens camera control*, a body of techniques that permit a user to manipulate a virtual camera by controlling and constraining features in the image seen through its lens. Rather than solving for camera parameters directly, constrained optimization is used to compute their time derivatives based on desired changes in user-defined controls. This effectively permits new controls to be defined independent of the underlying parameterization. The controls can also serve as constraints, maintaining their values as others are changed. We describe the techniques in general and work through a detailed example of a specific camera model. Our implementation demonstrates a gallery of useful controls and constraints and provides some examples of how these may be used in composing images and animations.

Keywords: camera control, constrained optimization, interaction techniques

1   Introduction

Camera placement and control play an important role in image composition and computer animation. Consequently, considerable effort has been devoted to the development of computer graphics camera models. Most camera formulations are built on a common underlying model for perspective projection under which any 3-D view is fully specified by giving the center of projection, the view plane, and the clipping volume. Within this framework, camera models differ in the way the view specification is parameterized. Not all formulations are equivalent—some allow arbitrary viewing geometries, while others impose restrictions. Even so, alternative models can be viewed to a great degree as alternative slicings of the same projective pie.

How important is the choice of the camera model's parameterization? Very important, if the parameters are to serve directly as the controls for interaction and keyframe interpolation. For example, the popular LOOKAT-/LOOKFROM/VUP parameterization makes it easy to hold a world-space point centered in the image as the camera moves without tilting. To do the same by manually controlling generic translation/rotation parameters would be all but hopeless in practice, although possible in principle.

The difficulty with using camera parameters directly as controls is that no single parameterization can be expected to serve all needs. For example, sometimes it is more convenient to express camera orientation in terms of azimuth, elevation and tilt, or in terms of a direction vector. These particular alternatives are common enough to be standardly available, but others are not. A good example involves the problem, addressed by Jim Blinn[3] of portraying a spacecraft flying by a planet. Blinn derives several special-purpose transformations that allow the image-space positions of the spacecraft and planet to be specified and solves for the camera position. The need for this kind of specialized control arises frequently, but we would rather not face the prospect of deriving and coding specialized transformations each time they do.

In short, camera models are inflexible. To change the controls, one must either select a different pre-existing model or derive and implement a new one. If this inflexibility could be removed, the effort devoted to camera control could be reduced and the quality of the result enhanced.

In this paper, we present a body of techniques, which we call *through-the-lens camera control*, that offer a general solution to this problem. Instead of a fixed set, the user is given a palette of interactive image-space and world-space controls that can be applied "on the fly," in any combination. For example, the image-space position of an arbitrary world-space point can be controlled by interactive dragging, or pinned while other points are moved. Image-space distances, sizes, and directions can also be

©1992   ACM-0-89791-479-1/92/007/0331 $01.50

controlled. Points can be constrained to remain within the image or within a specified sub-region. These and other image-space controls can be freely combined with direct world-space controls on camera position and orientation. The set of controls is extensible, with a general procedure for adding new ones.

Using through-the-lens control, the spacecraft/planet problem, and others of its kind, could be solved immediately and interactively: a point on the planet would be grabbed, dragged to its target location, then left pinned at that image point. The spacecraft would be similarly positioned and pinned. Residual degrees of freedom could be fixed by dragging additional points, or manipulating the camera in world space, while both image points remained nailed. All the while, the required camera motions would be computed automatically at interactive speed.

The principal technical obstacle to achieving this kind of control lies in the nonlinearity of the relationship between the desired controls and the underlying view specification. No general guaranteed procedure exists for solving nonlinear algebraic systems; in fact there may often exist no solution, or many. The direct approach—solving numerically for the camera parameters given the controls—is therefore unlikely to succeed.

The key to our approach is that we instead formulate the problem differentially—solving for the *time derivatives* of the camera parameters, given the *time derivatives* of the controls. For example, a point is dragged by specifying its velocity from moment to moment, rather than giving a final target position. When the camera is under interactive control, it falls to the user interface to convert user actions, such as pointer motions, into suitable velocity signals. In keyframe control, the velocity is calculated by taking the time derivative of the interpolating function. The use of differential control does not allow us to directly position the camera in global leaps, but instead provides a robust and accurate means of translating continuous adjustments of the controls into continuous motions of the camera. We are primarily interested in interactive control by grabbing and dragging, for which continuous motion is desirable, and with low-level camera control for animation, for which continuous motion is sufficient.

We formulate the problem of computing time derivatives of camera parameters as a simple constrained optimization. Once the derivatives have been computed, using them to update the camera's state over time reduces to the standard problem of solving a first-order ordinary differential equation from an initial value, for which good numerical methods abound (see Press *et. al.* [20] for a good practical introduction.)

An interesting feature of through-the-lens control is the new role in which it places the camera parameterization. Although we retain a fixed underlying camera model, the model's parameters no longer bear the burden of serving as user-level controls. In fact, the parameters may be completely hidden from the user. This leaves us free to choose a camera model on the basis of numerical well-behavedness and implementation convenience. Our preferred formulation, based on quaternion rotations, is a case in point: it is a very poor model by conventional criteria, since the four components of the quaternion would be exceedingly difficult to control directly. Yet it provides an ideal substrate for through-the-lens control because it allows free camera rotations without singularities or other artifacts. We avoid the well-known difficulties involved with interpolating quaternions for animation[22] by interpolating the controls instead.

The remainder of the paper is organized as follows: Following a discussion of related work, we develop the machinery of through-the-lens control in terms of a generic camera model, starting with the problem of controlling the image-space velocity of a single point, then generalizing to the full solution. We then present complete through-the-lens equations for our simple quaternion-based camera model. We describe our implementation and present examples, then conclude with a discussion of future work.

2   Related Work

As we noted in Section 1, standard computer graphics camera models are based on specialized transformations that specify the view as a function of parameters that are useful for interactive, procedural, or keyframed control. Earlier we discussed the standard LOOKAT/LOOKFROM model. An example of a more general viewing model currently in wide use is the PHIGS+ model[6]. In addition, a variety of special-purpose models such as Blinn's spacecraft flyby transformations [3] have been developed. Issues involved in using the LOOKAT/LOOKFROM model to navigate virtual spaces are considered by [16]. In [7], the LOOKAT/LOOKFROM model is embedded in a procedural language for specifying camera motions.

Much of the work on interactive camera placement in computer graphics has been concerned with direct control of the camera's position and orientation. The problem of developing intuitive controls for 3-D rotations is a difficult one[5], particularly when the input device is two-dimensional. Several researchers have addressed the problem through the use of use of 3-D interfaces, including six degree-of-freedom pointing devices[26, 25, 1] and more specialized devices such as steerable treadmills[4].

Problems involving the recovery of camera parameters from image measurements have been addressed in photogrammetry[1], computer vision, and robotics. All of these are concerned with the recovery of parameter values, rather than time derivatives. Algebraic solutions to specific problems of this kind are given in [18] and [9], while numerical solutions are discussed in [15, 10, 17]. In [24], constrained optimization is employed to position a

---

[1]Also see chapter 6 of [21] for amazing mechanical solutions to photogrammetry problems.

real camera, mounted on a robot arm, for the purpose of object recognition. Factors considered in the optimization include depth of field, occlusion, and image resolution.

Optimization techniques have been applied to the related problem of object placement in computer graphics. In [1] articulated figures are posed using penalty methods to meet positional goals. In [28], similar methods are employed for general object placement and control. The use of these methods for camera placement in animation is described in [30].

The differential control methods employed in this paper are formally more closely allied to the methods of constrained dynamic simulation described in [29, 2, 19, 31, 23] than to the positional optimization methods cited above. Some of the issues involved in adapting these methods to differential kinematic control are addressed in [13], while [27] considers their application to the design of free form surfaces, and [12] illustrates their use in a constraint-based drawing program.

3 The Machinery

In this section we introduce the basic mechanisms that support through-the-lens control, employing a simple constrained optimization formulation. Assuming that we have chosen a camera model to provide the fixed, underlying parameterization, we solve for the time derivatives of the parameters such that their mean squared deviation from a desired value is minimized, subject to the constraints imposed by the image-space controls. Setting the default values to zero yields a solution that minimizes the mean squared rate of change of camera parameters. Non-zero values can be used to support interactive dragging subject to the constraints imposed by other controls.

We begin by giving the relationship between a world-space point and its image-space counterpart, which we express in terms of a generic camera model. A specific quaternion-based model will be fully described in section 4. We give the coordinates of an image point $\mathbf{p}$ as

$$\mathbf{p} = \mathbf{h}(\mathbf{Vx}), \qquad (1)$$

where $\mathbf{x}$ is the world-space point that projects to $\mathbf{p}$, $\mathbf{V}$ is a homogeneous matrix representing the combined projection and viewing transformations, and $\mathbf{h}$ is a function that converts homogeneous coordinates into 2-D image coordinates, defined by

$$\mathbf{h}(\mathbf{x}) = \left[\frac{x_1}{x_4}, \frac{x_2}{x_4} \right],$$

where the x_i's are components of homogeneous point $\mathbf{x}$. The matrix $\mathbf{V}$ is some (for now unspecified) function of the camera model parameters, which we denote by a length-n vector $\mathbf{q}$. In practice, $\mathbf{V}$ would usually be computed as the product of several matrices, each a function of one or more of the parameters.

3.1 Camera motions and image point velocities.

Assuming for now that the world space point $\mathbf{x}$ is fixed, the image point $\mathbf{p}$ is entirely a function of the camera parameters $\mathbf{q}$. This is a nonlinear relationship because $\mathbf{h}$ is nonlinear, as in general is $\mathbf{V}(\mathbf{q})$. We obtain the expression for the image velocity $\dot{\mathbf{p}}$ by applying the chain rule:

$$\dot{\mathbf{p}} = \mathbf{h}'(\mathbf{Vx}) \left(\frac{\partial(\mathbf{Vx})}{\partial \mathbf{q}} \right) \dot{\mathbf{q}}, \qquad (2)$$

where $\mathbf{h}'(\mathbf{x})$ is the matrix representing the derivative of $\mathbf{h}(\mathbf{x})$, given by

$$\mathbf{h}'(\mathbf{x}) = \begin{bmatrix} \frac{1}{x_4} & 0 \\ 0 & \frac{1}{x_4} \\ 0 & 0 \\ -\frac{x_1}{x_4^2} & -\frac{x_2}{x_4^2} \end{bmatrix}, \qquad (3)$$

$\dot{\mathbf{q}}$ is the time derivative of $\mathbf{q}$, and $\partial(\mathbf{Vx})/\partial \mathbf{q}$ is the $4 \times n$ matrix representing the derivative of the transformed point $\mathbf{Vx}$ with respect to $\mathbf{q}$. We differentiate the point $\mathbf{Vx}$ rather than the matrix $\mathbf{V}$ to avoid differentiating a matrix with respect to a vector, which would give rise to a rank-3 tensor. In section 4, we give an example of how this derivative matrix can be computed.

For notational compactness we will define the $2 \times n$ matrix

$$\mathbf{J} = \mathbf{h}'(\mathbf{Vx}) \frac{\partial(\mathbf{Vx})}{\partial \mathbf{q}}, \qquad (4)$$

so that

$$\dot{\mathbf{p}} = \mathbf{J}\dot{\mathbf{q}}. \qquad (5)$$

Notice that equation 5 gives $\dot{\mathbf{p}}$ as a *linear* function of $\dot{\mathbf{q}}$, even though $\mathbf{p}$ is a nonlinear function of $\mathbf{q}$.

3.2 Controlling a single point

Having obtained $\dot{\mathbf{p}}$ as a function of $\dot{\mathbf{q}}$, we next consider the problem of controlling a single image point, i.e. solving for a value of $\dot{\mathbf{q}}$ that makes the image point assume a given velocity $\dot{\mathbf{p}} = \dot{\mathbf{p}}_0$. In practice the value for $\dot{\mathbf{p}}_0$ might be supplied by the user interface or might indicate the velocity on a keyframed motion path. Although the relation between $\dot{\mathbf{p}}$ and $\dot{\mathbf{q}}$ is linear, we cannot simply solve $\dot{\mathbf{p}}_0 = \mathbf{J}\dot{\mathbf{q}}$ for $\dot{\mathbf{q}}$ unless matrix $\mathbf{J}$ is square and of full rank, which in general it will not be.

The singularity of the matrix $\mathbf{J}$ reflects the fact that many distinct camera motions can cause a single point to move in the same way. One way to solve the problem might be to require the user to control enough points or other features to yield a square matrix. We choose a different option that offers far more flexibility: subject to the constraint that $\dot{\mathbf{p}} = \dot{\mathbf{p}}_0$, we minimize the magnitude of $\dot{\mathbf{q}}$'s deviation from a specified value $\dot{\mathbf{q}}_0$. Letting $\dot{\mathbf{q}}_0 = 0$ imposes a criterion of minimal change in the camera parameters. As we shall see later, the ability to choose other values makes it possible, for example, to drag image points and other features *subject to* the hard constraints.

The problem we now wish to solve is:

$$\text{minimize } E = \frac{(\dot{\mathbf{q}} - \dot{\mathbf{q}}_0) \cdot (\dot{\mathbf{q}} - \dot{\mathbf{q}}_0)}{2} \text{ subject to } \dot{\mathbf{p}} - \dot{\mathbf{p}}_0 = 0. \tag{6}$$

To qualify as a constrained minimum, $\dot{\mathbf{q}}$ must satisfy several conditions. First, of course, the constraint must be met, i.e.

$$\dot{\mathbf{p}}_0 = \mathbf{J}\dot{\mathbf{q}}.$$

At an unconstrained minimum, we would require that the gradient $dE/d\dot{\mathbf{q}}$ vanish. Instead, we require that it point in a direction in which displacements are prohibited by the constraints. This condition is expressed by requiring that

$$dE/d\dot{\mathbf{q}} = \dot{\mathbf{q}} - \dot{\mathbf{q}}_0 = \mathbf{J}^T \lambda,$$

for some value of the 2-vector λ of *Lagrange multipliers*. This equation simply states that the gradient of E must be a linear combination of the gradients of the constraints. Combining the two conditions gives

$$\mathbf{J}\mathbf{J}^T \lambda = \dot{\mathbf{p}}_0 - \mathbf{J}\dot{\mathbf{q}}_0, \tag{7}$$

which is a matrix equation to be solved for λ. Then the camera parameter derivatives are given by

$$\dot{\mathbf{q}} = \dot{\mathbf{q}}_0 + \mathbf{J}^T \lambda. \tag{8}$$

Finally, we must use the computed value of $\dot{\mathbf{q}}$ to update the camera state $\mathbf{q}$, a standard initial value problem. See Press *et. al.* [20] for a discussion of the issues and a good assortment of numerical methods for ordinary differential equations. The very simplest method, *Euler's method,* employs the update formula

$$\mathbf{q}(t + \Delta t) = \mathbf{q}(t) + \Delta t \dot{\mathbf{q}}(t).$$

Although easy to implement, Euler's method is notoriously unstable and inaccurate. Use it at your own risk! In the interactive loop of through-the-lens control, drawing and input are interleaved with solver steps.

3.3 General quadratic objective functions

The restricted form of the objective function given in equation 6 is often adequate, but can cause problems: when the controls do not fully determine the camera's state, the task of accounting for the remaining degrees of freedom falls to the objective function. For example, if the camera is able to respond to the motion of a controlled point by a combination of tracking and panning, the objective function determines how much of each will take place. Because the error norm of equation 6 is the Euclidean distance in the camera's parameter space, rather than being intrinsic to the world-space camera motion, the behavior depends in a somewhat haphazard way on the choice of camera parameterization, and could even depend, for example, on the choice of linear and angular units of measure!

To allow such behavior to be controlled in a more rational way we make a reasonably straightforward generalization, allowing E to be any quadratic function of $\dot{\mathbf{q}}$, having

the form

$$E = \frac{1}{2}\dot{\mathbf{q}}\mathbf{M}\dot{\mathbf{q}} + \mathbf{b} \cdot \dot{\mathbf{q}} + c,$$

where $\mathbf{M}$ is a matrix, typically symmetric and positive-definite, $\mathbf{b}$ is a vector, and c is a scalar, none of them depending on $\dot{\mathbf{q}}$. Since E is quadratic, the problem remains linear, although the matrix equation to be solved becomes a bit more complex. The gradient of $\mathbf{E}$ becomes

$$\frac{\partial E}{\partial \dot{\mathbf{q}}} = \mathbf{M}\dot{\mathbf{q}} + \mathbf{b}.$$

Denoting the inverse of $\mathbf{M}$ by $\mathbf{W} = \mathbf{M}^{-1}$, equation 7 assumes the form

$$\dot{\mathbf{p}}_0 = \mathbf{J}\mathbf{W}\mathbf{J}^T \lambda - \mathbf{J}\mathbf{W}\mathbf{b}. \tag{9}$$

It is also possible to solve for λ without obtaining the explicit inverse for $\mathbf{M}$ by forming a larger linear system (see [8].)

Under this general linear/quadratic formulation, the camera's response to controls can be decoupled from the parameterization, for instance by letting $\mathbf{M}$ be a *mass matrix* for the camera[13, 29, 31].

3.4 Multiple Points and Other Functions

Controlling more than one point involves a simple extension to the foregoing derivation. The matrix $\mathbf{J}$ depends on $\mathbf{x}$, so each point being controlled yields a distinct version of equation 5. We combine the m equations into a single one by concatenating the derivative matrices to form a $2m \times n$ matrix, and concatenating the image velocities to form a $2m$-long vector. From that point on, the derivation proceeds as above, to the solution of equation 7 for λ, which is now also a vector of length $2m$.

In addition to controlling image points directly, we would like to control functions of one or more points, such as image distance or orientation. In fact, to mix image-space and world-space controls we may want to control other functions of $\mathbf{q}$ that do not involve the image at all, such as object-to-camera distance. Conceptually, this is not a difficult generalization to make: in equation 5, we simply interpret $\mathbf{p}$ not as a literal point, but as the vector of quantities we wish to control. Matrix $\mathbf{J}$ must then give the derivative of each controlled quantity with respect to each camera parameter. In practice, performing the derivative evaluations, indexing and other bookkeeping, etc., can become quite complex. See [14, 29] for general-purpose schemes that facilitate the handling of this kind of matrix-assembly problem. Although our own implementations are based on such a scheme, the camera control problem is sufficiently restricted in scope that this certainly is not necessary.

Many through-the-lens controls, such as point-to-point distance, can be expressed as functions of several image points' positions. The labor involved in implementing such controls can be greatly reduced through through the use of the chain rule. For instance, consider a scalar function of two image points $f(\mathbf{p}_1, \mathbf{p}_2)$. The derivative of f with respect to $\dot{\mathbf{q}}$ is

$$\frac{df}{d\dot{\mathbf{q}}} = \frac{\partial f}{\partial \mathbf{p}_1}\mathbf{J}_1 + \frac{\partial f}{\partial \mathbf{p}_2}\mathbf{J}_2,$$

where $\mathbf{J}_1$ and $\mathbf{J}_2$ are the derivative matrices for $\mathbf{p}_1$ and $\mathbf{p}_2$, computed according to equation 4. The code that evaluates $\mathbf{J}$ for image points need only be implemented once. Thereafter, just derivatives with respect to image points need be treated anew for each control. These tend to be simple, and as an added advantage, they are independent of the choice of the underlying camera parameterization.

3.5 Constrained Dragging and Soft Controls

When controls are added dynamically by the user, it is entirely possible for inconsistencies to arise, either because the degrees of control exceed the camera's degrees of freedom, or because some controls are in conflict, e.g. trying to move one point in two directions. These problems can be handled gracefully by employing a least-squares method to solve the matrix equation—see for example the conjugate gradient solver described in [20]—so that the error due to the inconsistency is distributed uniformly over the controls, in a least-squares sense.

Although the least-squares solution avoids disaster when conflicts arise, we have found that it is very helpful to permit the user to drag points and other features *subject to* the constraints imposed by existing controls, so that conflicts can never arise. We achieve this behavior by incorporating the dragged point's desired behavior into the objective function, rather than using a "hard" constraint to control it. The constrained optimization solution then resolves any conflicts strictly in favor of the hard constraints. Thus, for example, a point whose range of motion is restricted by the controls will move freely up to the limit of its travel, but no further. A simple way to implement such "soft" controls is to specify the desired camera motion $\dot{\mathbf{q}}_0$ according to the formula

$$\dot{\mathbf{q}}_0 = k_c\mathbf{J}^T(\mathbf{p}_c - \mathbf{p}), \qquad (10)$$

where $\mathbf{k}_c$ is a constant and $\mathbf{p}_c$ is the position of the cursor in image coordinates. Using this value to drive the system is similar to attaching a rubber band between $\mathbf{p}_c$ and $\mathbf{p}$, inducing camera motion that causes $\mathbf{p}$ to "chase" $\mathbf{p}_c$. Inserting this value of $\mathbf{q}_0$ into equation 7 minimizes the mean squared difference between $\dot{\mathbf{q}}$ and $\dot{\mathbf{q}}_0$, subject to the constraints. Soft controls can be implemented more accurately, at the expense of greater complexity, by minimizing the squared difference between $\dot{\mathbf{p}}$ and a desired value $\dot{\mathbf{p}}_0$, subject to the constraints. To express this objective function, the general form given in equation 9 must be used.

A greatly simplified though much less powerful version of through-the-lens control is obtained by using soft controls only. Then, the constrained optimization of equation 6 collapses into an unconstrained optimization. For example, an image point could be dragged by using equation 10 directly to determine $\dot{\mathbf{q}}$.

3.6 Position Feedback

So far, we have cast the problem in terms of velocity control. The velocity signals that drive the control process may come from several sources. For example, during interactive dragging of a controlled image point, the velocity may represent an estimate of mouse velocity. In keyframing, the velocity represents the derivative of a known trajectory curve $\mathbf{p}_0(t)$. In both cases, position as well as velocity information is available. This extra information can be used to greatly improve tracking accuracy by preventing error accumulation and drift as velocity is integrated over time. We do this by the addition of a simple linear feedback term to our initial statement of the control requirement:

$$\dot{\mathbf{p}} = \dot{\mathbf{p}}_0 - k_f(\mathbf{p} - \mathbf{p}_0),$$

where k_f is a feedback constant, and $\mathbf{p}_0$ is the desired position for $\mathbf{p}$ at the current time. When $\mathbf{p}$ is on target, the feedback term vanishes, but if positional error exists, the velocity is biased in a direction that reduces the error. The feedback term carries straight through the derivation, leading to the following modified form for equation 7:

$$\mathbf{J}\mathbf{J}^T\lambda = \dot{\mathbf{p}}_0 + k_f(\mathbf{p}_0 - \mathbf{p}) - \mathbf{J}\dot{\mathbf{q}}_0. \qquad (11)$$

3.7 Tracking a moving point

Until now, we have assumed that the world-space point $\mathbf{x}$ is stationary. A small generalization makes it possible to accurately track a moving point. In keyframe animation, for example, this would allow moving points on objects to be tracked automatically. To make the generalization, we assume that the world-space point moves according to a known function $\mathbf{x}(t)$. In practice, we need only know the point's current position $\mathbf{x}$ and velocity $\dot{\mathbf{x}}$. Since $\mathbf{x}$ now depends on time, an additional term appears in equation 2, the chain-rule expression for $\dot{\mathbf{p}}$, accounting for the part of $\mathbf{x}$'s image velocity due to the motion of $\mathbf{x}$ itself:

$$\dot{\mathbf{p}} = \mathbf{h}'(\mathbf{V}\mathbf{x})\frac{\partial(\mathbf{V}\mathbf{x})}{\partial\mathbf{q}}\dot{\mathbf{q}} + \mathbf{h}'(\mathbf{V}\mathbf{x})\mathbf{V}\dot{\mathbf{x}} \qquad (12)$$

As before, the extra term carries through, adding an additional correction factor to the right hand side of equation 7, yielding

$$\mathbf{J}\mathbf{J}^T\lambda = \dot{\mathbf{p}}_0 + k_f(\mathbf{p}_0 - \mathbf{p}) - \mathbf{h}'(\mathbf{V}\mathbf{x})\mathbf{V}\dot{\mathbf{x}} - \mathbf{J}\dot{\mathbf{q}}_0. \qquad (13)$$

This formulation makes it possible to control the *image-space* motion of a point independently of its *world-space* motion. If the image point is pinned, the camera will move as necessary to maintain its position. Both the image point and the world point can be keyframed independently: the camera will move as required to achieve the desired image motion, regardless of the world-space motion of the point.

4   A Quaternion Camera

Having developed the through-the-lens equations in generic form, it remains to fill in the blanks. In the equations of the last section, the camera transformation was described in terms of an anonymous matrix $\mathbf{V}$ depending on an anonymous parameter vector $\mathbf{q}$. To proceed, we must say what the function $\mathbf{V}(\mathbf{q})$ actually is. Then we must formulate the equations that are required to evaluate the image point derivative matrix $\mathbf{J}$. If we limit ourselves to image-space controls that can be expressed purely as functions of point positions, then the matrices $\mathbf{V}$ and $\mathbf{J}$ tell us everything we need to know about the camera.

As we noted in section 1, through-the-lens control hides the underlying camera parameterization from the user, so that most of the criteria by which a conventional camera model would be judged do not apply. The model we present in this section is unusual in that a quaternion is used to represent the camera's orientation; we choose it because of the quaternion's ability to represent arbitrary rotations free of singularities and other artifacts. The equations of section 3 are compatible with any camera model. If you prefer another one, the derivation in this section can still serve as a template for the general procedure.

4.1   The View Matrix

Our model employs a translation to specify the Lookfrom point and a quaternion to specify orientation. The view matrix $\mathbf{V}$ called for by equation 1 is given by the matrix product

$$\mathbf{V} = \mathbf{P}(f)\mathbf{T}(t_x, t_y, t_z)\mathbf{Q}(q_w, q_x, q_y, q_z), \qquad (14)$$

where $\mathbf{P}$ is a matrix for perspective projection with focal length f, $\mathbf{T}$ is the matrix for translation by $[t_x, t_y, t_z]$, and $\mathbf{Q}$ is a *quaternion rotation matrix,* performing the rotation specified by the quaternion $\mathbf{q}$, with scalar part q_w and vector part $[q_x, q_y, q_z]$. The camera parameter vector $\mathbf{q}$ is the length-8 vector formed by concatenating the transformation parameters, $[f, t_x, t_y, t_z, q_w, q_x, q_y, q_z]$.

The perspective matrix is a simple one, placing the focal point at the origin and the image plane at distance f from the origin along the z-axis, lying parallel to the xy-plane:

$$\mathbf{P} = \begin{bmatrix} 1 & 0 & 0 & 0 \\ 0 & 1 & 0 & 0 \\ 0 & 0 & 1 & 0 \\ 0 & 0 & 1/f & 0 \end{bmatrix}.$$

The translation matrix is the standard one:

$$\mathbf{T}(t_x, t_y, t_z) = \begin{bmatrix} 1 & 0 & 0 & t_x \\ 0 & 1 & 0 & t_y \\ 0 & 0 & 1 & t_z \\ 0 & 0 & 0 & 1 \end{bmatrix}.$$

The quaternion rotation matrix is a bit more complex. The

form given in [22],

$$\mathbf{Q} = 2\begin{bmatrix} \frac{1}{2} - q_y{}^2 - q_z{}^2 & q_x q_y + q_w q_z & q_x q_z - q_w q_y & 0 \\ q_x q_y - q_w q_z & \frac{1}{2} - q_x{}^2 - q_z{}^2 & q_w q_x + q_y q_z & 0 \\ q_w q_y + q_x q_z & q_y q_z - q_w q_x & \frac{1}{2} - q_x{}^2 - q_y{}^2 & 0 \\ 0 & 0 & 0 & \frac{1}{2} \end{bmatrix}, \qquad (15)$$

assumes that the quaternion has unit magnitude, i.e. that

$$|\mathbf{q}| = \sqrt{q_w^2 + q_x^2 + q_y^2 + q_z^2} = 1.$$

Otherwise, $\mathbf{Q}$ is not a pure rotation, and shapes will be distorted. This constraint on $|\mathbf{q}|$ means that the camera has only seven true degrees of freedom. To enforce the constraint, it is not sufficient simply to normalize $\mathbf{Q}$ between iterations: in that case, the derivative matrix wouldn't "know" about the constraint, and the control solution would be incorrect. While it would be possible to add the constraint, in differential form, to the control solution, there is a much simpler alternative: in place of equation 15, we express $\mathbf{Q}$ in a form that incorporates the normalization, so that quaternions $\mathbf{q}$ and $\alpha \mathbf{q}$ specify the same transformation, for any scalar α. Under this scheme, we must still normalize $\mathbf{q}$ from time to time to prevent the accumulation of numerical errors. The modified version of $\mathbf{Q}$ is most simply expressed as the product

$$\mathbf{Q}_n = \frac{1}{|\mathbf{q}|^2}\hat{\mathbf{Q}},$$

where

$$\hat{\mathbf{Q}} = 2\begin{bmatrix} \frac{|\mathbf{q}|^2}{2} - q_y{}^2 - q_z{}^2 & q_x q_y + q_w q_z & q_x q_z - q_w q_y & 0 \\ q_x q_y - q_w q_z & \frac{|\mathbf{q}|^2}{2} - q_x{}^2 - q_z{}^2 & q_w q_x + q_y q_z & 0 \\ q_w q_y + q_x q_z & q_y q_z - q_w q_x & \frac{|\mathbf{q}|^2}{2} - q_x{}^2 - q_y{}^2 & 0 \\ 0 & 0 & 0 & \frac{|\mathbf{q}|^2}{2} \end{bmatrix}$$

4.2   Evaluating J

Employing the notation of section 3, the image coordinates corresponding to world point $\mathbf{x}$ are given by

$$\mathbf{p} = \mathbf{h}(\mathbf{V}\mathbf{x}) = \mathbf{h}(\mathbf{P}\mathbf{Q}_n\mathbf{T}\mathbf{x}).$$

The rows of $\mathbf{J}$ are formed by differentiating this expression with respect to each camera parameter in turn. To perform the differentiations, we note that each camera parameter influences exactly one matrix in the chain. Therefore, using the rule for differentiation of a product, the derivative of the chain with respect to a parameter is another chain, obtained by replacing the appropriate matrix by its element-by-element derivative. Thus, for example,

$$\frac{\partial \mathbf{V}\mathbf{x}}{\partial t_x} = \mathbf{P}\frac{\partial \mathbf{T}}{\partial t_x}\mathbf{Q}_n\mathbf{x},$$

and we obtain the row of $\mathbf{J}$ corresponding to t_x from

$$\frac{\partial \mathbf{p}}{\partial t_x} = \mathbf{h}'(\mathbf{V}\mathbf{x})\frac{\partial \mathbf{V}}{\partial t_x},$$

where $\mathbf{h}'(\mathbf{V}\mathbf{x})$ is as defined in equation 2, and where

$$\frac{\partial \mathbf{T}}{\partial t_x} = \begin{bmatrix} 0 & 0 & 0 & 1 \\ 0 & 0 & 0 & 0 \\ 0 & 0 & 0 & 0 \\ 0 & 0 & 0 & 0 \end{bmatrix}.$$

Differentiating each matrix with respect to each parameter on which it depends yields eight matrices in all. The matrix for $\partial \mathbf{T}/\partial \mathbf{t}_x$ is given above—the other two derivatives of $\mathbf{T}$ are likewise trivial. The derivative of $\mathbf{P}$ with respect to its only parameter, f, is

$$\frac{\partial \mathbf{P}}{\partial f} = \begin{bmatrix} 0 & 0 & 0 & 0 \\ 0 & 0 & 0 & 0 \\ 0 & 0 & 0 & 0 \\ 0 & 0 & -1/f^2 & 0 \end{bmatrix}.$$

The four derivatives of $\mathbf{Q}_n$ may be expressed compactly as

$$\frac{\partial \mathbf{Q}_n}{\partial q_w} = \frac{-2q_w}{|\mathbf{q}|^4}\hat{\mathbf{Q}} + \frac{2}{|\mathbf{q}|^2}\begin{bmatrix} q_w & q_z & -q_y & 0 \\ -q_z & q_w & q_x & 0 \\ q_y & -q_x & q_w & 0 \\ 0 & 0 & 0 & q_w \end{bmatrix},$$

$$\frac{\partial \mathbf{Q}_n}{\partial q_x} = \frac{-2q_x}{|\mathbf{q}|^4}\hat{\mathbf{Q}} + \frac{2}{|\mathbf{q}|^2}\begin{bmatrix} q_x & q_y & q_z & 0 \\ q_y & -q_x & q_w & 0 \\ q_z & q_w & -q_x & 0 \\ 0 & 0 & 0 & q_x \end{bmatrix},$$

$$\frac{\partial \mathbf{Q}_n}{\partial q_y} = \frac{-2q_y}{|\mathbf{q}|^4}\hat{\mathbf{Q}} + \frac{2}{|\mathbf{q}|^2}\begin{bmatrix} -q_y & q_x & -q_w & 0 \\ q_x & q_y & q_z & 0 \\ q_w & q_z & -q_y & 0 \\ 0 & 0 & 0 & q_y \end{bmatrix},$$

and

$$\frac{\partial \mathbf{Q}_n}{\partial q_z} = \frac{-2q_z}{|\mathbf{q}|^4}\hat{\mathbf{Q}} + \frac{2}{|\mathbf{q}|^2}\begin{bmatrix} -q_z & q_w & q_x & 0 \\ -q_w & -q_z & q_y & 0 \\ q_x & q_y & q_z & 0 \\ 0 & 0 & 0 & q_z \end{bmatrix}.$$

To evaluate $\mathbf{J}$, we need only implement functions that calculate each of these eight derivative matrices, along with the function that calculates $\mathbf{h}'(\mathbf{x})$. Standard matrix/vector operations are then used to produce the eight rows of $\mathbf{J}$.

5 Implementation and Examples

We have implemented through-the-lens control as part of a multi-view, direct manipulation testbed. The program is written in C++ on a Silicon Graphics Iris workstation and uses a toolkit which permits rapid evaluation of dynamically composed functions and their derivatives[14]. All of the examples in this paper can be specified interactively and run at interactive rates on a Silicon Graphics IRIS 4D/210 GTX.

We have experimented with a wide variety of through-the-lens controls including

- the position of a point on the screen,
- the distance between two points on the screen,
- the orientation of two points in the image,
- the ratio between two screen space distances.

All can be interactively specified and connected to vertices in the scene, can be made into hard or soft controls, can serve as constraints, and can be keyframed. Controls that do not have an obvious geometric method for direct manipulation, such as the last three on the list, can be connected to sliders.

The architecture of our system makes it easy to define new types of controls, although this must be done at compile time. Unlike finding new transforms, which entails solving systems of non-linear equations, defining new controls is easy to automate in a general and guaranteed manner since the only required mathematical manipulation is differentiation. We have built automatic code generation tools that facilitate defining new types of controls.

By adding the ability to place boundaries on the values of a control, we have been able to create several interesting through-the-lens features in our system, such as

- bounding a point within a region of the image,
- ensuring that an object does not become larger or smaller than a certain size,
- preventing an object from becoming too much bigger or smaller than another.

We use an active set technique[11] to extend the methods of section 3 to provide the capability of inequality constraints.

These through-the-lens controls work in concert with a variety of world-space controls. Because a camera is a first class object in our system, these controls can be applied to them as well as other objects in the scene. Multiple windows with cameras dynamically assigned to them make it easy to use world and image space controls together in composing an image.

Building on top of a general purpose facility for composing derivatives permits our implementation to exercise the full generality of the methods in section 3 by allowing us to solve simultaneously for camera and object parameters. Through-the-lens controls can therefore affect other objects in addition to the camera. Although removing the restriction that $\mathbf{x}$ does not depend on $\mathbf{q}$ does not require any change to the techniques presented, the pragmatic issues that arise in including parameters of objects other than the camera in $\mathbf{q}$ are beyond the scope of this paper. These issues are discussed in [14, 13, 29]. They permit a unified approach to controlling and constraining all objects, including cameras.

When the state vector includes objects besides the camera, through-the-lens controls provide a way to couple the camera and scene objects. If a point on an object is pinned to a particular place in the image, as the object moves the camera will also change to maintain the constraint. Changing the camera will similarly alter the object. If the camera is locked in place, the object is restricted to locations where its image satisfies the through-the-lens requirements. Adjusting a through-the-lens control can cause both the camera and the scene objects to change,

Figure 1: Multiple through-the-lens constraints: Multiple through-the-Lens point controls fixate two corners of the center cube. As the camera is translated along the faces of the cube (following the arrows on the floor), it rotates and zooms to maintain the constraints.

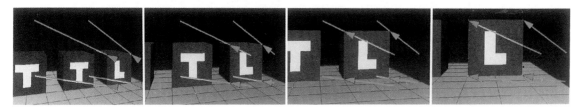

Figure 2: Through-the-lens keyframing: Through-the-lens controls are moved along keyframe paths. Each arrow grabs a corner of the cube and pulls it along a path in the image.

such controls permit manipulation of an object in terms of how it appears in the image. In a highly constrained environment, this can make it easy to achieve a desired effect when it is unclear how to do it by controlling the camera and other objects independently.

As a simple example of what through-the-lens controls can do, consider the role of the standard LOOKAT/-LOOKFROM/VUP camera model in our system. The ability to place points in the image and specify the orientations of line segments subsumes the need for this camera model. Although L/L/V is one of several camera models we have coded into our system[2], we typically prefer to use representations like the quaternion-based one in section 4 for their well-behavedness, using through-the-lens controls to point the camera. Even if the L/L/V representation is employed, the user is not restricted to specifying the view using these parameters.

The spacecraft example from the introduction exemplifies the use of through the lens controls to compose an image (Figure 3). Continuing with the example, the constraints used to position the spacecraft and planet can be maintained as the spacecraft flies past the planet to create a fly-by animation, either by coupling the state variables or using the tracking techniques of section 3.7. If the geometry of the scene isn't predetermined, through-the-lens control can help specify it. For example, consider creating a picture of the spacecraft flying by the planet and its moons. If we free the position of the craft, through-the-lens controls can move it so that its position in the image is maintained as we move the camera to find a view which shows the planets and the moons in a desirable manner.

Another use of through-the-lens controls is registering 3D models with photographs. This can be done by displaying a real image as a backdrop and pinning points on the synthesized image to their corresponding locations. Using

a least squares technique for overdetermined matrices can allow several points to be specified: the system will move towards the best fit (Figure 4). A viewing transform can be derived for registering 3 points[18], but through-the-lens techniques provide a general method for performing these manipulations.

6 Conclusion

As we gain more experience using through-the-lens control, we find more interesting controls and constraints to aid in the process of composing pictures and manipulating scenes. Other additions to through-the-lens manipulation might include using optimization and constraints to help compose images, developing an interface that makes it easier to specify both through-the-lens and world-space controls, inferring constraints to make manipulation easier, and providing a method of detecting and preventing unwanted occlusions. We are beginning to explore using through-the-lens techniques to connect 3D models to real photographs and live video. We are also considering how to use through-the-lens techniques to address issues in planning good camera motions for animations.

Through-the-lens techniques provide a method for manipulating the virtual camera by controlling and constraining image attributes. Interactive control techniques permit the user to control the virtual camera by directly manipulating the image as seen through the lens. The control techniques make it easy to enforce constraints on attributes of the image and scene. The techniques make it simple to implement a wide variety of constraints and controls.

Acknowledgements

This research was funded in part by Apple Computer, a fellowship from the Schlumberger Foundation, and an equipment grant from Silicon Graphics. We would like to thank Pete Wyckoff for the fractal planets, James Rehg

---

[2]Finding the derivatives of this matrix is not for the faint of heart — don't try it without a symbolic mathematics program.

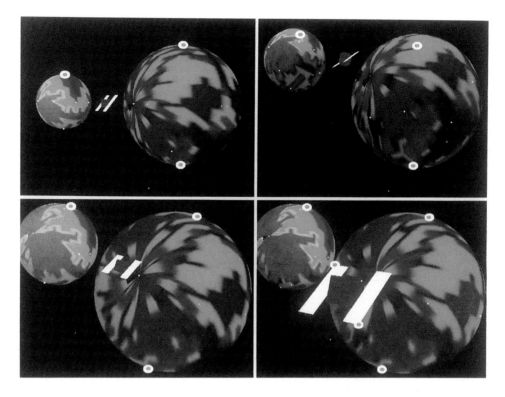

Figure 3: Composing an image with Though-the-Lens controls. Through-the-lens point controls are placed at the poles of the planet and the moon (upper left). The leftmost control is moved (upper right). The controls are adjusted further (lower left). After positioning the camera, through the lens controls are used to position the spacecraft (lower right).

Figure 4: Decorating the lab with Through-the-Lens controls: The rectangular polygon has the same dimensions as the tabletop. By interactively positioning the vertices to correspond with their respective corners, the virtual camera models the real camera.

and Michael Kass for providing some references, Steven Drucker and Tinsley Gaylean for helping renew our interest in camera placement, and Will Welch for providing caffeine and conversation.

References

[1] Norman Badler, Kamran Manoocherhri, and David Baraff. Multi-dimentional input techniques and articulated figure positioning by multiple constraints. In *Proceedings of the 1986 Workshop on Interactive 3d Graphics*, pages 151–170, October 1986.

[2] Ronen Barzel and Alan H. Barr. A modeling system based on dynamic constaints. *Computer Graphics*, 22:179–188, 1988. Proceedings SIGGRAPH '88.

[3] Jim Blinn. Where am I? What am I looking at? *IEEE Computer Graphics and Applications*, pages 76–81, July 1988.

[4] Frederick Brooks. Walkthough – a dynamic graphics environment for simulating virtual buildings. In *Proceedings of the 1986 Workshop on Interactive 3d Graphics*, pages 9–22, October 1986.

[5] Michael Chen, S. Joy Mountford, and Abigail Sellen. A study in interactive 3d rotation using 2d input devices. *Computer Graphics*, 22(4):121–130, August 1988. Proceedings SIGGRAPH '88.

[6] PHIGS+ Committee. Phigs+ functional description, revision 3.0. *Computer Graphics*, 22(3):125–215, 1988.

[7] Steven Drucker, Tinsley Gaylean, and David Zeltzer. CINEMA: a system for procedural camera movements. In *Proceedings of the 1992 Symposium on Interactive Computer Graphics*, pages 67–70, 1992.

[8] Roger Fletcher. *Practical Methods of Optimization*. John Wiley and Sons, 1987.

[9] Sundaram Ganapathy. Decomposition of transformation matrices for robot vision. In *International Conference on Robotics*, pages 130–139, March 1984.

[10] Donald Gennery. Stereo-camera calibration. In *Proc. DARPA Image Understanding Workshop*, pages 101–107, 1979.

[11] Phillip Gill, Walter Murray, and Margret Wright. *Practical Optimization*. Academic Press, New York, NY, 1981.

[12] Michael Gleicher. Briar - a constraint-based drawing program. In *CHI '92 Formal Video Program*, 1992. SIGGRAPH video review, in press.

[13] Michael Gleicher and Andrew Witkin. Differential manipulation. *Graphics Interface*, pages 61–67, June 1991.

[14] Michael Gleicher and Andrew Witkin. Snap together mathematics. In Edwin Blake and Peter Weisskirchen, editors, *Advances in Object Oriented Graphics 1: Proceedings of the 1990 Eurographics Workshop on Object Oriented Graphics*. Springer Verlag, 1991. Also appears as CMU School of Computer Science Technical Report CMU-CS-90-164.

[15] David Lowe. Solving for the parameters of object models from image descriptions. In *Proc. DARPA Image Understanding Workshop*, pages 121–127, 1980.

[16] Jock Mackinlay, Stuart Card, and George Robertson. Rapid controlled movement through a virtual 3d workspace. *Computer Graphics*, 24(4):171–176, August 1990.

[17] Chris McGlone. Automated image-map registration using active contour models and photogrammetric techniques. In *Proceedings of the SPIE, Volume 1070*, January 1989.

[18] Francis H. Moffitt. *Photogrammetry*. International Textbook Company, 1959.

[19] John Platt and Alan Barr. Constraint methods for flexible models. *Computer Graphics*, 22:279–288, 1988. Proceedings SIGGRAPH '88.

[20] William Press, Brian Flannery, Saul Teukolsky, and William Vetterling. *Numerical Recipes in C*. Cambridge University Press, Cambridge, England, 1986.

[21] K. Schwidefsky. *An Outline of Photogrammetry*. Pitman Publishing Corporation, first english edition, 1959.

[22] Ken Shoemake. Animating rotations with quaternion curves. *Computer Graphics*, 19(3):245–254, July 1985.

[23] Mark Surles. Interactive modeling enhanced with constraints and physics – with applications in molecular modeling. In *Proceedings of the 1992 Symposium on Interactive Computer Graphics*, pages 175–182, March 1992.

[24] Konstantinos Tarabamis, Roger Tsai, and Peter Allen. Automated senor planning for robotic vision tasks. In *Proceedings of th 1991 IEEE International Conference on Robotics and Automation*, pages 76–82, April 1991.

[25] Russell Turner, Francis Balaguer, Enrico Gobbetti, and Daniel Thalmann. Physically-based interactive camera motion using 3d input devices. In N. M. Patrikalakis, editor, *Scientific Visualiztion of Physical Phenomena: Proceedings of CG International 1991*, pages 135–145, Tokyo, 1991. Springer-Verlag.

[26] Colin Ware and Steven Osborne. Exploration of virtual camera control in virtual three dimensional environments. *Computer Graphics*, 24(2):175–184, March 1990. Proceedings 1990 Symposium on Interactive 3D Graphics.

[27] William Welch, Michael Gleicher, and Andrew Witkin. Manipulating surfaces differentially. In *Proceedings, Compugraphics '91*, September 1991. Also appears as CMU School of Computer Science Technical Report CMU-CS-91-175.

[28] Andrew Witkin, Kurt Fleischer, and Alan Barr. Energy constraints on parameterized models. *Computer Graphics*, 21(4):225–232, July 1987.

[29] Andrew Witkin, Michael Gleicher, and William Welch. Interactive dynamics. *Computer Graphics*, 24(2):11–21, March 1990. Proceedings 1990 Symposium on Interactive 3D Graphics.

[30] Andrew Witkin, Michael Kass, Demetri Terzopoulos, and Kurt Fleischer. Physically based modeling for vision and graphics. In *Proc. DARPA Image Understanding Workshop*, pages 254–278, 1988.

[31] Andrew Witkin and William Welch. Fast animation and control of non-rigid structures. *Computer Graphics*, 24(4):243–252, August 1990. Proceedings SIGGRAPH '90.

An Object-Oriented 3D Graphics Toolkit

Paul S. Strauss
Rikk Carey

Silicon Graphics Computer Systems
2011 North Shoreline Blvd.
Mountain View, CA 94039-7311
pss@sgi.com, rikk@sgi.com

Abstract

This paper presents an object-oriented toolkit for developers of interactive 3D graphics applications. The primary goal of the toolkit is to make it easier for programmers to create 3D graphics applications that employ direct manipulation techniques in addition to conventional 2D-widgets. Such techniques have generally been ignored in previous graphics packages and systems.

The toolkit provides a general and extensible framework for representing 3D scenes so that applications can integrate their data with graphical objects rather than having duplicate copies. A simple, integrated event model that enables direct interaction with 3D objects is also included.

CR Categories and Subject Descriptors

I.3.2 Graphics Systems; I.3.4 Graphics Utilities, Application Packages, Graphics Packages; I.3.6 Methodology and Techniques - Interaction Techniques; I.3.7 Three-Dimensional Graphics and Realism, Animation

Keywords

Interactive 3D graphics, object-oriented design, scene representation, direct manipulation.

Introduction

Writing interactive 3D graphics applications has traditionally been a tedious, time-consuming, and difficult task requiring a high level of expertise by the programmer. Because it has been so difficult, developers and researchers have either invented their own software abstractions above the low-level graphics commands or produced portable, "lowest common denominator" applications with little or no direct 3D interaction. The former choice yields short-term solutions that are rarely given sufficient design and implementation effort. The latter approach is more common in industry and results in disjoint user interfaces in which users view 3D areas but can interact only through remote user interface widgets or keyboard com-

mand languages.

A 3D graphics toolkit could facilitate writing interactive applications. A truly interactive 3D toolkit should provide a rich and extensible set of 3D objects and should support *direct manipulation*, allowing users to interact with those objects in the same window in which they appear. This technique is common in 2D graphics applications, yet it has rarely appeared in 3D applications. There are three fundamental areas in which a toolkit can enable the development of such interactive 3D programs:

- **Object representation**. Graphical data should be stored as editable objects and not just as collections of drawing primitives used to represent them. That is, applications should be able to specify *what it is* and not have to worry about *how to draw it*.

- **Interactivity**. An event model for direct interactive programming must be integrated with the representation of graphical objects.

- **Architecture**. Applications should not have to adapt to object representation or interaction policies imposed by the toolkit. Instead, the toolkit mechanisms should be used to implement the desired policies. Such flexibility should also be reflected in the ability to extend the toolkit when necessary.

Traditional 3D graphics application systems can be characterized as taking one of two approaches to object representation. GKS [3] and PHIGS+ [6] represent the *display list* approach in which objects are defined as sequences of drawing commands and cannot be treated as first-class 3D objects. Doré™ [1] and HOOPS™ [9] significantly improve the display list model by providing additional editing capabilities, but they still fall short of true 3D object representation.

Immediate mode libraries such as Iris GL™ [2], Starbase™ [7], and RenderMan™ [8] are streamlined drawing packages; they have no notion of retained or represented 3D objects (although GL and Starbase also support display lists). These libraries are focused on providing flexible and efficient interfaces to specific graphics devices or programs.

The main problem with both of these approaches is that they concentrate solely on the rendering or display aspects of application writing (a worthy task, especially considering advances in rendering hardware and algorithms during the 1970's and 1980's). However, rendering is only a small part of the task of writing an interactive application. 3D graphics packages, for the most part, have ignored user input; they often provide little more than gross-object picking. Furthermore, the programming models for these packages do not treat 3D objects as geometric, physical entities. Thus, previous systems are committed to display-oriented application development and provide little help for direct, 3D interaction support.

Another shortcoming of traditional graphics packages is that they proliferate the "duplicate database" problem. Applications store their objects in a form suited to their needs, but must convert them into structures required by the graphics package, which maintains an additional copy. Furthermore, graphics packages are typically closed systems that do not allow applications to add their own object geometries, properties, or operations.

There have been few published descriptions of 3D toolkits which attempt to solve the problems presented here. The InterViews [5] system successfully integrates rendering and interaction in the world of 2D graphics and text, but it does not extend to 3D. The Brown Animation Generation System [10] is one published system that successfully integrates abstract, 3D object representation and dynamics. It is designed primarily for animation but does include support for interactive techniques.

The toolkit described in this paper attempts to meet the needs described above. It defines an object-oriented framework for describing scenes containing 3D objects and operations on them. 3D objects are abstract representations that can render themselves when requested; they are not merely display lists. The methods by which objects are rendered can vary from machine to machine, but their representations are constant.

The framework of this toolkit is designed with application extensibility in mind. Application writers are able to add new, application-specific objects to the toolkit when necessary. By allowing application data to be incorporated into the toolkit, the need for duplicate databases is greatly reduced. Extensibility also includes object operations such as new rendering methods and geometric computations.

A simple, yet effective, model for handing events to 3D objects is integrated into the toolkit. Several interactive 3D objects are provided, allowing applications to add interactive operations, such as rotation, easily. This set of interactive objects is also extensible, and the toolkit provides several levels of support to make it easy for applications to create their own objects for direct interaction.

Overview

The 3D toolkit library consists of three main sections, as illustrated in Figure 1. Furthermore, there are two window system utility libraries built on top of the toolkit that provide window objects and handle event translation.

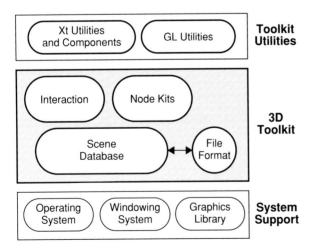

Figure 1. Overall toolkit architecture.

Each of the three toolkit sections provides a different level of pro-

gramming support. They are introduced here in order from low-level to high-level.

The foundation of the 3D toolkit is the *scene database*. It stores dynamic representations of 3D scenes as graphs (typically directed acyclic graphs) of objects called *nodes*. Various classes of nodes implement different geometries, properties, and database traversal behaviors. The database provides a set of *actions* that can be applied to scenes or parts of scenes; examples of actions are rendering, picking, computing a bounding box, handling an event, and writing to a file. The format and methods for storing scenes in files and retrieving them are defined by the database. Also included are objects for adding animation to scenes and for tracking changes to them.

The *interaction* section of the toolkit introduces event classes and "smart" nodes that process events. Event classes define an extensible set of abstract events such as `ButtonEvent` and `Location2-Event`. An example of a smart node is the `Selection` node, which provides an easy way for applications to maintain lists of selected objects. Selection tracks picking, supports various policies for replacing and extending selections, and graphically highlights selected objects. Another type of smart node is a *manipulator*, which responds to interaction events and edits other nodes in a database. A manipulator typically employs a surrogate object (e.g., bounding sphere or box) that represents the manipulator visually and provides a means for translating events into changes to the database. For example, the `Trackball` manipulator uses a bounding sphere around an object to modify the rotation of that object. Other manipulators perform object-specific functions, such as changing the illumination direction of a light source or dragging a vertex of a polyhedral shape. Manipulators provide an easy way for applications to incorporate direct 3D interaction.

The third section of the toolkit defines *node kits*, which make it easier to create structured, consistent databases. Each node kit object combines some scene database subgraph, attachment rules, and other policies into a single class. For example, the `SphereKit` is a wrapper around a sphere node that adds material, geometric transformation, and other properties in the correct place when needed. Node kits also allow programmers to create higher-level objects that encapsulate application-specific behavior.

Note that the 3D toolkit itself does not include any objects that represent windows on the display screen. This decision was made to ensure window system independence and greater portability. *Utility libraries* tied to specific window systems (such as X and GL) are built on top of the toolkit to provide convenience to application programmers. Each utility library provides a basic `RenderArea` object that maintains a resizable window that handles automatic redrawing, translates window system events into toolkit events, and distributes events to objects rendered in the window. Furthermore, the utility libraries can also provide a set of application-level *components* that implement common interactive functions. Examples of components are color editors, surface material editors, light source editors, and viewers, which process user interaction to edit cameras.

Architecture

The 3D toolkit is implemented in C++, which supports many of the object-oriented paradigms essential to extensible systems. C bindings are also provided, although much of the extensibility is not accessible from C.

Nodes

Each node in a scene database performs some specific function. There are *shape nodes* that represent geometric or physical objects (see Figure 7), *property nodes* that describe various attributes of those objects (see Figure 8), and *group nodes*, which connect other nodes into graphs and subgraphs. Other nodes, such as cameras and lights, are also provided. A representative sampling of node classes is given in Table 1.

Shape nodes:	Group nodes:
Cone	Group
Cube	Separator
Cylinder	Switch
FaceSet	Selection
IndexedFaceSet	Manipulator
IndexedLineSet	LayerGroup
IndexedTriangleMesh	Array
LineSet	MultipleCopy
NurbsCurve	
NurbsSurface	**Property nodes:**
PointSet	BaseColor
QuadMesh	Complexity
Sphere	Coordinate3
Text2	DrawStyle
Text3	Environment
TriangleStripSet	Font
	LightModel
Light/camera nodes:	Material
OrthographicCamera	MaterialBinding
PerspectiveCamera	Normal
DirectionalLight	NormalBinding
PointLight	Texture2
SpotLight	TextureCoordinate2
	Transform

Table 1. Some node classes.

Instance-specific information is stored within nodes in sub-objects called *fields*. Each node class defines some number of fields, each with a specific value type associated with it. For example, the `Cylinder` shape node contains two real-number (float) fields that represent the radius and height of a specific cylinder instance. Field objects provide a consistent mechanism for editing, querying, reading, writing, and monitoring instance data within nodes.

The set of nodes is designed to allow most of the high-volume data to be shared when possible. For example, coordinates and normal vectors are specified in separate (property) nodes that can be shared among various shapes. This scheme has the additional benefit of enforcing consistency of representation.

A variety of group node classes connect nodes into graphs. Each group node class determines if and how traversal of children is performed and how properties are inherited. A node typically inherits properties from its parent, and children of a group node usually inherit from prior siblings. Some groups provide inheritance from the group node to its parent, making insertion of properties in subgraphs simple. Other groups, such as `Separator` nodes, save state before and restore state after traversing children, isolating their effects from the rest of the graph.

These groups represent traditional, hierarchical grouping objects found in most 3D systems. However, other behaviors can be implemented. For example, the `Switch` node selects one of its children to traverse; this can be useful for implementing level-of-detail, for example. The `Array` node traverses its children multiple times, applying a transformation before each traversal to arrange the results in a 3D array.

Figure 2 depicts a scene graph whose rendered result appears in Figure 9.

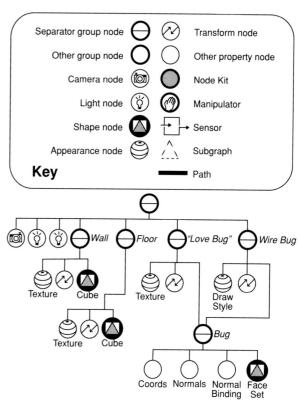

Figure 2. A simple scene graph.

Paths

A node may be a child of more than one group, allowing common subgraphs (multiple instances) to be shared. For example, a model of a bicycle may use a subgraph representing a wheel twice, with different transformation nodes applied to each instance of the wheel. This scheme can result in more compact and manageable scene representations in many cases. The downside is that it is not always possible to refer unambiguously to an object (such as the rear bicycle wheel) in the 3D scene simply by pointing to a single node. To remedy this problem, the toolkit supports *path* objects, which point to nodes in a chain from some node in the graph down to the node in question (see Figure 3). For example, performing a pick operation returns a path from the root of the graph to the shape node under the cursor, unambiguously indicating the object that was picked.

Note that a path actually defines a subgraph consisting of more than just the connected chain of nodes. The subgraph also includes all nodes (if any) below the last node in the chain and all nodes (typically to the left of the chain) that have an effect on these nodes. This definition is extremely important when performing graph editing such as cut-and-paste; all of the subgraph nodes are necessary to fully represent the selected object.

Actions

Objects called *actions* traverse scene graphs to perform specific operations, such as rendering, computing a bounding box, searching, or writing to a file. Several currently supported actions are listed in Table 2. An application performs an action on a scene in a database by applying it to a node in the scene graph, typically the root. Actions may also be applied to paths. The next section discusses the mechanism of applying actions in more detail.

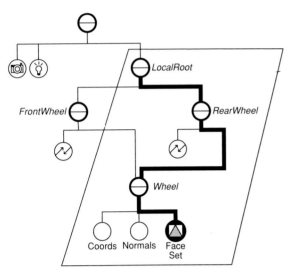

Figure 3. The *Wheel* node is multiply instanced, since it is a child of both *FrontWheel* and *RearWheel*. The path (heavy line) refers unambiguously from the local graph root to the shape defining the rear wheel. Within the parallelogram is the subgraph defined by the path.

CallbackAction	Generic scene traversal with user callbacks.
GLRenderAction	Renders objects in database.
GetBoundingBoxAction	Computes bounding box of scene or part of scene.
GetMatrixAction	Computes cumulative transformation matrix for object in scene.
HandleEventAction	Gives nodes in database a chance to handle an event.
RayPickAction	Returns frontmost object or all objects intersected by a ray cast into scene.
PrintAction	Produces PostScript primitives or other printable form of rendered scene.
SearchAction	Looks for specific node or type of node in database.

Table 2. Action classes.

The 3D toolkit is designed to be extensible in many areas. It is assumed that users will often extend the set of nodes to create new shapes, properties, manipulators (which are derived from nodes), and other classes. Similarly, it may be useful in some applications to create actions to perform new tasks while traversing a scene graph. Unfortunately, the standard virtual method table implementation in C++ makes this two-way extensibility very difficult: it is relatively easy to create a new node class that supports all of the standard actions, but it is not possible for application writers to add new action methods to existing standard node classes. This could be done by creating subclasses of all nodes that supported the new actions, but this is an unattractive solution.

To solve the two-way extensibility problem, the toolkit uses a two-dimensional virtual table to implement node/action methods. Each entry in the table is a method that implements a certain action for a particular node. Adding a new node is equivalent to adding a column to this table, whereas adding a new action involves adding a new row. For convenience, standard action methods are implemented as regular virtual functions on nodes.

This method lookup scheme is the justification for implementing

actions as separate objects. The resulting syntax for applying an action to a graph, `action->apply(node)`, is fairly easy to use and understand.

Applying Actions

Applying an action to a scene graph usually results in a traversal of the graph. Although group node subclasses are free to define their own traversal behavior, standard groups visit their children in left-to-right order. Therefore, scene graph traversal is usually depth-first.

Most actions require *state* to be accumulated during traversal. For example, when a shape node is encountered during rendering traversal, it may need to know the current material, set of coordinates, and drawing style. Each of these properties is stored in an *element* in the state. Typically, property nodes change one or more state elements, and shape nodes interpret the current values of the elements.

When a `Separator` node (a type of group) is encountered, traversal state is saved before visiting its children and is restored afterwards. Because this node is used very often in scene graphs to segregate objects, state saving and restoration must be efficient. The state puts off saving element values until those values are modified after the save; this "lazy" scheme avoids copying data unnecessarily.

Rendering and Picking

Because the toolkit is designed for interactive graphics applications, the action that performs rendering must be capable of interactive speeds. Therefore, the rendering methods built into nodes have been tuned for maximum performance. The toolkit can also boost rendering performance by caching state at crucial points. For example, once it has been determined how to render a subgraph, caching a display list can make the next traversal fast and easy. Caching is built into `Separator` nodes and can be activated by an application when desired. References to nodes used to build a cache are stored with it, so any changes to those nodes will automatically invalidate the cache. Additionally, it is possible to abort a rendering action during traversal; this is useful when implementing real-time applications and for minimizing the wait for event processing in interactive applications.

Some rendering features, such as texture mapping, are not implemented on all supported platforms. Users of the toolkit do not need to test whether a particular machine supports a feature; they can just specify the feature by inserting nodes in the scene database, and the toolkit does the rest. On architectures that do not support the feature, the toolkit can simulate it in software (if this would not greatly compromise interactive performance) or elide it.

Interactive applications require flexible and efficient picking. The `RayPickAction` can be used to find a path to the frontmost object under the cursor. If an application requires more information, it can query the action for more details, such as the world-space and object-space points of intersection and the surface normals at those points. Each shape node class can define additional, specific information that can be queried. For example, objects constructed from sets of vertices can return the face containing the intersection point and the edge and vertex closest to it.

Picking performance, like that of rendering, is improved by caching. `Separator` nodes automatically cache bounding boxes, which are used by the pick action for culling. This caching speeds picking enough to make locate highlighting (dynamic highlighting of the object under a moving cursor) possible.

Sensors

Sensor objects are used to track changes to nodes and to implement simple animation. There are two major types of sensors, each of which calls a user-defined callback function when triggered. A *data sensor* is attached to a node and is triggered when it detects changes to data in that node or any descendant node. These sensors can be used by an interactive editor to update sliders or other indicators whenever any other program element changes values used by the editor. A data sensor can also be attached to the root of a graph to track changes to the entire scene (e.g., to determine when to redraw).

The other type of sensor is a *timer sensor*, which is triggered at a specified time or at regular intervals. For example, an application can set a timer sensor to trigger 30 times a second to animate parts of a graph. Figure 4 illustrates how sensors can be connected to a scene database.

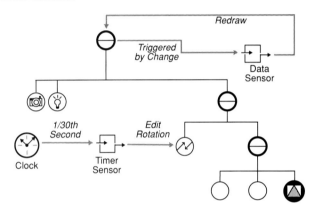

Figure 4. A scene graph with sensors attached. The data sensor at the top of the graph is triggered whenever a change is made to any node below the top; it is used to determine when to redraw the graph. The timer sensor connected to the clock fires at regular intervals, animating the rotation of the object at the lower right.

3D Event Model

The toolkit and utility libraries use a very simple algorithm to distribute user events to manipulators and other smart nodes. An event specific to the window system is generated as the result of some user action (mouse motion, keyboard button press, etc.) and is passed to the instance of the utility library's `RenderArea` object that corresponds to the window in which the event occurred. If the `RenderArea` is part of a component, the component might handle the event itself. For example, a viewer component might process all mouse motion to edit the position and orientation of a camera in the scene.

If the component does not process the event, the `RenderArea` translates the window system event into a toolkit event (independent of any window system) and distributes it to the nodes in the 3D scene. The `RenderArea` applies an instance of the `HandleEventAction` to the root node of the graph to distribute the event. This action performs a standard traversal of the graph. Any node that is interested in events may process the event and indicate that it has handled it. As with all other actions, each node class is free to define its own behavior when handling events.

Some nodes, such as manipulators, may be interested in mouse events only when the cursor is over their rendered objects. Such nodes may ask the `HandleEventAction` for a path to the object

under the cursor. To process this request, the action automatically performs a pick (using a `RayPickAction`) to determine this path; it is cached so further inquiries do not require additional picks. Therefore, pick correlation is performed only when requested, speeding up the event handling process.

Database traversal for the `HandleEventAction` stops as soon as a node is found to handle the event. Nodes that want to monitor events without ending the traversal can do so by omitting the step that marks the event as handled. Also, nodes that are interested in future events can perform a "grab," meaning that they will receive all events until further notice. Event grabbing is useful for processing mouse press-move-release sequences.

An example of the workings of the event model is illustrated in Figure 5.

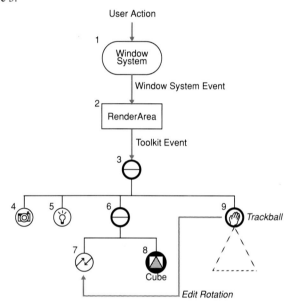

Figure 5. Event model example. (1) The window system processes a user action and produces a window system event. (2) The `RenderArea` associated with the window in which the action occurred translates the event into a toolkit event and passes it to a `HandleEventAction` which it applies to the root of its graph. (3) The root node of the graph passes the event to its children. (4)-(5) The camera and light nodes are not interested in events, and therefore they ignore this one. (6) The next child, a separator group, passes the event to its children. (7)-(8) The transform and cube nodes ignore the event. (9) The trackball manipulator checks if the event is a left-mouse-down, and, if so, determines whether the cursor is over the trackball object defined in its subgraph. If the cursor is over the object, the trackball grabs future events and indicates that it has handled the event. Subsequent events are sent immediately to the trackball manipulator, which processes mouse motion events and edits the rotation field in the transform node. This process continues until a left-mouse-up event is processed by the trackball, which then releases its grab.

Manipulators

The event model described above is designed to allow manipulators and other interactive nodes to be integrated easily into graphics applications. As an illustration, this section explores the implementation of the trackball manipulator (Figure 10) in more detail.

As mentioned earlier, the trackball manipulator places an invisible surrogate bounding sphere around the 3D object it is manipulating. The sphere is used to translate mouse motion into rotational changes to this object. Three cylindrical bands around the sphere make it easy to specify rotations constrained to the principal axes.

When a trackball is activated, it is given a path to the geometric transformation node it is to edit to achieve the rotation. The application inserts a `Trackball` node into its scene graph, ensuring that the trackball is rendered with the rest of the scene and that it is given an opportunity to handle events. The `Trackball` node (derived from `Separator`) has as children a scene graph that defines the surrogate sphere and constraint bands.

When a `Trackball` node is encountered during traversal by a `HandleEventAction`, the node checks if the event is a left-mouse-down. If so, it asks the action for the object under the cursor (computed by picking). If the cursor is over the trackball object, the node does two things. First, it announces to the action that it has handled the event, so traversal need not continue. Second, it performs a grab so that all future events will go directly to the trackball. The grab will be released when a left-mouse-up event is processed by the trackball. Each intervening mouse-motion event is processed by the trackball to compute rotational changes to its target object.

The toolkit includes many *simple* manipulators, each of which performs a single task, such as translation in one dimension or cylindrical rotation. Also in the toolkit are *compound* manipulators (such as the trackball) that combine several simple manipulators into a more complex, integrated tool. Figure 11 illustrates several manipulators.

Node Kits

Because the scene graph library is general enough to provide maximum performance and flexibility, it can often be confusing to novice users. There are no strict rules for forming scene graphs, so it is possible to create bizarre and sometimes meaningless collections of nodes unless some sort of structural guidelines are imposed. (This situation is reminiscent of assembly code and structured programming.) Furthermore, class-specific traversal and inheritance rules make it difficult to examine a scene graph and determine exactly how subgraphs of nodes relate to "objects" (chairs, bicycles) in the 3D scene.

Node kits provide one way to make these tasks easier by enforcing a consistent policy for database construction, editing, and inquiry. Each node kit effectively contains some structured subgraph of database nodes. A template associated with the node kit determines which nodes can be added when necessary, and where they should be added. For example, the `SphereKit` node represents a sphere object; its template allows a material, geometric transformation, and other properties to be inserted in the correct place when needed (Figure 6).

Another use of node kits is to define application-specific objects and semantics. For example, consider a flight simulation package that includes a variety of objects representing airplanes. Each of these airplanes consists of the same general scene graph structure (e.g., fuselage, wings, and landing gear) as well as some airplane-specific methods (e.g., *bank-left*, *raise-landing-gear*). To an application writer using this package, each type of airplane can be dealt with in a similar way. There is no need to know the details of the structure of the subgraph representing the landing gear to raise it, since there is a general method for doing so.

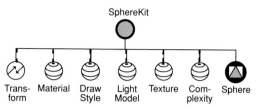

Figure 6. Sphere node kit. When an application creates an instance of the kit, a template of the above graph is constructed, opaque to the application. The application makes changes to the sphere only though the node kit. Nodes connected by dashed lines are created only when necessary. For example, applying a transformation to the node kit is implemented internally as a change to the transform node, which is created first if necessary.

Callbacks

No toolkit can ever be complete; users will always want to add something. One way to extend the set of objects provided by the toolkit is to derive new classes from existing ones. Although the toolkit is designed to make such extensions as easy as possible, sometimes an easier mechanism is useful. For this reason, several objects in the toolkit provide callback mechanisms for quick prototyping of new features.

The `Callback` node, for example, invokes a user-defined function whenever it is encountered during traversal for any action; this node makes it easy to introduce specialized behavior into a scene graph or to prototype new nodes without subclassing. Similarly, the `CallbackAction` allows functions to be called before and after each node encountered during traversal, giving them access to the current traversal state.

Other classes provide callbacks during various interactive processes, such as direct manipulation and selection of objects.

Conclusions and Future Work

The toolkit presented here is an attempt to make it easier for graphics application developers to design and implement 3D applications with direct interaction. The flexible and extensible 3D database makes it possible for applications to use only one representation of application data. By integrating interactive objects into the data with a simple event model, the toolkit allows applications to support direct manipulation of 3D data, which is often more friendly and intuitive than conventional widget-driven interfaces. Of course, the 3D toolkit still allows standard widgets to be integrated into applications in addition to the direct interfaces. Sample applications showing a variety of interactive techniques are shown in operation in Figure 12 through Figure 15.

An obvious direction for the future is extending the toolkit to have more nodes, actions, manipulators, and components. Chief among these are volumes, more 2D shapes, shape-specific manipulators, photorealistic rendering, and the ability to generate and return primitives (polygons, lines, etc.) for all shapes. This last feature can be used to implement radiosity, simulation, and analysis.

Other potential directions for the toolkit include:

Animation. Sensors provide the mechanism upon which to build more complex animation and constraint schemes. The toolkit could provide higher-level classes to facilitate the creation and storage of constrained, timed, and scripted motion.

Shared databases. Running distinct components or applications as separate processes requires databases to be stored in shared memory to avoid duplicating large amounts of data. The challenge is to design a means for exclusive access into shared memory that does not greatly compromise performance.

Acknowledgments

The other members of the team that designed, implemented, and documented the 3D toolkit are Thad Beier, Gavin Bell, Alain Dumesny, David Immel, Paul Isaacs, Howard Look, David Mott, Nick Thompson, and Josie Wernecke. Thanks to Derrick Burns for NURBS support, Paul Haeberli for help with printing algorithms, and Delle Maxwell for assistance with images and aesthetics.

Thanks to Wei Yen and Silicon Graphics for their support of the Iris Inventor™ 3D toolkit project [4].

References

[1]   *Doré Programmer's Guide, Release 5.0*, Kubota Pacific Computer, Incorporated, Santa Clara, Calif., 1991.

[2]   *Graphics Library Programming Guide*, Silicon Graphics Computer Systems, Mountain View, Calif., 1991.

[3]   International Standards Organization, *International Standard Information Processing Systems — Computer Graphics — Graphical Kernel System for Three Dimensions (GKS-3D) Functional Description*, ISO Document Number 8805:1988(E), American National Standards Institute, New York, 1988.

[4]   *Iris Inventor Programming Guide*, Silicon Graphics Computer Systems, Mountain View, Calif., 1992.

[5]   Mark Linton, Paul Caulder, John A. Interrante, Steven Tang, and John M. Vlissides, *InterViews Reference Manual, Version 3.0.1.*, Stanford University, October 1991.

[6]   PHIGS+ Committee, Andries van Dam, chair, "PHIGS+ Functional Description, Revision 3.0," *Computer Graphics*, **22**(3), pp. 125-218 (July 1988).

[7]   *Starbase Graphics Techniques and Display List Programmer's Guide*, Hewlett-Packard Company, Fort Collins, Colo., 1991.

[8]   Steve Upstill, *The RenderMan Companion*, Addison-Wesley, Reading, Mass., 1990.

[9]   Garry Wiegand and Bob Covey, *HOOPS Reference Manual, Version 3.0*, Ithaca Software, 1991.

[10]   Robert C. Zeleznik, D. Brookshire Conner, Matthias M. Wloka, Daniel G. Aliaga, Nathan T. Huang, Philip M. Hubbard, Brian Knep, Henry Kaufman, John F. Hughes, and Andries van Dam, "An Object-Oriented Framework for the Integration of Interactive Animation Techniques," *Computer Graphics (SIGGRAPH '91 Proceedings)* **25**(4) pp. 105-111 (July, 1991).

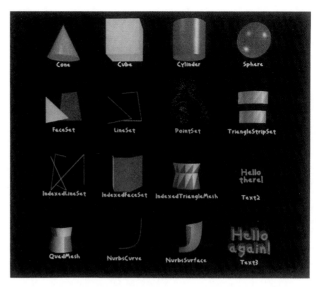

Figure 7. Examples of shape nodes provided by the toolkit.

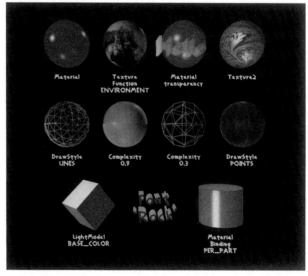

Figure 8. Examples of property nodes provided by the toolkit.

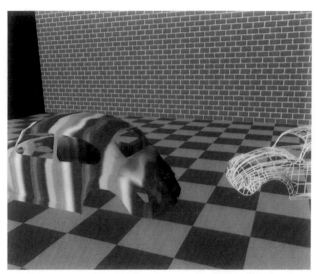

Figure 9. The result of rendering the scene graph in Figure 2.

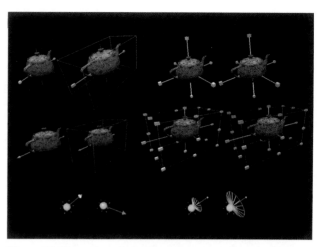

Figure 11. Examples of simple and compound manipulators. Each manipulator is shown in the inactive (left) and active (right) states. Clockwise, from upper left, the manipulators are: one-axis scale, jack, handle box, spot light, directional light, and one-axis translate.

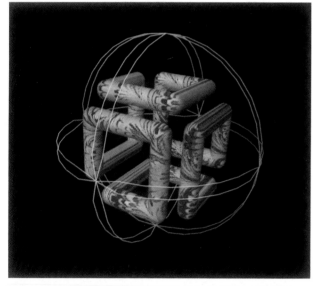

Figure 10. A trackball manipulator being used to rotate an object directly.

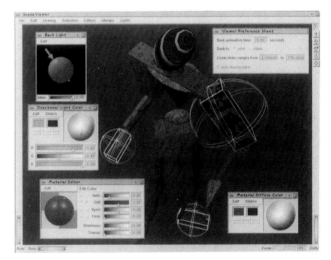

Figure 12. A sample application showing several forms of interaction. The large 3D window is a viewer component. Selected parts of the humanoid figure being viewed are highlighted with yellow bounding boxes. These parts are also enclosed by `Trackball` manipulators, which are used to rotate and scale objects directly. Other components in the figure are used to edit materials, light sources, and viewing options.

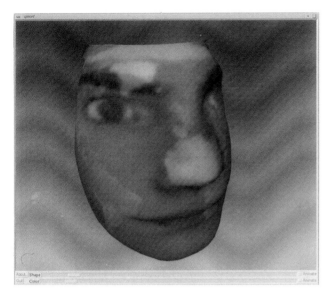

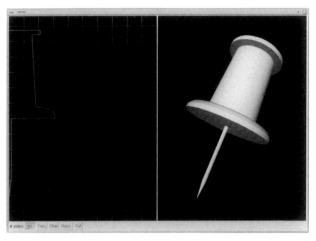

Figure 15. An application for creating objects of revolution. The same profile manipulator as shown in Figure 14 is used to edit the revolution profile.

Figure 13. A three-dimensional morphing application. Geometry and color/texture can be interpolated independently. (Thanks to Rick Pasetto for letting us morph his face.)

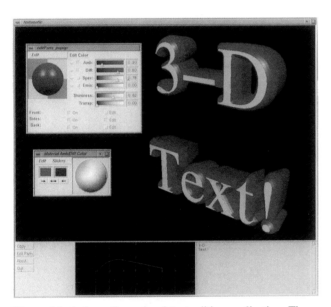

Figure 14. A three-dimensional text editing application. The small window at the bottom contains a profile curve manipulator which is used to extrude the 3D text.

Using Deformations to Explore 3D Widget Design

Scott S. Snibbe, Kenneth P. Herndon, Daniel C. Robbins,
D. Brookshire Conner and Andries van Dam

Brown University
Department of Computer Science
Providence, RI 02912
(401) 863-7693; {sss,kph,dcr,dbc,avd}@cs.brown.edu

CR Categories

H.5.2 [Information Interfaces and Presentation]: User Interfaces; Interaction Styles; Theory and Methods; I.3.5 [Computer Graphics]: Computational Geometry and Object Modeling; Curve, Surface, Solid, and Object Representations; I.3.6 [Computer Graphics]: Methodology and Techniques; Interaction Techniques

1   A 3D Interface for Deformations

We are developing a framework for creating interactive 3D environments for applications in design, education, and the communication of information and ideas [3]. Our most recent work focuses on providing a useful and powerful interface to such a complex environment. To this end we have developed *3D widgets*, objects that encapsulate 3D geometry and behavior, to control other objects in the scene [2]. We build 3D widgets as first-class objects in our real-time animation system. Because our system allows rapid prototyping of objects, we hope to enlarge today's surprisingly small vocabulary of 3D widgets that includes menus floating in 3D, gestural picking, translation and rotation, cone trees, and perspective walls.

As a way to focus on issues of 3D widget design, we have developed widgets to perform a particular task: applying high-level deformations to 3D objects [1]. The complexity of these operations makes numerical specification or panels of sliders difficult to use, and yet direct manipulation interfaces cannot provide meaningful feedback without fixing most parameters. In this video paper, we show a set of new 3D widgets to control deformations called *racks*.

A simple rack consists of a bar specifying the axis of deformation and some number of handles attached to the bar specifying additional deformation parameters. For example, a taper rack has two additional handles. Moving the ends of the handles towards or away from the axis bar changes the amount of taper of the deformed object; changing the distance between the handles changes the region over which the deformation is applied.

A more complex rack can have multiple handles specifying different deformations. The racks in Figures 1–3 all have handles for twisting (purple), tapering (blue), and bending (red) an object. The deformation range is the region between the twist and taper handles.

2   The Issues in 3D Widget Design

Many of the issues in designing 3D widgets are similar to those in designing a good 2D interface. However, good answers that serve in 2D are not necessarily good answers in more complex 3D environments. For example, two common 2D interface solutions are control panels (e.g., sliders, buttons, and menus) and the direct manipulation of objects (e.g., dragging files in the Macintosh Finder). A control panel for a deformation can require as many as a dozen sliders and thus consumes a great deal of screen real estate; it also artificially differentiates related parameters and does not provide good correlation to its 3D effects. In addition, although these controls may be arranged so that related sliders (say, for the three components of a vector) are logically grouped, users are rarely able to correlate changes in these controls with corresponding changes in the deformed objects.

A 3D direct manipulation interface to control the same deformation might be implemented in which the user clicks and drags the faces of an object. One problem with this approach is that most computer graphics objects look rigid, as though they do not permit deformation. Rigid objects appear to afford six degrees of freedom, three translational and three rotational, and direct manipulation techniques like virtual sphere rotation work very well because they exploit this apparent rigidity. To compensate for the lack of feedback in certain direct manipulation techniques, we can introduce tools that make additional degrees of freedom available; the rack is an example of such a tool. However, the widget's geometry, while possibly suggesting the kinds of actions that can be performed, may at the same time obscure the object of interest or unnecessarily complicate the scene. In addition to showing this tradeoff, we consider the following issues in widget design:

- Self-disclosure

  A widget whose geometry indicates its behavior is called *self-disclosing*. For example, a handle that twists an object can itself be a twisted object, thereby suggesting its action.

- Implicit versus explicit control of parameters

  Widgets usually explicitly control one or more parameters of an action. For example, a handle in a taper rack controls the amount that the object is tapered. A widget may simplify an action by implicitly controlling other parameters. For example, a widget can implicitly control the tesselation of objects by varying the tesselation with the amount of deformation. There is no handle to explicitly control the tesselation.

- Degrees of freedom

  A 3D environment offers multiple degrees of freedom that can hinder as well as help a particular operation. A tool can be made more effective by *removing* unnecessary degrees of freedom with constraints.

- Intended use

An impressionistic modeling tool for illustration or design requires only that the modeled object "look right." Tools designed for manufacturing and mechanical design, however, must set parameters to precise values and produce changes that are exactly reproducible.

3 Conclusions

The design space of 3D widgets is extremely large and unexplored. A great deal of experimentation, by both designers and users, is necessary before a common, useful, and powerful collection of 3D metaphors and widgets becomes as widespread as those of the 2D windows, icons, and mouse interfaces of today. By allowing the same power for widget development as it does for application development, our system provides the rapid prototyping environment necessary to explore this vast design space — a variant of a deformation widget can be built within a few hours, a completely new widget within days. We can now begin to look critically at 3D interface design and develop productive environments that use the power of 3D effectively.

In addition, we are now in the process of using our widgets to build more widgets, leading to a complete 3D interface construction set that will itself be a 3D interface. For example, the deformed handles of some of the widgets presented in the video paper were made with these very same widgets. We will also continue designing widgets, extending our existing designs to include animation, complex rendering techniques, and even simulation methods in order to explore, for example, physically based widgets.

Acknowledgments

This work was supported in part by the NSF/DARPA Science and Technology Center for Computer Graphics and Scientific Visualization. We also gratefully acknowledge the sponsorship of IBM, NCR, Sun Microsystems, Hewlett Packard and Digital Equipment Corporation. We also thank the members of the Brown University Graphics Group for their help and support, especially Bob Zeleznik, Nate Huang, and our visitor from Darmstadt, Frank Graf.

References

[1] Alan H. Barr. Global and local deformations of solid primitives. In *Proceedings of the ACM SIGGRAPH, Computer Graphics*, volume 18(3), pages 21–30, July 1984.

[2] D. Brookshire Conner, Scott S. Snibbe, Kenneth P. Herndon, Daniel C. Robbins, Robert C. Zeleznik, and Andries van Dam. Three-dimensional widgets. In *Proceedings of the 1992 Symposium on Interactive 3D Graphics*, pages 183–188, 1992.

[3] Robert C. Zeleznik, D. Brookshire Conner, Matthias M. Wloka, Daniel G. Aliaga, Nathan T. Huang, Philip M. Hubbard, Brian Knep, Henry Kaufman, John F. Hughes, and Andries van Dam. An object-oriented framework for the integration of interactive animation techniques. In *Proceedings of the ACM SIGGRAPH, Computer Graphics*, volume 25(4), pages 105–112, July 1991.

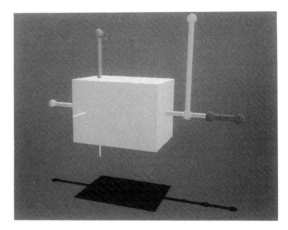

Figure 1: The starting configuration for a pink cube and a rack with twist (purple), taper (blue), and bend (red) handles.

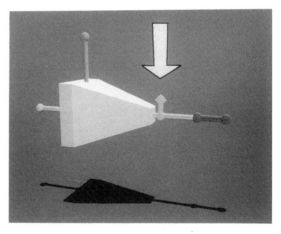

Figure 2: The taper handle is translated downward, tapering the cube. The deformation range is the region between the twist and taper handles.

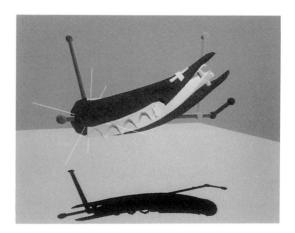

Figure 3: A pocketknife is twisted and bent with a rack.

Interactive Inspection of Solids: Cross-sections and Interferences

Jarek Rossignac, Abe Megahed, Bengt-Olaf Schneider

Interactive Geometric Modeling, IBM T.J. Watson Research Center

Abstract

To reduce the cost of correcting design errors, assemblies of mechanical parts are modeled using CAD systems and verified electronically before the designs are sent to manufacturing. Shaded images are insufficient for examining the internal structures of assemblies and for detecting interferences. Thus, designers must rely on expensive numerical techniques that compute geometric representations of cross-sections and of intersections of solids. The solid-clipping approach presented here bypasses these geometric calculations and offers realtime rendering of cross-sections and interferences for solids represented by their facetted boundaries. In its simplest form, the technique is supported by contemporary high-end graphics workstations. Its variations, independently developed elsewhere, have already been demonstrated. Our implementation is based on the concept of a cut-volume interactively manipulated to remove obstructing portions of the assembly and reveal its internal structure. For clarity, faces of the cut-volume which intersect a single solid are hatched and shaded with the color of that solid. Interference areas between two or more solids are highlighted. Furthermore, to help users find the first occurrence of an interference along a search direction, we have developed an adaptive subdivision search based on a projective approach which guarantees a sufficient condition for object disjointness. The additional performance cost for solid-clipping and interference highlighting is comparable to the standard rendering cost. An efficient implementation of the disjointness test requires a minor extension of the graphics functions currently supported on commercial hardware.

CR Categories and Subject Descriptions:
I.3.3 [Computer Graphics]: Picture/Image Generation—*Display Algorithms;* **I.3.5** [Computational Geometry and Object Modeling]: Solid Representation; **I.3.7** [Three-Dimensional Graphics and Realism]: Visible Surface Algorithms; **J.6** [Computer Aided Engineering]: Computer Aided Design.

Keywords: Cross-section, Clipping, Interferences.

Authors' address:
IBM Research, P.O. Box 704, Yorktown Heights, NY 10598.
Rossignac: jarek@watson.ibm.com, 914-784-7630.
Schneider: bosch@watson.ibm.com, 914-784-6002.

1. Introduction

Design errors discovered at the manufacturing or assembly stages result in expensive engineering changes and production delays. Manufacturers of mechanical goods have invested in advanced graphics hardware and in the solid modeling technology hoping that they will eliminate the need for clay models and drastically reduce the number of design errors prior to fabrication. Although designers can interactively visualize subsets of an assembly using shaded or wireframe pictures, they need cross-sections and interference highlights to understand how components fit together in tight assemblies. For example, the shaded image of the small assembly in Figure 1 may be produced in realtime on most high-end graphics workstations, but reveals neither the internal structures of the assembly nor the interferences between its components.

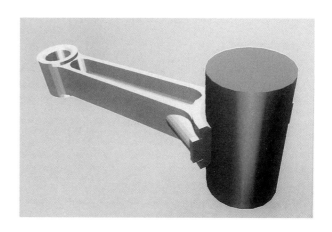

Figure 1. *A small mechanical assembly: The interference between the cylinder and the connecting rod is not apparent.*

The availability of an informationally complete solid modeling representation of each assembly component permits the automatic calculation of cross-sections and the calculation of interferences. Unfortunately, classical implementations of these functions rely on expensive geometric operations, which, when applied to models of industrial complexity, increase the system's response time far beyond tolerable limits for interactive sessions.

This paper describes new techniques for automatically: (1) **filling and shading multi-facetted cross-sections through solids**, (2) **identifying and highlighting areas of interference in a cross-section**, and (3) **positioning cross-sectioning planes at the beginning of interference or contact regions.**

The solid-clipping techniques presented here exploit existing graphics architectures in novel ways to create, in realtime, shaded images showing cross-sections, cut-outs, and interference regions. Cut-outs are discussed in Section 2. Interferences are addressed in Section 3. The result of a combination of these techniques is illustrated in Figure 2, where a portion of the assembly was cut away using a user-specified cut-volume and where the interference region between the two components was highlighted in red. Furthermore, the cross-section areas are hatched for clarity and the cut-away portions are indicated using transparent faces and silhouette lines.

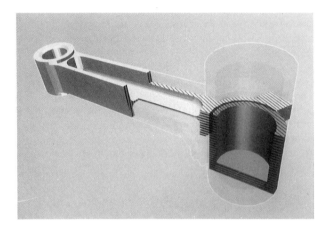

Figure 2. *Graphics inspection techniques*: A multi-facet cut-volume is removed to show the internal structure of the assembly. The resulting cross-sections are displayed in the appropriate color and hatched. Red areas indicate interferences.

These techniques are based on clipping planes and on auxiliary bit-planes that are manipulated during the standard surface scan-conversion to create and later exploit appropriate pixel-masks. They exhibit realtime performance for simple assembly models.

A solution similar to ours for cross-section filling and interference highlights has been independently developed at Silicon Graphics Inc. by Kurt Akeley in 1991 [1]. It is discussed in Section 3.1. Hewlett Packard's graphics library also offers filling and interference highlights, but no description of the underlying techniques is available. Since the manual mentions "the collection of capping edge data" and "cap polygons" [6], we conjecture that an approach different from ours is used.

The automatic detection of interferences is described in Section 3.2. Its requires feedback from the graphics hardware to the application. An efficient implementation of this feedback loop is not supported on commercially available workstations; thus we simulate it by a software inspection of the frame buffer.

2. Solid-clipping

This section describes a new technique for computing in realtime images of solids, or of assemblies of solids, from which user-controlled linear half-spaces or polyhedral cut-volumes have been subtracted. The technique leverages on the recent support of auxiliary clipping planes

and pixel-masks in the rendering pipeline of high-end graphics workstations [13].

Clipping planes are commonly used for surface-clipping, i.e. to trim the objects' faces prior to display. The difference between the solid-clipping technique presented in this section and the previously available surface-clipping is illustrated in Figures 3 and 4 using a single-face cut-volume, i.e. a volume bounded by a single clipping plane. Figure 3 shows the effect of the standard surface-clipping, which treats each solid as a hollow shell, because clipping planes do not fill pixels, but merely limit the extent of faces. The image is confusing, since the viewer must mentally reconstruct the areas where the clipping plane intersects the solids. Figure 4 shows the result of the new solid-clipping technique, which, in addition to clipping the solids' faces, also fills the regions of intersection between each solid and the clipping plane. These cross-section regions are hatched to visually differentiate them from other surfaces in the assembly.

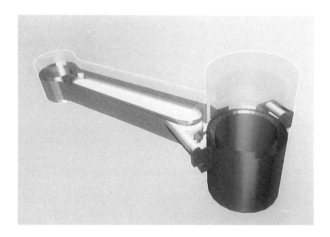

Figure 3. *Surface-clipping*: The standard surface-clipping technique correctly removes portions of the solids' faces, but does not fill in the cross-section areas.

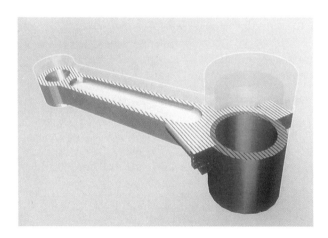

Figure 4. *Solid-clipping*: In addition to the surface clipping of Figure 3, the cross-section of each solid by the clipping plane is hatched and shaded using the color of the solid.

A standard way to produce the image of Figure 4 is to perform the Boolean difference operation between the solids and the cut-volume and to display the result. A slightly better approach combines surface clipping with the display of a cross-sections computed as the geometric intersection of the solid with a plane [7]. A CSG formulation of the result may also be used with special-purpose direct CSG rendering hardware [3-5, 11].

The technique described in this section provides an alternative which neither requires the hardware used for efficiently rendering CSG models nor any complex geometric intersection calculations. It works with any boundary representation for solids, provided that the scan-conversion method used by the graphics hardware satisfies the following parity condition.

When the entire solid fits between the front and the back clipping planes, each pixel is visited an even number of times during the scan-conversion of the solid's faces.

Early scan-conversion techniques did not guarantee the parity condition at pixels traversed by the projection of a common edge between two faces. A reliable implementation of the methods presented here requires a "true point-sampling" scan-conversion [9].

To establish which points of a clipping plane lie inside any given solid, we use the following property [14].

A point Q lies inside a bounded solid S if and only if Q is not on the boundary of S and if a semi-infinite line (ray) starting at Q intersects the boundary of S at an odd number of isolated transversal intersection points[1]. Since the result is independent of the direction for the ray, the viewing direction may be used. Suppose that the location of Q is stored in the z-buffer as Z(q), the depth of the pixel q corresponding to the projection of Q onto the screen.

Q lies in the interior of S if and only if the number of times q is visited during the scan-conversion of the faces of S with a depth greater than Z(q) is odd.

Furthermore:

A point Q, projecting on a pixel q and lying on a clipping plane C, is inside a solid S if and only if q is visited an odd number of times while scan-converting the faces of S after they have been clipped using C.

Note that all points Q of C that correspond to pixels of the screen may be classified during a single pass over S. We use the above property to construct a pixel mask (one bit per pixel), Mp, for the cross-section region where the clipping plane intersects any given solid. The process is illustrated in Figure 5.

When the outward normal of a cut-volume face points away from the viewer, it corresponds to a potential front face of the solid resulting from the cut. Therefore, we use the term **front clipping plane** when referring to the planes

containing such a back face of the cut-volume. We need to fill only the cross-sections of front clipping planes, because other (back) clipping planes are never visible.

To make the classification results consistent with the mathematical definition of the regularized difference between the original solid and the cut-volume [8], the clipping of faces coincident with the clipping plane must be performed using a "less than" depth test for clipping planes and a "less or equal" depth-test otherwise[2].

The technique assumes that the solids are not clipped by the back plane of the viewing volume. If the depth span of the object is known, it suffices to temporarily adjust the back plane. However, changes to the z-resolution may produce side-effects. It is also possible to set the perspective such that the back plane coincides with the horizon,[3] to guarantee that no object is clipped by the back clipping-plane.

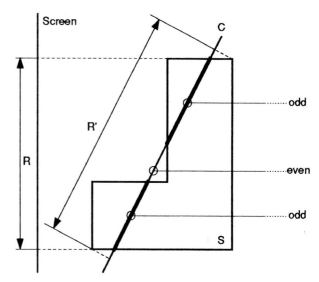

Figure 5. *Parity-based mask construction: The pixel-mask, Mp, for the intersection of plane C with solid S is computed by toggling the mask during the scan-conversion of the faces of S behind C. R is the projection of S onto the screen and R' the projection of S onto C.*

A high-level algorithm for rendering assemblies clipped by a cut-volume composed of a single half-space is presented below. It renders the cross-section through each solid using the color (surface properties) of that solid[4]. If C is a back clipping plane, the standard surface clipping approach may be used, otherwise, we proceed as follows.

Single-plane solid-clipping:

```
01   Activate C as a front clipping plane
02   For all pixels do Z=0, I=0, Mp=0
03   For each solid S do
04       Render all the faces of S toggling Mp
05       Deactivate C
06       Shade C and reset Mp where Mp==1
```

---

1. Tangential intersection cases, where the ray touches a primitive's boundary without crossing it, must be treated properly by the hardware scan-conversion, so as to ensure the correct parity at all pixels [9]. Cases where a one-dimensional subset of the ray lies on a face are ignored by scan-conversion procedures without compromising the parity condition.

2. Scan-conversion inaccuracies, which produce inconsistencies when displaying overlapping coplanar faces, may be addressed by introducing tolerances in the depth-test [11].

3. The screen lies exactly between the viewpoint and the horizon-plane of all the vanishing points.

4. Interference areas may exhibit color mixing unless the interference highlighting technique of the next section is used.

Line 02 resets the z-buffer (Z), the frame buffer (I), and the pixel mask (Mp). During the rendering of the faces of S (Line 04), the portions cut away by C or by the clipping planes of the viewing volume are discarded. The remaining portions are scan-converted and for each surface point s projecting on some pixel q, the following operations are performed: (1) toggle the parity mask Mp(q), (2) if the depth of s is smaller than the depth stored at q, update the z-buffer and the frame buffer at q. Note that both the front and the back faces of S must be scan-converted for the mask computation, although only the front faces need to be rendered.

The cross-section filling of Line 06 is performed using the color and surface properties of S, to distinguish the contribution of each solid to the cross-section. C is deactivated (Line 05) to prevent self-clipping.

The standard depth-test for hidden surface removal is used during the rendering of the faces of S (Line 04) and of the cross-section C (Line 06) to ensure that only visible faces in a scene are rendered. Consequently, **convex cut-volumes** may be produced using several passes through this algorithm for different clipping planes.

To render the cross-section using the standard scan-conversion with hidden-surface removal, a suitable face F_C on C must be constructed. As the clipping plane is manipulated interactively, F_C must be adjusted to always contain the cross-section area. We use a rectangle in C enclosing the orthogonal projection, R', of S onto C (Figure 5).

Polyhedral cut-volumes with concave edges defined as arbitrary Boolean combinations of half-spaces may be needed to better expose the internal structure of tight assemblies. An example is shown Figure 6. The remainder of this section presents an extension of the solid-clipping technique for such cut-volumes.

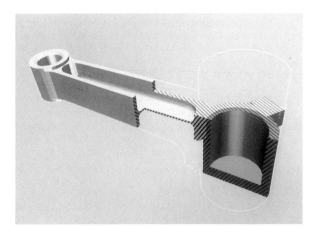

Figure 6. Solid-clipping with non-convex cut-volumes: Three clipping planes, $C_1, C_2,$ and $C_3,$ are used to define a compound cut-volume, $C_1 \cap (C_2 \cup C_3)$.

Although, the metaphor of a "cut-volume", v, interactively manipulated by the designer to remove obstructing portions of the assembly may be more intuitive than the notion of a "clipping volume", v', used to delimit the assembly through an intersection operation, both formulations are equivalent, since v' is the complement, $\bar{v}$, of v, and for any solid S, we have: $S - v = S \cap v'$.

Given a Boolean expression of v, it is straightforward to extract a disjunctive form[5] for v'. For example, if the linear half-space volumes are denoted v_i, the cut-volume $v = (v_1 \cup v_2) \cap (v_3 \cup v_4)$ yields the following disjunctive form of two products: $(\overline{v_1} \cap \overline{v_2}) \cup (\overline{v_3} \cap \overline{v_4})$ for v'.

The intersections of S with these convex clipping-products are processed one-by-one using the algorithm below. The image of the union of these intersections is composed via the standard z-buffer test.

```
Solid-clipping algorithm for a clipping-product:
01  For all pixels do Z=0, I=0, Mp=0
02  For each solid S do
03     For each clipping-product P do
04        Activate all the front clipping planes of P
05        Disable writing into the depth and frame buffers
06        Render all the faces of S toggling Mp
07        Select rendering color for S
08        Enable writing into the depth and frame buffers
09        Activate all the front and back clipping planes
10        Render the front faces of S
11        For each front clipping plane C in P do
12           Deactivate C
13           Shade C and reset Mp for pixels where Mp==1
14           Activate C
15        Deactivate all planes of P
```

In Line 06, the front and back faces of S are clipped against all the front clipping planes of a product and then scan-converted. Each time a pixel q is visited during that scan-conversion, its mask bit Mp(q) is toggled. The frame and z-buffers are never updated during that scan-conversion (see Line 05). After the execution of Line 06, the mask Mp corresponds to a cut-volume composed of only the front cutting planes of that product (see Figure 7). When the cross-sections are displayed for that product (Line 13), this mask is used in conjunction with the other front and back clipping planes to delimit the contribution of each front clipping plane.

Each front clipping plane is temporarily deactivated (Line 12) prior to display (Line 13) to avoid self-clipping. The portions of the front faces of S that lie within the clipping-product and are not hidden by previously rendered objects are rendered into the z-buffer and the frame buffer (Line 10). The rendering in Line 13 is performed using the standard z-buffer test.

An efficient implementation of the solid-clipping with composite cut-volumes requires: (1) a standard z-buffer, (2) an application-controlled set of clipping planes, (3) one bit-plane for the mask, and (4) facilities for programming the scan-conversion so as to toggle the bit-plane for each surface point and to use the mask as a condition for rendering. All these facilities are supported by commercially available graphics hardware for a limited number of application-controlled clipping planes.

---

5 The disjunctive form is a union of products, each product being the intersection of half-spaces.

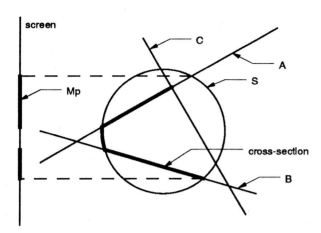

Figure 7. *Masking for a clipping-product: Two front clipping planes A and B and one back clipping plane C bound a clipping-product. Mp is constructed by scan-converting S clipped by A and B. The visible cross-sections are obtained by rendering A (clipped to B and C) and B (clipped to A and C) over pixels where Mp is 1.*

3. Interferences

Usually, a mechanical assembly must be free from interferences[6], but may contain lower-dimensional contact regions [7] between its components.

Intersections between pairs of solids may be computed in various ways. A geometric approach evaluates the boundary of the regularized Boolean intersection of the two solids. The existence of a single vertex in the intersection suffices to indicate interference. Efficient Null Object Detection techniques may be used, especially if the solids are in CSG form [10, 15]. Hardware architectures for testing interferences between triangulated boundaries have also been proposed [16]. Although asymptotically efficient computational geometry techniques for finding the minimum distance between two polyhedra are available [2], these numeric approaches are too expensive for interactive inspection and should be reserved for the final stages of the assembly verification.

Two hardware-assisted graphics techniques are relevant to interference detection: (1) a discretized (ray casting) approach reduces interference detection to a series of one-dimensional interval-intersection tests and is supported by special-purpose ray-casting hardware [3] and (2) the ability to automatically select and report which of the scan-converted objects interfere with an application-defined block provides a mechanism for eliminating unnecessary interference calculations. (Solids that are clearly disjoint from any solid S because they are disjoint from a box containing S may be efficiently identified that way.)

Geometric intersection techniques are too expensive. Ray-casting can be efficiently parallelized, but interactive

performance on an affordable platform has not been demonstrated. Boxing techniques provide only a necessary condition for interference. Consequently, the approach described in this section constitutes an important tool for detecting and displaying interferences. The first portion of this section focuses on an extension of the solid-clipping technique to highlight interferences in the cross-sections (Figure 9). The second portion presents a technique for automatically locating the beginning of interference regions along a user-specified search direction. This search facility is used interactively for two purposes: (1) to quickly and reliably establish that a particular region is free of interferences or (2) to automatically locate the first interference region and position the clipping plane at its beginning to facilitate the visual inspection of the extent of the interference. Subsequent interferences are located automatically by starting the search past the current interference region.

3.1 Highlighting interference areas

The algorithm for highlighting the interference is presented below in its simplified version for a **clipping product restricted to a single front clipping plane** C. The successive steps are illustrated in Figure 8. The algorithm computes a parity pixel mask, Mp, for the cross-section of the current solid, a cumulative (union) pixel mask, Mu, for the union of the cross-sections of all previously processed solids, and an intersection-mask, Mi. The cross-section of the solid, restricted to (Mp AND NOT Mu), is rendered with the solid's colors. The interference area is rendered at the end in a highlighted mode over Mi.

```
Algorithm for highlighting interferences:
01  For all pixels do Z=0, I=0, Mu=0, Mi=0, and Mp=0
02  For each solid S do
03      Activate C as a clipping plane
04      Scan S toggling Mp and rendering where Mu==0
05      Disable writing into z-buffer
06      Deactivate C
07      Render C where Mp==1 and Mu==0
08      For all pixels in R do
09          If (Mu==1 && Mp==1) Mi=1
10          If (Mp==1) Mu=1 and Mp=0
11      Enable writing into the z-buffer
12      Disable writing into z-buffer
13      Select color and style for the interference
14      Render R' on C for pixels where Mi==1
15      Enable writing into the z-buffer
16      Disable writing into the frame buffer
17      Render R' on C for pixels where Mu==1
```

In Line 04, all the front and back faces of S are clipped by C and then scan-converted. For each access to a pixel during that scan-conversion the pixel's parity mask, Mp, is toggled. Furthermore, if at that pixel the mask Mu is not set, the z-buffer and frame buffer are updated. (Note that this update is not necessary for the back faces of S.) Testing Mu prior to update avoids overwriting previously computed cross-sections for which the z-buffer has not yet been properly set.

---

6   The interference between two solids A and B is their regularized intersection: (A ∩*B). Regularization removes lower dimensional parts, thus, the regularized intersection is the closure of the interior of the intersection [8].

7   The contact between two solids is ((A ∩ B) − (A ∩*B)), the set theoretic difference between their set theoretic intersection and their regularized intersection.

In Line 07, the R' portion of C is rendered over pixels in the Mp mask, but out of the Mu mask, to fill the cross-section contribution of S. However, the z-buffer is not yet updated to the cross-section depth, so as to avoid depth-conflicts when filling in the interference region, Line 14. The z-buffer is correctly set in Line 17, without altering previously computed colors in the frame buffer. This technique of delaying the update of the z-buffer is used to make sure that when the interference area of the cross-section is filled, the surface depth is not compared to previously computed z-values from pixels on the same cross-sectioning plane. Such comparisons, when performed with limited numeric accuracy, produce inconsistent pixel colors across the overlap area.

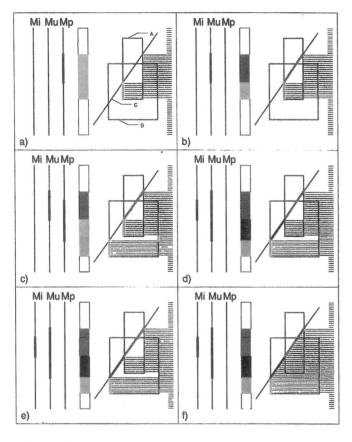

Figure 8. *Highlight construction*: *A 2D slice through the scene is used to explain the steps of the interference-highlighting algorithm. The interfering solids A and B are intersected by the clipping plane C. In the drawing the contents of the z-buffer is indicated by thin horizontal lines. The contents of the pixel-masks are shown using the thin vertical lines on the left. Asserted bits are shown by heavy lines. The contents of the frame buffer is indicated using colors in the vertical window on the left of each figure. Color lines on the contours of A, B, or C indicate, for each pixel, which surface has contributed to the frame buffer. (a) Solid A is scan-converted into the frame buffer and the z-buffer; the parity mask is constructed in Mp. (b) The contents of Mp is unioned into Mu. (c) Solid B is scan-converted into the frame buffer and the z-buffer; the parity mask is constructed in Mp. (d) Mi is asserted where Mp and Mu overlap. The contents of Mp is unioned into Mu. (e) The clipping plane is scan-converted into the frame buffer. Regions of interference are marked in red. (f) The clipping plane is scan-converted into the depth buffer.*

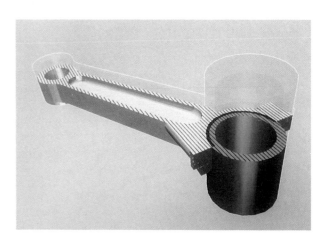

Figure 9. *Interference highlight*: *The solid-clipping technique of Figure 4 is enhanced by highlighting (in red) the cross-section regions where pairs of solids interfere. The portion of the assembly removed by the cut-volume is displayed in transparent mode.*

An elegant alternative was independently invented by Akeley [1]. It exploits the numeric increment operation on three stencil bits to implement our mask-combine operations (Lines 09 and 10). For each solid, Mp is computed as in our approach. Then the 3-bit counter (Mi,Mu,Mp) is incremented for pixels where Mp is set. The counter clamps to preserve Mi in case of overflow (i.e. when more than three solids are intersected by the same portion of the cross-section plane).

Using several parallel cross-section planes and only rendering interference areas, one can produce stacks of 2D cross-sections that indicate the extent and the shape of the 3D interference volume (see Figure 10). An algorithm for rendering **only the interference part**, i.e. the cross-section where the mask Mi was set may be obtained by eliminating the shading operations Lines 04, 07, and 17. It was used to produce the stacks of Figure 10.

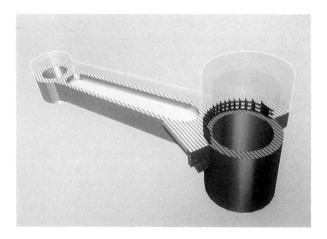

Figure 10. *Interference stacks*: *The interference visualization technique of Figure 9 is further enhanced with stacks of parallel cross-sections through the 3D interference region.*

3.2 Locating interference regions

This subsection is devoted to the automatic detection and location of interferences and contacts along a user-defined search direction and within a given search interval.

Without loss of generality, the search direction is chosen orthogonal to the cross-sectioning plane C. The search interval is confined to a slice between C and another plane C′ parallel to C. The location of C′ may be specified by the user or computed automatically from a bounding box, so as to extend past the entire assembly. The positions of C and C′ are indicated by the starting and ending parameters Z_{start} and Z_{end} along the search direction D.

Using a stack of parallel cross-sections evenly distributed between Z_{start} and Z_{end} and testing if any of them contains an interference region will not guarantee the detection of interferences, since these may occur between two consecutive cross-sections. The cost of testing a sufficient number of cross-sections to reduce the size (in depth) of possibly missed interferences is prohibitive.

Instead of such a discrete probing, the technique presented here uses the procedure "IntersectionFreeSlice" to compute a sufficient but not necessary condition for interference. If the answer is negative, the designer may be reassured immediately. Otherwise, the following algorithm recursively subdivides the search interval (Z_{start}, Z_{end}) until a user-defined maximum level (i.e. minimal slice thickness), L, is reached (in which case, the beginning of a possible interference region is returned) or until all branches of the search tree that correspond to positive test result have been explored (in which case there is no interference and Z_{end} is returned). The minimal slice thickness, the depth resolution, and the z-scaling factors control the accuracy of the test and define the ability to differentiate between interference and contact. The command Search(Z_{start}, Z_{end}, MI), where MI defines the maximum recursion level, starts the search. MI may be adjusted to ensure the desired accuracy. The parameters, Zs, Ze, and level define the current status of the recursion.

```
Algorithm for interval location:
01  Search (Zs,Ze,level)
02      If (IntersectionFreeSlice(Zs,Ze)) return Zend
03      If (level==L) return Zs
04      Zm=(Zs+Ze)/2
05      Zf=Search(Zs,Zm,level+1)
06      If (Zf!=Zend) return Zf
07      Else return Search(Zm,Ze,level+1)
```

A 2D bounding box around the discovered interference is used to position an arrow highlighting the potential interference region. The clipping plane C is automatically placed at the beginning of that interval, so that the user can inspect the area, then move C past the current interference, and finally resume the search.

The "IntersectionFreeSlice" test is implemented in the following algorithm by generating a mask Mp for the projection of the intersection of the current solid S with the slice and by testing if this mask intersects the Mu mask for the union of the projection of previously proc-

essed solids. The approach is based on the following property.

If the projections of the slices through the solids are disjoint, there is no interference within the slice.

```
IntersectionFreeSlice:
01  Activate C as a front clipping plane
02  For all pixels do Mu=0, Mi=0, Mp=0
03  For each solid S do
04      Scan-convert S toggling Mp
05      Activate C' as a back clipping plane
06      Scan-convert S forcing Mp=1
07      For all pixels in R do
08          If (Mu==1 && Mp==1) return 0
09          If (Mp==1) Mu=1 and Mp=0
```

To avoid missing thin interferences that fall between pixels, it suffices, as part of the shading of a solid, to draw the edges of each solid in lines 3 pixels wide. Each edge must be drawn twice to maintain the parity condition. (We simply draw the edges of each face after shading it.) On the other hand, to distinguish contact regions from true interferences, we apply a two-dimensional discretized morphological shrinking operation [12], i.e. a 3x3 filter over all pixels, to the mask Mi so as to remove interferences that are thinner than two pixels.

By acting on the scaling factor (i.e. the space distance corresponding to the inter-pixel resolution), one can adjust the thresholds between clearance, non-invasive contact, and true interference. By performing the "IntersectionFreeSlice" test twice (once with drawing the edges and once with eroding the mask) one can distinguish clearance (if both test return false), from contacts (if the results of both tests are different), from interferences (if both tests return true). However, searching true interferences (through mask erosion) for regions with oblique contact areas between overlapping faces of different objects forces the adaptive subdivision to visit all the branches of the search tree down to a depth corresponding to a slice thickness for which there is no interference between the projections of the solids.

The interference search automatically positions the cross-sectioning plane at the beginning of an interference region. The user examines the interference by moving the viewpoint and the clipping plane. The interfering objects may be selected by a graphic pick and the corresponding CAD models which require engineering changes may be identified. Facilities for interactively hiding some models or for producing exploded views also help decide which of the interfering parts must be redesigned.

The search algorithms described above require extensions to the functions supported by currently available graphics libraries and may also involve some hardware modifications. For example, Line 08 of the "IntersectionFreeSlice" algorithm requires a feedback from the buffer to the application. Such a feedback exists for reporting enclosing boxes around pixels traversed by the scan-conversion, but does not take into account any result of testing mask values for these pixels. This step is handled today by the application software which must inspect each pixel of Mi. Similarly, the erosion operation is also currently performed in software, which considerably reduces the performance of the search algorithm.

Nevertheless, except for regions where two or more objects are in contact, the search algorithm only visits a few branches of the search tree, and thus its software implementation requires the inspection of only a small number of pixel-masks within a limited domain (R).

Conclusion

Simple algorithms for displaying cross-sections through solids, for highlighting interference areas, and for automatically detecting interferences and contacts between solids have been presented. Because the additional cost for filling the cross-sections and for highlighting interference areas does not significantly exceed the original rendering cost, these algorithms exhibit realtime performance for small assemblies—with the exception of interference detection. They provide the engineering visualization techniques needed to replace the expensive clay models, traditionally used during the design-inspection phases, by electronic "virtual" solid models. The algorithms have been integrated in an experimental system developed by the Interactive Geometric Modeling group at IBM Research and have been successfully tested on industrial assembly models.

Acknowledgements

We are very grateful to Kurt Akeley for his comments on this paper and for allowing us to compare both his and our implementations. We also wish to thank Dan Brokenshire for pointing out the limitations of the standard clipping technique for solid modeling applications and for participating in the early phases of this work.

References

[1] Kurt Akeley, Silicon Graphics Inc.. Private communication subsequent to the SIGGRAPH review process. March 1992.

[2] David Dobkin and Herbert Edelsbrunner, Space Searching for Intersecting Objects. ACM & IEEE Sum. on Foundations of Computer Science, IEEE Computer Society Press, New York, NY, 387-392, 1984.

[3] John Ellis, Gershon Kedem, Rich Marisa, Jay Menon, and Herbert Voelcker, Breaking Barriers in Solid Modeling. CIME, pages 28-34, February 1991.

[4] Dave Epstein, Friderik Jansen, and Jarek Rossignac, Z-buffer Rendering from CSG: The Trickle Algorithm. Research Report, RC 15182, IBM T.J. Watson Research Center, Yorktown Heights, NY, December 1990.

[5] Jack Goldfeather, Steve Molnar, Greg Turk, and Henry Fuchs, Near Real-Time CSG Rendering Using Tree Normalization and Geometric Pruning. IEEE Computer Graphics and Applications, 9(3):20-28, May 1989.

[6] Starbase Reference Manual. "set_capping_planes" command. Hewlett Packard.

[7] Martti Mäntylä, An Introduction to Solid Modeling. Computer Science Press, Rockville, Maryland, 1988.

[8] Aristides Requicha and Robert Tilove, Mathematical Foundations of Constructive Solid Geometry: General Topology of Regular Closed Sets. Production Automation Project, Tech. Memo. No. 27a, Univ. of Rochester, June 1978.

[9] Jarek Rossignac, Accurate scanconversion of triangulated surfaces, in A. Kaufman, editor, Advances in Computer Graphics Hardware VI, Springer-Verlag, Berlin, 1992.

[10] Jarek Rossignac and Herbert Voelcker, Active Zones in CSG for Accelerating Boundary Evaluation, Redundancy Elimination, Interference Detection and Shading Algorithms. ACM Transactions on Graphics, 8(1):51-87, January 1989.

[11] Jarek Rossignac and Jeffey Wu, Correct Shading of Regularized CSG Solids Using a Depth-Interval Buffer. Eurographics Workshop on Graphics Hardware, Lausanne, Switzerland, September 1990.

[12] Jean Serra, Image Analysis and Mathematical Morphology. Academic Press, New York, 1982.

[13] Graphics Library—Reference Manual, Iris 4D VGX. Silicon Graphics, Inc., 1990.

[14] Robert Tilove, Line/Polygon Classification: A Study of the Complexity of Geometric Computation. IEEE Computer Graphics and Applications, 1(2):75-88, April 1981.

[15] Robert Tilove, A Null Object Detection Algorithm for Constructive Solid Geometry. Comm. ACM, 27(7):684-694, July 1984.

[16] Fujio Yamaguchi, A unified approach to interference problems using a triangle processor. Proceedings SIGGRAPH'85, 19(3):141-149, 1985.

A Collision-based Model of Spiral Phyllotaxis

Deborah R. Fowler

Department of Computer Science
University of Calgary
and University of Regina

Przemyslaw Prusinkiewicz

Department of Computer Science
University of Calgary

Johannes Battjes

Hugo de Vries Laboratory
University of Amsterdam

ABSTRACT

Plant organs are often arranged in spiral patterns. This effect is termed spiral phyllotaxis. Well known examples include the layout of seeds in a sunflower head and the arrangement of scales on a pineapple. This paper presents a method for modeling spiral phyllotaxis based on detecting and eliminating collisions between the organs while optimizing their packing. In contrast to geometric models previously used for computer graphics purposes, the new method arranges organs of varying sizes on arbitrary surfaces of revolution. Consequently, it can be applied to synthesize a wide range of natural plant structures.

CR Categories: I.3.5 [**Computer Graphics**]: Computational Geometry and Object Modeling: *Curve, surface, solid and object representation.* I.3.7 [**Computer Graphics**]: Three-Dimensional Graphics and Realism. J.3 [**Life and Medical Sciences**]: Biology.

Keywords: realistic image synthesis, modeling of plants, spiral phyllotaxis, flower head, cactus.

1 INTRODUCTION

Phyllotaxis, or a regular arrangement of organs such as leaves, flowers, or scales, can be observed in many plants. The pattern of seeds in a sunflower head and the arrangement of scales on a pineapple are good examples of this phenomenon. It is characterized by conspicuous spirals,

or *parastichies*, formed by sequences of adjacent organs composing the structure. The numbers of parastichies running in opposite directions usually are two consecutive Fibonacci numbers. The *divergence angle* between consecutively formed organs (measured from the center of the structure) is close to the Fibonacci angle of $360°\tau^{-2} \approx 137.5°$, where $\tau = (1+\sqrt{5})/2$ [3]. Computer simulation has shown that the quality of the pattern depends in a crucial way on this angle value [10, Chapter 4]. The intriguing mathematical properties have led to many models of phyllotaxis, which can be broadly categorized as *descriptive* and *explanatory* [9].

Descriptive models attempt to capture the geometry of phyllotactic patterns. Two models in this group, proposed by Vogel [12] and van Iterson [5, 8], characterize spiral arrangements of equally-sized organs on the surface of a disk or a cylinder, and have been applied to synthesize images of plant structures with predominantly flat or elongated geometry [7, 10]. Unfortunately, the assumptions that simplified the mathematical analysis of these models limited the range of their applications. In nature, the individual organs often vary in size, and the surfaces on which they are placed diverge significantly from ideal disks and cylinders. Spherically shaped cactus bodies provide a striking example, but even elongated structures, such as spruce cones, are not adequately described by the cylindrical model, which fails to characterize pattern changes observed near the base and the top of a cone.

A larger variety of organ sizes and surface shapes can be accommodated using explanatory models, which focus on the dynamic processes controlling the formation of phyllotactic patterns in nature. It is usually postulated that the spirals result from local interactions between developing organs, mechanically pushing each other or communicating through the exchange of chemical substances. Unfortunately, no universally accepted explanatory model has yet emerged from the large number of competing theories [9].

In this paper we propose a *collision-based* model of phyllotaxis, combining descriptive and explanatory components.

© 1992   ACM-0-89791-479-1/92/007/0361 $01.50

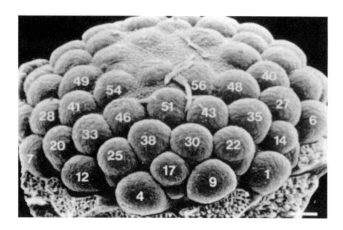

Figure 1: Microphotograph of a developing capitulum of *Microseris pygmaea*. Numbers indicate the order in which the primordia are formed. The scale bar represents $50\mu m$.

Section 2 presents the principle of this model and places it in the context of biological observations. Section 3 applies it to realistic image synthesis, using compound inflorescences (clusters of flowers) and cacti as examples. Section 4 concludes the paper with an analysis of the results and a list of open problems.

2 THE COLLISION-BASED MODEL

2.1 Morphology of a Developing Bud

Although phyllotactic patterns can be observed with the naked eye in many mature plant structures, they are initiated at an early stage of bud development. Consequently, microscopic observations are needed to analyze the process of pattern formation.

Figure 1 depicts a developing bud of *Microseris pygmaea*, a wild plant similar to the dandelion. The numbered protrusions, called *primordia*, are undeveloped organs that will transform into small flowers or *florets* as the plant grows. The primordia are embedded in the top portion of the stalk, called the *receptacle*, which determines the overall shape of the flower head (*capitulum*). The numbers in Figure 1 indicate the order in which the primordia are formed. The oldest primordium differentiates at the base of the receptacle, then the differentiation progresses gradually up towards the center, until the entire receptacle is filled. The divergence angle between position vectors of consecutive primordia approximates 137.5°.

2.2 Biological Origin of the Model

The collision-based model originates from a study of *numerical canalization* [13]. This term describes the phenomenon

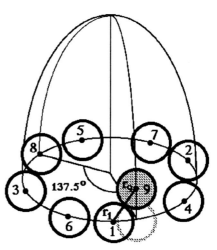

Figure 2: The collision-based model of phyllotaxis. Primordia are distributed on the receptacle using a fixed divergence angle of 137.5° and are displaced along the generating curves to become tangent to their closest neighbors. In the case shown, primordium 9 collided with primordium 1.

that in capitula of many plants, organs such as petals or bracts are more likely to occur in certain quantities than in others. Fibonacci numbers of organs, relating canalization to phyllotaxis, are found with a particularly high frequency.

We developed the computer model to simulate the effect of canalization in *Microseris* [2], and observed that it provides a flexible model of phyllotaxis, free of restrictions present in the previous geometric models. Specifically, it operates on receptacles of arbitrary shapes, and accommodates organs of varying sizes. In this paper, we extrapolate this collision-based model beyond its strict observational basis, to visualize phyllotactic patterns in a variety of plants.

2.3 The Proposed Model

The purpose of the model is to distribute primordia on the surface of the receptacle. The principle of its operation is shown in Figure 2. The receptacle is viewed as a surface of revolution, generated by a curve rotated around a vertical axis. Primordia are represented by spheres, with the centers constrained to the receptacle, and are added to the structure sequentially, using the divergence angle of 137.5°. The first group of primordia forms a horizontal ring at the base of the receptacle. The addition of primordia to this ring stops when a newly added primordium collides with an existing one. The colliding primordium is then moved along the generating curve towards the tip of the receptacle, so that it becomes tangent to its closest neighbor. The subsequent primordia are placed in a similar way — they lie on generating curves determined by the divergence angle, and are tangent to their closest neighbors. The placement of primordia terminates when there is no room to add another primordium near the tip of the receptacle.

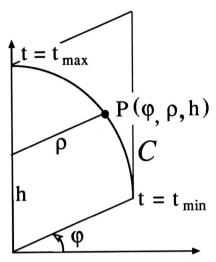

Figure 3: Variables used in the description of the collision-based model

2.4 Formalization

In order to calculate positions of consecutive primordia, we assume that the model is placed in a cylindrical coordinate system φ, ρ, h (Figure 3). The receptacle is described by the parametric equation $\rho = \rho(t)$, $h = h(t)$, and can be conceptualized as the result of the rotation of a generating curve $\mathcal{C}(\varphi = 0, \rho(t), h(t))$ around the axis h. In our implementation, $\mathcal{C}$ is specified as one or more Bézier curves [6]. Parameter t changes from t_{min}, corresponding to the base of the receptacle, to t_{max}, corresponding to the tip. Thus, a point P on the receptacle can be represented by a pair of numbers: $\varphi \in [0, 360)$ and $t \in [t_{min}, t_{max}]$. Assuming that the radii of consecutive primordia form a given sequence $\{r_0, r_1, r_2, \ldots\}$, the pattern generated by the collision-based model satisfies the following recursive formulae:

$$\begin{cases} \varphi_0 & = & 0, \\ t_0 & = & t_{min}, \end{cases}$$

$$\begin{cases} \varphi_{n+1} & = & \varphi_n + 137.5° = (n+1) \cdot 137.5°, \\ t_{n+1} & = & \min\{t \in [t_{min}, t_{max}] : (\forall i = 0, 1, \ldots, n) \\ & & \| P(\varphi_i, t_i) - P(\varphi_{n+1}, t) \| \geq r_i + r_{n+1}\}. \end{cases}$$

The expression $\| P(\varphi_i, t_i) - P(\varphi_{n+1}, t) \|$ denotes the Euclidean distance between the points $(\varphi_i, \rho(t_i), h(t_i))$ and $(\varphi_{n+1}, \rho(t), h(t))$. The formula for t_{n+1} has a simple interpretation — it specifies t_{n+1} as the smallest value of parameter t, for which the center of the newly added primordium $P(\varphi_{n+1}, t)$ will be separated by at least $r_i + r_{n+1}$ from the center of any previously placed primordium $P(\varphi_i, t_i)$. The angle φ_{n+1} at which the new primordium will be placed is fixed at $(n+1) \cdot 137.5°$.

In practice, the value t_{n+1} is computed using a binary search

of the interval $[t_{min}, t_{max}]$. The recursion ends when no value $t \in [t_{min}, t_{max}]$ satisfies the inequality:

$$(\forall i = 0, 1, \ldots, n) \| P(\varphi_i, t_i) - P(\varphi_{n+1}, t) \| \geq r_i + r_{n+1}.$$

A modification of the formula for t_{n+1} is useful when consecutive primordia decrease in size ($r_0 > r_1 > r_2 \ldots$). In this case, small primordium that should be positioned near the top of the receptacle may accidentally fit in a gap between much larger primordia near the base. This undesirable effect, distorting the phyllotactic pattern, can be avoided by limiting the maximum decrease of parameter t between consecutive primordia to a heuristically selected value δ. The change in the formula for t_{n+1} consists of replacing the constant value t_{min} by $t'_{min} = \max\{t_{min}, t_n - \delta\}$. We have found δ corresponding to the radius of the new primordium satisfactory in most cases.

2.5 Model Validation

The collision-based model describes the formation of a capitulum in a simplified way. The crudest assumption is that primordia emerge on an already developed receptacle, while in nature the differentiation is concurrent with the receptacle's growth. Despite this simplifying assumption, the placement of primordia resulting from the collision-based model corresponds closely to the microscopic observations.

3 APPLICATION TO COMPUTER GRAPHICS

3.1 Principles

Once the phyllotactic pattern has been formed in the early stages of bud development, the bud grows and develops into a mature flower head. The actual organs — florets or seeds — may have totally different shapes from the primordia, yet the original spiral arrangement will be retained.

The collision-based model is applied to image synthesis following a similar scheme: first the phyllotactic pattern is generated by placing spheres on a receptacle, then the spheres are replaced by realistic models of specific organs. In our implementation, the organs are constructed from Bézier surfaces.

For placement purposes, each organ is represented by a contact point and a pair of orthogonal vectors $\vec{v}$ and $\vec{w}$. The organ is translated to make its contact point match the center of the sphere that it will replace, then rotated to align the vectors $\vec{v}$ and $\vec{w}$ with the normal vector to the receptacle and the vector tangent to the generating curve. The radius of the sphere representing the primordium may be used to determine the final size of the mature organ.

Figure 4: Green coneflower

Figure 5: Daisies and chrysanthemums

Figure 6: Raspberry-os

3.2 Results

The first example, a model of green coneflower (*Rudbeckia laciniata*), is shown in Figure 4. The receptacle is approximately conical. The flower head includes three different types of organs: ray florets (with petals), and open and closed disk florets. The size of disk florets decreases linearly towards the tip of the cone.

Almost flat receptacles have been used to synthesize the composite flower heads shown in Figure 5, yielding similar results to the geometric models based on Vogel's formula [7, 10, 12].

The operation of the collision-based model on a spherical receptacle is illustrated in Figure 6, where individual berries of the multi-berry fruits are represented as intersecting spheres. A change of organs and proportions yields the flowers of buttonbush (*Cephalanthus occidentalis*), shown in Figure 7. In this case, the spherical receptacle is confined to the center of the inflorescence. The individual flowers, at the ends of long pedicels, form a ball with a much larger radius.

Figure 7: Flowers of buttonbush

Figure 8: Seed head of goatsbeard

Figure 9: A model of *Mammillaria geminispina*

Figure 10: Cauliflowers and broccoli

In goatsbeard (*Tragopogon dubius*), presented in Figure 8, the collision-based phyllotaxis model is used in a compound way, to capture the distribution of the seeds (*achenes*) on the receptacle, and to construct their parachute-like attachments. The same technique has been applied to model cactus *Mammillaria geminispina*, with a spiral arrangement of spine clusters on the cactus stem (Figure 9). The compound application of the phyllotaxis model has been exploited even further in the models of cauliflowers and broccoli (Figure 10). In this case, the receptacle carries clusters of compound flowers, which are themselves clusters of simple flowers approximated by spheres. Thus, the collision-based model has been applied here at two levels of recursion. In Figure 11, the model governs the positions of spine clusters and flowers, as well as the arrangement of spines in each cluster and petals in each flower.

Since the collision-based model provides a mechanism for filling an area with smaller components, it can be applied to other purposes than the simulation of phyllotaxis. For example, in Figure 12 it was used to place many single-stem plants in each pot. The soil surface was considered as a large, almost flat "receptacle", and the distribution of spherical "primordia" on its surface determined the position of each stem. As a result, the flower heads form dense clusters without colliding with each other.

3.3 Implementation

The modeling environment consists of two programs designed for Silicon Graphics workstations. An interactive editor of Bézier curves and surfaces is used to specify the shape of the receptacle and the organs. A generator of phyllotactic patterns distributes the organs on the receptacle according to the collision-based model.

The arrangement and display of primordia on the receptacle takes one to two seconds, making it possible to manipulate parameters interactively. After the desired pattern has been found, the generator outputs a set of transformation matrices that specify the position of each organ. The organs are incorporated into the final image by the renderer (the ray tracer `rayshade`) as instances of predefined objects. Instantiation makes it possible to visualize complex plant models, consisting of millions of polygons, using relatively small data files.

Figure 11: Table of cacti, including realistic models of the elongated *Mammillaria spinosissima*

Figure 12: Flower shop. The collision-based model controls the arrangement of plants in each pot.

From the user's perspective, the reproduction of a specific structure begins with the design of the receptacle. This is followed by the interactive manipulation of the primordia sizes, leading to the correct arrangement of parastichies. The total time needed to develop a complete structure is usually dominated by organ design.

4 CONCLUSIONS

This paper presents a biologically motivated collision-based model of phyllotaxis and applies it to the synthesis of images of different plants. The model employs local interactions between organs to adjust their positions on the underlying surface and can operate without modification on surfaces of diverse shapes. In contrast, purely geometric models of phyllotaxis used previously for computer graphics purposes [7, 10] have been limited to the surface of a disk or a cylinder.

Below we list several open problems, the solution of which could result in more robust and varied models.

- *Formal characterization of patterns generated by the collision-based model.* While most models of phyllotaxis were constructed to describe or explain the conspicuous spirals, the collision-based model originated from research on canalization. Consequently, it does not provide ready-to-use formulae relating the arrangement of parastichies to the geometry of the receptacle and the sizes of primordia. Such formulae would improve our understanding of the phenomenon of phyllotaxis, and provide additional assistance in building models of specific plants.

- *Analysis of the validity range.* Although the model operates correctly for various combinations of receptacle shapes and primordia sizes occurring in nature, one can easily produce input data for which it does not generate phyllotactic patterns. For example, this may happen if the receptacle has zones with a small radius of curvature, compared to the size of primordia, or if consecutive primordia vary greatly in size. The model could be therefore complemented by a characterization of the range of input data for which it produces nondistorted phyllotactic patterns.

Figure 13: Grape hyacinths

Figure 14: Inflorescences of water smartweed

- *Simulation of collisions between mature organs.* This is an important problem in the visualization of structures with densely packed organs, such as the inflorescences shown in Figures 13 and 14. In nature, individual flowers touch each other, which modifies their positions and shapes. This effect is not captured by the present model, since collisions are detected only for primordia. Consequently, the mature organs must be carefully modeled and sized to avoid intersections. This is feasible while modeling still structures, but proper simulation of collisions would become crucial in the realistic animation of plant development.

- *Comparison with related models.* Mechanical interactions between neighboring primordia were also postulated in other models of phyllotaxis. Adler [1] proposed a *contact-pressure* model which, in a sense, is opposite to ours: it uses constant vertical displacement of primordia and allows the divergence angle to vary, while we fix the divergence angle and let collisions control the displacement along the generating curves. Two other models explaining phyllotaxis in terms of mechanical interactions have been proposed recently by Van der Linden [11], and Douady and Couder [4]. A comparison and synthesis of these results is an open problem. Specifically, the incorporation of a mechanism for the adjustment of the divergence angle into the collision-based model may lead to structures better corresponding to reality, and provide a causal explanation for the divergence angle used. The comparison of phyllotactic models can be put in an even wider perspective by considering non-mechanical models, such as those based on reaction-diffusion [9].

Figure 15: Window sill — various phyllotactic patterns

In spite of its simplicity, the collision-based model captures a wide range of plant structures with phyllotactic patterns (Figure 15). It also illustrates one of the most stimulating aspects of the modeling of natural phenomena — the close coupling of visualization with ongoing research in a fundamental science.

Acknowledgements

This research was sponsored by an operating grant from the Natural Sciences and Engineering Research Council of Canada, and by a graduate scholarship from the University of Regina. The Canadian-Dutch cooperation was made possible by a SIR grant from the Dutch Research Organization (NWO). The images were ray-traced using the program `rayshade` written by Craig Kolb, in computer graphics laboratories at the University of Calgary and Princeton University. We are indebted to Craig for his excellent and well supported program, to Pat Hanrahan for providing Deborah with access to his research facilities at Princeton, and to Jim Hanan for recording the images at the University of Regina. Also, we would like to thank Jules Bloomenthal and Lynn Mercer for many helpful comments.

References

[1] I. Adler. A model of contact pressure in phyllotaxis. *Journal of Theoretical Biology*, 45:1–79, 1974.

[2] J. Battjes, K. Bachmann, and F. Bouman. Early development of capitula in *Microseris pygmaea* D. Don strains C96 and A92 (Asteraceae: Lactuceae). *Botanische Jahrbücher Systematik*, 113(4):461–475, 1992.

[3] H. S. M. Coxeter. *Introduction to Geometry*. J. Wiley & Sons, New York, 1961.

[4] S. Douady and Y. Couder. Phyllotaxis as a physical self-organized growth process. Manuscript, Laboratoire de Physique Statistique, Paris, 1991.

[5] R. O. Erickson. The geometry of phyllotaxis. In J. E. Dale and F. L. Milthrope, editors, *The Growth and Functioning of Leaves*, pages 53–88. University Press, Cambridge, 1983.

[6] J. D. Foley, A. Van Dam, S. K. Feiner, and J. F. Hughes. *Computer Graphics: Principles and Practice*. Addison-Wesley, Reading, Massachusetts, 1990.

[7] D. R. Fowler, J. Hanan, and P. Prusinkiewicz. Modelling spiral phyllotaxis. *computers & graphics*, 13(3):291–296, 1989.

[8] G. Van Iterson. *Mathematische und mikroskopisch-anatomische Studien über Blattstellungen*. Gustav Fischer, Jena, 1907.

[9] R. V. Jean. Mathematical modelling in phyllotaxis: The state of the art. *Mathematical Biosciences*, 64:1–27, 1983.

[10] P. Prusinkiewicz and A. Lindenmayer. *The Algorithmic Beauty of Plants*. Springer-Verlag, New York, 1990. With J. Hanan, F. D. Fracchia, D. R. Fowler, M. J. M. de Boer, and L. Mercer.

[11] F. Van der Linden. Creating phyllotaxis: The dislodgement model. *Mathematical Biosciences*, 100:161–199, 1990.

[12] H. Vogel. A better way to construct the sunflower head. *Mathematical Biosciences*, 44:179–189, 1979.

[13] C. H. Waddington. Canalization of development and the inheritance of acquired characteristics. *Nature*, 150:563–565, 1942.

Generative Modeling: A Symbolic System for Geometric Modeling

John M. Snyder
James T. Kajiya
California Institute of Technology
Pasadena, CA 91125

Abstract

This paper discusses a new, symbolic approach to geometric modeling called generative modeling. The approach allows specification, rendering, and analysis of a wide variety of shapes including 3D curves, surfaces, and solids, as well as higher-dimensional shapes such as surfaces deforming in time, and volumes with a spatially varying mass density. The system also supports powerful operations on shapes such as "reparameterize this curve by arclength", "compute the volume, center of mass, and moments of inertia of the solid bounded by these surfaces", or "solve this constraint or ODE system". The system has been used for a wide variety of applications, including creating surfaces for computer graphics animations, modeling the fur and body shape of a teddy bear, constructing 3D solid models of elastic bodies, and extracting surfaces from magnetic resonance (MR) data.

Shapes in the system are specified using a language which builds multidimensional parametric functions. The language is based on a set of symbolic operators on continuous, piecewise differentiable parametric functions. We present several shape examples to show how conveniently shapes can be specified in the system. We also discuss the kinds of operators useful in a geometric modeling system, including arithmetic operators, vector and matrix operators, integration, differentiation, constraint solution, and constrained minimization. Associated with each operator are several methods, which compute properties about the parametric functions represented with the operators. We show how many powerful rendering and analytical operations can be supported with only three methods: evaluation of the parametric function at a point, symbolic differentiation of the parametric function, and evaluation of an inclusion function for the parametric function.

Like CSG, and unlike most other geometric modeling approaches, this modeling approach is closed, meaning that further modeling operations can be applied to any results of modeling operations, yielding valid models. Because of this closure property, the symbolic operators can be composed very flexibly, allowing the construction of higher-level operators without changing the underlying implementation of the system. Because the modeling operations are described symbolically, specified models can capture the designer's intent without approximation error.

CR Categories: I.3.5 [Computer Graphics]: Computational Geometry and Object Modeling – curve, surface, solid, and object representations; geometric algorithms, languages, and systems

Additional Key Words: geometric modeling, parametric shape, sweep

1 Introduction

One way of representing a limited class of shapes uses sweeps. A sweep represents a shape by moving an object (called a generator) along a trajectory through space. The simplest sweeps are extrusions and surfaces of revolution, which sweep 2D curves. Sweeps whose generator can change size, orientation, or shape are called general sweeps. General sweeps that use 2D curve generators are called generalized cylinders [BINF71].

Several researchers have studied sweeps [GOLD83,CARL82b,WANG86, COQU87]. Barr's *spherical product* [BARR81], is an example of a sweep that uses a constant 2D curve generator with translation and scaling. Carlson [CARL82b] introduced the idea of varying the sweep generator. Wang and Wang [WANG86] explored sweeps of surfaces for use in manipulating numerically controlled milling machine cutter paths. Sweeps have been used in solid modeling systems for many years (e.g., GMSolid, ROMULUS). Lossing and Eshleman [LOSS74] developed a system using sweeps of constant 2D curves. Alpha_1, a modeling system developed at the University of Utah, has a much more sophisticated sweeping facility [COHE83].

One of the advantages of sweeps is their naturalness, compactness, and controllability in representing a large class of man-made objects. For example, an airplane wing is naturally viewed as an airfoil cross section which is translated from the root to the tip of the wing. At the same time its thickness is modified, it is twisted, swept back, and translated vertically according to other schedules. Two crucial questions remain concerning how sweeps fit into a general shape design and manipulation program:

- how can sweeps be specified by the human designer in a general and powerful way?

- what tools are appropriate to allow swept shapes to be rendered and simulated?

The generative modeling approach presented here extends the kinds of sweeps that can be conveniently specified, and provides high-level tools for their rendering and simulation. The approach specifies sweeps procedurally, in a fashion similar to other procedural specification methods in computer graphics: shade trees [COOK84], Perlin's texturing language [PERL85], and the POSTSCRIPT language [ADOB85].

A prototype system called GENMOD has been developed implementing these ideas, which includes a C interpreter, a curve editor, methods for several dozen primitive symbolic operators, and a multidimensional visualization library. While each piece of the system is fairly simple, we have found that combining all the pieces into a single system produces an extremely powerful geometric modeling tool.

2 Generative Modeling Overview

A *generative model* is a shape generated by the continuous transformation of a shape called the *generator*. As an example, consider a curve generator $\gamma(u)$: $\mathbf{R}^1 \to \mathbf{R}^3$, and a parameterized transformation, $\delta(p, v)$: $\mathbf{R}^3 \times \mathbf{R} \to \mathbf{R}^3$, that acts on points $p \in \mathbf{R}^3$ given a parameter v. A generative surface, $S(u, v)$, may be formed consisting of all the points generated by the transformation δ acting on the curve γ, i.e.,

$$S(u, v) = \delta(\gamma(u), v)$$

A cylinder is an example of a generative model. The generator, a circle in the xy plane, is translated along the z axis. The set of points generated as the circle is translated yield a cylinder. Mathematically, the generator and

©1992   ACM-0-89791-479-1/92/007/0369 $01.50

transformation for a cylinder are

$$\gamma(u) = \begin{pmatrix} \cos(2\pi u) \\ \sin(2\pi u) \\ 0 \end{pmatrix} \qquad \delta(p, v) = \begin{pmatrix} p_1 \\ p_2 \\ p_3 + v \end{pmatrix}$$

yielding the surface

$$S(u, v) = \delta(\gamma(u), v) = \begin{pmatrix} \cos(2\pi u) \\ \sin(2\pi u) \\ v \end{pmatrix}$$

2.1 Parametric Functions and the Closure Property

If a generator is expressed as a parametric function, then a generative model built by transforming this generator is also a parametric function. Generalizing from the cylinder example, let a generator be represented by the parametric function

$$F(x): \mathbf{R}^l \rightarrow \mathbf{R}^m$$

A continuous set of transformations can be represented as a parameterized transformation

$$T(p; q): \mathbf{R}^m \times \mathbf{R}^k \rightarrow \mathbf{R}^n$$

where $p \in \mathbf{R}^m$ is a point to be transformed, and $q \in \mathbf{R}^k$ is an additional parameter that defines a continuous set of transformations. The generative model is the parametric function [1]

$$T(F(x); q): \mathbf{R}^{l+k} \rightarrow \mathbf{R}^n$$

The ability to use a generative model as a generator in another generative model will be called the *closure property* of the generative modeling representation. The use of parametric generators and transformations yields closure because transformation of a generator can be expressed as a simple composition of parametric functions, resulting in another parametric function. In fact, the use of parametric generators and transformations blurs the distinction between generator and transformation. Both are parametric functions; the domain of a generator must be completely specified, while the domain of a transformation is partly specified and partly determined as the image of a generator.

2.2 Terminology

Let $F: \mathbf{R}^n \rightarrow \mathbf{R}^m$ be a parametric function with scalar variables $x_1, x_2, \ldots, x_n$, called the *parametric variables* or *parametric coordinates*. The number of parametric coordinates on which F depends, n, is called the *input dimension* of the parametric function. The number of components in the result of F, m, is called the *output dimension* of the parametric function. In this work, the domain of F is a rectilinear region of $\mathbf{R}^n$, called a *hyper-rectangle*, of the form:

$$[a_1, b_1] \times [a_2, b_2] \times \ldots \times [a_n, b_n]$$

Hyper-rectangles are convenient for sampling and integration of the parametric functions in a computer implementation. The image of F over a specified hyper-rectangle defines the shape of interest.

2.3 Operators and Methods

One way of specifying parametric functions is by selecting a set of *operators*. An operator is a function that takes parametric functions as input and produces a parametric function as output. For example, addition is an operator that acts on two parametric functions f and g, and produces a new parametric function, $f + g$. The addition operator is recursive, in that we can continue to use it on its own results or on the results of other operators, in order to build more complicated parametric functions (e.g., $(f + g) + h$).

Like the addition operator, all operators in the system are recursive; their results can be used as inputs to other operators. [2] Together with the closure

property of parametric generators, this recursive nature of operators yields a modeling system with closure. That is, the designer is not prevented from using any reasonable combination of operations to specify shapes. For example, the addition operator can be applied to parametric functions of any input dimension (e.g., curves or surfaces). It can also be applied to parametric functions of any output dimension, to perform vector addition, as long as the output dimension of its two arguments is identical.

Of course, it is not enough to represent parametric functions; we must also be able to compute properties about the parametric functions for rendering and analysis. Such computations can be implemented by defining a set of *methods* for each operator. One method evaluates the parametric function at a point in its parameter space. Other methods include symbolic differentiation of the parametric function and evaluation of an inclusion function (see [SNYD92a] for a discussion of inclusion functions). Section 3.2 discusses methods in more detail.

3 Symbolic Operators

3.1 Specific Operators

In this section, we examine specific operators that form a basis for a flexible variety of shapes. This set of operators will be used in Section 4 to show the capability of the generative modeling approach for combining such operators to build interesting shapes.

Elementary Operators   Elementary operators include constants, parametric coordinates, arithmetic operators, square root, trigonometric functions, exponentiation, and logarithm. [3] The constant operator represents a parametric function with a real, constant value, such as $f(x) = 2.5$. The parametric coordinate operator represents a particular parametric coordinate, such as $f(x) = x_2$, where x_2 is the second component of the parametric domain, in a global coordinate system. Arithmetic operators are addition, subtraction, multiplication, division, and negation of parametric functions. They are useful for such geometric operations as scaling and interpolation, and in many other more complicated operations. They can also be combined to represent bicubic patches, NURBS, and other parametric polynomials.

Other elementary operators are useful in special circumstances. The square root operator, for example, is useful to compute the distance between points. The sine and cosine operators are useful in building parametric circles and arcs.

Vector and Matrix Operators   Vector operators are projection, cartesian product, vector length, dot product, and cross product. Projection and cartesian product allow extraction and rearrangement of coordinates of parametric functions. Vector length, dot product, and cross product find many applications in defining geometric constraints on parameterized shapes.

Vector operator analogs of the arithmetic operators are also useful for geometric modeling. These operators include addition and subtraction of vectors, and multiplication and division of vectors by scalars. Matrix operators include multiplication and addition of matrices, matrix determinant, and inverse. Matrix multiplication is especially useful to define affine transformations, which are used extensively in simple sweeps (see Section 4.2). While these operators can be defined in terms of simple projection, cartesian product, and arithmetic operators, they are included as primitive operators for the sake of efficiency.

Differentiation and Integration Operators   The differentiation operator returns the partial derivative of a parametric function with respect to one of its parametric coordinates. This is useful, for example, in finding tangent or normal vectors on curves and surfaces.

The integration operator integrates a parametric function with respect to one of its parametric coordinates, given two parametric functions representing the upper and lower limits of integration. For example, the function

$$\int_{b(u)}^{a(u,v)} s(v, \tau) d\tau$$

---

[1] More precisely, the generative model is the set of points in the image of $T(F(x); q)$ over a domain $U \subset \mathbf{R}^{l+k}$.

[2] It should be noted that the result of an operator can not always be used as input to another operator. Operators may constrain the output dimension of their arguments (e.g., an operator may accept only a scalar function as an argument and prohibit the use of functions of higher output dimension). In special circumstances, it may be desirable to constrain other properties of operator arguments. For example,

the inversion operator expects its argument to be a monotonic scalar function. In this context, closure of the set of operators implies that an operator not arbitrarily prohibit any "reasonable" arguments, given the nature of the operator.

[3] GENMOD contains many more simple operators like these, listed in [SNYD92b].

can be formed by the integration operator applied to three parametric functions, where $s(v, \tau)$ is the integrand, $a(u, v)$ the upper limit of integration, and $b(u)$ the lower limit of integration. In general, parametric functions having any number of input parameters can be used as the integrand, or limits of integration. Integration can be used to compute arclength of curves, surface area of surfaces, and volumes and moments of inertia of solids.

Indexing and Branching Operators   A useful operation in geometric modeling is concatenation, the piecewise linking together of a collection of shapes. For example, the concatenation of the set of n curves $\gamma_1(u), \gamma_2(u), \ldots, \gamma_n(u)$, each defined over the parametric variable $u \in [0, 1]$, may be defined as

$$\gamma(u) = \begin{cases} \gamma_1(nu) & u \in [0, 1/n] \\ \gamma_2(nu - 1) & u \in (1/n, 2/n] \\ \vdots \\ \gamma_n(nu - (n-1)) & u \in ((n-1)/n, 1] \end{cases}$$

The concatenation of surfaces or functions with many parameters can be defined similarly, where the concatenation is done with respect to one of the coordinates. This kind of concatenation is *uniform* concatenation, because each concatenated segment is defined in an interval of equal length $(1/n)$ in parameter space. It is commonly used in defining piecewise cubic curves such as B-splines.

Uniform concatenation is implemented using an *indexing operator*, which takes as input an array of parametric functions and an index function that controls which function is to be evaluated. Given the same $\gamma_i(u)$ curves used in the previous example, and an index function $q(x)$, the index operator is defined as

$$\text{index}(q(x), \gamma_1(u), \ldots, \gamma_n(u)) = \gamma_{\lfloor q(x) \rfloor}(u)$$

where $q(x) = nu$ results in the uniform concatenation of the γ_i functions. In addition to the indexing operator, it is also useful to have a *substitution operator* to define uniform concatenation. The substitution operator symbolically substitutes a given parametric function for one of the parametric coordinates of another parametric function. For example, this can be used to represent $\gamma_i(nu - (i-1))$ given $\gamma_i(u)$, by substituting the function $nu - (i-1)$ for the parametric coordinate u.

The index operator is a special case of a *branching operator*, an operator that takes as input a sequence of conditional functions and evaluation functions. The result of the branching operator is the result of the first evaluation function whose corresponding conditional is true. This multiway branch operator can be used to define a *nonuniform* concatenation of parametric functions where each concatenated segment need not be defined on an equally sized interval. Branching operators are also useful for finding the minimum and maximum of a pair of functions, for defining deformations that act only on certain parts of space, and for detecting error conditions (e.g., taking the square root of a negative number, or normalizing a zero length vector).

Relational and Logical Operators   In order to support the definition of useful conditional expressions for the branching operators (and the constraint solution operator to be presented), we include the standard mathematical relational operators such as equality, inequality, greater than, etc., and the logical operators (such as "and", "or", and "not").

Curve and Table Operators   Curve and table operators allow shapes to be specified from data produced outside the system. The curve operator specifies continuous curves such as piecewise cubic splines, produced using an interactive curve editor. The table operator is used to specify an interpolation of a multidimensional data set (GENMOD implements both linear and bicubic interpolation). For example, a simulation program may produce data defined over a discrete collection of points on a solid. The table operator interpolates this data to yield a continuous parametric function.

Inversion Operator   Inversion of monotonic functions can be used, for example, to reparameterize a curve by arclength, as shown in Figure 1. Let $\gamma(t)$ be a continuous curve specifying the object's trajectory, starting at $t = 0$ and ending at $t = 1$. The arclength along γ, $\gamma_{\text{arc}}(t)$ is given by

$$\gamma_{\text{arc}}(t) = \int_0^t \|\gamma'(\tau)\| d\tau$$

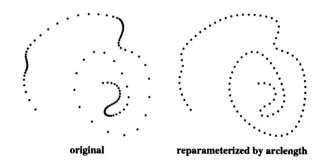

| original | reparameterized by arclength |

Figure 1: A parametric curve is reparameterized by arclength. Each dot represents a point on the curve along uniform increments of the curve's input parameter.

The integration and differentiation operators mentioned previously serve to define γ_{arc}. The reparameterization of γ by arclength, γ_{new}, is then given by[4]

$$\gamma_{\text{new}}(s) = \gamma\left(\gamma_{\text{arc}}^{-1}\left(s\,\gamma_{\text{arc}}(1)\right)\right)$$

This reparameterization involves the inversion of the monotonic arclength function, γ_{arc}.

Many other useful operations can also be formulated in terms of the inversion of monotonic functions, including the reparameterizing of curves and surfaces so that their parameters are matched by arclength, polar angle, or output coordinate to some other curve or surface. Inversion of monotonic functions in a single variable may be computed using fast algorithms, such as Brent's method [PRES86].

Constraint Solution Operator   The constraint solution operator takes a parametric function representing a system of constraints, and produces a solution to the constrained system or an indication that no solution exists. [5] Two forms of solution are useful: finding any point that solves the system, or finding all points that solve it, assuming there is a finite set of solutions. [6] The operator also requires a parametric function specifying the hyper-rectangle in which to solve the constraints.

For example, the constraint solution operator can be used to find an intersection between two planar curves. Let $\gamma^1(s)$ and $\gamma^2(t)$ be two curves in $\mathbf{R}^2$. These curves could be represented using the curve operator of Section 3.1, or any of the other operators. The appropriate constraint is

$$F(s, t) \equiv (\gamma^1(s) = \gamma^2(t))$$

which can be represented using the equality relational operator. The constraint solution operator applied to F produces a constant function representing a point, (s, t), where the two curves intersect. Such an operation can be used to define boolean operations on planar areas bounded by parametric curves, which we will use in the screwdriver tip example of Section 4.4.

The constraint system can also be solved over a subset of its parameters, to yield a non-constant parametric function. For example, the constraint system $\gamma^1(r, s) = \gamma^2(t)$ can be solved over s and t, resulting in a function that depends on r. The user therefore specifies not only a parametric function representing the constraint system, but also which parametric coordinates the system should be solved over, and which coordinates parameterize the system.

Constraint solution has application to problems involving intersection, collision detection, and finding appropriate parameters for parameterized shapes. A robust algorithm for evaluating this operator uses interval analysis, and is described in [SNYD92a].

---

[4]The s parameter of γ_{new} actually represents "normalized" arclength, in that s varies between 0 and 1 to traverse the original curve γ, and equal distances in s represent equal distances in arclength on the curve.

[5]Note that inversion operator of the previous section is a special case of the constraint solution operator.

[6]One form of the constraint solution operator produces a single solution, with an output dimension equal to the number of coordinates over which the constraint is solved. The other form returns the number of solutions as one output coordinate, followed by the solution points. The concatenated array of solution points is padded to some maximum length, n, specified by the user. Padding is done because parametric functions in GENMOD always have a fixed output dimension. The second form thus has output dimension $n + 1$.

Constrained Minimization Operator The constrained minimization operator takes two parametric functions representing a system of constraints and an objective function, and produces a point that globally minimizes the objective function, subject to the constraints. The operator also requires a parametric function specifying a hyper-rectangle in which to perform the minimization. The minimization operator has many applications to geometric modeling, including

- finding intersections of rays with surfaces

- finding the point on a shape closest to given point

- finding the minimum distance between shapes

- finding whether a point is inside or outside a region defined with parametric boundaries

A robust algorithm for evaluating parametric functions defined with the minimization operator uses interval analysis, and is described in [SNYD92a].

ODE Solution Operator The ODE operator solves a first order, initial value ordinary differential equation. It is useful for defining limited kinds of physical simulations within the modeling environment. For example, we can simulate rigid body mechanics, or find flow lines through vector fields. Figure 12 illustrates the results of the ODE operator for a simple simulation specified entirely in GENMOD.

Let f be a specified parametric function of the form

$$f(t, y_1, y_2, \ldots, y_n): \mathbf{R}^{n+1} \to \mathbf{R}^n$$

The ODE operator returns the solution $y(t)$ to the system of n first order equations

$$\frac{dy}{dt} = f(t, y)$$

with the initial condition

$$y(t_0) = y_0$$

Parameterized ODEs, in which f and y_0 (and thus the result y) depend on an additional m parameters $x_1, \ldots, x_m$, are also allowed. The user supplies the ODE operator with an indication of which parametric coordinates of f are the t and y_i variables, and which are the additional parameters x_i.

GENMOD implements the ODE operators using a Numerical Algorithms Group(NAG) ODE solver. Similar operators, for solution of boundary value problems and PDEs, are also useful in a geometric modeling environment, but have not been implemented in the present GENMOD system.

3.2 Operator Methods

Let P be an operator that takes n parametric functions as inputs and produces the parametric function $p = P(f_1, \ldots, f_n)$. A method for P is a function that can be evaluated by evaluating similar methods for the functions $f_1, \ldots, f_n$. A method on parametric functions is called *locally recursive for P* if its result on p is completely determined by the set of its results on each of the n parametric functions $f_1, \ldots, f_n$. Thus, a method to evaluate a parametric function at a point in parameter space is locally recursive for the addition operator because $f + g$ can be evaluated by evaluating f, evaluating g, and adding the result. A method to symbolically integrate a parametric function is not locally recursive for the division operator, because $\int f/g$ can not be computed given only $\int f$ and $\int g$. Generally, a locally recursive method can be simply implemented and efficiently computed.

We now examine specific methods useful in a geometric modeling system.

Evaluation at a Point Computation of points on a shape is necessary to approximate the shape for visualization and simulation. A method to evaluate a parametric function at a point in parameter space is locally recursive for most of the operators discussed previously. Several operators are exceptions: the integration, inversion, and ODE solution operators.[7] All three of these operators require their input parametric functions to be evaluated repeatedly over many domain points. For example, evaluation of the integration operator can be computed numerically using Romberg integration [PRES86,

pages 123–125], which adds evaluations of the integrand over many points in its domain.

Two forms of the evaluation method have proved useful: evaluation at a single, specified point in parameter space and evaluation over a multidimensional, rectilinear lattice of points in parameter space. Evaluation of a parametric function over a rectilinear lattice gives information about how the function behaves over a whole domain, and is useful in "quick and dirty" rendering schemes. Although evaluation over a rectilinear lattice can be implemented by repeated evaluation at specified points, much greater computational speed can be achieved with a special method, as we will see in the Appendix.

The evaluation methods return an error condition as well as a numerical result. The error condition signifies whether the parametric function has been evaluated at an invalid point in its domain (e.g., f/g where g evaluates to 0, or $\sqrt{h}$ where $h < 0$). A failure error condition is also returned when the constraint solution or constrained minimization operators are evaluated in a domain in which there are no solutions.

Differentiation The differentiation method is used to implement the differentiation operator introduced in Section 3.1. The differentiation method computes a parametric function that is the partial derivative of a given parametric function with respect to one of the parametric coordinates. The partial derivative is computed symbolically; that is, the partial derivative result is represented using the set of symbolic operators. For example, the partial derivative with respect to x_1 of the parametric function $x_1 + \sqrt{x_1 x_2}$ yields the parametric function $1 + x_2/(2\sqrt{x_1 x_2})$, which is represented with the addition, multiplication, division, square root, constant, and parametric coordinate operators.

Although the differentiation method is not locally recursive for most operators discussed previously, it is still relatively easy to compute. For example, the partial derivative of the parametric function $h = \cos(f)$ depends not only on the partial derivative of f, but also on f itself, since

$$\frac{\partial h}{\partial x_i} = -\sin(f)\frac{\partial f}{\partial x_i}$$

The differentiation method is therefore not locally recursive for the cosine operator, but may be computed simply if a sine operator exists. Similar situations arise for many of the other operators. Fortunately, it is a simple matter to extend a set of operators such that the set is closed with respect to the differentiation method, meaning that any partial derivative may be represented in terms of available operators.[8]

Evaluation of an Inclusion Function An inclusion function computes a hyper-rectangular bound for the range of a parametric function, given a hyper-rectangular domain. It is used in interval analysis algorithms to evaluate parametric functions defined with the constrained minimization and constraint solution operators. It is also useful to approximate shapes to user-defined tolerances, and compute CSG and offset operations. The uses and implementation of inclusion functions are fully discussed in [SNYD92a, SNYD92b].

Although an inclusion function computes a global property of a parametric function, it can often be computed using locally recursive methods. For example, an inclusion function method for the multiplication operator can be computed using interval arithmetic on the results of the inclusion functions for its parametric function multiplicands.

Other Methods Another useful method determines whether a parametric function is continuous or differentiable to a specified order over a given hyper-rectangle. Many times, algorithms for rendering and analysis require differentiability of input functions (e.g., multidimensional root finding methods). The differentiability operator can therefore be used to select whether an algorithm that assumes differentiability is appropriate, or if a more robust and slower algorithm must be used instead.

The differentiability/continuity method is locally recursive for most of the operators discussed previously, but there are exceptions. For example, the differentiability method for the division operator can not simply check that the two parametric functions being divided are differentiable. It must

---

[7]The derivative operator, and the constraint solution and constrained minimization operators are also exceptions. As we will discuss later, the evaluation method for the differentiation operator depends on the differentiation method, while the evaluation method for the constraint solution and constrained minimization operators uses the inclusion function method.

[8]For example, this implies that if the cosine operator is included in the set of primitive operators, then the sine operator must be included as well. Some operators, such as the constrained minimization operator, do not have analytically expressible partial derivatives. For these operators, the partial derivative must be computed numerically.

also check whether the denominator is 0 in the given domain. This can be accomplished using an inclusion function method.

Other operator methods, whose implementation is still a research issue, include determining whether a function $f: \mathbf{R}^n \rightarrow \mathbf{R}^n$ is one-to-one over a hyper-rectangle. A similar method is *degree*, defined as

$$d(f, D, p) = \text{cardinality} \{x \in D \mid f(x) = p\}$$

where $D \subseteq \mathbf{R}^n$.

3.3 Operator Libraries

While the primitive operators described in Section 3.1 form a powerful basis for a shape representation, they do not always match the operations the designer wishes to perform. In these cases, the designer can employ operators formed by composition of the primitive operators. The GENMOD system includes operator libraries which predefine hundreds of such higher level operators. The definitions of these operators are loaded from interpreted files when the program is first run, and can be dynamically modified and added to by the user.

For example, a simple but useful non-primitive operator is the linear interpolation operator, `m_interp`, whose GENMOD definition is[9]

```
MAN m_interp(MAN h,MAN f,MAN g)
{
    return f + h*(g-f);
}
```

The `MAN` type (for *manifold*) is the basic data structure in GENMOD, representing a parametric function. The `+`, `-`, and `*` operators have been overloaded to perform addition, subtraction, and multiplication of manifolds.

The `m_interp` operator takes three parametric functions as input: f and g are functions to be interpolated, and h is the interpolation variable. The parametric functions f and g can be of any input or output dimension, as long as they have equal output dimension. This allows linear interpolation between two curves, surfaces, or even higher dimensional shapes. [10]

The closure property of the generative modeling approach means that such non-primitive operators can be very powerful. For example, the `m_arc_2pt_height` non-primitive operator used in the next section forms a circular arc connecting two 2D points and having a specified height above their line of connection. The 2D points supplied as arguments to this operator need not be constants but can depend on parameters, allowing convenient definition of the spoon of Section 4.3.

4 Examples

This section presents examples of generative shapes and their specification in GENMOD. It is meant to show how the generative modeling approach leads a designer to think about shape, and the size of the domain of shapes that can be represented. Many other examples can be found in [SNYD92b].

4.1 Lamp Bases and Profile Products

A profile product [BARR81] is perhaps the simplest nontrivial generative surface. It is formed by scaling and translating a 2D cross section according to a 2D profile. More precisely, a profile product surface, $S(u, v)$, is defined using a cross section curve, $\gamma(u) = (\gamma_1, \gamma_2)$, and a profile curve, $\delta(v) = (\delta_1, \delta_2)$, where

$$S(u, v) = \begin{pmatrix} \gamma_1(u)\delta_1(v) \\ \gamma_2(u)\delta_1(v) \\ \delta_2(v) \end{pmatrix}$$

A profile product may be defined in the GENMOD language as follows:

---

[9] GENMOD's language is based on ANSI C, with several extensions. The extensions allow overloading of the C operators, in order to more naturally express parametric functions. Several additional operators were also added.

[10] The binary arithmetic operators in GENMOD can be used in two modes. If the two parametric function arguments have the same output dimension, the operation is performed separately for each component on the corresponding components of the two arguments. If the output dimension of one argument is 1, and the other greater than 1, then the operation is performed on each component of the multicomponent argument with the same value of the scalar argument. Thus, $f + g$ denotes vector addition of f and g when f and g have the same output dimension, but $f * 2$ scales each component of f by a factor of 2.

```
MAN cross = m_crv("cross.crv",m_x(0));
MAN profile = m_crv("profile.crv",m_x(1));
MAN lampbase = m_profile(cross,profile);
```

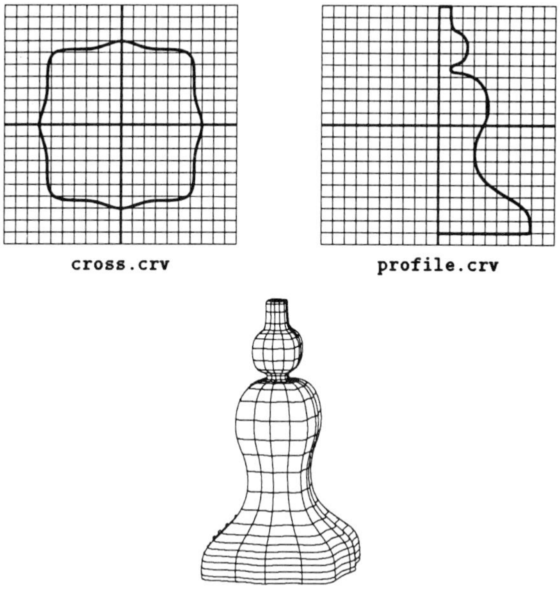

cross.crv   profile.crv

Figure 2: Lamp base example — A lamp base shape is represented by a profile surface. The GENMOD definition of a lamp base is shown, followed by graphs of the two curves (plotted between -1 and 1 in x and y) used in the definition, and a wire frame image of the shape.

```
MAN m_profile(MAN cross,MAN profile)
{
    return @(cross[0]*profile[0],
             cross[1]*profile[0],
             profile[1]);
}
```

The `@()` operator, a C extension in GENMOD's language, is the cartesian product operator, which, in this case, combines three scalar functions into a 3D point. The `[]` operator returns a single output coordinate of a parametric function. In keeping with C language convention (and unlike the mathematical notation used in the definition of $S(u, v)$), coordinate indexing is done starting with index 0 for the first coordinate, rather than index 1.

Figure 2 presents an example of a profile product surface for a lamp base shape. It uses the `m_profile` operator defined above, and the primitive curve operator `m_crv`. The curve operator takes the name of a file, produced using a curve editor program, and creates a parametric curve that is evaluated over the parametric function specified as its second argument. In this case, the shape of the cross section curve is specified in the file `cross.crv`, and is evaluated over `m_x(0)`, representing parametric coordinate x_0. The profile curve is evaluated over parametric coordinate x_1 (`m_x(1)`).

4.2 Impeller Blades and Affine Transformations

An affine transformation shape uses a 2D or 3D curve generator and a transformation represented by a linear transformation and a translation. Let $\gamma(u)$ be a 3D curve, $M(v)$ be a linear transformation on 3D space, and $T(v)$ be another 3D curve. An affine transformation surface, $S(u, v)$, is given by

$$S(u, v) = M(v)\gamma(u) + T(v)$$

One method of representing affine transformations is to use 4×4 matrices (homogeneous transformations), allowing the composition of affine transformations using simple matrix multiplies.

Figure 3 presents an example of an affine transformation representing the impeller blade of a centrifugal compressor. The `m_transform3d` non-primitive GENMOD operator takes a vector and applies an affine transformation to it. Note that because the matrix transforms the cross section by

```
MAI u = m_x(0);
MAI v = m_x(1);
MAI cross = m_crv("bladecros.crv",u);
MAI blade = m_transform3d(@(cross,0),
    m_transz(m_interp(v,-1,1)) *
    m_transx(-0.5) *
    m_rotz(pi*m_crv("bladerot.crv",v)[1]) *
    m_transx(0.5) *
    m_scalex(m_crv("bladexscl.crv",v)[1]) *
    m_scaley(m_crv("bladeyscl.crv",v)[1])
);
```

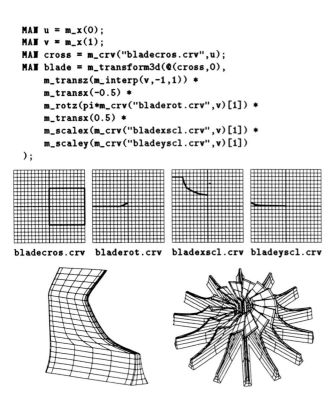

bladecros.crv   bladerot.crv   bladexscl.crv   bladeyscl.crv

Figure 3: Impeller blade example — An impeller blade surface is represented using an affine transformation. A square cross section in the xy plane, which forms the bottom of the blade, is scaled separately in x and y, translated in x, rotated around z, translated back in x, and translated up the z axis.

premultiplying it, transformations that affect the cross section first must appear last in the list of multiplied transformations. The **m_transz, m_rotz, m_scalex,** and **m_scaley** are non-primitive operators that produce 4×4 matrices representing translation along z, rotation around z, and scaling of the x and y axes, respectively. They are multiplied together to define the complete affine transformation applied to a square cross section.

4.3 Spoons and Closed Offsets

Curve offsetting can also be used to define a cross section with a given thickness that surrounds a given non-closed curve (see Figure 4). An offset curve of radius r around a 2D curve $\gamma(t)$ is given by

$$\gamma(t) + rn(t)$$

where $n(t)$ is the unit normal to the curve. The closed offset of a 2D curve $\gamma(t)$ of radius r can therefore be defined as the uniform concatenation of 4 curve segments: the offset curve of γ of radius r, the reversed offset curve of γ of radius $-r$, and two semicircles of radius r with centers at $\gamma(0)$ and $\gamma(1)$. The non-primitive GENMOD operator **m_closed_offset** creates the closed offset to a 2D curve (first argument), of a given radius (second argument).

Figure 5 shows a spoon whose cross section is formed using this technique. In this case, the curve that is offset is a circular arc whose end points and radius are varied.

4.4 Screwdriver Tips and CPG

Constructive planar geometry (CPG) is the analog of constructive solid geometry for 2D areas. It is a modeling operation that uses Boolean set operations on closed planar areas to produce new planar areas. Figure 6 shows some examples of CPG operations.

Many objects can be represented as surfaces where each cross section is a Boolean set subtraction of one closed area from another. The fact that

Figure 4: Defining a cross section using offsets and circular end caps — A closed cross section may be defined in terms of a non-closed curve by concatenating two offset curves and two circular end caps.

```
MAI u = m_x(0), v = m_x(1);
MAI shape = m_crv("shape.crv",v);
MAI bowl = m_crv("bowl.crv",v);
MAI bend = m_crv("bend.crv",v);
MAI p1 = @(-shape[1],0);
MAI p2 = @(shape[1],0);
MAI arc = m_arc_2pt_height(p1,p2,bowl[1],u);
MAI closed = m_closed_offset(arc,0.01);
MAI spoon = @(shape[0],closed[0],closed[1]+bend[1]);
```

shape.crv   bowl.crv   bend.crv

Figure 5: Spoon example – A spoon surface is formed using a cross section formed by the closed offset of an arc. The curve that is offset is deformed as it is extruded – its radius is increased to give the spoon its bowl, and its length is changed to shape the width of the spoon.

the two planar areas may be swept according to different schedules before being subtracted makes the operation more powerful. Figure 7 shows two screwdriver blade tips specified using CPG. The Phillips blade, for example, is specified by sweeping a circle with a varying radius, from which is subtracted a notch of varying size.

CPG operations require computation of the intersections between planar curves bounding the 2D regions. Often, the intersections between boundary curves can be computed analytically, such as for regions whose boundary is represented as a piecewise series of line segments. When intersections can not be analytically computed, the constraint solution operator can be used. The resulting segments can then be combined by concatenation as described in Section 3.1.

5 Rendering

Most methods of rendering shapes require approximation of the shape into units such as cubes, polygons, or line segments. Such approximation, in turn, require sampling – computation of points over the shape. Two sampling techniques are available in the GENMOD system: uniform sampling, used to quickly preview the shape, and adaptive sampling, used to obtain a more accurate approximation.

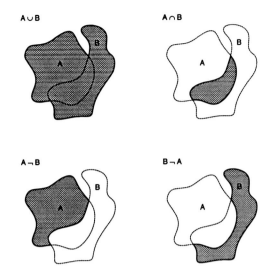

Figure 6: Constructive planar geometry – Two planar regions, A and B, are used in four binary CPG operations. We can compute the boundary of the result of a CPG operation by computing the intersections of the boundaries of the regions, dividing the boundaries into segments at these intersections, and concatenating appropriate segments.

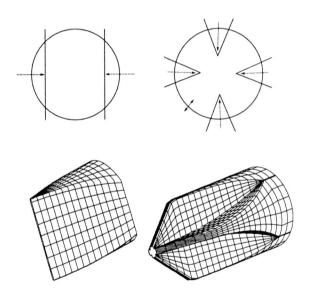

Figure 7: Screwdriver example – The tips of two screwdriver blades are constructed using CPG. The regular screwdriver on the left is generated using a cross section formed by subtracting two half-plane regions from a circle. The two half-planes are gradually moved toward each other as the cross section is translated to the tip of the screwdriver. The Phillips screwdriver on the right has a cross section formed by subtracting four wedge shaped regions from a circle. In this case, the wedge shaped regions are moved toward the circle's center as the cross section is translated to the tip of the screwdriver. while the circle is scaled down near the tip to yield a pointed blade.

5.1 Sampling

Uniform sampling of a parametric function involves evaluating the function over a rectilinear lattice of domain points. For each parametric coordinate x_i, we pick a number of samples, N_i. The parametric function S is then evaluated over the $\prod_{i=1}^{n} N_i$ samples given by

$$\left(a_1 + \frac{i_1(b_1 - a_1)}{N_1 - 1}, \ldots, a_n + \frac{i_n(b_n - a_n)}{N_n - 1} \right)$$

where a_i and b_i define the hyper-rectangular domain of the parametric function. Each of the indices i_j independently ranges from 0 to $N_j - 1$. This evaluation is done by calling the uniform evaluation method of S (from Section 3.2). Uniform evaluation can be optimized so that it computes much faster than simple evaluation at each point in the rectilinear lattice of domain points, as discussed in the Appendix.

Adaptive sampling can be used to generate approximations that satisfy criteria [VONH87], where the sampling density varies over the parameter space. Robust approximation techniques that use inclusion functions are discussed in [SNYD92b]. The simple "evaluation at a specified point" method is used to compute the samples. Such evaluation can be optimized using caching, as discussed in the Appendix.

5.2 Interactive Visualization

A *visualization method* takes a shape and produces a renderable object, or produces a transformation that can be applied to a renderable object. There are four kinds of interactively renderable objects in GENMOD: points, curves, planar areas, and surfaces. A point is rendered as a dot in 2D or 3D space. A curve is rendered as a sequence of line segments. A planar region is rendered as a single polygon formed by the interior of an approximated curve.[11] A surface is rendered as a collection of triangles. A transformation can be applied to any of the other renderable objects, transforming it via the 4x3 affine transformation

$$p \rightarrow Mp + T$$

where M is a 3×3 matrix and T is a 3D vector.

Each of the visualization methods expects a shape of a given output dimension (e.g., a function $S(u, v)$ must have output dimension three to be used as input to the surface visualization method). Each visualization method also expects an input dimension at least as large as the intrinsic input dimension of the shape. For example, a function $C(t)$: $\mathbf{R} \rightarrow \mathbf{R}^3$ can be used in the curve visualization method, as can $D(t, s)$: $\mathbf{R}^2 \rightarrow \mathbf{R}^3$, since C and D have input dimension at least 1. On the other hand, a constant function is not appropriate for the curve method, nor is a function of a single coordinate appropriate for the surface method. The following table shows the number of intrinsic input parameters and output parameters of GENMOD's visualization methods:

name	intrinsic dim.	output dim.
point	0	2 or 3
curve	1	2 or 3
planar area	1	2 or 3
surface	2	3
transformation	0	12

Functions that have an input dimension greater than the visualization method's intrinsic dimension (e.g., a surface that deforms in time) are still valid input to the visualization method. The extra input coordinates, called *variable input parameters*, can be visualized with two techniques: *animation* or *superimposition*. The shapes are first sampled at various points in the variable input parameter space. Superimposition combines these shape instances in a single image, while animation renders the instances one at a time, according to the values of graphics input devices.

As an example, consider a parameterized family of 3D lines, $L(t, u, v)$ defined as

$$L(t, u, v) = S(u, v) + tV(u, v)$$

where $S(u, v)$ represents the line origin, and $V(u, v)$, the line direction. The t parameter is the intrinsic parameter of the line; u and v are variable input parameters. This family of lines can be visualized by superimposition as in Figure 8, resulting in an image containing a 2D family of line segments. Alternatively, the u and v parameters can be animated, resulting in an image of a single line segment which interactively changes as the user controls, say, two dials. The user could also superimpose the u parameter and animate v, resulting in a 1D family of line segments that changes in response to a single dial. Visualization methods therefore require an argument specifying which of the variable input coordinates are to be superimposed, and which are to be animated.

---

[11]The curve must not self intersect, and must lie in a plane. Planar regions are convenient for forming end caps of generalized tubes, where the tube cross-section is bounded by an arbitrary planar curve. Surfaces can also be used for this purpose, but are less convenient, since they require a 2D parameterization of the region's interior, rather than a simple boundary curve.

Figure 8: Visualization of a vector field defined over a surface – A parametric function of input dimension 2 and output dimension 6 can be visualized by rendering a surface, representing the vector field origin, and a set of line segments, representing the vector field direction. The line segments were drawn with the curve visualization method with the two variable input parameters, representing the vector's origin, superimposed.

GENMOD's interactive visualization methods approximate shapes using uniform sampling. The number of samples to be evaluated in each parametric coordinate is specified as an argument to the visualization method. Sampling is precomputed for all the shape's input coordinates, including the variable input coordinates. For example, the surface visualization method takes samples which form a set of 2D grids, one for each value of the variable input parameters. Let $S(u, v, t)$ be a time-varying surface, uniformly sampled with n_u samples in u, n_v samples in v, and n_t samples in t. The uniform samples of S thus form a collection of n_t 2D grids, each $n_u \times n_v$, representing S at a single t value. For each 2D grid, we form a collection of triangles, simply by forming two triangles for each adjacent group of four uv samples.

This scheme has the advantage that real-time animation is possible, even when the shape is represented using complicated functions. The disadvantage is that large amounts of memory is used in storing the precomputed samples, and the modeler must choose the sampling densities before the shape is visualized.

5.3 High Quality Visualization

Visualization methods using adaptive sampling are also available, but are more useful to communicate to outside programs (such as simulation or high-quality rendering programs) than as interactive tools. Parametric surfaces can also be visualized by direct ray tracing, rather than by approximating the shape, using constrained minimization [SNYD92a].

6 The GENMOD System

A block diagram of the GENMOD system is shown in Figure 9. Versions of GENMOD have been developed on a Silicon Graphics IRIS 4D-80GTB and an HP 9000/800 graphics workstation.

Like the Alpha_1 system, GENMOD is based on an interpreted, general purpose language (ANSI C), to allow flexible and interactive shape design. The language allows calls to a substrate of compiled code, which does the bulk of the computation. Typically, only the interface routines, which create GENMOD manifolds and initiate rendering and simulation, need be interpreted. Nevertheless, the full power of an interpreted language is often useful, especially in a research environment.

A curve editor is used to produce curve files for use in the `m_crv` operator. Currently, it supports several types of piecewise cubic curves. The curve editor can be run as a separate task, or run under the direction of GENMOD, allowing the user to see shapes change as the curves they depend on are edited. This mode of operation has proved to be an extremely convenient means of creating models for our computer graphics animations.

The sampling and approximation library provides modules to adaptively approximate parametric shapes according to user-specified criteria. The li-

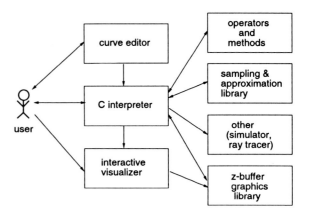

Figure 9: The GENMOD system.

brary also includes algorithms to approximate implicitly defined curves and surfaces, and compute trimming operations on parametric surfaces. These algorithms are described in [SNYD92b].

6.1 GENMOD Manifolds

A *manifold* (type **MAN** in the examples) is the basic type in the GENMOD system, representing a parametric function. A manifold is recursively defined as the application of a symbolic operator to a set of manifolds which are used as its inputs. A manifold stores the following data:

- a list of parametric coordinate indices on which the function depends

- the input and output dimension of the parametric function

- a reference to the top-most operator of the manifold tree (including the operator's methods)

- operator-specific data which includes references to other manifolds used as inputs to the operator. For example, the binary arithmetic operators store a pointer to their two input manifolds. The constraint solution operator stores pointers to the manifolds that define the constraint system, the manifolds which define the region in which to solve the constraint system, and a list of the parametric coordinates over which to solve the constraint system.

6.2 Shape Analysis in GENMOD

The GENMOD system allows many forms of analysis to be computed on parametric shapes. These include finding volume, moments of inertia, and other physical properties of shapes, which can be computed using the integration operator. Collisions between moving shapes can be computed using the constraint solution operator. Such operations are useful in computing rigid body simulations of shapes both for physically-based computer graphics animation and for mechanical CAD. Moreover, the results of such operations are not merely "outputs" of the modeling program, but can be used in further modeling operations allowing us to find, for example, the parameter of a parameterized surface such that its surface area equals a given constant.

The constraint and minimization operators allow a powerful level of analysis not possible with other modeling techniques. For example, parameterized families of shapes can be designed and a particular instance can be selected whose parameter solves a system of constraints. In practice, the complexity of the constraint systems is sometimes limited by the computer's speed. On the other hand, we have successfully used constraint solution and constrained minimization operators in a wide variety of applications including approximating implicit curves and surfaces, direct ray tracing of parametric shapes, and feasible/optimal parameter selection for small (5 or fewer constraint variables) constraint systems.

7 Conclusions

The generative modeling approach represents a shape as the image of a parametric function over a hyper-rectangle in $\mathbf{R}^n$. Parametric functions are built using a set of symbolic operators. Associated with each operator is a set of methods, which perform all the primitive shape computations needed by the rendering and analysis tools.

What is the advantage of such a representation? First, the representation is sufficient for shapes of different dimensionality. It can represent both curves and surfaces, shapes parameterized by time or other variables, and shapes embedded in space of any number of dimensions. The ability of GENMOD to represent and visualize such multidimensional shapes has been indispensable in many projects, such as the modeling of combed teddy bear fur used in [KAJI89] (Figure 11), the modeling of elastic volumes using networks of masses and springs, and the modeling of time-dependent surfaces used in the 1988 SIGGRAPH Film and Video Show animation "Going Bananas" (Figure 10).

Second, the representation is high-level. Shapes can be defined using sophisticated operators such as integration, differentiation, and constraint solution. Unlike simple representations such as polyhedra and NURBS, the representation can be matched to a high-level interface without conversions or approximation error. Third, the representation is extensible. Extension is accomplished by adding new primitive operators, with a few attendant methods. We have added operators many times in the development of GENMOD, most recently an operator which allows bicubic interpolation through 3D data [LAID92] (see Figure 13). Once an operator is defined, it can be combined with any of the other operators already in the system to make new shapes, because of the closure property of the generative modeling approach.

The interface advocated here is an interpreted language, essentially a textual specification of the operators used in the representation. With a language interface, the human designer can construct non-primitive operators such as the profile product or linear interpolation operators. The designer can use and build libraries of such operators, using combinations of the primitive and non-primitive operators. Augmented with such libraries, the modeling interface can be quite complex and powerful, while the basic implementation of the system (i.e., the primitive operators and methods) remains simple.

Acknowledgments

Many thanks are due to Al Barr, for his support and encouragement of the publication of this research. This work was funded, in part, by IBM, Hewlett-Packard, and the National Science Foundation.

References

[ADOB85]   Adobe Systems Incorporated, *PostScript Language Reference Manual*, Addison-Wesley, Reading, Massachusetts, 1985.

[BARR81]   Barr, Alan H., "Superquadrics and Angle Preserving Transformations," *Computer Graphics*, 15(3), August 1981, pp 11-23.

[BARR86]   Barr, Alan H., "Ray Tracing Deformed Surfaces," *Computer Graphics*, 20(4), August 1986, pp. 287-296.

[BINF71]   Binford, T., in *Visual Perception by Computer, Proceedings of the IEEE Conference on Systems and Control*, Miami, FL, December 1971.

[CARL82b]   Carlson, W.E., *Techniques for Generation of Three Dimensional Data for use in Complex Image Synthesis*, Ph.D. Thesis, Ohio State University, Sept. 1982.

[COHE83]   Cohen, E., "Some Mathematical Tools for a Modeler's Workbench," *IEEE Computer Graphics and Applications*, 5(2), pp. 63-66.

[COOK84]   Cook, Robert L., "Shade Trees," *Computer Graphics*, 18(3), July 1984, pp. 223-232.

[COQU87]   Coquillart, S. "A Control Point Based Sweeping Technique," *IEEE Computer Graphics and Applications*, 7(11), 1987, pp. 36-45.

[FRAN81]   Franklin, W.F. and Alan H. Barr, "Faster Calculation of Superquadrics," *IEEE Computer Graphics and Applications*, 1(3), 1981, pp. 41-47.

[GOLD83]   Goldman, R.N., "Quadrics of Revolution," *IEEE Computer Graphics and Applications*, 3(2), 1983, pp. 68-76.

[KAJI89]   Kajiya, James T., and Timothy L. Kay, "Rendering Fur with Three Dimensional Textures," *Computer Graphics*, 23(3), July 1989, pp. 271-280.

[LAID92]   Laidlaw, David, J. Snyder, A. Woodbury, and A. Barr, "Model Extraction using Classification," manuscript in progress.

[LOSS74]   Lossing, D.L., and A.L. Eshleman, "Planning a Common Data Base for Engineering and Manufacturing," *SHARE XLIII*, Chicago, IL, Aug. 1974.

[PERL85]   Perlin, Ken, "An Image Synthesizer," *Computer Graphics*, 19(3), July 1985, pp. 287-296.

[PRES86]   Press, William H., Brian P. Flannery, Saul A. Teukolsky, and William T. Vetterling, *Numerical Recipes*, Cambridge University Press, Cambridge, England, 1986.

[SNYD91]   Snyder, John, *Generative Modeling: An Approach to High Level Shape Design for Computer Graphics and CAD*, Ph.D. Thesis, California Institute of Technology, 1991.

[SNYD92a]   Snyder, John, "Interval Analysis for Computer Graphics," to be published in Siggraph 92.

[SNYD92b]   Snyder, John, *Generative Modeling for Computer Graphics and CAD: Symbolic Shape Design Using Interval Analysis*, to be published by Academic Press, July 1992.

[THOM85]   Thompson, Joe F., Z.U.A. Warsi, and C. Wayne Mastin, *Numerical Grid Generation*, North-Holland, New York, 1985.

[VONH87]   Von Herzen, Brian P. and Alan H. Barr, "Accurate Sampling of Deformed, Intersecting Surfaces with Quadtrees," *Computer Graphics*, 21(4), July 1987, pp. 103-110.

[WANG86]   Wang, W.P. and K.K. Wang "Geometric Modelling for Swept Volume of Moving Solids," *IEEE Computer Graphics and Applications*, 6(12), 1986, pp. 8-17.

Appendix – Sampling Speedups

Uniform Sampling Speedup using Table Lookup   A substantial speedup of uniform parametric evaluation can be accomplished by constructing evaluation tables for subfunctions, where a subfunction is a subtree in the tree of symbolic operators representing a parametric function [FRAN81]. For example, let $f: \mathbf{R}^3 \rightarrow \mathbf{R}$ be the function:

$$f(x_1, x_2, x_3) = (x_1 x_2 + x_2 x_3)e^{x_2}$$

which we wish to uniformly sample using n_i samples for each x_i. This can be done by evaluating f at each of the $n_1 n_2 n_3$ lattice points in parameter space. Alternatively, we can construct evaluation tables for the subfunctions $f_1(x_1, x_2) = x_1 x_2$, $f_2(x_2, x_3) = x_2 x_3$, and $f_3(x_2) = e^{x_2}$, so that these subfunctions are not reevaluated at each lattice point. Here is a table of the number of operations required for the two methods of evaluating f:

function	* ops	+ ops	e^x ops
evaluation point by point			
$f = (x_1 x_2 + x_2 x_3)e^{x_2}$	$3n_1 n_2 n_3$	$n_1 n_2 n_3$	$n_1 n_2 n_3$
evaluation using tables			
$f_1 = x_1 x_2$	$n_1 n_2$	0	0
$f_2 = x_2 x_3$	$n_2 n_3$	0	0
$f_3 = e^{x_2}$	0	0	n_2
$f = (f_1 + f_2) * f_3$	$n_1 n_2 n_3$	$n_1 n_2 n_3$	0
total	$n_1 n_2 n_3 + n_1 n_2 + n_2 n_3$	$n_1 n_2 n_3$	n_2

The table shows that substantial computational savings result when the lower-dimensional subfunctions are evaluated and stored in tables. In general, **evaluation tables should be constructed for each subfunction that has an input dimension smaller than its parent.** For example, the subfunction e^{x_2}, of input dimension 1, should be tabulated because its parent function f has input dimension 3. Such a subfunction should be tabulated at the lattice points of its particular input variables (e.g., evaluations from the subfunction e^{x_2} are stored in a 1D table of size n_2, while evaluations from the subfunction $x_1 x_2$ are stored in a 2D table of size $n_1 \times n_2$).

Adaptive Sampling Speedup Using Caching   Adaptive sampling can be enhanced by caching the last computed value of a subfunction. Both the input point and the subfunction result are stored. If, in a future evaluation, the input point matches the cached point (or the subfunction is input dimension 0), then the cached function result may be used without reevaluation. Candidate subfunctions are those that have lower input dimension than their parent, or that are repeated (i.e., shared subexpressions). Caching can be used for inclusion function evaluation as well as point evaluation.

Caching is especially useful in cases such as when an integrand contains a subfunction that is not dependent on the parameter of integration, when a subfunction of input dimension 0 is defined using computationally expensive operators (e.g., $x_1 + \int g(x_2)dx_2$), or when the same subfunction is used many times.

Figure 11: Animation Example. The figure shows a frame from the 1988 Siggraph film "Going Bananas" in which every object was specified using an early version of the GENMOD program. The movement and deformation of several characters in the animation were also defined using time-varying functions. Rendering was accomplished with a separate ray tracing program using polygons produced by GENMOD.

Figure 12: Teddy Bear Example. The GENMOD program was used to model both the surfaces forming the skin of the bear, and the way in which the fur was "combed" over the skin. The bear was rendered using the technique described in [KAJI89].

Figure 13: ODE Solution. The figure shows the results of the ODE solution operator to compute the trajectory of a point mass in the gravitational field of three fixed masses.

Figure 14: Modeling a Jade Plant from MR Data. The jade plant surface was modeled by extracting an isosurface through interpolated magnetic resonance (MR) data, using GENMOD's implicit surface approximation.

Modeling seashells

Deborah R. Fowler

Department of Computer Science
University of Calgary
and University of Regina
Canada

Hans Meinhardt

Max-Planck-Institut
für Entwicklungsbiologie
7400 Tübingen, Germany

Przemyslaw Prusinkiewicz

Department of Computer Science
University of Calgary
Alberta, Canada T2N 1N4

(Authors listed alphabetically)

ABSTRACT

This paper presents a method for modeling seashells, suitable for image synthesis purposes. It combines a geometric description of shell shapes with an activator-inhibitor model of pigmentation patterns on shell surfaces. The technique is illustrated using models of selected shells found in nature.

CR Categories: I.3.5 [**Computer Graphics**]: Computational Geometry and Object Modeling: *Curve, surface, solid and object representation.* I.3.7 [**Computer Graphics**]: Three-Dimensional Graphics and Realism. J.3 [**Life and Medical Sciences**]: *Biology.*

Keywords: realistic image synthesis, modeling of natural phenomena, seashell, logarithmic helico-spiral, sweep representation, reaction-diffusion pattern model.

1 INTRODUCTION

The beauty of shells invites us to construct their mathematical models. The motivation is to synthesize realistic images that could be incorporated into computer-generated scenes and to gain a better understanding of the mechanism of shell formation. The latter objective was crisply justified by Raup, the pioneer of computer modeling of shell morphology [28]:

> Successful simulation provides confirmation of the underlying models as valid descriptions of the actual biological situation;
> Unsuccessful simulation shows flaws in the postulated model and may suggest the changes that should be made in the model to correct the flaws;
> Non-occurring forms, perhaps intermediate between actual species, may be simulated and thus may lead to a better understanding of the relationships between the real forms.

In this paper, we propose a modeling technique that combines two key components: a model of shell shapes derived from a descriptive characterization by d'Arcy Thompson [31], and a reaction-diffusion model of pigmentation patterns originated by Meinhardt [17]. The results are evaluated by comparing models with the real shells.

Historically, the logarithmic spiral, capturing the essence of the shell shape, was first described in 1638 by Descartes [31, page 754] and applied to characterize shell coiling by Moseley [21]. By the beginning of the twentieth century, it was observed in many artificial and organic forms [4]. Moseley's characterization was supported experimentally and popularized by Thompson [31], who presented careful measurements of a wide variety of taxonomic and functional types of shells, and showed their conformity with the logarithmic model.

The application of computers to the visualization and analysis of shell shapes was originated by Raup. In the first paper devoted to this topic [27], he presented two-dimensional plots of longitudinal cross-sections of shells as a form of blueprints that may assist a person who is drawing shell forms. Subsequently, Raup extended his model to three dimensions [29], and visualized shell models as stereo pairs, using a wire-frame representation [28].

Kawaguchi [15] developed the first shell model intended specifically for computer graphics purposes. He enhanced the appearance of shell models using a polygon mesh instead of a wire frame. Similar representations were used subsequently by Oppenheimer [23], and Prusinkiewicz and Streibel [26]. Pursuing a different approach, Pickover [24, 25] approximated shell surfaces using interpenetrating spheres, placed at carefully chosen distances from each other and rendered using periodically altering colors to create the appearance of a ribbed surface with stripes.

The recent work on the modeling of shells has been characterized by an increased attention to detail. Illert [14] introduced Frenet frames [3, 7] to precisely orient the opening of the shell. His model also captured a form of surface sculpture. Cortie [5] allowed for independent tilting of the opening in three directions, presented models with the apertures defying simple mathematical description, and extended the range of surface ornamentations captured by the model.

Our model of shell geometry is similar to that originated by Raup and culminating in the work of Cortie. It enhances previous models by applying free-form parametric curves (in the Bézier form) to capture the shape of shell aperture. However, the most conspicuous improvement results from the incorporation of pigmentation patterns into the models.

Mathematical modeling of pigmentation patterns was pioneered in 1969 by Waddington and Cowe [35], who reproduced patterns of *Oliva porphyria* using cellular automata. A similar formalism was applied by Baker and Herman [1], and Wolfram [37]. According to Murray [22, page 506], these models had no basis in the underlying biological processes involved in the mollusc's growth. In 1984, Meinhardt introduced a biologically-motivated reaction-diffusion model [17], subsequently refined with Klinger [18, 19, 20]. Ermentrout, Campbell and Oster [8] proposed an alternative model employing neural nets. These two models share the basic mathematical concepts of short-range activation and long-range inhibition, and consequently yield similar patterns. We employ Meinhardt's model in our implementation.

From the computer graphics perspective, the use of reaction-diffusion processes [11, 16, 33] for image synthesis purposes was pioneered by Turk [34], and Witkin and Kass [36]. They focused on patterns defined by the distribution of morphogens in two-dimensional surfaces. In contrast, pigmentation patterns in shells are formed only along the growing edge of a shell. The second dimension results from the deposition of new shell material, which continually changes the position of the growing edge over time. Thus, the pattern on a shell can be viewed as a record of what has happened at the growing edge during the life span of a particular animal. This dynamic aspect sets the pigmentation patterns in shells apart from the reaction-diffusion models previously considered in computer graphics.

The organization of the paper follows the main division of the topic into the modeling of shell shapes (Section 2) and the generation of pigmentation patterns (Section 3). The results are evaluated in Section 4, which is concluded with a list of open problems.

2 MODELING SHELL GEOMETRY

In Chapter XI of *On Growth and Form* [31], d'Arcy Thompson provided a detailed description of shell geometry, supported by measurements of selected shells. Some of his observations are quoted below in a slightly edited form.

> The surface of any shell may be generated by the revolution about a fixed axis of a closed curve, which, remaining always geometrically similar to itself, increases its dimensions continually. [...] Let us imagine some characteristic point within this closed curve, such as its centre of gravity. Starting from a fixed origin, this characteristic point describes an equiangular spiral in space about a fixed axis (namely the axis of the shell), with or without a simultaneous movement of translation along the axis. The scale of the figure increases in geometrical progression while the angle of rotation increases in arithmetical, and the centre of similitude remains fixed. [...] The form of the generating curve is seldom open to easy mathematical expressions.

Our modeling method is derived from this description.

2.1 The helico-spiral

The modeling of a shell surface starts with the construction of a logarithmic (equiangular) helico-spiral $\mathcal{H}$ (Figure 1). In a cylindrical coordinate system (shown in Figure 1 as embedded in the Cartesian xyz system) it has the parametric description [6]:

$$\theta = t, \quad r = r_0 \xi_r{}^t, \quad z = z_0 \xi_z{}^t. \tag{1}$$

Parameter t ranges from 0 at the apex of the shell to t_{max} at the opening. The first two equations represent a logarithmic spiral lying

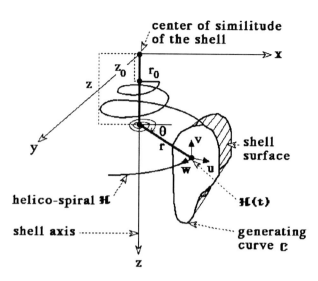

Figure 1: Construction of the shell surface

in the plane $z = 0$. The third equation stretches the spiral along the z-axis, thus contributing a helical component to its shape.

Distances r and z are exponential functions of the parameter t, and usually have the same base, $\xi_r = \xi_z = \xi$. As a result, the generating helico-spiral is self-similar, with the center of similitude located at the origin of the coordinate system xyz. Given the initial values θ_0, r_0, and z_0, a sequence of points on the helico-spiral can be computed incrementally using the formulae:

$$\begin{aligned}
\theta_{i+1} &= t_i + \Delta t &= \theta_i + \Delta\theta, \\
r_{i+1} &= r_0 \xi_r^{t_i} \xi_r^{\Delta t} &= r_i \lambda_r, \\
z_{i+1} &= z_0 \xi_z^{t_i} \xi_z^{\Delta t} &= z_i \lambda_z.
\end{aligned} \tag{2}$$

While the angle of rotation θ increases in arithmetic progression with the step $\Delta\theta$, the radius r forms a geometric progression with the scaling factor $\lambda_r = \xi_r^{\Delta t}$, and the vertical displacement z forms a geometric progression with the scaling factor $\lambda_z = \xi_z^{\Delta t}$. In many shells, parameters λ_r and λ_z are the same. Variations of shell shapes due primarily to different parameters of the helico-spiral are shown in Figure 2. They correspond closely to the shell types identified by d'Arcy Thompson [32, page 192].

2.2 The generating curve

The surface of the shell is determined by a generating curve $\mathcal{C}$, sweeping along the helico-spiral $\mathcal{H}$. The size of the curve $\mathcal{C}$ increases as it revolves around the shell axis. The shape of $\mathcal{C}$ determines the profile of the whorls and of the shell opening. In order to capture the variety and complexity of possible shapes, we construct the generating curves from one or more segments of Bézier curves [9]. The impact of the generating curve on the shape of a shell is shown in Figures 3 and 4.

2.3 Incorporation of the generating curve into the model

The generating curve $\mathcal{C}$ is specified in a local coordinate system uvw. Given a point $\mathcal{H}(t)$ of the helico-spiral, $\mathcal{C}$ is first scaled up by the factor $\xi_c{}^t$ with respect to the origin O of this system, then rotated and translated so that the point O matches $\mathcal{H}(t)$ (Figure 1). The axes uvw are used to orient the generating curve in space. The

2.4 Construction of the polygon mesh

In the mathematical sense, the surface of the shell is completely defined by the generating curve C, sweeping along the helico-spiral $\mathcal{H}$. Nevertheless, we represent this surface as a polygon mesh for rendering purposes. The mesh is constructed by specifying $n + 1$ points on the generating curve (including the endpoints), and connecting corresponding points for consecutive positions of the generating curve. The sequence of polygons spanned between a pair of adjacent generating curves is called a *rim*.

The reaction-diffusion equations describing pigmentation patterns, to be discussed in Section 3, can be solved the easiest way if the (one-dimensional) space in which they operate is discretized uniformly. This corresponds to the partition of the rim into polygons evenly spaced along the generating curve. A suitable partitioning method was described by Bartels and Hardtke [2] and is summarized below.

Let $C(s) = (u(s), v(s), w(s))$ denote a parametric definition of the curve C in coordinates uvw, with $s \in [s_{min}, s_{max}]$. The length of an arc of C is related to an increment of parameter s by the equations:

$$\frac{dl}{ds} = f(s), \qquad (4)$$

$$f(s) = \sqrt{\left(\frac{du}{ds}\right)^2 + \left(\frac{dv}{ds}\right)^2 + \left(\frac{dw}{ds}\right)^2}. \qquad (5)$$

The total length L of C can be found by integrating $f(s)$ in the interval $[s_{min}, s_{max}]$:

$$L = \int_{s_{min}}^{s_{max}} f(s) ds. \qquad (6)$$

Inversion of the equation (4) yields:

$$\frac{ds}{dl} = \frac{1}{f(s)}. \qquad (7)$$

Given the initial condition $s(0) = s_{min}$, this first-order differential equation describes parameter s as a function of the arc length l. By numerically integrating (7) in n consecutive intervals of length $\Delta l = \frac{L}{n}$, we obtain a sequence of parameter values $s_0 = s_{min}, s_1, s_2, \ldots, s_n = s_{max}$, representing the desired sequence of $n + 1$ polygon vertices equally spaced along the curve C. The effect of the reparametrization of the generating curve is shown in Figure 6.

The same figure reveals unequal spacing of polygon vertices between adjacent generating curves. The polygons are stretched horizontally in the wide central portions of the shells, and squeezed near the top and the bottom. This effect is due to the differences in the lengths of the trajectories traced by different points on the generating curve in equal time intervals. A reparametrization of trajectories by their arc length would yield a uniform distribution of vertices along each trajectory, but the benefits of such operation are not certain. Specifically, it is not clear whether the progress of the reaction-diffusion process along a trajectory depends directly on its length, the progress of time, or a combination of both factors. In the context of *Nautilus pompilus* this problem has been discussed by Meinhardt and Klinger [18].

2.5 Modeling the sculpture on shell surfaces

Many shells have a sculptured surface. Common forms of sculpturing include ribs parallel to the direction of growth or to the

Figure 6: The effect of the reparametrization of the generating curve. In the left shell, mesh vertices are spaced along the generating curve using constant increments of the parameter s. In the right shell, the increments of parameter s have been adjusted to divide the generating curve into segments of equal length. As a result, texture distortion along the generating curve has been eliminated.

generating curve. Both types of ribs can be easily reproduced by displacing the vertices of the polygon mesh in the direction normal to the shell surface.

In the case of ribs parallel to the direction of growth, the displacement d varies periodically along the generating curve. The amplitude of these variations is proportional to the actual size of the curve, thus it increases as the shell grows. Sample applications of this technique are depicted in Figures 7, 8, and 9.

The periodic displacement along the generating curve could be incorporated into the curve definition, but we chose to capture the displacement independently from the overall shape of C. This approach is more flexible and can be easily extended to other sculptured patterns. For example, oblique ribs oriented diagonally with respect to the generative curve (as in *Strigilla carnea* [18]) result from a gradual incrementation of the phase of the periodic displacement during the shell's growth.

Ribs parallel to the generating curve are obtained by periodically varying the value of the displacement d according to the position of the generating curve along the helico-spiral $\mathcal{H}$. As previously, the amplitude is proportional to the current size of the generating curve. Examples are shown in Figure 10. The two shells on the right side have ribs parallel to the generating curve. The shells on the left display latticed sculpturing, obtained by superimposing ribs parallel to the generating curve and to the direction of growth.

3 GENERATION OF PIGMENTATION PATTERNS

Pigmentation patterns constitute an important aspect of shell appearance. We propose to capture them using a class of reaction-diffusion models developed by Meinhardt and Klinger [17, 18, 19, 20]. A summary of this approach is presented below in order to make our description of shell modeling complete.

Pigmentation patterns in shells show enormous diversity. From the perspective of mollusc evolution, this diversity is attributed to the lack of selective value of any particular pattern. In many cases, the animals live burrowed in sand, or are active at night. Sometimes the pattern is invisible as long as the animal is alive, due to a covering

Figure 2: Variation of shell shapes resulting from different parameters of the helico-spiral. Leftmost: turbinate shell ($z_0 = 1.9$, $\lambda = 1.007$). Top row: patelliform shell ($z_0 = 0$, $\lambda = 1.34$) and tubular shell ($z_0 = 0.0$, $\lambda = 1.011$). Bottom row: spherical shell ($z_0 = 1.5$, $\lambda = 1.03$) and diskoid shell ($z_0 = 1.4$, $\lambda = 1.014$). Values of $\lambda = \lambda_r = \lambda_z$ correspond to $\Delta\theta = 10°$.

Figure 3: Variation of the shell shape resulting from different generating curves. From left to right: turreted shell, two fusiform shells, and a conical shell.

simplest approach is to rotate the system uvw so that the axes v and u become respectively parallel and perpendicular to the shell axis z. If the generating curve lies in the plane uv, the opening of the shell and the growth markings (such as the ribs on the shell surface) will be parallel to the shell axis. However, many shells exhibit approximately *orthoclinal* growth markings, which lie in planes normal to the helico-spiral $\mathcal{H}$ [14]. This effect can be captured by orienting the axis w along the vector $\vec{e}_1$, tangent to the helico-spiral at the point $\mathcal{H}(t)$. The curve is fixed in space by aligning the axis u with the principal normal vector $\vec{e}_2$ of $\mathcal{H}$. The unit vectors $\vec{e}_1$ and $\vec{e}_2$ can be calculated using the following formulae [3]:

$$\vec{e}_1 = \frac{\vec{\mathcal{H}}'(t)}{|\vec{\mathcal{H}}'(t)|}, \quad \vec{e}_3 = \frac{\vec{e}_1 \times \vec{\mathcal{H}}''(t)}{|\vec{e}_1 \times \vec{\mathcal{H}}''(t)|}, \quad \vec{e}_2 = \vec{e}_3 \times \vec{e}_1. \quad (3)$$

Symbols $\vec{\mathcal{H}}'(t)$ and $\vec{\mathcal{H}}''(t)$ denote the first and the second derivative of the position vector $\vec{\mathcal{H}}(t)$ of the point $\mathcal{H}(t)$, taken with respect to the parameter t. Vectors $\vec{e}_1$, $\vec{e}_2$ and $\vec{e}_3$ define a local orthogonal coordinate system called the *Frenet frame*. It is considered a good reference system for specifying orientation, because it does not depend on the parametrization of the helico-spiral $\mathcal{H}$ or on the coordinate system in which it is expressed [7]. The Frenet frame is not defined in the points with zero curvature, but a helico-spiral has no such points ($\mathcal{H}''(t)$ is never equal to zero). The impact of the orientation of the generating curve is illustrated in Figure 5. The opening of the real shell and the ribs on its surface lie in planes normal to the helico-spiral. This is properly captured in the model in the center, which uses Frenet frames to orient the generating curve. The model on the right incorrectly aligns the generating curve with the shell axis.

In general, the generating curve need not be aligned either with the shell axis or with the Frenet frame. In the case of non-planar generating curves, it is even difficult to define what the "alignment" could mean. It is therefore convenient to be able to adjust the orientation of the generating curve with respect to the reference coordinate system. We accomplish this by allowing the user to specify a rotation of the system uvw with respect to each of the axes $\vec{e}_1$, $\vec{e}_2$, and $\vec{e}_3$.

Figure 4: A photograph [12, page 97] and a model of *Thatcheria mirabilis* (Miraculous Thatcheria). The unusual shape of this shell results from the triangular generating curve. Photograph by courtesy of The Natural History Museum, London, England.

Figure 5: A photograph [12, page 47] and two models of *Epitonium scalare* (Precious Wentletrap). Photograph by courtesy of Ken Lucas, Biological Photo Service, Moss Beach, California.

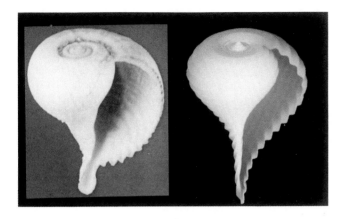

Figure 7: A photograph [30, entry 326] and a model of *Rapa rapa* (Papery Rapa) showing surface sculpturing with the ribs orthogonal to the generating curves. The shape of ribs in the model is captured by a sine function uniformly spaced along the edge of the shell.

Figure 9: Surface sculpturing with the ribs orthogonal to the generating curves. A photograph [30, entry 128] and three models of *Turritella nivea* illustrate the effect of the decreasing frequency of the modulating function.

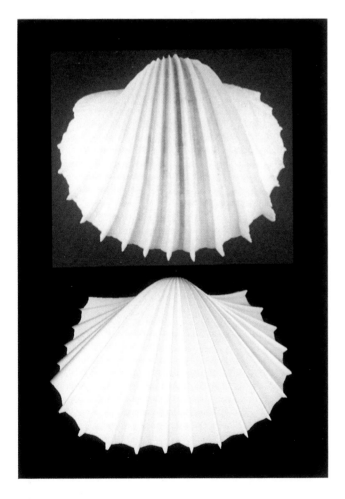

Figure 8: A photograph [30, entry 22] and a model of *Cardium costatum* (Ribbed Cockle)

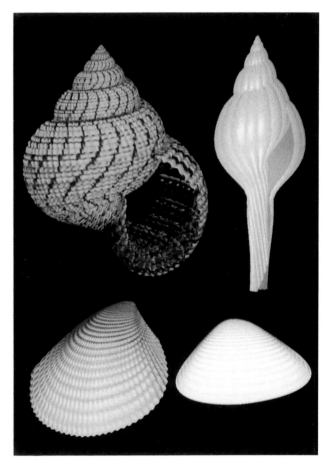

Figure 10: Surface sculpturing with the ribs parallel to the generating curve (right) and with a lattice of ribs (left)

by non-transparent layers. Consequently, there is no evolutionary pressure giving a preference to specific patterns.

The diversity of the patterns, which may differ in details even between shells of the same species, suggests a morphogenetic mechanism general enough to encompass large specimen-to-specimen and species-to-species variations. We assume that it is of the reaction-diffusion type [11, 16, 33]. Pigment deposition is under the control of a substance, called the *activator*, which stimulates its own production through a positive feedback mechanism, or *autocatalysis*. In order for a pattern to be formed, a mechanism is also needed for suppressing the production of the activator in the neighborhood of the autocatalytic centers. This prevents the activator from spreading over the entire substrate. Thus, the pattern is formed as a result of the antagonistic interaction between short-range activation and long-range inhibition.

Harrison [13] points out that reaction-diffusion is not a single model, but the cornerstone of a whole spectrum of models, differing in the number and characteristics of the reacting substances. This observation remains true for the models of pigmentation patterns in shells. We do not capture all possible patterns in a single system of equations, but modify it according to the specific pattern. Generally, we group our models into two basic categories distinguished by Gierer and Meinhardt [11]: activator-substrate, and activator-inhibitor.

3.1 The activator-substrate model

The inhibitory effect may result from the depletion of the substrate required to produce the activator. A possible interaction is described by the following equations:

$$
\begin{aligned}
\frac{\partial a}{\partial t} &= \rho s \left(\frac{a^2}{1 + \kappa a^2} + \rho_0 \right) - \mu a + D_a \frac{\partial^2 a}{\partial x^2} \\
\frac{\partial s}{\partial t} &= \sigma - \rho s \left(\frac{a^2}{1 + \kappa a^2} + \rho_0 \right) - \nu s + D_s \frac{\partial^2 s}{\partial x^2}
\end{aligned}
\tag{8}
$$

The activator, with the concentration a, diffuses along the x-axis at the rate D_a and decays at the rate μ. Similarly, the substrate, with the concentration s, diffuses at the rate D_s and decays at the rate ν. The substrate is produced at a constant rate σ. Production of the activator is an autocatalytic process, proportional to a^2 for small activator concentrations. This process can take place only in the presence of the substrate, and decreases its amount. Parameter ρ is the coefficient of proportionality. The autocatalysis can saturate at high activator concentrations, at the level controlled by the parameter κ. Parameter ρ_0 represents a small base production of the activator, needed to initiate the autocatalytic process.

Figure 11 shows the application of equations (8) to the formation of stripes parallel to the direction of shell growth. In order to start the pattern formation process, parameter ρ is subject to small random fluctuations (less than 2.5% of its average value) for the individual cells. The pattern that emerges after the initial transition is stable in time, but periodic in space. This periodicity is achieved by setting the range of inhibition (determined by the diffusion and decay rates of the substrate) to a fraction of the total length of the growing edge.

In order to solve the equations and generate the images, the growing edge is divided into cells of length Δx. In the planar representation of the pattern on the left side of Figure 11, the cells correspond to a horizontal row of pixels. In the shell on the right the cells correspond to the polygons on the growing edge. The equations are solved using the forward Euler method [10] (a FORTRAN code is included in the paper [19]. We ignore the effect of the gradual increase of polygon size resulting from the rim's growth.

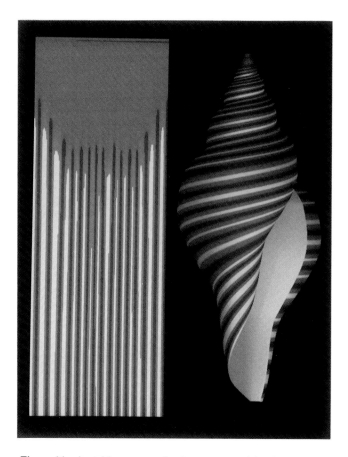

Figure 11: A stable pattern of stripes generated by the activator-substrate model using equations (8), with $\rho = 0.01 \pm 2.5\%$, $\rho_0 = 0.001$, $\mu = 0.01$, $D_a = 0.002$, $\sigma = 0.015$, $\nu = 0$, $D_s = 0.4$, and $\kappa = 0$

Concentrations of the activator corresponding to fixed time intervals Δt determine colors of cells in the consecutive rows or rims.

The generation of stripes using the activator-substrate model is interesting from the theoretical perspective, since it illustrates the emergence of a pattern from an almost uniform initial distribution of substances (the solid area in the upper part of the planar representation in Figure 11). The development of a pattern in a homogeneous medium motivated the original definitions and studies of the reaction-diffusion models [11, 33]. In order to demonstrate their practical usefulness for the synthesis of shell images, we must consider more complex patterns than stripes.

Figure 12 shows a photograph and a model of *Amoria undulata*. The pattern consists of wavy lines that, on the average, run in the direction parallel to the growing edge. This direction is partially obscured by the large amplitude of the waves. The periodic character of the pattern in the direction of the helico-spiral is a manifestation of the oscillations of the activator concentration over time. In the activator-substrate model they are known to occur for $\sigma < \mu$ [17]. In order to generate lines of undulating shape, we assume that the activator-substrate process is regulated by an external factor, which modulates the substrate production σ according to a periodic (sine) function of cell position, $\sigma = \sigma(x)$. Undulations occur, since in regions with higher σ oscillations are faster than in regions with lower σ values. The coherence of the lines is maintained by the diffusion of the activator. Higher diffusion constants force better synchronization between the neighboring cells, yielding lines that follow the orientation of the growing edge more closely.

Figure 12: A photograph [30, entry 222] and a model of *Amoria undulata* (Waved Volute). Generated using equations (8), with $\rho = 0.1 \pm 2.5\%$, $\rho_0 = 0.005$, $\mu = 0.1$, $D_a = 0.004$, $\sigma_{max} = 0.012$, $\nu = 0$, $D_s = 0.0$, and $\kappa = 1$.

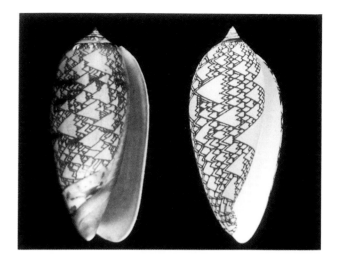

Figure 14: A photograph [30, entry 83] and a model of *Oliva porphyria*. Generated using equations (9), with $\rho = 0.1 \pm 2.5\%$ $\rho_0 = 0.0001$, $\mu = 0.1$, $D_a = 0.015$, $\sigma = 0.0002$, $\nu = 0.014$, $D_h = 0.0$, $\rho' = 0.1$, $\eta = 0.1$, $h_0 = 0.1$, and $\kappa = 0.25$.

Figure 13: A photograph [30, entry 132] and a model of *Volutoconus bednalli* (Bednall's Volute). Generated using equations (8), with $\rho = 0.1 \pm 2.5\%$, $\rho_0 = 0.0025$, $\mu = 0.1$, $D_a = 0.01$, $\sigma_{max} = 0.11$, $\nu = 0.002$, $D_s = 0.05$, and $\kappa = 0.5$.

Volutoconus bednalli, shown in Figure 13, displays a variant of the same mechanism. In this case, the function $\sigma(x)$ periodically exceeds the decay constant of the activator, producing stripes of cells with permanently high activator concentration. The oscillating patterns between these stripes can be viewed as traveling waves that annihilate each other as they meet.

3.2 The activator-inhibitor model

Propagation of colliding waves is the essential feature of the pigmentation pattern of *Oliva porphyria*, presented in Figure 14. The oblique lines represent waves of activator concentration, traveling along the growing edge. As previously, colliding waves extinguish each other. In Figure 14, this corresponds to an element of the pattern in the shape of the symbol $<$. Another element of this pattern is a branch that occurs when an activated point of one wave spontaneously

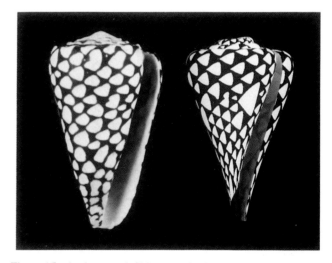

Figure 15: A photograph [30, entry 240] and a model of *Conus marmoreus* (Marble Cone)

neously initiates another wave, traveling in the opposite direction. Observation of the shell indicates that the number of traveling waves is approximately constant over time. This suggests a global control mechanism that monitors the total amount of activator in the system, and initiates new waves when its concentration becomes too low. This mechanism can be captured using the following system of equations:

$$
\begin{aligned}
\frac{\partial a}{\partial t} &= \frac{\rho}{h + h_0}\left(\frac{a^2}{1 + \kappa a^2} + \rho_0\right) - \mu a + D_a \frac{\partial^2 a}{\partial x^2} \\
\frac{\partial h}{\partial t} &= \sigma + \rho \frac{a^2}{1 + \kappa a^2} - \frac{\nu}{c} h + D_h \frac{\partial^2 h}{\partial x^2} \\
\frac{dc}{dt} &= \frac{\rho'}{x_{max} - x_{min}} \int_{x_{min}}^{x_{max}} a\, dx - \eta c
\end{aligned}
\tag{9}
$$

The first two equations represent an activator-inhibitor system. As with the activator-substrate model, production of the activator is an autocatalytic process. The activator also catalyzes the production of its antagonist, the inhibitor h, which in turn decreases the production of the activator proportionally to $1/(h+h_0)$. We postulate that this process is globally regulated by a hormone c, which monitors the total amount of activator along the growing edge. The hormone diffuses much faster than the remaining substances, thus its concentration along the growing edge is assumed to be constant. A small number of traveling waves yields a small concentration of the hormone, which accelerates the decay of the inhibitor h. The concentration of the activator increases and at some points reaches the threshold at which new waves are formed. This is a self-regulating process, where the hormone c provides a negative feedback maintaining the number of traveling waves at an approximately constant level.

The model of *Conus marmoreus*, shown in Figure 15, is similar to that of *Oliva*. The pigment producing process is controlled by another reaction-diffusion process, instead of a hormone. Models of several other patterns are presented in detail by Meinhardt and Klinger [18, 19].

4 CONCLUSIONS

This paper presents a comprehensive model of seashells, suitable for computer imagery purposes. The model combines separate results described in the existing paleontological, biological, and computer graphics literature into a single model, capable of generating relatively realistic images of many shells. The overall shape of a shell is determined by the parameters of the helico-spiral and the generating curve. The sculpturing is obtained by periodically displacing vertices of the polygon mesh representing the shell surface. Attention is given to details, such as the orientation of the axial ribs and the shell opening, and prevention of distortions of the sculptured and pigmented patterns. Pigmentation is simulated using reaction-diffusion models. A comparison of the results with the photographs of real shells shows good correspondence of the shapes and the patterns. This is important both from the visual perspective and from the viewpoint of the applications of the models to biology. Direct observation of phenomena such as the postulated flow of a hormone in *Oliva* is difficult, and agreement of synthetic images with reality indirectly supports the models. Realistic visualization makes such comparisons more convincing.

Comparisons with the real shells also reveal shortcomings of our models, leading to problems open for further research:

- *Proper modeling of the shell opening.* The sweeping of a uniformly growing generating curve along the helico-spiral produces a strictly self-similar surface that can be mapped into itself by a scaling and a rotation around the shell axis [6, 31]. In real shells, the lips at the shell opening often display a departure from self-similarity. *Strombus listeri*, on the left side of Figure 16, provides a striking example of this phenomenon, although to a lesser extent it also occurs in other shells, such as *Volutoconus bednalli* and *Oliva porphyria* (Figures 13 and 14). The modeling of the shell opening requires further investigation.

- *Modeling of spikes.* The model of shell sculpture, based on the perturbation of the surface in the direction of the normal vector, is an appropriate technique for reproducing relatively small ridges. It does not capture large modifications of the shape, such as spikes in *Murex pecten* and extrusions in *Chicoreus spectrum* (Figure 16). The incorporation of these structures into the models remains an open problem.

- *Capturing the thickness of shell walls.* We represent a shell wall as a single surface, albeit its two sides are rendered

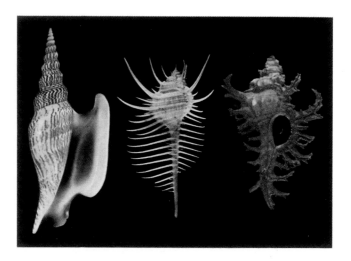

Figure 16: Photographs [30, entries 113, 276 and 29] of three shells that exemplify the main limitations of the present model. From left to right: *Strombus listeri* (Lister's Conch), *Murex pecten* (Venus Comb Murex), and *Chicoreus spectrum* (Ghost Murex).

differently. In reality, the wall has some thickness, which should be reproduced to properly visualize the edge of the shell opening.

- *Alternatives to the integrated model.* The integration of pigmentation patterns into the shell model is an appealing feature from the biological perspective, since it is consistent with the developmental nature of the models. Unfortunately, it also leads to large polygon meshes, necessary to capture the intricacies of the patterns. In our implementation, the meshes may consist of millions of polygons. This creates rendering problems, because the renderer may impose limits on the maximum size of the mesh. Separate generation of the shell shape and the pigmentation pattern, combined into a single image using texture mapping, may represent a preferable approach.

- *Improved rendering.* A comparison of the photographs of real shells with the synthetic images of their models exhibits the need for a better rendering technique. Specifically, it could capture the anisotropic highlights, the translucency of shell walls, and the darkening inside the shell opening.

Solutions to all of these problems seem to be achievable. They should improve our understanding of the forms and patterns of shells, and bring us closer to photorealism.

Acknowledgements

This research was sponsored by an operating grant from the Natural Sciences and Engineering Research Council of Canada, and by a graduate scholarship from the University of Regina. We are indebted to Pat Hanrahan for providing Deborah with the access to his research facilities at Princeton, and to Jim Hanan for recording the images at the University of Regina. Photographs of real shells included in Figures 7, 8, 9, 12, 13, 14, 15, and 16 are reproduced with the kind permission of Giuseppe Mazza. We would like to thank the anonymous referees for many useful comments on the first version of this paper.

References

[1] R. Baker and G. T. Herman. Simulation of organisms using a developmental model, parts I and II. *Int. Journal of Bio-Medical Computing*, 3:201–215 and 251–267, 1972.

[2] R. Bartels and I. Hardtke. Speed adjustment for key-frame interpolation. In *Proceedings of Graphics Interface '89*, pages 14–19, 1989.

[3] W. Bronsvoort and F. Klok. Ray tracing generalized cylinders. *ACM Transactions on Graphics*, 4(4):291–303, 1985.

[4] T. A. Cook. *Curves of Life*. Dover Publications, New York, 1979. Originally published in 1914, by Constable and Company, London.

[5] M. B. Cortie. Models for mollusc shell shape. *South African Journal of Science*, 85:454–460, 1989.

[6] H. S. M. Coxeter. *Introduction to Geometry*. J. Wiley & Sons, New York, 1961.

[7] M. do Carmo. *Differential Geometry of Curves and Surfaces*. Prentice Hall, Englewood Cliffs, 1976.

[8] B. Ermentrout, J. Campbell, and G. Oster. A model for shell patterns based on neural activity. *The Veliger*, 28:369–388, 1986.

[9] J. D. Foley, A. Van Dam, S. K. Feiner, and J. F. Hughes. *Computer Graphics: Principles and Practice*. Addison-Wesley, Reading, Massachusetts, 1990.

[10] L. Fox and D. F. Mayers. *Numerical Solution of Ordinary Differential Equations*. Chapman and Hall, London, 1987.

[11] A. Gierer and H. Meinhardt. A theory of biological pattern formation. *Kybernetik*, 12:30–39, 1972.

[12] N. R. Gordon. *Seashells: A Photographic Celebration*. Friedman Group, New York, 1990.

[13] L. G. Harrison. What is the status of the reaction-diffusion theory thirty-four years after Turing? *Journal of Theoretical Biology*, 125:369–384, 1987.

[14] C. Illert. Formulation and solution of the classical seashell problem. *Il Nuovo Cimento*, 11 D(5):761–780, 1989.

[15] Y. Kawaguchi. A morphological study of the form of nature. *Computer Graphics*, 16(3):223–232, 1982.

[16] H. Meinhardt. *Models of Biological Pattern Formation*. Academic Press, London, 1982.

[17] H. Meinhardt. Models for positional signalling, the three-fold subdivision of segments and the pigmentation patterns of molluscs. *J. Embryol. exp. Morph.*, 83:289–311, 1984. Supplement.

[18] H. Meinhardt and M. Klinger. A model for pattern formation on the shells of molluscs. *Journal of Theoretical Biology*, 126:63–89, 1987.

[19] H. Meinhardt and M. Klinger. Pattern formation by coupled oscillations: The pigmentation patterns on the shells of molluscs. In *Lecture Notes in Biomathematics*, volume 71, pages 184–198. Springer-Verlag, Berlin, 1987.

[20] H. Meinhardt and M. Klinger. Schnecken- und Muschelschalen: Modellfall der Musterbildung. *Spektrum der Wissenschaft*, pages 60–69, August 1991.

[21] H. Moseley. On the geometrical forms of turbinated and discoid shells. *Philosophical Transactions of the Royal Society of London*, pages 351–370, 1838.

[22] J. D. Murray. *Mathematical Biology*. Springer-Verlag, Berlin, 1989.

[23] P. Oppenheimer. Real time design and animation of fractal plants and trees. *Computer Graphics*, 20(4):55–64, 1986.

[24] C. A. Pickover. A short recipe for seashell synthesis. *IEEE Computer Graphics and Applications*, 9(6):8–11, 1989.

[25] C. A. Pickover. *Computers and the Imagination*. St. Martin's Press, New York, 1991.

[26] P. Prusinkiewicz and D. Streibel. Constraint-based modeling of three-dimensional shapes. In *Proceedings of Graphics Interface '86 — Vision Interface '86*, pages 158–163, 1986.

[27] D. M. Raup. Computer as aid in describing form in gastropod shells. *Science*, 138:150–152, 1962.

[28] D. M. Raup. Modeling and simulation of morphology by computer. In *Proceedings of the North American Paleontology Convention*, pages 71–83, 1969.

[29] D. M. Raup and A. Michelson. Theoretical morphology of the coiled shell. *Science*, 147:1294–1295, 1965.

[30] B. Sabelli. *Guide to Shells*. Simon & Schuster, New York, 1979. Edited by H. S. Feinberg.

[31] d'Arcy Thompson. *On Growth and Form*. University Press, Cambridge, 1952.

[32] d'Arcy Thompson. *On Growth and Form, Abridged Edition*. University Press, Cambridge, 1961.

[33] A. Turing. The chemical basis of morphogenesis. *Philosophical Transactions of the Royal Society of London B*, 237:37–72, 1952.

[34] G. Turk. Generating textures on arbitrary surfaces using reaction-diffusion. *Computer Graphics*, 25(4):289–298, 1991.

[35] C. H. Waddington and J. Cowe. Computer simulations of a molluscan pigmentation pattern. *Journal of Theoretical Biology*, 25:219–225, 1969.

[36] A. Witkin and M. Kass. Reaction-diffusion textures. *Computer Graphics*, 25(4):299–308, 1991.

[37] S. Wolfram. Cellular automata as models of complexity. *Nature*, 311:419–424, 1984.

Graphics Software Architecture for the Future

Chair:
Andries van Dam, Brown University

Panelists:
Salim Abi-Ezzi, Sun Microsystems Computer Corporation
Carl Bass, Ithaca Software
Rikk Carey, Silicon Graphics
Mark Tarlton, Microelectronics and Computer Technology Corporation

Advances in hardware processing power, user interfaces, multithreaded operating systems and integrated media have fueled demand for graphics applications that take advantage of these capabilities. Ambitious software projects, however, have exposed the limitations of existing graphics APIs. These limitations include their inability to deal with multiple media and their synchronization as well as other aspects of time-critical and interactive computing.

In this panel architects of well-known graphics Application Programmer Interfaces (APIs) discuss the limitations of existing architectures and outline the characteristics and design tradeoffs of future systems. These systems will be able to exploit concurrent processing, time-critical modeling, and object-oriented programming to achieve new levels of expressiveness and intereactivity.

Salim Abi-Ezzi:

The high processing power and networking capabilities that will be available in affordable desktop machines in the mid nineties will enable a new breed of distributed applications characterized by much more powerful and effective human-machine interfaces. These applications will treat the user as a realtime participant of the computing system. These new generation user interfaces will employ time-critical computation, present audible and visual data, and allow the time-critical sensing of human gestures for intimate interaction. A prototype application will be group telecollaboration over a network with a shared whiteboard.

This breed of application requires an integrated media framework. Central to this framework is the notion of time-critical computing. Time-critical computing, in a sense, suggests a new view of computer science in which the definition of correctness of a computation requires that the computation be completed within a specified deadline. Time-critical computing requires specifying the timeliness of computations to the operating system, which then must deploy elaborate scheduling of resources to satisfy these needs. Furthermore, in cases of resource overload, it is perfectly acceptable to gracefully degrade the quality of a computation — obtaining an approximation to the actual result, in order to honor a deadline. In addition, it is essential to achieve time-critical computing in a general purpose, multi-tasking, and networked computer environment, and not in special purpose systems. Only in this way can we maintain compatibility with the existing body of software.

3D graphics (and conceivably 3D audio) systems are essentially synthetic media systems that make use of highly interactive and compact mathematical models, which unfold into media streams under intense computations. This is in contrast to presampled media systems, based on the reception, compression, transmission, and decompression of media streams. While time is implicit with presampled media, 3D graphics systems must incorporate explicit time modeling to achieve the synchronization and fusion between synthetic media and other media streams.

An important challenge in the nineties will be the development of an integrated media framework that provides:
* Time-critical computing across a network.
* Rules and hooks for uniform and well integrated media-specific APIs.
* Synchronization and fusion/mixing of different media streams.
We propose that future 3D graphics systems incorporate time as a first class concept — to play a part as an equal media system in this emerging framework.

Carl Bass:

Existing graphics subsystems have succeeded in simplifying the task of building traditional applications. They have overcome problems of portability, provided a reasonably high level of abstraction, and learned to coexist symbiotically with window systems, all without sacrificing high performance. More recently, systems which can be easily extended and modified by users are appearing, thereby overcoming some of their inflexibility.

All of these systems, however, are variants of display list technology. Designed to simplify the task of building applications using synthetic 3D graphics, these models imply that the same program organization and methods of user interaction are suitable for all graphics applications. While these techniques have served the graphics community well for over ten years, they are being stretched by the the size and complexity of today's applications. In addition, they appear to be inadequate for dealing with new issues such as multimedia, time-critical computing, and asynchronous user input.

The primary goal of our work is to simplify and modularize interactive applications. To do this, we have adopted a programming paradigm based on multiple, simultaneous, independent, and distributed threads of control. Such a system, which allows for control of and communication between "actors", offers a significantly more expressive paradigm that greatly simplifies the task of building and maintaining interactive applications. And, as a fortuitous side effect, this model of computation is easily and efficiently distributed on the emerging class of multiprocessing hardware.

This technique, although promising, is still severely hampered by the technology offered on today's popular computing platforms. In particular, the currently available languages, operating systems, and models of distributed computing are not yet sufficient for supporting these new techniques.

Rikk Carey:

3D application development remains in the domain of experts and enthusiasts. It has not yet bloomed into a mainstream technology for everyday application and user interface development. One reason for this limited growth is that the computational and rendering requirements of 3D are beyond the performance capabilities of most machines. The other major reason for the slow proliferation of 3D into the mainstream is that software libraries available today do not provide a programming model that is appropriate for widespread use by developers not familiar with 3D graphics programming. The latest generation of RISC-based workstations and personal computers seem quite capable of handling the 3D performance issue. As the hardware gets faster, software will become the critical factor in the further growth of 3D application development.

Currently available 3D software libraries are of two types. *Hardware drawing libraries,* such as Iris Graphics Library and Starbase, provide pixel and graphics primitive drawing commands as a software layer above hardware devices (typically a frame buffer). *Structured drawing libraries*, such as *Phigs+, HOOPS, and Doré*, provide structured drawing commands that are abstracted one level above the hardware interface.

The next generation of 3D software toolkits will be *object-based* rather than *drawing-based*. They will be composed of extensible sets of editable 3D objects that perform a variety of operations. Rendering will be one of the many operations that each object implements. The 3D objects will be building blocks that lend themselves to programmer customization through techniques such as subclassing.

An essential element of future 3D toolkits is the interaction model for 3D. 3D objects will be analogous to 2D widgets in that they can be grouped by other objects into hierarchies and that they can receive and process events. This will result in an interaction model that is a super-set of the existing 2D window-based approach. Note that this capability will be an intrinsic behavior of each 3D object; interaction behavior is not implemented as part of the application. Thus, a new class of 3D objects can be created that include *live* objects. For example, these objects might include a *trackball* object — a transparent sphere that rotates other objects when fiddled with by an input device, and a *mannequin* object — an articulated hierarchy which has built-in joint rotations and limits, that can be edited with an input device. These objects blur the boundary between application and data.

Generalizing the object model makes it possible to create application-specific objects that are subclassed from or composed of other objects. These application-specific objects also include application-level semantics, as well as rendering and computations (for example, *Render()* and *GetBoundingBox()*). For example, a *PieChart* object that implements all of the intrinsic operations such as rendering, and picking, could also have a function *GetNumberOfPieSlices()* which returns the number of pie slices.

An important result of the next generation of object-oriented 3D toolkits is that the programming model will more closely match the problem being solved. When writing applications the programmer need not worry about the details of the rendering or input control (this is handled mostly by the objects). It is like choosing parts from a hardware store and assembling them to achieve the desired results, and sometimes having to build custom parts when the store does not have what you need.

Future object-oriented toolkits will blur the current distinctions between 2D, 3D, windows, and user interface programming. New object-oriented systems will treat all of these as similar objects that perform rendering, picking, event handling, animation, grouping, geometry computations, and other intrinsic functions. The programmer's task will be primarily focused on solving the application problems, rather than spending inordinate amounts of time on the graphics and user interface implementation. Furthermore, creating 3D objects that have physical behavior will be much easier and thus more prevalent. Applications will rely less on indirect panel-driven user interfaces and instead provide direct manipulation 3D user interfaces that behave much like objects in the real world.

Mark Tarlton:

As we consider the requirements for next generation graphics systems, we must look beyond the usual technical requirements of rendering quality, performance, features, etc. Ease of use will be a critical factor as interactive 3D is applied to new application areas. While advances in hardware is making interactive 3D graphics systems more affordable, the expense of developing applications which incorporate interactive 3D is still quite high. One reason for this is existing APIs to graphics require a high degree of graphics programming expertise to use. What is needed instead, is a foundation for interactive graphics that enables individuals who are not computer graphics sophisticates to easily incorporate dynamic 3D imagery into their applications — applications that may be highly interactive and imagery that is driven by the application data.

To address this need, we've tried to do two things: first, reduce the complexity inherent in dynamic visual applications through greater modularity of application elements, and second, hide device dependent issues of rendering from the application developer.

The resulting architecture provides a representation system for graphics, time-based activities, and event-driven processes. This representation system builds upon standard object-oriented programming languages to provide an extensible foundation for interactive visual applications. The methodology encourages application development through modeling. That is, the developer uses objects to represent elements of the application or of the resulting visualization, and controls them through their attributes and relationships with other objects. The screen presentation is then produced by a device-specific interpreter.

The tradeoffs that we have made are: first, ease of use is provided at the expense of pixel-level control of the final image, and second, performance is maintained at the expense of making the interpreters less portable.

Summary:

The goal of this panel is to lend insight into the future directions of software architecture. The panelists share the belief that building an interactive graphics application today is still needlessly difficult due to the relatively low level support provided by today's APIs. The panel hopes to share different strategies for simplifying this process so that developers can focus on building new, complex and exciting applications.

Further Reading:

Cunningham, S., N. Knolle Craighill, M. Fong and J.R. Brown, eds., *Computer Graphics Using Object-Oriented Programming*, Wiley, 1992.

Lorensen, W., M. Barry, D. McLachlan, and B. Yamrom, "An Object-Oriented Graphics Animation System," General Electric TIS Report #86CRD067, June 1986. (reprinted in SIGGRAPH '87 course notes, Object-Oriented Geometric Modeling and Rendering)

Northcutt, J. D. and E. M. Kuerner, "System Support for Time-Critical Applications," Second International Workshop on Network and Operating System Support for Digital Audio and Video, Heidelberg, Germany, Nov 1991.

Tarlton, M. A. and P. N. Tarlton, "A Framework for Dynamic Visual Applications" Proceedings of 1992 Symposium on Interactive 3D Graphics, ACM Press, 29 March - April1 1992.

Wisskirchen, P., *Object-Oriented Graphics: From GKS and PHIGS to Object-Oriented Systems*, Springer-Verlag, 1990.

From "Le Musée Imaginaire" to Walls Without Museums

Co-Chairs:
Greg Garvey, Concordia University
Brian Wallace, The Computer Museum

Panelists:
Rene Paul Barilleaux, Madison Art Center
Vincent Bilotta, Advance Multi-Media Systems
Eric Hoffert/Gavin Miller, Apple Computer
Masahiro Kawahata, Tepia High Technology Pavilion
Dan Sandin, University of Illinois at Chicago
Rand Wetherwax, multimedia composer-performer

Goals and principal issues of the panel

This panel will address the emerging reality of the virtual museum and the resulting implications that must confront artists, curators, critics, art consumers, collectors, hardware manufacturers, software multimedia developers, and interface designers in the creation, exhibition and dissemination, collection, and conservation of computer graphic art.

Background and rationale for the panel

Digital representation of computer graphic art, coupled with the spread of new display media, changes the terms of any discussion of image output, realization, exchange, or conservation. No longer necessarily a one-of-a-kind, precious object, computer graphic art may theoretically may be downloaded from a network on demand and displayed or printed wherever suitable output or display devices exist.

"Smart displays" will seamlessly blend in with existing architecture, require little or no maintenance, can be remotely activated by the casual passerby without requiring a push of a button or the use of a physical input device, will be responsive to multiple users, requires no manual, and will of course be robust. The goal is to preserve the kind of experience that the casual viewer has in an art gallery or museum. Hence such a display does not require the user/viewer to wear a data glove, eye phones: no encumbrances are necessary for interaction. The foregoing implies developing new Human Interface Guidelines for such technology. In this new environment, art makers and consumers must conceive of and execute new transactions which will ultimately redefine our notion of the museum.

Brian Wallace

Has the museum ever or always been a repository of unique, canonical works? Does each new art medium reinforce or challenge existing ideas about reproduction, appropriation, and originality? Why repeatedly and digitally reproduce and redistribute a tiny, anointed fragment of the world's history of art? Is it imperative that contemporary art partake of the new(est) technologies?

Greg Garvey

A variety of technologies can now be employed to sense the viewer's distance from a displayed image and thereby initiate changes to the observed image in a multitude of ways such as viewpoint, scale or resolution such that the act of viewing becomes the active exploration of the viewing space. We should see in the near future the development of 'smart' flat panel displays that will interactively change because of the actions of the viewer. This interaction can be modelled on the choreography of observation that a typical viewer of paintings, still photography, 3D sculpture, or installations performs when viewing the object of desire from a multiplicity of angles, distances and viewpoints. What remains to be seen is whether the aesthetic integrity of still 2D and 3D imagery will be preserved or replaced by an MTV barrage of images or even a new aesthetic not yet manifest.

Rene Paul Barilleaux

Rene Paul Barilleaux recently organized the first exhibition of holography at the Whitney Museum of American Art. While Barilleaux's focus is on contemporary art, his particular interests center on non-traditional and technology-based media. He will explore the work of contemporary artists who use the computer in combination with other materials and techniques to create hybride forms—derived from graphics, sculpture, photography, video, holography and audio art. His presentation will examine works by Judith Yourman, Alan Rath, Yasumasa Morimura, Robert Russett, Dean Randazzo and Liz Phillips. Barilleaux will focus on how the computer is a part of the creative process for some artists, and a part of the final creation or presentation for others. Emphasis will be placed on how each artist uses technology-based tools to develop a concept as opposed to only manipulating media in technically sophisticated ways.

Vincent Bilotta

The industrial revolution begat the "designer," a creator of ideas, divorced from execution. This attitude reinforced the class structure of industrialism and framed a dualist aesthetic that shaped the architecture, artifacts and art we live with. The nature of digital tools challenge our aesthetic premises that are so rooted in the industrial attitudes with which we value objects and concepts. By placing emerging technologies and applications in a historical context, we may consciously evaluate how our social, emotional and spiritual needs are best met and choose our direction.

What are the peer relationship in a virtual environment? What will institutional and individual personas look like in a flexible reality? Will we drop the distinction between information and entertainment, adopting a "medieval" relationship to ideas? The institutions we build to organize and present our culture will evolve with our application of technology. By promoting a dialogue on the ecology of these issues, we are better fitted to build a domain we can live with. Our institutions, such as museums and galleries, will be redefined by the change in our relationship to representative cultural objects.

Eric Hoffert/Gavin Miller

The Virtual Museum is an interactive, electronic museum. Users can move from room to room of the museum, and select any exhibit in each room for more detail and examination. The museum uses real-time video decompression for the display and interaction with very high-quality computer animation. The museum rendering was created on the Macintosh using a 3D architectural modeling tool, previewed using a real-time radiosity motion-planner and rendered with texture mapping and radiosity. The museum experience was built by extending the functionality of both Hypercard, an interactive media program, and QuickTime, a digital multimedia extension for system software.

Careful attention was paid to the museum aesthetics; antique frames hold the paintings, classical music accompanies some exhibits and historical artwork was used. The experience of wandering through the museum permits 3D navigation of a highly realistic-looking space. In addition, the user can select any 3D object or artifact in the museum to trigger movement to another 3D space, to examine an exhibit in animated form, or to play a digital movie or soundtrack.

We have developed a version of the Virtual Museum which can run at both CD-ROM and T-1 data rates, and interaction with the museum can be over an Ethernet network from a media server. It is hoped that the museum will eventually be appropriate as a consumer-oriented on-line experience, to be dialed up and selected from a variety of electronic museums, both real and virtual, from an international broadband network of the future.

Masahiro Kawahata

We are living in a society where information occupies an important position and where conspicuous advances are being made in the collection, processing, transmission, display, and consumption of information. Tokyo's Tepia High Technology Pavilion showcases new technologies and the ways they are integrated into daily life.

The recent High-tech Art Planning (HARP) exhibition at the Tepia Pavilion focused on future human communication by introducing frontier technologies that closely connect industrial society and culture with broad human relationships. Several exhibits address the question: what kind of visual space will be produced if HDTV images are used to create a visual environment? A high-definition electronic hanging scroll and a virtual garden, both situated in a Japanese style room, place emerging technology at the service of traditional images. Exhibit-goers had overwhelmingly positive responses to the room.

Future exhibitions and reseach will examine the impact of new and emerging communications technologies on the potential for the "Intelligent City" to become the "Creative City".

Dan Sandin

Museums function as the repository of original objects. Historically museums have utilized new technologies such as photography, infrared images, and x-rays to preserve, document, and catalog these original objects. For instance, the use of high quality color printing and color photography has not replaced the primary role of displaying original works but has spawned beautifully illustrated art books, and massive slide libraries, both of which form alternative methods of disseminating information about original objects.

Most electronic media have no identifiable original object. The perfect and easy copying of information specifying the work makes the concept of a unique original inapplicable. The extensive photographic print collections in some art museums could be considered a model for the role of museums in the electronic arts. These collections are composed of a limited number of originals, and there is considerable effort and skill required to make each copy.

Electronic media will not displace traditional media in museums. Work will always be produced which befits the museum format (art media do not become outmoded). In addition, new distribution techniques, owing little to museums, will be developed to carry the cultural information. Moreover, it is misleading to use museums as a model or even a metaphor for thinking about the distribution techniques and channels for new electronic media. The museum of tomorrow will be like the museum of today. The electronic art of tomorrow will be on your desk top.

Rand Wetherwax

Rand Wetherwax has created several interactive multimedia-based pieces. The most notable release to date is <<Sunlight on Silver>>, Graham Nash's interactve B & W photography gallery. This elegant

CD-ROM includes B & W photography, text, music, and voiceovers. It is currently being expanded to include Quick Time JPEG compression, video and image creation tools. This work, its capabilities, and the future of multimedia galleries will be explored and discussed.

Summary statement

The disembodiment of computer graphic art moves the artistic encounter out of the traditional gallery or museum into a new electronic venue. As colonizers of this virtual space, computer graphic artists are already examining virtuality's promise of increased availability and accessibility of images. These developments herald a re-formulation of the aesthetic and commodity status of images and image-making. Andre Malraux's "Le Musee Imaginaire," his "museum without walls" situated in cyberspace, may come to be revealed to us as "walls without museums." How will these walls accommodate our visual tradition? How will these walls define a new multimedia paradigm of human computer interaction?

Additional Reading:

Baudrillard, Jean, "Beyond the Vanishing Point of Art," in *Post-Pop Art* , edited by Paul Taylor, MIT Press, Cambridge, MA, 1989.

Benjamin, Walter, "The Work of Art in the Age of Mechanical Reproduction," in *Illuminations*, New York:Schocken, 1969.

Boswell, Peter. *Alan Rath* (exhibition brochure). Minneapolis: Walker Art Center, 1991.

Brill, Louis M., ed. "Holography as an Art Medium," *Leonardo*, 22, nos. 3 and 4 (1989).

Burnett, Christopher , *The Information Machine: Computers, Photography and Simulation at the 1964 Worlds Fair*, hypertext document and privately printed book; Charlestown, MA 1988-91.

Bush, Vannevar, "As We May Think," in *Endless Horizons*, Public Affairs Press, Wahington, D.C., 1946.

Curran, Paul J., *Principles of Remote Sensing*, New York: Longman, 1985.

Donato, Debora Duez, "Review of an exhibition of works by Alan Rath," in <<*New Art Examiner*>>, New Art Association, Chicago, IL., April 1992.

Gideion, Sigfried, *Mechanization Takes Command*.

Gips, Terry, ed. "Computers and Art: Issues of Content," *Art Journal*, Fall 1990, Vol. 49 No. 3.

Hoffert, Eric, with Gavin Miller, Shenchang Eric Chen, Sally Ann Applin, Dean Blackketter, Elizabeth Patterson, Steve Rubin, Derrick Yim, Jim Hanan. *The Virtual Museum*. Proceedings of the Imagina '92 Conference (Monaco, France), February 1992.

Kawahata, Masahiro, "Information and Cities: From Intelligent City to Creative City," in *Journal of New Cities*, Tokyo, 1991.

Krueger, Myron, *Artificial Reality*, Reading, Mass., Addison-Wesley, 1983.

Landow, George P., *Hypertext; The Convergence of Contemporary Critical Theory and Technology*, Johns Hopkins University Press, Baltimore, MD, 1992.

Leonardo, supplemental issues (1989-90), SIGGRAPH Art Show Catalog and essays.

Malraux, Andre, *Museum without Walls*, New York: Doubleday, 1967.

McLuhan, Marshall, *Understanding Media: the Extensions of Man*, New York: McGraw-Hill, 1965.

Miller, Gavin, Eric Hoffert, Shenchang Eric Chen, Sally Ann Applin, Dean Blackketter, Elizabeth Patterson, Steve Rubin, Derrick Yim, Jim Hanan. "The Virtual Museum: Interactive 3D Navigation of a Multimedia Database," *The Journal of Visualization and Animation*, to appear.

Mumford, Lewis, *Technics and Civilization*.

Mhire, Herman, ed. *Robert Russett: A Retrospective Survey* (exhibition catalog). Lafayette, Louisiana: University Art Museum, University of Southwestern Louisiana, 1989.

Reveaux, Tony. *Graphite Ground* (exhibition brochure). Madison, Wisconsin: Madison Art Center, 1989.

Sharp, Isabella , "Virtual Reality: The Uses of Techno-Utopia," in *1-800 Magazine*, Techne Group, Inc., Amherst, MA, Spring/Summer 1992.

Trembly, William and Eben Gay, Head Quarters, room-size, responsive computer-generated evnironment; Massachusetts College of Art, Boston, MA, 1992.

Wilson, Beth, ed. *1990 catalog of programs*. San Francisco: New Langton Arts, 1991.

Wright, Beryl J. *Yasumasa Morimura* (exhibition brochure). Chicago: Museum of Contemporary Art, 1991.

Youngblood, Gene, "Computer Art as a Way of Life," *Send*, no. 8 (Fall 1983).

What Will Gigabit Networks Do for Visualization?

Chair: Steve Wolff, National Science Foundation

Panelists:
Gary Demos, DemoGraFX
Robert Kahn, Corporation for National Research Initiatives
Robert W. Lucky, AT&T Bell Laboratories

The High Performance Computing and Communications (HPCC) federal initiative, as well as private sector initiatives in the telecommunications industry, are creating an entirely new environment for visualization and graphics. HDTV, video-on-demand, multimedia services, video teleconferencing, visual tele-science, and remote control of supercomputers will be widely available with the federally-supported National Research and Education Network (NREN) and with advanced network services in the private sector. The panel brings together visionaries who paint a picture of the opportunities these changes are bringing to visualization and graphics professionals.

Implications of Merging Digital Television, Communications, and Computing

Chair:
Branko J. Gerovac, Digital Equipment Corp. / MIT Media Laboratory

Panelists:
W. Russell Neuman, Massachusetts Institute of Technology
Bruce Sidran, MCC First Cities
Greg Thagard, CST Entertainment Imaging
Larry Irving, House Telecommunications Subcommittee

In the last couple of years, television, communications, and computing are increasingly converging to a common set of underlying digital technologies — the clear and rapid move to computational digital image representation and digital communication. The technologies are improving at an increasingly rapid rate.

The convergence represents more than simply derivative technologies that are useful across industries. Instead, an impending interplay and merger of the industries, products, and services themselves is being recognized that will foster innovation and will stimulate rapid development in the utility and diversity of products and services.

The move to a digital basis for HDTV has been a pivotal driving force. The four leading proponents in the FCC HDTV trials are digital. Though the FCC decision has yet to be made, it is virtually assured that the outcome will be digital compression and digital transmission. Already, this seemingly simple outcome is enabling cable television and terrestrial broadcast to propose expanding the number of NTSC television channels by a factor of 4 to 5 as a coexisting alternative to single channel HDTV. The additional capacity opens up alternatives for a broad variety of information services, and it exposes the need to consider flexible, interactive communications protocols and network services.

The next pivotal technology will be communications. An emerging vision is toward a interactive, open access, interoperable, global communications infrastructure. Such an infrastructure would provide universal realtime access as the telephone, high bandwidth as cable television into the home, and a variety of interactive services as computer networks.

The implications of this are forcing people to think about new ways to address problems in the delivery of education, health care, advertising, industrial competitiveness, etc. To the SIGGRAPH audience, this means visual communication and visualization available to the whole of the population.

Toward an Open Communications Infrastructure

Regulators, by their nature, are cautious and conservative. They would prefer to avoid making decisions if at all possible. They would urge the television, telecommunications, computer and publishing industries to go off in a room, work out all the necessary concessions for digital interoperability and bring back a done deal for the regulators to cautiously approve. We argue in this paper that this traditional posture of regulatory forbearance proves to be highly counterproductive and will unintentionally slow down an otherwise natural process of technological evolution.

We outline the benefits of a proactive federal policy for open communications infrastructure based on fully competitive provision of all local and national communications services. We propose lifting all regulatory distinctions between wireline and wireless communications services, between narrowband and broadband, between broadcast and switched communications services, and between content and conduit.

In our view, the key to regulatory reform is breaking the policy gridlock caused by slow demise of the last monopoly, local telephony. A special opportunity lies in the concept of personal communications services (PCS). Wireless microcell and cellular technologies have a very special property. They lack the scale economies of wireline technologies. One need not invest billions to wire up an entire city in order to compete with the local exchange carrier for stationary service. One can profitably start small and build as business expands.

The most fundamental principle of common carriage is that scale economies in service provision make regulated monopoly more efficient than competition. Wireless access to the local loop represents much more than the convenience of a pocket telephone, it represents an opportunity to bring a second revolution to telecommunications regulation, the prospect of an aggressive gameplan to establish meaningful competition in local exchange service provision with the goal of deregulating the telecommunications industry in its entirety.

Computer and cable industries would like to provide enhanced voice, data and video services via wire and spectrum. They would like to provide telephone services without turning into regulated telephone companies. It is a most reasonable request. In return, however, we need to get used to the fact that the newly unregulated telephone companies will become major players in computational video.

First Cities: A National "Mall" for Electronic Commerce

There are very few events in the history of business that forever change the nature of the marketplace. The world is in the midst of such a change. The "information highways" of the future are being built that will radically change the way people live, work, and play. The businesses that take advantage of the revenue opportunities that are emerging — that survive and prosper — will be those companies that have helped shape and define this evolving marketplace. First Cities is designed to give participating companies that competitive edge.

First Cities is aimed at expanding the market for consumer information services by providing a national market-building trial for interactive multimedia information services based on scalable, extensible and open delivery systems. First Cities provides valuable market assessment and feedback while engendering the new business relationships that will serve as the underpinnings of this evolving marketplace.

The First Cities program is planned to include at least 200,000 users clustered in several sites, serving as community testbeds for multi-resolution equipment and services interconnected by an intelligent network. By supporting many communications technologies, the First Cities network will, in effect, be independent of transport technology. Applications will be delivered by a variety of technologies, including cable TV, fiber, wireless and twisted copper pair. The companies participating in this effort have the opportunity to test equipment, technologies, applications and services while building an expanded market for information services.

The greatest competitive business opportunity for the information industry today is the emergence of universal multimedia information networking, and its impact will be enormous.

The 1990s will see a virtual explosion of global digital networking. This networking infrastructure will support a new generation of products, services and capabilities that will forever change the nature of newspapers, periodicals, book publishing and all information services; of television, broadcasting, movies and other forms of entertainment; of education; of advertising; of shopping; of work; of travel and tourism; of business integration and computerized commerce, including manufacturing; of financial institutions; and of government.

Entertainment on demand, interactive games, shopping, electronic publishing, teleconferencing, health care and education: these and many more products and services can be conducted across networks. Today's network technology, made possible by advances in telecommunications, computing, video, and imaging, will bring these services literally to the consumer's doorstep. For businesses supplying goods and services, the emergence of this network is providing unprecedented business opportunities today.

This network will affect all companies involved in the production,

delivery and display of audio, data and visual information. Today's strategic decisions by programming, broadcast, advertising, cable, telephone and electronics manufacturing companies will determine their roles in the domestic and international multi-resolution systems marketplace and set the foundation for a multi-billion dollar global industry.

First Cities gives participants an opportunity to perfect and showcase their products and services, test customer reactions and build markets rapidly. It will also provide feedback to network designers and technology developers, as well as to participating communities. It will result in open, visible evidence of the economic impact of ubiquitous multimedia interactive networks. First Cities is the only national testbed designed to give this type of feedback to a broad range of participants.

Integrating Digital into Film

The real world applications of digital image technology are expanding. We are seeing the convergence of video and film, thanks to the resolution independence of the digital domain, and the impact is profound. Within the digital environment, filmmakers are compositing material from a variety of sources, from computer graphics to live action, from matte painting to miniatures. The traditional barriers among media are breaking down, and the opportunities are tremendous.

Digital techniques are transforming image production in a variety of ways. The visual effects field is being dramatically affected in motion pictures, commercials, rock videos and "ride films." Digital effects provide an economical and faster alternative to traditional optical effects, and offer a way to reduce the cost of a motion picture or television program without sacrificing image quality.

The technology can be used to solve a variety of image production problems. For scenes filmed with puppets or actors on wires, costly hand rotoscoping is a thing of the past. Today's digital approach even makes it easy to remove wires when models are in front of moving backgrounds, which makes it possible to shoot more complex scenes. It has also been demonstrated that this technology can achieve unprecedented effects, like removing whole objects from a scene. The creative possibilities of this have just begun to be tapped.

The same techniques which the visual effects supervisor will use to create new looks will also be the salvation of editors. The old cliché "we'll fix it in post" is no longer wishful thinking. Currently digital techniques are ideal for scratch and blemish removal, and useful for correcting common mistakes, such the shadow of a boom microphone intruding on a scene, or unsightly telephone pole in the background. Rather than incur the cost of re-shooting, a filmmaker can salvage a flawed scene.

The same flexibility exists in the area of color. Digital technology makes it easy to do color correction and film restoration without costly chemical procedures, and also offers intriguing creative options. It is possible not only to transform black and white images into color, but also to alter the look of an existing color scene, applying color directly on objects as they move. Sophisticated methods for determining the luminance of different objects in a scene makes it possible to treat film footage with a whole range of color effects, from highly realistic to a stylized, hyper-real effect.

The challenge ahead is not to attract users to this technology, but to develop the standard that will facilitate its use. Just as film is a common medium with recognized standards, we need the same for digital imagery.

We can take a lesson from the current debate over HDTV, which is really just a transitional medium between today's NTSC standards and the film quality standard we ultimately want. What HDTV debate reveals is that we need to design an extensible system — and digital clearly gives us that ability. The only thing we've yet to develop is a commonalty of purpose, and a recognition that a huge global audience is waiting for us to succeed.

Design, Creativity & Process

Chair:
Renée LeWinter, Odyssey Communications

Panelists:
Terrence G. Heinlein, Wentworth Institute of Technology
Frank Romano, Computer Artist
Robb Wyatt, Telezign
Joe Shingelo, Telezign
Graham Walters, Pacific Data Images

This panel examines the current state of computer graphics hardware and software and its future development from the perspective of the designer. Panelists explore how their individual areas of design — in print, architecture, broadcast design and in high-end R&D applications — are impacted by current technology. They review the successes and failures, effects of the developer on design process and creativity, and possible directions for new hardware and tool development.

Panel Overview
The panel members are in agreement that to reach the next level of development — one that incorporates an expert level of user knowledge — would require a full partnership between developer and designer, if the new products are well targeted to the needs of the design community.

Several issues need to be acknowledged and discussed. These include: a) the increased complexity of software products targeted to the design market and their lengthened learning curves, b) the minimal participation of designers in the first stages of hardware and software development, c) the general lack of understanding of the creative process, d) the need for greater modularity and integration of hardware and software across platforms, and e) the implications of hardware and software development on the "look and feel" of a design.

Each member of the panel was asked to suggest additional readings on these issues. Each was hard pressed to name an article or publication which dealt with the topics discussed in this panel presentation. It seemed that no one publication or book easily came to mind which would be readily accessible for follow-up reference. Clearly we need to bring this issue from the back burner. Many products coming onto the market seem to lack a clear understanding of what was needed to support the designer. What was the basis for the choices developers made in product creation and marketing? What were their reference sources? Whose expertise did the products represent?

Renee LeWinter:Impact on Technology on Design Style, Design Process and Creative Thinking
Using examples from the development of type manufacturing and page composition, panel organizer I will present a short overview on the impact of technology on design style, design process and creative thinking.

Terrence G. Heinlein: Computer-based Constraints on The Design Process
Graphics software for architects is largely developed by non-architects; graphic software in the construction industry is most used by architects. This division between the developers and the appliers results in programs and their utilization which are separate from the needs of architecture and society.

The computer, especially in CAD applications, has allowed the designer to view and proceed through the typical architectural design process with much greater speed. But at what cost? Although speed is gained, the effect on design decision making and the design process has not always been positive. Prior to CAD, the designer had more time to step back, to consider the design of individual pieces, and ponder the relationship of these individual parts to the final design. This process supported an architect's ability to go beyond standard situations and still be able to present clearly defined solutions to the client. Currently, although progress is being made, the repertoire of the CAD programs are still sufficiently limited to make this issue a major problem.

Secondly, the computer can create problems as well when the design is modeled. In determining what will be rendered and how that information will be displayed, the program can present misinformation to the architect. The architect needs to see displayed more than massing solids and voids. The computer environment should be able to provide for intelligent real time feedback. Future programs should allow the architect to input major design parameters and flag the architect when a design decision is not within specifications. This will permit a much more informed process and will also facilitate the teaching of architectural design.

Frank Romano: Usage Trends for the Design Community
Design and creativity must also link to the real world of process and production. Developers often do not understand the users of their tools. As programs and systems advance to include more sophisticated capabilities, additional burdens are placed upon the creative professional who uses them.

My presentation will focus on platforms and programs that are impacting the creative process. An overview will be presented on the U.S. community for design and creative professionals, with statistics on technology usage and current and projected trends. This data will show how new approaches are being assimilated by the design community and the problems that face users.

Design and creative professionals work in almost every business entity in the American market, from corporate offices, to printing and publishing organizations, to art studios, advertising agencies, packaging, and lastly as individuals. They are the pivotal group in the development of total electronic approaches to information dissemination, as camera-ready art is replaced by computer-ready art.

Robb Wyatt: Digital Information and What It Means to the Designer
My discussion will center upon the interface of digital workstations (including a discussion of the Macintosh and how it is affecting the interaction of print and video media). This discussion will be supported by a demonstration showing certain projects as they pass through all stages of development (print, Macintosh, and high-end animation). The benefits and problems of further modularity and

integration of software components will be explored and what impact this has had on the industry process and design style.

Joseph Shingelo: Development from the Perspective of a User of Turnkey Systems

My discussion will focus on technological hardware and software developments from the turnkey system users' point of view. New and unique software tools are constantly being created and packaged into turnkey systems. However it is difficult for facilities such as Telezign to take full advantage of all these developments as they hit the market. Small companies with thirty to forty employees — a studio equipped with four to five 3D workstations and a crew of five 3D specialists, can find their resources stretched and profitability decreased trying to support these systems.

The investment and commitment to one software package, especially, is so great because of the initial set-up costs. Also, studios have to factor in the cost of supporting licensing and maintenance for each package across a small network of workstations. These costs included in overhead charges can negatively impact the ability of a studio to remain competitive.

Additionally, second packages are often not totally integrated to work with the previously installed software. This adds additional rework time in production and additional staff training. Given the complexity of many programs, it is difficult for staff to quickly become professionally proficient in a software product. Several months of hands-on experience are needed. Access then is not as practical as it could be, forcing a negative impact on creative decision making and aesthetic style. It becomes more difficult to create a unique look for a client.

Graham Walters: Building a Successful Artist/Developer Relationship

This presentation will discuss, from Pacific Data Image's (PDI's) experience, the components that contribute to the success of a artist/developer relationship.

The animation production process at PDI is perhaps unique because of the company's significant investment in in-house software. Initially, eleven years ago, there was no alternative to developing in-house software. Now a significant body of commercial software exists which is quite successful in areas such as keyframed rigid body animation. However, the changing nature of PDI's work requires techniques which do not exist in commercial software and cannot be trivially integrated into available systems.

Our experience from developing our own software is that it takes several iterations of development, use, feedback and redesign for the artist/machine interface to mature. By writing our own software it has been possible for us to take advantage of the tight communication between our production and R&D groups. While the resources available at commercial software houses allow them to develop cleaner and more robust tools for those portions of the production process which has become standard, the current length of the development cycle in these companies does not allow for as tight a feedback loop as is necessary to satisfy the high-end community.

Summary

The question should not be "Who controls creativity: Developer or designer?" But rather, how can we increase participation by designers in the development process? If computer graphics is to mature and evolve, there needs to be greater flexibility for intuitive design. Intuitive design is based upon a body of knowledge, built-up over time and applied through creative problem solving and reflects the expertise of both developer and designer. From this partnership, exciting directions and new products can evolve that will be mutually beneficial for supporting old markets and opening up new avenues of opportunity for the industry.

Research Topics in Virtual Reality

Chair:
Linda Nonno, Los Alamos National Laboratory

Panelists:
Grigore Burdea, Rutgers-The State University of New Jersey
S. Kicha Ganapathy, AT&T Bell Laboratories
Stephen Jacobsen, The University of Utah
Joseph Rosen, Dartmouth-Hitchcock Medical Center

Virtual Reality is at the top of the "food chain". It is a technology that feeds from a variety of other fields — graphics, sensory interfaces, robotics, and psychology to name a few. Yet, it is also a field in its own right, characterized by a tight coupling of human factors and the enabling technologies. This panel presents a brief survey of research work in the field from laboratories that have not been heard from in the past. The intent is to produce a fresh look at the depth and variety of the ever evolving field that is Virtual Reality.

Telerobotics: Grigore Burdea
The Rutgers Portable Dexterous Master with Force Feedback, a telerobotic system interfaced through gloves such as the Dataglove, will be presented. An experimental distributed system and supporting software will be discussed. The results of interactive computer simulation using the Dexterous Master will also be covered. These simulations provide virtual force feedback under elastic and plastic object deformations.

Telecommunications: S. Kicha Ganapathy
The potential impact of Virtual Environment technology on the telecommunications industry will be addressed. The opportunities, obstacles, and challenges faced in translating this potential into reality will be presented.

Telerobotics: Stephen Jacobsen
The continuing goal of the Center for Engineering Design (CED) and Sarcos Incorporated (SI) is the generation of effective and economic portals through which both sensory (visual and acoustic) and physical (force and position) information can be dynamically interchanged between an operator and a remote virtual world.

The CED and SI have developed, over the past two decades, a number of interfaces which permit people to effectively and intuitively control machines which include many actuated movements.

- Initial work in the area of prosthetics produced the Utah Artificial Arm (UA), which has been in commercial production for a decade. The UA includes an interface which translates muscle-generated Electro Myographic Signals (EMG) into command inputs for hand closure and elbow flexion, and in some cases wrist rotation and humeral rotation.
- For the control of the Utah/MIT Dexterous Hand, two masters have been developed for the dynamic measurement of finger position. The first system, a series of instrumented linkages, was commercialized as the EXOS Master. The second, which incorporates improvements to guarantee more reliable measurement of the true angular position at each joint, is about to enter production.
- In the TOPS program, a fully actuated, force reflective hand and arm master was developed as part of an advanced telerobotic system intended for undersea use. The master includes 22 powered and instrumented joints in an anthropomorphic configuration which conveniently attaches to a human arm, hand, torso, and head.
- Current efforts on the Utah Dexterous Arm (UDA) include the integration of state-of-the-art sensors, actuators and controllers into interface systems that permit people to carry out challenging tasks in remote or synthetic environments. The new system uses high bandwidth actuation, very high performance multiplexed sensors and advanced control algorithms to achieve necessary characteristics with reasonable economy.

Surgical Simulation: Joseph Rosen
Surgical simulation, like flight simulation, allows the user to be trained to perform a complex task using an interactive computer environment. This interactive environment has progressed from a two-dimensional screen to a three-dimensional virtual environment. The surgeon can perform life-like operations on an electronic patient in a virtual operating room. The patient model is programmed to respond in a manner analogous to its real-world counterpart. In addition, the patient model serves as a basis for analysis of the procedure in order to provide objective feedback about the likely outcome. This allows the surgeon to explore many options, and perform an operation multiple times in different ways to choose the operation with the best outcome.

Summary
Virtual Reality draws from a number of other fields, yet is characterized in its own right by a tight coupling of human factors and enabling technologies. This characteristic has fostered a variety of innovative research. This panel attempts to present a very brief, but nonetheless diverse, overview of some of the current research efforts undertaken in the field of Virtual Reality.

Progress Report from the Global Village

Chair:
Hank Grebe, AT&T Bell Labs

Panelists:
Marc Canter, Canter Technology
Denise Caruso, Editor of Digital Media: A Seybold Report
Oliver Jones, PictureTel
Mitchell Kapor, Electronic Frontier Foundation
Timothy Onosko, Entertainment Industry Consultant

Technology visionaries address the issues of delivering high technology tools to the average global villager. The panelists present demos and discuss current and future trends in consumer electronics, multimedia computing, electronic networks, and telephony.

Panel Background:

"pity this busy monster, mankind, not. Progress is a comfortable disease." e. e. cummings, *One Times One*, 1944.

This panel addresses emerging trends, such as the current blurring between computers, telecommunications and consumer electronics. Maintaining a focus on the ever-expanding, media-engulfing hybrid blob that is multimedia is a constant challenge to technology developers. Progress reports on the diverse media components of multimedia must be frequently updated.

This panel brings together five leaders within their areas of specialization in technology journalism, consumer electronics and computer science. All of the panelists share a common talent for grasping the unfolding events of cutting edge technology, in some cases have participated in shaping them.

They will discuss and forecast important technological developments and the impact of emerging products and services which the public should expect to gain access to by the mid 90's. Each in their own way, the panelists have striven to bring the latest technologies closer to the average end-user.

Panel Goals and Issues:

Accompanying the introduction and convergence of new technologies into the mainstream are issues concerning standardization, delivery and distribution, licensing, government regulation and funding, and general accessibility. The mission of the panel is to describe and analyze where we are and where we are going with emerging tools such as ISDN, electronic networks, optical discs, and interactive multimedia computing.

Numerous technological predictions of the past have proven to be late in arriving, or appear only in isolated pockets. What scientific, political and logistical hurdles need to be made in order to progress toward these future visions? Some futuristic notions, such as "the paperless society" may only be a mythical ideal. Which pathways to the future are worth following? Or, upon which pathways into the future are we being led?

What are the obstacles confronting fast, easy to use, affordable network and multimedia services such as ISDN? What new services and interfaces should we expect to be delivered on digital HDTV? Where is the entertainment industry going as movie theaters give way to video tape, cable television, and other newer services? Will rewrite-able optical disks such as Kodak's Photo CD, become the next home recording medium? What is the extent of new technologies' impact on an international, global level? What are the bright spots and black holes in new technology?

The panel will offer their proactive views on technology futures and answer questions from the attendees during the concluding portion of the session.

Mitchell Kapor

The deployment of speedy, ubiquitous, affordable public communications infrastructure in the near-term, such as ISDN, would create an open platform for information entrepreneurship and would spur the development and acceptance of new information services to the public at large.

Oliver Jones

(1) "multimedia" (whatever that is) is great because it's visually compelling, etc. (2) PCs (generic, not any particular type) are great because they empower the end user. (3) entertainment media is wonderful, and precanned multimedia is wonderful, but it doesn't empower the end user—an hour of canned "instructional" multimedia material takes 300-800 hours of skilled labor. (4) video telephony is great because it allows the illusion of personal presence over great distances. (5) the marriage of the video telephone and the PC provides a framework in which "multimedia" can work in a way which allows all end-users to be producers as well as consumers (like net news or email, ideally).

Denise Caruso

Digital technology, once considered exotic and of limited utility, has become pervasive as air. At a rapid clip, the media of communication — print, graphic arts, sound, music, photography, video, film, animation — are being digitized and are becoming part of the datastream.

The move to a world of all-digital media is progressing at an astonishing pace, and applications based on digital technology are cutting to the quick in the industries upon which our society is based. The convergence of publishing, computing, entertainment, consumer electronics and telecommunications is full of vast possibilities, but also raises troubling ethical and practical questions about the integrity of digital information and those who use and process it.

Marc Canter

This year at the CD-ROM conference, Bill Gates proclaimed that he needed two CD-ROMs to implement a decent multimedia content piece. Next year it will take 4 CD-ROMs, and the year after that 10 CD-ROMs. The world will soon discover that CD-ROMs are far too small to fit all the multimedia information we want to distribute.

The only choice is fiber delivery (or some other form of electronic delivery). To get beyond the Catch-22 of waiting for broadband B-ISDN (150 Mbps) infra-structure, we must build simulation systems today that can help us solve tomorrow's problems. By focusing on issues like audience interaction, how many clicks per second does it take to keep a customer interested and happy, and what other sorts of interactivity can we develop besides shooting, killing, driving and flying, we can develop algorithms today that will be useful in the future, when a typical fiber-caster will be sending the same multimedia information into 10 million homes.

Once the grisly bloodbath of multimedia players wars are completed, we'll have a standard data format, and set of chips that will be ubiquitous and cheap. Then we can focus on the real question, "How can we make each of those 10 million customers feel like they're individually interacting with the fiber-casted information?"

Timothy Onosko

1) Among the next megahit products will be an acceptable-quality video-telephone at $500 or less and an under-$1000 video projector with the resolution of 16mm film. "Megahit" is defined as a product that produces that "I've gotta have that" lust.

2) Virtual reality will continue to be a media fantasy. Everybody knows that VR really requires future generations of a) computing power, b) huge capacity storage, c) high-definition display technology, none of which is here, yet. Nonetheless, a video game company will soon introduce a "virtual reality" headset for home entertainment and kids will love it.

3) Computer-generated movie effects will be joined by computer graphics characters and even sets and locations. Each new level of development in computer graphics movies will be showcased in its own blockbuster movie. We've already seen the first of these, "Terminator 2".

4) In five years we'll still be talking about multimedia as a future trend because nobody knows what it is or what it's supposed to do. The entertainment industry, not the computer software or hardware industries, will determine whether multimedia will ever be viable, because that's who stands to profit.

Hank Grebe

This should prove to be a lively group of speakers, with opportunities for questions and debate. Everyone has their own crystal ball. Yet, as focused as a vision might be, fate often proves the outcome to be something unforeseen. We can only try and make the best guess.

It's an exciting time to be alive. Amidst all the technological wonders, the world has devastating social and economic problems to overcome (as I write this, Los Angeles is cleaning up after the Rodney King riots). In bringing together these proponents for responsible, effective use of technology, it is my hope that their statements will provide insights for strategic planners and managers. Our leaders, whether they be corporate, financial, educational or governmental, need to be computer literate and technologically attuned in order to commit to decisions that beneficially lead us into the 21st century.

For growth and progress to be made, inventors, innovators and entrepreneurs need support, from start-up ventures on up to the corporate level. Through synergetic discussions and collaborative efforts such as this, we can encourage time and capital to be invested with prudence, resulting in a higher percentage of developers and end-users coming up as winners.

References:

Books

Ambron, Sueann, *Learning with Interactive Multimedia*, Microsoft Press, 1990.

Barlow, John, *Crime and Puzzlement*, Whole Earth Review, June, 1990. (available via anonymous FTP from ftp.eff.org in /pub/ EFF/papers)

Benedikt, Michael, Ed. *Cyberspace: First Steps*, MIT Press, 1991.

Czikszentmihalyi, Mihalyi, *Flow: The Psychology of Optimal Experience*, Harper & Row, 1990.

Gilder, George, *Life After Television*, Whittle Direct Books, 1990.

Jones, Oliver, *Introduction to the X Window System*, Prentice-Hall, 1989.

Lambert, S. and Ropiequet, S., *The New Papyrus*, Microsoft Press, 1986.

Markoff, John and Hafner, Katie, *Cyberpunk: Outlaws and Hackers on the Computer Frontier*, Simon & Schuster, 1991.

Reingold, Howard, *Virtual Reality*, Summit Books, 1991.

Wright, Benjamin, *The Law of Electronic Commerce*, Little, Brown, 1991.

Periodicals

Digital Media: A Seybold Report, published monthly by Seybold Publications.

Electronic

USENET newsgroup: comp.org.eff.news (an electronic Internet newsgroup)

Special Session: SIGKids Learning Laboratory

Chair: Coco Conn, Homer & Associates

Panelists:
Judy Sachter, IBM
Roy Pea, Northwestern University
Peter Rowley, The Ontario Institute for Studies in Education/CSILE
Stephen Long, Creating With Technology

The SIGGRAPH '92 SIGKids Learning Lab is where junior and senior high school students present computer graphics projects they have worked on since the beginning of the year, with assistance of local volunteer mentors. This Special Session looks at the workings of SIGKids and the use of technology in the classroom from various points of view: research, industry, student and teacher.

Overview:

This year, SIGKids has invited a group of computer-using junior and high school students to spend a week at the SIGGRAPH '91 conference in Chicago. Technology teachers were targeted at schools in the Chicagoland area and were sent applications. Students with a good working knowledge of computers were asked to fill out the applications and answer the following questions: Names of students with whom you will collaborate, Project description, What hardware and software will you use to create your project, What hardware and software will you use to demo your project, Past experience with computers (hardware and software). All applications were accepted.

At SIGGRAPH, the students are giving presentations of their projects, attending a panel and paper session, visiting a workshop, the film show and the art show. Guest speakers are presenting 20-30 minute 'tutorials' to the students on topics such as: CGI & music videos, programming & graphics, the evolution of the artist, artificial life programming, understanding motion for animation, multimedia, rendering, and many more. During the week, students are keeping journals on CSILE, an educational collaborative hypermedia system developed at the Ontario Institute for Studies in Education, and documenting their visit on video, interviewing SIGGRAPH '92 attendees, vendors, presenters, each other, and visiting students.

The SIGKids Learning Lab has computers for student demos, a video table with Video 8 playback and record decks, and a multimedia table. In the multimedia area the students will begin putting together all the elements of their research and data gathering.

The students have been working on their projects since the beginning of the year. Software companies have donated graphics programs to the students (Alias, Autodesk, Virtus, Inc., Macromedia, Virtual Reality Studio, LCSI, Electronic Arts, Paradigm Software, and Broderbund). U.S. Robotics donated 9600 baud modems to help get the students on-line. In most cases mentors have been provided where the students needed help in new areas. Students have met at local facilities and institutions (Argonne National Laboratory, Editel Chicago, Institute for Learning Sciences at Northwestern, and the Electronic Visualization Laboratory at the University of Illinois at Chicago).

These meetings were an opportunity for the students to talk, interact, help each other, meet mentors and ask questions. Teachers, mentors and friends and family were always welcome. Tours showed them the work being done in the commercial and research worlds. In some cases they shifted focus and took on new topics. They knew that their experience would be shared by students all over the country once the videos were edited.

Local teachers were contacted through ICE (Illinois Computing Educators) and TEMA (Teachers of Electronic Media in Art). These teachers and their students were also invited to participate in the SIGKids Learning Lab. Schools in Ontario, Salt Lake City, Rowland High School, New York City, and Hawaii also worked on projects for SIGKids. Paradigm Software worked with students in Cambridge, who built LEGO plotters to create 3D computer graphics using Object Logo. The SIGKids Showcase area shows hardware and software uses in education. Almost all demos are given by the students.

Videos sent from schools and educators and researchers, including the videos the students are making at the conference, will play all week long. A resource computer is available in the SIGKids area to all conference attendees to input information about education and technology issues.

Roy Pea

As multimedia technology proliferates, we must explore some central learning questions. Whereas movies separate directors and viewers, the technology of interactive multimedia can unite creators and viewers in much the same way as the technology of writing unites writers and readers. Society might come to regard multimedia literacy as essential as writing is today. A major challenge has been to design tools that young learners can use to create multimedia communications. These tools enable students to become multimedia composers, not just consumers. (I use the term "composer" rather than "author" because it correctly implies that creating multimedia involves designing an arrangement of parts.)

Learners need to control computer-controlled multimedia to communicate their own understanding of information. Multimedia objects (text, pictures, video clips, and so forth) are important building blocks for developing and conveying a student's understanding, for several reasons:

1. Multimedia communication is similar to face-to-face communication.
2. Multimedia is less restricted than written text. Many people come to understand text better with broader media support for its interpretation.
3. Multimedia can place abstract concepts in a specific context (for example, refraction in physics might be depicted in a film on lens and light behavior).
4. Multimedia allows for individual selection of preferred sensory channels for learning.
5. Multimedia coordinates diverse external representations (with distinctive strengths) for different perspectives.

Creating multimedia composition tools for young learners is no small challenge. It means more than letting learners make choices among predefined options. Consider how students go about scholarly research. They develop a critical synthesis to summarize literature or film, craft a compelling argument, and carefully weigh pros and cons. In short, they construct meaning from cultural artifacts, a process similar to composing multimedia interpretations. Unless students start composing their own multimedia interpretations, multimedia "educational materials" will be "delivered" to students, just as books are now. We might find the 21st century recapitulating extant problems with texts in education, which promote an "authority-centered" epistemology.

Today's book report or research paper is one place to start thinking about multimedia composing. With these assignments, students typically underuse research resources, are limited to written text as their final product, and lack opportunities for presenting and discussing that product with a critical community (that is, teachers and peers). When we extend these assignments to connect with large, user-extensible multimedia databases, collaborative activities, and interactive presentations to reactive audiences, then we come closer to a culturally-based learning activity centered on students' constructing and communicating their understanding.

Judy Sachter

What do children learn from using 3D computer graphics? How do different children think about space and develop strategies for constructing, transforming, and displacing objects? What is confusing to children in this process? What strategies do they use to solve spatial problems? How do children overcome obstacles? When and how do they ask for help? How do they choose their frame of reference? What are the gender differences in spatial problem solving? Computer graphics provides us with a window into the process of constructing knowledge, designs and ideas.

3-D computer graphics allows several aspects of spatial cognition to come together in coherent spatial learning environment. Children learn about Euclidean and projective space while creating images and animation. They actively use these concepts through perceptual and cognitive exploration and spatial problem solving.

5th grade children explored a microworld in which they manipulate transformations and views of objects through a command language. They specify the transformation using positive and negative numbers and decimal fractions, which are solidly bound to the Cartesian coordinate system and visual feedback. This system offers multiple representations of spatial concepts through visual, verbal, and formal modes. The integration of these different representations is designed to enhance children's understanding of spatial concepts, as well as make this environment accessible for children of a variety of styles.

In school mathematics, children have to memorize a definition for a point and a polygon, but it means nothing to them. When they create objects in 3D, they need these mathematical concepts to create and manipulate real images. In this virtual world the children are not intentionally learning these concepts but are actively using them for manipulating objects in space through doing art, animation, Euclidean mathematics, geometry, and decimal fractions; they are examining space, creating mental imagery, and using 3-D computer graphics.

Peter Rowley

The goal of the Computer-Supported Intentional Learning Environments (CSILE) Project at OISE is to build (a) an instructional theory driven by cognitive science research into collaborative learning processes and expert knowledge organization, and (b) a collaborative educational hypermedia system which supports fine-grained sharing of a wide spectrum of classroom information, including rough work, wonderings about a new area, plans for tackling problems, and finished projects. The theory is constructivist, placing emphasis on student expression of pre-existing knowledge and their explicit articulation and revision of theories about a domain (e.g. gravity). The design of the system is based on the theory, and in turn provides support for classroom experiments to test its predictions. It has been in daily use, in grades one to thirteen, over the past six school years.

The design of the CSILE system walks a fine line between supporting its constructivist theory of instruction and providing a comfortable starting point for students, and particularly teachers, who are accustomed to traditional school practices. We argue that, in general, interfaces that aim to stimulate learning of expert processes must pay attention to this balance. A corollary is that interfaces that do not have this developmental attitude run the risk of perpetuating, and potentially solidifying (via increased efficiency), current task

structures (e.g., classroom procedures) that are ineffective or detrimental.

Stephen Long: Creating with Technology

The mission of Creating With Technology is to enable and empower children and adults to express themselves confidently and creatively in a technological world.

The electronic information space is as vast as our astronomical universe. The educator today is like the space pilot learning to navigate the stars for the first time at the speed of light. What are the resources and how do we use them? Where are the guiding stars? What strategies shall we use to navigate? In multimedia, no longer can we think of computers as dumb machines capable only of regurgitating our input. Now we communicate with a social and cultural intelligence, a subject-object which embodies the genius of individuals and groups who have thought abut computers, communication, science and art and stored their information for us in hardware and software. In this super-rich environment we hope to contribute our own genius to the conversation.

Did televising or computers revolutionize the classroom? Not as single media. But the integration of video, audio, computers, print and communications already has changed the roles of the participants, curricula and methodologies. For one thing the classification of the curriculum into subjects has completely broken down. The only content now is hypermedia. In the finite Newtonian universe, we created curricula, what was to be learned. Working with our technological, cultural subject-object intelligences (multimedia computers) in a post Einsteinian time, we create a learning process to discover what we need to know for our journey out of the galaxy.

Afterward: Coco Conn

At SIGGRAPH '87, SIGKids first presented a group of 4th to 12th grade students. Today those students still talk about that experience and its impact. SIGGRAPH is breaking new ground by giving students and teachers a voice and a platform while everyone else is talking about 'fixing' our schools. We will gain a better insight on how we teach and learn. Letting students use media to express what they understand about a subject is our window into their minds.

References

Scardamalia, M. and Bereiter, C., "Higher Levels of Agency for Children in Knowledge Building: A Challenge for the Design of New Knowledge Media," *J. Learning Sciences*, 1,1, pp. 37–68, 1991.

Papert, S., *Mindstorms: Children, Computers, and Powerful Ideas*, Basic Books, 1980.

Piaget, J. & Inhelder, B., *The Child's Conception of Space*, Norton & Co., New York, 1967.

Sachter, J.E., Kids N' Space: Exploration intospatial cognition of children, Unpublished doctoraldissertation, MIT Media Laboratory, Cambridge, MA, 1990.

Harel, I. & Papert, S., *Constructionism*, MIT MediaLaboratory, Cambridge, MA, 1991.

Sachter, J.E., "Different Styles of Exploration andConstruction of 3-D Spacial Knowledge in a 3-D ComputerGraphics Microworld," 1990, *Constructionism*, ed: Harel, I. &Papert, S., MIT Media Laboratory, Cambridge, MA, 1991.

Pea, R.D., E. Boyle, and R. de Vogel, "Design spaces for Multimedia Compositing Tools," in *Designing for Learning*, B. Bowen, ed., Apple Computer Press, Cupertino, CA, 1990.

Hollan, J., E. Hutchins, and D. Norman, "DirectManipulation Interfaces," in *User-Centered System Design*, D. Norman and S. Draper, eds., Lawrence Erlbaum Associates, Hillsdale, NJ, 1987.

Pea, R.D., *Human-Machine Symbiosis: Exploring Hypermedias New Cognitive and Cultural Technologies*, Institute for Research Learning, Palo Alto, CA.

Mills, M., and R.D. Pea, "Mind and Media in Dialog," to be published in *Full Spectrum Learning*, K. Hooper and S. Ambron, eds., Apple Press, Cupertino, CA.

Pea, R.D., and E. Soloway, "Mechanisms for Facilitating a Vital and Dynamic Education System: Fundamental Roles for Education Science and Technology," Rept. to the Office of Technology Assessment (National Tech. Information Service Rept. PB 88–194 634/AS), 1987.

Debating Multimedia Standards

Chair:
Rita Brennan, Apple Computer, Inc.

Panelists:
Phil Dodds, Interactive Multimedia Association
Jim Green, Intel Corporation
Brian Knittel, Silicon Graphics Corporation
Brian Markey, Digital Equipment Corporation

The panel presents a perspective and comparison of emerging industry standards for integrated media, both de facto and chartered by a standards committee. Panelists active in championing new multimedia standards, such as those based on HyTime, QuickTime, UNIX media, Application Programmer Interfaces (APIs), and PC multimedia standards, describe the architectural models, implementation trials and tribulations, and future of these emerging standards. Audience participation is expected and encouraged in the debate on whether committee standards groups, trade associations, user groups, or platform vendors are driving the new media integration standards.

What Can We Do to Bring the Multimedia Fledgling Out of its Nest?: Rita Brennan

Within the last five years or so, the potential of multimedia has been recognized by the computer industry, and long before that was recognized by the artists' community. Just as artists have long used various tools to create their works, such as paints, pencils, papers, fibers, and even music and text to achieve a desired effect, now media developers and designers hope to use computer systems to achieve similar effects.

Unfortunately, while computers have the potential to empower the artist and aid in the process, media designers and the users of their work are discovering that working on the computer can sometimes be more time consuming and frustrating than working without one. Perhaps it is because the tools are not adequate, or the system is inefficient in its execution of a program. It is our contention, however, that most problems arise when a previously created work cannot be integrated into the overall project or new component. This incompatibility is particularly noticeable in group projects, where individuals with talents come together to create a single multimedia work, but find it impossible, or at best difficult, to integrate their work with others.

Let's call this the interchange issue. This is one problem that multimedia standards should be able to solve. Another scenario involving interchange is the "existing arts" issue. Without digressing into copyright and ownership issues, users have available to them today thousands (millions?) of examples of media data that could potentially be reused in a modern multimedia environment.

What is necessary to make the multimedia industry soar? It could be being able to retrieve and interchange new and existing types of data that can then be integrated easily into a designer or user's work. The interchange issue impacts all computer platforms, networks, and application developers. Along with the interchange issue, the multimedia community may or may not benefit from standardized APIs, databases, and all-assuming architectures.

This panel is comprised of experts in each of these multimedia areas, who are in consensus about some multimedia issues and not others. We expect a lively debate amongst the panelists as well as with the audience. The debate will focus not on whether standards for multimedia should be developed and supported, but rather on who should be driving the standards initiative, so as not to repeat the mistakes of traditional standards initiatives.

The speakers of this panel are all proponents of multimedia standards; all have very different views about how to achieve standards in a timely manner so that the industry and users may deem them useful, and what the standards should address first and foremost. The experiences of Phil Dodds, Jim Green, Brian Knittel, Brian Markey and myself will hopefully provide new insight into the behind-the-scenes operations of the multimedia standards world.

Your feedback could be just what the industry needs to move multimedia standards forward.

Standards Must be Timely to be Useful: Brian Knittel

Standards are only useful if consensus can be achieved rapidly. Many standards are obsolete by the time they arrive. Just like real products, they have a window of opportunity, and the development of standards should be treated like product development.

Politics should be relegated to the objective setting phase and divorced from the technical arena. When political issues arise during the technical development phase, the process gets lengthy and the standard becomes bloated, and results are not achieved.

Standards in multimedia can help the industry mature more rapidly - but only if they arrive before the technology has changed radically.

What is Appropriate to Standardize and What is not?: Brian Markey

Multimedia and hypermedia pose a unique opportunity to be the first standards-driven software technology. Many groups, both formal and ad hoc, are working on multimedia-related standards.

It is my belief that formal standards, which include well-defined mechanisms of checks and balances, offer the best hope for usable standards. The development of vendor-driven ad hoc standards will likely proceed and many such standards will gain wide acceptance. But lacking formalism in definition, these vendor-driven standards are likely to contribute to further pluralism in hardware and software platforms.

The marketplace tends to react to standards in one of two ways: standards either act as a catalyst for new products and technologies or they are ignored. Obviously, the developers of standards would prefer that their work was a positive influence. With this in mind, most standards bodies eventually wrestle with the question "what is appropriate to standardize and what is not?". In the software arena, where progressive thought is the norm, standardizing applications semantics or processing models is shunned. Bold and often unanticipated methods arise in a marketplace that's free from the constraints of standardized mediocrity.

While standards bodies typically do not define applications, they do define certain elements of the framework, such as the data interchange formats that applications will use. This facilitates the software vendor's desire to create innovative products, while allowing users the flexibility of open environments and shared information. HyTime is one standard that allows this kind of flexibility.

Format Standards and the Environments They Apply to: Phil Dodds

Companies that produce multimedia platforms can be considered as providing a contiuum from 'low-end' consumer platforms, to home/education based platforms, through the desk-top (home->business), and then to enterprise-wide environments:

Consumer—>Home—>Desk Top—>Enterprise-wide

When you look at how companies are positioned and marketed, those at the left side of this continuum are platforms that are content or "title" driven. Hence, great interest accrues to who will win the format wars. Toward the right side, however, workstation and network-oriented companies are interested in common system services at this end of the spectrum to support client-server environments. They will adopt anyoneUs data stream provided it works.

In the middle you have today's Desk Top group who want to own their APIs (system services) so as to control their software vendors. They are increasingly willing to support common formats, but only if it does not threaten their APIs.

Lessons to be learned from the Consumer Electronics Industry: Jim Green

The computer industry should take a page out of the book used by the consumer electronics industry. Specifically, the energizing multimedia industry should standardize on the formats for media and content (e.g., everyone's players can play the same CD's), and for connectivity. Once this is accomplished, all the players can then compete over price/performance and features.

Currently the multimedia industry is playing a dangerous and self-absorbed role. The party line of major system providers goes something like this: "We are working on our own technology. As soon as it's done, we will open it up and make it a standard." This lack of cooperation among key players with users will result in a multiplicity of formats, not standards. It is my position that early cooperation during the development of these formats is critical to our success.

References
"Comparison of IMP and QuickTime", Brian Knittel for the Chinatown Group: A Technical Working Group of the Interactive Multimedia Association, September, 1991.

"Definitions of Device Control Matrix and Methods," The Chinatown Matrix Committee, April, 1991.

"Hypermedia Marketplace Prepares for HyTime and MHEG," Brian Markey, *Proceedings of USENIX-Summer '91 Proceedings.*

"QuickTime Movie Resource Format" *Apple Computer, Inc.,* January, 1991.

"IMA Compatibility Project Proceedings," Volume 1 Issue 1, September, 1991.

"IMA Architectural Framework," James Green and Phil Corman, April, 1992.

"A Multimedia Class Hierarchy," James Green for the Architecture Technical Working Group, September, 1991.

Visualization in Computational Biology

Chair:
Sidney Karin, San Diego Supercomputer Center

Panelists:
Mark Ellisman, University of California at San Diego
Robert Langridge, University of California at San Francisco
Klaus Schulten, University of Illinois at Urbana-Champaign
John Wooley, National Science Foundation

A New Look on Life

Computational biology, from biochemistry to ecology, is producing some of the most exciting new applications of scientific visualization. This panel of experts in the field will discuss the visual and computational philosophies behind the dazzling portraits of molecules at work as well as brain cells in health and illness They talk about visualizing how blood circulates, bones knit, plants grow, and populations interact. Life scientists are pioneering new ways to see problem and to process, on scales from the microscopic to the global, and are finding new ways to use the tools of computation, both locally and globally.

Computational Biology: New Star in the Computational Cosmos

Computational science is exploring the new world of questions that can only be asked because high-performance computing and communications are developing so rapidly. Scientific visualization, often described as a new way of seeing numbers, has become a critical component of computational science. While we are used to computer simulations and visualizations of the numbers associated with the processes of physics, the application of these techniques to biology is emerging as one of the most exciting new arenas for visualization.

The processes of biology are complex and subtle in and of themselves, and on top of that, they are enmeshed in and conditioned by the larger order of nature and life. Computational biology, from biochemistry to ecology, is the field that is producing some of the most exciting new applications of scientific visualization. The web of influence and consequence always extends beyond the process under study, and the visions and visualizations reflect that fact as they cope with the world beyond the edges of the screen.

The experts on this panel have opened new avenues of thought as they pioneered biological applications of scientific visualization. They will discuss how visualization animates important areas of biological research and how it facilitates insights not otherwise available.

For them, the High Performance Computing and Communications (HPCC) Initiative opens a new era in biology. Interaction among scientists—collective thought—is accelerated by the HPCC era and its supercomputers and supernetworks. For biologists concerned with the complexity and interactivity of processes on all scales, the new tools mean not only more inter-scientist interaction, but more inter-process interaction. Biological and medical experimentation can conquer the limits of local constraints and poor statistics, as the laboratory, the clinic, and the fields and forests are interconnected.

Combining Microscope and Computer to Visualize Human Cells: Mark Ellisman

The Microscopy and Imaging Research Resource at the University of California at San Diego is a national biotechnology resource for high voltage electron microscopy and image analysis. Dr. Ellisman will discuss how the revolutionary tools of high-voltage electron microscopes and computers housed at the Microscopy and Imaging Research Resource are used by researchers at UCSD and locations throughout the world. The visualization and high-speed communications equipment, combined with a microscope that can be used via computer, are aiding scientists in finding causes and treatments for diseases ranging from cardiovascular disorders through Alzheimer's and other disorders of the nervous system.

National Supercomputer Centers' Role in Bioscience Research: Sid Karin

The San Diego Supercomputer Center at the University of California at San Diego, a National Science Foundation-sponsored center, is providing researchers a full-spectrum computational science and engineering environment. Dr. Karin will discuss the center's new initiative in computational biology, also funded by NSF, which includes projects with Professor Ellisman's lab, with human genome researchers, with ecological researchers, and with the Computational Center for Macromolecular Structure (CCMS), a joint project of the Chemistry Department and SDSC at UCSD, and Scripps Research Institute.

SDSC's computational science and scientific visualization assets recently played a major role in the CCMS's successful solution of the complete three-dimensional structure of a protein kinase, key for a whole family of enzymes, and Dr. Karin will discuss this effort as an example of the role of visualization in computational biology.

Directions in Macromolecular Graphics: Robert Langridge

The developments in computer graphics hardware which made it such a powerful tool for computational molecular biology were:

    1) Interactive, real time, three dimensional rotation (1964).
    2) Time-sliced (tachistoscopic) stereo (1970).
    3) Real time vector color systems (1979).

I regard all these attributes as essential for research on complex molecular structures and interactions. However, the developments in computer graphics which have gained the most attention in the last ten years have been in the realm of "realistic" representation of objects and scenes, developments which at present only have value in molecular biology research in the production of illustrations for publications or lectures ("realism" in molecular displays have often meant realistic displays of plastic models of molecules - models which merely simulate those which can be built on the lab bench and which make minimal use of the freedom which computer graphics provides).

It is possible to provide items 2) and 3) for static representations of biological molecules, but most day-to-day research demands the ability to manipulate the molecules in three dimensions and in real time (that is the USERS real-time, not the molecular time being simulated). While I would be one of the first to use a system which provided real time, interactive three dimensional ray traced images of arbitrary objects, the equipment to do this is not here yet, and until it is, the representation of molecules in the classical chemical way as lines for covalent bonds, with clouds of points or meshes as surfaces, meets the needs of the practicing chemist or molecular biologist, though it is often convenient to switch between the real-time (usually vector) interactive display and the shaded "realistic" display.

I feel equally dubious about the PRESENT value of Virtual Reality systems. While such systems are undoubtedly valid subjects for computer graphics research, they are nowhere near being superior to the now orthodox stereo, real-time, interactive (color, of course), workstation.

Having said all this, I must emphasise that molecular graphics systems are far from satisfactory for the average user who is more interested in the science to be done than in the computer, an individual who I have described as "aggressively apathetic" about computers. Not only does he or she not know about computers, he or she does not WANT to know. The provision of smooth user interfaces is as big a problem in this field as it is in all areas where users expect the interaction with the computer to be tuned to their areas of expertise - the chemist wants to do chemistry, not computer science. Aside from the interface itself, satisfactory means have yet to be found for the analysis of the dynamics of macromolecular interactions - a problem which will become more acute as the speed of the associated computers increases by orders of magnitude over the next few years. Chemical complexity is not merely three dimensional, it extends into the time domain.

I will illustrate my remarks with examples of work over the last three decades, most recently by my colleagues at UCSF on inhibitors of a protein crucial in the maturation of the AIDS virus — HIV-1.

Interactive Molecular Simulations: Klaus Schulten
Dr. Schulten will discuss recent advances in interactive simulation. Any molecular configuration takes about 100 femtoseconds to stabilize, and the latest parallel machines will make this sort of calculation in about 10 seconds. This opens the prospect for researchers to interact with molecular simulations in real time, changing geometries, folding patterns, a molecule's response to induced stresses, and scenarios in which molecules dock and bind to other molecules. He will discuss plans for virtual reality interfaces to this sort of interactive computation, illustrating the possibilities that will be opened up when scientists can participate in the life of the molecule.

Research Initiatives in Computational Biology: John Wooley
Dr. Wooley's background is in structural biology and microscopy, specializing in cell metabolism. He will discuss the way in which visualization and high-speed communications figure in a number of new initiatives funded by the NSF. These include efforts to model physiological processes, to develop properly structured databases for different kinds of biological data—including interactive visual databases, and to understand some of the special challenges posed for mathematics by biological phenomena. He posits a new topological enterprise, that takes advantage of visualization, will be required to describe and categorize newfound complexities in well-known biological processes.

Visualization on the Bioscience Frontier
Biologists, it has been said, work very close to the frontier between bewilderment and understanding in a discipline so complex, messy, and richly various that it mirrors life itself. The members of this panel take you to this frontier and show you some of computational science's newest and most exciting applications of scientific visualization.

References
Lander, E.S., R. Langridge, D.M. Saccocio, "Computing in Molecular Biology: Mapping and Interpreting Biological Information," *Computer*, Vol. 24, No. 11, Nov. 1991.

Huang, C.C., E.F. Pettersen, T.E. Klein, T.E. Ferrin, and others, "Conic — A Fast Renderer for Space-Filling Molecules with Shadows," *Journal of Molecular Graphics*, Vol. 9., No. 4:230+, Dec. 1991.

Shifman. M.A., A. Windemuth, K. Schulten, P.L. Miller, "Molecular Dynamics Simulation on a Network of Workstations Using a Machine-Independent Parallel Programming Language," *Computers and Biomedical Research*, Vol. 25, No. 2:168-180, April 1992.

Treutlein, H., K. Schulten, A.T. Bruner, M. Karplus, and others, "Chromophore Protein Interactions and the Function of the Photosynthetic Reaction Center — A Molecular Dynamics Study," *Proceedings of the National Academy of Sciences of the United States of America*, Vol. 89, No. 1:75-79, Jan. 1992.

Hessler, D., Young, S.J., Carragher, B.O., Martone, M., Hinshaw, J.E., Milligan, R.A., Masliah, E., Whittaker, M., Lamont, S. and Ellisman, M.H. (1992) *SYNU: Software for Visualization of Three-Dimensional Biological Structures.* Microscopy,. 1 (in press)

Mercurio, P.J., Elvins, T.T., Young, S.J., Cohen, P.S., Fall, K.R. and Ellisman, M.H. (1992) "The distributed laboratory: An interactive visualization environment for electron microscopy and three-dimensional imaging." *CACM* (in press)

Masliah, E., Ellisman, M., Carragher, B., Mallory, M., Young, S., Hansen, L., DeTeresa, R. and Terry, R. (1992) "3-Dimensional analysis of the relationship between synaptic pathology and neuronal threads in Alzheimer disease." *J. Neuropath. and Exptl. Neurol.* (in press)

Rowlands, N., Price, J., Kersker, M. and Ellisman, M. (1992) "Design and calibration of an IVEM for general 3D imaging of non-diffracting materials." *Proceedings of the Annual Meeting of the Electron Microscopy of America.*

Ellisman, M.H., Martone, M., Soto, G., Masliah, E., Hessler, D., Lamont, S. and Young S. (1992) "Computer aided methods for 3-D visualization of serial sections and thick biological specimens." *Proceedings of the Annual Meeting of the Electron Microscopy of America.*

Soto, G.E., Martone, M.E., Lamont, S., Young, S.J., Deerinck, T.J., and Ellisman, M.H. (1992) "Three-dimensional reconstruction of large subcellular structures: A method for combining axial tilt tomography with serial thick sections." *Soc. Neurosci. Abstr.*

Kingsbury, David T., "Computational biology for Biotechnology: Part I The role of the computational infrastructure," *Trends in Biotechnology*, Vol 7, p. 82-87,1989.

Wooley, John C., "Computational biology for Biotechnology: Part II Applications of scientific computing in biotechnology, " *Trends in Biotechnology*, Vol 7, p. 126-132, 1989.

Artificial Life

Chair:
Steven Levy, *Macworld*

Panelists:
Chris Langton, *Los Alamos National Laboratory and Santa Fe Institute*
Przemyslaw Prusinkiewicz, *University of Calgary*
Craig Reynolds
Karl Sims, *Thinking Machines*
Larry Yaeger, *Advanced Technology Group, Apple Computer, Inc.*

Artificial Life is a new science dedicated to duplicating the emergent mechanics of biology *in silico*. The potential advantages are overwhelming. Living systems are the most intricate and efficient machines known. If we could understand and utilizing their techniques, we would obviously reap tremendous benefits. Yet the intimiating complexity of living systems is such that so far, even with the most powerful computers, it is difficult to match even the abilities of the most simple organism.

Artificial life suggests a solution. Instead of trying to simply duplicate the effects of living systems, artificial life researchers attempt to build these behaviors from the bottom-up, much in the style that nature itself uses. A typical artificial life approach begins with a biological behavior—these have included reproduction, evolution, foraging, and locomotion—and attempts the extract simple local rules behind that behavior. When the rules are applied in software, computational agents display the emergent behavior.

Panelist Christopher Langton, the organizer of the 1987 Los Alamos conference which kick-started the field, and perhaps the field's chief theorist, puts it another way.

> Essentially, artificial life is merely a consequence of the universal observation that distinct physical systems can be organized to exhibit identical behaviors. If non-biological parts can be put together in such a way that they exhibit the same collective dynamical behavior as "living" things, it seems perfectly legitimate to attribute "life" to the dynamical behavior, rather than to its material substrate, and to call these artifacts "alive" as well.

It is endlessly fascinating to speculate on the implications of creating an artificial being that actually *lives*. At the least this accomplishment would be a historic occasion. The appearance of artificial life-forms also would raise some disturbing questions, ranging from the potential civil rights of information organisms, to the spectre of freely evolving computer viruses who develop immunities to anti-viral software.

Those attending the SIGGRAPH artificial life panel, however, might well ask what this has to do with computer graphics. The answer comes from the emergent behaviors made possible by artificial life techniques. These can be exploited to replicate complex images and behaviors found in nature—using the same mechanisms that nature itself employed to bring them about.

For instance, one of the classic artificial life experiments was panelist Craig Reynolds' creation of flocking "boids"—birdlike constructs given three simple rules. When each boid executed this local behavior, the aggregation of boids miraculously duplicated the flocking behavior seen in groups of birds. As Reynolds explains, this technique, which most recently has been used to animate flocks of bats in the movie *Batman Returns*, not only enhances versimilitude, but amplifies an individual artist's efforts:

> While still an experimental technique, behavioral animation in the style of artificial life suggests the possibility that animated characters can be made to automatically script (improvise?) their own actions. Self-directed, autonomous characters of this sort can be used to create complex background action for computer animation by serving as "extras" or "bit players". Because the animation of these characters is automated, it becomes practical to use hundreds or even thousands of them in a scene. Increasing the population does not add to the animator's workload as it would with manually keyframed motion control.

Other computer graphics researchers use artificial life technqiues to generate not behaviors but highly complex graphics. Some of the more impressive examples have come from the "virtual laboratory" of panelist Przemyslaw Prusinkiewicz, who uses a formal grammar, L-Systems, to generate realistic botanic forms.

Developmental processes of plants can be captured by using the formalism of L-systems, introduced in 1968 by Lindenmayer as a theoretical framework for studying the development of simple multi-cellular organisms, and subsequently applied to investigate higher plants and plant organs. After the incorporation of geometric features, plant models expressed using L-systems became detailed enough to allow the use of computer graphics for realistic visualization of plant structures and developmental processes. Computer-aided visualization of these structures, and the processes that create them, joins science with art.

Prusinkiewicz will illuminate this by discussing his recent work, involving a mathematical analysis of biological pattern formation, the relationship between L-systems and reaction-diffusion models, and new results with modeling seashells.

While the mathematical formalism of L-Systems (and other such techniques such as fractal geometry and the "graftals" of Alvy Ray Smith) has proven effective in producing natural forms, the execution of the system is in the *spirit* of biological processes, but not closely parallel to any specific computational process found in nature. Other computer artists have hewn more closely to mechanisms of biology itelf. Panelist Karl Sims of Thinking Machines has used the rules of evolution as a means of very quickly producing intricate images. Sims has conducted several experiments with his brand of "artificial evolution" in several ways, creating 3D plant structures, procedurally generated pictures and textures, 3D objects defined by parametric equations, and dynamical systems described by differential equations. Some of the results of his digital Darwinism have been instrumental in creating the images in the animations "Panspermia" and "Primordial Dance." He explains:

> Simulations of life and life-like processes can be a powerful approach for creating complex and interesting worlds that would be difficult to achieve using traditional methods. These methods have potential as powerful tools for exploring procedural models and achieving flexible complexity with a minimum of user input and knowledge of details. Complex virtual worlds can be generated that might not easily be designed or even understood by humans alone.

Sims's comment underlines how quickly experiments in artificial life have arrived at the frontiers of our biological and computational knowledge. As the work of panelist Larry Yaeger of Apple Computer demonstrates, the creations of artificial life techniques are often sufficiently interesting—and relevant to biological counterparts—to themselves qualify as objects of study. In other words, we can learn from our creations. Yaeger has created PolyWorld, an artificial ecology running on Silicon Graphics machines that has generated species that, after a period of generations, evolve neural networks that allow them to expoit their environment—and each other. Yaeger explains:

> By utilizing both the method (natural selection) and the tools (assemblies of neuronal cells) used in the creation of natural intelligence, PolyWorld is an attempt to take the appropriate first steps towards modeling, understanding, and reproducing the phenomena of intelligence. For while one of the grand goals is certainly the developement of a functioning human level (or greater) intelligence in the computer, it would be an only slightly less grand acheivement to evolve a computational Aplysia that was fully knowable—fully instrumentable, and, ultimately, fully understandable—to let us know we are on the right path.

The early indications that artificial life might be a fertile breeding ground for useful images—and viable life-forms—raises innumerable questions, a few of which our panel will consider. How broadly can artificial life techniques be used to produce useful work? What are the limitations? What are the problems in creating truly autonomous organisms? How can a bottom-up approach satisfy two seemingly exclusive goals: creating organisms which display novel behaviors, and creating organisms who do what we want them to do?

I hope that the this first SIGGRAPH panel on artifical life will not only serve as an introduction to a powerful new tool but also provide a glimpse of a science which may expand the boundaries of natural history—changing its creators in the process.

BACKGROUND MATERIAL AND REFERENCES:

Christopher G. Langton, ed., *Artifical Life*. Santa Fe Institute Studies in the Sciences of Complexity Vol. VI. Reading, MA: Addison-Wesley, 1989.

Chris Langton, Charles Taylor, J. Doyne Farmer, Steen Rasmussen, ed., *Artificial Life II*. Santa Fe Institute Studies in the Sciences of Complexity Vol. X. Reading, MA: Addison-Wesley, 1992.

Steven Levy, *Artificial Life: The Quest for a New Creation*. New York: Pantheon, 1992.

Przemyslaw Prusinkiewicz and Aristid Lindenmayer, *The Algorithmic Beauty of Plants*. New York: Springer-Verlag, 1990.

Craig Reynolds, "Flocks, Herds, and Schools: A Distributed Behavioral Model," *Computer Graphics* 21:4 (July 1987), p. 25.

Karl Sims, "Artificial Evolution for Computer Graphics," *Computer Graphics* 25:4 (July 1991), pp. 319–328.

Karl Sims, "Interactive Evolution of Dynamical Systems," in *Proceedings of the First European Conference on Artificial Life* Cambridge: MIT Press, 1982.

Special Session: SIGGRAPH Town Hall Meeting

Chair:
Donna Cox, Panels Chair '93

Panelists:
Loren Carpenter, Pixar
Steve Cunningham, director for publications, ACM SIGGRAPH
Rich Ehlers, panels chair, SIGGRAPH '93
Jim Kajiya, papers chair, SIGGRAPH '93
Alyce Kaprow, design show chair, SIGGRAPH '93
Adele Newton, conference planning committee chair, ACM SIGGRAPH
Simon Penny, art show chair, SIGGRAPH '93
Jamie Thompson, electronic theater chair, SIGGRAPH '93
Robert L. Judd and Mark Resch, co-chairs, SIGGRAPH '93

This special session focuses on how to participate more effectively in SIGGRAPH venues, such as papers, panels, courses, electronic theater, and art show. The panel provides important information about how to volunteer, prepare venue proposals, and plan SIGGRAPH presentations.

Recent surveys indicate that many conference attendees believe that the SIGGRAPH organization and conferences are run by insiders. Some individuals believe that preference is given when selecting certain types of technical papers, films and videos, and courses. The panelists discuss these concerns and encourage audience questions about SIGGRAPH, both the conference and the organization.

3D Graphics Standards Debate: PEX versus OpenGL

Chair: James Foley, Georgia Institute of Technology
Organizer: Bill Glazier, Silicon Graphics

Panelists:
Kurt Akeley, Silicon Graphics
Murray Cantor, IBM Corporation
Mark Goldstein, SDRC
Marty Hess, Sun Microsystems
Jeff Stevenson, Hewlett Packard

As the price of graphics hardware falls, three dimensional graphics will likely become a mainstream workstation, and perhaps PC, technology. Three dimensional visualization will emerge from it's niche of technical and scientific uses into broader applications, such as the user interface, business graphics and presentations, and the visualization of information from application domains. A single software API level standard may need to emerge to allow ISV's to take advantage of this new hardware potential.

Historically, software developers with 3D graphics requirements had two paths from which to choose. They could follow the proprietary graphics API path, typically with vendor specific, higher performance, more fully featured API's such as SGI's GL, HP's Starbase, and Sun's XGL. Or, they could choose portable API's developed by international standards bodies, such as GKS and PHIGS. Application developers with a high performance requirement typically followed the first path - and absorbed the extra costs of porting and supporting the different platform's graphics environments. Customers for whom portability and cost were most important selected the international standard approach, but suffered in performance in some cases.

The ISV and end user community today are demanding an API that provides the best of both worlds: portability, openness, and performance. Companies with an interest in traditionally proprietary API's and those whose strategy is based on the historically open standards are rushing to evolve their technology to meet these needs.

PEX is a 3D technology based on the PHIGS ANSI and ISO standard. The X Consortium, the governing organization for PEX, is defining an API for PEX, PEXlib, which will offer a standardized approach for low level graphics rendering. PEXlib holds the promise of high performance 3D immediate mode rendering in an X environment, something PHIGS has lacked. Several PEX supporters have established a PEX interoperability center, to help vendors and ISV's ensure portability across different PEX implementations. A traditional criticism of the PHIGS and PEX standards is individual companies have implemented vendor specific versions which made portability difficult.

Silicon Graphics, the company with the leading proprietary API, recently announced it would license its IRIS Graphics Library to the computer industry. OpenGL, the publicly available version of this technology, has been rearchitected to become vendor neutral. OpenGL is a rendering only API with all of the advanced graphics features from earlier releases. SGI has created a governing organization, the Architecture Review Board composed of 6 PC and workstation companies, in an attempt to create a level playing field for all licensees.

Companies are just now taking sides in the debate. This panel will allow hardware and software companies to argue the technical and nontechnical issues and answer the tough questions. Can PEXlib overcome its linkage with PHIGS, and address the portability problems? Can either architectural body move quickly to evolve and enhance their interface as new needs arise? Can OpenGL be effectively implemented on non-SGI systems, and is the governing process for OpenGL fundamentally fair to the rest of the industry? The next year is the critical time frame for the market to sort out which approach holds better promise as a high performance, portable, open standard. Standards debates always prove lively and emotional - we expect nothing less from our panelists.

Kurt Akeley:
The world is waiting for a 3D graphics standard that:

1. Exists on multiple platforms with different window systems and operating systems.
2. Provides an immediate mode interface, yet also supports server-side display lists for precomputation and data caching.
3. Integrates image manipulation and geometry comands into a single whole that transcends both traditional image processing and graphics capabilities.
4. Is well enough defined and tested that applications really do work on various platforms.
5. Evolves quickly to track graphics capabilities and requirements.

OpenGL is currently the best answer to these expectations. In particular, the OpenGL X extension, formally GLX, is superior to the PEX Extension accessed through the PEXlib API. Whereas PEX derives from PHIGS, a largely failed graphics toolkit, OpenGL derives from the Silicon Graphics IRIS GL, one of the most successful graphics API in the computer workstation industry. It inherits a mature and complete set of graphics capabilities, including texture mapping, antialiasing, atmospheric effects, and image composition. Furthermore, OpenGL is designed to be window system independent, while PEX can exist only in the X Window system. OpenGL in the Microsoft Windows NT environment will accelerate the merging of the workstation and personal computer worlds.

While OpenGL is licensed by Silicon Graphics, it is controlled by an Architecture Review Board with members from six different companies. This small board facilitates timely review of the specification, which was released in its initial form on 1 July of this year. Included in this first release is a comprehensive conformance suite designed to insure vendor compliance with the specification, and have application portability across multiple platforms. OpenGL implementations are expected from many companies within the next 12 months.

Marty Hess:
My position is based upon my long standing belief and promotion of "useful standards" (no, that is NOT an oxymoron) for the graphics industry, in particular the 3D graphics industry. Furthermore, I believe in the need for such standards offering distributed, interoperable solutions within a heterogenous, user definable operating environment.

Specifically, the PEX 3-D graphics protocol extension to the X11 Window System, and the PEXlib low-level library interface to PEX, is currently the best possible solution to these needs in today's graphics systems environment. This comes from designing PEX to efficiently support not only the PHIGS ISO standard, but a substantial variety of other 2-D and 3-D graphics API's as well, in an efficient, flexible, and extensible manner.

My position is presented in two parts:

The first part defines what it means to be a "useful standard," — technology which is widely available without burden, strategically-backed by major computer industry vendors and IHV's/ISV's, and commercially available in large volume, preferably from more than one source — yet solve all the technically oriented problems as well.

The second part will argue for PEX and PEXlib as good technical solutions, sighting existing PEX based products, and then argue on each of the points why PEX is already a "useful standard" today by the definition given previously.

Jeff Stevenson:

Many have observed the wide-spread success of the X Window System, and in particular, the Xlib library in the area of 2D graphics. Many 2D graphics applications on workstations have moved to Xlib as their porting interface. There are many benefits to this, the most important being a portable, standard, dependable interface for development and maintainence of 2D graphics applications.

Many would like to see 3D graphics develop in the same way. Given the success of the X Window system, it is clear that whatever interface is chosen for 3D, it must integrate well with X. Furthermore, with the emergence of client/server computing, the interface must be capable of interoperability in a heterogenous environment. The PEX protocol has demonstrated its ability to meet these requirements, as shown at SIGGRAPH '91 where 10 vendors, all running PEX display servers, were able to share remote applications across platforms.

PEXlib is an effort to leverage the capabilities of the PEX protocol to a more portable, standard, dependable interface for 3D graphics. Of course, many applications may not wish to develop at such a low level. This will give rise to the opportunity for development of 3D toolkits on top of PEXlib, much in the way that toolkits were developed for PEXlib. This will result in a small set of widely accepted toolkits that, when combined with direct access to PEXlib for actual rendering, will provide a powerful, yet flexible, standard interface for 3D graphics.

PEX and PEXlib have also demonstrated the support necessary to make PEX a widely-available standard. And, the definition is open to everyone which levels the playing field to ensure that everyone has equal opportunity to develop products based on the standard.

Murray Cantor:

There are two points of view to consider when judging whether a graphics API is to be preferred as a standard: the ISV and the workstation customer. It is my position that OpenGL is superior to the current PEXlib draft 5.1 in meeting the needs of both groups.

The ISV, when programming to a standard, needs entirely predictable behavior from all implementations of that standard. The application developer cannot afford long term to have multiple versions of code, each for a different workstation. This requires that identical functionality be made available on all implementations (no subsetting) and none of the behavior be left to the implementor. The real strength of X, at least until recently, was that it met the above criterion. For the requirement of consistency to be met by an API, it needs to be fully specified with none of the behavior to be "implementation dependent". Further, it needs to have a complete reference implementation. PEXlib 5.1 does not meet this requirement. Subsetting is permitted, some behavior is left to the implementor, and no full functioned reference implementation exists. OpenGL has none of these deficiencies.

It is much easier for a workstation developer to provide a customers a cost effective robust implementation of OpenGL than PEXlib. PEX has more code to implement and optimize. OpenGL, including the Utility Library, provides more useful functionality with fewer calls (OpenGL has less than 200, PEX more than 800). Further, there is much state in PEX (bundle tables, attribute state flags) that many feel provide little benefit to the programmer, but are a burden to the workstation developer.

This burden is not only in code development but in testing. More state results in very large numbers of test cases. All of this leads to cost that must be passed on to the customer. The OpenGL approach of making the graphics resource more explicit with just enough state to use the resource results in a much easier development and testing effort, making it easier to provide the customer with a quality implementation. It should be noted that OpenGL has a complete sample implementation (like X) so that the workstation developer can focus on performance, not functionality.

OpenGL is a superior platform to PEXlib for providing application developers and workstation customers a quality and cost effective solution.

Mark Goldstein:

SDRC, as the developer of a leading mechnical design automation product, is faced with the challenge of supporting a wide variety of 3D graphics environments over numerous workstation platforms. This task is currently accomplished by developing a unique graphics support layer for each workstation platform. This layer leverages each workstation vendor's "strategic" graphics API, which provides first access to new graphics hardware and features. This strategic API typically provides the best performance as well. Although there are a number of downsides to this approach, our customers are not willing to accept compromises in features, hardware support, or performance that would result from a least common denominator approach to 3D graphics.

The emergence of a 3D graphics standard across multiple hardware platforms would simplify the support effort required for this custom graphics layer and the incorporation of new graphics hardware. However, to be successful in accomplishing this task, the 3D API must meet the difficult requirement of being both a true multi-vendor standard while at the same time providing the flexibility to evolve with new graphics capabilities in a timely manner.

To be truly effective, we believe a 3D API standard must address the following issues:

- The graphics API must be architecture independent (i.e., not better suited for one hardware platform over another)
- The API must be strategic to several leading workstation suppliers. Being strategic implies the preferred method to obtain an optimal balance between performance, features, and hardware support.
- The evolution of the API must not be constrained by formal standards development processes (ANSI, ISO)
- The API licensing mechanism must provide a level playing field from a business perspective
- The API and its controlling party must support a process whereby extensions can be added by various vendors and these extensions eventually be incorporated into the standard API.
- The API must support a robust query mechanism which allows the application to sense the capabilities and relative performance of these capabilities on a particular device.
- The API must support window system interaction cleanly (i.e., graphics restore, color resource sharing, etc.)
- The API must provide low level graphics control to the application. If higher levels of graphics control can be used by the application, graphics toolkits developed on top of the base API can support these needs.
- The API must support immediate mode graphics, retained mode graphics, and a graceful combination of both.
- The API has the same level of integration in a distributed environment as in a local environment.

Graphics Education for Computer Science

Chair: Nan Schaller, Rochester Institute of Technology

Panelists:
Albert Bunshaft, Advanced Graphics Hardware Development, IBM
Toby Howard, University of Manchester, UK
Wilf LaLonde, Carleton University Canada
Dino Schweitzer, U.S. Air Force Academy
Carolyn Wasikowski, Minnesota Supercomputer Center
Zhigang Xiang, Queens College

Over the past decade, there have been major advances in the computer graphics field: in computer graphics techniques, the trend towards object-oriented programming, and availability of relatively inexpensive, high-resolution graphics hardware and sophisticated rendering packages. This suggests that a reevaluation of the traditional computer graphics syllabus is appropriate. Panelists from industry as well as academia attempt to begin this process.

Overview:

The "Computing Curricula 1991" report from the ACM/IEEE-CS Joint Curriculum Task Force (Allen B. Tucker, ACM Press/IEEE Computer Society Press) suggests the incorporation of a graphics course into the core of the computer science curriculum. Its syllabus is traditional. However, over the past decade, there have been major advances in the computer graphics field. It is the intent of this panel to explore the effects that these advances should have on how graphics is taught. (Note: Each of the educators on the panel teaches non-traditional graphics courses.) Some of the issues to be discussed are:

- What role should graphics play in a computer science curriculum? Should it be integrated throughout the curriculum? Should computer graphics courses really be part of the core courses in computer science curricula or should they be electives?
- What should computer science students learn from a computer graphics course? Should they learn how to construct graphics packages, how to use them, or both? What kinds of graphics or rendering packages should they be exposed to?
- What topics should be emphasized in such course(s): rendering or basic techniques, graphics systems or algorithms, or interactive techniques?
- What role should scientific visualization and interdisciplinary collaboration play?

Toby Howard

The view of the computer science department at the University of Manchester is that graphical interfaces are so much a part of modern computing systems that all students in computing disciplines need to know about them. Therefore, our students all do a first year graphics course, but thereafter, graphics and related courses are options.

In the first year, the emphasis is on graphical interfaces. This material is integrated with a course on databases. We use the Simple Raster Graphics Package (Foley, Van Dam, et al.) together with a local graphical toolkit. The students design and build a graphical interface to a database system. Some of the database entries are digitised images. In order to teach some aspects of analysis and design, we teach basic 2-D graphics, task analysis, and the development of conceptual models.

In the second year, a human computer interface course is available that has a bias towards software tools. It covers conceptual design, task analysis, dialogue modeling techniques, user interface design principles, more graphics, window system architectures, and advanced 3-D interfaces.

Traditional graphics courses covering advanced image synthesis are offered to third year students and also at the graduate level.

Wilf LaLonde

Smaller universities cannot compete with large well-funded universities that provide expensive equipment and a half dozen computer graphics courses. They are better off providing one or two highly focused courses with clear independent objectives rather than comprehensive survey courses.

At Carleton, we have developed an Interactive Computer Animation course with some novel features. The course focuses on 2-D character control, bitblt graphics, obstacle intersection, character design, world design, special effects, etc..

How can such a course be valuable to students? First, the course is taught using Smalltalk, providing the students with valuable experience in an application of object-oriented technology. Second, the course develops an interactive 2-D system from scratch. We develop the system on-line; i.e., we bring a development machine into class, and we design the interactive system together.

The course also plays a number of important secondary roles: (1) It teaches object-oriented analysis, design, and implementation, and highlights the importance of prototyping. In this way, it is complementary to a software engineering course. (2) It develops a complete working system and is, in this way, complimentary to compiler construction courses. (3) It encourages students to develop solutions on their own and gives them the confidence to tackle difficult problems.

Dino Schweitzer

The introductory graphics course at the U. S. Air Force Academy is unique in two respects.

First, a set of visualizations of computer graphic concepts has been developed for use in the classroom. These are specifically designed to support lecture material and are used interactively during class. Design considerations include: the ability to set up "what if" scenarios, displaying algorithms at the conceptual level, consistency of visual representations, and the ability to backup a step in an algorithm. Some of the areas covered by the visualizations include: 2-D and 3-D transformations, clipping, viewing transformations, line drawing algorithms, and shading algorithms.

Second, ray tracing, a topic usually reserved for advanced courses in the discipline, is taught. Teaching ray tracing offers several advantages. First, it is a simple algorithm. The primary algorithm is easy for students to understand and can be coded in a few hundred lines. Second, it requires no special hardware resources such as a large Z-buffer. Third, it does not require separate viewing or perspective transformations. But, perhaps the biggest advantage is the motivation that the students gain by producing impressive images with transparency, shadows, and reflection.

Zhigang Xiang

Graphics has traditionally been presented to computer science students with an emphasis on vector graphics. Introduction to color and illumination models is often delayed until the end of the term. This approach needs to change in order to keep up with the rapid growth of the field. Computer science students should be exposed to issues such as light versus color, local versus global illumination, and modeling versus rendering in a systematic way. Understanding the intrinsic mechanisms and underlying principles of the science provides a solid foundation for the students to enrich their learning with techniques and tools for generating sophisticated images.

We have re-organized our course material (partial support for this work was provided by the National Science Foundation ILI program through grant #USE-9152523) around the theme that computer graphics is the simulation of optical phenomena on display surfaces that typically consist of discrete pixels. Discussion of illumination models including Phong and ray-tracing precedes and guides discussion of other topics. Such a "reversal" of the traditional curriculum is feasible because rasterization and clipping algorithms are not prerequisites for illumination models. This approach makes the students' learning process a more natural, goal-oriented activity.

Albert Bunshaft

The IBM Graphics Systems organization is responsible for the design and development of computer graphics subsystems, including the development of programming tools and libraries, low level system software, on-board microcode, and graphics hardware. Lead programmers and engineers must be expert in system design. Job responsibilities require a working knowledge of computer graphics and span a wide range of technical areas. The ideally prepared professional for one of these jobs has a strong basic education in computer science and/or engineering. Today, most applicants with a bachelors degree have taken a computer graphics related course

as part of their undergraduate curriculum. Rarely though do these courses give the new hire the skills needed to perform their duties.

It is my opinion that all computer science graduates should have some formal education in computer graphics. Graphical interfaces dominate the modern world of computing. At a minimum, students should be taught the basic concepts and techniques used in these systems. The concepts of a bit-mapped display and the algorithms for manipulating these systems should be covered. Students should also be required to learn a common user interface design system like Motif. These topics and other basic graphics concepts should be incorporated throughout the curriculum.

Carolyn Wasikowski

The breadth and continually-changing nature of the computer graphics industry make it impossible to teach students all the specifics they will need to know after graduation. Instead, computer graphics courses should be designed to give students the tools that they will need in order to continue learning on their own: (1) an understanding of the basic vocabulary and current techniques, and (2) the ability to research new techniques, e.g., knowledge of journals and other sources of technical information. These skills could be taught in a single introductory course, while elective courses could give students the opportunity to learn more about particular topics.

As part of my job, I interview potential employees for the Graphics and Visualization Department. The first thing I look for is enthusiasm, and a willingness to learn. The second thing is their knowledge base: Do they have a basic understanding of the work to be done and exposure to major programming projects involving independent research?

Summary:

It is the panel's hope that the ensuing discussion will provide insight and guidance for those who have been struggling with these issues on their own. Our goal is to encourage others to begin thinking creatively about the role of graphics in computer science. We hope to foster an active exchange of ideas which can then be used to redefine the standards for computer graphics syllabi.

Beyond Gouraud-Shaded Polygons...Where Will Graphics Hardware Go Next?

Chair:
Douglas Voorhies, Silicon Graphics Computer Systems

Panelists:
Kurt Akeley, Silicon Graphics Computer Systems
Nick England, Sun Microsystems, Inc.
Fred Kitson, Hewlett-Packard Labs
Turner Whitted, Numerical Design, Ltd.

Graphics hardware has been evolving at a breathtaking rate. Many new ideas, not restricted to a narrow focus on zillions of simple polygons/second, may differ considerably from what you expect. The same technology seen in hot-box workstation CPUs permits analogous improvements in graphics hardware. How has this opportunity been seized? What will you soon be able to do at your desk that you could not do before?

This panel summarizes recent ideas and projects which push the hardware envelope. Attendees gain a clearer idea of what is now possible in hardware, what to expect from commercial products in the short term, and what new avenues of exploration have become reasonable.

Overview:
Where does the future of graphics hardware lie? Over the short term, recent momentum makes the path clear. Both general-purpose and specialized approaches will succeed.

General purpose CPUs are becoming fast enough and will have graphics enhancements added so that a modest collection of such processors can provide high performance graphics with a very rich feature set, including imaging, video, advanced rendering, etc. Specialized hardware will still be able to outperform such devices, but may be cost-effective only for real-time applications.

Vendors have been pushing hard on improved rasterizing performance and algorithms, such as texture mapping, anti-aliasing, etc. When the whole screen can be filled with such "high-quality" polygons, we will have attained the next generation of rendering hardware (after wireframe and shaded polygons). By going to this next step in realism without losing "real-time" performance, 3-D rendering will become far more mainstream, with experimental user interfaces (e.g. virtual reality) and casual visualization becoming practical. Texture especially offers a visual richness which aids surface perception and offers a powerful degree of freedom for data visualization.

Somewhat farther out, tremendous bandwidth improvements will be achieved when the rendering engine and pixel memory are merged on the same chip. In such a configuration, entire spans of a texture-mapped polygon might be rendered in parallel on a single chip, or entire polygons might be rendered as in Pixel Planes.

The currently dominant architecture for display systems focuses on "engines," typically featuring a geometric processor whose output is fed to a raster processor, the "predictable pipeline of polygon processing" [Reghbati88]. The components used to implement these two elements vary widely but the basic structure has remained unchanged for over 15 years. Within the bounds of this structure, designers of display hardware have provided advanced local shading features, texture mapping, transparency, and other elements of systems that display realistic images. However display software, and more recently applications, have begun to make greater use of global and procedural shading effects. The traditional structure doesn't support this.

There have been proposals, e.g. [Clark92], for new architectures to accelerate advanced shading effects. In research environments, machines with a lot of parallelism also lend themselves to a wide range of rendering effects [Fuchs89] [Potmesil89] even though they retain some of the conventional structure. A key element of these highly parallel display processors is recognition that advanced shading effects are predominantly geometric and are not handled effectively in processors which are optimized for image operations. In the end, these approaches reduce to hooking up a bunch of general purpose computing elements to speed up graphics operations.

So eventually our "engine" focus will give way to an "interconnection" focus; tasks which are not specialized or which require machines with extreme random-access bandwidth may be done on general-purpose massively-parallel multiprocessors. Global illumination, path planning, and teleologically-based modeling fall into this category. It is not clear whether graphics hardware will evolve to directly attack such global problems, or whether general-purpose massively-parallel processors will get there first. Perhaps the resulting machine would be the same!

This raises the fundamental question of whether there is anything at all unique about graphical display processing that merits a special architecture in the long term. Graphical display is, even for the most esoteric rendering methods, sufficiently specialized that it can be more readily accelerated by special purpose architectures than by a collection of current general purpose computers with general connectivity. It is clear, though, that designers of graphics hardware systems have not identified the new primitive elements of the next generation architectures. Should it be a ray? Should it be a NURBS surface? Or perhaps it should be a solid "texture"? And in the longest term, the physics of photons bouncing around a 3-D volume resembles countless other physical phenomena, and so future simulation machines whose structure parallels these problems may subsume graphics with ease.

Interconnection at the network level, when cost-effective for the casual transfer of high-resolution images at real-time rates, may give rise to RISC-based client workstations which can display images from a centralized "Visual Media Server." Such a central resource could have scalable RISC horsepower and extensive multimedia database storage as well as high bandwidth connections for fiber or wireless connections. Such a scheme can amortize the expense of specialized media processing and access, network connection, and utilization of the processors. The server can also orchestrate distributed processing of the clients as well as its own commodity parallel processors. Many applications, such as Finite Element Analysis and Physically-based Modeling require short periods of extremely high floating point performance (e.g. solving differential equations) as well as graphics. A high speed network can engender the transparent access to advanced graphics and image processing with the price/ performance advantage

There is much work to be done in examining the trade-offs made in distributing the graphics/imaging tasks. This distribution may be at several levels, among geometry or rasterizing chips, or among whole renderers, or within a heterogeneous network of various resources. Traditional graphics has been "embarrassingly parallel," with little communications between processors of polygons or pixels. Future machines may tackle far more difficult problems.

Unfortunately there seems to be very little hardware research work going on in universities (with the sole exception of UNC). The last non-commercial, non-UNC hardware paper in the SIGGRAPH proceedings was in 1984! Why is this? Does it matter that universities have essentially abandoned graphics hardware exploration? To the extent that university research competes with the torrid pace of commercial product design, it is of decreased value. But by putting the current state-of-the-art in perspective and by going far beyond it, attacking problems whose solution is far from commercially viable, they can play a leading role.

References:

[Clark92] Clark, James H., "Roots and Branches of 3-D," *Byte*, v. 17, no. 5, May 1992, pp. 153-164.

[Fuchs89] Fuchs, Henry, et al, "Pixel-Planes 5: A Heterogeneous Multiprocessor Graphics System Using Processor-Enhanced Memories," *Proceedings* of SIGGRAPH '89, July 1989, pp. 79-88.

[Potmesil89] Potmesil, Michael, and Eric M. Hoffert, "The Pixel Machine: A Parallel Image Computer," *Proceedings* of SIGGRAPH '89, July 1989, pp. 69-78.

[Reghbati88] Reghbati, H. K. and A. Lee, *Tutorial: Computer Graphics Hardware -Image Generation and Display*, IEEE Computer Society Press #753, 1988.

From Perception to Visualization

Chair:
Nahum D. Gershon, The MITRE Corporation

Panelists:
Richard Mark Friedhoff, Visicom Corporation
Margaret S. Livingstone, Harvard Medical School
Vilayanur S. Ramachandran, University of California at San Diego
Robert L. Savoy, The Rowland Institute for Science

Visualization is the process of transforming information into a visual form, enabling users to observe the information. Knowledge of the way the brain and the visual system perceive information can be used to greatly improve the visualization process and its results.

This panel will address this issue — what could be learned from visual perception to help us improve the visualization process. The panel will discuss how understanding visual perception could help the user improve existing visualization methods or create innovative new ways to represent the data visually. Visual perception areas to be discussed include perception of depth, motion, symmetry, color, shape, visual illusions, and internal visualization.

Conscious and Preconscious Processing in Visualization: Richard Mark Friedhoff

Visualization should be defined as the substitution of preconscious visual competencies and machine computation for conscious thinking. This definition appears to apply to most, if not all, instances in which data is rendered as imagery, including scientific, medical, and design visualization. In each case, visualization replaces ad hoc or improvised, consciously-mediated algorithms with preconscious, hard-wired algorithms resident in the physiology of the visual system. The distinction between conscious thinking and preconscious visual processing is easy to define qualitatively, and is already useful in 1) choosing problems for visualization, 2) directing the visualization process and 3) evaluating the quality of a visualization. Nonetheless much remains to be accomplished before we can define preconscious processing more formally and reconcile the perspective of the scientist interested in understanding visualization with that of the visual physiologist or psychophysicist.

Perception and Visualization. Practical Aspects: Nahum D. Gershon

Data represented in a visual form is used for visual analysis of data and for scanning data for existence of desired features. Researchers and analysts examining data displays would like to detect regions of specified data values (e.g., high, medium, or low), their locations, and shapes. The problem of detecting the existence of patterns, locations, and shapes can be difficult, especially in low resolution browse sets where one would like to be able to scan large quantities of fuzzy data as fast as possible and detect features efficiently.

Understanding human visual perception provides us with ways to improve the visualization process and to create new ways to represent data visually. For example, perception of shape and symmetry of an object embedded in the data depends on the orientation of the object relative to the viewer. This means that when scanning data for familiar shapes and symmetries of features, one has to look at the data from different orientations. To allow viewing the data from different orientations, developers should create fast algorithms for orienting data on the screen.

Detection of features present in fuzzy data could be difficult not only because the data is fuzzy but also because current display devices are inefficient. However, if one could use the flexibility of display devices to feed information through preattentive visual processes, one would enable the user to perceive the desired information efficiently and fast. Methods discussed are based on the sensitivity of the human visual system to motion and the ease at which electronic display devices could change their display.

Art, Illusion, and the Visual System: Margaret S. Livingstone

Seeing is much more complicated than most people realize. It is tempting to think of vision as just another way of making a picture. However, no camera or computer system can match the ability of the human visual system to make sense of an infinite variety of images. That ability is made possible by the brainUs capacity to simultaneously process huge amounts of information.

Recent studies suggest that form, color, and spatial information are processed along three independent pathways in the brain. That explains why certain images can create surprising visual effects. Taking into account these characteristics of the visual system could vastly improve the perceptual quality of displayed images.

What Could Be Learned from Perception?: Vilayanur S. Ramachandran

Computers have provided us with new ways of creating visual images from abstract and non-abstract data. Reaching out to the fields of visual physiology, psychophysics, and cognitive psychology could not only explain why human vision is so efficient, but also how to create better images and what could be the limitations of particular representations. The knowledge acquired from perception research on motion correspondence, stereopsis, perception of transparency, derivation of shape from shading and illusory boundaries, color, and recovering 3-D structure from motion are examples of areas which are relevant to the visualization process.

Perception and Internal Visualization: Robert L. Savoy

How does a glimmer of an idea become an invention? Does it make sense to ask where "perception" ends and Rinternal visualizationS begins? Inventors have always used external visual images to help themselves create, and have used whatever technology is available, from the stick-in-the-sand to color CRTs. Whether making images from their own perceptual systems to observe, or making images to communicate with others, they have implicitly understood the need to match the attributes of the images to the capabilities and natural facilities of the human visual systems that process those images.

The power of computer-controlled visual displays gives us an opportunity to go beyond this "impedance matching" at the lowest levels of perception in the visual system. Perhaps it is possible to tailor visual displays to systematically resonate with whatever processes are involved in internal visualization. Because the visual system is, in all probability, intimately involved with our highest problem solving and creative abilities, addressing those human capabilities more directly has a great potential payoff. The panelist will present a "butterfly collection" of facts from a range of psychological research — in human visual perception, in primate neurophysiology, in patients with brain damage, and in the ubiquitous use of visual thinking in problem solving — to titillate your internal visualization systems with regard to these issues.

Afterword

Visual perception, no matter how distant it seems to be from computer-based visualization, is an integral part of the visualization process. As long as there is a human interface link in the chain for transferring information from the computer to the viewer, understanding how humans perceive visual information could help improve the quality and effectiveness of the visualization product.

References

R. M. Friedhoff, *Visualization: The Second Computer Revolution*, W.H. Freeman, New York (1991).

R.M. Friedhoff, "Conscious and Preconscious Processing in Visualization," *Proceedings of the Image Society 1992*, The Image Society, Tempe, AZ (1992).

N. D. Gershon, "Visualizing 3-D PET Images", *IEEE Computer Graphics and Applications*, September 1991, 11–13.

N. D. Gershon, "Enhanced Visualization of Multi-Dimensional Structures. Applications in Positron Emission Tomography and Climate Data", *Proceedings of Visualization '91*, pp. 188–192, IEEE Computer Society Press, Washington, DC (1991).

M. S. Livingstone, "Art, Illusion, and the Visual System," *Scientific American*, January 1988, 78–85.

S. Pinker (ed.), *Visual Cognition*, The MIT Press, Cambridge, MA (1985).

V. S. Ramachandran, "Visual Perception in Humans and Machines," in *AI and the Eye*, Blake, A., and Troscianko, T. (eds), pp. 21–77, John Wiley & Sons, New York (1990).

J. M. Wolfe (ed.), *The Mind's Eye*, Readings from Scientific American, W. H. Freeman, New York (1986).

Color Space Wars

Chair:
Robert L. Cook, Light Source Computer Images, Inc.

Panelists:
Jacob Aizikowitz, Electronics for Imaging
Don Carli, Mills Davis, Inc.
Ed Giorgiani, Eastman Kodak Company
Ed Granger, Light Source Computer Images, Inc.
Maureen C. Stone, Xerox Corporation

For years, people have been promising that color on the desktop is just around the corner. The choice of color space is an important part of making this promise a reality. But which color space is best is the source of much contention. Is XYZ the ultimate standard? Are there better alternatives? With audience participation, the discussions should prove lively.

Data Compression for Multimedia Systems

Chair:
Gregory K. Wallace, Digital Equipment Corporation, Chairman, ISO JPEG committee

Panelists:
Bernd Girod, Academy of Media Arts, Germany
Didier J. LeGall, C-Cube Microsystems, Chairman, ISO MPEG Video Committee
Hans-Georg Musmann, Universität Hannover, GERMANY, Chairman, ISO MPEG Audio Committee

Modern data compression techniques can reduce the data rates of good-quality audio and video streams to the point of manageability within commonplace networks and storage devices. But are the new international data compression standards JPEG, MPEG, and Px64 premature for this active area of research? Leaders in the research, commercialization, and standardization of multimedia data compression provide insights on this key issue.

Panel Overview:

The raw data rates of even modest-quality digital video and audio, which approach 100 Mbit/sec and more, tend to overwhelm commonplace networks and storages devices. Fortunately, data compression techniques can make these rates manageable, and the new international standards JPEG, MPEG, and Px64 enable both interoperability and economies of scale.

But are these standards premature for this active area of research? Will other techniques such as wavelets or sub-band coding yield practically superior results in the near future?

Leaders in the research, commercialization, and standardization of multimedia data compression provide insights on these key issues, whose outcome will influence how quickly multimedia capabilities are deployed.

The panelists' collective experience includes: fundamental research in data compression systems based on the Discrete Cosine Transform (DCT), sub-band coding, wavelets, and other methods; chairmanship of the JPEG, MPEG-Video, and MPEG-Audio standards committees; leadership roles in the commercialization of these technologies.

Each speaker will give a 10-minute introduction, either to one of these standards or to an alternative area of data compression research, and then state a position with regard to the expected longevity of these standards. The format of this panel is nominally the "comparison" category, but some healthy controversy is bound to be precipitated.

Position Statements:

Greg Wallace:

The ISO JPEG standard for still images is based on the 8x8 (two-dimensional) Discrete Cosine Transform (DCT), followed by psycho-visual quantization and statistical coding. With final ISO approval expected in Summer 1992, JPEG has already been widely embraced as the computing industry's standard encoding method for high-quality grayscale and color continuous-tone images for the computing industry. While other techniques may eventually prove to be incrementally superior for certain niche applications, JPEG will be the dominant continuous-tone still image datatype for at least the next 10 years.

Didier J. LeGall:

Both the CCITT Px64 standard for video teleconferencing and the ISO MPEG Video draft standard achieve compression by employing the two-dimensional DCT to reduce spatial redundancy, and motion compensation to reduce temporal redundancy. MPEG Video extends motion estimation to bidirectionally interpolated frames. The MPEG-Video design has achieved the practical state-of-the-art required of an international video compression standard for a variety of applications.

Although theoretical advantages are sometimes claimed for techniques such as wavelets and sub-band coding, there is little experimental evidence to suggest that such methods would be superior to the MPEG-Video design in the context of an "industrial-strength" international standard.

Hans-Georg Musmann:

In MPEG Audio, Layers I and II implement a filterbank which creates 32 subband representations of the input audio stream which are then quantized and coded under the control of a psychoacoustic model. In Layer III additional frequency resolution is provided by the use of a hybrid filterbank. The resulting digital audio bit-rate reduction technique supports several bit-rates covering a range from intermediate to compact disc quality. This latter quality can be obtained at a total bit-rate of 256 kbit/s for a stereophonic program.

MPEG Audio has achieved a successful transfer of state-of-the-art audio data compression methods from the research environment to an industry standard. While further progress is made in the research arena, MPEG Audio will be an important industry standard for the next several years.

Bernd Girod:

Data compression is a key technology to integrate moving images and sound into multimedia systems. While the emerging ISO and CCITT standards are clearly important for fostering the commercialization of this industry, it is important that university and other research not be de-emphasized. There is unrealized potential awaiting via further research into known methods such as vector quantization and wavelets.

Furthermore, there is enormous long-term potential in studying radically different approaches to multimedia data compression, based on fundamental research into areas such as image understanding and complex scene synthesis. Research breakthroughs in these areas could radically change the role of multimedia data compression in computing and communication systems.

References:

On JPEG, MPEG-Video, Px64, and Scalability: See articles by Wallace, LeGall, Liou, and Lippman, in the April 1991 *Communications of the ACM* (vol. 34, no. 4), devoted to Digital Multimedia Systems.

On MPEG-Audio: Karlheinz Brandenburg, Gerhard Stoll, et. al., "The ISO/MPEG-Audio Codec: a Generic Standard for Coding of High Quality Digital Audio", 92nd AES Convention, March 24-27, 1992, Audio Engineering Society Preprint No. 3336.

On Wavelets and Sub-band Coding: Olivier Rioul and Martin Vetterli, "Wavelets and Signal Processing", IEEE SP Magazine, October 1991, pp. 14-38.

Index

Cover Image Credits

Front cover

"Silver Box and Candles"
Copyright © 1992, Lawrence Berkeley Laboratory
Reference: *"Measuring and Modeling Anisotropic Reflection,"* Gregory J. Ward, p. 271

Title image

"Candidate vertex sets for tiling minimal surface"
Spots on a minimal surface show the positions of three nested vertex sets, used for creating versions of the model at different levels of detail in a manner that allows smooth interpolation between these versions. The surface model was created by James T. Hoffman using his adaptive meshing algorithm; the mathematical description is due to Celso Costa, David Hoffman and William Meeks III.
Reference: *"Re-Tiling Polygonal Surfaces,"* Greg Turk, p. 62

Back cover, top left

"Table of cacti"
Copyright © 1992, Deborah R. Fowler, Przemyslaw Prusinkiewicz, and Johannes Battjes
Reference: *"A Collision-based Model of Spiral Phyllotaxis,"* Deborah R. Fowler, Przemyslaw Prusinkiewicz, and Johannes Battjes, p. 366

Back cover, top right

"Seashell models"
Copyright © 1992, Deborah R. Fowler, Hans Meinhardt, and Przemyslaw Prusinkiewicz
Reference: *"Modeling Seashells,"* Deborah R. Fowler, Hans Meinhardt, and Przemyslaw Prusinkiewicz, p. 381

Back cover, middle left

"Black Nylon Cushion"
Copyright © 1992, Stephen H. Westin/Cornell University
Reference: *"Predicting Reflectance Functions from Complex Surfaces,"* Stephen H. Westin, James R. Arvo, and Kenneth R. Torrance, p. 263

Back cover, middle right

"NO SKINNYHACKING"
Copyright © 1992, Silicon Graphics Computer Systems Inc.
Artist: Carl Korobkin
Projective texture mapping is used to simulate the effect of a slide projector illuminating arbitrary surfaces in an environment.
Reference: *"Fast Shadows and Lighting Effects Using Texture Mapping,"* Mark Segal, Carl Korobkin, Rolf van Widenfelt, Jim Foran, and Paul Haeberli, p. 252

Back cover, bottom left

"Illumination with Intensity Law"
Reference: *"Illumination from Curved Reflectors,"* Don Mitchell and Pat Hanrahan, p. 290

Back cover, bottom right

"Intersection of a Sphere and Kummer's Quartic With 16 Double Points."
Copyright © 1992, AT&T Bell Laboratories
This Kummer surface has 16 double points, the maximum for a quartic. Twelve, the cusps apparent in the picture, are the vertices of a cuboctahedron. The others are on the plane at infinity of projective 3-space, at the points where the surface's eight arms, here truncated by intersection with a sphere, meet in pairs. Thanks to Don Mitchell for the malachite and cloud textures.
Reference: *"Interval Arithmetic and Recursive Subdivision for Implicit Functions and Constructive Solid Geometry,"* Tom Duff, p. 138

Local Groups Currently Operating

LocalGroupChairs@siggraph.org

California

Bay Area
Bruce McDiffett
P.O. Box 3553
Santa Clara, CA 95055
(415) 599-2054

Los Angeles
Coco Conn
2207 Willetta Avenue
Hollywood, CA 90068
(213) 466-3813 (H)
(213) 962-1662 (W)
coco@siggraph.org

San Diego
Mike Amron
2334 Galahad Rd.
San Diego, CA 92123
(619) 277-5699

Colorado

Denver/Boulder
Dave Miller
14 Inverness Drive East
Suite A100
Englewood, CO 80112
(303) 799-6766 (W)

Florida

North Central Florida
Millard Pate
Micron/Green
1240 N.W. 21st Ave.
Gainesville, FL 32609
(904) 376-1529
(904) 376-0466 (FAX)

Orlando
Christopher Stapleton
10151 University Blvd., Box 221
Orlando, FL 32817
(407) 894-3641 (H)

Georgia

Atlanta
Anita Critz
P.O. Box 250382
Atlanta, GA 30325
(404) 785-2911
(404) 436-6092(W)

Illinois

Chicago
Christine Oster
3810 N. Oakley, Apt. 1
Chicago, IL 60618
(312) 583-4636

Massachusetts

New England
Peter Ash
P.O. Box 194
Bedford, MA 01730
(617) 646-1632
pash@umb.edu

Minnesota

Minneapolis/St. Paul
Mark Feyereisen
16650 Marystown Rd.
Shakopee, MN 53379
(612) 445-2492 (H)
(612) 893-1800 (W)
(612) 893-0077 (FAX)

New Jersey

Princeton
Douglas Dixon
P.O. Box 1324
Princeton, N.J. 08525
(609) 936-7686 (W)
(609) 936-7900 (FAX)
drd@provax.intel.com

New Mexico

Rio Grande
Ray Elliott
P.O. Box 8352
Albuquerque, NM 87198
(505) 667-1449 (W)
(505) 672-3389 (H)
(505) 665-4361 (FAX)
rle@laln.gov

New York

New York City
Tim Binkley
School of Visual Arts
209 East 23rd Street
New York, NY 10010
(212) 645-0852

Texas

Dallas
Ken Schwarz
P.O. Box 800691
Dallas, TX 75380-0691
(214) 575-6433 (W)
(214) 437-5146 (H)
schwarz@utdallas.edu

Houston
Frank Taylor
McDonnell-Douglas
Space Systems
16055 Space Centre Blvd.
Houston, TX 77062
(713) 283-4278 (W)
(713) 283-4020 (FAX)

Washington, D.C.

Washington, D.C
Paul Lipsky
Image Communications
1420 Spring Hill Road, Suite 400
McLean, VA 22102
(703) 532-3917
(703) 848-0770 (FAX)

Canada

Vancouver
Bruce Sinclair
P.O. Box 33986, Postal Station D
Vancouver, BC V6J 4L7
(604) 731-8117 (W)
bruce@van.wti.com

Toronto
John Faichney
Personnae
36 Sullivan Street
Toronto, M5T 1B9
(416) 596-7421 (W)
(416) 596-7836 (H)

France

Paris
Alain Chesnais
#2 Rue Henre Matisse
59300 Aulnoy-les-Valenciennes
France
[33] 27-30-18-10
[33] 27-42-52-00 (FAX)

United Kingdom

London
Greg Moore
27 Sinclair House
Sandwish Street
London, WC1H 9PT
[81] 368-1299 ext. 7475
gregg1@clus.mdx.ac.uk

U.S.S.R.

Moscow
Yuri Bayakovski
Keldysh Institute of Appl. Maths
Miusskaya Sq., 4
Moscow, 125047 Russia
[7] (095) 250-7817
[7] (095) 972-0737 (FAX)
yumbay@keldysh.msk.su

Local Groups Steering Committee

lgsc@siggraph.org

Lou Katz, chair
Metron Computerware, Ltd.
3317 Brunell Drive
Oakland, CA 94602
(510) 814-7000 (W)
(510) 814-7026 (FAX)
(510) 530-8870 (H)
(510) 530-5841 (FAX)
lou@siggraph.org

Maureen Jones, local groups
startup assistance
255 West 90th Street
New York, NY 10024
(212) 787-0151
(516) 267-6159

Len Breen, overseas liaison
CASCAAD, Faculty of Art
and Design
Middlesex Polytechnic
Cat Hill, Barnet
Herfordshire, EN4 8HT
[44] 81 36 81 299 ext. 5134
[44] 81 44 09 541 (FAX)
[44] 71 24 20 551 (H)
len1@clus.mdx.ac.uk

Ed Council, member at large
Timberfield Systems
34 Salem End Road
Suite 3B
P.O. Box 2345
Framingham, MA 01701
(508) 872-0796
(508) 875-0521 (FAX)
council@siggraph.org

Jeff Jortner, member at large
P.O. Box 5178
Albuquerque, NM 87185
(505) 265-8616 (H)
(505) 845-7556 (W)
(505) 845-7442 (FAX)
jortner@siggraph.org

---

*Local groups editor for
Computer Graphics*
Susan Mair
University Computing Services
University of British Columbia
6356 Agricultural Road
Vancouver, B.C., V6T 1Z2 Canada
(604) 822-3938
(604) 822-5116 (FAX)
mair@siggraph.org

Local groups coordinator
Judy Granat
ACM
1515 Broadway, 17th Floor
New York, NY 10036
(212) 869-7440
(212) 944-1318 (FAX)
granat@acmvm.bitnet